PUBLIC LAW

PUBLIC LAW

Text, Cases, and Materials

SIXTH EDITION

Andrew Le Sueur

LLB (Lond), PFHEA, FRSA, Bencher of the Middle Temple
Emeritus Professor,
Essex Law School, University of Essex

Maurice Sunkin

KC (Hon), LLB (Lond), LLM (Lond), PhD (Essex), Barrister, of the Middle Temple
Emeritus Professor of Public Law and Socio-Legal Studies
Essex Law School, University of Essex

Jo Eric Khushal Murkens

LLB (Lond), PhD (EUI), Barrister, of the Inner Temple
Professor, LSE Law School
London School of Economics and Political Science

OXFORD
UNIVERSITY PRESS

OXFORD
UNIVERSITY PRESS

Great Clarendon Street, Oxford, OX2 6DP,
United Kingdom

Oxford University Press is a department of the University of Oxford.
It furthers the University's objective of excellence in research, scholarship,
and education by publishing worldwide. Oxford is a registered trade mark of
Oxford University Press in the UK and in certain other countries.

Third Edition 2016
Fourth Edition 2019
Fifth Edition 2023

Published in the United States of America by Oxford University Press
546 Fifth Avenue, New York, NY 10036, United States of America

British Library Cataloguing in Publication Data
Data available

Library of Congress Control Number: 2026937180

ISBN 9780198983880

Printed in the UK by Bell & Bain Ltd., Glasgow

The manufacturer's authorized representative in the EU for product safety is
Oxford University Press España S.A. of Parque Empresarial San Fernando de Henares,
Avenida de Castilla, 2 – 28830 Madrid (www.oup.es/en or product.safety@oup.com).
OUP España S.A. also acts as importer into Spain of products made by the manufacturer.

FSC
www.fsc.org
MIX
Paper | Supporting
responsible forestry
FSC® C007785

To our families, partners, and friends

PREFACE

Public law remains one of the most fast-moving and contested fields of legal study. Over the past decade, the United Kingdom's constitutional landscape has been reshaped by major developments: the continuing aftershocks of leaving the European Union; ongoing debates about the territorial constitution and the future of devolution; sustained political interest in replacing or revising the Human Rights Act 1998; and intense scrutiny of how the state uses its powers, from immigration control to policing of public protest. These debates matter because they affect how government remains accountable, how people experience the state in their daily lives, and how the constitution adapts to social and political change.

There is much written on public law and an ever-growing range of key texts for university courses on the subject, including on constitutional and administrative law, as it is often referred to: the big textbooks, shorter works, and a number of 'text, cases, and materials' books. For us, it is this latter type which provides an ideal medium for an account of the legal aspects of the United Kingdom constitution. There are three main reasons. First, it gives students a chance to read at first hand the analysis and arguments of academics and participants in the constitution, most aspects of which are contested: the extracts convey the debates and disagreements most effectively. In selecting the materials for use in this book and adding our commentaries we have attempted to focus on subjects that are in the mainstream of the majority of public law or constitutional and administrative law courses in the United Kingdom. We have focused on *legal* aspects of the constitution, not least because most users of the book will be studying public law as a core area of their undergraduate *law* studies, but we hope that non-lawyers will also find the book of value.

A second reason for a text, cases, and materials approach is that it is good for presenting case studies that breathe life into the law. In this book, we use case studies to look at a variety of constitutional issues and episodes, including the use of the prerogative to deploy the armed forces and to prorogue Parliament (both in Chapter 10); the attempted use of delegated legislation to control public protest (Chapter 13); in relation to the use of delegated legislation and administrative justice we look at the Windrush scandal (Chapters 13 and 16); and in relation to the Human Rights Act 1998, the interaction of school uniform policies and rights to manifest religion, anti-terrorism legislation in the United Kingdom, and prisoner voting (all in Chapter 22). The case studies are designed to encourage readers to 'drill down' into specific constitutional goings-on to see how general principles and processes operate in a particular context and to gain an understanding of the law that is difficult to achieve when using other types of book.

A third reason is that the text, cases, and materials approach provides students with access to key sources of law and other materials. This book, for example, provides readers with a carefully selected range of extracts from important statutes and leading judgments, as well as from materials drawn from a wide range of official reports. In our commentary we explain these extracts and seek to place them in their context.

The best way to learn about constitutional law is to become engaged in the issues. Recognising that this cannot be done passively, throughout the book we invite readers to 'pause for reflection' and pose questions that are intended to prompt readers to check their understanding and to critically reflect on what they are reading. In this way we hope that the book will be a valuable resource that will complement the work of lecturers and teachers.

Any book of this length requires an organized structure, although we do not assume that all readers will use the chapters in the order in which they are presented. The book is divided into five Parts. Part I deals with constitutional fundamentals and covers core matters including the legislative supremacy of Parliament (Chapter 3), the Rule of Law (Chapter 4), separating and balancing powers (Chapter 5), and Multilevel Governance (Chapter 6). Part II deals with Executive Functions. It includes chapters on the Government (Chapter 8), Accountability (Chapter 9), and the Prerogative (Chapter 10). Part III concerns legislative functions and covers Primary Legislation (Chapter 12) and Delegated Legislation (Chapter 13). Part IV concerns Judicial and Dispute Resolution functions and considers the Judiciary (Chapter 15), Administrative Justice (Chapter 16), Judicial Review, which now extends to four Chapters (Chapters, 17, 18, 19, and 20); and human rights protection in the UK, in two Chapters (Chapter 21 and 22). Part V deals with the European Union covering the Institutions of the EU (Chapter 23) and Joining and Leaving the EU (Chapter 24).

The book was finalized in December 2025. The online resources that accompany this book will enable us to provide regular updates for students studying our changing constitution.

Andrew Le Sueur
Maurice Sunkin
Jo Eric Khushal Murkens
December 2025

NEW TO THIS EDITION

The whole text has been updated to include the principal developments since the 5th edition in October 2022.

- Chapter 1 has been substantially rewritten. A new section (1.5) outlines the rise and decline of the British Empire and considers how colonialism has shaped the United Kingdom's constitutional arrangements. This responds to growing recognition that public law cannot be understood without addressing the histories that have influenced its development. The opening extract, taken from Wendy Williams' *Windrush Lessons Learned Review* (2020), illustrates how limited awareness of the UK's colonial past can affect present-day policy and decision-making.
- Chapter 3 on parliamentary supremacy has a new section (3.8) examining its relationship with the British Empire. The doctrine underpinned the UK Parliament's authority to legislate for many colonial territories, though the way this authority was exercised varied across the Empire. After independence, most successor states adopted written constitutions that constrain legislative power, marking a clear shift away from parliamentary supremacy as the organizing principle of their constitutional systems.
- Chapter 4 on the Rule of Law includes extracts from recent publications, including JUSTICE's 2023 report *The State We're In: addressing threats and challenges to the rule of law.* The principle of legality receives fuller treatment and we explore the implications of automated and AI-decision-making—is this a friend or foe of the rule of law?
- Chapter 6 on Multilevel Governance has been substantially expanded to cover English devolution, including detailed analysis of the English Devolution and Community Empowerment Bill 2024–25, Metro Mayors, and combined authorities with updated statistics and maps. It also includes new material on Section 35 of the Scotland Act and its first use in 2023 (Gender Recognition Reform Bill).
- In the previous edition, Chapter 7 dealt with Protecting Rights. The key issues that were dealt with in that chapter are now in Chapters 20 and 21. This allows more space to be devoted to the practical enforcement of human rights in the UK.
- Chapter 9 (Accountability) has been rewritten to make clearer links with other foundational principles. A new case study (Section 9.6) on the parliamentary dimensions of the Windrush scandal is included, complementing the case study in Chapter 16, which focuses on the administrative justice aspects of the harms and redress sought by members of the Windrush generation.
- Chapter 10 (Prerogative Powers) explains prerogative powers and brings together in one chapter the case study on *R (Miller) v Secretary of State for Exiting the European Union* [2017] UKSC 5 and the case study on the use of prerogative powers to deploy the armed forces. As well as underlining the practical importance of the prerogative these case studies illustrate the challenges facing those seeking to reform prerogative powers.
- Chapter 12 (Primary Legislation) has been substantially rewritten, emphasizing this topic's links to foundational principles. It provides a clearer account of pre-legislative consultation, including the use of referendums and the significance of manifesto commitments.
- Chapter 13 (Delegated Legislation) includes a new case study on the Public Order Act 1986 (Serious Disruption to the Life of the Community) Regulations 2023, which were controversial in Parliament and held to be unlawful in the courts.

- Chapter 16 (Administrative Justice, Tribunals, and Ombuds) updates the case study on the Windrush scandal highlighting the importance of administrative justice.
- Chapters 17, 18, 19, and 20 provide an extended and updated treatment of judicial review to reflect the growing political and constitutional importance of this area. There are now four chapters discussing the foundations, importance, and use of judicial review (Chapter 17); the grounds of judicial review (Chapters 18 and 19), and prevention and exclusion of judicial review (Chapter 20).
- Chapter 21 (Protecting Rights: Using Human Rights in the UK Courts) updates the law and practice in this area, taking into account new empirical evidence, for instance Lewis Graham's studies on judicial behaviour and Section 3 usage. It includes analysis of the Supreme Court's restrictive turn under Lord Reed's leadership, including discussion of *Elan-Cane*, *Elgizouli*, as well as a new section (20.5.5) on common law constitutional rights and the HRA. Finally, it discusses the impact of legislation, such as the Illegal Migration Act 2023, Safety of Rwanda Act 2024, and Victims and Prisoners Act 2024, on the HRA.
- Chapter 22 retains three case studies on the protection of human rights concerning school uniforms and the right to manifest one's religion; terrorism; and prisoner voting.
- Chapter 23 provides a streamlined account of the EU institutions.
- Chapter 24 on joining and leaving the EU is updated to include the Retained EU Law (Revocation and Reform) Act 2023, which converted retained EU law into 'assimilated law' and removed its special constitutional status and supremacy over conflicting UK legislation. It includes updated coverage of the Northern Ireland Protocol including the Windsor Framework (February 2023) with its Green Lane/Red Lane system, Stormont Brake mechanism, and modified ECJ role. It also discusses *Lipton v BA Cityflyer* [2024] to show how the UK Supreme Court disagreed over retained EU law.

ACKNOWLEDGEMENTS

As with the previous editions, this book is a team effort. We thank those whose words we have extracted and curated in our efforts to paint a picture of the UK Constitution as a dynamic and contested system. The whole OUP team have been superbly supportive. We are grateful to Lucy Hyde for her work as copy editor, and to those, including our students, who have provided us with feedback and suggestions for improving the book. We owe special thanks to Mark Sandford, for research help. As always we thank our partners, families, and friends who were generous with their patience. We are, of course, responsible for any errors and omissions in the book.

SOURCE ACKNOWLEDGEMENTS

Grateful acknowledgement is made to all the authors and publishers of copyright material which appears in this book, and in particular to the following for permission to reprint material from the sources indicated:

Crown copyright material and public sector information are reproduced under the Open Government Licence v3.0. Parliamentary copyright material is reproduced under the Open Parliament Licence v3.0.

Blogs: Extracts from A.L. Young, 'The Draft Fixed-term Parliaments Act 2011 (Repeal) Bill: Turning Back the Clock?', U.K. Const. L. Blog (4th Dec. 2020) (available at https://ukconstitutionallaw.org/); Mark Elliott, 'A New Approach to constitutional adjudication? Miller 11 in the Supreme Court', *Public Law for Everyone*, September 24, 2019 (www.publiclawforeveryone.com); J. Tomlinson, N. Coakley, and R. Gambroudes, 'It's a trap! The changing dynamics of executive engagement with judicial review', *UK Const. L. Blog* (28th July 2022) (available at https://ukconstitutionallaw.org/).

Cambridge University Press: extracts from N.W. Barber, 'Prelude to the Separation of Powers' [2001] 60 Cambridge Law Journal 59, 71–2; H.W.R. Wade, 'The basis of legal sovereignty' [1955] 13 Cambridge Law Journal 172, 174, 187–8; C.J.S. Knight, 'Bi-polar sovereignty restated' [2009] 68 Cambridge Law Journal 361, 362, 365–6; A. Moravcsik, 'The origins of human rights regimes: Democratic delegation in postwar Europe' (2000) 54 International Organization 217, 238.

Hart, Bloomsbury: extracts from E.C. Page, *Governing by Numbers* (2001, Oxford: Hart Publishing), pp. 20–1.

ICLR: extracts from the Law Reports: *Appeal Cases* (AC), *Queen's Bench Division* (QB), and *Weekly Law Reports* (WLR).

JUSTICE: extracts from A British Bill of Rights: Informing the Debate—The Report of the JUSTICE Constitution Committee (2008, London: JUSTICE), pp. 55–6; Ann Abraham, The Parliamentary Ombudsman and Administrative Justice: Shaping the Next 50 Years, JUSTICE, Tom Sargant Memorial Annual Lecture, October 2011.

Oxford University Press: extracts from A. Tomkins, *Public Law* (2003, Oxford: OUP), pp. 46–7, 50. Extracts from P. Cane and J. Conaghan (eds) *The New Oxford Companion to Law* (2008, Oxford: OUP): Andrew Le Sueur, 'Accountability' pp. 7–8; Maurice Sunkin, 'Crown' pp. 286–7; C. Saunders, 'Entrenchment of Constitutions and Legislation' pp. 382–3; T. St J. Bates, 'Legislation' p. 726. Extracts from P. Cane and J. Conaghan (eds) *The New Oxford Companion to Law* (2009, Oxford: OUP): R. Baldwin, 'Legislation, types of' p. 721. Extracts from D. Feldman (ed.) *English Public Law*, 2nd edn (2009, Oxford: OUP): A.T.H. Smith, 'Offences against the state', in ch. 27, p. 1161; A. Le Sueur, 'The Nature, Powers, and Accountability of Central Government', para. 3.09, 3.12–3.14. Extracts from Jowell and D. Oliver (eds) *The Changing Constitution:* The 6th edn (2007, Oxford: OUP): A. Le Sueur, 'Courts, Tribunals, Ombudsmen, ADR: Administrative Justice, Constitutionalism and Informality', p. 333. The 7th edn (2011, Oxford: OUP): D. Oliver, 'Reforming the United Kingdom Parliament' ch. 7, p. 172. The 8th edn (2015, Oxford: OUP): D. Oliver, 'Regulating Politics in Government' ch. 11, p. 318. The 9th edn (OUP 2019): B. Dickson, 'Devolution in Northern Ireland' p. 247; R. Rawlings, 'The Welsh Way/Y Ffordd Gymreigi' pp. 297–298; A. McHarg, 'Devolution in Scotland' pp. 272–273; M. Elliott, 'Parliamentary Sovereignty in a Changing Constitutional Landscape' p. 38. Extracts from D. Hodson (et al) (eds) *The Institutions of the European Union*, 5th edn (2021, Oxford: OUP): U. Puetter, 'The Council of the European Union: co-legislator, coordinator, and executive power' pp. 82–83; A. Ripoll Servent and O. Costa, 'The European Parliament: powerful but fragmented' p. 145; F. Mérand, 'The European Commission: the cabinet and the services' p. 200; U. Puetter, 'The Council of the European Union:

co-legislator, coordinator, and executive power' p. 102; L. van Middelaar and U. Puetter, 'The European Council—the Union's supreme decision-maker' p. 75.

Oxford University Press Journals: extracts from Aileen Kavanagh, 'The role of parliamentary intention in adjudication under the Human Rights Act 1998' [2006] Oxford Journal of Legal Studies 26(1): 179; M. Sunkin, L. Platt, T. Landman, and K. Calvo, 'Judicial review litigation as an incentive to change in local authority public services in England & Wales' (2010) Journal of Administration Research and Theory, 20:I, 243–260.

Palgrave Macmillan: extracts from S.L. Greer, 'Whitehall', in R. Hazell (ed.) *Constitutional Futures Revisited: Britain's Constitution to 2020* (2008, Basingstoke: Palgrave Macmillan), ch. 8, p. 125; A.V. Dicey, *Introduction to the Study of the Law of the Constitution* (1885; 10th edn 1959, London: Macmillan & Co), pp. 406–10 (Chapter XIII 'Relation between Parliamentary Sovereignty and the Rule of Law').

Policy Exchange: extracts from the Judicial Power Project. London, 2019: John Finnis, The unconstitutionality of the Supreme Court's prorogation judgment; Martin Loughlin, The Case of Prorogation, The UK Constitutional Council's ruling on appeal from the judgment of the Supreme Court. London, 2016: Graham Gee: extracts from G. Gee, 'A Tale of Two Constitutional Duties: Liz Truss, Lady Hale, and Miller'.

Public Law Project: extracts from R. Thomas and J. Tomlinson, 'The Digitalisation of Tribunals: What we know and what we need to know' [2018] Public Law Project.

Thomson Reuters (Professional) UK Limited: extracts from N.W. Barber, 'Laws and constitutional conventions' (2009) 125 Law Quarterly Review 294, 294; Richard Rawlings, 'Concordats of the Constitution' (2000) 116 Law Quarterly Review 257, 258, 279; Jeffrey Jowell, 'Parliamentary sovereignty under the new constitutional hypothesis' [2006] Public Law 562, 578; Eric Barendt, 'Separation of powers and constitutional government' [1995] Public Law 599, 603–4; Harry Woolf, Jeffrey Jowell and Andrew Le Sueur, *de Smith's Judicial Review* (2007, London: Sweet & Maxwell), paras 5-044–5-045; Rodney Brazier, '"Monarchy and the Personal Prerogatives": a personal response to Professor Blackburn' [2005] Public Law 45, 45–6; Robert Hazell, 'Time for a new convention: parliamentary scrutiny of constitutional bills 1997–2005' [2006] Public Law 247, 246; D. Oliver, 'Improving the Scrutiny of Bills: The Case for Standards and Checklists' [2006] Public Law 219, 219–20, 226–7; David Feldman, 'Parliamentary Scrutiny of Legislation and Human Rights' [2002] Public Law 323, 324–7; Ann Abraham, 'The ombudsman and "paths to justice": a just alternative or just an alternative?'[2008] Public Law 1, 2–3; Nick O'Brien, 'Ombudsmen and social rights adjudication' [2009] Public Law 466, 468–9; Robert Thomas, 'Administrative Justice, Better Decisions, and Organisational Learning' [2015] Public Law, 111, at 112–114 and 131–133; D. Mead, 'Outcomes aren't all: Defending process-based review of public authority decisions under the Human Rights Act' [2012] *Public Law* 61, 76–8.

Every effort has been made to trace and contact copyright holders prior to publication. If notified, the publisher will undertake to rectify any errors or omissions at the earliest opportunity. We have used AI tools to generate first drafts of some figures which we have then redrawn and revised.

OUTLINE TABLE OF CONTENTS

DETAILED CONTENTS

TABLE OF CASES

TABLE OF LEGISLATION

TABLE OF UK STATUTES

References are to page numbers. The abbreviation 'n' indicates a footnote.

TABLE OF UK STATUTORY INSTRUMENTS

References are to page numbers. The abbreviation 'n' indicates a footnote.

TREATIES AND CONVENTIONS

References are to page numbers. The abbreviation 'n' indicates a footnote.

EUROPEAN UNION DIRECTIVES

EUROPEAN UNION REGULATIONS

PART I

CONSTITUTIONAL FUNDAMENTALS

1

MAPPING PUBLIC LAW

CENTRAL ISSUES

1. What is a constitution—and what does it do? A constitution organizes state power, sets limits on public bodies powers, and protects rights. Most countries express these rules in a single text, but the United Kingdom builds them from many sources.
2. Why is the UK unusual? The UK has no single constitutional document. Its rules lie across statutes, court judgments, and political conventions. This flexibility allows rapid change through ordinary Acts of Parliament but also raises questions about how executive and legislative power is controlled.
3. How did the UK reach this point? The constitution evolved through centuries of bargaining and pressure. It reflects gradual reform rather than a revolution with a single constitution-making moment.
4. Should the UK codify its constitution? Some favour a single written text for clarity and control of power; others value the adaptability of an uncodified system. The debate continues over which better serves democracy.
5. Whose voices and experiences shape the constitution? Modern constitutional study asks whose interests it protects and whose knowledge it ignores. Questions of devolution, diversity, and decolonization invite a broader understanding of power, identity, and constitutional change.

1.1 UNDERSTANDING PUBLIC LAW AND THE UK CONSTITUTION

Public law sets the legal and constitutional framework for state action.[1] It defines what governments[2] and legislatures[3] may do and places limits on how they exercise those powers. It also allows people to challenge official decisions in the courts.[4] Constitutional systems therefore exist not only to organize

[1] Definition: the state is the enduring structure of public authority in a country. It continues beyond changes in government and acts through institutions such as parliament, the government, courts, and public officials. There is disagreement on whether it always acts in the general public interest or reflects the power of particular groups.

[2] Part II of this book. [3] Part III of this book. [4] Part IV of this book.

the state but to restrain it. They limit power, protect rights, and defend democracy—guarding against both misuses of authority and the excesses of majority rule, when leaders claim to act for 'the people' but erode the rule of law.[5] Striking the right balance is difficult: constitutions must stop the abuse of power while still protecting free speech and political participation, so that dissent and criticism can flourish without weakening the safeguards of democracy itself.

> **PAUSE FOR REFLECTION**
>
> Around the world, some political leaders claim to speak for 'the people' while criticizing courts and lawyers as obstacles to democracy. How can constitutions protect fair government and the rights of minorities without stopping people from expressing strong political opinions? When does political disagreement become a threat to fairness and equality before the law?

In the United Kingdom, public law forms a broad and evolving system that links parliaments, governments, and the courts with the rights and expectations of the public. Before exploring how the system operates, Part I of this book introduces the foundational features of the UK constitution. This chapter provides an overview. Chapter 2 explores what we call the constitutional rule book. The following chapters consider the system's core principles: the legislative supremacy of the UK Parliament (Chapter 3); the concept of the rule of law (Chapter 4); how different forms of state power are kept separate and balanced (Chapter 5); and the UK's multilevel character (Chapter 6).

> **PAUSE FOR REFLECTION BOXES AND QUESTIONS: HOW TO USE THEM**
>
> Throughout this book you'll find Pause for Reflection boxes and questions. These features encourage you to think and reason both as a lawyer and as an active citizen—testing ideas, using real cases and materials, and forming your own arguments. In line with national expectations for first-year undergraduate law study, they build the skills that matter: understanding key principles, using evidence well, explaining and evaluating law in context, and reflecting on how it affects people's lives.

1.1.1 PUBLIC LAW, POLITICS, AND POWER

Like all branches of law, public law can be described and divided in different ways. Most university courses distinguish between *constitutional law*—which studies the basic structures of the state, such as Parliament, the executive, and the courts—and *administrative law*, which examines how public authorities make decisions and how those decisions can be challenged or reviewed. Since the Human Rights Act 1998, the protection of human rights has become central to both areas. However it is organized, public law provides the framework through which the state exercises and is held accountable for its power. Before turning to those institutions, we need to understand the territory they govern—the geography and history that give the United Kingdom its constitutional identity.

[5] See Neil Walker, 'Populism and Constitutional Tension' (2019) 17 *International Journal of Constitutional Law* 515 https://doi.org/10.1093/icon/moz027; Richard Bellamy, 'Political Constitutionalism and Populism' (2023) 50 *Journal of Law and Society* (Suppl) S7 https://doi.org/10.1111/jols.12401

1.1.2 TERRITORIAL BORDERS

This book is about the public law system of the *United Kingdom of Great Britain and Northern Ireland* (the UK). Great Britain comprises England, Wales, and Scotland. Together with Northern Ireland, these make up the four constituent parts of the UK. Occasionally we will look beyond the UK to other countries whose constitutional arrangements shed light on how the British system works.

Since 1998, the UK state has become less centralized. The UK Parliament has devolved substantial powers to Wales, Scotland, and Northern Ireland. Each now has its own elected institutions with authority to make laws and take executive action across many areas of public policy. The distribution of powers is asymmetric: England has no separate parliament or government for the whole country. Chapter 6 examines how these devolution and local government arrangements operate in practice and how they shape relationships among the different parts of the United Kingdom.

The UK government is responsible for two groups of smaller territories that are not part of the United Kingdom, and which have high degrees of internal self-government: the fourteen British Overseas Territories[6] and the Crown Dependencies of the Isle of Man, Jersey, Guernsey, Alderney, and Sark. These relationships show that the United Kingdom's constitutional reach extends beyond its shores, connecting its laws and institutions with issues of sovereignty, defence, and international responsibility.

1.1.3 MAKING AND REMAKING OF THE UNION

The United Kingdom's full title—The United Kingdom of Great Britain and Northern Ireland—and the existence of the British Overseas Territories show how the constitution has been shaped by centuries of expansion, union, and separation.

From a constitutional point of view, the Union developed in three main stages. First, England and Wales were joined under the Laws in Wales Acts 1536 and 1543, which annexed Wales to the English Crown and brought it under English law and administration. Second, Scotland shared a monarch with England from 1603. In 1706–07 the Scottish and English Parliaments enacted parallel Acts of Union giving legal effect to the Treaty of Union and creating the Kingdom of Great Britain. The new country had a single Parliament at Westminster but retained Scotland's separate legal and church systems. Third, Ireland—long under English control—entered a legislative union with Great Britain through parallel Acts of Union passed by the Irish and British Parliaments in 1800, forming the United Kingdom of Great Britain and Ireland. This sequence of legislative unions shows that the UK was created through political agreement and statute, not by a single founding constitutional document.

The United Kingdom has never been a settled union. Each nation has its own history of resistance, loyalty, and change.

In Wales, the Tudor Acts of Union in the sixteenth century incorporated Welsh territory into the English legal and administrative system, abolishing its separate political institutions and making English the language of law and government. Welsh identity nevertheless persisted through community life, religion, and cultural traditions. By the late twentieth century, organized campaigns for self-government led to devolution and the creation of a national assembly (now called the Senedd) whose competences over domestic policy have expanded steadily since 1999.

In Scotland, the 1707 Union created a shared Parliament at Westminster but preserved distinct Scottish legal, religious, and educational institutions, leaving a long-running debate about autonomy. Devolution

[6] In order of population size they are: Cayman Islands, Bermuda, Turks and Caicos Islands, British Virgin Islands, Gibraltar, St Helena, Ascension and Tristan da Cunha, Montserrat, and Pitcairn Islands, plus some that have no resident population.

following a referendum in 1997 established a Scottish Parliament with substantial law-making powers. The 2014 independence referendum resulted in a vote to remain in the United Kingdom, yet arguments about Scotland's constitutional future continue to shape its political landscape.

In Ireland, centuries of British rule produced repeated movements for self-government. Following the Irish War of Independence (1919–21), the island was partitioned: the Irish Free State became a self-governing dominion and later an independent republic, while Northern Ireland remained part of the United Kingdom. The decades of violence known as the Troubles (late 1960s–1998) concluded with the 1998 Good Friday Agreement, implemented chiefly through the Northern Ireland Act 1998. That settlement created devolved, power-sharing institutions. It also provides for a future referendum on Irish unity (often called a 'border poll') if the Secretary of State concludes that a majority would likely vote in favour.

Today, attitudes towards the Union vary across the four nations. Most people in England and Wales favour the current constitutional arrangements, whereas opinion in Scotland is more evenly split. In Northern Ireland, support differs markedly between communities, broadly aligning with unionist and nationalist traditions.[7] The Union's future therefore depends not only on legal structures and constitutional traditions but on the continuing consent of the populations it brings together.

PAUSE FOR REFLECTION

These prompts encourage you to consider how constitutional law, national identity, and democratic consent interact in shaping the modern Union.

- The United Kingdom emerged through several Acts of Union rather than a single constitutional document. What benefits and drawbacks arise from constructing a constitution through ordinary legislation rather than one codified text?
- The Northern Ireland Act 1998 makes Northern Ireland's place in the UK contingent on continuing popular consent. Should a similar principle apply to all four nations, and how might it be expressed or administered?
- England makes up the majority of the UK's population yet has no separate parliament or government. What tensions does this create within a multi-nation state, and how might they be addressed?

1.2 WHAT IS A 'WRITTEN CONSTITUTION'?

The UK constitution has grown through political practice, the enactment of ordinary legislation, and development of the common law rather than a single founding document. Its core features—the Union, parliamentary supremacy, the rule of law, and the balance between central and devolved government—have evolved over time. To see why this gradual and 'unwritten' approach makes the UK distinctive, we now turn to the written constitutions found in most other countries.

Most people live in countries that have a single text called something like 'The Constitution' or 'The Basic Law'.[8] Historian Linda Colley describes how 'single document constitutions', which sought to

[7] National Centre for Social Research, *British Social Attitudes 39: Broken Britain?* (Report, NatCen Social Research, 22 September 2022); Katy Hayward and Ben Rosher, *Bordering on a Poll? Attitudes in Northern Ireland on the Constitutional Question* (ARK Research Update 165, ARK 2025) 2–3.

[8] We adopt Anthony King's distinction between using a capital 'C' for written texts, and lowercase 'c' when referring to constitutional systems: see A. King, *Does the United Kingdom Still Have a Constitution?* (Sweet & Maxwell 2001), p. 3.

constrain government and protect rights, 'proliferated exponentially and in connected waves across multiple frontiers' with a surge after the First World War (1918) and even more after the Second World War (1945).[9] Three countries missed out on this process so have no such text (the United Kingdom) or a text that is not comprehensive (Aotearoa New Zealand[10] and Israel).

We'll see in Chapter 2 that academics disagree over how fundamental the difference is between countries with a single text and those that do not have one. For practical lawyers, one difference is in the methods we must use to find the main rules of the constitutional system. In countries which have 'The Constitution', that document systematically sets out basic rules for how the country is governed. Most can be printed as a booklet, slim enough to be slipped comfortably into a pocket. Many of these codified constitutional texts share similar headings: typically, there are sections on the executive (which may include a president, prime minister, monarch, emperor, governor-general, the cabinet, etc), the legislature (which may be called a chamber of deputies, a senate, a parliament, etc), the judiciary (which may include a supreme court, a constitutional court, etc), and on the fundamental rights of individuals (for example, freedom of expression, the right to fair trials, etc).

1.2.1 THE LIFE CYCLE OF A CODIFIED CONSTITUTION

A codified Constitution, like any living document, can be born, amended, and replaced. The average lifespan of codified constitutional texts is only 17 years,[11] though some have lasted for much longer (such as the Constitution of the USA dating back to 1789). Although the United Kingdom has never adopted a codified Constitution, British activists, lawyers and officials have drafted constitutions for many other parts of the world. As historian Linda Colley observes, '*During the centuries in which they invested in overseas empire, powerful and exploratory Britons regularly drafted constitutions for different groups of settlers and colonised peoples—a habit that continued until the 1970s*'.[12] These exported models often reflected British ideas about law, government, and civilization, shaping institutions that newly independent states later sought to reform or decolonise. British writers were also among early activists and theorists advocating constitutional rights and controls. In *Rights of Man* (1791–2), Thomas Paine argued that a constitution should be '*the act of a people constituting a government*', not a grant of power from rulers. Drawing on the example of the United States, he presented written constitutions as foundations for democratic government, designed to limit the authority of those in power. Mary Wollstonecraft argued that women, like men, were rational beings entitled to equal rights of citizenship. Her *Vindication of the Rights of Woman* (1792) challenged their exclusion from the political and constitutional rights that men claimed for themselves.

Birth. New constitutions usually emerge at moments of profound political change—such as independence, the end of war, the collapse of a regime, or a peaceful transition to democracy. The process of drafting a new constitution is often led by a specially convened constituent assembly or constitutional convention, which is dissolved once the text is agreed. The draft is then typically submitted to the people for approval in a referendum, giving the constitution democratic legitimacy. In recent

[9] L. Colley, *The Gun, the Ship and the Pen: Warfare, Constitutions and the Making of the Modern World* (Profile Books 2021) p. 3.

[10] Aotearoa is the Māori name for New Zealand and is increasingly used in bilingual form as part of efforts to recognize te reo Māori as an official language under the Māori Language Act 1987 and to acknowledge the constitutional significance of Te Tiriti o Waitangi (the Treaty of Waitangi).

[11] T. Ginsburg, Z. Elkins, and J. Melton, 'The Lifespan of Written Constitutions', www.law.uchicago.edu/alumni/magazine/lifespan accessed 15 November 2025.

[12] L. Colley, *The Gun, the Ship and the Pen: Warfare, Constitutions and the Making of the Modern World* (Profile Books 2021) p. 212.

decades, international actors such as the United Nations, the World Bank, and regional organizations have also promoted constitution-building as part of post-conflict reconstruction and governance reform, linking it to goals such as stability, economic development, and the protection of human rights.

Amendment. Constitutions may need revision to reflect social change or to correct institutional weaknesses. Proposals for amendment can come from many sources: political leaders, legislatures, social movements, or citizen campaigns. Ireland's 2015 referendum, which inserted a guarantee of marriage equality into its Constitution, shows how popular mobilization can align constitutional text with contemporary values. Many systems require a super-majority in the legislature, a popular referendum, or—in federal states—approval from a proportion of regional governments. These hurdles entrench the Constitution, protecting it from change by a simple majority and insulating it from day-to-day political pressure. Some constitutions are more difficult to amend than others: in Australia, for example, only eight of forty-four proposed constitutional amendments have been approved by referendum since 1901, making the Commonwealth Constitution one of the more rigid democratic constitutions in practice.

Replacement or 'death'. Constitutions can end in very different ways. Some collapse after a coup—for example, Chile's 1925 Constitution was effectively set aside following the 1973 military takeover and replaced under General Pinochet with the 1980 Constitution. Others are replaced through democratic reform. In France, the 1958 referendum brought the unstable Fourth Republic to a close and established the Fifth Republic, illustrating how a new constitutional text can stabilize government by redefining executive authority. Current debate about a possible Sixth Republic shows that even written constitutions must adapt to shifting political conditions.

1.2.2 CONSTITUTIONAL SUPREMACY

In most countries the codified Constitution stands as the highest form of law. Symbolically, this status appears in oaths of office and in national 'Constitution Days,' which celebrate the authority of the state's founding text. Constitutions also express shared political values. In many states they are treated as a source of national identity and moral authority, invoked in public life and education. In South Africa, for example, the 1996 Constitution is regarded as the founding text of democracy and a moral compass after apartheid, a 'birth certificate' for the newly democratized country.[13]

Substantively, constitutional supremacy means that all branches of government are bound by the Constitution and that courts—a Supreme Court or Constitutional Court—have the authority to strike down laws or executive actions that conflict with it. This principle expresses the idea that governmental power is both created and limited by law. The Constitution provides the ultimate legal standard against which the actions of legislatures and governments are measured. When courts enforce that standard, by requiring officials to act lawfully or by declaring legislation unconstitutional, they give practical effect to the rule of law. Yet constitutional supremacy brings its own challenges. Every Constitution must be interpreted and applied to concrete situations, and those interpretations often carry political implications.

In some systems, concerns have been raised that courts charged with enforcing the constitution are exercising political rather than purely legal judgment. In the United States, the Supreme Court has often been criticized for reflecting deep partisan divisions. During the Trump administration, the Senate confirmed three conservative justices in quick succession, a shift widely viewed as entrenching

[13] H. Ebrahim and L. Miller, 'Creating the Birth Certificate of a New South Africa', ch. 5 in L. Miller (ed), *Framing the State in Times of Transition: Case Studies in Constitution Making* (United States Institute of Peace 2010) https://www.usip.org/sites/default/files/Framing%20the%20State/Chapter5_Framing.pdf accessed 15 November 2025.

a durable ideological majority. In *Dobbs v Jackson Women's Health Organization* (2022), the Court overturned *Roe v Wade* (1973) and *Planned Parenthood v Casey* (1992), thereby ending federal constitutional protection for abortion rights. The decision left each of the 50 states free to determine its own abortion laws.[14] Because all three Trump-appointed justices joined the majority, many commentators argued that *Dobbs* demonstrated how the composition of the Supreme Court—and the political dynamics of judicial appointment—can shape constitutional interpretation with far-reaching social consequences. The case shows how, in systems of constitutional supremacy, the boundary between law and politics can be difficult to maintain.

EXERCISE

Visit the Constitute project website www.constituteproject.org, which provides English-language access to over 200 constitutions from around the world.

Select two countries (avoiding the United Kingdom, Aotearoa New Zealand, and Israel as these have 'unwritten' constitutional systems). Aim to choose countries from different regions or with different constitutional histories (e.g. one postcolonial and one European).

- Compare and contrast how each constitution addresses two of the following areas:
    - The executive: How is the head of government selected? What powers do they hold?
    - The legislature: Is it unicameral or bicameral? What are its law-making powers?
    - The judiciary: Is there a constitutional or supreme court? How is judicial independence protected?
    - Basic rights: What fundamental rights are protected?
- Use the search tool on the website to help locate relevant sections (e.g. search for 'judiciary' or 'freedom of expression').
- Present your findings as a short comparison table or a paragraph (150–200 words), highlighting key similarities and differences.

1.3 CONSTITUTIONS AS SYSTEMS

A constitutional system is not only a text but a living structure of institutions and practices. A written Constitution may not provide a complete picture of how a country's constitutional system actually operates. This is an important point. In many cases, the codified text is limited in scope: it may omit significant rules[15] or fail to reflect how power is exercised in practice.[16] To understand a country's constitutional arrangements fully, it is necessary to look beyond the codified text to examine the wider

[14] *Dobbs v Jackson Women's Health Organization* 597 US 215 (2022). The case addressed whether the Due Process Clause of the Fourteenth Amendment—which prohibits states from depriving any person of 'life, liberty, or property, without due process of law' and has been interpreted to protect certain unenumerated fundamental rights—encompasses a constitutional right to terminate a pregnancy.

[15] Famously, the Constitution of the USA adopted in 1789 does not explicitly state that the US Supreme Court has power to invalidate laws made by Congress that breach the constitution. The Court held that it had a power of judicial review of legislation in 1803 in *Marbury v Madison*, 5 US 137.

[16] e.g. Art. 1 of the Constitution of Cyprus provides that 'the State of Cyprus is an independent and sovereign Republic with a presidential regime, the President being Greek and the Vice-President being Turk elected by the Greek and the Turkish Communities of Cyprus respectively'. The post of vice-president has remained vacant since 1974, following the political division of the island and the withdrawal of Turkish Cypriot participation in central government.

constitutional *system*. This broader view includes judicial decisions—especially those from courts responsible for interpreting the constitution—as well as ordinary legislation that may carry constitutional significance. Political customs and informal practices also play a crucial role in controlling how institutions behave, how conflicts are resolved, and how principles such as accountability and the rule of law are upheld in day-to-day government.

In thinking about a constitutional systems, we can identify several basic functions that are needed in modern, democratic countries. The system should provide institutions of the state. Typically, these fall into the categories of executive (government), legislature, and judiciary. We explore the separation of powers in Chapter 5.

The system should define the relationship between institutions. For example, where there is a bicameral legislature, we need to know about the respective powers of the upper and lower chambers. Another example is the power of the judiciary: does it have authority to invalidate laws made by the democratically elected legislature that contravene the constitution? Almost all the chapters in this book consider constitutional relationships. Professor Anthony King draws a useful distinction between two types of institutional relationships. Some constitutions tend towards 'power sharing', with 'pluralist and fragmented' layers of government, proportional electoral systems, governments by coalitions of political parties based on negotiated compromises, and a constitutional court empowered to strike down legislation. 'Power hoarding' systems are characterized by single party 'winner takes all' governments, weaker local and regional layers of government, and less powerful constitutional courts.[17]

The system should define, protect, and encourage a culture in which people's basic rights are respected. This upholds individual human dignity and is an important way in which the power of state institutions is limited. Most countries with codified Constitutions list the 'constitutional', 'basic', or 'fundamental' rights. We explore rights protection in Chapter 4, as an aspect of the Rule of Law.

In some systems power is shared between national and sub-national levels, each with its own constitution. In the United States, for example, there is a federal constitution for the country as a whole and separate constitutions for each of the fifty states. Canada, Australia, and Nigeria are similar multi-tier systems in which the national constitution regulates relations between the federal government and the component units. By contrast, countries such as France, Jamaica, China, and Japan are unitary states, governed by a single constitutional framework. The United Kingdom occupies a distinctive position between these models: since 1998, the UK Parliament has devolved substantial powers to institutions in Scotland, Wales, and Northern Ireland, creating an asymmetrical form of devolution that gives each nation a measure of self-government without making the UK a fully federal state.

Taking stock, we can say that the term 'constitution' is capable of being used in different ways, as Dr Geoffrey Marshall (1929–2003) explains:

G. Marshall, 'The Constitution: Its Theory and Interpretation', in V. Bogdanor (ed.) *The British Constitution in the Twentieth Century* (2004, Oxford: OUP for the British Academy), ch. 2, p. 31

> Four distinguishable senses of 'constitution' [. . .] would be:
>
> (a) the combination of legal and non-legal (or conventional) rules that currently provide the framework of government and regulate the behaviour of the major political actors;
>
> (b) a single instrument promulgated at a particular point in time and adopted by some generally agreed authorisation procedure under the title 'constitution' (or equivalent rubric such as 'basic law');

[17] A. King, *Does the United Kingdom Still Have a Constitution?* (Sweet & Maxwell 2001) pp. 7–12.

(c) the totality of legal rules, whether contained in statutes, secondary legislation, domestic judicial decisions or binding international instruments or judicial decisions, that affect the working of government;

(d) a list of statutes or instruments that have an entrenched status and can be amended or repealed only by a special procedure.

These are not mutually exclusive definitions: a country may have a constitution in some or all of these senses. The United Kingdom has a constitution in meanings (a) and (c), but not (b) and (d). Some scholars are sceptical whether it makes much difference whether or not there is a 'single instrument' (or 'capital C' constitution), as Anthony King argues:

A. King, *Does the United Kingdom Still Have a Constitution?* (2001, London: Sweet & Maxwell), p. 3

Constitutions [. . .] are never—to repeat, *never*—written down. They might possibly in principle be written down, but in practice they never are. There are, of course, written documents called Constitutions—with a capital 'C'—but they are never, ever coextensive with all of a country's most important rules regulating the relations between different parts of government and those between the government and the people. Constitutions as defined here ['*A constitution is the set of important rules that regulate the relations among the different parts of the government of a given country and also the relations between the different parts of the government and the people of the country*'] and the written documents called Constitutions overlap to a greater or lesser degree. Of course they do: all capital-C Constitutions have at least *some* bearing on how the countries that have them are actually governed. But capital-C Constitutions and small-c constitutions are never the same thing, and sometimes the relationship between the two is quite tenuous (even if, in a given country, the capital-C Constitution is taken seriously).

1.4 SHOULD THE UNITED KINGDOM ADOPT A CODIFIED CONSTITUTION?

So far in this chapter, we have seen that the United Kingdom is unusual in lacking a single, codified Constitution. The union of England, Wales, Scotland, and Northern Ireland rests on historic political settlements given legal effect through Acts of Parliament. Rather than constitutional supremacy, the system rests on the principle of the legislative supremacy of the UK Parliament, which may make and unmake law without restriction from a higher-level code (as we explore in Chapter 3). The United Kingdom is often said to have an 'unwritten constitution', but as we will see in Chapter 2, nearly all its core roles appear in written sources—just not gathered into one, superior text.

1.4.1 PAST OPPORTUNITIES FOR CONSTITUTION DRAFTING IN BRITAIN

There have been several points in British history where the country might have adopted a written constitution. One early landmark was Magna Carta, a charter of liberties issued by King John in 1215 under pressure from rebellious barons. Although it is sometimes described—anachronistically—as an early 'written constitution', Magna Carta is often invoked in modern political debate as a symbol of the rule of law and the idea that rulers are not above the law. As historian Nicholas Vincent puts it, '*The merest glance at the newspapers or at modern political debate reveal the semi-mythical status that Magna Carta still commands in England and the English-speaking world*'.[18] Some provisions of the 1297 version of Magna Carta remain on the statute book today, but they reflect the values of a feudal society, not the framework of a modern constitution.

Another major turning point was the English Civil War and the wider Wars of the Three Kingdoms (1642–51), a series of conflicts across England, Wales, Scotland, and Ireland in which royalist and Parliamentarian forces fought over authority, religion, and the constitution. The wars were devastating: historians estimate that roughly 200,000 people died from fighting, famine, and disease. The upheaval tested the balance of power between Crown and Parliament and stimulated new thinking about government and rights. Among the most radical groups were the Levellers, who argued for government based on popular consent, wider suffrage, and equality before the law.[19] Charles I was tried and executed for treason in 1649, and England (with Wales) was subsequently governed as a Commonwealth before Oliver Cromwell became Lord Protector under the Instrument of Government (1653), often regarded as an early written constitution. The experiment ended with the Restoration of the monarchy in 1660, but it left enduring debates about representation and the limits of executive authority. [20]

A generation later, the Bill of Rights 1688 in England and Wales—formally titled, '*An Act declaring the rights and liberties of the subject and settling the succession of the crown*'—placed legal limits on the power of the new monarchs, William III and Mary II.[21] Geoffrey Lock has called it '*the prime candidate for being regarded as the basic constitutional document of the United Kingdom, in so far as there is one*'. [22] However, it falls far short of providing a comprehensive constitutional code. In Scotland, the Claim of Right 1689 served a similar purpose. It stated that the monarch was subject to the law and affirmed some principles of due process.[23] However, it too is a limited document and incudes anti-Catholic provisions that would not be acceptable in a modern, inclusive constitution.[24]

In the nineteenth century, the working-class Chartist movement campaigned for a more democratic political system, calling for universal male suffrage, annual Parliaments, and a secret ballot.

[18] See N. Vincent, *Magna Carta: A Very Short Introduction* (OUP 2012) p. 2.

[19] A radical current within the Parliamentarian army and London political circles that advocated political reform, wider religious liberty, and equality before the law. The Putney Debates of 1647, in which army officers and elected soldiers' representatives discussed the franchise and the principle of government by consent, are often seen as one of the earliest recorded English discussions of democratic constitutional ideas—though the Levellers' proposals were not adopted.

[20] A radical movement within the Parliamentarian army that demanded political reform, religious tolerance, and equality before the law. In debates held at Putney, soldiers and officers argued over who should have the right to vote and how far government should rest on the consent of the governed; it was one of the earliest public discussions of democratic constitutional ideas in England.

[21] The events known as the Glorious Revolution (1688–89) saw Parliament invite Dutch-born William of Orange and his wife Mary to replace King James II, who was unpopular for his Catholic faith, his efforts to rule without Parliament, and his maintenance of a standing army in peacetime. The transfer of power in England was largely bloodless (James fled to France) but in Ireland and Scotland there was armed resistance as the new regime secured control. Mary was James' daughter.

[22] See G. Lock, 'The 1689 Bill of Rights' (1989) XXXVII *Political Studies* 540.

[23] See D. Edward, 'Scotland's Magna Carta: the Claim of Right and the common law' (2015) 6 *The UK Supreme Court Yearbook* 8.

[24] Definition: Anti-Catholic laws were rules that discriminated against people who belonged to the Roman Catholic Church, a major branch of Christianity. In the UK, such laws were introduced after the sixteenth-century break from the Pope's authority. They were designed to stop Catholics from holding public office or becoming monarch. Even today, the monarch must be Protestant and cannot be Catholic, under the terms of the Act of Settlement 1701. Most other anti-Catholic laws have now been repealed or reformed.

Had its demands been achieved through revolutionary change, Britain might have moved towards a codified constitution, but the movement was suppressed and its petitions rejected. Democratic reform instead proceeded gradually through legislation. The Representation of the People Act 1832 (the 'Great Reform Act') abolished many 'rotten boroughs'—constituencies with very small electorates—and extended the vote to more property-holding men. The Second Reform Act of 1867 enfranchised large numbers of urban working-class men, followed by the Third Reform Act of 1884, which extended voting rights to agricultural labourers. Some women could vote in local elections from 1869, but universal suffrage was not achieved until 1928, after decades of campaigning by suffragists and suffragettes, when women gained the same voting rights as men in parliamentary elections.

So far in the twenty-first century, adopting a written constitution has not been a major item on the UK-wide political agenda. The larger UK political parties do not support such a move.[25]

1.4.2 THE CASE FOR A CODIFIED CONSTITUTION

During the 2010–15 Parliament, the House of Commons Political and Constitutional Reform Committee undertook an inquiry into the pros and cons and implications of codifying the British constitution. The committee worked closely with academics at King's College London to develop proposals, held several oral evidence sessions, and consulted on different options. In their Second Report, the committee set out a short summary of the case for change and the case for retaining the status quo, written by Professor Robert Blackburn.

House of Commons Political and Constitutional Reform, *A New Magna Carta?*, Second Report of 2014–15 (HC 463), p. 19

> The case for a written constitution is that it would enable everyone to know what the rules and institutions were that governed and directed ministers, civil servants and parliamentarians in performing their public duties. The sprawling mass of common law, Acts of Parliament, and European treaty obligations, surrounded by a number of important but sometimes uncertain unwritten conventions, is impenetrable to most people, and needs to be replaced by a single document of basic law dictating the working and operation of government in the United Kingdom easily accessible for all. Furthermore, it has become too easy for governments to implement political and constitutional reforms to suit their own political convenience, and entrenched procedures to ensure popular and parliamentary consent are required that necessitate a written constitution. The present 'unwritten constitution' is an anachronism riddled with references to our ancient past, unsuited to the social and political democracy of the 21st century and future aspirations of its people. It fails to give primacy to the sovereignty of the people and discourages popular participation in the political process. A written constitution would circumscribe the boundaries of the British state and its relationship with Europe and the world. It would become a symbol and expression of national identity today and a source of national pride.

The Committee also outlined three 'illustrative blueprints' or 'basic models' for a written constitution. These usefully show that the options are more nuanced than 'written' or 'not written'.

[25] Among the smaller UK-wide parties, both the Liberal Democrats and the Green Party have expressed support for a written constitution. The Scottish National Party (SNP) has also argued for a written constitution, but only in the context of an independent Scotland. Reform UK has not advocated a codified constitution and generally focuses its constitutional proposals on sovereignty, institutional accountability, and public administration rather than formal codification.

House of Commons Political and Constitutional Reform, *A New Magna Carta?*, Second Report of 2014-15 (HC 463), p. 7

(a) Constitutional Code—a document sanctioned by Parliament but without statutory authority, setting out the essential existing elements and principles of the constitution and workings of government.

(b) Constitutional Consolidation Act—a consolidation of existing laws of a constitutional nature in statute, the common law and parliamentary practice, together with a codification of essential constitutional conventions.

(c) Written Constitution—a document of basic law by which the United Kingdom is governed, including the relationship between the state and its citizens, an amendment procedure, and elements of reform.

1.4.3 THE CASE AGAINST A CODIFIED CONSTITUTION

Some commentators explain the UK's resistance to codification in terms of what has been called the 'conservative disposition'—a general preference for continuity, tradition, and gradual change. Political philosopher Michael Oakeshott described this as a tendency to value 'the familiar to the unknown,' especially in matters of government. From this perspective, the British constitution's flexibility is not a weakness but a strength. It reflects an evolutionary political culture that trusts long-standing practice over abstract design. For those with this view, attempts to fix the constitution in a single text risk importing unnecessary rigidity and undermining the adaptability that has historically contributed to the system's stability.[26] In the following extract, a parliamentary committee sets out the case for retaining the current uncodified arrangements.

House of Commons Political and Constitutional Reform, *A New Magna Carta?*, Second Report of 2014-15 (HC 463), p. 24

The case against a written constitution is that it is unnecessary, undesirable and un-British. The fact that the UK system of government has never been reduced to a single document is an indication of the success of the Westminster system of parliamentary democracy and the stability it has brought to the country. This contrasts with most other countries whose written constitutions were the product of revolution or independence. The unwritten nature of the constitution is something distinctively British, it reminds us of a great history, and is a source of national pride. Contrary to claims that it is out of date, it is evolutionary and flexible in nature, more easily enabling practical problems to be resolved as they arise and individual reforms made, than would be the case under an entrenched constitutional document. While some are concerned about the supposed existence of an 'elective dictatorship' and inadequate checks and balances in the political system, there is in fact a wide range of considerable pressures exerted upon ministers seeking to make controversial changes. A written constitution would create more litigation in the courts, and politicise the judiciary, requiring them to pass judgement on the constitutionality of government legislation, when the final word on legal matters should lie with elected politicians in Parliament, not unelected judges. There are so many practical problems inherent in preparing and enacting a written constitution, there is little point in considering the matter. As a public policy

[26] See further Graham Gee and Grégoire Webber, 'A Conservative Disposition and Constitutional Change' (2019) 39 *Oxford Journal of Legal Studies* 526.

proposal it lacks [sic] any depth of genuine popular support and, especially given the massive amount of time such a reform would entail, it is a very low priority even for those who support the idea. An attempt to introduce one would be a distraction and might well have a destabilizing effect on the country.

In March 2015, the committee published a final report.

House of Commons Political and Constitutional Reform, *Consultation on a New Magna Carta?*, Seventh Report, Session 2014–15 (HC 599)

55. In our original report we presented the arguments for and against constitutional codification and a written constitution, to assist those considering the matter to make up their minds one way or the other. While the balance of views expressed to us favours some form of codification in general, and a written constitution in particular, we do not propose here to endorse or to amend one particular model or blueprint. Our purpose has been to set out the arguments and to illustrate how codification might be achieved.

56. As Professor Blackburn has made clear in his paper on the design and implementation of a codified constitution, the initiative for codification lies with the executive. The involvement, for the first time, of a parliamentary committee in inquiring into the basis of the UK's constitutional arrangements and illustrating options for codification has received a broad welcome. The practical illustrations we have provided, together with the informed commentaries on the exercise, should serve as a resource for an incoming administration which has constitutional codification as a policy priority: much of the practical work of examination and description of the existing constitutional arrangements has been achieved.

57. As vital as the debate about whether and how to codify the constitution is the debate about what constitutional arrangements it is desirable to codify. The three illustrations of models of codification which we published have been grounded in practical politics and the maintenance, as far as possible, of the status quo: where the written constitution blueprint described elements of reform, it did so on the basis of existing proposals for reform. We deliberately did not set out to propose constitutional codification allied with radical constitutional reform, but we recognise that an element of constitutional change may well be necessary in any process of codification. Moreover, we recognise that the broadest possible public debate about constitutional alternatives must form the basis of any process of large-scale constitutional change which genuinely seeks the engagement and consent of the public.

EXERCISE: A CITIZENS' ASSEMBLY ON A WRITTEN CONSTITUTION

Imagine the United Kingdom decides to hold a nationwide Citizens' Assembly to consider whether the UK should adopt a written (codified) constitution. You have been selected to represent your region. Before the Assembly begins its discussions, participants are invited to write a short personal reflection (around 300–400 words) setting out their initial thoughts on the question. In your reflection:

- Define and explain what a written constitution is, and how it differs from the UK's existing arrangements.

- Select and analyze the strongest arguments for and against adopting one, explaining why you find them persuasive.
- Compare and illustrate your reasoning with one or two examples from other countries or from the UK's constitutional history.
- Evaluate and conclude with your own considered view: should the UK move towards a codified constitution, and why? In doing so, consider how different nations and communities across the UK—and people whose rights or identities might be affected by reform—might view the issue.

1.5 UNDERSTANDING THE RISE AND FALL OF THE BRITISH EMPIRE

In 2020, the UK Government commissioned an independent review by Wendy Williams into the Windrush scandal. Thousands of long-term UK residents from Commonwealth countries[27] who had arrived legally as children in the decades after the Second World War were wrongly classified as illegal immigrants by the Home Office. Lacking formal paperwork, they lost jobs and housing, were denied welfare benefits and healthcare, and in some cases were detained or removed to countries they had not visited since childhood. Williams recommended that the Home Office ensure civil servants understand Britain's colonial history.

Independent Review by Wendy Williams, *Windrush Lessons Learned Review,* March 2020, HC 93, p. 139

Tell the stories of empire, Windrush and its legacy

The Windrush scandal was in part able to happen because of the public's and officials' poor understanding of Britain's colonial history, the history of inward and outward migration, and the history of black Britons. A lack of institutional memory or comprehensive understanding of the impact of the complex immigration situation created by successive legislative changes, set against an unwillingness or inability to learn from past mistakes, or to engage with experts and local communities, has compounded this situation. Officials need to understand the past to inform the present and the future of immigration policy.

In September 2024, responding to this recommendation, the Home Office published *The Historical Roots of the Windrush Scandal: Independent Research Report*. This online publication is a valuable resource for anyone seeking to understand how empire and colonisation continue to shape British society. It is included in our Further Reading at the end of this chapter. The United Kingdom's constitutional system cannot be understood without considering the history and legacy of empire. This section offers a concise overview of key developments that are particularly relevant to constitutional change.

For over three centuries, British law and government extended far beyond *Great Britain and Ireland*. From 1801 to 1922, Ireland was formally part of the United Kingdom; yet many historians argue that Ireland was governed in ways that closely resembled colonial rule, shaped by settlement,

[27] The Commonwealth of Nations is a voluntary association of 56 countries, most of which have historical links to the former British Empire, and it developed in its modern form from the 1949 London Declaration.

coercion, and economic and cultural control. Understanding this dual character is important, because it influenced later imperial policies elsewhere and continues to inform debates about identity and constitutional history.[28]

At its height in the early twentieth century, the British Empire governed around 400 million people—roughly a quarter of the world's population—through a system in which London acted as the imperial centre.[29] The Westminster Parliament legislated for many colonies, the Crown appointed governors and exercised executive authority, and the Judicial Committee of the Privy Council was the final court of appeal for much of the empire. The character and consequences of the empire remain the subject of continuing debate.

The empire was never a single or uniform structure. A small group of colonies—Canada, Australia, New Zealand, and South Africa—became dominions, exercising extensive self-government under the Crown through political systems modelled on Westminster institutions. Their autonomy was affirmed by the Statute of Westminster 1931, which confirmed that no dominion laws would be invalid because of inconsistency with an Act of the United Kingdom. In these territories, European settlers established new political orders that displaced and marginalized Indigenous peoples through violence, dispossession, and policies of assimilation. In Britain, the dominions were often presented as evidence of imperial success, yet their histories reveal profound inequalities of power that continue to inform debates about sovereignty, reconciliation, and constitutional identity.

India occupied a particularly complex place within the empire. It was governed first by the East India Company and, after 1858, directly by the British Crown, alongside hundreds of semi-autonomous princely states. From the late nineteenth century, Indian reformers, lawyers, and political organizations—including the Indian National Congress, founded in 1885—pressed for fuller participation in government. British administrators responded with limited constitutional reforms that introduced advisory and representative institutions, enabling only a small number of Indian members to influence policy. The Government of India Act 1919 created provincial legislatures with Indian ministers responsible for certain areas of administration, and the Government of India Act 1935 went further by providing for elected provincial governments and a proposed federal system, although the federal scheme was never brought into force. These measures projected an image of partnership while retaining British control over defence, finance, and external affairs. Coercion and state violence also remained central to imperial rule, exemplified by the Jallianwala Bagh (Amritsar) massacre of 1919, which strengthened demands for full independence. The escalating conflict between imperial authority and movements for self-rule ultimately ended British rule in 1947, when India gained independence and the subcontinent was partitioned into India and Pakistan.

Elsewhere, colonies were administered directly from London through governors and imperial officials. In many territories—particularly in parts of Africa and the Caribbean—British administrators relied on local intermediaries, such as traditional rulers or appointed chiefs, to collect taxes, enforce laws, and maintain order. Across these regions, imperial rule introduced legal and administrative systems designed to advance British political and economic interests. Law often formalized racial hierarchy, differentiating Europeans from colonized peoples in rights, legal status, and access to justice. Christianity also formed part of the imperial project: missionaries established schools, courts, and churches that promoted certain ideas of education and morality while supporting British authority and cultural norms. This interaction of religion, law, and empire reshaped local governance and family life in ways that continue to have visible effects today.

[28] See J. Ohlmeyer, 'Laboratory', in *Making Empire: Ireland, Imperialism, and the Early Modern World* (OUP 2023; online edn, Oxford Academic, 24 August 2023) https://doi.org/10.1093/oso/9780192867681.003.0005 accessed 16 October 2025.

[29] For an introduction, see A. Jackson, *The British Empire: A Very Short Introduction* (Oxford University Press 2013) and T O Lloyd, *The British Empire 1558–1995* (Oxford University Press 1996).

The empire's decline was gradual but irreversible. Two world wars weakened Britain's global position and strengthened movements for independence. India and Pakistan became independent in 1947, followed by a wider process of decolonization across Africa, the Caribbean, and Asia. After 1945, international recognition of the right of peoples to self-determination—set out in the Charter of the United Nations 1945—gave additional momentum to these movements and helped frame independence as a legal as well as political process. The transfer of sovereignty took different forms, including Acts of Parliament, Orders in Council, and negotiated constitutions. In 1949, the Commonwealth of Nations emerged as a voluntary association of states that were, at least in principle, equal in status. The Judicial Committee of the Privy Council continued and in some cases still continues to serve as the final court of appeal for several Commonwealth states and for the UK's remaining Overseas Territories.

Empire building was always contested. Throughout the nineteenth century, politicians, writers, and activists argued over its moral, political, and economic foundations, and these debates continue today.[30] Some scholars, such as Nigel Biggar, contend that although British rule caused serious harm, it also introduced legal and administrative practices—including certain understandings of the rule of law—and therefore requires what he calls a measured 'moral reckoning' rather than outright condemnation.[31] Others, including Caroline Elkins, reject this balance-sheet view.[32] They argue that the violence, dispossession, and racial hierarchy embedded in imperial systems make such weighing impossible. Their work, along with post-colonial and critical race theorists, highlights how imperial legacies persist in global inequality and racialized patterns of policing, imprisonment, and economic disadvantage. As public lawyers, the task is not to resolve these historical disputes but to recognize how arguments about empire continue to shape law, governance, and constitutional language.

Empire-building also relied on constitutional law. Ideas that still shape UK public law—such as parliamentary supremacy, the rule of law, and the Crown's prerogative powers—were carried into colonial administrations and used to organize government across the empire. British officials claimed that these principles promoted order and civilization, yet they were also invoked to justify conquest and racially structured systems of authority.[33] In many territories, the spread of British law curtailed or displaced Indigenous legal traditions and reshaped existing systems of power.

Writing in 2025, Vidya Kumar noted that '*there has been very little engagement with race, racism, colonisation and empire in UK public law textbooks*'.[34] The movement to address this gap is often described as 'decolonizing the curriculum'. As Folúké Adébísí explains, this phrase covers a wide spectrum of activity, from work 'that merely *acknowledges* the colonial nature of the discipline [of law]' to more radical political efforts that seek 'to *disrupt* and *dismantle* the colonial nature of the world'.[35]

[30] Nicholas Owen, 'Critics of Empire in Britain' in Andrew Porter (ed), *The Oxford History of the British Empire: The Nineteenth Century* (OUP 1999) 188.

[31] Nigel Biggar, *Colonialism: A Moral Reckoning* (William Collins 2025); Niall Ferguson offers a similar perspective, finding benefits in the spread of relatively incorrupt administration and commercial infrastructure: Niall Ferguson, *Empire: How Britain Made the Modern World* (Allen Lane 2003).

[32] Caroline Elkins, *Legacy of Violence: A History of the British Empire* (Random House 2022); Alan Lester, 'Time to Throw Out the Balance Sheet?' *Snapshots of Empire* (Blog, 26 January 2016) https://blogs.sussex.ac.uk/snapshotsofempire/2016/01/26/time-to-throw-out-the-balance-sheet/ accessed 16 October 2025.

[33] Definition: *race* refers to social, not biological, ways of classifying people by perceived physical or cultural traits. Such classifications have long reinforced hierarchies of power. *Racialized* describes the process by which people are defined or treated through these socially created ideas of race, highlighting that inequality arises from institutions and social practice, not from nature.

[34] Vidya Kumar, 'Race and UK Public Law' [2025] *Public Law* 201, 202.

[35] Folúké Adébísí, *Decolonisation and Legal Knowledge: Reflections on Power and Possibility* (Bristol University Press 2024) p. 11.

She warns that decolonization in law schools should not become a tick-box exercise and encourages academics and students '*to do something, personal, provable, and practical toward decolonisation*'.[36]

Understanding colonial legacies helps us make sense of how the UK's public institutions and legal ideas developed. Many features of today's constitution—including the Home Office, immigration controls, policing structures, and forms of executive power—took shape while Britain governed a global empire. Courts also continue to deal with issues that have their roots in that history, such as citizenship, nationality, and the status of overseas territories. Seeing these connections helps us understand that public law has changed over time and was shaped by unequal power relationships as well as democratic reform. This historical awareness provides helpful context for studying concepts like parliamentary sovereignty,[37] the rule of law,[38] and accountability,[39] and encourages a more informed discussion about how state power affects different communities today.

PAUSE FOR REFLECTION: WHOSE KNOWLEDGE COUNTS?

Decolonising the curriculum encourages teachers and students to reconsider where legal ideas come from and whose perspectives are represented. When we study 'British' public law today, what questions about inclusion, authority, and the distribution of power should we keep in mind?

1.6 LOOKING BACK, LOOKING AHEAD

The UK's constitution continues to evolve. Recent debates over withdrawal from the European Union,[40] the Human Rights Act, public standards, and the distribution of power between Westminster and the devolved nations show that constitutional law is never fixed. These disputes raise the same enduring questions: who should hold power, how should it be checked, and in whose interests? They remind us that core principles—accountability, fairness, and respect for the rule of law—must be renewed by each generation and tested in new circumstances. Studying public law is therefore not only about the past but about shaping how power is used, shared, and restrained in the future.

In the next chapter we turn to 'the rule-book'—the main legal sources of the UK constitution—and consider how this complex, evolving system of statutes, conventions, and judicial decisions fits together.

[36] Folúké Adébísí, *Decolonisation and Legal Knowledge: Reflections on Power and Possibility* (Bristol University Press 2024) pp. 137, 136. In that spirit, we recognize that earlier editions of this book paid limited attention to the dynamics of racialization and colonialism. In explaining features of the modern British constitution, we did not sufficiently address how the legacies of the British Empire continue to shape public law. In this edition we have sought to be more attentive to those legacies, drawing on the work of scholars who have developed research, teaching, and institutional change in collaboration with their students. The pedagogic project of decolonization is ongoing: it depends on sustained dialogue, reflection, and shared learning. See, for example, Dave S.P. Thomas and Suhraiya Jivraj for the Decolonise University of Kent Collective (eds), *Towards Decolonising the University: A Kaleidoscope of Empowered Action* (Counterpress 2020); LSE Change Makers, *Diversifying and Decolonising the Law Curriculum: Full Report 2020–21* (London School of Economics and Political Science 2021) https://info.lse.ac.uk/current-students/part-of-lse/assets/documents/Change-makers/research-archive/2020-21/26b-Diversifying-Decolonising-Full-Report.pdf accessed 10 October 2025; Hannah Gibson and Kyle Jerro, '*Decolonising the curriculum at Essex: What? Why? How*' (University of Essex Blog, 11 June 2020) https://www.essex.ac.uk/blog/posts/2020/06/11/decolonising-the-curriculum-at-essex-what-why-how

[37] See Chapter 3 (section 3.8). [38] See Chapter 2 (section 2.3.1). [39] See Chapter 9.

[40] The UK left the European Union in 2020 after a 2016 referendum, ending more than forty years of shared law-making with other European countries.

FURTHER READING

Loughlin, M., *The British Constitution: A Very Short Introduction* (2013, OUP). A concise but sophisticated introduction.

King, J., 'The democratic case for a written constitution' (2019) 72 *Current Legal Problems* 1. Argues that codification would strengthen democratic accountability by clarifying constitutional norms and protecting core values from political erosion.

Murkens, J. E. K., 'A written constitution: A case not made' (2021) 41 *Oxford Journal of Legal Studies* 965. Assesses different proposals for a written constitution and problematizes the process of constitution-making.

Gordon, R., *Repairing British Politics: A Blueprint for Constitutional Change* (2024, 2nd edn, Hart Publishing). Sets out arguments for and against a written constitution and presents a working draft of a possible model.

Adébísí, F., *Decolonisation and Legal Knowledge: Reflections on Power and Possibility* (2023, Bristol University Press). Explores how colonial legacies continue to shape what counts as legal knowledge, calling for a more globally inclusive approach to legal education.

Wheatle, S. and O'Loughlin, E. (eds), *Diverse Voices in Public Law* (2024, Bristol University Press). Addresses how constitutional structures and reforms affect different communities, with a focus on inclusivity and critical scholarship.

Home Office, *The Historical Roots of the Windrush Scandal: independent research report* (2024) https://www.gov.uk/government/publications/the-historical-roots-of-the-windrush-scandal

2

THE CONSTITUTIONAL RULEBOOK

CENTRAL ISSUES

1. Where do the United Kingdom's constitutional rules come from? The UK has no single written constitution, so its fundamental rules appear in Acts of Parliament, judicial decisions, and constitutional conventions. International treaties are also influential. Understanding how these sources fit together is key to understanding how the constitution operates.
2. What makes a statute 'constitutional'? Some Acts of Parliament—such as the Human Rights Act 1998 and the Scotland Act 1998—shape how public power is organized and limited. Do courts treat these differently from ordinary legislation?
3. To what extent can the common law act as a constitutional safeguard? Judges have long developed principles like access to justice and fairness through case law. Should we see these as part of an unwritten 'common law constitution'?
4. Why do conventions matter if they are not law? Many of the most important constitutional rules—such as collective ministerial responsibility or the monarch's political neutrality—exist only as conventions. What gives them authority, and what happens when they are ignored?
5. How does international law influence the UK constitution? Treaties such as the European Convention on Human Rights or the Good Friday Agreement bind the UK internationally, but Parliament remains sovereign. How should conflicts between international obligations and domestic law be resolved?
6. Who should be trusted to uphold the constitution—politicians or judges? Political constitutionalists emphasize Parliament and elections; legal constitutionalists give greater weight to courts and rights. Which approach offers stronger protection for democracy and the rule of law in an uncodified system?

2.1 THE UK CONSTITUTION'S MULTIPLE SOURCES

In Chapter 1, you learned that the United Kingdom does not have a codified Constitution. To understand what that means in practice, it helps to see how the Supreme Court itself describes the nature of the UK's constitutional order. In *Miller* (a case about whether the government could trigger the legal process for leaving the EU without an Act of Parliament), the Court set out the main sources of constitutional authority and highlighted how they have emerged over time. The following passage introduces this idea in the Court's own words.

R (on the application of Miller) v Secretary of State for Exiting the European Union
[2017] UKSC 5, [40]

Unlike most countries, the United Kingdom does not have a constitution in the sense of a single coherent code of fundamental law which prevails over all other sources of law. Our constitutional arrangements have developed over time in a pragmatic as much as in a principled way, through a combination of statutes, events, conventions, academic writings and judicial decisions. Reflecting its development and its contents, the UK constitution was described by the constitutional scholar, Professor AV Dicey, as 'the most flexible polity in existence' – *Introduction to the Study of the Law of the Constitution* (8th ed, 1915), p. 87.

This chapter will help you locate, interpret, and evaluate the sources of constitutional rules. By the end, you should be able to explain how they interact to structure the state, limit power, and uphold fundamental rights.

A good starting point is *The Cabinet Manual*, published by the government in 2011 to set out clearly in one place '*the internal rules and procedures under which the Government operates*'. It is regarded as an authoritative guide to parts of the constitution, but it has no legal force.[1] In the following extract, it explains the sources of the constitution.

Cabinet Office, *The Cabinet Manual*, 1st edn (2011, London: Cabinet Office), p. 2

The UK does not have a codified constitution. There is no single document that describes, establishes or regulates the structures of the state and the way in which these relate to the people. Instead, the constitutional order has evolved over time and continues to do so. It consists of various institutions, statutes, judicial decisions, principles and practices that are commonly understood as 'constitutional'. The UK does not have a constitutional court to rule on the implications of a codified constitution, and the sovereignty of Parliament is therefore unrestrained by such a court [. . .]

2.1.1 CONFLICTS OVER RULES, RIGHTS, AND PRINCIPLES

The UK constitutional system is not static. Even when most standards are clear, disagreement and contestation are part of how public law develops. Such disagreements often reveal deeper questions about who has the power to define and enforce the rules that govern state authority.
Conflicts may arise for different reasons.

[1] In 2021, the House of Lords Constitution Committee issued a report: *Revision of the Cabinet Manual*, 6th Report of Session 2021–22, HL Paper 34. This noted that 'As a matter of constitutional principle, ensuring adherence to the content of the Manual, in general terms, will ultimately be a matter for the Prime Minister' and recommended when a new edition is published, the Prime Minister should make clear 'the duty on all ministers to adhere to the constructional principles in the Cabinet Manual' (paras 19–20). The Constitution Committee called for an updated version to be published after every general election.

Sometimes there is disagreement about the *content of a rule, right, or principle*—what it means or what it should mean.[2] For example, in 2013 the UK Supreme Court had to decide whether it could hold part of a hearing in closed session, excluding one party, while the justices examined highly sensitive evidence about national security.[3] This went to the heart of constitutional principles about fair trials and open justice. All nine Justices sat; a majority accepted that a closed session was legally possible in exceptional circumstances, while others dissented, warning that it risked undermining public confidence in the courts.

Controversy may also arise about *who* should have power to make, change, interpret, or repeal a rule, right or principle. For instance, after the 2016 referendum on leaving the European Union, a dispute arose over whether the government could, on its own, notify the EU of the UK's intention to withdraw (under Article 50 of the Treaty on European Union), or whether Parliament had to give express legal authority to government to do this through an Act. The issue reached the courts. Both the Administrative Court and, on appeal, the Supreme Court held that such authorisation was required from Parliament. The courts' decision provoked strong reactions. Some newspapers attacked the judges as 'enemies of the people' for interfering in politics. Yet the case illustrates the judiciary's constitutional duty to ensure that the government acts within the limits of the law. In the following extract, the Administrative Court explains the legal foundation for that duty and how the ordinary courts approach constitutional questions.[4]

R. (on the application of Miller) v Secretary of State for Exiting the European Union

[2016] EWHC 2768 (Admin), Lord Thomas of Cwmgiedd CJ, Sir Terence Etherton MR and Sales LJ, [18]

> The United Kingdom does not have a constitution to be found entirely in a written document. This does not mean there is an absence of a constitution or constitutional law. On the contrary, the United Kingdom has its own form of constitutional law, as recognised in each of the jurisdictions of the four constituent nations. Some of it is written, in the form of statutes which have particular constitutional importance [. . .] Some of it is reflected in fundamental rules of law recognised by both Parliament and the courts. There are established and well-recognised legal rules which govern the exercise of public power and which distribute decision-making authority between different entities in the state and define the extent of their respective powers. The United Kingdom is a constitutional democracy framed by legal rules and subject to the rule of law. The courts have a constitutional duty fundamental to the rule of law in a democratic state to enforce rules of constitutional law in the same way as the courts enforce other laws.

The *Miller* litigation underlined a basic feature of the UK constitution: government is subject to law. Courts ensure that ministers and public bodies act within the limits set by Acts of Parliament and the common law, and this legal accountability is an important strand of the rule of law.[5] At the same time, the scope of that judicial role is contested. Political constitutionalists argue that, in a parliamentary system, many constitutional questions are better resolved through political processes rather than by judges.

[2] In public law, a rule is a clear, binding instruction that applies in set situations (for example, that a bill must receive Royal Assent before it becomes an Act). A right is an entitlement that a person or group can rely on, such as freedom of expression or the right to a fair hearing. A principle is a broader guiding idea—like the rule of law or fairness—that helps courts and officials interpret and apply rules and rights in particular cases.

[3] *Bank Mellat v HM Treasury (No 1)* [2013] UKSC 38; and see further Chapter 22.

[4] *R (Miller) v Secretary of State for Exiting the European Union* [2017] UKSC 5.

[5] See Chapter 4.

Even more fundamentally, there is disagreement over who made and who would have power to change a rule that is the central feature of the UK constitution: parliamentary supremacy. As we will see in Chapter 3, some judges and academics contend that this is a common law rule that the judiciary alone could change; another school of thought is that any modification to the principle would require a broad consensus across the judiciary, Parliament, and government.

2.1.2 OVERVIEW OF SOURCES

Taking stock, in the United Kingdom's uncodified constitutional rulebook, where should you look for '*the set of important rules*' that form the constitutional framework? Some of the answers are in Table 2.1.

Table 2.1 Sources of constitutional rules in the United Kingdom

Source of rule	Who makes the rule	Process by which rule is made	Where to find the rules
Acts of Parliament	Members of the House of Commons (elected) and House of Lords (unelected)	Government lawyers draft bills; both Houses scrutinize and amend them; a bill becomes law once it has completed the legislative process and received Royal Assent	www.legislation.gov.uk. Rules of constitutional importance contained in Acts of Parliament often need explanation from textbooks, academic articles, and other expert commentary.
The common law	Judges of the higher courts in England and Wales, Scotland, Northern Ireland, and the UK Supreme Court	Judges decide cases and give written reasons. Over time, these decisions build up a body of binding legal rules and principles.	The National Archives (https://caselaw.nationalarchives.gov.uk/) or law reports. Because the volume is large, students benefit from using textbooks or other guides.
Constitutional conventions	Politicians and civil servants	Developed through consistent practice, where people behave in a certain way because they believe they ought to. Conventions are considered binding but are not enforced by courts.	There is no official list of all conventions. *The Cabinet Manual* is a good starting point, www.gov.uk/government/publications/cabinet-manual. Textbooks and academic writing are essential for understanding them.
International treaties ratified by the United Kingdom	Diplomats (politically neutral officials) working on behalf of the government	The UK government negotiates treaties with other states or international bodies. A treaty only affects domestic law if Parliament incorporates it into an Act.	www.gov.uk/guidance/uk-treaties. Useful commentary is found in textbooks and academic writing.

In the rest of this chapter, we examine each of these sources in turn—how they work, how they interact, and how they shape the balance between government power and individual rights.

2.2 CONSTITUTIONAL STATUTES

'The statute book' refers to all the Acts of Parliament that have received Royal Assent—the final stage of the legislative process—and which are in either force or awaiting commencement.[6] In the absence of a codified Constitution, Acts of Parliament are the highest form of law in the United Kingdom. This section develops the discussion in three stages. First, it identifies which statutes can be regarded as constitutional. Second, it explores what follows from that classification. Finally, it considers how suitable it is for a country's constitutional rules to appear within in Acts of Parliament.

2.2.1 IDENTIFYING CONSTITUTIONAL STATUTES

In 2003, a parliamentary committee was appointed to examine proposals for new emergency powers allowing ministers to make regulations to disapply or amend Acts of Parliament in response to threats of serious harm to human welfare, the environment, or national security arising from war or terrorism. The committee warned that such sweeping powers, '*in the wrong hands, ... could be used to remove all past legislation which makes up the statutory patchwork of the British constitution*'.[7] Its report identified twenty-one statutes that it regarded as forming 'the fundamental parts of constitutional law', the last of which was the draft bill then under scrutiny. The resulting Civil Contingencies Act 2004 provides in section 23 states that emergency regulations may not be made in relation to that Act itself or to the Human Rights Act 1998. Here is the committee's list of constitutional statutes:

1. Magna Carta 1297
2. Bill of Rights 1688
3. Crown and Parliament Recognition Act 1689
4. Act of Settlement 1700
5. Union with Scotland Act 1707
6. Union with Ireland Act 1800
7. Parliament Acts 1911–49
8. Life Peerages Act 1958
9. Emergency Powers Act 1964
10. European Communities Act 1972 (repealed in 2020)
11. House of Commons Disqualification Act 1975
12. Ministerial and Other Salaries Act 1975
13. British Nationality Act 1981
14. Supreme Court Act 1981 (now called the Senior Courts Act 1981)
15. Representation of the People Act 1983
16. Government of Wales Act 1998

[6] See Chapter 12.

[7] Joint Committee on the draft Civil Contingencies Bill, First Report of 2002–03 (HL Paper 184/HC Paper 1074), para. 183.

17. Human Rights Act 1998
18. Northern Ireland Act 1998
19. Scotland Act 1998
20. House of Lords Act 1999
21. Civil Contingencies Act 2004.

The committee offered no definition of what counts as constitutional and noted that '*the Minister argued that it is not possible to define a category of constitutional legislation which ought to be protected by amendment*'. Arguably, there are some omissions from the committees list, for example the Freedom of Information Act 2000, or any legislation dealing with the structure and powers of local authorities. Since the committee's report, further Acts that may be viewed as constitutional have been enacted, for example:[8]

22. Constitutional Reform Act 2005
23. Tribunals, Courts and Enforcement Act 2007
24. Parliamentary Standards Act 2009
25. Constitutional Reform and Governance Act 2010
26. Localism Act 2011
27. Recall of MPs Act 2015
28. House of Lords (Expulsion and Suspension) Act 2015
29. Scotland Act 2016
30. Wales Act 2017
31. European Union (Notification of Withdrawal) Act 2017
32. European Union (Withdrawal) Act 2018
33. European Union (Withdrawal Agreement) Act 2020
34. Dissolution and Calling of Parliament Act 2022
35. Safety of Rwanda (Asylum and Immigration) Act 2024 (repealed in 2025)
36. House of Lords (Hereditary Peers) Act 2025
37. Public Office (Accountability) Act 2026
38. English Devolution and Community Empowerment Act 2026

In both Parliament and the courts, the identification of constitutional statutes has often followed a 'you know it when you see it' approach, rather than seeking to apply a technical definition. Academic writers have attempted to bring more precision, though there is no unanimity in definitions.[9] Tarunabh Khaitan observes that Acts may use the term 'constitution' in their short title, pointing to the Constitutional Reform Act 2005 and the Constitutional Reform and Governance Act 2010.[10]

[8] This list reflects the authors' own judgement rather than any official classification. Your lecturers may take a different view, and you are encouraged to compare and debate alternative selections.

[9] See further: A. Blick, D. Howarth and N. le Roux, *Distinguishing Constitutional Legislation: A Modest Proposal* (The Constitution Society 2014); J. McGarry and S. Spence, 'Constitutional statutes – roots and recognition' (2020) 41 *Statute Law Review* 378; A. Psygkas, 'The United Kingdom's Statutory Constitution' (2020) 40 *Oxford Journal of Legal Studies* 449.

[10] A *short title* is the official name by which an Act of Parliament may be cited, usually given in the final section of the Act (for example, 'This Act may be cited as the Constitutional Reform Act 2005').

He notes that 'There is no requirement that a statute must come packaged and labelled as "constitutional" to be recognised as such'. But is using the 'constitutional' in the short title sufficient?

Tarunabh Khaitan, '"Constitution" as a statutory term' (2013) *Law Quarterly Review* 589, 596-7

> ... a Parliamentary characterisation of a statute as constitutional is likely to be relevant to—although not determinative of—judicial determination of its status. However, both statutes [he is referring to the Northern Ireland Act 1998 and the Scotland Act 1998] were passed recently, around the same time as the judges had begun carving a special category of 'constitutional statutes'. In using the term in titles of these two statutes, Parliament is unlikely to have been aware of a legally distinct category of constitutional statutes, let alone any intention to characterise them as such. Thus, while Parliamentary characterisation of these statutes as constitutional may dispose judges to use special interpretive approaches towards their provisions, it will be unlikely, without more, to persuade them that it should also be immune from implied repeal.

What would a workable definition look like? David Feldman suggests that '*constitutional legislation establishes state institutions and confers functions, responsibilities and powers on them. Such legislation constitutes the state and lays out its structure. . . . [T]he key function of a constitution is (in my view) to constitute the state and its institutions and confer functions, powers and duties on them*'.[11] Ahmed and Perry argue that this is 'over inclusive', since it would classify legislation such as the Coroners and Justice Act 2009 and the Crown Prosecution Service Inspectorate Act 2000 as constitutional—when few would regard them in that way. They propose the following alternative.

Farrah Ahmed and Adam Perry, 'Constitutional statutes' (2017) *Oxford Journal of Legal Studies* 461, 471

> ... our definition of a constitutional statute is easy to state. A constitutional statute is a statute at least a part of which (1) creates or regulates a state institution; and (2) is among the most important elements of our government arrangements, in terms of (a) the influence it has on what state institutions can and may do, given our other governing norms; and (b) the influence it has on what state institutions can and may do, through the difference it makes to our other norms. Simplifying a bit, a constitutional statute is a statute that is about state institutions and which substantially influences, directly or indirectly, what those institutions can and may do.

Feldman, and Ahmed and Perry, define constitutional statutes mainly by looking at institutions, not at the rights of individuals. In *Thoburn v Sunderland City Council*, discussed in the next section, Laws LJ shifts the focus to the relationship between the state and its citizens, and to how constitutional statutes help to protect fundamental rights.[12]

[11] D. Feldman, 'The nature and significance of "constitutional" legislation' (2013) 129 *Law Quarterly Review* 343, 350.
[12] [2002] EWHC 195 (Admin), [2003] QB 151.

2.2.2 WHAT FOLLOWS FROM CLASSIFYING A STATUTE AS CONSTITUTIONAL?

Having explored what counts as a constitutional statute, we now need to ask: so what? What difference does it make if a bill—or the Act that results from it—is regarded as *constitutional*? To answer this, we need to consider the implications for both Parliament and the courts.

Let's start with Parliament. It might seem reasonable to expect constitutional bills to receive enhanced scrutiny as they progress through the legislative process. The House of Lords Constitution Committee goes further, arguing that Parliament should be able to scrutinise a draft bill and suggest improvements before the start of the formal lawmaking process: '*Significant constitutional legislation should be subject to pre-legislative scrutiny. This requirement should be departed from only in exceptional circumstances*'.[13] By convention, bills of first-class constitutional importance have their committee stage on the floor of the House of Commons chamber, allowing all MPs to take part rather than leaving scrutiny to a smaller Public Bill Committee.[14] Successive governments, however, have resisted the idea that there is a clearly defined category of constitutional legislation. In 2011, the Deputy Prime Minister (Liberal Democrat MP Nick Clegg), responding to another House of Lords Constitution Committee recommending that '*a clear and consistent process should apply to all significant change*', wrote:

Deputy Prime Minister, The Government Response to the House of Lords Constitution Committee Report 'The Process of Constitutional Change' Cm 8181 (2011) paras 2–3

> The Government notes that the Committee does not offer a definition of 'constitutional'. The Government sees this as a significant problem in introducing a special process for 'constitutional' legislation. There is a further difficulty in that the origins of 'constitutional' legislation may vary greatly. For example, a proposal may have been included as a direct manifesto commitment on which a new Government was elected.[15] By contrast, something like the response to the parliamentary expenses scandal needed to be done quickly.[16] There would have been no public understanding if the then Government had suggested that it needed to do two years research and public consultation before deciding what to do about the MPs' expenses regime. Not all constitutional change is discretionary; some is driven, as in all policy areas, by events.

This exchange highlights a recurring tension in UK constitutional practice: while many argue that constitutional measures deserve special handling, governments often prioritise political expediency and flexibility over procedural safeguards.

[13] House of Lords, *Legislative standards of the Constitution Committee: 2017–2024* (May 2025) p.5 https://committees.parliament.uk/publications/47701/documents/249210/default/ accessed 20 October 2025.

[14] See Chapter 12.

[15] Mr Clegg was probably referring to two Liberal Democrat manifesto commitments on constitutional reform that were carried into the 2010 coalition agreement with the Conservatives. The first was to introduce fixed-term Parliaments, removing the Prime Minister's discretion to call a general election. This led to the Fixed-term Parliaments Act 2011, which proved unworkable and was later repealed by the Dissolution and Calling of Parliament Act 2022. The second was to replace the first-past-the-post voting system for the House of Commons with the Alternative Vote. That proposal was rejected by 68 per cent of voters in the referendum held in 2011.

[16] The MPs' expenses scandal in 2009 exposed widespread misuse of parliamentary allowances by Members of Parliament, leading to resignations, criminal prosecutions, and major reforms to the system of expenses and oversight.

Turning to the courts: what follows from classifying a statute as constitutional? A good starting point is a landmark judgment by Laws LJ's in 2002. The case arose from the so-called 'metric martyrs', greengrocers convicted for selling produce solely in imperial units (pounds and ounces). They argued that the Weights and Measures Act 1985 had impliedly repealed section 2(2) of the European Communities Act 1972, so that ministers lacked authority to make metrication regulations under that section.[17] Laws LJ rejected this idea.

Thoburn v Sunderland City Council
[2002] EWHC 195 (Admin), [2003] QB 151

Laws LJ

62. We should recognise a hierarchy of Acts of Parliament: as it were 'ordinary' statutes and 'constitutional' statutes. The two categories must be distinguished on a principled basis. In my opinion a constitutional statute is one which (a) conditions the legal relationship between citizen and State in some general, overarching manner, or (b) enlarges or diminishes the scope of what we would now regard as fundamental constitutional rights. (a) and (b) are of necessity closely related: it is difficult to think of an instance of (a) that is not also an instance of (b). The special status of constitutional statutes follows the special status of constitutional rights. Examples are the Magna Carta, the Bill of Rights 1689, the Act of Union, the Reform Acts which distributed and enlarged the franchise, the [Human Rights Act 1998], the Scotland Act 1998 and the Government of Wales Act 1998. The [European Communities Act 1972, 'the ECA'] clearly belongs in this family. It incorporated the whole corpus of substantive Community rights and obligations, and gave overriding domestic effect to the judicial and administrative machinery of Community law. It may be there has never been a statute having such profound effects on so many dimensions of our daily lives. The ECA is, by force of the common law, a constitutional statute.

This judgment introduced an important qualification to the traditional doctrine of parliamentary supremacy. By recognising a distinct category of *constitutional statutes*, Laws LJ held that such Acts cannot be impliedly repealed by ordinary legislation: they can only be repealed or amended by express words.

More broadly, courts have considered whether a statute's constitutional status justifies a modified approach to interpretation. This question has arisen especially in relation to the Acts establishing devolution in 1998. In *Robinson v Secretary of State for Northern Ireland*, the issue was whether the election of the First Minister and Deputy First Minister two days after the six-week deadline in the Northern Ireland Act 1998 was valid. The House of Lords (before the creation of the UK Supreme Court) held that it was. Lord Bingham stated: '*The 1998 Act does not set out all the constitutional provisions applicable to Northern Ireland, but it is in effect a constitution. So to categorise the Act is not to relieve the courts of their duty to interpret the constitutional provisions in issue. But the provisions should, consistently with the language used, be interpreted generously and purposively, bearing in mind the values which the constitutional provisions are intended to embody*'.[18] In more recent cases, however, the UK Supreme Court has downplayed the practical consequences of an Act's constitutional status.[19]

[17] We look at implied repeal in more detail in Chapter 3.

[18] *Robinson v Secretary of State for Northern Ireland* [2002] UKHL 32, [11].

[19] *In the matter of an application by James Hugh Allister and others for Judicial Review* [2023] UKSC 5. See further M. Elliott and N. Kilford, 'Nothing to See Here? *Allister* in the Supreme Court' (2024) 28 Edinburgh Law Review 95; K. Majewski, '*Re Allister*: The End of "Constitutional Statutes"?' UKCLA Blog, 21 February 2023, https://ukconstitutionallaw.org/2023/02/21/kacper-majewski-re-allister-the-end-of-constitutional-statutes/ accessed 20 October 2025.

These are important but complex questions about how far courts can or should treat some Acts as having constitutional status. For now, it is enough to recognise that this remains an area of continuing debate rather than settled doctrine.

2.2.3 ARE ACTS OF PARLIAMENT A GOOD SOURCE FOR CONSTITUTIONAL RULES, RIGHTS, AND PRINCIPLES?

So far, we have identified some of the principal examples of constitutional statutes and looked at why it matters that certain Acts of Parliament are recognised as constitutional statutes. We now turn to a more evaluative question: is it desirable for rules of a constitutional character to be contained in Acts of Parliament? Three broad answers can be given.

First, reformers who advocate a codified Constitution generally answer no. They argue that the most important constitutional rules should appear in a higher form of law that cannot be amended or repealed by an ordinary majority in Parliament. On this view, a codified Constitution would set out the state's fundamental institutions, rights, and procedures for change, and would require special approval—perhaps by super-majority in Parliament or referendum—before alteration. The claim here is that constitutional rules should be protected from short-term political pressures and be grounded in specific popular consent, for example through a referendum.

Second, some commentators regard the common law as a better repository for fundamental constitutional principles than legislation made by what they see as transient or politically motivated governments. As section 2.3 explores, this perspective stresses the role of the courts in recognising and refining enduring principles—such as the rule of law, access to justice, and procedural fairness—that exist independently of political control from the majority of the House of Commons.

Third, there is an answer that favours leaving constitutional rule-making to the ordinary political process. 'Political constitutionalism' is the label given to a set of ideas and practices that values highly the role of politicians and the political process in the British constitution. People who have this viewpoint say that major decisions affecting the life of the nation should be debated and decided in Parliament (not in courtrooms) and Parliament (not the courts) should have the final say on the content of the constitutional rule book. The notion of democracy that underpins this is *majoritarianism*. The views of the majority, as reflected in the composition of the House of Commons, should be decisive. Parliament is therefore, by its procedures and composition, well equipped to hold good-quality debates on legislation and inquiries into government action.

PAUSE FOR REFLECTION

Before going further into the debate about where constitutional authority should lie, consider this question: who should have the power to introduce a right as significant as the right of same-sex couples to marry?

1. In England and Wales, this right was created by legislation—the Marriage (Same Sex Couples) Act 2013—passed through the ordinary processes of parliamentary democracy.
2. In Ireland, it came about through constitutional change. Following a referendum in 2015, Article 41 of the Irish Constitution was amended to state that 'marriage may be contracted in accordance with law by two persons without distinction as to their sex'.
3. In the United States, the right was recognised by the judiciary. In *Obergefell v Hodges* 576 US 644 (2015), the Supreme Court held that the Fourteenth Amendment to the US Constitution implicitly protects the right of same-sex couples to marry.

How do these different routes—legislative, constitutional amendment, and judicial interpretation—compare in terms of democratic legitimacy, stability, and protection of minority rights?

A deep vein of scepticism about the constitutional role of the judiciary runs through political constitutionalist thinking. In his controversial book *The Politics of the Judiciary* (1977), J.A.G. Griffith (1918–2010)—a leading exponent of political constitutionalism—used a selection of cases (on areas such as race relations, trade union law, police powers, and students) to advance an argument that judges in Britain, by reason of their upper-class background—private schools and Oxbridge degrees—and their institutional position in society, *necessarily* had a strong ideological bias towards 'established authority' and views associated with the Conservative Party at that time. In other words, they routinely ruled against trade unionists, demonstrators, students, and so on. In Griffith's view, judges could not be seen as politically neutral and they were not effective guardians of individual liberty against the state. This was not a criticism of individual judges, but an analysis of the institutional role played by the judiciary. In the follow extract, Graham Gee revisits Griffith's work to clarify its core claim: that constitutional limits on government should arise primarily through politics, not the courts.

G. Gee, 'The political constitutionalism of J.A.G. Griffith' (2008) 28 *Legal Studies* 20, 28 (footnotes omitted)

[. . .] Griffith is not troubled by limiting government per se, but rather by limiting government through judicially imposed constraints, and even then he is troubled only by certain judicially imposed constraints. On my reading, Griffith's political constitutionalism is just that: a *political* model of *constitutionalism*. And any model of constitutionalism must include an account of the norms creating, structuring and defining the authority of the governing institutions, including an explanation as to how those norms *constrain* the power of those institutions. For Griffith, politics, and in particular the parliamentary process, should create, structure and define the authority of the governing institutions, including imposing constraints on those institutions. That is to say, politics, and to some extent law, should (and do in fact) constrain the governing institutions.

Griffith was a Left-leaning academic, but political constitutionalism has cross-party appeal. Conservatives and others on the Right in British politics have attached great weight to the principle of parliamentary supremacy and the central place of Parliament in the constitutional system. The ability of the national Parliament to legislate free from unnecessary legal constraints from the European Union (EU) was a defining view of many on the Right who supported the United Kingdom's withdrawal. Since then, another body of law and court—the European Convention on Human Rights, the European Court of Human Rights, and the Human Rights Act 1998—have become a target for criticism.

Politicians in both Labour and Conservative governments have expressed frustration at what they see as judicial 'activism' and the mission-creep of courts. In 2025, Shabana Mahmood MP, then the Lord Chancellor and Secretary of State for Justice in the Labour government, gave a speech in which she called for reform of the European Convention on Human Rights (ECHR) and approach to its interpretation by the European Court of Human Rights.

Rt Hon Shabana Mahmood MP, Lord Chancellor speech at the Council of Europe, 18 June 2025

There is a growing perception – sometimes mistaken, sometimes grounded in reality – that human rights are no longer a shield for the vulnerable, but a tool for criminals to avoid responsibility. That the law too often protects those who break the rules, rather than those who follow them. This tension is not new. The Convention was written to protect individuals from the arbitrary power of the state. But in today's world, the threats to justice and liberty are more complex. They can come from technology, transnational crime, uncontrolled migration, or legal systems that drift away from public consent.

Mahmood went on to say that '*If judges are being asked to solve political problems that parliaments avoid, we weaken both institutions*'.

Political constitutionalists see no value and many dangers in the United Kingdom adopting a codified Constitution. In the following extract, Martin Loughlin warns against the idea that the text(s) of a constitution can provide all the answers needed to resolve conflicts.

M. Loughlin, 'Constitutional Law: The Third Order of the Political', in N. Bamforth and P. Leyland (eds) *Public Law in a Multi-layered Constitution* (2003, Oxford: Hart Publishing), ch. 2, pp. 48–9

Although advocating a more formal separation of powers, Montesquieu[20] also recognised the political character of the exercise, believing that, provided each of these roles is properly acknowledged, the three branches of government 'are constrained to move by the necessary motion of things'. With the emergence of constitutional legalism, however, came the belief that solutions to these intrinsically political matters are to be found in, or through, the text. Consequently, whenever—as has been the case in all modern states—the executive has acted to fill those spaces which exist within all constitutional documents, this has been the occasion for disapprobation.

The error of constitutional legalism is of a most basic kind, that of mistaking the part for the whole. Such legalism fails properly to acknowledge the provisional character of constitutional arrangements and that 'the development and acceptance of a constitutional framework can occur only as the contingent result of irresolvable conflict'. Indeed, this must be so, because its object—the activity of governing—is interminable. The arrangements of governing are in a permanent state of disequilibrium, since 'the system has never been designed as a whole, and such coherence as it possesses is the product of constant readjustment of its parts to one another'. What Michael Oakeshott [1901–90, a philosopher] calls 'the system of superficial order' is, of course, always 'capable of being made more coherent'. And while this can often be a useful and positive exercise, 'the barbarism of order appears when order is pursued for its own sake and when the preservation of order involves the destruction of that without which order is only the orderliness of the ant-heap or the graveyard'.

[20] See Chapter 5 for more on Montesquieu and separation of powers theory.

PAUSE FOR REFLECTION

1. In your own words, what makes an Act of Parliament 'constitutional' according to Laws LJ in *Thoburn v Sunderland City Council*? How does his definition differ from academic definitions?
2. Select one of the 38 constitutional Acts of Parliament listed in section 2.2.1. Find it on UK Government's official legislation website: legislation.gov.uk. Identify a provision you think most clearly limits government power or protects individual rights, and explain briefly why.
3. Do you agree that Parliament should have power to create, amend or abolish constitutional rules, rights, and principles through legislation? Give one argument for and one against this view.

2.3 CONSTITUTIONAL RULES IN THE COMMON LAW

Let's now move on to explore a second source of constitutional rules: the written judgments of the higher (or 'senior') courts.[21] Judges have contributed to the development of constitutional principles and rights. The following are some examples.

- '*It is a long-established principle of the English common law that, subject to certain exceptions and statutory qualifications, the defendant in a criminal trial should be confronted by his accusers in order that he may cross-examine them and challenge their evidence*': *R v Davis* [2008] UKHL 36, [5], Lord Bingham (discussed further in Chapter 4).
- '*[T]he executive cannot in law abrogate the right of access to justice, unless it is specifically so permitted by Parliament; and this is the meaning of the constitutional right*'—in a case about the lawfulness of a decision to raise court fees: *R v Lord Chancellor, ex parte Witham* [1998] QB 575, [24], Laws LJ (discussed further below).
- '*It is a general principle of the common law that a lawful sentence pronounced by a judge may not retrospectively be increased*': *Pierson v Secretary of State for the Home Department* [1998] AC 539, Lord Steyn.
- '*In rejecting the use of torture, whether applied to potential defendants or potential witnesses, the common law was moved by the cruelty of the practice as applied to those not convicted of crime, by the inherent unreliability of confessions or evidence so procured and by the belief that it degraded all those who lent themselves to the practice*': *A v Secretary of State for the Home Department* [2005] UKHL 7, [11]–[12], Lord Bingham of Cornhill, holding the prohibition of evidence received through torture 'more aptly categorized as a constitutional principle than as a rule of evidence'.
- '*At common law, any subject of the Crown has the right to enter and remain in the United Kingdom whenever and for as long as he pleases*': *R (on the application of Bancoult) v Secretary of State for Foreign and Commonwealth Affairs (No 2)* [2008] UKHL 61, [44], Lord Hoffmann.

[21] See M. Elliott and K. Hughes (eds), *Common Law Constitutional Rights* (2020); T.R.S. Allan, 'Constitutionalism at Common Law: the Rule of Law and Judicial Review' (2023) 82 *Cambridge Law Journal* 236.

The list could go on but these illustrations are sufficient to demonstrate the point that judges in the United Kingdom, drawing on precedent, enunciate rules of a constitutional character in their judgments. But there are also many cases in which the courts have rejected arguments for a common law rights, for example:

- In *Elgizouli v Secretary of State for the Home Department* [2020] UKSC 10, a majority of the UK Supreme Court held that there was no common law rule prohibiting the UK government from sharing information about a suspected terrorist with the US government where the information might facilitate the imposition of the death penalty.
- In *For Women Scotland Ltd v The Scottish Ministers* [2025] UKSC 16, the UK Supreme Court confirmed that the 'common law of England and Wales did not recognise the possibility of a person becoming a different gender from their gender at birth'.

Because the common law develops through judicial decisions, it remains open to the courts to recognise new rights as legal principles evolve. As Shreya Atrey explains in the next extract, this flexibility allows the common law to adapt to changing understandings of justice and equality.

S. Atrey, 'A Common Law Principle of Racial Equality?'
[2025] *Public Law* 215, 215

> . . . a handful of cases . . . engage with common law to attack racial discrimination. These cases invoke racial equality as a matter of rationality or reasonableness rather than constitutional or statutory law. Their presence prompts a question. What is the status of racial equality at common law? . . . although racial equality is not an independent ground of judicial review, its invocation in other grounds generates the possibility of addressing racial discrimination matters of governance and of general importance. Although this possibility has not yet been activated, it continues to be raised in judicial review cases. In principle, this leaves open the door to activating something like a common law principle of racial equality, especially in cases which prove unwieldy under statutory law either because of its formal limits or because of the way in which it is applied under the Equality Act 2010 and the Human Rights Act 1998.

Atrey concludes by saying that if lawyers do not pursue development of this principle, '*the commitment to racial equality in the UK remains half-hearted if considered a matter of statutory protection alone; thus lacking broader constitutional significance as a matter of rule of law and democracy*' (p. 222).

2.3.1 IS THE COMMON LAW A GOOD SOURCE FOR CONSTITUTIONAL RULES, RIGHTS, AND PRINCIPLES?

Building on the fact that over many years the courts have recognised certain constitutional principles and rights, some judges and academics identify a 'common law constitution' and favour 'legal constitutionalism'. This is a rival to political constitutionalism. Legal constitutionalists favour a prominent role for law, legal processes, and judges in regulating the constitutional system (whereas political constitutionalists prefer prominent roles for politicians and the political process). In the absence of a codified Constitution, many legal constitutionalists welcome the creative development of the common law as a way of ensuring that legal values permeate the current constitutional system. Strategically, they see the common law as a defence against government and even Parliament reducing basic rights or undermining constitutional principles.

If judges' constitutional role were confined to interpreting and applying Acts of Parliament in a mechanistic way ('the Act states ministers must do X, the minister has not done X, so the minister has acted unlawfully'), politicians and political constitutionalists would have little to criticise. Judges, in that scenario, are merely ensuring that the intention of Parliament is respected and acted upon. But judges have not (just) been mechanistic and their contribution to constitutional rule-making has become controversial.

Judges have been creative in using the common law to establish limitations on government. We have seen that the courts have identified various common law fundamental rights. The development of the grounds of judicial review is another area where the courts have been creative, though this has created recurring tension between ministers of all political parties and the courts.[22] Successive governments and parliaments have sought to limit judicial intervention by enacting legislation designed to oust or restrict the role of the courts.[23] In 2025, for example, the Labour government announced plans to introduce new procedural restrictions on individuals and campaign groups seeking judicial review of major infrastructure projects, such as proposals to build nuclear power stations.[24]

Common law constitutionalism also makes a much deeper claim about the common law. Whereas Acts of Parliament are made by 'here-today, gone-tomorrow' politicians,[25] the common law constitution, based on precedent and tradition, embodies 'some form of latent wisdom'.[26] This idea rests partly on the fact that judges have been developing constitutional rules for a very long time: we still make references to seventeenth- and eighteenth-century case law. For example, in the landmark judgment *Entick v Carrington* (1786) the Lord Chief Justice held that the king's messengers trespassed on Entick's land when they entered his house to search for seditious papers without specific legal authority to do so.[27] From a still earlier period, we have the *Case of Proclamations* in which Lord Chief Justice Coke laid down the principle that the king could only make new laws through Parliament.[28] The development of common law rules is generally incremental, with rules emerging through lines of precedent as fact-situations are distinguished from each other. It is seen as a virtue that judges are 'independent', meaning (in this context) that judges are not involved in the rough and tumble of party political debate. Common law rules emerge through a more refined, principled, and rational process of legal argumentation. Moreover, the common law is claimed to embody substantive values that favour individual liberty. Consider the following extract from the judgment in a case in which the court held that the government had acted unlawfully when it increased court fees without making proper provision for people (such as benefit claimants) of limited financial means.

R v Lord Chancellor Witham
[1997] EWHC Admin 237, [1998] QB 575

Laws LJ

12. The common law does not generally speak in the language of constitutional rights, for the good reason that in the absence of any sovereign text, a written constitution which is logically and legally prior to the power of legislature, executive and judiciary alike, there is on the face of it no hierarchy of rights such that any one of them is more entrenched by the law than any other. And if the concept of a constitutional right is to have any meaning, it must surely sound in the protection which the law affords

[22] See Chapters 17, 18, 19 and 20 on judicial review.
[23] See Chapter 20 (Exclusion and Limitation of Judicial Review).
[24] M. Fouzder, 'Starmer vows to take on "Nimbys" with JR curbs' *The Law Society Gazette*, 23 January 2025 https://www.lawgazette.co.uk/news/starmer-vows-to-take-on-nimbys-with-jr-curbs/5122117.article?utm_ accessed 19 October 2025.
[25] This phrase comes from an interview of a politician by TV journalist Sir Robin Day in 1982. The minister he was interviewing stormed out.
[26] See A. Vermeule, 'Common law constitutionalism and the limits of reason' (2007) 107 Columbia Law Review 1482, who rejects the claim that the common law is a repository of such latent wisdom.
[27] *Entick v Carrington* (1765) 19 St Tr 1029.
[28] *Case of Proclamations* (1611) 12 Co Rep 74.

to it. Where a written constitution guarantees a right, there is no conceptual difficulty. The State authorities must give way to it, save to the extent that the constitution allows them to deny it. There may of course be other difficulties, such as whether on the constitution's true interpretation the right claimed exists at all. Even a superficial acquaintance with the jurisprudence of the Supreme Court of the United States shows that such problems may be acute. But they are not in the same category as the question: do we have constitutional rights at all?

13. In the unwritten legal order of the British State, at a time when the common law continues to accord a legislative supremacy to Parliament, the notion of a constitutional right can in my judgment inhere only in this proposition, that the right in question cannot be abrogated by the State save by specific provision in an Act of Parliament, or by regulations whose *vires*[[29]] in main legislation specifically confers the power to abrogate. General words will not suffice. And any such rights will be creatures of the common law, since their existence would not be the consequence of the democratic political process but would be logically prior to it.

Unpicking Laws LJ's reasoning, there are three elements. First, the common law, created by the judiciary, predates legislation: common law rights are 'logically prior' to Parliament and majoritarian democracy. Second, the courts recognise that Parliament has power to interfere with common law rights (the principle of parliamentary supremacy).[30] But, third, the courts will permit Parliament to do this only if clear words are used in an Act of Parliament.[31]

Some judges (supported by sympathetic academics) have suggested that, in an extreme situation, they would be prepared to develop the common law to overturn what most people regard as *the* central rule of the British constitution: parliamentary supremacy. The concept of parliamentary supremacy is that Acts of Parliament are the highest form of law in the United Kingdom and judges have no power to question their validity. Consider the following academic writing by Sir John Laws.[32]

Sir John Laws, 'Law and democracy'
[1995] *Public Law* 72, 84

Now it is only by means of compulsory law that effective rights can be accorded, so that the medium of rights is not persuasion, but the power of rule: the very power which, if misused, could be deployed to subvert rights. We therefore arrive at this position: the constitution must guarantee by positive law such rights as that of freedom of expression, since otherwise its credentials as a medium of honest rule are fatally undermined. But this requires for its achievement what I may call a higher-order law: a law which cannot be abrogated as other laws can, by the passage of a statute promoted by a government with the

[29] Definition: '*vires*' means 'power'. A paraphrase of what Laws LJ means is: the common law right, here the right of access to the court, cannot be taken away except by clear words in an Act of Parliament or in secondary legislation. We look at secondary legislation in Chapter 13. In essence, it is law made by the government with relatively little involvement from Parliament.

[30] See Chapter 3.

[31] The *principle of legality* is a common law presumption that Parliament does not intend to interfere with fundamental rights or constitutional principles unless it does so using clear and express language. It allows courts, when interpreting statutes, to protect basic rights against inadvertent or ambiguous legislative encroachment. See *R v Secretary of State for the Home Department, ex p Simms* [2000] 2 AC 115 (HL).

[32] You have already read extracts from Sir John's judgments in *Thoburn* and *Witham* earlier in this chapter For further insight into his constitutional thinking, see John Laws, *The Constitutional Balance* (Hart Publishing, 2021), a collection of his essays and lectures published posthumously.

necessary majority in Parliament. Otherwise the right is not in the keeping of the constitution at all; it is not a guaranteed right; it exists, in point of law at least, only because the government chooses to let it exist, whereas in truth no such choice should be open to any government.

The democratic credentials of an elected government cannot justify its enjoyment of a right to abolish fundamental freedoms. If its power in the state is in the last resort absolute, such fundamental rights as free expression are only privileges; no less so if the absolute power rests in an elected body. The byword of every tyrant is 'My word is law'; a democratic assembly having sovereign power beyond the reach of curtailment or review may make just such an assertion, and its elective base cannot immunise it from playing the tyrant's role.

Common law constitutionalists see the courts and legally enforceable rights as keys to creating conditions under which the state's power is limited. Parliamentary control of government is regarded as ineffective—the reality, it is said, is that government controls Parliament (rather than the other way around). The principle of parliamentary supremacy is therefore too weak to be an effective restraint on government. It provides no guarantee for fundamental rights or the rights of minorities.

Faith placed in the common law as a constitutional safeguard deserves closer scrutiny. Common law constitutionalism often assumes that judge-made rules, rights and principles tend to promote fairness and protect individuals and communities; but the history of the common law tells a more complex story. During Britain's imperial expansion, it served as a key instrument of colonial rule.[33] Recognising this history complicates the idea that the common law has always advanced justice.

One striking example concerns land rights—a core constitutional issue. In the 1889 case *Cooper v Stuart*, the Judicial Committee of the Privy Council in London held that common law applied in the Australian colony of New South Wales.[34] The rationale was that the territory was *terra nullius*—a land 'practically unoccupied, without settled inhabitants or settled law'. As Eddie Synot and Roshan de Silva-Wijeyeratne argue, this shaped Australia's constitutional framework and '*stood as the legal authority for Australian nationhood for over a century*'. This legal fiction erased from view the more than one million Aboriginal people who had lived in Australia for thousands of years before European settlement. By treating them as legally invisible, the decision enabled the Australian constitution to be '*developed without legitimate consideration for the rights of First Nations*'.[35]

PAUSE FOR REFLECTION

Imagine that Parliament repeals the Human Rights Act 1998 and passes a new law making criticism of Ministers a criminal offence punishable by up to ten years' imprisonment.

1. What do political constitutionalists mean when they say that Parliament should have the final word on constitutional questions?
2. How would that view apply to this example? Would a political constitutionalist think the courts could do anything about such an Act?
3. How might a common law constitutionalist respond differently, and on what legal or moral grounds?
4. Which approach do you find more persuasive, and why? What does your answer suggest about the balance between democracy and the rule of law in the UK constitution?

[33] See Chapter 1.

[34] *William Cooper v The Honourable Alexander Stuart (New South Wales)* [1889] UKPC 16; (1889) 14 App Cas 286.

[35] See E. Synot and R. de Silva-Wijeyeratne, 'Constitutional Foundations: The Persistent Myth of *Cooper v Stuart*' ch. 3 in N. Watson and H. Douglas (eds), *Indigenous Legal Judgments* (Routledge 2021), p. 37.

2.4 CONSTITUTIONAL CONVENTIONS

Having looked at Acts of Parliament and the common law as sources of constitutional rules, we can now turn to constitutional conventions. *The Cabinet Manual*'s description of the UK constitution makes plain the importance of 'constitutional conventions' as a source of rules.[36] It defines conventions as '*rules of constitutional practice that are regarded as binding in operation but not in law*'. Among the conventions discussed in the *Manual* are:

(a) '*By convention, the Sovereign does not become publicly involved in party politics of government.*'

(b) '*The roles of the Prime Minister and Cabinet are governed largely by convention.*'

(c) '*By modern convention, the Prime Minister always sits in the House of Commons.*'

(d) '*There is a convention that an individual will be a minister only if they are a Member of the House of Commons or the House of Lords.*'

(e) '*By convention, Cabinet and Cabinet committees take decisions which are binding on members of the Government.*'

(f) '*The two Houses of Parliament acknowledge various conventions governing the relationship between them, including in relation to primacy of the House of Commons,* . . . .'

(g) '*In 2011, the Government acknowledged that a convention had developed in Parliament that before troops were committed the House of Commons should have an opportunity to debate the matter and said that it proposed to observe that convention except when there was an emergency and such action would not be appropriate.*'

This is not an exhaustive list but illustrates that many of the United Kingdom's most important constitutional rules take the form of political understandings rather than law. Conventions help ensure that the constitution functions smoothly by guiding the conduct of those who exercise public power, even though they lack formal legal status.

It is easy enough to identify rules set out in the form of legislation, because they have been made according to a defined process and are published in a prescribed format.[37] Similarly, we know that a legal rule in a judgment exists because it is written by a judge at the conclusion of formal court procedures. But how do we identify rules in the form of conventions? Professor Sir Ivor Jennings (1903–65) suggested a three-part test.

Sir Ivor Jennings, *The Law and the Constitution*, 5th edn (1959, London: University of London Press), pp. 134–5

It is clear, in the first place, that mere practice is insufficient. The fact that an authority has always behaved in a certain way is not warrant for saying that it ought to behave in that way. But if the authority itself and those connected with it believe that they ought to do so, then the convention does exist. This is the ordinary rule applied to customary law. Practice alone is not enough. It must be normative. [. . .] Similarly, the fact that the Sovereign has once behaved in a certain way does not bind him to act in that way. [. . .] Something more must be added. As in the creation of law, the creation of a convention must

[36] See F. Ahmed, R. Albert, and A. Perry, 'Judging constitutional conventions' (2019) 17 *International Journal of Constitutional Law* 787; N. Barry, N. Miragliotta, and Z. Nwokora, 'The dynamics of constitutional conventions in Westminster democracies' (2019) 72 *Parliamentary Affairs* 664; S. Stephenson, 'Constitutional conventions and the judiciary' (2021) 41 *Oxford Journal of Legal Studies* 750.

[37] See Chapter 12.

be due to the reason of the thing because it accords with the prevailing political philosophy. It helps to make the democratic system operate; it enables the machinery of the State to run more smoothly; and if it were not there, friction would result. Thus, if a convention continues because it is desirable in the circumstances of the constitution, it must have been created for the same reason. We have to ask ourselves three questions: first, what are the precedents; secondly, did the actors in the precedents believe that they were bound by the rule; and thirdly, is there a good reason for the rule? A single precedent with a good reason may be enough to establish the rule. A whole string of precedents without such a reason will be of no avail, unless it is perfectly certain that the persons concerned regarded them as bound by it.

Let's apply this test. First, consider the monarch's power to grant Royal Assent to bills that have completed their passage through Parliament. It is said to be a constitutional convention that Royal Assent must always be granted. Is this true? Step (a): there are clear precedents: Royal Assent is routinely granted and has not been withheld since the eighteenth century. Step (b): does the monarch regard himself as bound by the rule? We can assume so. Step (c): there is a good reason—a constitutional justification—for the rule. Withholding Royal Assent (for example, because the monarch had a moral objection to something in the bill) would be undemocratic. Conclusion: there is a convention.[38]

The second element in the Jennings' test is helpful in distinguishing conventions from mere practices that, although routinely followed, do not really serve any 'good reason' relevant to the functioning of the state and which could be changed without being thought to breach a constitutional rule. An example of a practice that should not be regarded as constitutional convention is that ministers' official papers are transported in special red, leather-covered despatch boxes. This has happened since the nineteenth century (step (a)). In 2015, the Prime Minister decided that they would be phased out and replaced by electronic tablet devices; he seemed not to consider continued use of red boxes to be a binding rule (step (b)). Anyway, there is no 'good reason' (step (c)), constitutionally speaking, for having red boxes. Conclusion: there is no convention, it was merely a practice.

While Jennings viewed conventions as 'bottom-up' rules inferred from political practice, some are deliberately created 'from above'. The Ministerial Code—issued by the Prime Minister and updated by the Cabinet Office—illustrates this more formal approach to defining standards of behaviour. Similar written understandings, often called memoranda of understanding or concordats, set out how different institutions should cooperate in practice. Examples include the 2018 agreement between the Ministry of Justice and the Welsh Government on consultation and information-sharing,[39] and an earlier understanding between the Lord Chief Justice and the Lord Chancellor clarifying their respective roles after the reform of that ancient office.[40] Such documents have no legal force: they express principles of trust and cooperation rather than binding obligations. Even so, some—like the judiciary–executive concordat—have come to be treated as documents of constitutional importance because they stabilise relationships during institutional change.

Concordats and other 'soft-law' instruments occupy an ambiguous constitutional space.[41] They show how an uncodified constitution can evolve by negotiation and administrative practice rather

[38] Matters may be somewhat more complicated. If you want to delve deeper, see N.W. Barber, 'Can Royal Assent be refused on the advice of the Prime Minister?', UK Constitutional Law Blog, 25 September 2013.

[39] Ministry of Justice and Welsh Government, *Concordat between the Ministry of Justice and the Welsh Government* (March 2018) https://www.gov.uk/government/publications/concordat-between-the-ministry-of-justice-and-the-welsh-government accessed 17 October 2025.

[40] House of Lords Select Committee on Constitutional Reform Bill, *First Report* (Session 2003–04) Appendix 6: The Lord Chancellor's Judiciary-Related Functions: Proposals (the 'concordat') https://publications.parliament.uk/pa/ld200304/ldselect/ldcref/125/12514.htm.

[41] R. Rawlings, 'Concordats of the constitution' (2000) 116 *Law Quarterly Review* 257.

than by legislation or precedent. Yet their deliberately informal character raises questions about accountability and power: if they depend on goodwill rather than law, what happens when that goodwill breaks down? Critics worry that top-down conventions risk concentrating authority in those who draft and interpret them, while others see them as a flexible way of maintaining cooperation within a complex, devolved system.[42]

2.4.1 CONVENTIONS AND LAWS DISTINGUISHED

This section explores how conventions differ from legal rules, and whether that distinction remains useful in understanding how the constitution operates. Albert Venn Dicey, who was Vinerian Professor of English Law at Oxford from 1882 to 1909, drew a sharp distinction between laws 'in the strictest sense' and constitutional conventions. The difference between the two categories lay, he stressed, in the role of the courts in relation to enforcement of failures to comply with the rules.

A.V. Dicey, *Introduction to the Study of the Law of the Constitution* (1885; 10th edn 1959, London: Macmillan & Co.), pp. 23–4

> [... T]he rules which make up constitutional law, as the term is used in England, include two sets of principles or maxims of a totally distinct character.
>
> The one set of rules are in the strictest sense 'laws', since they are rules which (whether written or unwritten, whether enacted by statute or derived from the mass of custom, tradition, or judge-made maxims known to common law) are enforced by the courts; these rules constitute 'constitutional law' in the proper sense of that term, and may for the sake of distinction be called collectively 'the law of the constitution'.
>
> The other set of rules consist of conventions, understandings, habits, or practices which, though they may regulate the conduct of several members of the sovereign powers, of the Ministry, of the officials, are not in reality laws at all since they are not enforced by the courts. This proportion of constitutional law may, for the sake of the distinction, be termed the 'conventions of the constitution', or constitutional morality.

He also made clear that the distinction was not related to whether the rules were 'written' or 'unwritten', because many constitutional conventions are expressed in 'printed rules'. He included in the category of conventions '*the whole of our parliamentary procedure*', which he said '*is nothing but a mass of conventional law*'.

The idea that it is possible, or helpful, to draw a clear dividing line between rules in the form of laws and those in the form of conventions has long been questioned. Jennings argued that '*there is not distinction of substance or nature*' between laws and conventions, although he went on to say that it is '*important from the technical angle*' to know into which category a rule falls. More recently, N.W. Barber argues that we should view laws and conventions not as separate categories of rules, but as a spectrum.

[42] A. Perry and A. Tucker, 'Top-down constitutional conventions' (2018) 81 *Modern Law Review* 765; A. McHarg, 'Reforming the United Kingdom constitution: law, convention and soft law' (2008) 71 *Modern Law Review* 853.

N.W. Barber, 'Laws and constitutional conventions' (2009) 125 *Law Quarterly Review* 294, 294

> The difference between law and convention is one of degree: laws and conventions should be placed upon a spectrum of types of social rules, a spectrum gradated in terms of the formalisation of rules. Laws lie at the most formalised end of this spectrum, but there is no single, definable, point at which rules shift from being conventions into being laws. Alongside this argument, it will be contended that conventions can become laws through judicial intervention, and that conventions can 'crystallise' into laws over time by becoming increasingly formalised.

Barber goes on to consider the *Ministerial Code*, the set of rules governing the conduct of ministers issued by the Prime Minister.[43] He argues that '*The focus of political attention on the Code suggests the emergence of a new convention: one of the rules of ministerial responsibility now places a duty on Ministers to follow the rules set out in the Code. Failure to do so will lead to political censure and may end with the Minister leaving office*'. Barber argues that the Code has become more like law over the years, and '*possesses many of the characteristic features of a legal system*'.

Barber's point that conventional and legal rules can be viewed as a spectrum rather than two distinct categories is illustrated by the Sewel convention (named after the government minister who announced the proposed rule). The rule could be found written in various places, including in the following guidelines used by officials when they are preparing bills.

Cabinet Office, *Guide to Making Legislation* (2025), p. 131

> Parliament remains sovereign, but will 'not normally' pass primary legislation in areas of devolved or transferred competence without legislative consent and agreement from the devolved legislatures. This is known as 'the Sewel Convention'.

In the early years of devolution, the Sewel convention was a principle agreed by politicians, without any legal backing. But as part of ongoing development of the devolution settlement, the Scotland Act 2016 added the following words to s. 28 of the Scotland Act 1998: '*But it is recognised that the Parliament of the United Kingdom will not normally legislate with regard to devolved matters without the consent of the Scottish Parliament*'. Similarly, section 107 of the Wales Act 2017 was amended to state: '*But it is recognised that the Parliament of the United Kingdom will not normally legislate with regard to devolved matters without the consent of the Assembly.*' Did these statutory words change the nature of the Sewel rule? The House of Lords Constitution Committee, reviewing the proposed new words to be added to the Scotland Act, thought not.

House of Lords Constitution Committee, *Proposals for the devolution of further powers to Scotland*, Tenth Report, Session 2014–15 (HL Paper 145)

> 72. Although in this way the Sewel convention will be put on a statutory footing, the measure seems to have only symbolic significance, consolidating the idea that Scottish devolution is a permanent arrangement, the terms of which will not be changed unilaterally by the UK Parliament. Aside from

[43] See Chapter 9.

the general rule that Parliament is unable to bind its successors [. . .], the use of the word 'normally' (which is unusual in legislation and is undefined) seems to make clear that Parliament will still have the legal power to legislate for Scotland, even on devolved matters, without the consent of the Scottish Parliament. Therefore, it can be said that the new provision will recognise the existence of the Sewel convention rather than turn it into a legally binding principle.

In other words, Parliament chose to acknowledge the existence of the Sewel Convention within statute but without surrendering its legal sovereignty. The convention continues to have political, rather than legal, force.[44]

2.4.2 LEGAL ENFORCEMENT OF CONSTITUTIONAL CONVENTIONS

This section considers whether conventions, though political in nature, can ever be recognised or enforced through legal proceedings. What happens if a political actor ignores or breaches a constitutional convention? Usually, the response takes the form of political rather than legal consequences: ministers may face criticism in Parliament, pressure from the media, or loss of public confidence. The political actor can be said to be acting 'unconstitutionally'. But are there circumstances when a breach of a convention may also be 'unlawful', and subject to adjudication and enforcement in the courts? The orthodox answer is no. Conventions are not legally binding rules but political understandings that guide behaviour. The UK Supreme Court confirmed this during litigation relating to the United Kingdom's withdrawal from the EU, holding that the Sewel convention creates a political expectation rather than a legal duty, even though it was referred to in an Act of Parliament.

R (on the application of Miller) v Secretary of State for Exiting the European Union
[2017] UKSC 5, [141], [144], [146]

141. . . . It is well established that the courts of law cannot enforce a political convention. In *Re Resolution to Amend the Constitution* [1981] 1 SCR 753, the Supreme Court of Canada addressed the nature of political conventions. In the majority judgment the Chief Justice (Laskin) and Dickson, Beetz, Estey, McIntyre, Chouinard and Lamer JJ stated at pp. 774 to 775: 'The very nature of a convention, as political in inception and as depending on a consistent course of political recognition by those for whose benefit and to whose detriment (if any) the convention developed over a considerable period of time is inconsistent with its legal enforcement'. [. . .]

142. Attempts to enforce political conventions in the courts have failed. Thus in *Madzimbamuto v Lardner-Burke* [1969] 1 AC 645, the Judicial Committee of the Privy Council had to consider a submission that legal effect should be given to the convention which applied at that time that the UK Parliament would not legislate without the consent of the government of Southern Rhodesia on matters within the competence of the Legislative Assembly. In its judgment delivered by Lord Reid the Board stated at p 723 that: 'That is a very important convention but it had no legal effect in limiting the legal power of Parliament. It is often said that it would be unconstitutional for the UK Parliament to do certain things, meaning that the moral, political and other reasons against doing them are so strong that most people would regard it as highly improper if Parliament did these things. But that does not mean that it

[44] See Chapter 6 (section 6.4.1).

is beyond the power of Parliament to do such things. If Parliament chose to do any of them the courts could not hold the Act of Parliament invalid.' [...]

146. Judges therefore are neither the parents nor the guardians of political conventions; they are merely observers. As such, they can recognise the operation of a political convention in the context of deciding a legal question (as in the Page 48 Crossman diaries case – *Attorney General v Jonathan Cape* Ltd [1976] 1 QB 752), but they cannot give legal rulings on its operation or scope, because those matters are determined within the political world. As Professor Colin Munro has stated, 'the validity of conventions cannot be the subject of proceedings in a court of law' (1975) 91 LQR 218, 228.

The court added, that the words 'But it is recognised that the Parliament of the United Kingdom will not normally legislate with regard to devolved matters without the consent of the Scottish Parliament' inserted into the Scotland Act 1998 did not seek '*to convert the Sewel Convention into a rule which can be interpreted, let alone enforced, by the courts; rather, it is recognising the convention for what it is, namely a political convention, and is effectively declaring that it is a permanent feature of the relevant devolution settlement*' (para.148).

As the UK Supreme Court observed referring to the Crossman Diaries case, courts are not precluded from recognising conventions where this is necessary to decide a case.[45] Doing so may involve hearing evidence and defining the scope of a convention. This occurred in *Evans v Information Commissioner*[46], where journalist Rob Evans sought to use the Freedom of Information Act 2000 to obtain copies of the so-called 'black spider memos'—handwritten letters sent by the then Prince of Wales (now King Charles III) to government ministers engaging in advocacy on a range of public policy issues, including farming and the environment. In deciding whether the Information Commissioner had acted lawfully in finding that that disclosure would be against the public interest, the Upper Tribunal (Administrative Appeals Chamber) received oral and written evidence from two academic experts and examined several constitutional conventions in detail. These included the tripartite convention (that the monarch has a right to be consulted, to encourage, and to warn their government); the cardinal convention (that the monarch must act on the advice of ministers); and the education convention (which allows the heir to the throne to be instructed in the business of government in preparation for their future role). The Tribunal made it clear that its task was limited to making factual findings about these conventions and determining their scope as part of deciding whether disclosure of the letters would be contrary to the public interest under the Act. The *Evans* case shows that while courts cannot enforce conventions, they may need to recognise and interpret them to resolve related legal questions.

Although the courts have settled the principle that constitutional conventions are not legally enforceable, some scholars have challenged the traditional view that the courts should never enforce

[45] In *Attorney General v Jonathan Cape Ltd* [1976] QB 752, the government sought an injunction to prevent publication of the diaries of a former Cabinet minister, Richard Crossman MP. It argued that disclosure would undermine the convention of collective Cabinet responsibility by revealing confidential discussions. The court held that constitutional conventions are not legally enforceable and that there were no sufficient grounds at common law, such as breach of confidence, to restrain publication.

[46] [2012] UKUT 313 (AAC). In a twist, the UK Government issued a certificate under the Freedom of Information Act that in effect overrode the Upper Tribunals ruling. The UK Supreme Court held that this was unlawful: *R (on the application of Evans) v Attorney General* [2015] UKSC 21. The letters sent by Prince Charles are available online https://www.theguardian.com/uk-news/ng-interactive/2015/may/13/read-the-prince-charles-black-spider-memos-in-full accessed 22 October 2025.

conventions. They argue that the distinction between law and convention is more fluid than orthodox accounts suggest. The following extract is the conclusion drawn by Professor Trevor Allan at the end of a discussion of the Supreme Court of Canada's judgment in *Re: Resolution to amend the Constitution*.[47] The Federal Government of Canada wanted to repatriate the Canadian constitution. Up to that point, the statute law that formed the basis of Canada's constitution was an Act of the UK Parliament (the British North America Act 1867), reflecting Canada's history as a dominion of the United Kingdom. Some provinces in Canada were opposed to the repatriation proposals and challenged the planned resolution of the two Houses of Parliament in Canada (which was to be in the form of an address to the Queen, requesting this reform). The provinces opposed to the change argued that any amendment to the constitutional system could not occur without the consent of the provinces of Canada. The majority of the court accepted that there was a convention that provinces consent, but held that the powers of the two Canadian Houses of Parliament were unlimited as a matter of law. Allan disagreed with this approach.

T.R.S. Allan, 'Law, conventions, prerogative: Reflections prompted by the *Canadian Constitutional Case*' (1986) 45 *Cambridge Law Journal* 305

The present argument envisages that the validity of a statute might properly give way, in an extreme case, to the force of convention. On one view, the fundamental nature of the convention threatened in the Canadian patriation case would justify that result. Such a result would obviously be rare. There is no reason, however, why legal remedies should not be granted in support of a convention, where that convention enjoys a firm foundation in principle. In substance, the Crossman Diaries case acknowledged that possibility.[48] As a source of law, a constitutional convention could rarely prevail over the explicit terms of an Act of Parliament: legislative supremacy is itself a major component of our conventional morality. [. . . T]he authority of Parliament to legislate for Canada could not be constrained—as a matter of English law—by any convention requiring dominion consent. It does not follow, however, that convention may not be an important source of law governing the interpretation of statute, or influencing the development of the common law. As a practical matter, the enforcement of any particular convention must normally involve the application of existing legal doctrine in order to provide a suitable remedy. The equitable doctrine protecting matters of confidence, in Crossman, and the rules of natural justice, in GCHQ, were harnessed to supply a legal remedy for breach of convention.[49] The sharp law/convention dichotomy, however, neglects the sense in which recognition of convention by the courts has a normative aspect. It imports an application of political principle. The traditional orthodoxy is worth contesting because it obscures the important sense in which constitutional morality is a legitimate source of law. It rests on a separation of legal from political principle which, in the last analysis, cannot be sustained.

In the following extract, Farrah Ahmed, Richard Albert, and Adam Perry argue that courts should, in some circumstances, enforce a specific category of constitutional conventions, which they label 'power-shifting conventions'. They give as an example that the monarch has legal power to dismiss

[47] [1981] 1 SCR 753.

[48] In *Attorney-General v Jonathan Cape Ltd* [1976] QB 752, the government attempted to suppress the publication of *Diaries of a Cabinet Minister*, an account of life as a government minister by Richard Crossman MP, on the grounds that it breached the constitutional conventions that Cabinet proceedings are confidential and of collective ministerial responsibility.

[49] In the *GCHQ* case (*Council of Civil Service Unions v Minister for the Civil Service* [1985] AC 374), trade unions—which had, in the past, always been consulted on changes to terms and conditions of employment—sought judicial review of a unilateral decision by the Prime Minister Mrs Thatcher to ban workers at an intelligence-gathering agency from belonging to an independent trade union.

ministers but *by convention* this is exercised only on the Prime Minister's advice. If the monarch purported to dismiss a minister for personal reasons, judicial intervention to enforce the convention 'would uphold rather than disrupt, the constitutional allocation of power'. The common law ground of judicial review known as legitimate expectation would provide the doctrinal basis for this.[50]

F. Ahmed, R. Albert, and A. Perry, 'Enforcing Constitutional Conventions' (2020) 17(4) *International Journal of Constitutional Law* 1146, 1159

> Under the doctrine of legitimate expectations, if a public body engages in a practice of acting in some way sufficient to generate a social rule, then the court will provide a remedy if that body breaches that rule, unless there is good reason to the contrary. Power-shifting conventions are social rules. Providing a remedy for the breach of a rule is a form of enforcement. The doctrine of legitimate expectations provides a legal foundation for enforcing these power-shifting conventions. We acknowledge that the doctrine has not so far been used in this way and would need to be extended. But to extend the existing doctrine to the closely analogous context of constitutional conventions accords with the role of the common law judge as agent of incremental legal development. [. . .]
>
> Here, then, is the role we see for judges. By enforcing power-shifting conventions, judges uphold the legitimate allocation of power—legitimate, not according to judges but according to constitutional actors. In our vision, judges act as executors of the will and judgment of constitutional actors. Constitutional actors decide who can legitimately wield power; judges execute their decisions. To fulfil this role, judges need only do what they currently do in many other contexts when they enforce the social rules with which public actors bind themselves. Judges therefore have an executive role to play in giving effect to widely shared judgments of who can legitimately exercise power, and they can do so using doctrinal tools they already have available to them.

The study of constitutional conventions highlights the hybrid nature of the UK constitution. Many of its most important rules depend on shared understandings rather than legal commands. Courts may recognise conventions when necessary to decide legal questions, but their enforcement remains primarily political. Debates about whether judges should go further reveal how the boundary between law and politics remains fluid, and how the constitution ultimately depends on both legal rules and the self-restraint of those who exercise power.

PAUSE FOR REFLECTION

Constitutional conventions are political rules rather than laws. They depend on good faith and shared understanding rather than on court enforcement. If a government were to breach a major constitutional convention should the courts intervene to protect the principle at stake, or should enforcement remain a matter of political accountability?

What would be gained or lost if judges began enforcing conventions?

Reflect on whether the current balance between political accountability and judicial oversight remains appropriate in today's constitutional climate.

[50] See Chapter 19, section 19.4 on legitimate expectations generally.

2.5 INTERNATIONAL TREATIES

A final place to look for rules relevant to the United Kingdom's constitutional order is in treaties—formal agreements between states that create binding obligations in international law.[51] Treaties cover a wide range of topics, from trade and the environment to taxation and human rights. Some have profound constitutional consequences, shaping how public power is exercised within the UK, and it is those that we are interested in. Examples include:

- European Convention on Human Rights 1950 (ECHR), introduced enforceable human rights standards for individuals; ECHR rights were later incorporated into UK law by the Human Rights Act 1998.
- Treaty of Rome 1957 (and later EU treaties), which established the European Economic Community and subsequently the European Union (EU), of which the United Kingdom was a member from 1973 to 2020.
- The Belfast (or Good Friday) Agreement 1998, consisting of a political agreement among Northern Ireland's parties and the British–Irish Agreement between the UK and Irish governments, and international treaty that underpins the peace settlement and devolved institutions.
- The EU–UK Withdrawal Agreement 2020 which set the terms for the United Kingdom's exit from the EU, including the Northern Ireland Protocol, with major implications for trade and the UK Parliament's law-making powers.[52]

2.5.1 TREATIES AND GOVERNMENT

Treaty making is a function of government. The negotiation and signature of treaties are exercises of the royal prerogative, carried out by ministers with advice from officials, on behalf of the Crown.[53] Ratification—the final confirmation of consent to be bound—creates obligations under international law but has no automatic effect in domestic law.

The *Ministerial Code* recognises the '*overarching duty on ministers to comply with the law, including international law and treaty obligations, and to protect the integrity of public life*'.[54] The boundaries of that duty have been tested in recent years. In 2020, the Secretary of State for Northern Ireland, Brandon Lewis MP, conceded that a bill under consideration did '*break international law in a very specific and limited way*'.[55] The Attorney General, Suella Braverman MP, told an angry House of Commons that '*Parliamentary supremacy means it is entirely constitutional and proper for Parliament to enact legislation, even if it breaches international treaty obligations*'.[56] The relevant clauses in the

[51] 'International law' includes two main sources. *Treaties* are formal agreements between states that create binding obligations once ratified—the focus of this chapter. *Customary international law* arises from the consistent practice of states accepted as legally required; examples include the prohibition of torture and diplomatic immunity. In the UK, treaty obligations take effect in domestic law only when incorporated by Parliament, but rules of customary international law are generally regarded as part of the common law unless displaced by statute or binding precedent (see *Trendtex Trading Corporation v Central Bank of Nigeria* [1977] QB 529 (CA)).

[52] See Chapter 24. [53] On prerogative powers, see Chapter 10.

[54] *Ministerial Code* (Cabinet Office, 13 October 2025) para 1.6.

[55] For background, see House of Commons Library, *The United Kingdom Internal Market Bill 2019–21* (Briefing Paper No.9003, 2020) p.63 https://researchbriefings.files.parliament.uk/documents/CBP-9003/CBP-9003.pdf accessed 18 October 2025.

[56] HC Deb 24 September 2020, vol 680, col 1124.

United Kingdom Internal Market bill would have allowed ministers to make regulations overriding parts of the Northern Ireland Protocol, a binding element of the EU-UK Withdrawal Agreement. Following strong criticism from Parliament, lawyers, and the European Commission, the clauses were withdrawn before the bill became law.

A later controversy concerned the Conservative government's plan to transfer some asylum seekers to Rwanda. Under section 5 of the Safety of Rwanda (Asylum and Immigration) Act 2024, ministers had discretion to decide whether the United Kingdom would comply with interim measures issued by the European Court of Human Rights; this was never tested, however, as under the incoming Labour government, Parliament repealed this provision in 2025. Critics argued that this power would have allowed ministers to disregard the UK's obligations under international law and more broadly that the whole scheme was contrary to international law.[57]

PAUSE FOR REFLECTION

Parliament is legally supreme, but the UK is also bound by the international treaties it has signed. If Parliament passes a law that breaches those treaties, is that an acceptable use of sovereign power—or does it undermine the rule of law and the UK's credibility in international affairs? How might your answer differ if the treaty concerned fundamental rights, such as those protecting children, refugees, or the environment?

2.5.2 TREATIES AND PARLIAMENT

The UK Parliament oversees treatymaking and implementation in two ways: by scrutinising treaties before ratification and by incorporating treaty obligations into domestic law.

Under Part 2 of the Constitutional Reform and Governance Act 2010 (CRAG), most treaties must be laid before Parliament for 21 sitting days before they can be ratified by the Government. Either House may object. If the House of Commons passes a resolution against ratification, the Government cannot proceed unless it lays the treaty again and explains its reasons. The House of Lords has established an International Agreements Committee to examine all treaties subject to the CRAG procedure. In 2025, the Committee called for reform to address what it described as an accountability gap, noting that the current 21-day timeline 'simply does not allow Parliament to conduct an in-depth evidence-based review of a significant treaty'.[58]

Constitutional systems differ in how treaties become part of domestic law. In monist systems, international law and domestic law are seen as part of a single legal order, so a ratified treaty automatically forms part of the national legal order and may be applied by courts. In dualist systems, such as the United Kingdom, treaties take effect in domestic law only if Parliament enacts legislation to that effect. The constitutional rationale is that Government cannot create or change domestic law without parliamentary approval. There are three main models of incorporation:[59]

- Direct incorporation occurs when an Act of Parliament reproduces the wording of a treaty, makes it binding on public authorities, and allows individuals to rely on it in legal proceedings. The Human Rights Act 1998, which gives effect to the European Convention on Human Rights, is an example.

[57] Joint Civil Society Statement on the Rwanda Bill for Second Reading in the House of Lords (2024) https://www.amnesty.org.uk/joint-civil-society-statement-rwanda-bill?utm_ accessed 18 October 2025.

[58] House of Lords International Agreements Committee, *Treaty Scrutiny in Westminster: Addressing the Accountability Gap*, 10th Report of Session 2024–26, HL Paper 168.

[59] See Kasey McCall-Smith, Incorporating Human Rights in Scotland, 'Different Models of Incorporation' https://www.law.ed.ac.uk/research/research-projects/incorporating-human-rights-in-scotland accessed 19 October 2025.

- Indirect incorporation happens when an Act of Parliament refers to a treaty and requires public authorities to take it into account or avoid breaching it, without creating directly enforceable rights. For instance, section 2 of the Asylum and Immigration Appeals Act 1993 provides that nothing in the immigration rules shall lay down any practice which would be contrary to the 1951 Geneva Convention relating to the Status of Refugees.
- Piecemeal incorporation describes situations where Parliament gives effect to parts of a treaty, often without referring to it directly. Obligations under the 1982 UN Convention on the Law of the Sea (UNCLOS), for example, underpin the Territorial Sea Act 1987, the Continental Shelf Act 1964 (as amended), and the Marine and Coastal Access Act 2009.

If the UK Government decides that a treaty should take effect in domestic law, it is normally for the UK Parliament to pass the necessary legislation. Since devolution in 1998, however, the devolved governments and legislatures have sometimes taken different approaches to incorporation. The United Nations Convention on the Rights of the Child 1989 (UNCRC) illustrates this. The United Kingdom ratified the Convention in 1991, but successive UK Governments have taken the view that formal incorporation is unnecessary. As a result, the UNCRC has no direct or indirect effect in England or at the UK level, and the same applies in Northern Ireland. The other two nations have taken a different stance.

In Scotland, the United Nations Convention on the Rights of the Child (Incorporation) (Scotland) Bill 2021 sought to make the UNCRC directly enforceable in Scots law. The UK Supreme Court held that Scottish Parliament did not have legislative competence to require Scottish courts to 'read down' provisions in UK Acts of Parliament to make them compatible with the UNCRC, or to declare them incompatible with UNCHR rights.[60] After amendment, the UNCRC (Incorporation) (Scotland) Act 2024 was enacted, giving children enforceable rights against Scottish public authorities within devolved areas. In Wales, the Rights of Children and Young Persons (Wales) Measure 2011 uses indirect incorporation: it requires Welsh ministers to have 'due regard' to the UNCRC when exercising their functions, but UNCRC rights are directly enforceable in the Welsh courts.

PAUSE FOR REFLECTION

Children's rights under the UNCRC are protected differently in different parts of the UK. What is the constitutional logic behind this variation? How does it reflect the design of the UK's devolved system of government, and what tensions might arise between international obligations accepted by the UK as a whole and domestic legal diversity within it? (Chapter 6 explores devolution in more detail).

2.5.3 TREATIES AND THE COURTS

When a treaty has been incorporated—directly or indirectly—courts will apply the terms of the relevant statute. The more difficult question is how courts treat treaties that have *not* been incorporated. First, when a court is interpreting an ambiguous word or concept in domestic legislation, courts will presume that Parliament intended the law to conform to the United Kingdom's international law obligations.[61]

[60] *Reference by the Attorney General and the Advocate General for Scotland* [2021] UKSC 42.

[61] *R v Secretary of State for the Home Department, ex parte Brind* [1991] 1 AC 696, 747, 760. For examples, see *Cheney v Conn (Inspector of Taxes)* [1968] 1 WLR 242, discussed in Chapter 3 and *Moohan and another v Lord Advocate (Advocate General for Scotland intervening)* [2014] UKSC 67, [2015] AC 901.

Second, provisions in an unincorporated treaty may also give rise to a ground of judicial review known as legitimate expectation.[62] The principle is that if the United Kingdom has made clear international commitments—such as by ratifying a treaty—it may be unfair for the Government to act in a way that contradicts those commitments at home. The courts have occasionally treated such conduct as breaching a legitimate expectation, although the law in this area continues to develop.[63]

More fundamentally, at least one senior judge has suggested that the restrictions placed on the courts by the 'dualist' approach are unjustified. In 2015, the UK Supreme Court heard a case in which it was argued that the government's policy of having a 'benefits cap' was incompatible with the UNCRC. The benefit cap reduced an unemployed person's housing benefit if their total entitlement to welfare benefits (including child benefit) was more than the net median earnings of working households. Three single mothers challenged the lawfulness of the cap, contending that it would have a disproportionate impact on children in larger families. Article 3.1 of UNCRC which states '*In all actions concerning children [. . .] the best interests of the child shall be a primary consideration*'. The UNCRC had not been incorporated into domestic law. The majority followed orthodox dualist thinking, holding that art. 3.1 of the UNCRC could not be directly relied upon—it was not part of domestic law. Giving a minority judgment, Lord Kerr JSC took a radical line:

R (SG) v Secretary of State for Work and Pensions (Child Poverty Action Group intervening)
[2015] UKSC 16

254. I consider that the time has come for the exception to the dualist theory in human rights conventions foreshadowed by Lord Slynn in *Lewis* [2001] 2 AC 50 and rather more firmly expressed by Lord Steyn in *In re McKerr* [2004] 1 WLR 807 to be openly recognised. This can properly be done in relation to such conventions without espousing the complete abandonment of the theory advocated by some of the commentators referred to above [not included in this extract].

255. If Lord Steyn is right, as I believe he is, to characterise the rationale for the dualist theory as a form of protection of the citizen from abuses by the executive, the justification for refusing to recognise the rights enshrined in an international convention relating to human rights and to which the United Kingdom has subscribed as directly enforceable in domestic law is not easy to find. Why should a convention which expresses the United Kingdom's commitment to the protection of a particular human right for its citizens not be given effect as an enforceable right in domestic law?

256. Standards expressed in international treaties or conventions dealing with human rights to which the United Kingdom has subscribed must be presumed to be the product of extensive and enlightened consideration. There is no logical reason to deny to United Kingdom citizens domestic law's vindication of the rights that those conventions proclaim. If the Government commits itself to a standard of human rights protection, it seems to me entirely logical that it should be held to account in the courts as to its actual compliance with that standard. This is particularly so in the case of the UNCRC. On its website UNICEF has stated: 'The CRC is the basis of all of UNICEF's work. It is the most complete statement of children's rights ever produced and is the most widely-ratified international human rights Treaty in history'.

257. I therefore consider that article 3.1 of the UNCRC is directly enforceable in United Kingdom domestic law. A primacy of importance ought to have been given to the rights of children in devising the Regulations which bring the benefits cap into force. For the reasons given by Baroness Hale DPSC, I have concluded that this has not taken place.

[62] See Chapter 19, section 19.4.
[63] *R v Secretary of State for the Home Department, ex parte Ahmed* [1999] Imm AR 22 (CA).

In a 2021 judgment, the UK Supreme Court confirmed that it would be constitutionally inappropriate for a court to apply an unincorporated treaty (again, the UNCRC) as the treaty was not part of the law of the United Kingdom[64]—though as noted above, the position is now different in Scotland and Wales.

PAUSE FOR REFLECTION

Which of the following statements do you prefer?

(a) The dualist system respects democracy; it would be wrong for national law to recognize rules made by government in treaty-making that have not been approved by Parliament.

(b) The dualist system is wrong in principle: if the government has made promises about individual rights to other governments in a treaty, it is unfair if citizens cannot benefit from those rights in national courts.

2.6 CONCLUDING COMMENTS

In this chapter, we have seen that constitutional rules come from several sources—Acts of Parliament, the common law, conventions, and international treaties—which together form the framework of the United Kingdom's uncodified constitution. Behind the question of where the United Kingdom's constitutional rules come from—and whether they should be brought together in a single written document—lies a continuing debate between political and common law constitutionalists. Each takes a distinct view of how democracy works and of the role law should play in limiting state power (see Table 2.2).

Table 2.2 Political and legal constitutionalism compared

Topic	Political constitutionalists	Legal constitutionalists
Parliamentary supremacy (see Chapter 3)	Regard parliamentary sovereignty as the foundation of the constitution. Elected representatives, not judges, should have the final say on the laws under which people live.	Regard unconstrained parliamentary power as a threat to liberty. The constitution should impose legal limits on what Parliament may do.
Rule of law (see Chapter 4)	Emphasise *rule by law*: government must act according to law but the content of law is for Parliament to decide.	Support a *substantive* rule of law that protects rights and upholds constitutional principles enforceable by the courts.
Separation of powers (see Chapter 5)	Give priority to political accountability through Parliament and elections.	Emphasise judicial and legal checks to ensure power is exercised lawfully and fairly.
Devolution (see Chapter 6)	See devolution mainly as a political settlement managed through negotiation between governments.	View devolution as part of a wider legal framework that distributes and limits power between the centre and the devolved nations.

[64] *R (SC) v Secretary of State for Work and Pensions* [2021] UKSC 26.

We revisit these perspectives at several points in Part I. The remaining chapters in Part I examine in more detail some of the functions of and principles underpinning the constitutional system: parliamentary supremacy (Chapter 3), the rule of law (Chapter 4), separating and balancing powers (Chapter 5), and devolution (Chapter 6).

QUESTIONS

1. List the main sources of the United Kingdom's constitutional rules. Which of these do you think has the greatest practical influence on how the British state operates today, and why?
2. In a country without a single written Constitution, what does it mean to describe an action or law as 'unconstitutional'? Give one example. What does it mean to say something that happens in the constitutional system is 'unlawful'?
3. Imagine a researcher from outside the United Kingdom studies only Acts of Parliament to understand how the UK constitutional system works. What would they learn, and what would they miss by ignoring the common law, conventions, and international treaties?
4. Compare constitutional conventions with legal rules. How does each guide behaviour? What happens if either is broken?
5. In the following situation, identify the different institutions involved—Parliament, the courts, the government, and the public—and discuss how each contributes to (or challenges) democracy in this situation. In *Chahal v United Kingdom* (1997) 23 EHRR 413, the European Court of Human Rights (the international court which adjudicates on the ECHR) held that a person may not be deported to a country where he or she will face a real risk of torture or inhuman or degrading treatment. This ruling is binding on the UK government in international law. In 2001, the government proposed legislation to enable ministers to order that foreign nationals suspected of involvement in terrorism be detained in prison without charge or trial in cases in which it was not possible (because of the *Chahal* ruling) to remove them from the United Kingdom. That legislation was passed by Parliament as the Anti-terrorism, Crime and Security Act 2001 (although many MPs were opposed to the proposals). In 2004, judges of the United Kingdom's highest court held that those provisions were incompatible with the ECHR on the grounds that they were disproportionate and discriminatory: see *A v Secretary of State for the Home Department* [2004] UKHL 56. The government responded to this ruling by introducing legislation to repeal the relevant parts of the 2001 Act and create a different way of monitoring suspects (through 'control orders'). In October 2005, 79 per cent of people questioned in a survey in London said that deporting or excluding non-UK citizens who encourage terrorism is acceptable.
6. After studying Table 2.2 above, which approach—political constitutionalism or legal constitutionalism—do you find most persuasive, and why? Can you think of a current issue that illustrates your view?

FURTHER READING

Cabinet Office, *The Cabinet Manual: A Guide to the Laws, Conventions and Rules on the Operation of Government* (2011, London: Cabinet Office).

Jowell, J. and O'Cinneide, C. (eds), *The Changing Constitution*, 9th edn (2019, Oxford: OUP).

Kavanagh, A., *The Collaborative Constitution* (2023, CUP).

Loughlin, M., *The British Constitution: A Very Short Introduction* (2013, Oxford: OUP).

Wheatle, S. and O'Loughlin, A. (eds), *Diverse Voices in Public Law* (2024, Bristol University Press).

Young, A. L., *Democratic Dialogue and the Constitution* (2017, OUP).

3

THE LEGISLATIVE SUPREMACY OF THE UK PARLIAMENT

CENTRAL ISSUES

1. In the United Kingdom, parliamentary supremacy means that courts must treat Acts of Parliament as legally authoritative and cannot refuse to apply them, even where legislation appears inconsistent with fundamental rights or constitutional principles. The usual justification centres on democratic legitimacy: any limits on what Parliament may enact should be imposed by elected representatives and, ultimately, by voters.
2. Some commentators argue that parliamentary supremacy reflects a historically English understanding of constitutional authority and sits uneasily with the political traditions and evolving systems of government in Scotland, Wales, and Northern Ireland.
3. At one level, parliamentary supremacy can be described through a series of legal rules. These include the enrolled bill rule, which prevents courts from examining how legislation was enacted inside Parliament; and the rule that international treaties cannot override a statute.
4. The source of the doctrine is contested. It is neither created by statute nor explained by constitutional convention, and commentators disagree on whether it originates in the common law or stands as a constitutional principle of its own kind.
5. A practical consequence often attributed to parliamentary supremacy is that Acts of Parliament cannot be entrenched—that is, made harder to amend or repeal because of their subject matter or importance. Whether this is an absolute rule remains a matter of debate.
6. A further practical issue is implied repeal. Under the usual approach, if two statutory provisions conflict, the later one prevails. This can be problematic where the earlier statute deals with matters of constitutional significance, raising questions about whether all Acts should be treated as equally open to repeal by implication.
7. The doctrine of parliamentary supremacy was closely bound up with the structures of the British Empire. The Imperial Parliament at Westminster claimed legal authority to legislate for many territories under British control. As these territories achieved independence, most rejected parliamentary supremacy as a model for their new constitutions and instead adopted systems based on constitutional supremacy.
8. The Human Rights Act 1998 sought to preserve parliamentary supremacy by allowing courts to issue declarations of incompatibility, rather than to invalidate legislation that conflicts with ECHR rights. How far this approach reshapes the practical balance between Parliament and the courts remains contested.

3.1 INTRODUCTION

Imagine Parliament passes a law saying that every social-media platform must hand over users' private messages to the police on request. Many people would think this is a serious intrusion into personal privacy. You might expect the courts to step in. But if the Act is clearly worded, judges cannot strike it down. In the United Kingdom's constitutional system, Parliament has the legal authority to make any law it chooses. That is the core idea behind parliamentary supremacy.[1]

This chapter explores the principle of parliamentary supremacy it in two ways. First, we focus on the legal rules: what supremacy means in practice, and how the courts apply it. Then we turn to a bigger question: is this principle still defensible today? As you saw in Chapter 2, public lawyers often disagree about how the constitution should work. Legal constitutionalists argue that law—especially the common law or a future written constitution—should limit state power. Political constitutionalists are more sceptical of courts and put their trust in democracy, insisting that elected politicians, not judges, should have the final say. Parliamentary supremacy lies at the heart of this debate. For its defenders, it ensures democratic control over lawmaking. For its critics, it leaves dangerous gaps in the protection of rights and freedoms and basic constitutional principles.

Within the United Kingdom, only the UK Parliament has legal supremacy; the devolved legislatures have defined limits to their lawmaking powers. The Scottish Parliament and Senedd Cymru/Welsh Parliament operate under a reserved-powers model: they may legislate on any matter unless it is reserved to Westminster by the relevant devolution Acts.[2] Northern Ireland's settlement is more intricate, dividing matters into excepted, reserved and transferred groups, but the core principle is similar: the Assembly can legislate only within the fields of competence set out in statute. The UK Supreme Court may rule that a provision of devolved legislation is outside competence, in which case it has no legal effect.

Parliamentary supremacy also does not prevent the courts from quashing delegated legislation made by ministers if it exceeds, or is otherwise incompatible with, the powers granted by Parliament.[3]

3.2 PARLIAMENTARY SUPREMACY AS A SET OF RULES

Professor Dicey presented parliamentary supremacy as a central virtue of the British constitution, and his classic formulation remains a useful starting point for understanding the doctrine.

A.V. Dicey, *Introduction to the Study of the Law of the Constitution* (1885; 10th edn 1959, London: Macmillan & Co.), pp. 39–40

> The principle of Parliamentary sovereignty means neither more nor less than this, namely, that Parliament [. . .] has, under the English constitution, the right to make or unmake any law whatever; and, further, that no person or body is recognised by the law of England as having a right to override or set aside the legislation of Parliament.

[1] We use the term 'parliamentary supremacy' in this chapter. Some writers instead use 'parliamentary sovereignty'. The two are generally treated as equivalent in contemporary scholarship, though a few commentators distinguish them in narrow theoretical terms. For present purposes, the terms can be read interchangeably.

[2] See Chapter 6. [3] See Chapter 13.

> A law may, for our present purpose, be defined as 'any rule which will be enforced by the Courts'. The principle then of Parliamentary sovereignty may, looked at from its positive side, be thus described: Any Act of Parliament, or any part of an Act of Parliament, which makes a new law, or repeals or modifies an existing law, will be obeyed by the Courts. The same principle, looked at from its negative side, may be thus stated: There is no person or body of persons who can, under the English constitution, make rules which override or derogate from an Act of Parliament, or which (to express the same thing in other words) will be enforced by the Courts in contravention of an Act of Parliament.

Dicey's definition was considered by a House of Commons select committee in 2010:

House of Commons European Scrutiny Committee, *The EU Bill and Parliamentary Sovereignty*, Tenth Report, Session 2010–11, vol. I (HC 633)

What is meant by Parliamentary sovereignty?

23. In the light of the evidence submitted to the inquiry we concluded, agreeing with Professor Bradley, that the term 'Parliamentary sovereignty' bears a number of meanings which can get confused. We prefer to use the term the 'legislative supremacy of Parliament' in this Report for the reasons so clearly set out by Professor Bradley: 'Dicey's Law of the Constitution made famous the phrase 'the sovereignty of Parliament', but a more exact term for the legal doctrine is 'legislative supremacy', whereby the power of the [King]-in-Parliament to legislate is subject to no legal limitations, and the courts have no power to review the validity of Acts of Parliament. This doctrine is always considered to be subject to the limitation that Parliament is unable to bind its successors (a matter to which I return briefly below). An advantage of using the term supremacy rather than sovereignty is that it enables the supremacy of EU law to be balanced against the supremacy of national law.'

Dicey's famous summary captures the essence of parliamentary supremacy, but it leaves many of the practical details unstated. Modern case law and constitutional practice reveal a fuller set of rules that shape how the doctrine operates today. If we tried to express those rules in the familiar language of an Act of Parliament, they might read along the following lines.

Note: this is the authors' own illustrative summary.

1 Legislative authority of Parliament

(1) It is recognized that the Parliament of the United Kingdom of Great Britain and Northern Ireland (referred to in this section as 'the UK Parliament') is sovereign.[4]

(2) The UK Parliament may—

  (a) make, amend and repeal laws, known as Acts of Parliament, and

  (b) define the procedures and formal requirements for an enactment to constitute an Act of Parliament.

[4] These words are used in European Union (Withdrawal Agreement) Act 2020, s. 38.

(3) For the avoidance of doubt, it is declared that a provision in an Act of Parliament may—

(a) alter the common law, whether prospectively or retrospectively[5]

(b) be inconsistent with the United Kingdom's obligations under international law

(c) conflict with principles of human rights recognised by domestic or international law;[6]

(d) restrict or exclude the jurisdiction of a court,[7]

provided that Parliament's intention to do so is expressed in clear and unambiguous terms. The interpretation of such terms is a matter for the courts.

(4) It is recognized that

(a) the UK Parliament will not normally legislate with respect to devolved matters without the consent of the Scottish Parliament, Senedd Cymru, or Northern Ireland Assembly[8]

(b) This principle, known as the Sewel Convention, is a political convention and does not create a legally enforceable restriction.

(5) It is affirmed that judgments, decisions and interim measures of the European Court of Human Rights—

(a) do not form part of domestic law unless incorporated by an Act of Parliament, and

(b) do not limit the authority of the UK Parliament to legislate.[9]

2 Express repeal and entrenchment

(1) Any provision contained in an Act of Parliament ('Act A') may be repealed or amended by a later Act of Parliament ('Act B').

(2) Subsection (1) does not apply[10] where Act A includes an express entrenchment provision, stating that all or part of the Act may only be amended or repealed—

(a) following a specified parliamentary procedure that differs from the ordinary legislative process, or

(b) with the approval of a majority of voters in a referendum held for that purpose.

(3) Act B may amend or repeal such a provision only if it complies with the requirements specified in Act A.

(4) For the purposes of this section, an entrenchment provision shall not be presumed effective unless clearly and unambiguously expressed.

3 Implied repeal

(1) Where a provision contained in a later Act of Parliament ('Act D') is irreconcilable with a provision in an earlier Act ('Act C'), the earlier provision shall be treated as repealed to the extent of the inconsistency.

(2) Subsection (1) does not apply[11] where—

(a) Act C is a constitutional statute, and

(b) there is no clear indication in Act D that Parliament intended to repeal or modify Act.

[5] See *R (Evans) v Attorney General* [2015] UKSC 21, [52].

[6] *R v Secretary of State for the Home Department* [2000] 2 AC 115, 131 (Lord Hoffmann).

[7] On ouster clauses, see Chapter 20.

[8] Words similar to these are used in the Scotland Act 1998, s. 28, the Government of Wales Act 2006, s. 107, and Northern Ireland Assembly Standing Order 42A; this is known as the Sewell Convention.

[9] The Conservative government led by Boris Johnson published a Bill of Rights Bill in 2022, designed to replace the Human Rights Act 1998; it was withdrawn. These words are like those used in clause 1(3).

[10] Many people would disagree with this formulation of the rule, as discussed in Section 3.6 (Entrenchment).

[11] See *Thoburn v Sunderland City Council* [2002] EWHC 195 (Admin), [60]–[67].

(3) For the purposes of the section, an Act of Parliament is a constitutional statute if it—
   (a) governs the legal relationship between individual and state in a general or foundational way, or
   (b) protects or restricts a fundamental constitutional right.
(4) A constitutional statute may only be amended by express and unambiguous words in a later Act of Parliament.
(5) Nothing in this section prevents Parliament from enacting legislation that expressly overrides a constitutional statute, but courts shall not infer such an intention from general or ambiguous language.

4 Courts are subject to parliamentary supremacy

(1) It is the constitutional duty of the courts to interpret, apply and give effect to Acts of Parliament.
(2) No court or tribunal may decline to apply a provision of an Act of Parliament on the basis that it is invalid or unconstitutional, unless the UK Parliament has expressly authorized such a course.[12]
(3) Courts retain the power to determine whether a purported Act of Parliament is validly enacted under the terms of the Parliament Acts 1911 and 1949.[13]
(4) It is recognized that the European Court of Human Rights may find that legislation enacted by the UK Parliament is incompatible with the European Convention on Human Rights, and may award just satisfaction to victims of such breaches.[14]
(5) In accordance with section 4 of the Human Rights Act 1998, a UK court may make a declaration of incompatibility if satisfied that a provision of an Act of Parliament is incompatible with a Convention right; such a declaration does not affect the validity, continued operation, or enforcement of that provision.
(6) Parliament may, by express and unambiguous language, limit or exclude the jurisdiction of a court to review decisions or interpret certain provisions, but general words shall not be taken to oust judicial review or displace the courts' constitutional role, except where clearly intended.[15]

5 Government is subject to parliamentary supremacy[16]

(1) Ministers must act in accordance with Acts of Parliament.
(2) Ministers may not exercise prerogative powers in a manner that overrides, contradicts, or frustrates any provision of an Act of Parliament, whether express or implied.[17]
(3) Any delegated legislation made by a Minister is unlawful if it exceeds the scope of authority granted by an Act of Parliament, or is otherwise inconsistent with the enabling Act.[18]

[12] See *R (Public Law Project) v Lord Chancellor* [2016] UKSC 39, [20].

[13] See discussion of *Jackson and others v Her Majesty's Attorney General* [2005] UKHL 56 in Chapter 19.

[14] See Chapter 4. [15] See Chapter 20.

[16] This section reflects the constitutional principle that the executive—meaning government ministers—derives legal authority from Parliament and cannot override legislation through the use of prerogative powers or delegated legislation. This principle has been confirmed in cases such as *R (Miller) v Secretary of State for Exiting the European Union* [2017] UKSC 5 and *R (UNISON) v Lord Chancellor* [2017] UKSC 51.

[17] See for example *R. (Miller) v Secretary of State for Existing the European Union* [2017] UKSC 5, [25] ('An important aspect of the fundamental principle of parliamentary sovereignty is that primary legislation is not subject to displacement by the Crown through the exercise of its prerogative powers'). On prerogative powers, see Chapter 10.

[18] On delegated legislation see Chapter 13.

3.3 WHAT THE COURTS SAY ABOUT PARLIAMENTARY SUPREMACY

How have courts defined their constitutional role in relation to Acts of Parliament? The dominant view has long been straightforward: judges recognise Acts of Parliament as binding law and have no authority to strike them down or not apply them in a case. In a brief period around the turn of the millennium, several judges made obiter comments in judgments and extra-judicial writing that common law constitutional rights and principles might, in exceptional circumstances, place limits on Parliament's authority. Those comments generated academic interest but were never tested in practice, and later case law has not built on them. More recent decisions of the Supreme Court, particularly under Lord Reed's presidency, have instead reaffirmed a restrained approach that treats parliamentary supremacy as a settled legal principle.

3.3.1 PARLIAMENTARY PROCEDURE IS NON-JUSTICIABLE

Mr Pickin, a campaigner to keep a railway line open in Somerset, sought to argue that a private Act of Parliament[19] should be set aside because allegedly fraudulent statements had been made during the parliamentary proceedings. Lord Reid explained that courts cannot question how Parliament makes its laws—even if fraud is alleged. Once a law has been passed, courts must apply it, no matter what happened during its passage.

British Railways Board v Pickin
[1974] AC 765, 782, 787–8

Lord Reid

In earlier times many learned lawyers seem to have believed that an Act of Parliament could be disregarded in so far as it was contrary to the law of God or the law of nature or natural justice but since the supremacy of Parliament was finally demonstrated by the Revolution of 1688 any such idea has become obsolete [. . .].

The function of the Court is to construe and apply the enactments of Parliament. The Court has no concern with the manner in which Parliament or its officers carrying out its Standing Orders perform these functions. Any attempt to prove that they were misled by fraud or otherwise would necessarily involve an enquiry into the manner in which they had performed their functions in dealing with the Bill which became the British Railways Act 1968. [. . .]

For a century or more both Parliament and the Courts have been careful not to act so as to cause conflict between them. Any such investigations as the Respondent seeks could easily lead to such a conflict, and I would only support it if compelled to do so by clear authority. But it appears to me that the whole trend of authority for over a century is clearly against permitting any such investigation.

This approach is known as the 'enrolled Bill rule': once a Bill has passed through the formal stages and received Royal Assent, it is treated as valid law, regardless of how it got there.

Can the enrolled Bill rule be circumvented by an early challenge to legislation before it receives Royal Assent? In *R (A) v Secretary of State for the Home Department* [2022] EWHC 360 (Admin), a

[19] On the distinction between private and public Acts, see Chapter 12.

group of asylum seekers challenged aspects of the consultation process leading to the Nationality and Borders Bill, introduced in the Commons in July 2021.[20] The court held that intervening in the legislative process would breach parliamentary privilege and cut across the constitutional separation of powers.[21] In short, parliamentary proceedings are a no-go area for the courts.

3.3.2 ACTS OF PARLIAMENT PREVAIL OVER INTERNATIONAL LAW

As we saw in Chapter 2, the United Kingdom's ratification of an international treaty does not, by itself, make its obligations or rights enforceable in domestic law; incorporation requires an Act of Parliament. Even where a treaty has been incorporated, that does not mean that another Act of Parliament can be struck down or not applied in a case for conflicting with the treaty.

Mr Cheney, a peace campaigner, argued that a tax imposed under statute was unlawful because some of the revenue would fund nuclear weapons in breach of an international treaty obligation. The court held that, whatever the use of the revenue and whatever the content of international law, the courts must still apply the statute tax law passed by Parliament. International obligations—whether incorporated or unincorporated—cannot override clear primary legislation unless Parliament has expressly given them that effect.

Cheney v Conn (Inspector of Taxes)
[1968] 1 WLR 242, 244–5

Ungoed-Thomas J

The submission is that the assessments are invalid because it is to be taken that what is collected will be, in part, applied in expenditure on the armed forces and devoted to the construction of nuclear weapons with the intention of using those weapons if certain circumstances should arise. It is conceded for the purposes of this case that a substantial part of the taxes for the years that I have mentioned was allocated to the construction of nuclear weapons. The issue therefore becomes whether the use of [tax] for the construction of nuclear weapons, with the intention of using them should certain circumstances arise, invalidates the assessments.

[. . .] I shall deal first with the relationship of statute law to international law and international conventions.

First, international law is part of the law of the land, but it yields to statute. That is made clear by the case of *Collco Dealings Ltd v Inland Revenue Commissioners*, where Viscount Simonds, quoted with approval, and in accordance with the decision of the House of Lords in that case, *Maxwell on the Interpretation Of Statutes* (10th edn), p 148. I quote: 'But if the statute is unambiguous, its provisions must be followed even if they are contrary to international law.' It is therefore very understandable why the taxpayer in this case relies primarily, at any rate, not on a conflict between international law in general and the statute, but on the conflict between the [Geneva Conventions] Act of 1957, and its reference to ratification, and another statute, the Finance Act 1964. Secondly, conventions which are ratified by an Act of Parliament are part of the law of the land; and, thirdly, conventions which are ratified, but not by an Act of Parliament, which would thereby give them statutory force, cannot prevail against a statute in unambiguous terms. [. . .]

It is, I may add, the [King] in Parliament and not the [King] independently of Parliament, acting as the executive through the cabinet, who makes what is law in this land.

[20] See Chapter 12, Section 12.4.3. [21] See Chapter 4.

The most significant incorporation of treaty rights in recent years is the Human Rights Act 1998, which makes rights from the European Convention on Human Rights part of national law. As we explore in Chapter 21, the Act was designed expressly to preserve parliamentary supremacy. Where a court concludes that a provision in an Act of Parliament is incompatible with the European Convention on Human Rights, the only remedy is a declaration of incompatibility, which leaves the provision's legal validity untouched and does not alter the outcome of the case. As Lord Hoffmann observed, '*Parliamentary sovereignty means that Parliament can, if it chooses, legislate contrary to fundamental principles of human rights*'.[22] The constraints on Parliament are political rather than legal, and the HRA does not alter that basic constitutional position.

For the avoidance of doubt, the rule that international treaty obligations cannot override Acts of Parliament does not prevent Parliament from requiring ministers or other public bodies to comply with those obligations. For example, section 2 of the Asylum and Immigration Appeals Act 1993 provides that '*Nothing in the immigration rules. . . shall require or authorise any person to act in a manner which is contrary to the Refugee Convention*'. That provision is a direct statutory instruction that the immigration rules—and those applying them—must operate consistently with the Convention. But the immigration rules are delegated legislation, not primary legislation, so when the courts enforce section 2 they are ensuring compliance with the 1993 Act itself, not questioning the validity of a statute in the way Mr Cheney sought to do.

3.3.3 DETERMINING WHETHER AN ACT HAS BEEN MADE LAWFULLY UNDER THE PARLIAMENT ACTS

In 2004, pro-hunting campaigners brought judicial review proceedings arguing that the Hunting Act 2004, which banned hunting certain wild mammals with dogs, was not a valid Act of Parliament. At first sight, inviting a court to rule on the validity of an Act looks like a direct challenge to parliamentary supremacy and the enrolled bill rule discussed above. But the claim raised a different kind of question, and for that reason was allowed to proceed.

The claim rested on the unusual parliamentary history of the Hunting Act. The House of Lords, acting in its legislative capacity, had blocked the passage of the Hunting Bill. In response, the government relied on the rarely used Parliament Acts 1911 and 1949. These Acts allow certain bills passed by the House of Commons to become law without the approval of the Lords if specified statutory conditions are met.[23] The challenge focused on the status of the 1949 Act itself. The claimants argued that it was not a valid Act of Parliament because it had been enacted using the alternative procedure created by the 1911 Act, and that this procedure did not authorise amendments to its own scope. Because the 1949 Act was invalid, the claimants argued so too was the Hunting Act.

This challenge required the Appellate Committee of the House of Lords to decide a narrow but important question: what counts as a properly enacted Act of Parliament when Parliament has itself created more than one lawful route for passing legislation? The issue was therefore quite different from Pickin. Pickin concerned allegations about what happened *inside* Parliament during the passage of a Bill, which the courts treat as non-justiciable. Jackson was about something else: whether the statutory conditions laid down in the Parliament Acts had been satisfied. Parliament had chosen to define, in legally binding terms, the circumstances in which a bill could become law without the Lords' consent. Once Parliament sets such legal conditions, it is for the courts to interpret those

[22] *R v Secretary of State for the Home Department, ex parte Simms, R v Secretary of State for the Home Department, ex parte O'Brien* [1999] UKHL 33.

[23] See Chapter 12.

conditions, just as they would interpret any other Act. On that basis, the court held that it was not questioning parliamentary supremacy at all. It was giving effect to Parliament's own instructions about how the alternative legislative procedure operates. The Law Lords upheld the validity of the 1949 Act and, therefore, the Hunting Act. Several members of the court offered broader reflections on parliamentary sovereignty and the nature of Acts passed under the Parliament Acts procedure, but on the central point they were unanimous: provided the statutory requirements in the Parliament Acts are met, legislation enacted under that procedure is a valid Act of Parliament. The courts can interpret those statutory requirements, but they will not inquire into the internal workings of either House.

3.3.4 OBITER DICTA ON WHETHER PARLIAMENTARY SUPREMACY MAY BE SUBJECT TO EXCEPTIONS

In the late 1990s and early 2000s several judicial observations—made in obiter dicta and in extra-judicial writing and speeches—suggested, at least in theory, that constitutional principles such as the rule of law might qualify Parliament's legislative authority in exceptional circumstances. The next extract comes from what is often regarded as the high-water mark of that debate. The case concerned whether a Scottish statute dealing with asbestos-related injuries fell within the Scottish Parliament's legislative competence. Although the court held that it did, Lord Hope used the opportunity to explore a broader question: whether the sovereignty of the UK Parliament is truly absolute, or whether there might be circumstances, however rare or extreme, in which a court could recognise limits on Parliament's authority.

AXA General Insurance Ltd v HM Advocate
[2011] UKSC 46

Lord Hope

50. The question whether the principle of the sovereignty of the United Kingdom Parliament is absolute or may be subject to limitation in exceptional circumstances is still under discussion. For Lord Bingham, writing extrajudicially, the principle is fundamental and in his opinion, as the judges did not by themselves establish the principle, it was not open to them to change it: *The Rule of Law*, p. 167. Lord Neuberger of Abbotsbury, in his Lord Alexander of Weedon lecture, *Who are the masters now?* (6 April 2011), said at para. 73 that, although the judges had a vital role to play in protecting individuals against the abuses and excess of an increasingly powerful executive, the judges could not go against the will of Parliament as expressed through a statute. Lord Steyn on the other hand recalled at the outset of his speech in *Jackson*, para. 71, the warning that Lord Hailsham of St Marylebone gave in *The Dilemma of Democracy* (1978), p 126 about the dominance of a government elected with a large majority over Parliament. This process, he said, had continued and strengthened inexorably since Lord Hailsham warned of its dangers. This was the context in which he said in para. 102 that the Supreme Court might have to consider whether judicial review or the ordinary role of the courts was a constitutional fundamental which even a sovereign Parliament acting at the behest of a complaisant House of Commons could not abolish.

51. We do not need, in this case, to resolve the question how these conflicting views about the relationship between the rule of law and the sovereignty of the United Kingdom Parliament may be reconciled. The fact that we are dealing here with a legislature that is not sovereign relieves us of that responsibility. It also makes our task that much easier.

The tide appears to have turned. Commentators have observed that under the leadership of President Lord Reed, the Supreme Court is affirming orthodox understandings of parliamentary supremacy. Writing in 2024, Lewis Graham discussed this trend.

L. Graham, 'Has the UK Supreme Court become more restrained in public law cases?' (2024) 87(5) *Modern Law Review* 1073, 1082

. . . it is clear that over the last few years the Court has adopted a particularly muscular conception of parliamentary sovereignty, no longer some background constitutional principle but in some cases almost a distinct legal tool in and of itself, the application of which has resulted, amongst other things, in greater limitations upon devolved governments, a stunting of the development of the common law, and a severely limited scope for review of legislation under the HRA.

We return to this in discussion in relation to the Human Rights Act.[24]

3.4 A DIFFERENT APPROACH IN SCOTLAND AND WALES?

Some scholars argue that parliamentary supremacy is a distinctively English idea, and that it had no clear counterpart in the constitutional traditions or trajectory of Scotland or Wales. This raises important questions about whether a single principle can—or should—define the authority of UK Parliament across the whole United Kingdom. In the following extract, Gavin Little shows how these ideas have shaped legal debate north of the border.

G. Little, 'Scotland and parliamentary sovereignty' (2004) 24 *Legal Studies* 540, 540, 543–4

In the context of Scottish constitutional reform, unionists have often viewed parliamentary sovereignty as an important symbol of Westminster's claim to political supremacy over Scotland. Importantly, however, the idea that an alternative concept of popular sovereignty operates in Scotland, whilst obviously of great significance to nationalists, also has a broad, non-party-political currency north of the border. [. . .]

[. . . I]t should be noted that Dicey's arguments have attracted criticism in the Scottish courts. For Scottish constitutional lawyers, the issue of parliamentary sovereignty has historically and conceptually been associated with important questions regarding the legal status of the Treaty of Union of 1707 between Scotland and England. Can the Treaty of Union, which created a new entity, the Parliament of Great Britain, and, inter alia, purports to guarantee the continued existence of certain historic Scottish institutions, prevail over inconsistent Acts of Parliament as a form of fundamental or higher law? Was, in JDB Mitchell's phrase, the UK Parliament 'born unfree'? As is well known, the status of parliamentary sovereignty was considered in the Scottish courts by Lord Cooper of Culross in the 1953 case of *MacCormick v The Lord Advocate*. The pursuer in the action was John MacCormick, who was then a leading figure in Scottish politics and the campaign for Scottish Home Rule. He challenged the new Queen's title as 'Elizabeth the Second' on the basis that it was, inter alia, incorrect historically (there has

[24] See Chapter 21.

never been an Elizabeth the First in Scotland), and in conflict with Article I of the Treaty of Union. In his decision, Lord Cooper stated:

> The principle of unlimited sovereignty of Parliament is a distinctly English principle which has no counterpart in Scottish constitutional law. It derives its origin from Coke and Blackstone, and was widely popularised during the nineteenth century by Bagehot and Dicey [. . .] Considering that the Union legislation extinguished the Parliaments of Scotland and England and replaced them by a new Parliament, I have difficulty in seeing why it should have been supposed that the new Parliament of Great Britain must inherit all the peculiar characteristics of the English Parliament but none of the Scottish Parliament, as if all that happened in 1707 was that Scottish representatives were admitted to the Parliament of England. That is not what was done.

Little concludes that 'Whatever may have motivated Lord Cooper's comments on sovereignty, it must be recognised that their legal significance is unclear and open to question'.

These constitutional tensions are not limited to academic debate. In 2019, the Scottish Parliament commented on the European Union (Withdrawal Agreement) Bill, reaffirming a long-standing view within Scottish legal tradition that sovereignty resides with the people, not with Parliament. This stands in contrast to the orthodox UK position, where legal supremacy is said to lie with the Crown in Parliament—a view that, as the Scottish Parliament noted, has never been fully accepted in Scotland.[25] Similarly, the Welsh Government has questioned whether the traditional doctrine of parliamentary supremacy still provides a sound foundation for an evolving multi-nation constitution.

Welsh Government, *Reforming our Union: Shared Governance in the UK*, 2nd edn (2021), p. 9

Whatever its historical origins, the United Kingdom is best seen now as a voluntary association of nations taking the form of a multi-national state, whose members share and redistribute resources and risks amongst themselves to advance their common interests.

Wales is committed to this association, which must be based on the recognition of popular sovereignty in each part of the UK; Parliamentary sovereignty as traditionally understood no longer provides a sound foundation for this evolving constitution.

PAUSE FOR REFLECTION

1. Are there any legal limits on what the UK Parliament can do when making laws? Consider how courts have described parliamentary sovereignty. Can they ever refuse to apply an Act of Parliament?
2. What political factors can limit Parliament's law-making power in practice? Think about examples where public protest, opposition in Parliament, or the prospect of an election have caused the government to change or drop proposed legislation.

[25] Scottish Parliament, *Legislative Consent Memorandum: European Union (Withdrawal Agreement) Bill* (2019) para. 43.

3.5 WHAT IS THE SOURCE OF PARLIAMENTARY SUPREMACY?

So far, we have looked at the rules that govern what the UK Parliament can do, and how courts respond to legislation. But where do these rules actually come from? In the absence of a written constitution, the UK's constitutional principles are found in a range of sources.[26] To understand the legal status of parliamentary supremacy, we now need to consider which of these sources give it authority.

So, where do the rules of parliamentary supremacy fit—are they found in statute, common law, or do they belong in a category of their own? This is not just an academic question. If these rules are part of the common law, then the courts may, in principle, be able to develop or even revise them—just as they do in areas like contract or tort. But if parliamentary supremacy is something more fundamental or politically rooted, then judicial innovation may not be legitimate. Understanding where these rules come from is key to understanding whether—and how—they might evolve.

3.5.1 STATUTE LAW?

At present, the basic rules of parliamentary supremacy are not set out in any single Act of Parliament. But could they be? Some commentators argue that this would be constitutionally impossible. This next section explores that argument—and asks whether parliamentary supremacy is the kind of principle that can be declared by Parliament itself, or whether doing so would assume precisely the authority that is in question. Salmond argues that not all rules of law come from other legal sources. At some point, the legal system must rely on an ultimate rule that doesn't come from statute or case law. Parliamentary supremacy, he says, is one of those rules—it exists because the legal system assumes it does.

Sir John Salmond, *Jurisprudence*, 12th edn (1966, London: Sweet & Maxwell), p. 111

> All rules of law have historical sources. As a matter of fact and history they have their origin somewhere, though we may not know what it is. But not all of them have legal sources. Were this so, it would be necessary for the law to proceed *ad infinitum*, in tracing the descent of its principles. It is requisite that the law should postulate one or more first causes, whose operation is ultimate and whose authority is underived [. . .] The rule that a man may not ride a bicycle on the footpath may have its source in the by-laws of a municipal council; the rule that these by-laws have the force of law has its source in an Act of Parliament. But whence comes the rule that Acts of Parliament have the force of law? This is legally ultimate; its source is historical only, not legal [. . .]. It is the law because it is the law, and for no other reason that it is possible for the law itself to take notice of. No statute can confer this power upon Parliament, for this would be to assume and act on the very power that is to be conferred.

Barendt notes that even if Parliament were to assert its own legislative supremacy in a statute, such a provision would be merely declaratory. It would not *create* Parliament's authority, because the authority of an Act already depends on the underlying rule that Acts of Parliament are legally binding. A statutory statement of supremacy cannot supply its own constitutional foundation; to do so would be circular.

[26] See Chapter 2.

E. Barendt, *An Introduction to Constitutional Law* (1998, Oxford: OUP), p. 87

Naturally, Parliament could declare by an Act of Parliament that it is legally sovereign and that it has unlimited entitlement to enact any legislation it likes. But such a declaratory statute would not add anything to its legislative capacity. Parliament can hardly confer constitutional authority on itself by its own enactment.

None of this, however, prevents Parliament from asserting its own legislative supremacy in statute. For example, section 28 of the Scotland Act 1998 (as amended) states that the devolution of powers to the Scottish Parliament does not affect the power of the UK Parliament to legislate for Scotland.[27] The provision also sets out the Sewell convention, that the UK Parliament 'will not normally legislate with regard to devolved matters without the consent of the Scottish Parliament'.[28] Similarly, section 38 of the European Union (Withdrawal Agreement) Act 2020 declares that 'the Parliament of the United Kingdom is sovereign.' However, such provisions are regarded as declaratory rather than legally enforceable. They serve as political affirmations of constitutional principles rather than as sources of new legal authority.[29]

3.5.2 COMMON LAW?

If the rules of parliamentary supremacy are neither created nor fully defined by statute, does it follow that they are part of the common law? Some scholars argue that parliamentary supremacy is a rule created by the courts themselves as part of the common law. If this is true, then courts could also limit or revise that rule in future cases.

E. Barendt, *An Introduction to Constitutional Law* (1998, Oxford: OUP), pp. 86–7 (footnotes omitted)

What is the source of the United Kingdom Parliament's legislative authority and what is the scope of that power? The short answer is that the source of its legislative authority is the common law, the uncodified rules of law formulated by judges when they decide particular cases. Further, it is for the courts to determine the scope of that authority. They must decide, for instance, whether Parliamentary legislative authority prevails over or gives way to inconsistent rules of European Community law [. . .]. It is largely for this reason the United Kingdom constitution can be described, among other things, as a common law constitution. The law reports are full of statements to the effect that it is the duty of the courts to give effect to enactments of Parliament, or that they cannot be challenged for infringing some fundamental right or the rules of international law. For example, a court easily rejected the argument that it was unconstitutional for Parliament to introduce the offence of incitement to racial hatred, because the law limited the fundamental right to freedom of speech. Judges have emphasized that the United Kingdom Parliament has unlimited legislative supremacy, or that it is sovereign.

It is therefore the courts, rather than Parliament itself, which have formulated the principle which is the corner-stone of the uncodified constitution of the United Kingdom.

[27] See Chapter 6. [28] See Chapter 2.

[29] G. Cowie (House of Commons Library), *Withdrawal Agreement Bill: Sovereignty, Special Status and the Withdrawal Agreement* (2019).

Barendt's view reflects a broader school of thought that treats parliamentary supremacy as a doctrine recognised and shaped by the courts—raising the possibility that judges could, in principle, revise or limit it if constitutional circumstances demand.

3.5.3 A CONSTITUTIONAL CONVENTION?

Some might wonder whether parliamentary supremacy is best understood as a constitutional convention. But that view can be quickly dismissed. One of the key features of conventions is that they are not legally enforceable—yet parliamentary supremacy is applied, and its rules are enforced, by the courts. This makes it fundamentally different from a non-legal political practice.

3.5.4 SOME OTHER CATEGORY OF NORM?

Some commentators argue that parliamentary supremacy does not fit neatly into any standard legal category. Instead, they suggest it stands in a class of its own. As we have seen, Sir John Salmond (1862–1924)[30] wrote that it '*is legally ultimate; its source is historical only, not legal [. . .]. It is the law because it is the law.*' Professor William Wade (1918–2004)[31] suggested that it is the 'ultimate *political* fact'. In the following extract, Wade sets out why he believed the principle lies beyond both statutory and common law foundations.

H.W.R. Wade, 'The basis of legal sovereignty' (1955) 13 *Cambridge Law Journal* 172, 174, 187–8 (footnotes omitted)

> An orthodox English lawyer, brought up consciously or unconsciously on the doctrine of parliamentary sovereignty stated by Coke and Blackstone, and enlarged upon by Dicey, could explain it in simple terms. He would say that it meant merely that no Act of the sovereign legislature (composed of the [King], Lords and Commons) could be invalid in the eyes of the courts; that it was always open to the legislature, so constituted, to repeal any previous legislation whatever; that therefore no Parliament could bind its successors; and that the legislature had only one process for enacting sovereign legislation, whereby it was declared to be the joint Act of the Crown, Lords and Commons in Parliament assembled. He would probably add that it is an invariable rule that in case of conflict between two Acts of Parliament, the later repeals the earlier. If he were then asked whether it would be possible for the United Kingdom to 'entrench' legislation—for example, if it should wish to adopt, a Bill of Rights which would be repealable only by some specially safeguarded process—he would answer that under English law this is a legal impossibility: it is easy enough to pass such legislation, but since that legislation, like all other legislation, would be repealable by any ordinary Act of Parliament the special safeguards would be legally futile. This is merely an illustration of the rule that one Parliament cannot bind its successors. It follows therefore that there is one, and only one, limit to Parliament's legal power: it cannot detract from its own continuing sovereignty. It is tempting to add that Parliament's power is therefore inalienable, but that is to anticipate a question which must be investigated later on. For, leaving that point aside, we

[30] After studying law at UCL, Salmond returned to New Zealand where he held posts as Solicitor General and as a judge.
[31] Wade's academic career was spent at the universities of Oxford and Cambridge. His biographer noted: '*The confidence and clarity of Wade's vision of the law could sometimes come across as cocksure. But it was always logical, principled, and practical.*'

> have already entered the area of controversy. Even the proposition that English law knows no means of 'entrenching' sovereign legislation, which most English lawyers would accept as a self-evident truth, has been questioned or denied by leading authorities. [. . .]
>
> [I]f no statute can establish the rule that the courts obey Acts of Parliament, similarly no statute can alter or abolish that rule. The rule is above and beyond the reach of statute [. . .] because it is itself the source of the authority of statute. This puts it into a class by itself among rules of common law, and the apparent paradox that it is unalterable by Parliament turns out to be a truism. The rule of judicial obedience is in one sense a rule of common law, but in another sense—which applies to no other rule of common law—it is the ultimate *political* fact upon which the whole system of legislation hangs. Legislation owes its authority to the rule: the rule does not owe its authority to legislation. To say that Parliament can change the rule, merely because it can change any other rule, is to put the cart before the horse. For the relationship between the courts of law and Parliament is first and foremost a political reality.

Goldsworthy offers a different view. He says parliamentary supremacy is based on agreement—among judges, Parliament, and government—that Acts of Parliament are the highest law. This means courts cannot change the doctrine on their own. But it also means Parliament cannot unilaterally entrench its own powers.

J. Goldsworthy, 'Abdicating and limiting Parliament's sovereignty' (2006) 17 *King's College Law Journal* 255, 261

> [. . .] the doctrine of parliamentary sovereignty is constituted by a consensus among the senior officials of all branches of government. It was not (as history confirms) made by the judges alone. Its content is fixed by official consensus, and it is unclear insofar as there is no consensus. It cannot be changed unilaterally by any one branch of government, unless it is part of the consensus that it can be so changed, and there is little evidence that it is. Of course, any change to a rule of recognition must start somewhere: someone has to initiate the requisite change in consensus. The courts can attempt to initiate change, but they can succeed only if the other branches of government are willing to accept it.

Goldsworthy suggests that it would be wrong for the courts to alter parliamentary supremacy because '*they could impose all kinds of limits on Parliament's authority without any democratic input*'.[32] But, equally, it would be wrong for Parliament to attempt to do so: '*[I]f Parliament had such authority, a political party with temporary control of both Houses could protect its partisan policies, enacted into law, from amendment or repeal by majorities in future Parliaments, which would also be undemocratic.*'[33]

3.5.5 THE DEBATE ABOUT THE SOURCE OF PARLIAMENTARY SUPREMACY

In 2010, a House of Commons select committee examined the long-standing debate about where the legislative supremacy of Parliament comes from. The inquiry was prompted by wider concerns about the impact of EU law and judicial power on parliamentary authority. Drawing on evidence from

[32] J. Goldsworthy, 'Abdicating and limiting Parliament's sovereignty' (2006) 17 King's College Law Journal 255, 261.
[33] Ibid.

leading scholars, the committee explored whether supremacy is grounded in statute, common law, or a more fundamental constitutional principle.

House of Commons European Scrutiny Committee, *The EU Bill and Parliamentary Sovereignty*, Tenth Report, Session 2010–11, vol. I (HC 633)

Acts of Parliament v the common law

25. On one side of the debate are those who argue that the absolute sovereignty of Parliament as understood by Dicey remains unqualified, or at least should remain unqualified, by recent constitutional reforms or change in judicial climate. So Parliament can legislate however it chooses, for example to stop judicial review by the High Court. And if it did so, the judges would have to observe the terms of such legislation so long as they were unambiguously expressed. As Professor Tomkins says at paragraph 6 of his written evidence:

> What the doctrine establishes is the legal supremacy of statute. It means that there is no source of law higher than—i.e. more authoritative than—an Act of Parliament. Parliament may by statute make or unmake any law, including a law that is violative of international law or that alters a principle of the common law. And the courts are obliged to uphold and enforce it.

The late Lord Bingham was emphatic that judges should be subservient to the legislative supremacy of Parliament, as quoted here in the written evidence of Professor Tomkins:

> It has to my mind convincingly been shown that the principle of parliamentary sovereignty has been recognised as fundamental in this country not because the judges invented it but because it has for centuries been accepted as such by judges and others officially concerned in the operation of our constitutional system. The judges did not by themselves establish the principle and they cannot, by themselves, change it.

Professor Jeffrey Goldsworthy, who submitted written evidence and whose book on Parliamentary sovereignty was described by Lord Bingham as 'magisterial', is also a notable proponent of this view.

26. On the other side of the debate are those whose view is that the sovereignty of Parliament is a construct of the common law. As such it is open to revision by the courts in circumstances where, say, a court has to reconcile contradictory statutory provisions, or a higher law, such as a fundamental human right, is violated. Professor Allan, who subscribes to this view, explained it as follows:

> The nature and scope of legislative supremacy are matters of common law in the sense that they are questions to be resolved, necessarily, by the courts in order to determine contested and doubtful cases. Such cases depend for correct resolution on consideration of all the pertinent reasons. The present context, concerning the implications of British membership of the EU, vividly illustrates the dependence of Parliament's continuing legislative authority on judicial interpretation of the nature of the UK legal order, viewed as a whole.
>
> The Thoburn judgment provides a good illustration of the operation of the common law constitution. In seeking to accommodate the European doctrine of the primacy of EU law with the supremacy of Parliament, as a matter of domestic constitutional law, Lord Justice Laws made—or rather proposed—a very modest change to the general rule permitting implied repeal: it would be necessary for Parliament expressly to amend or repeal the ECA before it could be overridden by a later statute.

Professor Craig shared Professor Allan's belief that Parliamentary sovereignty was a construct of the common law and that 'it was not beyond peradventure' that the courts would disapply a statutory provision which was violative of fundamental rights. In answer to a question from the Chairman, Professor Craig reconfirmed his previously stated view that the legislative supremacy of Parliament was ultimately to be decided by the courts as being 'derived from normative arguments of legal principle, the content of which can and will vary across time'. He also reconfirmed that 'on this view, there is no a priori inexorable reason why Parliament merely because of its very existence must be regarded as legally omnipotent', a view which he shared with Professor Allan.

Professor Bradley expressed a 'qualified belief in Parliamentary sovereignty'. Underpinning the evidence of all three witnesses was the view that Parliament could not be supreme—that is, having the capacity to make any law whatsoever—simply by dint of being Parliament: a further, normative justification was required. A corollary of this view was that the courts could in extreme cases, for example where the rule of law was infringed, disapply the offending provision of an Act of Parliament.

PAUSE FOR REFLECTION

1. Which of the following best describes the source of parliamentary supremacy?
   (a) A rule of common law developed by the courts.
   (b) A fundamental political fact accepted by all branches of government.
   (c) Something else? (Explain your view.)
2. Could Parliament abolish or limit its own supremacy? For example, could it pass a law giving the courts power to strike down future Acts that violate basic rights?
3. Could the courts limit parliamentary supremacy on their own? Could judges decide that, under the common law, they now have the power to disapply Acts of Parliament that seriously breach constitutional principles or fundamental rights?

Table 3.1 summarises the three views on the source and nature of parliamentary supremacy.

Table 3.1 Three views on the source and nature of parliamentary supremacy

Question	Wade (Continuing Sovereignty)	Jennings (Self-Embracing Sovereignty)	Goldsworthy (Constitutional Practice / Consensus)
What is the source of parliamentary supremacy?	A constitutional fact accepted by courts and officials, not created by ordinary legal rules.	A legal rule recognised by the courts: Parliament's authority comes from legislation enacted in the proper legal form.	A constitutional doctrine grounded in long-standing practice and broadly accepted by the courts and political institutions.
Can Parliament bind its successors?	No, attempts to entrench legislation would be legally ineffective.	Possibly—Parliament may impose binding 'manner and form' requirements if it legislates clearly.	Possibly—but only if entrenchment becomes part of accepted constitutional practice and is recognised by the courts.

(continued)

Table 3.1 Continued

Question	Wade (Continuing Sovereignty)	Jennings (Self-Embracing Sovereignty)	Goldsworthy (Constitutional Practice / Consensus)
Can the courts change the doctrine of supremacy?	No—the courts must uphold the existing doctrine unless a constitutional rupture occurs.	Yes—courts may apply new validity rules if Parliament changes the legal form.	Only as part of an evolution in wider constitutional practice; not through judicial action alone.
Key metaphor or idea	'Ultimate constitutional fact.'	Courts recognise 'what is made in the proper legal form.'	A Hartian 'rule of recognition' shaped by established constitutional practice.
Implications for constitutional change	Fundamental change would require a constitutional rupture rather than incremental development.	Change can occur gradually through legal development and institutional practice.	Change occurs when constitutional practice evolves and the courts are willing to recognise the shift.

3.6 ENTRENCHMENT: CAN AN ACT OF PARLIAMENT BE MADE THAT BINDS FUTURE PARLIAMENTS?

Some countries make it harder to change constitutional laws by using special procedures—like supermajorities or referendums. The UK doesn't usually do this, but some proposals have tried. This section explores what those options might look like. There are three key questions about entrenchment in the UK constitution:

(a) When, and why, might it be desirable to make an Act of Parliament harder to repeal or amend?

(b) What legal or procedural mechanisms could be used to entrench legislation?

(c) Is entrenchment even possible within the framework of parliamentary supremacy?

These questions are the subject of considerable legal debate. Some commentators argue that entrenchment is fundamentally at odds with the idea that Parliament cannot bind its successors. To begin, the following extract from Cheryl Saunders offers a clear explanation of what entrenchment means, and how it works in other constitutional systems.

C. Saunders, 'Entrenchment of Constitutions and Legislation', in P. Cane and J. Conaghan (eds) *The New Oxford Companion to Law* (2008, Oxford: OUP), pp. 382–3

Entrenchment subjects the constitution or legislation to which it applies to an alteration procedure that is more difficult than that for ordinary laws. In extreme cases, it may prevent alteration altogether. Mechanisms for entrenchment typically range from requirements for special parliamentary majorities to use of the referendum. Typically, the provision that prescribes the special alteration procedure is itself entrenched, to prevent it from being altered by ordinary law, thus circumventing the effect of entrenchment.

There is no constitutional obstacle to entrenchment in states in which prevailing political theory accepts that the people is sovereign and can confer a system of government on itself. Difficulty may arise, however, where, as in the United Kingdom, theory assigns legal sovereignty to the parliament. There are at least two possible understandings of what sovereignty involves in this context. First, it might mean that the legislative authority of the current parliament can never be constrained by legislation of an earlier parliament, making entrenchment impossible. Second, it might mean that the authority of a current parliament extends even to protecting its own legislation from future change, albeit at a cost to the authority of later parliaments. In *The Concept of Law*,[34] H.L.A. Hart described the distinction as being between 'continuing' and 'self-embracing' sovereignty.

The former remains the orthodox understanding in the United Kingdom, favoured by A.V. Dicey and some early twentieth-century case law. The latter applies in most other countries in the British constitutional tradition. Comparison is complicated by the colonial origins of the constitutional arrangements in these states. Nevertheless, it is increasingly difficult to reconcile continuing sovereignty with actual practice in the United Kingdom, and the question should be regarded as unsettled.

Its resolution is affected by various factors. First, an entrenching provision that prescribes the manner or the form in which amending legislation must be passed can be understood as altering the composition or the procedures of a future parliament for this purpose, rather than limiting parliamentary authority. This line of thought reconciles the possibility of entrenchment with the continuing view of parliamentary sovereignty, although in a highly artificial way. Second, the Parliament Acts of 1911 and 1949 have already altered the composition of Parliament for some purposes. While these Acts make legislation easier, rather than more difficult, it has been held that they create an additional primary legislation-making procedure, and some judicial comments offer further encouragement to the possibility of entrenchment. Third, acceptance of entrenchment would have implications for the rule that courts will not look behind an Act of Parliament to examine the procedure by which it was made.

3.6.1 THE DESIRABILITY (OR OTHERWISE) OF ENTRENCHING LEGISLATION

One argument in favour of entrenchment is that it could help protect fundamental constitutional principles and rights from being easily repealed by future governments. This idea is not new. During the negotiations leading up to the 1707 union between England and Scotland, there was a strong desire to preserve the Protestant religion 'in all times coming'. This concern was reflected in the Union with Scotland Act 1706, which attempted to entrench the status of the Church. In more recent debates, some have proposed entrenching a UK Bill of Rights to give stronger and more lasting protection than the current Human Rights Act 1998. However, others are more sceptical. In 2008, a parliamentary committee examined whether entrenchment would be desirable or appropriate in the context of the UK's constitutional tradition.

Joint Committee on Human Rights, *A Bill of Rights for the UK?*, 29th Report, Session 2007–08 (HL 165-I/HC 150-I)

233. A number of witnesses to our inquiry addressed the question of whether a Bill of Rights should be entrenched. They expressed a range of views. Some favoured entrenchment in order to ensure the superiority of a Bill of Rights and protect it from easy amendment by Parliament. One witness suggested

[34] (1961, Oxford: OUP).

that entrenchment is required to protect the power of the UK courts to adjudicate upon claimed violations of human rights and ensure an effective remedy.

234. On the other hand, other witnesses suggested that entrenchment may not be desirable. Professor Harlow opposed entrenchment because in her view the common law combined with parliamentary sovereignty allows rights to be easily updated as society changes, although she recognised that this could also mean that rights may be swept away more easily.

235. We are not in favour of entrenching a UK Bill of Rights against future amendment or repeal by requiring that any such amendments or repeal must satisfy a special procedure, such as approval by a special parliamentary majority or by the people in a referendum. In our view such forms of entrenchment are not compatible with our tradition of parliamentary democracy which has carefully preserved the freedom of each Parliament to legislate according to its view of the public interest.

This extract highlights how deeply divided expert opinion remains on the question of entrenchment—reflecting a broader tension between the desire to safeguard constitutional principles and the commitment to parliamentary flexibility.

3.6.2 HOW MIGHT ENTRENCHMENT BE ACHIEVED?

If entrenchment is possible in the UK constitutional system, what techniques might be used?

One method sometimes used is to include a declaration that a particular Act, or part of it, is intended to remain permanently in force. In the example below, the focus is on substance rather than process: those negotiating the Union of England and Scotland sought to guarantee that the position of the Protestant religion would remain a 'fundamental and essential' element of the new constitutional settlement.

Union with Scotland Act 1706, art. XXV, s. V (emphasis added)

That the said Act passed in this present Session of Parliament intituled An Act for securing the Church of England as by Law established and all and every the matters and things therein contained And also the said Act of Parliament of Scotland intituled Act for securing the Protestant Religion and Presbyterian Church Government with the Establishment in the said Act contained *be and shall for ever* be held and adjudged to be and observed as Fundamental and Essential Conditions of the said Union And shall *in all times coming* be taken to be and are hereby declared to be essential and fundamental parts of the said Articles and Union And the said Articles of Union so as aforesaid ratified approved and confirmed by Act of Parliament of Scotland and by this present Act And the said Act passed in this present Session of Parliament intituled an Act for securing the Church of England as by Law established And also the said Act passed in the Parliament of Scotland intituled Act for securing the Protestant Religion and Presbyterian Church Government are hereby enacted and ordained to be and continue *in all times coming* the complete and entire Union of the two Kingdoms of England and Scotland.

Subsequent history shows that such provisions were not legally entrenched. A straightforward illustration is the alteration of Scotland's representation in the House of Commons. Article XXII of the 1706 Act fixed Scotland's entitlement at 45 MPs, yet later Parliaments repeatedly revised that number as the electoral system evolved. This demonstrates that even provisions once treated as foundational could be amended or replaced. The language of constitutional permanence has resurfaced in modern legislation—for example, in the 'permanence clauses' inserted by the Scotland Act 2016 and the Government of Wales Act 2006—but these sections also acknowledge that they do not limit the UK Parliament's continuing power to legislate.[35] Whether they amount to anything more than political statements remains contested.

A second way would be to make future legislation dependent on a referendum. Consider the following provision, originally included in the Northern Ireland Constitution Act 1973.

Northern Ireland Act 1998, s. 1

1 Status of Northern Ireland

(1) It is hereby declared that Northern Ireland in its entirety remains part of the United Kingdom and shall not cease to be so without the consent of a majority of the people of Northern Ireland voting in a poll held for the purposes of this section in accordance with Schedule 1.

(2) But if the wish expressed by a majority in such a poll is that Northern Ireland should cease to be part of the United Kingdom and form part of a united Ireland, the Secretary of State shall lay before Parliament such proposals to give effect to that wish as may be agreed between Her Majesty's Government in the United Kingdom and the Government of Ireland.

Put simply, section 1 prevents the UK Parliament legislating to transfer the territory of Northern Ireland to Ireland unless a referendum is held and produces a majority in favour of that change.

A third option would be to require a special parliamentary procedure before amendment or repeal could take place. For example, this might involve a super-majority in the House of Commons, rather than a simple majority. Another possibility would be to require that both the House of Commons and the House of Lords agree to the change. This would represent a departure from the usual position under the Parliament Acts 1911 and 1949, which allow a bill to become law even if the House of Lords objects, provided certain conditions are met.[36]

3.6.3 IS IT POSSIBLE TO ENTRENCH LEGISLATION IN THE UK CONSTITUTIONAL SYSTEM?

A fundamental constitutional question in the United Kingdom is whether Parliament can entrench legislation—either by placing substantive limits on what future Parliaments may do, or by introducing procedural requirements that must be followed to change the law. Legal opinion on this issue is divided. At first glance, the idea seems paradoxical. If Parliament has the power to limit its own future actions, then it appears to no longer possess full legal supremacy. As Dicey famously put it: 'A sovereign power cannot, while retaining its sovereign character, restrict its own powers by any particular enactment.' But equally, if Parliament cannot limit its own future actions, then its law-making power might also be seen as incomplete.

[35] See Chapter 6.

[36] See further Justice, *A British Bill of Rights: Informing the Debate—The Report of the Justice Constitution Committee* (2008, London: Justice), pp. 55–6 https://files.justice.org.uk/wp-content/uploads/2015/07/06170839/A-British-Bill-of-Rights.pdf accessed 16 November 2025.

As noted by Cheryl Saunders in the extract above, two broad schools of thought have emerged. The first—often referred to as the 'no entrenchment' view—is associated with theorists such as Dicey and Wade. On this view, Parliament cannot bind its successors: each Parliament must remain free to make or unmake any law. Supporters of this approach acknowledge that a radical constitutional transformation (a 'Big Bang' moment), such as a revolution or judicial assumption of constitutional review, might change this. But unless or until such a transformation occurs, they maintain that Parliament's legislative supremacy remains absolute. Sir William Wade, for example, rejected the idea of an entrenched Bill of Rights on precisely these grounds.

H.W.R. Wade, *Constitutional Fundamentals*, 32nd Hamlyn Lectures (1980, London: Stevens), pp. 24–5

> I approach this [. . .] as a purely technical problem of legislation: how can our legislative machinery be made to deliver these particular goods? In any normal situation there is no need for any question, since Parliament is omnipotent. But the one inherent limit on its omnipotence, which is the consequence of that omnipotence itself, is that the Parliament of today cannot fetter the Parliament of tomorrow with any sort of permanent restraints, so that entrenched provisions are impossible. That, at any rate, appears to be the view of the legal establishment.

The core idea behind the theory of continuing parliamentary supremacy is that Parliament's power to legislate using the ordinary procedures is, in Wade's words, 'indestructible by legislation'. In other words, one Parliament cannot use legislation to limit the legislative powers of its successors. Even if an Act sets out a special procedure or attempts to place a substantive limit on future law-making, a later Act can override it. The courts will apply the later statute—because it reflects Parliament's most recent intention. Wade acknowledged that 'it is always for the courts, in the last resort, to say what is a valid Act of Parliament'. But this should not be read as a licence for judicial innovation. He did not mean that judges can unilaterally change the fundamental rules for recognising legislation. Instead, he saw judges as guardians of the orthodox principle of parliamentary supremacy, ensuring that no Parliament could bind the hands of a future one. On this central point, Wade argued, the famously flexible British constitution is, in fact, rigid.

By contrast, supporters of a different theory of parliamentary supremacy argue that *entrenchment is possible*—without the need for a dramatic 'Big Bang' transformation of the UK legal system. This is often described as the 'self-embracing', 'manner and form', or 'new' approach to sovereignty.

One of the leading figures associated with this view was Sir Ivor Jennings. He challenged the traditional view that Parliament can never limit its future powers. He argues that if Parliament sets up special procedures for changing a law, courts might treat those rules as binding—unless and until Parliament follows the proper steps to change them.

Sir Ivor Jennings, *The Law and the Constitution*, 5th edn (1959, London: University of London Press), pp. 152–4 (emphasis in original)

> 'A sovereign power cannot, while retaining its sovereign character, restrict its own powers by any particular enactment,' says Dicey [. . .]. This is a perfectly correct deduction from the nature of a supreme power. If a prince has supreme power, and continues to have supreme power, he can do anything, even to the extent of undoing the things which he had previously done. If he grants a constitution,

> binding himself not to make laws except with the consent of an elected legislature, he has power immediately afterwards to abolish the legislature without its consent and to continue legislating by his personal decree.
>
> But if the prince has not supreme power, but the rule is that the courts accept as law that which is made in the proper legal form, the result is different. For when the prince enacts that henceforth no rule shall be law unless it is enacted by him with the consent of the legislature, the law has been altered, and the courts will not admit as law any rule which is not made in that form. Consequently a rule subsequently made by the prince alone abolishing the legislature is not law, for the legislature has not consented to it, and the rule has not been enacted according to the manner and form required by the law for the time being.
>
> The difference is this. In the one case there is sovereignty. In the other, the courts have no concern with sovereignty, but only with the established law. 'Legal sovereignty' is merely a name indicating that the legislature has for the time being power to make laws of any kind in the manner required by the law. That is, a rule expressed to be made by the [King], 'with the advice and consent of the Lords spiritual and temporal, and Commons in this present Parliament assembled, and by the authority of the same,' will be recognised by the courts, *including a rule which alters this law itself.* If this is so, the 'legal sovereign' may impose legal limitations upon itself, because its power to change the law includes the power to change the law affecting itself.

Debate between these competing theories of parliamentary supremacy continues among constitutional scholars. Much academic commentary seeks to assess which theory—Wade's continuing supremacy or Jennings's self-embracing model—offers the more persuasive account of how sovereignty operates in the UK legal system today.[37]

PAUSE FOR REFLECTION

Suppose the government is concerned about the growing popularity of a campaign to abolish the monarchy. It proposes a bill that would provide that the monarch must remain head of state unless all of the following conditions are met:

1. At least three-quarters of all MPs vote in favour of the change;
2. Both the House of Commons and the House of Lords vote in favour of the change;
3. At least 70 per cent of voters support the change in a national referendum; and
4. Any amendments to this bill are subject to the same requirements.

Consider both Wade's and Jennings's views on entrenchment. What would each theorist say?

3.6.4 AN ALTERNATIVE TO ENTRENCHMENT: A NEW JUDICIAL OATH?

Sir William Wade offers a creative solution: rather than changing parliamentary supremacy through law, it might be possible to reinforce key constitutional values by updating the oath judges swear when they take office. '*The only trouble at present is that the existing form of oath gives no assurance*

[37] See, e.g., M. Gordon, 'The conceptual foundations of parliamentary sovereignty: Reconsidering Jennings and Wade' [2009] Public Law 519 (Gordon is a supporter of Jennings); M. Gordon, *Parliamentary Sovereignty in the UK Constitution: Process, Politics and Democracy* (2015); for a contrary view see J. Goldsworthy, 'The "manner and form" theory of parliamentary sovereignty' [2021] Public Law 568.

of obedience to statutes binding later Parliaments', he wrote. arguing 'If we should wish to adopt a new form of constitution . . . all that need be done is to put the judges under oath to enforce it'.[38] Wade's suggestion that a revised judicial oath might offer an alternative to formal entrenchment raises the question whether symbolic commitments can shape constitutional outcomes.

3.7 IMPLIED REPEAL

Another important aspect of parliamentary supremacy concerns the rules on 'implied repeal'. These technical rules reflect deeper views about the nature of sovereignty and the constitution. Given the vast volume of UK statute law—spanning tens of thousands of pages—it is perhaps inevitable that, from time to time, Parliament enacts two statutes that are inconsistent with one another. Despite the efforts of parliamentary counsel o draft legislation carefully, such clashes occasionally arise. If the courts are unable to resolve the inconsistency through interpretation, and it is accepted that the conflict cannot be reconciled, then the doctrine of implied repeal is applied: the later Act takes precedence and is treated as having repealed the earlier one to the extent of the inconsistency.

At first glance, the rules on implied repeal may seem disarmingly straightforward. The basic principle is that where two statutes are in conflict, the later provision is treated as legally binding. In such cases, Parliament is understood to have *impliedly repealed* the earlier provision by enacting the later one. As Laws LJ put it, '*The rule is that if Parliament has enacted successive statutes which on the true construction of each of them make irreducibly inconsistent provisions, the earlier statute is impliedly repealed by the later.*'[39]

However, this rule does not necessarily work well in all contexts. Some Acts of Parliament—particularly in the absence of a codified constitution—are widely understood to lay down the ground rules of the UK's constitutional system.

In the next extract, (the 'metric martyrs' case), the court explained that some Acts of Parliament are so important they cannot be repealed by accident. Later laws must clearly say if they are changing earlier constitutional statutes. Laws LJ identifies examples of such Acts and proposes a way to determine whether a statute qualifies as a 'constitutional statute'. If the ordinary rule of implied repeal were applied to these, Parliament might unknowingly erode core constitutional principles—by enacting later legislation that conflicts with them, even if unintentionally. Laws LJ therefore argued, in a now widely accepted view, that *constitutional statutes are immune from implied repeal.* They can be amended or repealed only through express words—Parliament must make its intention unmistakably clear. In *Thoburn*, the constitutional statute in question was the European Communities Act 1972 (later repealed by section 1 of the European Union (Withdrawal) Act 2018). Although that Act has now been repealed, the principles in *Thoburn* remain of enduring importance. The case itself arose in an unexpected context. Local authority officers had sought to enforce laws requiring certain goods—such as fruit, vegetables, and fish—to be sold in metric rather than imperial measures. This led to legal action against traders who refused to comply, including Steven Thoburn, one of the so-called 'metric martyrs'. In deciding the case, Laws LJ referred to earlier decisions such as the *Factortame* litigation, which had established the primacy of EU law (a doctrine that no longer applies post-Brexit). For our purposes, however, *Thoburn* is most significant for what it says about the idea of constitutional statutes and the limits of implied repeal.

[38] H.W.R. Wade, *Constitutional Fundamentals*, 32nd Hamlyn Lectures (1980, London: Stevens), pp. 37–8.
[39] *Thoburn v Sunderland City Council* [2002] EWHC 195 (Admin), [37].

Thoburn v Sunderland City Council

[2002] EWHC 195 (Admin)

Laws LJ

59. [. . .] Parliament cannot bind its successors by stipulating against repeal, wholly or partly, of the ECA [that is, the European Communities Act 1972]. It cannot stipulate as to the manner and form of any subsequent legislation. It cannot stipulate against implied repeal any more than it can stipulate against express repeal. [. . .] The conditions of Parliament's legislative supremacy in the United Kingdom necessarily remain in the United Kingdom's hands. But the traditional doctrine has in my judgment been modified. It has been done by the common law, wholly consistently with constitutional principle.

60. The common law has in recent years allowed, or rather created, exceptions to the doctrine of implied repeal: a doctrine which was always the common law's own creature. There are now classes or types of legislative provision which cannot be repealed by mere implication. These instances are given, and can only be given, by our own courts, to which the scope and nature of Parliamentary sovereignty are ultimately confided. The courts may say—have said—that there are certain circumstances in which the legislature may only enact what it desires to enact if it does so by express, or at any rate specific, provision.

[. . .] In the present state of its maturity the common law has come to recognise that there exist rights which should properly be classified as constitutional or fundamental: see for example such cases as *Simms* [2000] 2 AC 115 per Lord Hoffmann at 131, *Pierson v Secretary of State* [1998] AC 539, *Leech* [1994] QB 198, *Derbyshire County Council v Times Newspapers Ltd.* [1993] AC 534, and *Witham* [1998] QB 575. And from this a further insight follows. We should recognise a hierarchy of Acts of Parliament: as it were 'ordinary' statutes and 'constitutional' statutes. The two categories must be distinguished on a principled basis. In my opinion a constitutional statute is one which (a) conditions the legal relationship between citizen and State in some general, overarching manner, or (b) enlarges or diminishes the scope of what we would now regard as fundamental constitutional rights. (a) and (b) are of necessity closely related: it is difficult to think of an instance of (a) that is not also an instance of (b). The special status of constitutional statutes follows the special status of constitutional rights. Examples are the Magna Carta, the Bill of Rights 1689, the Act of Union, the Reform Acts which distributed and enlarged the franchise, the HRA, the Scotland Act 1998 and the Government of Wales Act 1998. The ECA clearly belongs in this family. It incorporated the whole corpus of substantive Community rights and obligations, and gave overriding domestic effect to the judicial and administrative machinery of Community law. It may be there has never been a statute having such profound effects on so many dimensions of our daily lives. The ECA is, by force of the common law, a constitutional statute.

63. Ordinary statutes may be impliedly repealed. Constitutional statutes may not. For the repeal of a constitutional Act or the abrogation of a fundamental right to be effected by statute, the court would apply this test: is it shown that the legislature's actual—not imputed, constructive or presumed—intention was to effect the repeal or abrogation? I think the test could only be met by express words in the later statute, or by words so specific that the inference of an actual determination to effect the result contended for was irresistible. The ordinary rule of implied repeal does not satisfy this test. Accordingly, it has no application to constitutional statutes. I should add that in my judgment general words could not be supplemented, so as to effect a repeal or significant amendment to a constitutional statute, by reference to what was said in Parliament by the minister promoting the Bill pursuant to *Pepper v Hart* [1993] AC 593. A constitutional statute can only be repealed, or amended in a way which significantly affects its provisions touching fundamental rights or otherwise the relation between citizen and State, by unambiguous words on the face of the later statute.

64. This development of the common law regarding constitutional rights, and as I would say constitutional statutes, is highly beneficial. It gives us most of the benefits of a written constitution, in which fundamental rights are accorded special respect. But it preserves the sovereignty of the legislature and

> the flexibility of our uncodified constitution. It accepts the relation between legislative supremacy and fundamental rights is not fixed or brittle: rather the courts (in interpreting statutes, and now, applying the HRA) will pay more or less deference to the legislature, or other public decision-maker, according to the subject in hand. Nothing is plainer than that this benign development involves, as I have said, the recognition of the ECA as a constitutional statute.

At the time, the approach taken by Laws LJ in *Thoburn* was seen as unconventional. Traditionally, legal commentators maintained that all Acts of Parliament were equal in status: there were no distinct categories of statute in UK law. On this view, legislation such as the Dentists Act 1984 or the Dangerous Dogs Act 1991—which have no constitutional significance—stood on the same legal footing as statutes like the Human Rights Act 1998 or the Parliament Acts, which clearly play a foundational role in the UK's constitutional framework.

The *HS2* case raised a difficult question: what happens when two constitutional laws conflict? The court was asked to choose between a key UK constitutional rule (free speech in Parliament) and an EU rule about environmental planning. The judges avoided making a final decision—but they highlighted the complexity of having multiple sources of constitutional law. In *R (HS2 Action Alliance Ltd) v Secretary of State for Transport*, the UK Supreme Court referred to the '*important insights into potential issues in this area*' that could be found in Laws LJ's 'penetrating discussion' in *Thoburn*[40]—endorsing the new approach. But whereas in *Thoburn* the clash was between a constitutionally important statutory provision (in the European Communities Act 1972) and an ordinary one (rules on metrication), in *HS2* the potential conflict was between two constitutionally important provisions. These were (a) art. 9 of the Bill of Rights 1689—a key principle of the British constitution—which prohibits courts from reviewing parliamentary proceedings so as to protect free speech in Parliament and (b) an EU directive, which before Brexit would normally have a higher status over conflicting national law, laying down procedures for assessing the environmental impact of infrastructure projects—in this case, the plans to build a major new railway line. In the UK some major infrastructure projects receive planning permission through the enactment of a 'hybrid' Act of Parliament rather than by decision-making of a local authority or government minister. The Supreme Court ultimately held that the hybrid bill procedure did comply with EU requirements. As a result, it was unnecessary for the court to go against art. 9 of the Bill of Rights by delving deeply into the detail of how Parliament would consider environmental issues during the hybrid procedure.

However, the case raised a profound constitutional question: what should happen when two instruments of high constitutional status appear to conflict? The Court noted the 'important insights into potential issues in this area' offered by Laws LJ in his 'penetrating discussion' in *Thoburn v Sunderland City Council* [2002] EWHC 195 (Admin). But unlike *Thoburn*, where the clash was between a constitutionally significant statute (the European Communities Act 1972) and an ordinary one (concerning metrication), *HS2* posed a more complex scenario—one involving two norms of constitutional magnitude. While the issue was not resolved definitively, the judges' obiter remarks suggest a judicial willingness to engage with constitutional pluralism in the UK context. This case thus illustrates the evolving nature of the UK's constitutional order, especially in the face of overlapping domestic and international legal commitments.

[40] *R (HS2 Action Alliance Ltd) v Secretary of State for Transport* [2014] UKSC 3, [208].

R (HS2 Action Alliance Ltd) v Secretary of State for Transport
[2014] UKSC 3

Lord Neuberger and Lord Mance (with whom Lady Hale, Lord Kerr, Lord Sumption, Lord Reed, and Lord Carnwath agreed)

206. Under the European Communities Act 1972, United Kingdom courts have also acknowledged that European law requires them to treat domestic statutes, whether passed before or after the 1972 Act, as invalid if and to the extent that they cannot be interpreted consistently with European law: *R v Secretary of State, Ex p Factortame Ltd (No 2)* [1991] 1 AC 603. That was a significant development, recognising the special status of the 1972 Act and of European law and the importance attaching to the United Kingdom and its courts fulfilling the commitment to give loyal effect to European law. But it is difficult to see how an English court could fully comply with the approach suggested by the two Advocates General without addressing its apparent conflict with other principles hitherto also regarded as fundamental and enshrined in the Bill of Rights. Scrutiny of the workings of Parliament and whether they satisfy externally imposed criteria clearly involves questioning and potentially impeaching (i.e. condemning) Parliament's internal proceedings, and would go a considerable step further than any United Kingdom court has ever gone.

207. The United Kingdom has no written constitution, but we have a number of constitutional instruments. They include Magna Carta, the Petition of Right 1628, the Bill of Rights and (in Scotland) the Claim of Rights Act 1689, the Act of Settlement 1701 and the Act of Union 1707. The European Communities Act 1972, the Human Rights Act 1998 and the Constitutional Reform Act 2005 may now be added to this list. The common law itself also recognises certain principles as fundamental to the rule of law. It is, putting the point at its lowest, certainly arguable (and it is for United Kingdom law and courts to determine) that there may be fundamental principles, whether contained in other constitutional instruments or recognised at common law, of which Parliament when it enacted the European Communities Act 1972 did not either contemplate or authorise the abrogation.

208. We are not expressing any view on whether or how far article 9 of the Bill of Rights would count among these, but the point is too important to pass without mention. We would wish to hear full argument upon it before expressing any concluded view. It is not a point upon which the parties before us proposed to make any submissions until it was raised by the Court. We were then told that the attention of the Parliamentary authorities (and we deliberately use a vague expression) had been drawn to this appeal, and they elected not to be represented. If and when the point does fall to be considered, the Parliamentary authorities may wish to reconsider whether they should be represented, and, particularly if they still regard that course as inappropriate, it may well be the sort of point on which the Attorney General should appear or be represented. Important insights into potential issues in this area are to be found in their penetrating discussion by Laws LJ in the Divisional Court in *Thoburn v Sunderland City Council* [2002] EWHC 195 (Admin), [2003] QB 151, (The Metric Martyrs case), especially paras 58–70, although the focus there was the possibility of conflict between an earlier 'constitutional' and later 'ordinary' statute, rather than, as here, between two constitutional instruments, which raises yet further considerations.

209. As it is, however, we have come to the conclusion that the step mentioned in paras 200 and 206 above is one which the European legislature in this instance clearly provided by article 1(4) (formerly 1(5)) need not and should not be taken, and which the European Court of Justice has not endorsed. The Court of Justice's more limited approach in this respect is also borne out by an examination of the objectives of the Directive. Nothing in the Directive suggests that it is aimed at excluding either political involvement or reasoning based on political policy decisions from planning decisions. On the contrary, the recognition that projects may legitimately be approved by specific legislative act constitutes express recognition of the legitimacy of such factors.

210. The appellants' case, that the Parliamentary process will be tainted by considerations such as whipping or collective ministerial responsibility or simply by party policy, amounts to challenging the whole legitimacy of Parliamentary democracy as it presently operates. There would doubtless be a similar problem in most, probably all, the democracies of the Union. Finally, we note that article 10 TEU itself recognises that, in a Union 'founded on representative democracy', whose citizens are directly represented in the European Parliament, '[p]olitical parties at European level contribute to forming European political awareness and to expressing the will of citizens of the Union.' This, though it may at present be largely aspirational in so far as it refers to pan-European political parties, undermines any suggestion that the ordinary workings of political democracy can or should be seen as suspect under article 1(4) of the EIA [Environmental Impact Assessment] Directive.

211. In the upshot, there is, as Lord Reed concludes, no basis under the EIA Directive for the wide-ranging review of Parliamentary process advocated by the appellants, whether this be to assess the quality of the consideration given in Parliament or the extent to which the members of either House will be free of party influence when deciding how to vote; and we further agree that this is clear to a point where is no need for a reference to the European Court of Justice.

This suggested that the principle of EU law supremacy—requiring courts (during the UK's EU membership) to give effect to EU law over conflicting national law—might not always hold in such absolute terms. In exceptional cases, where the national rule in question is itself of constitutional importance, the courts might choose to prioritise it, resisting the automatic application of the EU measure. The *HS2* case thus hinted at a more nuanced approach, recognising that not all national laws stand on the same constitutional footing.

PAUSE FOR REFLECTION

1. Laws LJ's rule in *Thoburn* requires a distinction to be made between constitutional and ordinary statutes. What criteria does Laws LJ suggest? Are those criteria objective or subjective? Can you think of cases or examples where classification might be controversial?
2. Using the test proposed by Laws LJ, analyse whether the following Acts are likely to be 'constitutional' or 'ordinary' statutes. For each, consider: does the Act condition the legal relationship between the individual and the state in a fundamental way? Does it concern fundamental rights or the structure of government?
   (a) An Act imposing a new tax;
   (b) an Act making it compulsory for children to receive education;
   (c) an Act establishing the National Health Service; and
   (d) an Act creating a new criminal offence.
3. In *HS2*, the Supreme Court suggested that there may be 'fundamental principles, whether contained in other constitutional instruments or recognised at common law', that Parliament does not intend to override unless it states this explicitly. How might a court identify whether Parliament intended to preserve or override such fundamental constitutional principles? What sources might be used to determine that intention—e.g. the wording of the statute, its context, legal traditions, or parliamentary debates? Should the courts be cautious about assuming Parliament intends to override constitutional norms?

In 2023, the Supreme Court confirmed that even 'constitutional statutes' can be modified by later Acts of Parliament—provided Parliament uses clear and specific wording.[41].

3.8 PARLIAMENTARY SUPREMACY AND THE BRITISH EMPIRE

The doctrine of parliamentary supremacy was deeply entangled with the theory and practice of imperial rule.[42] When the Westminster Parliament legislated beyond the United Kingdom, it was often described as the Imperial Parliament. Dicey captured this outlook when he wrote that it was 'in possession of absolute sovereignty throughout every part of the British Empire'.[43]

The colonies of Canada, Australia, New Zealand, Newfoundland and the Union of South Africa—often described as settler-dominated or white-settler colonies, though each had long-established Indigenous populations whose political authority was displaced by British rule—were the first to acquire extensive self-government through their own legislatures, and to be known as 'dominions' rather than 'colonies'. Initially, laws passed by these bodies were controlled by executive veto powers exercised by British-appointed Governors and Lieutenant-Governors, and by review through the Judicial Committee of the Privy Council. Colonial judges, treating Imperial statutes as supreme, sometimes struck down local legislation that conflicted with Acts of the UK Parliament. To regulate the disruptive impact of the practice, the Imperial Parliament enacted the Colonial Laws Validity Act 1865, which confirmed that any law properly made by a colonial legislature would be valid unless it was repugnant to an Act of the UK Parliament *that expressly extended to that colony*. For 50 years, that arrangement worked but there were growing demands in the Dominions for greater legislative autonomy. This pressure led to the Statute of Westminster 1931, which recognised Dominion legislative independence by providing that Acts of the UK Parliament would no longer apply to them unless they formally requested and consented to such legislation. This marked the beginning of the end of Westminster's claim to legislative supremacy beyond the United Kingdom itself.

This story covers only the Dominions and does not reflect the wider range of relationships that made up the British Empire. Across Africa, Asia, the Caribbean and the Pacific, the level of local autonomy varied greatly. British officials often worked from the Victorian idea that societies could be ranked on a scale from 'primitive' to 'civilized'. This hierarchy, now recognised as racist, was used to argue that some peoples were not 'ready' for self-government. It shaped imperial policy for much of the nineteenth and early twentieth centuries and influenced how firmly the Imperial Parliament's supremacy was asserted in each territory, from directly administered Crown colonies to protectorates and partially self-governing regions.

India was by far the largest and most populous territory governed by Britain. The Government of India Acts were a series of statutes through which the Imperial Parliament reshaped the constitutional structure of British India. The Act of 1858 transferred control of India from the East India

[41] *In the matter of an application by Allister and others for Judicial Review* [2023] UKSC 5; see further K. Majewsk, 'Re Allister: The End of "Constitutional Statutes"?' UK Constitutional Law Association Blog, 21 February 2023 https://ukconstitutionallaw.org/2023/02/21/kacper-majewski-re-allister-the-end-of-constitutional-statutes/ accessed 16 November 2025.

[42] See Chapter 1.

[43] A. V. Dicey, *Introduction to the Study of the Law of the Constitution*, 8th edn (Liberty Fund reprint, orig.1915), 24–25. For further, D. Lino, 'Albert Venn Dicey and the Constitutional Theory of Empire' (2016) 36(4) *Oxford Journal of Legal Studies* 751; and D. Coffey, 'Constitutional law and empire in interwar Britain: universities, liberty, nationality and parliamentary supremacy' (2020) 71 NILQ 193.

Company to the British Crown, establishing direct rule through the Viceroy and Secretary of State for India. Later Acts, such as those of 1909 and 1919, introduced limited legislative representation but left key areas of government under British control. The Government of India Act 1935 went further by creating a federal framework and expanding provincial autonomy, yet ultimate authority remained with the British Governor-General. These statutes illustrate how Westminster used its legislative supremacy to redesign the constitutional arrangements of a major colony without democratic consent. India and Pakistan gained full independence in 1947.

The next four decades saw a rapid unravelling of British rule as territories in the 1950s (for example Ghana and Malaya), 1960s (for instance Jamaica and Trinidad and Tobago) and 1970 and 80s (Belize, Vanuatu, and Zimbabwe) gained independence. Their post-independence constitutions almost always placed legal limits on legislative power and authorised courts to enforce those limits. In theory, some new states could have carried forward Westminster's model of parliamentary supremacy. In practice, only Aotearoa New Zealand did so through its gradual constitutional separation from the United Kingdom, maintaining an uncodified system in which Parliament remains legally supreme. With that exception, newly independent states adopted written constitutions, displacing parliamentary supremacy with constitutional supremacy. In the following extract, Hamid Ghany outlines how this shift took place in the Commonwealth Caribbean.[44]

H. Ghany, 'The Commonwealth Caribbean: Legislatures and democracy', ch. 3 in N. Baldwin, *Legislatures of Small States: A Comparative Study* (2013, Routledge), p. 25

All of the constitutions of the Commonwealth Caribbean countries have a bill of rights in them, which is a chapter that recognizes, declares and protects fundamental human rights and freedoms. In 11 countries, the bill of rights has been influenced by the European Convention on Human Rights 1950, while Trinidad and Tobago has been influenced by the Canadian Bill of Rights 1960. The constitutional effect of this is to permit the individual to challenge the State on the ground of human rights violations being a constitutional infringement. The courts are used as the vehicle of challenge, and the judiciary has the constitutional power to overturn executive or judicial action and parliamentary will in order to redress such infringements.

Courts have not hesitated to invalidate Acts of Parliament that conflict with Caribbean constitutions. In *Northern Construction Ltd v Attorney General* [2000] 1 AC 1, a statutory ouster clause in Trinidad and Tobago was struck down, and in *Hinds v The Queen* [1977] AC 195 parts of Jamaica's Gun Court Act were held unconstitutional for breaching the separation of powers. In both cases the rulings came from the Judicial Committee of the Privy Council—the final court of appeal for those states and composed largely of senior UK judges—so post-independence constitutional limits on legislative power were still being enforced from London.[45]

South Africa was among the last former British colonies to establish a democratic constitutional order, doing so in the 1990s as apartheid came to an end following decades of internal resistance and international pressure.[46] Ending parliamentary supremacy of the South African Parliament was

[44] Antigua and Barbuda, the Bahamas, Barbados, Belize, Dominica, Grenada, Guyana, Jamaica, St Kitts–Nevis, St Lucia, St Vincent and the Grenadines, and Trinidad and Tobago.

[45] Several Caribbean countries have since adopted the Caribbean Court of Justice as their highest court, but Jamaica and Trinidad and Tobago continue to retain the Privy Council.

[46] South Africa remained a Dominion until 1961, when it left the Commonwealth and became the Republic of South Africa.

essential to dismantling a system that had enabled the apartheid legislature to enact discriminatory laws without meaningful constitutional restraint. The 1994 interim constitution introduced an entrenched bill of rights and replaced the old doctrine of parliamentary supremacy with a system in which legislative action must be justified against constitutional standards. In the following extract, Etienne Mureinik describes this shift as a movement from a 'culture of authority' to a 'culture of justification'.

E. Mureinik, 'A bridge to where - introducing the Interim Bill of Rights' (1994) 10 *S Afr J on Hum Rts* 31, pp. 31–2

What the bridge is from is a culture of authority. Legally, the apartheid order rested on the doctrine of Parliamentary sovereignty. Universally, that doctrine teaches that what Parliament says is law, without the need to offer justification to the courts. In South Africa, since Parliament was elected only by a minority, the doctrine taught also that what Parliament said was law, without a need to justify even to those governed by the law. The effect of these teachings, at the apogee of apartheid, was to foster an ethic of obedience. The leadership of the ruling party commanded Parliament, Parliament commanded its bureaucracy, the bureaucrats commanded the people. [. . .]

If the new Constitution is a bridge away from a culture of authority, it is clear what it must be a bridge to. It must lead to a culture of justification—a culture in which every exercise of power is expected to be justified; in which the leadership given by government rests on the cogency of the case offered in defence of its decisions, not the fear inspired by the force at its command. The new order must be a community built on persuasion, not coercion.

There is a striking irony in the global history of parliamentary supremacy. Britain used this doctrine to justify its authority across a large empire, yet most states that emerged from that empire chose a different constitutional model. Their experience of rule from London made a system of concentrated and unreviewable legislative power unattractive for new democracies. As independence constitutions took hold, parliamentary supremacy that had once been projected across much of the world shrank to a far smaller geographical and political footprint.

PAUSE FOR REFLECTION

If so many former colonies rejected parliamentary supremacy in favour of constitutions that limit legislative power, what might this suggest about the strengths and weaknesses of the UK model today?

3.9 REASSERTING PARLIAMENTARY SUPREMACY: CRITIQUES OF THE HUMAN RIGHTS ACT

The Human Rights Act 1998, though designed to preserve parliamentary supremacy, is seen by critics as undermining the traditional relationship between courts and Parliament in the UK constitutional system, to the detriment of the public interest.[47] Their concern is not with the idea of rights, but with

[47] See Chapter 21.

who should decide how rights are balanced against other public interests. A prominent example of this view appears in work by public law scholars associated with the think tank Policy Exchange.

R. Ekins, S. Laws, and C. Casey, *The Impact of the Human Rights Act 1998 in Twenty-Five Cases* (2024, Policy Exchange), pp. 16–7

We flatly deny that the merits of Parliament's lawmaking choices must be, or should be, subject to judicial supervision. The undoubted moral importance of human rights does not sanctify human rights law, viz. the jurisdiction of courts, domestic or European, to decide how the ECHR, and Convention rights in domestic law, should be understood and applied. There is no good reason to accept that judges have any competence or skill set that gives them special insight into whether legislation or policy is necessary in a democratic society, fulfils a compelling state interest, or strikes a proportionate or otherwise appropriate balance between an individual's claim and the public good to be achieved by a relevant measure under challenge or between different competing Convention rights or other rights. Rather, there is good reason to be sceptical that any of these types of questions can be answered by what we would typically consider legal learning or lawyerly skills, precisely because they involve decisions in respect of which there are no scales and metrics available suitable to the judicial role and its typical competences and would typically be made in proceedings in which only the claimant's interests were properly represented. Decisions concerning the proportionality and necessity of legislation, in truth, involve a kind of moral and practical evaluation and reasoning that judges and lawyers are neither responsible nor institutionally equipped for. Giving judges the power to review statutes for their consistency with the open-ended and morally laden language typical of a bill of rights thus risks converting courts into largely unaccountable legislative bodies in permanent law-reform session to make retrospective changes in the law, while the subjects of the law are left unable to know what law will be taken to apply to their conduct.

This critique reflects a broader constitutional anxiety: that the Human Rights Act enables unelected judges to reshape public policy in ways that may weaken political accountability.[48] From this perspective of political constitutionalism, parliamentary supremacy is not simply a historical doctrine but a safeguard of democratic legitimacy. It ensures that decisions with significant social, moral and financial consequences are made by elected representatives rather than by courts. Supporters of this view argue that judges lack the institutional mandate and public accountability to resolve complex choices about issues such as national security, social welfare, taxation or public spending. Such choices, they contend, are inherently political and should remain primarily with Parliament.

Others take a different view of the Human Rights Act and the role of the courts. Legal constitutionalists argue that weak-form review enhances, rather than undermines, democracy. On this account, requiring ministers to justify legislation against Convention rights helps to ensure that decisions affecting fundamental values are made openly and with clear reasons. The declaration of incompatibility mechanism leaves the final word with Parliament, but it also enables courts to signal when legislation appears to conflict with basic rights, creating space for political debate and public scrutiny. Supporters of this position see judicial involvement not as a threat to democratic decision-making but as a safeguard against arbitrary or discriminatory use of legislative power. They suggest that democratic accountability is strengthened when Parliament must confront rights concerns directly and explain why it is departing from them.

[48] See Chapter 9.

PAUSE FOR REFLECTION

Given that under the Human Rights Act, the UK Parliament retains the final say after a declaration of incompatibility, does the power to grant declarations of incompatibility reinforce parliamentary supremacy by prompting clearer justification, or does it nonetheless give judges too much influence over decisions that should remain with elected representatives?

3.10 CONCLUDING COMMENTS

This chapter has examined parliamentary supremacy from several angles: its traditional legal rules, the way courts have applied those rules, and the competing theories that seek to explain its constitutional foundations. We have seen that, while the courts continue to treat Acts of Parliament as legally supreme, some judicial dicta have hinted at possible limits in exceptional circumstances, although recent decisions under Lord Reed's leadership point towards a firmer reassertion of parliamentary supremacy as the foundational rule of the UK constitution.

In Chapter 4, we turn to the rule of law. This principle offers a distinct way of thinking about how power should be exercised and controlled, sometimes in opposition to the idea of parliamentary supremacy. Understanding the rule of law will help explain how courts approach their constitutional role and how they respond when legislation or executive action appears to fall short of these basic requirements.

FURTHER READING

Allan, T. R. S., *The Sovereignty of Law: Freedom, Constitution, and Common Law* (2013, Oxford: OUP).

Kavanagh, A., *The Collaborative Constitution* (2022, Cambridge: CUP), ch. 5.

Prabhat, D., 'The Begum Case, Discretion and Parliamentary Sovereignty: Unmaking the Constitutional Subject', in S. Wheatle and E. O'Loughlin (eds), *Diverse Voices in Public Law* (2023, Bristol: Bristol University Press), ch. 7.

Young, A. L., *Parliamentary Sovereignty and the Human Rights Act* (2009, Oxford: Hart).

4

THE RULE OF LAW

CENTRAL ISSUES

1. The 'rule of law' is widely acknowledged to be an essential component of a good constitution: it is a principle that is concerned with constraining governmental action. First articulated in the nineteenth century, it has become increasingly frequently used by academics, politicians, and judges during the twentieth century.
2. Academics disagree about how to define the rule of law. Some argue it should be 'content-free', dealing only with the form of law and the procedures by which law is made. Others favour a 'content-rich' meaning, so that the substance of laws should have to comply with fundamental rights. Dicey's influential three-limb explanation of the rule of law continues to be a point of reference despite strong criticism. Some academics take a sceptical stance, doubting whether it is possible or desirable to have an agreed definition of the rule of law.
3. There is general agreement that all three arms of the state—the judiciary, Parliament, and government—have a shared responsibility for upholding the role of law, though each institution has a distinct role.
4. Courts uphold the rule of law through their everyday adjudication of disputes. This chapter uses the statutory interpretation technique known as the principle of legality to explore the tensions that can arise between parliamentary supremacy and the judicial protection of fundamental common law rights and basic constitutional standards.
5. Parliament has the power, through Acts of Parliament, both to safeguard the rule of law and to weaken it. In recent years, improved parliamentary procedures provide more systematic checks on government proposals that deliberately or inadvertently breach rule of law principles. But parliamentary supremacy means that Parliament can, if it chooses, legislate contrary to fundamental principles of human rights and the rule of law.
6. Within government, various office-holders are responsible for ensuring respect for the rule of law. Among these, the Lord Chancellor's role is regarded as being of particular importance. Radical reforms to the office of Lord Chancellor made in 2005 are thought by some to have weakened the ability of this office to protect the rule of law even though s. 1 of the Constitutional Reform Act 2005 declares that the reforms do not adversely affect the existing constitutional principle of the rule of law or the Lord Chancellor's role in relation to that principle. There is debate on whether increasing use of automated and AI-decision-making in public administration helps or hinders the rule of law.

4.1 INTRODUCTION

The rule of law has long been regarded as a central feature of the UK constitution. Even so, its definition, content, and practical demands continue to be debated. In 2023, JUSTICE—the cross-party law reform and human rights organization—published a report that used recent legislation and government practice to illustrate areas where, in its assessment, the rule of law had been placed under pressure.[1] The report began by emphasizing that the rule of law is not an abstract ideal but sits alongside parliamentary supremacy as one of the constitution's core principles. Its overall conclusion was blunt: developments in policy and lawmaking in recent years had created conditions in which the rule of law was, in its view, at risk.

JUSTICE, *The State We're In: Addressing Threats and Challenges of the Rule of Law* (2023) paras 7.1–7.2

7.1 The rule of law has been critiqued for being an overly broad, amorphous term, difficult to define in a way that resonates with politicians, let alone the public. While a precise definition may be contested, its core features – access to justice, equality before the law, and controls on the exercise of discretion – are of vital importance to a well-functioning democracy. Underpinning each of these concepts should be human rights, as the late Lord Bingham, esteemed judge and author of *The Rule of Law* rightly observed. This is vital, both for the public at large, who expect the state to behave in a responsible manner, and to ensure due respect for the rights of society's most marginalised.

7.2 The value of the rule of law shines most brightly when we consider a world in its absence. A state that neither respects nor adheres to this principle can impose obligations but is itself unbound by any. The universality of human rights, in recognition of each person's inherent dignity, is supplanted by privileges afforded to the few. Onerous rules apply to some but not others. Challenging the validity of these rules, for example through a court, is rendered wholly ineffective because the judicial system is neither independent nor impartial.

The rule of law is widely recognised as bringing a range of benefits. The World Justice Project (WJP)—an independent, multidisciplinary organization concerned with strengthening the rule of law worldwide—highlights the wide social and economic benefits of adherence to the rule of law: it is associated with 'increased investment and economic growth, more jobs, higher incomes, and greater tax receipts—which can enable more and better government services that further underpin the rule of law. It's a virtuous cycle from which everyone benefits'.[2] The WJP collects global data and ranks jurisdictions on rule of law performance; in 2025, it placed the United Kingdom fourteenth out of 143 countries.

Though elements of the rule of law in the United Kingdom have deep historical roots, the idea as we now understand it began to take shape during the nineteenth century; through the twentieth century it has become an increasingly common reference point for academics, judges, lawyers, and politicians. Comparable though not identical ideas exist in other countries: in Germany, for example, the term used is *Rechtsstaat* ('recht' means 'law', 'staat' means 'state'); in France, *l'Etat de droit*.

This chapter explores the rule of law through two basic questions. First: how is the rule of law defined? As we see in Section 4.2, 'Defining the Rule of Law', Lord Bingham proposed a definition that

[1] JUSTICE, *The State We're In: Addressing Threats and Challenges of the Rule of Law* (2023) https://files.justice.org.uk/wp-content/uploads/2023/08/31123029/JUSTICE-The-State-Were-In-Addressing-Threats-Challenges-to-the-Rule-of-Law-September-2023.pdf accessed 18 November 2025.

[2] World Justice Project https://worldjusticeproject.org/ accessed 18 November 2025.

quickly became influential. Underlying his definition are, however, ideological controversies, which need to be explored.

Second: how is the rule of law protected? If the rule of law is going to make a practical contribution to better government it has to be respected and implemented. In the United Kingdom, we will see in Section 4.3, 'Practical Protection of the Rule of Law', that different constitutional actors are involved: the courts using a variety of techniques; Parliament; and within the executive. An emerging issue is the extent to which automated and AI-based decision-making helps or hinders the rule of law.

4.2 DEFINING THE RULE OF LAW

As a starting point, we need to work out what 'the rule of law' means. One approach is to understand the rule of law as a list of essential characteristics relating to law and legal process that ought to exist in a good constitutional system. A now classic attempt at this is by Lord Bingham (1933–2010) who was successively Master of the Rolls, Lord Chief Justice of England and Wales, and the Senior Law Lord. In a lecture subsequently elaborated on in a book, he argued that '*the core of the existing principle is [. . .] that all persons and authorities within the state, whether public or private, should be bound by and entitled to the benefit of laws publicly and prospectively promulgated and publicly administered in the courts*'.[3] He then went on to identify and discuss eight 'sub-rules':

(1) '*The law must be accessible and so far as possible intelligible, clear and predictable.*'

(2) '*Questions of legal right and liability should ordinarily be resolved by application of the law and not the exercise of discretion.*'

(3) '*The laws of the land should apply equally to all, save to the extent that objective differences require differentiation.*'

(4) '*Ministers and public officers at all levels must exercise the powers conferred on them in good faith, fairly, for the purpose for which the powers were conferred, without exceeding the limits of such powers and not unreasonably.*'

(5) '*The law must afford adequate protection of fundamental rights.*'

(6) '*Means must be provided for resolving, without prohibitive cost or undue delay, bona fide civil disputes which the parties themselves are unable to resolve*'.

(7) '*Adjudicative procedures provided by the state should be fair.*'

(8) '*The rule of law requires compliance by the state with its obligations in international law as in national law.*'

Coming from the pen of one of the United Kingdom's most respected judges, it is not surprising that this checklist quickly became influential. The European Commission on Democracy through Law ('the Venice Commission') adopted it in its 2011 report on the rule of law.[4] The Bingham Centre for the Rule of Law, based in London and named after Lord Bingham, is an organization of lawyers, academics, and judges '*devoted to identifying rule of law issues in national, regional and international systems and seeking to analyse, establish and promote the rule of law's fundamental qualities*'.[5] Against

[3] 'The rule of law' (2007) 66 Cambridge Law Journal 67, 69 (the published version of the lecture); *The Rule of Law* (2010, London: Allen Lane), p. 37.

[4] European Commission for Democracy through Law (Venice Commission), *Report on the Rule of Law* (Adopted by the Venice Commission at its 86th plenary session, Venice, 25–26 March 2011).

[5] http://binghamcentre.biicl.org/.

this background, it may seem tempting simply to agree that Lord Bingham's criteria form a definitive statement of what the rule of law is in the twenty-first century. To do so would, however, ignore several important disagreements.

4.2.1 CONTENT FREE OR CONTENT RICH?

The first academic and political controversy goes to the heart of what should be included within the notion of the rule of law.

On one view, the rule of law should only be about the form of law and the procedures by which law is made. These aspects of the rule of law map onto Lord Bingham's sub-rules 1, 2, 6, and 7. This view does not prescribe any content for legal rules. In his 1977 article advocating this understanding, the legal philosopher Joseph Raz argued strongly against '*the promiscuous use made in recent years of the expression "the rule of law"*'.[6] He offered a 'very incomplete' list of the '*principles that can be derived from the basic idea of the rule of law*', which can be summarized as follows: all laws should be prospective, open, and clear; laws should be relatively stable; the making of particular laws (particular legal orders) should be guided by open, stable, clear, and general rules; the independence of the judiciary must be guaranteed; the principles of natural justice must be observed—meaning procedural fairness in decision-making by public officials; the courts should have review powers over the implementation of other principles; the courts should be easily accessible; and the discretion of the crime-preventing agencies should not be allowed to pervert the law. Raz draws the following conclusions.

J. Raz, 'The rule of law and its virtue' (1977) 93 *Law Quarterly Review* 195, 210–11

Conformity with the rule of law is a matter of degree, and though other things being equal, the greater the conformity the better—other things are rarely equal. A lesser degree of conformity is often to be preferred precisely because it helps realisation of other goals.

In considering the relations between the rule of law and the other values the law should serve it is of particular importance to remember that the rule of law is essentially a negative value. It is merely designed to minimise the harm to freedom and dignity which the law may cause in its pursuit of its goals however laudable these may be. Finally regarding the rule of law as the inherent excellence of the law means that it fulfils essentially a subservient role. Conformity to it makes the law a good instrument for achieving certain goals, but conformity to the rule of law is not itself an ultimate goal. This subservient role of the doctrine shows both its power and its limitations. On the one hand if the pursuit of certain goals is entirely incompatible with the rule of law then these goals should not be pursued by legal means. But on the other hand one should be wary of disqualifying the legal pursuit of major social goals in the name of the rule of law. After all the rule of law is meant to enable the law to promote social good, and should not be lightly used to show that it should not do so. Sacrificing too many social goals on the altar of the rule of law may make the law barren and empty.

So Raz argues for a negative, content-free, 'thin' version of the rule of law. If this is correct, then it is possible to say that an evil legal system (for example, one based on race or religious discrimination) could nonetheless be regarded as respectful of the rule of law if it conformed to required forms and processes. A law removing the right to vote from members of a religious minority could

[6] 'The rule of law and its virtue' (1977) 93 Law Quarterly Review 195, 196.

be described as 'undemocratic' and 'wrong' but if the law was passed according to normal parliamentary procedures, was published and accessible to all, and if there was adequate access to the courts for people who want to argue that they were not a member of that minority, then it could be rule of law-compliant.

A content-free rule of law also takes little account of social and economic equality between people—what matters is formal equality. The French writer Anotole France captures this in his bon mot: '*The law, in its majestic equality, forbids the rich and the poor alike to sleep under bridges, to beg in the streets, and to steal bread.*' So the rule of law is not concerned with socio-economic rights, such as rights to food, housing, health, and education. Only if economic equality directly impinges on one of the basic elements of the content-free rule of law, such as access to the courts, does it become relevant. A judge's quip that '*In England, justice is open to all—like the Ritz hotel*' is frequently invoked a century after it was made whenever cuts to public funding of litigation (legal aid) are proposed.[7] In Lord Bingham's words, '*denial of legal protection to the poor litigant who cannot afford to pay is one enemy of the rule of law*'.[8]

Why do some people believe that it is a good idea to confine the rule of law to formal matters and steer clear of the substance of the law? Professor Paul Craig (not himself a supporter of this content-free version of the rule of law) gave the following explanation to the House of Lords Constitution Committee.

P. Craig, 'The Rule of Law', A paper for the House of Lords Constitution Committee, Sixth Report, Session 2006–07 (HL 151), 'Relations between the Executive, the Judiciary and Parliament', p. 101

The rationale for restricting the rule of law in this manner is as follows. We may all agree that laws should be just, that their content should be morally sound and that rights should be protected within society. The problem is that if the rule of law is taken to encompass the necessity for 'good laws' in this sense then the concept ceases to have an independent function. There is a wealth of literature devoted to the discussion of the meaning of a just society, the nature of the rights which should subsist therein, and the appropriate boundaries of governmental action. Political theory has tackled questions such as these from time immemorial. To bring these issues within the rubric of the rule of law would therefore rob this concept of an independent function. Laws would be condemned or upheld as being in conformity with, or contrary to, the rule of law when the condemnation or praise would simply be reflective of attachment to a particular conception of rights, democracy or the just society. The message is therefore that if you wish to argue about the justness of society do so by all means. If you wish to defend a particular type of individual right then present your argument. Draw upon the wealth of literature which addresses these matters directly. It is however on this view not necessary or desirable to cloak the conclusion in the mantle of the rule of law, since this will merely reflect the conclusion which has already been arrived at through reliance on a particular theory of rights or the just society.

In the following extract, Ronald Dworkin challenges the idea of a content-free rule of law (which he derides as a 'rule book conception') and puts forward an alternative 'rights' conception.

7 The Ritz Hotel is one of the most luxurious and expensive in London.

8 T. Bingham, *The Rule of Law* (2010, London: Allen Lane), p. 85.

R. Dworkin, 'Political Judges and the Rule of Law', in *A Matter of Principle* (1985, Oxford: OUP), ch. 1, pp. 11–12 (abridged)

There are, in fact, two very different conceptions of the rules of law, each of which has its partisans. The first I shall call the 'rule book' conception. This insists that, so far as is possible, the power of the state should never be exercised against individual citizens except in accordance with rules explicitly set out in a public rule book available to all. The government as well as ordinary citizens must play by these public rules until they are changed, in accordance with further rules about how they are to be changed, which are also set out in the rule book. The rule-book conception is, in one sense, very narrow, because it does not stipulate anything about the content of the rules that may be put in the rule book. It insists only that whatever rules that may be put in the rule book must be followed until changed. Those who have this conception of the rule of law do care about the content of the rules in the rule book, but they say that this is a matter of substantive justice, and that substantive justice is an independent ideal, in no sense part of the ideal of the rule of law.

I shall call the second conception of the rule of law the 'rights' conception. It is in several ways more ambitious than the rule-book conception. It assumes that citizens have moral rights and duties with respect to one another, and political rights against the state as a whole. It insists that these moral and political rights be recognized in positive law, so that they may be enforced *upon the demand of individual citizens* through the courts and other judicial institutions of the familiar types, so far as this is practicable. The rule of law on this conception is the ideal of rule by an accurate public conception of individual rights. It does not distinguish, as the rule-book conception does, between the rule of law and the substantive justice; on the contrary it requires, as part of the ideal of law, that the rules in the rule book capture and enforce moral rights.

Dworkin goes on to argue that the 'rights' conception of the rule of law is far more demanding than the simple 'rule-book' view. The rule-book model asks only whether officials follow the rules laid down in advance. By contrast, the rights conception can fail in several ways: the state may recognise too few rights, fail to enforce rights against itself, misunderstand what rights people have, or enforce them unfairly so that disadvantaged groups struggle to secure them in practice. Because of this, the rights conception captures a thicker, justice-oriented vision of legality.

He adds that the two models can coexist: any society is better if officials follow clear rules, and also better if its institutions protect the rights people hold. But the models differ in their moral weight. A society that routinely ignores its own rules cannot be just, however enlightened its aims. Yet strict compliance with unjust rules plainly does not produce justice. The rights conception reverses this: a society that scores well on protecting and enforcing rights will almost certainly be just, even if it is poorly run.

Lord Bingham's definition of the rule of law (discussed at the start of this section), is clearly not content-free. To comply with the rule of law as he defines it, there needs to be adherence to various formal and procedural aspects but additionally his sub-rules 5 and 8 require laws to comply with human rights. Human rights norms include requirements about the substance of the law, for example freedom of expression and freedom of association. Bingham's fuller account of the rule of law can be seen in the concerns raised by the JUSTICE report discussed at the start of this chapter, and it also informed the approach of the Attorney General appointed when the Labour government took office in 2024.

Lord Hermer KC 'The Rule of Law in an Age of Populism', The 2024 Bingham Lecture (14 October 2024) https://www.gov.uk/government/speeches/attorney-generals-2024-bingham-lecture-on-the-rule-of-law

I want to be clear that by the rule of law, I do not just mean rule by law; a purely procedural and formal conception that populists and authoritarians can themselves so often use as a cloak of legitimacy.

One of Lord Bingham's great contributions was to promote a more substantive conception of the rule of law, including the idea that the law must afford adequate protection of fundamental human rights. I too believe that human rights - both at the level of principle, and in practice through how they are enforced - are an essential element of the rule of law and a stable democratic culture. As well as recognising and protecting the dignity of all, they guarantee the essential rights and freedoms which underpin our system.

Far from being at odds with democracy, as some populists would have us believe, the rule of law is the bedrock on which it rests. What good is democracy - indeed, can democracy exist - without the right to free and fair elections or freedom of speech, guaranteed by the right of access to the courts and an independent judiciary? And I would go further. Democracy, in my view, is inextricably related to the rule of law, properly understood. For what good is the rule of law without democracy, which confers essential legitimacy on the rules that govern the relationship between citizen and state?

Hermer went on to warn in his speech that '*Parliamentary sovereignty is one of the fundamental features of our constitution and the ultimate legal authority of Parliament to make or unmake any law is crystal clear. However, viewing the rule of law through this distorting lens of ultimate decision-making authority alone risks mistaking it for a purely formal, and thin, conception of "rule by law"*'.

PAUSE FOR REFLECTION

Which version of the rule of law do you prefer and why: content-free or content-rich?

4.2.2 DICEY AND HIS CRITICS

So far our exploration of definitions has focused on modern debates between content-free and content-rich conceptions of the rule of law. We now need to turn to a much earlier account that still carries significant authority as well as attracting criticism—that of A.V. Dicey (1835–1922). One Canadian academic has suggested that continuing to analyse Dicey's work '*is to belabour a horse which is thought to have died so long ago, after assaults so numerous and savage, that humane considerations might dictate another line of investigation*'.[9] Even so, Dicey's lasting influence on British public law means his ideas cannot be ignored. For Dicey, the rule of law was a distinctively British achievement, which he believed set the United Kingdom apart from other constitutional systems.

[9] H.W. Arthurs, 'Rethinking administrative law: A slightly Dicey business' (1979) 17 Osgoode Hall Law Journal 1, 4.

A.V. Dicey, *Introduction to the Study of the Law of the Constitution* (1885; 10th edn 1959, London: Macmillan & Co.), pp. 187–95

When we say that the supremacy or the rule of law is a characteristic of the English constitution, we generally include under one expression at least three distinct though kindred conceptions.

We mean, in the first place, that no man is punishable or can be made to suffer in body or goods except for a distinct breach of law established in the ordinary legal manner before the ordinary courts of the land. [. . .]

We mean in the second place not only that [. . .] no man is above the law, but that [. . .] every man, whatever his rank or condition, is subject to the ordinary law of the realm [. . . that . . .] every official, from the Prime Minister down to a constable or a collector of taxes, is under the same responsibility for every act done without legal justification as any other citizen. [. . .]

We may say [thirdly] that the constitution is pervaded by the rule of law on the ground that the general principles of the constitution (as for example the right to personal liberty, or the right of public meeting) are [. . .] the result of judicial decisions determining the rights of private persons [. . .].

One early critique of Dicey came from Sir Ivor Jennings (1903–65). Jennings was a socialist who welcomed the increasing government regulation of business, social security provision, and shared none of Dicey's hostility to the interventionist state. Jennings' own book (*The Law and the Constitution*[10]) criticized the whole scope of Dicey's analysis, arguing that Dicey failed to deal with the *powers* of government: Dicey '*seemed to think that the British constitution was concerned almost entirely with the rights of individuals*'.[11] In fact, even when Dicey was writing, central and local government had considerable discretionary legal powers to carry out all sorts of functions from the compulsory purchase of land to restricting overseas trade. Jennings' assessment was that Dicey '*honestly tried [. . .] to analyse [the constitution], but, like most, he saw the constitution through his own spectacles, and his own vision was not exact*'.[12]

In Appendix II of his book, Jennings considers Dicey's theory of the rule of law. In relation to Dicey's first meaning (the absence of arbitrary and discretionary powers), Jennings explains that what Dicey really meant was that 'wide administrative or executive powers are likely to be abused *and therefore ought not to be conferred*'.[13] But the discretionary powers of ministers and local authorities were as much part of the 'regular' law of the land as any others. And while, of course, occasional abuse of power might occur, this was no reason for not conferring discretionary powers on officials. These powers were used to ensure socially progressive goals such as minimum standards of health and safety in workplaces and the clearing of slum housing. This, Jennings said, was of no interest to Dicey:

Sir Ivor Jennings, *The Law and the Constitution*, 5th edn (1958, London: University of London Press), pp. 310–11

Dicey [. . .] was much more concerned with the constitutional relations between Great Britain and Ireland than with the relations between poverty and disease on the one hand, and the new industrial system on the other. In internal politics, therefore, he was concerned not with the clearing up of the nasty industrial sections of towns, but with the liberty of the subject. In terms of powers, he was concerned with police powers, and not with other administrative powers.

[10] (1st edn 1933, 5th edn 1958). [11] *The Law and the Constitution* (5th edn 1958), p. 55.
[12] Ibid, p. 316. [13] Ibid, p. 307.

In relation to Dicey's second definition of the rule of law (equality before the law), Jennings flatly denied that there was any equality between the rights and duties of an official and that of an ordinary person. Dicey surely realized this, but had chosen to ignore the public law position of officials, for example the duty of local authorities to provide education to children and the powers of the tax inspectors to demand information. Dicey was only writing about the position in tort law—not public law. While it was true that generally officials could be sued personally by an aggrieved citizen for a tortious act or omission in the course of their duty, Jennings' withering retort was that *'this is a small point upon which to base a doctrine called by the magnificent name of "rule of law", particularly when it is generally used in a very different sense'*.[14]

Lastly, Jennings questioned Dicey's proposition that the rule of law meant that 'the constitution is *the result* of the ordinary law of the land' rather than a constitutional code. Jennings could not see Dicey's point.

Sir Ivor Jennings, *The Law and the Constitution*, 5th edn (1958, London: University of London Press), p. 314

I do not understand how it is correct to say that the rules are the consequence of the rights of individuals and not their source. The powers of the Crown and of other administrative authorities are limited by the rights of individuals; or the rights of individuals are limited by the powers of the administration. Both statements are correct; and both powers and rights come from the law—from the rules.

QUESTIONS

1. What assumptions are made by Dicey and Jennings, respectively?
2. Dicey's ideas about the rule of law continue to be quoted by academics, judges, and official bodies. Should they be, or do Jennings' arguments so dent Dicey's definition of the rule of law that we should stop referring to it?

4.2.3 SCEPTICAL VIEWS

So far, we have considered two academic controversies about the rule of law: whether it is content-free or content-rich; and whether Dicey's groundbreaking writings on the subject withstand later criticisms. There is a third controversy. Some academics take the sceptical view that the rule of law is not a useful concept.

In the following extract, John Griffith (1918–2010)—a leading political constitutionalist of his generation, based at the LSE—berates what he saw as the extravagant and politically partisan use of the idea of 'the Rule of Law' (note the capital letters) in the 1970s by campaigners for incorporation of the ECHR into English law and other developments of which he disapproved.

[14] Ibid, p. 312.

J.A.G. Griffith, 'The Political Constitution' (1979) 42 *Modern Law Review* 1, 15

[In recent years] 'the law' has been raised from its proper and useful function as a means towards ends (about which it is possible to have differing opinions) to the level of a general concept. On this view, individual rules of law may be good or bad but 'the law' is undeniably good and must be upheld or chaos will come again. There is more than a suspicion of slight [*sic*] of hand here. For nobody, except committed anarchists, suggests that 'the law' should be dispensed with.

The ground is then shifted slightly and what becomes sacred and untouchable is something called the Rule of Law. The Rule of Law is an invaluable concept for those who wish not to change the present set-up. A person may be said not to be in favour of the Rule of Law if he is critical of the Queen, the Commissioner of the Metropolitan Police, the Speaker of the House of Commons or Lord Denning. Statutes may be contrary to the Rule of Law [. . .] but the common law, it seems, can never be. Objection to the rules of international law in their application to the United Kingdom is wholly excusable on proper occasions. Defiance of regulations and directives emanating from Brussels may often be accounted as a positive virtue.

If the Rule of Law means that there should be proper and adequate machinery for dealing with criminal offences and for ensuring that public authorities do not exceed their legal powers, and for insisting that official penalties may not be inflicted save on those who have broken the law, then only an outlaw could dispute its desirability. And Bracton is a thirteen-century authority in its support. But when it is extended to mean more than that, it is a fantasy invented by Liberals of the old school in the late nineteenth century and patented by the Tories to throw a protective sanctity around certain legal and political institutions and principles which they wish to preserve at any cost. Then it is become a new metaphysic, seeming to resolve the doubts of the faithful with an old dogma.

More recently, Martin Loughlin (also of the LSE) expresses doubts on different grounds. The European Commission for Democracy through Law (the Venice Commission) invited Loughlin to prepare a discussion paper for their deliberations on the meaning of the rule of law.

M. Loughlin, 'The Rule of Law in European Jurisprudence', Study 512/2009 (Venice Commission, 2009)

There is every reason to accept that the rule of law must be a mere slogan and that, however laudable its underlying intentions, the goal of achieving a 'government of laws and not of men' is one that is incapable of realization. One reason is that since in the modern era law is universally acknowledged to be a human creation, it cannot be placed above human will: law cannot therefore be placed above a 'government of men'. A second is that laws cannot be said to rule, for the obvious reason that ruling involves action and, in themselves, laws do not act. The rule of law, it would appear, is merely a rhetorical expression, and this conviction is reinforced by virtue of its intrinsic ambiguity: the ubiquity of usage of the expression, 'the rule of law', is matched only by the multiplicity of its meanings. [. . .]

[. . . P]recision in public law might demand abandonment of these concepts altogether in favour of a less charged investigation into the nature of the relationship between state, constitution, governing and law. The difficulty is that the very ubiquity of the expression demands that it be examined, especially for the purposes of revealing its underlying values, determining whether any coherent account of the general concept can be assembled, and assessing the force of the claim that it is a foundational element of the discipline. In this paper [written for the Venice Commission], the origins of these expressions in English, German and French thought will be examined, and an argument made about the coherence of the directing idea. My argument will be that although a coherent formulation of the general concept can be devised, that this formulation is entirely unworkable in practice. Consequently, the rule of law cannot be conceived as amounting to a foundational concept in public law. So far as it has utility, it must be deployed with precision, especially because, precisely because it is unrealizable, it is susceptible to being used for ideological purposes. The main value of the concept, it would appear, concerns its aspirational quality. But acceptance of this quality must be tempered by recognition that the extent to which the directing idea can—and should—be realized remains an essentially political task.

QUESTIONS

1. What do you think Griffith means when he says that the rule of law is a fantasy '*invented by Liberals of the old school in the nineteenth century*'? Who might he have in mind?
2. Does Griffith approve of a content-free rule of law, or is he against the whole idea?
3. Do you agree with Loughlin's conclusion that '*the rule of law cannot be conceived as amounting to a foundational concept in public law*'?
4. What would be the implications of adopting the standpoint that the rule of law is 'a mere slogan'?

4.3 PRACTICAL PROTECTION OF THE RULE OF LAW

Having considered the main debates about how the rule of law should be defined, we now turn to a second question: how is it protected in practice. A helpful way into this issue is provided by a 2023 speech by the Attorney General and a 2017 UK Supreme Court judgment.

Victoria Prentis KC MP, 'The Rule of Law and Effective Government', speech at the Institute for Government, 10 July 2023

Who is responsible for upholding the rule of law?

Given that the rule of law is so fundamental to our society, this raises a question. Who is responsible for upholding the rule of law? Parliament, the Executive (in the form of Ministers) and the Judiciary all have vital roles to play in this. And much in the way that each parent plays their own role and brings their own strengths to that role, so too do Parliament, the Executive and the courts.

Parliament determines what the law will be, and the powers that are granted to the Government and to other public bodies. The scrutiny of legislation by both houses improves lawmaking.

The Executive must act in accordance with their powers - whether statutory or prerogative - and these must not be exercised arbitrarily.

Finally, an independent judiciary ensures that government exercises its powers in accordance with the law. Judges rightly uphold the work of government when it acts within its powers and prevent overreach when it does not.

Each of these branches of government contribute, in their own right, to the rule of law and effective government. However, . . . these branches contribute to the rule of law in their own right and in relationship to one another.

***R* (on the application of UNISON) *v* Lord Chancellor**
[2017] UKSC 51, Lord Reed JSC, para 68

At the heart of the concept of the rule of law is the idea that society is governed by law. Parliament exists primarily in order to make laws for society in this country. Democratic procedures exist primarily in order to ensure that the Parliament which makes those laws includes Members of Parliament who are chosen by the people of this country and are accountable to them. Courts exist in order to ensure that the laws made by Parliament, and the common law created by the courts themselves, are applied and enforced. That role includes ensuring that the executive branch of government carries out its functions in accordance with the law. In order for the courts to perform that role, people must in principle have unimpeded access to them. Without such access, laws are liable to become a dead letter, the work done by Parliament may be rendered nugatory, and the democratic election of Members of Parliament may become a meaningless charade. That is why the courts do not merely provide a public service like any other.

Read together, the two extracts take noticeably different routes into the same territory. The Attorney General stresses that the rule of law works only when Parliament, ministers, and the courts each carry out their constitutional responsibilities and recognise the limits of their own authority. Lord Reed's account is more tightly focused on legal structure. He underlines that the rule of law depends on courts being able to apply and enforce Parliament's laws, and that this requires effective access to justice. The contrast is therefore one of emphasis: the Attorney General highlights cooperation between constitutional actors, while Lord Reed concentrates on the legal conditions that make the system function at all.

PAUSE FOR REFLECTION

Both extracts point to the importance of each institution doing its job properly. But in practice, do some bear heavier burdens than others when the rule of law comes under strain?

4.3.1 THE JUDICIARY AS GUARDIANS OF THE RULE OF LAW

In the broadest sense, the work of courts and tribunals supports the rule of law across all forms of legal proceedings from commercial litigation to family disputes, and from criminal cases to consumer claims. This links directly to Bingham's 'sub-rules' that people should have access to procedures for resolving genuine disputes without prohibitive cost or undue delay, and that state-provided adjudication must be fair. Judicial independence is separate constitutional principle, but it provides the essential conditions in which judges give effect to the rule of law.[15]

For present purposes, the most relevant role played by the courts is their responsibility for protecting fundamental rights and ensuring that executive power is exercised within established legal limits. Throughout this book, we examine topics that bear directly on how the judiciary act as guardians of the rule of law. Early on, we saw that Acts of Parliament and the common law set the basic framework for government—while acknowledging that other features are regulated by non-legal constitutional conventions.[16] The devolution settlement is set out in statute and places the UK Supreme Court as the final arbiter on compliance with the distribution of powers laid out in the devolution

[15] See Chapter 15. [16] See Chapter 2.

Acts.[17] Since the 1960s, the courts have developed common law grounds of judicial review, and refined techniques of statutory interpretation, creating a detailed set of legal standards against which the lawfulness of executive power can be accessed based on illegality, irrationality and procedural impropriety.[18] The Human Rights Act 1998 added further tools for judicial scrutiny.[19] Supporters of legal constitutionalism see these developments as strengthened the rule of law.[20] Critics adopting a more political constitutionalist view argue that judicial control has expanded too far, limiting executive freedom of action in ways that do not always serve the public interest,[21] in some contexts calling for judicial review to be excluded or limited.[22]

This section now turns to examine a technique the courts have developed for giving practical effect to the rule of law: an approach to statutory interpretation known as the 'principle of legality'. This body of case law shows how parliamentary supremacy and the rule of law interact in practice, and tensions that sometimes arise. Judges recognise Parliament's authority to change the law, but they also ensure that important rights or foundational constitutional principles are not overridden unless Parliament has chosen to do so in clear and explicit terms.

Before turning to the principle of legality, it is important to recall how courts normally interpret Acts of Parliament. Statutory interpretation begins with the ordinary meaning of the words Parliament has enacted, read in their immediate context and in light of the statute's overall purpose. Only once that baseline is clear can we understand what the principle of legality adds. In the following extract, Lord Hodge DPSC explains this default approach, which remains the starting point for all cases involving the interpretation of legislation.

R (on the application of Project for the Registration of Children as British Citizens) v Secretary of State for the Home Department

[2023] AC 255, Lord Hodge DPSC, para 29 (with whom the majority agreed)

> The courts in conducting statutory interpretation are 'seeking the meaning of the words which Parliament used': *Black-Clawson International Ltd v Papierwerke Waldhof-Aschaffenburg* AG [1975] AC 591, 613 per Lord Reid. More recently, Lord Nicholls of Birkenhead stated: 'Statutory interpretation is an exercise which requires the court to identify the meaning borne by the words in question in the particular context' (*R v Secretary of State for the Environment, Transport and the Regions, Ex p Spath Holme Ltd* [2001] 2 AC 349, 396). Words and passages in a statute derive their meaning from their context. A phrase or passage must be read in the context of the section as a whole and in the wider context of a relevant group of sections. Other provisions in a statute and the statute as a whole may provide the relevant context. They are the words which Parliament has chosen to enact as an expression of the purpose of the legislation and are therefore the primary source by which meaning is ascertained. There is an important constitutional reason for having regard primarily to the statutory context as Lord Nicholls explained in *Spath Holme*, p. 397: 'Citizens, with the assistance of their advisers, are intended to be able to understand parliamentary enactments, so that they can regulate their conduct accordingly. They should be able to rely upon what they read in an Act of Parliament'.

[17] See Chapter 6.
[18] See Chapters 17 (the role of judicial review), 18 (grounds of illegality and irrationality), 19 (ground of procedural fairness), and 20 (excluding and limiting judicial review).
[19] See Chapter 21. [20] See Chapter 2, section 2.3.1.
[21] See Chapter 2, section 2.2.3. [22] See Chapter 20.

In the following extract, Lord Hoffmann sets out what has become the classic formulation of the principle of legality.

R v Secretary of State for the Home Department, Ex p Simms
[2000] 2 AC 115, 131, Lord Hoffmann (emphasis added)

> Parliamentary sovereignty means that Parliament can, if it chooses, legislate contrary to fundamental principles of human rights . . . The constraints upon its exercise by Parliament are ultimately political, not legal. But the principle of legality means that Parliament must squarely confront what it is doing and accept the political cost. *Fundamental rights cannot be overridden by general or ambiguous words.* This is because there is too great a risk that the full implications of their unqualified meaning may have passed unnoticed in the democratic process. In the absence of express language or necessary implication to the contrary, the courts therefore presume that even the most general words were intended to be subject to the basic rights of the individual.

The principle of legality can be expressed in four steps. Step 1 is to identify the fundamental common law right said to be in issue. Step 2 is to interpret the legislation said to restrict that right. If Parliament has used clear words, the court must give effect to them. The court cannot 'disregard an unambiguous expression of Parliament's intention',[23] and where there are 'provisions of a detailed, specific and unambiguous character'[24] that restrict a right, the court will implement this. Under parliamentary supremacy, Parliament may restrict or remove rights, and the court's constitutional duty is to uphold what Parliament has decided. Step 3 applies where the statutory wording is general or unspecific: in such cases, 'the courts should be slow to impute to the legislature an intention to override' the right.[25]

To see how the principle of legality works to protect rights, let's look at *R v (on the application of N3 and another) v Secretary of State for the Home Department* [2025] UKSC 6. The Home Secretary exercised the power in section 40(2) of the British Nationality Act 1981 to make an order depriving an individual of British citizenship on national security grounds. The power could only be used if the Home Secretary was satisfied that the person would not be made stateless. Step 1: the Supreme Court confirmed that 'the status of citizenship is a fundamental status at common law'. Step 2: the relevant provisions of the 1981 Act were unclear about whether a person ceased to be a British citizen immediately upon the making of a deprivation order, or only once any appeal against the order had been finally determined. Step 3: applying the principle of legality, the Court held that the individual who brought a successful appeal must be treated as having remained a British citizen throughout the appeal proceedings. This finding had significant practical consequences. The claimant had become a parent during that period, and if they were still a British citizen at the time of the child's birth, the child would also acquire British citizenship.

The approach embodied in the principle of legality has been applied not only where fundamental common law rights are in play, but also where a basic constitutional principle is at stake. *R (on the application of Evans) v Attorney General* [2015] UKSC 21 concerned a long running attempt by a *Guardian* journalist to obtain, under the Freedom of Information Act 2000, letters written by Prince Charles to ministers on issues such as environmental standards and farming. Because of his distinctive handwriting, the correspondence became known as the 'black spider memos'. After the Upper Tribunal

[23] *Ahmed v HM Treasury (Nos 1 and 2)* [2010] UKSC 2, [117].
[24] *R (on the application of Gillan) v Commissioner of Police for the Metropolis* [2006] UKHL 12, [15].
[25] *R (on the application of N3 and another) v Secretary of State for the Home Department* [2025] UKSC 6, [66].

ordered disclosure, the Attorney General invoked the rarely used ministerial veto in section 53 of the Act. This allowed the Attorney General to certify that disclosure need not occur if he had, 'on reasonable grounds, formed the opinion' that the information should be withheld. The Court of Appeal, and later a majority of the Supreme Court, held that the Attorney General's certificate was unlawful. The judgments in the Supreme Court are complex and rest on different strands of reasoning. For the majority, Lord Neuberger emphasized that section 53 could not be interpreted as giving a member of the executive the power to overturn a judicial decision merely because they disagreed with it. To read the provision in that way, he explained, would cut across fundamental constitutional principles without Parliament having spoken clearly.

R (on the application of Evans) v Attorney General
[2015] UKSC 21, [51]–[52], Lord Neuberger

51. A statutory provision which entitles a member of the executive (whether a Government Minister or the Attorney General) to overrule a decision of the judiciary merely because he does not agree with it would not merely be unique in the laws of the United Kingdom. It would cut across two constitutional principles which are also fundamental components of the rule of law.

52. First, subject to being overruled by a higher court or (given Parliamentary supremacy) a statute, it is a basic principle that a decision of a court is binding as between the parties, and cannot be ignored or set aside by anyone, including (indeed it may fairly be said, least of all) the executive. Secondly, it is also fundamental to the rule of law that decisions and actions of the executive are, subject to necessary well established exceptions (such as declarations of war), and jealously scrutinised statutory exceptions, reviewable by the court at the suit of an interested citizen.

Lord Wilson dissented. In his view, the Court of Appeal and Supreme Court majority went beyond interpretation and effectively rewrote section 53, relying on constitutional principles at the expense of the words enacted by Parliament. He argued '*parliamentary sovereignty, emblematic of our democracy*' (para 168) required the court to respect the breadth of the power Parliament had chosen to confer.

This disagreement in *Evans* helps bring the principle of legality into focus. The majority relied on it to limit the reach of a broadly framed statutory power; the dissent warned against using constitutional principles to narrow legislation beyond what its wording can bear. Subsequent case law reinforces the majority's basic point: legality guides interpretation but does not permit courts to disapply Acts of Parliament. Where Parliament truly intends to authorize an intrusion on fundamental rights or constitutional norms, it must do so expressly. The courts cannot set aside Acts of Parliament, but they can substantially limit their legal effect through interpretation where Parliament has not spoken clearly.

PAUSE FOR REFLECTION

Principle of legality cases often involve a minister—politically accountable to Parliament—being prevented by the courts from carrying out a policy the government considers to be in the public interest. In your own words, explain why it may be legitimate for a court to block a minister's decision in these circumstances.

4.3.2 PARLIAMENT AS A GUARDIAN OF THE RULE OF LAW

How legislation is made, and its quality, is a rule of law issue.[26] Parliament has the power, though legislation, both to protect and promote the rule of law and to undermine it, consciously or inadvertently. The principle of parliamentary supremacy leads to Parliament, not the courts, having the final say on the validity of provisions in Acts of Parliament that offend the rule of law. Dicey thought it unlikely that Parliament would undermine the rule of law, as he explains:

A.V. Dicey, *Introduction to the Study of the Law of the Constitution* (1885; 10th edn 1959, London: Macmillan & Co.), pp. 406–10 (Chapter XIII, 'Relation between Parliamentary Sovereignty and the Rule of Law')

The sovereignty of Parliament and the supremacy of the law of the land—the two principles which pervade the whole of the English constitution—may appear to stand in opposition to each other, or to be at best only counterbalancing forces. But this appearance is delusive; the sovereignty of Parliament, as contrasted with other forms of sovereign power, favours the supremacy of the law, whilst the predominance of rigid legality throughout our institutions evokes the exercise, and thus increases the authority, of Parliamentary sovereignty.

The sovereignty of Parliament favours the supremacy of the law of the land.

That this should be so arises in the main from two characteristics or peculiarities which distinguish the English Parliament from other sovereign powers.

The first of these characteristics is that the commands of Parliament (consisting as it does of the Crown, the House of Lords, and the House of Commons) can be uttered only through the combined action of its three constituent parts, and must, therefore, always take the shape of formal and deliberate legislation. The will of Parliament can be expressed only through an Act of Parliament. [. . .]

The second of these characteristics is that the English Parliament as such has never, except at periods of revolution, exercised direct executive power or appointed the officials of the executive government.

No doubt in modern times the House of Commons has in substance obtained the right to designate for appointment the Prime Minister and the other members of the Cabinet. But this right is, historically speaking, of recent acquisition, and is exercised in a very roundabout manner; its existence does not affect the truth of the assertion that the Houses of Parliament do not directly appoint or dismiss the servants of the State; neither the House of Lords nor the House of Commons, nor both Houses combined, could even now issue a direct order to a military officer, a constable, or a tax-collector; the servants of the State are still in name what they once were in reality—'servants of the Crown'; and, what is worth careful notice, the attitude of Parliament towards government officials was determined originally, and is still regulated, by considerations and feelings belonging to a time when the 'servants of the Crown' were dependent upon the King, that is, upon a power which naturally excited the jealousy and vigilance of Parliament.

Hence several results all indirectly tending to support the supremacy of the law. Parliament, though sovereign, unlike a sovereign monarch who is not only a legislator but a ruler, that is, head of the executive government, has never hitherto been able to use the powers of the government as a means of interfering with the regular course of law; and what is even more important, Parliament has looked with disfavour and jealousy on all exemptions of officials from the ordinary liabilities of citizens or from the jurisdiction of the ordinary Courts; Parliamentary sovereignty has been fatal to the growth of 'administrative law.' The action, lastly, of Parliament has tended as naturally to protect the independence of the judges, as that of other sovereigns to protect the conduct of officials. It is worth notice that

[26] See Chapters 11, 12, and 13.

Parliamentary care for judicial independence has, in fact, stopped just at that point where on a priori grounds it might be expected to end. The judges are not in strictness irremovable; they can be removed from office on an address of the two Houses; they have been made by Parliament independent of every power in the State except the Houses of Parliament.

In recent years, Parliament has put in place procedures that help ensure that Acts of Parliament comply with rule of law principles—or, at least, if they do not then Parliament legislates knowingly. Examples of this is the work of the House of Lords Constitution Committee (which reviews bills for compliance with all constitutional principles) and the Joint Committee on Human Rights (which, as its name suggests, focuses on compliance with human rights and in particular the ECHR).[27]

There is no doubt, however, that if an Act of Parliament clearly enacts legislation in conflict with rule of law principles, the role of the courts is limited. Parliament may enact legislation to abolish or limit a fundamental right that has been recognised by the common law.

This was demonstrated in 2008 when, shortly after the House of Lords reasserted a rule of the common law that defendants in criminal trials have a right to confront their accuser, Parliament abolished that rule. In *R v Davis*,[28] the accused stood trial for shooting two people dead at a New Year's Eve party in London. Witnesses were reluctant to come forward. The police assured them that their identities would be protected if they were to give evidence in court. The judge made an order allowing witnesses to use pseudonyms, to be hidden behind screens in court, to have their voices mechanically distorted, and to bar Davis' counsel from asking questions that might enable any of them to be identified. Davis was convicted. He appealed on the ground that he did not receive a fair trial because the anonymity arrangements prevented his counsel from cross-examining the witnesses.

R v Davis [2008] UKHL 36

Lord Bingham of Cornhill

5. It is a long-established principle of the English common law that, subject to certain exceptions and statutory qualifications, the defendant in a criminal trial should be confronted by his accusers in order that he may cross-examine them and challenge their evidence. This principle originated in ancient Rome [. . .]. But in continental Europe the principle was greatly attenuated in early mediaeval times and the procedure of the Inquisition, directed to the extirpation of heresy and the preservation of society, depended heavily on evidence given secretly by anonymous witnesses whom the suspect was denied the opportunity to confront. In England, where proof of crime depended on calling live evidence before a jury to convince it of a defendant's guilt, there was no room for such procedures. But concern as to national security and intimidation of witnesses did lead to reliance on secret, anonymous evidence and evidence not adduced in court, and thus to departures from the rule of confrontation, notably in the Court of Star Chamber and in common law trials for treason, as notoriously at the trial of Sir Walter Raleigh. The Court of Star Chamber, popular at first, came over time to attract the same popular loathing as the Inquisition, its procedures regarded as foreign, cruel, oppressive and unfair. It was promptly abolished by the Long Parliament in 1641, and steps were taken [. . .] to bring the procedure of treason trials into line with that required at common law. [. . .] The practice of confronting defendants with their accusers so that the latter may be cross-examined and the truth established was recognised by such

[27] See Chapter 12. [28] [2008] UKHL 36.

> authorities as Sir Matthew Hale [. . .] Blackstone [. . .] and Bentham [. . .]. The common law right to be confronted by one's accusers was included within the colonial constitutions of several North American colonies [. . .] and other states adopted similar declarations at the time of independence. By the sixth amendment to the United States constitution adopted in 1791 it was provided that 'In all criminal prosecutions, the accused shall enjoy the right [. . .] to be confronted with the witnesses against him [. . .]'. The rule has been strictly applied: in *Alford v United States* 282 US 687 (1931) a conviction was quashed where a government witness had been excused from answering a question about where he lived.

The House of Lords held that the trial judge had no power to make the anonymity order that he did: it infringed an important common law right. Reaction to this ruling in some sections of the news media was unfavourable (and in the following example, ludicrously overblown).

***The Sun*, 'Anarchy is unleashed'**, 25 June 2008

> Barmy Law Lords were last night accused of unleashing anarchy by barring anonymous witnesses in court trials. Worried police warned that dozens of terrorists and murderers will walk free unless the judges' ruling is swiftly overturned by the Government. They fear Britain could witness unrestrained violence like the slaughter in Zimbabwe.

Within a few weeks of the judgment, a bill was fast-tracked through Parliament designed to allow judges to make wide-ranging anonymity orders.

Criminal Evidence (Witness Anonymity) Act 2008, s. 1

> **1. New rules relating to anonymity of witnesses**
>
> (1) This Act provides for the making of witness anonymity orders in relation to witnesses in criminal proceedings.
>
> (2) The common law rules relating to the power of a court to make an order for securing that the identity of a witness in criminal proceedings is withheld from the defendant (or, on a defence application, from other defendants) are abolished.
>
> (3) Nothing in this Act affects the common law rules as to the withholding of information on the grounds of public interest immunity.

From a constitutional perspective, what happened following the *Davis* case was not particularly controversial. Although a common law right was abolished, the scheme set out in the 2008 Act required trial judges to exercise their new powers in such a way as to ensure that there would be a fair trial that complies with the requirements of Art. 6 of the ECHR (part of domestic law following the Human Rights Act 1998). The House of Lords, in their judgment, had indeed suggested that Parliament should consider the whole area. There was cross-party support for the new scheme replacing the common law right.

It is, however, possible to imagine different and more contentious circumstances in which a court seeks to protect a common law right and Parliament responds by seeking to overturn it. As we saw in Chapter 3, orthodox accounts of parliamentary supremacy state that Parliament may make and unmake any law. It has, however, been argued that Parliament's sovereign power is not absolute and that certain inherent constitutional limitations on its power exist. The thrust of the argument is that since Parliament derives its sovereignty from the constitution, the scope of its sovereignty is delineated by the constitution and by the basic principles of the constitutional system. This means that Parliament cannot claim sovereign power to subvert the basic principles upon which its very sovereignty is based. It cannot, for example, enact legislation that is contrary to essential notions of democracy or rights that are fundamental.

T.R.S. Allan, *Law, Liberty, and Justice* (1994, Oxford: OUP), p. 282

> A parliamentary enactment whose effect would be the destruction of any recognizable form of democracy—for example, a measure purporting to deprive a substantial section of the population of the vote on the grounds of their hostility to government policies—could not consistently be applied by the courts as law. Judicial obedience to the statute [. . .] could not coherently be justified in terms of the doctrine of parliamentary sovereignty, since the statute would violate the political principle which the doctrine itself enshrines.

Allan argues that limitations on Parliament do not imply a conflict between the rule of law and democratic principle. On the contrary, since both ideas flow from a basic moral commitment to democracy, they are both necessary and each supports the other. Sir John Laws (a Court of Appeal judge) took a similar approach in his academic writing.

Sir John Laws, 'Law and Democracy' [1995] *Public Law* 72

> [A]s a matter of fundamental principle [. . .] the survival and flourishing of a democracy in which basic rights (of which freedom of expression may be taken as a paradigm) are not only respected but enshrined requires that those who exercise democratic, political power must have limits set to what they may do: limits which they are not allowed to overstep. If this is right, it is a function of democratic power itself that it be not absolute.

The constitution, he goes on to argue, must guarantee such rights as freedom of expression '*since otherwise its credentials as a medium of honest rule are fatally undermined*'. This requires a 'higher-order law', which cannot be abrogated by a statute promoted by a government with the necessary majority in Parliament. It is, he argues, the constitution rather than Parliament that is sovereign. These are issues to which we shall return at various points in this book. Remember that in Chapter 3, we noted that in recent years the UK Supreme Court case law points towards a firmer reassertion of parliamentary supremacy as the foundational rule of the UK constitution.

The power of Parliament to legislate contrary to fundamental rights and rule of law principles remains even after the enactment of the Human Rights Act 1998, which assumes that Parliament may pass legislation that is incompatible with Convention rights.[29] A minister introducing a bill may '*make a statement to the effect that although he is unable to make a statement of compatibility the government nevertheless wishes the House to proceed with the Bill*' (s. 19). A court which subsequently

[29] See further Chapter 21.

determines that a provision of an Act of Parliament is not compatible with a Convention right may make only a 'declaration of incompatibility' which '*does not affect the validity, continuing operation or enforcement of the provision in respect of which it is given*' (s. 4).

PAUSE FOR REFLECTION

What justifications are there for permitting Parliament to abolish rights regarded as 'constitutional' or 'fundamental' by the courts?

4.3.3 GOVERNMENT AS A GUARDIAN OF THE RULE OF LAW

Few governments have escaped criticism—in Parliament, in the courts, in the news media—that some of their policies or decisions are unlawful. As we have just seen, one of the constitutional functions of the judiciary is to adjudicate in cases where it is alleged that ministers acted outside the law. In most situations where this happens, nobody doubts the good faith of the minister; there is simply disagreement, based on different but reasonably held interpretations of the law, about whether the minister has breached a principle of public law.

4.3.3.1 Political Leadership to Support the Rule of Law

The premiership of Boris Johnson MP (2019–22) raised a number of concerns about adherence to the rule of law. The principle that laws apply equally to everyone came under particular scrutiny during the 'partygate' investigations. Police inquiries into social gatherings in No.10 Downing Street during the 2020–21 Covid restrictions resulted in 126 fixed penalty notices issued to 83 people, including the Prime Minister and the Chancellor of the Exchequer. The episode generated considerable public criticism and prompted unusually direct comment in Parliament about the importance of political leaders modelling compliance with the law.

A separate issue concerned Lord Bingham's final precept: that the state should comply with its international legal obligations. The EU–UK Withdrawal Agreement of 2020, agreed and ratified by the Johnson government, included the Northern Ireland Protocol. The Protocol avoided a hard border on the island of Ireland but required checks on goods moving from Great Britain to Northern Ireland. As practical and political difficulties emerged, the government proposed legislation—the United Kingdom Internal Market Bill—that would have enabled ministers to disapply parts of the Protocol unilaterally. Critics described this as a clear breach of international law. The government replied that parliamentary supremacy allowed Parliament to legislate inconsistently with treaty commitments, but the most contentious clauses were removed before Royal Assent. The episode prompted the resignations of the Advocate General for Scotland and the Treasury Solicitor.[30] Tensions continued. The Northern Ireland Protocol Act 2022 gave ministers further powers to depart from the UK's treaty obligations, with the government invoking the international law doctrine of necessity. These events brought renewed attention to the question of how far executive reliance on parliamentary supremacy can be reconciled with the rule of law's expectation that the state should honour its international commitments.

These events point to a wider issue about how political leadership shapes the rule of law. Formal safeguards—statutory limits, judicial review, the work of law officers, the Lord Chancellor, and parliamentary committees—sit within a broader constitutional culture. In a system that gives significant

[30] See Chapter 8.

authority to ministers and rests on parliamentary supremacy, much depends on those in high office showing a consistent commitment to legality and to the UK's international obligations. When political leaders appear willing to push at, or work around, those limits, public confidence in the rule of law can weaken even if the courts and Parliament continue to perform their institutional roles. By contrast, clear signals from ministers that legal boundaries matter can help reinforce the culture of compliance on which an uncodified constitution depends.

PAUSE FOR REFLECTION

To what extent does the effectiveness of the rule of law depend on legal rules and formal systems, and how much depends on the attitudes and behaviour of those who govern?

4.3.3.2 Rule of Law in the Age of Automated and AI-based Decision-making

In Chapter 8 (section 8.3), we will look in more detail at the growing use of computer-based and AI-supported systems in public administration. Commentators increasingly debate whether AI in public administration threatens core rule-of-law values or might, in some settings, help to realize them. Stephen Daly captures both sides of this discussion in the extract below.

S. Daly, 'Artificial Intelligence, the Rule of Law and Public Administration: The Case of Taxation' (2024) 83(3) *Cambridge Law Review* 437, pp. 442–3 (footnotes omitted)

The Rule of Law too is said to be under threat. Proponents of thicker accounts have argued that AI technologies are problematic because they could lead to the 'domination' of humans. AI power, if unchecked, could diminish respect for the Rule of Law. As AI imperils fundamental rights, some authors argue that to the extent that this materialises, the Rule of Law too is undermined. With respect to thinner accounts, important Rule of Law values, such as transparency and accountability, predictability and consistency, and equality before the law could be attenuated. Where AI technology is opaque, humans subjected to decisions negatively affecting their interests are denuded of the possibility of challenging those decisions to ensure that they had been arrived at correctly. The focus overwhelmingly is on how the Rule of Law provides a good reason to limit technology's capabilities.

These claims are not disputed here. But it needs to be appreciated that these technologies can also be used to assist governments in meeting various Rule of Law demands. For instance, the Rule of Law encourages public authorities to make swift and consistent decisions and to achieve high levels of compliance with the underlying rules, whether that is through assisting citizens in complying with their legal obligations or enjoying their legal rights, or through being more effective in the execution of public functions. AI can be harnessed to satisfy these Rule of Law demands.

Daly's analysis can be linked to several of Lord Bingham's sub-rules. When an AI system is difficult to understand or its reasoning cannot be explained, the basic expectation that the law should be accessible and predictable is harder to meet. If a system is trained on biased or incomplete data, it may also put pressure on the commitment to equality before the law. Automated tools raise further questions about whether public power is being exercised within proper limits, especially if officials cannot demonstrate that the technology is operating on lawful and relevant criteria. At the same time, Daly's extract reminds us that well-designed systems can help public bodies act more consistently and handle decisions more efficiently—outcomes that sit comfortably with Bingham's focus on predictability and the effective administration of justice. The central challenge is to make sure that the use of AI strengthens, rather than undermines, these core elements of the rule of law.

> **PAUSE FOR REFLECTION**
> Automated and AI-based decision making: friend or foe of the rule of law?

4.3.3.3 The Rule of Law Duties of the Law Chancellor

Within central government, the ministerial office of Lord Chancellor has special responsibility for the rule of law and independence of the judiciary. To understand the Lord Chancellor's role, and why the system may not be working well, we need to compare and contrast this ministerial role before and after reforms were introduced by the Constitutional Reform Act 2005.

Before 2005, the Lord Chancellor was always a senior lawyer affiliated to the governing party. Lord Mackay of Clashfern was the last of the traditional Conservative holders of the office, serving for a decade from 1987 to 1997. Before his appointment by Margaret Thatcher, he had practised law in Scotland and served as Lord Advocate, the senior Scottish law officer. When Tony Blair became Prime Minister, he appointed Lord Irvine of Lairg, a leading barrister, who held the post for six years.

These pre-2005 Lord Chancellors combined an unusual concentration of roles. They were cabinet ministers; they headed the department responsible for the courts and tribunals; they acted as the presiding officer of the House of Lords; they served as head of the judiciary and oversaw judicial appointments; and, when time allowed, they sat as members of the Appellate Committee of the House of Lords to hear cases. No Lord Chancellors went on to be hold other ministerial posts. Critics said that this arrangement breached basic principles of separation of powers.[31] Supporters said that it worked well in practice and that the cabinet benefited from having a senior legal figure at the table able to defend the rule of law.

In 2004, Tony Blair announced what appeared to be a sudden and far-reaching package of constitutional reforms. The Government proposed to abolish the office of Lord Chancellor, replace the House of Lords Appellate Committee with a new, separate Supreme Court, and establish an independent judicial appointments system for England and Wales. Strong resistance in Parliament led to the office of Lord Chancellor being retained, but only in a fundamentally altered form. The holder of the office would no longer sit as a judge, serve as head of the judiciary, take a direct role in judicial appointments, or preside over the House of Lords. Notably, the requirement that the Lord Chancellor be legally qualified was removed. These changes were given statutory effect by the Constitutional Reform Act 2005.

Since then, Lord Chancellors have typically served for much shorter periods. Between 2010 and 2024, during the Coalition and subsequent Conservative administrations, eleven people held the role, several of whom were not legally trained. The office is now combined with that of Secretary of State for Justice, a portfolio that includes responsibility for the prison system. A number of recent Lord Chancellors have also moved on to other senior ministerial positions, including Liz Truss MP, who later became Prime Minister. Some commentators argue that these patterns leave the modern Lord Chancellor with less time, authority, or incentive to champion rule of law concerns within government.

[31] See Chapter 5.

In what ways does—or did—the Lord Chancellor help to promote the rule of law inside government? Consider this extract from evidence given to a select committee by Lord Mackay, who was opposed to the reforms.

Oral Evidence to the House of Lords Select Committee on the Constitutional Reform Bill, 20 April 2004, QQ 277-8

Lord Mackay of Clashfern: [. . . T]he Lord Chancellor is [. . .] in the Cabinet and in the Cabinet his job is to ensure that the Cabinet decides and takes executive action in accordance with the law, but he is not the legal adviser. I think there have been mistakes in the past when the Lord Chancellor has assumed the task of advising the Government about the law. That is not the Lord Chancellor's function; the Lord Chancellor is a judge and it would be improper for him, in fact, to act as legal adviser in that sense. The legal adviser is the Attorney General, but the Lord Chancellor's job is to see that if an issue arises which requires legal advice is taken, because often non-lawyers do not appreciate—naturally enough, because they are not lawyers—there is a legal question involved.

Q278 Lord Holme of Cheltenham [a Liberal Democrat peer]: It is the difference between generic advice that the Government is generally acting or not within the law, and specific advice on specific issues.

Lord Mackay of Clashfern: It is really a responsibility to see, if the law is unclear in an area, that it is clarified by advice before the Cabinet proceeds. If the law is clear then the Lord Chancellor will note that situation. He is the best qualified to realise whether or not there is a risk in what the Cabinet are proposing from the point of view of the law, and to see that the minister, whoever it is, that is making the proposal takes the appropriate legal advice.

As the Constitutional Reform Bill went through Parliament in 2004–05, the idea emerged that the bill should contain an express reference to the rule of law. Finding the right form of words proved difficult. Ministers and others were concerned that if too much was said in a clause about the rule of law, the Lord Chancellor might become subject to judicial review if he or she were to fail in the duty. Some ministers would have preferred the bill to say nothing about the rule of law. But in December 2004, as the bill neared the end of its passage in the House of Lords, the government put forward an amendment, which was enacted as follows.

Constitutional Reform Act 2005, s. 1

1 The rule of law

This Act does not adversely affect—

(a) the existing constitutional principle of the rule of law, or

(b) the Lord Chancellor's existing constitutional role in relation to that principle.

Lord Falconer, the new Lord Chancellor, explained the government's thinking.

House of Lords Hansard, 20 December 2004, cols 1538–9

Lord Falconer of Thoroton: My Lords, we have had several useful debates on the rule of law. Perhaps I may summarise the position which I think we reached. We all agreed that we do not want to change the Lord Chancellor's existing role in relation to the rule of law. That role goes further than simply respecting the rule of law in discharging his ministerial functions. It includes being obliged to speak up in Cabinet or as a Cabinet Minister against proposals that he believes offend the rule of law. That role does not require him proactively to police every act of government. The role is not one that is enforceable in courts.

In the debate on this issue at Report stage, the noble Lord, Lord Kingsland [the Conservative front-bench spokesman], supported by the noble Lord, Lord Goodhart [the Liberal Democrat front-bench spokesman], sought reassurance that the Government's previous amendment covered the Lord Chancellor's 'constitutional duty to speak up in Cabinet'. I think that that was the only issue between us. Amendment No. 1 [set out above] provides such clarity.

The new draft also avoids any possibility of inadvertently infringing on the Lord Chancellor's existing statutory duty regarding the rule of law. Perhaps I can draw attention particularly to the speech on Report of the noble and learned Lord, Lord Mackay of Clashfern, in which he referred specifically to the *Witham* case.[32] I think that the new wording puts this issue beyond any doubt whatever. I have discussed it fully with the noble Lords, Lord Kingsland and Lord Goodhart, and I think that they are content.

The legality of the Government's conduct is no less crucial to the rule of law than the matters within the Lord Chancellor's remit. The ministerial code requires all Ministers to consult the Attorney-General on issues involving legal considerations.[33] The Attorney-General is the authoritative source of legal advice within the Government.

The Government have listened very carefully to all the concerns raised in previous stages and shown their willingness to meet those concerns and to engage in constructive debate. I think that we can now be satisfied that not only do we now share the same objectives, but that the draft before us successfully achieves those objectives. I beg to move.

Lord Goodhart: My Lords, during the tripartite discussions between the noble Lord, Lord Kingsland, the noble and learned Lord the Lord Chancellor and myself it became apparent that we were agreed on the principle that we should continue with the existing standard of the rule of law and with the existing constitutional responsibility of the Lord Chancellor to uphold it. We had some difficulty in finding a form of words acceptable to us all, but I am satisfied with the form of words in the amendment. Therefore, I am happy to support the amendment.

Lord Tebbit [a former minister in Margaret Thatcher's Cabinet]: My Lords, the adverb 'adversely' clearly qualifies the verb 'affect'. Is it intended to strengthen or to weaken the impact of that verb?

Lord Falconer of Thoroton: My Lords, the words 'does not adversely affect' make it clear that the Bill does not affect, one jot, the duty of the Lord Chancellor in relation to the rule of law.

Lord Tebbit: My Lords, I understand that that is the intention, but would it not be clearer—or less clear—if the adverb 'adversely' was left out?

Lord Falconer of Thoroton: My Lords, we humbly thought it made it clearer.

Lord Tebbit: My Lords, I apologise for being more dense than usual.

[32] In the judicial review case *R v Lord Chancellor, ex parte Witham* [1998] QB 575, the High Court held that there was a common law constitutional right of access to a court, which the Lord Chancellor had breached when he made secondary legislation removing exemption from court fees for people on low incomes.

[33] On the *Ministerial Code*, see Chapter 9. This express requirement was removed when Gordon Brown (Prime Minister 2007–10) revised the Code in 2007.

A year after the CRA 2005 came into force, a parliamentary select committee considered how the rule of law should be defined.

House of Lords Select Committee on the Constitution, *Relations between the Executive, the Judiciary and Parliament*, Sixth Report, Session 2006–07 (HL Paper 151)

23. Section 1 of the CRA states that 'This Act does not adversely affect (a) the existing constitutional principle of the rule of law, or (b) the Lord Chancellor's existing constitutional role in relation to that principle'. This provision begs several questions, the first of which is what the 'rule of law' actually means. To assist our understanding of this term, we commissioned a paper from Professor Paul Craig, Professor of English Law at the University of Oxford (Appendix 5).

24. Although Professor Craig shed much light on the matter, it is apparent that despite its inclusion in the statute book, the rule of law remains a complex and in some respects uncertain concept. Professor Craig drew our attention to three different meanings. First, 'a core idea of the rule of law [. . .] is that the government must be able to point to some basis for its actions that is regarded as valid by the relevant legal system'. This is, however, too limited so, secondly, the rule of law requires that legal rules 'should be capable of guiding one's conduct in order that one can plan one's life'. In other words, legal rules should meet a variety of criteria, including that they should be prospective, not retrospective; that they should be relatively stable; and that there should be an independent judiciary. Professor Craig told us that some commentators regard these 'formal' attributes of law to be necessary but not sufficient. So a third meaning of the rule of law held by some is that it encompasses substantive rights, thought to be fundamental, which can be 'used to evaluate the quality of the laws produced by the legislature and the courts'.

25. Lord Falconer [Lord Chancellor 2003–07] told us that 'the rule of law includes both national and international law as far as I am concerned, therefore if we remained in breach of the European Convention then we would be in breach of international law. I think the rule of law also goes beyond issues such as specific black letter law. I think there are certain constitutional principles which if Parliament sought to offend would be contrary to the rule of law as well. To take an extreme example simply to demonstrate the point, if Parliament sought to abolish all elections that would be so contrary to our constitutional principles that that would seem to me to be contrary to the rule of law. The rule of law goes beyond specific black letter law; it includes international law and it includes, in my view, settled constitutional principles. I think there might be a debate as to precisely what are settled constitutional principles but it goes beyond, as it were, black letter law' (Q 8).

26. On the question of who is responsible for upholding the rule of law, the Lord Chief Justice [Lord Phillips of Worth Matravers 2005–07] told us that 'it is the role of the judiciary, in practice, to uphold the rule of law, to apply the rule of law, to enforce the rule of law, and to do that they have to be independent of outside influence. Insofar as it is the Lord Chancellor's job to uphold the rule of law, this must be very largely a job of ensuring that our independence is observed. Equally, there must be occasions in government where a question may arise as to whether the conduct that the Government is contemplating is or is not in accordance with the rule of law, and there, I would imagine, the Lord Chancellor would have a role to play in his capacity as a minister' (Appendix 8, Q 7). In relation to the rule of law and the HRA, the Lord Chief Justice explained that if a court made a declaration of incompatibility 'it would be open to the Government to say, 'the court has ruled that this is contrary to the Human Rights Act. Notwithstanding that, we do not intend to comply with the Human Rights Act on this point' and that would be contrary to what I would call rule of law'. That would, however, be the end of the argument 'because Parliament is in that field supreme' (Appendix 8, QQ 9, 10).

In 2022, the House of Lords Constitution Committee started a further inquiry into the effectiveness of the office Lord Chancellor as a guardian of the rule of law within government. In its evidence, the Bar Council was doubtful that the system was working well: '*Since May 2015 [to 2020] there have been six Lord Chancellors. Such a rapid turnover is undesirable in an office intended to uphold the fundamental and timeless concept of adherence to the rule of law across Government*'; the Bar Council added '*In 2017, the Lord Chief Justice was correct when he said that the then Lord Chancellor [Liz Truss MP, who went on to become prime minister] was "constitutionally absolutely wrong" for not publicly backing the judges who had been described as "Enemies of the People" after deciding that the Government would require Parliamentary consent to give notice of the UK's withdrawal from the European Union*'.[34] In their report, the Constitution Committee recommended that '*The Lord Chancellor should fulfil a wider, cross-departmental, role in defending the rule of law and educating his or her colleagues on its importance. Historically, the office has fulfilled that role, there is already a statutory duty and, unlike the Law Officers, the Lord Chancellor is a full member of the Cabinet. We note that none of the former Lord Chancellors we spoke to expressed any qualms about performing a wider role*'.[35]

Taken together, these points suggest that the Lord Chancellor's ability to act as a guardian of the rule of law depends as much on the person holding the office as on the statutory framework. Continuity, experience, and the confidence to challenge colleagues when necessary all matter. The Constitution Committee's recommendations reflect a wider view that the Lord Chancellor should play an active, cross-government role in explaining and defending the rule of law. Whether the changes made in 2005 have helped or hindered that goal remains an open question in current discussions about how the executive supports constitutional principles.

QUESTIONS

1. What is the significance of s. 1 of the Constitutional Reform Act 2005? What assumptions does it make?
2. The Ministry of Justice is preparing a public guide to the UK constitution to help people understand their rights and responsibilities. You have been asked to draft a definition of the rule of law in no more than 150 words. Before you begin, the ministry also asks you to reflect briefly on the choices involved in defining the rule of law. In shaping your definition, consider:
   - which features you think should be included;
   - which features you would leave out;
   - and how far those decisions reflect legal principle, practical considerations, or underlying political values.

   Prepare a short note (no more than 150 words for the definition plus up to 100 words of explanation) responding to this request.
3. A series of coordinated terrorist attacks in the United Kingdom has resulted in mass casualties, with around 10,000 people killed and many thousands more injured. Intelligence

[34] The Bar Council—written evidence (RLC0018), House of Lords Constitution Committee inquiry into the Role of the Lord Chancellor and the Law Officers (March 2022).

[35] House of Lords Constitution Committee, *The roles of the Lord Chancellor and the Law Officers*, 9th Report of Session 2022–23, HL Paper 118, para. 102.

assessments warn of further imminent attacks. In response, Parliament enacts the Authorization to Torture (Exceptional Circumstances) Act, which provides:

(1) A police officer does not act unlawfully by inflicting severe pain or suffering on a person if the officer:

(a) has reasonable grounds for suspecting that the person is, or has been, involved in terrorism-related activity;

(b) believes that obtaining information through such methods is necessary to protect the public from an imminent risk of terrorism; and

(c) acts during a period in which the Secretary of State has issued a declaration of emergency for the purposes of this section, approved by the House of Commons.

(2) This Act is to be interpreted, applied and enforced notwithstanding any incompatibility with international human rights law, customary international law, or the common law.

(3) The Human Rights Act 1998 does not apply to this Act.

A declaration of emergency has been made. Person X is being held by the police and is currently being subjected to torture under the authority of the Act. X's lawyer applies to the High Court for an injunction to prevent any further mistreatment. The case comes before a judge. You are the judge's judicial assistant. They ask you to prepare a brief note outlining the legal options open to the court in determining how to treat the Authorization to Torture (Exceptional Circumstances) Act.

4.4 CONCLUDING COMMENTS

This chapter has examined the rule of law, in particular its definition and some of the main ways in which the institutions of the British constitution seek to protect it. While there continues to be academic and political debate about the best definition of the rule of law, or whether the rule of law is a valuable concept, there is no doubt that a broad idea of the rule of law has become implanted in British constitutional thinking and practice—though adherence to basic rule of law principles is continually tested.

FURTHER READING

Bingham, T., *The Rule of Law* (2010, London: Allen Lane).

European Commission for Democracy through Law (Venice Commission), *Report on the Rule of Law* (Adopted by the Venice Commission at its 86th plenary session, Venice, 25–26 March 2011).

Jowell, J., 'The Rule of Law', in J. Jowell and C. O'Cinneide (eds) *The Changing Constitution*, 9th edn (2019, Oxford: OUP), ch. 1.

JUSTICE, *The State We're In: Addressing Threats and Challenges of the Rule of Law* (2023) https://files.justice.org.uk/wp-content/uploads/2023/08/31123029/JUSTICE-The-State-Were-In-Addressing-Threats-Challenges-to-the-Rule-of-Law-September-2023.pdf.

5

SEPARATING AND BALANCING POWERS

CENTRAL ISSUES

1. A basic task for a constitutional system is to determine how power is to be distributed across different institutions and public office-holders—separation of powers. A three-part division between executive, legislative, and judicial functions has dominated constitutional thinking and practice since the eighteenth century. More recently, a fourth type of function, responsible for integrity in the state, has been recognised.
2. The UK version of separation of powers sees a strong overlap between the executive and legislature, with the leader of the majority party in the House of Commons becoming Prime Minister.
3. The best way to understand separation of powers in the United Kingdom is to look at examples in action. The chapter examines which institution(s) should be responsible for deciding how long people convicted of murder serve in prison; the replacement of the Appellate Committee of the House of Lords with the UK Supreme Court; and whether civil servants should have power to confiscate passports and driving licences or whether this should be a judicial function.
4. There is debate about the purpose of separation of powers. On one version, it protects individual liberty by ensuring that too much power is not concentrated into the hands of one person or institution. In another, it is said to promote efficiency, by ensuring that appropriate institutions make decisions.
5. Legal rules and constitutional conventions regulate the day-to-day relationships between Parliament, government, and the judiciary. The chapter examines how parliamentary privilege rules constrain the use of parliamentary materials in litigation.

5.1 INTRODUCTION

One of the main tasks of a constitutional system is to determine which institutions and office-holders have power and responsibility for carrying out public functions. This chapter looks at the traditional division between 'executive',[1] 'legislative',[2] and 'judicial' roles[3]—a three-part distinction that is

[1] See Chapters 7–10. [2] See Chapters 11–13. [3] See Chapters 14–22.

central to much thinking about the constitutional principle of separation of powers (and around which we have structured this book).

Lord Mustill recognises the tripartite model in the following extract, in a case concerning all three institutions. Parliament had passed a law, ministers had decided not to bring it into force, and the court had to rule whether that was lawful.

R v Secretary for the Home Department, ex parte Fire Brigades Union
[1995] 2 AC 513, 567

> It is a feature of the peculiarly British conception of the separation of powers that Parliament, the executive and the courts each have their distinct and largely exclusive domain. Parliament has a legally unchallengeable right to make whatever laws it thinks fit. The executive carries on the administration of the country in accordance with the powers conferred on it by law. The courts interpret the laws, and see that they are obeyed.

Lord Mustill refers to 'the peculiarly British conception', often described as Westminster-style democracy or the Westminster model. In the United Kingdom, executive and legislature are closely connected—indeed, institutionally fused. The leader of the majority party in the House of Commons becomes Prime Minister and heads the executive. This fusion shapes how separation-of-powers principles operate in practice, since it reduces the institutional distance between the bodies that make law and those that implement it.[4]

There is increasing recognition that some state functions do not fit neatly into the classic executive–legislature–judiciary model. Scholars sometimes refer to these as 'fourth-branch' or 'integrity' institutions, because they are designed to safeguard accountability, rights, and ethical standards across government. Examples include the National Audit Office, which supports Parliament by scrutinizing how public money is spent; the Information Commissioner's Office, which regulates data protection, privacy, and freedom of information; and the Equality and Human Rights Commission, which promotes and enforces equality law and human rights standards. These bodies wield public power yet sit at arm's length from ministers, and their independent status is now seen as part of the UK's wider constitutional architecture.[5] Tarunabh Khaitan, who calls these types of body 'guarantor institutions', argues that their effectiveness is determined by their expertise/capacity, independence, and accountability.

T. Khaitan, 'Guarantor (or the So-Called "Fourth Branch") Institutions', ch. 35 in J. King and R. Bellamy (eds), *Cambridge Handbook of Constitutional Theory* (CUP, 2024)

> The three—relatively thin and pro tanto—design principles that I have argued for in this chapter demand that the design of any guarantor institutions should seek to ensure that it has:
>
> i. Sufficient expertise and capacity to perform its functions effectively;
> ii. Sufficient independence from political, economic, or social actors with an interest in frustrating the relevant norm it is meant to guarantee; and
> iii. Sufficient accountability to bodies with an interest in upholding the relevant norm.

[4] For further discussion of the Westminster model, see V. Bogdanor, *The New British Constitution* (Hart 2009); P. Norton, 'Is the Westminster System of Government Alive and Well?' (2022) 9 J Int'l & Comp L 1.

[5] On arm's length bodies, see Chapter 8.

These principles are developed from real world examples of guarantor institutions (or institutions that have the potential to act as guarantors), although it is quite possible that no single extant guarantor satisfies all of them. These principles are conditionally normative: if a constitution wishes to effectively guarantee a specific non-self-enforcing norm, it should take these principles seriously when designing an institution to guarantee the relevant norm. They also suggest that political independence and political accountability of guarantor institutions need not trade off against each other: the group they need independence from overlaps with, but is not the same as, the group who they should owe accountability to.

Whether there are three or four types of power, at the heart of the idea of separation of powers is the proposition that there are different *kinds* of public function that:

(a) ought to be distinguished from each other; and
(b) ought either to be exercised by different institutions or personnel, or somehow 'balanced' to prevent an overconcentration of power in the hands of a single person or institution.

Some commentators are, however, sceptical about stressing *separation*, preferring instead to highlight the need for institutions to work together, as Ralf Dahrendorf, a political scientist, explains in the next extract.

R. Dahrendorf, 'A confusion of powers: Politics and the rule of law' (1977) 40 *Modern Law Review* 1, 11–12 (footnotes omitted)

Like the division of labour, the separation of powers is a very theoretical concept indeed. It is above all a concept, and not a fact; what we see is not the division of labour, but its combination in the co-operative structure of organisations; it is not the separation of powers, but their co-ordination and sometimes their confusion. It is useful to think of government, parliament and the judiciary as separate functions; it may to some extent be important to institutionalise this separateness, for example by safeguarding the independence of the judiciary; but the theoretical separation of powers is merely the preface to the main volume of practical problems of how the different and possibly separate powers should be co-ordinated.

James Madison [1751–1836, one of the founding fathers of the USA] saw this even more clearly than Montesquieu[6] himself, who of course realised that the powers of legislature and executive in Britain were anything but separate. Like Montesquieu, Madison preferred the term 'distribution of power' and proceeded to look for 'the sense in which the preservation of liberty requires that the three great departments of power should be separate and distinct.' And this seems quite clear to Madison, as it does to common sense, that it does not make sense to assume 'that the legislative, executive and judiciary departments should be wholly unconnected with each other'; on the contrary, the real question is how they are 'connected and blended.'

Dahrendorf's emphasis on coordination rather than strict separation may reflect his experience in European Union institutions, where he served as a German-nominated Commissioner from 1970 to 1979.[7] In that setting, effective governance relies on shared authority and continual cooperation. His point encourages us to look beyond rigid boundaries and focus on how public bodies actually work together.

[6] See extract C. de Secondat (Baron de Montesquieu), *L'Esprit des Lois* in Section 5.4 below.

[7] See Chapter 23. An EU Commissioner is a politically appointed office-holder, nominated by national governments and approved by the European Parliament, who leads an EU policy portfolio and works in the interests of the Union rather than any single state.

5.2 PRACTICAL SCENARIOS

If this all sounds rather abstract, consider the following practical scenarios. These are situations in which disagreements have erupted over whether the 'wrong person' or 'wrong institution' was carrying out the public function in question.

5.2.1 RELEASING MURDERERS, WHO DECIDES: A MINISTER, A JUDGE, PARLIAMENT?

When a court passes a life sentence on a person convicted of murder, who should have power to order for how long the person must remain in prison for the purposes of punishment before being eligible for release 'on licence' (if he or she is no longer a danger to the public)? Should a government minister—a politician accountable to Parliament and influenced by public opinion—have this function, or should it be exercised by the judiciary, or should Parliament lay down rules in legislation? Section 61(1) of the Criminal Justice Act 1967, passed when the death penalty for murder was abolished in the United Kingdom, gave the function to the Home Secretary. The power was re-enacted, in slightly modified form, in s. 29 of the Crime (Sentences) Act 1997. Anthony Anderson, serving life imprisonment for two murders, brought a judicial review challenge. After conviction, the trial judge set the minimum time to be served before Anderson could apply for parole at 15 years; six years later, the Conservative Home Secretary increased that to 20 years. His legal team argued that ministers were too easily swayed by public opinion and the tabloid press to make fair decisions.

R v Secretary of State for the Home Department, ex parte Anderson
[2002] UKHL 46

Lord Steyn

39. In a series of decisions since *Doody* in 1993 [. . .], the House of Lords has described the Home Secretary's role in determining the tariff period to be served by a convicted murderer as punishment akin to a sentencing exercise. In our system of law the sentencing of persons convicted of crimes is classically regarded as a judicial rather than executive task. Our constitution has, however, never embraced a rigid doctrine of separation of powers. The relationship between the legislature and the executive is close. On the other hand, the separation of powers between the judiciary and the legislative and executive branches of government is a strong principle of our system of government. The House of Lords and the Privy Council have so stated: *Attorney-General for Australia v The Queen and the Boilermakers' Society of Australia* [1957] AC 288, 315; *Liyanage v The Queen* [1967] 1 AC 259, 291; *Hinds v The Queen* [1977] AC 195; *Duport Steels Ltd v Sirs* [1980] 1 WLR 142, 157B. It is reinforced by constitutional principles of judicial independence, access to justice, and the rule of law. But the supremacy of Parliament is the paramount principle of our constitution. Whatever arguments there were about the precise nature of the Home Secretary's role in controlling the release of convicted murderers, Parliament had the power to entrust this particular role to the Home Secretary. It did so unambiguously by enacting section 29 of the 1997 Act and its precursors. While a series of House of Lords' decisions have revealed concerns about the compatibility of the operation of the system with the rule of law, the lawfulness in principle of the Home Secretary's role was not in doubt.

40. The question is now whether the Home Secretary's decision-making power over the terms to be served by mandatory life sentence prisoners is compatible with a later statute enacted by Parliament,

namely the Human Rights Act 1998 by which Parliament incorporated the European Convention on Human Rights into the law of the United Kingdom. Article 6(1) of the Convention, so far as it is material, provides: 'In the determination of his civil rights and obligations or of any criminal charge against him, everyone is entitled to a fair and public hearing within a reasonable time by an independent and impartial tribunal established by law.' [. . .]

51. The power of the Home Secretary in England and Wales to decide on the tariff to be served by mandatory life sentence prisoners is a striking anomaly in our legal system. It is true that Parliament has the power to punish contemnors by imprisonment. This power derives from the medieval concept of Parliament being, amongst other things, a court of justice: see *Erskine May: Treatise On The Law, Privileges, Proceedings and Usages of Parliament*, 22nd edn (1997), p. 131 et seq. Subject to this qualification, there is in our system of law no exception to the proposition that a decision to punish an offender by ordering him to serve a period of imprisonment may only be made by a court of law: *Blackstone's Commentaries on the Laws of England*, 2001, vol. 1, [. . .] para. 137. It is a decision which may only be made by the courts. Historically, this has been the position in our legal system since at least 1688. And this idea is a principal feature of the rule of law on which our unwritten constitution is based. It was overridden by Parliament by virtue of section 29 of the 1997 Act. Now the duty to decide on the compatibility of that statutory provision with article 6(1) has been placed by Parliament on the courts under the Human Rights Act. [. . .]

The House of Lords held that section 29 of the Crime (Sentences) Act 1997 was incompatible with Article 6 ECHR because allowing the Home Secretary to set the tariff for a mandatory life sentence breached the requirement of an independent and impartial tribunal. The tabloid press criticized the Anderson judgment. The Labour government, reluctantly, introduced a bill that became the Criminal Justice Act 2003, transferring responsibility for setting minimum terms to judges and placing tariff decisions fully within the judicial sphere. But Home Secretary David Blunkett also announced further changes: Parliament would create new sentencing guidelines, arguing that parliamentary accountability was 'fundamental to confidence in the criminal justice system in our democracy'.[8] This approach has persisted. The Police, Crime, Sentencing and Courts Act 2022, for example, made a whole-life order the starting point for the premeditated murder of a child. And in September 2025, after a dispute between the government and the independent Sentencing Council over proposals for pre-sentence reports for certain racial groups, the Labour government announced plans to amend the law so that the Council could not issue new guidelines without the Justice Secretary's approval.[9] The current constitutional settlement therefore continues to involve Parliament and the executive in setting the sentencing framework, while judges make the individualized decisions.

PAUSE FOR REFLECTION

Why was it constitutionally problematic for ministers, rather than judges, to decide how long a person convicted of murder must serve before becoming eligible for release?

[8] For example, S. Doughty, 'Lords give 215 murderers hope of early release' *Daily Mail*, 26 November 2022, p. 5.

[9] R. Comerford, 'Justice secretary to get power to veto sentencing guidance' *BBC News*, 2 September 2025 https://www.bbc.co.uk/news/articles/cn848g3ll09o accessed 27 November 2025.

5.2.2 TOP COURT: FROM PARLIAMENTARY COMMITTEE TO SUPREME COURT

A second scenario is the background to the creation of the UK Supreme Court. Until 30 September 2009, the United Kingdom's highest court—the Appellate Committee of the House of Lords—operated as a committee of one of the Houses of Parliament. The court's professional judges—the Lords of Appeal in Ordinary—were peers. The court's hearings were held in committee rooms in Parliament; and judgments were delivered in the chamber of the Lords. The Law Lords' not only shared accommodation with parliamentarians but took part in some aspects of the House of Lords' legislative and scrutiny work when not sitting as judges, including chairing a select committee on scrutiny of EU legal proposals. Some Law Lords would sit in the chamber to hear debates on significant bills. This was, by world standards, an unusual constitutional arrangement; but there was broad consensus that the Law Lords were effective and independent judges.

In 2003, the Labour government decided that there should be an institutional separation of the 'judicial business' from the legislative and scrutiny of the work of the House of Lords, with judicial functions transferred to a newly created Supreme Court. The government's thinking is set out in the following extract from a consultation paper issued by the department responsible for the reforms.

Department for Constitutional Affairs, *Constitutional Reform: A Supreme Court for the United Kingdom* (July 2003), para. 3

It is not always understood that the decisions of the 'House of Lords' are in practice decisions of the Appellate Committee and that non-judicial members of the House never take part in the judgments. Nor is the extent to which the Law Lords themselves have decided to refrain from getting involved in political issues in relation to legislation on which they might later have to adjudicate always appreciated. The fact that the Lord Chancellor, as the Head of the Judiciary, was entitled to sit in the Appellate and Judicial Committees and did so as Chairman, added to the perception that their independence might be compromised by the arrangements. The Human Rights Act, specifically in relation to Article 6 of the European Convention on Human Rights, now requires a stricter view to be taken not only of anything which might undermine the independence or impartiality of a judicial tribunal, but even of anything which might appear to do so. So the fact that the Law Lords are a Committee of the House of Lords can raise issues about the appearance of independence from the legislature. Looking at it from the other way round, the requirement for the appearance of impartiality and independence also increasingly limits the ability of the Law Lords to contribute to the work of the House of Lords, thus reducing the value to both them and the House of their membership.

The need to separate judges from Parliament was not accepted by everyone. Giving evidence to the House of Commons Constitutional Affairs Committee after the government announced their reform plans, Lord Lloyd of Berwick, a retired Law Lord, made the following statement to MPs.

House of Commons Constitutional Affairs Committee, Judicial Appointments and a Supreme Court (Court of Final Appeal), First Report, Session 2003–04 (HC 48-I), para. 20

Since it is the judges who have to decide whether ministers are breaking the law or exceeding their powers or whatever it may be, it is obviously vital that the judiciary and the executive should be separate and distinct. But there has never been a reason—not one that I can see—why the judges and the legislature should be distinct and separate.

The Constitutional Reform Act 2005 created the statutory framework for a new, fully independent Supreme Court. In October 2009 the Law Lords—renamed Justices of the Supreme Court—left the House of Lords and moved across Parliament Square to their new home in Middlesex Guildhall. From that point, the Supreme Court began operating as the UK's separate final court of appeal.

PAUSE FOR REFLECTION

The Law Lords were widely regarded as an effective and independent final court, producing judgments that influenced legal developments around the world. Was it justified to disrupt a well-functioning institution in order to align the system more closely with a constitutional principle?

5.2.3 CIVIL SERVANTS IMPOSING PENALTIES ON PARENTS

This third scenario is about designing a system for applying pressure on non-resident parents (usually fathers) to pay child maintenance. The government decided on a policy of confiscating non-payers' passports and driving licences as a sanction. Who, in such a scheme, was to make decisions? Was it objectionable on constitutional grounds for a civil servant (civil servants are responsible for the administration of central government and work within the executive) working in the Child Maintenance and Enforcement Commission (CMEC, as it then was) to have these powers? When the idea was proposed, the government and the House of Lords Constitution Committee disagreed about this.

House of Lords Constitution Committee, Welfare Reform Bill, Ninth Report, Session 2008–09 (HL 79)

8. We remain of the view, expressed in our December 2007 report [which criticized previous proposals], that it is constitutionally unsatisfactory for CMEC and its contractors—rather than the courts—to have a sanction power to withdraw a person's right to hold a passport. The freedom to travel to and from one's country is a constitutional right of such significance that restricting this right as a punishment demands rigorous examination by an independent and impartial judge.

9. In recent years, there has been a notable transfer of sanction powers from the courts to the executive. In recent reports and correspondence with ministers, we have sought to ensure that where the executive is conferred with coercive sanction powers there are safeguards for ensuring fair procedures are followed and that there is an effective appeal to the courts to ensure judicial oversight. In relation to the present bill, we acknowledge that a person who is disqualified by CMEC from holding a passport would have a right of appeal to a court and that if such a right of appeal is exercised, the disqualification will be suspended until the appeal is determined. The possibility of an appeal does not, however, answer the prior question: is the sanction power one which the executive, rather than the courts, should be allowed to exercise.

10. In the present bill, the Government seek to transfer sanction powers from the courts to civil servants in relation to passports and driving licences. It should be noted that the Child Maintenance and Other Payments Act 2008 created other sanction powers, including the imposition of curfew orders and an associated power to search premises and confiscate any money found. Curfew orders and search powers are, under current arrangements, made and authorised by the courts following an application by CMEC. While the Government have not proposed that the executive should have power to impose curfew orders or search premises without reference to the courts, we are concerned that an unintended change in the constitution is occurring in which the executive is acquiring ever more powers to impose

> sanctions and punish people that a generation ago would have been regarded as falling within the remit of the courts. A line needs to be drawn around the type of power that civil servants can appropriately exercise and those for which judges should be responsible. In our view, suspending a person's right to hold a passport, because of its impact on a constitutional right, should fall into the latter category (along with powers to impose curfew orders and order searches of premises).

Criticism of an executive-based sanctions mechanism led ministers to drop that element of the Welfare Reform Bill. A revised model appeared a few months later in the Child Maintenance and Other Payments Act 2008, under which civil servants could apply to a magistrates' court for an order disqualifying a non-resident parent from holding or obtaining a passport or driving licence, but only the court may impose the sanction. Use of these powers has been modest: in the quarter ending September 2024, for example, there was one passport disqualification order and two driving-licence disqualifications.

5.2.4 TAKING STOCK

The conclusion that can be drawn from these three scenarios is that far from being dry, abstract, textbook topics, debates about what kind of institution or person exercises different public functions take place regularly. These examples also show that the way in which powers are allocated and separated is often a contentious matter.

Questions as to who in the constitutional system had decision-making power in relation to the United Kingdom leaving the European Union came to the UK Supreme Court in two cases brought by Gina Miller, a political activist.[10] In *Miller 1*, the issue was whether the UK government could use non-statutory prerogative powers to serve notice on the EU (as required by Article 50 of the EU Treaty) or whether Parliament needed to authorize this under an Act of Parliament. The court held that ministers could not invoke prerogative powers[11] and Parliament had to enact legislation—the European Union (Notification of Withdrawal) Act 2017—granting statutory power to the government to serve the notice. In *Miller 2* the issue was whether the prime minister could use non-statutory prerogative power to 'prorogue' the UK Parliament: The Prime Minister Boris Johnson MP had sought temporarily to suspend Parliament from sitting for several days to prevent MPs and peers from debating and possibly voting against the government as it tried to negotiate a fresh withdrawal agreement with the EU. The court held that he could not do so as this would frustrate Parliament in carrying out its constitutional responsibilities in holding the government to account.[12]

5.3 INSTITUTIONAL SEPARATION OR PERSONNEL SEPARATION?

Before going further in analysing the UK position, it helps to be clear about what is being separated. Does the doctrine require executive, legislative and judicial authority to be housed in different institutions, or is the central concern about individuals avoiding conflicting roles?

[10] On the process of EU withdrawal generally, see Chapter 24.

[11] *R (Miller) v Secretary of State for Exiting the European Union* [2017] UKSC 5.

[12] *R (Miller) v Prime Minister (Lord Advocate intervening)* [2019] UKSC 41.

In its *institutional* form (applied in few, if any, constitutional systems), the concept of separation of powers suggests that these three functions must be exercised by completely different institutions: legislation should only be made by legislative bodies (parliaments); executive functions should only be carried out by governments (ministers and civil servants); and courts alone should be responsible for judicial functions. In practice, in many constitutional systems, institutions exercise functions from more than one of the categories: for example, the government may have rule-making powers (a legislative function).

In its *personnel* form, the idea of separation of powers stresses that a single person should not exercise more than one of the functions. For example:

- a person who is a member of the executive branch (a minister or an official) should not also be a member of the judiciary or of the legislature;
- a person who is a member of the judiciary should not simultaneously be a member of the legislature (Parliament) or the government (as a minister or official); and
- a person who is a member of the legislature (an MP) should not be a judge or a member of the executive (as a minister or civil servant).

We will see shortly that the UK constitutional system does not match up to all of these requirements (which leads some commentators to suggest that the separation of powers is not particularly important in the United Kingdom).

There is one very obvious way in which the United Kingdom—along with many other major constitutional systems around the world—does not fit the 'personnel separation' model: ministers (who exercise executive functions) are *required* to be members of the legislature (Parliament), in which they have a dominant role in the legislative process.[13] There is therefore an important distinction to be made between presidential systems (in which executive and legislature are separate—as in the USA, Mexico, and Brazil) and parliamentary systems (in which they are not—as in the United Kingdom, Ireland, Australia, Canada, and the Netherlands).

It is often stressed that the separation of powers does not aim only, or mainly, to separate different functions, but to ensure that there are 'checks and balances' within the constitution so that power is not overly concentrated in one institution. For example, if the legislature were to delegate some law-making powers to ministers, the courts (exercising their judicial function) should have powers to review whether those powers are lawfully exercised in accordance with the intention of the legislature.

In Chapter 2, the debate between political and legal constitutionalism was introduced in the context of the principles of parliamentary supremacy and the rule of law. It should be no surprise that the tensions surface again in relation to debates over the meaning and application of the doctrine of separation of powers. Political constitutionalists tend to downplay the role of courts: as we see shortly, Tomkins, for example, argues that it is wrong in the English constitutional set-up to view the judiciary as a 'third branch'.[14] Legal constitutionalists, on the other hand, tend to be keen on using the idea of separation of powers to bolster the importance of the courts as a major 'check and balance' on the institutions that carry out the other two functions (legislative and executive).

5.4 WHAT IS THE POINT OF SEPARATING POWERS?

There are three main reasons why theorists and more practically minded people have been interested in the idea of separation of powers.

[13] See extract W. Bagehot, *The English Constitution* in Section 5.4 below.

[14] See extract A. Tomkins, *Public Law* in Section 5.5 below.

(a) First, it may be thought of as a template for the design of a constitutional system. If a country is starting from scratch (after a revolution of some kind, for example), the idea of separation of powers offers guiding principles on allocating legislative, executive, and judicial functions to various kinds of institution.

(b) Second—and this is a view taken in different centuries by Baron Montesquieu (1689–1755) and Eric Barendt, in the extracts that follow—the point of separation of powers may be to protect liberty. The gist of the idea is that if too much of one kind of power is concentrated in the hands of one person or institution, there is more of a risk of that power being abused to curtail freedom than if the powers are kept distinct or if there is a system of 'checks and balances'.

(c) Third, we will see that N.W. Barber argues that '*it is efficiency, not liberty, which is at the heart of separation of powers*'. If the various types of power are allocated sensibly to the right kind of institution, it is more likely to be exercised efficiently.

Montesquieu (Charles-Louis de Secondat) was a French aristocrat who travelled widely in Europe, who lived in England for two years in 1729–31, and who had great knowledge of the ancient Roman and Greek civilizations. The overarching theme of his book *The Spirit of Laws*, on which he worked for 20 years, was to examine how judgements should be made about the qualities of laws and systems of government (which he classified as 'republican', 'aristocratic', and 'despotic'). In that part of his book entitled 'Of the laws that form political liberty, with regard to the constitution', he describes a picture under the heading 'Of the constitution of England' that bore no resemblance to the *actual* arrangements then (or now), so presumably his aim was to outline an idealized system.

C. de Secondat (Baron de Montesquieu), *L'Esprit des Lois [The Spirit of the Laws]* (1748), Book XI, ch. VI, p. 181

Of the constitution of England

In every government there are three sorts of power; the legislative; the executive, in respect of things dependent on the law of nations; and the judicial, in regard to things that depend on the civil law.

By virtue of the first, the prince or magistrate enacts temporary or perpetual laws, and amends or abrogates those that have been already enacted. By the second, he makes peace or war, sends or receives embassies, establishes the public security, and provides against invasions. By the third, he punishes criminals, or determines the disputes that arise between individuals. The latter we shall call the judicial power, and the other simply the executive power of the state.

The political liberty of the subject is a tranquillity of mind, arising from the opinion each person has of his safety. In order to have this liberty, it is requisite the government be so constituted as one man need not be afraid of another.

When the legislative and executive powers are united in the same person, or in the same body of magistrates, there can be no liberty; because apprehensions may arise, lest the same monarch or senate should enact tyrannical laws, to executive them in a tyrannical manner.

Again, there is no liberty, if the power of judging be not separated from the legislative and executive powers.

Were it joined with the legislative, the life and liberty of the subject would be exposed to arbitrary control; for the judge would then be the legislator. Were it joined to the executive power, the judge might behave with all the violence of an oppressor.

There would be an end of every thing, were the same man, or the same body, whether of nobles or of the people to exercise those three powers, that of enacting the laws, that of executing public resolutions, and that of judging the crimes and differences of individuals.

Compare this with Bagehot's analysis 120 years later. Walter Bagehot (1826–77) qualified as a lawyer, but went into business as a journalist and founded *The Economist* magazine. In his view, the nineteenth-century British constitution was characterized by the fusion, not the separation, of powers—with the Cabinet at the epicentre.

W. Bagehot, *The English Constitution* (1867; 1963, London: Fontana/Collins), pp. 68–9

A Cabinet is a combining committee—a *hyphen* which joins, a *buckle* which fastens, the legislative part of the State to the executive part of the State. In its origins it belongs to one, in its functions it belongs to the other. [. . .]

The fusion of the legislative and executive functions may, to those who have not much considered it, seem but a dry and small matter to be the latent essence and effectual secret of the English constitution; but we can only judge of its real importance by looking at a few of its principal effects, and contrasting it very shortly with its great competitor, which seems likely, unless care be taken, to outstrip it in the progress of the world. That competitor is the Presidential system. The characteristic of it is that the President is elected from the people by one process, and the House of Representatives by another. The independence of the legislative and executive powers is the specific quality of Presidential government, just as the fusion and combination is the precise principle of Cabinet government.

Having noted that Dicey says almost nothing about separation of powers, in the next extract, Eric Barendt takes issue with Sir Ivor Jennings' analysis in *The Law and the Constitution* (1959). He notes that Jenning's central objection was that the supposed differences between the three functions are illusory. For Jennings, the separation principle cannot explain why a particular task should belong to one branch rather than another because, as he saw it, there are no material distinctions to ground such an allocation. The contrast often drawn between judicial and administrative decisions illustrates the point. Jennings accepted that it is usually preferable for certain decisions to be taken by bodies that follow formal legal procedures—'impartial tribunals considering a case in public and on the evidence'—rather than by officials implementing a policy agenda. But he argued that this preference does not show that any category of decision is *inherently* judicial. For Barendt, the differences are procedural rather than substantive, and therefore cannot sustain a strict separation of powers.

E. Barendt, 'Separation of powers and constitutional government' [1995] *Public Law* 599, 603–4 (footnotes omitted)

Jennings did admit that the legislative function may be identified as that of making 'general rules of law', but it did not much matter that in practice in the U.K. (as in other countries) ministers issue a lot of general rules under delegated legislative authority. There would only be tyranny if all laws were made in this way, or, he might have added, if they were made by the executive without any legislative authority at all. Moreover, he concluded that the separation principle was irrelevant as a safeguard against bureaucracy or tyranny; what prevented that was democratic control through the House of Commons and the party system.

Geoffrey Marshall shares Jennings' view that it is impossible to define with precision the separate functions of government and consequently determine to whom their performance should be allocated. Moreover, it is the universal practice for governments to enjoy massive delegated legislative authority. Another of his points is that while most jurisdictions regard the independence of the judicial branch as sacrosanct, there is frequently (as in the U.K.) at least partial fusion of the legislative and executive branches. Finally, on some versions of the separation principle, e.g. the partial separation of powers found in the United States, constitutional judicial review is appropriate to check the legislative and executive branches, while it would be an unwarrantable violation of it according to the pure theory. The judiciary would then be interfering with the discharge by the legislature or executive of its functions. Marshall's conclusion is that the doctrine is far too imprecise and incoherent to be of any use in the analysis or critique of constitutions: '[i]t may be counted little more than a jumbled portmanteau of arguments for policies which ought to be supported or rejected on other grounds'. But he does not explain what these other arguments might be.

Finally, the separation of powers principle arguably amounts to a constraint on legislative supremacy. For that reason alone English commentators are generally reluctant to take the principle too seriously. It would require, for example, the courts to strike down criminal law statutes which retrospectively amended the law to deal with a particular incident. For such legislation would be viewed as a usurpation of the judicial function or an interference with the independence of the judiciary, whose role is to apply general rules and principles framed for all contingencies. [. . .]

Barendt goes on to respond to Jennings's well-known scepticism about the coherence of the separation of powers by arguing that Jennings overstates the difficulty. It is possible, he suggests, to describe in broad terms what counts as a legislative, executive, or judicial function, and to expect courts to police those boundaries. Jennings was right that the theoretical criteria can be unclear and that borderline cases exist, but Barendt insists that courts can still make principled distinctions. For example, decisions affecting personal rights have historically been treated as 'inherently suitable for judicial resolution'; by contrast, the allocation of benefits or other public goods can legitimately be left to administrative authorities. Some written constitutions make this explicit. Article 66 of the French Fifth Republic Constitution states that 'the judicial authority, guardian of the liberty of the individual, ensures respect for this principle'. The French Constitutional Council has used this to strike down legislation granting the police wide discretionary inspection powers, because the scheme lacked safeguards and meaningful judicial oversight. English courts, although operating in an uncodified system, have taken a similar line: they are reluctant to read statutes as allowing administrative bodies to reach final decisions on questions of legal liability, such as tax.

Courts also distinguish between legislative functions and those that are executive or judicial. Broadly, the legislative function concerns the creation of general rules with prospective effect. But for Barendt, the real weakness in the Jennings/Marshall critique is its focus on classificatory purity. The central purpose of the doctrine is not accurate labelling; it is the diffusion of power so as to prevent arbitrary government. Functional allocation is a means to that end, not the end itself. Misallocations may produce inefficient outcomes, but they do not necessarily imperil the constitutional structure unless they concentrate power in a way that threatens liberty.

This becomes clearest when looking at administrative agencies, Barent explains. Many bodies routinely exercise more than one type of power: they issue rules, craft policies, and determine individual cases. This is true of many independent regulators in the United States and, in the UK, of local authorities and various national agencies. On a strict functional view, this ought to be constitutionally suspect. Barendt argues that this is the wrong lens. What matters is not that agencies mix functions, but whether their design creates excessive concentrations of authority. The key questions are institutional: who appoints and removes members; who directs the body's work; and—crucially—whether judicial review remains available for the more adjudicative decisions. A separation of powers problem arises if, for instance, a minister can both appoint the agency's members and instruct it in detail while its decisions affecting individual rights are insulated from meaningful court supervision. The difficulty here,

Barendt suggests, is not that an 'executive agency carried out judicial functions', but that its structure 'create[s] or reinforce[s] a concentration of power in the hands of the government'.

Nicholas Barber disagrees with Barendt's thesis that the main rationale for separation of powers is to protect liberty. In the next extract, he argues instead that the purpose of the doctrine is *efficiency*.

N.W. Barber, 'Prelude to the separation of powers' (2001) 60 *Cambridge Law Journal* 59, 71–2 (footnotes omitted)

Separation of powers is a distinctively constitutional tool. It addresses itself to the authors of the constitution; it enjoins them to match function to form in such a way as to realise the goals set for the state by political theory. Having decided that a particular goal ought to be striven after in a society, the doctrine then focuses our attention on the manner by which it may be achieved. At this stage in the article the political assumptions that lie behind the broad understanding of the separation of powers must be thickened up. Whereas in the earlier part of the article all that was assumed was the thin assumption that powers should be allocated to the institution which was best placed to execute them, further assumptions must now be made about what factors may make an institution good at undertaking certain tasks. Again, though, these assumptions are weak ones. They merely indicate issues of significance, they do not necessarily require the prioritisation of one factor over the others. Separation of powers encourages us to consider various interconnected structural factors that affect the competency of institutions in the performance of their tasks. First, the composition and skills of an institution must be examined: the knowledge and experience of the actors within it. Secondly, the scope of the institution's information-gathering powers may be of interest; some bodies are better than others at gathering different types of information. Thirdly, the manner of the institution's decision-making process may be significant; some issues may lend themselves well to expert decision-making, others will be better allocated to amateur processes which have the virtues of openness and inclusivity. This point leads on to a fourth consideration: the vulnerability of the institution to outside pressures. Whether this is considered an advantage or a danger will depend both on the particular issue before the decision-maker and on our understanding of the nature and importance of citizens' participation in decision-making. As this fourth consideration shows, this thin understanding of separation of powers rests on a slippery slope.

Barber goes on to acknowledge that structural questions about allocating functions inevitably connect to broader issues of legitimacy. They point, he says, towards 'richer, thicker, normative theories' concerned with rights and democracy, and these concerns are just as relevant to a full account of the separation of powers as the institutional points made earlier. He argues, however, that it is useful to resist moving too quickly into a comprehensive normative theory. By concentrating on more 'uncontroversial factors', we can identify reasons for and against giving a function to a particular branch that are common to all versions of the doctrine. Yet Barber stresses that these reasons are necessarily limited: on their own they cannot deliver a 'conclusive answer' to where a function should finally sit.

5.5 'CROWN VS PARLIAMENT' SEPARATION

So far, we have been examining the idea of a separation of powers between executive, legislative, and judicial powers. Adam Tomkins takes issue with this approach in two respects and, in its place, puts forward a 'Crown versus Parliament' thesis. His main objection is that this tripartite division does not reflect the historical development of the English constitution. The executive–legislative–judicial model emerged from the writings of Montesquieu (as we saw previously) and was influential in the planning of the US Constitution—but is not a good fit for England. He also prefers the term separation 'of power' rather than 'of powers', because '*it is not so much that discrete functions of powers are allocated to separate bodies, but that constitutional authority—power—is divided between the Crown and Parliament*'.[15]

In the following extract, Tomkins refers to the English Civil War (1641–51). This was a series of bitter armed conflicts between supporters of Charles I (an adherent to the notion of the 'divine right of kings') and the parliamentary forces led by Oliver Cromwell. Charles I attempted to rule without convening Parliament, resorting to a variety of means to raise revenue (such as 'ship money') to run the country without parliamentary approval for general taxation. In 1649, Charles I was executed for treason. For 11 years, the country was ruled without a king; monarchy was restored in 1660 when Charles II became king.

A. Tomkins, *Public Law* (2003, Oxford: OUP), pp. 46–7 (footnotes omitted)

The Civil War, of course, was fought not between three powers separate but equal, but between two. On the one side there was the Crown, and on the other stood Parliament. Just as the war was fought between parliamentarians and royalists, so too were the peace settlements of 1660–1662 and 1689–1700 negotiations between the forces of Parliament on the one hand and of the Crown on the other. Now, it is one thing to sketch an historical argument to the effect that seventeenth century constitutionalism was based on a separation of power between the Crown and Parliament; it is quite another to take the argument further and to suggest that contemporary public law continues to reflect this historical division. But such is precisely the issue that we will now explore: in what sense may it be argued that contemporary English public law is based on a separation of power between the Crown and Parliament, a separation derived from England's political history?

The argument presented here will be that the separation of power in today's English public law does indeed continue to reflect its seventeenth century heritage. The separation of power English-style, it will be argued, is and remains a confrontational, bi-partisan, bi-polar separation, between the only two powers the constitution has ever recognized as enjoying any degree of sovereign authority, namely the Crown, and Parliament. Every constitutional actor falls on one side or the other of this great divide, in that all constitutional actors ultimately draw their power from either the Crown or from Parliament. This is a separation of power which is designed to facilitate accountability [. . .]. As with Magna Carta so too with the Bill of Rights and the Act of Settlement: the purpose of these instruments is to find ways of holding the power of the Crown to some form of constitutional or parliamentary account. This stands in some contrast to the classical, eighteenth century understanding of the separation of powers, which, as Madison made clear, was designed not to facilitate constitutional accountability, but to safeguard liberty.

In short, the key to understanding power in England is not the separation of power between legislature, executive, and judiciary, but that between the Crown and Parliament. Tomkins presents the following evidence to support his thesis.

(a) First, he cites parliamentary supremacy—that is, Acts of Parliament '*represent the legal moment when the two sovereign authorities of England come together and agree: Parliament on the one hand, the Crown on the other*'.[16] 'The Crown' here refers to Royal Assent.[17]

(b) Second, there is the constitutional convention that ministers—Tomkins stresses that they are *ministers of the Crown*—are accountable to Parliament.[18] Ministers are 'the monarch's advisers'

[15] A. Tomkins, *Public Law* (2003, Oxford: OUP), p. 46, fn 24.
[16] Ibid, p. 48.
[17] On Royal Assent, see Chapter 12.
[18] On ministerial accountability, see Chapter 9.

and their '*oath of allegiance is to the Crown, and they may exercise considerable royal prerogative power on behalf of the Crown*'.[19] In order for ministers to be accountable to Parliament, '*the English version of the separation of powers* requires *that ministers simultaneously be parliamentarians*'.[20]

(c) Third, Tomkins points to what he calls '*the tortuous relationship of the law to the Crown*' and deals at some length with the case of *M v Home Office*.[21] The question in that case was whether a minister (the Home Secretary) could be held to be in contempt of court for failing to respect undertakings given to a court that an asylum seeker would not be removed from the United Kingdom until the court had time to consider a judicial review challenge to the lawfulness of the rejection of his asylum application. Eventually, the House of Lords held that English law permitted the Home Secretary to be found liable for this contempt in his official capacity. Tomkins concludes: '*What this case shows [. . .] is that even as recently as the 1990s the courts in England have found it exceptionally difficult to subject the Crown and its sovereign authority to the rule of law.*'

Where, in Tomkins' 'Crown versus Parliament' thesis, are the courts? He says (acknowledging that this is a controversial proposition) that '*the courts are in some sense part of, or dependent upon, the Crown, and are not independent of it*'.[22]

A. Tomkins, *Public Law* (2003, Oxford: OUP), p. 55 (footnotes omitted)

A few words of clarification on this important point are called for here. First, it should be made clear what the argument is not saying. It is no part of the present argument to claim that individual judges can be removed from office by mere royal whim, as James I and Charles I thought 400 years ago. The Act of Settlement put a stop to that in 1701. Neither is it being argued here that in disputes involving the Crown the courts will always or necessarily hold for the Crown. Such a thesis would be bound to fail [. . .]. What the argument here is suggesting, however, is that the judiciary derives its constitutional power ultimately from that of the Crown. Unlike the position under Article III of the US Constitution, or under Article 220 (formerly Article 164) of the EC Treaty, for example, in English law there is no independent source of judicial authority. The English judiciary is not the third branch of the State, separate yet equal, as is the case in the United States. In England the judiciary is, properly conceived, neither entirely separate nor entirely equal: it is not fully separated (even now) from the Crown, and it remains subservient to it as a source of authority.

What does Tomkins mean when he says that the judiciary 'remains subservient' to the Crown? Chapter 15 examines the various ways in which the British constitution seeks to ensure the constitutional principle of the independence of the judiciary—including making it hugely difficult for a senior judge to be removed from office (a vote in the Commons and the Lords is required), the new judicial appointments commissions working at arm's length from ministers, and the statutory duties of ministers to respect judicial independence. While there may be practical restraints on *ministers* of the Crown interfering with the judiciary, there are, however, strong formal and symbolic ties between the judicial system and the Crown (meaning, in this context, not ministers, but an abstract idea of constitutional authority). The royal heraldic symbols hang behind the judges in most courts.[23] The judicial oath (or for non-religious people, affirmation) of office also reflects this intimate link (see Box 5.1) not yet amended after King Charles III acceded to the throne in September 2022.

[19] Tomkins (n 4), pp. 49–50. [20] Ibid, p. 50. [21] [1994] 1 AC 377. [22] Tomkins (n 4), pp. 54–5.
[23] Not, however, in the UK Supreme Court, which uses its own badge.

BOX 5.1 JUDICIAL OATHS/AFFIRMATIONS

Under the Promissory Oaths Act 1868, judges take two oaths or affirmations—one of allegiance and a specifically judicial one. The following are the words used by those who choose to affirm.

I, _______________ , do solemnly sincerely and truly declare and affirm that I will be faithful and bear true allegiance to His Majesty King Charles the Third, His Heirs and Successors, according to Law.

I, _____________, do solemnly sincerely and truly declare and affirm that I will well and truly serve our Sovereign Lord King Charles the Third in the office of _____________, and I will do right to all manner of people after the laws and usages of this Realm without fear or favour affection or ill will.

5.6 INTERACTIONS BETWEEN PARLIAMENT, THE EXECUTIVE, AND JUDGES

So far, we have approached the separation of powers in two ways: as a model for organizing public authority, and as a source of political tension when one part of the state believes another has gone too far. We now look more closely at how the UK gives practical effect to this idea. A wide set of constitutional rules—some found in legislation, others operating as conventions or established practices—shape how those who exercise legislative, executive, and judicial authority interact with one another.

5.6.1 CAN MEMBERS OF PARLIAMENT BE JUDGES?

Statutory rules state that MPs and peers are not eligible to serve as full-time members of the judiciary, and vice versa.[24] There is, however, no prohibition in England and Wales on MPs or peers holding part-time judicial appointments (for example, as a deputy High Court judge or lay magistrate), and some legally qualified MPs and peers have done so.[25]

PAUSE FOR REFLECTION

Should MPs or peers ever sit as judges, even on a part-time or voluntary basis? Think about how this might affect public confidence in judicial independence, but also how it might help Parliament understand the justice system better. Where should the line be drawn?

5.6.2 CAN JUDGES PARTICIPATE IN THE LEGISLATIVE PROCESS?

The short answer is: it's complicated. Until 2009, senior judges who had been conferred with a peerage—the 12 Lords of Appeal in Ordinary and some other senior judges—were entitled to sit and vote during the House of Lords' legislative work, although few did so. Eyebrows were raised

[24] House of Commons Disqualification Act 1975, Sch. 1; Constitutional Reform Act 2005, s. 137.

[25] For example, Conservative MP Andy Carter sat as a magistrate during the 2019–2024 Parliament. In the same period, Karl McCartney MP also served as a magistrate, but was issued with a formal warning by the Judicial Conduct Investigations Office for referring to his position as a magistrate in an electoral leaflet: see BBC News, 'Karl McCartney: MP warned over election leaflet', 18 January 2021 https://www.bbc.co.uk/news/uk-england-lincolnshire-55706044 accessed 26 November 2025. Lord Carlile of Berriew KC sat as a Deputy High Court Judge 2001–16 while a Liberal Democrat peer in the House of Lords.

when two Law Lords (Lords Scott of Foscote[26] and Hoffmann[27]) voted against proposals contained in the Hunting Bill—a piece of legislation on which the Law Lords were later to rule. Because they had expressed pro-hunting views through voting during the passage of the bill through Parliament, Lords Scott and Hoffmann were unable to be members of the nine-judge panel of Law Lords in *Jackson v Attorney General*.[28] Taking part in the appeal would have breached Art. 6 of the ECHR (on fair trials), which prohibits a person who has participated in the legislative process from subsequently adjudicating on issues under that legislation.[29] The European Court of Human Rights takes the view that an accumulation of functions—in the legislative and then judicial roles—gives rise to doubts regarding the impartiality of the judge (viewed from an objective point of view). Up to October 2009, Law Lords also took part in the political scrutiny work of the House of Lords, such as chairing the European Union (EU) Select Committee Subcommittee E, which examined proposals in the area of EU law and institutions. All of these roles came to an end with the transfer of the House of Lords' 'judicial business' to the UK Supreme Court and the consequential statutory disqualification of the judges of the Supreme Court from participating in the work of Parliament.[30]

Although serving judges cannot now participate *directly* in the legislative process for making Acts of Parliament,[31] they nonetheless may have an interest in commenting on legislative proposals, as a senior judge explains to MPs in the following extract.

House of Commons Justice Committee, Oral Evidence, 2 July 2008

Q42 Alun Michael [a Labour MP]: Obviously there is an interplay between the role of the judiciary and the role of Parliament in legislation. How do you think that relationship or the connection between those roles can and should be developed, especially if we are looking at a more structured sentencing framework in the future?

Lord Phillips of Worth Matravers [the then Lord Chief Justice of England and Wales]: The relationship between judges and Parliament in relation to legislation is a tricky area. It first arises when legislation is being proposed where my view is that judges have a valid advisory role in relation to the implications on running the justice system of the legislation that is proposed and we frequently comment, 'If you introduce that, it is going to impose a substantial demand on judicial resources because it is going to lead to appeals in this area or that area', that is a perfectly legitimate area in which judges should be advising. We should not be involved in advising in relation to policy which is a matter ultimately for Government and Parliament. If you then ask what interrelationship should there be between judges and Parliament in relation to the act of sentencing and the implications sentencing has, I think the answer must be it is for Parliament to legislate and for judges to do their best to apply the legislation in accordance with its provisions and that is what is happening.

Judges occasionally appear before parliamentary committees to give evidence on bills and draft bills. Robert Hazell and Juliet Wells are of the opinion that the main purpose of this is 'educational': '*Judges comment on Bills can draw attention to constitutional standards and legal principles, they can point to gaps in the law, they can warn about poorly drafted provisions likely to cause difficulties in the courts*'.[32]

[26] 12 March 2001. [27] 19 March 2002, 21 October 2003, and 26 October 2004. [28] [2005] UKHL 56.

[29] *McGonnell v United Kingdom* (2000) 30 EHRR 289 (a case concerning the Bailiff of Guernsey, an ancient office that combined the role of presiding officer of the island's legislature with being chief justice).

[30] Constitutional Reform Act 2005, s. 137. [31] See Chapter 12.

[32] R. Hazell and J. Wells, 'Judicial input into parliamentary legislation' [2018] Public Law 106; and Judicial Executive Board, *Guidance to Judges on Appearances before Select Committees* (2012) https://www.judiciary.uk/wp-content/uploads/JCO/Documents/Guidance/select_committee_guidance.pdf accessed 27 November 2025.

Judges have also made suggestions for legislative reform in the news media. For example, interviewed on BBC Radio 4, Lord Justice Sedley suggested that the whole population of the United Kingdom and all visitors should have their DNA recorded on a national database—prompting a government spokesman to say that this would create '*huge logistical and bureaucratic issues*' and civil liberty concerns.[33]

Judges also have a formal role in the making of delegated legislation[34] about court procedures. For example, s. 45 of the Constitutional Reform Act 2005 provides that '*The President of the Supreme Court may make rules (to be known as "Supreme Court Rules") governing the practice and procedure to be followed in the Court.*' While these rules are drafted by the President (no doubt in close collaboration with civil servants in the Ministry of Justice), it is not possible for the President (who is not an MP) to initiate the formal legislative process, so under s. 46 this is a role carried out by the Lord Chancellor (a minister and MP).

5.6.3 CAN JUDGES ADJUDICATE ON PARLIAMENTARY MATTERS?

Three bodies of law structure how the courts and Parliament relate to one another. One is parliamentary supremacy, discussed in Chapter 3, which defines the respective powers of the courts and the Crown-in-Parliament over primary legislation. A second, relevant here, is the law of parliamentary privilege. Its core statutory source is article 9 of the Bill of Rights, enacted at the time of the Glorious Revolution as the modern constitutional monarchy took shape.[35]

Bill of Rights 1688, Article IX

That the Freedome of Speech and Debates or Proceedings in Parlyament ought not to be impeached or questioned in any Court or Place out of Parlyament.

In private law, article 9 prevents anybody being sued for defamation for anything said in Parliament. As the government puts it, '*Freedom of speech in Parliament is of fundamental importance. Parliament should be a forum for free and frank debate, and Members of both Houses should be able to raise issues without having to agonise over the exact form of words used to guard against legal action*'.[36] Alongside the statutory guarantee, a linked body of common law—known as Parliament's 'exclusive cognisance'—recognises the right of each House to regulate its internal affairs free from external interference.[37] As the Supreme Court put it in *R v Chaytor* [2010] UKSC 52, exclusive cognisance refers to the 'exclusive right of each House to manage its own affairs without interference from the other or from outside Parliament'. In navigating these constraints, the courts have had to determine when it is appropriate for litigants and judges to rely on material from Parliament—such as statements recorded in *Hansard*, or reports and other publications produced by parliamentary committees.

5.6.3.1 Interpreting Acts of Parliament

One use of parliamentary material arises when a court interprets a provision in an Act of Parliament. The court's primary focus is the statutory text, read in its legal and factual context. But the landmark

[33] BBC News, 'All UK "must be on DNA database"', 5 September 2007. [34] Chapter 13.

[35] See Chapter 1 (section 1.4.1). [36] HM Government, *Parliamentary Privilege* (2012), Cm 8318, para 45.

[37] E. Lui, 'Piercing the Parliamentary Veil against Judicial Review: The Case against Parliamentary Privilege' (2022) 42(3) *Oxford Journal of Legal Studies* 918.

decision in *Pepper v Hart* [1993] AC 593 relaxed the earlier prohibition on consulting *Hansard* if three criteria are present: (i) the legislation must be ambiguous, obscure, or its natural meaning would lead to absurdity; (ii) the extract from *Hansard* the court examines is focused on the minister or other promoter of the bill; and (iii) the parliamentary material is itself sufficient clear to be helpful.[38] From a separation-of-powers perspective, this might appear counter-intuitive: why should the executive's explanation matter more than Parliament's collective will? Its practical value, however, is in preventing the executive from advancing in litigation an interpretation inconsistent with what ministers told Parliament the legislation would mean.

Is *Pepper v Hart* compatible with article 9 of the Bill of Rights? In 1999, a parliamentary committee considered this question and concluded that it was.

Joint Committee on Parliamentary Privilege, Volume 1—Report and Proceedings (April 1999), HL 43-I, HC 214-I, para 45

> Parliament must be vigilant in protecting its freedom of speech. Any departure by the courts from hitherto accepted practice must be scrutinised thoroughly to see whether, as a matter of principle and practice, it is justifiable. Applying that test the Joint Committee is of the view that the development outlined above in *Pepper v Hart* is unobjectionable. This use of parliamentary proceedings is benign. The Joint Committee recommends that Parliament should not disturb the decision in *Pepper v Hart*. However, it is important that this specific court decision should not lead to any general weakening of the prohibition contained in article 9.

A study by Lewis Graham has accessed the impact of *Pepper v Hart*, concluding that while it was rarely invoked it was an important feature in statutory interpretation.

L. Graham, '30 Years of Pepper v Hart: an empirical review' (2025) 46 *Statute Law Review* 1, 12

> The legacy of *Pepper v Hart* is . . . a balanced one: it has not led to judges becoming completely overwhelmed by invitations to consider Hansard, but equally it has not, as others have feared, died off and become completely irrelevant. Rather, it occasionally provides assistance to judges in circumstances where it is considered that the strict criteria laid down in *Pepper* are satisfied. It remains an important, if relatively rarely invoked, element of modern statutory interpretation.

5.6.3.2 Assessing the Proportionality of an Act of Parliament

Since the Human Rights Act 1998, courts may be asked to assess whether a provision in an Act of Parliament is a proportionate restriction on a qualified Convention right, such as freedom of expression or the right to respect for privacy. This is a distinct exercise from interpreting the statute's meaning. In *Wilson v First County Trust Ltd (No. 2)* [2003] UKHL 40, the House of Lords recognised that proportionality analysis may require courts to look beyond the words of the statute.

[38] See Chapter 11 (section 11.4.3), Chapter 4 (section 4.3.1), and for a critical perspective from the judiciary, see Lord Steyn, '*Pepper v Hart*: A re-examination' (2001) 21 Oxford Journal of Legal Studies 66.

Wilson v First County Trust Ltd (No. 2) [2003] UKHL 40, Lord Nicholls of Birkenhead

62. The legislation must not only have a legitimate policy objective. It must also satisfy a 'proportionality' test. The court must decide whether the means employed by the statute to achieve the policy objective is appropriate and not disproportionate in its adverse effect. This involves a 'value judgment' by the court, made by reference to the circumstances prevailing when the issue has to be decided. It is the current effect and impact of the legislation which matter, not the position when the legislation was enacted or came into force. [. . .]

63. When a court makes this value judgment the facts will often speak for themselves. But sometimes the court may need additional background information tending to show, for instance, the likely practical impact of the statutory measure and why the course adopted by the legislature is or is not appropriate. Moreover, as when interpreting a statute, so when identifying the policy objective of a statutory provision or assessing the 'proportionality' of a statutory provision, the court may need enlightenment on the nature and extent of the social problem (the 'mischief') at which the legislation is aimed. This may throw light on the rationale underlying the legislation.

64. This additional background material may be found in published documents, such as a government white paper. If relevant information is provided by a minister or, indeed, any other member of either House in the course of a debate on a Bill, the courts must also be able to take this into account. The courts, similarly, must be able to have regard to information contained in explanatory notes prepared by the relevant government department and published with a Bill. The courts would be failing in the due discharge of the new role assigned to them by Parliament if they were to exclude from consideration relevant background information whose only source was a ministerial statement in Parliament or an explanatory note prepared by his department while the Bill was proceeding through Parliament. By having regard to such material the court would not be 'questioning' proceedings in Parliament or intruding improperly into the legislative process or ascribing to Parliament the views expressed by a minister. The court would merely be placing itself in a better position to understand the legislation.

65. To that limited extent there may be occasion for the courts, when conducting the statutory 'compatibility' exercise, to have regard to matters stated in Parliament. It is a consequence flowing from the Human Rights Act. The constitutionally unexceptionable nature of this consequence receives some confirmation from the view expressed in the unanimous report of the parliamentary Joint Committee on Parliamentary Privilege (1999) (HL Paper 43-I, HC 214-I), p. 28, para 86, that it is difficult to see how there could be any objection to the court taking account of something said in Parliament when there is no suggestion the statement was inspired by improper motives or was untrue or misleading and there is no question of legal liability.

66. I expect that occasions when resort to Hansard is necessary as part of the statutory 'compatibility' exercise will seldom arise. The present case is not such an occasion. Should such an occasion arise the courts must be careful not to treat the ministerial or other statement as indicative of the objective intention of Parliament. Nor should the courts give a ministerial statement, whether made inside or outside Parliament, determinative weight. It should not be supposed that members necessarily agreed with the minister's reasoning or his conclusions.

67. Beyond this use of Hansard as a source of background information, the content of parliamentary debates has no direct relevance to the issues the court is called upon to decide in compatibility cases and, hence, these debates are not a proper matter for investigation or consideration by the courts. In particular, it is a cardinal constitutional principle that the will of Parliament is expressed in the language used by it in its enactments. The proportionality of legislation is to be judged on that basis. The courts are to have due regard to the legislation as an expression of the will of Parliament. The proportionality of a statutory measure is not to be judged by the quality of the reasons advanced in support

of it in the course of parliamentary debate, or by the subjective state of mind of individual ministers or other members. Different members may well have different reasons, not expressed in debates, for approving particular statutory provisions. They may have different perceptions of the desirability or likely effect of the legislation. Ministerial statements, especially if made ex tempore in response to questions, may sometimes lack clarity or be misdirected. Lack of cogent justification in the course of parliamentary debate is not a matter which 'counts against' the legislation on issues of proportionality. The court is called upon to evaluate the proportionality of the legislation, not the adequacy of the minister's exploration of the policy options or of his explanations to Parliament. The latter would contravene article 9 of the Bill of Rights. The court would then be presuming to evaluate the sufficiency of the legislative process leading up to the enactment of the statute.

5.6.3.3 Using Parliamentary Material as Evidence of Truth

A third setting in which a court may be asked to examine Hansard or parliamentary committee transcripts or reports is when a litigant seeks to use that as evidence. In *R (on the application of ALR, by their litigation friend ASG) and others v Chancellor of the Exchequer*, several children and their parents challenged the legality of the government's decision to impose value added tax (VAT) on private school fees, including children attending religious schools and with special educational needs. In a long judgment, the Administrative Court dismissed the claim for judicial review. Some of the claimants wanted to rely on two parliamentary committee reports, one from the Women and Equalities Committee and the other a 'value for money' report by the National Audit Office, that had been formally published by the Public Accounts Committee. The Speaker of the House of Commons objected to the use of the reports to establish factual matters that were in dispute between the parties. The Administrative Court was sympathetic with the claimants.

R (on the application of ALR, by their litigation friend ASG) and others v Chancellor of the Exchequer [2025] EWHC 1467 (Admin), Annex B: Article 9 of the Bill of Rights 1689 and Parliamentary Privilege

79. If the matter were unconstrained by authority, we would question whether any of the doctrinal rationales for Article 9 justify reading the prohibition on 'questioning or impeaching' so broadly as to prohibit any factual disagreement with the evidence given to, or indeed the conclusions reached by, a select committee. In principle, we find it hard to imagine that a witness or report author would be deterred from giving full and frank evidence by the prospect that a court, while not attaching criminal or civil liability or questioning the good faith of the witness or report author, might disagree with a factual conclusion. This is particularly so in the case of a professional witness or report author, such as those responsible for the preparation of NAO Value for Money reports, who must be assumed to encounter reasoned disagreement with their views routinely and be robust enough to tolerate it. The suggestion that the content of a select committee's own factual conclusions might be affected if the courts were able to consider them alongside other evidence and (if appropriate) reject them seems to us even more far-fetched.

80. Looking at the matter through the lens of the separation of powers, we find it difficult to see why a reasoned disagreement with the factual evidence given by a witness or report author, or indeed by a committee itself, should be regarded as interfering with the functions of the committee or as failing to accord respect to it, or to Parliament as a whole. Indeed, it might be argued that a rule

requiring a court to adopt an attitude of studied ignorance towards the evidence given to or conclusions reached by a select committee itself manifests a certain lack of respect for the important work performed in the public interest by those committees and by those who give evidence and report to them.

81. However, this point is now covered by authority. In [*Office of Government Commerce v Information Commissioner* [2008] EWHC 774 (Admin), [2010] QB 98 ('*OGC*')], Stanley Burnton J expressly considered whether the prohibition on challenging the 'veracity' of proceedings in Parliament included any challenge to the 'accuracy' of things said as part of such proceedings. We agree with him that the Privy Council in *Prebble v Television New Zealand* [1995] 1 AC 321 and the House of Lords in *Hamilton v Al Fayed [2001] UKHL 395* made clear, by endorsing the [Australian Parliamentary Privileges Act 1987] as reflective of the scope of Article 9, that the answer was 'yes'. We agree with Stanley Burnton J that, given the clarity of the views expressed in these authorities, it does not matter whether the point was part of the ratio of either decision. . . . On the present state of the authorities, we consider that it is too late for a change of course other than by the Supreme Court.

Clearly, the Administrative Court was frustrated by the current state of the law preventing a litigant referring to parliamentary materials for establishing a contested fact, but until the law is changed by the Supreme Court, the Administrative Court was bound by precedent.

PAUSE FOR REFLECTION

Amit, bringing a judicial review claim, wants to rely on Hansard and a select committee report for three different purposes. First, to support his argument about the meaning of a phrase in an Act of Parliament. Second, to help show that the provision is incompatible with Convention rights because it is disproportionate. Third, to prove a factual point. In your own words, summarise the rules governing when courts may use parliamentary material for each of these purposes.

5.6.4 CAN MEMBERS OF PARLIAMENT DISCUSS JUDGES AND JUDGMENTS?

Just as the courts are careful not to intrude into parliamentary proceedings, so too does Parliament try to steer away from undue interference with courts and judges. The *sub judice* rule requires that MPs should not seek to bring up in debates, questions, and motions cases that are pending or being heard by a court. The House of Commons Standing Order 42A provides that '*The Speaker, or the chairman, may direct any Member who breaches the terms of the sub judice resolution of the House to resume his seat.*' The rationale for this rule is that discussion of a case may have a prejudicial effect and may prevent the parties to the civil or criminal case from having a fair trial. There is, however, a discretion for the Speaker and Lord Speaker to allow discussion if it is in the national interest.

More broadly, parliamentarians are expected to be careful in any criticisms that they make of judges or judgments, as the following extract explains.

Joint Committee on Parliamentary Privilege, First Report, Session 1998–99 (HL 43-I/HC 214-I)

Parliament and the judiciary

226. Much of this report is necessarily concerned with the relationship between Parliament and the courts. The effective working of the constitution depends on the courts being ever sensitive to the need to refrain from trespassing upon the province of Parliament or even appearing to do so, and on Parliament being similarly sensitive to the need to refrain from trespassing upon the province of the courts. This is generally recognised by both institutions. This relationship would not be helped if judges were to make unnecessary or exaggerated critical comments on the actions of politicians, or if politicians use parliamentary privilege to attack particular judicial decisions or the character of individual judges.

227. So far as Parliament is concerned, both Houses consider opprobrious reflections on members of the judiciary to be out of order unless made on motion. In the Commons 36 motions critical of judges or seeking their removal have been tabled since 1961. None has been debated.

228. Occasionally statements or actions by members of Parliament may merit judicial criticism. Likewise, judicial decision or comment may merit criticism by members of Parliament. It is important for both institutions that such criticism is made in measured terms. In all cases members should pause to consider before tabling motions which often receive wide publicity. We agree with the Lord Chief Justice of England that a tradition of mutual reticence serves the country best.

This is not to say that parliamentarians cannot inquire into how courts interpret and apply legislation. In an interesting development, the Joint Committee on Human Rights reported twice on what it saw as the wrong approach adopted by the courts in deciding that private care homes were not covered by the Human Rights Act 1998.[39] These reports were influential in encouraging Parliament to reverse the effect of a House of Lords' decision that had maintained a narrow approach to the meaning of '*function of a public nature*'.[40] Parliamentary investigations into how courts are handling legislation may become more frequent in the future as procedures for post-legislative scrutiny are put in place.[41]

5.6.5 WHAT IS THE RELATIONSHIP BETWEEN MINISTERS AND JUDGES?

We discuss in Chapter 17 the statutory duties of ministers to uphold the independence of the judiciary and the role of the Lord Chancellor (a minister) in defending that independence. As we will see, ministers have, on occasion, been outspokenly critical of individual judges, the judiciary as a whole, and particular judgments.

5.6.6 WHAT IS THE ROLE OF THE EXECUTIVE IN PARLIAMENT?

In a system of parliamentary government, there is no separation between 'the legislature' and 'the executive'; on the contrary, ministers are *required* to be members of Parliament. As we discuss elsewhere, while this arrangement can be justified as enabling Parliament to hold ministers to account on a regular basis, the danger is that those parliamentarians who are ministers dominate the work of

[39] Joint Committee on Human Rights, *The Meaning of Public Authority under the Human Rights Act*, Seventh Report, Session 2003–04 (HL 39/HC 382); Ninth Report, Session 2006–07 (HL 77/HC 410).

[40] See Chapter 21. [41] See Chapter 12.

Parliament. This is especially so in relation to the legislative process. As we see in Chapters 9 and 10, the executive (ministers and civil servants) have dominant roles in the making of both primary and delegated legislation. Whereas some legislatures take the lead in developing policy and drafting legislation, the role of the UK Parliament is largely reactive: its role is to scrutinize and then approve (or reject) proposals from the government. There are few opportunities for members of the legislature—whether MPs or peers—who are not members of the government to initiate legislation and see it through to enactment: few private member's bills reach the statute book.

There are, however, some limited legal constraints on the executive. A cap is placed on the total number of MPs who can serve as ministers.[42] Civil servants, members of the armed forces, police officers, and a long list of holders of public offices are disqualified from being MPs by s. 1 of the House of Commons Disqualification Act 1975. Except for ministers (who receive a salary on top of their MPs' salary), there is also a general prohibition on an MP '*holding an office or place of profit under the Crown*' (s. 1(4)). This provides a procedural device for an MP's resignation: he or she is appointed, temporarily, to an office of the Crown and is thereby disqualified from sitting in the Commons.[43]

QUESTIONS

1. What are the rival explanations of the purpose of separation of powers? Which do you find most convincing?
2. In relation to each of the following rules, explain the constitutional rationale and whether it is contained in legislation or a constitutional convention.
   (a) Ministers must be members of one of the Houses of Parliament.
   (b) Judges cannot sit or vote as a member of either House of Parliament.
   (c) In relation to legislation, judges '*should not be involved in advising in relation to policy which is a matter ultimately for Government and Parliament*'.
   (d) Civil servants cannot be members of either House of Parliament.
3. To what extent can it be said that separation of powers is an important principle in the UK constitution?

5.7 CONCLUSION

This chapter has shown that separation of powers is not a single fixed model but a set of principles used to organize and control public authority. The United Kingdom's arrangements mix elements of separation and fusion: ministers sit in Parliament, courts maintain independence while engaging with legislation in limited ways, and some functions now lie with independent integrity bodies. Practical disputes over sentencing, the creation of the Supreme Court and administrative sanctions reveal how questions about the 'right' decision-maker arise in real settings, not just in theory. Competing explanations—protecting liberty, preventing concentrated power, improving efficiency and ensuring

[42] See Chapter 8.

[43] The offices to which MPs are appointed are 'Crown Steward and Bailiff of the three Chiltern Hundreds of Stoke, Desborough and Burnham' or 'Steward of the Manor of Northstead'.

accountability—help to illuminate these debates. The chapter's final sections examined the rules and conventions that shape everyday relations between Parliament, government and the judiciary, showing how the UK manages tensions between institutions while preserving a workable constitutional balance.

Chapter 6 now turns to look at another function of the constitution—distributing power between different levels of government.

FURTHER READING

Beatson, J., *Key Ideas in Law: The Rule of Law and the Separation of Powers* (2021, Hart Publishing)

Kavanagh, A., *The Collaborative Constitution* (2023, Cambridge University Press).

Vile, M. C. J., *Constitutionalism and the Separation of Powers*, 2nd edn (1998, Indianapolis, IN: Liberty Fund).

6

MULTILEVEL GOVERNANCE WITHIN THE UNITED KINGDOM

CENTRAL ISSUES

- Constitutional systems distribute executive and legislative power through three main approaches: unitary states concentrate authority at the centre; federal systems create distinct sovereign entities within the nation; devolution delegates power while preserving national sovereignty.
- The United Kingdom emerged from a union of separate nations but operated as a highly centralized state until 1998, with major decisions taken by the UK government and Parliament.
- Devolution since 1998 has transferred executive and legislative powers to Northern Ireland, Scotland, and Wales through founding Acts that have undergone extensive amendment, creating complex technical frameworks that pose interpretive challenges for the courts.
- England remains without devolved government or parliament despite constituting the UK's largest component. Some local-level executive devolution has occurred, but comprehensive solutions to the 'English Question' of territorial governance remain elusive.

6.1 INTRODUCTION

6.1.1 MODELS OF TERRITORIAL GOVERNANCE

The United Kingdom has a population of about 68.2 million and a land area of about 242,000 km^2. This polity contains three nations (England, Scotland, Wales) plus Northern Ireland, which is better characterized as a region rather than a separate country, province, or nation. The UK encompasses three distinct legal systems (England and Wales; Scotland; Northern Ireland), recognises six territorial identities (British, English, Irish, Northern Irish, Scottish, Welsh), and acknowledges seven indigenous languages under the Council of Europe's regional or minority languages charter (Welsh, Gaelic, Irish, Scots, Ulster Scots, Cornish, and Manx). Given this institutional, legal, and cultural complexity, what constitutional system should regulate the distribution of executive and legislative power across the UK's territories?

Unitary states concentrate decision-making in central institutions. Countries like France and Japan operate effectively as unitary states where territory broadly aligns with political identity. The UK's political tradition reflects its origins as a unitary state. Core constitutional principles—parliamentary supremacy, rule of law, cabinet government, parliamentary democracy, ministerial responsibility, judicial independence, and constitutional convention—originated during the late nineteenth century when the UK was seen as homogeneous and unified.

Federalism divides sovereignty constitutionally between national and regional governments. The Forum of Federations identifies 25 federal countries representing 40 per cent of the world's population, including Germany and the United States.[1]

K.C. Wheare, *Modern Constitutions* 2nd edn (1966, Oxford: OUP), p. 19

In a federal constitution, the powers of government are divided between a government for the whole country and governments for parts of the country in such a way that each government is legally independent in its own sphere. The government for the whole country has its own areas of powers and it exercises them without any control from the governments of the constituent parts of the country, and these in their turn exercise their powers without being controlled by the central government. In particular, the legislatures of the whole country have limited powers and the legislatures of the states or provinces have limited powers.

Federal systems uphold three main commitments. Distinct territories voluntarily agree to shared rule through central government with joint decision-making powers where all territories are represented. Political autonomy exists over regional affairs. Mutual checks operate between different levels of government. Although federal arrangements vary considerably, the core principle consistently emphasizes power-sharing, cooperation, and negotiation over centralization and dominance.

Devolution represents a third constitutional option. The term derives from Latin meaning '*to roll down*'. While devolution is similar federalism in distributing power across levels of government, it operates through different mechanisms.

Devolution involves the unidirectional transfer of legislative or executive power from central authority to a subordinate regional authority, unlike federalism's constitutionally protected division of sovereignty. Vernon Bogdanor identifies devolution's three defining characteristics: '*the transfer to a subordinate elected body on a geographical basis, of functions at present exercised by Parliament. These functions may be either legislative, the power to make laws, or executive, the power to make decisions within an already established legal framework*'.[2]

Central institutions retain ultimate authority under devolution. Devolved systems preserve the centre's unilateral power to reclaim transferred powers when deemed necessary, while maintaining ultimate legislative power over devolved areas. This creates hierarchical rather than coordinate relationships between governmental levels.

Devolution operates through ordinary national legislation rather than through constitutional frameworks protecting territorial autonomy. This provides flexibility but creates vulnerability, as devolved arrangements depend on central political goodwill rather than constitutional protection. Italy, Spain, and the United Kingdom exemplify European devolution models adapted to particular territorial circumstances.

[1] http://www.forumfed.org/countries/.

[2] V. Bogdanor, *Devolution* (1979, Oxford: OUP), p. 2.

6.1.2 THE UNITED KINGDOM AS A UNION STATE: HISTORICAL ORIGINS AND LEGAL TENSIONS

The United Kingdom defies simple constitutional categorization. It is best understood as a 'union state'—a constitutional form reflecting its origins in the gradual amalgamation of previously separate territories across the eighteenth and nineteenth centuries. This historical process of state formation created constitutional tensions that continue to shape contemporary territorial governance.

Wales was incorporated through conquest. The Kingdom of England brought the Welsh principality under control by thirteenth-century military conquest, then incorporated, united and annexed it under Henry VIII's Laws in Wales Acts 1535–42. These Acts abolished Welsh law, creating a single realm with English as the sole administrative language.[3]

Scotland resisted conquest but accepted union. After failed military campaigns, unification began when James VI of Scotland became James I of England (1603), culminating in the Treaty of Union 1706. The 1707 Acts of Union ratified this Treaty, creating the Kingdom of Great Britain with what J.D.B. Mitchell called a 'skeletal' constitution.[4] This settlement was contradictory: Scotland retained distinct legal, educational, and ecclesiastical systems. Its supreme courts remain expressly preserved '*in all time coming*' (Article XIX of the Treaty of Union) and beyond UK Supreme Court criminal jurisdiction today. Yet the Union was officially 'incorporating': Scottish laws became subject to alteration by the new Parliament of Great Britain, which effectively continued English parliamentary procedures (Article XVIII of the Treaty of Union).

This constitutional settlement embedded lasting tensions between Scottish institutional autonomy and English parliamentary dominance, tensions that continue to shape contemporary devolution debates and constitutional politics.

Ireland experienced incorporation without safeguards. The 1801 Act created the United Kingdom of Great Britain and Ireland, but unlike Scotland, Ireland received no constitutional protections. While Irish laws nominally remained, they were '*subject only to such alterations and regulations from time to time as circumstances may appear to the Parliament of the United Kingdom to require*' (Article 8 of the Act of Union (Ireland) 1800). Ireland gained Westminster representation (100–105 MPs) but lost its own parliament entirely.

This constitutional position created lasting tensions, leaving Ireland without either Wales's complete integration or Scotland's protected autonomy.

J. Kendle, *Federal Britain: A History* (1997, London: Routledge), p. 19

> Nothing could have as dramatically or as plainly underscored the 'colonial' status of Ireland in English eyes as the manner of its incorporation. Nor did its future administration soften that condition. Ireland was administered as a separate unit within the United Kingdom—quite unlike Scotland and Wales—with a lord lieutenant and chief secretary as heads, respectively, of government and administration. This structure was unique in the empire. Nowhere else was a province or a territory or a colony represented in the imperial parliament nor was any other part of the British Isles administered in so obviously colonial style. This novel arrangement reflected Ireland's particular status. Sitting as close as it did to British shores, it represented a strategic threat to the safety of the larger island containing England, Scotland

[3] The Welsh Language Act 1967 allowed the Welsh language to be used in legal proceedings in Wales, and the Welsh Language Act 1993 for the first time established parity between the Welsh and English languages in the conduct of public business in Wales.

[4] J.D.B. Mitchell, *Constitutional Law* (1964: Edinburgh: W. Green & Son), p. 75.

and Wales. The British government simply could not contemplate the possibility of a self-governing, and therefore unpredictable, Ireland. For safety's sake, if for nothing else, it had to be brought under central control – under the supreme authority of the Westminster Parliament.

Union formation created a constitution embodying contradictory principles. The constitutional settlement reflects Scotland and England's merger as equals, yet operates through Westminster and Whitehall's legal and political dominance while requiring pragmatic management of regional autonomy. These underlying tensions shape contemporary constitutional law and practice, generating competing interpretations of the UK's territorial arrangements.

One constitutional reading emphasizes the UK's intrinsic bias toward power concentration.[5] This interpretation traces its intellectual roots to Thomas Hobbes' *Leviathan* and its vision of absolute sovereign authority. It privileges centralization through sovereignty, ultimate legislative authority, enforceability, uniformity, and unity. This Hobbesian legacy underpins both the unitary state tradition and the British political tradition that emphasized parliamentary supremacy, collective responsibility, majoritarian decision-making through first-past-the-post elections, and weak judicial review until the late twentieth century.

The constitution may equally operate as a power-diffusion mechanism. This alternative understanding conceives the United Kingdom not as unitary and centralized but as a multiregional and plurinational state. Such a state encompasses multiple nations and diffuse institutions such as regional parliaments and governments while embracing plural constitutional forms (unitary, union, devolved, quasi-federal) and plural national identities.[6]

This pluralistic reality manifests in citizens' diverse self-identification: some identify as British, others as both British and Scottish or Welsh, while in Northern Ireland some identify exclusively as British or Irish. Where power-concentrating constitutionalism would impose uniform legal measures from a supreme Parliament, power-sharing constitutionalism might utilize the UK government's convening authority to reconcile territorial management, intergovernmental relations, policy divergence, and cultural differences through collective deliberation rather than centralized imposition.

The tension between these approaches—centralized majoritarianism versus decentralized consensualism—operates throughout the UK constitution, generating both fundamental and practical questions. The fundamental questions concern Westminster Parliament's legal supremacy, exemplified by the constitutional status of the Acts of Union. Can these foundational Acts constitute fundamental law overriding ordinary legislation? This question echoes *Thoburn v Sunderland City Council*, where Laws LJ identified the Acts of Union among '*constitutional statutes*', including the Bill of Rights 1689, Human Rights Act 1998, and Constitutional Reform Act 2005, that cannot be impliedly repealed.

The constitutional status of the Union settlement divides English and Scottish legal thought. A.V. Dicey, representing orthodox English constitutionalism, argued that the Acts of Union were 'fundamental' only in being 'important' rather than constituting 'supreme law'. This position faces vigorous rejection from Scottish constitutional lawyers like T.B. Smith and Lord President Cooper of

[5] Brian Barry, *Political Argument* (1965, London: Routledge & Kegan Paul), p. 237; A. King, *The British Constitution* (2009, Oxford: OUP), chs. 3 and 14; V. Bogdanor, *The New British Constitution* (2009, Oxford: Hart), chs. 1–2; A. Lijphart, *Patterns of Democracy: Government Forms and Performance in Thirty-Six Countries*, 2nd ed. (2012, New Haven, CT: Yale University Press), ch. 2.

[6] M. Keating, *Plurinational Democracy: Stateless Nations in a Post-Sovereignty Era* (2001, Oxford: OUP); A. King, *The British Constitution* (2009, Oxford: OUP), chs. 4 and 14; V. Bogdanor, *The New British Constitution* (2009, Oxford: Hart), chs. 3–9.

the Court of Session, who advocate for the Acts' special constitutional status. This scholarly divide reflects deeper tensions about whether the UK constitution operates through power-concentrating or power-sharing principles. These tensions continue to shape contemporary debates on devolution and territorial governance.

A.V. Dicey, *Introduction to the Study of the Law of the Constitution* 10th edn (1885; 10th edn 1959, London: Macmillan), p. 145

In England we have laws which may be called fundamental or constitutional because they deal with important principles (as, for example, the descent of the Crown or the terms of union with Scotland) lying at the basis of our institutions, but with us there is no such thing as a supreme law, or law which tests the validity of other laws. There are indeed important statutes, such as the Act embodying the Treaty of Union with Scotland, with which it would be political madness to tamper gratuitously; there are utterly unimportant statutes, such, for example, as the Dentists Act, 1878, which may be repealed or modified at the pleasure or caprice of Parliament; but neither the Act of Union with Scotland nor the Dentists Act, 1878, has more claim than the other to be considered a supreme law. Each embodies the will of the sovereign legislative power; each can be legally altered or repealed by Parliament; neither tests the validity of the other. Should the Dentists Act, 1878, unfortunately contravene the terms of the Act of Union, the Act of Union would be pro tanto repealed, but no judge would dream of maintaining that the Dentists Act, 1878, was thereby rendered invalid or unconstitutional. The one fundamental dogma of English constitutional law is the absolute legislative sovereignty or despotism of the King in Parliament. But this dogma is incompatible with the existence of a fundamental compact, the provisions of which control every authority existing under the constitution.

Dicey's view reinforces the power-hoarding model of the UK constitution. But this approach has been challenged by Scottish legal thinkers, who argue that the Acts of Union enjoy a special, entrenched status.

T.B. Smith, 'The Union of 1707 as Fundamental Law' [1957] *Public Law* 99, 109–10

I find myself . . . quite unable to accept the view of those English constitutional lawyers who hold that the terms of Union have no more force than an ordinary Act of Parliament. [. . .] I consider that the terms of Union (in their final form) as eventually agreed between England and Scotland, though set out in statute form, are in fact fundamental law – and have the force of a constituent document. Every schoolboy knows that the British Constitution has no fundamental written basis; but in my view every schoolboy has been misinformed. I have reached this view after much anxious thought and research; but considerations of space compel me to state this view very briefly.

The fallacy of regarding the terms of Union as mere legislation is largely, I think, due first to regarding the pre-Union English Act 6 Anne c. 11 as the Act of Union, and thus overlooking the fact that. as a mere legislative Act, it could and can have no effect outside England. It is not a United Kingdom statute, and strictly the Scottish courts could not notice it judicially as an Act of Parliament. Secondly, it has been assumed without justification that the British Parliament is the English Parliament with Scottish members admitted; and that its powers are those of the former English Parliament.

The argument that all Acts of Parliament, including the Acts of Union, enjoyed the same status, and were subject to either express or implied repeal by subsequent ordinary legislation, was further tested by a Scottish judge, Lord President Cooper. The following Scottish case concerned the designation of Queen Elizabeth as Elizabeth II in Scotland, when Queen Elizabeth I (who reigned from 1558–1603) had only been Queen of England, not of Scotland or the United Kingdom. The question was whether this amounted to a breach of the Act of Union 1707.

MacCormick v Lord Advocate

1953 S.C. 396, 411, *per* Lord President Cooper

> The principle of the unlimited sovereignty of Parliament is a distinctively English principle which has no counterpart in Scottish constitutional law. It derives its origin from Coke and Blackstone, and was widely popularized during the nineteenth century by Bagehot and Dicey, the latter having stated the doctrine in its classic form in his Law of the Constitution. Considering that the Union legislation extinguished the Parliaments of Scotland and England and replaced them by a new Parliament, I have difficulty in seeing why it should have been supposed that the new Parliament of Great Britain must inherit all the peculiar characteristics of the English Parliament but none of the Scottish Parliament, as if all that happened in 1707 was that Scottish representatives were admitted to the Parliament of England. That is not what was done. Further, the Treaty and the associated legislation, by which the Parliament of Great Britain was brought into being as the successor of the separate Parliaments of Scotland and England, contain some clauses which expressly reserve to the Parliament of Great Britain powers of subsequent modification, and other clauses which either contain no such power or emphatically exclude subsequent alteration by declarations that the provision shall be fundamental and unalterable in all time coming, or declarations of a like effect. I have never been able to understand how it is possible to reconcile with elementary canons of construction the adoption by the English constitutional theorists of the same attitude to these markedly different types of provisions.

Recall from Chapter 3 that Dicey's doctrine of parliamentary supremacy empowered Parliament to '*make or unmake any law whatever*'[7] while preventing any other person or body from overriding parliamentary legislation. This legal absolutism finds institutional expression in the UK's constitutional flexibility: as the Kilbrandon report observed, '*no special procedures are required to enact even the most fundamental changes in the constitution*'.[8]

Dicey acknowledged practical limitations to this theoretical supremacy. His recognition that tampering with the Act of Union would constitute '*political madness*' reveals the distinction between legal capacity and political prudence. These political constraints—electoral consequences, constitutional morality, and practical governance considerations—operate alongside formal legal authority to shape parliamentary behaviour.

[7] A.V. Dicey, *Introduction to the Study of the Law of the Constitution* 10th edn (1959, London: Macmillan), pp. 39–40.

[8] Royal Commission on the Constitution 1969–73 (1973 Cmnd 5460), the Kilbrandon Commission, (para. 56).

T.B. Smith and Lord President Cooper mounted a significant challenge to Diceyan orthodoxy. They argued that parliamentary supremacy represents a '*quintessentially English doctrine*' propagated by English scholars (Coke, Blackstone, Bagehot, Dicey) with '*no counterpart in Scottish constitutional law*'. From this perspective, Dicey's evolutionary account of British constitutional development tells only half the story.

If Great Britain's 1707 formation constituted a '*revolution by consent*',[9] Smith and Cooper contended, legal impediments to altering the Acts of Union must exist. The Union settlement's provisions guaranteeing Scottish institutions '*in all time coming*' suggest constitutional entrenchment rather than ordinary legislation. Parliament was therefore '*born unfree*',[10] constrained by the Union legislation's status as '*fundamental law*' overriding subsequent ordinary Acts.

This position appears heretical given the constitutional centrality of '*whatever the Crown in Parliament enacts is law*'.[11] The power-concentrating constitutional conception enjoys support from mainstream academic literature, judicial precedent, and institutional practice. Westminster has never acknowledged constitutional constraints on its authority, and no court has invalidated ordinary legislation for breaching the Acts of Union.

Smith and Cooper's critique anticipated later constitutional developments. Devolution and the protection of human rights have challenged key elements of Dicey's constitutional understanding, with judicial attitudes evolving from orthodox assumptions about unitary parliamentary authority. Scottish Law Lord Hope's dicta in *Jackson* echoed Cooper's 1953 challenge to '*untrammelled and unitary*' parliamentary supremacy.

This judicial evolution suggests that the constitutional tensions identified by Scottish scholars may be gaining legal recognition, potentially transforming the UK's territorial constitution through gradual judicial reinterpretation rather than formal constitutional amendment.

R (Jackson) v Attorney General

[2005] UKHL 56; 1 AC 262, *per* Lord Hope [104]

> Our constitution is dominated by the sovereignty of Parliament. But Parliamentary sovereignty is no longer, if it ever was, absolute. It is not uncontrolled in the sense referred to by Lord Birkenhead LC in *McCawley v The King* [1920] AC 691, 720. It is no longer right to say that its freedom to legislate admits of no qualification whatever. Step by step, gradually but surely, the English principle of the absolute legislative sovereignty of Parliament which Dicey derived from Coke and Blackstone is being qualified.

Devolution has altered the constitutional landscape by establishing multiple legislatures, diffusing executive power, and creating new intergovernmental relations. This chapter explores the allocation of public power within power-sharing constitutional arrangements.

The technical complexity of these arrangements reflects a broader constitutional tension. While legal and political solutions have emerged to govern at three levels (Table 6.1), the fundamental

[9] T.B. Smith, 'The Union of 1707 as fundamental law', 111.
[10] J.D.B. Mitchell, *Constitutional Law* (1964, Edinburgh: W. Green & Son), pp. 54–9.
[11] H.L.A. Hart, *The Concept of Law* (1994, Oxford: Clarendon Press), p. 148.

Table 6.1 Distribution of executive and legislative power

Level	Powers defined by	Main government and legislative institutions	Examples of areas of competence	Types of legislation made
Local	Localism Act 2011; Local Government Act 1972 and numerous subject-specific Acts	Local authorities	Social services; planning; refuse; libraries; social housing (see Section 6.6)	By-laws
Devolved (also in some contexts known as 'regional', 'sub-national')	(a) Northern Ireland Act 1998 (b) Scotland Act 1998 as amended by the Scotland Act 2012 and Scotland Act 2016 (c) Government of Wales Act 2006 as amended by the Wales Act 2017	(a) Northern Ireland Executive, Northern Ireland Assembly (b) Scottish Government, Scottish Parliament (c) Welsh Government, Senedd Cymru (Welsh Parliament)	See Section 6.3	(a) Acts of the Northern Ireland Assembly plus delegated legislation (b) Acts of the Scottish Parliament plus delegated legislation (c) Act of Senedd Cymru (Welsh Parliament), plus delegated legislation
National (also known as 'central')	In theory, the UK Parliament has unlimited legislative competence (and may confer competence on any matter to ministers)	HM Government (ministers, departments, executive agencies, etc) UK Parliament	UK tax; defence; national security; citizenship; border control; currency; international relations; the Crown; the UK Parliament	Acts of the UK Parliament Delegated legislation

conflict between Westminster supremacy and devolved governance remains unresolved. These tensions manifest in contemporary legislation, UK Supreme Court cases (Section 6.4), governance arrangements (Section 6.5), and extensive commentary.

Three questions drive this analysis: To what extent does the power-concentrating constitution remain the default conception? Are power-sharing mechanisms sufficiently robust for an increasingly devolved state? Do the fundamentals of the UK constitution require reassessment? See Figure 6.1.

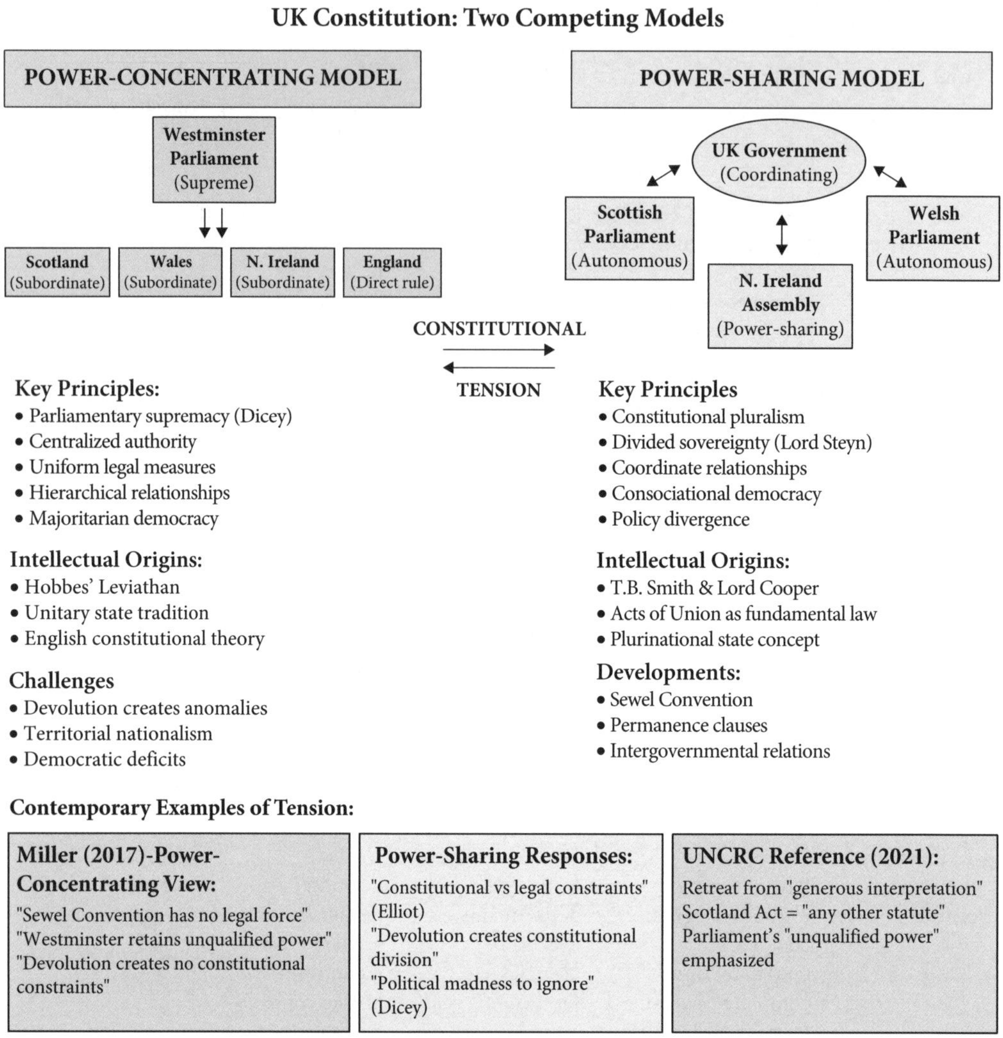

Figure 6.1 UK Constitution: Two competing models

QUESTIONS

1. Should the Acts of Union be treated as constituent documents with binding force on Parliament today? Consider: if they are merely ordinary statutes, how do we explain the creation of a joint Parliament and the continuing protection of Scotland's distinct legal system? If they are fundamental law, what are the implications for parliamentary supremacy?
2. Could Westminster unilaterally alter the constitutional status of Scotland, Wales, or Northern Ireland through ordinary legislation? What legal and political constraints might apply to such decisions?
3. If the UK adopted a written constitution, how might it reconcile Westminster supremacy with devolved governance? Should such a constitution entrench devolution arrangements, and if so, how?

6.2 THE POLITICS OF DEVOLUTION: FROM CENTRALIZATION TO CONSTITUTIONAL PLURALISM

The transition from constitutional possibility to political reality illustrates how the competing principles of power concentration and power sharing have operated in practice since the late twentieth century.

Until the late twentieth century, the United Kingdom operated as a highly centralized political unit, with policy-making and law-making concentrated in Whitehall and Westminster. This centralization reflected broader constitutional assumptions about British political uniformity. A typical scholarly view held that '*most of the generalizations that can be made about politics in England and Wales apply with only minor qualifications to Scotland, and for most practical purposes it is reasonable to treat the northern kingdom simply as part of a united political unit called Great Britain*'.[12] Such assumptions embodied the power-concentrating constitutional tradition, treating territorial diversity as constitutionally insignificant.

The first serious challenge to this centralized orthodoxy came in 1978 when James Callaghan's Labour government attempted to establish devolved institutions in Scotland and Wales. The Scotland Act 1978 and Wales Act 1978 represented a constitutional innovation, though their architects recognised that any such change would require popular legitimacy beyond parliamentary approval.

Both Acts mandated referendums with demanding thresholds: at least 40 per cent of the registered electorate must approve devolution. This requirement proved decisive. In Scotland, while 51.6 per cent of voters supported devolution, this represented only 32.9 per cent of the electorate, falling short of the statutory threshold. Wales rejected devolution entirely. Both Acts were consequently repealed, and the incoming Conservative government abandoned territorial decentralization for eighteen years.

Labour's 1997 electoral victory commenced devolution through constitutional sequencing. Within months of taking office, the new government published White Papers outlining devolution proposals and held referendums before introducing detailed legislation to Parliament. This reversed the 1978 approach by securing popular consent for the principle before parliamentary deliberation on specifics. Both Scotland and Wales voted for devolution. Elections for the Scottish Parliament and the National Assembly for Wales were held in May 1999, and power transfers were completed shortly thereafter.

As Secretary of State for Wales Ron Davies observed, that 'devolution is a process, not an event'—a phrase that captured the 1998 settlement's evolutionary character. The devolution Acts represented initial stages rather than final destinations, establishing frameworks for continuing constitutional development. Labour's 1997 manifesto framed this approach: '*a sovereign Westminster Parliament will devolve power to Scotland and Wales. The Union will be strengthened and the threat of separatism removed*'.

This strategy aimed beyond administrative decentralization toward political reengineering. The transfer of powers connected to aspirations for more consensual, participatory politics in Scotland and Wales. Yet the primary objective remained preserving rather than transforming the Union, seeking to '*kill nationalism stone dead*' through constitutional accommodation rather than confrontation, as Shadow Scottish Secretary George Robertson predicted in 1995.

The tension between these objectives—territorial autonomy versus Union preservation—would prove central to the subsequent evolution of devolution and to the constitutional conflicts examined throughout this chapter.

[12] A. Birch, *The British System of Government* (1967, London: Allen & Unwin), p. 15.

6.2.1 THE NORTHERN IRELAND PEACE SETTLEMENT AND CONSOCIATIONALISM

While Scotland and Wales experienced relatively smooth devolutionary transitions, Northern Ireland's path to self-government reflects a more complex and troubled constitutional history. The relationship between England and Ireland has been difficult across centuries, connected to the British Empire's rise, expansion, and decline. The constitutional connections between these territories and Northern Ireland's position between competing national allegiances require examination.

Until 1800, Ireland existed as a separate kingdom under the English Crown. The post-Union period saw growing demands for constitutional autonomy, culminating in the Irish Home Rule movement, which campaigned from the late nineteenth century through World War I for self-government within the United Kingdom of Great Britain and Ireland.

Conservative pro-Unionists viewed Home Rule as a threat to the British constitutional order. A.V. Dicey articulated this opposition: '*the movement in favour of the Parliamentary Independence of Ireland constitutes, whether its advocates recognize the fact or not, a demand for fundamental alterations in the whole Constitution of the United Kingdom ... I entertain the firmest conviction that any scheme for Home Rule in Ireland involves dangerous if not fatal innovations on the Constitution of Great Britain*'.[13] Despite this resistance, successive Liberal governments under Gladstone and Asquith pursued Home Rule legislation.

The Government of Ireland Act 1914, enacted through the Parliament Act 1911, represented the culmination of these efforts. World War I's outbreak led to immediate suspension, and subsequent events, particularly the Easter Rising 1916, ensured the Act never took effect.

The Irish War of Independence (1919–21) and Anglo-Irish Treaty (1921) changed the constitutional landscape. Rather than implementing Home Rule for a unified Ireland, British policy embraced partition. Ireland became a self-governing dominion (the Irish Free State covering 26 counties), while Northern Ireland (the remaining six counties) exercised its option to withdraw from Ireland and remain within the United Kingdom.

Between 1922 and 1972, Northern Ireland operated the UK's first experiment in territorial devolution. The Government of Ireland Act 1920 established institutions resembling other Empire dominions: a Northern Ireland Parliament empowered 'to make laws for the peace, order, and good government of Northern Ireland' (s. 4), an Executive Committee headed by a prime minister, and a governor general representing the Crown. This arrangement mirrored constitutional developments in Canada, Australia, and New Zealand, reflecting the imperial context within which early devolution operated.

This experiment failed due to systemic discrimination and mounting sectarian violence. Conflict between nationalist communities (favouring Irish reunification) and unionist communities (supporting continued Union) rendered power-sharing impossible. The UK government suspended devolved institutions in 1972, formally abolishing them through the Northern Ireland Constitution Act 1973.

From 1972 to 1998, Northern Ireland experienced direct rule through the Northern Ireland Office and Secretary of State for Northern Ireland, with Westminster making laws for the territory. This reversion to centralized control demonstrated devolution's fragility when constitutional arrangements lack cross-community support and institutional legitimacy.

The peace process that emerged from this institutional collapse gradually culminated in the Belfast Agreement signed in April 1998. This development would establish Northern Ireland as a laboratory for constitutional innovation, creating power-sharing arrangements that went beyond traditional devolution models to address the territory's divided society.

[13] A.V. Dicey, *England's Case Against Home Rule* 2nd edn (1886, London: Murray), p. vii.

B. Dickson, 'Devolution in Northern Ireland' in J. Jowell and C. O'Cinneide, *The Changing Constitution* 9th edn (2019, Oxford: OUP), p. 247

The Belfast Agreement of 1998 was a hugely important milestone in the history of Northern Ireland. It was the culmination of political talks which had been initiated in the late 1980s, a few years before the ceasefires announced by the main republican and loyalist paramilitary organizations in 1994. The IRA's ceasefire was breached in 1996, when bombs were exploded at Canary Wharf in London and in Manchester's city centre, but it was reinstated shortly after Labour, led by Tony Blair, won the UK general election in 1997. Unionists and nationalists each won an important victory in the Agreement. The former obtained a repetition of the statutory guarantee that the status of Northern Ireland as a part of the United Kingdom would not change without the consent of a majority of the people living in Northern Ireland,[14] and also a pledge by the Irish Government that Articles 2 and 3 of the Irish Constitution would be re-worded to ensure that they reflected more accurately the current political reality that Northern Ireland is a separate jurisdiction from the Republic of Ireland. Nationalists, on the other hand, won the right to share in the governance of Northern Ireland, not only through having one of their representatives as the joint head of the Northern Ireland Executive but also through being guaranteed a number of Ministries in that Executive proportionate to the size of their electoral vote; they also secured the establishment of a North-South Ministerial Council at which matters with an obvious all-Ireland dimension, such as trade, food safety, waterways and coastal fisheries would be discussed.

Northern Ireland's power-sharing arrangements transcend conventional devolution through two distinctive characteristics that reflect both the territory's divided society and its position between two sovereign states. These innovations have created constitutional mechanisms with implications extending beyond Northern Ireland itself.

Northern Ireland's devolution is linked to a comprehensive peace process that encompasses paramilitary weapons, prisoner releases, human rights protections, and equality provisions. Unlike the administrative transfers characterizing Scottish and Welsh devolution, Northern Ireland required political processes addressing decades of violent conflict and systematic discrimination.

This necessity produced Northern Ireland's autochthonous constitution—arrangements that required acceptance by all parties rather than imposition by external authority. The resulting Agreement exhibits both internal and external dimensions, combining consociational and confederal characteristics that distinguish it from traditional devolutionary models.

The Agreement's consociational core mandates cross-community executive power-sharing through institutional design. Assembly Members must designate as British unionists, Irish nationalists, or 'others', ensuring ethnic representation within the legislative process. The Northern Ireland Executive operates under a diarchy: the First Minister and Deputy First Minister are elected together by the largest Unionist and Nationalist groups respectively, share equal powers, and must resign together if either steps down.

This institutional architecture prevents majoritarian dominance while ensuring that both communities participate in governance. The Deputy First Minister's equal status demonstrates the Agreement's commitment to power-sharing rather than token representation.

[14] Versions of this guarantee were included in s. 1(2) of the Northern Ireland Act 1949 and s. 1 of the Northern Ireland Constitution Act 1973.

The Agreement's confederal dimension operates through inter-governmental institutions.[15] The North-South Ministerial Council provides a cross-border forum for all-Ireland matters with executive functions, acknowledging economic and cultural connections while respecting political division.

Two east-west institutions balance British and Irish influences. The British-Irish Council promotes '*the harmonious and mutually beneficial development of the totality of relationships among the people of these islands*' through representatives from Irish and UK governments, all UK devolved governments, and dependent territories (Guernsey, Jersey, Isle of Man). The British-Irish Intergovernmental Conference facilitates '*bilateral co-operation at all levels on all matters of mutual interest within the competence of the UK and Irish Governments*'.[16]

The Agreement's international legal character further distinguishes it from domestic devolution arrangements. Simultaneous referendums in Ireland (95 per cent support) and Northern Ireland (72 per cent support) provided democratic legitimacy, while implementation through the Northern Ireland Act 1998, Northern Ireland Assembly Act 1998, and Irish constitutional amendment created binding legal obligations. This corpus of interconnected domestic and international instruments constitutes what Lord Bingham described as effectively '*a constitution*',[17] both because of its comprehensive character and fundamental legal status.

Northern Ireland's constitutional developments raise questions about whether they represent regional accommodation, symbolic gestures, or point towards a reconfiguration of the UK constitution itself. The Agreement's innovations—mandatory power-sharing, international legal guarantees, confederal institutions—challenge traditional assumptions about British sovereignty and territorial governance.

Northern Ireland Act 1998

1. Status of Northern Ireland

(1) It is hereby declared that Northern Ireland in its entirety remains part of the United Kingdom and shall not cease to be so without the consent of a majority of the people of Northern Ireland voting in a poll held for the purposes of this section in accordance with Schedule 1.

(2) But if the wish expressed by a majority in such a poll is that Northern Ireland should cease to be part of the United Kingdom and form part of a united Ireland, the Secretary of State shall lay before Parliament such proposals to give effect to that wish as may be agreed between Her Majesty's Government in the United Kingdom and the Government of Ireland.

The Belfast Agreement establishes Northern Ireland's constitutional position through the principle of consent embedded in the Northern Ireland Act 1998. The British government is legally obliged under domestic legislation to enter negotiations on Irish unity if the majority consent condition in s. 1(2) is met. This principle of consent becomes a constitutional guarantee that distinguishes Northern Ireland from Scotland and Wales, where the British government recognises no legal right to independence.

[15] B. O'Leary, 'The Belfast Agreement and the British-Irish Agreement: Consociation, Confederal Institutions, a Federacy, and a Peace Process', in A. Reynolds (ed.), *The Architecture of Democracy: Constitutional Design, Conflict Management, and Democracy* (2002, Oxford: OUP), p. 293–356.

[16] The Belfast Agreement: An Agreement Reached at the Multi-Party Talks on Northern Ireland, Cm 3883, April 1998, Strand Three, pp. 14–16.

[17] *Robinson v Secretary of State for Northern Ireland* [2002] UKHL 32, [2002] NI 390, per Lord Bingham [11].

This constitutional asymmetry reflects Northern Ireland's position as a territory whose sovereignty depends on continuing popular consent rather than Westminster's political discretion. Unlike Scottish or Welsh independence, which would require Westminster's political agreement, Irish unification possesses legal recognition as a legitimate constitutional outcome contingent solely on Northern Ireland's electorate.

The Belfast Agreement emerged within a broader constellation of UK constitutional reform. It coincided with commitments to Scottish and Welsh devolution and domestic implementation of the European Convention on Human Rights. This constitutional moment represented territorial decentralization alongside enhanced rights protection, altering the UK's governing arrangements.

These devolution arrangements sought to reconcile three political concerns that had previously been considered incompatible. First, achieving consociational power-sharing in Northern Ireland through cross-border institutions and violence reduction measures. Second, accommodating Scottish and Welsh nationalist grievances through devolution—a concern welcomed by nationalists who believed it would facilitate rather than prevent independence. Third, preserving the Union and traditional British political arrangements: parliamentary supremacy, majoritarianism, and centralized administration.

The tension between these objectives explains subsequent trajectories. Devolution developed rapidly in Scotland and Wales, where institutional stability enabled incremental expansion of power. Northern Ireland's power-sharing arrangements have proved more fragile, periodically collapsing due to political disagreements and underlying constitutional tensions.

These developments have generated pressures on Unionism and the British political tradition. Scottish independence movements, rising territorial nationalism, and EU withdrawal have challenged assumptions about constitutional stability and territorial loyalty that underpinned the original devolution settlements. Rather than strengthening the Union as intended, devolution has created centrifugal forces that continue to strain the UK's territorial constitution.

Devolution, designed to accommodate territorial diversity while preserving Union unity, has instead highlighted the tensions between these objectives—tensions that continue to shape contemporary constitutional politics across the United Kingdom.

6.2.2 POLITICAL ORIGINS OF WELSH DEVOLUTION

Welsh devolution exemplifies constitutional evolution through incremental institutional development. Since 1998, Wales has experienced four distinct constitutional settlements,[18] each representing progressive expansion of self-government from administrative devolution toward legislative autonomy.

The initial settlement emerged from a narrow referendum victory under the Government of Wales Act 1998. Wales became a distinct political entity through its National Assembly, but one that departed significantly from conventional constitutional architecture. The Assembly combined executive functions with legislative and scrutiny activities, effectively operating without a separate 'government'.

The Assembly exercised only secondary law-making powers in specified areas (agriculture, fisheries, education, housing, highways) that had previously been held by the Secretary of State for Wales. This represented administrative devolution rather than self-government, with Wales acquiring responsibility for implementing policies made elsewhere.

The Government of Wales Act 2006 initiated the second settlement by formally separating executive and legislative functions. This created the Welsh Government as a distinct entity while enhancing the Assembly's legislative capacity to enact, amend, and scrutinize primary legislation.

[18] R. Rawlings, 'The strange reconstitution of Wales' [2018] *Public Law* 62–83, 63–5; Lord Lloyd-Jones, 'Wales: Law in a Small Nation', in D. Clarry (ed.), *The UK Supreme Court Yearbook 2018–19 Vol.10i* (2021, London: Appellate Press, 2021), pp. 1001–121, 1106.

Constraints remained: 'Assembly Measures' operated under a conferred powers model limited to 20 specified policy areas. Wales could legislate, but only within predetermined boundaries that maintained Westminster's ultimate control over the scope of devolved competence.

The 2006 Act anticipated further development through legislative enhancement. Following the March 2011 referendum, where 63 per cent of voters supported full primary law-making powers within those 20 jurisdictional areas, Wales achieved legislative devolution. The Silk Commission's 2012 recommendations for enhanced tax-raising powers, implemented through the Wales Act 2014, added fiscal dimensions to legislative autonomy.

The fourth phase marked constitutional restructuring through the Wales Act 2017's shift from conferred to reserved powers. Influenced by the Silk Commission's second report (March 2014) and the Scottish independence referendum's aftermath, this development aligned Welsh devolution more closely with Scotland's framework.

Under Schedule 7A of the Government of Wales Act 2006, the Assembly now enjoys power over any policy area not specifically reserved to the UK, reversing the previous presumption in favour of central control. While some reserved powers differ from Scotland's arrangements, the structural similarity represents Wales's constitutional maturation.

The 2017 Act also provided new constitutional foundations. Section 1(1) establishes the Assembly and Welsh Government as '*a permanent part of the United Kingdom's constitutional arrangements*', while s. 1(3) declares they '*are not to be abolished except on the basis of a decision of the people of Wales voting in a referendum*'. The May 2020 renaming to 'Senedd Cymru' or 'Welsh Parliament' symbolically reinforced this constitutional elevation.

Lord Lloyd-Jones acknowledges the 2017 Act's intention to create stable, enduring devolution, but notes that '*it remains to be seen how long this fourth settlement will last in its present form, in particular having regard to the consequences of the United Kingdom's withdrawal from the European Union*'.[19] This observation highlights how external constitutional changes, EU withdrawal foremost among them, continue to challenge devolutionary arrangements, suggesting that Welsh constitutional evolution may not yet have reached its final form.

R. Rawlings, 'The Welsh Way/Y Ffordd Gymreigi', in J. Jowell and C. O'Cinneide, *The Changing Constitution* 9th edn (2019, Oxford: OUP 2019), pp. 297–8

> [We are witnessing] the emergence of a distinct Welsh Government approach to constitutional reform, not only for the sub-state polity itself, but also, under the banner of a 'new Union', for the UK as a whole. This entails an increasingly advanced form of quasi-federalism: most obviously with a view to navigating a famously uncodified constitution in a period of great unsettlement, close and creative engagement with federal-type ideas of enabling unity while guaranteeing diversity. Cast in terms of the UK as a multi- pluri-national state, and of the gradual development in the UK territorial constitution of a multi-level political system, 'new Union' thinking naturally challenges and runs up against a central government mind-set long conditioned by the doctrine and practice of Parliamentary Sovereignty. At one and the same time, the approach fits with a long tradition of federal-type thinking in the UK, notably revivified in recent years; the familiar difficulties of establishing a fully-fledged federal system in the UK, more especially the sheer dominance of England; and is all the more significant for being propounded by official actors.

[19] Lord Lloyd-Jones, 'Wales: Law in a Small Nation', in D. Clarry (ed.), *The UK Supreme Court Yearbook 2018–19 Vol.10i* (2021, London: Appellate Press), pp. 1001–121, 1107.

6.2.3 POLITICAL ORIGINS OF SCOTTISH DEVOLUTION

Scottish devolution's trajectory illustrates the constitutional changes from administrative decentralization within a unitary state to legislative autonomy within a devolved arrangement. This evolution reveals both the capacity of devolution for institutional development and the enduring tensions between territorial self-government and Union preservation.

From 1885 to 1999, the UK government decentralized extensive governmental functions to Scotland through the Scottish Office. This represented administrative convenience rather than constitutional autonomy: the Scottish Office remained staffed by central government officials, controlled by the Secretary of State for Scotland, and subject to Westminster's governmental majority.

This arrangement exemplified decentralization within unitary states—redistributing administrative powers while maintaining central supervision. Unlike devolution, which transfers authority to democratically accountable institutions, decentralization merely relocates bureaucratic functions without creating self-government.

The Scotland Act 1998 reversed these governance dynamics while expressly amending the 1707 Union settlement (s. 37). The Act created a unicameral Scottish Parliament operating under reserved powers, enabling primary legislation in all areas not explicitly reserved to Westminster. The Scottish Government, comprising ministers appointed by the First Minister and accountable to the Scottish Parliament, assumed responsibility for devolved policy areas.

Under the Scotland Act, law and policy in devolved areas became independent from Westminster politics, determined instead by Scottish electoral outcomes and political decisions. Most Scottish Office functions were transferred to the new Scottish Executive (later the Scottish Government), which completed the institutional alterations.

Devolution served dual purposes—territorial autonomy and Union consolidation. Section 28(7) of the Scotland Act explicitly preserves Westminster's authority: the Scottish Parliament's devolved powers '*do not affect the power of the Parliament of the United Kingdom to make laws for Scotland*'. While technically unnecessary given Parliament's inherent legislative supremacy, this provision symbolically reasserted central authority.

Westminster's practical constraints derive from the Legislative Consent (Sewel) Convention, under which Westminster would not normally legislate on devolved matters without Scottish Parliament consent (see s.6.4.1). This convention operates through political restraint rather than legal limitation, preserving formal supremacy while enabling practical cooperation.

The 2008 Calman Commission reviewed devolution's first decade, concluding it had been '*a real success*' while recommending enhanced tax-raising powers. The Scotland Act 2012 implemented these recommendations, enabling the Scottish Parliament to set income tax rates and bands for Scottish taxpayers (though personal allowances remain reserved) while relaxing borrowing restrictions.

The SNP's 2011 electoral majority intensified pressure for constitutional change by demanding an independence referendum. The September 2014 referendum produced an ambiguous outcome: 55 per cent chose Union retention, interpreted as both Union validation and a status quo rejection.

Pre-referendum promises by Conservative, Labour, and Liberal Democrat leaders pledged that rejecting independence would deliver '*faster, safer, and better change than separation*', making the Scottish Parliament 'permanent' with '*extensive new powers*'.[20] The Smith Commission subsequently recommended statutory recognition of the Sewel Convention alongside further devolution of powers.[21]

[20] 'The Vow', *Daily Record* 16 September 2014.

[21] *Report of the Smith Commission for Devolution of Further Powers to the Scottish Parliament* (2014), p. 22.

The question of whether Scotland could hold another independence referendum without Westminster consent remained unresolved until 2022. When the UK government refused to grant another Section 30 order, the Scottish Government drafted a Scottish Independence Referendum Bill, and the Lord Advocate referred its competence to the UK Supreme Court. In *Reference by the Lord Advocate*,[22] the Court unanimously held that legislation providing for an independence referendum relates to the reserved matters of '*the Union of the Kingdoms of Scotland and England*' and '*the Parliament of the United Kingdom*'.[23] Even though a referendum would have no immediate legal consequences, the Court recognised it as 'a political event with important political consequences' that had 'more than a loose or consequential connection' with parliamentary supremacy.[24] This ruling confirmed that Scottish independence referendums require Westminster's explicit consent, reinforcing the constitutional hierarchy within devolved arrangements.

The post-referendum commitments materialized through the Scotland Act 2016 and the Wales Act 2017. The 2022 Supreme Court ruling established definitive legal boundaries around Scottish constitutional aspirations, confirming that fundamental constitutional change requires Westminster consent regardless of devolved institutional development.

P. Petkar, 'Cracking a nut with a sledgehammer: the Lord Advocate's Reference on a second Scottish independence referendum in constitutional context' (2024) 75(2) *Northern Ireland Legal Quarterly* 370–383, 383.

> From a political perspective, the Court's judgment is undoubtedly a significant roadblock in the pathway to independence outlined by the Scottish Government in June 2022. In strict legal terms, it confirms that there is no free-standing constitutional pathway to secession for Scotland that does not involve the consent of the UK Government of the day, distinguishing Scotland from the position of Northern Ireland and reinforcing the complex and tailored nature of the UK's devolution settlement. The Court's reasoning, however, threatens to open a series of constitutional Pandora's boxes, with implications that stretch beyond the question of competence. It brings into focus the relationship between sub-state and UK-level institutions within the UK constitution, the voluntary nature of the union and the way in which power is actually distributed under Scotland's contemporary devolution settlement. It remains to be seen whether, in future cases on the Scottish Parliament's legislative competence, the Court will further develop this line of reasoning or indeed step back from it to reorient Scotland's devolution settlement towards the principle of subsidiarity on which it claims that devolution settlement is based.

Scotland's constitutional evolution demonstrates how devolution can develop from administrative convenience through legislative autonomy toward quasi-federal arrangements, while simultaneously revealing the persistent tensions between territorial self-government and constitutional unity that continue to shape UK territorial governance.

QUESTIONS

1. Why is Northern Ireland's power-sharing arrangement constitutionally distinct from Scottish and Welsh devolution? Consider the role of the peace process, equality provisions, and international dimensions.

[22] [2022] UKSC 31. [23] At [57]. [24] At [82].

2. The Belfast Agreement combines 'consociational' and 'confederal' elements. Explain what each term means and how the Agreement demonstrates both characteristics through its institutional arrangements.
3. Welsh devolution has evolved through four distinct phases since 1998. What should characterize a possible fifth phase? Consider powers, institutions, and constitutional status.
4. The 2022 Supreme Court ruling in *Reference by the Lord Advocate* established that Scotland cannot hold an independence referendum without Westminster consent. Analyse this decision in the context of the competing constitutional narratives examined in this chapter. Does the ruling demonstrate the continued dominance of the 'power-concentrating' constitutional model, or can it be reconciled with 'power-sharing' approaches to territorial governance?

6.3 THE TECHNICAL FRAMEWORK FOR DEVOLUTION

Multilevel governance operates through complex legal technicalities and practical realities. These arrangements are intricate, but this analysis focuses on the main institutional features rather than exhaustive detail.

UK devolution operates asymmetrically, with territories exercising varying forms and degrees of power. Scotland, Wales, and Northern Ireland possess legislatures and executives capable of primary law-making within their competencies. England lacks comparable devolved institutions.

English devolution follows a different trajectory through Metro Mayors—directly elected leaders of city regions like Greater Manchester, Liverpool City Region, and the West Midlands, introduced under the Cities and Local Government Devolution Act 2016. These arrangements remain limited to executive powers over housing, transport, planning, and policing, falling short of legislative devolution elsewhere (see Section 6.6).

Westminster's response through English Votes for English Laws (EVEL) proved unsuccessful, operating from 2015–20 before abandonment. English governance from Westminster remains highly centralized, creating constitutional tensions within the Union's architecture (see Section 6.6).

This institutional diversity requires systematic examination of how power operates across different devolutionary models.

6.3.1 TWO MODELS OF POWER ALLOCATION

Any system allocating powers between national and sub-national government faces two design choices:

(a) **Reserved powers model**: Define powers exercised at the national level, with sub-national units possessing all remaining authority; or

(b) **Conferred powers model**: Define sub-national powers specifically, with all other authority remaining at the national level.

These models create different presumptions about where authority resides and affect how competence disputes are resolved. Despite their different power-sharing architectures, all three devolution settlements impose similar general restrictions on devolved institutions. Devolved governments and legislatures cannot legislate or take executive action contrary to retained EU law or Convention rights under the European Convention on Human Rights. These constraints ensure constitutional coherence across the UK's territorial constitution while preserving space for policy innovation within devolved competences.

6.3.2 POLICY DIVERGENCE: INNOVATION AND INTEGRATION CHALLENGES

Devolution's practical operation produces a basic consequence: different policies, authorized by different laws, are now implemented across the United Kingdom's constituent territories. This shift from uniform policy toward regional approaches brings decision-making closer to communities, enabling them to tailor policies to local needs and preferences.

This policy differentiation represents the core purpose of devolution. Rhodri Morgan, Welsh First Minister from 2000–9, envisioned devolution providing 'a "living laboratory", in which different approaches to common problems can be worked out and applied'.[25] Contemporary examples demonstrate this laboratory in action: Scotland provides free long-term elderly care while England and Wales have rejected this approach; university tuition fees operate in England and Wales but not Scotland; and school performance information systems differ markedly, with Wales using a National School Categorisation System while England relies on league tables measuring performance through different metrics.

Policy divergence creates practical complications within the UK's highly integrated economy, society, transport networks, and business supply chains. The Coronavirus pandemic illustrated these tensions. While the UK government managed most economic support measures, health and education remained devolved to Scotland, Wales, and Northern Ireland. Initially, the four governments coordinated their response, making lockdown decisions jointly. This cooperation proved temporary as divergent approaches emerged. Lockdown restrictions were eased at different times and through different mechanisms across the UK's territories, creating confusion for businesses and citizens operating across territorial boundaries.

These coordination challenges demonstrate that policy divergence requires management through intergovernmental discussion, information sharing, and joint decision-making where policies intersect across territorial boundaries (see further Section 6.5).

6.3.3 SCOTLAND

The Scottish Parliament and Scottish Government operate under the reserved powers model, possessing authority over all 'matters' not expressly 'reserved' to the United Kingdom. This creates a presumption in favour of devolved competence, with Westminster retaining only specifically enumerated powers.

Schedule 5 of the Scotland Act 1998 establishes this reservation framework through two categories. 'General reservations' encompass core state functions: the constitution, regulation of political parties, foreign affairs, the civil service, defence, and treason. These reflect powers typically associated with national sovereignty and external relations.

'Specific reservations' are organized under detailed 'heads' covering: financial and economic matters; home affairs; trade and industry; energy; transport; social security; regulation of the professions; employment; health and medicines; media and culture; and miscellaneous matters (including judicial remuneration and equal opportunities). This comprehensive framework attempts to delineate where Westminster authority ends and Scottish competence begins.

Devolution has proven dynamic rather than static, with Scottish powers expanding since 1998. The Scotland Act 2012 extended tax powers to the Scottish Parliament, moving beyond the original administrative devolution toward fiscal autonomy. The Scotland Act 2016 represented a more substantial

[25] Speech to the National Centre for Public Policy, Swansea, December 2002.

transfer, conferring enhanced law-making powers and executive functions over income tax rates and bands, welfare, equal opportunities, abortion law, and onshore oil and gas extraction licensing.

This evolutionary process has changed Scotland's fiscal position. Once fully implemented, the revenue-raising powers granted by these Acts will enable the Scottish Parliament to raise almost 50 per cent of its budget,[26] creating what one authority describes as '*wider fiscal devolution than in many federal states, including Switzerland, often thought of as the most decentralized federal democracy in the world*'.[27] This development represents a shift from administrative devolution toward something approaching fiscal federalism, even within the UK's formally unitary constitutional structure.

6.3.4 NORTHERN IRELAND

Northern Ireland operates under a constitutional framework that reflects both its political circumstances and gradual evolution toward fuller devolution. Section 4 of the Northern Ireland Act 1998 establishes a tripartite categorization of powers: 'excepted matters' intended never to be devolved; 'reserved matters' which may be devolved in the future but currently remain with Westminster; and 'transferred matters' already devolved to the Northern Ireland Assembly and Executive.

Schedule 2's excepted matters encompass core state functions permanently retained by Westminster, reflecting both constitutional principle and Northern Ireland's particular circumstances. These include sovereign powers (the Crown, UK Parliament, international relations, defence, and control of weapons of mass destruction) alongside matters of UK-wide application such as nationality, immigration, asylum, UK taxation, and national insurance. This category also reflects Northern Ireland's specific constitutional position through inclusions like the Northern Ireland Constitution Act 1973 and the office of the Advocate General for Northern Ireland (the UK government's principal legal adviser on Northern Ireland law).

Schedule 3's reserved matters fall between Westminster's powers currently exercised and those potentially transferable to Northern Ireland in the future. These encompass diverse areas, including navigation, civil aviation, postal services, minimum wages, financial services, telecommunications, and human genetics. This category provides constitutional flexibility and enables the gradual expansion of devolved competence as political conditions permit.

'Transferred matters' under section 4 constitute the operational core of Northern Ireland devolution. The Northern Ireland Executive's ministerial departments span: education; enterprise, trade, and investment; health, social services, and public safety; social development; employment and learning; justice; environment; culture, arts, and leisure; regional development; and agriculture and rural development.

The devolution of justice and policing powers in April 2010 was particularly significant, given the sensitivity of these functions within Northern Ireland's divided society.[28] This transfer demonstrated both the maturation of the peace process and the deepening of devolved governance beyond the original 1998 settlement.

Northern Ireland's tripartite model provides constitutional flexibility absent from the binary arrangements in Scotland and Wales. The reserved matters category enables incremental power transfers as political consensus develops, while excepted matters provide constitutional certainty about Westminster's permanent role. This graduated approach reflects both the peace process's evolutionary character and the need for adaptable governance arrangements within Northern Ireland's constitutional circumstances.

[26] House of Commons Library, *Scotland: Public Spending and Revenue*, 13 September 2021, p. 13.
[27] V. Bogdanor, *Beyond Brexit: Towards a British Constitution* (2019, London: I.B. Tauris), p. 181.
[28] Northern Ireland Act 2009 and the Department of Justice Act (Northern Ireland) 2010.

6.3.5 WALES

Welsh devolution exemplifies constitutional adaptation through successive reforms since 1998. Unlike Scotland's relatively stable reserved powers model, Wales has experienced systematic restructuring of its devolutionary framework, culminating in the current constitutional settlement that mirrors Scottish arrangements while reflecting Wales's distinct trajectory.

From 1998 to 2017, Welsh devolution operated under a conferred powers model that granted the National Assembly authority to make laws only on specifically enumerated subjects. This restrictive approach initially limited the Assembly to secondary legislation, with primary law-making powers developing gradually. Laws were first designated 'Assembly Measures' (2006–11) before acquiring the enhanced status of 'Acts of the Assembly,' reflecting the incremental expansion of legislative competence.

The conferred subjects encompassed: agriculture, forestry, animals, plants, and rural development; ancient monuments and historic buildings; culture; economic development; education and training; environment; fire and rescue services; food; health and health services; highways and transport; housing; local government; public administration; social welfare; sport and recreation; tourism; town and country planning; water and flood defence; and the Welsh language. Reflecting Wales's bilingual character, all legislation is drafted in both English and Welsh.

The Wales Act 2017 restructured Welsh devolution by abandoning the conferred powers model in favour of reserved powers similar to Scotland's. The Government of Wales Act 2006, Schedule 7A now employs the concepts of 'reservation', 'exception', and 'carve out' to define the Assembly's jurisdictional limits. This represents a more flexible approach that presumes devolved competence except where specifically reserved.

This restructuring included matters of constitutional importance that were reserved to Westminster: the constitution; public service; political parties; the single legal jurisdiction of England and Wales; tribunals; foreign affairs; and defence. Section 1 of the 2006 Act was amended to declare that '*The Assembly established by Part 1 and the Welsh Government established by Part 2 are a permanent part of the United Kingdom's constitutional arrangements*'. This language echoes the permanency clause included in the Scotland Act 2016.

The National Assembly also acquired fiscal powers, gaining authority to vary income tax rates by ten pence in the pound. This represented a shift toward fiscal devolution, though more limited than Scotland's extensive revenue-raising capabilities.

Wales's evolution from conferred to reserved powers represents more than technical restructuring. It signifies constitutional maturation from administrative devolution toward legislative autonomy. This development positions Wales closer to Scottish levels of self-government while maintaining its distinct institutional character, demonstrating how devolutionary arrangements can adapt to changing political circumstances and constitutional expectations (see Table 6.1).

- 'Central government' (not a technical legal term) and the UK Parliament is responsible for policy matters affecting the whole of the United Kingdom.
- Regional or 'devolved' governments and legislatures were created in 1999 for three parts of the country: Northern Ireland, Scotland, and Wales. This decentralized structure is said to be 'asymmetrical' because there is no government or legislature for England (the largest part of the United Kingdom, with 84 per cent of the population). Since 1999, the devolved institutions have gained greater powers.

- At local level, there are 382 principal councils (317 within England, 22 within Wales, 32 within Scotland and 11 within Northern Ireland) with roughly 20,000 elected councillors providing political leadership. The overall structure of local government is complex. In most of England, responsibility for council services is split between two tiers—county and district. Larger towns, cities, and some counties have one level of local government for all services—the unitary authority. If all tiers of local government in England are counted (including town, parish, community, neighbourhood, and village councils with relatively few powers), there are around 12,800 local councils across the entirety of the UK.

QUESTIONS

1. Compare the conferred powers model and the reserved powers model as methods of allocating competence between Westminster and devolved institutions. What are the practical implications of each approach for devolved legislatures and for resolving competence disputes?
2. Why was devolution implemented asymmetrically across Scotland, Wales, and Northern Ireland, with different institutional arrangements, powers, and timelines? Was this differentiated approach constitutionally appropriate or would a more uniform model have been preferable?
3. Northern Ireland's tripartite power structure includes 'reserved matters' that may be devolved in future, unlike the binary arrangements in Scotland and Wales. Does this intermediate category represent constitutional wisdom given Northern Ireland's circumstances, or does it create unnecessary complexity and uncertainty about the scope of devolved authority?

6.4 THE CONSTITUTIONAL STATUS OF DEVOLUTION

The 2014 Scottish Independence referendum triggered constitutional reforms. The Scotland Act 2016 and Wales Act 2017 made two changes to the principal devolution statutes: the Scotland Act 1998 and the Government of Wales Act 2006. First, they addressed the UK Parliament's authority to legislate on devolved matters. Second, they established the devolved institutions as 'permanent'.

These changes crystallize the central tension explored in Section 6.1.2: has the UK constitution retained its monolithic foundations rooted in power concentration and parliamentary supremacy, or can a power-sharing conception accommodate divided authority within devolved governance? Do these reforms represent continuity with established British political tradition, or do they signal the gradual erosion of legislative supremacy and a constitutional rupture?

Each change requires detailed examination, beginning with the statutory recognition of the Sewel Convention.

6.4.1 THE SEWEL CONVENTION: LEGAL SYMBOL OR CONSTITUTIONAL PRINCIPLE?

The statutory formulation of the Sewel Convention is set out in the amended Scotland Act 1998, which now explicitly recognises Westminster's constitutional restraint.

Scotland Act 1998 (as amended by the Scotland Act 2016)

28 Acts of the Scottish Parliament[29]

[...]

(7) This section does not affect the power of the Parliament of the United Kingdom to make laws for Scotland.

(8) But it is recognised that the Parliament of the United Kingdom will not normally legislate with regard to devolved matters without the consent of the Scottish Parliament

The first change concerns a convention named after Lord Sewel, the Minister of State in the Scotland Office, who shepherded the Scotland Bill through the House of Lords in 1998. During a July 1998 debate, Lord Sewel acknowledged that while devolution preserved the UK Parliament's ability to legislate for Scotland, '*we would expect a convention to be established that Westminster would not normally legislate with regard to devolved matters in Scotland without the consent of the Scottish Parliament*'.[30]

This political understanding became institutionalized. By 2001, the Sewel Convention was formally incorporated into the Memorandum of Understanding between the UK government and devolved administrations. Devolution guidance notes subsequently expanded their scope, recognising that the convention applies whenever Westminster legislation would expand or diminish devolved legislative or executive powers.[31]

This development raises questions about constitutional conventions. As non-legal rules of political behaviour, conventions bind political actors through acceptance rather than judicial enforcement. The Sewel Convention exemplifies this characteristic, operating through Westminster's self-restraint. But the 2016 and 2017 Acts placed this convention on a statutory footing.

This statutory recognition prompts a constitutional question: does placing the Sewel Convention in statute merely enhance its visibility, or does it transform a political convention into a legally enforceable principle? The answer has implications for understanding parliamentary supremacy in the devolved constitution.

House of Lords Select Committee on the Constitution, 'Proposals for the devolution of further powers to Scotland', 10th Report of Session 2014–15, March 2015

72. Although [by way of s. 28(8)] the Sewel convention will be put on a statutory footing, the measure seems to have only symbolic significance, consolidating the idea that Scottish devolution is a permanent arrangement, the terms of which will not be changed unilaterally by the UK Parliament. Aside from the general rule that Parliament is unable to bind its successors [...], the use of the word 'normally' (which is unusual in legislation and is undefined) seems to make clear that Parliament will still have the legal power to legislate for Scotland, even on devolved matters, without the consent of the Scottish Parliament. Therefore, it can be said that the new provision will recognise the existence of the Sewel convention rather than turn it into a legally binding principle.

[29] See also Government of Wales Act 2006, s. 107(5); Northern Ireland Act 1998, s. 5(6).

[30] Lord Sewel, HL Deb, vol. 592, col. 791 (21 July 1998).

[31] Cabinet Office, *Devolution Guidance Notes 8–10*, available at https://www.gov.uk/government/publications/devolution-guidance-notes

We need to distinguish carefully between what the statute *says* and what it *means*. According to the text, the statute *recognises* that Westminster will not *normally* legislate on matters that fall within devolved competence without the consent of the Scottish or Welsh legislatures. It does not stipulate that the UK Parliament is disabled from legislating on devolved matters without such consent. The House of Lords Select Committee report stresses that its new statutory footing only has '*symbolic significance*' and does not transform the Convention into a '*legally binding principle*'.

Understanding the provision's meaning requires a broader constitutional context. Judicial interpretation has begun to challenge orthodox constitutional assumptions. This emerging jurisprudence provides background for assessing the Sewel Convention's statutory recognition.

Judicial interpretation has evolved towards treating devolution legislation as constitutionally distinct. In *Thoburn*, Laws LJ classified the devolution Acts as '*constitutional statutes*' subject to express repeal only.[32] Lord Steyn in *Jackson* argued that the Scotland Act 1998 pointed to '*a divided sovereignty*', adding that '*the classic account of the doctrine of the supremacy of Parliament, pure and absolute as it was, can now be seen to be out of place in the modern UK*'.[33] Lord Bingham in *Robinson* described the Northern Ireland Act 1998 as a 'constitution' requiring interpretation '*generously and purposively, bearing in mind the values which the constitutional provisions are intended to embody*'.[34] Lord Hope in *Imperial Tobacco* reinforced this approach, observing that the Scotland Act should be interpreted purposively as '*a generous settlement of legislative authority*'.[35] This judicial evolution culminated in the Smith Commission's 2014 recommendation for statutory recognition of the Sewel Convention alongside the devolved institutions' permanence.

These developments reveal devolution legislation pulling in contradictory directions. The legislation expressly preserves Westminster's power-concentrating capacity to enact laws for Scotland, Wales, and Northern Ireland. Simultaneously, a competing strand of constitutional thought, traceable to T.B. Smith and Lord President Cooper, advocates power-sharing and diffusion, favouring '*generous and purposive*' interpretation while viewing Dicey's account of parliamentary supremacy as parochially English and anachronistic.

This tension between orthodox and revisionist constitutional thinking provides context for understanding how the statutory Sewel Convention operates in practice. The UK Supreme Court's engagement with these issues in *Miller (No. 1)* illustrates that tension. While the case concerned the question whether the UK government required parliamentary authorization to trigger Article 50, the Northern Ireland references forced the Court to consider whether devolved consent was needed under the Sewel Convention, given the EU withdrawal's implications for devolved policy areas and institutional powers. The Court's analysis reveals how statutory recognition affects the Convention's constitutional status.

R (Miller) v Secretary of State for Exiting the European Union
[2017] UKSC 5; [2018] AC 61

> 151. In reaching this conclusion we do not underestimate the importance of constitutional conventions, some of which play a fundamental role in the operation of our constitution. The Sewel Convention has an important role in facilitating harmonious relationships between the UK Parliament and the devolved legislatures. But the policing of its scope and the manner of its operation does not lie within the constitutional remit of the judiciary, which is to protect the rule of law.

[32] *Thoburn v Sunderland CC* [2003] QB 151, 189.

[33] *Jackson v Attorney-General* [2005] UKHL 56, [2006] 1 AC 262, 302, para. [102]; see also Lord Hope [104].

[34] *Robinson v Secretary of State for Northern Ireland* [2002] UKHL 32, [2002] NI 390, 398 [11]. See also per Lord Hoffmann at [25].

[35] *Imperial Tobacco Ltd v Lord Advocate (Scotland)* [2012] UKSC 61; 2013 SCLR 121 [51].

The UK Supreme Court's analysis constitutes a balancing act. The Court expressly recognises the '*fundamental role*' of the Sewel Convention '*in facilitating harmonious relationships*' between the centre and the regions, acknowledging that the Convention performs a constitutional function within devolutionary arrangements.

This recognition comes with limitations. As a matter of law, the Court maintains that UK Parliament's legislative authority remains unaffected by either the devolution legislation or the Sewel Convention. This distinction reflects an asymmetry in judicial approach: power-concentrating assumptions of the constitution attract judicial protection, while power-diffusion mechanisms are relegated to political convention.

This judicial position might suggest an impasse between parliamentary supremacy and the constitutional principles necessary for territorial governance. Such a reading oversimplifies the constitutional dynamics at work. The apparent deadlock dissolves when we recognise that legal and constitutional constraints operate on different planes.

This understanding builds upon constitutional thinking that stretches back to Dicey himself. Recall that even Dicey acknowledged practical limitations on parliamentary power, describing it as '*political madness to tamper [with the Act of Union] gratuitously*'. Modern constitutional scholars have developed this insight further, distinguishing between what Parliament may legally do and what it should constitutionally do. Mark Elliott's analysis exemplifies this approach, offering a framework that reconciles formal legal supremacy with substantive constitutional constraints:

M. Elliott, 'Parliamentary Sovereignty in a Changing Constitutional Landscape', in J. Jowell and C. O'Cinneide (eds) *The Changing Constitution*, 9th edn (2019, Oxford: OUP) p. 38

> The reason why it is politically difficult (but not necessarily impossible) for the UK Parliament to ride roughshod over the devolved institutions is rooted in deeper constitutional principles. That such principles are not enshrined in a written constitution does not detract from the appropriateness of regarding them as constitutional—indeed, as constitutionally fundamental—in character. Understood thus, the devolution schemes may not affect a legal division of authority between the UK legislature and its devolved counterparts, but this is not incompatible with the view that the devolution schemes effect a constitutional division of authority. As a result, it is entirely plausible to imagine UK legislation that might be lawful (because it cannot be otherwise) but unconstitutional (because it breaches fundamental principles such as those that are institutionalized by the Sewel convention). In this way, the devolved competences set out in the devolution legislation can properly be regarded as benchmarks by reference to which the constitutionality—as distinct from the legal validity—of UK legislation may be assessed.

6.4.2 PERMANENCE CLAUSES AND PARLIAMENTARY LIMITS

The second major change introduced by the post-2014 devolution legislation concerns the explicit designation of devolved institutions as 'permanent' within the UK's constitutional architecture—a development that challenges parliamentary supremacy more directly than the Sewel Convention.

The concept of 'permanence' in constitutional law raises questions about the nature of parliamentary sovereignty. If Parliament is indeed unbound by legal limits when it enacts legislation, as Dicey asserted, can it simultaneously declare certain institutions to be permanent? This apparent paradox is expressed in s. 63A of the Scotland Act 1998:

Scotland Act 1998 (as amended by the Scotland Act 2016)

63a Permanence of the Scottish Parliament and Scottish Government[36]

(1) The Scottish Parliament and the Scottish Government are a permanent part of the United Kingdom's constitutional arrangements.

(2) The purpose of this section is, with due regard to the other provisions of this Act, to signify the commitment of the Parliament and Government of the United Kingdom to the Scottish Parliament and the Scottish Government.

(3) In view of that commitment it is declared that the Scottish Parliament and the Scottish Government are not to be abolished except on the basis of a decision of the people of Scotland voting in a referendum.

The statutory language merits closer analysis. The text recognises the devolved institutions as 'a permanent part' of the UK's constitution, with the stated purpose being '*to signify the commitment*' to this permanence. Furthermore, it declares that the devolved institutions '*are not to be abolished*' without a referendum.

This formulation deliberately evokes historical constitutional guarantees. The provision recalls the Treaty of Union 1707's promises to endure '*forever after*' (Article I) and '*in all time coming*' (Article XIX)—language that T.B. Smith and Lord President Cooper argued created binding constitutional constraints on parliamentary power. The historical parallel is not coincidental; it represents a conscious attempt to ground contemporary devolution in Scotland's constitutional tradition.

These linguistic choices raise questions about parliamentary sovereignty. Does permanent constitute procedural entrenchment, protecting devolved institutions from abolition without referendum? If so, has Parliament effectively limited its own supreme authority? The implications reach beyond technical legal analysis to the heart of UK constitutional doctrine.

The immediate answer appears straightforward: devolution remains compatible with parliamentary supremacy and broader British constitutional tradition. Parliament retains its theoretical capacity to repeal any legislation, including provisions declaring institutions 'permanent'. This orthodox response, while legally correct, may obscure more complex constitutional dynamics at work.

The permanence provision may serve as more than political symbolism. While formally preserving parliamentary supremacy, it could, in practice, constrain its exercise through constitutional expectations about appropriate parliamentary behaviour.

House of Lords Constitution Committee, Sixth Report, Scotland Bill, November 2015

31. [Section 63A (1) of the Scotland Act 1998] seems to strengthen this argument. First, [. . .] it does not say that the Scottish Parliament and Government are 'recognized' as permanent, but states boldly that they are permanent. Secondly, sub-section [s. 63A(2)] signifies the commitment of

[36] See also Government of Wales Act 2006, s. A1.

> the Parliament and Government of the United Kingdom to the Scottish Parliament and the Scottish Government. On the one hand, this might serve to weaken the effect of the section as a whole: if the purpose of the section is to 'signify the commitment', then that might be taken to mean that it is not the purpose of the section to (among other things) prevent the UK Parliament from going back on that commitment. But another reading, and the one seemingly more consistent with the overall thrust of the new section seen in the light of the Vow, the Smith Commission and subsequent events, is that this is indeed an explicit attempt to make clear what is intended by the Clause as a whole; sub-section (2) is in effect an aid to interpretation that affirms Parliament's commitment to the permanence of the Scottish institutions.
>
> 32. It has long been a fundamental tenet of the UK constitution that Parliament is sovereign and that no Parliament can bind its successors. But while it has always been highly implausible in political terms, if not absurd, to consider a scenario in which Parliament might unilaterally attempt to abolish the Scottish Parliament, there is now a stronger legal argument that such a move might be interpreted by the courts as no longer valid. The most significant provision is sub-section [s. 63A(3)]. This introduces a step by which Parliament appears to make its own legislative competence contingent upon an intervening stage, namely a referendum result in Scotland in favour of abolition of the Scottish Parliament. This new clause may be seen as something of a half-way house; a contingent rather than an absolute form of self-limitation. It is not that Parliament cannot abolish the Scottish Parliament, but that it has circumscribed the conditions under which it may do so by creating the referendum requirement.
>
> 33. It is uncertain whether or not the courts would recognize such a contingent self-limitation, but it is at least arguable that they would [see *Jackson v Attorney General* (2006) 1AC 262] Parliament has legislated previously to alter the process by which legislation is to be made, notably in the Parliament Acts [1911 and 1949] [which created internal procedural changes to the passage of legislation].

The House of Lords Constitution Committee's analysis builds upon established constitutional theory to support this interpretation. Drawing on the 'manner and form' theory of parliamentary supremacy explored in Chapter 3, the Committee argues for '*a contingent rather than absolute form of self-limitation*'. Parliament ought to constrain future action by requiring specific procedures, in this case a referendum, before devolved institutions can be abolished.

While courts might not confidently prioritize the Scotland Act 1998 over a hypothetical 'Abolition of the Scottish Parliament Act 20XX', the constitutional landscape has shifted. The argument for procedural entrenchment has gained credibility through the accumulation of judicial precedents (*Thoburn*, *Jackson*, *Robinson*) and the post-2014 legislative reforms that explicitly recognise devolution's permanence. This evolution suggests that what once seemed constitutionally implausible may now merit judicial consideration.

This constitutional evolution faces resistance from judicial orthodoxy. McCrudden and Halberstam exemplify scholarly frustration with the courts' conservative approach to the constitutional significance of devolution. Their critique targets the UK Supreme Court's treatment of devolution in *Miller*, which they argue perpetuates outdated constitutional assumptions despite devolution's transformative impact.

The authors contend that the Court approached devolution from a conservative premise: assuming a power-concentrating constitution characterized by unitary state structures, centralized executive authority, and unqualified legislative supremacy. From this perspective, devolution's innovations since 1998 appear symbolic rather than constitutionally significant. McCrudden and Halberstam's criticism encompasses both the Court's explicit reasoning and its silences about devolution's constitutional implications:

C. McCrudden and D. Halberstam, '*Miller* and Northern Ireland: A Critical Constitutional Response', in *The UK Supreme Court Yearbook 2016-2017 Vol. 8.* (2018, London: Appellate Press), pp. 299–343, 337

What is missing from the Court's analysis [in *R (Miller) v Secretary of State for Exiting the European Union*], an analysis that was conservative even from pre-1972 standards, is any recognition that something fundamental occurred with the enactment of the statutes devolving powers to the Scottish Parliament and the Northern Ireland and Welsh Assemblies. There is no recognition that Parliament had overseen a transformation of the UK constitution, whilst preserving its ultimate authority, and no understanding that one major effect of these changes was to create a multi-level system of government, in which there is a complex relationship between the institutions of the devolved nations, the central Government, and the EU, and that this complex relationship requires to be managed in ways that Dicey would hardly relish.

The analysis of both the Sewel Convention and permanence provisions reveals a tension in contemporary constitutional discourse. UK constitutional debate is increasingly marked by a fault line between legal limits to parliamentary supremacy (what Parliament cannot do) and moral or political limits (what Parliament ought not to do). This distinction proves essential for understanding how devolution challenges traditional constitutional orthodoxy while remaining within established legal frameworks.

All the commentators examined—from the House of Lords Constitution Committee to academic critics like McCrudden, Halberstam, and Elliott—accept Dicey's negative limb of parliamentary supremacy: no person or body may override or set aside an Act of the UK Parliament. Their constitutional challenge targets instead the positive limb asserting Parliament's absolute legislative supremacy.

This scholarly re-examination is especially urgent in the context of devolution. As McCrudden and Halberstam argue, devolution has 'transformed' the UK constitution, while Elliott contends it has created '*a constitutional division of authority*' that demands recognition. These changes generate new constitutional expectations about appropriate parliamentary behaviour.

The practical implications become clear when we consider Parliament's theoretical power to abolish devolved institutions. While legally possible, such unilateral action would violate emerging constitutional norms. Parliament ought not to '*unilaterally attempt to abolish the Scottish Parliament*'—a scenario the House of Lords Constitution Committee branded 'absurd', echoing Dicey's own recognition that tampering with the Act of Union 1707 would constitute 'political madness'.

This convergence of opinion reflects growing recognition that underlying constitutional principles within the unwritten constitution create substantive, if not legally enforceable, constraints on parliamentary action. These principles affirm Parliament's commitment to both the Sewel Convention and the permanence of devolved institutions, transforming what might once have been political promises into constitutional obligations that responsible governance must respect.

The constitutional tension between legal orthodoxy and devolutionary innovation extends beyond these reforms. This dynamic emerges in the UK Supreme Court's interpretation of the competence provisions that define devolved powers. The tension becomes evident in the Court's approach to s. 29 of the Scotland Act 1998, which establishes that '*An Act of the Scottish Parliament is not law so far as any provision of the Act is outside the legislative competence of the Parliament*'.

While this provision might appear straightforward, its interpretation reveals the deeper constitutional currents examined here. The Supreme Court's recent engagement with this section in the *UNCRC* case demonstrates how judicial attitudes toward devolution continue to reflect the broader constitutional fault line between power-concentrating and power-sharing conceptions of the UK constitution.

6.4.3 DEVOLUTION AND THE COURTS

The constitutional tensions examined throughout this chapter find their clearest expression in the judicial interpretation of devolution legislation. The courts' evolving approach reveals competing visions of devolved competence and the balance between Westminster supremacy and territorial autonomy.

Early cases established a framework respecting devolved democratic processes. *AXA General Insurance v Lord Advocate*[37] concerned a challenge by insurance companies to Scottish legislation expanding asbestos-related compensation, arguing it violated their human rights and exceeded devolved competence. The Supreme Court rejected these challenges, with Lord Hope articulating judicial restraint: '*The democratic process is liable to be subverted if, on a question of political or moral judgment, opponents of an Act achieve through the courts what they could not achieve through Parliament*'.[38] Meanwhile, *Martin v Most*[39] questioned whether the Scottish Parliament could legislate on executing judicial warrants. This was ostensibly a devolved justice matter that could have affected reserved criminal law. The case demonstrated the practical complexity of competence boundaries, showing how seemingly devolved matters could intersect with reserved areas and requiring careful analysis of the cross-border effects of legislation.

Following these early cases, courts developed a more expansive approach. In *Robinson v Secretary of State for Northern Ireland*,[40] the House of Lords characterized devolution legislation as effectively '*a constitution*' requiring '*generous and purposive*' interpretation. This approach was reinforced in *Imperial Tobacco v Lord Advocate*,[41] where the Supreme Court described the Scotland Act as '*a generous settlement of legislative authority*'.

Constitutional tensions crystallized in 2021 when the Scottish Parliament attempted ambitious constitutional legislation incorporating the United Nations Convention on the Rights of the Child (UNCRC) into Scottish law. The UNCRC Bill drew on the architecture of the Human Rights Act 1998, with key provisions (ss. 19–21) establishing mechanisms for protecting rights. First, an interpretative obligation requiring Scottish law '*so far as it is possible to do so . . . be read and given effect in a way which is compatible with the UNCRC requirements*'. This mirrors the HRA's s. 3 duty. Second, judicial powers to issue a '*strike down declarator*' against incompatible existing legislation and an 'incompatibility declarator' against future legislation, echoing the HRA's s. 4 mechanism. Crucially, these provisions would have applied not only to Acts of the Scottish Parliament but to all legislation operating in Scotland, including Acts of the UK Parliament. This meant that a devolved legislature was, in effect, seeking to subject Westminster legislation to judicial reinterpretation and challenge within devolved territory.

This innovation prompted immediate resistance from the UK government. Under s. 33 powers in the Scotland Act 1998, the UK government referred the Bill's competence to the UK Supreme Court, challenging provisions requiring UNCRC compliance of all legislation, including Westminster Acts, and judicial discretion to strike down or declare Westminster legislation incompatible.

The Supreme Court adopted a restrictive approach that departed from earlier jurisprudence. Rather than applying '*generous and purposive*' interpretation, the Court declared that the Scotland Act '*must be interpreted in the same way as any other statute*' according to the '*ordinary meaning of the words*'.[42] The Court held that requiring judicial reinterpretation, which might conflict with Parliament's

[37] [2011] UKSC 46. [38] Lord Hope at [49]. [39] [2010] UKSC 10. [40] [2002] UKHL 32.

[41] [2012] UKSC 61.

[42] *Reference by the Attorney General and the Advocate General for Scotland—United Nations Convention on the Rights of the Child (Incorporation) (Scotland) Bill* [2021] UKSC 42; (2021) SCLR 629.

intention, would modify s. 28(7) of the Scotland Act 1998, which seeks to preserve Westminster's legislative power. Consequently, ss. 19–21 violated s. 29's competence requirements: '*A provision which required the courts to modify the meaning and effect of legislation enacted by Parliament would plainly impose a qualification upon its legislative power*'.[43]

This reasoning has attracted academic criticism, with commentators identifying shifts from generous constitutional interpretation toward restrictive formalism.

M. Elliott and N. Kilford, 'Devolution in the Supreme Court: Legislative supremacy, Parliament's "unqualified" power, and "modifying" the Scotland Act', U.K. Const. L. Blog (15 October 2021)

> The cumulative effect is a highly unconvincing judgment that reads the Scottish devolution settlement unnecessarily narrowly — an outcome that the Court prepares the ground for at the outset of its judgment when it says that the Scotland Act 'must be interpreted in the same way as any other statute' and according to its 'ordinary words' [7]. This approach completes the retreat from *Robinson v Secretary of State for Northern Ireland*, in which it was said that devolution legislation should be 'interpreted generously and purposively', moving instead towards a more limited conception of devolution that diminishes it by virtue of an interpretation of the underlying legislation which is far from favourable towards the devolved institutions.

The judicial evolution from expansive interpretation (*Robinson*, *Imperial Tobacco*) through democratic deference (*AXA*) to restrictive formalism (*UNCRC Reference*) reflects the deeper tension between power-concentrating and power-sharing constitutional models examined throughout this chapter. This shift toward restrictive interpretation represents a constraint on devolved competence and may signal broader judicial skepticism about territorial autonomy within the UK's constitutional framework—a theme to which we will return in Section 24.6.2.

6.4.4 SECTION 35 OF THE SCOTLAND ACT

These constitutional dynamics materialized in January 2023 when the UK government exercised Section 35 of the Scotland Act 1998 for the first time since devolution began. Secretary of State Alister Jack prevented the Gender Recognition Reform (Scotland) Bill from proceeding to Royal Assent, arguing that the legislation would adversely affect the operation of UK-wide equality law, and specifically the Equality Act 2010 (a reserved matter). This intervention represented a defining moment in devolution's evolution, demonstrating the UK Government's retained constitutional authority to veto devolved legislation that impacts reserved competences. The Scottish Government's immediate challenge through judicial review ultimately failed when the Court of Session ruled in December 2023 that the UK government had acted lawfully,[44] with the Scottish Government subsequently deciding not to appeal. Beyond its immediate legal significance, the Section 35 episode signifies the enduring tension between devolved autonomy and Westminster supremacy, illustrating how the formal preservation of UK parliamentary authority continues to constrain Scottish legislative independence despite 25 years of devolutionary practice.

[43] *Reference by the Attorney General and the Advocate General for Scotland—United Nations Convention on the Rights of the Child (Incorporation) (Scotland) Bill* [2021] UKSC 42; (2021) SCLR 629 [28], per Lord Reed.

[44] *Re Scottish Ministers' Petition* [2023] CSOH 89.

Chris McCorkindale and Aileen McHarg, '*Rescuing the Gender Recognition Reform (Scotland) Bill?* The Scottish Government's Challenge to the Section 35 Order', U.K. Const. L. Blog (25 April 2023)

Indeed, the way in which this dispute is resolved could well represent a watershed moment in the history of devolution. The GRR Bill has been remarkable for the extent to which opponents have sought to make use of arguments about devolved competence throughout the legislative process, and of the opportunities that the devolution legislation affords for 'forum-shifting' from the Scottish to the UK level, where their criticisms of the Bill have found a more receptive political audience. This kind of 'weaponisation' of decision-making constraints is no doubt inevitable in any system of constitutionally-limited and multi-level government. Nevertheless, the UK courts have in the past shown themselves to be sensitive to the fact that, as Lord Hope has said, 'the democratic process is liable to be subverted if, on a question of political or moral judgment, opponents of an Act achieve through the courts what they could not achieve through Parliament' (AXA, [49]). As this case makes its way through the courts, we hope that judges will be equally alive to the dangers to Scottish democracy – and indeed to the central constitutional purpose of devolution – of allowing policy choices allocated to the devolved level to be too easily overturned by the UK Government.

QUESTIONS

1. Has devolution transformed the UK's territorial constitution or merely created administrative decentralization within an essentially unitary framework? Consider both institutional changes and evolving constitutional principles.
2. The Sewel Convention's statutory recognition in 2016–17 raises questions about the relationship between political conventions and legal rules. Does this development represent constitutional change or symbolic recognition? What are the implications for parliamentary supremacy?
3. What is the constitutional significance of declaring devolved institutions 'permanent'? Does this language create meaningful constraints on Westminster's legislative authority, or does it remain subordinate to parliamentary supremacy?
4. The UK Supreme Court's approach in the UNCRC reference emphasized that Westminster has 'unlimited power' and that devolution statutes should be interpreted like 'any other statute'. How does this compare with earlier judicial approaches to devolution legislation, and what are its implications for the constitutional balance between Westminster and devolved institutions?

6.5 INTERGOVERNMENTAL RELATIONS

Any system of decentralized governance requires the constitution to operate as a coordination mechanism. Without effective intergovernmental machinery, even carefully crafted legal frameworks risk dysfunction and conflict.

The UK has developed institutions and procedures to manage relationships between the national level and devolved administrations, as well as to enable dialogue between the political units themselves. These intergovernmental relations (IGR) have formed part of what Peter Hennessy termed the '*hidden wiring*'[45] of the UK's territorial constitution since 1998. The UK approach differs from federal systems, relying heavily on ad hoc, informal, and bilateral relationships rather than formal constitutional structures.

This informal approach faces inherent disadvantages. The asymmetrical character of devolution—with different powers for Scotland, Wales, and Northern Ireland, plus no devolved government for England—complicates coordination efforts. As parliamentary analysis concluded: '*The absence of formal and effective inter-governmental relations mechanisms has been the missing part of the devolution settlement ever since devolution was established in 1998*'.[46]

Despite their informal character, IGR provide dispute resolution mechanisms between the UK government and devolved administrations. They create forums for joint decision-making in shared or overlapping policy areas. Both functions are important given the interconnected nature of modern governance. For Northern Ireland, IGR assumes additional international significance through the Belfast Agreement's cross-border institutions.

6.5.1 FOUR PHASES OF DEVELOPMENT

The development of IGR since 1998 reveals how constitutional practice adapts to changing political circumstances. Four distinct phases emerge, each shaped by different challenges and political configurations:

- **Phase One: The Honeymoon Period (1999–2007):** The initial phase benefited from stability. Labour Party dominance across the British, Scottish, and Welsh governments created a shared devolutionary vision and minimized territorial conflict. Economic prosperity further reduced friction points. Northern Ireland's direct rule from Westminster (2002–7) following Assembly suspension meant policy divergence remained minimal across the UK.
- **Phase Two: Political Pluralization (2007–16):** The UK's Conservative-Liberal Democrat coalition government (2010–15) coincided with nationalist parties gaining power in the devolved territories: the SNP formed its first Scottish Government, while Plaid Cymru entered a coalition with Welsh Labour. This period encompassed the Scottish independence referendum, the Smith Commission, and the resulting legislation.
- **Phase Three: Crisis and Reform (2016–22):** EU withdrawal and the Coronavirus pandemic exposed IGR's inadequacies.[47] These challenges demanded coordination at a time when political divergence was greatest. Lord Dunlop's 2019 assessment concluded that 'the IGR machinery is no longer fit for purpose and is in urgent need for reform'.[48] This phase demonstrated that informal arrangements cannot withstand major constitutional stress.

[45] Peter Hennessy, *The Hidden Wiring: Unearthing the British Constitution* (1995, London: Weidenfeld & Nicolson).
[46] House of Commons Public Administration and Constitutional Affairs Committee, *Devolution and Exiting the EU: Reconciling Differences and Building Strong Relationships*, Eighth Report of Session 2017–19, 31 July 2018, [25].
[47] House of Commons Public Administration and Constitutional Affairs Committee, *Devolution and Exiting the EU: Reconciling Differences and Building Strong Relationships*, Eighth Report of Session 2017–19, 31 July 2018, [122].
[48] Cabinet Office, *Review of UK Government Union Capability*, November 2019, p. 31.

N. McEwen, M. Kenny, J. Sheldon, and C. Brown Swan, 'Intergovernmental relations in the UK: Time for a radical overhaul?' (2020) 91(3) *The Political Quarterly* 632–40, 639

As debates intensify over the constitutional futures of Scotland and Northern Ireland, it may seem a little quixotic to stress—as we do—the importance of a little known, barely visible system of meetings which bring together the different administrations that together govern the UK. However, improving relationships between the UK's network of governments could do much to mitigate territorial tensions, as well as making an important contribution to the legitimacy and functionality of governance across the UK. In the short to medium term, a system of joint decision-making may support the UK's prospective departure from the EU's regulatory regimes. As powers come back from Brussels, there is greater risk of significant internal disruption to the workings of the UK's economy without cooperation and at least some coordination in areas such as animal health, food labelling, and trade.

The need for more cooperative and productive relationships between different tiers of government has been further highlighted by the [Coronavirus pandemic in 2020]. In this emergency situation, intergovernmental working and coordination have been taking place within the context of the Civil Contingencies Committee (COBR) and associated Cabinet Sub-Committees, and not within the [Joint Ministerial Committee] structure where they normally happen. This major crisis has thrown into sharp relief the importance of productive working relationships between all levels of government, and has also reminded politicians and publics of some of the profound, shared interests that continue to exist within the UK—and would do so whatever the constitutional arrangements between these territories. It is in the interests of all governments in the UK—despite their considerable political differences—to work together to devise a set of procedures that would help them make better decisions in concert as and when necessary.

The Joint Ministerial Committee (JMC) that is mentioned in the extract comprises ministers from the UK and devolved governments. The JMC system was set up in 1999, and its terms of reference are set out in the following Memorandum of Understanding.

Memorandum of Understanding and Supplementary Agreements: Between the United Kingdom Government, the Scottish Ministers, the Welsh Ministers, and the Northern Ireland Executive Committee, October 2013

Supplementary Agreement A1.2

Collaborative working will be founded on the following principles:

a. to consider non-devolved matters which impinge on devolved responsibilities, and devolved matters which impinge on non-devolved responsibilities;
b. where the UK Government and the devolved administrations so agree, to consider devolved matters if it is beneficial to discuss their respective treatment in the different parts of the United Kingdom;
c. to keep the arrangements for liaison between the UK Government and the devolved administrations under review; and
d. to consider disputes between the administrations.

The formal IGR structure centres on the Joint Ministerial Committee (JMC), comprising ministers from the UK and devolved governments. The gap between institutional design and operational reality reveals the limitations of informal constitutional arrangements.

Despite the Memorandum of Understanding requiring JMC meetings at least annually, practice has fallen short of this commitment. During Phase I's period of stability (2002–8), when Labour governments shared power across the UK, no formal summit meetings occurred between the four governments. The absence of meetings during this period suggests that shared party control masked rather than resolved the need for systematic intergovernmental coordination.

The Scottish National Party's 2007 electoral victory in Scotland changed this dynamic. Since then, the JMC has convened more frequently, but scheduling remains entirely at the UK government's discretion. This arrangement reflects the power imbalance within the UK's territorial constitution. The Memorandum explicitly limits the JMC's authority, describing it as *'a consultative body rather than an executive body, and so will reach agreements rather than decisions. It may not bind any of the participating administrations, which will be free to determine their own policies while taking account of JMC discussions'*.

6.5.2 CONSTITUTIONAL REFORM: THE FOURTH PHASE

Recognition of these structural inadequacies prompted comprehensive review. The fourth phase of IGR development began in 2022 following joint examination by the UK government and devolved administrations. The resulting reforms represent an attempt to move beyond the ad hoc arrangements that had characterized the previous two decades, with new IGR structures designed to enable all four administrations to build more stable and sustained intergovernmental relationships.

Cabinet Office, Review of Intergovernmental Relations, January 2022

Principles for intergovernmental relations

Collaborative working will be founded on the following principles:

- maintaining positive and constructive relations, based on mutual respect for the responsibilities of the governments and their shared role in the governance of the UK
- building and maintaining trust, based on effective communication
- sharing information and respecting confidentiality
- promoting understanding of, and accountability for, their intergovernmental activity
- resolving disputes according to a clear and agreed process.

The 2022 reforms establish a three-tier structure designed to address previous ad hoc arrangements. Unlike earlier IGR mechanisms, these structures operate on non-statutory foundations but with explicit commitments to regular engagement rather than crisis-driven meetings. Overall accountability remains vested in the UK's senior political leadership: the Prime Minister, the First Ministers of Scotland and Wales, and Northern Ireland's First Minister and Deputy First Minister.

The new architecture creates systematic coordination through three institutional levels. At the apex, the Prime Minister and Heads of Devolved Governments Council provide strategic oversight. The middle tier comprises the Interministerial Standing Committee (IMSC) for cross-cutting policy issues, the Finance Interministerial Standing Committee (F:ISC) for fiscal coordination, and additional time-limited committees. The operational foundation consists of interministerial groups (IMGs) focused on particular policy areas.

Early experience reveals persistent limitations. While 2023 saw increased meetings within IGR structures, most interministerial meetings still occur outside these structures, and in some policy areas have occurred less frequently than envisaged or not at all. The arrangements rely on each administration's active participation, particularly the UK Government's, something Welsh and Scottish Governments previously suggested was lacking.

The non-statutory character provides flexibility but lacks legal enforceability, remaining vulnerable to political discretion. Northern Ireland Executive instability (2022–24) demonstrated how territorial political crises undermine multilateral coordination.

Labour's 2024 manifesto promised a 'reset' in UK-devolved relations, but success depends on government decisions and devolved executives' responses. Despite institutional improvements, the emphasis on regular engagement represents progress from crisis-driven approaches, yet structural asymmetries persist. Political goodwill rather than institutional design remains the main determinant of IGR effectiveness, with deeper constitutional tensions about central authority versus territorial autonomy remaining unresolved.

QUESTIONS

1. What mechanisms are needed for effective intergovernmental cooperation in a devolved state? Consider how the UK should address the challenges of asymmetric devolution, competing political objectives, and power imbalances between Westminster and the devolved administrations. Assess whether the 2022 IGR reforms provide sufficient institutional foundation for building sustainable intergovernmental trust, or whether further constitutional changes are required.
2. The informal, 'hidden wiring' character of IGR since 1998 reflects broader features of the UK's constitutional system. Explain why IGR mechanisms were not formally entrenched in the original devolution legislation. What does this reveal about how the UK approaches constitutional design and institutional development?

6.6 THE ENGLISH QUESTION(S)

While executive and legislative powers have been decentralized to new institutions in Wales, Scotland, and Northern Ireland, England lacks its own parliament or government despite constituting over 80 per cent of the UK's population. This anomaly generates the 'English Question' or 'West Lothian Question', constitutional challenges that the 2024 Labour Party manifesto acknowledged by promising to '*deepen devolution settlements for existing Combined Authorities*' and to '*widen devolution to more areas*'.[49]

The first challenge concerns institutional design: what arrangements should govern England? England cannot simply replicate the Scottish, Welsh, or Northern Irish model with a single devolved government and parliament. Such symmetrical federalism would prove unworkable given England's demographic and economic dominance. As constitutional analysis concludes: '*the overwhelming size of England is a major obstacle and likely source of instability. [. . .] Federalism does not . . . provide a solution to the tensions in the UK's territorial constitution*'.[50]

[49] The Labour Party Manifesto 2024, p. 40.

[50] House of Lords Select Committee on the Constitution, 'The Union and Devolution', 10th Report of Session 2015–16, HL Paper 149, 25 May 2016, ch. 6 [274–5].

An alternative approach would divide England into eight or nine regions, each with executive powers and elected assemblies. This regional solution lacks political support. The decisive rejection of an elected regional assembly in the 2004 referendum in North-East England effectively ended consideration of this approach. No current proposals exist for equipping English regions with legislative powers.

6.6.1 THE LOCAL ALTERNATIVE: METRO MAYORS AND COMBINED AUTHORITIES

English devolution has developed through localized, executive-focused arrangements. London pioneered this approach through the Greater London Authority (GLA), which comprises the directly-elected Mayor of London and 25 London Assembly members. Despite coinciding with Scottish, Welsh, and Northern Irish devolution, the GLA's powers remain limited compared with a focus on economic development and environmental improvements. The GLA lacks influence over health, education, social care, arts, and culture—policy areas central to territorial devolution elsewhere—and possesses no legislative powers.

This London model has expanded across England through Metro Mayors and combined authorities as a form of local government reorganization rather than territorial devolution (see Map 6.1). Beginning with the Greater Manchester Combined Authority in 2011, which covers 10 local authorities and 2.8 million people and has jurisdiction over policing, health, transport, and housing, this model expanded through the Cities and Local Government Devolution Act 2016. As of May 2025, fourteen areas have combined authority mayors, covering over half of England's population.[51] The English Devolution and Community Empowerment Bill 2024–25 aims to extend this model further: six mayoral combined authorities are expected to hold initial elections in 2026–27 (Sussex, Hampshire, Essex, Norfolk & Suffolk in 2026; Cumbria, Cheshire & Warrington in 2027).[52] These developments represent a significant expansion of devolved governance, though arrangements remain executive-focused rather than legislative.

The Levelling-up and Regeneration Act 2023 addressed geographical limitations of existing arrangements while enhancing operational effectiveness. The Act's central innovation created combined county authorities—institutional models designed for non-metropolitan areas with two-tier local government structures. Unlike existing combined authorities, which require membership from all local authorities within their area, combined county authorities comprise only upper-tier authorities. This streamlined membership acknowledges that the original model, developed for urban areas like Greater Manchester, may be unwieldy in rural areas, where county-level coordination is more appropriate.

The legislation introduced operational improvements, including streamlining proposal processes for establishing combined authorities, reducing consent requirements for constitutional changes, enabling local authorities to adopt directly-elected leadership models more rapidly, and enhancing democratic accountability. The Act permitted directly-elected mayors to adopt titles reflecting local character, moving beyond the uniform 'mayor' designation.

[51] https://www.instituteforgovernment.org.uk/explainer/regional-mayors-devolution [last updated June 2025].

[52] M. Sandford, 'The English Devolution and Community Empowerment Bill 2024–25', House of Commons Library, Research Briefing, 20 August 2025, p.13.

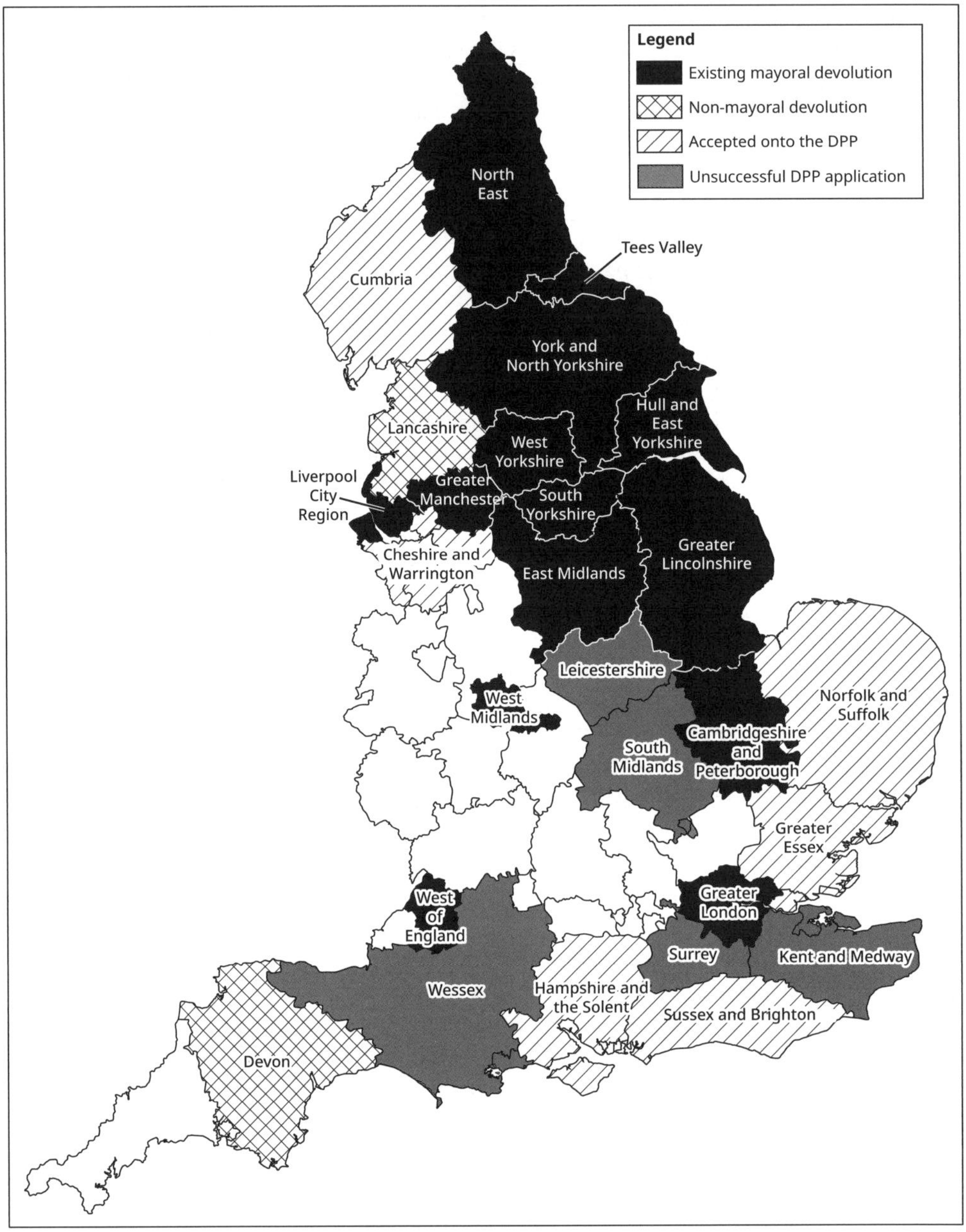

Map 6.1 Metro mayors and regional mayors in England

Labour's English Devolution and Community Empowerment Bill 2024–25 represents a systematic attempt to extend and standardize mayoral governance across England. The Bill creates a three-tier structure of 'strategic authorities':

- **Foundation strategic authorities**: non-mayoral combined and county authorities with basic powers;
- **Mayoral strategic authorities**: areas with directly-elected mayors and enhanced powers (e.g. the Greater London Authority);

- **Established mayoral strategic authorities**: authorities demonstrating strong track records and consolidated budgets with greater flexibility. Six authorities already qualify: Greater Manchester, West Midlands, Liverpool City Region, South Yorkshire, West Yorkshire, and North-East.

The government's long-term goal is for established mayoral strategic authorities to be established across England—authorities with elected mayors, proven track records, and enhanced powers including integrated settlements.[53]

The Bill introduces several major reforms. It extends the general power of competence to strategic authorities, allowing them to do anything an individual can do (unless specifically prohibited by law). It creates statutory duties requiring authorities to collaborate with each other. Significantly, the Bill mandates that all two-tier areas (with both county and district councils) must reorganize into single-tier unitary authorities. It also abolishes the committee system of local government, that require all councils to adopt the leader-and-cabinet model.

Additionally, the Bill amends the Localism Act 2011 to give all mayoral strategic authorities powers to establish mayoral development corporations—bodies that can drive large-scale regeneration projects in designated areas. These corporations can acquire land, provide infrastructure, and assume planning powers within their designated zones.

These reforms represent the most systematic approach to English territorial governance since devolution began in 1998. However, they remain within local government structures rather than pursuing legislative devolution comparable to that in Scotland, Wales, and Northern Ireland. English devolution continues to develop through executive leadership and strategic coordination rather than through devolved parliaments with law-making powers (see Map 6.2).

6.6.2 THE LEGISLATIVE CHALLENGE: ENGLISH VOTES FOR ENGLISH LAWS

Beyond territorial governance challenges, asymmetric devolution generates constitutional problems concerning Westminster's legislative procedures. How should the UK Parliament handle bills that apply only to England when devolution has altered the territorial scope of parliamentary authority?

The issue stems from devolution's asymmetric character. MPs representing Scottish, Welsh, and Northern Irish constituencies retain the right to vote on England-only legislation at Westminster. Yet English MPs possess no reciprocal influence over comparable policy areas in Scotland, Wales, and Northern Ireland, where legislative authority has transferred to devolved institutions. This creates a democratic anomaly: Scottish, Welsh, and Northern Irish representatives can shape English domestic policy on matters in which English MPs have no voice in their own constituencies.

The McKay Commission established in 2013 recommended that '*Decisions taken in the Commons which have a separate and distinct effect for England (or England-and-Wales) should normally be taken only with the consent of a majority of MPs sitting for constituencies in England (or England-and-Wales)*'.[54] This principle offered a procedural solution addressing English concerns while preserving Westminster's formal unity.

The resulting English Votes for English Laws (EVEL) system operated from 2015–20, implemented through House of Commons Standing Orders rather than primary legislation. The procedure required the Speaker to certify whether bills related exclusively to England, triggering an additional committee stage where only English MPs could participate. This Grand Committee possessed theoretical veto power over England-only measures.

[53] Ibid. 22–23. [54] http://tmc.independent.gov.uk/.

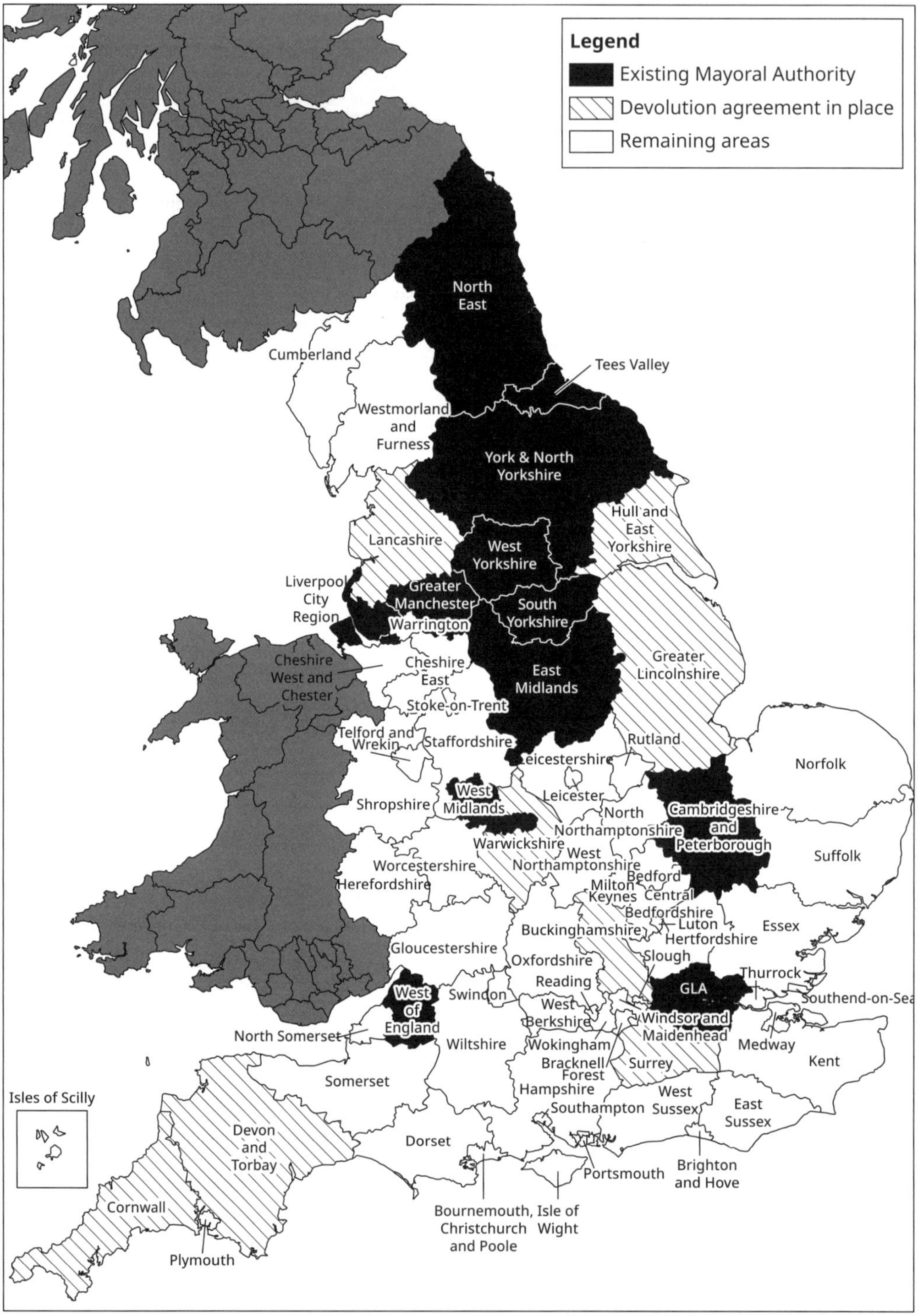

Map 6.2 Map of current English devolution landscape, December 2024

EVEL's practical impact proved negligible. The veto power was never exercised during the procedure's five-year existence. With English constituencies comprising 82 per cent of all Westminster seats and Conservative government control over most English constituencies, the Grand Committee rarely faced legislative disputes. EVEL added procedural complexity without addressing the underlying constitutional tensions it purported to resolve.

V. Bogdanor, *The Crisis of the Constitution* (2015, London: The Constitution Society), p. 23–4

[EVEL] is a separatist proposal, whose effect would be to separate two systems of government—the English and the Scottish—which need to be brought together if the Union is to be strengthened. It is no accident that the SNP has a settled policy of not voting on 'English' laws for it is an openly separatist party, favouring the separation of the Scottish and English systems of government. It is odd to find some Unionists seeking to follow suit. Devolution, while in my view an overdue and necessary reform, has made many English politicians believe that Scotland is another country with which they need not concern themselves. But constitutional reform should aim to link the various parts of the United Kingdom, and in particular the Scottish and English systems of government together, not to separate them. [. . .]

It is in any case a fallacy to believe that the English voice is not heard at present. Of the 650 constituencies represented at Westminster, 533 are English. England remains the dominant nation. She has no need to beat the drum or blow the bugle. If she does, the devolution settlement will be strained to breaking point. The existence of the United Kingdom rests on restraint by the dominant nation. Unionists, therefore, should continue to be guided by Disraeli's famous dictum that England is governed not by logic but by Parliament.

QUESTIONS

1. Why has English devolution developed through executive-focused Metro Mayors rather than legislative devolution comparable to Scotland, Wales, and Northern Ireland? Consider England's demographic dominance, the challenges of territorial scale, and the implications for the UK's constitutional balance.
2. What is the case for establishing a directly-elected English legislature operating under a reserved powers model? Consider the benefits for democratic representation and territorial balance against the challenges of England's size, economic dominance, and the risk of creating a rival to Westminster.
3. Was EVEL a reasonable response to legitimate English concerns about asymmetric devolution, or did it reflect flawed understanding of the Union's constitutional dynamics? Consider both its theoretical justification and practical operation between 2015 and 2020, and whether its abolition in 2021 represented recognition of practical failure or abandonment of English constitutional interests.
4. Could federalism solve the UK's territorial constitutional tensions? Consider both the advantages of formal constitutional equality between England, Scotland, Wales, and Northern Ireland, and the practical obstacles posed by England's overwhelming size and economic dominance. Drawing on comparative federal systems, assess whether federalism could strengthen the Union or whether England's dominance makes federal solutions inherently unstable.

Vernon Bogdanor's criticism proved accurate. He argued that the scheme rested on erroneous assumptions about the Union and reinforced rather than resolved English constitutional dominance within Westminster. Rather than strengthening territorial balance, EVEL highlighted England's overwhelming numerical superiority and the futility of procedural fixes for constitutional asymmetries.

EVEL was suspended in 2020 and formally abolished in 2021, leaving the English Question's legislative dimension unresolved. The failed experiment demonstrates the difficulty of managing England's dual role as both the UK's largest component nation and the territorial remainder after devolution.

6.7 CONCLUDING COMMENTS

Over the past two decades, the United Kingdom has transitioned from a formally centralized state into a complex system of multilevel governance. The establishment and evolution of devolved institutions in Scotland, Wales, and Northern Ireland have created distinct political communities with legislative autonomy, reflecting the UK's character as a plurinational state rather than a single, homogeneous entity.

These institutional developments coexist uneasily with legal orthodoxy. Westminster formally retains unlimited authority to legislate on devolved matters and override devolved decisions. While recent statutes declare Scottish and Welsh institutions 'permanent' and provide statutory recognition for the Sewel Convention, these developments have not displaced parliamentary supremacy. Recent judicial decisions, particularly in *Miller* and the *UNCRC Bill Reference*, have adopted restrictive interpretations of devolved competence, abandoning the '*generous and purposive*' approach advocated in earlier cases like *Robinson* in favour of narrow legalism that emphasizes Westminster's formal authority.

This legal conservatism occurs alongside persistent weaknesses in intergovernmental coordination. Despite recent reforms, intergovernmental relations remain informal and dominated by the UK government, while each territory faces distinct constitutional pressures. Northern Ireland's power-sharing arrangements remain fragile and prone to periodic collapse; Wales continues to adapt to its reserved powers framework; Scottish politics centres on unresolved independence questions; and English devolution remains piecemeal and executive-focused, reinforcing constitutional asymmetry.

The tension between political pluralism and legal centralism generates ongoing instability within the UK's territorial constitution. Contemporary constitutional debate has moved beyond traditional questions of union versus federation toward the question of whether existing structures can accommodate mounting pressures from territorial nationalism, policy divergence, and competing constitutional visions.

Devolution could be the most significant constitutional development since the exapansion of the franchise, yet structural weaknesses render the Union increasingly fragile. The convergence of EU withdrawal, demographic shifts in Northern Ireland, persistent independence movements in Scotland, and England's anomalous constitutional position could lead to constitutional instability. Constitutional arrangements remain contested, uneven, and contingent—shaped by political choices and institutional practices rather than fixed legal principles. Whether long-term stability emerges through a written constitution, federal settlement, enhanced pluralism, or alternative arrangements remains an open question.

N.W. Barber, *The United Kingdom Constitution: An Introduction* (2021, Oxford: OUP), pp. 224–5

The creation of the devolved assemblies in three of the constituent territories of the UK is certainly the most important constitutional development of the last twenty years, and is arguably the most significant since the expansion of the franchise in the early twentieth century. This is the area in which the major constitutional crises of the next few decades will arise, generated by the unstable nature of the devolution settlement. A number of factors have combined to put the survival of the Union under pressure. First, the elements that served to unite the UK have weakened. In her book on the birth of the UK, *Britons*, the historian Linda Colley identifies a combination of elements that bound the UK together. She picks out the shared Protestantism of England, Wales, and Scotland, the economic benefits that the emerging Empire offered to people within those regions, and the external threat posed by France, as factors that drew these territories together during the eighteenth and early nineteenth centuries. All of these factors dissipated during the second half of the twentieth century, a period that, probably not coincidentally, showed a renewed interest in Scottish and Welsh nationalism. Secondly, Brexit and, in Northern Ireland, long-term demographic changes have put pressure on the Union. Both Scotland and Northern Ireland voted against Brexit, and if those regions wished to rejoin the EU, they would need to leave the Union. Whilst in Northern Ireland the Protestant section of the population, which has tended to support the Union, is shrinking whilst the Catholic section, which has tended to support Irish unification, is growing. Finally, the structure of the 1998 devolution settlement is flawed: the opportunity to have a UK wide conversation in the late 1990s about a new regional structure was missed, with England left out of the scheme. The lack of regional representation for England means this territory is governed by the UK legislature and executive, a disparity that might, one day, become problematic. All of these factors have served to render the Union more fragile, and it is likely that one or more of the UK's constituent territories will leave the Union over the next twenty or so years.

FURTHER READING

Dickson, B., 'Devolution – Northern Ireland', in J. Jowell and C. O'Cinneide (eds) *The Changing Constitution*, 9th edn (2019, Oxford: OUP), ch. 9.

Keating, M. *Plurinational Democracy: Stateless Nations in a Post-Sovereignty Era* (2001, Oxford: OUP).

McEldowny, J., 'A Federal UK?', in J. Jowell and C. O'Cinneide (eds) *The Changing Constitution*, 9th edn (2019, Oxford: OUP), ch. 14.

McHarg, A., 'Devolution – Scotland', in J. Jowell and C. O'Cinneide (eds) *The Changing Constitution*, 9th edn (2019, Oxford: OUP), ch. 10.

McHarg, A. (2018). 'Unity and Diversity in the United Kingdom's Territorial Constitution', in M. Elliott, J. Varuhas, and S. Stark (eds.), *The Unity of Public Law? Doctrinal, Theoretical and Comparative Perspectives* (2018, Hart Publishing).

Rawlings, R., 'Devolution – Wales', in J. Jowell and C. O'Cinneide (eds) *The Changing Constitution*, 9th edn (2019, Oxford: OUP), ch. 11.

PART II

EXECUTIVE FUNCTIONS

7

INTRODUCTION TO EXECUTIVE FUNCTIONS

CENTRAL ISSUES

1. The 'executive functions' carried out by various bodies in the United Kingdom will be examined in Chapters 8, 9, and 10. As we saw in Chapter 5 in relation to the concept of separation of powers, in very broad terms, the 'executive function' may be defined as the powers of government to decide issues of policy, to raise and spend public money, and to implement decisions. Our focus is on the institutional and legal frameworks that make these activities possible.
2. Constitutions have a twin role in relation to executive functions: they *enable* executive action (by providing institutional and procedural frameworks for decision-making) and they also *constrain* it (to ensure that it stays within what is permitted by law and to make governments accountable for their actions).
3. One persistent theme is that there is, in the United Kingdom, an imbalance of power. Critics say that UK central government controls Parliament too much. Reforms are being introduced to allow the UK Parliament to have better opportunities to call ministers to account.
4. Another theme is the fragmentation of executive functions. In recent decades, some aspects of executive power have moved from UK central government to the devolved administrations in Scotland, Wales, and Northern Ireland (as we saw in Chapter 6).

7.1 FACTS AND THEMES

This Chapter is an overview of the main ideas and facts that will be covered in Chapter 8 (Government of the United Kingdom), Chapter 9 (Accountability), and Chapter 10 (Prerogative Powers).

7.1.1 WHAT IS THE 'EXECUTIVE FUNCTION'?

An obvious starting point is to work out what is meant by the 'executive function'. Consider carefully what Professors Craig and Tomkins say in the following extract.

P. Craig and A. Tomkins, 'Introduction', in P. Craig and A. Tomkins (eds) *The Executive and Public Law* (2006, Oxford: OUP), p. 1

Executive power is the power of governments. It is the legal authority vested in, and exercised by, for example, prime ministers, presidents, cabinets, and councils. It is the political power that all those who embark on a career in politics dream of wielding. It is the power to set policy, to take action, and to implement the law. In the great theory of the separation of powers that has hovered over western constitutional thinking since the mid eighteenth century, the preserve of the executive is to *do*. While the role of the legislature is to speak and that of the judiciary is to judge, governments *act*.

Few would deny that, at the opening of the twenty-first century, governments have become the most powerful organs of nation states. They determine the direction, if not always the detail, of domestic policy. They decide how public money should, and should not, be spent. Foreign policy is made almost entirely by governments. And control of military power is likewise the preserve of the executive. Whatever the truth of the claim that, in this era of apparent globalization, states are no longer the only or even the most powerful units of political power, within nation states governments still retain very considerable power. This is not to say that their power can never be checked. Governments may rule, but they do not always rule supreme. In democracies the personnel of the executive is subject to the verdict of the electorate; the policies of the executive may be subject to political or parliamentary accountability; and the legality of executive action may be reviewed by the courts of law.

In relation to the United Kingdom, executive functions are not carried out by a single institution. We will see in Chapter 8 that a range of official bodies throughout the United Kingdom are, as a matter of law or constitutional convention, responsible for carrying out executive functions. In order to understand the significance of this dispersal of functions, it is helpful to go back to the idea of devolution introduced in Chapter 5. There, we saw the debate over the future of the centralized nation state.

As we explore in some detail in Chapter 8, the United Kingdom can be said to have a system of 'parliamentary government' (meaning that ministers who give political leadership to 'the executive' *must* be members of one or the other of the Houses of Parliament). As Professor Munro explains in the following extract, this does not mean that Parliament *governs* in the sense of carrying out executive functions. The UK Parliament does, however, have a key role in *scrutinizing* the exercise of executive functions.

C.R. Munro, *Studies in Constitutional Law*, 2nd edn (1999, London: Butterworths), pp. 324–5 (footnotes omitted)

As John Stuart Mill said, 'there is a radical distinction between controlling the business of government, and actually doing it'. England had unhappy experience of a Parliament's efforts to govern the country in 1648 and 1649 when the Long Parliament proved to be so inefficient, intolerant, and meddlesome, as to provoke Cromwell's further intervention. That experience was perhaps in Mill's mind when he expressed the view that a representative assembly was 'radically unfit' to govern. In practice, the parliamentary body is not organised in such a way as would enable it to execute foreign policy or implement domestic policies. When it is said that we have 'parliamentary government', this must be understood as referring not to government by Parliament, but by an executive drawn from and accountable to Parliament.

7.1.2 WHAT IS THE ROLE OF A CONSTITUTION IN RELATION TO EXECUTIVE FUNCTIONS?

As Craig and Tomkins explain in the first extract in this Chapter, the executive function involves determining public policy (domestic and foreign), allocating public finance (raised by taxation or borrowed), and controlling military force. But what is the role of a constitution in this context? The answer is one that we have examined several times before—namely, that there is a dual aspect to constitutions.

- They *enable* governments by providing a framework for policy-making and implementation—we want governments to be able to take action in the public interest.
- A constitution also seeks to *constrain* executive power—ensuring that executive functions are carried out in accordance with the rule of law and in an accountable way.

Looking at executive functions from this perspective, it is possible to identify several overlapping 'constitutions', as follows.

(a) There is, first, the uncodified constitution of the whole of the United Kingdom, in which both law and constitutional conventions are important. Critics suggest that the uncodified nature of the UK constitution and its heavy reliance on convention create an insufficiently robust set of constraints on the power of government. Looked at from the other side of the coin, we can say that the principle of parliamentary supremacy is strongly *enabling* of the UK government—because a government that has a majority in the House of Commons will often find it possible to develop and implement policies without rigid rules on how the process takes place or the content of the policies. (You may find it helpful to look back at the survey of the debate between 'political constitutionalists' and 'legal constitutionalists' at the start of Chapter 3.)

(b) The 'devolution Acts'—the Scotland Act 1998, the Northern Ireland Act 1998, and the Government of Wales Act 2006—provide a framework for the operation of the devolved governments.

7.1.3 ASYMMETRY IN THE UK CONSTITUTION

When thinking about executive functions in the United Kingdom, it is important to keep in mind that the policy of devolution has led to new executive bodies being created in Scotland, Wales, and Northern Ireland, but not for the whole of England.

7.2 GOVERNMENTS AT A GLANCE

Boxes 7.1, 7.2, 7.3, and 7.4 and Figures 7.1, 7.2, 7.3, and 7.4 contain a summary of the basic constitutional and legal aspects of the various executive bodies considered in Chapters 8, 9, and 10.

BOX 7.1 THE NORTHERN IRELAND EXECUTIVE

Figure 7.1 No. 10 Downing Street
Source: © Oversnap/istockphoto.com.

Name: Her Majesty's Government (HMG) or 'central government'. The terminology of 'the Crown' may also be used in some contexts.

Main website: www.gov.uk/government/organisations/prime-ministers-office-10-downing-street.

Head of government: the Prime Minister (who also holds the title 'First Lord of the Treasury').

Other members of government:

- Chancellor of the Exchequer;
- Secretaries of State (no fixed number; in recent years, approximately 16);
- Lord Chancellor (post held by Secretary of State for Justice);
- Junior ministers.

Collective meetings of the government: in the Cabinet, usually on Thursday mornings at No. 10 Downing Street, but may meet at other times and places. Numerous Cabinet committees meet at other times.

Source of legal powers: Acts of Parliament; prerogative powers (in relation to some executive functions); 'the third source'.

Sources of legal advice:

- The Attorney General and Solicitor General, collectively known as 'the Law Officers', in relation to whole-UK, and England and Wales legal matters (online at www.gov.uk/government/organisations/attorney-generals-office).

- The Advocate General for Scotland in relation to issues of Scottish Law (online at www.gov.uk/government/organisations/office-of-the-advocate-general-for-scotland).
- The Advocate General for Northern Ireland (same person as the Attorney General of England and Wales—see Justice (Northern Ireland) Act 2002) advises on issues of Northern Ireland law.
- The Government Legal Profession (online at www.gov.uk/government/organisations/civil-service-government-legal-profession), including the Government Legal Department (previously called the Treasury Solicitor's Department) (online at www.gov.uk/government/organisations/government-legal-department).
- The First Treasury Counsel (colloquially known as 'the Treasury Devil'), a barrister in private practice who is instructed to represent the government in the most important litigation and to advise on matters of legality.

Principal government departments: these may be reorganized and renamed by the Prime Minister from time to time. In January 2023, the main departments were:

- Her Majesty's Treasury;
- the Department for Work & Pensions;
- the Department of Health & Social Care;
- the Department for Education;
- the Ministry of Defence;
- the Department for Housing, Communities & Local Government;
- the Home Office;
- the Department for Transport;
- the Department for Business & Trade;
- the Ministry of Justice;
- the Department for Environment, Food & Rural Affairs;
- the Department for Energy Security and Net Zero;
- the Foreign, Commonwealth and Development Office;
- the Department for Digital, Culture, Media & Sport; and
- the Department for Business & Trade.

Executive agencies: most departments have several agencies and public bodies that advise ministers or implement policy and deliver services—for example, the Department for Transport (based in London SW1, near to Parliament and No. 10 Downing Street) has 23 agencies and public bodies including:

- the Driver and Vehicle Licensing Agency (based in Swansea);
- the Vehicle Certification Agency (based in Bristol);
- the Maritime and Coastguard Agency (Southampton).

Civil service: the Home Civil Service; the Diplomatic Service.

BOX 7.2 THE SCOTTISH GOVERNMENT

Figure 7.2 Scottish Government Building, Victoria Quay, Leith, Edinburgh
Source: © Benjamin Brock/Wikipedia (CC-BY-SA 3.0)

Name: the Scotland Act 1998, s. 44, creates 'the Scottish Government'. The members of the Scottish Government may be referred to collectively as 'the Scottish Ministers'.

Main website: www.gov.scot.

Head of government: the First Minister (Scotland Act 1998, ss 45–47)

Other members of government:

- '*The First Minister may, with the approval of Her Majesty, appoint Ministers from among the members of the Parliament*': Scotland Act 1998, s. 47.
- Junior Scottish Ministers: Scotland Act 1998, s. 49.
- The two Scottish Law Officers—the Lord Advocate and the Solicitor General for Scotland: Scotland Act 1998, s. 44.

Source of legal powers: the Scotland Act 1998, as amended, provides a constitutional framework; other executive powers stem from Acts of the UK Parliament and Acts of the Scottish Parliament; some specific prerogative powers.

Sources of legal advice: the Lord Advocate and Solicitor General for Scotland (Scotland Act 1998, s. 48).

Principal ministers (in October 2025):

- Deputy First Minister and Cabinet Secretary for Economy and Gaelic;
- Cabinet Secretary for Education and Skills;
- Cabinet Secretary for Justice and Home Affairs;

- Cabinet Secretary for Health and Social Care;
- Cabinet Secretary for Finance and Local Government;
- Cabinet Secretary for Climate Action and Energy;
- Cabinet Secretary for Rural Affairs, Land Reform and Islands;
- Cabinet Secretary for Transport;
- Cabinet Secretary for Social Justice;
- Cabinet Secretary for the Constitution, External Affairs and Culture.

Civil service: '*The Scottish Ministers may appoint persons to be members of the staff of the Scottish Administration*' (Scotland Act 1998, s. 51).

BOX 7.3 THE WELSH GOVERNMENT

Figure 7.3 The Welsh Government Building at Cathays Park, Cardiff

Name: the Welsh Government (in Welsh: *Llywodraeth Cymru*), established by the Government of Wales Act 2006, s. 45 (as amended)

Main website: www.gov.wales

Head of government: the First Minister for Wales (in Welsh: *Prif Weinidog*) (Government of Wales Act 2006, ss. 46–47).

Other members of government: (limited to 12 members in total)

- The Welsh Ministers (*Gweinidogion Cymru*): Government of Wales Act 2006, s. 48.
- The Deputy Welsh Ministers (*Dirprwy Weinidogion Cymru*): Government of Wales Act 2006, s. 50.

- The Counsel General to the Welsh Government (*Cwnsler Cyffredinol i Lywodraeth Cymru*): Government of Wales Act 2006, s. 49.

Source of legal powers: the Government of Wales Act 2006 provides a constitutional framework; various Acts of the UK Parliament; legislation made by the National Assembly for Wales.

Sources of legal advice: the Counsel General to the Welsh Government and lawyers in the Legal Services Department.

Cabinet Secretaries (in October 2025):

- Deputy First Minister and Cabinet Secretary for Climate Change and Rural Affairs
- Cabinet Secretary for Housing and Local Government
- Cabinet Secretary for Housing and Local Government
- Cabinet Secretary for Finance and Welsh Language;
- Cabinet Secretary for the Economy, Energy and Planning;
- Cabinet Secretary for Social Justice, Trefnydd [Leader of the House] and Chief Whip;
- Cabinet Secretary for Transport and North Wales;
- Cabinet Secretary for Education.

Civil service: '*The Welsh Ministers may appoint persons to be members of the staff of the Welsh Government*' (Government of Wales Act 2006, s. 52).

BOX 7.4 THE NORTHERN IRELAND EXECUTIVE

Figure 7.4 Stormont, Northern Ireland Executive and Assembly
Source: © Robert Mayne/istockphoto.com.

Name: the Northern Ireland Executive—strictly speaking the 'Executive Committee' of the Northern Ireland Assembly (see Northern Ireland Act 1998, s. 20: '*There shall be an Executive Committee of each Assembly consisting of the First Minister, the deputy First Minister and the Northern Ireland Ministers*').

Main website: http://www.northernireland.gov.uk/.

Heads of government: the First Minister and Deputy First Minister: Northern Ireland Act 1998, s. 16.

Other members of government: the First Minister and the deputy First Minister acting jointly determine the number and the functions of 'ministerial offices' (Northern Ireland Act 1998, s. 18) and junior ministers (Northern Ireland Act 1998, s. 19).

Source of legal powers: the Northern Ireland Act 1998 provides a constitutional framework; Acts of the UK Parliament; Acts of the Assembly; '*the prerogative and other executive powers of Her Majesty in relation to Northern Ireland shall be exercisable on Her Majesty's behalf by any Minister or Northern Ireland department*' (Northern Ireland Act 1998, s. 23).

Sources of legal advice: the Attorney General for Northern Ireland (Justice (Northern Ireland) Act 2002) and staff.

Civil service: Northern Ireland Civil Service.

8

GOVERNMENT OF THE UNITED KINGDOM

CENTRAL ISSUES

1. Executive power in the United Kingdom is dispersed across a range of institutions—including the monarch, ministers, civil servants, and arm's-length bodies—whose authority rests on a mix of legal rules, prerogative powers, and constitutional conventions.
2. Legality and legitimacy are distinct but connected questions. Government must act within the powers granted by Parliament and the common law, but it must also be able to justify why those powers should be accepted.
3. The monarchy still plays a formal constitutional role, regulated by conventions. Understanding the distinction between the monarch as an individual and 'the Crown' as a legal and institutional concept is essential for making sense of how executive authority is constituted.
4. Ministers remain the core of the executive. Their powers derive from both Parliament and the Crown, and they are answerable to Parliament for the conduct of their departments. But modern government relies heavily on civil servants exercising powers in ministers' names and on public bodies operating at arm's length from political control.
5. Mechanisms exist to restrain government influence over Parliament—for example statutory limits on the number of ministers who may sit in the Commons—but party discipline and government control of parliamentary time shape how far these checks work in practice.
6. Arm's-length bodies now exercise extensive regulatory and oversight functions. Their independence protects certain decisions from day-to-day political pressure, but it also raises constitutional questions about democratic accountability and ministerial responsibility.
7. Automated and interface-first systems increasingly shape how public decisions are made and experienced. These technologies offer speed and consistency but introduce new concerns about transparency, fairness, and whether traditional models of accountability remain adequate.

8.1 OVERVIEW OF UK GOVERNMENT

If you've read the previous chapters, you already know quite a lot about how the UK government fits within the wider constitutional system. The following short recap brings together some of the key ideas you have encountered about where government power comes from, the legal limits on its use, and how it connects with other constitutional institutions.

2. The Constitutional Rulebook	The government operates within a framework of legislation, common law, conventions, and constitutional principles rather than a single written constitution.
3. Legislative supremacy of the UK Parliament	Parliament is the supreme law-making authority. The government may act only when authorised by Parliament through statute or through prerogative powers that Parliament has not limited or replaced.
4. The Rule of Law	Ministers, officials and other public bodies must act within the legal powers given to them. Through judicial review, the courts ensure that they remain within the 'four corners' of these powers.
5. Separating and balancing powers	Government forms the executive arm of the state, distinct from Parliament and the courts. The constitution relies on checks and balances to prevent any one part of the state—especially the executive—from dominating the others.
6. Multilevel governing within the UK	The UK government shares authority with devolved governments, local authorities, and other public bodies. Power is spread across several levels rather than concentrated entirely at Westminster and Whitehall.

At first sight, the array of office-holders and institutions can seem like a bewildering machine (see Figure 8.1). To keep the discussion focused on core features of central government, this chapter looks at four main parts of the institutional jigsaw: the monarchy (section 8.2), ministers (section 8.3), civil servants (section 8.4), arm's-length bodies (section 8.5), and automated decision-making (section 8.6). These cover the core of what is meant by 'UK government' and provide a framework for exploring key constitutional ideas about where executive power comes from, how it is organized, and how it operates in practice. The list is not exhaustive. It does not, for example, cover the police, the armed forces, the National Health Service, local authorities, or the devolved administrations in Scotland, Wales, and Northern Ireland.

Government is more than a collection of offices and laws; it is the practical expression of authority. Before we look in detail at who holds power and how it is exercised, it is worth pausing to ask a more basic question: what gives any person or institution with executive power the right to govern?

PAUSE FOR REFLECTION

When you think about people in positions of authority—whether ministers, judges, or civil servants—what questions come to mind about their power and responsibility? What makes you accept (or doubt) that their authority is legitimate?

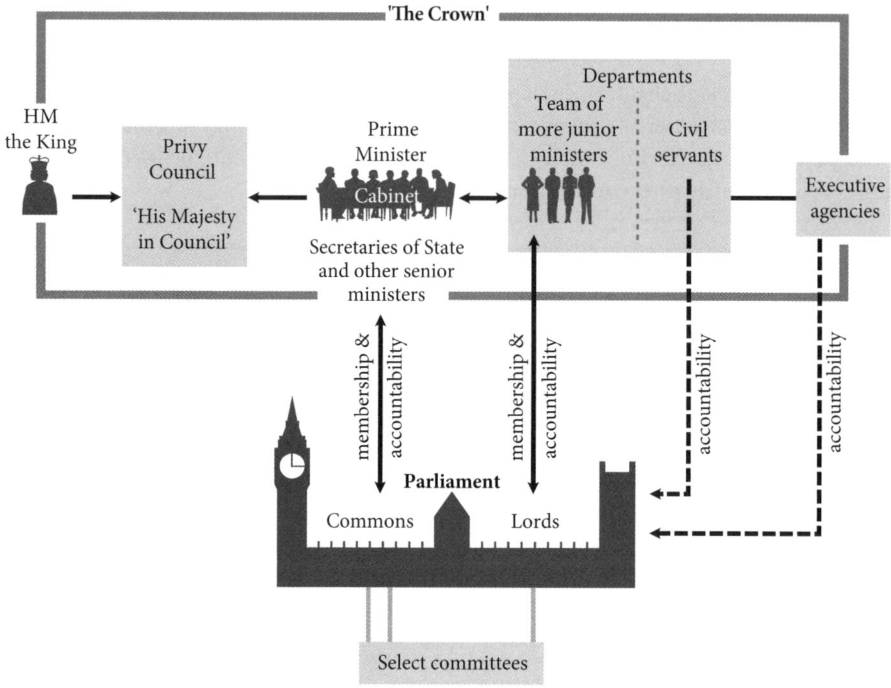

Figure 8.1 Institutions of UK government

Tony Benn (1925–2014). a long-serving Labour MP, often asked what makes power legitimate in a democracy. During a debate on the European Parliamentary Elections Bill, he set out 'five democratic questions'.

House of Commons Hansard, 16 November 1998, col. 319

> The House will forgive me for quoting five democratic questions that I have developed during my life. If one meets a powerful person [. . .] one can ask five questions: (i) what power do you have; (ii) where did you get it; (iii) in whose interests do you exercise it; (iv) to whom are you accountable; and, (v) how can we get rid of you?

These are sharp constitutional questions. For lawyers, the first two—what power do you have? and where did you get it?—raise issues of legality: what sources of law authorise the exercise of governmental power? In most countries, the answers would start with 'those powers conferred by the Constitution'. In the absence of a codified constitution in the United Kingdom,[1] a longer answer is needed: in general terms, those who govern have such powers as are conferred by Acts of Parliament, prerogative powers (in the case of some ministers and the monarch), and the common law.[2] The chapters in Part II will continue to map these out in more detail.

[1] See Chapter 1. [2] On prerogative and common law powers, see Chapter 10.

The remaining questions—in whose interests, to whom accountable, and how can we get rid of you?—concern legitimacy: the broader claim that power should be accepted as rightful. In a good constitution, it is not enough for those who govern to say, 'the law gives us power to govern' (*legality*); they must also implicitly or expressly make a claim as to why their powers to govern ought to be accepted, and that claim must be accepted by most of the people most of the time. This is the idea of *legitimacy*.

A. Le Sueur, 'People as "Users" and "Citizens": The Quest for Legitimacy in British Public Administration', in M. Ruffert (ed.) *Legitimacy in European Administrative Law* (2011, Groningen: Europa Law Publishing), ch. 3, p. 30 (footnotes omitted)

> Many academic studies of legitimacy of public authority preface their analysis with a warning that the concept of legitimacy is 'problematic' or 'contested'. [. . . C]onditions of legitimacy may encompass normative and empirical perspectives. Normative perspectives seek to provide moral reasons for citizen's acceptance of, acquiescence in or engagement with government decision-making: what entitles a public authority to act? Empirical perspectives seek to measure people's sentiments—their opinions and beliefs—about governance: why people accept (if they do) that a public authority is entitled to act.
>
> Conditions of legitimacy exist if, for good reason, people have confidence in administrative processes and respect and accept decisions of public authorities, even though they may disagree with some individual determinations. The notion of 'diffuse support' is important: people may be willing to comply with determinations even when they disagree with them; 'specific support' relates to particular determinations. If conditions of legitimacy exist, winners and losers—in individual decisions and in broader political debates—should accept the outcome. Legitimacy is therefore closely related to, but extends beyond, the idea of public compliance or consent. Compliance in a legitimate system is based on reason and principle not merely 'a matter of lingering habit, or expediency, or necessity'.

By the end of this chapter, you should have a clear picture of who exercises executive power in the United Kingdom, the main legal sources that enable them to do so, and how these powers are organized within the machinery of government. You will see how authority is distributed between the monarchy, ministers, civil servants, and arm's length bodies, and how their work is constrained and supported by rules, conventions, and political practices. The discussion that follows invites you to think critically about why these arrangements command public acceptance and how far they promote effective, responsible, and trusted government.

8.2 THE MONARCHY

It makes constitutional sense to begin with the monarchy. Although news and social media often portray members of the Royal family as celebrities, the monarch remains central to the legal structure of government. Historically, all executive and judicial power was exercised in the monarch's name, and traces of that heritage remain everywhere: in the title 'His Majesty's Government', in the names of government departments such as His Majesty's Revenue and Customs, and in the many official acts carried out formally by the monarch or under royal authority. Understanding the role of the Crown is therefore the starting point for understanding how government power is constituted in the United Kingdom.

King Charles III is head of state of the United Kingdom and, as of 2025, of 14 other Commonwealth realms.[3] The number of countries recognising the monarch as their head of state has declined significantly over time—from more than 30 in the mid-twentieth century—as many have become republics with elected heads of state, most recently Barbados in 2021. Debates about the role of the monarchy in these states are connected to questions of colonial history, national identity, and constitutional self-determination. Such themes continue to shape contemporary discussions about whether to retain or replace the monarch as head of state.

8.2.1 HISTORICAL DEVELOPMENT OF MONARCHY

The monarchy is hereditary. Today, members of the Mountbatten-Windsor family constitute the royal family.[4] Succession to the Crown is governed by statute: under the Act of Settlement 1700 and the Succession to the Crown Act 2013 it extends to all legitimate, Protestant[5] descendants of Sophia, Electress of Hanover, a German princess.[6] Buckingham Palace publishes a list showing only the first 25 individuals in line, although in principle several hundred people remain eligible.

Government based on hereditary monarchy stretches back for centuries, but events and ideas in the seventeenth century were decisive in shaping modern understandings of kingship. In the seventeenth century, the Stuart monarchs James I and Charles I clashed with Parliament over the scope of royal authority, especially taxation. Monarchs claimed a divine right to rule: authority derived directly from God. In today's secular and democratic society, that claim is untenable. The ensuing civil war ended in Charles I's execution in 1649. The country was ruled without a monarch from then until the restoration of the monarchy in 1660. But tensions between the Crown and Parliament soon re-emerged culminating in the Glorious Revolution of 1688. Parliament declared that James II had abdicated and invited his daughter Mary and her husband William of Orange to rule jointly, subject to the Bill of Rights 1689. The analysis of these events by legal historian F.W. Maitland was, '*it was extremely difficult for any lawyer to make out that what had then been done was lawful*',[7] but it was the start of a *constitutional* monarchy. The Act of Settlement 1700 further limited royal power and determined the line of succession, ensuring that the monarch could not be Roman Catholic and could not remove judges except with the agreement of both Houses of Parliament.

The Hanoverian succession in 1714, when the Crown passed to George I of the German House of Hanover under the Act of Settlement, brought a new dynasty to the British throne. Monarchs reigned for life until 1936, when Edward VIII abdicated after the government, led by the Prime Minister, made clear that it could not support his proposed marriage to Wallis Simpson, an American divorcée. Parliament enacted the Declaration of Abdication Act 1936, confirming that his brother became George VI and excluding Edward and any descendants (in fact he had none) from the line of succession.

[3] Beyond the United Kingdom, the monarch has a separate constitutional identity in each realm, often described as 'the King in right of . . .'. For example, in Australia Charles III is the King in right of Australia, exercising powers defined by the Australian Constitution.

[4] The family name Mountbatten-Windsor was adopted by Queen Elizabeth II and Prince Philip in 1960 to denote their direct descendants, combining the Queen's family name, Windsor, with Prince Philip's surname, Mountbatten.

[5] 'Protestant' refers to the branch of Christianity that separated from the Roman Catholic Church in the sixteenth century. Protestant churches reject the authority of the Pope and emphasize individual interpretation of the Bible and direct relationship with God.

[6] Sophia was the granddaughter of King James VI of Scotland and I of England. She never became queen herself, having died shortly before Queen Anne, but her son succeeded to the throne as King George I in 1714.

[7] F.W. Maitland, *The Constitutional History of England* (1908, Cambridge: Cambridge University Press), p. 283.

Reforms introduced by the Succession to the Crown Act 2013 modernized the eligibility rules for becoming monarch: removing male primogeniture and ending the prohibition on the monarch marrying a Roman Catholic. Corresponding legislation was enacted in the Commonwealth realms that retain the monarch as head of state.[8] However, the changes left untouched the rule that the monarch must themselves be Protestant. This preserves the long-standing constitutional link between the Crown and the established Church of England: the monarch is both head of state and Supreme Governor of the Church. But retaining a religious test for the office in an increasingly secular and multi-faith society raises questions about whether a hereditary institution shaped by earlier political and religious settlements can fully reflect the diversity of the United Kingdom today.

Queen Elizabeth II's long reign ended with her death on 8 September 2022. Her eldest son acceded immediately as King Charles III and was formally proclaimed by the Accession Council at St James's Palace, televised for the first time. Parliament met in special session to express condolences and pledges of loyalty, and the coronation in May 2023 served as both a formal act of state and a public and religious ritual expressing the Crown's continuing place in the UK's constitutional and national life.

Legislation makes reference to 'the Royal family', though the term is not defined in statute.[9] The Royal family comprises the monarch's close relatives who undertake public and ceremonial duties in support of the Sovereign. Some members are designated Counsellors of State by the Regency Act 1937 (as amended), enabling them to perform most royal functions when the monarch is temporarily unavailable—for example, when abroad or unwell. Certain members have withdrawn from public roles: the King's younger son, Prince Harry, and his wife stepped back from official duties in 2020; in 2025 the King exercised prerogative powers to remove the titles of Prince and Duke from his brother Andrew Mountbatten-Windsor following allegations of misconduct. Both remain in the line of succession, as do their children, which is determined by statute.

For centuries, the maxim 'the King can do no wrong' has formed part of the common law, though its meaning has changed over time.[10] One aspect is the procedural rule that the monarch cannot be sued or prosecuted in their personal capacity: the sovereign is immune from criminal proceedings, civil actions, and judicial review. This personal immunity does not shield the government from legal challenge. Acts done in the name of the Crown are carried out by ministers and officials, and it is they—rather than the monarch—who may be sued under the Crown Proceedings Act 1947 or subject to judicial review. Thus, when a challenge was brought in 2019 to the government's decision to suspend ('prorogue') Parliament for several weeks during the process of the United Kingdom's withdrawal from the European Union, it was the advice given to Queen Elizabeth II by Prime Minister Boris Johnson MP that was subject to judicial review, not the Queen's formal act of prorogation. In law, the monarch must act on ministerial advice, and it is that advice—rather than the sovereign's authorization—that is reviewable.[11]

PAUSE FOR REFLECTION

The United Kingdom, like several other European democracies such as Sweden, Norway, the Netherlands, Belgium, and Spain, retains a hereditary head of state. What are the advantages and disadvantages of constitutional monarchy in the 2020s? Think about constitutional principles such as accountability, continuity, equality, and the rule of law.

[8] See N. Parpworth, 'The Succession to the Crown Act 2013: Modernising the Monarchy' (2013) 76(6) Modern Law Review 1070.

[9] Crown Proceedings Act 1947 s. 40; Sovereign Grants Acts 2011 and 2022.

[10] See M.-F. Fortin, *The King Can Do No Wrong: Constitutional Fundamentals, Common Law History, and Crown Liability* (OUP 2024).

[11] *R (on the application of Miller) v The Prime Minister* [2019] UKSC 41.

8.2.2 THE MONARCH AND MINISTERS

The relationship between the monarch and ministers is governed almost entirely by prerogative powers and constitutional convention.

One of the monarch's most important powers is to appoint the Prime Minister. Where the result of a general election gives one political party a clear overall majority in the Commons, the convention is straightforward: the monarch invites the leader of that party to become Prime Minister and form the government. The same applies between general elections when the governing political party replaces its leader: once a new leader is chosen through the party's internal procedures, the outgoing leader is expected to resign as Prime Minister, allowing the monarch to invite the new party leader to form a government.

A potentially more complicated scenarios is where there is a hung Parliament after a general election, meaning no single party has an overall majority in the House of Commons. This occurred after the 2010 general election, when the Conservatives had the largest number of MPs but not an overall majority, leading to the formation of a coalition government with the Liberal Democrats. A priority for the outgoing Prime Minister (Labour's Gordon Brown MP), senior civil servants, and the Queen's senior officials was to insulate the monarchy from political controversy while the Conservatives and Liberal Democrats negotiated a coalition agreement. A parliamentary committee subsequently noted 'Government formation takes place within a constitutional framework which is largely unwritten and based on precedent', concluding 'constitutional processes were broadly clear and worked well'.[12] When *The Cabinet Manual* was published the following year, it included the following statement.

Cabinet Office, *The Cabinet Manual,* 1st edn (2011, London: Cabinet Office) (footnotes omitted)

The principles of government formation

2.8 Prime Ministers hold office unless and until they resign. If the Prime Minister resigns on behalf of the Government, the Sovereign will invite the person who appears most likely to be able to command the confidence of the House to serve as Prime Minister and to form a government.

2.9 Historically, the Sovereign has made use of reserve powers to dismiss a Prime Minister or to make a personal choice of successor, although this was last used in 1834 and was regarded as having undermined the Sovereign. In modern times the convention has been that the Sovereign should not be drawn into party politics, and if there is doubt it is the responsibility of those involved in the political process, and in particular the parties represented in Parliament, to seek to determine and communicate clearly to the Sovereign who is best placed to be able to command the confidence of the House of Commons.

As the Crown's principal adviser this responsibility falls especially on the incumbent Prime Minister, who at the time of his or her resignation may also be asked by the Sovereign for a recommendation on who can best command the confidence of the House of Commons in his or her place.

2.10 The application of these principles depends on the specific circumstances and it remains a matter for the Prime Minister, as the Sovereign's principal adviser, to judge the appropriate time at which to resign, either from their individual position as Prime Minister or on behalf of the government. Recent examples suggest that previous Prime Ministers have not offered their resignations until there was a situation in which clear advice could be given to the Sovereign on who should be asked to form a government. It remains to be seen whether or not these examples will be regarded in future as having established a constitutional convention.

[12] House of Commons Political and Constitutional Reform Committee, *Lessons from the process of government formation after the 2010 general election,* Fourth report of session 2010–11, vol 1, HC 258, paras 6–7.

There was a hung Parliament again after the 2017 general election. The incumbent Prime Minister Theresa May MP was able to remain in office by reaching a confidence-and-supply agreement with the Democratic Unionist Party of Northern Ireland. The Queen played no active role in this process. The episode confirmed the convention that government formation is a matter for party negotiations, not royal intervention.

The incoming Prime Minister has an audience with the King at Buckingham Palace (or another royal residence). The appointment becomes official when the new Prime Minister 'kisses hands' with the King, a symbolic gesture now made by handshake rather than an actual kiss. Other ministers recommended by the Prime Minister are appointed in the same way, usually in rapid succession over the following days. They receive seals of office (in the case of senior ministers such as Secretaries of State) or letters patent. Most ministers are not required by law to take an oath on appointment, although some—such as the Lord Chancellor—do so under specific statutory provisions.[13] Most senior ministers are also appointed to the Privy Council (if they are not already members), which enables them to take part in the formal business of government conducted in the King's name.[14]

The monarch is kept fully informed of government business through weekly confidential meetings with the Prime Minister: former Prime Ministers have described these audiences as frank and wide-ranging. The monarch also receives daily written briefings from officials, including Cabinet papers and reports from British ambassadors abroad. As Rodney Brazier explains, the monarch's influence now operates through a small set of conventional rights.

R. Brazier, 'The Monarchy', in V. Bogdanor (ed.) *The British Constitution in the Twentieth Century* (2003, Oxford: British Academy/OUP), ch. 3, p. 78

A sovereign exercises influence in governmental matters by using conventional attributes famously summarised by Bagehot as the right to be consulted, to encourage and to warn ministers. That formulation has occasionally been rendered as the rights to *advise*, to encourage and to warn, but a sovereign cannot offer advice nor support action, counsel against proposed action without knowing what ministers are doing. Perhaps, therefore, it is more accurate, albeit more prolix, to say that the sovereign has five conventional rights rather than three—to be informed, to be consulted, to advise, to encourage and to warn. A right of information would embrace even those cases where the sovereign is not expected to take any action, but is merely being made aware of what is happening. A right to be consulted, however, necessarily involves the notion that the sovereign may wish to express a view about the subject-matter, or indeed may have to exercise a prerogative power in order to give legal effect to it. Personalities and relationship affected the giving of information and of consultation to a degree.

The main characteristic of a constitutional monarchy in the British sense, settled since the end of Queen Victoria's reign, is that the monarch acts only on the advice of ministers. In law, a range of executive powers are exercised in the monarch's name. For example, section 23(2) of the Constitutional Reform Act 2005 provides that the justices of the UK Supreme Court are appointed by the monarch by 'letters patent' (an official document), but a recommendation for appointment may only be made by the Prime Minister (section 26). The King's Speech at the State Opening of Parliament setting out session's legislative programme is drafted entirely by the government. Most prerogative

[13] Constitutional Reform Act 2005 section 17: 'I, [name], do swear that in the office of Lord High Chancellor of Great Britain I will respect the rule of law, defend the independence of the judiciary and discharge my duty to ensure the provision of resources for the efficient and effective support of the courts for which I am responsible. So help me God.'

[14] Section 8.2.3.

powers—including those relating to foreign affairs, defence, and the civil service—are exercised by ministers on behalf of the Crown.[15]

> **PAUSE FOR REFLECTION**
>
> If the monarch's power to appoint the Prime Minister comes from the royal prerogative, what ensures that this power is exercised according to democratic principles rather than personal choice? How do constitutional conventions achieve this in practice?

8.2.3 THE CONCEPT OF 'THE CROWN'

So far, the discussion has focused on the monarch as an individual. The legal and constitutional concept of the Crown, however, is broader and more complex. It refers not only to the person of the monarch but also to the state and the institutions through which public power is exercised. The next extract explores how this concept has developed and why it is central to understanding executive authority in the United Kingdom.

M. Sunkin, 'Crown', in P. Cane and J. Conaghan (eds) *The New Oxford Companion to Law* (2008, Oxford: OUP), pp. 286–7

> The expression 'The Crown' has institutional and symbolic meanings. Institutionally it refers to both the monarch and the executive branch of government, and it symbolizes the formal location of authority within the UK's constitution. In both these senses the Crown presents difficulties for commentators and much disagreement exists as its precise meaning. These disagreements can have important practical constitutional implications, not least because the Crown (in its institutional sense) possesses significant privileges and immunities, including from judicial process.
>
> First, then, the Crown in its institutional sense: Lord Diplock said that 'the Crown' means 'the government' and includes 'all of the ministers and parliamentary secretaries under whose direction the administrative work of government is carried on': *Town Investments Ltd v Department of the Environment* (1978). Professor Sir William Wade considered this 'extraordinary'. He wrote that '[I]n truth, "the Crown" means simply the Queen, though the term is usually confined to her political or constitutional capacity' (M. Sunkin and S. Payne (eds), *The Nature of the Crown* (Oxford: OUP, 1999), 24). There can be no doubt that 'the Crown' extends to the monarch in her official capacity, but it is impossible to confine the Crown to the Queen. In particular, this is because circumstances exist in which the Crown's powers are exercised by ministers as agents of the Crown, so that their decisions are decisions of the Crown. Examples include the exercise of the prerogative of mercy by the Home Secretary and the disposition of the armed forces by the Prime Minister and the Secretary of State for Defence.[[16]] However, such situations are comparatively rare and most powers exercised by ministers are not Crown powers but powers conferred upon ministers specifically, usually by statute. In such situations ministers are members of Her Majesty's Government and serve the Crown: but they do not act as the Crown itself. For this reason, while Lord Diplock's statement may be colloquially correct, it is almost certainly inaccurate from a strictly legal perspective.

[15] See Chapter 10. [16] On prerogative powers over military deployment, see Chapter 10.

Turning to the Crown in its symbolic sense: in their leading textbook on Constitutional Law, Professors Bradley and Ewing say that: 'It is still formally the case that executive power in the United Kingdom is vested in the Crown however little this may reflect the reality of modern government' (A.W. Bradley and K.D. Ewing, *Constitutional and Administrative Law* (London: Pearson, 14th edn, 2007, 242)). In reality executive power is vested not in the Crown but in the government by virtue of its ability to command the political support of Parliament that derives from electoral success. So what sense is there in saying that formally executive power vests in the Crown? The essential answer is rooted in the fact that the monarch is the longest established source of power in the UK. While over the centuries its powers to dispense justice, to legislate, and to govern have been transferred to other institutions, the Crown continues to symbolize the continuity of a system in which those who exercise power do so because they have constitutional authority to do so.

8.2.4 THE PRIVY COUNCIL

The concept of the Crown embraces not only the monarch but also the institutions through which executive authority is exercised. One of the oldest of these institutions is the Privy Council, a body that formally advises the Sovereign. The term 'His Majesty in Council' is used to describe certain acts carried out by the monarch in this capacity. Such business often takes place at one of the monarch's monthly meetings with a small group of ministers, usually no more than four, at a royal palace.

The Privy Council as a whole consists of more than 700 members; there is no limit on the number. They include senior politicians and retired politicians, senior judges, and senior members of the Church of England. The number of politician Privy Counsellors is much larger than the number of current ministers because appointment is for life and some senior opposition politicians are also appointed. Appointments are, in some cases, honorific, but in the case of currently serving ministers, they are functional. At any given time, however, the executive functions of the Privy Council are carried out by the monarch and members of the current government. Privy Counsellors are referred to as 'Right Honourable'. In his diary entry for 22 October 1964, the Rt Hon. Richard Crossman MP describes rather irritably what happened after his appointment as Minister for Housing and Local Government when he was required to be sworn in as a member of the Privy Council.

A. Howard (ed.) *Diaries of a Cabinet Minister: Selections, 1964–70* (1979, London: Hamish Hamilton), p. 31

[. . . L]ast Monday we new ministers were summoned to the Privy Council offices to rehearse the ceremony of becoming a Privy Councillor. I don't suppose anything more dull, pretentious, or plain silly has ever been invented. There we were, sixteen grown men. For over an hour we were taught how to stand up, how to kneel on one knee on a cushion, how to raise the right hand with the Bible in it, how to advance three paces towards the Queen, how to take the hand and kiss it, how to move back ten paces without falling over the stools—which had been carefully arranged so that you did fall over them. Oh dear! We did this from 11.10 to 12.15. At 12.15 all of us went out, each to his own car, and we drove to the Palace and there stood about until we entered a great drawing-room. At the other end was this little woman with a beautiful waist, and she had to stand with her hand on the table for forty minutes while we went through this rigmarole. We were uneasy, she was uneasy. Then at the end informality broke out and she said, 'You all moved backwards very nicely,' and we all laughed. And then she pressed a bell and we all left her. We were Privy Councillors: we had kissed hands.

At its monthly meetings, the Privy Council no longer has any deliberative or consultative function. Its regular formal meetings are mainly to confer validity on documents and decisions that have already been agreed upon in Cabinet or by a government department. They are accordingly short; nobody sits down.

The Privy Council is responsible for an eclectic range of executive and legislative matters. It advises the monarch on the exercise of prerogative and statutory powers through formal instruments known as Orders in Council and Orders of Council, which may be legislative, executive, or judicial in nature.[17] It approves changes to the constitutions and by-laws of chartered professional bodies, and oversees certain statutory appointments. It also plays a constitutional role in relation to the Crown Dependencies and British Overseas Territories, where Orders in Council are sometimes used to give effect to local legislation. Finally, through the Judicial Committee of the Privy Council, it serves as the final court of appeal for some Commonwealth countries and overseas territories.

The Lord President of Council is the government minister who is head of the Privy Council Office (a department that deals with administrative matters relating to the Privy Council). The Lord President may be either a member of the House of Commons or the House of Lords. In the following extract, taken from a House of Lords debate, the government sets out its view of the role of the Privy Council in rather glowing terms.[18]

House of Lords Hansard, 12 May 2009, col. 1009

The Lord President of the Council (Baroness Royall of Blaisdon): [. . .] I take huge pride in the fact that I am a privy counsellor, and indeed that I am Lord President of the Council.

The Privy Council dates back to at least the 13th century. It formerly ran the whole Government, along with the Exchequer. The Cabinet is a committee of the Privy Council, which is why all Cabinet Ministers have to be privy counsellors too. Some modern departments were originally boards of the Privy Council, such as the Board of Trade and the Board of Education.

These days the Privy Council is simply another way of saying 'Ministers collectively'. It is a thoroughly modern example of joined-up government which provides a highly effective means of dispatching a great deal of public business. The Privy Council approves amendments to the byelaws and statutes of chartered institutions. It also approves rules made by the statutory registration councils responsible for the medical and certain other professions, and it makes instruments of government for higher education corporations. In addition, it makes certain appointments to statutory bodies. [. . .]

On prerogative business, where there is no legislation allocating the responsibility to a particular Minister, the council provides a mechanism for giving ministerial advice to the Queen, as constitutionally the Queen acts only on such advice. On statutory business, where the use of 'the Privy Council' rather than 'the Secretary of State' in an Act enables more than one government department to be involved, it allows joined-up government. It also enables the devolved Administrations to be involved, as the First Ministers are all privy counsellors.

Writing for the law reform charity JUSTICE, Patrick O'Connor KC—a veteran criminal and civil liberties lawyer—offered a forthright critique of the Privy Council.

[17] Orders in Council are made by the monarch on ministerial advice, either under statute (as delegated legislation) or under the royal prerogative. Orders of Council are made by Privy Counsellors without the monarch's approval, usually for administrative matters such as professional regulation. See https://privycouncil.independent.gov.uk/orders/ accessed 12 November 2025.

[18] For a more critical assessment, see P. O'Connor, *A Justice Report: The Constitutional Role of the Privy Council and the Prerogative* (2009, London: Justice).

Patrick O'Connor, The Constitutional Role of the Privy Council and the Prerogative (JUSTICE 2009) p. 36

The Privy Council is a dysfunctional body. There is no rationale which can justify the eclectic range of its work. It currently ranges from being in part 'synonymous with government', to an independent court: from a forum for the monarch's real remaining personal prerogative powers, to a theatre for benign historic ceremonial. This has all arisen by historical accident, and has never been analysed rationally. Do the charters of universities and professional associations have to be administered by the same body as produces the laws of Guernsey, and proclaims bank holidays and our coinage? Does Parliament have to be dissolved by the same body as approves royal marriages, closes burial grounds and approves pensions for the marine personnel in Hong Kong?

He concluded staying '*fundamental consideration should be given to the future role, and even continued existence, of the Privy Council*' (p. 38). However, this is unlikely to become a political priority for any government in the foreseeable future.

8.2.5 WHAT FUTURE FOR THE MONARCHY?

In 2025, opinion polls suggest two-thirds of UK residents think the United Kingdom should continue as a monarchy, though there is somewhat lower support from younger people.[19] The political parties that have formed governments in recent years all support the continuation of monarchy. What, if any, legitimacy claims can be made for a hereditary head of state?

Roger Scruton (1944–2020) was a leading British philosopher and public thinker who wrote widely on politics, culture, and beauty from a conservative perspective. He believed that national institutions carry moral and emotional meaning that reaches beyond their practical use. In *England: An Elegy* (2000), his meditation on what he saw as the fading of England's historic culture, Scruton treats the constitutional monarchy as a living symbol of continuity and belonging. The passage below expresses his view that the Crown stands 'above politics', giving voice to the nation's history and linking each generation to those who came before and those still to come.

Roger Scruton, *England: An Elegy* (Chatto & Windus 2000) p. 188

The constitutional monarchy is the light above politics, which shines down on the human bustle from a calmer and more exalted sphere. Not being elected by popular vote, the monarch cannot be understood as representing the interests only of the present generation. He or she is born into the position, and also passes it on to a legally defined successor. The monarch is in a real sense the voice of history, and the very accidental way in which the office is acquired emphasises the grounds of the monarch's legitimacy, in the history of a place and a culture. This is not to say that kings and queens cannot be mad, irrational, self-interested or unwise. It is to say, rather, that they owe their authority and their influence precisely to the fact that they speak for something other than the present desires of present voters, something

[19] Matthew Smith, 'Royal family favourability trackers, August 2025' (YouGov 2025) https://yougov.co.uk/politics/articles/52737-royal-family-favourability-trackers-august-2025 accessed 24 October 2025.

vital to the continuity and community which the act of voting assumes. Hence, if they are heard at all, they are heard as limiting the democratic process, in just the way that it must be limited if it is to issue in reasonable legislation. It was in such a way that the English conceived their Queen, in the sunset days of Queen Victoria. The sovereign was an ordinary person, transfigured by a peculiar enchantment which represented not political power but the mysterious authority of an ancient 'law of the land'. When the monarch betrays that law — as, in the opinion of many, the Stuarts betrayed it — a great social and spiritual unrest seizes the common conscience, unrest of a kind that could never attend the misdemeanours of an elected president, or even the betrayal of trust by a political party.

But there are critics of the institution. In *Abolish the Monarchy*, Graham Smith (CEO of the campaign organisation Republic) makes the case against the institution: it is wrong in principle, and it does not work in practice, he argues.

Graham Smith, *Abolish the Monarchy: Why we should and how we will* (Penguin 2023), p. 100.

If, like most people in the UK, you believe in democracy, equality and the rule of law, then it is unprincipled and wrong to support the continuation of the monarchy. This isn't just because principles have some theoretical value. Principles also have very real meaning in terms of how we are governed and the society we live in. There's a reason we put great store in political equality, the right to speak in opposition to those in power and the need for accountability to the electorate. Because without those things we suffer oppression, arbitrary and unjust rule and a general suppression of our rights. Principles don't just exist in the world of the theoretical, they matter in our day-to-day lives. To undermine our principles is a problem. As if to prove a point, it is notable how quick the police were to arrest even the most harmless protester in the days after the Queen's death, suggesting that, when it comes to the monarchy, free speech is cancelled out by deference. Symon Hill was arrested for simply shouting, 'Who elected him?' as he walked past the Oxford accession ceremony. Barrister Paul Powlesland tweeted on the Monday after the King's accession: 'Just went to Parliament Square & held up a blank piece of paper. Officer came & asked for my details. He confirmed that if I wrote "Not My King" on it, he would arrest me under the Public Order Act because someone might be offended.'

Smith's critique therefore poses the question of whether hereditary monarchy can ever be reconciled with democratic principle. His argument emphasizes the incompatibility between inherited power and political equality, whereas Nicholas Barber's more cautious analysis in the next extract approaches the issue from the perspective of constitutional function. For Barber, the test is not only moral but practical: whether the monarchy still serves a unifying role that no other institution could easily replace.

N.W. Barber, 'What's the Point of Constitutional Monarch?' (2024) 69 *The American Journal of Jurisprudence* 189, 203–4

When the monarch is succeeding in providing a point of identification for a significant portion of state members, and is not a significant cause of alienation for others, it might be a mistake to unsettle this position. We cannot be sure that alternative mechanisms of identification will be equally efficacious, indeed, as there are many forms of republic to choose from, the process of choice could alienate, creating winners and losers in the debate. More broadly, the act of removing a monarch who does have support, even minority support, will be destabilizing. The contents of those elements of the state which ground identification are often hard, or impossible, to rationally defend, in that they establish an emotion connection with the state rather than provide a rational argument for our support. This emotional connection is, nevertheless, exceptionally important in securing the support of state members for state institutions and for shaping the ways state members interact with each other. The principled arguments against monarchy show that a state must ensure that there are other ways of grounding this identification, and that it be possible to be member of the state without supporting the monarchy. Constitutional monarchies, with their paired leadership [for example, with the Prime Minister], often accomplish this, providing a republican narrative that runs alongside the monarchical. State members can then ground their identification with the state on differing parts of the constitutional order. This is, though, a fragile argument for the maintenance of monarchy. When monarchy is working well, and it can work well for a long time, it is an asset to the constitution, but its mode of selection renders it a time-limited constitutional form. Whereas democracy provides a standing argument for republican institutions, even when those institutions are functioning poorly, when monarchy functions poorly the reasons for including it within the constitution disappear. As Bagehot put it, a good monarchy is invaluable, but a bad monarchy is irreparable.

PAUSE FOR REFLECTION

The extracts you have read present three very different ways of thinking about monarchy. Roger Scruton sees the Crown as a stabilising symbol of continuity and belonging, its authority drawn from history rather than the ballot box. Graham Smith argues that this same feature—the absence of democratic accountability—makes monarchy indefensible in a modern state committed to equality and the rule of law. Nicholas Barber offers a middle ground: monarchy may have value when it helps unify the community, but its hereditary nature means that value is always temporary. Reflect on these competing claims.

- Can a hereditary institution ever sit comfortably within a democratic constitution?
- Is emotional attachment to tradition a legitimate reason for retaining a form of government?
- What other institutions or practices might provide the same sense of continuity and shared identity if the monarchy were abolished?

8.3 MINISTERS

The Crown represents the state, but it is ministers who exercise most of the political power in its name. When we speak of 'His Majesty's Government', we are describing this system: ministers, led by the Prime Minister, who govern on the monarch's behalf. Some of their authority comes from the royal prerogative—the residue of powers historically exercised by the monarch, such as foreign affairs or defence.[20] But most modern ministerial powers are conferred by Acts of Parliament, which specify what a minister may do, though many Acts delegate further law-making powers to ministers.[21] Ministers therefore operate at the intersection of two constitutional traditions: the ancient powers

[20] See Chapter 10 (Prerogative Powers).
[21] See Chapter 12 (Primary Legislation) and Chapter 13 (Delegated Legislation).

of the Crown and the democratic authority of Parliament. Understanding how these powers coexist, and how ministers are held to account for their use, is central to understanding executive power in the UK constitution.

Cabinet Office, *The Cabinet Manual*, 1st edn (2011, London: Cabinet Office), p. 2 (footnotes omitted)

Constitutional convention is that executive power is exercised by the Sovereign's government, which has a democratic mandate to govern. Members of the Government are normally Members of the House of Commons or the House of Lords and the Government is directly accountable to Parliament. The government of the day holds office by virtue of its ability to command the confidence of the House of Commons. Elections are held at least every five years to ensure broad and continued accountability to the people. Election candidates can stand independently but they usually represent political parties, and party numbers in the House of Commons determine the composition of the Government.

8.3.1 THE PRIME MINISTER

The Prime Minister is the central figure in the UK government. The Prime Minister is head of government—distinct from the monarch, who is head of state—and must be a sitting MP in the House of Commons. Yet, viewed strictly in legal terms, the Prime Minister holds surprisingly few statutory powers. The office exists by constitutional convention rather than by statute: there is no single Act of Parliament that defines its functions or authority. The Prime Minister's ability to act depends mainly on prerogative powers exercised in the monarch's name—such as appointing ministers, conducting foreign affairs, and advising on the dissolution of Parliament—which are examined in more detail in Chapter 10. The Prime Minister's wider influence arises from political leadership, control of the Cabinet, and the ability to shape the legislative and policy agenda, rather than from legal powers alone.

Although the Prime Minister's legal powers are limited, political authority is extensive. The office combines leadership of the government, control over Cabinet business, and influence over the policy agenda and public communication. Scholars often debate whether the Prime Minister should still be seen as *primus inter pares*—the first among equals in Cabinet—or as occupying a more presidential role, exercising dominant personal authority within the executive.[22] The succession of Conservative Prime Ministers between 2016 and 2022—Theresa May, Boris Johnson, Liz Truss, and Rishi Sunak—illustrates how swiftly prime-ministerial authority can weaken when support within Parliament and the governing party falls away. When a change of party leadership occurs between general elections, there is no constitutional convention requiring a fresh general election. In some circumstances, the governing party's internal rules may mean that only one candidate comes forward, as occurred when Rishi Sunak succeeded Liz Truss, and no vote of party members takes place at all.

The constitutional takeaway is that the Prime Minister's authority depends less on legal powers than on political circumstances. The office demonstrates how convention and political control can create real constitutional power without statutory definition. Understanding the Prime Minister's

[22] See further A. Blick and G. Jones, *Premiership: The Development, Nature and Power of the Office of the British Prime Minister* (Societas 2010).

role therefore requires thinking about the interaction between law, politics, and accountability: the law provides only the framework, while the day-to-day operation of government depends on confidence in the Commons and support within the governing party.

PAUSE FOR REFLECTION

If the office of Prime Minister rests mainly on convention rather than law, what—if anything—limits how a Prime Minister may use their authority? Think about the role of Cabinet support, party confidence, and parliamentary scrutiny. Do these political checks offer enough restraint in the absence of clear legal limits?

8.3.2 DEPARTMENTAL MINISTERIAL TEAMS

Apart from the Prime Minister, the most senior ministers in the UK system are known as Secretaries of State. In law, there is a single office of 'Secretary of State', shared by around 15 senior politicians chosen by the Prime Minister and formally appointed to office by the monarch. The Prime Minister may designate a 'First Secretary of State' to emphasize his or her status in the government and may also create the post of deputy Prime Minister, though there is no legal requirement to do so. Each Secretary of State is supported by a team of junior ministers—Ministers of State and Parliamentary Under-Secretaries of State—appointed by the Prime Minister to take responsibility for specific areas within the department's portfolio.

Acts of Parliament are usually drafted to confer executive and delegated law making powers on 'the Secretary of State', as in the following example.

National Health Service Act 2006, s. 1

(1) The Secretary of State must continue the promotion in England of a comprehensive health service designed to secure improvement—
 (a) in the physical and mental health of the people of England, and
 (b) in the prevention, diagnosis and treatment of illness. [. . .]

(2) The Secretary of State retains ministerial responsibility to Parliament for the provision of the health service in England.

In some cases, legislation expressly requires the Secretary of State to act personally, particularly where decisions impact on fundamental rights. For example, section 13(5) of the Immigration Act 1971 provides that a person may be excluded from the United Kingdom on the ground that it is conducive to the public good only by 'the Secretary of State (and not by a person acting under his authority)'. Similarly, under section 30 of the Investigatory Powers Act 2016, decisions about interception of communication warrants must be 'taken personally by the Secretary of State'.

Unless an Act expressly imposes such a requirement, powers conferred on the Secretary of State may generally be exercised by other ministers within the department. For instance, delegated legislation made under powers granted to the Secretary of State is often signed by the junior minister responsible for the relevant policy area.[23] However, context matters. In *R v Adams* [2020] UKSC 19, the UK Supreme Court held that interim custody orders (ICOs) in Northern Ireland—commonly described as 'detention without trial'—that had been signed in the 1970s by a junior minister (a Minister of State) rather than the Secretary of State, were invalid. The court found that, given the wording of the Detention of Terrorists (Northern Ireland) Order 1972, the impact of ICOs on individual liberty, and limited number of people affected, the Secretary of State should have exercised the power personally.[24]

Many ministers have a 'parliamentary private secretary' (PPS). PPSs are other MPs in the governing party who act as the ministers' 'eyes and ears' in the Commons and assist ministers with parliamentary work (for example, arranging meetings with MPs). Being a PPS, which carries no salary on top of that of an MP, is regarded as being a stepping stone to appointment as a junior minister. PPSs are not part of the government, but they are expected to be active supporters of government policy.

There is also a more recent debate as to whether the 'centre of government'—meaning the Prime Minister, the Cabinet Office, and HM Treasury—have assumed too much power in relation to other departments (for example, by imposing targets of various kinds).[25] From a constitutional perspective, a concern that grows out of these developments is that the Prime Minister is insufficiently accountable to Parliament.

A House of Commons inquiry into the implications of the 2010–15 Conservative–Liberal Democrat Coalition government's aim of significantly reducing the cost of government suggested there were three areas of work for ministers.

House of Commons Select Committee on Public Administration, *Smaller Government*, Seventh Report, Session 2010–12 (HC 530)

[. . . W]e have formulated our own account of what we believe the proper role of a minister is. These functions can be grouped in terms of the bodies with which ministers have a relationship: Government, Parliament, and the public.

Within Government

21. Within Government, a minister . . . fulfils three key tasks. The first is to set policy priorities. This is their primary function. Ministers are responsible for setting the policy and providing leadership to their department to ensure their objectives are met. Once policy is set it is the job of civil servants to ensure that the outcomes are delivered. . . ..

22. This does not mean that when policy has been set the minister will have no further involvement with it; the implementation of policies can be as politically sensitive as the policy decision itself. It is not possible to draw a line through the policy process after which no more ministerial involvement is required. The process of designing and implementing a scheme can raise issues that require a minister

[23] R. Ekins and S. Laws, *Mishandling the* Law (Policy Exchange 2020) p. 38; and see Chapter 13 below.

[24] After his release, Gerry Adams became a leading Irish republican politician, serving as president of Sinn Féin from 1983 to 2018 and playing a central role in the Northern Ireland peace process. The Supreme Court's judgment in his case was politically and legally controversial.

[25] House of Lords Constitution Committee, *The Cabinet Office and the Centre of Government*, Fourth Report, Session 2009–10, HL Paper 30; National Audit Office, *The Cabinet Office and HM Treasury: The Centre of Government,* Session 2014–15, HC 171.

to make further political judgements. In such a situation, civil servants should present ministers with a range of options about how the policy could be implemented, the minister should make a decision and then the civil servants act on that instruction.

23. The second function that a minister must perform within government is to negotiate on behalf of their department, in cabinet committees, in bilateral meetings and in formal meetings of the Cabinet, as well as with the Treasury about their spending programmes. . . .

24. Thirdly, ministers must also ensure those charged with running the department, their senior civil servants, are able to do so, but they should not personally manage the department. ....

Answering to Parliament

Ministers must also discharge certain duties in Parliament. They must be accountable to the legislature through answering oral and urgent questions, opening and responding to debates and appearing before select committees. Ministers must also explain and justify their legislative proposals as they go through Parliament.

The public face of Government

Acting as the public face of Government is an important ministerial function. Ministers need to get outside their departments and meet a wide range of stakeholders to ensure that their policy decisions reflect the reality on the ground; and to guard against them getting captured by their department's own agenda. Attending public events, while essential to ensure that ministers keep in touch with the issues affecting the people they serve, will necessarily compete with other demands on their time. Ministers must prioritise the numerous demands on their time to ensure that their energy is directed to where it is best spent.

PAUSE FOR REFLECTION

Why does it matter whether a decision is taken personally by the Secretary of State or by a junior minister or official? Consider how this affects accountability to Parliament, responsibility to the courts, and public trust in the decision-making process.

8.3.3 MINISTERS MUST BE IN PARLIAMENT

The United Kingdom has a system of *parliamentary government*. So, whereas some constitutional systems (such as that of the USA) separate the executive and legislative branches so that members of the executive cannot sit in the legislature, the UK takes the opposite approach. By convention, all government ministers must be members of either the House of Commons or the House of Lords. In 2024–5, there were 120 ministers, of whom 28 were in the House of Lords.

This convention limits the Prime Minister's choice of ministers to Members of Parliament and peers, although on occasion an individual has been appointed as a minister and then promptly nominated for a peerage to meet the requirement. For example, in July 2024, James Timpson, chief executive of the Timpson retail group of shoe repair shops and a leading advocate for prisoner rehabilitation, was appointed Minister of State for Prisons, Probation and Reducing Reoffending and was rapidly created a life peer to enable him to serve in the House of Lords. The rationale is that ministers must be directly accountable to Parliament. Their membership of one of the two Houses enables Parliament to question, debate with, and, if necessary, criticise the ministers responsible for government policy and administration.

Things *might* have turned out differently. As Sir Maurice Amos (1872–1940) explains, there was a moment of opportunity in the early eighteenth century that might, had it been taken, have established a constitutional system in which the ministers were not excluded from Parliament, giving Britain a system of separation of powers.

Sir Maurice Amos, *The English Constitution* (1930, London: Longmans, Green & Co.), pp. 65-6 (footnotes omitted)

[. . .] Ministers are Members of Parliament and generally, in modern times, of the House of Commons; and [. . .] Ministers are chosen from that party which has a majority in that House. These two facts, taken together, are of primary importance. It is only because Ministers are Members of Parliament, entitled to vote and speak, sharing the corporate life and the traditional feelings of the House to which they belong, taking a continuous and prominent part in all its business, familiarly known by daily association to friends and foes alike, and, last but not least, both leading and depending on the votes and cheers of the party which is in the ascendancy, that it is possible to bring about that intimate union between the management of Parliament and the management of the executive administration which is the essence of Cabinet government. It is a striking fact that it was almost by chance that at a critical moment in the development of the Constitution, Ministers of the Crown were not excluded from the House of Commons. When the Act of Settlement was passed in 1701, to take effect when the anticipated change of dynasty should be realised, so great was the fear of the corrupting influence of the Crown, that it was provided that 'after the said limitation (of the Crown to the House of Hanover) shall take effect, no person who has an office or place of profit under the King or receives a pension from the Crown shall be capable of serving as a Member of the House of Commons.' This drastic provision was so amended in 1706, before it came into force, as to permit of Ministers becoming Members of the House of Commons if they had been elected, or re-elected, after appointment. If the original plan had been carried into effect and had remained law, it is impossible to calculate what our Government would have become: it certainly could not have developed as it has done. Either the Parliament and the Crown must have remained in a relationship of perpetual loggerheads—which it is impossible to conceive; or Parliament must have dwindled to impotent subserviency; or possibly, again, some awkward arrangement, difficult to picture, would have been worked out by which the Departments of State became the secretariats of standing committees composed of unofficial Members of Parliament—some such arrangement as would exist in America if the President were eliminated. From this choice of uninviting paths we were delivered by 'that remarkable system which combines unity, steadfastness, and initiative in the executive, with the possession of supreme authority alike over men and measures in the House of Commons'.

PAUSE FOR REFLECTION

What difference does it make that ministers sit in Parliament? Consider how direct accountability through questions, debates, and select committees strengthens parliamentary control, but also how close links between the executive and legislature might weaken the separation of powers. How would the UK constitution function if, like the United States, ministers could not be MPs or peers?

8.3.4 RESTRAINING GOVERNMENT INFLUENCE OVER PARLIAMENT

The close connection between government and Parliament raises practical questions about how many ministers should sit in the legislature. If too many MPs hold ministerial and PPS posts, there are fewer independent backbenchers available to question and challenge the government, making parliamentary scrutiny of bills and policy less effective.

The House of Commons Disqualification Act 1975 caps the number of ministers who may sit in the House of Commons at 95; there is no restriction on the number of ministers in the House of Lords. The Ministerial and Other Salaries Act 1975 limits the number of ministers (across both Houses) who may receive a salary to 109, including 21 Cabinet ministers plus the Lord Chancellor.[26] In 2010, a select committee called for reforms to reduce the number of ministers.[27]

A statutory cap on the number of ministers who may sit in the House of Commons has not, many critics argue, prevented governments from exerting excessive influence over Parliament. Party organization is central to that influence. Each major party ensures that its MPs are well coordinated—attending key debates and voting in divisions. For a government to function effectively, it must secure the support of its party's MPs and peers, and discourage public dissent. This is done through the system of whips, who issue instructions on how and when to vote. A three-line whip indicates the strongest requirement, and serious defiance can lead to suspension or expulsion from the party, making re-election unlikely. Around twenty MPs and peers serve as government whips, appointed by the Prime Minister to salaried posts. The Chief Whip, formally the Parliamentary Secretary to the Treasury, sits in the Cabinet.

Party discipline is less pronounced in the work of select committees, where MPs generally operate on a cross-party basis in scrutinising government policy. [28] However, select committee reports are advisory: their findings and recommendations are not binding on the government.

The government also effectively controls the timetabling of business in the House of Commons, as specified in the House of Commons Standing Orders.

House of Commons Standing Orders

Arrangement and Timing of Public and Private Business

14. (1) Save as provided in this order, government business shall have precedence at every sitting.

(2) Twenty days shall be allotted in each session for proceedings on opposition business, seventeen of which shall be at the disposal of the Leader of the Opposition and three of which shall be at the disposal of the leader of the second largest opposition party; and matters selected on those days shall have precedence over government business [. . .].

While allowing opposition parties some opportunities to choose the subjects of debate on the floor of the chamber and enabling backbench MPs of all parties opportunities to initiate short debates, Standing Order 14 gives government the upper hand. There have been calls for reform,

[26] See further, C. Rhodes and C. Watson, 'Limitations on the number of ministers' (House of Commons Library 2021) https://assets-learning.parliament.uk/uploads/2021/12/Limitations-on-the-Number-of-Ministers.pdf accessed 13 November 2025.

[27] House of Commons Public Administration Select Committee, *Too Many Ministers?* Ninth Report, Session 2009–10 (HC 457); and *Smaller Government: What Do Ministers Do? Further Report*, Fiftieth Report, Session 2010–12 (HC 1540).

[28] See Chapter 9.

including making a House of Commons business committee—which would feature representatives of all the main political parties—responsible for deciding what is debated and on what votes are taken.[29]

As we see in Chapters 12 and 13, government control over legislative processes is an area of concern to many parliamentarians. In November 2021, a House of Lords committee issued the 'stark warning' that '*the balance of power between Parliament and government has for some time been shifting away from Parliament, a trend accentuated by the twin challenges of Brexit and the COVID-19 pandemic. A critical moment has now been reached when that balance must be re-set: not restored to how things were immediately before these exceptional recent events but re-set afresh.*'[30]

8.3.5 CABINET

From a narrow legal perspective, there is little to say about the Cabinet: it is a committee of the Privy Council; it has no independent legal personality or legal powers. Like the Prime Minister, it can be described as 'a creature of convention'. From a broader constitutional perspective, it is, however, of considerable importance.

A. Le Sueur, 'The Nature, Powers, and Accountability of Central Government', in D. Feldman (ed.) *English Public Law*, 2nd edn (2009, Oxford: OUP), paras 3.12–3.14 (footnotes omitted)

It is the gathering of senior ministers, typically 20 or so in number, normally once a week at 10 Downing Street, though it may meet at any time and location. Much work is done through a plethora of committees and subcommittees, some of which include officials as well as ministers. The Cabinet Secretariat, part of the department called the Cabinet Office, supports the work of the Cabinet. Ministers often meet each other outside the formal structures of Cabinet. Although the Cabinet is composed entirely of members of the House of Commons and House of Lords, more particularly the leading members of the majority party in the Commons, it is not a committee of Parliament. Decisions taken in Cabinet and its committees nevertheless exert significant control over Parliament, as it is a Cabinet committee that decides upon and manages the legislative agenda in each annual session of Parliament. The organization of the forthcoming week's business in Parliament is discussed at the preceding Thursday's Cabinet meeting.

The relative powers of the Prime Minister and the Cabinet have been the subject of much analysis and debate. For some, the 'central directing instrument of government, in legislation as well as in administration, is the Cabinet [. . .] It is the Cabinet which controls Parliament and governs the country.' For another, the 'post-war epoch has seen the final transformation of Cabinet Government into Prime Ministerial Government'. Still others relate the role and importance of the Cabinet to the leadership styles of particular Prime Ministers. What is indisputable is that the Prime Minister has considerable control over the agenda of the Cabinet itself and the number, membership and terms of reference of Cabinet committees. The Prime Minister presides over the Cabinet and any Cabinet committees of which he is a member. The Prime Minister may also exercise prerogative powers without prior reference to Cabinet. It is equally clear, however, that the Cabinet is the source of a Prime Minister's political authority: without the support of Cabinet colleagues, a Prime Minister cannot continue in power for long.

[29] See, e.g., Hansard Society, *Representative Democracy Briefing Paper 1: House of Commons Reform* (June 2009), available at www.hansardsociety.org.uk; Select Committee on Reform of the House of Commons, *Report: Rebuilding the House*, First Report, Session 2009–10 (HC 111).

[30] House of Lords Secondary Legislation Scrutiny Committee, *Government by Diktat: A Call to Return Power to Parliament*, 20th Report of Session 2021–22 (HL Paper 105), p. 2.

Decisions made or ratified by Cabinet and its committees are given legal effect through the statutory or prerogative powers of individual ministers or, if no legal basis exists, the relevant minister will introduce a bill in Parliament.

QUESTIONS

1. What roles do ministers have in the constitutional system?
2. From a constitutional perspective, what are the pros and cons of the convention that requires all ministers to be members of one or other House of Parliament?
3. Does the government have too much influence over the House of Commons?

8.4 THE CIVIL SERVICE

Every government depends on a large administrative system to put political decisions into effect and implement routine tasks such as collecting tax, paying welfare benefits, and controlling borders. This section explores how the civil service performs that task and why it is constitutionally significant. Ministers rely on politically neutral officials to carry out the day-to-day business of government, exercising powers that are legally those of the Crown or are conferred by statute. Under the Carltona principle, decisions made by officials within their authorised responsibilities are treated in law as the decisions of the minister. The civil service is bound by long-standing principles of impartiality and accountability, now given statutory recognition in the Constitutional Reform and Governance Act 2010 and the Civil Service Code. Together, these arrangements help to maintain the balance between political leadership and professional administration within the executive branch of the constitution.

8.4.1 HISTORICAL DEVELOPMENT OF THE CIVIL SERVICE

During the nineteenth century, ideas about the organization of government changed, and new techniques and structures of public administration were introduced. In 1853, two senior civil servants, Sir Stafford Northcote and Sir Charles Trevelyan, conducted a wide-ranging review of administration. Their admirably short 20-page report was the impetus for transforming the British civil service.

S.H. Northcote and C.E. Trevelyan, *Report on the Organization of the Permanent Civil Service,* Presented to both Houses of Parliament by Command of Her Majesty (1854, London)

That the Permanent Civil Service, with all its defects, essentially contributes to the proper discharge of the functions of Government, has been repeatedly admitted by those who have successively been responsible for the conduct of our affairs. All however, who have had occasion to examine its constitution with care, have felt that its organisation is far from perfect, and that its amendment is deserving the most careful attention.

It would be natural to expect that so important a profession would attract into its ranks the ablest and the most ambitious of the youth of the country; that the keenest emulation would prevail among those who had entered it; and that such as were endowed with superior qualifications would rapidly rise to distinction and public eminence. Such, however, is by no means the case. Admission into the Civil Service is indeed eagerly sought after, but it is for the unambitious, and the indolent or incapable that it is chiefly desired. [. . .]

It may be noticed in particular that the comparative lightness of work, and the certainty of provision in case of retirement owing to bodily incapacity, furnish strong inducements to the parents and friends of sickly youths to endeavour to obtain for them employment in the service of Government [. . .]

The general principle [. . .] which we advocate is, that the public service should be carried on by the admission into its lower ranks of a carefully selected body of young men [. . .]

Upon a review of the recommendations contained in this paper, it will be seen that the objects we have principally in view are these:—

1. To provide, by a proper system of examination, for the supply of the public service with a thoroughly efficient class of men.
2. To encourage industry and foster merit, by teaching all public servants to look forward to promotion according to their deserts, and to expect the highest prizes in the service if they can qualify themselves for them.
3. To mitigate the evils which result from the fragmentary character of the Service, and to introduce elements of unity, by placing the first appointments upon an uniform footing, opening the way to the promotion of public officers to staff appointments in other departments than their own, and introducing into the lower ranks a body of men (the supplementary clerks) whose services may be made available at any time in any office whatever.

It remains for us to express our conviction that if any change of the importance of those which we have recommended is to be carried into effect, it can only be successfully done through the medium of an Act of Parliament. The existing system is supported by long usage and powerful interests; and were any Government to introduce material alterations into it, in consequence of their own convictions, without taking the precaution to give those alterations the force of law, it is almost certain that they would be imperceptibly, or perhaps avowedly, abandoned by their successors, if they were not even allowed to fall into disuse by the very Government which had originated them. A few clauses would accomplish all that is proposed in this paper, and it is our firm belief that a candid statement of the grounds of the measure would insure its success and popularity in the country, and would remove many misconceptions which are now prejudicial to the public service.

Traditionalists viewed these proposals with hostility when they were first published—some even seeing in them 'the seeds of republicanism', because objective examinations (rather than Crown discretion) were to determine who was appointed to the civil service. But public outrage over the lives lost in the Crimean War due to administrative inefficiencies helped to prepare the ground for the adoption of the proposals. In 1870, when Gladstone was Prime Minister, a new civil service Order in Council (a piece of primary legislation made under the royal prerogative)[31] was made implementing most of the proposals in the Northcote–Trevelyan report. The civil service that emerged during this period was, however, far from socially representative. Women, people from minority ethnic backgrounds (in the age of the British Empire), and those from working-class communities were largely excluded from senior posts. Modern diversity and inclusion strategies aim to address the legacy of these historic patterns.[32]

[31] See Chapter 10.

[32] At permanent secretary level, the first woman appointed was Evelyn Sharp, who became Permanent Secretary at the Ministry of Housing and Local Government in 1955. Sir Suma Chakrabarti was the first British Asian permanent secretary, appointed to lead the Ministry of Justice in 2007. Dame Sharon White became the first Black person appointed as a permanent secretary when she took up the post of Second Permanent Secretary at HM Treasury in 2013.

Not all public officials are civil servants. The police are organized into local constabularies rather than forming part of the civil service, preserving their operational independence from ministers. Members of the armed forces are Crown servants under military command, not civil servants, reflecting the constitutional principle of civilian control of the military. Judges are office-holders whose independence requires complete separation from the executive, and parliamentary staff serve the two Houses rather than the government. Employees of local authorities and of public bodies such as the BBC, regulators such as Ofcom, and NHS trusts are also outside the civil service, ensuring that their work can be carried out at arm's length from ministers while still subject to public accountability.

8.4.2 SIZE AND STRUCTURE OF THE CIVIL SERVICE

There are two main bodies of civil servants: about 500,000 (full-time equivalents) who serve in the Home Civil Service and around 17,500 in the Diplomatic Service. The size of the Civil Service grew after 2016, reflecting preparations for the United Kingdom's withdrawal from the European Union, the transfer of responsibilities previously exercised by EU institutions, and the additional pressures created by the Covid-19 pandemic. Each department is led by a Permanent Secretary, the most senior civil servant, who supports the minister, oversees day-to-day operations, and manages the departmental budget.

The term 'Whitehall' is often used to refer collectively to UK government departments, after the London street where some are located. Although people often speak of 'the civil service' as a single, uniform organization, the Institute for Government emphasizes that it is better understood as a collection of different professions and organizations, each with its own functions, cultures, and capacities.

J. Worlidge et al, *Whitehall Monitor 2024* (Institute for Government 2024) p. 11

> A more useful way to understand why departments have grown or shrunk is to look at changes in the *types* of work that civil servants do, or the 'profession' to which they belong. All civil servants belong to a profession. Some, most obviously the policy profession, are 'cross-departmental' – common to all departments. We classify others, such as the international trade, tax and intelligence analysis professions, which are mostly confined to one department, as 'departmental professions'. Prison officers, asylum caseworkers and Jobcentre Plus staff, meanwhile, are part of the operational delivery profession – which makes up more than half of the entire civil service.

The Institute for Government's analysis highlights how varied the UK civil service actually is, yet the constitutional principles governing it remain uniform. These are set out clearly in the Cabinet Manual, which defines the civil service's role, its relationship with ministers, and the standards of impartiality that underpin it.

8.4.3 CONSTITUTIONAL POSITION OF THE CIVIL SERVICE

In some countries, senior civil servants are political appointments that change when a new government or president takes office. In the United States, for example, each incoming administration appoints thousands of officials to senior posts to ensure that those implementing policy share the government's political outlook. This model can promote policy coherence but often sacrifices continuity and institutional memory and risks politicising the administration.

The United Kingdom has chosen a different approach. Its civil service is permanent and politically impartial. Ministers change, but senior officials remain, providing professional expertise and administrative continuity across governments. This arrangement helps to ensure that the machinery of government remains stable, that public administration is not disrupted by changes in political leadership, and that ministers are supported by experienced, non-partisan advisers who can serve governments of any party.

Part 1 of the Constitutional Reform and Governance Act 2010 placed the regulation of the civil service on a statutory footing for the first time; it was previously based on prerogative powers. An independent body, the Civil Service Commission, is responsible for ensuring that appointments on merit on the basis of fair an open competition. The Minister for the Civil Service—a ministerial post held by the Prime Minister has power to manage the civil service and to publish a code of conduct. The Foreign Secretary has similar powers in relation to the diplomatic service.

Cabinet Office, *The Cabinet Manual*, 1st edn (2011, London: Cabinet Office) (footnotes omitted)

The Civil Service

7.1 Civil servants are servants of the Crown. The Civil Service supports the government of the day in developing and implementing its policies, and in delivering public services. Civil servants are accountable to ministers, who in turn are accountable to Parliament.

The role of ministers and officials

7.2 Ministers are required to uphold the political impartiality of the Civil Service and not ask civil servants to act in any way that would conflict with the Civil Service Code or the requirements of the Constitutional Reform and Governance Act 2010. Ministers also have a duty to give fair consideration and due weight to informed and impartial advice from civil servants, as well as to other considerations and advice in reaching policy decisions.

7.3 In addition, civil servants should not be asked to engage in activities likely to call into question their political impartiality or give rise to the criticism that resources paid from public funds are being used for party political purposes.

When a minister wishes to pursue a policy that senior civil servants believe falls outside the standards of regularity, propriety, value for money, or feasibility, the department's accounting officer (normally the permanent secretary) may request a ministerial direction. This is a written instruction in which the minister formally takes responsibility for the decision. The direction is sent to the Comptroller and Auditor General (the head of the National Audit Office, responsible for auditing government departments and reporting to Parliament) and is usually published. For example, in April 2022, the Home Office Permanent Secretary, Matthew Rycroft, sought a ministerial direction from the Home Secretary (Priti Patel MP) to proceed with the Migration and Economic Development Partnership with Rwanda. He concluded that the policy, part of the Conservatives' plan to send asylum seekers there, did not meet the usual value-for-money test and therefore required formal ministerial instruction.[33]

[33] Home Office, Letter from Matthew Rycroft to Rt Hon Priti Patel, 13 April 2022 https://www.gov.uk/government/publications/migration-and-economic-development-partnership-ministerial-direction/letter-from-matthew-rycroft-to-rt-hon-priti-patel-accessible accessed 14 November 2025.

Occasionally, senior civil servants have resigned in protest at government policy. Jonathan Jones resigned as permanent secretary of the Government Legal Service in 2020 after the Conservative government introduced the UK Internal Market Bill, which included clauses empowering ministers to breach international treaty obligations. His departure was widely reported as a protest against a policy he believed was unlawful and incompatible with the civil service's obligation to uphold the rule of law.[34]

8.4.4 THE CARLTONA PRINCIPLE

When civil servants perform official functions, they do so 'in the name of' their minister rather than under delegated powers. As the following extract from *JOYS*—an official guide to judicial review written for government officials—explains, their authority derives from the constitutional principle that the acts of departmental officials are legally treated as the acts of the minister.

Government Legal Department, *The Judge Over Your Shoulder*, 6th edn (2022)

> 2.45 As far as departments of central government are concerned, the courts accept that ministers cannot possibly personally make every decision made in their name, and that officials in government departments may act on their behalf. This is known as the Carltona principle after the leading case (*Carltona Ltd v Commissioners of Works* [1943] 2 All ER 560). Theoretically, legally and constitutionally, there is no unlawful delegation in these circumstances because the acts of officials are the acts of their ministers and the ministers remain accountable to Parliament for those acts. The Carltona principle applies to both statutory and non-statutory powers.

The Carltona principle ensures that ministers remain politically and legally responsible for what their officials do. It connects administrative efficiency with accountability: officials can act in the minister's name, but ministers must answer to Parliament and, if necessary, to the courts for those acts. As Lord Reed stated in *R (on the application of Bourgass) v Secretary of State for Justice* [2015] UKSC 54, the principle is not one of delegation but 'Rather, the principle is that a decision made on behalf of a minister by one of his officials is constitutionally the decision of the minister himself'.

There are limits on the application of the Carltona principle. As discussed above, some Acts of Parliament require executive decisions to be made personally by the Secretary of State where the action would have profound impact on individual liberty.[35]

8.5 ARM'S LENGTH BODIES

Arm's-length bodies (ALBs) carry out many significant public functions. The include regulators such as Ofcom and Ofgem; rights and oversight bodies such as the Equality and Human Rights Commission; non-ministerial departments such as HM Revenue and Customs; and large service-delivery

[34] R. Hogwarth, 'Jonathan Jones's resignation points to wider questions about breaking international law', Institute for Government blog, 8 September 2020 https://www.instituteforgovernment.org.uk/article/comment/jonathan-joness-resignation-points-wider-questions-about-breaking-international-law accessed 14 November 2025.

[35] Section 8.3.2.

organizations such as NHS England. These bodies come in several forms—non-ministerial departments, executive agencies, non-departmental public bodies, and public corporations—but they rest on the same constitutional idea: some decisions must be made by people who can act without political pressure. Regulation, rights protection, and the enforcement of tax and competition laws often require judgments that may frustrate ministers or impose limits on government. Insulating those decisions from political pressure helps maintain fairness, protects against misuse of state power, and supports public confidence in the integrity of the system.

At first sight, this sits uneasily within a system where ministers are normally responsible for the exercise of public power. ALBs are part of government yet lie outside the ordinary chain of command. Their design aims to ensure that ministers cannot direct how statutory tasks are carried out or predetermine outcomes. That distance gives ALBs their value, but it raises familiar constitutional concerns about legitimacy and accountability.

8.5.1 APPOINTING ALBS

Peter Riddell, a former Commissioner for Public Appointments, argues that '*The public appointments system rests on two, at times, apparently contradictory principles — ministerial responsibility and selection by merit. . . . In reality, as with so much in public life, the answer lies in a balance between the principles*'.[36] Ministers make many ALB appointments, and are accountable for them, but within a framework of safeguards. A published *Governance Code on Public Appointments* sets out principles and procedures, appointment panels usually include at least one independent member, and the Commissioner for Public Appointments oversees compliance with the Code and investigates complaints. In addition, House of Commons select committees may hold public pre-appointment hearings with the preferred candidate for the most senior roles and issue non-binding reports for ministers to consider before making a final decision.

Independent reviews suggest the public appointments system is more transparent than in the 1990s, but several weaknesses persist. A study by the Institute for Government highlights slow and inconsistent appointment processes.[37] Several reviews have also highlighted the need to improve diversity among public appointees, noting persistent under-representation of people from minority ethnic and lower socio-economic backgrounds in senior roles. Concerns about politicisation have also surfaced. A high-profile example arose in 2021 when Conservative ministers encouraged Paul Dacre, former editor of the Conservative-supporting *Daily Mail*, to reapply for the post of Ofcom chair (the senior non-executive leader of the UK communications regulator) after an initial panel reportedly judged him unsuitable for appointment, prompting a public debate about whether the process had been tilted in his favour.[38] The role ultimately went to Lord Michael Grade, a Conservative peer and former chair of the BBC Governors.

House of Commons pre-appointment hearings increased openness around the most senior public appointments, and committees have, at times, prompted candidates to withdraw or forced departments to think again. But their influence is limited: committees cannot block appointments, and

[36] P. Riddell, 'The public appointments system is under strain: it needs more clarity and transparency' *The Constitution Unit Blog*, 16 May 2021 https://constitution-unit.com/2021/05/16/the-public-appointments-system-is-under-strain-it-needs-more-clarity-and-transparency/ accessed 14 November 2025.

[37] M. Gill and G. Dalton, *Reforming public appointments* (Institute for Government 2022).

[38] J. Waterson, 'Paul Dacre will get second chance to apply for Ofcom chair, ministers confirm' *The Guardian* 27 October 2021 https://www.theguardian.com/media/2021/oct/27/paul-dacre-will-get-second-chance-to-apply-for-ofcom-chair-ministers-confirm accessed 14 November 2025.

ministers can proceed despite critical reports.[39] The process improves scrutiny, but it acts as a modest rather than decisive check on ministerial power.

8.5.2 CONSTITUTIONAL ROLE OF ALBS

ALBs perform a wide range of public functions in the modern UK constitutional system: regulating communications and energy markets, enforcing tax and competition law, protecting equality and data rights, and overseeing aspects of public services.[40] These tasks often require technical assessments and decisions that may run counter to short-term political pressures. Independence helps to preserve the integrity of these judgments. During the 2021–22 energy crisis, for example, Ofgem raised the energy price cap despite strong political pressure to hold bills down, arguing that a failure to adjust the cap would threaten the stability of the supply market. In 2023, the Competition and Markets Authority blocked Microsoft's proposed acquisition of Activision Blizzard (a major video-game publisher), despite wider political pressure to present the UK as open to large tech investments, on the ground that the merger risked harming competition in the cloud-gaming market.

This independence raises the classic question *quis custodiet ipsos custodes?*—'who will guard the guards?'. ALBs are insulated from ministers, but they remain subject to several forms of oversight. The Treasury scrutinises budgets; many bodies operate within framework documents agreed with their sponsoring department; and most publish annual reports and accounts that select committees may examine. In 2022, for instance, the House of Commons Business, Energy and Industrial Strategy Committee issued a strongly critical report on Ofgem's handling of energy market regulation.[41]

Judicial review provides further oversight. Courts assess whether ALBs act within their legal powers and follow fair procedures. For example, Liberty started legal proceedings to argue that the EHRC's consultation on changes to its Code of Practice—triggered by the Supreme Court's ruling that the Equality Act 2010 uses biological rather than certificated sex—was too short and procedurally unfair.[42]

PAUSE FOR REFLECTION

Arm's-length bodies are designed to protect specialist and sometimes sensitive decisions from day-to-day political pressure. Yet they exercise significant public power and are not directly elected. After reading this section, ask yourself: does the UK strike the right balance between independence and accountability for ALBs—or are the safeguards either too weak or too constraining?

[39] See R. Hazell, T. Hursit, H. Mehta, and P. Waller, *Improving Parliamentary Scrutiny of Public Appointments* (UCL Constitution Unit 2017). In 2009, the Children, Schools and Families Committee declined to endorse the government's preferred candidate for Children's Commissioner for England, noting that although professionally competent, the nominee showed too little determination to assert the role's independence or champion children's rights (Eighth Report of Session 2008–09, HC 998, para 18). The minister confirmed the appointment regardless.

[40] Cabinet Office, *Classification of Public Bodies* (2023) https://assets.publishing.service.gov.uk/media/5a74d700e5274a59fa715592/Classification-of-Public_Bodies-Guidance-for-Departments.pdf accessed 14 November 2025.

[41] House of Commons Business, Energy and Industrial Strategy Committee, *Energy pricing and the future of the energy market*, Third Report of Session 2022–23, HC 236 https://committees.parliament.uk/publications/23255/documents/169712/default/ accessed 14 November 2025.

[42] *R (on the application of National Council for Civil Liberties) v Equality and Human Rights Commission* [2025] EWHC 1504 (Admin). Permission to proceed with a judicial review claim was refused, the court holding that the EHRC had met its equality duties and had allowed sufficient time for consultees to respond. Liberty's appeal to the Court of Appeal was unsuccessful: you can view the hearing here: https://www.judiciary.uk/live-hearings/national-council-for-civil-liberties-claimant-appellant-v-equality-and-human-rights-commission-defendant-respondent/ accessed 14 November 2025.

8.6 AUTOMATED AND AI-BASED DECISION-MAKING

Public bodies no longer rely only on people to make decisions. To help make sense of the different technologies discussed in this section, the following box summarizes three distinct but overlapping developments in modern public administration.

BOX 8.1 THREE FORMS OF TECHNOLOGY IN MODERN PUBLIC ADMINISTRATION

Automation

- Uses fixed, pre-programmed rules to make decisions.
- Example: calculating tax based solely on information entered on a form.
- Main concern: errors in coding or rules applied too rigidly.

Artificial intelligence

- Uses statistical models to identify patterns and generate predictions or recommendations.
- Example: a model predicting the likelihood of benefit fraud.
- Main concerns: biased or incomplete data, opaque reasoning, difficulties in explaining outcomes.

Interface-first bureaucracy

- The user's main interaction with the state is through a digital interface, even before speaking to a person.
- Example: managing a Universal Credit claim entirely through an online account.
- Main concerns: accessibility, digital exclusion, and design choices that shape how users behave or understand their rights.

These three developments interact. Decisions taken at the interface feed automated and AI-based systems, while those systems determine what users see next and how their claims are judged.

Since the 1990s, government departments have built computer systems that calculate tax, assess benefits, and process large volumes of routine applications. These early systems for automated decision-making, with little or no human involvement, followed fixed rules and replaced tasks once carried out by civil servants.

Today's landscape looks quite different. Increasingly, a person's first contact with government is not with a civil servant or a paper form but through an online interface—usually a website or app. Researchers describe this as an 'interface-first' bureaucracy: users must navigate a digital system before they can speak to a human being. In welfare administration, for example, most Universal Credit claimants manage their entire claim through an online account rather than by phone or face-to-face meetings.[43] This matters because interface design can influence both outcomes and user experience.

[43] J. Meers, S. Halliday, and J. Tomlinson, 'An "interface first" bureaucracy: Interface design, universal credit and the digital welfare state' (2024) 59 Soc. Policy. Admin. 119.

Decisions about how information must be entered, the order of questions, whether explanations are available, and how evidence can be uploaded can affect how long an application takes, how easy it is to correct mistakes, and how confident claimants feel about their rights. Poorly designed systems risk creating barriers for people with limited digital access or skills.

Alongside this shift in the front-end of administration, more sophisticated systems now operate behind the scenes. Many public bodies use algorithmic and AI-based systems to analyse large datasets, identify patterns, and generate predictions or recommendations from them. Profiling tools generate predictions about individuals based on their own characteristics and those of people with similar profiles. These systems can highlight potential fraud risks, signal unusual immigration claims, or flag cases for closer human review. Machine-learning models can adapt their behaviour as they are exposed to more examples, which makes their internal logic harder to interpret. Generative systems—those able to produce new content such as draft letters, summaries of evidence, or recommended outcomes—are already being used to support tasks such as triaging applications.[44]

Governments often emphasize the potential public benefits of automation: lower costs, faster processing, and more consistent decisions. The following extract by Cary Coglianese and Alicia Lai summarises research that appears to support this optimistic view.

C. Coglianese and A. Lai, 'Assessing Automated Administration', ch. 23 in J. Bulluck et al (eds), *The Oxford Handbook of AI Governance* 462, 464 (references omitted)

Studies have shown that algorithms can more accurately recall memorized content than humans can. They can also do better than humans in terms of predictive accuracy. Research indicates that, if applied to bail decisions, machine learning algorithms could be expected to reduce crime rates substantially, even with no change in the rate of jailing—or, alternatively, they could reduce jailing rates up to 42 percent with no change in crime rates. If used by environmental regulators to select industrial facilities to inspect for compliance with water pollution regulations, machine-learning algorithms could help increase the identification of violators by as much as 600 per cent.

Automated systems may also promote greater uniformity of decision-making, especially for tasks that currently necessitate repeated judgments involving multiple individuals, such as decisions concerning taxation, immigration, status, or benefits eligibility. The alternative to automation, namely, the training and overseeing human decision-makers can be costly and ineffective or both. But a uniform algorithmic system that applies nationwide may feasibly achieve more consistent results across individual states. Furthermore, when errors rise or biases are discovered, automated systems that rely on a common algorithm may be easier to modify and fix than to re-train a large number of human decision-makers.

Some commentators have argued that automation could strengthen the rule of law.[45] The following extract explains this early optimism.

[44] See generally J. Bright et al, 'Generative AI is already widespread in the public sector: evidence from a survey of UK public sector professionals' (2025) 6(1) Digit. Gov. Res. Pract. 2.1 https://dl.acm.org/doi/pdf/10.1145/3700140 accessed 14 November 2025.

[45] See also the discussion in Chapter 4.

A. Le Sueur, 'Robot Government: Automated Decision-making and its Implications for Parliament', ch. 9 in A. Horne and A. Le Sueur (eds), *Parliament: Legislation and Accountability* (Hart 2016) (footnotes omitted)

Empirical socio-legal studies show that human officials may fail to operate in complete conformity with rules laid down in legislation when making decisions about individuals. There are various possible reasons for this, including lack of awareness of relevant rules or misunderstanding what they require, professional administrative cultures in which legal rules are only one of a number of competing pressures, and uncertainties built-in to the particular legal rules being applied.

Automated decision-making may achieve more consistent implementation of the formal rules approved by Parliament than can be offered by human officials. Automation based on the application of objective criteria holds out the promise of legal certainty (like cases are treated identically), the elimination of bias, ensuring that no irrelevant considerations are taken into account, and that all relevant factors are included. To this extent, automation can be regarded as enhancing the rule of law. Moreover, it can be contended that the outcome will always be right. Discussing automated decision-making in 1997, De Mulder and van Noortwijk suggest 'If a computer programme that has been designed by the legislative power has come up with a decision, and given that the input has been correct, such a decision would be exactly according to the law and it would arguably not need to be subject to any form of appeal'.

The proposition that automated decision-making guarantees error-free conclusions is however open to doubt. Some early and small-scale empirical studies have identified mistakes in computer-generated decisions – though they also show examples where automation led to fewer errors. It would be constitutionally dangerous to assume that 'the computer is always right'; even more worrying is the idea (no doubt attractive to government) that automation may require less provision to be made for citizens to challenge decisions.

Le Sueur's argument highlights a central point. Automated systems may avoid some of the weaknesses associated with human decision-making—such as inconsistency, unconscious bias, or misunderstanding of legal rules. However, they introduce new risks. Automated tools often rely on data that may be incomplete, outdated, or biased. Profiling may reproduce long-standing inequalities embedded in the data used to train the model. Errors may be difficult for users to detect, and it can be challenging to obtain a clear explanation of how a system reached a particular conclusion. These developments raise familiar constitutional concerns in a new setting. Transparency becomes harder when key steps take place inside models that few officials can interpret. Fairness may be affected if certain groups are disproportionately represented or excluded in the data used to train systems. Accountability becomes more complex when outcomes depend on a mixture of human judgment, programmed rules, and algorithmic predictions.

A further constitutional question relates to how long-standing principles of administrative law apply when a computer makes a decision. Under the Carltona principle, a decision made by an authorised civil servant is constitutionally treated as a decision of the Secretary of State. It is not yet settled whether this reasoning extends to decisions made directly by computer systems. Parliament first addressed this in the Social Security Act 1998, section 2, which provides that certain decisions may be made not only by an officer acting under the Secretary of State's authority but also by a computer for which that officer is responsible. This recognised that computers were no longer merely tools but were, in effect, performing the role of decision-maker. Despite the growing use of automated tools, provisions of this kind remain uncommon in Acts of Parliament, leaving uncertainty about how automated systems sit within traditional principles of constitutional responsibility.

Another area of concern is accessibility. Digital systems assume that users have stable internet access, appropriate devices, and the skills to navigate online services. In practice, many people—including older users, people with disabilities, low-income households, and those for whom English is not a first language—encounter real obstacles when trying to use these systems. These difficulties are not minor irritations. When some groups find public services harder to access, the principle of fairness is put under strain. Where digital exclusion mirrors wider social and economic inequalities, automated systems may reinforce those inequalities rather than reduce them. Protecting constitutional legitimacy in an interface-first administrative state therefore requires public bodies to ensure that digital reforms do not leave particular communities at a disadvantage.

One commonly suggested safeguard is to 'keep a human in the loop': requiring a civil servant to check or confirm automated recommendations. In the extract below, Andrew Murray explains why this safeguard may not always work in practice.

A. Murray, 'Automated Public Decision Making and the Need for Regulation' (2024) 3(3) LSE Public Policy Review 1, 8

The challenge of algorithmic confirmation bias is that even when a human is in the loop, they will often defer to algorithmic recommender systems on the basis that the computer cannot be wrong (see the Post Office Horizon Inquiry). We need to ensure that the human remains empowered. This is likely to start with algorithmic literacy campaigns for public decision- makers, but in terms of governance means that the law ensures human decision-makers are encouraged to challenge algorithmic recommendations, for example, by requiring them to give reasons for their decisions, protecting whistle-blowers . . . and periodically auditing or reviewing the actions of decision-makers.

The Post Office Horizon scandal concerned thousands of sub-postmasters who were wrongly accused of theft or false accounting because of faults in the Horizon IT system used to record transactions. Despite repeated reports of errors, the system's outputs were treated as reliable, leading to wrongful prosecutions, convictions, and significant financial and personal harm.[46] Murray's argument points to a broader challenge. Even where a human official signs off a decision, meaningful oversight may be limited if they do not feel equipped—or permitted—to question an algorithmic output.

PAUSE FOR REFLECTION

- Automated systems promise speed and consistency, but they also shift some decision-making power from people to computers. Based on what you have read in this section, do these tools strengthen or weaken the constitutional values of transparency, fairness, and accountability?
- What safeguards should Parliament require before such systems are used more widely in public administration?

[46] Post Office Horizon IT Inquiry—Official Website: https://www.postofficehorizoninquiry.org.uk/

8.7 CONCLUDING COMMENTS

This chapter has outlined how executive authority in the United Kingdom is distributed across a range of institutions: the monarchy, ministers, the Cabinet, civil servants, and arm's-length bodies. Although their powers derive from different legal sources—statute, prerogative, and common law—they operate within a constitutional framework that emphasizes both legality and legitimacy. Understanding who exercises executive power, how they are appointed, and the conventions that shape their relationships is essential for assessing how the modern state functions.

At several points, we have also noted emerging pressures on this framework: the changing role of the monarchy, the concentration and fragility of prime-ministerial authority, the constitutional significance of civil service impartiality, the rise of independent regulators, and the impact of automated and interface-first decision-making. These themes all raise a central question: how are those who wield executive power held to account? Chapter 9 turns to that question directly.

FURTHER READING

Hazell, R. and Morris, B. (eds), *The Role of Monarchy in Modern Democracy: European Monarchies Compared* (2022, Hart).

Poole, T., 'The Executive in Public Law' in J. Jowell and C. O'Cinneide (eds) *The Changing Constitution*, 9th edn (2019, Oxford: OUP), ch. 7.

Thomas, A. et al, *A New Statutory Role for the Civil Service* (2022, Institute for Government).

Wallner, P., *Understanding Whitehall* (2014, London: UCL Constitution Unit).

Young, A. L., *Democratic Dialogue and the Constitution* (2017, Oxford: OUP).

9

ACCOUNTABILITY

CENTRAL ISSUES

1. Accountability is a core constitutional idea, but its meaning varies across political, legal, and administrative settings. Understanding who must justify decisions—and on what terms—depends on context and on competing models of political and legal constitutionalism.
2. Individual ministerial responsibility remains a key convention linking ministers to Parliament. Its scope now spans truthful parliamentary statements, departmental conduct, and ministers' personal behaviour, but enforcement depends heavily on political judgement and the Prime Minister's discretion.
3. Collective cabinet responsibility underpins the government's public unity, yet suspensions, conscience votes, and high-profile breaches reveal its fragility and the pressures placed on the convention by referendums, coalition politics, and internal party conflict.
4. Civil servants exercise substantial delegated power, but remain accountable to Parliament only through ministers. Select committee scrutiny, Accounting Officer duties, and the Osmotherly Rules shape this indirect accountability in practice.
5. Parliament's tools—select committees, questions, and debates—provide structured routes for scrutiny. Media investigation and independent reviews can also expose failings. The case study on the Windrush scandal illustrates how accountability operates in practice.

9.1 OVERVIEW

Accountability is often claimed to be a constitutional principle as significant as the rule of law or parliamentary supremacy. It is one of the main ways in which those who exercise public power are expected to justify their actions; but the term itself is elastic and used in many different ways. Tony Wright, a former MP who has written extensively on Parliament and government, captures how the concept has evolved.

T. Wright, 'The Politics of Accountability', ch. 5 in M. Elliott and D. Feldman (eds), *The Cambridge Companion to Public Law* (2015, Cambridge University Press), p. 96 (footnotes omitted)

Accountability has recently been described as 'the uber-concept of modern times'. In politics it has certainly become ubiquitous. There are daily demands for someone or something to be 'held to account'. The routine response to a whole range of political issues is a call for 'more accountability'. Yet this political usage of the word is relatively recent. What began life as the language of the counting house, as dry as financial dust, has been converted into the stock language of the political and constitutional arena. Even more interestingly, what was once a means by which medieval monarchs could count the assets of their subjects has been transformed into the means whereby modern citizens can hold to account those who rule them.

The modern use of the term can still be vague. As Jonathan Fox notes in the following extract, accountability is now applied to a wide range of political, administrative, and legal problems. Understanding its meaning therefore requires us to pay close attention to context.

J. Fox, *Accountability Keywords*, Accountability Working Paper 11 (2022, Accountability Research Centre), p. 8

Accountability is often treated as a magic bullet, an all-purpose solution to a very wide range of problems—from corrupt politicians or the quality of public service provision to persistent injustice and impunity. The concept is a very broad umbrella that has become shorthand to refer to diverse efforts to address problems with the exercise of power. This raises the question of 'what counts' as accountability. In practice, the usual answer is either fuzzy— 'you know it when you see it'—or is limited to sectoral silos or specific contexts.

This chapter focuses on accountability within a particular setting: the relationship between the UK Parliament and the central executive. It examines how ministers and civil servants are expected to explain and justify their conduct to Parliament, and how Parliament exercises oversight in practice. This is not a complete account of accountability across the whole constitution—we do not look for instance at the police, National Health Service, devolved administrations, or local authorities.

9.2 ACCOUNTABILITY IN ITS CONSTITUTIONAL SETTING

This section introduces accountability as a constitutional idea rather than just a political slogan. It starts to place parliamentary, judicial, and institutional scrutiny in historical and theoretical context, helping us understand why different bodies hold the executive to account in different ways.

John Stuart Mill (1806–1873), one of the most influential liberal thinkers of the nineteenth century and briefly an MP, is best known for his definition of liberty as protection from excessive state and social power, but he advanced many other ideas. Writing in 1861, he argued that Parliament's core function was not to run the country but to supervise those who did. The next extract is a helpful starting point for understanding today's assumptions about the role of Parliament.

J.S. Mill, *Considerations on Representative Government* (1861, Parker, Son, and Bourn), p.104

> Instead of the function of governing, for which it is radically unfit, the proper office of a representative assembly is to watch and control the government; to throw the light of publicity on its acts; to compel a full exposition and justification of all of them which any one considers questionable; to censure them if found condemnable, and if the men who compose the government abuse their trust, or fulfil it in a manner which conflicts with the deliberate sense of the nation, to expel them from office, and either expressly or virtually appoint their successors. This is surely ample power, and security enough for the liberty of the nation.

This view places accountability—not executive decision-making—at the heart of Parliament's constitutional purpose. But Parliament is not the only forum in which government power is supervised. The courts have long made clear that political accountability to Parliament does not replace legal accountability to the judiciary. Lord Diplock's well-known statement in the following extract explains the distinction.

Commissioners of Inland Revenue v National Federation of Self-Employed and Small Business Ltd
[1981] UKHL TC_55_133 at 170 (Lord Diplock)

> It is not, in my view, a sufficient answer to say that judicial review of the actions of officers or departments of central government is unnecessary because they are accountable to Parliament for the way in which they carry out their functions. They are accountable to Parliament for what they do so far as regards efficiency and policy, and of that Parliament is the only judge; they are responsible to a court of justice for the unlawfulness of what they do, and of that the court is the only judge.

The constitutional picture is therefore a balance. Some questions are legal and appropriate for judicial review; others are political and may be non-justiciable, meaning the courts treat them as inappropriate for legal intervention even though Parliament can still hold ministers to account. Drawing the boundary between these spheres is not mechanical and remains contested. This takes us back to the distinction, introduced in Chapter 2, between political constitutionalism and legal constitutionalism. Political constitutionalists see elected bodies—especially Parliament—as the primary check on government. Legal constitutionalists place greater weight on the courts and judicially enforceable standards. Both traditions help explain why accountability in the UK is dispersed across multiple institutions.

In recent decades both forms of accountability have grown more structured. Parliament's creation of departmental select committees has strengthened its scrutiny of ministers, civil servants, and public bodies.[1] Meanwhile, the courts have developed more demanding standards of judicial review,[2] and the Human Rights Act 1998 has required clearer legal justification for many forms of executive action.[3]

Alongside Parliament and the courts, a number of bodies are sometimes described as the 'integrity' or 'watchdog' branch. They do not make or apply law in the traditional sense, but they monitor the behaviour of public authorities using established standards and processes. Examples include

[1] See section 9.5.1 below. [2] See Chapters 17–20. [3] See Chapter 21.

the Parliamentary Commissioner for Standards, who investigates MPs' conduct and interests; the National Audit Office, which audits public expenditure on behalf of Parliament; and the Civil Service Commission, which protects merit-based appointment and investigates alleged breaches of the Civil Service Code. These institutions broaden the landscape of accountability beyond politics and law.

Yet the modern appetite for accountability has its critics. In her 2002 BBC Reith Lectures, the philosopher Onora O'Neil—an academic known for her work on ethics, political philosophy, and public trust—argued that increasingly elaborate accountability mechanisms can create unintended harms. From the 1980s onwards, successive governments introduced managerial reforms often described as the 'New Public Management'. Public services became subject to detailed performance targets, audits, and inspection regimes, aiming to make organizations more efficient and more accountable for measurable results. By the early 2000s this targets-and-audit culture was deeply embedded across health, education, welfare, and policing. O'Neil's lecture challenges aspects of this managerial approach, but also questions other modern developments—including expansive rights claims and demands for ever-greater transparency—which, she argues, can unintentionally erode trust.

O. O'Neil, 'Lecture 1: A Question of Trust', BBC Reith Lectures 2002, transcript.

We may not have evidence for a crisis of trust: but we have massive evidence of a culture of suspicion. Let me briefly join that culture of suspicion, ... My first suspicion falls on one of our most sacred cows: the human rights movement. We fantasise, in my view irresponsibly, that we can promulgate rights without thinking carefully about the counterpart obligations, and without checking whether the rights we favour are consistent, with one another let alone set feasible demands on those who have to secure them for others. My suspicions fall secondly on our new conceptions of accountability, which superimpose managerial targets on bureaucratic process, burdening and even paralysing many of those who have to comply. My suspicions fall thirdly on the new ideal of the information age: transparency, which has marginalised the more basic and important obligation not to deceive. My suspicion falls finally on our public culture, which is so often credulous about its own standards of communication and suspicious of everyone else's. We need, I think, genuine rights, genuine accountability, genuine efforts to reduce deception, and genuine communication but we may be pursuing distorted versions of each of them.

Perhaps claims about a crisis of trust are mainly evidence of an unrealistic hankering for a world in which safety and compliance are total, and breaches of trust are eliminated. Perhaps the culture of accountability that we are relentlessly building for ourselves actually damages trust rather than supporting it. Plants don't flourish when we pull them up too often to check how their roots are growing: political institutional and professional life too may not go well if we constantly uproot them to demonstrate that everything is transparent and trustworthy.

PAUSE FOR REFLECTION

Think about the different institutions discussed in this section—Parliament, the courts, and the various watchdog bodies. Each claims to hold the executive to account, but they do so in different ways and for different reasons. Do these forms of accountability complement one another, or do they sometimes compete?

Consider also O'Neil's warning about the unintended consequences of expanding rights claims, transparency demands, and managerial targets. How do we strike a balance between ensuring that public power is scrutinized and avoiding systems that become so burdensome that they limit trust, judgement, or effective government?

9.3 INDIVIDUAL MINISTERIAL RESPONSIBILITY

The previous section introduced the idea of accountability, and how it operates within the wider constitutional framework. We now turn to a more specific and practical expression of that idea, situated at the point where government and Parliament meet: individual ministerial responsibility.

9.3.1 SCOPE OF THE RULES ON INDIVIDUAL MINISTERIAL RESPONSIBILITY

The standards associated with individual ministerial responsibility are constitutional conventions, not legal rules.[4] Although the convention long predates any formal written statement, the modern expression of it can be found in two key sources—one parliamentary the other from government.

The first source is the set of identical resolutions adopted by the House of Commons and the House of Lords in March 1997. Parliament acted in response to the Arms to Iraq affair, in which the export of military-related equipment to Iraq had been permitted contrary to stated government policy. When several businesspeople were prosecuted for breaching export controls, it emerged during their trial that ministers and officials had known about, and in some respects allowed, the exports. The trial collapsed, and a public inquiry led by Sir Richard Scott (the Scott Report, 1996) criticized ministers for failing to give Parliament a full and accurate account of policy and practice. Though the issues were debated in Parliament, no minister resigned. The controversy prompted both Houses to restate formally the standards expected of ministers, and the resolutions remain a clear parliamentary articulation of the convention.

House of Commons Hansard, 19 March 1997, col. 1046

(1) Ministers have a duty to Parliament to account, and be held to account, for the policies, decisions and actions of their Departments [. . .];

(2) It is of paramount importance that Ministers give accurate and truthful information to Parliament, correcting any inadvertent error at the earliest opportunity. Ministers who knowingly mislead Parliament will be expected to offer their resignation to the Prime Minister;

(3) Ministers should be as open as possible with Parliament, refusing to provide information only when disclosure would not be in the public interest, which should be decided in accordance with relevant statute [. . .];

(4) Similarly, Ministers should require civil servants who give evidence before Parliamentary Committees on their behalf and under their directions to be as helpful as possible in providing accurate, truthful and full information in accordance with the duties and responsibilities of civil servants as set out in the Civil Service Code.

The second source is the *Ministerial Code*, issued by the Prime Minister at the start of each administration. As Michael Gordon observes, the *Ministerial Code* has evolved from an internal—and initially secret—document into a public statement of the ethical and procedural standards expected of ministers.[5]

[4] See Chapter 2.

[5] M. Gordon, 'Labour's Ministerial Code and Political Standards Reform', U.K. Const. L. Blog (5th December 2024) (available at https://ukconstitutionallaw.org/).

The Code is not approved by Parliament and can be amended at any time by the Prime Minister. This reflects its political character and the discretion the Prime Minister retains over the appointment and dismissal of ministers.

Cabinet Office, *Ministerial Code* (October 2025)

1. Ministers of the Crown

General principle

1.1 Ministers of the Crown are expected to maintain high standards of behaviour and to behave in a way that upholds the highest standards of propriety.

1.2 Ministers are expected to embody the principles of public service and to set a positive example as they govern in the national interest. Ministers should recognise that as office-holders, they are held to the highest possible standards of proper conduct, and ensure that they are living up to those standards in their words and actions.

1.3 Ministers are responsible for their own behaviour, and are ultimately accountable to the Prime Minister for their conduct under this Code.

The Seven Principles of Public Life

1.4 Ministers are expected to adhere to the Seven Principles of Public Life (also known as the 'Nolan Principles'), which are set out by the Committee on Standards in Public Life and apply to all public office holders:

a. Selflessness . . .

b. Integrity . . .

c. Objectivity . . .

d. Accountability . . .

e. Openness . . .

f. Honesty . . .

g. Leadership . . .

The remainder of the Ministerial Code develops these expectations in more practical terms. It explains how ministers should manage their official and political roles, how they must use public resources, and the standards that apply to their dealings with Parliament, civil servants and the public. It also sets out rules on appointments, conflicts of interest, and the use of government information. Later sections describe the role of the Independent Adviser on Ministerial Standards and the process for investigating alleged breaches. Together, these provisions aim to translate the broad principles in the opening section into day-to-day standards of conduct for ministers in office.

The Ministerial Code reinforces the link between its requirements and Parliament's expectations. It notes that 'ministers must also comply at all times with the requirements which Parliament itself has laid down in relation to the accountability and responsibility of ministers' (para 1.7). Although both the parliamentary resolutions and the Ministerial Code restate the core expectations of individual ministerial responsibility, they do so in different domains.

First, the focus of the resolutions is on ensuring that ministers account to Parliament for departmental policy and performance. The 1997 resolutions focus on the minister's relationship with Parliament: providing truthful information, correcting mistakes promptly, and ensuring civil servants give full and accurate evidence to committees. This reflects the convention's historical emphasis on public accountability through statements, questions, and committee hearings. Where there is a breach, an apology may suffice. For example, in 2018 the Minister for Pensions Esther McVey MP, made an apology in the chamber for making inaccurate assertions about the roll-out of the new Universal Credit programme. But on occasion, ministers have felt obliged to resign—as Home Secretary Amber Rudd's 2018 did in relation to the Windrush scandal (see the case study below).

A second domain, covered by the *Ministerial Code*, is that ministers must maintain appropriate standards in the departmental workplace. In 2020, an investigation by the Independent Adviser on Ministerial Standards found that Home Secretary Priti Patel MP had behaved in a way that met the definition of bullying and therefore breached the Code, but she remained in post after Prime Minister Boris Johnson declined to apply any sanction. Along similar lines, Dominic Raab MP resigned as Deputy Prime Minister and Justice Secretary in 2023 after an independent inquiry concluded that he had acted in an intimidating or undermining manner towards officials, breaching the Code. In 2021, Matt Hancock MP resigned as Health Secretary after CCTV footage showed him breaching Covid-19 social-distancing rules with an adviser in the departmental office, conduct the Prime Minister accepted was incompatible with the standards expected under the Ministerial Code.

The third domain, also covered by the Ministerial Code, is where a minister's conduct in their personal life the fall below the 'the highest possible standards of proper conduct'. In 2025, Deputy Prime Minister and Housing Secretary Angela Rayner MP resigned after the Independent Adviser on Ministerial Standards found that, although she had acted with integrity, she had breached the Ministerial Code by failing to obtain the specialist tax advice necessary to determine that a seaside apartment she purchased should have been treated as a second home for Stamp Duty Land Tax purposes; Rayner immediately resigned. Resignations may also take place if politically expedient, even if there has been no finding of wrong-doing under the Code. In August 2025, Rushanara Ali MP resigned as Homelessness Minister after being accused of hypocrisy for ending a tenants' contract in order to sell a house she owned and then, when the house did not sell, re-listing the property for rent at a higher price within six months, conduct that clashed with reforms she was helping to take through Parliament in the Renters' Rights Bill. Although she maintained that she had complied with all legal requirements, she accepted that remaining in office would be a distraction and therefore stepped down.

Two important areas fall outside the scope of the convention of individual ministerial responsibility.

First, ministers are not generally expected to answer to Parliament when a court, in judicial review proceedings, rules that they or their department have acted unlawfully. At first glance this may seem inconsistent with the Ministerial Code, which states that it should be read against the background of ministers' duty to comply with the law and to protect the integrity of public life (para 1.6). In practice, however, adverse judicial review findings do not normally trigger ministerial apologies or resignations, whether the court has identified illegality, procedural impropriety, or unreasonableness. A rare attempt to invoke individual ministerial responsibility in this context occurred in September 2019, when Jeremy Corbyn MP, then Leader of the Opposition, called on Prime Minister Boris Johnson MP to resign following the UK Supreme Court's ruling that his advice to prorogue Parliament was unlawful, and the SNP's Westminster leader Ian Blackford MP pressed for a vote of no confidence. Johnson did ultimately resign, but not until July 2022 and for unrelated reasons. A rationale for placing adverse court rulings beyond the reach of the convention of individual responsibility is that most successful judicial reviews concern technical or procedural errors rather than personal wrongdoing or misjudgment, and the courts make clear that unlawfulness does not imply bad faith. Moreover, requiring resignations in every such case would blur the line between legal accountability in the courts and political accountability in Parliament, and would make modern government very hard to run.

A second important limit on the convention of individual ministerial responsibility is that, in modern practice, ministers are not expected to resign simply because their department has experienced a serious operational or policy failure. The classic exception is Lord Carrington's resignation as Foreign Secretary in 1982 after Argentina invaded the Falkland Islands, when he accepted responsibility for his department's failure to anticipate events. In the same year, after an intruder managed to enter the Queen's bedroom in a major security breach, the Home Secretary William Whitelaw MP reportedly offered to resign, but the Prime Minister declined to accept it. Since then, although there have been many significant administrative failures, none has led directly to a minister stepping down under the convention. A minister's association with a failing department may weaken their political position and prompt removal in a reshuffle, but that reflects political judgement rather than the operation of a constitutional rule.

9.3.2 ENFORCEMENT THE RULES ON INDIVIDUAL MINISTERIAL RESPONSIBILITY

9.3.2.1 Felt accountability: Why ministers abide by the rules

Why do ministers, in practice, usually follow the convention of individual ministerial responsibility when there is no legal sanction for breaking it? Most do, most of the time, which raises a deeper question about what actually drives compliance. Conventional explanations focus on external pressures—scrutiny from Parliament, the media, party leaders and public opinion. These forces do not, however, tell the whole story. A less visible part of the picture lies in ministers' internal motivations: how they anticipate evaluation, how they interpret expectations, and how they judge their own conduct. Research in organizational psychology, often overlooked by public law textbooks, examines these 'felt accountability' dynamics, showing that individuals often behave as though they will be called to account because they believe their actions could be evaluated by an audience that matters to them, even if no formal sanction is guaranteed.[6]

That said, there will always be occasions when ministers fall short of the expectations set by the convention. How such situations are handled depends on the two roles a minister simultaneously occupies: as a parliamentarian (an MP or a peer) and as a member of the government. Each role is governed by its own code of behaviour—the Parliamentary Code of Conduct and the Ministerial Code—and although these frameworks are distinct, they overlap in several ways that shape how ministerial error or wrongdoing is addressed.

9.3.2.2 Parliamentary enforcement of individual ministerial responsibility

Each House has procedures for investigating and ruling on alleged breaches of its rule of conduct, but these apply only to members' parliamentary behaviour, not to their actions as ministers. In the Commons, the Parliamentary Commissioner for Standards (an independent public office-holder) investigates alleged breaches of the House of Commons Code of Conduct and related rules by MPs, reports their findings to the Committee on Standards, and advises on the operation of the standards system. These mechanisms cannot be used where the allegations concern ministerial duties, but they can apply to matters arising solely from a minister's role as a parliamentarian. For example, in 2014 the Commissioner investigated Maria Miller MP's claims for parliamentary expenses and the Committee on Standards concluded that she should repay money and apologise to the House, which she did in a brief statement; and although the case did not relate to her ministerial responsibilities, she resigned from the Cabinet a few days later.

[6] See Y. Fan, 'Accountability in Public Organization: A Systematic Literature Review and Future Research Agenda' (2025) 25 *Public Organisation Review* 295, 298 for an overview.

An issue that sits at the intersection of parliamentary and ministerial standards is the duty on ministers to avoid misleading Parliament. In the most serious case, where a minister is alleged to have deliberately given an untrue statement, the Commons could in theory consider the matter by way of a substantive motion, allowing a debate and vote; however, this procedure has not been used against a minister for misleading the House since the Profumo affair in 1963, and the precise sanction that would follow is uncertain.[7] The much more common situation is that a minister inadvertently provides inaccurate information. This occurs with some regularity, and the established practice is that the minister corrects the record at the earliest opportunity—either by a statement to the House or, if the error was made in a select committee, by writing to the committee to amend or clarify their evidence.

9.3.2.3 Prime Ministerial enforcement of the Ministerial Code

Where an allegation concerns a breach of the Ministerial Code, it is handled within government rather than by Parliament. Since 2006, successive Prime Ministers have appointed a part-time ethics adviser (now called the Independent Adviser on Ministerial Standards). This is a non-statutory office, established under the Prime Minister's prerogative power to manage the Cabinet. The Adviser's role is to investigate alleged breaches of the Code and advise the Prime Minister on whether the Code has been broken; the Adviser cannot impose sanctions.

The office came under particular strain during Boris Johnson MP's premiership, when two Independent Advisers resigned. In November 2020, Sir Alex Allan advised that the Home Secretary, Priti Patel MP, had breached the Code by shouting and swearing at civil servants in her team. Johnson issued a statement saying that he noted Allan's findings, but concerns had not been raised with Patel at the time and she had apologized for inadvertently causing upset. Johnson concluded that, taking all factors into account, his own assessment was that the Code had not been breached.[8] Allan resigned in protest. In June 2022, Allan's successor, Lord Geidt, resigned after being asked to advise on measures that he considered might involve a deliberate or purposeful breach of the Code in relation to the government's international trade obligations.

Reforms introduced in late 2024 by Prime Minister Keir Starmer MP increased the Adviser's operational independence. The updated Ministerial Code and revised terms of reference allow the Adviser to begin investigations without the Prime Minister's prior consent and require the publication of their advice, although the Prime Minister continues to decide the outcome and any consequences. The Adviser's findings remain advisory and not binding; the Patel case is a clear example of a Prime Minister rejecting an adverse finding.

For political constitutionalists, the current arrangements strike an acceptable balance: there is a public code of ministerial conduct, greater transparency than in the past, and accountability ultimately lies with the Prime Minister, who holds the constitutional prerogative to appoint and dismiss ministers. Legal constitutionalists take a different view, arguing that the system gives the Prime Minister too much discretion and leaves standards enforcement without meaningful independence or legal accountability; they favour stronger, rules-based mechanisms, potentially including statutory powers for the Adviser or enhanced parliamentary oversight.

[7] A. Lilly, 'Misleading parliament and correcting the parliamentary record' Institute for Government, 13 April 2022 https://www.instituteforgovernment.org.uk/explainer/misleading-parliament-correcting-record accessed 15 November 2025.

[8] The First Division Association (FDA), the trade union for senior civil servants, challenged this in a judicial review claim. The Administrative court refused the application: *R (on the application of FDA) v Prime Minister* [2021] EWHC 3279 (Admin).

9.3.2.4 Sanctions for breaching individual ministerial responsibility

What sanctions does a minister face if they are found to have breached the Parliamentary resolution or the Ministerial Code?

When faced with adverse findings from the Independent Adviser on Ministerial Standards, some ministers have recognized that the right thing to do is resign immediately. It is customary for an outgoing minister to write a letter to the Prime Minister, for the Prime Minister to respond—and for the correspondence to be published.

On occasion, the Prime Minister removes a minister from office against their will. This happened in 2019 when Prime Minister Theresa May MP dismissed Defence Secretary Gavin Williamson MP, saying there was 'compelling evidence suggesting your responsibility for the unauthorised disclosure' and 'no other credible version of events' relating to unauthorized disclose of information about plans to use Chinese telecoms company, Huawei, in developing the infrastructure of the UK's 5G network; Williamson denied he was the source of the leak. In 2025, Prime Minister Kier Starmer MP dismissed junior health minister Andrew Gwynne for posting sexist and racist comments on a WhatsApp group.[9]

Whether by resignation or dismissal, removal from ministerial office has significant financial implications for an ex-minister. A Secretary of State will stop receiving their ministerial salary (£72,454 a year), which is paid in addition to the MP's basic salary (£93,904 in 2025). Former ministers may claim a severance payment of £16,876, but this is not available if the departure follows a 'serious breach of the Ministerial Code'.

A resignation for breaching the Ministerial Code does not prevent a Prime Minister from returning a minister to Cabinet. A notably quick turnaround occurred in October 2022, when Suella Braverman MP resigned as Home Secretary after admitting she had sent a draft ministerial statement on immigration policy from her personal email to another MP. Despite this breach, she was reappointed to the same post just six days later. As we see in the Windrush case study, Amber Rudd MP resigned as Home Secretary in April 2018; she returned to the Cabinet as Secretary of State for Work and Pensions in November that year.

9.4 ACCOUNTABILITY OF CIVIL SERVANTS TO PARLIAMENT

Up to this point, we have focused on ministers who breach the Ministerial Code through their own acts or omissions. That gives only part of the picture. Ministers are frequently reshuffled by the Prime Minister or leave roles after elections. On average, they remain in a particular department for around two years, though recent governments have seen even shorter tenures.[10] Ministers therefore rely on civil servants for analysis, advice, and the day-to-day work of implementing the government's programme within the law; and the officials provide the continuity and institutional memory that allow departments to function over time.[11] At the front line, it is civil servants who exercise discretion as 'street-level bureaucrats', taking administrative decisions that directly affect individuals.

[9] J. Nevett, 'Minister sacked over WhatsApp messages faces standards probe' *BBC News*, 21 February 2025 https://www.bbc.co.uk/news/articles/cj4ndry4k54o accessed 20 November 2025.

[10] P. Walker, 'Post-2019 UK cabinet ministers last average of eight months, study finds' *The Guardian* 17 March 2024 https://www.theguardian.com/politics/2024/mar/17/cabinet-ministers-last-average-of-eight-months?utm accessed 21 November 2025.

[11] See Chapter 8.

When something goes wrong, it can be difficult to distinguish a minister's political responsibility from shortcomings in the advice or operational decisions made by officials. One illustration came in autumn 2022, when the Manston migrant processing centre (a former military base in Kent) became severely overcrowded, with some people held for weeks in a facility intended for stays of less than 24 hours.[12] Independent inspectors reported numbers far beyond the site's capacity, inadequate conditions and cases of disease. The episode exposed weaknesses on both sides of the accountability relationship. Civil servants were responsible for running the centre, forecasting capacity, arranging onward accommodation and ensuring compliance with legal limits on detention, but the pressures on the system were not addressed in time. Ministers, meanwhile, were answerable to Parliament for the overall performance of the Home Office and for ensuring that sufficient accommodation and resources were available. Disputes later arose about what information ministers had received, and when, as different accounts emerged about warnings given within the department. The episode showed how severe operational pressures can leave ministers accountable for outcomes they did not directly manage, while civil servants remain responsible for the day-to-day systems and decisions that shaped the conditions on the ground.

More broadly, the Institute for Government has noted that relations between the Labour government and the civil service in Prime Minister Starmer's first year (2024-25) were marked by mutual frustration, with ministers finding the pace of administrative change far slower than expected;[13] this was a continuation of a pattern of 'strained relations between ministers and officials and poor morale'.[14] The report observed that officials struggled to generate workable policy options at the speed ministers wanted, while ministers were sometimes unclear about priorities or hesitant to make decisions that would unblock delivery. This combination created an atmosphere in which Starmer's own description of inheriting a 'managed decline' reflected deeper structural constraints on a government seeking to move quickly through the existing administrative machinery.

Against this background, the central constitutional question becomes how responsibility should be allocated: when should only ministers answer to Parliament for the work of government, or are there circumstances when civil servants should themselves be directly accountable?

The complexities of departmental life were discussed during the House of Lords debate on the ministerial accountability in March 1997 (see section 9.3.1 above). Peers with experience as ministers and MPs acknowledged how difficult it was to reconcile the traditional doctrine of individual ministerial responsibility with the scale and complexity of modern administration.[15] Lord Renton argued that ministers could not reasonably be held responsible for every minor decision taken in large departments. Viscount Cranborne agreed, accepting that conscientious ministers should understand the essentials of their department's work, but that no minister could know everything. Both stressed that Parliament must apply judgement when assessing responsibility, because party politics inevitably shapes how accountability is pursued. The exchange revealed a tension that remains unresolved.

The *Cabinet Manual* presents the orthodox view succinctly: '*Civil servants are accountable to ministers, who in turn are accountable to Parliament*'.[16] This suggests that ministers, not officials, bear the constitutional public duty to explain and justify what happens within their departments.

[12] BBC News, 'Manston migrant centre: What were the problems?' 21 December 2022 https://www.bbc.co.uk/news/explainers-63456015 accessed 20 November 2025.

[13] A. Thomas et al, 'A reset squandered: the civil service in Labour's first year: Keir Starmer's "tepid bath of managed decline" jibe soured relations between ministers and officials' 30 June 2025 https://www.instituteforgovernment.org.uk/comment/one-year-labour-civil-service accessed 20 November 2025.

[14] S. Kaye, 'Reform analysis: The Maude review', *Re:State*, 14 November 2023 https://re-state.co.uk/react/reform-analysis-the-maude-review/ accessed 20 November 2025.

[15] House of Lords Hansard, 20 March 1997, cols 1057–8.

[16] On the constitutional status of the Cabinet Manual, see Chapter 2.

The approach is reinforced by the Osmotherly Rules, named after the civil servant who produced the first version in 1980.[17] These rules set out the government's internal guidance on how officials should give evidence to select committees.[18] They emphasize that officials appear before committees not in a personal capacity but as representatives of their ministers. They are expected to be as helpful as possible and to disclose any information that would not be exempt under the Freedom of Information Act. They may explain the rationale, objectives and effects of government policy, but they must not offer personal opinions that would compromise the political impartiality of the Civil Service. The rules also highlight the distinctive position of 'Accounting Officers'. Permanent Secretaries—the most senior civil servant in each department—hold this role and have a personal responsibility to explain to the Public Accounts Committee (the House of Commons committee responsible for examining value for money) how their departments have used public money, and whether spending meets principles of regularity, propriety, value for money and feasibility. 'Senior Responsible Owners' for major projects may also be called upon to explain delivery, reflecting the growing emphasis on professional project management across government. In practice, the distinction between appearing as a minister's representative and accounting for one's own decisions is not always straightforward. The more technical, operational or specialist the subject under scrutiny, the harder it becomes for ministers alone to provide an adequate explanation.

In 2012, the House of Lords Constitution Committee published a report on the accountability of civil servants.[19] On the basic constitutional framework, the Committee was unequivocal: '*the convention that ministers are constitutionally responsible for all aspects of their departments' business is an essential principle underlying the arrangements that enable Parliament properly to perform its function of holding the Government to account. The convention is clear, straightforward and leaves no gaps*' (para 12). The Committee went to say, '*We maintain our view that there is no constitutional difference between the terms responsibility and accountability*' (para 17). In its response, the government disagreed.

Government response to the Lords Constitution Committee's report on the Accountability of Civil Servants (undated)

The Government believes that there is an important distinction between ministerial accountability for all that a department does and the limits to the direct personal responsibility of Ministers for the actions of their department. The Government welcomes the Committee's acknowledgement that Ministers canno sensibly be held responsible for absolutely everything which goes on in the department in the sense of having personal knowledge and control of every action taken.

One of the Committee's recommendations proved controversial. It argued that select committees should, in rare cases, be able to criticize named civil servants when there were 'strong grounds' for doing so:

[17] Cabinet Office, *Giving evidence to Select Committees—Guidance for Civil Servants* (October 2014) https://assets.publishing.service.gov.uk/media/5a7ea981ed915d74e6225ad7/Osmotherly_Rules_October_2014.pdf accessed 20 November 2025.

[18] We explore select committees below.

[19] House of Lords Constitution Committee, *The accountability of civil servants*, 6th Report of Session 2012–13, HL Paper 61.

House of Lords Constitution Committee, *The Accountability of Civil Servants*, 6th Report of Session 2012–13, HL Paper 61, para 99

We are conscious that select committees are not disciplinary tribunals and do not contain the safeguards that employees are entitled to in a disciplinary process. However, when the evidence a committee receives leads it to conclude that a particular civil servant has been at fault, that committee should not be precluded from expressing criticism and, in extreme cases, recommending that the department consider appropriate disciplinary procedures.

Other select committees have made little use of this practice.

PAUSE FOR REFLECTION

Operational errors can have far-reaching consequences. In 2007, a junior HM Revenue and Customs official sent two unencrypted and untracked discs by courier that contained the details of every child in the UK and their parents' bank information to another site. The package never arrived, resulting in a major loss of sensitive personal data. Who should be held accountable, and in what way? The courier firm with no record of receiving the package? The official who sent it? HMRC's Permanent Secretary (the most senior civil servant)? A government minister?

Would your assessment of accountability change if you learned that middle-rank civil servants had adopted a policy—driven by budget constraints—of not encrypting discs as standard practice? Or that, even in 2007, sending data on physical discs rather than using secure online transfer was outdated? Or that HMRC's management structure had become so complex that lines of responsibility were blurred?

9.5 COLLECTIVE CABINET RESPONSIBILITY

Having looked at the constitutional convention of individual ministerial responsibility and the extent to which civil servants are accountable to Parliament, we turn now to consider the convention of collective ministerial responsibility. This convention links the Cabinet's decision-making to democratic accountability: if the government is to be answerable to Parliament and the public for its policies, it must present those policies as the agreed position of all serving ministers. Collective responsibility therefore requires unity in public, even when ministers have disagreed in private. A statement of how the government understands this convention is set out in the *Ministerial Code*.

Cabinet Office, *Ministerial Code* (October 2025)

Collective responsibility

General principle

5.1. The principle of collective responsibility requires that ministers should be able to express their views frankly in the expectation that they can argue freely in private while maintaining a united front when decisions have been reached. This in turn requires that the privacy of opinions expressed in cabinet and ministerial committees, including in correspondence, should be maintained. [. . .]

Collective responsibility

5.3. The internal process through which a decision has been made, or the level of committee by which it was taken, should not be disclosed. Neither should the individual views of ministers or advice provided by civil servants as part of that internal process be disclosed. Decisions reached by the cabinet or ministerial committees are binding on all members of the government. They are, however, normally announced and explained as the decision of the minister concerned. On occasion, it may be desirable to emphasise the importance of a decision by stating specifically that it is the decision of His Majesty's Government. This, however, is the exception rather than the rule. Ministers also have an obligation to ensure decisions agreed in cabinet and cabinet committees (and in write rounds) are implemented. Ministers should take special care in discussing issues which are the responsibility of other ministers, consulting ministerial colleagues as appropriate.

5.4. Matters wholly within the responsibility of a single minister and which do not significantly engage collective responsibility need not be brought to the cabinet or to a ministerial committee unless the minister wishes to inform their colleagues or to have their advice. No definitive criteria can be given for issues which engage collective responsibility. The cabinet secretariats can advise where departments are unsure, however, the final decision rests with the Prime Minister. When there is a difference between departments, it should not be referred to the cabinet until other means of resolving it have been exhausted. It is the responsibility of the initiating department to ensure that proposals have been discussed with other interested departments and the outcome of these discussions should be reflected in the memorandum or letter submitted to the cabinet or a cabinet committee.

A minister who feels unable to support government policy is expected to resign from office. It is not possible for ministers simultaneously to remain in office and to seek to disagree or disassociate themselves from the collective view of the government. Ministers who resign in these circumstances may make a personal statement on the floor of the Commons.

9.5.1 SUSPENDING OR MODIFYING THE CONVENTION

One enduring issue that has divided political parties—the United Kingdom's membership of the European Union—has tested the convention of collective responsibility for more than 50 years. Ahead of the 1975 referendum, the Cabinet was split on the issue of continued membership: Labour Prime Minister Harold Wilson MP had to introduce an 'agreement to differ' that permitted ministers to campaign on either side of the referendum. In 1977, James Callaghan (Labour prime minister) allowed ministers to take different views on direct elections to the European Parliament. The same happened in advance of the 2016 referendum.[20] The government's official position was to support continuing UK membership, but Conservative Prime Minister David Cameron lifted collective responsibility to permit some ministers to campaign to leave. His successor, Theresa May MP, reasserted collective responsibility as the UK negotiated the terms of its departure leading to several resignations. Michael Gordon diagnosed this as 'the Brexit unanimity crisis', writing '*Remarkably, these examples included five resignations from within the Cabinet, six resignations from within the Department for Exiting the European Union, the department leading negotiations with the EU—including two Secretaries of State, Davis and Raab —and May's successor as Prime Minister, the then Foreign Secretary Boris Johnson. May had to resign as PM*'.[21]

[20] See Chapter 24.

[21] M. Gordon, 'Ministerial irresponsibility in the UK Government: constitutional accountability after Theresa May and Boris Johnson' [2024] Public Law 414, 418.

M. Gordon, 'Ministerial irresponsibility in the UK Government: constitutional accountability after Theresa May and Boris Johnson' [2024] Public Law 414, 421 (footnote omitted)

From one perspective it might be argued that ministers resigning on the basis of disagreement with the government's Brexit policy was a sign of the convention working: ministers were simply following the traditional advice of Lord Salisbury, and exiting government when they could no longer accept or defend its key policy. There were other examples of resignations on the basis of such disagreements over government policy under Theresa May. Greg Hands resigned from government in 2018 in opposition to plans for a third runway at Heathrow Airport, on the basis of a promise made to his constituents to vote against the policy. And Tracey Crouch resigned in 2018 over a government u-turn regarding the implementation of limits on gambling using 'Fixed Odds Betting Terminals'. Crouch's resignation was successful in pressuring the government to return to its original plans. Yet what marks Brexit out in particular as producing a crisis of collective responsibility is the sheer volume of resignations, the diametrically opposed political objectives of the ministers resigning, and the strategic timing of many of these announcements, which were designed to attack government policy as much as to free ministers from their obligations to support it. These were not simply occasional or isolated breaches of the unanimity rule, but the complete and sustained absence of collective agreement within the government.

The collective responsibility convention has been suspended or modified on other issues. During the Conservative–Liberal Democrat government 2010–15, the coalition agreement between the parties permitted ministers to have publicly different views on various topics, including the 2011 referendum on the alternative voting system for general elections (supported by the Liberal Democrats, opposed by the Conservatives). 'Special arrangements' were also put in place to allow ministers who had obtained the prior approval of the Prime Minister to set out their personal opinions on the proposed plan for a third runway at Heathrow Airport (though other members of the Cabinet were subject to the normal rules of collective responsibility). During the 2022 Conservative party process to replace Boris Johnson MP as leader of the party (and Prime Minister), there was blatant disregard for the convention of collective responsibility as some leadership candidates disclosed discussions in Cabinet and sought to distance themselves from government decisions despite still being serving ministers.

Some issues, often those with a strong moral dimension, are treated by party leaders as 'votes of conscience'. Ministers and other MPs are then free to speak and vote according to their own judgement, without being bound by collective responsibility. This approach was used for the 2025 Assisted Dying Bill, introduced by a backbench MP, in which Labour ministers took differing public positions and the government was neutral.

PAUSE FOR REFLECTION

Can collective responsibility really be regarded as a convention if governments across several decades have been able to choose to suspend it and individual ministers disregarded it during the Conversative leadership election in 2022?

Collective responsibility is meant to present a unified government to the public, even when ministers disagree in private. After reading this section, do you think this expectation still makes sense in a political environment where disagreement is common and often public? And when, if ever, should ministers be allowed to express dissent without having to resign?

9.5.2 CONFIDENCE IN GOVERNMENT

Collective ministerial responsibility is important in terms of ensuring that there is effective accountability to Parliament. The government needs to defend its policies—and if the House of Commons were to lose confidence in the government as a whole, then the Prime Minister would, under a constitutional convention, be obliged to ask the monarch to exercise her prerogative power to dissolve Parliament, triggering a general election.

Writing in 1967, Geoffrey Marshall and Graeme Moodie said that '*The defeat of any substantial bill is nowadays regarded as a loss of confidence [. . .] governments now regard it as politically incumbent upon them to avoid defeat in the Commons on any issue whatsoever.*'[22] Their criticism of this rigidity was well founded. Contemporary practice is more flexible: governments have been defeated on significant elements of their own legislation without any serious suggestion that they should resign. For example, in November 2005 the Commons rejected the proposal to allow terrorist suspects to be detained without charge for 90 days, leading the Labour government to withdraw the measure. More recently, in January 2019, the Commons voted down Theresa May's proposed Withdrawal Agreement with the European Union—the largest government defeat in modern parliamentary history—yet the government continued in office.

Occasionally, the House of Commons debates a motion of 'no confidence' in the government (or, if tabled by the government, a motion of 'confidence'). The last time a government was defeated on such a motion was on 28 March 1979. James Callaghan's Labour government lost by one vote, triggering a general election. After the division, the Prime Minister made the following statement.

House of Commons Hansard, 28 March 1979, cols 589–90

> Mr James Callaghan: Mr Speaker, now that the House has declared itself, we shall take our case to the country. Tomorrow I shall propose to Her Majesty that Parliament be dissolved as soon as essential business can be cleared up, and then I shall announce as soon as may be—and that will be as soon as possible—the date of Dissolution, the date of the election and the date of meeting of the new Parliament.
>
> Mrs Margaret Thatcher [Leader of the Conservative Party]: As the Government no longer have authority to carry on business without the agreement of the Opposition, I make it quite clear that we shall facilitate any business which requires the agreement of the Opposition so that the Dissolution can take place at the very earliest opportunity and the uncertainty ended.

A vote of no confidence will normally bring down a government only when it lacks a secure Commons majority. Minority and small-majority administrations are therefore more exposed to this form of parliamentary control.

A different scenario arises when a Prime Minister loses the confidence of their own parliamentary party. In July 2022, Boris Johnson MP announced that he would resign as leader of the Conservative Party after an unprecedented wave of ministerial resignations, including several Cabinet ministers, ministers attending Cabinet, and dozens of junior ministers and parliamentary private secretaries. This left him unable to maintain effective collective responsibility or command the support of his parliamentary party. An internal leadership contest followed, producing Liz Truss MP as his successor and the new Prime Minister. Similarly, in 2019 Theresa May MP resigned as Prime Minister after sustained opposition within her party to her approach to government negotiations to withdraw from

[22] G. Marshall and G. Moodie, *Some Problems of the Constitution*, 4th edn (1967, London: Hutchinson University Library), p. 62.

the European Union, despite surviving a formal confidence vote under Conservative Party rules and a separate confidence motion in the Commons brought by the Opposition. In both cases, the transition of Prime Minister occurred without a general election.

These episodes illustrate an important constitutional point. There is no convention requiring a general election when the governing party changes its leader. A new Prime Minister can take office without seeking an immediate mandate from the electorate, provided the governing party retains the confidence of a majority in the House of Commons.

> **QUESTION**
>
> Scenario: Tricia Trout, the Secretary of State for Animal Welfare, tells a radio interviewer that her department will publish a consultation paper in a few weeks' time on whether angling should be made unlawful. Peter Pike MP, a junior minister in the Foreign, Commonwealth and Development Office, is taken by surprise. Speaking to a journalist later that day, he comments: 'This is a bonkers initiative from a department that is out of touch with reality.' His remark appears on the front page of a national newspaper.
>
> Question: Based on what you have learned about collective and individual ministerial responsibility, consider two issues. Has the Secretary of State acted consistently with the Ministerial Code? And has the junior minister breached the requirement to maintain a united public position on government policy? What should the Prime Minister do?

9.6 PARLIAMENT'S ACCOUNTABILITY FUNCTION

This section examines three practical ways in which Parliament today carries out its accountability role: select committees, ministerial questions, and debates. The idea that scrutiny is central to Parliament's purpose is not new. As noted at the start of this chapter, John Stuart Mill wrote in 1861 that the proper office of a representative assembly is '*to watch and control the government; to throw the light of publicity on its acts; to compel a full exposition and justification of all of them which any one considers questionable; to censure them if found condemnable*'[23]. That description still captures an important part of Parliament's work.

9.6.1 SELECT COMMITTEES

Before the 1980s, there was a rather ramshackle collection of House of Commons committees (see Figure 9.1) of backbench MPs responsible for scrutinizing the work of some government departments and various areas of policy. A more comprehensive system of 'select' committees—a better name would be 'scrutiny' committees—was introduced in 1979. Now, every major department has a corresponding select committee, typically comprising between 11 and 15 MPs reflecting the party-political composition of the House of Commons as a whole. Distinct from these 'departmental' select committees is the influential Public Accounts Committee, which scrutinizes public expenditure rather than policy. Chairs of committees are elected by secret ballots of MPs, with some chairs now achieving a public profile for their committee's work in the news media.

[23] John Stuart Mill, *Considerations on Representative Government* (Parker, Son, and Bourn 1861), p. 104.

Figure 9.1 A House of Commons select committee

The role of select committees is advisory and their methods of work inquisitorial. The relevant department is obliged to respond to committee reports, but there is no obligation to accept their findings. Committees devise a programme of topics on which they wish to conduct inquiries. Some inquiries have a much wider focus than what happened within government: for example, the 2011 inquiry by the Culture, Media and Sport Committee into phone hacking took evidence from Rupert Murdoch and the police.

Each committee is assisted by a clerk (who will normally take a lead in drafting a report for MPs to consider) and a small number of other staff. Specialist advisers, often academics, may be appointed to help the committee to identify suitable witnesses and to draft questions for MPs to ask. The questioning to which ministers may be subjected at an appearance before a select committee is far more rigorous and sustained than is the case when ministers appear 'at the despatch box' to answer oral questions on the floor of the chamber. Ministers can, and do, however refuse to appear before select committees. For example, in July 2022 the evening before she was due to go before the Home Affairs Committee, Home Secretary Priti Patel MP said she would not attend the session, which was likely to cover questions about government policy to deport asylum seekers to Rwanda, delays in processing passport applications, and policing. During 2019, when he was Prime Minister, Boris Johnson MP three times at short notice cancelled planned appearances before the Liaison Committee (made up of the chairs of all the select committee).

The role of chair of a select committee can be a demanding one and the MPs elected to this role receive a payment on top of their MPs' salary. The methods of working will vary according to the requirements of the inquiry, but usually include a public call for written evidence and several oral evidence sessions with key witnesses—including the relevant minister and senior civil servants.

Most of the time, select committees can work in a consensual, cross-party manner rather than dividing along party political lines. They provide an oasis of non-party activity in an institution that is otherwise dominated by the cut and thrust of party politics.

Several research projects carried out in recent years have sought to understand the operation and effectiveness of select committees.

- A 2011 study by researchers at UCL Constitution Unit sought to measure the impact select committees have on government policy. The report concluded that '*we almost invariably end up with a mixed picture. The select committees are influential, but not all of the time.*' Data analysed in the study showed that '*roughly 40% of committee recommendations were accepted and implemented by government, though two thirds of recommendations calling for a medium or large policy change ultimately failed*'.[24]
- The Institute for Government ('a think tank working to make government more effective') in a 2015 report recommended that '*committees ought to spend more time cultivating their "softer" sources of influence, such as expertise and relationships, and be less quick to resort to their formal status and powers. For their part, government departments should remember that it is in their own interests to help committees develop their multiple sources of influence*' and that committees should '*adopt a nuanced understanding of impact, which recognises that long-term influence, which may be difficult to measure, can be just as important as short-term impacts which are more readily attributable to committee activity*'.[25]
- In 2017, a report published by The Constitution Society (an 'independent, non-party educational foundation') concluded that the '*powers afforded to committees are still limited, and the impact of their work is frequently undermined by inadequate or tardy government responses. Reliance on government cooperation ensures that select committees remain the "underdogs"*' and warned that '*piecemeal development has also led to concerns about committees taking on too much work. As one respondent warned, commentators should be careful not to view select committees as a panacea, particularly amidst calls for committees to have a greater say in pre-legislative scrutiny work*'.[26]

There are also select committees in the House of Lords. Unlike most of the House of Commons' select committees, they do not shadow the work of particular government departments, but instead have remits to cover general topics. The House of Lords' Constitution Committee scrutinizes all government bills and also conducts thematic inquiries into broader constitutional issues.

Time—too little, critics say—is allowed for committee reports to be debated on the floor of the respective House.

9.6.2 PARLIAMENTARY QUESTIONS

Parliamentary questions (PQs) to ministers may be asked orally and in written form by MPs and peers. All questions must conform to certain guidelines, and MPs and peers may seek advice from parliamentary officials to ensure that they comply with these guidelines.

[24] M. Russell and M. Benton, *Selective Influence: the policy impact of House of Commons select committees* (2011, London: UCL Constitution Unit), p. 96.

[25] H. White, *Select Committees under Scrutiny: the impact of parliamentary committee inquiries on government* (2015, London: Institute for Government).

[26] L. Atkinson, *House of Commons Select Committees and the UK Constitution* (2017, London: The Constitution Society).

MP's Guide to Procedure, UK Parliament (November 2025)

You can ask a minister an oral question in the Chamber, or you can ask a written question. Questions are submitted through the Table Office.

All questions must:

- seek information or press for action
- be about something a minister is responsible for
- be based on fact, not speculation
- use neutral language and not contain unnecessary information
- not ask for information which is readily available
- not refer to a case that is active in the UK courts

In the Commons, the first hour of business in the chamber on weekdays is devoted to ministers answering oral questions from MPs. There is a rota, so that the ministerial team from each department must appear before the chamber every few weeks. There are always more MPs wanting to ask questions than can be accommodated in the time available, so MPs enter a ballot and are able to ask their question—followed by one or more 'supplementary' questions—only if they win a slot. Ministers have advance notice of some questions, but time is also set aside for 'topical' questions on any relevant subject.

Since 1961, there has been a practice of the Prime Minister answering oral questions weekly when the House of Commons is sitting—known as the Prime Minister's Questions (PMQs). Initially, this happened twice weekly for 15 minutes, but since 2003, the practice has been for the Prime Minister to appear before the Commons for 30 minutes at noon on Wednesdays. This gladiatorial contest between the Prime Minister, the leaders of the Opposition parties, and other MPs is normally rowdy, with the Speaker often intervening to try to keep order. PMQ sessions are widely reported, and to this extent are an important opportunity for the Commons to call the government to account publicly. Questions posed by MPs can cover international and national issues but also local ones, such as threatened closures of hospitals. MPs from the governing party called on to ask question often use this as an opportunity to praise the government. The shouting, grandstanding, and political point scoring leave little room for serious analysis of government policy and conduct.

Many thousands of written PQs are tabled in Parliament each year and ministers' responses (drafted on behalf of ministers by civil servants) are published in Hansard. Concerns have been expressed as to how effective written PQs are in calling the government to account. Criticisms include that there are delays in providing answers, that answers are sometimes incomplete and irrelevant, and that answers are not given on the grounds that the cost of researching the answer would be disproportionate (currently, the threshold is £850).

The fundamental purpose of the convention of individual ministerial responsibility is that it provides an important means of drawing information into the public domain. The obtaining of information, by MPs on behalf of their constituents, lies at the heart of the scrutiny process: the public accountability of government is a necessary and basic characteristic of any democratic system and ill-informed debate will not be effective. More generally, the openness and accountability of government is required by the fourth and fifth principles of public life set out by the Committee on Standards in Public Life, which have been incorporated into the *Ministerial Code*. However, where ministers refuse to provide information, the complaints of Westminster MPs that there are no sanctions recall Hobbes' axiom that, 'Covenants without the sword are but words'.

9.6.3 DEBATES ON THE FLOOR OF THE HOUSE

Debates on the floor of the Commons and the Lords are a further way in which the government is called to account for its policies and alleged failings, and for Parliament to discuss matters of public interest. In Chapter 12, we will see that much debating time is taken up with discussion of bills—the government's proposals for legislation—but debates also focus on how the government is conducting its policy and executive functions. During 2025, opposition day debates included the hospitality sector, Stamp Duty Land Tax, and welfare spending. In 'adjournment debates', the House is not called on to come to any specific conclusion and there is no vote at the end of deliberations. Debates may be initiated by the government, by leaders of the opposition parties (20 days are allocated for this purpose every year), or by backbench MPs (for the final 30 minutes of every day).

Since 1999, to make more time for debates initiated by backbench MPs and select committees, there has been a 'parallel chamber' in which the House of Commons may sit simultaneously in the main chamber and another debating room known as 'Westminster Hall'.

QUESTIONS

1. If you were an MP, would you prefer to serve as a junior minister or to chair a select committee? Which role do you think offers greater influence, and why?
2. Alex Average is a newly elected MP. Imagine that you are a clerk in the Table Office. She asks for advice on the following draft parliamentary question: 'Will the minister confirm that he has read recent reports in [a local newspaper] about the unlawful treatment of people in my constituency during allotment evictions,[27] and will he take action?'. How would you advise her on how to frame this question so that it meets parliamentary rules on language, responsibility, and scope?

9.7 CASE STUDY: WINDRUSH SCANDAL

This final section uses the Windrush scandal to draw together the different forms of accountability discussed in the chapter. It shows how policy choices, legislation, administrative systems, and frontline decision-making can combine to produce serious and lasting harm, particularly for people with limited access to legal advice or political influence.[28] It also highlights how multiple accountability routes can operate at once. As you read, consider what this reveals about how accountability works in practice.

9.7.1 ABOUT THE WINDRUSH SCANDAL

Between 1948 and 1973, several hundred thousand people from Caribbean territories that were, at the start of this period, part of the British Empire migrated to the United Kingdom, often travelling

[27] Allotments are small plots, often owned by local authorities, that are rented to local residents for growing fruit and vegetables.

[28] For personal accounts of the impact of the failures on individuals, see Policy Lab, 'Video: experiences of members of the Windrush Generation' (Home Office, undated) https://youtu.be/xEJksQpWkaE (an 8-minute video) and A. Gentleman, '"Lambs to the slaughter": 50 lives ruined by the Windrush scandal' *The Guardian*, 19 March 2020 https://www.theguardian.com/uk-news/2020/mar/19/lambs-to-the-slaughter-50-lives-ruined-by-the-windrush-scandal accessed 24 November 2025.

with their children. The UK government and many employers were actively recruiting workers to address post-war labour shortages, and people from the Caribbean were encouraged to take up those opportunities. They became known as the 'Windrush generation', named after the ship *HMT Empire Windrush*, which arrived in 1948. Under the nationality and immigration law in force at the time, many of these adults and children were Citizens of the United Kingdom and Colonies and were entitled to live and work in the UK without restriction.

Problems began to emerge for members of the Windrush generation during the 2010s, when changes to immigration law and policy—aimed at creating a 'hostile environment' for people living unlawfully in the UK—required employers, landlords, and public bodies to check documentary evidence that a person had a legal right to live and work in the United Kingdom. Many long-term residents from the Windrush generation, who had lawfully lived and worked in the UK for decades, did not have the paperwork now demanded and found it difficult or impossible to obtain it. As a result, some lost jobs and housing, and were refused access to NHS treatment or welfare support. Hundreds were detained or threatened with removal, and more than 80 people were unlawfully removed to countries they had not lived in since childhood.

By 2013, community leaders in the UK were becoming aware that these were not isolated administrative glitches but part of a wider pattern of administrative action. It was estimated that up to 57,000 individuals could be affected by Home Office policies. The UK government refused to engage with those expressing concerns about the emerging injustices and unlawful actions, including governments from several Caribbean states and British Overseas Territories.

9.7.2 THE GOVERNMENT ACKNOWLEDGES A PROBLEM, AT LAST

By Spring 2018, the UK Government could no longer deny the existence and scale of the emerging scandal. The news media, notably *The Guardian*, started to cover stories.[29] On 16 April, Amber Rudd MP, who had been Home Secretary since 2016, came to the House of Commons to answer an urgent question by backbench Labour MP, David Lammy.

House of Commons Hansard, Windrush Children (Immigration Status), Vol 639, 16 April 2018

> I recognise the concerns of some people in the Windrush generation, and I would not want anyone who has made their life in the UK to feel unwelcome or to be in any doubt of their right to remain here. As my right hon. Friend the Prime Minister has already made clear, there is absolutely no question about their right to remain, and I am very sorry for any confusion or anxiety felt.

Rudd went on to outline several measures the Home Office would take to assist people without documentation, including establishing a dedicated team of civil servants to resolve cases and waiving the fees that would normally apply to applications to regularise their status. If the government had hoped that this announcement would draw a line under the issue, it did not.

Political pressure on the government intensified in the days that followed. On 17 April 2018, Prime Minister Theresa May made a televised apology to Caribbean leaders at a meeting in London, saying she was 'genuinely sorry for any anxiety caused'.[30] Back in Parliament, the House of Commons

[29] The Guardian's investigation of the Windrush scandal, led by Amelia Gentleman, was awarded the Paul Foot Award for investigative and campaigning journalism in 2018.

[30] BBC News, 'Windrush generation: Theresa May apologises to Caribbean leaders', 17 April 2018 https://www.bbc.co.uk/news/uk-politics-43792411 accessed 24 November 2025.

Home Affairs Committee, chaired by Labour MP Yvette Cooper, launched an inquiry on Windrush Children. On 25 April 2018, Rudd appeared before he Home Affairs Select Committee to give oral evidence as part of its Windrush Children inquiry. She was questioned by Cooper. One line of questioning was about whether targets had been set for the number of people that officials should seek to deport from the United Kingdom. Rudd denied there were such targets.

Home Affairs Committee, Oral evidence: Windrush Children, HC 990, Wednesday 25 April 2018, Ordered by the House of Commons to be published on 25 April 2018

Chair: Targets for removals. When were they set?

Amber Rudd: We do not have targets for removals.

Q86 **Chair:** But you did?

Amber Rudd: What are you referring to?

Q87 **Chair:** We have just heard in the previous evidence that in the Home Office there are regional targets for net removals. [Before Rudd came into the committee, it heard evidence from a specialist legal practitioner group, a trade union, and a campaign organisation].

Amber Rudd: I did not hear the testimony. I am not sure what shape that might be in. If you are asking me if there are numbers of people we expect to be removed, that is not how we operate. I know we are talking about Windrush here, who are legal migrants, but where there are people who are here illegally it is right that we do try to remove them.

On the wider Windrush crisis, Rudd said '*I look back with hindsight and I'm surprised I did not see the shape of it sooner*', adding '*I bitterly, deeply regret that I didn't see it as more than individual cases that had gone wrong that needed addressing. I didn't see it as a systemic issue until very recently*'.[31]

The following day in the chamber of House of Commons, backbench Labour MP Diane Abbott was given permission to ask an urgent question ('To ask the Home Secretary if she will make a statement about the use of removal targets in the Home Office'.) Rudd gave the following answer.

House of Commons Hansard, Home Office Removal Target Volume 639: debated on Thursday 26 April 2018

Yesterday, I gave evidence to the Select Committee on Home Affairs about the Windrush generation—the people who contributed so much and who should never have experienced what they have. These people are here legally and should never have been subjected to any form of removal action; and, as I told the Home Affairs Committee yesterday, I have seen no evidence that that has happened. [. . .]

I have never agreed that there should be specific removal targets and I would never support a policy that puts targets ahead of people. The immigration arm of the Home Office has been using local targets for internal performance management. These were not published targets against which performance was assessed, but if they were used inappropriately, then I am clear that this

[31] A. MacAskill, 'Amber Rudd "deeply regrets" failing to spot scale of Windrush migrant problem', *Reuters*, 26 April 2018 https://www.reuters.com/article/world/amber-rudd-deeply-regrets-failing-to-spot-scale-of-windrush-migrant-problem accessed 14 November 2025.

> will have to change. I have asked officials to provide me with a full picture of the performance measurement tools which were used at all levels, and I will update the House, and the Home Affairs Committee, as soon as possible.

Abbott responded saying *'The [union leader who gave evidence before Rudd at the Committee hearing] later confirmed that the target this month was 8,337, with targets on posters in regional centres. When Lord Carrington resigned over the Falklands, he said that it was a matter of honour. Is it not time that the Home Secretary considered her honour and resigned?'* Rudd responded:

> I would like to make the very clear distinction between legal and illegal migrants. The right hon. Lady talks about the Windrush cohort. We have already established that the Windrush cohort is here legally. This Government are determined to put this right, which is why I put in the new measures to ensure that that happens.
>
> I believe that I have addressed the issue of targets, referring to the fact that some offices are working with them. Unfortunately, I was not aware of them, and I want to be aware of them, which is why I am now putting in place different measures to ensure that that happens.

9.7.3 THE HOME SECRETARY RESIGNS

Two days later, *Guardian* journalists revealed that Rudd had written to Prime Minister Theresa May in 2017, saying that she intended to increase deportation by 10 per cent, which the *Guardian* commented was 'seemingly at odds with her recent denials that she was aware of deportation targets'.[32] Within hours, Rudd resigned. Her letter to the Prime Minister, and the reply, were widely published.

> Dear Prime Minister,
>
> It is with great regret that I am resigning as home secretary. I feel it is necessary to do so because I inadvertently misled the Home Affairs Select Committee over targets for removal of illegal immigrants during their questions on Windrush.
>
> Since appearing before the select committee, I have reviewed the advice I was given on this issue and become aware of information provided to my office which makes mention of targets. I should have been aware of this, and I take full responsibility for the fact that I was not. [. . .]

The Prime Minister appointed Sajid Javid MP as the new Home Secretary. Within hours, he came to the House of Commons to respond to an urgent question, again from Diane Abbott MP. He acknowledged that the difficulties faced by 'long-standing pillars of the community' should never have occurred, remarking that 'it could be my mum, my brother, my uncle or even me'.[33] He was the first person from a minority ethnic background to hold the office of Home Secretary.

The government established two schemes to assist those affected. One provided formal documentation confirming a person's lawful status and right to live permanently in the United Kingdom; more than 17,000 people obtained documentation through this route. The other was a compensation scheme. Over 8,800 claims were submitted, but, as discussed below, the scheme attracted sustained criticism for delays and limited awards.

[32] H. Stewart et al, 'Amber Rudd resigns hours after Guardian publishes deportation targets letter', *The Guardian*, 30 April 2018.

[33] House of Commons Hansard, 30 April 2018, vol 640 col 35.

9.7.4 FURTHER ACCOUNTABILITY ACTIVITY

Since 2018, there have been numerous inquiries. In June 2018, the Joint Committee on Human Rights examined the use of immigration detention, reviewing Home Office files relating to two members of the Windrush cohort who had been wrongly detained. The committee identified a 'catalogue of errors' in the handling of these cases, including misapplication of the law on immigration status, the unlawful and inappropriate use of detention powers, and a culture that failed to treat people with basic respect and dignity. It called for 'fundamental change in the law, culture and procedures to protect human rights in the work of the Home Office'.

In July 2018, the House of Commons Home Affairs Committee concluded that 'there was a clear lack of oversight of the system as a whole, meaning that the Government did not recognise systemic problems as they arose'. The committee also made a series of recommendations to improve the documentation and compensation schemes.

In November 2018, the National Audit Office, which scrutinises public spending and the performance of government departments, examined the Home Office's information management and casework systems. It made a series of recommendations aimed at reducing the risk of similar problems recurring. In March 2019, the House of Commons Public Accounts Committee followed up on the NAO's report. It found that the Home Office had ignored early warning signs and there was 'a dereliction of duty for the Department not to monitor the impact of its compliant environment policy on vulnerable members of our society'.

In November 2020, the Equality and Human Rights Commission, the statutory body responsible for enforcing equality and human rights laws in Great Britain, found that the Home Office had not complied with the public sector equality duty. That duty requires public authorities to consider how their policies and decisions affect people with different protected characteristics. The Commission concluded that the Home Office failed to meet this obligation when developing and implementing the 'hostile environment' policy that triggered many of the Windrush problems.

Outside parliament, in March 2020, the 'Windrush Lessons Learned Review' commissioned by Sajid Javid when he was Home Secretary reported. The project was led by Wendy Williams, HM Inspector of Constabulary and Fire & Rescue Services.

Windrush Lessons Learned Review Independent review by Wendy Williams (March 2020, HC 93). p.7

> ... despite the scandal taking the Home Office by surprise my report sets out that what happened to those affected by the Windrush scandal was foreseeable and avoidable.
>
> The causes of the Windrush scandal can be traced back through successive rounds of policy and legislation about immigration and nationality from the 1960s onwards, the aim of which was to restrict the eligibility of certain groups to live in the UK.
>
> The 1971 Immigration Act confirmed that the Windrush generation had, and have, the right of abode in the UK. But they were not given any documents to demonstrate this status. Nor were records kept. They had no reason to doubt their status, or that they belonged in the UK. They could not have been expected to know the complexity of the law as it changed around them. But over time those in power forgot about them and their circumstances, which meant that when successive governments wanted to demonstrate that they were being tough on immigration by tightening immigration control and passing laws creating, and then expanding the hostile environment, this was done with a complete disregard for the Windrush generation.

> A range of warning signs from inside and outside the Home Office were simply not heeded by officials and ministers. Even when stories of members of the Windrush generation being affected by immigration control started to emerge in the media from 2017 onwards, the department was too slow to react. The report identifies the organisational factors in the Home Office which created the operating environment in which these mistakes could be made, including a culture of disbelief and carelessness when dealing with applications, made worse by the status of the Windrush generation, who were failed when they needed help most.

The Williams Review made 30 recommendations, all of which were initially accepted by the government, and work on implementation began. By January 2023, however, the then Home Secretary, Suella Braverman MP, announced that three recommendations would not be taken forward, including proposals for a programme of reconciliation events and the creation of a Migrants' Commissioner.

After the 2024 general election, the incoming Labour government appointed a Windrush Commissioner to oversee further implementation of the Williams Review and the compensation scheme. As of 31 July 2024, 8,828 compensation claims had been submitted, but only 2,634 had resulted in payments.

In November 2018, little more than six months after she resigned, Rudd returned to the Cabinet when Theresa May appointed her Secretary of State for Work and Pensions. In September 2019, after Boris Johnson became Prime Minister, she resigned from the Cabinet and left the Conservative parliamentary party, explaining that she could not support the government's approach to the United Kingdom's withdrawal from the European Union. Her departure at that point also provides an example of the conventions on collective ministerial responsibility, which we discuss in the next section. She did not contest the 2019 general election and has since worked mainly in the private sector.

9.7.5 WHAT THE WINDRUSH SCANDAL SHOWS

The Windrush scandal shows how multiple accountability mechanisms can operate simultaneously, sometimes reinforcing each other, but sometimes failing to prevent serious injustice until considerable harm has already occurred. The episode also highlights the contribution of investigative journalism. Reporting by *The Guardian* played a critical role in bringing individual stories to public attention, prompting parliamentary action and forcing ministers to address the issue. It is a reminder that accountability does not operate only through formal constitutional channels; the media can shine a light on administrative practices that would otherwise remain obscure.

The Windrush episode shows how responsibility for serious administrative failure can be dispersed across a department in ways that make the convention of individual ministerial responsibility difficult to operate in practice. Junior officials followed procedures that were poorly designed and inadequately supervised; senior civil servants failed to act on warning signs, appreciate the cumulative impact of casework decisions, or the impact of growing complexity in legislation and policy; and ministers set the political direction, approved policies that created a 'hostile environment', and relied on advice that did not convey the scale of harm being caused. Amber Rudd's resignation demonstrates that the convention can still provide a mechanism for political accountability when a minister misleads Parliament. Yet the scandal also exposes its limits: systemic problems persisted for years without correction, and attributing responsibility to a single minister risks obscuring the organizational culture, internal oversight failures, and policy choices that contributed to the injustice.

The Williams Review has had a more substantial and lasting effect than the select committee reports. While committees quickly exposed serious failures and pressed ministers for explanations, their ability to secure reform was limited by the familiar constraints on parliamentary scrutiny: short inquiry windows, incomplete information, and limited investigatory powers. The Williams Review, by contrast, had ministerial backing, extensive access to internal material, and the time to produce a comprehensive diagnosis of the legal, cultural, and administrative causes of the scandal. Its recommendations initially shaped the Home Office's reform agenda and have remained the main reference point for subsequent change, even after some were later dropped. The implication is that meaningful institutional reform in major scandals often depends less on Parliament's continuous oversight and more on whether ministers choose to commission, endorse, and act on independent reviews—raising a wider question about the limits of parliamentary influence over departmental culture and long-term corrective action.

9.8 CONCLUDING COMMENTS

This chapter has considered how key government office holders are called to account, focusing on the work of the UK Parliament. To continue reading about government, turn to Chapter 10, which considers how UK government ministers and the Crown exercise prerogative powers.

FURTHER READING

Fox, J., *Accountability Keywords* (2022, Accountability Research Centre).

Gentleman, A., *The Windrush Betrayal* (2019, Guardian Faber)

Norton, P. (Lord Norton of Louth), 'Parliament: The Best of Times, the Worst of Times?', in J. Jowell and C. O'Cinneide (eds) *The Changing Constitution*, 9th edn (2019, Oxford: OUP), ch. 6.

10

PREROGATIVE POWERS

CENTRAL ISSUES

1. A fundamental principle of the constitution is that executive action must be based on legal foundations.
2. Most public bodies are 'creatures of statute' established by an Act of Parliament. Statute provides their legal powers. The Monarch and Ministers in the UK government are in a different position, because the legal foundation for some of their specific actions is 'prerogative power', that is to say power that was originally exercised by the Monarch before the modern parliamentary system was established.
3. There are fewer opportunities to hold ministers to account when government uses its prerogative powers than when it exercises powers conferred by statute. Prerogative powers may therefore be thought to be out of step with modern constitutional requirements.
4. Judicial control over the legality of the exercise of prerogative powers has increased in recent years, but some important types of action are regarded by the courts as 'non-justiciable' and are effectively free from judicial oversight.
5. While most prerogative powers have now been replaced by statutory powers, prerogative powers remain important, including in relation to the conduct of the United Kingdom's foreign affairs and the deployment of its armed forces.
6. Two aspects of the prerogative that have been particularly significant in recent years will be discussed. The first concerns entry into, and exiting from, treaty relationships (see *R (Miller) v Secretary of State for Exiting the European Union*[1]). The second concerns the prorogation and dissolution of Parliament (*R (Miller) v Prime Minister; Cherry and others v Advocate General for Scotland*[2]). These decisions raise important questions about the court's willingness to review the legality of actions taken by government using prerogative power. The prorogation case will be discussed as a mini case study.
7. Many argue that the remaining prerogative powers should be abolished or placed on a statutory footing. While progress has been made in this regard reform has not been easy. The challenges are particularly evident in the context of attempts to reform the prerogative power to deploy armed forces abroad. This will be examined as a second mini case study.

[1] [2017] UKSC 5 (*Miller 1*). See further Chapter 24.

[2] [2019] UKSC 41 (*Miller 2*).

10.1 INTRODUCTION: SOURCES OF LEGAL AUTHORITY

Before considering prerogative powers in more detail, we need to understand the legal context in which they exist. As we have already seen, it is a fundamental principle of the constitution that public bodies must have legal authority for their actions. This requirement is basic to the rule of law,[3] and is laid down in cases such as *Entick v Carrington*.[4]

In countries with written constitutions, the text of the written constitution may provide a direct legal foundation for actions of public bodies. Without such a foundation in the United Kingdom, there are two main sources of legal authority on which a public body may seek to rely.

(a) *Statute law*—the vast majority of public bodies trace their legal powers to statutes or delegated legislation made under statutes.[5] All local authority powers stem from legislation,[6] as do the powers of the Scottish Government, the Welsh Government, and Northern Ireland Executive.[7] These bodies are therefore sometimes described as 'creatures of statute', because they have only those powers that are expressly or implicitly conferred on them by statute law.

(b) *Prerogative powers*—The Monarch and UK government ministers also possess certain prerogative powers. We will examine the controversy over how these powers should be defined later in this chapter. For now, we can say that prerogative powers are a set of specific legal powers that remain from the period when the Monarch governed the country that are accepted by the courts as part of the common law. They may be exercised only by the Monarch and UK government ministers acting in the name of 'the Crown'.

The use and continued existence of prerogative powers has been a matter of deep controversy for many years. Because prerogative powers are not conferred by Parliament and have not been subject to the same level of parliamentary discussion as have statutory provisions (and because government need not obtain the formal approval of Parliament before using them), many question whether it is appropriate for government to have prerogative powers. They argue that the remaining prerogative powers should either be abolished or placed on a statutory footing. As we will see, achieving such reform has not always been straightforward.

10.1.1 PREROGATIVE AND STATUTORY POWERS COMPARED

Before going any further, consider the main differences between executive power that is authorized by statute and that which is authorized by prerogative powers (see Box 10.1).

BOX 10.1 SUMMARY OF DIFFERENCES BETWEEN STATUTORY AND PREROGATIVE POWERS

	Statutory powers	Prerogative powers
Source	Created by Parliament	Residual executive powers, predating the development of Parliament in its modern form
Parliament's role	Parliament debates, scrutinizes, and approves legislation conferring statutory powers	Parliament's role is reactive, calling ministers to account for the way prerogative power has been exercised

[3] See Chapter 4. [4] (1765) 19 St Tr 1030, discussed in Chapter 4.
[5] On primary and delegated legislation, see Chapters 12 and 13. [6] See Chapter 6. [7] See Chapter 6.

	Statutory powers	Prerogative powers
Method of creating new powers	New statutory powers are created in every session of Parliament, as and when bills containing executive powers receive Royal Assent	No new prerogative powers can be created—it is '*350 years and a Civil War too late*' for that (*per* Diplock LJ, *BBC v Johns* [1965] Ch 32, 79)
Place in hierarchy of legal rules	Acts of Parliament are normally considered to be the highest form of law, although they may be repealed or amended by later Acts of Parliament	Prerogative powers are part of the common law and so may be abolished or restricted by Act of Parliament
Judicial review	Legality of exercise of executive powers conferred by statute may be subject to judicial review, unless the subject matter is 'non-justiciable'	Since 1984, exercise of prerogative powers may be subject to judicial review, unless the subject matter is 'non-justiciable'
	The legal limits of statutory powers is determined by statutory interpretation	Since prerogative powers are not based on statute there is no text to interpret. This makes it more difficult to determine the legal limits of prerogative powers.[8]

PAUSE FOR REFLECTION

Drawing on the points listed in Box 10.1 (and others that you can think of), list the main constitutional advantages and disadvantages of prerogative powers as compared with statutory powers from the points of view of (a) government and (b) Parliament.

10.1.2 A 'THIRD SOURCE' OF AUTHORITY?

There is a school of thought (sometimes advanced by government, and accepted by some scholars and judges) that, in addition to statutory or prerogative powers, UK government also possesses general common law power to do whatever private individuals can do, without needing express statutory or prerogative authority. B.V. Harris refers to these as the 'third source' of legal authority for government action (the other two being statute and the prerogative).[9] The idea that there are such powers is often referred to as the 'Ram doctrine', after the government lawyer who set out an explanation for their existence in a memorandum in 1945.[10] While it is uncontentious that government has the ability do

[8] *R (Miller) v Prime Minister; Cherry and others v Advocate General for Scotland* [2019] UKSC 41, para. 38.

[9] B.V. Harris, 'The "third source" of authority for government' (1992) 108 *Law Quarterly Review* 626; B.V. Harris, 'The "third source" of authority for government revisited' (2007) 123 *Law Quarterly Review* 225.

[10] Sir Granville Ram was First Parliamentary Counsel between 1937 and 1947. See further A. Lester and M. Weaitt, 'The use of ministerial powers without parliamentary authority: The Ram doctrine' [2003] Public Law 415. See also *Malone v Metropolitan Police Commissioner* [1979] Ch 344 where Sir Robert Megarry V-C held that because no law prevented telephone tapping the police were free to secretly listen to and record Mr Malone's telephone conversations; see also discussion of the doctrine in *R (on the application of Hooper) v Secretary of State for Work and Pensions.* [2005] UKHL 29 and *R (on the application of Shrewsbury and Atcham BC) v Secretary of State for Communities and Local Government.* [2008] EWCA Civ 148.

'anything ancillary to its explicit functions',[11] it is doubtful that this deserves to be called a doctrine, a term that suggests a special legal status. The Select Committee on the Constitution, for example, has said that: '*[T]he description of the common law powers of the Crown encapsulated by the phrase "the Ram doctrine" is inaccurate, and should no longer be used.*'[12] The key point is that it should now be assumed that government can only do what is permitted by statute or prerogative.

10.2 PREROGATIVE POWERS

Ministry of Justice, The Governance of Britain, Cm 7170 (July 2007), para. 20

> In most modern democracies, the government's only powers are those granted to it by a written constitution or by the legislature. A distinguishing feature of the British constitution is the extent to which government continues to exercise a number of powers which were not granted to it by a written constitution, nor by Parliament, but are, rather, ancient prerogatives of the Crown. These powers derive from arrangements which preceded the 1689 Declaration of Rights and have been accumulated by the government without Parliament or the people having a say.

In the following extract from his judgment in the *Miller 1* case Lord Neuberger provides a brief summary of the history.

R (Miller) v Secretary of State for Exiting the European Union
[2017] UKSC 5

> **Lord Neuberger**
>
> 41. Originally, sovereignty was concentrated in the Crown [. . .] Accordingly, the Crown largely exercised all the powers of the state [. . .] However, over the centuries, those prerogative powers, collectively known as the Royal prerogative, were progressively reduced as Parliamentary democracy and the rule of law developed. By the end of the 20th century, the great majority of what had previously been prerogative powers, at least in relation to domestic matters, had become vested in the three principal organs of the state, the legislature (the two Houses of Parliament), the executive (ministers and the government more generally) and the judiciary (the judges). It is possible to identify a number of seminal events in this history, but a series of statutes enacted in the twenty years between 1688 and 1707 were of particular legal importance. Those statutes were the Bill of Rights 1688/9 and the Act of Settlement 1701 in England and Wales, the Claim of Right Act 1689 in Scotland, and the Acts of Union 1706 and 1707 in England and Wales and in Scotland respectively. (Northern Ireland joined the United Kingdom pursuant to the Acts of Union 1800 in Britain and Ireland).

10.2.1 DEFINING PREROGATIVE POWERS

Before going further let us try to define what prerogative powers are. Here we need to be cautious because although prerogative powers have been exercised for centuries there has been much debate

[11] Sir Stephen Sedley, in evidence to the Select Committee on the Constitution, *The pre-emption of Parliament*, Select Committee on the Constitution, 13th Report of Session 2012–13, para. 56.

[12] *The pre-emption of Parliament*, Select Committee on the Constitution, 13th Report of Session 2012–13, para. 60.

among commentators about how they should be defined and the meaning of the '*royal prerogative*' remains '*far from clear-cut*'.[13] Certainly, there is no single, accepted definition of the prerogative and the various definitions that are offered appear to conflict with each other. One reason for the uncertainty is that the prerogative has been changing as it has evolved over the years and definitions that might have been appropriate in the past might not be appropriate today.[14] That said, two main definitions of the royal prerogative are widely used (see Box 10.2).

BOX 10.2 DEFINITIONS OF THE ROYAL PREROGATIVE

- **Dicey**: '*The residue of discretionary or arbitrary authority, which at any given time is legally left in the hands of the Crown*': A.V. Dicey, *Introduction to the Study of the Law of the Constitution* (1885; 10th edn 1959, London: Macmillan & Co.), p. 424.
- **Blackstone**: When referring to the royal prerogative, '*We usually understand that special pre-eminence which the King hath, over and above all other persons, and out of the ordinary course of the common law, in right of his regal dignity. [. . . It]must be in its nature singular and eccentrical; that it can only be applied to those rights and capacities which the King enjoys alone, in contradistinction to others, and not to those he enjoys in common with any of his subjects*': William Blackstone, *Commentaries on the Laws of England*, 1765–69.

Dicey's definition tells us that royal prerogative powers are those discretionary powers that the Crown retains because they have not been abolished by Parliament or replaced by statutory powers—hence the reference to *residual* powers. The problem with this definition is that while it tells us that prerogative powers are discretionary and residual, it tells us nothing about the nature of the powers themselves. For example, it tells us nothing about how, if at all, they differ from powers conferred on the executive by statute.

Blackstone's definition, by contrast, does say something about the nature of the powers themselves. His view is that prerogative powers are special in that (in his eighteenth-century language) they are '*singular and eccentrical*'. By this, Blackstone means that these are powers that only the monarch or the Crown[15] can possess. Powers that ordinary people have, such as the power to make contracts, to employ people, or to establish trust funds to distribute money, are, according to this definition, not prerogative powers. By contrast, no one apart from the Crown has the legal authority to dissolve Parliament or to deploy the United Kingdom's armed forces abroad.

Since Parliament can abolish prerogative powers or place them on a statutory footing, we can summarize Blackstone's definition by saying that prerogative powers are those powers of the Crown that:

(a) have not been abolished by Parliament or placed on a statutory footing; and

(b) are exclusive to the Crown in the sense that they are powers ordinary people do not possess.

Professor Wade accepts Blackstone's definition, but argues that a further condition must be added—that is, the requirement that prerogative powers must have legal consequences in UK domestic law: '*[T]he prerogative consists of legal power—that is to say, the ability to alter people's rights, duties or status under the laws of this country.*'[16] If action does not affect legal rights under UK law, it should not, according to Professor Wade, be considered to have been taken by virtue of the prerogative.

[13] S. Payne, 'The Royal Prerogative', in M. Sunkin and S. Payne (eds) *The Nature of the Crown* (1999, Oxford: OUP), p. 78.

[14] See, e.g., Lord Reid's judgment in *Burmah Oil Company v Lord Advocate* [1965] AC 75, 99–100.

[15] For an explanation of the concept of the 'Crown' see Chapter 8.

[16] Sir William Wade, *Constitutional Fundamentals*, revised edn (1989, London: Stevens and Sons), p. 58.

It seems then that, according to Wade, certain decisions that are generally assumed to be based on the prerogative are actually 'spurious prerogatives' and not really exercises of prerogative power at all. Decisions by a minister of the Crown, such as that challenged in *Council of Civil Service Unions v Minister for Civil Service* (the *GCHQ* case)[17] to alter the terms and conditions on which civil servants work should not be considered to be prerogative decisions, because similar decisions could be made by any employer. Interestingly, for the same reason, Wade also argues that the power of the Crown to appoint and dismiss government ministers is not a prerogative power. It is '*nothing else than the power which all legal persons have at common law to employ servants or agents*'.[18]

Moreover, since Wade says that prerogative decisions must affect rights, he argues that a decision by the UK government to commit the United Kingdom to an international treaty would not be an exercise of prerogative power: entry into treaties cannot, by itself, alter rights in domestic UK law. Similarly, according to Wade, the granting of passports is not a prerogative power, because ' *[a] passport has no status or legal effect at common law whatever*'.[19]

Sebastian Payne criticizes this aspect of Wade's approach as follows.

S. Payne, 'The Royal Prerogative', in M. Sunkin and S. Payne (eds) *The Nature of the Crown* (1999, Oxford: OUP), pp. 84–5

> [E]very act will have a legal effect somewhere along the line, for instance the giving away of money by the Crown will, [. . .] have the legal effect of entitling 'the recipient to retain the money'. The granting of a passport will have the legal effect of entitling that person to use the passport [. . .]. Even a treaty that has not been incorporated into domestic law may lead to a particular interpretation of a statute on the presumption that legislation would not be passed in contravention of our treaty obligations unless expressly stated.

Payne is surely correct,[20] but it is nonetheless important to understand that one implication of Wade's approach is to narrow the range of decisions that fall within the prerogative discretion of the executive and potentially beyond the reach of judicial review. This was especially important before the House of Lords held in the *GCHQ* case that prerogative powers can be reviewed in the same way as statutory powers.

This brief discussion illustrates some of the problems involved in defining the royal prerogative and in identifying which powers of the executive properly fall within its scope.[21]

10.2.2 THE MAIN PREROGATIVE POWERS

Having looked at definitions let us now turn to consider some of the actual prerogative powers. In March 2004, the House of Commons PASC produced an influential report, *Taming the Prerogative*. This surveyed the use of the prerogative powers and strongly argued the case for reform. We shall turn to the question of reform later, but for the moment it is valuable to see what the PASC had to say about the scope and nature of prerogative powers. The following extract from *Taming the Prerogative*

[17] [1985] AC 374., discussed later in this chapter and also in Chapter 18. [18] Ibid, p. 60. [19] Ibid, p. 63.

[20] See also *R(Miller) v Secretary of State for Exiting the European Union* [2017] UKSC 5, *per* Lord Neuberger, paras [52]–[53].

[21] See also Lord Reid's judgment in *Burmah Oil v Lord Advocate*, [1965] AC 75.

identifies three groups of prerogative powers, of which the third—prerogative powers of government ministers—is the one on which the Committee focused its attention.

House of Commons Public Administration Select Committee, Taming the Prerogative: Strengthening Ministerial Accountability to Parliament, Fourth Report, Session 2003–04 (HC 422) (emphasis added and footnotes omitted)

Defining the Ministerial prerogative

4. In preparing for our inquiry we identified three main groups of prerogative powers. This informal division allowed us to concentrate mainly on those prerogative powers which give executive authority to Ministers [. . .] The three areas are described in the following paragraphs.

5. **The Queen's constitutional prerogatives are the personal discretionary powers which remain in the Sovereign's hands.** They include the rights to advise, encourage and warn Ministers in private; to appoint the Prime Minister and other Ministers; to assent to legislation; to prorogue or to dissolve Parliament; and (in grave constitutional crisis) to act contrary to or without Ministerial advice. In ordinary circumstances The Queen, as a constitutional monarch, accepts Ministerial advice about the use of these powers if it is available, whether she personally agrees with that advice or not. That constitutional position ensures that Ministers take responsibility for the use of the powers.

[. . .]

7. **The legal prerogatives of the Crown, which The Queen possesses as the embodiment of the Crown.** There are many such prerogatives which are legal (rather than constitutional) in character. Several are historical remnants, such as the Crown's rights to sturgeon, certain swans, and whales, and the right to impress men into the Royal Navy. But two legal prerogatives have more modern legal significance, namely, the principle that the Crown (or the state) can do no wrong, and that the Crown is not bound by statute save by express words or necessary implication. Many of these legal prerogatives have been amended by parliamentary legislation; others are in need of reform; some others may be obsolete. [. . .]

8. **Prerogative executive powers** [. . .]Historically, the Sovereign by constitutional convention came to act on Ministerial advice, so that prerogative powers came to be used by Ministers on the Sovereign's behalf. As Ministers took responsibility for actions done in the name of the Crown, so these prerogative powers were, in effect, delegated to responsible Ministers. But Parliament was not directly involved in that transfer of power. This constitutional position means that these prerogative powers are, in effect though not in strict law, in the hands of Ministers. Without these ancient powers Governments would have to take equivalent authority through primary legislation. As with the legal prerogatives just outlined, the connection between these powers and the Crown, or The Queen, is now tenuous and technical, and the label 'royal prerogative' is apt to mislead. [. . .] It makes more sense to refer to these powers not as 'royal prerogative' but as 'Ministerial executive'.

[. . .]

Ministers' uncertain powers

12. [. . .]Ministers still have very wide scope to act without Parliamentary approval. Perhaps more surprisingly [. . .]Parliament does not even have the right to know what these powers are. Ministers have repeatedly answered parliamentary questions about Ministers' prerogative powers by saying that records are not kept of the individual occasions on which those powers are used, and that it would not be practicable to do so. Ministers have also said that it would be impossible to produce a precise list of these powers, and have asserted that, as Rt Hon John Major put it when he was Prime Minister 'It is for

individual Ministers to decide on a particular occasion whether and how to report to Parliament on the exercise of prerogative powers'. Further uncertainty over the scope of Ministerial power is caused by the Ram doctrine. [See above.]

13. Ministers are certainly accountable to Parliament for the use of prerogative powers just as for things done under statutory or common law authority. But they are only accountable after the event. The United Kingdom is typical of states which permit Ministers to use certain powers without parliamentary approval, but it is highly unusual among democracies in having neither a codified constitution nor having made such express grants of power by the legislature.

For the most part we focus on the exercise of prerogative powers by government ministers. However, as the above extract shows, prerogative powers are also still exercised by the monarch, including the power to assent to Bills that have been passed by Parliament and to dissolve and prorogue Parliament. This latter power came to prominence when in 2019 the legality of the decision to prorogue Parliament was successfully challenged in the courts.[22] Because of its interest and importance we will deal with this issue as a case study later in the Chapter.

Responding to concern about the uncertain scope and extent of prerogative powers, the government undertook a survey of central government departments and agencies with a view to obtaining an overview of areas in which prerogative powers are exercised. This was the first time such an exercise had been undertaken and its results are to be found in the Ministry of Justice's *Review of the Executive Royal Prerogative Powers: Final Report* (October 2009).

Ministry of Justice, The Governance of Britain, Review of the Executive Royal Prerogative Powers: Final Report (October 2009)

17. The extent of prerogative powers has never before been explored or codified on a systematic basis within Government. [. . .] Sixty-four departments and agencies were asked to identify prerogative powers used to perform executive functions, the exercise of which had effectively been delegated to Ministers. The results of this survey are set out in the Annex to this report [see the following extract].

[. . .]

19. The scoping exercise was intended to identify extant prerogative powers, whether or not they had fallen into disuse [. . .] The resulting list of prerogative powers, appended as the Annex to this report, is divided into the following main categories:
    a) prerogative powers exercised by Ministers;
    b) executive constitutional/personal prerogative powers exercised by the Sovereign;
    c) legal prerogatives of the Crown, such as Crown immunity (to the extent that it continues to exist in view of the Crown Proceedings Act 1947) and
    d) archaic prerogative powers, most of which are either marginal (relating to small, specific issues or largely superseded by legislation), or no longer needed.

The following extract from the Annex lists the ministerial prerogative powers that were identified in the survey; it does not list the constitutional or personal prerogatives of the monarch, the powers exercised by the Attorney General, the legal prerogatives of the Crown, and other archaic prerogative powers.

[22] *R (on the application of Miller) v Prime Minister* [2019] UKSC 41.

Ministry of Justice, The Governance of Britain, Review of the Executive Royal Prerogative Powers: Final Report (October 2009), Annex ('Ministerial prerogative powers')

Government and the Civil Service

Powers concerning the machinery of Government including the power to set up a department or a non-departmental public body

Powers concerning the civil service, including the power to appoint and regulate most civil servants

Power to prohibit civil servants and certain other crown servants from issuing election addresses or announcing themselves, or being announced as, a Parliamentary candidate or a Prospective Parliamentary candidate

Power to set nationality rules for 'non-aliens'—British, Irish and Commonwealth citizens—concerning eligibility for employment in the civil service

Power to require security vetting of contractors working alongside civil servants on sensitive projects

Powers concerning the Office of the Civil Service Commissioners, the Security Vetting Appeals Panel, the Office of the Commissioner for Public Appointments, the Advisory Committee on Business, the Civil Service Appeal Board and the House of Lords Appointments Commission, including the power to establish those bodies, to appoint members of those bodies and the powers of those bodies

Justice system and law and order

Powers to appoint Queen's Counsel [now King's Counsel]

The power to make provisional and full order extradition requests to countries not covered by Part 1 of the Extradition Act 2003

The prerogative of Mercy

Power to keep the peace

Powers relating to foreign affairs

Power to send ambassadors abroad and receive and accredit ambassadors from foreign states

Recognition of states

Governance of British Overseas Territories

Power to make and ratify treaties

Power to conduct diplomacy

Power to acquire and cede territory

Power to issue, refuse or withdraw passport facilities

Responsibility for the Channel Islands and Isle of Man

Granting diplomatic protection to British citizens abroad

Powers relating to armed forces, war and times of emergency

Right to make war or peace or institute hostilities falling short of war

Deployment and use of armed forces overseas

Maintenance of the Royal Navy

Use of the armed forces within the UK to maintain the peace in support of the police or otherwise in support of civilian authorities (e.g. to maintain essential services during a strike)

The government and command of the armed forces is vested in Her Majesty

Control, organisation and disposition of armed forces

Requisition of British ships in times of urgent national necessity

Commissioning of officers in all three armed forces

Armed forces pay

Certain armed forces pensions which are now closed to new members

War pensions for death or disablement due to service before 6 April 2005 [. . .]

Crown's right to claim Prize (enemy ships or goods captured at sea)

Regulation of trade with the enemy

Crown's right of angary, in time of war, to appropriate the property of a neutral which is within the realm, where necessity requires

Powers in the event of a grave national emergency, including those to enter upon, take and destroy private property

The Annex goes on to list various other miscellaneous ministerial prerogatives, such as the power to establish corporations by royal charter and to amend existing charters (for example, that of the British Broadcasting Corporation (BBC) was laid before Parliament in July 2006 and is periodically reviewed[23]).

QUESTIONS

1. Go through the list of ministerial prerogative powers and place them into three categories: extremely important; important; unimportant. Explain why you have classified them as you have.
2. According to the Public Administration Select Committee, how are ministers accountable to Parliament for the exercise of their prerogative powers? What are the main limitations on accountability?

10.2.3 THE MONARCH'S CONSTITUTIONAL PREROGATIVES

The ministerial prerogative powers are the most important group of prerogative powers in terms of the day-to-day work of government and it is upon this group of prerogatives that this Chapter focuses, although as we see when looking at the case study on the prorogation of Parliament there are overlaps between government actions and the prerogative powers of the monarch. While the monarch is not involved in making day-to-day executive decisions, as head of state the King continues to exercise constitutional prerogatives that are of considerable importance to the smooth running of the system as a whole. In Chapter 8, we examined the constitutional status of the monarch and the meaning of the term 'the Crown'.[24] Several examples of the monarch's prerogative powers are considered in other chapters:

- formally appointing government ministers, including the Prime Minister (see Chapter 8);
- making 'prerogative legislation' in the form of Orders in Council (see Chapter 13, Section 2(c), 'Orders in Council'); and
- giving Royal Assent to Bills (see Chapter 12).

In exercising these powers, the monarch will act in accordance with convention and on the advice of government ministers.

10.2.4 CROWN IMMUNITY

'The Crown' enjoys immunities and exemptions from the law. An Act of Parliament is presumed not to bind the Crown unless it expressly or by clear implication provides that it does so (for example, the Planning Act 2008, s. 226, states that '*This Act binds the Crown [. . .]*', then lists some ways in which

[23] The current mid-term review must be completed between 2022 and 2024.

[24] See extract M. Sunkin, 'Crown' in Chapter 8, at p. 200.

the application of the Act is modified). It is for this reason that the King, in his private capacity, is not liable to pay tax although does so on a voluntary basis. [25]

Prior to the enactment of the Crown Proceedings Act 1947 the Crown was immune from actions in tort.[26] And there is still a general common law rule that the Crown and 'emanations of the Crown' are immune from prosecutions for criminal offences (whether statutory or at common law). This is reflected in the legal maxim: 'The Crown can do no wrong.' For example, until the immunity was expressly removed in relation to the National Health Service (NHS) the NHS could not be prosecuted for serious breaches of health and safety law.[27] In 2001, an employee of the Royal Mint (at the time, an executive agency of HM Treasury) was killed at work. In a subsequent inquiry, a parliamentary select committee report stated that '*it is unacceptable that the Mint should hide behind Crown immunity*'. The following extract from evidence published with the report explains the legal background in more detail.

House of Commons Select Committee on Public Accounts, Royal Mint Trading Fund 2001-02 Accounts, 14th Report, Session 2002–03 (HC 588), Minutes of Evidence, Appendix 2: Supplementary memorandum submitted by HM Treasury

Crown Immunity from Prosecution

The Public Accounts Committee asked HM Treasury for a note on the Government's policy towards the Crown's immunity from prosecution in the context of the tragic fatality at the Royal Mint. [. . .]

What is "Crown immunity"?

Crown immunity means that emanations of the Crown are not susceptible to prosecution for offences either created by statute or of the common law. It is more difficult to define precisely what is meant by an "emanation of the Crown", but it is clear that ministers and their departments are included. Crown immunity is today primarily an issue of the criminal law. The Crown Proceedings Act 1947 substantially reduced the Crown's immunity from civil proceedings.

It is important to be clear about what Crown immunity does not protect the executive from. It does not afford any protection from investigation, for example by the Health and Safety Executive in the Royal Mint context. In the case of legislation relating to food and health and safety, the law applies to the Crown, but the Crown cannot be prosecuted under it. Instead a system of Crown censure and Crown notices is used, publicising the inspectors' findings. The HSE investigation into the Mint resulted in Crown censure. Crown immunity also does not grant protection to individuals from prosecution. In the Mint case, a thorough investigation by Police and HSE concluded that no Director or Manager could be prosecuted. Crown immunity also does not give protection from a civil claim. In this particular case the Mint has already written to the representatives of the deceased to confirm admission of liability and asking them to provide details of the quantum of their claim (a schedule of dependency).

[. . .]

HM Treasury

December 2002

[25] Memorandum of Understanding on Royal Taxation, HM Treasury July 2023.

[26] For a recent example see *Malone v Ministry of Defence* [2022] ICR 478 in which it was held that Crown immunity prevented a soldier bringing a claim against the Ministry of Defence in relation to an employment matter, even when the issue was presented as if it were a tort claim.

[27] The NHS and Community Care Act 1990 removed Crown immunity from NHS premises.

Before leaving Crown immunity it may be noted that the Crown's immunity must be contrasted with other immunities which may be permitted by the law, such as the so-called 'combat immunity', whereby there is no common law liability for negligence in respect of acts or omissions on the part of those who are engaged in armed combat.[28]

10.2.5 THE PREROGATIVE CANNOT BE USED TO CHANGE THE COMMON LAW AND CANNOT REMOVE RIGHTS

An important limiting feature of prerogative power is that it cannot be used to change the law, for example by removing people's rights, unless an Act of Parliament clearly permits this. This important constitutional issue was central to the UK Supreme Court's decision in the *Miller 1* case concerning whether the executive could rely on prerogative power to withdraw from the EU. The UK Supreme Court accepted that the executive can enter into and exit from treaties. However, it held that this power cannot be used to change the UK's domestic law. Exiting from the EU would, the majority said, alter UK domestic law and would remove rights that had been created by EU law. Since the prerogative cannot be used to do these things the executive had to obtain the authority of an Act of Parliament in order to issue notification of the UK's intention to leave the EU. The majority rejected the government's argument that statutory authority had been given in the European Communities Act 1972. The main principles are stated by Lord Neuberger in the following extracts from his judgment.

R (Miller) v Secretary of State for Exiting the European Union
[2017] UKSC 5

Lord Neuberger

44. In the early 17th century *Case of Proclamations* (1610) 12 co rep 74, Sir Edward Coke CJ said that "the King by his proclamation or other ways cannot change any part of the common law, or statute law, or the customs of the realm". Although this statement may have been controversial at the time, it had become firmly established by the end of that century. In England and Wales, the Bill of Rights 1688 confirmed that "the pretended power of suspending of laws or the execution of laws by regall authority without consent of Parlyament is illegall" and that "the pretended power of dispensing with laws or the execution of laws by regall authoritie as it hath beene assumed and exercised of late is illegall". In Scotland, the Claim of Right 1689 was to the same effect [. . .].

45. The Crown's administrative powers are now exercised by the executive, ie by ministers who are answerable to the UK Parliament. However, consistently with the principles established in the 17th century, the exercise of those powers must be compatible with legislation and the common law. Otherwise, ministers would be changing (or infringing) the law, which, as just explained, they cannot do.

Lord Neuberger continued to explain that joining and leaving treaties will affect international relations and international law but will not normally affect UK internal or domestic law. This is because the UK system is dualist in character,[29] it recognizes a distinction between two systems of law, one operating at the international level and one operating within the UK at the domestic level. While prerogative powers can alter the UK's international legal obligations they cannot, without Parliament's approval, alter UK's domestic law. In relation to EU law when Parliament enacted the

[28] See *Smith and others (FC) (Appellants) v The Ministry of Defence (Respondent)* [2013] UKSC 41.

[29] See Chapter 2, Section 2.5 International Treaties.

European Communities Act 1972 it enabled rights created by EU law to become part of UK domestic law. Leaving the EU would therefore alter UK domestic law and rights under EU law would be lost. The prerogative could only be used to have these effects if this is clearly permitted, in this case by the European Communities Act 1972. Lord Neuberger continued as follows.

R (Miller) v Secretary of State for Exiting the European Union
[2017] UKSC 5

Lord Neuberger

86. [. . . T]he EU Treaties [. . .] are a source of domestic law, and they are a source of domestic legal rights [. . .] Accordingly, the Royal prerogative to make and unmake treaties, which operates wholly on the international plane, cannot be exercised in relation to the EU Treaties, at least in the absence of domestic sanction in appropriate statutory form. [. . .] the proper analysis is that, unless [the European Communities Act 1972] positively created such a power in relation to those treaties, it does not exist. Once one rejects the contention that section 2 accommodates a ministerial power to withdraw from the EU Treaties (as to which see paras 79 and 84 above), it is plain that the 1972 Act did not create such a power of withdrawal [. . .].

Following the judgment Parliament enacted the European Union (Notification of Withdrawal) Act 2017, which authorized the government to give notice of the UK's withdrawal from the EU.

10.2.6 PREROGATIVE AND STATUTE

10.2.6.1 New prerogative powers cannot be created

Earlier in the chapter, we identified some differences between prerogative and statutory powers (see Box 10.1). One point made was that while Parliament regularly confers new statutory powers on government and other public bodies, new prerogative powers cannot be acquired by the executive. The executive can only claim to possess prerogative powers if these powers are already recognized by the common law. The principle was summarized by Diplock LJ (as he then was) in *BBC v Johns*, a case in which the Court of Appeal rejected the BBC's claim to be an 'emanation of the Crown' and thus entitled to be immune from paying income tax.

BBC v Johns
[1965] Ch 32, 79

Diplock LJ

Mr Bucher has submitted that because wireless telegraphy and telephony were new inventions the Crown had a prerogative right to a monopoly of their use and has chosen to exercise this monopoly as respects broadcasting [. . .] through the instrumentality of the BBC. This contention involves adopting what he describes as a modern [. . .] view of the scope of the prerogative. But it is 350 years and a civil war too late for the Queen's courts to broaden the prerogative. The limits within which the executive government may impose obligations or restraints upon citizens of the United Kingdom without any statutory authority are now well settled and incapable of extension.

10.2.6.2 Relationship between prerogative and statutory powers

We have already seen that prerogative powers cannot be used to alter domestic law. Nor can such powers be used so as to conflict with, or frustrate, primary legislation. Parliament can limit or abolish prerogative powers. It may also decide that the power should be retained, but placed on a statutory footing. Parliament can also revive a prerogative power, as has happened in relation to the power to dissolve and call a new Parliament.

Dissolution and Calling of Parliament Act 2022

2 Revival of prerogative powers to dissolve Parliament and to call a new Parliament

(1) The powers relating to the dissolution of Parliament and the calling of a new Parliament that were exercisable by virtue of Her Majesty's prerogative immediately before the commencement of the Fixed-term Parliaments Act 2011 are exercisable again, as if the Fixed-term Parliaments Act 2011 had never been enacted.

[. . .]

Occasionally, situations arise in which Parliament has not abolished a prerogative power, but has enacted legislation that conflicts with the prerogative in some way. Where this happens, can government choose to use the prerogative rather than the statutory provisions?

The situation is illustrated by the decision in *Attorney General v De Keyser's Royal Hotel*.[30] This case concerned the requisitioning of a hotel in London during the First World War. The government had two ways in which it could requisition the hotel: by using a prerogative power and by exercising powers conferred by a statute. The difference was that, under the prerogative, compensation did not have to be paid to the owner, whereas under statute, it did. Could the government choose to use its prerogative powers and save money? Both the Court of Appeal and the House of Lords held that the government had to use the statutory powers.

Attorney General v De Keyser's Royal Hotel
[1920] AC 508, 526

Lord Dunedin

[. . . I]t is certain that if the whole ground of something which could be done by the prerogative is covered by the statute it is the statute that rules. On this point I think the observation of the learned Master of the Rolls[31] is unanswerable. He says: 'What use would there be in imposing limitations if the Crown could, at its pleasure, disregard them and fall back on prerogative?'

Another situation is when a statute deals with the same general subject matter as a prerogative power, but, unlike in *De Keyser's Royal Hotel*, it is not clear that the use of the prerogative would be incompatible with the statute. The issue arose in the controversial decision in *R v Secretary of State for the Home Department, ex parte Northumbria Police Authority*.[32] In 1986, the Home Secretary sent a circular to

[30] [1920] AC 508. See also discussion of *R (Miller) v Secretary of State for Exiting the EU* in Chapter 24.
[31] Swinfen Eady MR, in the Court of Appeal: [1919] 2 Ch 197, 216.
[32] [1989] 1 QB 26.

all chief constables in England explaining that a central store for plastic bullets and CS gas would be set up, and that chief constables could buy this crowd-control equipment without having to obtain the permission of their local police authority (statutory bodies established to subject police forces to local accountability). Many police authorities were dismayed that this equipment could be purchased without their involvement and the Northumbria Police Authority unsuccessfully challenged the legality of the government's scheme. The Court of Appeal held that the Police Act 1964 permitted the establishment of a central store and the direct supply of this equipment to chief constables. It also said that the Home Secretary has prerogative power to '*maintain peace in the realm*', which included power to take precautionary steps to ensure that chief constables have access to a supply of crowd-control equipment. This power had not been removed by statutory provisions.

R v Secretary of State for the Home Department, ex parte Northumbria Police Authority
[1989] 1 QB 26, 43

Croom-Johnson LJ

[. . .] It is clear that the Crown cannot act under the prerogative if to do so would be incompatible with statute. What was said here is that the Secretary of State's proposal under the circular would be inconsistent with the powers expressly or impliedly conferred on the police authority by section 4 of the Police Act 1964. The Divisional Court rejected that submission for reasons with which I wholly agree; namely that section 4 does not expressly grant a monopoly, and that granted the possibility of an authority which declines to provide equipment required by the chief constable there is every reason not to imply a Parliamentary intent to create one.

The House of Lords also had to consider the relationship between prerogative and statutory powers in *R v Secretary of State for the Home Department, ex parte the Fire Brigades Union*.[33] In this case, the central question was whether the executive can use prerogative powers in a manner that effectively means that an Act of Parliament will not be brought into force. The Criminal Injuries Compensation Scheme was introduced in 1964 using what were claimed to be prerogative powers. In 1988, Parliament enacted the Criminal Justice Act 1988 in order to place the scheme on a statutory footing. Although the statute received the Royal Assent, the enacted provisions were only to come into effect '*on such day as the Secretary of State may [. . .] appoint*'.[34] No such day was appointed and the provisions therefore did not come into effect.

Eventually, in March 1994, the Home Secretary told Parliament that the non-statutory scheme would be modified in a way that would introduce a lower level of compensation payments than the Act envisaged. He also said that, in due course, the provisions of the Criminal Justice Act 1988 would be repealed. The Home Secretary's decision to reduce compensation was challenged by several trade unions, which believed that their members would be disadvantaged by the failure to implement the legislation. In a majority decision, the House of Lords held that it was an abuse of power for the Home Secretary to exercise his purported prerogative powers to introduce a system that would conflict with his continuing duty to bring the statutory scheme into force.[35]

[33] [1995] 2 AC 513. [34] Criminal Justice Act 1988, s. 171(1).

[35] See also *In the Matter of an Application by JR80 for Judicial Review* [2019] NICA 58 in which the Northern Ireland Court of Appeal held that while the department of the Executive Office in Northern Ireland had prerogative power to established an *ex gratia* scheme to compensate victims of historical institutional abuse even though statute did not establish such a scheme.

R v Secretary of State for the Home Department, ex parte the Fire Brigades Union
[1995] 2 AC 513, 551–2

Lord Browne-Wilkinson

It does not follow that, because the Secretary of State is not under any duty to bring the section into effect, he has an absolute and unfettered discretion whether or not to do so. So to hold would lead to the conclusion that both Houses of Parliament had passed the Bill through all its stages and the Act received the Royal Assent merely to confer an enabling power on the executive to decide at will whether or not to make the parliamentary provisions a part of the law. Such a conclusion, drawn from a section to which the sidenote is "Commencement," is not only constitutionally dangerous but flies in the face of common sense. [. . .] Surely, it cannot have been the intention of Parliament to leave it in the entire discretion of the Secretary of State whether or not to effect such important changes to the criminal law. In the absence of express provisions to the contrary in the Act, the plain intention of Parliament in conferring on the Secretary of State the power to bring certain sections into force is that such power is to be exercised so as to bring those sections into force when it is appropriate and unless there is a subsequent change of circumstances which would render it inappropriate to do so.

[. . .]

My Lords, it would be most surprising if, at the present day, prerogative powers could be validly exercised by the executive so as to frustrate the will of Parliament expressed in a statute and, to an extent, to pre-empt the decision of Parliament whether or not to continue with the statutory scheme even though the old scheme has been abandoned. [. . .] It is for Parliament, not the executive, to repeal legislation. The constitutional history of this country is the history of the prerogative powers of the Crown being made subject to the overriding powers of the democratically elected legislature as the sovereign body.

10.2.7 JUDICIAL REVIEW OF PREROGATIVE POWERS

If the government claims to exercise a prerogative power and its action is challenged in judicial review proceedings,[36] the courts will examine whether the claimed prerogative power exists and, if it is found not to exist will invalidate any action taken under the purported power.[37] Until 1984, if the courts were satisfied that the prerogative power existed, they would not review the way in which the power was used. Now in general the courts can review prerogative powers on the same grounds as they can review the way in which statutory powers are used.[38] As in the case of statutory powers, however, there may be occasions on which courts will not intervene because the subject matter of the power is regarded by the courts as 'non-justiciable' (in other words, the issues are not suitable for judicial determination).[39] These propositions have been established by two decisions of the House of Lords.

[36] See further B. Hadfield, 'Judicial Review and the Prerogative Powers', in M. Sunkin and S. Payne (eds) *The Nature of the Crown* (1999, Oxford: OUP), ch. 8.

[37] See, e.g., Lord Bingham in *Bancoult (No. 2)* [2008] UKHL 61.

[38] One difference is that when exercising prerogative powers government may refuse to depart from blanket policies: *R (on the application of Sandiford) v The Secretary of State for Foreign and Commonwealth Affairs* [2014] UKSC 44. See further Fettering Discretion Chapter 18. As a general rule the prerogative power to make or unmake treaties is not judicially reviewable: see *R Miller) v Secretary of State for Exiting the European Union*, [2017] UKSC 5, para 55.

[39] See further the Independent Review of Administrative Law, March 2021 considered the issue of justiciability, see esp. ch. 2. See also the case study on *Miller 2* later in the Chapter.

10.2.7.1 The *GCHQ* case

The first was the decision in *Council of Civil Service Unions v Minister for the Civil Service* (the *GCHQ* case).[40] In this case, the civil service unions challenged a decision taken by the Minister for the Civil Service (a ministerial post normally held by the Prime Minister, at that time Mrs Thatcher) that workers at the Government Communications Headquarters (GCHQ, the government's electronic eavesdropping organization responsible for collecting intelligence) could no longer belong to a trade union. The decision was taken under powers conferred on the minister by the Civil Service Order in Council 1982, which was a legislative instrument enacted by the Queen in Council by virtue of prerogative powers.[41]

The unions claimed that the courts could review the decision even though it had been taken under prerogative powers. They submitted that the decision had been unlawful because the government's failure to consult before the decision breached the workers' legitimate expectation of consultation and was therefore procedurally unfair. The government argued that prerogative powers could not be judicially reviewed. To the government's dismay Glidewell J granted the application for judicial review.

Council of Civil Service Unions v Minister for the Civil Service (the GCHQ case)
[1984] IRLR 309, 310

Glidewell J

I can see no reason in logic or principle why an exercise by a Minister of a power conferred by an Order in Council should not be subject to the same scrutiny and control by the courts as would be appropriate for the exercise of the same power if it had been granted by statute.

Having established that he could intervene, Glidewell J went on to emphasize the need for government to follow the correct and fair procedure required by the common law. In the circumstances, he held that the failure to consult prior to deciding to ban union membership was procedurally unfair. He therefore held that the minister had acted unlawfully.

The government immediately appealed and, before the Court of Appeal, presented an argument that had not been explicitly put to Glidewell J—namely, that the failure to consult was justified by the interests of national security. The Court of Appeal accepted this argument and reversed Glidewell J's decision. In November 1984, the House of Lords upheld the Court of Appeal. Their Lordships held that although the failure to consult was contrary to the principles of natural justice, the courts should not interfere with it because the decision had been taken on grounds of national security, something into which the courts could not inquire.

In many ways, the actual decision of the House of Lords is a typical example of the courts being anxious to defer to the executive when national security is said to be involved. The judgment is a

[40] [1985] AC 374; see further A. Le Sueur and M. Sunkin, *Public Law* (1997, London: Longman), ch. 2, which provides more background to the litigation and its implications. See also R. Drabble, 'Council of Civil Service Unions v Minister for the Civil Service [1984]: Reviewing the Prerogative' in S. Juss and M. Sunkin (eds) *Landmark Cases in Public Law* (2017, Oxford: Hart Publishing), ch. 2; H. Lanning and R. Norton-Taylor, *A Conflict of Loyalties: GCHQ 1984–1991* (1992, London: New Clarion); G. Drewry, 'The *GCHQ* Case: A failure of government communication' (1985) *Parliamentary Affairs* 371; K. Ewing, 'Prerogative–judicial review—national security' (1985) 44 *Cambridge Law Journal* 1: J.A.G. Griffith, 'Judicial decision-making in public law' [1985] *Public Law* 564; H.W.R. Wade, 'Procedure and prerogative in public law' (1985) 101 *Law Quarterly Review* 180.

[41] See Chapter 13.

landmark, however, not because of the actual outcome, but because of what their Lordships said about the potential scope of judicial review in relation to prerogative powers. Lords Scarman, Diplock, and Roskill indicated that the courts can, in principle, review the exercise of any prerogative powers, provided that the matter is suitable for judicial determination (that is, justiciable). Lords Fraser and Brightman were more cautious: while they would have been willing to review the decision to ban unions taken under powers delegated by the Order in Council, they were not willing, on this occasion at least, to say that courts could also review the legality of an Order in Council itself.

10.2.7.2 *Bancoult (No. 2)*

The second case is the decision in *R (on the application of Bancoult) v Secretary of State for Foreign and Commonwealth Affairs (No. 2)*.[42] This case concerned the Chagos Islands in the Indian Ocean, which, until 1965, were part of the British colony of Mauritius.[43] In that year, the islands were made a separate colony, known as the 'British Indian Ocean Territory' (BIOT). Following negotations between the UK and USA a joint military base was established on Diego Garcia, the main island in the BIOT. This required the removal of the population of the territory and, in 1971, the UK government, through the Queen in Council, made a piece of prerogative legislation known as the Immigration Ordinance 1971, which gave power to exile the population. Following this the islanders were forcibly removed. In 2000 Mr Bancoult (one of the islanders affected) successfully challenged the legality of the Ordinance (*Bancoult No. 1*).[44] The government stated that it accepted the court's ruling and would not appeal.

The government later decided, however, that resettlement of the islands was not feasible and that the territory was still wanted for defence purposes. Two further Orders in Council were therefore made by the Queen in Council on advice of the government.[45] These prevented the islanders from returning to the islands. Mr Bancoult once again claimed judicial review, this time challenging the two Orders in Council. Here Mr Bancoult was challenging Orders in Council themselves rather than executive actions taken under the Orders in Council, as in the *GCHQ* case. He argued that the right of abode was so fundamental that it could not be removed by the Crown in any circumstances; that the Crown's powers were limited to enacting legislation for the '*peace, order and good government*' of the territory; that the law had to be for the benefit of the inhabitants, and that the government's statement following *Bancoult (No. 1)* created a legitimate expectation that the Chagossians would be allowed to return to the islands. He was successful in both the Divisional Court[46] and the Court of Appeal.[47]

On appeal to the House of Lords, the government argued, among other things, that the courts had no power to review the validity of an Order in Council legislating for a colony, because it was primary legislation comparable to an Act of Parliament; that, in any case, the islanders did not have the fundamental rights that they claimed; and that there was no breach of a legitimate expectation that they would be allowed to return. The House of Lords accepted that courts can review the legality of Orders in Council and, to this extent, it developed the law beyond the *GCHQ* case. The following statement made by Lord Hoffmann represents the overall view of the House on this point.

[42] [2008] UKHL 61.

[43] See generally, Phillipe Sands, *The Last Colony: A Tale of Exile, Justice and Britain's Colonial Legacy*, (Weidenfeld and Nicolson, 2022).

[44] *R (on the application of Bancoult) v Secretary of State for Foreign and Commonwealth Affairs* [2001] QB 1067.

[45] British Indian Ocean Territory (Constitution) Order 2004 and the British Indian Ocean Territory (Immigration) Order 2004.

[46] [2006] EWHC 1038 (Admin).

[47] [2007] EWCA Civ 498, [2008] QB 365.

R (on the application of Bancoult) v Secretary of State for Foreign and Commonwealth Affairs (No. 2)
[2008] UKHL 61

Lord Hoffmann

35. [. . .]the fact that such Orders in Council in certain important respects resemble Acts of Parliament does not mean that they share all their characteristics. The principle of the sovereignty of Parliament, as it has been developed by the courts over the past 350 years, is founded upon the unique authority Parliament derives from its representative character. An exercise of the prerogative lacks this quality; although it may be legislative in character, it is still an exercise of power by the executive alone. Until the decision of this House in [the *GCHQ* case], it may have been assumed that the exercise of prerogative powers was, as such, immune from judicial review. That objection being removed, I see no reason why prerogative legislation should not be subject to review on ordinary principles of legality, rationality and procedural impropriety in the same way as any other executive action.

The majority (Lords Bingham and Mance dissenting) nonetheless refused to accept that the Orders in Council were unlawful. The main elements of the majority decision on the legality of the Orders in Council may be summarized as follows. The Orders in Council were not repugnant to the Chagossians' fundamental right of abode and to return to the islands. The right of abode was a creature of the law, not a constitutional right, and there was no basis for saying that the right of abode was so fundamental that the Crown's legislative powers simply could not touch it. Nor was there support for the proposition that, in legislating for a colony, either Parliament or Her Majesty in Council had to have regard only, or even predominantly, to the immediate interests of the inhabitants. In essence, the Chagossians' right of abode was purely symbolic, because there was no prospect of them being able to live on the islands in the foreseeable future. Having regard to the practical interests of the Chagossians, the decision to reimpose immigration control on the islands could not be described as unreasonable or an abuse of power. Moreover, there had been no clear and unambiguous promise to the effect that the Chagossians would be free to return to the islands even if they could not be resettled there and therefore no legitimate expectation had been created.[48]

In his dissenting judgment Lord Bingham considered that there was no prerogative power to exile an indigenous population from its homeland. In his view the orders were also irrational in the sense that there was no good reason for making them, the security arguments being weak and vague. He also said that just because the islanders' right of abode was of little practical value provided no justification for removing the right: the smaller its practical value the less reason to take it away. Also, in his view, the orders contradicted a clear representation by the made by the Government in November 2000, from which it could not resile without compelling reason, No such reason had been shown. [49]

In 2022 Chagossians, and their direct descendants[50], became eligible to claim British citizenship. In October 2023 the Governments of UK and Mauritius announced an agreement that sovereignty

[48] See further, M. Elliott and A. Perreau-Saussine, 'Pyrrhic public law: *Bancoult* and the sources, status and content of common law limitations on prerogative power' [2009] Public Law 697; also M. Cohn, 'Judicial review of non-statutory executive powers after *Bancoult*: A unified anxious model' [2009] Public Law 260. On legitimate expectations, see Chapter 18.

[49] Following this decision the Chaggosians took the matter to the ECHR, but their claim was held to be inadmissible: *Chagos Islanders v United Kingdom*, App 35622/04, (11 December 2012).

[50] E.g. someone's child, grandchild, great grandchild.

of the Chagos Islands was to be transferred to Mauritius.[51] Many islanders were against this fearing that moving sovereignty from the UK would reduce their chances of one day being able to return to their homeland and in March 2025 solicitors representing Chagossians indicated that they would bring legal proceedings should there be a signed agreement. On May 20 2025 the solicitors learned from the press that the signing of an agreement was imminent. They then made an urgent application for an interim injunction to delay the signing. Their application was dealt with by Goose J at 2.25 am on Thursday 22 May 2025. He granted a temporary stay until the arguments could be more carefully considered, which they were later that morning. Chamberlain J decided that the interim injunction should not be granted partly because the claimants were seeking to '*. . . prevent the Secretary of State from exercising the foreign affairs prerogative and from concluding a treaty. . .*'[52]

QUESTIONS

1. In relation to judicial review of prerogative powers, what is the significance of the decisions of the House of Lords in *GCHQ* and *Bancoult*?
2. '*Bancoult establishes the principle that courts can review primary legislation on the ground that the legislation conflicts with fundamental rights, although it also illustrates the uncertain nature of these rights.*' Do you agree?

10.2.8 MINI CASE STUDY: THE PROROGATION OF PARLIAMENT CASE: *MILLER 2*

In this mini-case study, we look at one of the most significant and controversial constitutional decisions taken by the UK Supreme Court. The case arose from the UK government's implementation of the 2016 referendum decision to withdraw from the EU. In September 2019, the Conservative government under Boris Johnson MP wanted to push ahead with withdrawal, if need be, even if no deal could be agreed with the EU on the 'divorce' arrangements. The House of Commons was not in favour of withdrawing without a deal. Against this background, and wanting to minimize opportunities for opponents of no deal to question the government, the Prime Minister advised the Queen to prorogue Parliament on a day between 9–12 September 2019 until 14 October 2019. Parliament was accordingly prorogued.

While Parliament is prorogued, neither House can meet, debate and pass legislation. Neither House can debate Government policy. Nor may members of either House ask written or oral questions of Ministers. They may not meet and take evidence in committees. In general, Bills which have not yet completed all their stages are lost and will have to start again from scratch in the next session of Parliament.[53]

[51] The International Court of Justice had previously given an Advisory Opinion that '*the United Kingdom is under an obligation to bring to an end its administration of the Chagos Archipelago as rapidly as possible*' *Chagos Islanders v United Kingdom* (App 35622/04) (11 December 2012) *International Court of Justice Advisory Opinion on Legal Consequences of the Separation of the Chagos Archipelago from Mauritius in 1965* (2019/2) 25 February 2019).

[52] *Beatrice Pompe v The Secretary of State for Foreign Commonwealth and Development Affairs v The Cabinet Office of the Prime Minister* [2025] EWHC 1489 (Admin), para 18.

[53] *R (Miller) v Prime Minister; Cherry and others v Advocate General for Scotland* [2019] UKSC 41, para. [2].

Challenges, including by Joanna Cherry MP (Scottish National Party Spokesperson on Justice) to the legality of the prorogation were brought in the Court of Session in Scotland. The Inner House held that the prorogation was unlawful because the Prime Minister's advice to the Queen was 'motivated by the improper purpose of stymying Parliamentary scrutiny of the executive'.[54] That decision was appealed to the UK Supreme Court. A similar challenge was brought by Mrs Gina Miller in the High Court. This was dismissed by the Divisional Court on the ground that the matter was not justiciable but that court allowed a leapfrog appeal directly to the UK Supreme Court. The two cases raised the same issues and were heard together. This was the first time that a UK top court had been asked to review the legality of a prorogation. Here it was asked in circumstances in which the political issues could not have been more intense. It was for these reasons that the UK Supreme Court consisted of all 11 Supreme Court justices. The unanimous judgment of the court was delivered by the President, Lady Hale, and the Deputy President, Lord Reed.

The decision to prorogue Parliament is a prerogative decision made by the monarch acting on the advice of the Privy Council. In practice, the advice is given by the Prime Minister as head of the government and the monarch accepts that advice.[55] The first key issue was whether the legality of the Prime Minister's advice to the Queen was justiciable.

Before deciding this issue, Lady Hale and Lord Reed stressed that the court was not concerned with when and on what terms the UK should leave the EU. They said that four points should be made clear at the outset.

R (Miller) v Prime Minister; Cherry and others v Advocate General for Scotland
[2019] UKSC 41

Lady Hale and Lord Reed

30. [. . .] First, the power to order the prorogation of Parliament is a prerogative power: that is to say, a power recognised by the common law and exercised by the Crown, in this instance by the sovereign in person, acting on advice, in accordance with modern constitutional practice. It is not suggested in these appeals that Her Majesty was other than obliged by constitutional convention to accept that advice. In the circumstances, we express no view on that matter. That situation does, however, place on the Prime Minister a constitutional responsibility, as the only person with power to do so, to have regard to all relevant interests, including the interests of Parliament.

31. Secondly, although the courts cannot decide political questions, the fact that a legal dispute concerns the conduct of politicians, or arises from a matter of political controversy, has never been sufficient reason for the courts to refuse to consider it. [. . .] almost all important decisions made by the executive have a political hue to them. Nevertheless, the courts have exercised a supervisory jurisdiction over the decisions of the executive for centuries. Many if not most of the constitutional cases in our legal history have been concerned with politics in that sense. [The *Case of Proclamations* (1611) 12 Co Rep 74 and *Entick v Carrington* (1765) 19 State Tr 1029 are cited as examples.]

[. . .]

[54] Ibid, para. 24.

[55] House of Commons Library Briefing Paper (No 8589, 11 June 2019). https://www.thetimes.co.uk/article/prime-minister-apologised-to-queen-after-court-verdict-6kcv28qgz. S. Theil, 'The Unconstitutional prorogation of Parliament' [2020] Public Law 529–47. Argues that there are circumstances in which, the monarch may reject ministerial advice to prorogue Parliament.

33. Thirdly, the Prime Minister's accountability to Parliament does not in itself justify the conclusion that the courts have no legitimate role to play. That is so for two reasons. The first is that the effect of prorogation is to prevent the operation of ministerial accountability to Parliament during the period when Parliament stands prorogued. [. . .] The second reason is that the courts have a duty to give effect to the law, irrespective of the minister's political accountability to Parliament. The fact that the minister is politically accountable to Parliament does not mean that he is therefore immune from legal accountability to the courts.

34. Fourthly, if the issue before the court is justiciable, deciding it will not offend against the separation of powers. [. . .] the court will be performing its proper function under our constitution. Indeed, by ensuring that the Government does not use the power of prorogation unlawfully with the effect of preventing Parliament from carrying out its proper functions, the court will be giving effect to the separation of powers.

[Lady Hale and Lord Reed then turn to the question of justiciability.]

35. [. . .] In the case of prerogative powers, it is necessary to distinguish between two different issues. The first is whether a prerogative power exists, and if it does exist, its extent. The second is whether, granted that a prerogative power exists, and that it has been exercised within its limits, the exercise of the power is open to legal challenge on some other basis. The first of these issues undoubtedly lies within the jurisdiction of the courts and is justiciable, as all the parties to these proceedings accept. [See *Council of Civil Service Unions v Minister for the Civil Service* [1985] AC 374.] The second of these issues, on the other hand, may raise questions of justiciability. The question then is not whether the power exists, or whether a purported exercise of the power was beyond its legal limits, but whether its exercise within its legal limits is challengeable in the courts on the basis of one or more of the recognised grounds of judicial review. In the *Council of Civil Service Unions* case, the House of Lords concluded that the answer to that question would depend on the nature and subject matter of the particular prerogative power being exercised. In that regard, Lord Roskill mentioned at p. 418 the dissolution of Parliament as one of a number of powers whose exercise was in his view non-justiciable.

36. Counsel for the Prime Minister rely on that dictum in the present case, since the dissolution of Parliament under the prerogative [. . .] is in their submission analogous to prorogation. They submit that prorogation is in any event another example of what Lord Roskill described as "excluded categories" [. . . It is . . .] important to understand that this argument only arises if the issue in these proceedings is properly characterised as one concerning the lawfulness of the exercise of a prerogative power within its lawful limits, rather than as one concerning the lawful limits of the power and whether they have been exceeded. [. . .]

37. Before reaching a conclusion as to justiciability, the court therefore has to determine whether the present case requires it to determine where a legal limit lies in relation to the power to prorogue Parliament, and whether the Prime Minister's advice trespassed beyond that limit, or whether the present case concerns the lawfulness of a particular exercise of the power within its legal limits. [. . .]

[Lady Hale and Lord Keen consider whether the current challenge concerns the legal limits of the prerogative power or the manner in which the power was exercised within those limits. They explain that the lawful limits of prerogative powers relating the operation of Parliament are to be determined by the fundamental principles of UK constitutional law.]

[. . .]

41. Two fundamental principles of our constitutional law are relevant to the present case. The first is the principle of Parliamentary sovereignty: that laws enacted by the Crown in Parliament are the supreme form of law in our legal system, with which everyone, including the Government, must comply. [. . .] Time and again, in a series of cases since the 17th century, the courts have protected Parliamentary sovereignty from threats posed to it by the use of prerogative powers, and in doing so have demonstrated that prerogative powers are limited by the principle of Parliamentary sovereignty. [. . .]

42. The sovereignty of Parliament would [. . .] be undermined as the foundational principle of our constitution if the executive could, through the use of the prerogative, prevent Parliament from exercising its legislative authority for as long as it pleased. That, however, would be the position if there was no legal limit upon the power to prorogue Parliament [. . .] An unlimited power of prorogation would therefore be incompatible with the legal principle of Parliamentary sovereignty.

[. . .]

45. [. . .] How, then, is the limit upon the power to prorogue to be defined, so as to make it compatible with the principle of Parliamentary sovereignty?

46. The same question arises in relation to a second constitutional principle, that of Parliamentary accountability [. . .]

48. That principle is not placed in jeopardy if Parliament stands prorogued for the short period which is customary, and as we have explained, Parliament does not in any event expect to be in permanent session. But the longer that Parliament stands prorogued, the greater the risk that responsible government may be replaced by unaccountable government: the antithesis of the democratic model. So the same question arises as in relation to Parliamentary sovereignty: what is the legal limit upon the power to prorogue which makes it compatible with the ability of Parliament to carry out its constitutional functions?

[. . .]

[Lady Hale and Lord Reed explain that when courts have considered claims that the exercise of statutory powers have impeded or frustrated the operation of constitutional principles they have held infringement to be unlawful unless a reasonable justification has been established. The same approach, they say, should be taken in relation to the exercise of prerogative powers.]

[. . .]

50. For the purposes of the present case, therefore, the relevant limit upon the power to prorogue can be expressed in this way: that a decision to prorogue Parliament (or to advise the monarch to prorogue Parliament) will be unlawful if the prorogation has the effect of frustrating or preventing, without reasonable justification, the ability of Parliament to carry out its constitutional functions as a legislature and as the body responsible for the supervision of the executive. In such a situation, the court will intervene if the effect is sufficiently serious to justify such an exceptional course.

51. [. . .] The court then has to decide whether the Prime Minister's explanation for advising that Parliament should be prorogued is a reasonable justification for a prorogation having those effects. The Prime Minister's wish to end one session of Parliament and to begin another will normally be enough in itself to justify the short period of prorogation which has been normal in modern practice. It could only be in unusual circumstances that any further justification might be necessary. Even in such a case, when considering the justification put forward, the court would have to bear in mind that the decision whether to advise the monarch to prorogue Parliament falls within the area of responsibility of the Prime Minister, and that it may in some circumstances involve a range of considerations, including matters of political judgment. The court would therefore have to consider any justification that might be advanced with sensitivity to the responsibilities and experience of the Prime Minister, and with a corresponding degree of caution. Nevertheless, it is the court's responsibility to determine whether the Prime Minster has remained within the legal limits of the power. If not, the final question will be whether the consequences are sufficiently serious to call for the court's intervention.

Conclusions on justiciability

52. Returning, then, to the justiciability of the question of whether the Prime Minister's advice to the Queen was lawful, we are firmly of the opinion that it is justiciable. As we have explained, it is well established, and is accepted by counsel for the Prime Minister, that the courts can rule on the extent of prerogative powers. That is what the court will be doing in this case by applying the legal standard which we have described. That standard is not concerned with the mode of exercise of the prerogative

power within its lawful limits. On the contrary, it is a standard which determines the limits of the power, marking the boundary between the prerogative on the one hand and the operation of the constitutional principles of the sovereignty of Parliament and responsible government on the other hand. An issue which can be resolved by the application of that standard is by definition one which concerns the extent of the power to prorogue, and is therefore justiciable.

[. . .]

55. Let us remind ourselves of the foundations of our constitution. We live in a representative democracy. The House of Commons exists because the people have elected its members. The Government is not directly elected by the people (unlike the position in some other democracies). The Government exists because it has the confidence of the House of Commons. It has no democratic legitimacy other than that. This means that it is accountable to the House of Commons—and indeed to the House of Lords—for its actions, remembering always that the actual task of governing is for the executive and not for Parliament or the courts. The first question, therefore, is whether the Prime Minister's action had the effect of frustrating or preventing the constitutional role of Parliament in holding the Government to account.

56. The answer is that of course it did. This was not a normal prorogation in the run-up to a Queen's Speech. It prevented Parliament from carrying out its constitutional role for five out of a possible eight weeks between the end of the summer recess and exit day on the 31st October. Parliament might have decided to go into recess for the party conferences during some of that period but, given the extraordinary situation in which the United Kingdom finds itself, its members might have thought that parliamentary scrutiny of government activity in the run-up to exit day was more important and declined to do so, or at least they might have curtailed the normal conference season recess because of that. Even if they had agreed to go into recess for the usual three-week period, they would still have been able to perform their function of holding the government to account. Prorogation means that they cannot do that.

[. . .]

[Lady Hale and Lord Reed turn to whether there was a reasonable justification for proroguing Parliament for the unusually long period of time . . .]

[. . .]

58. The next question is whether there is a reasonable justification for taking action which had such an extreme effect upon the fundamentals of our democracy. [. . .] We are not concerned with the Prime Minister's *motive* in doing what he did. We are concerned with whether there was a reason for him to do it. It will be apparent from the documents quoted earlier that no reason was given for closing down Parliament for five weeks. [. . .]

[. . .]

61. It is impossible for us to conclude, on the evidence which has been put before us, that there was any reason—let alone a good reason—to advise Her Majesty to prorogue Parliament for five weeks, from 9th or 12th September until 14th October. We cannot speculate, in the absence of further evidence, upon what such reasons might have been. It follows that the decision was unlawful.

[Lady Hale and Lord Reed next consider the appropriate remedy. They are willing to grant a declaration that the Prime Minister's advice to the Queen was unlawful, but consider whether they should declare that the prorogation that followed the advice was null and of no effect. They also rejected the government's argument that such a declaration would be contrary to Art. 9 of the Bill of Rights of 1688 which prevents courts questioning the legality of proceedings in Parliament. They did so because . . .]

68. The prorogation [. . .] cannot sensibly be described as a "proceeding in Parliament". It is not a decision of either House of Parliament. Quite the contrary: it is something which is imposed upon them from outside. It is not something upon which the Members of Parliament can speak or vote. [. . .] They have no freedom of speech. This is not the core or essential business of Parliament. Quite the contrary: it brings that core or essential business of Parliament to an end.

[. . .]

Having reached this conclusion the UK Supreme Court issued a declaration that the prorogation was unlawful and therefore a nullity. Since it had had not been prorogued Parliament resumed sitting the next day and the session was ended with a shorter period of prorogation from 8 October to 14 October 2019.[56]

As would be expected reactions to the decision were mixed. *The Guardian* described the decision as 'momentous';[57] the *Daily Mail* 'historic' and 'eviscerating'.[58] The *Sunday Times* reported that Boris Johnson rang the Queen and personally apologized for embarrassing her.[59]

Attitudes amongst academic commentators, predictably were also divided with those inclined towards a legal constitutionalist position applauding the judgment whereas judicial sceptics and political constitutionalists being extremely critical of the judgment. While the following extracts cannot present their full analysis and arguments, they provide a sense of some of the key positions taken by the authors and of the differences between the main approaches.

The first extract is from a paper written by Professor John Finnis for Policy Exchange's Judicial Power Project. It presents a court sceptic—political constitutional approach to the judgment which as we explain elsewhere[60] stresses that the UK's constitutional system is essentially political rather than legal in nature and that key controls on government should be rooted in the electoral system, rather than imposed by judges who are not politically accountable or competent to deal with political questions.

John Finnis, The unconstitutionality of the Supreme Court's prorogation judgment (Policy Exchange, Judicial Power Project, London, September 2019) (see also John Finnis, '"Changing the Ground Rules" of Our Constitution', (2021) 10 UK Supreme Court Yearbook 299–330)

Executive Summary

The Supreme Court's judgment in Miller/Cherry [. . .] holds that Parliamentary sovereignty needs to be judicially protected against the power of the Government to prorogue Parliament. But the Judgment itself undercuts the genuine sovereignty of Parliament by evading a statutory prohibition – art. 9 of the Bill of Rights 1689 – on judicial questioning of proceedings in Parliament.

The Judgment was wholly unjustified by law. What it protects is not the sovereignty of Parliament [. . .] but the practical opportunities of each House to pass Bills and scrutinise the Government – all redescribed as the "principle of Parliamentary accountability". Those constitutionally vital opportunities, and that principle, have been protected for over 300 years, without significant mishap, by constitutional conventions which are policed politically, ultimately by the electorate. In working with the principles of Parliamentary sovereignty and political accountability, our constitutional law has always [. . .] distinguished firmly between legal rules (justiciable) and conventions (non-justiciable). The

[56] See further, Graeme Cowie and Adam Cygan, *The Prorogation Dispute of 2019: One Year On*, House of Commons Library Briefing Paper, Number 9006, 24 September 2020.

[57] Owen Bowcott et al., 'Johnson's suspension of parliament unlawful, supreme court rules', *The Guardian*, 24 September 2019, https://www.theguardian.com/law/2019/sep/24/boris-johnsons-suspension-of-parliament-unlawful-supreme-court-rules-prorogue.

[58] Martin Robinson et al., 'Eleven Supreme Court judges rule UNANIMOUSLY that Boris Johnson's suspension of Parliament WAS unlawful—in historic ruling that sends Prime Minister's Brexit plans into chaos as Speaker Bercow vows to recall MPs "without delay"', *Daily Mail*, 24 September 2019 https://www.dailymail.co.uk/news/article-7497911/Supreme-Court-delivers-ruling-Boris-Johnson-broke-law.html.

[59] Tim Shipman, 'Prime minister apologizes to Queen after court verdict', *Sunday* Times, 29 September 2019, https://www.thetimes.co.uk/article/prime-minister-apologised-to-queen-after-court-verdict-6kcv28qgz.

[60] See Chapter 2.

Judgment offers no plausible reason for transferring the conventions about prorogation into the domain of justiciable law.

The reason it does offer for this transformation is that, in some "extreme hypothetical" circumstance, the power to prorogue might be used to frustrate Parliamentary scrutiny of the Government [. . .]. The longstanding constraints on such abuse, in the form of conventions, strict legal preconditions for expenditure on maintaining government, and accountability to the electorate at legally defined intervals, constraints regarded as sufficient for hundreds of years, are suddenly assessed to be "scant reassurance." [. . .]

Thus the Court suddenly assumes supreme responsibility for the maintenance and preservation of the pivot of the constitutional-political order. [. . .]

In relation to the operation of its newly self-bestowed power, the Court says that it involves no more than defining the "boundaries" of the proroguing power, as distinct from taking over its "mode of exercise". But the "legal standard" the Judgment invents to define those newly-legal boundaries is immediately deployed to review the mode of exercise. [. . .]

The Court's misconceived review, in turn, fails to apply the "standard's" main criterion, which looks to the effects of prorogation. The Judgment undertakes no serious review of effects. That would have shown that the impugned prorogation threatened nothing that Parliament could not rectify before the actual prorogation. Instead the Judgment faults the Government for providing no documented and, for the judges, sufficient reason for selecting "five weeks" rather than some lesser period which is not specified by the Judgment.

The Supreme Court's review of the decision to prorogue ignores most of the immediately relevant statutory and political constraints and contextualising factors, and illustrates the ineptitude of judicial forays into high politics. [. . .] The Judgment should be recognised as a historic mistake, not a victory for fundamental principle. The next Parliament should exercise its authentic law-making sovereignty to reverse the Judgment's misuse of judicial power. [. . .]

The second extract is from the introduction to a paper, also published by Policy Exchange in which Professor Martin Loughlin presents a response to the Supreme Court's decision in the form of a judgment of the (hypothetical) United Kingdom Constitutional Council hearing an appeal from the Supreme Court. The extract provides insight into some broader themes. In particular, Loughlin addresses the claim that the judgment marks a triumph of legality over politics. Like Finnis, Loughlin is concerned about judicial overreach, but in this extract he disputes that a line can be drawn between legality and politics and the implication that since courts are concerned with legality they are not political. For Loughlin, in constitutional cases judges are inevitably political actors. He argues that this can be seen in how courts make choices about the approach they take and the legal techniques they use: the ability to make political choices is particularly evident when courts draw on broad 'principles'. He says that the UK Supreme Court's decision, in effect, to establish itself as the ultimate guardian of fundamental constitutional principles, was itself a political decision.

Martin Loughlin, 'The Case of Prorogation The UK Constitutional Council's ruling on appeal from the judgment of the Supreme Court' (Policy Exchange, Judicial Power Project, London, 2019)

Introduction

The Supreme Court's declaration that the Prime Minister's decision to seek a five-week prorogation of Parliament was unlawful is of major constitutional significance. It is also highly controversial. Many, for obvious political reasons, will welcome the decision. Their views are eloquently expressed by Sir

Stephen Sedley, formerly of the Court of Appeal, who has suggested that the decision 'as much by its unanimity . . . as by its reasoning, has re-lit one of the lamps of the United Kingdom's constitution: that nobody, not even the Crown's ministers, is above the law'. [. . .]

I have argued elsewhere that constitutional interpretation involves an interplay between the relative authority of text, precedent, and principle. Constitutional review is such an intensely contested exercise because although lawyers have rigorous methods for interpreting texts, following precedents and balancing principles, they do not have any authoritative method for evaluating the relative importance of these different factors (Political Jurisprudence, OUP, 2017, esp. 4–7). This is an intractable difficulty. It makes constitutional review intrinsically political, not least because each of these factors expresses different conceptions of law. To suggest, as Sedley does, that the Supreme Court's judgment vindicates the law-based character of the British constitution begs the question: it assumes, without demonstrating it, the truth of the Court's conclusions.

The problem is: what conception of law drives the result? According to a traditional, common law understanding, law is a type of 'artificial reason' acquired through deep immersion in source-based legal materials and judges, the guardians of the law, maintain their independence as 'lions under the throne' by acknowledging that the law has its limits. That is, judges recognise a distinction between matters legal and matters political. On an alternative, modern, understanding, law is an expression of will of the sovereign authority and the Act of Parliament is the highest expression of law. In this respect, judges are the precision instruments of legislative intention. Recently, however, a third conception has become influential. This is a conception of law as a set of fundamental principles. In place of the common law as an expression of artificial reason acquired through practical experience or the modern sense of law as an expression of will, law-as-principle is the elaboration of a type of scholastic reason that limits the range of legitimate expressions of will by governing majorities.

Constitutional review is so contentious because the more the issue in dispute touches central questions about how political authority is constituted, the more the dispute turns on the relative authority of conflicting conceptions of law. The Supreme Court's judgment is a case in point. It sets aside clear precedents concerning justiciability, adopts creative reasoning to avoid being bound by legislative will expressed in the Bill of Rights, and asserts the authority of certain newly-minted 'constitutional principles'. The techniques of common law reasoning through precedents and statutory interpretation of Acts of Parliament are displaced by an assertion of the priority of principles. This conception of law has been gaining influence in judicial review, but now the Court has made a paradigmatic shift. It claims that, rather than consisting of a set of rules and practices, the British constitution rests on some overarching framework of constitutional principles of which the Court acts as guardian.

Many will welcome this manoeuvre. But we should not pretend that this is anything other than a political act. It is deceptive to claim that the judgment merely signifies that somehow 'the rule of law' has been vindicated.

[. . .]

The above extracts reflect examples of what was said about the judgment by those who are concerned about judicial overreach. By no means all commentators were critical of the judgment. Many welcomed it.[61] Professor Mark Elliott provided one of the first positive reactions to the judgment in his blog, *Public Law for Everyone*. The extract is from his conclusion.

[61] See, e.g., Professor Alison L Young, 'The Prorogation Case: Re-inventing the Constitution or Re-imagining Constitutional Scholarship?' in *The UK Supreme Court Yearbook* (2018–19), vol. 10, pp. 357–89; P.P. Craig, 'The Supreme Court, prorogation and constitutional principle' [2020] Public Law 248–77.

Mark Elliott, 'A new approach to constitutional adjudication? Miller II in the Supreme Court', Public Law for Everyone, 24 September 2019
https://publiclawforeveryone.com/2019/09/24/the-supreme-courts-judgment-in-cherrymiller-no-2-a-new-approach-to-constitutional-adjudication/

Conclusion: A new approach to constitutional adjudication or the application of established principles?

[. . .]

What, then, are we to make of this case? Is it a legal landmark, or is it an orthodox application of existing constitutional principle? It is both. The judgment affirms, articulates, clarifies, develops and applies fundamental principles governing the place of Parliament within the constitution and its relationship with the executive. [. . .] What renders the judgment a legal landmark is the willingness of the Court to take those principles to their logical conclusion in the face of a perfect storm of factors that, on the more superficial analysis favoured by the Divisional Court, appeared to close the door to judicial review. Thus the Supreme Court was prepared to draw inferences from, rather than relying exclusively on the formal core of, the principle of parliamentary sovereignty. It was willing to spell out the legal-constitutional implications of the political-constitutional principle of executive accountability to Parliament. It rejected the sloppy argument that because the issue had political implications it could not, at root, be a legal matter. It extended the principle of legality such that it now falls to be understood—as it always should have been—as a mechanism for giving concrete legal effect to fundamental constitutional principle, irrespective of whether the legal powers at stake are conferred by legislation or arise under the prerogative. And—crucially—the Court was prepared to take all of these steps simultaneously, with the result that what appeared, following the Divisional Court's judgment, to be an utterly hopeless case culminated in a powerfully reasoned and unanimous Supreme Court judgment.

This helps us to understand why the case is capable of being at once both rooted in orthodoxy *and* path-breaking. The Supreme Court was prepared to take a series of significant—but individually entirely legitimate—legal steps in circumstances that were politically extraordinary and that resulted in the transformation of fundamental principle into hard and novel limits on executive authority. In doing so, the Court does something that is both trail-blazing and mundane. It is trail-blazing because "forbidden" executive territory has been shown to be anything but by a Court prepared to treat fundamental principle as something that is neither a mere rhetorical flourish nor something arid and technical to be understood in isolation from the broader constitutional landscape in which it sits. Yet the judgment is simultaneously mundane because, in the final analysis, it stands for the most modest of constitutional propositions: that the UK is a democracy founded on parliamentary sovereignty, executive accountability, and the subjugation of government to law; that, from those basic constitutional facts of life, it follows that the government is not afforded an unfettered power to deny the legislature the opportunity to perform its vital constitutional role; and that questions about the legal scope of government power are questions of law for courts of law. Once those self-evident propositions are accepted, it becomes clear that judicial intervention in this matter is a realisation of, not an affront to, the separation of powers. Indeed, for the Court to have declined to play its part, and to have refused to determine and enforce the legal limits upon the government's authority to suspend Parliament, would have been nothing other than a dereliction of its constitutional duty.

QUESTIONS

1. Can you summarize the core legal principle established by *Miller 2*?
2. Do you agree with those who are critical of the judgment or those who see it as a positive constitutional development? Explain.
3. What key lessons do you draw from the case?
4. Was the Supreme Court correct to say that the legality of the Prime Minister's advice to prorogue Parliament was justiciable?
5. Do you agree with Professor Finnis that the judgment does not protect the sovereignty of Parliament as properly understood?
6. You hear two people discussing the *Miller 2* decision. One says that: 'The judgment shows how courts will invent fundamental constitutional principles in order to give themselves more power.' The other disagrees saying that: 'The judgment shows the courts applying fundamental constitutional principles in order to protect the constitution.' If you joined the discussion would you agree with one or other of these views, and if so which? If you would not agree with either, what would you say?
7. What would be the difference between asking the UK Supreme Court to review the legality of the monarch's decision to prorogue Parliament and asking the court to review the legality of the Prime Minister's advice to the monarch to prorogue Parliament. Is this a difference that matters?

10.2.8.1 Concluding comments

In this mini case study we have looked briefly at one of the most interesting and controversial court judgments in recent constitutional history. While the core of the judgment concerns the prerogative power to prorogue Parliament the case raises issues of importance across the constitutional system and of relevance to many chapters in this book, including the chapters on judicial review.[62] This is therefore a case study to which you will want to return. You may also want to research deeper into the issues.

10.3 REFORMING MINISTERIAL PREROGATIVES

In the final section of the Chapter we consider approaches to reforming the prerogative. Vociferous calls for reform of prerogative powers have been made since at least the 1980s and 1990s. In 1994, Jack Straw MP (who was later to serve in Labour governments as Home Secretary, Foreign & Commonwealth Secretary, Lord Chancellor, and Secretary of State for Justice), for example, wrote that the '*royal prerogative has no place in a modern western democracy [. . . the prerogative] has been used as a smoke-screen by Ministers to obfuscate the use of power for which they are insufficiently accountable*'.

As the following comments from William Hague MP (then a frontbench Conservative spokesman, he later became the Foreign Secretary 2010–14) show, there has been widespread consensus across the political parties that the use of prerogative powers fits uneasily in a modern democratic constitution.

[62] Chapters 17, 18, 19 and 20.

House of Commons Hansard, 15 May 2007, cols 485–93

Mr. Hague: In April 2003 the Right Hon. Tony Benn [a veteran left wing Labour MP who retired in 2001] and I, in what some regarded as a highly unusual alliance, made a joint presentation to the Public Administration Committee, calling for the whole of the royal prerogative now exercised by Ministers, including the power to conclude treaties, the right to reorganise Government Departments, and the administration of the honours system, as well as the power to enter armed conflict, to be brought under parliamentary scrutiny and control. [. . .] The Public Administration Committee came to a clear conclusion in 2004. [. . .] that "the prerogative has allowed powers to move from monarch to Ministers without Parliament having a say in how they are exercised. This should no longer be acceptable to Parliament or the people. [. . .] It is now time for this unfinished business to be completed."

Given the breadth of support for reform, including from those who became senior ministers, it might be thought that reformers would be pushing at an open door. But, of course, the situation is not that straightforward. It is one thing to call for reforms when in Opposition, but quite another to make changes when in government. Reforming the use of prerogative powers has proved to be an extremely complex matter—not least because the prerogative is used across a broad and diverse range of situations including decisions to go to war, the making of public appointments, decisions relating to passports, and the granting of honours. In *Taming the Prerogative*,[63] the PASC considered the case for reform to be 'unanswerable', but each of these areas raises distinct and difficult questions.

Here, we are at the heart of the constitutional system, where the imperatives of executive power, on the one hand, and the principles of democratic accountability, on the other, are inevitably in a state of tension. In this section, we draw in particular on the prerogative relating to the deployment of armed forces abroad, to explore how these tensions have affected the process of reform and nature of the solutions reached.

10.3.1 APPROACHES TO REFORM: PRAGMATISM OR PRINCIPLE?

Given these tensions, a basic question is how should reform be approached? In its 2004 report *Taming the Prerogative*, the PASC identified two broad options: one based on pragmatism and the other on principle. The pragmatic approach continues the long-standing practice of subjecting individual prerogative powers to parliamentary control on a case-by-case basis, perhaps relying on convention rather than statute depending on the circumstances. Reform based on principle calls for comprehensive legislation to subject prerogative powers in general to parliamentary control. The following extract is from the PASC's discussion of the virtues of each of these approaches.

[63] Public Administration Select Committee, *Taming the Prerogative: Strengthening Ministerial Accountability to Parliament*, Session 2003–04 (HC 422).

House of Commons Public Administration Select Committee, Taming the Prerogative, Strengthening Ministerial Accountability to Parliament, Fourth Report, Session 2003–04 (HC 422) (footnotes omitted)

The case for pragmatism

37. Lord Hurd[64] put to us the case for continued piecemeal and pragmatic extension of Parliamentary control: "I was brought up on a full diet of Edmund Burke and on the whole I believe the constitution evolves and is best looked at in the light of particular criticisms, particular mischiefs, that can be identified and then change made, rather than examining it on a philosophical basis, which rapidly turns artificial." [. . .]

39. He cited a number of individual examples in his own Ministerial experience where powerful practical and political considerations led government to subject the prerogative to much greater Parliamentary scrutiny: "every now and then a reform, a change, becomes clearly necessary. [. . .] two Acts of Parliament which put under statutory power or identity the three intelligence services: the Security Services Act 1989 and the Intelligence Services Act 1994. There were [. . .] very practical, cogent reasons which persuaded even the Prime Ministers of the day, and certainly the heads of the services, that this was a good and necessary move".

[. . .]

Putting democratic structures in place

[. . .]

45. Lord Lester set the argument in a broad constitutional context: "We were all brought up in our unwritten constitution to believe that there were two great principles to our constitution: one was parliamentary supremacy, that the executive was accountable to Parliament rather than to the king or queen; and, secondly, the principle of the rule of law, that public powers should be exercised according to the law. The difficulty about our unwritten, flexible, permeable, part monarchical and part parliamentary constitution is to make sure that those principles apply in practice".

46. Mr Hague also put the general case for a formal framework, telling us that "there is still a vast scope for extending parliamentary control of the royal prerogative". He cast doubt on the notion that a piecemeal approach to legislation was the most effective one, expressing his impatience "one problem with gradualism [. . .] it may not actually be sufficient. The other problem with gradualism is that it is not moving at all in some areas". [. . .]

EXERCISE

Summarize the main arguments for and against adopting a pragmatic and a principled approach to reform and explain which of these two approaches should be adopted and why?

The PASC's *Taming the Prerogative* report helped to frame the reform agenda. First, it strengthened the case for a move away from the pragmatism that has typified the approach to reform in the past. Second, it presented a cogent case for drawing a distinction between executive prerogatives in general which might be reformed by using generalized legislation and special situations that give rise to particular difficulties, such as the decision to deploy armed forces abroad. It is to this particularly difficult area that we now turn drawing on a second mini case study. We do so both because of its importance and because it provides a clear illustration of the complexities involved in reforming key elements of the working constitution.

[64] Lord Douglas Hurd served in the Conservative government as a Secretary of State for Northern Ireland from 1984 to 1985, as Home Secretary from 1985 to 1989, and as Foreign Secretary from 1989 to 1995.

10.3.2 MINI CASE STUDY: THE DEPLOYMENT OF ARMED FORCES ABROAD

The use of prerogative powers by government to deploy British armed forces abroad[65] is one of the most important and possibly controversial decisions that government can make.[66] As well as potentially resulting in death and injury to soldiers and civilians, deployments carry a huge financial cost and risks to national security. Despite its importance there is no set legal procedure that must be followed by ministers when deciding to deploy armed forces abroad and the government is under no *legal* obligation to obtain Parliament's consent, although by convention Parliament is able to debate and call ministers to account for actions they have taken. While in principle the power to deploy armed forces must be lawfully exercised and accord with international law,[67] in practice United Kingdom courts are likely to hold that the exercise of executive discretion in this context is non-justiciable.[68]

R v Jones and ors
[2006] UKHL 16

Lord Hoffmann

65. [. . .] the making of war and peace and the disposition of the armed forces has always been regarded as a discretionary power of the Crown into the exercise of which the courts will not enquire. [. . .] the reason why the courts cannot enquire is not the technicality that the powers form part of the royal prerogative. [. . .] It is because of the discretionary nature of the power itself. [. . .]

Here, then, is a matter of the gravest importance in relation to which formal legal and parliamentary controls are extremely limited. That said, wider political accountability may lead to electoral accountability and Prime Ministers have both benefitted and suffered at the hands of the electorate for their decisions to send British forces to fight.[69]

10.3.2.1 The convention that Parliament be involved

In Chapter 2, we examined the characteristics of constitutional conventions as a source of rules governing the behaviour of public bodies, noting that they are especially important in regulating how prerogative powers are exercised. In the following extract, Jack Straw, then Leader of the House,

[65] See further V. Fikfak and H. J. Hooper, *Parliament's Secret War, Hart Studies in Security and Justice* (2018, Oxford: Hart Publishing); House of Lords Constitution Committee, *Constitutional Arrangements for the Use of Armed Force*, Second Report, Session 2013–14 (HL Paper 46) (July 2013); L. Maer and O. Gay, *The Royal Prerogative*, House of Commons Standard Note 30 December 2009 SN/PC03861 (available at www.parliament.uk); C. Mills, House of Commons Library, Briefing Paper, *Parliamentary Approval for Military Action*, CBP 7166, 18 May 2018.

[66] Cf. deployment of armed forces within the UK, on which see House of Commons Library, Research Briefing 28 July 2022, Number 09601, by Louisa Brooke-Holland.

[67] International law permits the use of force in only three situations: for self-defence; if authorized by the Security Council acting under Chapter VII of the UN Charter exceptionally; or (arguably) to avert an overwhelming humanitarian catastrophe.

[68] *R v Jones and ors* [2006] UKHL 16; *Chandler v Director of Public Prosecutions* [1964] AC 763. Also *Smith and others (FC) (Appellants) v The Ministry of Defence (Respondent)* [2013] UKSC 41 on 'combat immunity' whereby there is no common law liability for negligence in respect of acts or omissions on the part of those who are actually engaged in armed combat.

[69] Margaret Thatcher is widely considered to have benefitted following the Falklands war and Tony Blair to have suffered as a consequence of his government's actions in Iraq.

explained to the Commons the government's view of what constitutional conventions govern decisions to deploy armed forces.

House of Commons Hansard, 15 May 2007, cols 492–7

> [Previous practice has] established a clear precedent for the future from which I do not believe there will be, or could ever be, a departure. Indeed, as my Right Hon. Friend the Prime Minister put it: 'The fact of the matter is that I cannot conceive of a situation in which a Government [. . .] is going to go to war—except in circumstances where militarily for the security of the country it needs to act immediately—without a full Parliamentary debate'.

In March 2011 the government once again accepted that a convention existed. The then Leader of the House of Commons, Rt Hon. Sir George Young MP, said:

> A convention has developed in the House that before troops are committed, the House should have an opportunity to debate the matter. We propose to observe that convention except when there is an emergency and such action would not be appropriate. As with the Iraq war and other events, we propose to give the House the opportunity to debate the matter before troops are committed.[70]

It is arguable that more recent events show the convention to be rather stronger than this and to require not only a debate in the House of Commons, but also that the approval of the House be obtained before armed forces are committed abroad.

The following extract from the House of Commons Political and Constitutional Reform Committee's report, *Parliament's Role in Conflict Decisions: a way forward*[71] summarizes the events in August 2013 when the House of Commons rejected a motion approving the government's proposed military intervention in Syria to stop the use of chemical weapons.

House of Commons Political and Constitutional Reform Committee, Parliament's Role in Conflict Decisions: a way forward, Twelfth Report, Session 2013-14 (footnotes omitted)

> [Following the rejection] the Prime Minister told the House:
>
> [. . .] I strongly believe in the need for a tough response to the use of chemical weapons, but I also believe in respecting the will of this House of Commons. It is very clear tonight that [. . .] Parliament, reflecting the views of the British people, does not want to see British military action. I get that, and the government will act accordingly.
>
> [The Committee continued . . .]
>
> 6. [. . .] The Prime Minister's decision to follow the views of the House in this matter was particularly significant. Although the government has only acknowledged a convention that the House should have the opportunity to debate conflict decisions, on this occasion the Prime Minister not only gave the House the opportunity to debate the matter, but deferred to the view it expressed. [. . .]

[70] HC Deb, 10 March 2011, col. 1066. The convention, as expressed by Sir George Young was subsequently written into the *Cabinet Manual* (1st ed. 2011).

[71] Twelfth Report, Session 2013–14 (HC 892).

It has been said that the government's decision to abide by the decision of the House was a significant indication of '*parliamentary sovereignty and a direct challenge to the royal prerogative on such matters*'.[72] Some have gone further to argue that the vote and the government's reaction to it indicate that there is now a convention not only that the government allow the House of Commons to debate and vote on proposed military interventions but also that the government must abide by the outcome of that vote. As Professor Gavin Phillipson, has put it:

> It may now be said with some confidence, therefore that, following the Syria episode, a constitutional convention exists to the effect that the government must, before, commencing any military action, permit a debate and vote in the House of Commons and abide by its result, subject to a narrow exception exists where truly urgent action is required.[73]

The 'narrow exception' is extremely important and occasions have occurred, and no doubt will continue to do so, when military action is taken without recourse to Parliament.[74]

10.3.2.2 Pros and cons of formalizing parliamentary involvement

While the main thrust of the reform agenda has been to strengthen Parliament's role in relation to the prerogative in general, and the deployment of armed forces in particular, there has been considerable debate around the best way forward. As we have seen broadly two schools of thought have emerged. Some believe that the current way of dealing with things is about right and any changes should be pragmatic and on a case-by-case basis. Others, however, seek more radical change. In the context of deployment decisions those taking the first approach are broadly content with relying on convention and practice whereas those taking the second approach would like to see a strengthened role for Parliament, and possibly also the courts, enshrined in statute. The case for and against ensuring 'full parliamentary scrutiny' of decisions on armed conflict was considered by the House of Lords Constitution Committee during its inquiry into the use of the prerogative. The following extract from the Committee's report summarizes what witnesses said were the benefits and drawbacks. The views are summarized in Box 10.3 and the extract from the report explains the points in more detail.

BOX 10.3 BENEFITS AND DRAWBACKS OF PARLIAMENTARY INVOLVEMENT IN DECISIONS ON ARMED CONFLICT

Benefits	Drawbacks
Increase legitimacy	Undermine operational effectiveness
Increase accountability	Shift responsibility from the executive
Improve decision-making	Lead to litigation
Improve morale	Undermine morale

[72] *Parliamentary Approval for Military Action*, House of Commons Briefing Paper 7166, 12 May 2018, Claire Mills, p. 4.

[73] G. Phillipson, '"Historic" Commons' Syria vote: the constitutional significance (Part I)' UK Constitutional Law Blog, 19 September 2013, http://ukconstitutionallaw.org. In December 2015 the government once again sought the approval of the House of Commons to military action in Syria. On this occasion MPs voted 397 to 223 in favour of permitting airstrikes against Islamic State militants in Syria.

[74] On 14 April 2018 without recourse to Parliament the UK, together with the United States and France, conducted air strikes against Syrian targets intended to '*degrade the Syrian Government's chemical weapon capabilities.*' *Parliamentary Approval for Military Action*, House of Commons Briefing Paper 7166, 18 May 2018, Claire Mills, p. 37.

House of Lords Constitution Committee, Waging War: Parliament's Role and Responsibility, Fifteenth Report, Session 2005-06 (HL Paper 236-I) (footnotes omitted)

The Benefits of Increasing Parliamentary Involvement

Legitimacy: source and exercise of the deployment power

37. A key concern over the current deployment power is one of constitutional principle: that Parliament should be the source of the Government's power and not the Crown. Lord Lester regarded the key question about the deployment power to be: "should it be Parliament that is Sovereign, to whom the executive is constitutionally accountable, or should it be the Monarch?" He considered it anomalous for the Crown to be able to exercise public powers without parliamentary authority, on the basis of mediaeval notions of kingship and through Crown Ministers. Mr Sebastian Payne agreed: "Parliament should be the source of Government's power," a position also taken by Professor McEldowney.

[. . .]

Increased accountability of decision-making

40. Several witnesses advocated greater parliamentary involvement on the grounds that the current deployment power lacks sufficient accountability or restraint. [. . .] it could be said that the ability of United Kingdom governments to use the royal prerogative power to engage in conflict is paradoxically less democratic than when the Monarch exercised the power personally. [. . .] Now, the Government [. . .] not only exercises the royal prerogative but also generally controls the House of Commons and therefore its power over finance [. . .]

"Better" decision-making

44. Other witnesses proposed that a change to the current deployment power was necessary because the highly personalised nature of the royal prerogative power leads to poor processes of decision-making. Clare Short told us that because the royal prerogative power is exercised by the Prime Minister alone [. . .] this can lead to decisions being taken in a "vacuum". A requirement for scrutiny by Parliament, she argued, might lead to better considered and prepared decisions [. . .]

The impact on military morale

45. Several witnesses suggested that more legitimate decision-making would result in greater support for deployment decisions among the public, senior military figures and serving troops.

Arguments Against Increasing Parliamentary Involvement

Undermining effectiveness of operations

49. Several witnesses regarded operational efficiency to be the key benefit of the present deployment arrangements, and one which could be undermined by greater parliamentary involvement in the process. Field Marshal Lord Vincent of Coleshill said that the success of many military operations relies on the need to maintain "secrecy, security and surprise".

Coalition-working

51. Mr Ingram told us that in his experience coalition partners liked to work with British units because the current process gave the Government the capacity to make quick decisions about deployments and to provide wide mandates for British forces.

Maintaining executive responsibility for action

52. We have heard evidence to suggest that the responsibility for taking the decision to deploy armed forces should very clearly rest with the executive and not be dictated by the immediate views and reactions of Parliament or of the people. The Government has clearly stated that "the power to deploy troops is an executive power. Such decisions are by their nature most suitable for the executive to take". [. . .]

Difficulties of informed decision-making

55. There was broad agreement that it is necessary to restrict some information in a potential deployment situation and an acknowledgement that this could compromise the ability of Parliament to make informed decisions about a given situation.

[. . .]

Legal impact of legislation

57. We have heard that if parliamentary involvement in the deployment decision was enshrined in legislation that required, for instance, prior parliamentary approval, this would require language tantamount to definitions of what is lawful and might lead to the legality of any deployment being challenged in the United Kingdom courts. Some witnesses raised concerns that this could lead to individual servicemen facing criminal prosecution for actions in an "unlawful" deployment.

Undermining morale

59. While we have heard evidence to suggest that greater parliamentary involvement in the deployment power would improve morale [. . .] we also heard contrasting evidence to suggest that it might actually undermine it. The Lord Chancellor and Secretary of State for Constitutional Affairs told us that any restriction on deployment might introduce an "unpredictable and damaging level of uncertainty" as to the legality of the actions of Armed Forces on the ground. Lord Boyce told us that the uncertainty that resulted from relying on Parliament's approval would be bad for morale. [. . .]

10.3.2.3 Weighing the arguments

Had you been a member of the House of Lords Constitution Committee, you would have needed to assess and weigh these arguments to form a view on whether or not it is desirable to increase Parliament's role and, if so, how. Looking over the arguments, some are based on constitutional principle and others are more practical in nature. How are arguments on principle and practice to be weighed against each other? Increasing the democratic legitimacy of decision-making is clearly important as a matter of principle, but does it outweigh risks to the operational effectiveness of military campaigns? Another problem that you would have faced is that of weighing conflicting opinions of experts. For example, we can see that senior military figures differed on whether parliamentary involvement would enhance or damage morale within the armed forces. How would you and your fellow committee members know which of these views is the more likely to be accurate? Without clear evidence, this is a question of judgement and approach.

QUESTIONS

1. You have been appointed to a parliamentary committee to consider reform of the powers by which armed forces are deployed abroad. As a member of such a committee would you favour greater parliamentary involvement in decisions to deploy armed forces or would you be against it?
2. It is suggested to you that the main options for reform are as follows.
   - Things continue as now, but that it should be recognized that the power to deploy armed forces derives from Parliament, rather than from the prerogative.
   - Government remains responsible for the decision, but must provide Parliament with a justification for its action. Parliament should be able to debate this justification and be critical, but Parliament should not be able to veto a decision of the government.
   - Subject to specific exceptions, government should send military forces abroad to fight only with the prior agreement of Parliament.

Do you agree that these are the main options? If not, what other options should be considered?

10.3.2.4 Recommendation of the Constitution Committee

The Committee made two central recommendations: one substantive, and the other relating to method or process. Its substantive recommendation was that Parliament should be involved as a matter of right and not only as a matter of executive largesse. Obviously influenced by those who feared the adverse consequences of using legislation to achieve this change, it nonetheless recommended that the change should be achieved by using convention rather than by using legislation.[75]

10.3.2.5 Government's response to these recommendations

The government response was brief and disagreed with the Committee:

Government Response to the House of Lords Constitution Committee's Report, Waging War: Parliament's Role and Responsibility, Cm 6923 (7 November 2006)

4. [We are] not presently persuaded of the case for [. . .] establishing a new convention determining the role of Parliament in the deployment of the armed forces. The existing legal and constitutional convention is that it must be the Government which takes the decision in accordance with its own assessment of the position. That is one of the key responsibilities for which it has been elected. But the matter needs to be kept under review.

[75] House of Lords Constitution Committee, *Waging War: Parliament's Role and Responsibility*, Fifteenth Report, Session 2005–06 (HL Paper 236-I).

10.3.2.6 The continuing need for reform

This is a matter that has continued to attract the attention of various parliamentary committees and views both within government and in Parliament have changed. One of the lessons for government has been that reform in this area as in other areas of constitutional law and practice is more complex than first appears. The following is from the report of the House of Commons Political and Constitutional Affairs Committee, *Parliament's Role in Conflict Decisions: A Way Forward.*

House of Commons Political and Constitutional Reform Committee, Parliament's Role in Conflict Decisions: A Way Forward, Twelfth Report, Session 2013–14 (HC 892) (March 2014)

When we asked Lord Wallace to update us on the Government's current position, he told us:

> The Government has an evolving position. This Government, like its predecessor, has discovered as it goes into it that this is a great deal more complex than one thought. The definition of armed conflict and the deployment of forces has all sorts of ragged edges, questions of urgency and secrecy come in [. . .]. We are in the process of discovering we need a strong convention but how we actually interpret it, let alone how we legislate on it or whether we should legislate on it, is a large question. Legislation and judicial review go together and the Government has become much more sensitive about judicial review of military action.

These statements indicate that the Government is not united on this matter, and does not have a clear position on the issue.

Graham Allen MP, when chair of the House of Commons Political and Constitutional Reform Committee, summarized the current situation by saying that '*to all intents and purposes, a Prime Minister has the same power over our forces as Henry V, although without the same obligation to lead them in person. Nearly six centuries after Agincourt, Parliament still has no formal or agreed role in the decision to war or the conduct and purposes of a war.*'[76]

Before he became Prime Minister Keir Starmer indicated that in his view legislation is needed to ensure that military action only takes place with the consent of the House of Commons. However such legislation has yet to be introduced and in October 2024, in response to UK involvement in defending Israel against Iranian missile and drone attacks, as Prime Minister, he said in the House of Commons that '*the whole House will understand that there will be occasions when it is important for a Government to act without first coming to this House.*'[77]

[76] Ibid.

[77] See *Military Action: Parliament's role*, Clair Mills, House of Commons Library, 14 October 2024, p 57. Here Clair Mills explains that in January, February and May 2024 parliamentary approval was not sought before military strikes on Houthi targets in Yemen, nor was retrospective approval obtained. In response to these events, Richard Foord, then Liberal Democrat Defence Spokesman, introduced a Private Members Bill that would have required parliamentary approval for military action subject to exemptions. The Bill had a second reading but fell when Parliament was dissolved in May 2024 for the general election.

QUESTIONS AND POINTS FOR REFLECTION

1. *'The process of reform of prerogative war powers, highlights the extent to which the UK constitution is based on convenience and convention rather than principle and law.'* Assess the accuracy of this statement.
2. *'Another lesson to be drawn from the government's approach to reform in this area is that government will only move forward with constitutional reform in an area as sensitive as the power to deploy armed forces if it can secure consensus. Here at least government follows but will not lead. This is as it should be.'* Discuss.
3. Should the power to deploy armed forces abroad be based on statutory provisions that require parliamentary approval for deployments or is the existing convention adequate? Explain your response.

10.3.2.7 Concluding comments on the mini case study

This mini case study has focused on another extremely important area in which prerogative power is still used. It has shown that despite many calls for reform of the prerogative achieving reform has proved extremely complex due largely to the tensions between the desire for accountability on the one hand and the need to allow government the freedom to act on the other. Whether Parliament should and will be given a greater role when armed forces are sent abroad to fight remain contentious questions. They are a further illustration of the relationships between law and practice in the UK's constitution.

10.4 A FINAL WORD ON THE CHAPTER

This Chapter has considered the nature and continuing importance of prerogative powers that are rooted in a system that predates the contemporary parliamentary democratic system. We have seen that questions remain regarding the definition of prerogative powers. But the issues extend beyond matters of definition. While there is widespread agreement that ministerial prerogative powers should be limited and that government should be accountable there is continuing debate about the most appropriate methods of accountability. Should these be based primarily on the political system or should they be based on law and policed by the courts, and if so on what principles? These are big issues to which we return, especially in Part IV of the book.

FURTHER READING

Cox, N., *The Royal Prerogative and Constitutional Law* (2021, Routledge).

Craig, R., *Royal Law: Prerogative Foundations* (2025, Bloomsbury).

Hazel R., and Foot, T., *Executive Power: The Prerogative, Past, Present and Future* (2022, Bloomsbury Publishing).

Tomkins, A., *The Crown* (2003, OUP, Clarendon Law Series).

Torrance, D., *The royal prerogative and ministerial advice* (House of Commons Library, 1 August 2025).

PART III

LEGISLATIVE FUNCTIONS

11

INTRODUCTION TO LEGISLATIVE FUNCTIONS

CENTRAL ISSUES

1. Legislation is central to the UK constitution: it gives legal authority to government action, regulates everyday life, and reflects the constitutional balance between Parliament, ministers, and the courts.
2. Understanding how legislation is made—both in Parliament and through delegated powers—is essential to understanding how law and politics interact in a parliamentary democracy.
3. Distinguishing between public, private, hybrid, primary, and delegated legislation helps explain the different forms and procedures through which laws are created and controlled.
4. Effective legal research requires the ability to find legislation, determine whether it is in force, and understand its background and purpose through preparatory materials and parliamentary records.

11.1 OVERVIEW

Legislation affects almost everything we do. The radio alarm that wakes us, the energy that powers it, the food we eat, and the safety standards of the transport we use—all depend on laws made by Parliament or by ministers using powers delegated to them. From the moment we start our day, legislation quietly orders daily life.[1]

Yet the process of making law is rarely tidy. Political compromise, limited scrutiny, and shifting priorities all leave their mark on the final text. Awareness of this is essential for lawyers, because the imperfections of the process often explain why legislation is ambiguous, inconsistent, or difficult to apply. As one saying (wrongly attributed to Otto von Bismarck) puts it, 'Laws, like sausages, cease to inspire respect in proportion as we know how they are made'. Understanding how

[1] For example, radio broadcasting is licensed under the Broadcasting Act 1996 and Communications Act 2003; electricity supply is regulated by Ofgem under the Electricity Act 1989; and even the label on a box of cornflakes must comply with the Food Safety Act 1990 and the Food Information Regulations 2014 (SI 2014/1855), which carry forward EU-derived consumer-labelling rules after the UK's withdrawal from the EU.

legislation is made reveals much about the United Kingdom's constitutional balance. It shows how the principles of parliamentary supremacy, the rule of law, and the separation of powers interact—sometimes harmoniously, sometimes in tension—as democratic ideals meet the political realities of government.

This chapter introduces the main terminology and skills developed further in Chapter 12 ('Primary Legislation') and Chapter 13 ('Delegated Legislation').

PAUSE FOR REFLECTION

Imagine a group of local farmers asking a lawyer for advice. They want to sell unpasteurised milk directly from their farm shops. Can they legally do so? Do they need a licence—and if so, who issues it? What hygiene rules would apply?

To answer, you would first need to *find* the relevant legislation. Where would you start? Which Acts, regulations, or agencies might be involved? How would you check whether those rules are still in force?

If the law prevents the farmers from selling the milk as they wish, who could they lobby to change it—ministers, civil servants, or Parliament itself?

Questions like these show why lawyers must know not only how legislation is made, but also how to locate and interpret it in practice.

11.1.1 PUBLIC AND PRIVATE LEGISLATION DISTINGUISHED

Public legislation—such as most Acts of Parliament—is general in nature. It sets out rules of law that apply to classes of people or situations rather than to named individuals.

A core constitutional principle is that Parliament does not legislate to punish or privilege particular persons. To do so would undermine the rule of law, which requires laws to be general, prospective, and publicly known. In earlier centuries, however, Parliament occasionally passed Acts targeting specific individuals. One notorious example is the Act for Poysoning 1531, promoted by Henry VIII, which declared the Bishop of Rochester's cook guilty of treason and ordered that he be boiled alive. Such 'bills of attainder' are no longer regarded as constitutionally acceptable. In modern times, the War Crimes Act 1991 was controversial because critics argued that it retrospectively targeted a small, though unnamed, group of no more than fifty individuals alleged to have committed war crimes in German-occupied territory during the Second World War.[2]

Not all Acts, however, are general in their application. Sometimes Parliament passes legislation directed at a particular body or local concern—for example, a university, a charity, a local authority, or a company. These are known as private Acts of Parliament. They usually confer powers, authorise works, or alter legal relationships that cannot conveniently be achieved through ordinary public legislation.

[2] Only three prosecutions were brought under the Act. Two were discontinued—one because the defendant was unfit to plead on medical grounds, and the other for lack of sufficient evidence. The third, Anthony Sawoniuk, was convicted of murder in 1999.

A bill that combines public and private elements is called a hybrid bill.[3] Infrastructure projects such as railways (HS2 and Crossrail) and public monuments fall into this category. Hybrid bills follow a special procedure. In addition to the usual parliamentary stages, they are examined by a committee before which people or organizations directly affected by the private provisions may petition Parliament and make representations—normally through legal counsel.

11.1.2 GOVERNMENT AND PRIVATE MEMBERS' BILLS DISTINGUISHED

Bills introduced in Parliament fall into two main categories: government bills and private members' bills. Government bills are promoted by ministers on behalf of the government and form part of its legislative programme, which is announced in the King's Speech at the opening of each parliamentary session. They account for the vast majority of Acts of Parliament.

By contrast, private members' bills are introduced by backbench MPs or members of the House of Lords who are not ministers. Success usually depends on an MP securing a place in the annual ballot, having a bill ready to present, and—crucially—obtaining at least tacit government support to secure time for debate and progression through Parliament. These bills allow individual parliamentarians to raise issues of public concern or to propose legal changes outside the government's legislative programme. Only a small proportion become law, but they can influence government policy or draw attention to emerging social questions. A recent example is the Terminally Ill Adults (End of Life) Bill, introduced in the House of Commons by Kim Leadbeater MP in 2024, which sought to legalise assisted dying for terminally ill adults. Two earlier landmark social reforms also began as private members' bills: the Abortion Act 1967, introduced by David Steel MP, and the Sexual Offences Act 1967, introduced by Leo Abse MP, which decriminalised homosexual acts between consenting adults in private in England and Wales.

11.1.3 PRIMARY AND SECONDARY LEGISLATION DISTINGUISHED

The terms *primary* and *secondary* (also known as *delegated* or *subordinate*) legislation are used frequently throughout this book, so it is helpful to begin by clarifying the difference. In broad terms, primary legislation is made by the legislative bodies of the United Kingdom: the UK Parliament; the Scottish Parliament; the Northern Ireland Assembly; and the Senedd Cymru/Welsh Parliament. These bodies make laws in the form of Acts (see Box 11.1).

By contrast, secondary legislation is law made by ministers or, in some cases, by other public authorities, under powers delegated to them by an Act of Parliament or an Act of a devolved legislature. The authority to make such legislation must always be granted by primary legislation. Box 11.2 summarises some of the main differences between primary and secondary legislation.

The devolved legislatures owe their existence to Acts of the UK Parliament and legislate within defined though broad statutory competences, ultimately subject to judicial control. For the purposes of the Human Rights Act 1998, section 21(1) classifies devolved Acts as 'subordinate legislation'; but the courts have consistently treated such Acts as primary in nature, reflecting the devolved legislatures' plenary law-making powers within their statutory limits.

[3] P. Evans, 'Hybrid Bills and Parliament: History, procedure and controversies', *Hansard Society Blog* 15 October 2023 https://www.hansardsociety.org.uk/blog/hybrid-bill-procedure-holocaust-memorial-parliament accessed 11 November 2025.

BOX 11.1 MAIN TYPES OF LEGISLATION

	United Kingdom	Scotland	Wales	Northern Ireland
Government responsible for initiating the making of most legislation	UK Government	Scottish Government	Welsh Government	Northern Ireland Executive
Primary legislation	Bills introduced to the UK Parliament become Acts of Parliament on receiving Royal Assent.	Bills introduced to the Scottish Parliament under s 28 of the Scotland Act 1998 become Acts of the Scottish Parliament on Royal Assent.	Bills introduced to Senedd Cymru/ Welsh Parliament under Pt 4 of the Government of Wales Act 2006 (as amended by the Wales Act 2017) become Acts of the Senedd Cymru on Royal Assent.	Bills introduced to the Northern Ireland Assembly under Pt II of the Northern Ireland Act 1998 become Acts of the Northern Ireland Assembly on Royal Assent.
Secondary legislation	Statutory Instruments (SIs) made by UK ministers under powers conferred by Acts of Parliament.	Scottish Statutory Instruments made by Scottish ministers under Pt VI of the Scotland Act 1998.	Welsh Statutory Instruments made by Welsh ministers under powers conferred by Welsh Acts and Measures.	Statutory Rules made by Northern Ireland departments under powers conferred by Acts of the Northern Ireland Assembly.

BOX 11.2 UK PRIMARY AND SECONDARY LEGISLATION COMPARED

UK primary legislation	UK secondary legislation
'Bills' contain the text of proposed legislation. They are made up of numbered 'clauses'	Also known as 'delegated' or 'subordinate' legislation, 'regulations', 'orders', and 'rules'
A bill is debated in each House of Parliament in turn, in a process involving a First Reading, Second Reading, Committee Stage, Report, and Third Reading	Can only be made if an Act of Parliament provides ministers with a power to legislate on a given topic
Once a bill is approved by both Houses of Parliament, in practice, it receives Royal Assent	Most instruments are made as statutory instruments under the Statutory Instruments Act 1949 (affirmative or negative procedure).
Thereafter, the legislation is known as an 'Act of Parliament' (or, more generically, 'a statute'). Clauses are known as 'sections'	Delegated legislation is scrutinized by several parliamentary committees, but most are not subject to any debate and (unlike bills) cannot be amended as they progress through Parliament

11.1.4 LEGISLATION AND DEVOLUTION

Although this book focuses on the institutions and processes of the United Kingdom as a whole, readers should be aware that the legislative systems of the devolved nations differ in structure and procedure.

Legislative powers have been conferred by the UK Parliament on the Scottish Parliament, the Northern Ireland Assembly, and the Senedd Cymru/Welsh Parliament since 1998. Devolution is not uniform: each legislature operates within its own constitutional framework and with different degrees of autonomy.[4]

In Wales, the principal framework is Part 4 of the Government of Wales Act 2006, as amended by the Wales Act 2017. This reform replaced the earlier 'conferred powers' model—under which the National Assembly could legislate only on specified topics—with a 'reserved powers' model, allowing the Senedd to legislate on all matters except those expressly reserved to Westminster.

In Scotland, the Scotland Acts 2012 and 2016 expanded the Scottish Parliament's powers first granted by the Scotland Act 1998 over areas such as taxation, welfare, and elections, reflecting a growing degree of legislative and fiscal autonomy.

In Northern Ireland, law-making powers were transferred to the Northern Ireland Assembly by the Northern Ireland Act 1998, forming part of the Belfast (Good Friday) Agreement. The Assembly has competence in a wide range of areas, including health, education, and justice, but its operation has at times been suspended during periods of political disagreement, when legislative powers temporarily return to Westminster.

All the devolution Acts state that the grant of legislative powers '*does not affect the power of the Parliament of the United Kingdom to make laws*' for those parts of the United Kingdom, though in relation to Wales and Scotland the devolution Acts were amended to add '*But it is recognised that the Parliament of the United Kingdom will not normally legislate with regard to devolved matters without the consent of the*' Senedd Cymru and the Scottish Parliament.[5]

11.2 THE USES OF LEGISLATION

For what purposes is legislation used? As we have seen, one of the main activities of government is to formulate and implement policy. In the case of the UK government, sometimes implementation can be achieved without new legislation (in cases in which there are sufficient powers authorizing executive action already on the 'statute book'[6]) or without any legislative backing (in which cases prerogative or 'third source' powers are used[7]). But the pressure for new legislation is constant. Ministers and their departments view it as an important activity, and there is competition within government to secure time for a department's bills in the crowded annual legislative programme. Outside government, pressure groups are constantly calling for new legislation in order to achieve the goals that they espouse (for example, better environmental protection and an end to cruelty to animals).

If you leaf through the statute book, you will see that legislation is in place for a wide range of purposes, including:

- to set out public law rights—for example, the Human Rights Act 1998, the Freedom of Information Act 2000, and the Equality Act 2010;
- to impose taxation—the government cannot perform executive functions without access to funds, and tax can be levied only through legislation;

[4] See Chapter 6. [5] See Chapter 2 (The Constitutional Rule Book—Conventions).
[6] Shorthand for all legislation; see www.legislation.gov.uk [7] See Chapter 10.

- to create powers for public bodies to take action—almost all public bodies created in recent years are 'creatures of statute', meaning that they have those powers (and only those powers) conferred on them by legislation;
- the regulation of commercial activity—one school of thought holds that there is simply too much legislation. In relation to the regulation of businesses, a cross-party consensus has emerged that 'red tape' (meaning legislation that imposes unnecessary bureaucracy) should be minimized. A programme of 'regulatory reform' was in operation for several years to review the regulatory requirements with which we could dispense;[8] and
- social control—traditionally, this has been through the creation of criminal offences; in more recent years, the courts have been empowered to make a wide range of preventative injunctions (such as antisocial behaviour orders).

QUESTIONS

1. Identify a piece of legislation that you would like to see repealed or amended. How would you set about achieving this?
2. Look at the output of over the last year or two at http://www.legislation.gov.uk/ukpga. What other reasons for making legislation can you suggest in addition to those we have listed?

11.3 SKILLS

Lawyers often need to locate, read, and interpret legislation quickly and accurately. The growth of online databases has made legal research easier, but finding the most up-to-date version of an Act or statutory instrument still requires care and attention to detail. This section outlines some of the key research skills you will need.

11.3.1 FINDING THE TEXT

The first step in working with legislation is to locate the text of the provision you need.

Parliament no longer issues paper copies of Acts or delegated legislation, but authorized versions can still be purchased from The Stationery Office Ltd (TSO), a private company licensed to reproduce official legislation. Prices vary according to length, and delivery may take several days. Until the early 2000s, lawyers relied mainly on printed bound and loose-leaf volumes to access legislation. The principal bound series were *Halsbury's Statutes of England and Wales* (Butterworths) and the official *Statutes in Force*. These provided authoritative, subject-arranged statements of the law but were quickly overtaken by amendments. Alongside them, practice-specific loose-leaf services—such as *Current Law Statutes*, *Sweet & Maxwell's Statutes Service*, and specialist collections in fields like housing, planning, and employment—were issued in ring-binders with replacement pages several times a year. These systems allowed practitioners to keep their paper libraries current in an era before online updating. Although most have now been discontinued or migrated to digital platforms, they remain useful for historical research and for tracing how statutory wording has evolved over time.

Today, almost all research on legislation is carried out electronically. The official, free, and authoritative source of UK legislation is the government website legislation.gov.uk, maintained by The

[8] See Chapter 13, on the Legislative and Regulatory Reform Act 2006.

National Archives. It allows readers to view the law as originally enacted, to see how it has been amended, and to check whether each provision is currently in force.

Commercial databases such as Westlaw and LexisNexis reproduce the same legislative content under licence but add features such as cross-references to cases, commentary, and updating alerts. These systems are widely used in universities and larger law firms and chambers, but because of cost smaller law practices and public-sector organizations often rely mainly on the official open-access sources.

Students and practitioners should be careful when using internet searches to find the law. Search engines rank results by popularity rather than legal authority and may lead to websites that reproduce incomplete or outdated material. Some sites summarise legislation inaccurately or omit amendments and commencement details. Others blur the boundaries between UK and overseas law. Even apparently trustworthy pages may provide commentary rather than the law itself. Relying on such sources risks citing provisions that have been repealed or never brought into force, which can lead to poor advice or loss of professional credibility.

AI tools carry different but related dangers. They can produce confident and polished explanations without checking the accuracy of the underlying law. Because they draw on patterns of text rather than verified sources, they may misstate, oversimplify, or invent details. They also lack the ability to confirm whether a statutory provision is current or in force. The responsible approach is to treat any AI output as a starting point, not as authority. Lawyers should always verify information on official or professionally maintained databases, confirm the status and date of each provision, and note precisely where the material was found.

PAUSE FOR REFLECTION

What could go wrong if you rely on an unofficial summary or an automated answer when advising a client, preparing an argument, or writing an exam answer? How can you check that the legislation you are using is both accurate and up to date?

11.3.2 WORKING OUT WHETHER THE LEGISLATION IS IN FORCE

A second task is to determine whether the legislation is actually in force—in other words, legally operative. An Act comes into force: (a) immediately after Royal Assent; or (b) on a specific date set out in the Act; or (c) the Act may leave the decision as to when a piece of legislation is to be given binding force to the government—in other words, while *Parliament* enacts legislation, *government* often decides whether it is legally binding in practice. When scenario (c) applies, government brings primary legislation into force by making a piece of delegated legislation often known as a 'commencement order'.[9]

The www.legislation.gov.uk website indicates whether a provision is in force and, if so, from what date. Commercial databases such as Westlaw and LexisNexis also include this information. Nonetheless, it is good practice to verify this for yourself by checking:

(a) the commencement section near the end of the Act;

(b) any schedules identifying provisions brought into force; and

(c) any relevant commencement order listed on *legislation.gov.uk*.

If no commencement order has been made, the provision is not yet in force. There may, however, still be plans to bring the provision into force. The responsible government department may publish information about its intentions in a policy paper, implementation update, or departmental press

[9] See Chapter 13.

release. Details may also appear in a ministerial statement or written parliamentary answer announcing the government's timetable for commencement.

Some sections of Acts remain dormant—passed by Parliament but not brought into force—for many years. A well-known example is section 1 of the Equality Act 2010, the 'public sector duty regarding socio-economic inequalities'. It requires ministers, local authorities, and other public bodies, when making strategic decisions, to consider how their powers could be used to reduce inequalities of outcome. The Act was passed under Gordon Brown's Labour government, but the subsequent Coalition and Conservative governments chose not to commence section 1, describing it as an unnecessary bureaucratic burden. The Welsh and Scottish governments later brought the duty into force in their respective jurisdictions, in 2018 and 2021. The Labour Party's 2024 general election manifesto pledged to commence the duty in England.[10]

We return to constitutional problems with commencement in Chapter 12 section 12.9.

PAUSE FOR REFLECTION

Why might different governments reach different decisions about commencement? How does this affect your understanding of how law and politics interact in the legislative process?

When advising a client, how could you make sure that the section of an Act you rely on is actually in force? What sources would you check to confirm this?

11.3.3 RESEARCHING WHAT WAS SAID AND DONE DURING THE LEGISLATIVE PROCESS

Once legislation has been enacted, lawyers often treat the text itself as the final word. The enrolled Act rule means that courts will not question whether a bill was properly passed through Parliament, although they may examine the validity of delegated legislation. There are, however, occasions when it is useful—or even necessary—to look back at what was said or done while a bill was being made law. This is known as researching the legislative history. It can help a lawyer understand the policy behind a provision, clarify ambiguous language, or prepare an argument about how a statute should be interpreted.

Courts usually interpret legislation purposively—that is, by asking what Parliament was trying to achieve. To discover that purpose, they may consult preparatory materials such as Green Papers and White Papers. Since 1999, bills have been accompanied by 'explanatory notes', drafted by officials in the sponsoring department. These notes aim to explain, in plain language and without argument, what the bill is intended to do and how it will operate. They are not formally approved by Parliament, but they are published alongside the bill and remain accessible after enactment. Courts sometimes refer to them as an aid to interpretation, particularly where they help to identify the purpose or context of the legislation, as Lord Steyn explains.

Westminster City Council v National Asylum Support Service
[2002] UKHL 38, [4]–[6], Lord Steyn

4. . . . The purpose is to help the reader to get his bearings and to ease the task of assimilating the law. . . .

[10] J. Meers, 'Enacting the socio-economic duty: inequalities of outcome and section 1 Equality Act 2010' (2025) 33(2) Journal of Poverty and Social Justice 221.

> 5. . . . Insofar as the Explanatory Notes cast light on the objective setting or contextual scene of the statute, and the mischief at which it is aimed, such materials are therefore always admissible aids to construction. They may be admitted for what logical value they have. Used for this purpose Explanatory Notes will sometimes be more informative and valuable than reports of the Law Commission or advisory committees, Government green or white papers, and the like. After all, the connection of Explanatory Notes with the shape of the proposed legislation is closer than pre-parliamentary aids which in principle are already treated as admissible [. . .]
>
> 6. If exceptionally there is found in Explanatory Notes a clear assurance by the executive to Parliament about the meaning of a clause, or the circumstances in which a power will or will not be used, that assurance may in principle be admitted against the executive in proceedings in which the executive places a contrary contention before a court.

Explanatory notes can be found on the www.legislation.gov.uk website.

In limited circumstances, the courts may also refer to statements made by ministers (but not other parliamentarians) in Parliament under the principle *in Pepper (Her Majesty's Inspector of Taxes) v Hart* [1993] AC 593, where Hansard was used to clarify the meaning of a tax provision. This marked a major departure from traditional rules of statutory interpretation. The decision was justified on the ground that ministerial explanations could clarify Parliament's intention and promote fairness in interpretation: it would be wrong for counsel representing the government in court to argue for an interpretation that conflicted with what the minister in charge of the bill had said in Parliament. However, the case has always been controversial. Critics argue that it blurs the constitutional boundaries between Parliament, the executive, and the courts. Under the principle of parliamentary supremacy, Acts of Parliament speak through their enacted text, not through ministers' speeches. Allowing courts to rely on what was said in debate risks giving legal effect to statements made by members of the executive during the legislative process, rather than to the words approved by Parliament as a whole. It may also privilege ministers' views over those of other MPs and peers who voted for the measure. There are also practical objections: parliamentary debates are often politically charged, inconsistent, and not designed as interpretative aids. Searching Hansard can be time-consuming, and the material found may reflect negotiation or political compromise rather than clear legal meaning. For these reasons, later cases while reaffirming the approach in *Pepper v Hart* have indicated that it should be applied sparingly, only when the statutory wording is ambiguous and the minister's statement is clear and authoritative.

Hansard is not available on the www.legislation.gov.uk website; instead you need to look at the 'Bills before Parliament' service at https://bills.parliament.uk.

PAUSE FOR REFLECTION

When approaching a new Act, should you read the statutory text first, or start with the explanatory notes? Each approach offers different insights: one shows what Parliament enacted, the other what the government says it meant. Which is the better starting point—and why?

11.4 WHERE TO GO FROM HERE

To learn about how bills are introduced, debated, and enacted as Acts of Parliament, turn to Chapter 12 on primary legislation.

To explore how ministers and other authorities make legally binding rules under powers delegated by Parliament, turn to Chapter 13 on delegated legislation.

12

PRIMARY LEGISLATION

CENTRAL ISSUES

1. Acts of Parliament are the primary vehicle for giving legal effect to government policy, and studying how they are made illuminates parliamentary supremacy, the rule of law, and separation of powers in practice.
2. Formally, the legislature is the King in Parliament; in practice, government dominates policy initiation, drafting, and the passage of bills through Parliament, while Parliament's core function is scrutiny and—exceptionally—veto.
3. Consultation can strengthen proposed legislation, whether through referendums, pre-legislative scrutiny of draft Bills, or routine public engagement exercises. Yet there is long-standing scepticism about how much these processes actually influence the final outcome.
4. Specialist lawyers in the Office of the Parliamentary Counsel convert a department's policy instructions into legislative text. Some bills take the form of 'skeleton' legislation, setting out broad powers but leaving key policy detail to be supplied later by delegated legislation; this approach raises constitutional concerns about transparency, scrutiny, and the proper balance between Parliament and the executive.
5. The formal stages—Second Reading, Committee, Report, and Third Reading—are accompanied by parallel committee scrutiny (e.g. Constitution Committee, Delegated Powers and Regulatory Reform Committee, Joint Committee on Human Rights). Evidence-taking in Public Bill Committees has helped on some bills, but agenda control and party discipline limit its impact; the Lords often influences detail, with disagreements resolved in 'ping-pong' and, rarely, via the Parliament Acts.
6. Post-legislative scrutiny examines whether Acts are operating as intended and identifies areas for revision or repeal. Although there is broad cross-party support for this form of review, its use remains uneven, and select committees often struggle to give it priority amid competing demands.
7. The quality of the statute book is itself a constitutional issue linked to the rule of law. Persistent concern about the growing length, complexity, and frequent amendment of Acts underline the need for clarity, coherence, and adequate scrutiny if legislation is to remain effective.

12.1 INTRODUCTION

This chapter explores how Acts of Parliament are made and how the legislative process gives practical effect to, and sometimes tests, the principles of parliamentary supremacy, the rule of law, and the separation of powers. It begins by explaining how policy proposals are turned into bills, outlining the roles of ministers, civil servants, and the Office of the Parliamentary Counsel. It then follows a bill's journey through Parliament—from pre-legislative scrutiny and formal stages in both Houses to Royal Assent and subsequent post-legislative review—showing how accountability operates at each stage and how weaknesses in process can affect the clarity, effectiveness, and legitimacy of primary legislation.

12.1.1 LEGISLATIVE PROCESS AND PARLIAMENTARY SUPREMACY

Parliamentary supremacy gives Acts of Parliament ultimate legal authority: once a bill has passed both Houses and received Royal Assent, it cannot be set aside by any court or any other public body.[1] Yet the legitimacy of this principle depends not only on the formal rule but also on the quality and fairness of the process that produces legislation. If bills are poorly drafted, insufficiently scrutinised, or passed without meaningful engagement with those affected, the authority of Parliament risks appearing hollow. This chapter shows that, although many parts of the legislative process function effectively, independent research and parliamentary committees continue to identify weaknesses in how legislation is prepared, examined, and reviewed.

As discussed in Chapter 3, A. V. Dicey distinguished between *legal sovereignty (or 'supremacy')*—the rule that Parliament may make or unmake any law—and *political sovereignty*, which lies with the electorate whose will Parliament is supposed to express.[2] That distinction raises an immediate question: how far does Parliament in the 2020s reflect the people it claims to represent? The House of Commons has undoubtedly become more diverse but still falls short of reflecting the UK population. Around 40 per cent of MPs are women and about 14 per cent are from minority ethnic backgrounds, compared with roughly 17 per cent of the population. Fewer than one in five MPs come from working-class occupations, and around 90 per cent hold university degrees—far higher than the national average. Nor does the composition of the Commons necessarily mirror the balance of political opinion across the country: the first-past-the-post electoral system rewards concentrated party support and often produces large parliamentary majorities from a minority of votes. Turnout at recent general elections has hovered around two-thirds of eligible voters, with participation lowest among younger people, renters, and those on lower incomes. This further limits how far the Commons reflects the views and experiences of the whole population. The range of voices heard in parliamentary evidence sessions during the legislative process reflects similar imbalances, as committees often turn to a familiar set of experts and organizations rather than those directly affected by proposed laws. The unelected House of Lords is less representative still: about 30 per cent of peers are women and around 6 per cent are from minority ethnic backgrounds, with most drawn from older, professional, and privately educated backgrounds.

Concerns about how representative Parliament is happen across the political spectrum. For some critics on the right, an unrepresentative legislature symbolises an unresponsive political establishment that frustrates the 'will of the people'.[3] For some on the left, it reflects deep structural inequalities

[1] See Chapter 3

[2] A. V. Dicey, *Introduction to the Study of the Law of the Constitution* (10th edn, Macmillan 1959).

[3] For example, Reform UK's 2024 manifesto *Our Contract with You* said, 'We are ruled by an out-of-touch political class who have turned their backs on our country' (p. 1).

in whose voices shape law and whose interests are heard.[4] From these contrasting perspectives, questions of representation and legitimacy remain central to how legislatures—and the UK's rule of parliamentary supremacy—are interpreted and defended in contemporary constitutional debate.[5]

PAUSE FOR REFLECTION

If Parliament's authority rests on its claim to represent the will of the people, what are the implications when participation is uneven and the voices shaping legislation come mainly from the same social and professional circles?

12.1.2 LEGISLATIVE PROCESS AND THE RULE OF LAW

As discussed in Chapter 4, a central difficulty in the British constitution is how to reconcile the doctrine of parliamentary supremacy with the principle of the rule of law. The idea that Parliament may make or unmake any law—even one that restricts fundamental rights—sits uneasily with the expectation that legislation should comply with basic standards of legality, fairness, and respect for individual liberty. In response, Parliament has developed structured procedures and constitutional standards intended to steer law-making away from such risks. Specialist committees in the House of Lords, including the Constitution Committee and the Joint Committee on Human Rights, play a central role in this work by identifying when bills raise rule-of-law concerns and by reminding parliamentarians of the constitutional principles at stake. The House of Lords can delay the passage of a bill before it receives Royal Assent, but if the government-controlled House of Commons insists, it can ultimately enact the bill without the Lords' consent.

Recent Acts of Parliament have raised concerns about their consistency with the rule of law and the protection of fundamental rights. The Public Order Act 2023 broadened police powers to restrict protest, leading to fears that its wide definitions could deter lawful demonstrations and free expression. The Illegal Migration Act 2023 curtailed access to asylum and judicial review for people arriving irregularly, with parliamentary committees warning that it may breach international obligations and weaken legal accountability. The Higher Education (Freedom of Speech) Act 2023, introduced to strengthen academic freedom, has been criticised for creating overlapping duties and potential conflicts with equality law. Taken together, these Acts show how parliamentary supremacy allows legislation to be enacted that may test the limits of the rule of law.

PAUSE FOR REFLECTION

Parliament can, in principle, pass any law it wishes. Does that make the rule of law vulnerable to oppressive political power, or does it show how flexible the UK constitution can be? As you read this chapter, consider what safeguards exist to prevent Parliament from using its supremacy in ways that undermine legality or fundamental rights.

[4] For example, the leader of the Green Party of England and Wales, Zack Polanski, railed against a 'political class poisoned by extreme wealth' in his speech to the party's conference in October 2025: Chris Jarvis, 'Zack Polanski delivers first speech to Green Party conference as the party's news new leadership' *Bright Green* (3 October 2025) https://bright-green.org/2025/10/03/zack-polanski-delivers-first-speech-to-green-party-conference-as-the-partys-new-leadership accessed 11 November 2025.

[5] For a political science exploration, see D. Judge and C. Leston-Bandeira, 'What it matters to keep asking why legislatures matter' (2021) 27(2) *The Journal of Legislative Studies* 155.

12.1.3 LEGISLATIVE PROCESS AND SEPARATION OF POWERS

The constitutional division of responsibilities between Parliament, the executive, and the judiciary is sometimes described in simple terms. As Lord Reed observed, '*in accordance with the principle of Parliamentary sovereignty, the Government and other public bodies can only exercise powers given to them by Parliamentary legislation . . . The courts can only decide the disputes before them, including disputes relating to the exercise of Government and other public power, in accordance with the law*'.[6] This captures the traditional understanding of the separation of powers: Parliament makes the law, the executive implements it, and the courts interpret and apply it.

In practice, however, modern law-making rarely conforms to this neat division. Almost all Acts of Parliament originate as government bills—drafted to give effect to government policy. Legislative drafting is an executive function carried out by around 50 specialist lawyers in the Office of the Parliamentary Counsel, based in Whitehall. (As we note in Chapter 13, delegated legislation is drafted within government departments.) Bills are not prepared by lawyers employed by Parliament. Government ministers—one in the Commons and one in the Lords—guide each bill through its stages. Most successful amendments made to bills are proposed by ministers rather than by other MPs or peers. The government also controls the timetable for debate and can curtail discussion, especially in the Commons, by using its majority to move a bill forward. As a result, some legislation receives only limited scrutiny.

Other constitutional systems draw sharper institutional boundaries. For example, in the United States, members of the executive branch may not sit in Congress, so the government cannot introduce or steer legislation directly. Bills are introduced by members of Congress, though many reflect proposals developed in the executive departments. Committees of the House of Representatives and the Senate play a dominant role in drafting, amending, and scrutinising legislation before it reaches the floor for debate.

A central theme of this chapter, and of Chapter 13, is that in the United Kingdom the executive plays a decisive role in law-making. To say that 'Parliament is the legislature' is formally true but substantially incomplete. The government initiates most policy, drafts most bills, determines the pace of parliamentary scrutiny, decides when Acts come into force, and makes extensive use of delegated legislation. Government is involved in every stage of the legislative process. Many critics—and occasionally governments themselves—argue that this concentration of control weakens Parliament's capacity to scrutinise and, where appropriate, resist the government's legislative agenda.

PAUSE FOR REFLECTION

If the government controls nearly every stage of the legislative process, is this evidence that the UK cannot be said to have a meaningful separation of powers? What practical reforms might help Parliament exercise more independent scrutiny of government-sponsored legislation?

If Parliament is meant to represent the people, what does it mean when large sections of the population—particularly younger voters, people on lower incomes, and those who rent rather than own homes—are less likely to vote in elections? How might this affect whose interests are heard when laws are made?

[6] Lord Reed (President of the UK Supreme Court), Response to a call for evidence produced by the Independent Review of Administrative Law Panel (2020) https://www.supremecourt.uk/uploads/iral_response_26_october_2020_019d602d30.pdf accessed 11 November 2025.

12.2 THE POLICY-MAKING PROCESS: OVERVIEW

The main purpose of legislation is to give legal backing to government policies. Political scientists have spilt much ink over the definition and characteristics of 'policy'.[7] For the purposes of this chapter, we can say that government policy is an authoritative determination by ministers and civil servants of what will be done about something. Examples of that 'something' include: the climate change crisis; ensuring that British manufacturing industry survives the economic downturn; the challenge of ensuring financial support for people during the Covid pandemic; dealing with antisocial behaviour; and so on.

S. James, *British Government: A Reader in Policy Making* (1997, London: Routledge), pp. 1–2

The Policy Making Process

What is a policy? The working definition [. . .] is: a course of action which the government has taken a deliberate decision to adopt. This should be distinguished from a government's philosophy. A government comes into office with a certain set of ideas and values—its philosophy—and the government's policies are the practical plans through which that philosophy is translated into practice. So the Labour government came to power in 1974 with a philosophical intent of great social equality; increasing state pensions was one way of contributing to that aim. [. . .] A policy may be painstakingly constructed over years, or cobbled together in hours. And it is made in different ways on different subjects: the decisive way in which the government devised—and then scrapped—unit fines contrasts with the bumbling prevarication over the 1964 race relations bill. None the less, it is possible to chart a 'policy process', the various stages through which a policy will pass as it develops.

James suggests that there are six stages, as follows.

(a) A subject becomes an issue.
(b) The issue gets onto the policy agenda. (Other authors may group these two stages together as 'policy initiation'.)
(c) The government investigates an issue.
(d) The government takes a decision.
(e) There follow the stages of legislation and legitimization.
(f) The final stage is that of policy implementation and review.

For now, we are interested in stages (a)–(d)—in other words, the things that happen before a bill is introduced to Parliament by the government. Of particular interest for us is what constitutional and legal constraints and incentives control these processes.

Policy-making takes place at many different speeds. Sometimes, the government feels the need to formulate a policy and seek to implement it quickly. For example, the Social Security (Up-Rating of Benefits) Bill was introduced in the House of Commons on 8 September 2021, to allow the Secretary of State for Work and Pensions for one year only not to increase old age pensions for the following

[7] For further insights, see P. Cairney et al, 'The state of British policymaking: How can the UK government become more effective?' (2024) 77 *Parliamentary Affairs* 837.

financial year to keep up with average weekly earnings, as earnings were soaring and the government decided that this would be unaffordable. The bill completed all its stages in the Commons on a single day (20 September) and in the House of Lords over 26 days and received Royal Assent on 17 November 2021. A spate of 'fast tracked' bills led the House of Lords Constitution Committee to conduct an inquiry into rapidly made legislation in 2008–09.[8] The Committee called for a requirement that ministers introducing bills in these circumstances should make a statement explaining why fast-tracking was thought necessary, what consultation there has been with interested parties, and other matters. The Committee also recommended that there should be a presumption in favour of bills that are being fast-tracked including a 'sunset clause', which would require the Act of Parliament to be debated and renewed after 18 months or some other specified period; it would continue in force only if that was approved by a positive vote. The Committee also recommended that bills that had been fast-tracked through Parliament should be subject to post-legislative scrutiny ideally within one year.[9]

Normally, the development of policy and legislation takes much longer—sometimes years.

B. Jones, D. Kavanagh, M. Moran, and P. Norton, *Politics UK* (2004, Harlow: Pearson), p. 597

> Each government decision has a long and complex provenance, but all must start somewhere. It is tempting to think that they originate, eureka-like, in the minds of single individuals, but they are more often the produce of debate or a general climate of opinion involving many minds. Policy initiatives, moreover, can originate in all parts of the political system. Setting the political agenda is a curiously elusive process. Items can be deliberately introduced by the government, and clearly it has many routes available to it, e.g. Tony Blair in the summer of 1999 announcing in an interview that fox hunting really would be banned. [. . .] The media too have enormous power to set the agenda: Michael Buerk's reports from Ethiopia detailing the scale of the famine that touched the nation and initiated assistance. [. . .]
>
> The public's role in policy making is usually limited to (the democratically vital function of) voting for a particular policy package at general elections. They do have other occasional opportunities, however, for example the referendums on the EC and Scottish and Welsh devolution [. . .], and pressures can be built up through lobbying MPs. Occasionally, events occur that create widespread public concern, and governments often take action in the wake of them. For example, legislation on dogs was enacted after a spate of attacks by dogs on children one summer in the 1980s, and after the Dunblane shootings of March 1996 handguns were banned. In many cases—as in the two just cited—such precipitate action, in reaction to the sudden rousing of public opinion, proves to be poorly framed and receives much criticism.

12.3 GOVERNMENT CONSULTATIONS

This section examines the government's legal and constitutional obligations to consult before introducing a bill to Parliament. Consultation matters because it affects both the quality and legitimacy of legislation: it enables those likely to be affected to contribute evidence and perspective, improves policy design, and helps ensure that new laws command public confidence. Yet the law draws important boundaries around when consultation is required, and how far the courts will intervene if it is inadequate.

[8] House of Lords Constitution Committee, *Fast-track Legislation: Constitutional Implications and Safeguards*, Fifteenth Report, Session 2008–09 (HL Paper 116).

[9] See later section 12.10 'Post-legislative scrutiny'.

12.3.1 REFERENDUMS ON CONSTITUTIONAL CHANGE

In countries with codified constitutions, amendments to the constitutional text often require approval in a referendum—a national vote on a specific question. The United Kingdom does not have a codified constitution, but referendums have nonetheless been used to test public consent before Parliament passes legislation to give effect to major constitutional change. By international standards, their use has been limited. Only three referendums have covered the whole UK: on membership of the European Communities in 1975, on replacing the House of Commons voting system in 2011, and on membership of the European Union again in 2016. Parliament has also legislated for referendums in particular parts of the UK, with questions on devolution, whether Northern Ireland (1973) or Scotland (2014) should leave the United Kingdom, and proposals for regional government in England. Under section 1 of the Northern Ireland Act 1998, the Secretary of State must order a border poll if it appears likely that a majority of voters in Northern Ireland would support leaving the United Kingdom to join a united Ireland.

When the UK government decides to hold a referendum, this must be authorised by an Act of Parliament. For example, the European Union Referendum Act 2015 provided the legal basis for the 2016 vote on the question, 'Should the United Kingdom remain a member of the European Union or leave the European Union?'. Part VII of the Political Parties, Elections and Referendums Act 2000 establishes the general legal framework for conducting referendums, including a requirement that the wording of the question be reviewed by the independent Electoral Commission. What the 2000 Act does *not* do is specify the circumstances in which a referendum should be held. In 2009–10, the House of Lords Constitution Committee examined this issue and, as the following extract shows, it was not persuaded that referendums are an inherently good idea.

House of Lords Constitution Committee, *Referendums in the United Kingdom* 12th Report of Session 2009–10, HL Paper 99, paras 62, 93–94

62. The balance of the evidence that we have heard leads us to the conclusion that there are significant drawbacks to the use of referendums. In particular, we regret the ad hoc manner in which referendums have been used, often as a tactical device, by the government of the day. Referendums may become a part of the UK's political and constitutional practice. Where possible, cross-party agreement should be sought as to the circumstances in which it is appropriate for referendums to be used.

93. [. . .] The UK's experience of referendums does not offer any consistency in terms of judging what constitutes a 'fundamental constitutional issue'.

94. Notwithstanding our view that there are significant drawbacks to the use of referendums, we acknowledge arguments that, if referendums are to be used, they are most appropriately used in relation to fundamental constitutional issues. We do not believe that it is possible to provide a precise definition of what constitutes a 'fundamental constitutional issue'. Nonetheless, we would consider to fall within this definition any proposals:

- To abolish the Monarchy;
- To leave the European Union; [This was before the 2016 referendum]
- For any of the nations of the UK to secede from the Union;
- To abolish either House of Parliament;
- To change the electoral system for the House of Commons;
- To adopt a written constitution; and
- To change the UK's system of currency.

This is not a definitive list of fundamental constitutional issues, nor is it intended to be.

In 2022, the Scottish Government sought to hold a second independence referendum without the consent of the UK government. The UK Supreme Court held that the Scottish Parliament lacks competence to legislate for such a vote because the Union between Scotland and England is a matter 'reserved' to Westminster under the Scotland Act 1998.[10] The judgment confirmed that any further independence referendum would require authorisation by an Act of the UK Parliament.

The question therefore remains: what principles or political expectations now govern when a referendum should be held? Lucy Atkinson and Andrew Blick have proposed a set of good-practice guidelines for the future use of referendums in the UK. The following extract summarizes the first three.

L. Atkinson and A. Blick, *Referendums and the Constitution* (2017, The Constitution Society), pp. 127–131 (abridged)

1. Referendums can enhance democracy, but they can also be detrimental to it. In the UK, the use of referendums has had both positive and negative democratic manifestations. In the context of UK democracy, they should be deployed sparingly. They should be used as a means of ensuring major changes take place on a basis of broader than usual consent; they should not be deployed purely for partisan purposes, or in a way that undermines democratic principles.

2. Referendums have generally been applied to decisions that can be regarded as constitutional in nature. But over what issues, precisely, should they be held? It is useful to distinguish between three categories when considering whether a referendum should be held on a particular subject. First, there are courses of action that should be embarked upon only after receiving approval in a referendum. They might be considered, in the UK context, entrenched. This category would include the abolition of the devolved institutions of Wales, Scotland or Northern Ireland; the creation of new devolved legislatures in England; and the secession of any part of the Union; all of which would necessarily be subject to approval in the territories concerned. Major transfers of sovereignty for the whole UK should be subject to popular votes across the entire country, though definitions of this kind of issue may be contested. Second, it is useful to consider whether there are matters over which a referendum should never be held. This group is most likely to involve personal freedom and the rule of law. To hold public votes on such subjects is to court the risk of populist violation of human rights. For instance, perhaps the status of the European Convention of Human Rights in UK law should not be the subject of a referendum; nor should the universal application of due process of law. The third category covers all those matters that do not fit in the first two. It is possible that a future government will encounter an issue – that may well be constitutional in nature, but not inevitably so – of such controversy or importance that it feels it should consult the public on the proper response. [. . .]

3. It is undesirable for a referendum to create a circumstance in which a UK government feels obliged to implement a major public policy with serious implications for its overall programme to which it and the UK Parliament (especially the House of Commons) were opposed. For this reason, referendums on major initiatives of this kind should generally take place because a government wants to embark upon them, not because it is seeking permission to avoid them. [. . .]

Atkinson and Blick go on to identify other principles, including that the binding or advisory nature of the result should be stated clearly from the outset; opportunities for government manipulation should be minimised; and, where the choice is particularly grave, thresholds or super-majorities may be appropriate. They conclude that referendums should never be regarded as producing mandates that override the ordinary principles of representative democracy and the rule of law.

[10] *Reference by the Lord Advocate on devolution issues under paragraph 34 of Schedule 6 to the Scotland Act 1998* [2022] UKSC 31.

While the use of referendums is now an established feature of UK constitutional practice, many constitutionally significant reforms have still been introduced without a public vote. These include the creation of the UK Supreme Court under the Constitutional Reform Act 2005, successive reforms to the composition of the House of Lords, and the incorporation of the European Convention on Human Rights through the Human Rights Act 1998.

PAUSE FOR REFLECTION

If a future government sought to repeal the Human Rights Act 1998 and withdraw from the Convention, should that decision be put to a referendum? What arguments can you think of for and against doing so?

12.3.2 MANIFESTO PLEDGES TO LEGISLATE

Public consultation through formal referendums on specific questions is rare and reserved for the most constitutionally significant legislative proposals. But public support for some legislative proposals may be tested through the general election manifesto of the political party that forms the government. For example, the Labour Party's 2024 manifesto pledged that '*Labour will legislate where the Conservatives have failed, overhauling the regulation of the private rented sector*', and the Labour Government went on to introduce the bill that became the Renters' Rights Act 2025. By contrast, some major reforms—including those of clear constitutional importance—have not been foreshadowed in any manifesto. The Labour Party's 2001 manifesto, for instance, said nothing about plans to create the UK Supreme Court, later established by the Constitutional Reform Act 2005.

Who is allowed to vote in referendums—residents rather than expatriates, citizens rather than long-term residents—also affects whose interests are represented when major constitutional decisions are made.

Manifesto pledges are political promises rather than legally binding commitments. As Lord Denning observed in a case concerning a local government manifesto: '*A manifesto issued by a political party—in order to get votes—is not to be taken as gospel. . . It may contain —and often does contain — promises or proposals that are quite unworkable*'.[11] Attempts to enforce manifesto commitments through the courts have consistently failed. In *JR83 (No 2) v The Prime Minister*, the Northern Ireland Court of Appeal rejected a judicial review challenge to Prime Minister Boris Johnson's decision to sign the EU Withdrawal Agreement and Northern Ireland Protocol.

JR83 (No 2) v The Prime Minister
[2021] NICA 49, Morgan LCJ

28. We do not accept that there is any legal limit to the power to ratify the treaty established by the promises contained in the Conservative manifesto. Such promises do not give rise to any legitimate expectation in law[[12]] and issues in relation to them are managed in the political rather than the legal

[11] *Bromley London Borough Council v Greater London Council* [1983] 1 AC 768. The pan-city local authority had issued a 180-page manifesto which included a commitment to cut bus and tube fares. The courts held that councillors acted unlawfully when they gave 'undue weight' to their manifesto commitments.

[12] On legitimate expectation as a ground of judicial review, see Chapter 19.

process. As Lord Bingham explained at paragraph 29 of *A v Secretary of State for the Home Department* [2005] 1 AC 68: 'The more purely political (in a broad or narrow sense) a question is, the more appropriate it will be for political resolution and the less likely it is to be an appropriate matter for judicial decision. The smaller, therefore, will be the potential role of the court. It is the function of political and not judicial bodies to resolve political questions'.

PAUSE FOR REFLECTION

General-election manifestos set out the policies a political party promises to pursue if it wins power. Yet, as the courts have made clear, such pledges are not legally enforceable. If a government fails to deliver a key manifesto commitment, what forms of accountability remain available? Are political promises ever so important that they should carry legal weight?

12.3.3 ROUTINE CONSULTATION BEFORE LEGISLATING

Even when a commitment to legislate appears in the governing party's general-election manifesto—and many policies do not—such pledges rarely provide the level of detail needed by those likely to be affected by the proposed law. Individuals, civil-society organizations, and interest groups therefore depend on opportunities to engage with government during the policy-development stage. Since 2000, the UK government has issued guidance to departments on when and how to conduct public consultations to inform policy design. The current *Consultation Principles* (Cabinet Office, 2018) set out eleven concise principles intended to make consultation processes more effective and transparent.[13] Among them are that consultations should be clear and concise, consultations should be informative, and consultations should last for a proportionate amount of time.

The approach of successive governments to public consultation has attracted criticism. In 2015, a House of Lords committee reviewing consultation practice found that, although many departmental consultations were effective and served both public and governmental needs, 'too many examples' remained where significant policy developments were preceded by 'poorly conceived consultation exercises'.[14] The committee's findings prompted the Government to revise its guidance, leading to publication of the current *Consultation Principles* in 2018.

Failure to follow the Consultation Principles or other consultation obligations before introducing a Bill to Parliament does not, in itself, provide a ground for legal challenge. In *R (on the application of A) v Secretary of State for the Home Department* [2022] EWHC 360 (Admin), a group of asylum seekers sought judicial review in relation to the Nationality and Borders Bill, introduced in the House of Commons in July 2021. The Home Secretary had earlier presented to Parliament a policy document announcing that a public consultation and engagement process would be undertaken. That process lasted six weeks. The claimants argued that the consultation arrangements were discriminatory under the Equality Act 2010 (for example, no provision was made for non-English speakers). They also claimed there was a breach of the 'Gunning principles', which are four common law requirements for a lawful consultation: it must occur when proposals are still at a formative

[13] Cabinet Office, *Consultation Principles* (19 March 2018) https://www.gov.uk/government/publications/consultation-principles-guidance/consultation-principles-2018 accessed 9 November 2025.

[14] House of Lords Secondary Legislation Scrutiny Committee, *Inquiry into Government Consultation Practice*, 22nd Report of Session 2014–15, HL Paper 98, para. 52.

stage; provide sufficient information for informed response; allow adequate time for responses; and require conscientious consideration of those responses before a final decision is made.[15] The aim of the litigation was to '*inform "Parliament", in dealing with the Bill, about what "weight" to attach to the (unlawful) consultation exercise*' (para. 6). Fordham J refused permission to continue with the judicial review claim.

R (on the application of A) v Secretary of State for the Home Department [2022] EWHC 360 (Admin), para. 26

> A declaration that an applicable legal standard was breached, in the consultation and engagement process culminating in the operative decisions as to the design of the Bill to introduce into Parliament, would, in my judgment, clearly constitute a breach of Parliamentary privilege and the constitutional separation of powers. [. . .] A declaration from a judicial review Court, declaring that the consultation which preceded the Bill and informed its design was unlawful would – even if the Court bent over backwards to make very clear that that was the scope and extent of its judgment and its declaration – clearly raise questions about whether some step ought to be taken in light of that conclusion of law by the Court.

Note that the same constitutional sensitivities do not arise when a claimed failure to consult lawfully concerns a minister exercising delegated legislative powers (see Chapter 13). In several cases, courts have quashed regulations as unlawfully made where a minister failed to comply with statutory or common-law consultation requirements.[16]

QUESTION

The Widget Manufacturers Association (WMA) is a trade body representing the interests of UK widget producers. A Bill has been introduced to Parliament to restrict the export of widgets to countries where the Secretary of State believes they could be used to facilitate human rights abuses against political opponents. The proposed restrictions go much further than the brief pledge on the issue in the governing party's general-election manifesto. Although the Government held a public consultation before introducing the Bill, the WMA believes it asked the wrong questions and ignored key economic impacts.

What advice would you give the WMA about the prospects of bringing a claim for judicial review, considering constitutional principles on consultation and the limits of review in relation to primary legislation? Would your answer be different if, instead of a Bill, the new rules were contained in draft delegated legislation?

[15] See Lord Woolf MR in *R (on the application of Coughlan) v North and East Devon Health Authority* [2001] QB 213 at 108, approving *R . v Brent LBC Ex p. Gunning* (1985) 84 LGR 168.

[16] See e.g. *R (on the application of The Associated Society of Locomotive Engineers and Firemen) v Secretary of State for Business and Trade* [2023] EWHC 1781 (Admin).

12.4 DRAFTING BILLS

In the United Kingdom, the drafting of government bills is a highly specialized and centralized process. Responsibility lies with a team of around fifty Parliamentary Counsel—government lawyers based in the Office of Parliamentary Counsel (OPC)—who prepare bills and advise departments. Drafting begins once a department issues formal 'instructions' setting out the policy to be implemented. Work is typically allocated to small teams, allowing collaboration and peer review.

The next extract, by Sir Geoffrey Bowman, a long-serving First Parliamentary Counsel, gives a rare insider's perspective on the craft of legislative drafting and the culture of precision, analysis, and clarity that underpins the OPC's work.

G. Bowman, 'Why is there a Parliamentary Counsel Office?' (2005) 26 *Statute Law Review* 69, 69, 81 (footnotes omitted)

Let me start with a homely insight into the drafter's mind. Some time ago a table in my room at work was sent away for french-polishing. When it came back it had a notice on it saying 'Nothing must be placed on this table.' I immediately thought that there were at least two things wrong. First, if nothing was to be placed on the table how did the notice get put onto it? And secondly, for how long was nothing to be put onto it? It defeats the object of a table if nothing can ever be put onto it. So I mentally redrafted the notice so that it read: 'Nothing (except this notice) must be placed on this table until such time as the french-polisher allows it.' But it does not stop there. What happens if the french-polisher dies or becomes ill or insane or goes out of business before he approves of the table's use? That may give you some idea of the slightly mad world that legislative drafters inhabit. [. . .]

The process of legislative drafting needs someone who will stand back; who will ruthlessly analyse the ideas; who will question everything with a view to producing something that stands up to scrutiny in Parliament and in the courts; who will break concepts down to their essential components; and who will then express them in easily digestible provisions and in language that is unambiguous, clear and simple. I think the Parliamentary Counsel Office achieves this by recruiting people with the right aptitude, and then by giving them a long and careful training. That is why we have a Parliamentary Counsel Office.

As for whether the job could be done by lawyers in private practice, it is interesting that there was an experiment in 1996 when part of the Finance Bill was drafted by private practitioners. It was not a success, and has not been repeated. As Daintith and Page say in their book *The Executive in the Constitution*: 'As well as being very expensive the contractors' work was thought to be opaque and "over-drafted".'

After researching the relevant field of law and analysing what it is the department seems to be seeking to achieve, drafting begins. Counsel hold meetings with department lawyers and officials as and when needed. Counsel see themselves as technicians rather than policy-makers. [. . .]

Bowman's reflections capture the analytical discipline and technical skill that remain the hallmarks of legislative drafting. While his account evokes the OPC's long tradition, legislative drafting is not static. Two decades on, the OPC and comparable offices in other jurisdictions are engaging with new technologies, including the use of artificial intelligence (AI) to enhance the efficiency and quality of drafting. As discussed in Chapter 8, the increasing use of automated decision-making in government raises important questions about how legislation itself is conceived and written.

Traditional drafting assigns powers and duties to public authorities—most often to ministers referred to in statutes as 'the Secretary of State'. In practice, officials usually exercise these powers on the minister's behalf under the Carltona principle, which treats their acts as legally those of the minister. Many decisions continue to be made through human review of paper or digital documents, while major or politically sensitive matters are taken personally by the minister, supported by civil service and legal advice. Alongside these established practices, interest is now growing in rules as code (RaC), an approach that seeks to express legislation simultaneously in natural language and in a computer-readable format. The next extract, by Rónán Kennedy, introduces this idea.

R. Kennedy, 'Rules as code and the rule of law: ensuring effective judicial review of administration by software' (2024) 16(1) *Law, Innovation and Technology* 170, 171–2.

Full implementations of RaC involve legislators, drafters and programmers working in close collaboration to develop a set of legal rules which are accompanied by software code which purports to entirely implement those rules in a form which can be re-used either as a stand-alone programme or incorporated into a larger system. RaC produces a human-language text as well as an official coded version. Technology is used as an aid to understanding both in drafting and in implementation, so that the drafters and policy-makers can verify that it operates as they expect. It can also involve government publishing this code in an openly-accessible application programming interface for re-use by third parties.

Kennedy notes studies suggesting that RaC can 'improve the alignment between intention and implementation, enable more modelling, speed up delivery, and improve consistency' (p. 175). Given the current capabilities of AI, RaC appears most effective for legislation involving highly structured, rules-based decision making, and less suited to open-textured standards such as 'reasonable', which are not easily reduced to code. Some commentators worry that widespread reliance on RaC could gradually shift legislative design towards rigid, rule-driven systems, reducing the space for human judgement. This concern is explored in the following extract from Andrew Le Sueur.

A. Le Sueur, 'Robot Government: Automated Decision-Making and its Implications for Parliament' ch. 9 in A. Horne and A. Le Sueur (eds), *Parliament: Legislation and Accountability* (2016, Hart Publishing), pp. 192–3

The 'rules versus discretion' debate is a long running conversation among administrative lawyers and policy makers. Most fields of administration have, over the years, included a mix of hard-edged rules leading to legal entitlements (e.g., no licence may be issued to a person who has an unspent criminal conviction) and issues on which professional judgement or discretion needs to be brought to bear because the power conferred on the administrator is flexible or open-textured (e.g., licensees must be a 'fit and proper person'). At different times, the political preferences for one or other approach have waxed and waned. The reality has usually been nuanced. As Titmuss explains 'Law and discretion are not separated by a sharp line but by overlapping zones. Exercising discretion may be a part of finding facts and applying law, and finding facts may be a part of exercising discretion'.

One hypothesis about automated decision-making is that it will provide an incentive for decision-making systems to be designed that emphasize hard-edged rules and reduce or eliminate the capacity of officials to provide personalised solutions. Computers have to work within the straightjacket of the algorithms with which they are programmed. This challenges the model described in 1980 (before the rise of automation) by Lipsky in his classic account, where he argued that 'The essence of street-level bureaucracies is that they require people to make decisions about other people. Street-level bureaucrats have discretion because the nature of service provision calls for human judgment that cannot be programmed and for which machines cannot substitute'.

PAUSE FOR REFLECTION

If laws were routinely written in both prose and computer code, how might this change the balance between legal certainty and administrative discretion? Would it enhance transparency and consistency—or risk narrowing law and policy to what can be expressed in code?

12.5 PRE-LEGISLATIVE SCRUTINY OF DRAFT BILLS

From time to time, the government publishes a draft version of a bill (usually as a Command Paper)[17] some months, or even years, before it a bill is formally introduced to Parliament. This process allows a parliamentary select committee—either a departmental committee or a specially appointed joint committee of both Houses—to take evidence from ministers, officials, and outside experts. The committee then reports on the draft, making recommendations that the government may consider before finalising the bill for introduction.

An example is the Draft Terrorism (Protection of Premises) Bill, often referred to as Martyn's Law. Published by the Conservative government in May 2023, the bill aimed to strengthen security and safety at public venues following the Manchester Arena terrorist attack in which Martyn Hett was one of the 22 people killed. The House of Commons Home Affairs Committee examined the draft, welcoming its purpose but raising significant concerns about the potential burden on small premises such as pubs and village halls. After the 2024 general election, the incoming Labour government introduced a revised bill, and the Terrorism (Protection of Premises) Act 2025 received Royal Assent in April 2025.

The following extract from the House of Commons Modernisation Committee sets out the main reasons why publishing draft bills for early scrutiny is regarded as good legislative practice.

House of Commons Modernization Committee, *The Legislative Process*, First Report, Session 1997-98 (HC 190), para. 20

There is almost universal agreement that pre-legislative scrutiny is right in principle, subject to the circumstances and nature of the legislation. It provides an opportunity for the House as a whole, for individual backbenchers, and for the Opposition to have a real input into the form of the actual legislation which subsequently emerges, not least because Ministers are likely to be far more receptive to suggestions for change before the Bill is actually published. It opens Parliament up to those outside affected by legislation. At the same time such pre-legislative scrutiny can be of real benefit to the Government. It could, and indeed should, lead to less time being needed at later stages of the legislative process; the use of the Chair's powers of selection would naturally reflect the extent and nature of previous scrutiny and debate. Above all, it should lead to better legislation and less likelihood of subsequent amending legislation.

[17] A Command Paper is an official document presented to Parliament by a government minister 'by Command of His Majesty'. It is used to publish a wide range of materials—such as government policy statements, White and Green Papers, treaties, and reports from independent inquiries. Command Papers are numbered sequentially (e.g. Cm 1234). Alternatively, draft clauses (not a whole bill) are sometimes more informally published on departmental websites for consultation.

While few disagree with the principle of pre-legislative scrutiny, the extent to which it is used has varied greatly. In practice, it tends to be reserved for less controversial measures or for complex technical legislation where early expert input is particularly valuable. The extract below from Andrew Kennon, a senior parliamentary official, explains some of the political and practical constraints.

A. Kennon, 'Pre-legislative scrutiny of draft Bills' [2005] *Public Law* 477, 479–80

No Bill that is highly controversial between the political parties has been subject to pre-legislative scrutiny. [. . .] Legislation starts in Whitehall. Within any department officials and Ministers have a list of subjects on which they would like to change the law. Ministers, with a weather eye on the vane above No.10 Downing Street, will have political priorities. Officials are also conscious of matters that need improving but which do not engage political attention. The Government's annual legislative programme needs to include high profile political measures. Limits on parliamentary time mean that the legislative programme of a couple of dozen Bills has to be split between the contentious and the non-contentious. Few departments would presume to claim more than one place in each category. [. . .]

It is against this background that the Government's tentative promise that 'the presumption [is] that Bills will be published in draft for pre-legislative scrutiny unless there is good reason otherwise' needs to be considered. It is unrealistic to expect that a Minister who stands a good chance of securing a place in the legislative programme for a high profile Bill will want to delay its enactment by going through the longer process of pre-legislative scrutiny. By definition, this sort of Bill has a political impetus that may overwhelm detailed scrutiny. An evidence-taking committee might be carried away by the political avalanche behind the Bill and not have time to look at the minutiae. The understandable combat between Government and Opposition on a key issue might leave the details unexamined.

The value of pre-legislative scrutiny has been recognised repeatedly in Parliament. In 2013, the House of Commons Political and Constitutional Reform Committee described it as 'one of the best ways of improving legislation and ensuring that it meets the quality standards that Parliament and the public are entitled to expect'.[18] The Committee recommended that the publication of bills in draft should become the default, with the government required to explain any decision not to do so. The government accepted the value of pre-legislative scrutiny but declined to make it mandatory.

Despite these calls, pre-legislative scrutiny remains used only sporadically. In a 2022 report, Jess Sargeant and Jack Pannell found that, since 1997, an average of only five draft bills have been published in each parliamentary session, compared with around 35 bills introduced directly without a draft. [19] They argue for a formal requirement to conduct pre-legislative scrutiny, citing Ireland's experience as an example of a more systematic and effective approach.

PAUSE FOR REFLECTION

If pre-legislative scrutiny improves the quality of law-making, why do governments so often choose to bypass it? Should Parliament insist that draft bills become the norm, even if this slows down the lawmaking process?

[18] Political and Constitutional Affairs Committee, *Ensuring Standards in the Quality*, First Special Report, Session 2013–14 (HC 85), paras 47 and 115.

[19] J. Sargeant and J. Pannell, *The legislative process: How to empower parliament* (Bennett Institute of Public Policy/ Institute for Government 2022) p.37.

12.6 THE PARLIAMENTARY YEAR

Between general elections, Parliament organizes its workload into 'sessions'. A session usually lasts for about a year, though it may be shorter or longer. Before each session, departments submit bids for bills they wish to include in the legislative programme. The Cabinet's Parliamentary Business and Legislation Committee reviews these bids, assessing their urgency, policy fit, and readiness before advising Cabinet on which to include.

Each session starts with the State Opening of Parliament, one of Westminster's great ceremonial occasions. The King attends the House of Lords, to which MPs are summoned. From the throne, the King reads out 'the King's Speech' written by the government, outlining its planned legislation in the coming session.

12.7 PARLIAMENTARY STAGES OF A BILL

Political scientists surveying democracies have suggested that there are three kinds of legislature.[20]

(a) First, there are those that can be described as 'policy-making' or 'transformative' because they have the capacity to develop policy of their own. The US Congress is one of the few that falls into this category.

(b) Second (and this is the category into which the UK Parliament falls), there are 'policy-influencing', 'reactive', 'arena', or 'legitimizing' legislatures. They operate to modify or reject proposals from government, but they do not develop their own policies. The emphasis is on debate and ratifying decisions made elsewhere (that is, in government). One practical reason for these legislatures not being able to take a lead in policy-making is simply that they lack the resources to do so. Parliamentarians do not have a large body of advisory civil servants or much time.

(c) Third, there are legislatures that have 'little or no policy effect': their role is essentially to assent to whatever policy is made by government.

As you read the next two extracts, consider into which category the authors would fit the UK Parliament.

P. Norton, *Parliament in British Politics* (2005, Palgrave Macmillan), pp. 61–2

In terms of their impact on public policy, three types of legislature can be identified: policy-making, policy-influencing, and those with little or no policy affect. Policy-making legislatures can involve themselves in the drawing up—the making—of policy. Policy-influencing legislatures have the formal capacity to amend, even to reject, measures of policy placed before them, but they are essentially dependent on government to put forward those measures. Even if they reject a measure, they look to government to formulate and bring forward a replacement. The legislature itself does not seek to generate—or make—policy. It lacks the political will, the institutional resources or even, in some cases, the constitutional power to do so. Legislatures with little or no policy effect exist mainly to give assent to measures laid before them.

[20] See, e.g., J.E. Schwarz 'Exploring a new role in policymaking: The British House of Commons in the 1970s' (1980) 74 American Political Science Review 23.

Philip Norton (a professor of government at Hull University who is also a Conservative member of the House of Lords) concludes that, for most of its history, the UK Parliament '*has not been a policy-making body*'. He explains that the UK Parliament has looked to the executive—first the monarch, then the monarch's government—to bring forward bills for it to consider. The UK Parliament is, he argues, '*a policy-influencing legislature*'. Political scientists have generally regarded the UK Parliament as having only a very weak influence on policy formation. Recent research, however, questions this view.

M. Russell, D. Gover, and K. Wollter, 'Does the executive dominate the Westminster legislative process?: Six reasons for doubt' (2015) 68 *Parliamentary Affairs* 1, 23

This article has presented summary results from the largest study of the legislative process at Westminster for 40 years. The resulting evidence suggests that the British parliament is far less dominated by the executive than is often assumed, and that it exerts a significant influence on government policy. Despite the various dismissive statements at the start of the article (just some of the many we could have cited), the empirical evidence simply does not back these up.

A key reason for Westminster's reputation as weak is that it exhibits few visible signs of conflict with the executive: government defeats in the House of Commons are very rare, and few non-government amendments are passed in either chamber. In contrast, many hundreds of government amendments are agreed in both each year. This creates an impression not only of parliamentary weakness, but of executive dominance, with ministers freely changing their own legislation even after it has been introduced. But a more careful look at the amendment process shows that this is a misleading picture. The majority of government amendments have little substance, while most substantive changes made inside parliament in fact follow pressure from non-government parliamentarians. Meanwhile, many non-government amendments serve purposes other than seeking immediate policy change, such as 'probing', signalling to groups outside parliament, embarrassing the government or creating policy markers for the future. Published figures thus give a false impression of non-government failure, as well as of government success. We have shown that significant changes to legislation were wrought in parliament, both under the Labour government 2005–2010 and the Conservative/ Liberal Democrat coalition [2010–2015].

Perhaps most importantly, however, parliament influences the shape of legislation long before it is introduced, and continues to influence policy implementation and future development once it has been formally passed. As Judge (1993) emphasized years ago, parliament sets the political parameters within which policy must be negotiated, even where the detailed discussions largely go on between government departments and interest groups. But this was a difficult argument to make without clear, empirical evidence of parliamentary policy influence. In exploring more tangibly the power of parliament, it is clearly not sufficient to scour the official record or trace changes made within the institution. Because parliament's greatest power is one of 'anticipated reactions', detecting this requires discussion with insiders (particularly from the executive) about behind-the-scenes negotiations.

A sketch of what the scrutiny process looks like from inside Parliament is provided by David Feldman, who as well as being an academic, had practical experience of parliamentary scrutiny during his time as legal adviser to the Joint Committee on Human Rights.

D. Feldman, 'Parliamentary scrutiny of legislation and human rights' [2002] *Public Law* 323, 324

The first and essential point to bear in mind is that parliamentary scrutiny of legislation is a part-time activity for parliamentarians. In the House of Commons, MPs have a large number of other functions. They represent constituencies, and rely on their support in the constituency—both in the local party and

> among the electorate at large—to have a chance of retaining the seat at the next election. As constituency representatives, MPs spend a great deal of their time answering letters and telephone calls from constituents, holding 'surgeries' in the constituency, and following up their grievances on their behalf by writing to ministers and other public authorities, asking parliamentary questions, or (more rarely) intervening on the floor of the House. They also open fêtes, visit hospitals, and so on. Much of their local reputation, and sometimes their prospects for re-election, will depend on how they deal with issues which are important to their constituencies. [. . .] Scrutinising legislation, by contrast, attracts little publicity (unless it is concerned with controversial issues such as sexuality or abortion). It requires a great deal of concentrated attention, and must take its place in the queue of activities vying for a member's time. Particularly if the member has little expertise in the field of policy and law with which the legislation is concerned, it is quite understandable that MPs tend to rely on the directions on voting given by the party's whips, rather than attempting to analyse all legislation in depth.

Feldman goes on to explain that in the House of Lords peers are not fulltime salaried members, so many have outside jobs and roles. While there is much expertise in the Lords, research support is limited. He concludes, '*the prevailing atmosphere in both Houses gives one the feeling that people are doing important things at great speed, with remarkably little support, and in physical conditions which are improving gradually as more space is made available, but which for most members of both Houses are still cramped, uncomfortable, and inconvenient*'.

Let us now move on to consider what happens from the point at which a bill is introduced to Parliament by the government (see Figure 12.1). The basic rule is that a bill needs to progress through various stages in the House of Commons and then the House of Lords—or vice versa. About half of the 30 to 40 government bills introduced in a parliamentary session start in the Commons and about half in the Lords. There is no real significance as to which House is chosen to start the bill off, except that 'Money Bills' (bills that deal only with taxation and government expenditure) always begin in the Commons.

You can follow the progress of bills through Parliament at https://bills.parliament.uk/ and see the various reprints of each bill, updated to include amendments.

12.7.1 FIRST READING

The First Reading marks the formal introduction of a bill to Parliament. The minister rises and says, 'I beg to move, That the [short title of the bill] be now read a first time'. After a few procedural steps, the bill is authorised for publication and made available in printed form and on Parliament's website. There is no debate on the bill's content at this stage.

12.7.2 PARALLEL COMMITTEE WORK

The First Reading of a bill signals the start of scrutiny not only in the main chambers but also by several specialist cross-party committees that examine different aspects of proposed legislation. Their work takes place in parallel with the bill's formal stages. The Committees aim to publish reports in time for the Second Reading in their House, to inform debate. The main committees in relation to bills are:

- House of Lords Constitution Committee, which considers the constitutional implications of all public bills and reports on those raising significant issues. It has published a compilation of the 'legislative standards' it applies when scrutinising bills.[21]

[21] House of Lords Constitution Committee, *Legislative standards of the Constitution Committee 2017–2024* (6 May 2025) https://committees.parliament.uk/publications/47701/documents/249210/default/ accessed 10 November 2025.

- House of Lords Delegated Powers and Regulatory Reform Committee, which assesses whether bills delegate powers appropriately and subject them to the right level of parliamentary control.
- Joint Committee on Human Rights (JCHR), which examines every bill for compatibility with the European Convention on Human Rights and other human rights standards.

12.7.3 SECOND READING

The Second Reading usually takes place two to four weeks after the First Reading. It is the first opportunity for Parliament to debate the bill's substance, focusing on its general principles and policy objectives rather than on individual clauses. The responsible minister introduces the bill, outlining its purpose and political rationale. An opposition spokesperson responds, after which backbench MPs

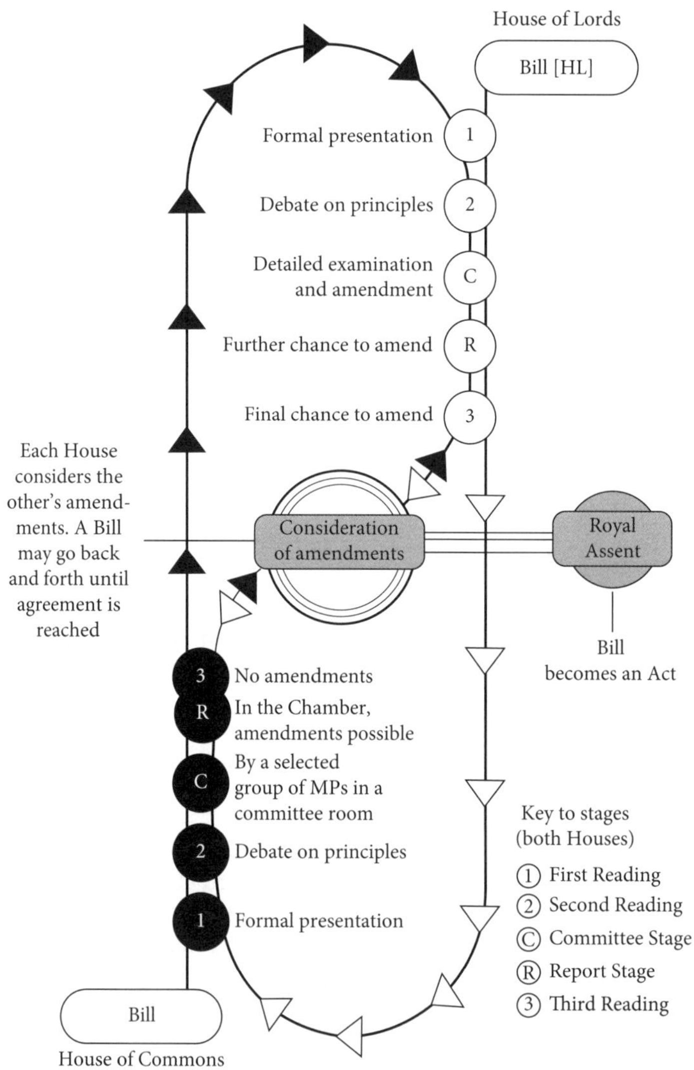

Figure 12.1 The legislative process

or peers may raise concerns about the bill's aims, likely effects, or political implications. At the end of the debate, the House votes on whether the bill should proceed to detailed scrutiny in committee. Debates are recorded in Hansard, Parliament's official transcript, which is publicly accessible online.

In the past century, only one government bill has failed to pass its Second Reading in the Commons. The Conservative government's Shops Bill 1986, which sought to liberalise Sunday trading hours, was defeated after many of its own backbench MPs voted against it. Following the vote the bill was withdrawn from the legislative programme.[22] By convention, the House of Lords does not vote down a government bill at Second Reading, especially if it implements a manifesto commitment. Known as the Salisbury-Addison Convention, this practice reflects the Lords' recognition of the elected Commons' primacy in giving effect to the government's legislative mandate.[23]

Research by Meg Russell and Daniel Gover shows that although governments almost always win the Second Reading vote, this stage still matters.[24] It helps define the political and policy framing of a bill, signals which provisions may face opposition, and can shape the amendments and concessions that follow. In the House of Lords, where governments lack a majority, Second Reading debates often provide an important platform for cross-party negotiation and expert input.

PAUSE FOR REFLECTION

If governments rarely lose a Second Reading vote, what makes this stage worth having? Is its value mainly symbolic, or does the early airing of concerns genuinely improve the quality of legislation that follows?

12.7.4 COMMITTEE STAGE

The Committee Stage usually starts two weeks later and is when detailed consideration of the policy and drafting of the bill occurs. Daniel Greenberg, a former member of the PCO, injects an air of realism as to what this means in practice in the following extract.

D. Greenberg, *Laying Down the Law: A discussion of the people, processes and problems that shape Acts of Parliament* (2011, Sweet & Maxwell), 33

> Although in theory every clause is scrutinised by Parliament, the scrutiny does not in practice extend to every provision in a meaningful way, and is carried out by persons who, and in circumstances which, make it impossible for the technicalities of each provision to be tested against the substantive policy to which it is designed to give effect.

In the Commons, this is normally in a Public Bill Committee of between 15 and 20 MPs (in proportion, party-politically, to the composition of the House as a whole). These committees are temporary: they are formed specifically to consider a bill and are dissolved at the end of that task (a few weeks or

[22] See A. Le Sueur and M. Sunkin, *Public Law* (Longman 1997) ch. 9.

[23] House of Lords Constitution Committee, *The Salisbury-Addison Convention*, 5th Report of Session 2017–19, HL Paper 28.

[24] M. Russell and D. Gover, *Legislation at Westminster: Parliamentary Actors and Influence in the Making of British Law* (OUP 2017) ch. 2.

months later). They are non-specialist: MPs chosen by the parties to serve on a committee will often have little expertise in the subject matter of the bill. They are also adversarial, operating as mini-debating chambers along party political lines. (In these three respects, Public Bill Committees differ from the permanent, specialist select committees that carry out accountability functions in the House of Commons).[25]

Since 2006, the committee's work begins with oral evidence sessions in which MPs hear from experts, campaign groups, and finally the minister in charge of the bill. A report for the Institute for Government asks how well this is working.

J. Sargeant and J. Pannell, *The Legislative Process: How to empower parliament*
(2022, Bennett Institute of Public Policy/Institute for Government), p. 7

> There is some evidence to suggest that reforms to permit public bill committees to take oral evidence from ministers, experts and civil society groups have improved their work. MPs can draw on oral evidence to strengthen their arguments and more successfully press the government for changes to bills. But oral evidence is taken on only a minority of bills – just 27% of all bills in the last five parliamentary sessions. And in addition, witnesses are often decided in an opaque manner, carved up between the opposition and the government, invited at the last minute, and rarely venture beyond the 'usual suspects'.

This pattern can mean that larger, well-resourced organizations dominate the conversation, while smaller community groups and people most directly affected by the proposed law struggle to be heard.

There is then clause-by-clause debate, with Opposition MPs seeking to argue that amendments should be made; very few, if any, of these amendments are agreed to by the Public Bill Committee (on which the governing party has a majority of members), because the government instructs the MPs of its party, who will form a majority of the committee, to vote against them. It is normal also for the government to make amendments: often they will be 'technical', to tidy up drafting points; sometimes, they will alter the policy of the bill slightly if the government has been convinced that it could be improved.

A small number of bills have their Commons committee stage taken in the main chamber, in a Committee of the Whole House (CWH). Robert Hazell traces the convention that Bills of 'first class constitutional importance' should be scrutinised in this way to 1945, when procedural reforms directed most bills going to what are now Public Bill Committees. This became an accepted convention, although, as Hazell notes, its boundaries were never clearly defined. He argues that while the convention allows more MPs to participate in debate, it limits time for detailed scrutiny. Bills considered in CWH receive fewer amendments and less line-by-line examination than those taken in Public Bill Committees.[26]

In the House of Lords, the Committee Stage normally takes place on the floor of the chamber, giving all peers interested in the bill an opportunity to table amendments seeking (in their view) to improve it. Under the Salisbury-Addison Convention, the Lords do not pass wrecking amendments that would undermine the core purpose of a bill introduced by the government to fulfil a manifesto commitment.

[25] See Chapter 9.

[26] R. Hazell, 'Time for a new convention: Parliamentary scrutiny of constitutional Bills 1997–2005' [2006] Public Law 247, 248.

12.7.5 REPORT AND THIRD READING

After the Committee Stage in the relevant house, there follow the Report and Third Reading stages. These stages often take place on the same day. They are further opportunities for MPs or peers (depending on in which House the bill is in at that time) to press for acceptance of their amendments and for the government to make its own amendments.

The government does not have a majority in the House of Lords, so controversial bills are often amended against ministers' wishes during the later stages of scrutiny. In 2023, for example, the Lords made 20 amendments to the Illegal Migration Bill despite government opposition. These included a provision that 'nothing in this Act shall require any act or omission' that conflicted with international treaties such as the UN Refugee Convention, and an amendment lowering the threshold for individuals to succeed in challenges to removal from the UK on the ground that it would expose them to 'serious harm'.

12.7.6 PING-PONG

Once the bill has been through both Houses, agreement needs to be reached on the final text that will be presented for Royal Assent. Where there is disagreement, a process informally known as 'ping-pong' begins, with proposed amendments and counter-amendments shuttling back and forth, until both Houses are willing to consent to the bill.

Although the House of Lords has the power to insist on its amendments, convention and political reality usually lead it to defer to the elected House of Commons, which has the final say on the content of legislation. For example, the 20 Lords' amendments made to the Illegal Migration Bill in 2023 against the government's wishes were overturned in the Commons.

12.7.7 INVOKING THE PARLIAMENT ACTS

The normal requirement is that a bill is passed by both the House of Commons and the House of Lords before it may receive Royal Assent. Four bills since 1949 have received Royal Assent under the terms of the Parliament Act 1911 (as amended in 1949), which permits Royal Assent to be given even though the Lords disagree with a bill: the War Crimes Act 1991, enabling prosecution of British citizens for Nazi war crimes even though they were not British at the time of the alleged atrocity; the European Parliamentary Elections Act 1999, introducing a new electoral system for elections to the European Parliament; the Sexual Offences (Amendment) Act 2000 equalizing the age of consent for gay and heterosexual teenagers; and the Hunting Act 2004, criminalizing fox hunting with dogs.

These constitutional arrangements are reflected in the Preamble to each Act. The first applies to an Act passed in the normal way.

> Be it enacted by The King's most Excellent Majesty, by and with the advice and consent of the Lords Spiritual and Temporal, and Commons, in this present Parliament assembled, and by the authority of the same, as follows:—

A second type of Preamble is used if Royal Assent is received under the terms of the Parliament Acts 1911 and 1949, when on a rare occasion the House of Lords refuses to pass a bill supported by the Commons.

> Be it enacted by The King's most Excellent Majesty, by and with the advice and consent of the Commons in this present Parliament assembled, in accordance with the provisions of the Parliament Acts 1911 and 1949, and by the authority of the same, as follows:—

12.7.8 ROYAL ASSENT, PRINTING, AND PUBLICATION

Royal Assent is the final stage of the legislative process. The grant of Royal Assent is a prerogative power of the monarch—although, by constitutional convention, it is always granted.[27]

After Royal Assent, the new Act of Parliament must be officially printed and published in print and online.[28] About six months later, one copy of the Act is printed on high-quality paper and is signed by the Clerk of the Parliaments (the senior official in the House of Lords) and lodged in the House of Lords Record Office. Benard Jackson explains that '*This is the copy to which the courts would seek access, in case of any doubt regarding the authenticity or text of a statute*'.[29]

12.8 BRINGING LEGISLATION INTO FORCE

After a bill has completed its passage through Parliament and received Royal Assent, the next step is for it to be brought into force.[30] Every Act contains a commencement provision towards its end. Some are very straightforward and say simply '*This Act comes into force on the day on which it is passed*' (that is, the day on which it received Royal Assent) or may specify a date; most are more complex. The commencement provision may grant power to a minister to bring sections into force by delegated legislation (something we look at in Chapter 13). Not knowing when new legislation is to be brought into force can be a major problem for businesses and citizens. Since 2008, a more coordinated approach has been taken, with the introduction of 'common commencement dates' twice a year.

A problem of a different sort arises if the government decides not to bring primary legislation into force. In 1993, the Home Secretary announced that he would not be bringing into force sections in the Criminal Justice Act 1988 that set out in statutory form the methods by which the Criminal Injuries Compensation Board calculates its payments to people who have suffered crime. (The Board had, in fact, been operating on a non-statutory basis since 1964.) Instead, he said, the government would instruct the Board to make future payments according to a tariff system set by the Home Office (which was going to reduce the amounts of compensation payable in many cases). The Law Lords, by a majority, held that the Home Secretary's decision was unlawful: although he was entitled to decide when to bring a section into force, he was not able to declare he would never do this and make rules contrary to the will of Parliament expressed in the Act. The government subsequently introduced its tariff scheme in a new Act.

R v Secretary of State for the Home Department, ex parte Fire Brigades Union and ors
[1995] 2 AC 513, 550

Lord Browne-Wilkinson

[. . . I]f the argument of the applicants is right, there must come a time when the Secretary of State comes under a duty to bring the statutory provisions into force and accordingly the court could grant mandamus against the Secretary of State requiring him to do so. Indeed, the applicants originally sought such an order in the present case. In my judgment it would be most undesirable that, in such circumstances, the court should intervene in the legislative process by requiring an Act of Parliament to be brought into effect.

[27] On prerogative powers, see Chapter 10.
[28] See Chapter 11 on using the official legislation.gov.uk website.
[29] B.S. Jackson, 'Who enacts statutes?' (1997) 18 Statute Law Review 177, 182.
[30] See also the discussion in Chapter 11 section 11.4.2 (Working out whether legislation is in force).

That would be for the courts to tread dangerously close to the area over which Parliament enjoys exclusive jurisdiction, namely the making of legislation.

In the absence of clear statutory words imposing a clear statutory duty, in my judgment the court should hesitate long before holding that such a provision as section 171(1) imposes a legally enforceable statutory duty on the Secretary of State.

It does not follow that, because the Secretary of State is not under any duty to bring the section into effect, he has an absolute and unfettered discretion whether or not to do so. So to hold would lead to the conclusion that both Houses of Parliament had passed the Bill through all its stages and the Act received the Royal Assent merely to confer an enabling power on the executive to decide at will whether or not to make the parliamentary provisions a part of the law. Such a conclusion, drawn from a section to which the sidenote is 'Commencement', is not only constitutionally dangerous but flies in the face of common sense. The provisions for bringing sections into force under section 171(1) apply not only to the statutory scheme but to many other provisions. For example, the provisions of Parts I, II and III relating to extradition, documentary evidence in criminal proceedings and other evidence in criminal proceedings are made subject to the same provisions. Surely, it cannot have been the intention of Parliament to leave it in the entire discretion of the Secretary of State whether or not to effect such important changes to the criminal law. In the absence of express provisions to the contrary in the Act, the plain intention of Parliament in conferring on the Secretary of State the power to bring certain sections into force is that such power is to be exercised so as to bring those sections into force when it is appropriate and unless there is a subsequent change of circumstances which would render it inappropriate to do so.

There is a second consequence of the power in section 171(1) being conferred for the purpose of bringing the sections into force. As I have said, in my view the Secretary of State is entitled to decide not to bring the sections into force if events subsequently occur which render it undesirable to do so.

But if the power is conferred on the Secretary of State with a view to bringing the sections into force, in my judgment the Secretary of State cannot himself procure events to take place and rely on the occurrence of those events as the ground for not bringing the statutory scheme into force. In claiming that the introduction of the new tariff scheme renders it undesirable now to bring the statutory scheme into force, the Secretary of State is, in effect, claiming that the purpose of the statutory power has been frustrated by his own act in choosing to introduce a scheme inconsistent with the statutory scheme approved by Parliament.

PAUSE FOR REFLECTION

Is there any constitutional problem with the executive deciding when legislation should be brought into force?

12.9 QUALITY AND EFFECTIVENESS OF LEGISLATION

At this point, the chapter turns from the process of how Acts of Parliament are made to the question of substance: does that process produce legislation that is well designed, clearly drafted, and effective in achieving its intended purpose? It is an important question because legislation gives practical effect to the rule of law—the principle that government acts must be lawful, clear, and predictable. If laws are poorly designed, they can undermine that principle by creating confusion, inconsistency, or uncertainty about rights and duties. High-quality legislation helps ensure that people can understand and comply with the law, that courts can interpret and apply it consistently, and that ministers and officials are held to clear legal standards. Assessing the quality and effectiveness of Acts of Parliament is therefore central not only to good governance but also to maintaining public confidence in the rule of law itself.

A study by a group of London School of Economics undergraduates, working with their professor, investigated whether there are distinctive features of the UK's law-making process that contribute to problems of legislative quality. To explore this question, they conducted a survey of 559 legal professionals.

LSE GV314 Group, 'Cobblers: Lawyers' views on the quality of legislation' (2024) 45 *Statute Law Review* 1

> The reason one might still hanker after a general definition of legislative quality derives from the desire to understand whether there are any broad features about the way law is made that make it more likely that defects, shortcomings, and infelicities, however defined, will be built into legislation, or at least not excluded from it. This is a particularly important point if one considers arguments by political scientists that the UK is especially bad at producing legislation. For King and Crewe the British politico-administrative system is especially 'blunder' prone. For Dunleavy the fact that the UK parliament passes what he claims to be the 'fastest law in the west' means legislation is often especially ill-thought through. Taking a wider comparative perspective, the UK 'majoritarian' form of policy making (where one party dominates the executive and legislative branch) leads to deficiencies in deliberating legislation that 'consensus' democracies such as those in Germany or Scandinavia tend to avoid.

Respondents to the survey—barristers, solicitors, and academics—identified the three most frequent problems with Acts of Parliament as their being 'unnecessarily unwieldy or complex', containing ambiguous wording, and leaving 'too much to be interpreted by secondary legislation, codes or other guidance or rules' (p. 5). The main consequences were said to be 'extra work in trying to work out what the legislation means' and 'compromising the quality of the advice lawyers can give their clients' (pp 11–12). The leading causes of poor legislative quality were lack of subject expertise among drafters, excessive amendment and regulatory layering, politically driven design, and laws becoming outdated (p. 13). The most popular remedies were greater attention to specialist legal input, wider consultation on drafting, and more resources for consolidation of the statute book (p. 14).

Dawn Oliver has argued that formal 'scrutiny standards' or checklists should guide both government and Parliament when developing and examining bills.[31] These would ensure attention to legal, constitutional, and procedural principles such as the rule of law, human rights, proper delegation of powers, and adequate consultation. Unlike many democracies, the UK often overlooks these safeguards, reflecting a divide between legal and political cultures. Oliver contends that adopting such standards would help Parliament uphold constitutional values, improve the quality of legislation, and reduce the amount of poorly conceived or overly complex law introduced by government.

Oliver and other academics working through the UCL Constitution Unit subsequently developed a detailed checklist, based on points raised by the House of Lords Constitution Committee in its reports on bills.[32] The authors explain that their project has three principal goals: (a) '*to draw attention to the*

[31] D. Oliver 'Improving the scrutiny of Bills: The case for standards and checklists' [2006] Public Law 219.

[32] J. Simson Caird, D. Oliver, and R. Hazell, *The Constitutional Standards of the House of Lords Constitution Committee*, 3rd edn (UCL Constitution Unit 2025) https://www.ucl.ac.uk/social-historical-sciences/sites/social_historical_sciences/files/constitutional-standards-third-edition.pdf accessed 10 November 2025.

normative foundations of the work of the Constitution Committee'; (b) '*to provide a potential resource for those involved in the legislative process*'; and (c) '*to contribute to the debate on the development of a code of general legislative standards that was begun by the House of Commons Select Committee on Political and Constitutional Reform*'. The following extract is of part of the section on the rule of law.

J. Simson Caird, R. Hazell, and D. Oliver, *The Constitutional Standards of the House of Lords Select Committee on the Constitution*, 3rd edn (UCL Constitution Unit 2017) (footnotes omitted)

1) The Rule of Law

1.1 Retrospective legislation

1.1.1 Enacting legislation with retrospective effect should be avoided.

1.1.2 Provisions that have retrospective effect should be drafted as narrowly as possible.

1.1.3 Individuals should not be punished or penalised for contravening what was at the time a valid legal requirement.

1.1.4 Laws should not retrospectively interfere with obligations when the liberty or criminal liability of the citizen is at stake.

1.1.5 Laws should not deprive someone of the benefit of a judgment already obtained.

1.1.6 Laws should not prevent a court from deciding pending litigation according to its merits on the basis of the law in force at the time when the proceedings were commenced.

1.1.7 Retrospective legislation should only be used when there is a compelling reason to do so.

1.1.8 A legislative power to make a provision which has retrospective effect should be justified on the basis of 'necessity', and not of 'desirability'.

The reference above to the '*development of a code of general legislative standards that was begun by the House of Commons Select Committee on Political and Constitutional Reform*' refers to an inquiry that led to a report called *Ensuring standards in the quality of legislation* published by the committee in May 2013. Quoting the Hansard Society with approval, the committee endorsed the view that '*There is no single cause for [. . .] deficient legislation. The explanation lies in a complex confluence of factors primarily related to volume, attitude, preparation and deliberation.*'[33] The committee recommended the adoption of a Code of Legislative Standards and the creation of a Joint Committee on Legislative Standards (with membership from the Commons and Lords). In its response a few months later, the government rejected both ideas. In May 2025, the House of Lords Constitution Committee did, however, take matters into its own hands and publish a set of legislative standards.[34]

12.10 POST-LEGISLATIVE SCRUTINY

So far, this chapter has examined how primary legislation is made. It began with pre-legislative scrutiny, when the government publishes a draft bill for consultation and parliamentary review, and then traced the stages of a bill's passage through Parliament. A final, often overlooked, phase comes later:

[33] House of Commons Political and Constitutional Reform Committee, *Ensuring standards in the quality of legislation*, First Report, Session 2013–14 (HC 85-I), p. 3.

[34] House of Lords Constitution Committee, *Legislative standards of the Constitution Committee 2017–2024* (6 May 2025) https://committees.parliament.uk/publications/47701/documents/249210/default/ accessed 10 November 2025.

post-legislative scrutiny, carried out a few years after an Act has come into force, allows Parliament to assess how effectively the law is working in practice. The experience of post-legislative scrutiny mirrors that of pre-legislative scrutiny: there is broad agreement that it is valuable, yet in practice its use remains uneven and inconsistent.

The idea of systematic post-legislative scrutiny was recommended by the Law Commission of England and Wales in 2006.

The Law Commission, *Post-legislative Scrutiny* (2006, Law Com No 302)

[. . . W]e understand post-legislative scrutiny to refer to a broad form of review, the purpose of which is to address the effects of the legislation in terms of whether the intended policy objectives have been met by the legislation and, if so, how effectively. However, this does not preclude consideration of narrow questions of a purely legal or technical nature.

The government's response was broadly positive. It agreed that departments responsible for implementing Acts of Parliament should prepare post-legislative memoranda, normally within three to five years of an Act's commencement, and that these documents would be submitted to the relevant departmental select committees. The expectation was that committees could use these memoranda as the basis for their own post-legislative inquiries. But reviewing the operation of post-legislative scrutiny in the UK Parliament, Tom Caygill argues that it 'remains limited as a form of scrutiny, at least from the perspective of committees launching inquires and publishing reports', suggesting that committees have found it difficult to prioritize post-legislative scrutiny work.[35]

PAUSE FOR REFLECTION

If a statute proves confusing or ineffective, who should take responsibility—the drafters, ministers, or Parliament?

12.11 CONCLUDING COMMENTS

This chapter has examined the legislative process for making primary legislation. We have seen that the executive (ministers, advised by civil servants and the PCO in drafting bills) has a central role in initiating legislative proposals and managing bills as they pass through Parliament. The function of Parliament (through debates on the floors of both chambers and the work of committees) is to scrutinize, and occasionally to exercise a power of veto, over government proposals. In the following extract, Stephen Laws suggests that the main function of Parliament's role '*is to provide political legitimacy*' for the implementation of (often controversial) government policy. Sir Stephen worked in the PCO for 37 years, ending his career as First Parliamentary Counsel.

[35] T. Caygill, 'The UK post-legislative scrutiny gap' (2020) 26 The Journal of Legislative Studies 387, 404.

Sir Stephen Laws, 'What is the parliamentary scrutiny of legislation for?', in A. Horne and A. Le Sueur (eds), *Parliament: Legislation and Accountability* (2016, Oxford: Hart Publishing), ch. 2, p. 27

At least one important function of Parliament in relation to legislation—maybe its principal function—is to provide political legitimacy for the implementation of what usually begins as a partisan proposal. The passage of legislation through the processes of the nation's principal institution for democratic debate is what turns a controversial political proposal into something authorised or required by law, and it does this by putting it in a form that can be accepted as a general rule by law-abiding members of society and applied by an impartial judiciary. So the constitutional processes for passing legislation for implementing a controversial policy proposal are, and need to be, processes that will work in practice to turn something politically contentious into something that attracts greater public acceptance and adherence.

To explore how Parliament delegates law-making powers to ministers and how those powers are exercised, turn now to Chapter 13. That chapter examines the different types of delegated legislation, the procedures used to scrutinise them, and the constitutional questions they raise about accountability and control.

FURTHER READING

Le Sueur, A. and Simson Caird, J., 'The House of Lords Constitution Committee' in A. Horne, G. Drewry, and D. Oliver (eds), *Parliament and the Law* (2013, Oxford: Hart Publishing), ch. 11.

Russell, M. and Gover, D., *Legislation at Westminster: Parliamentary Actors and Influence in the Making of British Law* (2017, OUP).

Sargeant, J. and Pannell, J., *The Legislative Process: How to empower parliament* (2022, Bennett Institute/Institute for Government).

Xanthaki, H., *Drafting Legislation: Art and Technology of Rules for Regulation* (2014, Hart).

13

DELEGATED LEGISLATION

CENTRAL ISSUES

1. Delegated legislation allows government to make law quickly and flexibly, but it also transfers power from Parliament to the executive. The constitutional question is where the balance should lie: how far should ministers be allowed to fill in the detail of Acts of Parliament, or even amend them, and at what point does delegation undermine parliamentary sovereignty?
2. Why is delegated legislation used so extensively—and when does delegation go too far? It is uncontroversial that ministers may rely on delegated powers to bring Acts into force and to fill in technical or administrative detail. However, many Acts have been criticised as *skeleton legislation*: they set out only broad objectives and leave ministers to decide key elements of policy and rules later by statutory instrument. This blurs the proper boundary between what should appear in primary legislation and what may be left to executive law-making.
3. Although statutory instruments are made in a minister's name, they are drafted and developed by civil servants and departmental lawyers. Ministers usually merely approve rather than be actively involved in designing content, though they remain constitutionally responsible for it.
4. Oversight of delegated legislation is carried out through a mix of affirmative and negative procedures and by specialist committees. In practice, debates are brief (if they happen at all) and amendments are not allowed—raising doubts about how effectively Parliament controls ministerial law-making.
5. Courts can review delegated legislation and quash it if it exceeds the powers granted by Parliament or breaches procedural or human-rights standards. This provides an important, though sporadic, check on executive rule-making that does not apply to Acts of Parliament themselves.
6. Concerns about the scale of delegated legislation have prompted calls for major reform. Proposals by the Hansard Society and others include clearer limits on what may be delegated and stronger parliamentary scrutiny procedures. These reforms aim to restore a constitutional balance between Parliament and the executive.

13.1 OVERVIEW

This chapter explains what delegated legislation is, why it is used, how it is controlled by Parliament and the courts, and what reforms have been proposed. It links these issues to the constitutional principles of parliamentary supremacy,[1] the rule of law,[2] and the separation of powers.[3] A case study on protest regulation illustrates how delegated legislation can raise constitutional controversy when ministers use broad powers to amend primary legislation, testing the limits of parliamentary control and judicial oversight.

Modern government could not function without delegated legislation—also known as subordinate legislation or secondary legislation. Many Acts of Parliament (primary legislation) grant ministers and other public authorities enabling powers to make legally binding rules, and the Acts that contain these powers are often referred to as 'parent acts'. For example, section 4 of the Data (Use and Access Act) 2025 states '*The Secretary of State or the Treasury may by regulations make provision requiring a data holder to publish business data or provide business data—(a) to a customer of the trade to whom the business data relates, or (b) to another person of a specified description*'. In other words, Parliament has authorised ministers to decide the detailed rules about when and how businesses must share commercially held data, rather than setting those requirements itself in the Act.

Studying delegated legislation therefore involves questions at two levels: what rule-making powers do Acts of Parliament confer, and what rules are actually made under them? Each year, around 1,200 to 1,400 pieces of delegated legislation are made—compared with fewer than 50 Acts of Parliament. This means that most of the detailed rules that shape everyday life for individuals and businesses are created not directly by Parliament, but by the executive.[4]

Most delegated legislation is made in the form of 'statutory instruments'. The parliamentary process of making SIs is regulated by the Statutory Instruments Act 1946. SIs may be called 'Orders', 'Regulations', or sometimes 'Rules'; there is no legal significance to the use of these titles—it is more to do with historical accident and drafting practices. The process begins when officials in a government department draft the text under an enabling power in an Act of Parliament. Departmental lawyers prepare the instrument, and a minister formally approves it by signing it—this is called 'making' the SI. Once made, the SI is laid before Parliament, meaning it is formally presented and published for scrutiny. The Statutory Instruments Act 1946 provides two main procedures:

- Negative procedure: the SI automatically becomes law unless either House objects within 40 sitting days. Almost all SI use this procedural route.
- Affirmative procedure: a draft SI must be debated and approved by both Houses before it can take effect.

Most SIs are considered by specialist committees that check their legality or policy merits, but Parliament cannot amend them; it can only approve or reject them. After the scrutiny period, the SI is published on the official legislation.gov.uk website and has the same legal force as an Act of Parliament.

Orders in Council are a type of statutory instrument. They differ from most other SIs in that they are made by the King in Council, rather than by a minister alone. Once any required parliamentary procedure has been completed, the draft Order is submitted for formal approval at a meeting of the

[1] See Chapter 3. [2] See Chapter 4. [3] See Chapter 5.

[4] This chapter focuses on delegated legislation made under powers conferred by Acts of the UK Parliament applying to the whole United Kingdom or to England. The devolved legislatures—the Scottish Parliament, Senedd Cymru (the Welsh Parliament), and the Northern Ireland Assembly—also confer powers on ministers and other bodies within their jurisdictions to make delegated legislation.

Privy Council—usually a brief, ceremonial occasion held at a royal residence and attended by a small group of senior ministers. The parent Act may require that a statutory instrument be made in the form of an Order in Council where the subject matter is of particular constitutional significance. In other cases, the form is retained for historical or procedural reasons.[5]

EXERCISE: FINDING STATUTORY INSTRUMENTS

Visit the official website legislation.gov.uk. Use the search or filters to find three statutory instruments (SIs) made in the last 12 months. For each SI, note: (i) its title and number (for example, SI 2025/1234), (ii) the minister or other public authority that made it, and (iii) its subject matter (try to include one that relates to business regulation and one on social rights such as housing or welfare benefits). Consider what your examples reveal about the kinds of issues dealt with through delegated legislation.

The quantity of delegated legislation made each year is widely regarded as a problem. As Hayley Hooper observes, '*ever increasing recourse to delegated legislation in a constitutionally unprincipled manner has featured in the activity of all governments, regardless of their political hue*'.[6] No one suggests that delegated legislation could be abolished. The constitutional issues are about where its limits lie, who exercises these powers, and how Parliament and the courts can hold the executive to account in this context. These questions engage with issues of parliamentary supremacy (Chapter 3), the rule of law (Chapter 4), and principles of separation of powers (Chapter 5). The Hansard Society—a leading independent research organization— warned in 2023 that '*Parliamentary control of delegated legislation is one of the most significant constitutional challenges of our time. At stake is democratic control of political power*'.[7]

The issues explored in this chapter are not unique to the United Kingdom, nor to an uncodified constitution, nor one founded on the principle of parliamentary supremacy. A comparative study found that Australia, Canada, India and New Zealand '*share the UK system's broad features: established mechanisms for technical scrutiny of delegated legislation, but scant tools for effective merits-based scrutiny*'.[8]

13.1.1 DELEGATED AND PRIMARY LEGISLATION COMPARED

Understanding delegated legislation is easier when it is compared directly with Acts of Parliament. Both are forms of law, but they differ sharply in how they are made, who makes them, and how far they can be scrutinised or challenged. Box 13.1 highlights the main procedural and constitutional distinctions between delegated and primary legislation.

[5] But not all Orders in Council are delegated legislation made under an Act of Parliament. Some are made under the royal prerogative—for example, those dealing with the governance of British Overseas Territories or certain national security matters. These prerogative Orders in Council are not statutory instruments and are not subject to parliamentary procedure: see Chapter 10.

[6] Hayley J. Hooper, 'Delegated Legislation in an Unprincipled Constitution' ch. 10 in R. Johnson and Y. Y. Zhu (eds), *Sceptical Perspectives on the Changing Constitution of the United Kingdom* (Hart Publishing 2023) p. 207.

[7] Hansard Society, *Proposals for a New System of Delegated Legislation* (Hansard Society 2023) p.1.

[8] T. Fleming and T. Ghazi, 'Parliamentary Scrutiny of Delegated Legislation: Lessons from Comparative Experience' (2023) 94(3) *The Political Quarterly* 412.

BOX 13.1 DELEGATED AND PRIMARY LEGISLATION COMPARED

	Delegated legislation	Primary legislation (Acts of Parliament)
Who makes it?	Ministers, with the approval of Parliament	The Crown in Parliament (House of Commons, House of Lords, Royal Assent)
By what procedure?	Varies All is subject to 'technical' scrutiny by the Joint Committee on Statutory Instruments The House of Lords Secondary Legislation Scrutiny Committee reports on significant legislation	Second Reading, Committee, Report, and Third Reading in Commons and Lords Scrutiny by Joint Committee on Human Rights and Constitution Committee
Is it amendable?	No: MPs and peers cannot suggest improvements	Yes: much of the debate is on amendments by MPs and peers
How long is the debate?	Most is not debated at all. If there is debate, it is strictly limited to 90 minutes	Varies according to importance and complexity—usually many days
Can the courts review it?	Yes: the courts may apply the normal grounds of judicial review.	Constitutional principle of parliamentary sovereignty prevents this (but the courts may make a declaration of incompatibility under the Human Rights Act 1998 or British Bill of Rights Act 2023)

Together, these contrasts show that while delegated legislation has the same legal force as an Act of Parliament, it receives far less democratic scrutiny—raising important questions about how parliamentary control over law-making is exercised in practice.

13.2 WHY IS DELEGATED LEGISLATION USED?

In what circumstances does Parliament delegate law-making powers to ministers? We can begin to answer this question by looking at some examples of enabling provisions in Acts.

13.2.1 BRINGING ACTS OF PARLIAMENT INTO FORCE

Some Acts of Parliament come into force as soon as they receive Royal Assent. Most Acts, however, require are more gradual approach. Officials may need training, computer systems may need to be developed, or businesses may need time to prepare for compliance. In such cases, it is common for an Act to give a minister the power to decide when the law should commence, and to bring it into effect by making a piece of delegated legislation (a 'commencement order').

For example, section 145 of the Renters' Rights Act 2025—landmark legislation improving protection for tenants—states '*(1) This Act comes into force on such day as the Secretary of State may by regulations made by statutory instrument appoint . . . (2) This Act comes into force for the purposes of making regulations on the day on which it is passed*'. The Act received Royal Assent on 27 October 2025; the government press release published on that day said, '*In the coming weeks, ministers will outline how the reforms will be rolled out*'. This illustrates how commencement powers enable ministers to control the timing and sequencing of major legislative reforms.

The use of delegated legislation to bring into force primary legislation is generally regarded as a sensible practical arrangement. It is regarded as acceptable to delegate this decision about *timing* to the government and commencement orders are normally subject to no parliamentary scrutiny procedure. An enabling provision creates a *power*, not a *duty*, to bring sections of an Act of Parliament into force—but as long as an enabling provision has not been repealed, there is a continuing obligation on the Secretary of State to consider whether to bring a statutory scheme into force and he or she must avoid doing anything that would undermine that obligation (for example, announcing that he or she will *never* bring it into force).[9]

Delegating this discretion to ministers has the consequence that sections of Acts, although appearing on the face of the 'statute book', are in fact never brought into force and so are not binding law. There are no statistics as to what proportion of the statute book is not in force, but it may not be too far-fetched to suggest 10 per cent, including some apparently important provisions. Arguably, this creates a tension with the constitutional principle of parliamentary sovereignty: Parliament has decided that the law should be X, but that is never turned into binding law because the government decides otherwise (even if, following the *Fire Brigades Union* case, they keep an open mind). There may also be tensions with ideals of openness and accessibility of law, which are aspects of the rule of law: citizens and legal advisers may struggle to work out whether a provision in an Act has been brought into force or not.

QUESTIONS

1. Explain how to work out whether a particular section of an Act of Parliament is or is not in force. What legislation would you need to consult? What databases would be helpful?
2. How easy or difficult is the task of tracking down commencement dates? Are the difficulties *practical* or *constitutional* (or both) in character?
3. What does this tell us about accessibility of the law — an aspect of the rule of law discussed in Chapter 4?

13.2.2 FRAMEWORK FILLING

Many Acts of Parliament set out a general framework, sometimes described as a skeleton, for the policies they are intended to achieve, leaving ministers to fill in detail through delegated legislation. This can go too far. In 1932, the Donoughmore Committee warned that Acts of Parliament containing 'only the barest general principles' could 'closely affect the rights and property of the subject' receiving 'little supervision from Parliament'.[10] MPs and peers scrutinising such a bill will not know enough about the substance of the rules that will subsequently be made by ministers. The concern persists today, as the authors in the following extract explain.

[9] *R v Secretary of State for the Home Department, ex parte Fire Brigades Union* [1995] 2 AC 513, discussed in Chapters 5 and 10.

[10] Report of the Committee on Ministers' Powers (Donoughmore Report), *Report* (Cmd 4060, 1932) pp. 51–52.

D. Lock, F. de Londras and P. Grez Hidalgo, 'Delegated legislation in the pandemic: further limits of a constitutional bargain revealed' (2023) 43 *Legal Studies* 695, 700 (footnotes omitted)

The problems identified by the Donoughmore Committee have not abated. Indeed, they have become more acute in the ninety years since its report was published. Continuing a trend that has been a concern for decades, a huge amount of delegated legislation continues to be made, . . . and delegated law-making is heavily relied on to address complex but constitutionally significant 'events' like Brexit, as well as issues with clear human rights and rule of law implications like deportation and asylum-related procedures, and changes to criminal law. There is an argument, then, that the 'exceptional' has become increasingly normalised; that secondary legislation is now routinely being used for purposes and in respect of issues that the Donoughmore Committee recognised as being ill-suited to delegation. At the same time, it is not at all clear that the safeguards the Donoughmore Committee called for operate effectively to maintain constitutional integrity in the light of this extensive use of delegated law-making.

We argue that these safeguards can be found in a three-part constitutional bargain on delegated law-making between the Executive and Parliament, comprised of proper limitation of delegation by Parliament, self-restraint on the part of the Executive, and meaningful scrutiny by Parliament. This way of conceptualising how to manage the long-standing tension between practicality and principle when it comes to delegated law-making clearly involves trade-offs. Robust limitation of delegation by Parliament may slow down policy responses by requiring more primary legislation to be passed before regulations can be produced. Meaningful parliamentary scrutiny may mean that regulations cannot immediately come into force. Executive self-restraint may limit policy, flexibility, dynamism, innovation or responsiveness. On the other hand, allowing delegation per se means that Parliament limits its capacity to influence and shape government action, making itself vulnerable to the extent of the Executive's commitment to self-restraint and accountability to Parliament. The constitutional bargain seeks not to resolve but to manage these tensions; to provide a framework to safeguard constitutional principle while enabling everyday governance.

The authors illustrate these tensions through a case study of the use of delegated legislation during the Covid-19 pandemic, when the UK government imposed a series of emergency restrictions—commonly called lockdowns and social-distancing measures—that limited movement, gatherings, and business operations, and closed schools to slow the spread of the virus and protect public health between 2020 and 2022. The parent Act for almost all these measures was the Public Health (Control of Disease) Act 1984, under which more than 580 statutory instruments were made. Although the circumstances of a national public health emergency were exceptional, they provided a major test of the constitutional limits and tensions surrounding the use of delegated legislation. The Speaker of the House of Commons expressed strong concern about how these powers were used.

Mr Speaker (Sir Lindsay Hoyle MP), 'Speaker's Statement', Hansard HC Deb, vol 681, col 331, 30 September 2020

The way in which the Government have exercised their powers to make secondary legislation during this crisis has been totally unsatisfactory. All too often, important statutory instruments have been published a matter of hours before they come into force, and some explanations of why important measures have come into effect before they can be laid before this House have been unconvincing; this shows a total disregard for the House.

The following year, the Lords Delegated Powers and Regulatory Reform Committee published a report looking at the constitutional problems of skeleton bills as part of a wider inquiry into the balance of powers between Parliament and government.

Delegated Powers and Regulatory Reform Committee, *Democracy Denied? The Urgent Need To Rebalance Power Between Parliament and the Executive,* 12th Report of Session 2021–22 (HL Paper 106), extracts from Chapter 4 (footnotes omitted and abridged)

Skeleton legislation

59. Skeleton – or framework – legislation may involve the entire bill or clauses within a bill. The first report of the Scrutiny of Delegated Powers Committee [in 1992] described a skeleton bill as one which contained so many significant delegated powers that the 'real operation [of the Act] would be entirely by the regulations made under it'. A few years later [in 1998], the Committee gave a more colourful description: they were bills which were 'little more than a licence to legislate and so give flesh to the "skeleton" embodied in the bill'.

60. The use of skeleton legislation has long been a source of significant concern. The Donoughmore Committee [in 1932] described how critics of skeleton legislation had argued that the practice had 'so far passed all reasonable limits, as to have assumed the character of a serious invasion of the sphere of Parliament by the Executive'. [. . .]

61. [. . .] in a letter dated 25 September 2020, this Committee, the Constitution Committee and the SLSC [Secondary Legislation Scrutiny Committee] wrote to the Government about 'the growing tendency for the Government to introduce skeleton bills, in which broad delegated powers are sought in lieu of policy detail'. The Committees complained that 'Parliament is being asked to pass legislation without knowing how the powers conferred may be exercised by ministers and so without knowing what impact the legislation may have on members of the public affected by it.'

63. Despite these strictures, the number of skeleton bills in recent years has grown markedly. [. . .]

65. The Lord President suggested that skeleton bills were more likely 'immediately after a general election, for the respectable reason that a Government has just got elected promising to do something and therefore they have an urgency to do it, to implement it'. This is, in our view, an example of a conflict between political expediency and principle. **The appropriate threshold between primary and secondary legislation should not be dependent on the exigencies of timing but should be founded on the overarching principle that the principal aspects of policy should be on the face of a bill and only its detailed implementation left to delegated legislation. There is a long-standing maxim that ignorance of the law excuses no-one but if Parliament is ignorant of the law passed in its name, then how can the public be expected to know and obey it.**

A 'skeleton legislation declaration'

66. **Skeleton legislation signifies an exceptional shift in power from Parliament to the executive and entails the Government, in effect, asking Parliament to pass primary legislation which is so insubstantial that it leaves the real operation of the legislation to be decided by ministers. As such, it will rarely be justifiable.**

67. **We recommend that: Should the Government introduce skeleton legislation, the delegated powers memorandum should make an explicit declaration that the bill is a skeleton bill or clauses within a bill are skeleton clauses.**

Such a declaration should be accompanied by a full justification for adopting that approach, including why no other approach was reasonable to adopt and how the scope of the skeleton provision is constrained.

[. . .]

69. There may, of course, be occasion where the DPRRC [Delegated Powers and Regulatory Reform Committee] may disagree with a department's conclusion that a declaration is not required. In these circumstances, the Committee may wish to invite a minister to attend an oral evidence session to justify his or her department's view. The Committee would then make a report to the House. In this event, it would, we believe, be helpful to the House—if time permitted—if the Committee were to make a report before second reading (rather than the usual practice of reporting before committee stage) so that the House can test the government's justification during the debate on second reading. We envisage that such a report would focus on the skeletal nature of the legislation only, with the Committee's more detailed analysis of delegated powers following in the usual way as a report before committee stage.

70. . . . **we propose that consideration should be given to the DPRRC having a 'scrutiny reserve', exercisable in exceptional circumstances only. A difference of opinion about whether a bill contains skeleton provision and requires a skeleton legislation declaration would amount to such an exceptional circumstance. This would allow the Committee time to take evidence from the minister and prepare a report before second reading.**

71. We are aware that the SLSC, in its parallel report, suggests that there may be a role for the Speakers in the two Houses in deciding whether a bill, or parts of a bill, should be declared skeletal. We look forward to the debate which will no doubt be promoted by this suggestion. [. . .]

74. **We support the SLSC's recommendation that the Government, together with the two Houses of Parliament and their Procedure Committees, should consider, following consultation, how the democratic deficit inherent in skeleton legislation can be remedied.**

The government did not accept these proposed reforms.

QUESTIONS

1. Why might governments prefer to pass skeleton or framework legislation rather than detailed Acts?
2. What constitutional risks arise when Parliament delegates broad law-making powers to ministers?
3. Lock, de Londras and Grez Hidalgo describe a 'constitutional bargain' between Parliament and the executive. What are its three parts, and do you think that bargain operates effectively today?

13.2.3 IMPLEMENTING UK WITHDRAWAL FROM THE EU

So far we have considered how delegated legislation is used for routine purposes—such as bringing Acts into force through commencement orders—and, more controversially, to give detailed effect to broad framework Acts. Another major and contested use occurred when the United Kingdom left the European Union in January 2020. Something had to be done with the large body of legislation derived from EU law that was in force in the UK—an issue we explore in more detail in Chapter 24. For the purposes of the present Chapter, it is notable that much of this was in the form of delegated legislation made by UK ministers under delegated law-making powers in the (now repealed) European Communities Act 1972 or other Acts. The European Union (Withdrawal) Act 2018 provided a new statutory basis for this body of 'retained' delegated legislation to continue in force in the domestic legal system, pending a review of what to do with each piece of legislation.

In 2021–2, the UK government ran a public consultation on whether each piece of retained legislation should remain unchanged, be repealed, be amended, or be replaced. The task of reviewing more than 2,400 pieces of legislation, much of it highly complex and technical (for example dealing with environmental standards or product safety) was formidable, requiring technical, policy-making, and legal expertise. In the then Conservative government's view, giving ministers delegated law-making powers was the only practical way to manage such a large and complex process.

Many parliamentarians disagreed. The House of Lords Delegated Powers and Regulatory Reform Committee (DPRRC), scrutinizing the European Union (Withdrawal) Bill in 2018, said that it gave 'unprecedented powers to Ministers and other public bodies to make changes to EU law' retained in domestic law, the 'law-making powers of Ministers are subject to little parliamentary scrutiny', and 'Ministers have powers to alter more than 60 years of EU law as applied to the United Kingdom if they consider it appropriate to deal with deficiencies arising from the United Kingdom's withdrawal from the EU'.[11] The House of Lords Constitution Committee also issued a report on the Bill.

House of Lords Constitution Committee, European Union (Withdrawal) Bill: Interim report, 3rd report, Session 2017–19 (HL Paper 19), para. 47

We are concerned about the delegated powers the Government is seeking in the European Union (Withdrawal) Bill. The number, range and overlapping nature of the broad delegated powers would create what is, in effect, an unprecedented and extraordinary portmanteau of effectively unlimited powers upon which the Government could draw. They would fundamentally challenge the constitutional balance of powers between Parliament and Government and would represent a significant—and unacceptable—transfer of legal competence. We stress the need for an appropriate balance between the urgency required to ensure legal continuity and stability, and meaningful parliamentary scrutiny and control of the executive.

This was followed by a further report by the DPRRC.

House of Lords Delegated Powers and Regulatory Reform Committee, European Union (Withdrawal) Bill, 12th report, Session 2017–19 (HL Paper 73), paras 3–4

3. We published an initial report on 28 September 2017 so that Members of Parliament could consider it during the Bill's passage in the House of Commons. Earlier in 2017, we had set out our expectations for the delegated powers in this Bill.
    - Ministers must not have unfettered delegated powers, nor the power to choose whichever procedure they like for statutory instruments made under the Bill.
    - Significant powers given to Ministers to amend or repeal Acts of Parliament by statutory instrument ('Henry VIII powers') must be fully explained and justified.
    - The Bill should not enable major changes to policy or establish new frameworks save where it is necessary to ensure that UK law continues to work properly on exit day.
    - Any time-limited delegated powers would need careful examination to see that they worked properly.

[11] House of Lords Delegated Powers and Regulatory Reform Committee, *European Union (Withdrawal) Bill*, 12th report of Session 2017–19 (HL Paper 73), paras 3–4.

4. The Bill does not meet our expectations on any of these matters.
   - The law-making powers of Ministers are subject to little parliamentary scrutiny. Apart from the small number of cases where statutory instruments must adopt the affirmative procedure, the Government have an unfettered choice as to which procedure to adopt. This is a radical departure from the norm and one that we regard as wholly unacceptable.
   - The Bill confers on Ministers wider Henry VIII powers than we have ever seen.
   - Ministers have powers to alter more than 60 years of EU law as applied in the United Kingdom if they consider it appropriate to deal with deficiencies arising from the United Kingdom's withdrawal from the EU. This goes much wider than the Government's White Paper commitment not to make major changes to policy beyond those that are necessary to ensure UK law continues to function properly from exit day.
   - Although time-limits apply to secondary legislation made by Ministers under clauses 7 to 9, they do not apply to secondary legislation made under other powers contained in the Bill, or to legislation made pursuant to secondary legislation (so-called tertiary legislation).

Despite such criticisms, the main delegated power in the bill appears unaltered in the European Union (Withdrawal) Act 2018, though the bill was amended to include several procedural safeguards.

European Union (Withdrawal) Act 2018, s. 8

(1) A Minister of the Crown may by regulations make such provision as the Minister considers appropriate to prevent, remedy or mitigate –

(a) any failure of retained EU law to operate effectively, or

(b) any other deficiency in retained EU law,

arising from the withdrawal of the United Kingdom from the EU.

These regulations 'may make any provision that could be made by an Act of Parliament' (s. 8(5)).

Under the 2018 Act, Parliament created new sifting committees in both Houses to examine proposed statutory instruments made under the Act. Their role was to decide whether a minister's proposal to use the negative procedure—where regulations automatically become law unless Parliament objects—should instead follow the affirmative procedure, which requires active approval. The idea was to strengthen scrutiny of the extensive delegated powers used to amend retained EU law. The Public Law Project (a justice charity) set up the SIFT project. This assessed how these committees worked in practice. It found that while the new process improved transparency, its impact was limited: the committees' recommendations were advisory only, and ministers often declined to follow them. This led researchers to question whether the mechanism genuinely enhanced parliamentary accountability or merely gave the appearance of scrutiny without constraining executive power.[12]

[12] Public Law Project, 'The Sift Project' https://publiclawproject.org.uk/current-projects-and-activities/brexit/the-sift-project/ accessed 6 November 2025.

PAUSE FOR REFLECTION

Supporters of the United Kingdom's withdrawal from the EU argued that it would allow the country to 'take back control' of its laws. Think about the meaning of 'taking back control' in light of what you have read. Who seems to have gained more control — Parliament or ministers — and why?

13.2.4 'HENRY VIII' CLAUSES

So far, we have looked at the use of delegated legislation for the purposes of: (a) bringing sections of Acts into force; (b) filling in framework Acts; and (c) implementing the UK's withdrawal from the EU. A fourth purpose may strike you as unusual: delegated legislation can be used *to amend or repeal Acts of Parliament*. Think about that for a moment: this is *secondary* legislation being used to change *primary* legislation. Enabling provisions that confer this surprising power on ministers have been dubbed 'Henry VIII' provisions, so called because some critics argue that if abused, Henry VIII powers contained in Acts of Parliament risk giving ministers powers to suspend parliamentary legislation such as were enjoyed by the notoriously autocratic Tudor king.

Why would Parliament wish to give ministers these powers? One answer is that they are useful for relatively small-scale fine-tuning to the reforms being introduced by the Act without the need to trouble Parliament with a bill. Often, minor problems come to light only after an Act has received Royal Assent. Many Acts contain an enabling clause like the following.

Bus Services Act 2025

39 Power to make consequential provision

(1) The Secretary of State may by regulations make provision that is consequential on this Act.

(2) Regulations under this section may amend, repeal or revoke provision made by or under an Act passed—

(a) before this Act, or

(b) later in the same session of Parliament as this Act.[13]

(3) The power to make regulations under this section includes power to make—

(a) consequential, supplementary, incidental, transitional or saving provision;

(b) different provision for different purposes.

(4) Regulations under this section are to be made by statutory instrument.

(5) A statutory instrument containing regulations under this section that amend or repeal provision made by an Act may not be made unless a draft of the instrument has been laid before and approved by a resolution of each House of Parliament.

(6) Any other statutory instrument containing regulations under this section is subject to annulment in pursuance of a resolution of either House of Parliament.

Provisions like this illustrate how Parliament balances practicality with oversight. By delegating limited law-making powers to ministers, it allows government to adjust and clarify legislation efficiently while still retaining control through procedures such as the affirmative and negative resolution processes.

[13] Without this wording, the rule of implied repeal (see Chapter 3) would normally mean that later Acts take priority over earlier ones, and a minister could not lawfully amend an Act passed after the parent Act itself.

The use of Henry VIII clauses for reasons other than minor consequential amendments remains controversial. In 1997, the House of Lords established a select committee—now known as the Delegated Powers and Regulatory Reform Committee—to monitor the inclusion of Henry VIII powers in bills. The committee reports any concerns to the House of Lords, so that peers may, if they agree, seek to amend the bill to remove or limit the power in question. Consider the following example of a Henry VIII clause with a wide reach.

Animal Welfare Act 2006, s. 1

1 Animals to which the Act applies

(1) In this Act, except subsections (4) and (5), 'animal' means a vertebrate other than man.

(2) Nothing in this Act applies to an animal while it is in its foetal or embryonic form.

(3) The appropriate national authority may by regulations for all or any of the purposes of this Act—

(a) extend the definition of 'animal' so as to include invertebrates of any description;

(b) make provision in lieu of subsection (2) as respects any invertebrates included in the definition of 'animal';

(c) amend subsection (2) to extend the application of this Act to an animal from such earlier stage of its development as may be specified in the regulations.

(4) The power under subsection (3)(a) or (c) may only be exercised if the appropriate national authority is satisfied, on the basis of scientific evidence, that animals of the kind concerned are capable of experiencing pain or suffering.

(5) In this section, 'vertebrate' means any animal of the Sub-phylum Vertebrata of the Phylum Chordata and 'invertebrate' means any animal not of that Sub-phylum.

The 'national authority' referred to is the Secretary of State in England and the Senedd Cymru/Welsh Parliament in Wales. The enabling provision has not yet been used to amend the 2006 Act.[14]

PAUSE FOR REFLECTION

1. How broad is the discretion conferred on ministers by this section 1 of the Animal Welfare Act?
2. Can you suggest any reasons why it was seen as impossible or undesirable to have a firm definition of 'animal' on the face of the Act?
3. What risks to parliamentary control arise when ministers are given powers to amend primary legislation?

Having considered why delegated legislation is used, we now turn to the process through which it is made.

[14] This is notable because the Animal Welfare (Sentience) Act 2022 created an expert committee to advise government on the welfare of animals. During its passage through Parliament, the committee's remit was extended—at a late stage—to include decapod crustaceans and cephalopod molluscs (such as crabs, lobsters, crayfish, octopus, and squid), following scientific evidence that these species are capable of experiencing pain and pleasure.

13.3 MINISTERS, CIVIL SERVANTS AND DEPARTMENTAL LAWYERS

Most Acts that confer delegated legislative powers state that the rule-maker is a minister. In practice, however, ministers are rarely involved in the detailed drafting of statutory instruments. As senior politicians, they focus mainly on overall policy direction rather than technical matters, relying on departmental officials and lawyers to prepare the text for signature. Ministers are more likely to take a close interest where a proposal is politically sensitive or controversial; but in routine or technical cases, they will normally act on officials' advice. Constitutionally, however, the minister remains responsible for the content of the instrument and answerable to Parliament for its making.

SIs are drafted by lawyers working in departments (not by the Parliamentary Counsel Office, which drafts bills). Drafting can therefore be described as decentralized. The Legislation Services at The National Archives publish an official guide directed at government lawyers and civil servants who do this work: *GLS Statutory Instrument Practice*.[15]

The role of ministers in the process of making SIs became a live issue in a judicial review challenge to an SI made under the Medicines Act 1968 prohibiting the sale for medicinal purposes of kava-kava, a plant-based tranquillizer, and another made under the Food Safety Act 1990 banning its use in foodstuffs. To 'make' the SI, the minister in the relevant department must sign the text produced by civil servants and government lawyers. But how much is the minister in question expected to know about the subject matter of the draft SI, or the reasons why it is being made? Is a ministerial signature just a rubber stamp for things done by officials?

R (On the Application of National Association of Health Stores) v Secretary of State for Health
[2005] EWCA CIV 154

Sedley LJ

1. [. . .] In each case the measure was authorised by a minister in the name of the Secretary of State [. . .]

2. The principal ground of challenge is that in each instance the minister authorised the measure in ignorance of the relevant fact that prohibition was opposed by a leading psychopharmacological authority, Professor Ernst, on cogent grounds which he had spelt out in a published meta-analysis. [. . .]

What knowledge does the law impute to Ministers?

23. The next question is altogether more profound. It is not answered, only broached, by the historic decision of this court [the Court of Appeal] in *Carltona Ltd v Commissioners of Works* [1943] 2 All ER 560. There the court was presented with an attempt to transpose a familiar doctrine of the law of agency—the rule that one who is delegated cannot himself delegate—into the field of public administration, treating the minister as the Crown's delegate. Lord Greene MR, with his compendious knowledge of public administration, recognised the inappropriateness of the argument and answered it by holding that in law . . . civil servants acted not on behalf of but in the name of their ministers.

24. *Carltona*, however, establishes only that the act of a duly authorised civil servant is in law the act of his or her minister. It does not decide or even suggest that what the civil servant knows is in law the minister's knowledge, regardless of whether the latter actually knows it. For the novel proposition that

[15] The National Archives, *Statutory Instrument Practice* 5th edn (2017) https://www.legislation.gov.uk/pdfs/StatutoryInstrumentPractice_5th_Edition.pdfaccessed 6 November 2025.

it is, Mr Cavanagh [counsel for the Department of Health] founds upon one sentence in Lord Diplock's speech in *Bushell v Secretary of State for the Environment* [1981] AC 75:

> The collective knowledge, technical as well as factual, of the civil servants in the department and their collective expertise is to be treated as the minister's own knowledge, his own expertise.

25. It is Mr Cavanagh's submission that this affords a complete answer, without resort to evidence, to the accusation that Lord Hunt [the junior minister] was inadequately informed about Professor Ernst's views when he signed the Order. The departmental knowledge, which included everything that was material about Professor Ernst and his report, was the minister's, even if the minister did not in fact know it. This argument, advanced below by Mr Philip Sales [counsel for the Department of Health at first instance], was accepted by Crane J [the judge in the Administrative Court]. He held:

> 72. It follows that information available to officials involved in advising a minster is information that can properly be said to be information taken into account by the minister. It was submitted by Mr. Thompson QC that this would mean that information known to any official in the department can be said to be known to the minister taking a decision. I do not think that follows. If on a challenge to a decision, it were to be asserted that the Secretary of State took into account such information, when in fact no official involved in the matter knew of it, that would in my judgment be an inaccurate assertion. Nor, for example, would it be an accurate assertion if the relevant information was buried in a file but not in fact considered by any official in the matter. However, it does not follow that the court will in the ordinary way investigate whether such an assertion is accurate.

26. In my judgment, and with great respect to Crane J, this part of his decision is unfounded in authority and unsound in law. It is also, in my respectful view, antithetical to good government. It would be an embarrassment both for government and for the courts if we were to hold that a minister or a civil servant could lawfully take a decision on a matter he or she knew nothing about because one or more officials in the department knew all about it. The proposition becomes worse, not better, when it is qualified, as Crane J qualified it and as Mr Cavanagh now seeks to qualify it, by requiring that the civil servants with the relevant knowledge must have taken part in briefing or advising the minister. To do this is to substitute for the *Carltona* doctrine of ordered devolution to appropriate civil servants of decision-making authority (to adopt the lexicon used by Lord Griffiths in *Oladehinde* [1991] 1 AC 254) either a de facto abdication by the lawful decision-maker in favour of his or her adviser, or a division of labour in which the person with knowledge decides nothing and the decision is taken by a person without knowledge.

27. In contrast to *Carltona*, where this court gave legal authority to the practical reality of modern government in relation to the devolution of departmental functions, the doctrine for which Mr Cavanagh contends does not, certainly to my knowledge, reflect the reality of modern departmental government. The reality, subject no doubt to occasional lapses, is that ministers (or authorised civil servants) are properly briefed about the decisions they have to take; that in the briefings evidence is distinguished from advice; and that ministers take some trouble to understand the evidence before deciding whether to accept the advice. I will come later in this judgment to the critical question of how much of the evidence the minister needs to know; but I cannot believe that anybody, either in government or among the electorate, would thank this court for deciding that it was unnecessary for a decision-maker to know anything material before reaching a decision.

28. Four years after *Bushell* was decided, the High Court of Australia had before it an issue akin to the issue before us. A minister had made an order affecting land rights in ignorance of a potentially crucial fact. The fact was known, however, within his department. It is of interest that the minister's counsel, David Bennett QC (now S-G), one of Australia's leading constitutional lawyers, did not attempt to advance the argument which has been advanced by Mr Cavanagh. He contended only that the minister could lawfully delegate fact-finding to officials, and that there was no evidence that the material fact had been overlooked at official level: in other words, he sought to refine *Carltona* into a doctrine of split or partial delegation.

29. The High Court [of Australia] rejected this endeavour. Gibbs CJ said:[16]

> Of course the Minister cannot be expected to read for himself all the relevant papers that relate to the matter. It would not be unreasonable for him to rely on a summary of the relevant facts furnished by the officers of his Department. No complaint could be made if the departmental officers, in their summary, omitted to mention a fact which was insignificant or insubstantial. But if the Minister relies entirely on a departmental summary which fails to bring to his attention a material fact which he is bound to consider, and which cannot be dismissed as insignificant or insubstantial, the consequence will be that he will have failed to take that material fact into account and will not have formed his satisfaction in accordance with law.

30. Mason J (as he then was) pointed out that what was being proposed was that 'the minister had power to delegate part of his decision-making function [. . .] to his department, and that he exercised this power by splitting the function, leaving his staff to decide what facts or matters would be taken into account.' Any delegation, he went on to point out, must first be lawful and secondly be shown to have been made. He made it clear that in that case (as in this) the issue was whether the decision-maker had omitted a consideration which was in the obligatory class of relevance.

31. The High Court was unanimous in rejecting the argument, both on principle and from convenience, that the minister could decide without actually knowing something which bore the requisite degree of relevance to his decision. [. . .].

32. In the light of this significant Australian decision one comes back to what Lord Diplock said in *Bushell*. The full passage reads:

> What is fair procedure is to be judged not in the light of constitutional fictions as to the relationship between the minister and the other servants of the Crown who serve in the government department of which he is the head, but in the light of the practical realities as to the way in which administrative decisions involving forming judgments based on technical considerations are reached. To treat the minister in his decision-making capacity as someone separate and distinct from the department of government of which he is the political head and for whose actions he alone in constitutional theory is accountable to Parliament is to ignore not only practical realities but also Parliament's intention. Ministers come and go; departments, though their names may change from time to time, remain. Discretion in making administrative decisions is conferred upon a minister not as an individual but as the holder of an office in which he will have available to him in arriving at his decision the collective knowledge, experience and expertise of all those who serve the Crown in the department of which, for the time being, he is the political head. The collective knowledge, technical as well as factual, of the civil servants in the department and their collective expertise is to be treated as the minister's own knowledge, his own expertise.

37. [. . .] The serious practical implication of the argument [advanced by counsel for the Department of Health] is that, contrary to what the decided English cases take for granted, ministers need know nothing before reaching a decision so long as those advising them know the facts. This is the law according to Sir Humphrey Appleby.[17] It would covertly transmute the adviser into the decision-maker. And by doing so it would incidentally deprive the adviser of an important shield against criticism where the decision turns out to have been a mistake.

38. The only authority Mr Cavanagh was able to produce which appeared to chime with his argument was a decision of Lord Clyde, sitting in the Outer House of the Court of Session, in *Air 2000 v Secretary*

[16] *Minister for Aboriginal Affairs v Peko-Wallsend Ltd* 1986) 162 CLR 24 at 30–31.

[17] Sir Humphrey Appleby is a fictional senior civil servant in the BBC television comedies *Yes Minister* and *Yes, Prime Minister* (1980–88). The character, known for his polished language and bureaucratic manoeuvring, has come to symbolise the shrewd, obstructive civil servant who skilfully controls ministers while appearing to serve them.

of State for Transport (No 2) [1990] SLT 335. Advice from the Civil Aviation Authority which by statute the Secretary of State was required to consider had been seen not by him but by an interdepartmental working party which advised him. Lord Clyde cited *Carltona* for the uncontroversial proposition that 'what is done by his responsible official is done by [the minister]'. However, while rejecting as 'too extreme' a submission that the mere physical delivery of the advice to the department was sufficient, Lord Clyde accepted that 'if it is given to an official who has responsibility for the matter in question, that should suffice'. If by this Lord Clyde meant that such receipt would amount in law to consideration by the Secretary of State, I would respectfully disagree. For the reasons I have given, it would be incumbent on such an official to ensure that either the advice or a suitable précis of it was included in the submission to the minister whose decision it was to be.

[Sedley LJ went on to consider the question 'Did the Minister leave relevant matter out of account in deciding to make the Order?' Sedley LJ looked at the evidence to see what was included and what omitted from the briefing papers prepared for the minister.]

60. But what in the end I am unable to accept is that the minister had less information than the law required. The test is the familiar public law test: was something relevant left out of account by him in taking his decision? [. . .]

62. Given the constitutional position as this court now holds it to be, a minister who reserves a decision to himself—and equally a civil servant who is authorised by him to take a decision—must know or be told enough to ensure that nothing that it is necessary, because legally relevant, for him to know is left out of account. This is not the same as a requirement that he must know everything that is relevant. Here, for example, much that was highly relevant was appropriately sifted by the Commission in formulating its advice and then distilled within the department in order to make a submission to the minister which would tell him what it was relevant (not simply expedient or politic) for him to know. What it was relevant for the minister to know was enough to enable him to make an informed judgment. This centrally included the Commission's advice and the reasons for it. It also included the fact of Professor Ernst's opposition and the essential reasons for it. All this he had.

The Court of Appeal dismissed the National Association's appeal. The Medicines for Human use (Kava-kava) (Prohibition) Order 2002 (SI 2002/3170) remains in force, prohibiting the sale, supply, and importation of Kava-kava for use in unlicensed medicines.

QUESTIONS

1. What differences are there between the way in which the text of a SI is created and the way in which the text of a bill is produced?
2. Summarize in a few sentences what the court held in the *National Association of Health Stores* case about the constitutional role of (a) officials and (b) ministers in making delegated legislation.

13.4 PARLIAMENT'S ROLE IN DELEGATED LEGISLATION

One of the rationales for delegated legislation is that it relieves Parliament of some of the burden of legislating. It is therefore not surprising that draft SIs receive far less scrutiny than bills. Some SIs—those that make commencement orders bringing sections of an Act into force—are subject to no parliamentary procedure at all; other draft SIs are subject to a range of oversight mechanisms, depending on the importance of the subject matter.

The enabling provision in the Act of Parliament under which the minister is authorized to make delegated legislation may specify that the SI is subject to the 'affirmative' procedure, meaning that the draft SI must be approved by Parliament before it comes into force. Unlike bills, the House of Commons and House of Lords cannot amend the SI only decline to approve the SI. This process applies to approximately one in five SIs.

Alternatively, the SI is subject to negative procedure and may be signed by the minister ('made') before being 'laid in Parliament'. The SI will come into force after 40 sitting days unless there is a motion in either House to annul it.

Three parliamentary committees (see Box 13.2) are concerned with reviewing enabling provisions in bills and, once the Act is in force, how ministers are exercising their delegated law-making powers. Most members of the committee have no legal expertise or training, but each committee carries out its work with the assistance of a lawyer on the parliamentary staff.

BOX 13.2 HOW PARLIAMENT SCRUTINIZES STATUTORY INSTRUMENTS

Name of committee	Remit
House of Lords Delegated Powers and Regulatory Reform Committee	Reports to the House of Lords on whether the provisions of any bill inappropriately delegate legislative power, or whether they subject the exercise of legislative power to an inappropriate degree of parliamentary scrutiny.
Joint Committee on Statutory Instruments	Scrutinizes all SIs and reports any concerns to the House of Commons and House of Lords. Does not assess the 'merits' of the SI.
House of Lords Secondary Legislation Scrutiny Committee	Scrutinizes all SIs laid before the House of Lords, examining the policy merits, and reporting on any concerns or if a SI subject to the negative procedure should be upgraded to the affirmative procedure.

The Joint Committee on Statutory Instruments (a committee of backbench MPs from the House of Commons and peers in the House of Lords) takes no view on the merits of the policy contained in the SIs, but instead considers whether each SI falls foul of any specified technical flaws, outlined in the Standing Orders of each House.

House of Commons Standing Order 151(1)(B), Statutory Instruments (Joint Committee)

[. . .]

(i) that it imposes a charge on the public revenues or contains provisions requiring payments to be made to the Exchequer or any government department or to any local or public authority in consideration of any licence or consent or of any services to be rendered, or prescribes the amount of any such charge or payment;

(ii) that it is made in pursuance of any enactment containing specific provisions excluding it from challenge in the courts, either at all times or after the expiration of a specific period;

(iii) that it purports to have retrospective effect where the parent statute confers no express authority so to provide;

(iv) that there appears to have been unjustifiable delay in the publication or in the laying of it before Parliament;

(v) that there appears to have been unjustifiable delay in sending a notification under the proviso to section 4(1) of the Statutory Instruments Act 1946, where an instrument has come into operation before it has been laid before Parliament;

(vi) that there appears to be a doubt whether it is intra vires or that it appears to make some unusual or unexpected use of the powers conferred by the statute under which it is made;

(vii) that for any special reason its form or purport calls for elucidation;

(viii) that its drafting appears to be defective;

or on any other ground which does not impinge on its merits or on the policy behind it; and to report its decision with the reasons thereof in any particular case.

In the House of Lords, the Secondary Legislation Scrutiny Committee and its subcommittees review all SIs and draft SI and other delegated legislation. Its work has increased with the quantity of delegated legislation made under the European Union (Withdrawal) Act 2018 and the Retained EU Law (Revocation and Reform) Act 2023.

House of Lords Secondary Legislation Scrutiny Committee[18]

(3) The grounds on which an instrument, draft or proposal may be drawn to the special attention of the House are—

(a) that it is politically or legally important or gives rise to issues of public policy likely to be of interest to the House;

(b) that it may be inappropriate in view of changed circumstances since the enactment of the parent Act;

(c) that it may imperfectly achieve its policy objectives;

(d) that the explanatory material laid in support provides insufficient information to gain a clear understanding about the instrument's policy objective and intended implementation;

(e) that there appear to be inadequacies in the consultation process which relates to the instrument.

It is extremely rare for Parliament to reject an SI, as the House of Lords Constitution Committee explains in the following extract.

[18] SLSC Terms of Reference (29 July 2024) https://committees.parliament.uk/committee/255/secondary-legislation-scrutiny-committee/content/120278/toref accessed 7 November 2025.

House of Lords Constitution Committee, *Delegated Legislation and Parliament: A response to the Strathclyde Review*, 9th Report of Session 2015-16, HL Paper 116

40. Parliament rejects statutory instruments extremely rarely. Only 17 statutory instruments have been rejected by the two Houses over the last 65 years out of nearly 170,000, including five instruments out of some 23,000 laid before Parliament since 1997. Since statutory instruments are, except in extremely unusual cases, unamendable by Parliament, that legislation is passed into law precisely as drafted by Government. There are obvious incentives for successive Governments to propose broad delegated powers that make it possible for ministers to pass significant policy decisions through Parliament without undergoing the full scrutiny afforded to primary legislation.

QUESTIONS

Visit the home pages of these committees on the UK Parliament website (www.parliament.uk): the Joint Committee on Statutory Instruments, the House of Lords Secondary Legislation Scrutiny Committee, and House of Lords Delegated Powers and Regulatory Reform Committee. Look at the most recent reports of each committee and note any statutory instruments (SIs) that they have drawn to the attention of the House.

1. What types of concerns—legal, procedural, or policy-related—do the committees most often raise?
2. Based on what you have read, how effective do you think parliamentary scrutiny of SIs is in practice?
3. Why might it matter that, unlike bills, draft SIs cannot be amended during their passage through Parliament?

13.5 JUDICIAL REVIEW OF DELEGATED LEGISLATION

The lawfulness of a piece of delegated legislation can be challenged through a claim for judicial review. This is so even where delegated legislation has been subject to affirmative procedure in Parliament, where it has been debated and expressly approved. The principle of parliamentary supremacy does not apply to delegated legislation.[19] The role of the court, when adjudicating on a challenge, is to ensure that the minister making the delegated legislation has done so lawfully. All of the grounds of judicial review[20] are potentially applicable: illegality (for example, the delegated legislation is outside the ambit of the enabling provision); procedural impropriety (for example, consultation was flawed or non-existent); irrationality (that is, the order defies logic or accepted moral standards); or that it violates a Convention right contrary to the Human Rights Act 1998.

Judicial review challenges to delegated legislation are rare—probably no more than one or two cases each year. Given that over a thousand statutory instruments are made annually, the courts play only a limited and occasional role in controlling ministerial power in this area. The following examples illustrate some of the few cases in which such challenges have succeeded. In one of its first cases, the new UK Supreme Court had to review the lawfulness of two pieces of delegated legislation that were

[19] See Chapter 3. [20] See Chapters 17–21.

designed to freeze the assets of suspected terrorists. The enabling provision relied on by the government was s. 1 of the United Nations Act 1946, which stated that if the UN Security Council called on the United Kingdom to implement measures, '*His Majesty may by Order in Council make such provision as appears to Him necessary or expedient for enabling those measures to be effectively applied, including (without prejudice to the generality of the preceding words) provision for the apprehension, trial and punishment of persons offending against the Order*'. The names of the three claimants appeared on a list drawn up by the UN as people being involved in terrorism. The UK government in turn designated them as people whose assets would be frozen under the orders. At no point was there any procedure for the claimants to challenge the UN or the government's determination, in clear contravention of basic principles of procedural fairness. The Supreme Court held that the orders were *ultra vires* as they fell outside the scope of s. 1 of the 1946 Act: the enabling provision was not sufficiently wide to permit ministers to interfere with fundamental rights to fair process.[21] Lord Phillips 'topped' and 'tailed' his judgment by reference to the constitutional framework in which the court was operating.

Ahmed and Ors v HM Treasury (JUSTICE intervening) (Nos 1 and 2)
[2010] UKSC 2

85. It is particularly appropriate that these should be the first appeals to be heard in the Supreme Court of the United Kingdom, for they concern the separation of powers. At issue is the extent to which Parliament has, by the United Nations Act 1946 delegated to the executive the power to legislate. Resolution of this issue depends upon the approach properly to be adopted by the court in interpreting legislation which may affect fundamental rights at common law or under the European Convention on Human Rights. [. . .]

157. Nobody should conclude that the result of these appeals constitutes judicial interference with the will of Parliament. On the contrary it upholds the supremacy of Parliament in deciding whether or not measures should be imposed that affect the fundamental rights of those in this country.

In response to the ruling, the government fast-tracked a bill through Parliament, which became the Terrorist Asset-Freezing (Temporary Provisions) Act 2010; this was subsequently replaced by the Terrorist Asset-Freezing etc. Act 2010. So, using primary legislation, the government now has power to implement UN Security Council measures on asset freezing. The primary legislation includes a right of appeal for the designated person.

In another high profile challenge to delegated legislation, the Public Law Project (PLP) questioned the lawfulness of a new government policy to have a 'residence test' for eligibility to civil legal aid—people living in the United Kingdom for less than 12 months would no longer be able to receive financial assistance for access to legal advice and representation. The government sought to achieve this through a statutory instrument (the draft Legal Aid, Sentencing and Punishment of Offenders Act 2012 (Amendment of Schedule 1) Order 2014). The UK Supreme Court accepted PLP's argument that the Act under which the Lord Chancellor purported to make the SI (the Legal Aid, Sentencing and Punishment of Offenders Act 2012 or 'LASPO') did not provide the power to do so: '*The exclusion of a specific group of people from the right to receive civil legal services in relation to an issue, on the ground of personal circumstances or characteristics (namely those not lawfully resident in the UK, Crown Dependencies or British Overseas Territories) which have nothing to do with the nature of the issue or services involved or the individual's need, or ability to pay, for the services, is simply not within*

[21] On the principle of legality, see Chapter 4.

the scope of the power accorded to the Lord Chancellor by section 9(2)(b) of LASPO, and nothing in section 41 undermines that contention'.[22]

Lord Neuberger set out the constitutional context for this conclusion.

R (On the application of the Public Law Project) v Lord Chancellor
[2016] UKSC 39

Lord Neuberger

20. The draft order, once formally made, would, of course, be secondary, or subordinate, legislation, unlike LASPO itself which, as a statute, is primary legislation. Primary legislation is initiated by a Bill which is placed before Parliament. To the extent that Parliament considers it appropriate, all or any of the provisions of a Bill can be subject to detailed scrutiny, discussion, and amendment in Parliament before being formally enacted as primary legislation; it is then formally approved by the monarch, whereupon it becomes a statute. In our system of parliamentary supremacy (subject to arguable extreme exceptions, which I hope and expect will never have to be tested in practice), it is not open to a court to challenge or refuse to apply a statute, save to the extent that Parliament authorises or requires a court to do so.

21. Subordinate legislation consists of legislation made by members of the Executive (often, as in this case, by Government ministers), almost always pursuant to an authority given by Parliament in primary legislation. The draft order in the present case would be a statutory instrument, which is a type of subordinate legislation which must be laid in draft before Parliament. Some statutory instruments are subject to the negative resolution procedure—ie they will become law unless, within a specified period, they are debated and voted down. Other statutory instruments, such as the draft order in this case, are subject to the affirmative resolution procedure—ie they can only become law if they are formally approved by Parliament—see subsections (6) and (7)(a) of section 41.

22. Although they can be said to have been approved by Parliament, draft statutory instruments, even those subject to the affirmative resolution procedure, are not subject to the same legislative scrutiny as bills; and, unlike bills, they cannot be amended by Parliament. Accordingly, it is well established that, unlike statutes, the lawfulness of statutory instruments (like other subordinate legislation) can be challenged in court. As Lord Diplock said in *F Hoffmann-La Roche & Co v Secretary of State for Trade and Industry* [1975] AC 295, 365, 'even though [subordinate legislation] is contained in an order made by statutory instrument approved by resolutions of both Houses of Parliament, . . . I entertain no doubt that the courts have jurisdiction to declare it to be invalid if they are satisfied that in making it the Minister who did so acted out with the legislative powers conferred upon him by the . . . Act of Parliament under which the order [was] purported to be made . . .'.

23. Subordinate legislation will be held by a court to be invalid if it has an effect, or is made for a purpose, which is ultra vires, that is, outside the scope of the statutory power pursuant to which it was purportedly made. In declaring subordinate legislation to be invalid in such a case, the court is upholding the supremacy of Parliament over the Executive. That is because the court is preventing a member of the Executive from making an order which is outside the scope of the power which Parliament has given him or her by means of the statute concerned. Accordingly, when, as in this case, it is contended that actual or intended subordinate legislation is ultra vires, it is necessary for a court to determine the scope of the statutorily conferred power to make that legislation.

24. Normally, statutory provisions which provide for subordinate legislation are concerned with subsidiary issues such as procedural rules, practice directions, and forms of notice; hence statutory instruments are frequently referred to as regulations. However, such statutory provisions sometimes permit more substantive issues to be covered by subordinate legislation, and, as is the case with section 9(2)(b) of LASPO, they sometimes permit subordinate legislation which actually amends the statute concerned (or even another statute), by addition, deletion or variation.

[22] *R (on the application of the Public Law Project) v Lord Chancellor* [2016] UKSC 39.

QUESTIONS

1. The courts have considerable powers to review delegated legislation—but how *effective* are judicial review claims in monitoring the lawfulness of delegated legislation? Think about how easy or difficult it is for a person to launch a judicial review claim.
2. What constitutional justifications are there for the courts having a role in reviewing delegated legislation when the parliamentary supremacy denies them such a role in relation to *primary* legislation?

13.6 CASE STUDY: REGULATING PROTEST AND THE LIMITS OF DELEGATED POWER

To see how parliamentary and judicial controls over ministerial power to make delegated legislation intersect, this case study looks at the Public Order Act 1986 (Serious Disruption to the Life of the Community) Regulations 2023 – controversial in Parliament and held to be unlawful in the courts.

Peaceful public protest is one of the hallmarks of a democratic society. It allows people to express their views and seek to influence government and Parliament. In recent years, protests in the United Kingdom have focused on issues such as the climate emergency, the conflict in Israel and Gaza, and the housing of asylum seekers in hotels. The right to protest has long been subject to legal regulation. The Public Order Act 1986 replaced several common law public order offences with a statutory framework giving the police powers to prevent disorder, protect property, and maintain public safety. The 1986 Act empowered the police to impose conditions on public processions and assemblies where an officer reasonably believes it may result in 'serious disruption to the life of the community'(though this was not defined).

In 2021–22, the Conservative Government introduced a Bill to expand police powers relating to public order, responding to widespread disruption caused by environmental protest movements such as Extinction Rebellion, Insulate Britain, and Just Stop Oil. The Bill provoked strong public debate. The human rights organization Liberty described it as 'a huge and dense piece of legislation with seriously worrying consequences'. It prompted demonstrations, a petition attracting nearly one million signatures, and criticism from a range of professional and civil society groups. The House of Lords removed several clauses, some of which were later reinserted by the House of Commons. One government amendment made in the Lords—defining the concept of 'serious disruption to the life of the community' in the Public Order Act 1986—was rejected and for procedural reasons could not be debated when the Bill returned to the Commons. The Bill was enacted as the Police, Crime, Sentencing and Courts Act 2022.

The 2022 Act amended the 1986 Act to confer on the Home Secretary a Henry VIII power to make regulations amending the meaning of 'serious disruption' in the Public Order Act 1986. In 2023 that power was exercised by a Minister of State in the Home Office, Chris Philp MP, to make the draft Public Order Act 1986 (Serious Disruption to the Life of the Community) Regulations. The government's stated aim was to clarify—and, in practice, to lower—the threshold for police intervention. The draft Regulations provided that police could impose conditions where the disruption was 'more than minor', included a non-exhaustive list of examples of serious disruption, required the police to consider the cumulative impact of repeated protests, and defined the term 'community'. In substance, the draft Regulations sought to achieve by delegated legislation what the government's unsuccessful amendment to the Bill had attempted to do through primary legislation.

The Regulations were subject to the draft affirmative procedure, meaning that they had to be approved by both Houses of Parliament before becoming law. Remember that Parliament is unable to amend draft delegated legislation. The House of Commons approved the Regulations on 12 June 2023, and the Lords debated them the following day.

The Lords Secondary Legislation Scrutiny Committee published a report just in time for the debate. This said 'Given the profile of the issue and the wide range of interested parties, the Home Office should, according to the Government's own Consultation Principles, have consulted more widely before bringing forward the proposals' and went to say:[23]

> 'As well as not justifying the substance of the provisions, the Home Office has not provided any reasons for bringing the measures back in the form of secondary legislation, which is subject to less scrutiny, so soon after they were rejected in primary legislation. We are not aware of any examples of this approach being taken in the past; the House may wish to verify this with the Minister. We believe this raises possible constitutional issues that the House may wish to consider.'

In the Lords, two motions were tabled by peers opposed to the draft Regulations: a 'fatal' motion to decline approval of the Regulations, and a 'non-fatal' (or 'regret') motion to allow them to pass while recording concern. Peers from across the House argued that the Regulations reintroduced measures previously rejected during the passage of the Police, Crime, Sentencing and Courts Bill, and that it was constitutionally improper to do so by delegated legislation. The Government contended that the Regulations merely clarified the law. After debate, the fatal motion was defeated and the regret motion agreed, meaning the Lords formally expressed disquiet but still approved the Regulations.[24]

The parliamentary process was not the end of the story. Ten days after the Lords debate, Liberty (formally The National Council for Civil Liberties) brought judicial review proceedings challenging the lawfulness of the Regulations. The Public Law Project (PLP) was granted permission to intervene in support of Liberty. In May 2024, the Administrative Court — sitting as a 'divisional court' of two judges—held that the Regulations were ultra vires (beyond the powers conferred on the Home Secretary).[25] The Divisional Court granted the Home Secretary leave to appeal to the Court of Appeal, said that the appeal should be expedited, and suspended its order that the Regulations be quashed until the outcome of the appeal.

Following the general election in July 2024, the new Labour Home Secretary Yvette Cooper MP appealed against the decision. The Court of Appeal dismissed the appeal and handed down its judgment in May 2025. The Court of Appeal upheld the Divisional Court's decision that the Home Secretary had acted ultra vires—beyond the powers granted by Parliament—when making the Regulations. The key issue was whether the Henry VIII provisions in the 1986 Act, inserted by the 2022 Act, conferred sufficiently wide powers to make the Regulations. There were in fact two enabling powers, in almost identical terms: section 12 (imposing conditions on public processions) and section 14 (imposing conditions on public assemblies). Each provided that 'The Secretary of State may by regulations amend' the section 'for the purposes of making provision about the meaning for the purposes of this section of— (a) serious disruption to the activities of an organisation which are carried on in the vicinity of' a public procession or assembly, 'or (b) serious disruption to the life of the community'.

Liberty successfully argued that the Regulations did more than merely 'make provision *about the meaning*' of the terms; they purported *to change the meaning* of the term 'serious disruption' by introducing a lower threshold of 'more than minor" disruption and adding new examples of what could amount to serious disruption, the Regulations went beyond what Parliament had intended in the enabling provision.

[23] House of Lords Secondary Legislation Scrutiny Committee, 38th Report of Session 2022-23, HL Paper 189, pp. 4–7.

[24] The Public Order Act 1986 (Serious Disruption to the Life of the Community) Regulations 2023 (SI 2023/655).

[25] *R (on the application of The National Council for Civil Liberties) v Secretary of State for the Home Department* [2024] EWHC 1181 (Admin).

R (on the application of The National Council for Civil Liberties) v Secretary of State for the Home Department
[2025] EWCA Civ 571, [47]–[49], Underhill LJ

> First, it is inherently unlikely that Parliament would have intended to grant by secondary legislation the power to amend the primary statute in a way which changed a criterion which was fundamental to the balance which it struck between the rights of individuals to protest and the rights of the community [. . .]
>
> Second, that consideration is reinforced by the nature of the rights with which the statute is concerned. Parliament is unlikely to have granted a right to interfere by secondary legislation with the balance which it had chosen to strike as regards fundamental rights. It is also relevant that breach of a condition imposed under sections 12 or 14 [of the 1986 Act] is a criminal offence.
>
> Third, I agree with the Divisional Court that it is relevant that we are here dealing with a Henry VIII power. . . . [T]here is (at least) an ambiguity: the Court is having to choose between a narrower and a broader interpretation (assuming for present purposes that both are available) of the phrase 'about the meaning'; and in accordance with the principles stated in [*R (Public Law Project) v Lord Chancellor* [2016] UKSC 39, considered above] it should accept the narrower.

Speaking after the Court of Appeal's judgment in May 2025, Shameen Ahmad, CEO of PLP, said 'We trust that this decisive victory for the rule of law and Parliamentary sovereignty will serve as a watershed moment for the Government. These restrictive protest laws should now be permanently abandoned and Henry VIII powers relegated to the annals of history where they belong'.[26]

The Home Secretary decided not to appeal to the UK Supreme Court. In March 2025, the campaign group Just Stop Oil—whose actions of non-violent direct action had been one of the main triggers for the 2023 Regulations—announced that it would end its public protests. It held a final march described as 'a defiant celebration of the effectiveness of civil resistance', noting that its central demand, to end new oil and gas licensing, had by then become government policy. The question of police powers to manage protest nevertheless remained politically live, particularly amid the large-scale pro-Palestine demonstrations that took place across the UK in 2024 and 2025. These events renewed debate about whether the police had adequate powers to deal with repeated and disruptive protests. In October 2025, the new Home Secretary, Shabana Mahmood MP, announced that 'the government will make these improvements by amending sections 12 and 14 of the Public Order Act 1986 to explicitly allow the police to take account of the cumulative impact of frequent protests on local areas when deciding whether to impose conditions on public processions and assemblies'.[27] This would be done by primary legislation. In substance, this returned the policy debate to where it had begun—with a proposal similar to the one the previous Conservative government had sought to implement.

[26] PLP, 'Court of Appeal dismisses Government's appeal over anti-protest laws' (2 May 2025) https://publiclawproject.org.uk/latest/court-of-appeal-dismisses-governments-appeal-over-anti-protest-laws/ accessed 8 November 2025.

[27] Home Office, 'New police powers to protect communities from disruption caused by protests' (5 October 2025) https://www.gov.uk/government/news/new-police-powers-to-protect-communities-from-disruption-caused-by-protests accessed 8 November 2025.

QUESTIONS

1. What constitutional principles are engaged when Parliament gives ministers the power to amend an Act of Parliament by delegated legislation?
2. How effective is parliamentary scrutiny under the draft affirmative procedure, given that members cannot amend draft instruments and debate time is limited?
3. The courts were able to strike down the Regulations, but they could not have done so if the same wording had appeared in primary legislation. Why is that? What does this difference reveal about the respective constitutional positions of Parliament, ministers, and the courts?

13.7 REFORM

Concerns about the scale and control of delegated legislation have grown steadily in recent decades. The balance between Parliament and the executive has been tested by the increasing use of wide enabling powers in Acts, which leave much of the substance of the law to be set out later in statutory instruments. This trend has been especially visible in emergency and fast-moving policy areas such as Brexit and the Covid-19 pandemic, when governments sought to legislate quickly and flexibly.

Critics argue that the cumulative effect has been to tilt the constitutional balance in favour of ministers, weakening Parliament's capacity to scrutinise and control the content of secondary legislation. A 2023 working paper by the Hansard Society—the leading independent research body on Parliament—offered a stark diagnosis of the scale of the problem and called for a fundamental overhaul of the system. The following extract summarises the Society's assessment of how delegated legislation has come to undermine the United Kingdom's constitutional arrangements.

Hansard Society, *Proposals for a New System of Delegated Legislation* (2023, Hansard Society), p. 1

What is the problem?

Over the last century, but increasingly in the last few decades, more and more extensive powers to make law have been delegated to Ministers while parliamentary control over the exercise of those powers has eroded, to the extent that it now undermines the constitutional balance between the executive and the legislature. This compromises the UK's system of parliamentary democracy.

This position has arisen for two principal reasons:

1. The shifting boundary between what should go in primary and what in delegated legislation

First, the dividing line between what should go in primary legislation made by Parliament and what should go in delegated legislation made by Ministers has shifted over the decades.

Although recent Governments have been especially widely criticised for their approach to delegated legislation, administrations of all political stripes over the last 30 years have pushed the boundaries of what constitutes an appropriate delegation of power, and Parliament has typically given way. The

Government's desire to legislate at speed in response to events – particularly during Brexit and the Covid pandemic – has further normalised the bypassing of proper policy development processes and the consequent inclusion of very broad powers in Bills. [. . .]

This links to the second problem.

2. Inadequate scrutiny procedures

Delegated legislation is not solely the preserve of the uncontroversial administrative and technical detail for which it was historically intended, and for which the parliamentary scrutiny procedures for SIs – particularly in the House of Commons – were designed nearly 80 years ago.

Principal matters of policy – including some of the most politically salient issues of the day – are now found in delegated legislation. However, the parliamentary scrutiny system is inflexible, so it rarely provides a satisfactory forum for Members to express their concerns about these laws that directly affect citizens.

The report makes a series of reform proposals, including:

- A Concordat on Legislative Delegation should be agreed between Parliament and Government to reset the boundary between primary and delegated legislation.
- A new Statutory Instruments Act should remove the existing scrutiny procedures applied by parent Acts to the use of delegated powers. In their place, a new single scrutiny procedure should apply to all SIs, in which Parliament can calibrate the level of scrutiny to the content of the Instruments.
- All SIs should be laid before Parliament in draft, other than in exceptional circumstances.
- A Parliamentary Office for Statutory Instruments (POSI) should be established as a joint department of both Houses of Parliament to analyse and produce briefings on SIs for MPs and Peers.
- A Joint Secondary Legislation Sifting Committee (JSLSC) should be established to determine which SIs require further scrutiny and approval by Parliament.
- In the House of Commons, motions to approve SIs should be amendable so that MPs can propose changes to an SI before it is approved.
- In the House of Lords, a new 'think again' procedure should be introduced so that Peers can ask the House of Commons to consider their concerns before an SI is approved.
- A 30-sitting-day 'safety window' should be introduced during which any parliamentarian could table a revocation motion against an SI after it had been made.
- A new urgent procedure should be introduced for use only in exceptional circumstances when the Government needs an SI to be made and come into force more quickly than is possible under the new standard scrutiny procedure.
- Parliament should publish draft SIs together with related materials on its website, bringing the SI publication process in line with that for primary legislation.

Taken together, these proposals amount to the most comprehensive blueprint for reform of delegated legislation in a generation. They aim to restore a clearer constitutional boundary between what should be enacted in primary legislation and what can properly be left to ministers, while equipping Parliament with the tools to scrutinise secondary legislation more effectively. Whether such reforms will be implemented remains uncertain: they would require both Houses, and the Government of the day, to accept limits on executive convenience in the interests of parliamentary accountability. Yet the Hansard Society's proposals have set a new benchmark for debate about how delegated law-making might be brought back within a framework that is both constitutionally balanced and democratically credible.

13.8 CONSTITUTIONAL IMPLICATIONS OF DELEGATED LEGISLATION

The extensive use of delegated legislation in the UK raises important issues for parliamentary supremacy (Chapter 3), the rule of law (Chapter 4), and the principle of the separation of powers (Chapter 5).

Delegated legislation tests what parliamentary supremacy means in practice. Parliament remains sovereign: it can make or unmake any law, including those that delegate power to ministers. Yet when wide law-making powers are granted through so-called 'skeleton' Bills, the ability of parliamentarians to scrutinise proposed laws effectively is reduced. Although various procedures exist for reviewing the resulting statutory instruments, numerous commentators have concluded that parliamentary control is limited. In substance, law-making authority often shifts to the executive. The issue is not that Parliament has lost its supremacy, but that it sometimes permits ministers to exercise it on its behalf.

There are also rule-of-law implications. The scale of delegated legislation and the limits on its scrutiny raise questions about transparency and legality. The rule of law requires that rules are made through proper procedures and are clear to those who must follow them. When significant policies are introduced through instruments that cannot be amended and are rarely debated, those safeguards weaken. The sheer complexity of the statute book further hinders public understanding of the legal rules that govern everyday and business life. While the courts ultimately determine whether a statutory instrument is lawful, the costs, risks, and lack of public awareness surrounding judicial review mean that this control operates only at the margins.

Delegated legislation also affects the balance between the legislature and the executive. Ministers now shape legal rules with the same force as Acts of Parliament, blurring the line between making and implementing the law. Effective parliamentary oversight—through committees, debate, and clear procedures—helps to keep that line intact and ensures that executive power remains answerable to Parliament. Debates about delegated legislation are therefore not only about efficiency but about the health of the constitutional separation of powers itself.

PAUSE FOR REFLECTION

These questions invite you to connect the chapter to the constitutional principles introduced earlier in the book.

1. How far does the current system of parliamentary scrutiny of delegated legislation preserve Parliament's claim to be the UK's supreme law-making body?
2. In what ways might the growing use of broad delegated powers undermine the accessibility and transparency that the rule of law requires?
3. Does the modern reliance on delegated legislation represent a practical necessity of government, or a constitutional imbalance between the executive and the legislature? Explain your view with examples.

FURTHER READING

Chng, K., 'Re-examining judicial review of delegated legislation' (2024) 44 *Legal Studies* 81.

Flemming, T. and Ghazi T., 'Parliamentary scrutiny of delegated legislation: Lessons from comparative experience' (2023) 94(3) *The Political Quarterly* 412.

Hansard Society, *Proposals for a New System for Delegated Legislation: a working paper for the Delegated Legislation Review* (2023, Hansard Society).

Hooper, H. J., 'Delegated Legislation in an Unprincipled Constitution', in R. Johnson R. and Zhu Y.Y. (eds), *Sceptical Perspectives on the Changing Constitution of the United Kingdom* (2023, Hart Publishing), 207.

PART IV

JUDICIAL AND DISPUTE RESOLUTION FUNCTIONS

14

INTRODUCTION TO JUDICIAL AND DISPUTE RESOLUTION FUNCTIONS

CENTRAL ISSUES

1. One of the main tasks of a constitution is to provide a justice system for resolving disputes arising from the enforcement, application, and interpretation of the law.
2. The public must have confidence that judges possess the necessary intellectual and personal skills, that the judiciary both broadly reflects society and is independent. The public must also be confident that the judiciary is capable of dealing impartially with disputes, including those involving government.
3. Systems of redress must be fit for their purpose. They must cater for the sort of problems or wrongs that people suffer; their procedures should be suitable; and adequate remedies should be provided when wrongs are suffered.
4. Within the United Kingdom, there are currently three distinct territorial jurisdictions: (a) England and Wales; (b) Scotland; and (c) Northern Ireland. Each has its own court system and head of judiciary.
5. The UK Supreme Court is the constitutional meeting point of the three jurisdictions and is the final court of appeal from most courts in the United Kingdom.
6. While the UK is no longer a member of the EU it remains a party to the European Convention on Human Rights and therefore the European Court of Human Rights (ECtHR) is still important within the United Kingdom.

14.1 THEMES AND ISSUES

This introduction to Part IV of the book is an overview of the main ideas, concepts, and facts that will be covered in this part of the book.

So far, we have considered the executive function—to make and implement policy—and the legislative function, by which policies become law. We now turn to the way disputes are resolved and the rule of law applied.

One of the main tasks of a constitutional system is to provide methods through which people can obtain definitive answers when they have disputes over the enforcement, application, and meaning of the law. It is the task of the various elements of the justice system to ensure that the law is interpreted and applied, and that these functions are performed in a manner that is fair, and is seen to be fair, to all concerned. These tasks fall upon all who are involved in the justice system, whether as non-lawyer (lay) members of tribunals and magistrates, as professional judges sitting in trial courts, or as senior judges in appellate courts.

It is vital that the public is confident that justice will be delivered by people of integrity who possess the necessary intellectual and personal skills. The public must also be confident that judges approach their task impartially as between the parties and that the judiciary, as an institution, is independent from the other branches of government. (This is particularly evident when they deal with disputes between individuals and the executive.)

Chapter 15 examines the constitutional position of judges within the United Kingdom, looking in particular at judicial independence and at the process by which judges are appointed. It also looks closely at the important matter of judicial diversity. Achieving a more diverse judiciary is now recognised to be an important goal: while there has been progress, this has been slow, and some argue that more radical steps are needed. As with many of the themes in this book, this is very much a live issue.

In Chapters 16–22 we are concerned with the main avenues of redress available for dealing with disputes involving public authorities. In Chapter 16, we look at redress mechanisms outside the court system—a terrain often referred to as the landscape of 'administrative justice'. This includes the work of ombuds and tribunals. (Note that, unless the context requires otherwise, in this book we tend to use the term ombuds instead of ombudsmen and ombud instead of ombudsman.) Chapters 17-20 are concerned with judicial review, the process by which people can challenge the legality of actions taken by public authorities; Chapter 21 examines the use of human rights arguments against these authorities. Chapter 22 provides three case studies on human rights protection, concerning: school uniforms; terrorism; and prisoner voting.

In these chapters, we return to some of the questions and controversies discussed in earlier parts of the book. The proper constitutional function of judges in a democracy continues to be the subject of academic and political debate. For some the greater role now played by the courts through the grounds of judicial review and protecting human rights, is a welcome counterweight to the previously overly 'political constitution'. For critics, judicial power is problematic: the judicial process is too limited and the judges are insufficiently accountable and representative to make it right to entrust them with powers to adjudicate about issues of social and political controversy.[1]

14.2 REDRESS MECHANISMS: ARE THEY FIT FOR PURPOSE?

As you read through this part of the book, ask yourself whether the systems of redress are fit for their purpose? Do they adequately respond to the sort of problems or wrongs that people suffer? Are the procedures that they use suitable? Do they provide adequate remedies?

Broadly speaking, the systems deal with three types of claim against public bodies. The first and probably most common situation occurs when someone claims a benefit or a service from a public authority and complains that the authority has made a mistake when dealing with their case: the complainant essentially says that the public authority has got it wrong and should make a more

[1] See discussion of legal and political constitutionalism in Chapter 2 and see also the mini case study on *Miller 2* in Chapter 10.

favourable decision. In practice, many complaints of this sort can be resolved quite quickly by the authority having another look at the case and checking to see whether a mistake has been made. If the claimed mistake is not rectified at this stage, there is often (although not always) a right to appeal against the authority's decision to a tribunal (or sometimes a court). We shall deal with such situations in Chapter 16.

Chapter 16 also deals with a second type of complaint, namely the situation in which someone claims to have been wronged by 'maladministration'—in other words, that the public body has behaved badly and has operated in a manner that falls below acceptable standards (for example, letters have been lost, questions are not answered, delays occur, mistakes have been made, and so on). Such administrative failings can cause injustice, and leave people feeling frustrated and angry, but they may not give rise to legal claims that can be taken to the courts. Complaints that injustice has been caused by maladministration can be taken to an ombuds, who may investigate and help to secure a remedy, as well as improvements in the way in which the public authority operates. There are now several ombuds in the public sector.

The third situation that we consider within the field of public law arises when claimants argue that a public body has failed to comply with the requirements of judicial review—that it has exceeded or abused its powers—or has breached human rights requirements. (Note that public bodies must also comply with obligations arising from the law or contract or tort, but this book does not deal with these branches of the law.) It is at this point that the senior courts may become involved. Typically, the legal arguments will be that the public authority has committed one or more (or a combination) of the following errors.

(a) It has misinterpreted or misunderstood the applicable law.
(b) It has abused its discretionary powers by, for example, taking into account irrelevant factors or failing to take account of relevant factors.
(c) It has made a procedural error or acted unfairly.
(d) It has acted incompatibly with 'Convention rights' contrary to s. 6 of the Human Rights Act 1998.

The first three of these arguments are considered in Chapters 18 and 19; the fourth is considered in Chapters 21 and 22.

While government can be expected to normally respect and comply with decisions of the courts there are circumstances in which government will seek to limit or even prevent the courts from dealing with matters, for example by asking Parliament to enact what are referred to as 'ouster' clauses that are intended to prevent (oust) judicial review. This situation raises some of the most difficult and controversial questions in UK constitutional law concerning potential conflict between key constitutional principles especially the supremacy of Parliament and the rule of law. These matters are dealt with in Chapter 20.

14.2.1 ARE THE PROCEDURES SUITABLE?

Procedures are important and getting procedures right is not easy. The achievement of proportionate dispute resolution (PDR) has been one of the goals of reform in recent years. Essentially, this means that public bodies should do all that they can to 'get it right' in the first place; if disputes do arise, then the procedures used should be suited to the dispute. Expensive court-like processes are not always necessary or desirable, and the drive for PDR has encouraged the development and use of alternatives to the courts, including mediation. In Chapter 16, we look more closely at the meaning and implications of PDR, and at some of the reasons why this concept is controversial.

The courts resolve disputes by using an adversarial process: the parties present their respective cases and show the weaknesses in the opposing case; an impartial judge then reaches a decision. This procedure has evolved over the centuries and has become the hallmark of the common law approach to adjudication in the courts. But this procedure is not suitable for resolving all disputes. As we shall see in Chapter 16, tribunals adopt a variety of procedures: some tribunals are very similar to courts in the way they deal with disputes; others are more inquisitorial in approach, with the tribunal chair and members taking the lead by asking questions; others still are far less formal and resemble a meeting around a table. In principle, procedures should suit the nature of the issues. Adversarial procedures may be suitable when the parties are represented by lawyers and in cases in which the arguments are focused on issues of law—but they are less suitable, or necessary, where one side is an ordinary person who is not represented and in cases in which the there are no major disputes about the law or the facts.

Ombuds do not use adversarial procedures, but are investigative in their approach. This means that they are in control of the matters to be examined, and they decide what evidence needs to be collected and what questions are to be asked. Inquisitorial approaches are considered much more suitable than adversarial procedures for investigating how public authorities have handled matters, not least because they are considered better at getting behind the accounts provided by public bodies while establishing trust and securing the cooperation of such bodies.

14.2.2 ARE REMEDIES ADEQUATE?

A further matter concerns remedies. One of the main questions to be asked about a system of redress is whether it provides suitable remedies when grievances or claims are upheld. For example, we shall see that there has been discussion about the inability of the Parliamentary and Health Service Commissioner (the PHSO or parliamentary ombuds—the organization responsible for investigating central government departments and agencies) to award legally enforceable remedies when it has upheld complaints that injustice has been caused by maladministration. Some see this as a fatal gap; others defend it on the grounds that this power would adversely affect the ombud's ability to work with departments. A related view is that the parliamentary ombuds should not be judged by its power to secure legally enforceable remedies for individuals, but rather by its broader role in achieving systemic changes. This disagreement illustrates the basic point that different people will see redress procedures in different ways. Claimants and their advisers will understandably judge procedures according to the outcomes that can be achieved for them; others will be more concerned about the general impact that bodies such as ombuds have on the wider machinery of government.

Similar issues arise in relation to judicial review. Often, people use the judicial review procedure because they want to force a public body to make a more favourable decision in their case—but judicial review is not well suited to achieving this outcome. Judicial review provides a legal check on the process by which decisions are taken and on whether the body has acted within its legal powers; it does not determine whether decisions of public bodies are right or wrong and it does not normally lead to judges replacing a challenged decision with their own decision. A successful judicial review claim will often result in a public authority being required to retake its decision: provided that the body follows the correct process, it may be able to make the same decision again. Unless this is explained to claimants, it can cause confusion and feelings of frustration.

There is an important difference here between a judicial review claim based on the common law and a case in which a claimant relies on the Human Rights Act 1998 (HRA) to establish that the public authority has infringed her or his Convention rights. Where the HRA is used, the court is concerned with whether the authority has infringed rights. If it has, this cannot be rectified by the authority simply looking at the decision again and then reaching the same decision following a better process. This is explained further in Chapters 21 and Chapter 22.

We shall see a further weakness of judicial review, as it operates in England and Wales, is that successful claimants do not have a right to any remedy: all remedies are discretionary. Moreover, successful claimants can only obtain damages in a very limited range of circumstances and not simply because a public authority has acted unlawfully in a public law sense. Similarly, in Chapter 21, we will see that while damages may be awarded for breaches of the HRA, the awards are often very low and there has been much criticism of the principles applied by the courts.

14.2.3 A SUMMARY

Box 14.1 summarizes some of the aspects of the discussion so far.

BOX 14.1 SUMMARY

	Independent	Binding decisions	Decision criteria	Method/procedure
Internal complaints/ reviews	No	Yes	Legality, merits, and maladministration	Inquisitorial; usually written
Ombuds	Yes	No	Maladministration	Inquisitorial; written
Tribunals	Yes	Yes	Legality and merits	Adversarial; inquisitorial; oral or written
Courts	Yes	Yes	Legality	Adversarial; oral occasionally written

Source: Based on table supplied in Tom Mullen, *The Way Forward: Final Report of the Administrative Justice Steering Group* (2009, Glasgow: Administrative Justice in Scotland), p. 39.

14.3 COURTS IN A MULTILEVEL SYSTEM

We need to say a word or two about the different jurisdictional 'systems' that are relevant to dispute resolution in the United Kingdom and the main courts that will be discussed in the following chapters (see Figure 14.1).

As a result of the United Kingdom's development as a union between formerly independent countries in the seventeenth century (the union of England and Wales with Scotland to create Great Britain) and in the early nineteenth century (the union of Great Britain and Ireland, to form the United Kingdom),[2] within the United Kingdom, there are three distinct territorial jurisdictions: (a) England and Wales; (b) Scotland; and (c) Northern Ireland. Each has its own court system and head of judiciary (see Box 14.2).

[2] See Chapter 6.

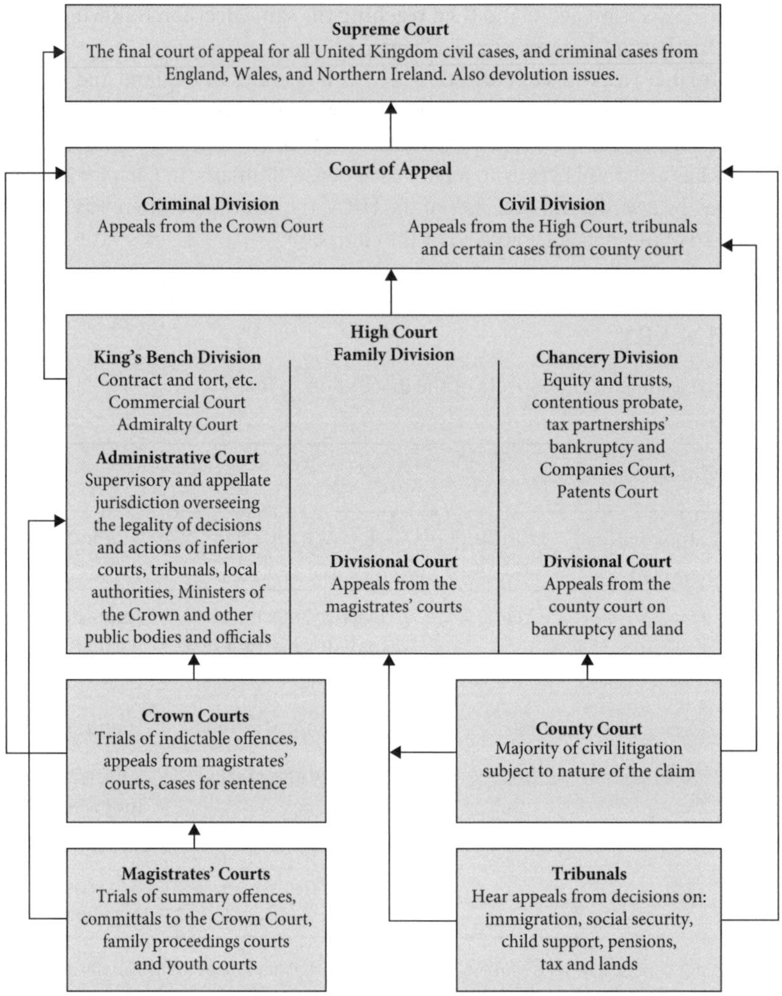

Figure 14.1 The organizational chart of the courts in England and Wales
Source: HM Court Service

BOX 14.2 HEADS OF THE JUDICIARY

England and Wales	Lord/Lady Chief Justice of England and Wales	Constitutional Reform Act 2005, s. 7
Scotland	The Lord/Lady President (of the Court of Session)	Judiciary and Courts (Scotland) Act 2008, s. 2
Northern Ireland	Lord/Lady Chief Justice of Northern Ireland	Justice (Northern Ireland) Act 2002, s. 12

The judges and heads of judiciary of the three jurisdictions carry out most of their work separately. Each head of the judiciary has their own channel of communication with the UK Parliament.

Constitutional Reform Act 2005, s. 5(1)

The chief justice of any part of the United Kingdom may lay before Parliament written representations on matters that appear to them to be matters of importance relating to the judiciary, or otherwise to the administration of justice, in that part of the United Kingdom.

Note that s. 5 is careful to make clear that 'matters' do not include those that are within the legislative competence of the Scottish Parliament or the Northern Ireland Assembly. In relation to devolved matters, the Lord/Lady President and the Lord/Lady Chief Justice of Northern Ireland have to look to their respective legislatures.

14.3.1 THE COURTS IN SCOTLAND

The following account of the courts in Scotland is taken from the 2009 report of the Scottish Civil Courts Review.

Report of the Scottish Civil Courts Review (2009), ch. 3

The Court of Session

2. The Court of Session is the highest civil court in Scotland. It sits in Edinburgh and has jurisdiction throughout Scotland. It is divided into the Outer House, which hears cases at first instance, and the Inner House, which deals mainly with appeals.

3. The Court deals with a wide range of civil matters including commercial, personal injury, property, taxation, and family cases. It alone can hear applications for judicial review [. . .].

The Outer House

9. In the Outer House cases are heard by a judge [known as a Lord/Lady Ordinary] sitting alone or, in certain cases, with a jury. There are currently 24 judges in the Outer House, most of whom also sit in the High Court of Justiciary, the supreme criminal court.

The Inner House

26. The Inner House hears appeals from the Outer House, sheriff court and certain tribunals and other bodies. It is divided into two Divisions: the First Division, presided over by the Lord President, and the Second Division, presided over by the Lord Justice Clerk; both Divisions are of equal authority. [. . .] Appeals are generally heard by a bench of three judges. On occasion, if a case is of particular difficulty or importance or if the Court has to consider overruling a binding authority, a larger bench will be convened.

[. . .]

28. A further appeal lies from the Inner House to the [UK Supreme Court].

The Sheriff Court

29. Scotland is divided into six sheriffdoms, each presided over by a sheriff principal who amongst his other duties hears appeals in civil matters and is responsible for the management of the sheriff courts

in his sheriffdom. The sheriffdoms are sub-divided into a total of forty-nine sheriff court districts, each with a court presided over by one or more sheriffs. In the larger urban areas, particularly Edinburgh and Glasgow, a number of resident and floating sheriffs hear a large volume of cases every day; in rural areas one sheriff may cover a number of courts and sit only on particular weekdays. [...]

30. Sheriff courts deal with civil, criminal and commissary matters. A wide range of civil matters are heard, including personal injury, contractual disputes, housing and family cases. If the sum sued for is £5,000 or less the action must be raised in the sheriff court; there is no upper limit. Criminal cases dealt with are either solemn (more serious cases involving trial on indictment before a sheriff sitting with a jury) or summary (less serious cases involving a trial where there is no jury).

14.3.2 THE COURTS IN ENGLAND AND WALES

Figure 14.1 provides an overview of the interaction between the courts discussed in this section.

14.3.2.1 The Magistrates' courts

Magistrates' courts deal with the less serious criminal cases and some civil matters.

14.3.2.2 The Crown Court

The Crown Court deals with more serious criminal cases, such as murder, rape, or robbery. It also handles cases on appeal and those referred to them by magistrates' courts. Trials are heard by a judge and a jury.

14.3.2.3 The County Court

The County Court sits in locations across England and Wales. It deals with civil matters, such as: claims for debt repayment, return of goods bought on credit, personal injury, and breach of contract; and family issues such as divorce or adoption; and housing disputes, including certain homelessness appeals from decisions of local housing authorities. Cases in the County Court are heard by a judge without a jury.

14.3.2.4 The High Court

The High Court sits in three divisions: the Chancery Division; the King's Bench Division; and the Family Division. Each Division has its own lead judge. The most important for constitutional lawyers is the King's Bench Division, which includes the Administrative Court. This handles judicial review claims. Until April 2009, claims for judicial review had to be made in London; they can now be dealt with in centres at Cardiff, Manchester, Birmingham, and Leeds.

14.3.2.5 The Court of Appeal

The Court of Appeal sits in London. It has a civil section (headed by the Master of the Rolls) and a criminal section (headed by the Lady Chief Justice). The Court of Appeal is staffed by Lords Justices of Appeal. The Civil Division hears appeals from the High Court, the County Court, and from certain tribunals.

14.3.3 WALES

Although Wales has had a devolved government system since 1998, with the National Assembly for Wales producing distinctively Welsh legislation,[3] it does not have its own system of courts and is not yet regarded as an entirely distinct *legal* jurisdiction separate from that of England.[4]

T. H. Jones and J. M. Williams, 'Wales as a jurisdiction' [2004] *Public Law* 78, 100 (footnotes omitted)

> Taken together with the law-making powers of the National Assembly, and the growing tendency of Parliament to legislate separately for Wales, developments within the legal system have given rise to the phenomenon of 'Legal Wales'. It would be a mistake to dismiss the significance of post-devolution changes on the basis that they do not amount to a jurisdiction that is more clearly separate from that of England, such as exists in Northern Ireland or Scotland. [. . .] Wales remains a jurisdiction that is emerging from the unified legal system of England and Wales. This is a process that deserves to be examined in its own terms. The trend towards greater differentiation in the public law area is likely to continue, whether or not the National Assembly gains primary legislative powers. Public bodies in Wales increasingly are going to be exercising powers that are different from their English counterparts.

14.3.4 THE COURTS IN NORTHERN IRELAND

The court system in Northern Ireland closely resembles that in England and Wales, although it has its own High Court judges and its own Northern Ireland Court of Appeal, which sits in Belfast.

14.3.5 THE UK SUPREME COURT

The constitutional meeting point of the three separate legal jurisdictions is the UK Supreme Court. This court serves as a final court of appeal from most courts in the three territorial jurisdictions—the exception being the High Court of Justiciary in Scotland, which is the final court of appeal for Scottish criminal cases. The UK Supreme Court is also the final arbiter of 'division of powers' questions that may arise under the devolution system.[5] As s. 41 of the Constitutional Reform Act 2005 makes clear, the status of the court differs according to whether it is acting as a final court of appeal from one of the territorial jurisdictions (when its judgments are formally binding only in the courts of the jurisdiction in question) or in relation to devolution adjudication (when the UK Supreme Court acts as a court of the whole United Kingdom).

[3] See Chapter 6.

[4] See Sarah Nason, 'Justice in Wales for the People of Wales', [2020] Edinburgh Law Review 297–304; T.H. Jones and J.M. Williams, 'Wales as a jurisdiction' [2004] Public Law 78; T. Hannant, 'Justifying a (Welsh) legal jurisdiction' [2019] Public Law 665. For an opinion piece arguing the case for a separate legal jurisdiction for Wales, see Dr Huw Evans, https://nation.cymru/opinion/the-case-for-a-separate-legal-jurisdiction-for-wales/

[5] See Chapter 6.

Constitutional Reform Act 2005, s. 41

41 Relation to other courts etc.

(1) Nothing in this Part is to affect the distinctions between the separate legal systems of the parts of the United Kingdom.

(2) A decision of the Supreme Court on appeal from a court of any part of the United Kingdom, other than a decision on a devolution matter, is to be regarded as the decision of a court of that part of the United Kingdom.

(3) A decision of the Supreme Court on a devolution matter—

(a) is not binding on that Court when making such a decision;

(b) otherwise, is binding in all legal proceedings.

(4) In this section 'devolution matter' means—

(a) a question referred to the Supreme Court under section 33 of the Scotland Act 1998 (c. 46) or section 11 of the Northern Ireland Act 1998 (c. 47);

(b) a devolution issue as defined in Schedule 8 to the Government of Wales Act 1998 (c. 38), Schedule 6 to the Scotland Act 1998 or Schedule 10 to the Northern Ireland Act 1998.

Jack Straw, Lord Chancellor and Secretary of State for Justice, *Supreme Court Opening Is Major Milestone for Government's Constitutional Reform*, 16 October 2009

The opening of the UK Supreme Court marks the culmination of a long—and very British—process of separating out the branches of the state. The official opening today finally delivers an idea which was first proposed by Gladstone in 1873, that the UK's highest court should be separated from Parliament.

The creation of this new British institution is a significant step in the evolution of British tradition, culture and history—the very groundwork for our constitution which has developed organically over centuries—and provides greater clarity by further separating the judiciary from the legislature, underlining the independence of our judicial system.

Situated in Parliament Square—one of the most historic and recognisable public spaces in the world—the Supreme Court sits alongside other key British institutions—Houses of Parliament, Westminster Abbey and the Treasury, further emphasising the clear and physical separation of powers.

This new institution will be much more visible than the one it replaces, providing greater access to the public than ever before. No longer will our highest court in the land be hidden at the end of a corridor in the House of Lords, but instead members of the public will be able to walk in off the street to see for themselves the work of our senior judiciary. [. . .]

15

THE JUDICIARY

CENTRAL ISSUES

1. Judges play a vital role in resolving legal disputes, interpreting and applying legislation, developing the common law, and supervising public authorities. Public confidence depends on judges being impartial, competent and fair, and on the judiciary being institutionally independent.
2. Judicial independence is protected by various guarantees including security of tenure and s. 3 of the Constitutional Reform Act 2005 which places duties on the Lord Chancellor and others to protect and maintain judicial independence.
3. How judges are appointed is also important. The process should satisfy the principles of independence, equality, and transparency. Judicial appointments should be on merit and ensure that the judges come from a diversity of backgrounds thereby supporting legitimacy and the quality of justice. There has been recent progress in achieving a more diverse judiciary but as we shall see, this remains a work in progress.
4. Judicial independence does not mean that judges must be unaccountable. Robust criticism of judgments is part of democratic debate. Inaccurate or intimidatory commentary, however, can undermine independence and the safety of judges.
5. Judges are sometimes asked to chair public inquiries and related bodies. These roles can serve the public interest but risk perceived politicisation, so safeguards are needed to protect judicial independence.

15.1 INTRODUCTION

15.1.1 THE ROLE OF THE JUDICIARY IN THE UNITED KINGDOM

Judges resolve disputes, interpret and apply legislation, develop the common law, and ensure public authorities act lawfully and respect human rights. Over the past three decades, expanded judicial review, the Human Rights Act 1998, and (historically) EU law have increased both the visibility and the constitutional weight of the judicial role. We therefore begin with who the judges are and how the system is structured, before turning to independence, accountability, appointments and diversity, media criticism, and the use of judges to chair inquiries. Each section asks what independence requires in practice and how far other constitutional values—transparency, diversity, free expression—can be accommodated without diluting it?

15.1.2 THE JUDICIARY: SOME FACTS AND FIGURES

In constitutional terms, the most important domestic judges sit in the United Kingdom's top court, the Supreme Court (until October 2009, the top court was the Appellate Committee of the House of Lords) and the 'higher', or 'senior', courts in each of the three territorial jurisdictions (see Box 15.1).[1] The judges of these courts make the most significant contribution to the development and exposition of the law, and decide the cases that are likely to be the most difficult and to have the greatest impacts.

BOX 15.1 HIGHER OR SENIOR COURTS IN THE THREE TERRITORIAL JURISDICTIONS

United Kingdom	United Kingdom Supreme Court (final court of appeal for civil cases across the UK and criminal cases from England & Wales and Northern Ireland. Scottish criminal appeals lie to the High Court of Justiciary.)
England and Wales	Court of Appeal—Civil and Criminal Divisions High Court (including the Administrative Court)
Scotland	Court of Session—Outer House (first instance) and Inner House (appellate). High Court of Justiciary (criminal)
Northern Ireland	Court of Appeal High Court; Crown Court

There are, however, many other judges handling the day-to-day work of the lower courts in each of the jurisdictions, including tribunal judges (and non-lawyers who serve on tribunals);[2] and the part-time lay magistrates (advised by legally qualified clerks) who, in England and Wales, deal with the bulk of criminal law matters. The following figures provide an indication of the number of judges as at 1 April 2025.

OFFICIAL STATISTICS, DIVERSITY OF THE JUDICIARY[3]

As at 1 April 2025 [. . .] there were:

- 3,578 court judges.
- 1,716 tribunal judges, with an additional 3,069 non-legal members of tribunals.
- 14,636 magistrates across England and Wales.

These figures provide an idea of the size of the judiciary. Surprisingly perhaps, the vast majority of judges are non-lawyers and, even among the legally qualified judges, the majority work on a part-time basis. From this perspective, the judiciary is a large and varied institution—but the figures in Box 15.2 show that, in terms of gender and ethnic composition, diversity is not yet a hallmark of the judiciary.

[1] https://www.judiciary.uk/ [2] On tribunals, see Chapter 16.

[3] https://www.gov.uk/government/statistics/diversity-of-the-judiciary-2025-statistics/diversity-of-the-judiciary-legal-professions-new-appointments-and-current-post-holders-2025-statistics--2

BOX 15.2 GENDER AND ETHNIC COMPOSITION OF THE JUDICIARY

Women

As at 1 April 2025 39 per cent of all court judges were women (14 percentage points higher than in 2015) and 54 per cent of tribunal judges were women. 28 per cent of judges in the High Court and above were women.[4]

In October 2023 Lady Carr, became the first woman Chief Justice of England and Wales, this was an institutional milestone relevant to judicial leadership, independence and the diversity agenda.

Asian and mixed ethnicity and Black and Other minority individuals

As at 1 April 2025, 12 per cent of judges were from ethnic minority backgrounds (including Asian, Black, Mixed and Other). 6 per cent were from Asian backgrounds (a 3 percentage point increase since 2015), 1 per cent were from black backgrounds (no overall change since 2015 and 1 per cent were from other ethnic minority backgrounds (no overall change since 2015).[5]

We shall return to the issue of diversity later in the chapter. Suffice to say, the above statistics indicate that while progress has been made much remains to be done.[6]

15.1.3 QUALIFICATIONS FOR BEING A JUDGE

Later, we shall consider the range of qualities and abilities that judges are expected to possess. Box 15.3 lists the main statutory qualifications.[7]

BOX 15.3 QUALIFICATIONS FOR JUDGES: CIRCUIT JUDGES AND ABOVE IN ENGLAND AND WALES

Position	Qualification
Justice of the UK Supreme Court	High judicial office for two years *or* 15 years as a 'qualifying practitioner'[8]
Lord/Lady Justice of Appeal (mainly sits in the Court of Appeal)	High Court judge *or* normally 7 years' right of audience in the High Court
High Court judge	Circuit judge for two years *or* normally 7 years' right of audience in the High Court
Circuit judges (mainly sit in the Crown Court and County Court)	Recorder *or* normally 7 years' right of audience in the Crown Court or County Court *or* other judicial office

[4] Official Statistics, Diversity of the judiciary, 2025 statistics. https://www.gov.uk/government/statistics/diversity-of-the-judiciary-2025-statistics/. The statistics provide a more detailed breakdown of these figures.

[5] Ibid.

[6] See K. Malleson, 'Diversity in the judiciary: The case for positive action' (2009) 36 Journal of Law and Society 376, 377; E. Rackley, 'A Short History of Judicial Diversity' (2023) *Current Legal Problems*, Vol 76, Issue 1, 265–296.

[7] Courts and Legal Services Act 1990, Pt III.

[8] Constitutional Reform Act 2005 (CRA 2005), s. 25(1). The term 'qualifying practitioner' is defined in s. 25(2).

15.1.4 RELATIONSHIPS WITH OTHER INSTITUTIONS

The principle of the separation of powers was discussed in Chapter 5. There we considered in general terms the relationship between the judiciary and Parliament and the executive. In that chapter, we cited the judgment of Lord Mustill in the *Fire Brigades Union* case. His comments are worth setting out once again.

R v Secretary for the Home Department, ex parte Fire Brigades Union
[1995] 2 AC 513, 567

Lord Mustill

It is a feature of the peculiarly British conception of the separation of powers that Parliament, the executive and the courts have each their distinct and largely exclusive domain. Parliament has a legally unchallengeable right to make whatever laws it thinks right. The executive carries on the administration of the country in accordance with the powers conferred on it by law. The courts interpret the laws, and see that they are obeyed. This requires the courts on occasion to step into the territory which belongs to the executive, not only to verify that the powers asserted accord with the substantive law created by Parliament, but also, that the manner in which they are exercised conforms with the standards of fairness which Parliament must have intended.

While Lord Mustill's statement sets out the general relationships between the three main branches of the constitutional system where the precise lines are to be drawn between the various domains can be intensely controversial. An obvious example was seen in relation to the *Miller 1* case, discussed later in the chapter and elsewhere in this book[9], which generated much debate on whether it was appropriate for the courts to decide if the executive had legal power to initiate the UK's withdrawal from the EU given the earlier referendum. Also, while Lord Mustill's statement explains that judges may be required to step into the executive domain, it says nothing about the ability of the executive or Parliament to step into the judicial domain.

The decision of the UK Supreme Court in *R (on the application of Evans) and another v Attorney General*[10] is an example of a case in which the executive claimed authority to overturn a judicial decision with which it disagreed, and thereby to enter the domain of the judiciary.[11] The case concerned correspondence between the then Prince of Wales and government ministers which the Upper Tribunal had decided to disclose in the public interest. The Attorney General claimed that statute gave him power to veto that decision and to prevent disclosure of the correspondence. Lord Neuberger said that the executive cannot 'set aside' court decisions. Note the two constitutional principles he identifies.

R (on the application of Evans) and another v Attorney General
[2015] UKSC 21

Lord Neuberger

52. [. . . S]ubject to being overruled by a higher court or [. . .] a statute, it is a basic principle that a decision of a court is binding as between the parties, and cannot be ignored or set aside by anyone, including (indeed it may fairly be said, least of all) the executive [. . . Second] it is also fundamental to

[9] See Chapter 24. [10] [2015] UKSC 21.

[11] For an analysis of the decision, see M. Elliott, 'A tangled constitutional web: The black-spider memos and the British constitution's relational architecture' [2015] *Public Law* 539.

> the rule of law that decisions and actions of the executive are, subject to necessary well established exceptions (such as declarations of war), and jealously scrutinised statutory exceptions, reviewable by the court at the suit of an interested citizen. [. . . The Attorney General's . . .] argument in this case, flouts the first principle and stands the second principle on its head. It involves saying that a final decision of a court can be set aside by a member of the executive (normally the minister in charge of the very department against whom the decision has been given) because he does not agree with it.

While Lord Neuberger does not specifically refer to the principle of judicial independence, it is clear that judicial independence would be flouted were the executive able to overturn judicial decisions with which they disagreed. We return to judicial independence in a moment, but first let us consider an example of a situation in which Parliament has been accused of trespassing into the judicial domain in relation to s. 19 of the Immigration Act 2014.[12]

Some of the terms of that section are set out below. You will see that the section indicates the factors to be considered by courts when deciding whether immigration decisions, such as decisions to deport, are compatible with Art. 8 of the ECHR and in particular whether they are justified as being in the public interest. As well as indicating factors to which courts must '*have regard*', the section also sets out factors which must be given '*little weight*' by judges. These include a private life established by a person '*while they were in the United Kingdom unlawfully or while their immigration status is precarious*'. It may be argued that while Parliament can legitimately set out the factors to be considered by judges, how much weight is to be attached to them is a matter for judges alone to decide.

Immigration Act 2014, s. 19

19. Article 8 of the ECHR: public interest considerations

After Part 5 of the Nationality, Immigration and Asylum Act 2002 insert—

Section 117A

(1) This [provision] applies where a court or tribunal is required to determine whether a decision made under the Immigration Acts—

(a) breaches a person's right to respect for private and family life under Article 8, and

(b) as a result would be unlawful under section 6 of the Human Rights Act 1998.

(2) In considering the public interest question [. . .]

117B [. . .]

(4) Little weight should be given to—

(a) a private life, or

(b) a relationship formed with a qualifying partner,

that is established by a person at a time when the person is in the United Kingdom unlawfully.

(5) Little weight should be given to a private life established by a person at a time when the person's immigration status is precarious.

[. . .]

[12] Which amended the Nationality, Immigration and Asylum Act 2002.

When scrutinizing the wording of the Immigration Bill 2013 (which became the 2014 Act), the Joint Committee on Human Rights described provisions intended to tell courts and tribunals that '*little weight*' should be given to certain considerations as '*a significant legislative trespass into the judicial function*'.[13]

The above issues concern the parameters of judicial independence: if judgments can be overturned by the executive and if Parliament can dictate what judgments are to be made by judges the judiciary will no longer be truly independent.

15.2 JUDICIAL INDEPENDENCE

The fundamental importance of judicial independence has been stated and restated many times. Here are three statements of its importance.[14]

Commonwealth Latimer House Principles, 1V

An independent, impartial honest and competent judiciary is integral to upholding the rule of law, engendering public confidence and dispensing justice.[15]

A and ors v Secretary of State for the Home Department; X and anor v Secretary of State for the Home Department
[2004] UKHL 56

Lord Bingham

42. [. . . T]he function of independent judges charged to interpret and apply the law is universally recognised as a cardinal feature of the modern democratic state, a cornerstone of the rule of law itself.

The Judiciary of England and Wales, 'Judges and the Constitution'

[. . . F]or hundreds of years the overriding principle of our legal system has been that judges are independent of government. That means they make their decisions without interference from the government or the executive. Judges also do not get involved with politics.[16]

[13] Joint Committee on Human Rights, Legislative Scrutiny: Immigration Bill, Eighth Report, Session 2013–14 (HL Paper 102, HC 935), para. 60. Another example was in s. 2(1) Safety of Rwanda (Asylum and Immigration) Act 2024. This told 'every decision-maker'(including judges) that Rwanda 'must conclusively be treated as a safe country'. This Act has now been repealed.

[14] See also, Art. 10 of the Universal Declaration of Human Rights, Art 6. of the ECHR; 2002 *Bangalore Principles*; *Mount Scopus Principles* of *International Standards of Judicial Independence*, 19 March 2008.

[15] Recent threats to judicial independence in Poland, Bulgaria, and Hong Kong have attracted widespread concern and condemnation, See, e.g., Jack Beatson, *The Rule of Law and the Separation of Powers* (2021, Oxford: Hart Publishing), p. 97.

[16] Available at www.judiciary.gov.uk. Lord Phillips of Worth Matravers discusses judges, the constitution, and judicial independence in a video and podcast interview, available at http://clients.westminster-digital.co.uk/judiciary. See also, Lord Neuberger in *R (Miller) v Secretary of State for Exiting the European Union* [2017] UKSC 5, at [3].

Of particular importance are the implications of judicial independence for:

(a) the institutional independence of the judiciary: i.e. the independence of the judiciary as a whole from the executive and Parliament; and

(b) the independence of individual judges to ensure the impartial application of the law to particular disputes.

We shall see that the concept of judicial independence continues to evolve as the key players in the constitutional system come to better understand how to balance independence with other demands, such as the call for the judiciary to be responsive to changes in society. It is often said that judicial independence does not require judicial isolation. This is true—but is independence compatible with greater judicial accountability? Is judicial impartiality possible if the judiciary is expected to reflect the wider community? The following extract from *The Governance of Britain: Judicial Appointments*, published by the Secretary of State and Lord Chancellor explains the value of judicial independence and what it means for the relationships between judges, the executive, the legislature, and the parties to a case.

Secretary of State for Justice and Lord Chancellor, *The Governance of Britain: Judicial Appointments*, Cm 7210 (October 2007), pp. 16–19

An independent judiciary

2.4 Judicial independence is vitally important to the rule of law, and in particular to public confidence in judges as a means of upholding the law. This in turn brings social and economic benefits. It enables people to be assured that when their rights are infringed, or when others' duties need to be enforced, the appropriate action will be taken. It assures people that justice will be done when a criminal allegation is made. It also helps to sustain international confidence in Britain as a stable country in which, and with which, it is safe to do business.

2.5 [. . .] It is important to be clear about the meaning of judicial independence—from whom or from what judges need to be independent.

The Executive

2.6 In a country operating under the rule of law, judges need to be independent of the executive. It must not be possible for the executive to require or improperly influence judges to decide cases in a particular way. Otherwise, there is an inevitable danger that the law could be used (or would be perceived as being used) to service the interests of the executive. Just as important, it is essential that the public has confidence that judges will interpret the law impartially and, where appropriate, stand up for the rights of individuals irrespective of the wishes or interests of the state.

The Legislature

2.7 The judiciary also needs to be independent of Parliament. Parliament (in particular the House of Commons) is the national body where the interests and views of the public are represented and with the ultimate power to make law. It is the duty of judges to decide cases within the limits of the law Parliament lays down. However, within those limits, it is in the interests of justice that the judiciary should be left free to decide cases, protected from political pressure to reach particular decisions in individual cases.

Parties to a case

2.8 It is also vital that judges be independent of the parties in a case. Most obviously, it means that no party to a case—including the Government, directly as a party in civil cases, and indirectly through the Crown as prosecutor in criminal cases—should be able to procure a favourable result by means of exerting improper influence. Further, it is a fundamental feature of the justice system that judges should be free from bias, and from perceptions of bias.

Securing independence

2.9 One of the most important ways of securing judicial independence is to ensure that the appointments process does not result in politically biased judges, or judges who are, or feel, beholden to the appointing body or person, or to any individual or organisation. [. . .]

2.10 There are a range of other factors—beyond the appointments process itself—that are vital to securing independence while a judge is in post. The first among these is security of tenure, ensuring that judges cannot be dismissed because they make unfavourable decisions against, or are unpopular with, Government. Judges are protected against threats of cuts to their salaries; against political pressure in relation to their judgments, for example by clear practices restricting what may be said publicly by the legislature or executive during ongoing legal proceedings; from intimidation; and may not generally be sued for the manner in which they discharge their responsibilities of office.

15.2.1 JUDICIAL INDEPENDENCE: A HISTORICAL PERSPECTIVE

Judicial independence[17] has not always been a feature of the constitutional system and some aspects have only been realized very recently. The basis of the modern system was laid by Art. 7 of the Act of Settlement 1701, which gave judges security of tenure, provided that judges hold office during 'good behaviour' and can only be removed by an address to the Crown by both Houses of Parliament.[18] It meant that the monarch could no longer act alone to remove judges because the monarch disliked their decisions.[19] This provision, now contained in s. 11(3) of the Senior Courts Act 1981, continues to protect the independence of the most senior judges, although the Lord Chancellor, with the concurrence of the Chief Justice, can remove less senior judges, including High Court judges, on grounds of misbehaviour or inability to perform their duties.[20]

Interestingly, while it was recognised that judges should be protected from the executive, there was no requirement that judges should be politically neutral, or that they should not be members of the legislature or the executive. Certainly, prior to Lord Haldane's time as Lord Chancellor (1912–15), it was common for judges to be appointed because of their politics and their party allegiance. Professor John Griffith, for example, quotes Lord Salisbury who, when Prime Minister in August 1895, wrote: '*That there is no clearer statute in [the unwritten law of our party system] than the rule that party claims should always weigh very heavily in the disposal of the highest [judicial] appointments.*'[21]

There have even been occasions when judges have served in government. Lord Cave, for example, served as Home Secretary for a short time at the end of the First World War while being a Law

[17] See further, Jack Beatson, *The Rule of Law and The Separation of Powers* (2021, Oxford: Hart Publishing), ch. 7. Also Lord Burnett of Maldon, 'Institutional Independence and Accountability of the Judiciary' The Lionel Cohen Lecture 2022, Hebrew University of Jerusalem, 30 May 2022, https://www.judiciary.uk/announcements/lionel-cohen-lecture-2022-lord-chief-justice/.

[18] Only one judge has been removed under Art. 7: Sir Jonah Barrington, in 1830 for embezzlement.

[19] As the Stuart kings had done. See further J.H. Baker, *An introduction to English Legal History* 5th edn (2019, Oxford: OUP), 117–78.

[20] 1760 legislation gave judges security of salary. But it did not secure their pensions and this continues to be a contentious issue.

[21] J.A.G. Griffith, *The Politics of the Judiciary*, 5th edn (1997, London: Fontana Press), p. 15.

Lord.[22] Although judges are not eligible to become members of the House of Commons[23] or speak in Parliamentary debates except on technical matters, until 2005 the Lord Chancellor combined judicial, executive, and legislative functions. Neither do we need reminding that the highest court in the system until the establishment of the UK Supreme Court was a committee of the legislature.

The modern relationships between the judiciary and the executive and Parliament must be understood against the backdrop of several key constitutional developments introduced by the Constitutional Reform Act 2005. In particular, as well as referring to the rule of law,[24] that Act:

- Created the UK Supreme Court so that the UK's top court is no longer the Appellate Committee of the House of Lords (part of the legislature) and is therefore institutionally independent of the legislature and executive.
- Modified the status and role of the Lord Chancellor so that the Lord Chancellor no longer exercises judicial functions, no longer chairs the House of Lords, and no longer heads the judiciary. The Lady Chief Justice of England and Wales now heads the judiciary in England and Wales, the Lord President of the Court of Session heads the judiciary in Scotland, and the Lord Chief Justice of Northern Ireland heads the judiciary in that part of the UK.
- Reformed judicial appointments and established the Judicial Appointments Commission.
- Reformed judicial discipline and established the Judicial Appointments and Conduct Ombudsman

Section 3 of the Constitutional Reform Act 2005 also provides the first statutory recognition of judicial independence and of duties upon the executive to maintain it.

15.2.2 STATUTORY GUARANTEES OF JUDICIAL INDEPENDENCE FROM THE EXECUTIVE

The reforms we have referred to were at least partly driven by a concern to create a greater separation between the judiciary and politicians (ministers and parliamentarians). An accompanying concern has been to achieve more explicit statements of the principle of judicial independence. These are now contained in three separate statutory provisions: the Constitutional Reform Act 2005, s. 3 the Judiciary and Courts (Scotland) Act 2008, s. 1 and the Justice (Northern Ireland) Act 2002, s. 1.

The three legislative provisions are an important step towards the codification of key constitutional principles, including the requirement for judicial independence, and a significant shift away from the traditional approach that left basic constitutional requirements to be protected by a rather loose combination of conventions, practices, and understandings (many of which, when tested, were found not to be very well understood).

We shall look more closely at the first and broadest of these provisions. As you read s 3, ask (i) who must defend independence? (ii) What 'special access' is ruled out? And (iii) when do issues concerning resourcing of the courts affect independence?

[22] T. Mohr, *Lord Cave, the British Empire and Irish Independence—A Test of Judicial Integrity* (2012) 12(2) Oxford University Commonwealth Law Journal 8.

[23] House of Commons Disqualification Act 1975, Sch. 1.

[24] See Chapter 4.

Constitutional Reform Act 2005, s. 3

Continued judicial independence

3 Guarantee of continued judicial independence

(1) The Lord Chancellor, other Ministers of the Crown and all with responsibility for matters relating to the judiciary or otherwise to the administration of justice must uphold the continued independence of the judiciary.

[...]

(2) The following particular duties are imposed for the purpose of upholding that independence.

(3) The Lord Chancellor and other Ministers of the Crown must not seek to influence particular judicial decisions through any special access to the judiciary.

(4) The Lord Chancellor must have regard to—

(a) the need to defend that independence;

(b) the need for the judiciary to have the support necessary to enable them to exercise their functions;

(c) the need for the public interest in regard to matters relating to the judiciary or otherwise to the administration of justice to be properly represented in decisions affecting those matters.

[...]

Independence, then, has guardians—especially the Lord Chancellor—who must defend it and recognise the need for the system to be resourced and supported .

15.2.2.1 The duties to maintain judicial independence

Section 3(1) of the CRA imposes a general duty on the Lord Chancellor, other government ministers, and '*all with responsibility for matters relating to the judiciary*' or '*the administration of justice*', to '*uphold the continued independence of the judiciary*'. It also imposes the following particular duties.

- Government ministers have the duty '*not to seek to influence particular judicial decisions through any special access to the judiciary*': s. 3(5) CRA.
- The Lord Chancellor has the duty '*to defend*' judicial independence: s. 3(6)(a) CRA.
- The Lord Chancellor must ensure that the judiciary has '*the support necessary to enable them to exercise their functions*': s. 3(6)(b) CRA.[25]

The significance and implications of the Lord Chancellor's duty to defend judicial independence have been considered by the House of Lords Select Committee on the Constitution. In the following extract, the Committee emphasizes the link between the rule of law and the independence of the judiciary, noting that the CRA imposes duties upon the Lord Chancellor to defend both.[26]

[25] The Lord Chancellor's duty to defend judicial independence is reflected in the following oath: '*I [...], do swear that in the office of Lord High Chancellor of Great Britain I will respect the rule of law, defend the independence of the judiciary and discharge my duty to ensure the provision of resources for the efficient and effective support of the courts for which I am responsible. So help me God*' (CRA 2005, s. 17).

[26] See also the HL Select Committee on the Constitution's report: *The Office of the Lord Chancellor*, December 2014, HL 75.

House of Lords Select Committee on the Constitution, *Relations between the Executive, the Judiciary and Parliament*, Sixth Report, Session 2006–07 (footnotes omitted)

39. [. . . T]he Lord Chancellor must ensure that the principle of judicial independence is not violated. His duty to 'defend' the independence of the judiciary is stronger than the duty of all other ministers to 'uphold' that independence, giving him a special enforcement role in relation to the rest of the government. Lord Lloyd of Berwick, a former Law Lord, told us that there were two key aspects to defending judicial independence. The first is 'where there is an attempt [. . .] by Government [. . .] to restrict [. . .] the jurisdiction of the courts', for example the proposed 'ouster' clause in the Asylum and Immigration (Treatment of Claimants, etc.) Bill in 2004.[27] In such cases, 'the Lord Chancellor's duty is absolute; he must point out in Cabinet that this would undermine the independence of the judiciary'. Even though the Lord Chancellor is no longer head of the judiciary, it is essential that he should remain a jealous guardian of judicial independence in Cabinet.

40. The second aspect of defending the independence of the judiciary, Lord Lloyd said, was dealing with ministers who attack individual judges. [. . .]

15.2.2.2 The Lord Chancellor and other members of the Executive must not seek to influence particular decisions by special access

If the government is a party to a case, it can, will, and should seek to present arguments to the court that are intended to persuade the judge(s) that its view of the facts and/or the law is correct and should be adopted. This is a normal part of adjudication. What government cannot do is seek 'special access' to judges in order to influence particular decisions.[28] This prohibition is intended to prevent attempts to influence judges beyond the transparency of the courtroom. But does it also prohibit government from seeking access to judges in order to obtain their opinion on the legality of government proposals, or other matters, before litigation arises? On one view, such access would be permissible and extremely useful. After all, if the government were able to obtain a judicial opinion on the legality of its proposals, this would enable government to amend its schemes in ways that may improve rights, and would save time and trouble later. It might even be argued that seeking the advice of judges at this stage would not offend the wording of s. 3, because it would not constitute an attempt to influence judges in relation to particular decisions.

That narrow interpretation, however, would not fully reflect the requirements of judicial independence. This can be illustrated by the following account given by Lord Phillips of Worth Matravers of the way in which senior judges reacted when the then Home Secretary, Charles Clarke, wanted to speak to the Law Lords about reforming the law relating to control orders under the counter-terrorism legislation.[29]

[27] See Chapter 22.

[28] Nor can the government, when a party to a case, seek to prevent the judges from seeing relevant material filed in the case. see *Privacy International v Foreign Secretary and others* [2020] UKIPTrib IPT 17, 86 CH. See further Jack Beatson, *The Rule of Law and the Separation of Powers* (2021, Oxford: Hart Publishing), p. 109.

[29] On which, see Chapter 22.

Lord Phillips of Worth Matravers, 'The Supreme Court and other constitutional changes in the UK', Address to the Members of the Royal Court, the Jersey Law Society, and the members of the States of Jersey, 2 May 2008 (footnotes omitted)

The public, and sometimes even politicians, do not always understand the importance of judicial independence. In 2006 Charles Clarke, the former Home Secretary gave evidence to the House of Lords Select Committee on the Constitution. The Prevention of Terrorism Act 2005 entitled the Home Secretary to make control orders for the restriction of the ambit of life of terrorist suspects. A series of Control Orders issued by Charles Clarke had been overturned by the court, and finally the House of Lords.

Charles Clarke vented his frustration at this before the Select Committee. He said—

> The judiciary bears not the slightest responsibility for protecting the public, and sometimes seems utterly unaware of the implications of their decisions for our security. I regard it as disgraceful that no Law Lord is prepared to discuss in any forum with the Home Secretary of the day the issues of principle involved in these matters. The idea that their independence would be corrupted by such discussions is risible [. . .] I strongly believe that the attitude of the Law Lords has to change. It fuels the dangerously confused and ill informed debate which challenges Britain's adherence to the European Convention on Human Rights. It is now time for the judiciary to engage in a serious and considered debate about how best to legally confront terrorism in modern circumstances.

Charles Clarke wanted the Law Lords to meet with him to discuss broad issues of principle. I can understand the frustration that the former Home Secretary feels on this point. But judges must not risk collusion with the executive when they are likely to be required to adjudicate on challenges to the actions of the executive.

[. . .]

15.2.2.3 Improper criticism of the judiciary by the Executive

As Lord Lloyd of Berwick explained to the House of Lords Constitution Committee, the duty to protect judicial independence requires judges to be protected from personal criticism by government ministers. The importance of this can be understood against the backdrop of criticism of judges following their decisions. In the mid-1990s, sections of the media launched attacks on the judges following several judicial review decisions that were unfavourable to the government. Andrew Le Sueur commented that these events suggested that it had become possible '*for ministers and their supporters to condemn unfavourable judicial review judgments in an unprecedentedly aggressive and confrontational manner*'. This, he said, upset the '*equilibrium in Britain's subtle uncodified constitution*'.[30]

Similar attacks on judges have continued. Following a decision by Collins J (as he then was) concerning the rights of asylum seekers to seek financial support under s. 55 of the Nationality, Immigration and Asylum Act 2002 that was unfavourable to the government,[31] David Blunkett, then Home Secretary, said in a radio interview that he was '*fed up with having to deal with a situation where Parliament debates issues and the judges then overturn them. I don't want any mixed messages going out so I am making it absolutely clear that we don't accept what Mr Justice Collins has said.*'[32]

This criticism was followed by personal attacks in the media, possibly based on Whitehall briefings.[33] Professor Bradley, for example, tells us that the *Daily Telegraph* said: '*One man's rulings have*

[30] A. Le Sueur, 'The judicial review debate: From partnership to friction' (1996) 31 *Government and Opposition* 8, 9, 24.
[31] *R (on the application of Q) v Secretary of State for the Home Department* [2003] EWHC 195 Admin.
[32] *The Times*, 20 February 2003.
[33] A. Bradley, 'Judicial independence under attack' [2003] Public Law 397, 401.

thwarted all moves to stem the tide of refugees [. . .] whenever the Government has been on the wrong end of an asylum ruling in recent years, Collins has often been the villain of the piece [. . .]. This particular judge is considered a serial offender in Whitehall.'[34]

The tabloids were more extreme in their comments. The *Daily Mail*, for example, referred to '*judges [. . .] who have it in for Britain [. . .] whose arrogance and perversity [is] setting the wishes of the people at nought and pursuing a liberal, politically correct agenda of their own*'.[35] Professor Bradley observes that '*it would be regrettable if similar recriminations were to occur whenever judges are exercising the functions that are entrusted to them by Parliament and which are essential in a democratic society that is committed to the rule of law*'.[36]

In the *Craig Sweeney* case, a judge was widely criticized for imposing a 12-year sentence on a convicted paedophile who had pleaded guilty to kidnapping a three-year-old girl and committing serious sexual offences on her while released on licence. The then Home Secretary, John Reid, said that the sentence was '*unduly lenient*' and did not '*reflect the seriousness of the crime*'. The Daily Express wrote that judges were '*deluded, out-of-touch and frankly deranged*' and that '*our legal system has not only lost touch with public opinion but with natural justice itself [. . .]*'. *The Sun* newspaper began a campaign to pressurize the government to sack judges who it claimed were guilty of being soft on '*killers, child sex beasts and rapists*'.

House of Lords Select Committee on the Constitution, *Relations between the Executive, the Judiciary and Parliament*, Sixth Report, Session 2006–07 (footnotes omitted)

49. The Sweeney case was the first big test of whether the new relationship between the Lord Chancellor and the judiciary was working properly, and it is clear that there was a systemic failure. Ensuring that ministers do not impugn individual judges, and restraining and reprimanding those who do, is one of the most important duties of the Lord Chancellor. In this case, Lord Falconer [the then Lord Chancellor] did not fulfil this duty in a satisfactory manner. The senior judiciary could also have acted more quickly to head off the inflammatory and unfair press coverage which followed the sentencing decision.

The Committee recommended that the *Ministerial Code* (the code of conduct and guidance on procedures for ministers, published by the Cabinet Office) should be revised to insert strongly worded guidelines setting out the principles governing public comment by ministers on individual judges.[37] The government agreed that ministers should not make '*inaccurate or ill-considered*' comments on the actions of any individual judge and to '*consider the committee's recommendations when the code is next revised*'.[38] However, to date the *Ministerial Code* has yet to be amended to include such a restriction on ministers.

More recently the Lady Chief Justice, felt it necessary to rebuke both Sir Keir Starmer, the Prime Minister, and Kemi Badenoch, the leader of the opposition, following their criticism of a immigration tribunal's decision that a family of refugees from Gaza were entitled to settle in the UK. [39] The

[34] Bradley notes that the term 'serial offender' also appeared in the *Daily Mail* and *News of the World*: ibid, 401. See also Lord Dyson's Third Annual Bailii Lecture on Criticising Judges 'Fair Game or off-limits?' (17 November 2014) https://www.judiciary.uk/wp-content/uploads/2014/11/bailli-critising-judges.pdf.

[35] A. Bradley, 'Judicial independence under attack' [2003] Public Law 397, 401.

[36] Ibid, 405.

[37] On the *Ministerial Code*, see Chapter 9.

[38] Baroness Royall of Blaisdon, House of Lords Hansard, 18 November 2008, col. 1125.

[39] This was the subject of an editorial in the Guardian newspaper: *The Guardian view on Labour and the constitution: respect judicial independence*, 19 February 2025.

issue was one of the matters raised by the House of Lords Constitution Committee during its annual meeting with the Lady Chief Justice. The committee's chair started by asking Lady Carr about her reaction to the Prime Minister's and the leader of the opposition's criticism of the tribunal's decision and whether 'there is a constitutional issue here which needs to be resolved satisfactorily'?

Constitution Committee Annual Evidence Session With The Lady Chief Justice,
26th February 2025

The Lady Chief Justice:. [. . .] I would say at the outset it is really important to understand that no one has ever suggested [. . .] that there should not be healthy, robust, open debate both in and outside Parliament, including criticism, if necessary, of judgments. That is fundamental. But the judicial process and judicial independence has to be respected at the same time. That's the fundamental point. So if judgments are wrong, you can appeal them. The judgment that was under discussion then is not the subject of appeal. But if judgments are wrong, there are routes of appeal. If the law is wrong, it is Parliament's prerogative to change it. So appropriate public debate inside and outside Parliament, based on fact, not misconception, is a sign of healthy democracy, it is a really important part of open justice . . . However, criticism of a judgment, debating a judgment, is one thing. Inaccurate reporting and the abuse of judges who cannot speak out to defend themselves is another. So the real trigger for my concern here . . .is, frankly, the dangers that arise out of inaccurate reporting. [. . .] to imply, for example, that a Palestinian family was allowed to settle in this country under the Ukrainian Family Scheme is simply wholly wrong. But, as a result of that headline and the publicity [. . .] there have been extraordinarily serious security threats. We are talking about judges being doorstepped. We have a death threat to a judge. [. . .] We have judges whose families live in fear, whose homes are targeted [. . .].

We return to the issues raised by Lady Carr when we look more closely at judicial accountability. We also return to media criticism of the judiciary later in the chapter in the context of the mini case study of the *Miller 1* decision.[40]

15.2.2.4 Independence and court resources

The final duty referred to in s. 3 does not concern judicial independence directly, but is addressed at ensuring that the courts are properly resourced and supported. Like other public services, the court system depends on public money distributed by the government: it costs to have courts, and to have judges and the necessary personnel to run the courts. But the government has to balance many factors when deciding how much to spend on the court system and this provision recognises that judicial independence may be undermined if the resources made available to the courts are insufficient.[41]

This provision came to the fore in the controversy that followed the government's announcement that it was to establish a Ministry of Justice, headed by the Lord Chancellor, with responsibility for both prisons and the court system. There was widespread concern, including among the judiciary, about the way in which the announcement had been made and criticism was especially levelled at the absence of consultation. But the judiciary was also concerned about the substance of the change. In particular, it was feared that, within the Ministry of Justice, there would be competition between the

[40] See Section 15.4.
[41] N. Browne-Wilkinson, 'The independence of the judiciary in the 1980s' [1988] Public Law 44.

needs of HM Prison Service and the needs of the administration of justice, and that this would present the Lord Chancellor with a conflict of interests that would make it difficult for him to meet the s. 3 CRA duty to support the court system.[42]

In the following evidence to the House of Lords Constitution Committee the Lady Chief Justice stresses the constitutional and practical importance of having a properly funded judicial system.

Constitution Committee Annual Evidence Session With The Lady Chief Justice,
26th February 2025

Lady Chief Justice

[. . .] it is important to recognise that the rule of law is not just about respecting constitutional boundaries, it is about a properly funded . . ., justice system. You could put it another way, the rule of law is not free. . . . [The] 25–26 budget . . .for the justice system, will be broadly around 1% of the health and social care budget, 2% of education and 3% of defence spending. Public funding for justice in England and Wales declined by 22% in real per person terms from 2009–10 to 2022–23 and over the same period overall government spending increased by 10% in real per person terms.

Can I emphasise at the outset that in making the case for proper funding of the justice system I am not in the business of simply asking for more money. [. . .] justice is referred to in the fiscal context often as an unprotected department, but in fact the courts and tribunals are protected [. . .] by law. Parliament imposed a statutory duty on the Lord Chancellor no less than three times in five years: the Courts Act 2003, the Constitutional Reform Act 2005, the Tribunal Courts and Enforcement Act 2007, to ensure that there is funding for the efficient and effective support of the courts and tribunals. [. . .] this statutory duty was relied on heavily by Lord Falconer, a former member of this committee, when the prisons and probation services were being brought under the umbrella of Ministry of Justice in 2007, and when it was suggested that the justice budget might need to be ring-fenced to protect it against the tensions that might arise, the answer was no, we have the statutory duty that I have just referred to. So it is a really important duty. [. . .]

[She went on to refer to the link between the rule of law and economic growth commenting that]

'[w]e cannot have economic growth without a stable and effective justice system.' We know that we have here the second largest legal sector in the world [. . .] And on this rests our country's reputation as a centre for justice and the rule of law, which is fundamental to our status as one of the world's leading financial centres [. . .]

It is not just about big businesses, is it? There is huge economic advantage in resolving disputes quickly, efficiently, and at proportionate cost for everyone, because if family disputes are resolved quickly then the children will be happier, they'll be healthier, they'll be less likely to commit crime, and they are more likely to get jobs, and their parents are likely to be working better and more productively at work. If employment and contract disputes are resolved quickly and at proportionate cost, then businesses can function with confidence and certainty

So in short, [. . .] The independent judiciary, the rule of law and an effective, properly resourced justice system are the constitutional pillars underpinning our economy, our democracy and society, and they are no less important to them than the NHS, education, and defence.

[42] See, e.g. Lord Phillips of Worth Matravers, 'The Supreme Court and other constitutional changes in the UK', Address to the Members of the Royal Court, the Jersey Law Society, and the members of the States of Jersey, 2 May 2008.

EXERCISE

You are an advisor to a parliamentary committee that is considering the judiciary's constitutional status and have been asked to draft brief note explaining:

- why judicial independence is important;
- the main requirements for achieving and maintaining judicial independence;
- whether it would it be appropriate for a member of the executive to ask judges to give their advice on the legality of a proposed change in the law and if not, why not?
- whether politicians and the media should be able to criticise both judges and judgments?
- the constitutional implications of Robert Jenrick MP's, (Robert Jenrick MP when the shadow justice secretary) announcement that if the Conservative Party forms the government at the next general election it will enact powers reenabling judges to be dismissed for being too activist and it would also abolish the Judicial Appointments Commission to give ministers a bigger role in appointing judges. [43]

15.3 JUDICIAL ACCOUNTABILITY

House of Lords Select Committee on the Constitution, *Relations between the Executive, the Judiciary and Parliament*, Sixth Report, Session 2006–07

> 27. Independence of the judiciary does not mean [. . .] and should not mean that the judiciary have to be isolated from the other branches of the State. Nor does it mean that the judiciary—individually and collectively—need to be insulated from scrutiny, general accountability for their role or properly made public criticisms of conduct inside or outside the courtroom.

There must be a balance between judicial independence and judicial accountability. We rightly expect those with power to be accountable for the way in which their power is exercised. The authority to decide cases, to determine the meaning of legislative provisions, to develop the common law, and to decide on the legality of government's actions, clearly carries very real and potentially controversial powers. We only have to consider the decisions of the courts on the legality of detention orders imposed under the Prevention of Terrorism Act 2005 and government's reaction to these, or more recently, the judges' decision that the executive lacked prerogative power to serve notice of the UK's intention to withdraw from the EU, to see that court decisions can affect contentious issues of public importance. But how are the requirements of judicial independence and judicial accountability to be reconciled? What forms of accountability are appropriate for judges and to whom should they account?

Professor Andrew Le Sueur has identified three schools of thought in relation to judicial accountability: the opponents to accountability; the reconceptualists; and the radicals. The opponents to judicial accountability, he has said, emphasize the need for judicial independence and argue that independence is not consistent with accountability. They say that the notion of an 'accountable judge' is an oxymoron. A judge cannot be both independent and accountable—at least if this means that he or she is to be accountable to those who are outside the court system.

[43] These proposals were announced by Robert Jenrick in a speech to the Conservative Party conference, in Manchester, October 2025.

The reconceptualists, says Le Sueur, agree with this basic point, but say that, within the context of 'self-policing', judges are accountable and that certain forms of accountability are part and parcel of the normal processes of judging.

A. Le Sueur, 'Developing mechanisms for judicial accountability in the UK'
(2004) 24 *Legal Studies* 73, 76

> Among the obvious activities that fall into this category are: the fact that most courts sit in public; the common practice of giving reasoned, written judgments; the possibility that judgments are appealable to a higher judicial body; and the scrutiny meted out to judgments (and judges) by a more-or-less well informed news media and scholarly work of academics.

Unsurprisingly, the radicals are not content with this and call for more and new forms of accountability. Le Sueur, for example, quotes Professor Keith Ewing as arguing that the challenge is '*to ensure that the judges as political actors are more fully accountable to the people over whom they govern, in a manner which enhances rather than undermines their independence [but this is] a tall order*'.[44]

One way of achieving greater accountability for judges has been suggested by Professor Bogdanor, who distinguishes between '*sacrificial accountability*' and '*explanatory accountability*' to Parliament. The former, he accepts, is appropriate in relation to government ministers, but not judges. The latter, however, is appropriate in relation to judges and does not conflict with the needs of judicial independence.

Professor V. Bogdanor, 'Parliament and the judiciary: the problem of accountability',
Sunningdale Lecture, 9 February 2006

> Must the judges be the single exception to the general rule of accountability? Let us distinguish between two different meanings of ministerial accountability to Parliament.
>
> The first meaning is one that we might call sacrificial accountability. This dictates that ministers take the credit for what goes right in their department, and the blame for what goes wrong, to the extent of resigning if something goes seriously wrong. Most ministers, of course, accept only the first part of this principle! Clearly, judges cannot be held accountable to Parliament in this sacrificial sense. They cannot be held to account for their decisions. If they were, this would make nonsense of the principle of the independence of the judiciary.
>
> [. . .]
>
> But it seems to me that there is no reason why judges should not regularly appear before Parliament, or rather before Select Committees of Parliament [. . .] to be cross-examined on their judicial philosophy. Indeed, in recent years, senior members of the judiciary, such as the [Lady] Chief Justice and the Master of the Rolls have appeared before Select Committees to answer questions on issues related to the machinery of Government, as it affects the judges. Judges cannot, of course, be expected to discuss particular judgements, nor matters which are likely to prove justiciable. Such matters would have to be explicitly excluded from the terms of reference of the relevant Select Committee. [This ensures that]. . . judges would become accountable to Parliament not in the first sense, the sacrificial sense, but in [. . .] the explanatory sense.

[44] K. Ewing, 'The Unbalanced Constitution', in T. Campbell, K. Ewing, and A. Tomkins (eds) *Sceptical Essays in Human Rights* (2001, Oxford: OUP), p. 117.

15.3.1 CRITICISM OF THE JUDICIARY IN THE MEDIA

Earlier in the chapter we discussed how improper criticism of judges by government ministers and politicians may be considered to undermine judicial independence. To say that serving government ministers should refrain from criticizing judges does not mean that judges should be immune from being criticized by others, including by ex-ministers or the media. Consider, for example, the decision in March 2012 taken by the then Northern Ireland Attorney General to commence proceedings for contempt of court against Peter Hain MP (now Lord Hain), a former Northern Ireland Secretary, in relation to passages in his memoir, *Outside In*, criticizing Judge Girvan's[45] decision in a 2006 judicial review case. The proceedings for contempt generated an all-party campaign to protect the freedom of MPs to comment on judgments, which led to the prosecution being dropped. The campaign also highlighted the more general question of whether there should be restrictions on free speech in order to prevent criticism of judges. In the House of Commons, David Blunkett MP (a former Labour Home Secretary who, as we have seen, has been very critical of judges) asked the Prime Minister the following question:[46]

> Does the Prime Minister share my concern at the actions of the Northern Ireland Attorney-General [. . .] to invoke contempt proceedings against the former Northern Ireland Secretary [. . .]? Should not respect for the independence of the judiciary be balanced with the rights of individuals to fair comment on that judiciary?

The Prime Minister replied:

> I do have a great deal of sympathy with what the Right Hon. Gentleman says. Parliamentary privilege, obviously and quite rightly, allows Hon. Members to express their views in Parliament. In terms of what is said outside Parliament, let me just say this: there are occasions, as we all know, when judges make critical remarks about politicians; and there are occasions when politicians make critical remarks about judges. To me, that is part of life in a modern democracy, and we ought to keep these things, as far as possible, out of the courtroom.

It is perhaps significant that the Prime Minister refers to situations in which judges have been critical of politicians. Lord Neuberger (when Master of the Rolls), has also commented that '*[M]utual respect between the judges and the politicians is essential [. . .] A judge can scarcely complain about ministers criticising him for the way he is doing his job if he criticises ministers for the way they are doing their jobs.*'[47] While some may see this to be a normal feature of democratic dialogue, Lord Neuberger considers there to be potentially serious consequences:

> [. . . I]f [judges and politicians] slang [*sic*] each other off in public, members of the judiciary and members of the other two branches of government will undermine each other, and, inevitably, the constitution of which they are all a fundamental part, and on which democracy, the rule of law, and our whole society rests.[48]

[45] Later Lord Justice Girvan: Lord Justice Girvan retired in 2015.
[46] Oral Answers to Questions, House of Commons Hansard, 18 April 2012, col. 317.
[47] Lord Neuberger MR, 'Where Angels Fear to Tread', Holdsworth Club Presidential Address, 2 March 2012, para. 37.
[48] Ibid, para. 37.

The above issues arose once again in the context of media reaction to the decision in the *Miller 1* case in which the courts held that the government could not rely on its prerogative powers to serve notice that the UK intended to leave the EU.[49] The aftermath to the High Court's decision raised the question whether there should be limits to press freedom to comment on and criticize judges? If so, where is the line to be drawn between legitimate criticism on the one hand and abuse of press freedom on the other? The aftermath also raised questions about the duty of the Lord Chancellor to protect judges from improper media comment. The saga is worth looking at more closely as a mini case study.

15.4 MINI CASE STUDY: THE *MILLER 1* CASE—INDEPENDENCE OF THE JUDICIARY; DUTIES OF THE LORD CHANCELLOR AND FREEDOM OF THE MEDIA

After the government lost the case in the High Court the *Daily Mail* carried a headline declaring the three judges in the case '*enemies of the people*'. The media also carried personal details of the judges including details of their sexuality.[50] Lord Neuberger, the then President of the Supreme Court, in an interview on BBC Radio 4's Today programme (16 February 2017) responded to this headline suggesting that such criticism undermines the judiciary:[51]

> If we undermine the judiciary, we are undermining the rule of law. The rule of law together with democracy is one of the two pillars on which our society is based [. . .] therefore, if without good reason the media or anyone else undermines the judiciary, that risks undermining our society.

Lord Neuberger also commented that politicians, including by implication the then Lord Chancellor, Elizabeth Truss MP, could have been '*quicker and clearer*' in defending the judiciary. While the former editor of the *Sunday Times*, Sir Harold Evans, said that he thought the *Daily Mail*'s headline '*was disgraceful. It was pure Trumpery*',[52] not all journalists agreed. Kelvin MacKenzie, a former editor of the *Sun*, told the BBC that Lord Neuberger was being '*overly sensitive*' and said judges '*cannot sit above argument or above criticism*':

> [Newspapers] certainly haven't undermined the rule of law [. . .] They have simply added to a debate going on outside the legal entity called the Supreme Court and there is nothing wrong with that. We call that free speech. Surely he is not indicating that free speech should have a limit in relation to the Supreme Court and a judgement [over Brexit] which had an enormous impact on a number of people?

Some lawyers also disagreed with the criticisms of the Lord Chancellor made by Lord Neuberger and others. In the following extract Professor Danny Nicol argues that far from threatening judicial independence, criticism of the judiciary in the press is a healthy sign of free speech that strengthens, rather than weakens, our system. [53]

[49] See also Chapter 10 and Chapter 24.

[50] The following *Guardian* article explores how the High Court judges in the case were individually '*attacked*'. https://www.theguardian.com/politics/2016/nov/04/enemies-of-the-people-british-newspapers-react-judges-brexit-ruling.

[51] https://www.bbc.co.uk/news/uk-38986228.

[52] Debate hosted by the Bureau of Investigative Journalism, reported by the *Press Gazette*, 1 March 2017: https://www.pressgazette.co.uk/enemies-of-the-people-lord-chancellor-liz-truss-says-it-would-be-dangerous-to-tell-daily-mail-want-to-print/.

[53] Professor Graham Gee agreed and argued that the Lord Chancellor had not breached her duty under s 3 of the Constitutionbal Reform Act 2005 in not doing more to protect the judges from media criticism: G. Gee, 'A Tale of Two Constitutional Duties: Liz Truss, Lady Hale, and Miller', Judicial Power Project, 28 November 2016.

D. Nicol, '"Enemies of the people", judicial independence and free speech', Judicial Power Project, 11 November 2016

[. . .] if the press cannot make forthright attacks on the judiciary then that casts doubt on everyone's freedom to do so; and that such a cocooning of the judiciary goes too far in infringing free speech.

The rationale for condemning the headlines is that they are so inflammatory as to undermine the independence of the judiciary. There's nothing wrong with criticising judges, so the story goes, but criticism must be couched in less extreme terms. Otherwise the judges may be intimidated into doing the bidding of the press which in this instance coincides with the wishes of the government. They will thereby lose their cherished freedom of judgment.

[. . .] this argument rather assumes that judges were independent in the first place. Yet as J.A.G. Griffith rather convincingly argues in *The Politics of the Judiciary* (1977) British judges cannot be politically neutral since they are constantly placed in positions where they are required to make political choices, which are presented as determinations of where the public interest lies. Their interpretation of the public interest, Griffith contends, is determined by the kind of people they are and the position they hold in our society. They are part of established authority, and so the judges tend to side with established authority. On Griffith's reading, therefore, the independence of the judiciary does not exist in any meaningful sense. It only exists if one inhabits an ivory tower in which one ignores the structure of capitalist society. The imperatives of that society constitute a far more profound violation of the independence of the judiciary than newspaper headlines.[. . .][54]

These themes were again addressed by the then Lord Chief Justice, Lord Thomas of Cwmgiedd, in a lecture later in the year.

'The judiciary within the state—the relationship between the branches of the state', Michael Ryle Memorial Lecture, 15 June 2017, paras 44–65 (footnotes omitted)

The RT Hon. The Lord Thomas of Cwmgiedd

[. . .] It is axiomatic that a liberal democracy rests upon free and vigorous media to inform the public of what goes on in Parliament, of what the Executive does or is considering doing, and of what the judiciary decides in court. It is the necessary means through which public debate is informed, and very often articulated. [. . .]

Mutual respect and support for the media to carry out its fundamental constitutional role is one of the underpinnings of open justice and its link to freedom of speech. Where the judiciary are concerned the freedom of the media, and freedom of speech, are inextricably linked with the constitutional principle of open justice. The media must be in a position to hear and understand what goes on in court: knowledge of proceedings is necessary if there is to be any speech about it. And they must then be free to report it. Debate must be rigorous, as it helps inform consideration by the Executive and Parliament over whether, and if so how and to what extent, the law needs to be revised or developed by Parliament. It is equally important because media and, through it, public scrutiny of the courts helps to ensure that justice is carried out properly, that arbitrary and unjust practices do not develop: that justice is done through being seen to be done.

[. . .]

[54] https://judicialpowerproject.org.uk/danny-nicol-enemies-of-the-people-judicial-independence-and-free-speech/.

judges must expect to be criticised in the media from time to time for their decisions, though [. . .] they cannot answer such criticism. However, the press is equally under a duty not to act in a way that undermines democracy through undermining the judiciary, Executive or Parliament. In this respect, it is therefore important to distinguish between criticism and abuse. Although the overwhelming majority of media journalists and commentators understand the difference, nonetheless the media have on occasions (rare though they be) subjected the judiciary to abuse, such as happened in November 2016 by labelling of judges as 'enemies of the people'—language used most commonly by totalitarian dictators. Such abuse is not simply an attack on the judges who made the decision; judges have undertaken to decide cases without fear or favour and must not be subjected to improper pressure of this kind. Moreover, such abuse is corrosive of public confidence in the judiciary and the rule of law and hence the other branches of the State. That is why it is so important to distinguish between criticism and abuse and for the media to properly respect the working of our constitution.

The House of Lords Select Committee on the Constitution revisited the various arguments discussed above in the context of the relationship between the judiciary and the government which it said '*was not helped by the furore*' around the *Miller 1* case.[55] After reviewing the views of the Lord Neuberger, Lord Thomas, and Liz Truss MP the Committee concluded as follows.

House of Lord Select Committee on the Constitution, *Judicial Appointments: Follow up*,
7th Report of the Session 2017-19, HL Paper 32

56. It is imperative that the independence of the judiciary is protected and that it is well-understood by the public. This does not impinge on the right of the free press to challenge or to criticise court judgments.

57. However, there is a difference between criticism and abuse; between challenging the content of a judgment and attacking the character and integrity of the judge handing down that judgment. In such cases, the Lord Chancellor's constitutional duty is clear—as stated in the oath of office, the Lord Chancellor must defend the independence of the judiciary. Should members of the judiciary suffer such personal attacks in future, we expect any person holding the office of Lord Chancellor to take a proactive stance in defending them publicly, as they are unable to defend themselves.

58. We welcome the new Lord Chancellor's commitment to be 'resolute and unflinching' in defending the independence of the judiciary.[56]

QUESTION

1. In your opinion was the *Daily Mail* headline declaring the judges who decided *Miller 1* in the High Court to be '*The Enemies of the People*' a legitimate expression of press freedom or an abuse of freedom that undermined the judiciary?

[55] House of Lord Select Committee on the Constitution, *Judicial Appointments: Follow up*, 7th Report of the Session 2017–19, HL Paper 32, para. 48.

[56] The government accepted these conclusions, see *The Government Response to the House of Lords Constitution Committee's 7th Report of Session 2017–19 Judicial Appointments: Follow up*, December 2017, Cmnd 9558, see esp. paras 29–32.

15.5 JUDICIAL IMMUNITY

Before moving on it may be noted that senior judges are absolutely immune from civil liability for what they say or do in the exercise of their judicial functions, even where malice is alleged. While the immunity has been justified as protecting the public interest in judicial independence some rightly argue that the immunity is too broad and should not protect judges who act with malice or personal animus. More broadly it has been argued that it is no longer appropriate for judges to have greater immunity than other professionals such as solicitors and doctors.[57]

15.6 IMPARTIALITY

Judges must be able to approach cases impartially on the basis of the evidence and legal arguments put to them. The requirement of impartiality demands that judges be free from overt or subtle pressures exerted on them by influences outside the courtroom. It also means that they cannot be connected with one or other of the parties in ways that could undermine the appearance of fairness. Independence and judicial impartiality therefore go hand in hand, and are both fundamental to people's confidence in the judicial system.[58]

While we expect our judges to be independent and impartial, we also expect them to be in contact with, and not isolated from, general trends in society. We expect judges to be aware of what is going on around them and capable of applying the law in a manner that strikes a chord with the rest of us. A balance must therefore be struck between the requirements of independence and the need for impartiality, on the one hand, and the desirability of judges to be in touch, on the other.[59]

In the following extract, the House of Lords Committee on the Constitution considers the extent to which judges should become embroiled in politically controversial issues. The Committee draws the distinction between the restraints that must be imposed on individual judges and the need for senior judges to speak on behalf of the judiciary as a whole in cases in which government policy may have an adverse impact upon the administration of justice.

Select Committee on the Constitution, *Relations between the Executive, the Judiciary and Parliament*, Sixth Report, Session 2006–07 (footnotes omitted)

52. Just as ministers ought to demonstrate restraint in commenting on the judiciary, so judges should (and generally do) avoid becoming inappropriately involved in public debates about government policy, matters of political controversy or individual politicians. [. . .]

53. However, the Lord Chief Justice, as head of the judiciary, and perhaps other senior judges with responsibility for specific parts of the justice system, are in a different position from that of other judges. On occasion, it is necessary for them to speak out publicly if a particular government policy is likely to have an adverse impact upon the administration of justice and ministers have failed to provide a satisfactory response during private consultations.

[57] See, Jack Beatson, *The Rule of Law and the Separation of Powers* (2021, Oxford: Hart Publishing), p. 102.
[58] See also Baroness Hale, *Gillies v Secretary of State for Work and Pensions (Scotland)* [2006] UKHL 2.
[59] See, *Guide to Judicial Conduct*, Courts and Tribunals Judiciary, July 2023.

54. Effective channels of communication between the executive and the senior judiciary are vital to ensure that the impact of government legislation or policy proposals upon the administration of justice is fully understood at an early stage. Such communications are facilitated in a variety of ways. [...] As Sir Igor Judge said, 'it is no longer [...] a concomitant of independence that judges should be isolated'.

[...]

56.... there are private meetings which take place between ministers and judges (especially the Attorney General, the Home Secretary—probably now the Secretary of State for Justice—and the Lord Chief Justice) to discuss the practicality of particular government policies in terms of the administration of justice. As Sir Igor Judge explained, 'week after week these sorts of discussions are going on at ministerial level [and] at official level' [...] If these meetings do not lead to satisfactory mutual understandings, it should be noted that the [Lady] Chief Justice can also in appropriate circumstances ask to see the Prime Minister.

QUESTION

'If government ministers are prevented from having "special access" to the judges surely judges should be prevented from having access to government ministers to discuss the impact of government policies on the administration of justice.' Do you agree with this statement, and if not, why not?

The above discussion concerns communication between the judiciary and government in relation to proposals to change policy or the law. Judicial involvement in non-judicial activities can also lead to problems in relation to the need for judges to be impartial in particular cases. For instance, a judge's impartiality may be questioned because they have an association with a particular organization or cause. One well-known example of this occurred when the House of Lords had to rehear an appeal involving the extradition of the ex-President of Chile, General Pinochet: Lord Hoffmann, one of the Law Lords who had sat in the first hearing, was held to be too closely associated with Amnesty International, one of the parties in the case.[60] Similar issues may also arise if a judge has expressed views in a non-judicial capacity, such as in talks or interviews with the media. If we expect judges to be part of society, at what point does their involvement in activities that are normal for most of us undermine their ability to act impartially as between the parties in a particular case? These issues have been considered by the courts in a number of cases over the years.

An example is the decision of the House of Lords in *Helow v Secretary of State for the Home Department and anor* (see the following extract). The appellant was a Palestinian who claimed asylum in the United Kingdom, having been actively involved in the Palestinian Liberation Organization (PLO). Her claim was unsuccessful, as was her appeal to an adjudicator. Permission to appeal further was refused by the Immigration Appeal Tribunal. She filed a further application seeking review of that refusal by the Court of Session in Scotland. The judge refused this application. Her lawyers subsequently discovered that the judge was a member of the International Association of Jewish Lawyers and Jurists and was a founder member of its Scottish branch. The appellant appealed to the House of

[60] *R v Bow Street Metropolitan Stipendiary Magistrate and ors, ex parte Pinochet Ugarte (No. 2)* [1999] 1 LRC 1; *Helow v Secretary of State for the Home Department and anor* [2008] UKHL 62.

Lords, contending that the Association had a '*strong commitment to causes and belief at odds with*' her own, and that the Association was anti-Palestinian, anti-Muslim, and antipathetic to the PLO and supportive of Israel. She argued that the judge was therefore disqualified from dealing with her case.

As can be seen from the following extracts, the basic test is said to be whether a fair-minded and informed observer, having considered the relevant facts, would conclude that there existed a real possibility that the judge was biased, by reason (in this case) of the judge's membership of the Association.[61] Applying this test, the House of Lords was unanimous in rejecting the argument and that judge was disqualified.

Helow v Secretary of State for the Home Department and anor
[2008] UKHL 62

Lord Mance

39. The basic legal test applicable is not in issue. The question is whether a fair-minded and informed observer, having considered the relevant facts, would conclude that there existed a real possibility that the judge was biased, by reason in this case of her membership of the Association [. . .] The question is one of law, to be answered in the light of the relevant facts, which may include a statement from the judge as to what he or she knew at the time, although the court is not necessarily bound to accept any such statement at face value, there can be no question of cross-examining the judge on it, and no attention will be paid to any statement by the judge as to the impact of any knowledge on his or her mind [. . .]

Lord Hope of Craighead

8. [. . .] The judge can be assumed, by virtue of the office for which she has been selected, to be intelligent and well able to form her own views about anything that she reads. She can be assumed to be capable of detaching her own mind from things that they contain which she does not agree with. This is why the complete absence of anything said or done by her to associate herself with the published material that the appellant complains of is so crucial to what the observer would make of this case. In the absence of anything of that kind there is no basis on which the observer would conclude that there was a reasonable possibility that the judge was biased.

Lord Rodger of Earlsferry

23. [. . .] Even lay people acting as jurors are expected to be able to put aside any prejudices they may have. Judges have the advantage of years of relevant training and experience. Like jurors, they swear an oath to decide impartially. While these factors do not, of course, guarantee impartiality, they are undoubtedly relevant when considering whether there is a real possibility that the decision of a professional judge was biased. Taking all these matters into account, I am satisfied that the fair-minded observer would not consider that there had been any real possibility of bias in Lady Cosgrove's case.

While Lord Walker of Gestingthorpe agreed he had more difficulty doing so. He stressed that: '*Those who take on the responsibility of judicial office have to exercise a measure of restraint in associating themselves publicly with controversial causes*'[62] and warned that '*the fair-minded and informed observer would be tending towards complacency if he treated the fact of having taken the judicial oath as a panacea*'.[63]

[61] See further Chapter 19. Also for an empirical study of whether the fair minded observer test reflects people's actual views, see A. Higgins and I. Levy, 'What the fair minded observer really thinks about judicial impartiality' (2021) Modern Law Review 811–841.

[62] *Helow v Secretary of State for the Home Department and anor* [2008] UKHL 62, [24].

[63] Ibid, [27].

QUESTIONS

1. Lord Mance says that there can be no question of subjecting a judge to cross-examination on her knowledge. Why do you think this is? Do you agree that judges should not be cross-examined when their impartiality is questioned?
2. Should a judge who is a member of motoring organizations such as the RAC or AA be disqualified from hearing cases concerning road accidents?

15.7 APPOINTING JUDGES AND DIVERSITY

The current system for making judicial appointments was created by the Constitutional Reform Act 2005. This established an independent Judicial Appointments Commission (JAC) for England and Wales with responsibility for recommending candidates when vacancies arise. Similar commissions exist in Scotland and Northern Ireland. A separate ad hoc selection commission is established to recommend candidates for appointment to the Supreme Court when vacancies arise. It is now accepted that the process by which judges are appointed should reflect the principles of judicial independence, transparency, effectiveness, diversity, and accountability. In the following extract from its report, *Judicial Appointments*, the House of Lords Constitution Committee explain the importance of these principles.

House of Lords Committee on the Constitution, *Judicial Appointments*, 25th Report, Session 2010–12 (footnotes omitted)

Constitutional Principles

14. [. . .] There was widespread agreement [amongst those who gave evidence to the committee] that the appointments process must [. . .] reinforce judicial independence. Judges in the United Kingdom should not be appointed through political patronage.

15. It is important not only that the judiciary act independently, but that they are seen to do so. This principle also extends to the appointments process. Lord Justice Toulson, Vice-Chairman of the JAC, noted that prior to the enactment of the CRA 'there was widespread public concern that judges were being appointed through cronyism and secret soundings. Nothing, really, could disabuse the public of that.' The establishment of the JAC was intended to put an end to such concerns. By operating in an open and transparent manner—for example, by advertising vacancies, specifying the criteria for appointment and publishing diversity statistics—the existence of an independent appointments commission is aimed at helping to ensure that no suspicion of political patronage remains.

16. As well as upholding independence and being open and transparent, the judicial appointments process must be effective. Assessment of professional competence must be central to the selection of judges in order to ensure the efficient delivery of justice. The CRA uses the term 'merit' to refer to these criteria [. . .] We received different views as to how merit ought to be understood and applied in judicial selection. Given the importance of the merit principle, it is important that there is clarity over its basic meaning [. . .].

17. Another principle relevant to judicial appointments is diversity. At one level this means that the process must be fair and non-discriminatory: by that we mean that it must continue to result in the appointment of high quality judges, but without the imposition of barriers against talented legal practitioners from any section of society. However, the issue of diversity goes further than this: we received evidence, with which we concur, arguing that diverse courts are better equipped to carry out the role of adjudicating than courts that are not diverse and that the public will have greater trust and confidence in a more diverse judiciary. [. . .]

18. The principle of accountability is also important. Judicial independence does not require that no-one be held accountable for the operation of the appointments process or perhaps even, in exceptional cases, for individual appointments. [. . .] the JAC and the Lord Chancellor are held to account [. . .] [t]hrough annual reports, a detailed website and appearances before parliamentary committees, the JAC provides regular accounts of its work to Parliament, ministers and the public. The Lord Chancellor's role in the appointments process is justified as necessary to secure accountability to Parliament through the usual convention of individual ministerial responsibility. Some of the evidence we received questioned the effectiveness of the current accountability mechanisms, leading to calls for Parliament to have a greater role in the appointments process.

[. . .]

15.7.1 THE APPOINTMENTS PROCESS PRIOR TO THE CRA

Prior to the CRA, appointment of judges was exclusively in the hands of the executive. Judges were (and still are) formally appointed by the King, acting on the advice of His Majesty's ministers, or by the Lord Chancellor on his behalf. In Scotland, the Lord Advocate would make recommendations to the Secretary of State for Scotland. In relation to the Law Lords and the most senior judges in the territorial jurisdictions, the monarch acted on the advice of the Prime Minister. Appointments to the High Court and to the Circuit Court were made by the monarch, on the advice of the Lord Chancellor. The Lord Chancellor appointed district judges, lay magistrates, and members of certain tribunals.

There were no open competitions for appointments to the High Court or to more senior positions. The Lord Chancellor—in those days, always a senior lawyer—decided whom to recommend for appointment after private consultations with the judiciary or senior members of the professions. This covert process was adopted by other Commonwealth countries, such as Australia, and was entirely different to the much more open approach used in the USA.[64] As Lord Justice Toulson told the House of Lords Select Committee on the Constitution, the process created '*widespread public concern that judges were being appointed through cronyism and secret soundings*'. The process was also considered to enable the judiciary to be an essentially 'self-perpetuating' institution.[65] Some of its consequences are summarized by Kate Malleson.

K. Malleson, 'Rethinking the merit principle in judicial selection' (2006) 33 *Journal of Law and Society* 126, 138 (footnotes omitted)

[. . .] The senior judiciary has traditionally been recruited from an extremely narrow group consisting of white, male barristers drawn from a small number of commercial chambers in London. The structural relationship between the bench and Bar, whereby judges have maintained strong links with their chambers, combined with the key role judges play in the selection system through the consultations process has meant that barristers joining such elite chambers as pupils have found themselves on a 'golden road' to judicial office?[66] They have been, effectively, the beneficiaries of a particularly pervasive and entrenched form of reverse affirmative action.

[64] Lecture given by Lord Clarke of Stone-cum-Ebony MR, 'Selecting judges: Merit, moral courage, judgment & diversity', 22 September 2009.

[65] J.A.G. Griffith, *The Politics of the Judiciary*, 5th edn (1997, London: Fontana Press), p. 22.

[66] The term was used by a judge to describe his career path from an elite chambers to the bench: K. Malleson and F. Banda, *Factors Affecting the Decision to Apply for Silk and Judicial Office*, Lord Chancellors Dept Research Series No. 2/00 (2000), p. 29 (citation in original).

The method of judicial appointment prior to the CRA patently failed to satisfy the fundamental principles to which we have referred.

15.7.2 THE PROCESS FOR APPOINTING JUDGES UNDER THE CRA

Judicial Appointments Commissions (see Box 15.4) now exist in each of the United Kingdom's jurisdictions. These operate at arm's length from government ministers. Their task is to carry out selection exercises when judicial vacancies arise and identify a single nominee whose name is put to the relevant government minister. The minister may accept the name, but has limited power to ask the commission in question to reconsider its selection or to reject it.

BOX 15.4 THE JUDICIAL APPOINTMENTS COMMISSIONS

Commission	Chair	Membership	To whom it makes recommendations	Legislative basis
Judicial Appointments Commission for England and Wales	Lay person	15—five judges, a barrister and solicitor, a legal tribunal member, a lay magistrate, and five lay people	Lord Chancellor	Constitutional Reform Act 2005, Pt 4
Judicial Appointments Board for Scotland	Lay person	10—five legal and five lay people	MSPs	Judiciary and Courts (Scotland) Act 2008
Northern Ireland Judicial Appointments Commission	Lord Chief Justice of Northern Ireland	13—five judges, a barrister and solicitor, and five lay people	Lord Chancellor (until such time as justice functions are devolved to the Northern Ireland Executive)	Justice (Northern Ireland) Acts 2002 and 2004
Ad hoc selection commission convened by the Lord Chancellor for vacancies on the UK Supreme Court	President of the UK Supreme Court	Five—two judges of the UK Supreme Court plus one member of each of the three territorial commissions (one of whom must be a lay person)	Lord Chancellor	Constitutional Reform Act 2005, ss. 25–31

15.7.2.1 Judicial Appointments Commission for England and Wales

In this section, we take a closer look at the work of the largest of the commissions—that of England and Wales.[67]

The JAC is an independent body (not an executive agency of a government department) consisting of 15 members, including the chair who must be a lay person. In addition to the chair there are six judges (including two tribunal judges); two practising lawyers; five lay members; and a non-legally qualified judicial member. Save for three of the judges who are selected by the Judges Council, a body broadly representative of the judiciary as a whole,[68] the members of the JAC are appointed by the Crown on the advice of the Lord Chancellor following open competition.

15.7.2.2 The selection process for judges in England and Wales

When a judicial vacancy arises the JAC starts a selection process. Vacancies are now advertised in the press and on the JAC website. The selection methods may involve a combination of activities such as interviews, written tests, and role play. Once the JAC has arrived at a selection decision, it reports this to the Lord Chancellor, if the appointment is to the High Court or above, or for all other appointments, to the Lady Chief Justice (for appointments to courts) or Senior President of Tribunals (for appointments to tribunals).[69] In practice, almost all recommendations are accepted and the person will be formally appointed.[70]

15.7.2.3 Appointments to the UK Supreme Court

Justices of the Supreme Court, including the President and Deputy President of the Court, are appointed by the monarch following the process set out in ss. 25–31 CRA. The minimum qualification for appointment is that the person has held judicial office for at least two years or has been a qualifying practitioner for at least 15 years (s. 25(1)). Lord Sumption, who served as a Supreme Court Justice between 2012 and 2018, of the Supreme was the first Supreme Court Justice not to have served as a full-time judge in the United Kingdom.

When appointing Justices of the Supreme Court, the monarch acts on the basis of a recommendation made by the Prime Minister (s. 26(1)), although the Prime Minister will invariably recommend the person notified by the Lord Chancellor. The real decisions about who should be appointed to the Supreme Court are made by the Supreme Court Selection Commission and the Lord Chancellor.

The UK Supreme Court Selection Commission is not a permanent body with its own staff—the relatively light workload would not justify this, so a commission is convened as and when required. When convened, a Supreme Court Selection Commission consists of: the President of the Supreme Court, a senior judge (who is not a Justice of the Supreme Court) from anywhere in the United Kingdom nominated by the President; one member of the JAC; one member of the Judicial Appointments Board for Scotland; and one member of the Northern Ireland Judicial Appointments Commission.[71] At least one of the people from the territorial appointments commissions must be a non-lawyer. Since the Crime and Courts Act 2013, if the appointment is of a new President of the Supreme Court the

[67] See further, Patrick O'Brien, 'The JAC for England and Wales: Reflecting on (Nearly) Two Decades' [2024] 8(2) *Irish Judicial Studies Journal* 167.

[68] The Judges Council informs and advises the Lady Chief Justice on matters relating to the judiciary and plays a significant role in the self-governance of the judiciary and thereby contributes to its independence: See J. Thomas, 'The judges council' [2005] Public Law 608.

[69] Prior to the Crime and Courts Act 2013, recommendations were made solely to the Lord Chancellor.

[70] The monarch formally appoints senior judges on the recommendation of the Lord Chancellor, or, in the case of the most senior judges, the Prime Minister.

[71] CRA 2005, Sch. 8.

out-going President is unable to be a member of the Commission and the Commission will be chaired by one of its lay members.

The Commission's initial selection task is to compile a shortlist of candidates from among those who have applied. The Commission then conducts a confidential consultation exercise in accordance with s. 27 CRA to gather views about the possible appointees (see Box 15.5).

BOX 15.5 SHORTLIST CONSULTEES

Consultee	Rationale for consultation
The Lord Chancellor	This politician has overall ministerial responsibility for judiciary-related matters in the United Kingdom
Senior judges who are not themselves candidates, including the judges of the Supreme Court. Lord Chief Justice, Master of the Rolls, the Lord President of the Court of Session, the Lord Chief Justice of Northern Ireland, and the heads of the various Divisions of the High Court	The UK Supreme Court hears appeals from the courts of appeal in the UK's three jurisdictions and it is important that the judges of those courts have confidence in anyone who is nominated to serve on the highest court
First Minister of Scotland	The senior politician in the Scottish Government. Although relatively few Scottish appeals are heard by the UK Supreme Court (four or five civil appeals and no criminal appeals), the court is responsible for adjudicating on devolution issues that may raise politically sensitive issues
First Minister for Wales	Wales is not a separate legal jurisdiction from England and there was no constitutional convention that one of the Law Lords was a Welsh judge (however that is defined). The rationale for consultation is therefore presumably because the UK Supreme Court may be called on to deal with devolution cases affecting Welsh affairs
Secretary of State for Northern Ireland	This still applies although responsibility for justice and policing have been devolved

Selection must be based on merit (s. 27(5) CRA). However, the merit principle is qualified to the extent that in making the selection, the Commission must ensure that '*between them the judges will have knowledge of, and experience in, the law of each part of the United Kingdom*' (s. 27(8)). By convention, two members of the United Kingdom's top court are from Scotland and—by a rather less well-established convention—one member has been from Northern Ireland. The Selection Commission must also have regard to any guidance given by the Lord Chancellor (s. 27(10)). Also, in relation to appointments to the Supreme Court where two candidates are of equal merit, s. 159 of the Equality Act 2010 (see Section 6(d)) does not apply. This, however, does not prevent the Commission from selecting one candidate rather than another in order to increase diversity amongst the Justices of the court.

Having identified its preferred nominee, the Commission reports the name of the person selected to the Lord Chancellor (s. 28). There is then a second round of consultation, with the Lord Chancellor seeking further views on the single name from very senior judges and from the consultees listed in Box 15.5. The Lord Chancellor may accept or reject the Commission's nomination, or ask the Commission to reconsider their nomination. Once a selection is complete, the Lord Chancellor notifies the Prime Minister, who passes the recommendation to the monarch, who makes the formal appointment.[72]

Prior to the CRA, advertisements for vacancies to the United Kingdom's top court were never seen and there would certainly never have been an advert seeking applications to become the senior Lord of Appeal in Ordinary (equivalent to the President of the UK Supreme Court). Now when vacancies for these positions arise they are always advertised. The following, for example, is the notice inviting applications to fill the vacancy following the retirement of Lord Hodge.

Judicial Vacancies at the Supreme Court of the United Kingdom[73]

As a result of the retirement of Lord Hodge in December 2025, applications are sought for the appointment of a Justice of the UK Supreme Court.

[. . .]

All those appointed to the Court need to be people of truly exceptional intellectual and legal ability, with sound judgment and decisiveness. The selection commission is looking for candidates who can show an ability to contribute to the collegiate decision-making of the Court, a sensitivity to the needs of different communities and groups and an ability and willingness to engage in the wider representational and leadership role of a Justice, together with an appreciation of the developing nature of the constitution and law in England, Scotland, Northern Ireland and Wales. The Supreme Court is required by statute to have judges with a knowledge of, and experience of practice in, the law of each part of the United Kingdom. For this recruitment, the selection commission is looking for a candidate with knowledge of, and experience of practice in, the law of Scotland.

The UK Supreme Court's commitment to diversity and inclusion is deeply rooted in its values. We recognise that diversity brings richness to the judiciary and we welcome applicants from all backgrounds. We support part-time and flexible working, subject to the needs of the Court.

[. . .]

15.7.3 JUDICIAL APPOINTMENTS AND CONDUCT OMBUDSMAN

The CRA also established the Judicial Appointments and Conduct Ombudsman (JACO) to provide redress for those dissatisfied with the way in which they were treated during a selection process in England and Wales, and to provide an element of independent oversight of the process.[74] The JACO is appointed by the monarch on the recommendation of the Lord Chancellor. The person appointed cannot have been a judge or practising lawyer. Previous service as a civil servant, a member of Parliament (MP), or with the JAC, or political activities may also make the person ineligible for appointment. Following an investigation, the JACO reports his or her findings, and any recommendations—including for the payment of compensation—to the Lord Chancellor, the JAC, and the complainant.[75] The Ombudsman may also investigate matters referred by the Lord Chancellor relating to the appointments process.

[72] The Constitutional Reform and Governance Bill introduced to Parliament in the 2009–10 Session proposed to remove the Prime Minister's role altogether. This provision was removed from the bill at the final stages.

[73] https://www.supremecourt.uk/news/judicial-vacancies.html.

[74] CRA 2005, s. 62, Sch. 13. On ombuds generally, see Chapter 16.

[75] The JACO is also responsible for investigating the handling of matters relating to judicial conduct and discipline.

15.7.4 THE NEED TO MAKE APPOINTMENTS BASED ON MERIT AND THE NEED FOR DIVERSITY

The JAC is under a statutory duty to select people of good character solely on merit.[76] In selecting on merit, the JAC must '*have regard to*' the need to '*encourage diversity in the range of persons available for selection*'.[77]

Constitutional Reform Act 2005, ss 63 and 64

63 Merit and Good character

[. . .]

(2) Selection must be solely on merit.

(3) A person must not be selected unless the selecting body is satisfied that he is of good character.

(4) Neither 'solely' in subsection (2), nor Part 5 of the Equality Act 2010 (public appointments etc), prevents the selecting body, where two persons are of equal merit, from preferring one of them over the other for the purpose of increasing diversity within—

(a) the group of persons who hold offices for which there is selection under this Part, or

(b) a sub-group of that group.[78]

64 Encouragement of diversity

(1) The Commission, in performing its functions under [. . .], must have regard to the need to encourage diversity in the range of persons available for selection for appointments.

(2) This section is subject to section 63.

Those appointed to become judges must have the qualities and abilities necessary for a judge. However, while s. 63 says that selection must be based solely on merit, the CRA does not define what constitutes 'merit' and the accepted requirements of 'merit' have altered over time.[79]

The most recent statement of the skills and abilities necessary for judicial office is set out in the following extract. As you will see it extends beyond abilities specifically associated with deciding disputes in accordance with the law to include the ability to adopt '*an inclusive approach to those with differences from themselves*' and to use or develop '*digital skills to the requisite standard.*'

[76] CRA 2005, s. 63. [77] CRA 2005, s. 64.

[78] Subsection (4) was added by the Crime and Courts Act 2013. This is often referred to as the 'tipping Provision'. See Graham Gee and Kate Malleson: *Judicial Appointments, Diversity and the Equal Merit Provision*, https://ukconstitutionallaw.org/2014/05/06/graham-gee-and-kate-malleson-judicial-appointments-diversity-and-the-equal-merit-provision/. See also the JAC's explanation of how the tipping provision is used: https://judicialappointments.gov.uk/equality-and-diversity/diversity-and-equality-measures/equal-merit/

[79] K. Malleson, 'Rethinking the merit principle in judicial selection' (2006) 33 *Journal of Law and Society* 126. See also *Judicial Diversity: Barriers and initiatives*, J. Barton-Crosby et al., National Centre for Social Research, Feb. 2025, p. 7.

Judicial Skills and Abilities Framework, Courts and Tribunals Judiciary 2025

Legal and judicial skills

- Possesses intellectual ability and analytical skills to the standard required for the role.
- Demonstrates legal skills and knowledge to the standard required for the role.
- Is able and willing to invest time in developing and maintaining skills and knowledge as appropriate for the role.
- Shows flexibility of approach: can apply skills and knowledge in unfamiliar or developing areas, as appropriate for the role.
- Clearly understands what is required for a fair hearing.
- Assimilates and organises pertinent information quickly.
- Identifies with clarity relevant issues of fact and law for decision.
- Reaches clearly reasoned, logical and concise decisions that weigh up relevant considerations.
- Demonstrates sound judgement and an appropriate level of decisiveness.

Communication skills and personal qualities

- Shows effective active listening skills, seeking to understand a party's case without prejudgement and with courtesy, sensitivity and appropriate patience.
- Demonstrates clear oral and written communication skills, in language appropriate for the forum and the particular circumstances.
- Adopts an appropriately authoritative approach that: inspires respect and confidence; o ensures both fairness, allowing proper participation by the parties, and an appropriate and efficient use of judicial resources.
- Adheres to the Bangalore Principles of independence, impartiality, integrity, propriety and equality of treatment, appreciating the importance of high standards of conduct and of maintaining public trust in the judiciary.
- Possesses sufficient resilience for the role and an ability to remain calm in challenging situations.
- Has a practical, common sense approach to problem-solving.
- Shows open-mindedness and self-awareness.

Effective working

- Is diligent and efficient, prioritising tasks appropriately and reaching timely decisions.
- Team work: has a collegiate approach; builds effective working relationships with colleagues taking full account of the Statement of Expected Behaviour.
- Takes an inclusive approach to those with differences from themselves.
- Is able and willing to challenge inappropriate behaviour by others.
- Uses or can develop digital skills to the requisite standard.

QUESTION

Are there any skills or abilities that judges should possess that are missing from the above list? If so, what are these?

Earlier in the chapter we considered recent statistics showing the percentages of judges who are women and/or come from black, Asian and minority ethnic communities. There is consensus that the need to further diversify the judiciary is now urgent. The following extract from the Constitution Committee's report, *Judicial Appointments* explains the importance of diversity.

House of Lords Select Committee on the Constitution, *Judicial Appointments*,
25th Report, Session 2010–12 (footnotes omitted)

Chapter 3: Diversity

68. [. . .] The judge [. . .]in England and Wales is stereotypically a white male from a narrow social background. Despite concerns raised over the last few decades, the proportion of women judges, black, Asian and minority ethnic (BAME) judges and others from under-represented groups has increased too slowly. Many of the causes for this appear to stem from the structures of the legal professions (barristers and solicitors) and the pool of available mid-career legal professionals eligible and interested in putting themselves forward for selection. However, other barriers arise as a result of the appointments process itself or of the structures of the courts and tribunals in which judges work.

69. The slow rate of change is not only a problem for those whose careers are affected; it is a problem for society as a whole. We examine in this chapter why diversity is important and what changes to the constitutional and legal framework might help to bring about a truly diverse judiciary. [. . .]

The constitutional significance of a diverse judiciary

70. [. . .] the concept of merit should [not] be narrowly focused on intellectual rigour. [. . .] Judging is a complex activity: it is necessary for judges to understand the wide array of concerns and experiences of those appearing before them. A more diverse judiciary can bring different perspectives to bear on the development of the law and to the concept of justice itself.

71. None of our witnesses argued that increasing diversity risks reducing the quality of the current judiciary. [. . .]

72. We consider it our responsibility to refute any notion that those from under-represented groups make less worthy candidates than the stereotypical white male. Indeed, we believe that increasing the pool of talent available will lead to an increased number of meritorious candidates from which to select. [. . .]

73. Justice, fairness and equality are central values in the law which should be reflected in the composition of the judiciary itself. Judges are independent of Parliament and the executive, but they should not stand apart from the society in which they adjudicate: the public must have confidence in the judges who make the decisions which affect their day to day lives. This is less likely to be the case 'if you have tribunal after tribunal with three members, all of whom are white men, particularly if that does not reflect the applicants coming through.' People appearing before a court must trust the judges to make decisions based on fairness: levels of trust will be greater if the judiciary itself is seen to have been fairly appointed. As Lady Justice Arden argued: 'People may well have more confidence that their concerns have been taken into account if the judiciary reflects more of a cross-section of society.'

74. A more diverse judiciary would not undermine the quality of our judges and would increase public trust and confidence in the judiciary.

The argument that diversity should improve the quality of judicial decisions is not new. Professor John Griffith, for example, argued that a diverse judiciary would be more open to arguments for change than a judiciary that was overwhelmingly male, white, and socially elite.

J. A. G. Griffith, *The Politics of the Judiciary*, 5th edn (1997, London: Fontana Press), pp. 7–8

When people like the members of the judiciary, broadly homogeneous in character, are faced with [political cases . . .] they act in broadly similar ways. It will be part of my argument to suggest that behind these actions lies a unifying attitude of mind, a political position, which is primarily concerned to protect and conserve certain values and institutions.

It has also been argued that having more female judges would make a difference. The following extract is taken from an article written by Madam Justice Bertha Wilson, who, in 1982, became the first woman judge on the Canadian Supreme Court.

Madam Justice Bertha Wilson, 'Will women judges really make a difference?'
(1990) 28 *Osgoode Hall Law Journal* 507, 512–15

[. . . S]tudies show overwhelming evidence that gender-based myths, biases, and stereotypes are deeply embedded in the attitudes of many male judges, as well as in the law itself. Researchers have concluded that gender difference has been a significant factor in judicial decision-making, particularly in the area of tort law, criminal law and family law: Further many have concluded that sexism is the underlying premise of many judgments in these areas, and that that is not really surprising having regard to the nature of the society in which the judges themselves have been socialized.

[. . . T]here are probably whole areas of the law on which there is no uniquely feminine perspective [. . . T]he principles and underlying premises are so firmly entrenched and so fundamentally sound that no good would be achieved by attempting to reinvent the wheel. In some other areas of the law, however, a distinctly male perspective is clearly discernible. It has resulted in principles that are not fundamentally sound and that should be revisited when the opportunity presents itself.

Baroness Hale has commented that '*it would be very surprising*' if these observations were not also applicable in the United Kingdom, '*given the restricted social, educational and professional background of most of our judges*'.[80] There is then some support for the view that diversity may affect the quality of decisions taken by judges, although Baroness Hale says that she is worried and sceptical about arguments based on the '*individual judges' ability or even willingness to make a difference*'.[81]

As we have seen, the House of Lords Select Committee on the Constitution argued that people are more likely to have confidence in a diverse judiciary. Baroness Hale relates this to democratic legitimacy.

Dame Brenda Hale, 'Equality and the judiciary: Why should we want more women judges?'
[2001] *Public Law* 489, 502–3 (footnotes omitted)

In a democratic society, in which we are all equal citizens, it is wrong in principle for that authority to be wielded by such a very unrepresentative section of the population. As individuals, my colleagues are a remarkably diverse bunch, but I do not need to rehearse the facts about how unrepresentative

[80] Dame Brenda Hale, 'Equality and the judiciary: Why should we want more women judges' [2001] Public Law 489.
[81] Ibid, 501. See also, Rachel J Cahill-O'Callaghan, 'Reframing the judicial diversity debate: personal values and tacit diversity' (2015) 35(1) Legal Studies 1–29.

they are: not only mainly male, overwhelmingly white, but also largely the product of a limited range of educational institutions and social backgrounds. [. . .] This matters because democracy matters. The judiciary may or should be independent of government and Parliament but ultimately we are the link between them both and the people. We are the instrument by which the will of Parliament and government is enforced upon the people. We are also the instrument which keeps the other organs of the state, the police and those who administer the laws, under control. [. . .]

15.7.4.1 How is greater judicial diversity to be achieved?

It has been clear for some time that achieving greater diversity requires a range of reforms and initiatives. As far back as 2010 the Lord Chancellor's Advisory Panel on Judicial Diversity, chaired by Baroness Rabbi Julia Neuberger made 53 recommendations. Its key messages are summarized in the following extract.

Report of the Advisory Panel on Judicial Diversity, February 2010, pp. 4–6

2. [. . . T]here is no quick fix to moving towards a more diverse judiciary. This will come as no surprise to those who have worked to promote diversity over recent years.

4. The message from our research and consultations is consistent with research and experience in other jurisdictions: we will achieve significant transformation if, and only if, diversity is addressed systematically—not only within the appointments process, but throughout a legal and judicial career, from first consideration of the possibility of joining the judiciary to promotion at the most senior level.

5. Delivering a more diverse judiciary is not just about recruiting talent wherever it may be found, important though that is, but about retaining talent and enabling capable individuals to reach the top.

[. . .]

These recommendations have been supported by the government, the legal professions, parliamentary committee, and the judiciary and a number of steps have been, and are being, taken.[82] A recent study undertaken by the National Centre for Social Research, commissioned by the Ministry of Justice, examined the continuing barriers to achieving greater diversity and the initiatives that are needed. Here is an extract from the report's findings regarding the initiatives that still needed.

J. Barton-Crosby et al., 'Judicial diversity: Barriers and initiatives' (2025) Feb *National Centre for Social Research*, pp. 7–8

Summary of findings: Initiatives promoting diversity

1. Initiatives within the wider legal professions
    - Initiatives focused on reducing barriers to diversity at entry to the legal profession concentrate on overcoming barriers related to social mobility, and include insight schemes for school and university students, work experience placements, and targeted outreach events.

[82] See. e.g., Judicial Diversity Forum—Priorities and Actions for 2025, 04 February 2025.

- Initiatives targeting barriers to retention and progression of under-represented groups within the legal professions focus on making employees feel recognised, represented, and supported in their workplace.

2. Initiatives to promote diversity [. . .]
   - Initiatives . . .[to] . . .focus . . . on encouraging under-represented individuals to apply for judicial appointment by providing potential applicants with greater insight into the role of a judge and how the judicial application process works, as well as preparing candidates with the skills and competencies required for success (i.e. judicial appointment).
   - At the application and selection stages of judicial appointment, activities centre on eliminating discrimination and ensuring fair and transparent processes. For example, name-blind sifting of applications; 'equality proofing' of selection materials to ensure appropriate content and tone; diversity checkpoints to monitor the progression of under-represented groups throughout the selection process; and use of the equal merit principle at both shortlisting and final decision-making.
   - Schemes to retain under-represented individuals once appointed to the judiciary include salaried part-time working and the introduction of options for flexible working.

15.7.4.2 Conclusion on judicial diversity

Achieving judicial diversity remains a work in progress, especially in relation to the senior judiciary. For example, while there is currently a Lady Chief Justice (Lady Carr) only two of the twelve UK Supreme Court judges (Lady Rose and Lady Simler) are women. Despite improvements some remain pessimistic about the rate of progress. Research from the LSE, for example, has indicated that: '*Many reforms that were heralded with much fanfare as promoting diversity have had little impact.*'[83]

QUESTIONS

1. Can you summarize the arguments for having a more diverse judiciary? Which of these do you consider to be the most compelling?
2. The Youth Justice and Criminal Evidence Act 1999 prevented defendants in rape trials from relying on evidence of the woman's sexual past to throw doubt on whether she consented to sex. In a case in 2001, it was argued that an all-male appeal court could not impartially decide where the balance lies between the right of male defendants in a rape case to a fair trial and the rights of their female accusers to privacy and dignity. This argument failed—but, in your view, did it have any substance?
3. In your view, what further steps should be taken to achieve a more diverse judiciary? Would you, for example, be in favour of having a quota of judicial appointments of people from underrepresented groups? For further discussion on this, see The HL Constitution Committee's report on *Judicial Appointments*, 25th Report, Session 2010–12, paras 102–8.

[83] http://www.lse.ac.uk/News/Latest-news-from-LSE/2017/12-December-2017/Reforms-to-increase-the-number-of-female-judges-have-had-little-impact; M. Blackwell, 'Starting out on a judicial career: gender diversity and the appointment of Recorders, Circuit Judges and Deputy High Court Judges 1996–2016.' (2017) 44(4) Journal of Law and Society 586–619.

15.7.5 EXECUTIVE INVOLVEMENT IN APPOINTING JUDGES

The appointments process must reflect the need for judicial independence from the executive and the legislature, but this does not necessarily mean that the executive should have no role in the appointment of judges. Arguments in favour of the executive being involved in the appointment of judges were set out by the then Secretary of State for Justice and Lord Chancellor in his 2007 report, *Governance of Britain.*

Secretary of State for Justice and Lord Chancellor, *The Governance of Britain: Judicial Appointments*, Cm 7210 (October 2007), pp. 32–3 (footnote numbers in original altered or omitted)

> 4.13 First and foremost, the Government has responsibility for the justice system overall, including the efficiency and effectiveness with which justice is delivered via the courts, and the level to which they are resourced. [. . .]
>
> 4.14 Some have argued that a role for the executive in the appointments process, at least in relation to senior appointments, is essential to maintaining the executive's confidence *in* the senior judiciary.[84] The Lord Chief Justice commented in a recent speech that: '[. . .] The senior judiciary today have, to some extent, to work in partnership with government. It would, I think, be unfortunate if a Chief Justice were appointed in whose integrity and abilities the Government had no confidence.'[85]
>
> 4.15 If the executive were completely removed from decisions on appointments, this would increase separation between the executive and judiciary. However, a side-effect of this might be that the Lord Chancellor would cease to operate so effectively as a bridge between the judiciary and Government. There would also be a risk that the Lord Chancellor would be seen as less inclined to defend the judiciary against criticism [. . .]
>
> 4.16 Further, reducing or removing the executive's role would reduce or remove the 'long-stop' mechanism in the CRA, whereby the JAC's individual recommendations can be challenged. [. . . I]ts existence means that the JAC's ability to recommend selections to individual vacancies is capable of being subject to some degree of scrutiny. [. . .]
>
> 4.17 The executive plays a wider constitutional role in appointments. In our constitution, The [Monarch] directly appoints Ministers, the more senior judges and other public office-holders. It is a constitutional convention that The [Monarch] does so on the advice of the Prime Minister or other Ministers, rather than by exercising [his or] her own discretion. This is so that Ministers can be held to account for those decisions. This fact provides a rationale for retaining a role for Ministers in the process. For their advice to be meaningful, it can be argued that a Minister should have at least some say in the recommendation.
>
> 4.18 Ministers are accountable to Parliament for the decisions they make and for the advice they give to The [Monarch]. Therefore, they need to be able to defend it. To defend it, they must be confident in it, and therefore, arguably, they should be able to question the decision that was made, or at the very least to have some leverage over or ability to question the overall process. If the role of Ministers were further reduced or removed entirely, an alternative mechanism for providing that accountability would need to be found.

The government went on to say that the executive's role in appointing judges could be reduced by limiting or removing the Lord Chancellor's ability to reject a candidate selected by the JAC or to require the JAC to reconsider a selection. Another possibility is that the Lord Chancellor's involvement

[84] E.g., Professor Robert Hazell, UCL Constitution Unit, Evidence to the Select Committee on the Constitutional Reform Bill, 6 April 2004.

[85] Commonwealth Law Conference Speech, Nairobi, 12 September 2007.

could be made formal only. Likewise, the Prime Minister's role in appointing the most senior judges could be removed. However, further reducing the role of the Lord Chancellor and the involvement, albeit normally only formal, of the Prime Minister has potential costs in terms of accountability.

15.7.6 PARLIAMENT'S ROLE IN APPOINTING JUDGES

As we have seen, one of the motivations for setting up judicial appointments commissions in the United Kingdom was to demonstrate that individual appointments are not subject to political influences—but what about accountability? In the old systems of judicial appointments, the Lord Chancellor was, in principle, answerable to the UK Parliament for the appointments made (although, in practice, this rarely if ever happened). In some other constitutional systems, an element of accountability for appointments is secured by giving the legislature a say—even a veto—in the process.

The UK Parliament plays no direct role in the appointment of the judiciary, although MPs and peers may—through questions and debates—require the Lord Chancellor to account for judicial appointments. Parliamentary select committees can also question the members of the JAC and explore matters arising from its annual report or reports by the JACO. Compared with the mechanism for judicial appointments in other systems, parliamentary involvement is already '*minimal*' and could hardly be reduced.[86] Moreover, while the Lady Chief Justice of England and Wales and other senior judges do now appear before parliamentary committees to answer questions relating to the judiciary, individual judges are not accountable to Parliament in the way that ministers are.[87]

The system in the United Kingdom contrasts with that of some other jurisdictions—most markedly, the USA, where in some states judges are directly elected and remain in office depending on their performance.[88] Also appointments by the President of Supreme Court Justices are subject to the 'advice and consent' of the Senate and the views of appointees, including their political views, are openly examined at confirmation hearings that are widely reported in the media. The intense controversy surrounding President Trump's nominations of Brett Kavanaugh to the US Supreme Court, and the heated hearings before the Senate Judiciary Committee, is perhaps the most graphic example of the difference between the low key appointments process to the UK Supreme Court and the potentially very high profile process for appointing members of the US Supreme Court.[89]

The House of Lords Select Committee on the Constitution heard evidence on whether Parliament should have a greater role in relation to individual judicial appointments, either in the form of pre-appointment hearings, or in the form of post-appointment hearings of the sort now used to question new governors and deputy governors of the Bank of England, and other members of the bank's Monetary Policy Committee.

House of Lords Select Committee on the Constitution, *Judicial Appointments*, 25th Report, Session 2010–12 (footnotes omitted)

38. It is the responsibility of Parliament to establish the statutory framework for the judicial appointments process. Parliament also has an accountability role to play in overseeing the process and reviewing the success or failure of its operation. To what extent should Parliament or parliamentarians be

[86] *Governance of Britain*, para. 4.33. [87] See Chapter 9.

[88] See, e.g., https://www.nytimes.com/2008/05/25/world/americas/25iht-judge.4.13194819.html.

[89] See also R. Cornes, 'Appointing Supreme Court Justices in the United States and United Kingdom: What role for the legislator?' [2009] Public Law 836–8, discussing the appointment of Judge Sonia Sotomayor to the US Supreme Court.

involved in individual appointments? And how best can Parliament hold the Lord Chancellor and the JAC to account for the operation of the process?

Pre-or Post-Appointment Hearings

39. We received evidence arguing that candidates for some senior judicial posts should be subject to a pre-appointment hearing before a parliamentary committee. Professor Robert Hazell [. . .] and Professor Kate Malleson [. . .] set out the arguments in favour of such hearings as follows:

- hearings act as a check on political patronage, help to ensure that independent and robust candidates are appointed and add to the appointee's legitimacy;
- Parliament has the power to scrutinise all acts of the executive—appointments of senior judges are an important exercise of ministerial discretion and should be subject to parliamentary scrutiny which is a useful check against political bias;
- Parliament nowadays has little contact with the judges: the senior judges are largely unknown to MPs; Supreme Court Justices will be unknown to the Lords now that the law lords have departed—through dialogue, political and judicial actors can better understand the constraints under which the other operates; and
- the judges should meet the body vested with the constitutional power to dismiss them.

40. A number of witnesses focused the case for some form of pre-appointment hearing on the increasingly complex role of the senior judiciary and the legitimate role for Parliament to consider candidates' competing judicial philosophies. Individual decisions made by judges impact on policy and determine the interpretation of legislation enacted by Parliament. Some witnesses argued that in respect of legislation such as the Human Rights Act 1998, and in the development of judicial review, the judiciary has a wide margin in which to develop the law and that Parliament has a legitimate interest in the manner in which this is done. [. . .]

43. The weight of our evidence was against pre-appointment hearings for UK judges. Professor Brice Dickson [. . .] stressed the ability of Parliament to overturn individual judicial decisions, whilst Lord Kerr, [. . .] described such hearings as 'the complete antithesis of the preservation of judicial independence'. The benefits of pre-appointment hearings in respect of senior public appointments are many, but the relationship between Parliament and the judiciary is a unique one. [. . .] Judges must be independent of both the executive and Parliament: it is imperative that they remain one step removed from the political process.

44. Our witnesses also raised more immediate concerns about pre-appointment hearings. It would be difficult to limit the questioning of candidates to matters of general judicial philosophy and approach. There is a real danger that questions might touch on specific issues that could come before the courts or on candidates' individual political positions. [. . .] Some witnesses were concerned that hearings would act as a disincentive to many potential candidates. There is a further question of what impact criticism of a candidate, explicit or implicit, might have on his or her future public standing.

45. Pre-appointment hearings 'would also risk undermining the public's confidence that the senior judiciary is appointed strictly on merit and having regard to integrity and independence.' Roger Smith, [then] Director of JUSTICE, thus described the proposal as 'a quagmire into which no one would want to go.'

46. We are against any proposal to introduce pre-appointment hearings for senior members of the judiciary. However limited the questioning, such hearings could not have any meaningful impact without undermining the independence of those subsequently appointed or appearing to pre-judge their future decisions. In the United Kingdom, judges' legitimacy depends on their independent status and appointment on merit, not on any democratic mandate.

The Committee went on to discuss post-appointment hearings but found little support for these and concluded that they would serve no useful purpose, except in relation to the Lady Chief Justice and the President of the Supreme Court who undertake leadership roles for which they can properly be held to account.[90]

An alternative way of securing parliamentary involvement in judicial appointments is to enable parliamentarians to sit as members of selection panels for senior judicial appointments. In their evidence to the House of Lord Select Committee on the Constitution, both Lord Justice Etherton (as he then was) and Baroness Hale argued for this on the grounds that *'politicians have the legitimacy of being elected'*,[91] and it would be a *'a small step towards increasing the democratic accountability of the process'*.[92] Baroness Hale also argued that it *'would reduce the potential for "cloning"'*.[93] Others, including Lord Phillips and Lord Neuberger, disagreed, essentially on the ground that it would be undesirable to allow political criteria to become part of the appointments process.[94] The Committee agreed with this, concluding that *'[T]here is no useful role that parliamentarians can play that could not be played by lay members on selection panels.'*[95]

QUESTIONS

1. What are the main arguments for and against executive and parliamentary involvement in judicial appointments?
2. Would you be in favour of candidates having to appear at pre-appointment hearings before a select committee of MPs? If you were an MP, what would be the main questions that would you ask a candidate for senior judicial office?
3. What, if any, changes to the current system of judicial appointments would you like to see?

15.8 THE USE OF JUDGES TO CHAIR PUBLIC INQUIRIES

In the United Kingdom, as in some other countries, judges are sometimes called upon to undertake activities outside the courtroom, including chairing bodies such as the Law Commission and public inquiries into a wide range of matters including examining alleged failings by ministers and officials, and the causes and implications of accidents.[96] Some examples of public inquiries chaired by judges are given in Box 15.6.

BOX 15.6 EXAMPLES OF PUBLIC INQUIRIES CHAIRED BY JUDGES

- Lord Denning's inquiry into the Profumo affair[97] focused on the relationship between John Profumo, a Conservative Secretary of State for War, and Christine Keeler, a prostitute who had slept with a Soviet naval attaché.

[90] *Judicial Appointments*, para. 48. [91] Ibid, para. 49. [92] Ibid, para. 49. [93] Ibid, para. 49.
[94] Ibid, paras 50, 51. [95] Ibid, para. 52.
[96] The main legislation governing public inquiries set up by UK government ministers is the Inquiries Act 2005. See, The Rt Hon. Lord Thomas of Cwmgiedd, 'The future of public inquiries' [2015] Public Law 224. More generally on inquiries see E.Ireton, 'Public Inquiries: irreconcilable interests and the importance of managing expectations' *Journal of Social Welfare and Family Law* Vol 45, 2023, 212–233.
[97] *The Security Service and Mr Profumo*, Cmnd 2152 (September 1963).

- Lord Scarman's 1981 inquiry into the riots in Brixton, South London.[98]
- Lord Taylor's inquiry into the Hillsborough disaster, in which 95 standing spectators at a football match were crushed to death and over 400 were seriously injured.[99]
- Sir Richard Scott's inquiry into 'the arms for Iraq affair' led to a report that was highly critical of ministers and of the Attorney General, and generated considerable political and legal debate.[100]
- Sir William Macpherson's inquiry into the death of Stephen Lawrence.[101]
- Lord Hutton's inquiry into the circumstances surrounding the death of Dr Kelly.[102]
- Lord Saville's inquiry into the events surrounding the deaths that occurred in Londonderry on Sunday 30 January 1972, referred to as 'Bloody Sunday'.
- Sir Martin Moore-Bick chaired the public inquiry into the circumstances leading up to and surrounding the fire at Grenfell Tower on 14 June 2017.
- Sir Brian Langstaff chaired the infected blood inquiry into the circumstances in which people treated by national Health Services in the United Kingdom were given infected blood and infected blood products. [103]
- Sir Wyn William chaired the inquiry into the Post Office Horizon IT scandal.[104]
- Baroness Hallett currently chairs *UK Covid-19 Inquiry and its* continuing modules and hearings.

Inquiries are often used to examine and report on matters of great concern and controversy. That being so there has been serious debate around whether it is right to use judges as inquiry chairs given that this may damage both the reputation of individual judges and the judiciary in general.[105]

15.8.1 SHOULD JUDGES BE CALLED UPON TO CHAIR INQUIRIES?

Three reasons are given for using judges to chair inquiries:

(a) because they are considered to possess the skills necessary for running inquiries, such as handling the questioning of witnesses and conducting proceedings fairly;

(b) because of their independence and neutrality, especially from the government, they confer authority and legitimacy on the inquiry process and on its findings—a quality to which Professor Jowell has referred as '*symbolic reassurance*';[106] and

(c) because they are available and it is relatively easy to transfer them from their normal judicial duties.

[98] *The Scarman Report, The Brixton Disorders, 10–12 April* (1981, Manchester: Pelican Press).
[99] *The Hillsborough Stadium Disaster, Interim Report*, Cm 765 (December 1989); *Final Report*, Cm 962 (May 1990).
[100] *The Scott Report*, Cm 115 (February 1996).
[101] *Report of the Stephen Lawrence Inquiry*, Cm 4262-I (February 1999).
[102] *Report of the Inquiry into the Circumstances Surrounding the Death of Dr David Kelly*, HC 247 (January 2004).
[103] *Infected Blood Inquiry, The Report*,20 May 2024, HC 569-1.
[104] The Post Office (Horizon System) Offences Act 2024 resulted in the Parliamentary mass-quashing of convictions following the inquiry's revelations.
[105] See further, Jack Beatson, *The Rule of Law and The Separation of Powers* (2021, Oxford: Hart Publishing), esp. pp. 111–14.
[106] Select Committee on Public Administration, *Government by Inquiry*, First Report, Session 2004–05 (HC 51-1), para. 42.

In the following extract the Select Committee on Public Administration questions whether these reasons are compelling while noting the risks in using judges in this way.

Select Committee on Public Administration, *Government by Inquiry*, First Report, Session 2004–05 (HC 51-1) (footnotes omitted)

44. [. . .] Mr Justice Beatson noted that the 'skills' argument is strongest where the task of the inquiry is solely to find facts. It is less compelling where issues of social or economic policy with political implications are involved'. [. . .]

46. [. . .] Lord Woolf made [the] point [that], 'today, judges do not often have any insight into the workings of the public service'. Hence Mr Justice Beatson concludes: 'Given the political nature of the British constitution, judicial skills may not necessarily be the most appropriate where an inquiry concerns the relationship between the government and Parliament'. [. . .]

47. The notion of judges as above the political process has also begun to be challenged. The growth of public law in recent years has made this more apparent as judges have come to play an increasing role in determining cases which raise political and constitutional issues. [. . .]

48. The authority of the judiciary, itself seen as a valuable import into an inquiry, risks being damaged by its aftermath. Those who do not agree with an inquiry's conclusions may not perceive it as independent and objective, regardless of whether the chair is a member of the judiciary. [. . .]

49. Such criticisms have the potential to damage the reputation of the individual judge, and Mr Justice Beatson considers that 'perceived deficiencies [. . .] whether procedural or substantive, will follow a judge back to the bench'. [. . .] As Professor Jowell suggested, this may have a 'corrosive effect on public trust in the judiciary'. [. . .]

The Committee's view was that there is value in using senior judges to chair '*fact-finding inquiries which are at a distance from government*', but it said that judges should not be required to chair inquiries into issues at the centre of government, which are, by their nature, politically contentious and require an understanding of how government works.[107]

The government responded by publishing its own consultation paper, *Effective Inquiries*,[108] in which it said that the most important criteria for a chair are independence and skills or experience appropriate for the task. In some cases, this will require a judge or senior lawyer and, in others, it may be more appropriate to appoint a non-judicial chairman.[109]

QUESTIONS

Do you think it is right to use judges to chair public inquiries into controversial and potentially politically sensitive matters? If judges are used for these purposes what, if anything, should be done to protect them from being drawn into matters that may damage the perceived independence of the judiciary?

[107] At para. 57. [108] DCA, CP 12/04, May 2004. [109] At para. 49.

15.9 CONCLUDING COMMENTS

Developments over the past two decades or so have increased the constitutional importance of the judiciary. This has highlighted the need for a clearer understanding of what judicial independence means, and how it is to be achieved and maintained. Judges have become increasingly involved in matters of controversy, both in relation to their role as judges and when called upon to perform other activities, such as chairing inquiries. While few, if any, judges are household names (or celebrities), the profile of the judiciary and of individual judges is now much higher than it was a generation or so ago. While there is a need to ensure that judges maintain, and are seen to maintain, their impartiality and independence judges should not be disconnected from society: as well as independence there needs to be appropriate accountability. As the judicial role has become more visible maintaining public confidence in the judiciary has grown in importance. Public confidence will not be maintained if judges are perceived to be an out-of-touch, white-male-dominated elite; as we have seen, progress is being made towards achieving greater diversity, but this is very much still a work in progress.

FURTHER READING

Gee, G., Hazell, R., Malleson, K., and O'Brien, P., *The Politics of Judicial Independence in the UK's Changing Constitution* (2015, Cambridge: Cambridge University Press).

Graham, L., *Judicial Individuality on the UK Supreme* (2025, Oxford: Hart Publishing).

Griffith, J. A. G., *The Politics of the Judiciary*, 5th edn (1997, London: Fontana Press).

Malleson, K. and Russell, P., (eds) *Appointing Judges in an Age of Judicial Power: Critical Perspectives from Around the World* (2006, Toronto: University of Toronto Press).

Malleson, K., 'Values Diversity in the United Kingdom Supreme Court: Abandoning the "don't-ask-don't-tell" policy' (2022) 49(1) *Journal of Law and Society* 3–22

Monaghan, C., 'Controversial judicial decisions and security of tenure: Reflections on Trump v United States, the Miller litigation, and the attempt to remove Sir John Donaldson in the 1970s' (2024) 29(3) *Judicial Review* 1.

Rackley, E., 'A short history of judicial diversity' (2023) *Current Legal Problems*, Vol 76, Issue 1, 265–296.

Shetreet, S. and Turenne, S., *Judges on Trial*, 2nd edn (2013, Cambridge: Cambridge University Press).

WEBSITES

The Judicial Appointments Commission	https://judicialappointments.gov.uk
The Judiciary of England and Wales	www.judiciary.gov.uk/
The Judicial Power Project	https://judicialpowerproject.org.uk/project/
The UK Supreme Court	https://www.supremecourt.uk/
Judicial Diversity Initiative	https://judicialdiversityinitiative.org/

16

ADMINISTRATIVE JUSTICE: TRIBUNALS AND OMBUDS

CENTRAL ISSUES

1. When public bodies make decisions about people's rights and entitlements—like benefits, housing or immigration decisions-these decisions must be correct, lawful and fair. If people are dissatisfied, they should be able to have decisions reconsidered and have access to independent bodies that are able to ensure that the required standards have been met.
2. Access to the courts is a fundamental right, but most people do not take their cases to court. Instead, complaints are often handled within the public body, through independent tribunals, or by ombuds.[1]
3. These alternative routes are a vital part of the UK's 'administrative justice' system.
4. It is important that disputes are resolved by the most appropriate procedures as quickly and as cheaply as possible. These requirements may be summarized by the requirement for 'proportionate dispute resolution' (PDR) and the need to get 'things right first time'.
5. Some worry that informal processes—like internal reviews or online appeals—may save time but risk weakening important legal protections. These tensions may increase as government and justice systems become more digital.
6. This chapter explains the administrative justice system, focusing on how decisions are made, the role of tribunals and ombuds, and what happens when things go wrong. It ends with the Windrush case study to show how serious the consequences of administrative failure can be.

[1] Unless the context requires otherwise, in our text we use the term 'ombud' (singular) and ombuds (plural) as generic terms instead of ombudsman or ombudsmen. See V. Bondy and M. Doyle, 'What's in a Name? A discussion paper on ombud terminology' in M. Hertogh and R. Kirkham (eds) *Research Handbook on The Ombudsman* (2018, Cheltenham: Elgar), ch. 26.

16.1 INTRODUCTION

PAUSE FOR REFLECTION

Imagine that you have just been told that your application for disability benefits has been rejected. You rely on those benefits to pay your bills, afford transport to medical appointments, and buy food. But the letter says you don't qualify—even though your doctor sent in a medical report and your situation hasn't changed. You try calling the helpline, but you're passed between departments. You feel invisible. Powerless. You're sure a mistake has been made. But what can you do? Who can you turn to?

This chapter explores the part of the constitutional system that deals with everyday justice—when people challenge government decisions that affect their homes, health, income, or immigration status. Often, these challenges don't go to court. They go through a range of other processes: complaints, appeals, tribunals, ombuds. We call this the system of administrative justice—and it's a part of public law that most people encounter long before they consider ever setting foot in a courtroom.

Government ministers and officials make countless decisions that are directly concerned with people's rights and entitlements in matters as diverse as claims for welfare benefits and pensions, the provision of services, rights to stay in the country, liability to pay taxes, and so on. A constitutional system should provide ways in which people can question such decisions and seek redress if errors and wrongs occur. This requirement is basic, but what does it actually entail and what are the redress mechanisms available within the UK system?

Lawyers will tend to think in terms of access to courts and the availability of legal remedies—and in particular judicial review. This is of undoubted importance; judicial review and the main legal arguments that can be addressed to courts are examined in the following chapters. Using courts, however, is a last resort: the courts are only part of the picture—and some would say a very small part. Certainly, only a tiny proportion of disputes between individuals and public bodies ever reach the courts.

In this chapter, we consider the main ways in which disputes between individuals and public bodies are resolved outside the court system in what is widely referred to as the landscape of 'administrative justice'.

16.1.1 THE IMPORTANCE OF 'ADMINISTRATIVE JUSTICE'

The expression 'administrative justice' indicates that the day-to-day administration of government must satisfy requirements of justice and that the delivery of justice is not the sole responsibility of civil or criminal courts. The use of the term 'justice' in this context also indicates that 'just' or 'good' administration is a matter of constitutional necessity rather than government largesse. The Ministry of Justice has acknowledged the constitutional significance of administrative justice and its impact on individuals' lives. The following extract, taken from a strategic planning document, emphasizes why a well-functioning administrative justice system matters for both people and public institutions.

Ministry of Justice, *Administrative Justice and Tribunals: A Strategic Work Programme 2013–2016*, December 2012, p. 5

[1] Public institutions make many decisions on behalf of central and local Government which concern the rights or entitlements of individuals. Some of these decisions—such as whether someone is eligible for benefits or whether they should be allowed to remain in the country—have a profound effect on people's lives. [. . .] the complexity, number and variety of individual circumstances and requirements can mean that [. . . mistakes are made . . .].

[2] With this complexity in mind, it is important that we have a system which is able to examine individual circumstances, rule on the validity of decisions where necessary and seek to correct systemic issues where they are identified. It is important to the individuals in question [. . .] it is also important to public institutions themselves, since if they are incorrectly discharging Parliament's intentions then this may have wider implications and costs. The system of administrative justice plays a vital role for individuals in their interactions with the state and in ensuring they have confidence in the administration of decisions and in their achieving redress when decisions are incorrectly made.

This passage underlines that administrative justice is not simply a question of individual redress, but a structural requirement to ensure public bodies act within the law and according to Parliament's intent.

Ann Abraham, who served as Parliamentary and Health Services Ombudsman between 2002 and 2011 also emphasized the real-world significance of administrative justice. Her remarks help highlight how administrative processes affect people's everyday experiences.

A. Abraham, 'The Parliamentary Ombudsman and Administrative Justice: Shaping the Next 50 Years', JUSTICE, Tom Sargant Memorial Annual Lecture, October 2011

Administrative Justice: Why it Matters

[. . . L]et me remind you why [Administrative Justice] matters. Administrative justice can sometimes seem the poor relation by comparison with the civil, criminal and family justice regimes. Yet citizens are just as likely, if not more likely, to come across administrative justice issues in their ordinary lives than civil or even family justice issues. The outcomes of decision making by a wide-range of public bodies on a daily basis affect family incomes, jobs, healthcare, housing, education and much, much more.

Administrative justice, then, concerns the way in which public bodies deal with the rights and interests of individuals, and the provision of redress when things go wrong.[2]

[2] For further discussion of the definition of administrative justice see 'Administrative Justice as a Field of Study' in M. Hertogh, R. Kirkham, R. Thomas, and J. Tomlinson (eds), *The Oxford Handbook of Administrative Justice* (2022, Oxford: OUP), pp. xv–xxviii.

16.1.2 THE 'SYSTEM' OF ADMINISTRATIVE JUSTICE

A statutory definition of the 'administrative justice system' is found in the Tribunals, Courts and Enforcement Act 2007. This definition captures the very wide range of decision-making and redress mechanisms across government.

Tribunals Courts and Enforcement Act 2007, Sch. 7, para. 13(4)

In this paragraph 'the administrative justice system' means the overall system by which decisions of an administrative or executive nature are made in relation to particular persons, including—

(a) the procedures for making such decisions,

(b) the law under which such decisions are made, and

(c) the systems for resolving disputes and airing grievances in relation to such decisions.

Such is the breadth and diversity of matters falling within the statutory definition that the term 'system' cannot be taken literally. The truth is that there is no single coherent institutional structure of administrative justice equivalent to the systems of civil or criminal justice that are focused on the civil and criminal courts. On the contrary, the landscape of administrative justice is, in reality, populated by distinct institutions that have different access requirements, responsibilities, ways of operating, and powers. Research by the UK Administrative Justice Institute (UKAJI) confirms the fragmented nature of the administrative justice landscape. The next extract outlines this complexity.

UK Administrative Justice Institute, *A Research Roadmap for Administrative Justice, 2018*, p. 6 https://administrativejusticeblog.files.wordpress.com/2018/02/final-ukaji_research_roadmap_web.pdf

[W]hile many talk about the 'system' of administrative justice, in reality there is no single system but instead a diverse range of processes and procedures concerned with a spectrum of issues, many of which are of key importance such as social security, education, housing, immigration, and health. It includes initial decision-making and the mechanisms for challenging those decisions. The bodies involved include legislatures, government departments, courts and tribunals, ombuds and complaint handlers across the jurisdictions of the UK. This is a complex, fragmented, and poorly understood landscape.

This analysis helps explain why users often struggle to navigate the system, and why reform efforts have focused on improving coherence and accessibility.

One explanation for the complexity of the system lies in its historical development. The following extract from the Scottish Consumer Council summarises the ad hoc evolution of redress mechanisms in the UK.

Administrative Justice Steering Group of the Scottish Consumer Council, *Administrative Justice in Scotland: The Way Forward*—*The Final Report* (2009, Glasgow: Consumer Focus Scotland)

3.21 The development of grievance machinery in the UK has been largely ad-hoc and resulted in the proliferation of bodies and procedures. At the end of the twentieth century, there was no overall system of administrative justice within either Scotland or the UK, and no serious attempt had ever been made to construct one. Tribunals in particular exhibited the effects of piece-meal evolution, there being a large number of specific tribunals each hearing appeals from different administrative agencies, and lacking a common approach on a range of important matters such as qualifications of members, rules of procedure, and whether there was a further right of appeal from the tribunal to a higher tribunal or to the courts. However, the tendency to proliferation of mechanisms was a general one exhibited also by ombudsmen and other complaints procedures. Like tribunals, these mechanisms for redress lacked a common approach to their function of providing redress of grievances. However, the last decade has been a period of great change in administrative justice and rationalisation and system design has been put firmly on the agenda. [. . .]

As this extract shows, much of the administrative justice system has developed reactively, rather than through planned design—a theme that recurs throughout this chapter.

A result of the ad hoc proliferation has been to make the administrative justice system potentially extremely difficult for users to navigate.[3] It also means that while some aspects of a problem can be handled by one institution or process, other aspects must be handled elsewhere. As we shall see later in the chapter the complexity of the system has remained one of the key issues that reformers have been trying to tackle in order to improve access to administrative justice and the overall coherence of the system. The case study on the Windrush scandal considered later in the chapter also underscores the importance of thinking beyond the administrative justice system.

16.1.2.1 The need for oversight of the administrative justice system

The main purpose of the statutory definition of the administrative justice system[4] was to delineate the scope of the responsibilities undertaken by the Administrative Justice and Tribunals Council (AJTC) to provide oversight of the administrative justice system.

The AJTC, and its Scottish and Welsh Committees, were an important influence and their annual reports and publications provide a wealth of information on developments in administrative justice. Nonetheless, despite widespread opposition, including from the House of Commons Public Administration Select Committee, the AJTC was abolished in 2013 as part of the then government's 'bonfire of the quangos' (a policy designed to cut public expenditure by reducing the number of public bodies). Subsequently, the Ministry of Justice established the Administrative Justice Forum (AJF), a body of experts with an independent chair, to advise it on administrative justice matters. The AJF was only a temporary measure and ceased to operate in 2017. Such was the perceived need

[3] For example, the authors of The House of Commons Library Briefing Paper on *The Parliamentary Ombudsman: Role and Proposals for Reform*, Briefing Paper No. CBP7496 (21 June 2018), esp. p. 15.

[4] S. Nason, 'Oversight of Administrative Justice Systems', in M. Hertogh, R. Kirkham, R. Thomas, and J. Tomlinson (eds), *The Oxford Handbook of Administrative Justice* (2022, Oxford, OUP), ch. 8.

for some oversight of this important area of the justice system that in 2014 a new research institute, The UK Administrative Justice Institute (UKAJI) was established to help pull together research and thinking from across the administrative justice landscape[5] and in July 2018 the Administrative Justice Council (AJC) was established as a non-statutory advisory body. The AJC is currently chaired by Lord Justice Dingemans, the Senior President of Tribunals, and is supported by the Ministry of Justice.[6] While the AJC is valuable it cannot completely fill the gap left by the abolition of the AJTC. It is not a statutory body and has no statutory powers; nor does it possess the resources of the AJTC. This means that there is currently no independent body with statutory powers and status able to provide effective and comprehensive oversight of administrative justice across the United Kingdom.

16.1.3 PERSPECTIVES ON ADMINISTRATIVE JUSTICE

For lawyers dispute resolution work is focused on the courts. This is very much a top down view of the system in which courts set precedents and establish legal standards that are intended to inform decision-making elsewhere in the system, so that decision-makers in public bodies, with the help of their lawyers, can learn from court judgments. In this way, it is expected that legal precedents will lead to improvement in the quality of decision-making.

Another way of viewing the system reflects how members of the general public experience administrative justice. In practice, people will come into contact with the administrative justice system whenever:

- decisions about their rights and interests are taken by officials;
- they want to have decisions looked at again by officials in the body concerned or to complain about the way in which their case has been handled;
- they want to appeal to an independent tribunal or complain to an ombud; or
- they seek further recourse to the courts.

A third, and perhaps a more dynamic, way of viewing the system is one that reflects the idea that complaints can do more than lead to the resolution of an individual grievance; they can also alert decision-makers to systemic problems within the organization and lead to overall improvements for the benefit of many others. Indeed, organizations are encouraged to view complaints in this positive light rather than to respond defensively to them.

This model is summarized in Figure 16.1, taken from the Administrative Justice and Tribunals Council's *Developing the Administrative Justice Landscape*.[7]

16.1.4 PRINCIPLES OF ADMINISTRATIVE JUSTICE

While the above perspectives provide different ways of looking at what the system of administrative justice does, they tell us little about how the system should work and provide no criteria for assessing whether the system is working properly and whether changes are needed. One way

[5] https://ukaji.org/. UKAJI has now been replaced by a broader research initiative, the Constitutional and Administrative Justice Initiative based the University of Essex. See https://essexlawresearch.blog/category/administrative-justice/:

[6] https://www.judiciary.uk/related-offices-and-bodies/advisory-bodies/administrative-justice-council/

[7] https://justice.org.uk/ajc/.

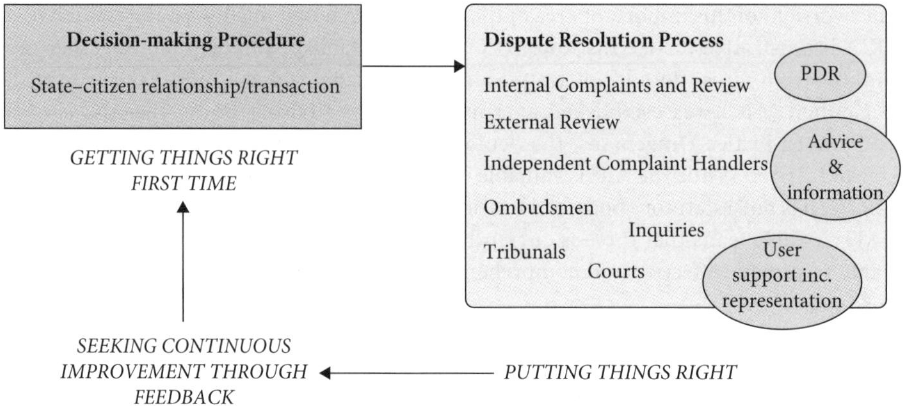

Figure 16.1 How complaints can influence the decision-making process

of approaching issues such as these is to look at the principles that the system should respect. Inevitably there are different ways of presenting these but the following summary provided by the Ministry of Justice gives an insight into what that government department regards as being the important principles to be satisfied by the system, namely principles concerning fairness, accessibility, and efficiency.

Ministry of Justice, *Administrative Justice and Tribunals: A Strategic Work Programme 2013–2016*, December 2012, p. 9

14. We believe that administrative justice should be underpinned by three key principles: *fairness, accessibility* and *efficiency*. [. . .]

15. In ensuring **fairness**, we expect the system to provide impartial and timely routes of complaint and redress which uphold the law. Fairness should be enshrined in all decision making and dispute resolution processes, and is preserved finally in the potential for an individual to seek redress through either a tribunal or court.

16. The systems that uphold justice in administrative decision making should also be **accessible**. Processes should, as far as possible, be understandable and navigable to the lay person. People should be helped to understand the decisions that have been taken about them, and provided with proportionate and transparent means of redress that empower them to resolve their problems as quickly as possible. The structures and procedures used within administrative justice and tribunals should recognise the needs of users.

17. Lastly, the administrative justice and tribunals system should aim to be **efficient**. This means incentivising state decision-making bodies to make correct and soundly-based decisions in the first instance and, where disputes arise, to provide proportionate forms of redress to allow parties to resolve their differences as quickly and simply as possible. [. . .]

These principles serve as benchmarks for evaluating the system, although, as we shall see, achieving them in practice can be challenging.

16.1.5 PROPORTIONATE DISPUTE RESOLUTION (PDR)

In the above extract the Ministry of Justice refer to the need for forms of redress that are proportionate. This is normally taken to include such matters as helping people to avoid problems and legal disputes in the first place and if problems do arise, providing ways of resolving disputes as quickly and cost-effectively as possible without recourse to tribunals or courts. Where tribunals and courts are used, they must also be cost-effective. The following extract sets out the rationale for this approach.

Secretary of State for Constitutional Affairs and Lord Chancellor, *Transforming Public Services: Complaints, Redress and Tribunals*, Cm 6243 (July 2004)

Proportionate Dispute Resolution

2.2 Our strategy turns on its head the [. . .] traditional emphasis first on courts, judges and court procedure, and second on legal aid to pay mainly for litigation lawyers. It starts instead with the real world problems people face. The aim is to develop a range of policies and services that, so far as possible, will help people to avoid problems and legal disputes in the first place; and where they cannot, provides tailored solutions to resolve the dispute as quickly and cost effectively as possible. It can be summed up as 'Proportionate Dispute Resolution'.

This move towards proportionate dispute resolution reflects a broader strategy to manage disputes more efficiently—but not without raising constitutional concerns.

16.1.6 CLASHING VALUES: INFORMALITY AND CONSTITUTIONALISM

Few will object to the idea of improving the quality of decision-making and developing tailored solutions to problems, thereby reducing the problems people face and where problems remain enabling people to resolve them early without needing to use the courts.[8] But this is an ambitious project and not entirely unproblematic—especially if it involves discouraging or even preventing people from using the courts and limits the ability of judges from developing standards that could improve the quality of administrative justice. Andrew Le Sueur, for example, has argued that the emphasis on informality may come at the expense of constitutional values. The extract below explores this tension between informal resolution and the rule of law.

A. Le Sueur, 'Courts, Tribunals, Ombudsmen, ADR: Administrative Justice, Constitutionalism and Informality', in J. Jowell and D. Oliver (eds) *The Changing Constitution*, 6th edn (2007, Oxford: OUP), p. 333

What has been suggested [. . .] is that there are two currents—changes associated with the promotion of constitutionalism and changes designed to implement values associated with informality. It is paradoxical that just at a time when courts and tribunals, traditionally the arenas for adjudication by judges, are being put on new and firmer constitutional footings so—simultaneously—there are attempts to steer disputes away from them. If the 'informalization' project is as successful as its supporters hope, fewer cases will be decided by judges finding facts and applying the law, and more by civil servants and third-parties through negotiation, mediation, early neutral evaluation and so on.

[8] Sometimes referred to as 'fitting the forum to the fuss', see F. Sander and S. Goldberg, 'Fitting the forum to the fuss' (1994) 10 Negotiation Journal 49.

This highlights a central theme of the chapter: that improving efficiency must not come at the cost of justice, legal standards, or individual rights.

> **QUESTIONS**
>
> Is it acceptable to sacrifice some legal formality in order to resolve disputes more quickly and cheaply? Who might benefit—and who might lose out—when justice becomes more 'informal'?

16.2 INITIAL DECISION-MAKING

It is perhaps self-evident that justice is served when decisions are made correctly in the first place. This also has advantages for the public bodies in question. In the following extract Professor Robert Thomas explains why it is important for decisions to be made correctly and the reasons why this often does not happen.

R. Thomas, 'Administrative justice, better decisions, and organisational learning'
[2015] 111 *Public Law* 112–14, 131–33 (footnotes omitted)

What does getting it right mean?

Making correct decisions is an essential principle of good administration. It involves collecting information relevant to the decision-making task and then applying the legal rules or standards to produce a decision that corresponds with the facts and is well-reasoned and robust. Decision-makers must assess the evidence and exercise sound judgment. [. . .]

There are several reasons why government should make correct decisions. First, administrators exercise considerable power over people's lives; any error or inefficiency in the handling or outcome of such decisions will be potentially distressing for the individuals concerned. . . . Poor decisions create unnecessary anxiety for individuals who ultimately succeed in challenging them. As appeal rights have increasingly been limited or curtailed, it is important to make good initial decisions. Secondly, poor decisions generate unnecessary costs and delay when they are challenged. [. . .] Thirdly, decision-making is an essential part of implementing policy, such as awarding people their entitlements. If government is to accomplish its policy goals (administering benefits, collecting taxes, determining immigration status), as approved by Parliament, then good decisions are required. Fourthly, correct decisions enhance the legitimacy of government agencies and their decision-making processes. Poor decision-making carries a reputational risk for agencies and can undermine public confidence in government as a whole and its legitimacy. Such problems are exacerbated if government repeats the same mistakes rather than learning from them.

[Thomas considers why so many decisions are not right first time and provides the following reasons drawn from the experience of those concerned with decision making in the context of social security.]

The President of social security appeal tribunals has repeatedly raised concerns about decision-making by the Department for Work and Pensions (DWP). The following themes have emerged from the President's reports: many decisions were overturned because the tribunal elicits additional information from appellants at appeal hearings; there was no consistent evidence to show that cases are effectively reconsidered before coming to tribunals; and there was confusion on the part of decision-makers about the appropriate evidential weight to be given to medical reports. Noting that there has been 'no significant improvement in the quality of administrative decisions coming before appeal tribunals', the President has highlighted the need for reforms, such as: collecting all relevant evidence and . . .[greate] . . .willingness to reconsider challenged decisions. Tribunals should be there to deal with the difficult cases; straightforward claims should be decided properly by initial decision-makers. But, in practice, too much of the time of tribunals is devoted to undertaking the initial fact-finding and decision-making for which the government agency is responsible.

Thomas's account shows that good administration requires more than legal compliance—it demands investment in staff training, feedback mechanisms, and a willingness to learn from mistakes.[9]

QUESTIONS

1. If you were responsible for advising on how initial decision-making could be improved, what steps would you suggest are taken?
2. Why do you think problems with the quality of initial decision-making have persisted?

16.3 ACCESSING THE ADMINISTRATIVE JUSTICE 'SYSTEM'

It is considered good administrative practice (and it may be a legal requirement) for public bodies to provide complaints procedures; they should also be willing to look at decisions again if those affected are dissatisfied. Indeed, for most welfare benefits there is a requirement that before cases are taken to tribunals they must be reconsidered (mandatory reconsideration) by the Department of Works and Pensions.[10] Internal procedures of this sort may enable problems to be resolved relatively quickly, and with minimum expense and trouble. However, internal procedures do not have the independence of tribunals, ombuds, or the courts and there are also concerns that the requirement that decisions be reconsidered before an appeal to a tribunal may operate as an obstacle to deter people from appealing.[11]

PAUSE FOR REFLECTION: HOW TO COMPLAIN ABOUT HOSPITAL TREATMENT?

A friend who knows that you are interested in law tells you that they are unhappy with how they were treated when recently visiting their local English hospital. They ask you whether they can complain and if so, what the procedure is? You decide to do some research and you first look at what NHS England say about complaints in their website. What do you find and how helpful is this?

Even though internal procedures are relatively accessible, it cannot be assumed that people will always complain or appeal when decisions are wrong (or, for that matter, that people will complain or appeal only against wrong decisions). In all probability, a significant proportion of wrong decisions are not questioned or challenged.

[9] See further R. Thomas and J. Tomlinson, 'A different tale of judicial power: Administrative review as a problematic response to the judicialisation of tribunals' (2019) Public Law 537–62; M. Hertogh, R. Kirkham, R. Thomas, and J. Tomlinson (eds), *The Oxford Handbook of Administrative Justice*, (2022, Oxford: OUP), chs 1 and 2.

[10] https://www.gov.uk/mandatory-reconsideration. See further: D. Cowan, A. Dymond, S. Halliday, and C. Hunter, 'Reconsidering mandatory reconsideration' [2017] Public Law 215–34.

[11] The compatibility of internal procedures with the independence requirement in Art. 6(1) ECHR has been questioned in the UK courts and in the European Court of Human Rights. In *Begum (Runa) v Tower Hamlets LBC* [2003] UKHL 5, it was held that internal reviews are compatible with Art. 6 of the ECHR because judicial review provides a sufficient element of independence; in *Tsfayo v UK* [2006] ECHR 981, it was held that judicial review does not provide a sufficient element of independence when internal review decisions are based on the credibility of the claimant—something that cannot be tested in judicial review proceedings; in *Ali v United Kingdom* (2016) 63 EHRR 20 it was held that Art. 6 did not guarantee a right to have the judicial body substitute its opinion for that of the decision-maker.

There are many reasons why people may not complain, including that they may not have access to advice or appropriate support, that they may believe there to be no point trying to question decisions of officials, that the process may seem too arduous, or that they may be deterred by the fear that complaining may have adverse repercussions for their future relationship with the public body.[12]

Failure to use complaints procedures is very common even in cases, as in homelessness, in which there is a right to have an adverse initial decision by a local housing authority reviewed internally by the local authority.[13] Professors David Cowan and Simon Halliday[14] open their study of internal reviews in homelessness cases with an illustration.

D. Cowan and S. Halliday, *The Appeal of Internal Review* (2003, Oxford: Hart Publishing), p. 1

Shortly before Christmas 2000, Andrew Holt applied with his girlfriend, Pamela McKenzie, to Brisford Council for somewhere to live. Andrew was 35 years old, Pamela was 29. Both had histories of drug use but had recently been through detoxification programmes. They each also suffered from other medical problems. They were unemployed and in receipt of welfare benefits. They were sleeping rough and were desperate to get off the streets as winter was setting in. Pamela was pregnant. Not long after making their housing application, however, Pamela tragically died in a fire. Andrew continued in his application for housing, but was eventually rejected as not having a 'priority need' as a homeless person. He was informed that he could have this refusal reviewed by a senior officer. There were no other housing options available to him and he was desperate for housing. During our taped interview with him he took hold of the microphone and pleaded for help from Brisford Council:

> I'll tell you what, keep this for the record, yes? Keep this one for the record and I'll tell 'em this then, I'll speak into your microphone: [Brisford] Council, will you please help me out? Will you please give me some permanent accommodation? Thank you very much. I would appreciate it. I will pay the rent. I will pay the bills and you know, I will be an absolutely model citizen. I will be an absolute model of a tenant for you, thank you very much. There you go.

However, Andrew never pursued his grievance with the Council. He did not take up the opportunity to have his decision reviewed internally, and so lost his right to have the decision reviewed subsequently in court.

The interesting and, in our view, surprising and worrying thing about this is that Andrew's reaction to the refusal of help, despite his desperate plight, is by far the normal response. The vast majority of homeless applicants specifically, and welfare applicants in general, fail to challenge adverse decisions despite their continuing sense of need. Surprisingly little is known about why citizens do not challenge adverse decisions from government agencies. [. . .]

QUESTIONS

1. What lessons about administrative justice can be learnt from this account? How could government and others respond to these lessons?
2. What remedies or procedures might have been available to Andrew Holt?

[12] H. Genn, *Paths to Justice* (1999, Oxford: Hart Publishing).
[13] *Begum (Runa) v Tower Hamlets LBC* [2003] UKHL 5, [2003] 2 AC 430.
[14] With C. Hunter, P. Maginn, and L. Naylor.

16.4 TRIBUNALS

Tribunals (the term 'tribunal' is used because these bodies typically have three members, a chair and two others) adjudicate upon a wide range of disputes between individuals and public bodies involving matters as diverse as social welfare issues, questions involving the liberty of people detained under the mental health legislation, immigration and asylum cases, special education needs and disability, and disputes over the value of property for the purposes of assessing liability to local taxes. They also deal with private disputes: for example, employment tribunals handle conflicts between employers and employees.

In *Cart*, Lady Hale offered a wide-ranging summary of the development, purpose, and diversity of tribunal systems. Her remarks provide a valuable overview of how tribunals differ from courts.

R (Cart) v Upper Tribunal
[2011] UKSC 28

Lady Hale

[11] One of the most important and controversial features of the development of the legal system in the 20th century was the creation and proliferation of statutory tribunals separate from the ordinary courts. Mostly they were set up to determine claims between an individual and the state—to war pensions, to social security benefits, to immigration and asylum, to provision for special educational needs, to be released from detention in a psychiatric hospital, against the refusal or withdrawal of licences or approvals to conduct certain kinds of business, for the determination of liability to direct and indirect taxation, for compensation for compulsory purchase and so on. In some instances, they were set up to adjudicate upon statutory schemes, generally those which modified what would otherwise be an ordinary contractual relationship between private persons—between employer and employee or between landlord and tenant of residential property.

[12] These jurisdictions were—and remain—very diverse. The subject matter can range from liability to VAT or entitlement to performing rights or the price of leasehold enfranchisement, which can be worth millions of pounds, to the amount of weekly means-tested benefits or war pensions entitlement, which may be worth only a few pounds at a time but may mean a great deal to the claimants involved and to others like them. The judiciary, also, could—and still can—be very diverse, ranging from seconded High Court judges . . . to fee-paid part-timers from a great variety of legal professional backgrounds. In many cases, tribunals also had—and still may have—members who were not legally qualified but had other professional qualifications or experience which was particularly suited to the subject matter of the claim. Some had single tier structures, some with and some without a right of appeal to the High Court or Court of Appeal. Some had two tier structures with their own appellate tier, again with or without a right of appeal to the High Court or Court of Appeal.

[13] But in general these tribunal systems shared some common characteristics. They were set up by statute to administer complex and rapidly changing areas of the law. Their judges were expected to know this law without having to have lawyers for the parties to explain it to them. Their members were expected to have relevant expertise or experience in the subject matter of the dispute, not only so that they would be able to adjudicate upon factual issues without the help of lawyers for the parties, but also so that the parties could feel confident that the overall balance of the panel (for example between employers and employees) would produce impartial results. Their procedures were also tailored to the subject matter of the dispute and they were not bound by the technical rules of evidence. While legal representation was common in those tribunals where large sums of money were at stake, and latterly

in mental health review tribunals where personal liberty was at stake, the original expectation in most tribunals was that people would not need representation, or could be helped by specialist non-lawyer representatives. In theory, therefore, the respective roles of the tribunal and the parties were rather different from their roles in the ordinary courts. The tribunal was more than a neutral referee before whom each party was expected to lay out all the material necessary to decide the case for the judge to choose which he preferred [. . .]. In general, this diverse specialism was regarded as a strength rather than a weakness, although the concomitant lack of legal aid in almost all tribunals was regretted by those who saw the benefits which skilled representation could bring.

[14] However, another feature of these tribunal systems was more controversial. They were mostly resourced and administered by whichever Department of State was responsible for the statutory scheme in question, rather than by the Department which was responsible for the administration of justice in the ordinary courts. This led to fears that they were not, or at least were not seen to be, sufficiently independent of those sponsoring Departments. The Department may have seen the independence and expertise of the tribunals as an integral part of the proper administration of a statutory scheme which was designed to bring certain benefits to the people. But others may have feared that they were simply accomplices with the Department in denying to claimants the benefits which were properly theirs. In between these two extremes, there might well be a perceived risk that the tribunals would be more inclined to accept the Departmental view of what the law was, rather than an alternative view which was more favourable to the claimant or taxpayer or whomever.

This extract clarifies the distinctive features of tribunals and sets the stage for understanding their role within the administrative justice landscape.

16.4.1 THE GROWTH OF TRIBUNALS

As Lady Hale indicates, modern tribunals can be traced to the major social reforms introduced by the Liberal government in the early twentieth century—particularly the introduction of pensions for the elderly[15] and National Insurance.[16]

The courts could have been used to deal with disputes arising from these schemes, but they were considered too expensive and too formal. There was also a fear that judges would sabotage the schemes, either because they were innately conservative or because they were out of touch with the needs of ordinary people, and would be unable to approach them in a balanced and sensitive way.[17]

Nonetheless, some argued that it was wrong to bypass the courts. Lord Hewart, a former Lord Chief Justice, for example, argued that 'administrative' tribunals (as they were referred to at the time) were, at best, a necessary evil established to save courts from being overwhelmed and, at worst, a subversion of the rule of law.[18] He considered that the use of administrative tribunals undermined the rule of law because these bodies were established, and largely controlled, by the government departments with whom individuals were in dispute.

[15] Old Age Pensions Act 1908. [16] National Insurance Act 1911.

[17] H. Street, *Justice in the Welfare State*, 2nd edn (1975, London: Stevens), p. 9; B. Abel-Smith and R. Stevens, *In Search of Justice* (1968, London: Allen Lane), p. 111. See generally J.A.G. Griffith, *The Politics of the Judiciary*, 5th edn (1997, London: Fontana Press).

[18] Lord Hewart, *The New Despotism* (1929, London: Ernest Benn).

This concern raised critical questions about how tribunals should be viewed and where they should fit: should they be part of the administrative system operated by government departments to resolve disputes internally, or should they be part of the justice system that was independent of government?

16.4.1.1 The Franks Committee report

This question was considered by the Franks Committee in its 1957 report.[19] The Committee had been established following the Crichel Down affair (1954) which involved poor government handling of land that had been compulsorily purchased during wartime and then mismanaged.[20] The affair had nothing specifically to do with tribunals, but allegations of corruption and departmental wrongdoing fanned public concern about the behaviour of government and its treatment of individuals, including the absence of redress against government wrongdoing.

Despite the submissions of government to the contrary, the Franks Committee was clear that tribunals should be part of the justice system and independent of government departments. It stressed that tribunals should possess three basic characteristics: openness, fairness, and impartiality.

The Franks Committee, *Report of the Committee on Administrative Tribunals and Enquiries*, Cmnd 218 (1957)

The Choice Between Tribunals and Courts of Law

38. [. . . T]ribunals have certain characteristics which often give them advantages over the courts. These are cheapness, accessibility, freedom from technicality, expedition and expert knowledge of their particular subject [. . .].

Tribunals as Machinery for Adjudication

40. Tribunals are not ordinary courts, but neither are they appendages of Government Departments. Much of the official evidence [. . .] appeared to reflect the view that tribunals should properly be regarded as part of the machinery of administration, for which the Government must retain a close and continuing responsibility. Thus, for example, tribunals in the social service field would be regarded as adjuncts to the administration of the services themselves. We do not accept this view. We consider that tribunals should properly be regarded as machinery provided by Parliament for adjudication rather than as part of the machinery of administration. The essential point is that in all these cases Parliament has deliberately provided for a decision outside and independent of the Department concerned [. . .]

To satisfy the principles of openness, fairness, and impartiality, the Franks Committee recommended that:

- those who chaired tribunals should be legally qualified;
- members of tribunals should not be chosen by departments;
- hearings should normally be in public;
- individuals should normally have the right to legal representation;

[19] *Report of the Committee on Administrative Tribunals and Enquiries*, Cmnd 218 (1957).

[20] *Report of Sir Andrew Clark into the Disposal of Land at Crichel Down*, Cmnd 9176 (1954); D.N. Chester, 'The *Crichel Down* case' (1954) 32 Public Administration 389.

- legal aid should be available;
- tribunals should give reasons for their decisions;
- there should be a right of appeal on '*fact, law and merits*' from tribunals to courts; and
- tribunals should be supervised by an independent body to be known as the 'Council on Tribunals'.

The main thrust[21] of these recommendations was subsequently implemented by the Tribunals and Inquiries Acts 1958, amended in 1992. A later report of the Scottish Consumer Council reflects on the legacy of Franks, noting its influence on the shape and perception of tribunal justice.

Scottish Consumer Council, *Administrative Justice in Scotland: The Way Forward*—*The Final Report of the Administrative Justice Steering Group* (2009, Glasgow: Consumer Focus Scotland)

3.9 The significance of Franks can be summarised as follows. First, as the specific recommendations above indicate, the most important legacy of Franks has been its encouragement of the judicialisation of tribunals. Second, however, Franks also promoted the idea that tribunals were different from courts in important respects notably their informality and accessibility. The assumption that tribunals are more user-friendly than courts has had important policy consequences, including [. . .] limitations on the availability of legal aid for tribunals. Third, Franks did nothing to restrain the proliferation of tribunals. Although recommending that proposals for any new tribunals should be referred to the suggested Councils, Franks also said that there was little scope for amalgamation of tribunals, and proliferation has continued until very recently.

As the final comment in this extract indicates, in the decades following Franks, the number of tribunals grew phenomenally.[22] By 2006, there were 70 different tribunal jurisdictions each established at different times for different reasons. Some—such as those concerned with social security, employment, asylum, tax, land registration, and mental health—were handling over half a million cases a year, whereas others did very little, if anything. The haphazard growth and the variety of tribunals highlighted the absence of any system. Moreover, with the enactment of the Human Rights Act 1998, there was concern that, despite the post-Franks reforms, tribunals remained insufficiently independent of government to satisfy the requirements of Art. 6 of the European Convention on Human Rights (ECHR). In response to these concerns, in 2000, the government commissioned Sir Andrew Leggatt, a former Lord Justice of Appeal, to conduct a wide-ranging review of tribunals.

The Leggatt Report was published in August 2001,[23] along with a government consultation paper.[24] The report was critical of the haphazard way in which tribunals were being established to meet the needs and convenience of departments, and said that 'users' often found tribunal procedures to be daunting and intimidating. Significantly, it stressed the need to increase the independence of tribunals and to establish a more coherent system. To achieve this, the Leggatt Report called for a new independent 'Tribunal Service', analogous to the Courts Service, to take over the management of tribunals from departments. It also recommended the creation of a single two-tier tribunal structure under the leadership of a senior judge.

[21] Legal aid has never been extended to more than a handful of tribunals.

[22] M. Adler, 'Tribunal reform: Proportionate dispute resolution and the pursuit of administrative justice' (2006) 69 Modern Law Review 958, 959, quoting Harlow and Rawlings.

[23] Sir Andrew Leggatt, *Tribunals for Users: One System, One Service* (2001, London: HMSO).

[24] Lord Chancellor's Department, *Tribunals for Users: A Consultation Paper* (2001, London: HMSO).

The main elements of the Leggatt Report were implemented by the Tribunals, Courts and Enforcement Act 2007 which established a new system for tribunals under the leadership of a senior judge, the Senior President of Tribunals.[25] The Tribunals Service joined the Courts Service in the HM Courts and Tribunals Service, an integrated agency of the Ministry of Justice created in April 2011.

The main elements of the current tribunal system are summarized in the following account by Sir Robert Carnwath (as he then was), the first Senior President of Tribunals.

Sir Robert Carnwath, 'Tribunal justice: A new start'
[2009] 48 *Public Law* 50–2 (footnotes omitted)

The Tribunals, Courts and Enforcement Act 2007 [TCEA]

Part 1 of the TCEA provided the framework for the creation of the new tribunal structure. [. . .]

Section 1 confirms the place of the tribunal judiciary as part of the independent judicial system of the country, protected by the same statutory guarantees of independence as their court colleagues.[26] It thus confirms the place of tribunals as part of the judicial system, rather than as an appendage of the administration. Section 2 creates the new post of Senior President of Tribunals . . .[whose] . . . responsibilities extend to non-devolved tribunals throughout the United Kingdom. The appointment is made by the Lord Chancellor with the concurrence of the Lord Chief Justice for England and Wales and his counterparts in Scotland and Northern Ireland.

The statutory functions of the Senior President are modelled in many respects on those of the Lord Chief Justice under the Constitutional Reform Act 2005. They confer wide-ranging responsibility for judicial leadership, including training, welfare and guidance of the tribunal judiciary, and for representing their views to Parliament and to ministers. [. . .]

The Act creates two new tribunals: the First-tier Tribunal and the Upper Tribunal. They will each be divided into 'Chambers', each with its own Chamber President [ss. 3–7 TCEA]. [. . .] The intention is that most existing tribunal jurisdictions, first-instance and appellate, will in due course be transferred into one or other of the new tribunals, so as to create a comprehensive two-tier structure.

The current chambers of the First-tier and Upper-tier Tribunals are shown in Figure 16.2.

Note that the new structure excludes tribunals that sit only in Scotland, Wales, or Northern Ireland.

16.4.2 CONSTITUTIONALISM VS PROPORTIONATE DISPUTE RESOLUTION: A CLASH OF VALUES?

Earlier, we referred to Le Sueur's argument that, in the area of administrative justice, tension exists between two sets of values: those rooted in constitutionalism and those rooted in concepts such as PDR. The implication is that constitutionalism is rooted in principles such as the rule of law,[27] whereas the goals of PDR are motivated by pragmatic considerations such as the desire to save money and achieve efficiency gains that gives a lower priority to the quality of fairness and rights to access the courts.

[25] Currently Lord Justice Lindholm.

[26] Section 1 TCEA extends the duty (in Constitutional Reform Act 2005, s. 3) upon the Lord Chancellor and other ministers to respect the continued independence of the judiciary to tribunal chair and members.

[27] On constitutionalism, see Chapter 2.

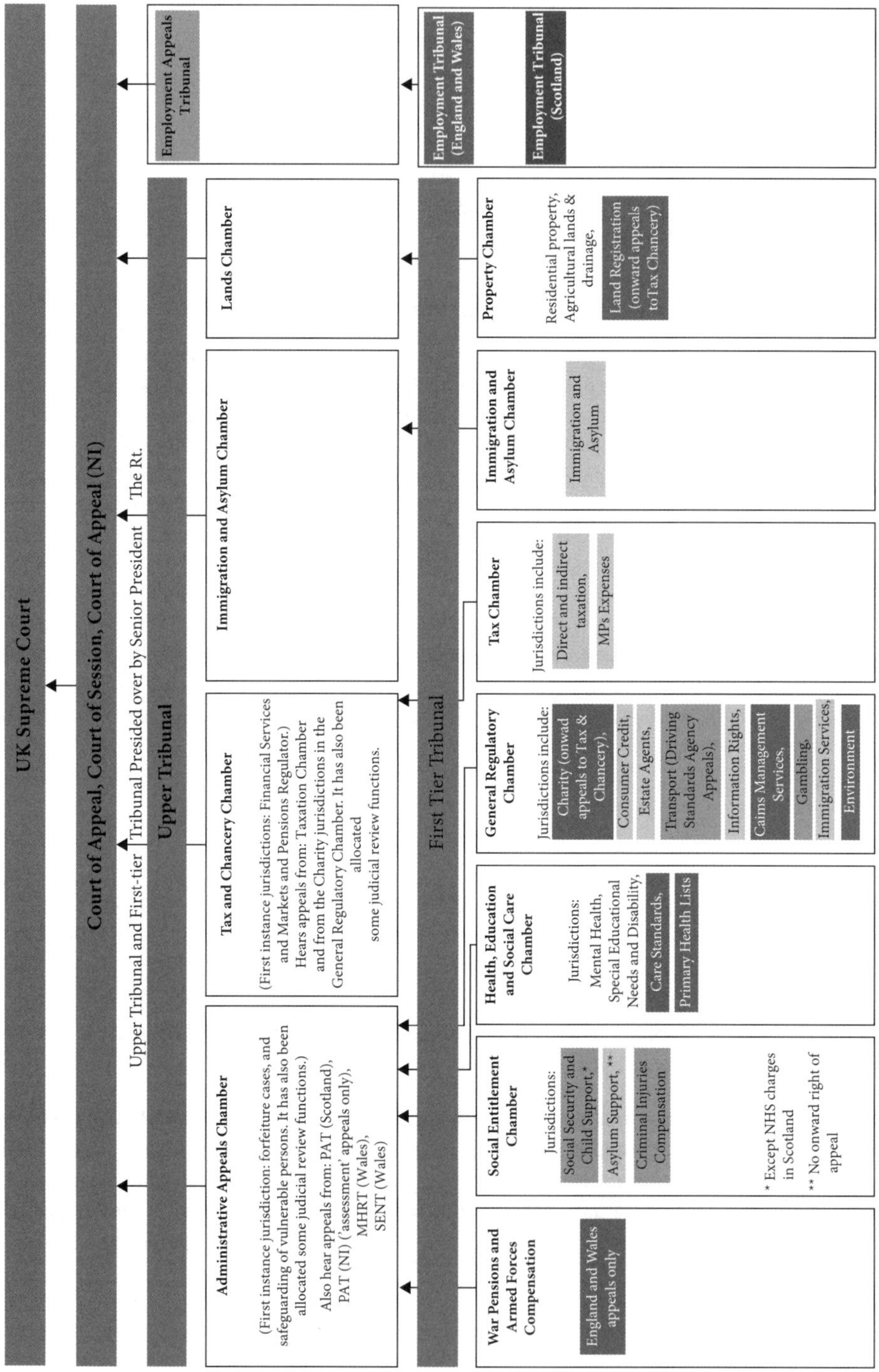

Figure 16.2 The current chambers of the First-tier and Upper-tier Tribunals

There can be no doubt that the tribunal system furthers the aims of constitutionalism insofar as it provides a statutory structure for tribunals that ensures their independence from government and enables coherence that was previously lacking. It places the tribunal judiciary on the same constitutional footing as judges in the civil and criminal justice systems.[28] Also, it should make it easier to develop standards that can be applied across the main tribunal jurisdictions, while recognising the specialist needs of the different Chambers. Those favouring a 'legal constitutionalists' approach are likely to see these developments as being positive.

But some argue that there is tension between these developments and the establishment of a system of tribunals that is separate from the courts and free to develop its own approaches that could compromise standards and the quality of justice.[29]

In recent years, especially as a result of the Covid pandemic, much of the debate around these matters has focused on whether tribunals should be able to dispense with the type of formal oral hearings typically used in courts and instead make greater use of written procedures or digital online hearings.[30]

16.4.2.1 Digitalization of tribunals

Even before Covid struck the Ministry of Justice and the HM and Courts and Tribunals Service (HMCTS) had embarked on a programme of reform aimed at introducing greater digitalization across the justice system, including tribunals.[31] In the context of the Social Security Tribunal, for instance, the:

> aim is to resolve social security appeals through a variety of methods—including 'continuous on-line hearings'. A key idea is that greater use of digital technology will bring the judge and the parties together at a much earlier stage to resolve cases in the most appropriate way, whether via a hearing or through an online exchange and decision. The overall aim is to devise a flexible system which initially retains the confidence of all parties and the judiciary, then moves on to becoming the accepted standard for resolving disputes, while at the same time being significantly more efficient in terms of time and resources.[32]

As tribunals increasingly use digital technology, questions have arisen about access, fairness, and the risk of exclusion. Professors Thomas and Tomlinson have critically examined these developments.[33]

[28] On the independence of the judiciary, see Chapter 15.

[29] It was in order to underpin the independence of tribunals that no automatic right of appeal from the Upper Tribunal to the courts was allowed. See further discussion of *R (Cart) v Upper Tribunal* [2011] UKSC 28 in Chapter 20.

[30] On the fairness of written as to opposed to oral hearings see G. Richardson and H. Genn, 'Tribunals in transition: Resolution or adjudication?' [2007] Public Law 116, 126; see also the of *Osborn v Parole Board* [2013] UKSC 61 in Chapter 18.

[31] Ministry of Justice, *Transforming Our Justice System* (2016); *Guidance Modernising Courts and Tribunals: Benefits of Digital Services*, (24 March 2025), https://www.gov.uk/guidance/modernising-courts-and-tribunals-benefits-of-digital-services

[32] R. Thomas and J. Tomlinson, *The Digitalisation of Tribunals: PLP/UKAJI Research Paper*, 5 April 2018, p. 6. On digital exclusion, see also *Preventing Digital Exclusion from Online Justice*, (2018, JUSTICE).

[33] See also N. Byrom, *Digital Justice: HMCTS Digital Strategy and Delivering Access to Justice* (2019, The Legal Education Foundation), https://research.thelegaleducationfoundation.org/research-learning/funded-research/digital-justice-hmcts-data-strategy-and-delivering-access-to-justice-report-and-recommendations. Also, Naomi Creutzfeldt, 'The digitalisation of tribunals and vulnerability' [2024] *Public Law* 211

R. Thomas and J. Tomlinson, *The Digitalisation of Tribunals: PLP/UKAJI Research Paper*, 5 April 2018, pp. 26–7 (footnotes omitted)

Access to justice

Much of the HMCTS digitalisation agenda is centred upon improving access to justice. This is often linked to familiar notions of the attractions of [online dispute resolution], i.e. that digital systems can create lower-cost and more convenient solutions for users. The intended reforms may well enhance access to justice but there are also risks here. One such risk is 'digital exclusion'—the concern that by putting services online we may exclude as much as a fifth of the population from them. [. . .] Some people cannot afford internet access. Some . . .have access at a library or some other place, but their access—in terms of time and convenience—is likely to be less than those who have their own at-home connection. Beyond this, connection quality and coverage varies drastically across the UK. These sorts of difficulties raise a range of possible issues in the context of online tribunals.

Online procedures

There are sure to be questions around fair procedures in online tribunals. [. . .] Online processes [. . .] promise huge changes in tribunals. This raises a host of questions. One prominent example [. . .] is the possible use of video technology in evidence-gathering. How much weight ought to be given to such evidence is a controversial question. There are also a range of questions about how these developments may be seen through the prism of the common law principles of procedural fairness. [. . .] there is also the issue of determining which cases are handled under online procedures. Are there some types of cases that would not be appropriate for ODR? If so, which types of cases? And how would those cases be identified—through a blanket policy or on a case by case basis? To what extent will the choice rest with individuals, the public body being challenged or the tribunal? What approach will be taken when cases raise issues of the appellant's credibility? (It is often assumed that it is preferable to assess credibility if the appellant appears in person.) There is a fine balance to be struck here. Too cautious of an approach means attempts at digitalisation will leave us with only a very expensive case management system. Too liberal of an approach will lead to unsuitable cases being determined through online procedures. More broadly, there may be challenges vis-à-vis translating traditional values of administrative justice to the digital sphere. Such values include transparency, fairness, participation etc. A key question will be how these values—along with traditional values of public law, such as judicial independence, open justice etc.—can be effectively respected into the digital sphere? This also raises a major dilemma of modern administration: the role of the private sector. The expanding role of the private sector has been a key feature of the debate around public administration and law in the last 30 years. What the role of the private sector will be in the online tribunals system—both in terms of design and operation—is an important question.

Thomas and Tomlinson raise vital questions about the future of administrative justice in a digital world and the fairness of online procedures especially for those who lack digital literacy or access. These are issues to which should also be borne in mind when we consider the grounds of judicial review and especially procedural impropriety in Chapter 19.

QUESTIONS

1. Should we be concerned about the movement to modernize the justice system by (a) seeking to ensure that tribunals adopt procedures that are less formal than those typically used in courts and (b) by making greater use of digital technologies such as online dispute resolution and virtual hearings?
2. What might be the main advantages and disadvantages flowing from the digitalization of tribunals?

16.5 OMBUDS

Whereas tribunals adjudicate between parties and reach binding decisions on the facts or law in the particular case, ombuds typically investigate complaints about the way in which the administration has handled a matter, and report their findings and make recommendations. The following extract explains how ombuds differ from courts and tribunals in both approach and power.

Administrative Justice Steering Group of the Scottish Consumer Council, *Administrative Justice in Scotland: The Way Forward*—*The Final Report* (2009, Glasgow: Consumer Focus Scotland)

3.15 Ombudsmen represented a new type of machinery for handling complaints which were not considered suitable for the courts primarily because they were complaints of deficiencies in administration rather than of illegality. Before the advent of ombudsmen, such complaints were not covered by statutory grievance machinery, but could be pursued by elected representatives using parliamentary and local government procedures. The most distinctive features of ombudsmen were, first, that they followed an investigative approach rather than the adversarial adjudicative approach employed by the courts, and, second, that they had power to recommend remedies for citizens, but no powers to enforce them.

16.5.1 THE MAIN OMBUDS

Ombuds are now widely used both in the public and the private sectors to investigate complaints and resolve disputes.[34] The following are the principal public sector 'ombuds'. Note that not all bodies referred to as being 'ombuds' or 'ombudsmen' are called 'ombuds' or ombudsmen.[35]

[34] The Ombudsman Association provides information on the many ombudsmen and complaint-handlers, see: https://www.ombudsmanassociation.org/find-ombudsman

[35] Note also the Service Complaints Ombudsman for the Armed Forces; New Homes Ombudsman, https://www.scoaf.org.uk/; Housing Ombudsman dealing with social housing: https://www.housing-ombudsman.org.uk/.

16.5.1.1 The Parliamentary and Health Service Ombudsman

The Parliamentary and Health Service Ombudsman (PHSO) is actually two ombuds:

- the Parliamentary Commissioner for Administration, established by the Parliamentary Commissioner Act 1967; and
- the Health Service Commissioner, which derives most of its powers from the Health Service Commissioners Act 1993.

The same person—currently, Paula Sussex CBE—holds both offices and, for many purposes, they can be treated as a single institution. They share the same home page, available at https://www.ombudsman.org.uk/.

16.5.1.2 Local Government and Social Care Ombudsman

The Local Government and Social Care Ombudsman can look at complaints about council services no matter who provides them. See further https://www.lgo.org.uk.

16.5.1.3 Public Services Ombudsman for Wales

The Public Services Ombudsman for Wales was established by the Public Services Ombudsman (Wales) Act 2005. It deals with complaints concerning a wide range of bodies in Wales including the Welsh Assembly government, the National Assembly for Wales Commission, local authorities, and health authorities: the website for the Public Services Ombudsman for Wales is now: https://www.ombudsman.wales/.

16.5.1.4 The Scottish Public Services Ombudsman

The Scottish Public Services Ombudsman (SPSO) was established by the Scottish Public Services Ombudsman Act 2002. Like its Welsh counterpart, the SPSO can consider complaints against a broad range of public bodies. It can be found at www.spso.org.uk/.

16.5.1.5 The Northern Ireland Ombudsman

The office of the Northern Ireland Ombudsman covers three bodies: Northern Public Services Ombudsman, The Northern Ireland Judicial Appointments Ombudsman and the Northern Ireland Local Government Commissioner for Standards. The website for the Northern Ireland Public Services Ombudsman is https://nipso.org.uk/.

16.5.2 THE PRINCIPAL CHARACTERISTICS OF THE PUBLIC SECTOR OMBUDS

Typically, the public sector ombuds possess the following characteristics.

- They are independent of the bodies that they may investigate.
- They investigate complaints that 'maladministration' has caused 'injustice'.[36]

[36] The local government ombuds can also investigate complaints arising from the provision of services or a failure to provide services. The Health Service Ombudsman has a wider remit to investigate complaints about hardship or injustice caused by failures in service provision. This ombud can also investigate exercises of clinical judgement: Health Service Commissioner Act 1993, s. 3. Unlike other UK ombuds services, the PHSO cannot undertake own initiative investigations (see further Section 16.5.10 on reform)).

- They operate through investigatory powers (rather than by adjudication, as in the case of courts and tribunals).
- They cannot force public bodies to comply with their findings and recommendations.

In this chapter, we focus on the PHSO.

16.5.3 THE PARLIAMENTARY AND HEALTH SERVICE OMBUDS

16.5.3.1 A short history

The Parliamentary Commissioner for Administration (PCA), established by the Parliamentary Commissioner Act 1967 (PCA 1967), was the first ombud in the United Kingdom. The concept of an 'ombudsman' (meaning 'grievance-handler') had, however, been used in Sweden since 1809, when the Swedish Ombud was created to investigate allegations that the government had been improperly trying to influence civil servants. The concept was adopted into the United Kingdom to improve redress against government, especially when the courts could not be used. We noted earlier that the Crichel Down affair (1954) acted as a catalyst for the establishment of the Franks Committee; it also stimulated interest in the creation of an ombud.[37]

The most influential call for an ombud came in a report by JUSTICE in 1961 (the Whyatt Report).[38] The proposal that a new institution be established to deal with complaints about central government was controversial. Many members of Parliament (MPs) feared that it would detract from their role as complaints-handlers for their constituents and others. It was also feared that an ombud able to look into the work of central government departments would undermine the doctrine of ministerial responsibility. With these concerns in mind, the Whyatt Committee proposed a Parliamentary Commissioner who would strengthen the House of Commons and support MPs vis-à-vis central government. For an initial period of five years, while the body was bedding in, citizens would have to route their complaints to MPs, who would then refer them to the Parliamentary Commissioner. The substance of the proposal was finally adopted by Wilson's Labour government with the enactment of the Parliamentary Commissioner Act 1967.

The Act, however, did not meet all of the Whyatt Committee's recommendations. In particular, while Whyatt had recommended that the MP filter should be temporary, the Act made it permanent and it has been retained, except in relation to complaints relating to the Victims' Code[39], despite many calls for its removal. Nor was any attempt made to link the parliamentary ombud to the courts or to tribunals—indeed, the ombud was prevented from handling matters that could be dealt with by the courts. The fact that decisions of the parliamentary ombuds were not to be legally enforceable was also criticized, as was the range of functions that fell beyond its jurisdiction. The Act, for example, prevented the parliamentary ombuds from examining complaints arising from the government's commercial transactions or involving civil service personnel matters.[40] We shall return to these matters later in the chapter, suffice to say here that because of these limitations some said that rather than an 'ombudsman', the Act had created an 'ombudsmouse'.[41]

[37] For a history, see R. Gregory and P. Giddings, *The Ombudsman, the Citizen and Parliament* (2002, London: Politico's Publishing).

[38] Sir J. Whyatt, *The Citizen and the Administration: Redress of Grievances* (1961, London: Justice).

[39] See Victims and Prisoner Act 2024, s 27 which came in force in January 2025.

[40] PCA 1967, Sch. 3.

[41] W. Gwyn, 'The British PCA: Ombudsman or ombudsmouse?' [1973] 35 Journal of Politics 45.

Despite these criticisms, the Act created a new type of institution that could significantly strengthen the ability of MPs and Parliament in relation to the administration, and it established a model that has been widely adopted by the other public service ombuds, as well as by the private sector.

16.5.3.2 The Parliamentary and Health Service Ombudsman in practice: Some facts and figures

In the following extract, a previous PHSO, Ann Abraham, provides an idea of the scale and range of the work done by the public sector ombuds. Although she is referring to the work of the PHSO nearly twenty years ago her general observations remain relevant, including for example her summary of the remedies that may be secured following ombuds investigations. In this context, she notes that public bodies normally comply with the recommendations of ombuds and makes the interesting point that compliance with ombuds recommendations is '*almost certainly far higher than compliance with judgments imposed by the civil courts*'.

A. Abraham, 'The ombudsman and "paths to justice": A just alternative or just an alternative?'
[2008] 1 *Public Law* 2–3 (footnotes omitted)

Between them, public sector ombudsmen handle complaints about all the main public services delivered in England, Northern Ireland, Scotland and Wales. [. . .concerning. . .] a wide range of government departments and agencies, with the biggest repeat customers being HM Revenue and Customs . . . Jobcentre Plus, the Child Support Agency, the Pension Service, and the Immigration and Nationality Directorate (IND), as it then was. [. . .] The remedies achieved as a result of PHSO investigation are equally diverse. In some cases, the remedy is pecuniary: a payment of £335 by the IND for a postal fee unnecessarily incurred; compensation from Jobcentre Plus for £18,000 arrears of income support, late payment of benefit, lost entitlement to free school meals and help with school uniforms; remittance by the Revenue of an overpayment of £7,500; reimbursement by the Disability and Carers Service of £9,500 to cover lost disability allowance plus interest over a four year period.

In others, it is non-pecuniary: a trust-wide audit of clinical records and the institution of training in the handling of MRSA positive patients; the review of a decision by a Primary Care Trust to refuse funding of continuing care; improvement of supervision, ward staffing levels and skill mix in the management of patients with dementia and poor communication; provision of weekend senior medical cover and better transfer procedures within a Primary Care Trust.

[. . .]

Compliance rates with the PHSO's recommendations are very high, and almost certainly far higher than compliance with judgments imposed by the civil courts. [. . .] There is no indication that the inability to make binding recommendations impairs the PHSO's ability to deliver substantive justice.

PAUSE FOR REFLECTION

Given that decisions of ombuds are generally not legally enforceable, why might it be that ombuds recommendations appear to be better complied with than are court judgments? Is it because there is more respect for the ombuds than for civil courts? Is it to do with the way in which ombuds work? Is it because ombuds have a higher level of understanding of public administration than judges? Is it because their procedures are able to secure the involvement, cooperation, and trust of public bodies? These are important questions and we will return to them later.

For up-to-date figures on the number and types of complaints made you should look at the annual reports of the ombuds. These can be found on the relevant websites. You will see from the PHSO's Annual Report for 2024–5, for example, that during that year the PHSO received 123,987 enquiries and reached decisions on 37,454 complaints. The PHSO made 1,274 recommendations, including 436 apologies, 336 compensation payments to make up for financial losses or to recognise the impact of errors, and 353 recommendations to improve services. Recommendations were complied with in 1,156 closed complaints and were not complied with in three cases.[42]

16.5.4 EXAMPLES OF INVESTIGATIONS

16.5.4.1 The *Sachsenhausen* case (1967)

The first major investigation undertaken by the parliamentary ombudsman was into complaints by former British servicemen who had been held within the Sachsenhausen concentration camp by the Nazis during the Second World War. They complained that they had been unfairly treated by the Foreign Office when it rejected their application for compensation. The ombud found that the complainants had been victims of injustice caused by maladministration and persuaded the Foreign Office to pay them compensation. As Richard Kirkham says, this outcome gave Parliament and the media early notice of the potential importance of the ombud.[43]

A rather different investigation was used by the then parliamentary ombuds, Ann Abraham, to illustrate how that ombud gives practical effect to human rights principles of fairness, respect, equality, dignity, and autonomy. The example concerns Mr R.

A. Abraham, The Parliamentary Ombudsman and Administrative Justice: Shaping the Next 50 Years, JUSTICE, Tom Sargant Memorial Annual Lecture, October 2011

> Mr R has learning disabilities and a mental health condition. He went overseas on holiday to stay with some family friends. His parents had intended to travel with him but were unable to do so because of his father's ill health. This was the first time that Mr R had travelled abroad alone. On his return he was stopped at his local airport by two trainee customs officers because he was carrying a large amount of tobacco. He was then interviewed about his trip abroad, how it had been funded, and the tobacco. Contrary to the UK Border Agency's own guidance, the customs officers did not check at the start of the interview whether Mr R was fit and well, or whether he had any medical condition they needed to be aware of. Nor did they ask him to read and sign the notes of the interview. If they had done, they would have discovered that Mr R could not read or write. The officers strip-searched Mr R—at one point leaving him naked. One of the reasons given for the strip-search was that Mr R appeared *'nervous'* and *'evasive'* when questioned. Although Mr R had referred to his disabilities and one of the officers had written *'Mental health problems, disability'* in his notebook, the officers simply continued with the interview and the search. No drugs were found. Mr R was eventually allowed to leave, but the tobacco he had been carrying was seized.
>
> My investigation found that the UK Border Agency had not had regard to Mr R's disability rights in the way that it had carried out its functions. As soon as Mr R referred to his disabilities, the customs officers should have stopped the interview and re-arranged it so that an appropriate adult could be present. Instead they

[42] Parliamentary and Health Service Ombudsman, *Annual Report and Accounts 2021–2025*, HC 998, p. 43.

[43] Dr R. Kirkham, *The Parliamentary Ombudsman: Withstanding the Test of Time*, Fourth Report, Session 2006–07 (HC 421, March 2007), p. 6.

had pressed on regardless, they had failed to follow the Agency's own interviewing protocols, which might have helped them to identify Mr R's disabilities and deal with him appropriately as a vulnerable adult.

An appropriate adult should have been able to explain that Mr R's difficulties in answering questions were due to his learning disabilities and not evidence of evasive behaviour. Not only was it unlikely that the encounter would have progressed so far as a strip search, but Mr R would have had the support and protection he was entitled to in what for him was a terrifying situation. Not surprisingly, he never wanted to go near an airport again.

We upheld the complaint. The UK Border Agency apologised to Mr R and paid him £5,000 compensation for the distress, humiliation and anxiety they had caused him.

In an attempt at restorative justice we asked the Agency to explore with Mr R and his mother what they might do to enable Mr R to feel comfortable using his local airport in future.

The Agency also agreed to review the disability awareness training provided to their customs officers, with a particular emphasis on identifying non-visible disabilities such as learning disabilities and mental health conditions.

So a good example of the Ombudsman providing redress for the individual—and also recommending systemic improvements for a wider public benefit.

The following summarizes some of the many other important investigations undertaken by the parliamentary ombuds.[44]

Examples of Parliamentary and Health Service Ombudsman Investigations

12 July 2005 [A Debt of Honour]

The PHSO published a report concerning complaints about the administration of an *ex-gratia* scheme for compensation for surviving members of British groups who had been interned by the Japanese during the Second World War. Following an inquiry by the Select Committee, the Government eventually accepted the PHSO's findings and implemented those of her recommendations that had initially been rejected.

In September 2011 the PHSO told the Government to 'hang its head in shame' after its report, *Defending the Indefensible*, highlighted repeated failings by the Ministry of Defence to treat fairly a family who were interned by the Japanese during the Second World War. Ann Abraham described this as: 'The worst example I have seen, in nearly nine years . . . of a government department getting things wrong and then repeatedly failing to put things right or learn from its mistakes.' She said that her report should be required reading for every aspiring senior civil servant.[45]

September 2013 [Time to Act: Severe Sepsis - *rapid diagnosis and treatment save lives*]

This was the first report on clinical practice published by the Health Service Ombud.[46] It concerned ten cases where patients did not receive the treatment they urgently needed. In every case the patient died but may not have done so had they received better care. In her Foreword to the report the ombud said that:

> We want complaining to make a difference and so we are publishing our first clinical report. [. . .] The Ombudsman can support the drive for a patient-centred NHS by shining a light on issues

[44] For further recent examples you can browse and search for decisions on the PHSO website: https://www.ombudsman.org.uk/

[45] See *Annual Report for 2011–2012*.

[46] Time to Act: Severe sepsis—rapid diagnosis and treatment save lives, September 2013: [https://www.ombudsman.org.uk/sites/default/files/2016-08/FINAL_Sepsis_Report_web.pdf].

raised with us by patients and their families. We would like to thank the families in this report who have allowed us to tell their stories. The crucial lessons to be learnt from this report all derive from concerned people raising complaints about the care received by their loved ones, and pursuing that complaint with us when they do not receive a satisfactory outcome. In doing so they are performing a valuable public service. We know that many do not complain because they feel it will make no difference. Our job is to make sure it does.

October 2020 – June 2021 [Windrush]

Mr R applied to remain in the UK via the Windrush Scheme in May 2018. Mr R had his own house and was a qualified tradesman. Since 2014, he has lost everything, being unable to provide documents which prove he has lived in the UK since before 1973. The PHSO found failings in the way the UK Visas and Immigration (UKVI) had handled the case, including unjustified delays giving incorrect advice.[47]

In another case the PHSO found that the UKVI had wrongly classified the complainant's late father, a victim of the Windrush scandal, as having no immigration status in the UK when he in fact had indefinite leave to remain. The PHSO determined that the way UKVI had dealt with the application and the subsequent complaint was maladministration. The PHSO further recommended systemic changes to ensure justice for Windrush victims.[48]

July 2021 Women's state pension

The PHSO found that the Department for Work and Pensions (DWP) had failed to adequately communicate the effects of changes to the age at which women become entitled to a state pension, which meant that women had been given insufficient notice of the changes.[49] This led to a special report to Parliament in March 2024.[50]

June 2024 Student Loans Company

The PHSO upheld Mrs R's complaint following the failure of the Student Loans Company to cancel her Advanced Learner Loan. The PHSO said that the complaint revealed a systematic failing that has impacted on a significant number of other students and found that the Student Loan Company had not done enough 'to put right the impact of its errors on Mrs R, or improve its services to prevent the risk of similar impact on other students'. They recommended the payment of a financial remedy to put right the distress caused to Mrs R.[51]

[47] *Final Investigation Report—UK Visas and Immigration*, PHSO, October 2020. See further below.

[48] https://www.ombudsman.org.uk/publications/investigation-uk-visas-and-immigrations-handling-windrush-mans-status, and see further below.

[49] https://www.ombudsman.org.uk/publications/womens-state-pension-age-our-findings-department-work-and-pensions-communication-0.

[50] Women's State Pension age: our findings on injustice and associated issues, Parliamentary and Health Service Ombudsman, Report Presented to Parliament 21 March 2024, HC 638.

[51] Decision dated 26 June 2024, see https://decisions.ombudsman.org.uk/search.

16.5.5 THE JURISDICTION OF THE PARLIAMENTARY OMBUD

The parliamentary ombud can deal with complaints against any of the bodies specifically listed in Sch. 2 to the PCA 1967.[52] This extends to all of the departments of central government and most other public bodies, but the list is not exhaustive. It is updated as new bodies are created and old ones abolished, or when decisions are made to extend the ombud's jurisdiction. Nonetheless, it has been observed that '*this method of proceeding is hardly transparent and it may help to explain why so many complaints to the PCA fall outside his [sic] jurisdiction*'.[53]

16.5.6 COMPLAINANTS MUST HAVE SUSTAINED 'INJUSTICE IN CONSEQUENCE OF MALADMINISTRATION'

The task of the parliamentary ombud is to investigate complaints that 'injustice' has been caused by 'maladministration' on the part of the public body concerned (s. 5(1)(a) PCA 1967). The terms 'injustice' and 'maladministration' were not defined in the Act, but were left to be interpreted and developed by the ombuds. 'Injustice' has been interpreted broadly. Sedley J (as he then was) said that it is not limited to types of injury that are '*redressible in a court of law*' and extends, for example, to '*the sense of outrage aroused by unfair or incompetent administration, even where the complainant has suffered no actual loss*'.[54]

'Maladministration' is a 'highly flexible concept'[55] that focuses on administrative errors that affect the *manner* in which decisions are reached and the *manner* of their implementation, rather than only the merits of decisions.[56] Richard Crossman MP—who, as the leader of the House of Commons at the time, steered the Parliamentary Commissioner Bill through the Commons—explained 'maladministration' by listing the type of wrongdoing that might be covered. His list (known as 'the Crossman catalogue') mentioned: bias; neglect; inattention; delay; incompetence; ineptitude; perversity; turpitude; and arbitrariness.[57]

In the following extract, Richard Kirkham (in an official report published by the PHSO) assesses the way in which the 'maladministration' test has been interpreted. He shows that while the test may have been intended to steer the ombud away from criticizing the merits of decisions, it has not prevented the ombudsman from exploring the merits of decisions or from criticizing unreasonable decisions. He also considers the overlap between 'maladministration' and legal grounds for challenging decisions.[58]

[52] By PCA 1967, s. 4(1) the ombudsman's jurisdiction extends to the '*government departments, corporations and unincorporated bodies*' listed in Sch. 2 to the Act.

[53] C. Harlow and R. Rawlings, *Law and Administration*, 3rd edn (2009, Cambridge: Cambridge University Press), p. 532. During 2011–12 there were 23,846 inquiries, of which 2,794 concerned matters that were beyond the PO's remit: Annual Report of the PHSO, *Moving Forward*, 2011–12 (HC 251, July 2012).

[54] *R v Parliamentary Commissioner for Administration, ex parte Balchin (No. 1)* [1998] 1 PLR 1, 11.

[55] M. Seneviratne, *Ombudsmen: Public Services and Administrative Justice* (2002, London: Butterworths), pp. 40–5; also M. Seneviratne, 'Updating the Local Government Ombudsman' [2008] Public Law 627, 630–2.

[56] PCCA 1967, s. 12(3) provides '*that nothing in this Act authorises or requires the Commissioner to question the merits of a decision taken without maladministration*'.

[57] See also Carnwath LJ, *R (Equitable Members Action Group) v HM Treasury and ors* [2009] EWHC 2495 (Admin), [36]; *R v Local Commissioner, ex parte Bradford Council* [1979] 1 QB 287, 311–12.

[58] See further extract set out below from *R (Rapp) v Parliamentary and Health Service Ombudsman* [2015] EWHC 1344 (Admin).

R. Kirkham, *The Parliamentary Ombudsman: Withstanding the Test of Time*, Fourth Report, Session 2006–07 (HC 421, March 2007), pp. 7–8 (footnotes omitted)

Although most ombudsman investigations focus on administrative procedures, this does not mean that ombudsmen cannot investigate the merits of decisions of public authorities. The 1967 Act left a degree of flexibility on the issue. Section 12(3) prevents the PO from questioning 'the merits of a decision taken *without* maladministration' (added emphasis). This implies that where a decision is taken *with* maladministration then the PO can legally consider the merits of the decision. More controversially, an administrative decision that is wholly unreasonable to most rationally minded people is a clear example of maladministration. Either way, the PO is entitled to explore the merits of a particular administrative decision during the course of an investigation. Were this not the case, it would often be impossible to come to a conclusion as to whether maladministration or an injustice had occurred.

The relationship between maladministration and tests of legality was also explained by Andrews J.

R (Rapp) v Parliamentary and Health Service Ombudsman
[2015] EWHC 1344 (Admin)

Andrews J

[38] i) The Ombudsman has no duty to determine questions of law. He/she is not acting as a surrogate of the court in determining whether there has been unlawful conduct, but rather, investigating a complaint of maladministration [. . .].

ii) Maladministration is a different concept from unlawfulness; consequently [. . .] the Ombudsman is not constrained by the legal principles which would apply if they were determining whether that conduct was unlawful;

iii) Unlawfulness is neither a precondition of, nor concomitant to a finding of maladministration; there may be maladministration without unlawfulness, and vice versa. [. . .]

The nature of maladministration has been developed by the PHSO and given a more positive twist with the enunciation of six basic 'principles of good administration', which should be respected by public bodies in all that they do. Identification of these principles reflects how the PHSO can build on the experience gained when dealing with individual complaints to improve the general quality of public administration. This proactive role is an important feature of ombuds, and one that tribunals and courts are less well equipped to perform. Richard Kirkham argues that this is a '*step to be encouraged*' and is evidence of the way in which the PHSO has matured: ' *[I]n terms of the development of administrative law more generally, it could represent the beginning of one of the most important innovations in recent years.*'

Parliamentary and Health Service Ombudsman, *Principles of Good Administration*, February 2009

1 Getting it right
2 Being customer focused
3 Being open and accountable
4 Acting fairly and proportionately
5 Putting things right
6 Seeking continuous improvement

[The core requirements of each of the principles are also set out. For example, getting it right involves:]

- Acting in accordance with the law and with regard to the rights of those concerned.
- Acting in accordance with the public body's policy and guidance (published or internal).
- Taking proper account of established good practice.
- Providing effective services, using appropriately trained and competent staff.
- Taking reasonable decisions, based on all relevant considerations.

[Acting fairly and proportionately involves:]

- Treating people impartially, with respect and courtesy.
- Treating people without unlawful discrimination or prejudice, and ensuring no conflict of interests.
- Dealing with people and issues objectively and consistently.
- Ensuring that decisions and actions are proportionate, appropriate and fair.[59]

16.5.7 RESTRICTIONS AND EXCLUSIONS

A major criticism of the PCA 1967 has been that it contains too many restrictions and limitations. One leading authority said that the effect of these was to exclude most of the matters about which people complain.[60] Certainly, there is a long list of matters that cannot be investigated,[61] including:

- action taken in matters affecting relations between the UK government and any other government, or any international organization of states or governments;
- action taken by the Secretary of State relating to extradition;
- action taken for the purposes of investigating crime or of protecting the security of the state, including action so taken with respect to passports;
- the commencement or conduct of civil or criminal proceedings before any court in the United Kingdom, or of proceedings before any international court or tribunal;
- action taken by administrative staff of any court or tribunal taken at the direction of any person acting in a judicial capacity;

[59] PHSO also has a 'Service Charter' setting out how it will deal with complaints: https://www.ombudsman.org.uk/making-complaint/how-we-deal-complaints/our-service-charter.

[60] H. Street, *Justice in the Welfare State*, 2nd edn (1975, London: Stevens), p. 116.

[61] PCA 1967, Sch. 3.

- any exercise of the prerogative of mercy;
- action taken in matters relating to contractual or other commercial transactions of government;
- action taken in respect of personnel matters relating to service personnel or civil servants; and
- the grant of honours, awards, or privileges within the gift of the Crown.

The exclusion of the government's commercial transactions and civil service personnel matters have been the most controversial exclusions.

Parliamentary and Health Service Ombudsman, *The Parliamentary Ombudsman: Withstanding the Test of Time*, Fourth Report, Session 2006–07 (HC 421, March 2007), p. 11 (footnotes omitted)

The need for these exclusions has been regularly questioned by, amongst others, Parliamentary select committees. They have been justified on the basis that the core role of the PO is 'to investigate the complaints against government by the governed and not against government in its role as employer or customer'. It is also arguable that in these areas alternatives, such as the courts, are usually more appropriate. Nevertheless, in an era when private sector provision has become an increasingly important feature of governance, the exclusion of contractual and commercial arrangements needs to be monitored to ensure that this governance technique is not used as a means by which to prevent accountability.

16.5.8 THE RELATIONSHIP BETWEEN THE PARLIAMENTARY OMBUD AND THE COURTS

Section 5(2) of the PCA 1967 provides that the parliamentary ombud shall not conduct an investigation when the person aggrieved has, or had, a remedy in any court of law or a tribunal.[62] This is one of the least satisfactory features of the Act. Since the 1960s, judicial review has expanded to such an extent that many complaints of maladministration could now give rise to judicial review proceedings and a strict interpretation of this restriction could add a significant obstacle to complainants who would be forced to resort to the courts. Fortunately, the Act allows the ombud discretion to deal with complaints if satisfied that, in the particular circumstances, it is not reasonable to expect the complainant to seek legal redress and this discretion seems to be regularly used. For example, in the *Debt of Honour* case,[63] the ombud undertook an investigation, despite a previous decision of the Court of Appeal in *Association of British Civilian Internees: Far Eastern Region (ABCIFER) v Secretary of State for Defence*.[64] The importance of the discretion to investigate even in cases in which legal proceedings are possible may also be illustrated by *Anufrijeva v Secretary of State for the Home Department*.[65] In this case, the Court of Appeal recognised that maladministration in meeting housing and welfare needs could lead to a breach of Art. 8 ECHR and to a claim for damages. This was a positive step in the development of human rights law, but if applied rigidly it could have had the negative effect of limiting

[62] Section 5(2). In *R v Local Commissioner, ex parte Bradford Council* [1979] 1 QB 287, 310, Lord Denning MR said that Parliament was '*at pains*' to ensure that the Ombudsman should not conduct an investigation that '*might trespass in any way on the jurisdiction of the courts of law or of any tribunals*'.

[63] *'A Debt of Honour': The Ex Gratia Scheme for British Groups Interned by the Japanese During the Second World War*, Fourth Report, Session 2005–06 (HC 324).

[64] [2003] QB 1397. [65] [2003] EWCA Civ 1406, [2004] QB 1124.

access to the ombud, which is not what the court intended. Here then the decision highlighted the need for a flexible approach to s. 5(2) that reinforces the value of ombud in the protection of human rights.

It is clear that ombuds investigations must be conducted in accordance with the principles of judicial review and that decisions of the ombuds may be challenged by judicial review.[66] For example, in *Cavanagh and ors v Health Service Commissioner*[67] the Court of Appeal held that the ombud has power to investigate only particular complaints and may not undertake investigations 'at large' into matters about which there has been no complaint. While the ombud was investigating a complaint brought by a parent of a disabled child about the way in which the child was being treated, the ombud commissioned her own experts to look into a variety of matters that had not been directly raised by the complaint. On the basis of her wider investigation the ombud rejected the complaint and criticized various people including doctors. The court stressed that while the ombud has wide investigative powers, she is unable to '*expand the ambit of a complaint beyond what it contains, nor to expand her investigation of it beyond what the complaint warrants*'.[68] The court also said that investigations must be conducted in accordance with the common law requirements of fairness and was particularly concerned that the doctors who had been criticized only knew about the full nature of the criticisms when they saw her draft report, to which they did not have a full chance to respond.[69]

Ombud investigations may also be used to help to mount litigation against the body about which a complaint has been made. *Congreve v Home Office*[70] is a well-known example. The case concerned the renewal of television licences. Anticipating an increase in the licence fee, Congreve (and 20,000 others) bought a new licence before the increase took effect and before his old licence had expired. The Home Office, hoping to prevent a loss of revenue, at first demanded an extra £6 from these 'overlappers'. It then changed its position and said that the new licences would be revoked early. Some of those affected complained to the ombud who, after an investigation, said that injustice had been caused by maladministration.[71] Armed with this finding, Congreve successfully challenged the Home Office in the courts.[72]

Here, we are primarily concerned with the way in which ombuds may be used and their powers, but we should also note in passing that there is another dimension that has to do with access to the courts. As we shall see in Chapter 17, claimants for judicial review have to bring their claim within three months and they also have to show that they have exhausted other available remedies such as appeals to tribunals and resort to ombuds; they may be refused permission to seek judicial review if they have not done so.[73] This can present potential claimants with a dilemma in cases where failure to complain to an ombuds may prevent a judicial review claim but a complaint to an ombuds may cause delay that could also prevent a judicial review claim.

While requirements such as these may be justified, they underscore the complexities that face ordinary people when deciding whether and how to complain against official action and they highlight the need for flexibility across different procedures for example to enable matters to be easily transferred from courts or tribunals to ombuds or vice versa.

[66] The first time that a decision of the PHSO was quashed, and twice sent back for reconsideration, was in the *Balchin* saga: see, e.g., *R (Balchin and ors) v Parliamentary Commissioner for Administration* [1996] EWHC Admin 152, [1999] EWHC Admin 484.

[67] [2005] EWCA Civ 1578.

[68] Per Lord Justice Sedley at [16].

[69] See *Miller v Health Service Commissioner for England* [2018] EWCA Civ 144.

[70] [1976] QB 629.

[71] Parliamentary Commissioner for the Administration, Seventh Report, Session 1974–75, para. 38.

[72] The decision of the Administrative Court in *Elias v Secretary of State for Defence* [2005] EWHC 1435 (Admin) was probably partly responsible for the Ministry of Defence's decision to accept the ombudsman's recommendations in the *Debt of Honour* case (see p. 437).

[73] *R (Cowl) v Plymouth City Council* [2002] 1 WLR 803.

Later in the chapter we shall return to recommendations aimed at improving the overall coherence of the administrative justice system, including the relationships between the current public sector ombuds.

16.5.8.1 Accessing the Parliamentary ombud

Normally people cannot complain directly to the Parliamentary ombudsman about UK government departments or other UK public organizations. The complaint must be routed through an MP.[74] As we have seen, the Whyatt Committee proposed that the 'MP filter', as it is known, should be in place for only an initial five years. Many were disappointed when the PCA 1967 made the MP filter a permanent feature and this has continued to be one of the most criticized aspects of the Act.

Originally, two arguments were used to justify the MP filter. One was that it protects the role of MPs in relation to their work helping their constituents—but it has been said that this argument '*is barely credible today*'.[75] Only a small proportion of constituency work is associated with the use of the ombud and there is evidence that MPs themselves do not consider the filter to be necessary. A survey of MPs conducted jointly by the PO and the Public Administration Select Committee, for example, found that 66 per cent of MPs questioned favoured removal of the filter.[76]

The second justification for the MP filter was the expectation that it would protect the ombud from being inundated by complaints. While it is difficult to know whether there would have been significantly more complaints without the filter, there has in any case been long-term concern that the PHSO has been underused—in part because the PHSO has had a low public profile.

In addition, it is now widely accepted that the MP filter acts as a deterrent to complainants and in recent years many, including the Public Administration Select Committee and the PHSO, have argued in favour of its removal.[77] In the following extract Professor Robert Thomas reinforces the case for reform in the light of the data on the numbers of complaints referred by MPs to the PHSO during the years 2016–2022.

The operation of the MP filter for complaining to the Parliamentary and Health Service Ombudsman, *Robert Thomas*, Essex Constitutional and Administrative Jusice Initiative Blog, 16 February 2023[78]

> [. . .] In the six years for which we have data, the percentage of MPs who referred no complaints to the PHSO exceeded 10 per cent of all MPs in the House of Commons. It is a consistent trend in the data that a significant proportion of MPs do not refer complaints to the PHSO. These are not the same 10 per cent of MPs from one year to the next. Nonetheless, this is a sizeable proportion of MPs elected to the House of Commons.

[74] PCA 1967, s. 5(1)(a). There is no MP filter for the Health Service ombud. Complaints relating to the Victims' Code of Practice may be made directly to the PHSO without reference to an MP: see Victims and Prisoner Act 2024, s 27 which came in force in January 2025.

[75] Dr R. Kirkham, *The Parliamentary Ombudsman: Withstanding the Test of Time*, Fourth Report, Session 2006–07 (HC 421, March 2007), p. 12.

[76] Parliamentary and Health Service Ombudsman, *Summary Results of the Survey of Members of Parliament on the Work of the Ombudsman*, cited in Kirkham, ibid, p. 24, fn. 68. See also, *Report on the Consultation on Direct Access to the Parliamentary Ombudsman*, November 2011.

[77] Public Administration Select Committee, *Annual Report of the Parliamentary Ombudsman*, Fourth Report, Session 1999–2000 (HC 106), para. 6; The Administrative Justice and Tribunals Council Response to the Law Commission's Consultation Paper, *Administrative Redress: Public Bodies and the Citizen*. See Dame Julie Mellor, 'Quango Unchained', 24 June 2014. See further below.

[78] https://essexcaji.org/2023/02/16/the-operation-of-the-mp-filter-for-complaining-to-the-parliamentary-and-health-service-ombudsman/

What are the implications of this data? It is . . . important to recall that the justification for having the MP filter is that it enables MPs to perform their constitutional function of scrutinising central government and holding it to account. However, if around 10 per cent of MPs do not refer any complaints to the ombudsman, then it is really questionable whether the MP filter is fit for purpose. [. . .]

The data does not tell us why a significant proportion of MPs do not any refer complaints or why some MPs refer one complaint whereas other MPs refer more complaints. It does not tell us about the regional variation or types of complaints or demographic factors involved. More work would be required to explore these issues.

However, the variations are striking and unsettling. This seems to be a major contradiction at the centre of how the MP filter actually works in practice. Many MPs do not refer any complaints at all and many only refer a small number of complaints. In light of this, it is difficult to see how MPs use the filter effectively to hold government to account.

[. . .] it stretches credibility to suppose that people in the constituencies of those 10 per cent of MPs who do not refer complaints do not experience the same type of faulty administration and poor public services in their interactions with central government and related public bodies which would justify a complaint to the ombudsman... Further, the data demonstrates that many other MPs do indeed refer a fair number of complaints to the PHSO. There is a substantial and undesirable degree of inconsistency in how the MP filter works in practice.

[. . .]

Matters become somewhat more concerning if we bear in mind that there are no formal criteria by which MPs decide whether or not to refer complaints to the ombudsman. This seems completely out of step with contemporary standards and expectations of administration and public decision-making.

[. . .]

In conclusion, there is good reason for the significant concern about the operation of the MP filter in practice. The MP filter should be removed – or replaced by a twin-track approach through complaints can be referred by MPs and people can also lodge their complaints directly with the ombudsman. In 2016, the Government accepted the need to remove the MP filter. However, that was in 2016 and nothing happened. The Government's Bill did not proceed. The above data concerns what has happened and not happened in the years after 2016. Clearly, the problems with the MP filter have continued. What is required is reform of the PHSO in order to improve and widen the ability of people to access it directly and without the requirement that complaints be referred by an MP.

16.5.8.2 Investigatory powers

The PHSO has very broad investigatory powers, which are contained in s. 8 of the PCA 1967. These powers are equivalent to those of the courts in relation to the attendance and examination of witnesses, and ministers and officials are required to furnish information and provide documents that are relevant to investigations. In some respects, the ombud's powers are significantly greater than those of the courts. For example, s. 8(3) in effect says that the Crown cannot prevent the ombud from having access to documents on grounds of public interest immunity.[79] These powers are important, but it is widely argued that, in order to be an effective investigator of complaints, the ombud must be able to rely on the cooperation of those being investigated.

[79] Note, however, that there are limits imposed by s. 8(4) (dealing with Cabinet proceedings) and (5) (dealing with privilege other than public interest immunity).

Parliamentary and Health Service Ombudsman, *The Parliamentary Ombudsman: Withstanding the Test of Time*, Fourth Report, Session 2006–07 (HC 421, March 2007), pp. 7–8 (footnotes omitted)

Investigatory Powers

One of the key reasons why the PO has become accepted as an important redress mechanism has been the Office's ability to produce independent, well reasoned and accurate reports. It is highly doubtful that this could have been achieved without the strong investigatory powers created in the 1967 Act. [. . .] This level of access to information gives to the work of the PO enhanced credibility and enables the Office to take on with confidence even politically sensitive investigations. On the other hand, the PO has periodically had cause to complain to Parliament that the government has been slow to comply with requests for information. Under the 1967 Act, the PO could tackle this problem through legal proceedings, but to achieve successful outcomes the PO is reliant on maintaining good relations with the government.

16.5.8.3 Reports, findings, and recommendations

Following an investigation, the PHSO reports its findings and may make recommendations. A report must be sent to the relevant MP, the principal officer of the department or authority concerned, and to any other person alleged in the complaint to have taken or authorized the action of which complaint has been made.[80] The ombud cannot force compliance with its findings, nor can it compel adoption of its recommendations—although government can only reject ombud findings if there are 'cogent reasons' for doing so.[81]

If there has been a finding of injustice caused by maladministration and it appears to the ombud that the matter has not been, or will not be, remedied, the Parliamentary ombudsman's ultimate formal power is to make a special report before Parliament.[82] This places the matter in the public and political arena, and it is here that the government must explain why it has not accepted the ombud's findings.

As we saw earlier, despite the absence of enforcement powers, non-compliance with the findings of the parliamentary ombud is extremely rare and this, therefore, does not seriously impede the ombud's effectiveness.[83] Richard Kirkham argues that, when discussing whether the absence of enforcement power is a weakness, account must be taken of three factors. The first is that the vast majority of findings are respected—although, in some cases, it seems that the ombud has had to make considerable efforts to persuade government departments. In the following extract, Kirkham explains the other two considerations.[84]

[80] PCA 1967, s. 10(1).

[81] *R (Bradley) v Department of Works and Pensions* [2007] EWHC 242 (Admin), see extract, R. Kirkham, B. Thompson, and T. Buck, 'When putting things right goes wrong: Enforcing the recommendations of the Ombudsman', in the next section.

[82] PCA 1967, s. 10(3). As at January 2025 the Parliamentary ombudsman had made nine special reports to Parliament.

[83] Parliamentary and Health Service Ombudsman, *The Parliamentary Ombudsman: Withstanding the Test of Time*, Fourth Report, Session 2006–07 (HC 421, March 2007), Foreword, p. 1.

[84] See also R. Kirkham, B. Thompson, and T. Buck, 'When putting things right goes wrong: Enforcing the recommendations of the Ombudsman' [2008] Public Law 510, 521–30.

R. Kirkham, *The Parliamentary Ombudsman: Withstanding the Test of Time*, Fourth Report, Session 2006–07 (HC 421, March 2007), p. 13 (footnotes omitted)

A second consideration is the principal reason why the PO lacks enforcement powers. . . . Ombudsmen are given almost total access to information and people within public bodies, and possess a very broad remit with which to investigate public sector activity. Given the potential depth of such investigations, the consequences of an ombudsman's report can have a huge impact on the design of future policy. Recognition of the potentially sensitive nature of the ombudsman's work is one of the reasons why ombudsman schemes tend to leave the power of implementation in the hands of the public authority concerned. Political accountability between the decision-maker and the electorate for the consequences of an ombudsman's report is thereby maintained. Arguably, another important benefit of this arrangement is that because public authorities know that they retain control of their decision-making, they are more likely to be encouraged to participate constructively in the investigation. It is this fear that powers of legal enforcement would radically alter the hitherto cooperative nature of the ombudsman's work that best explains why most ombudsmen are reluctant to go down this route.

Building on this understanding, a third point needs to be taken on board. As public authorities retain the final decision to provide redress, for the purposes of Article 6 of the European Convention of Human Rights, it is unlikely that the investigations and reports of the PO could be considered determinations of civil rights. Were the PO to possess powers of enforcement, this position could change. Such a development would almost certainly force the Office to reconsider its working practices. This could mean the increased use of formal hearings and more frequent legal representation. If this were the case, then the whole ethos and rationale of the ombudsman institution would be severely challenged and it is possible that many of the benefits would be lost.

Ann Abraham stressed that ombuds operate in ways that are different from courts and tribunals, on the one hand, and from systems based on mediation or negotiation, on the other. Unlike courts, '*ombudsman practice* [. . .] *has always prized its relative informality, its common sense approach to evidence, its inquisitorial process and its capacity to do justice in the individual case, unfettered by the burden of binding precedent*'.[85] She argues that an ombud will also have available a range of devices that are both capable of securing justice for the individual complainant and 'crucially' of facilitating systemic change.[86]

These themes are developed by Nick O'Brien when he compares the approaches of courts and ombuds in the context of disputes over social rights issues.

N. O'Brien, 'Ombudsmen and social rights adjudication'
[2009] 466 *Public Law* 468–9 (footnotes omitted)

If the court process can be characterised by its relative formality, expense, delay, complexity and rule-dominated qualities, the ombudsman process is by contrast relatively informal, free to both parties at the point of delivery, relatively quick, unfettered by complex rules of evidence or process, and normative in its application of principle rather than in the imposition of rules. There are, however, three specific aspects of ombudsman practice that are especially salient to the issue of their suitability for social rights adjudication. These aspects are their inquisitorial process, their functional flexibility, and their deliberative form of decision-making.

[85] A. Abraham, 'The ombudsman and "paths to justice": A just alternative or just an alternative?' [2008] Public Law 1, 4.
[86] Ibid, 5.

[. . .] In the context of human rights (and especially social rights) adjudication, [the] inquisitorial process in principle gives the ombudsman an advantage when it comes to . . . harnessing the sort of evidence needed to weigh the balance of priorities in what will frequently be disputes about indeterminate and open-ended positive obligations on a public authority. Advantage is gained too on the issue of citizen access, since in most cases it is the ombudsman who carries the burden of gathering evidence and . . . frames argument and shapes conclusions. In the course of conducting that balancing exercise, the ombudsman effectively counters any inequality of arms that might otherwise diminish the fairness of the process. Free to both parties at the point of delivery, the public sector ombudsman is rarely as passive as a conventional court in amassing and harnessing evidence or in articulating the key points at issue.

It is also a feature of the ombudsman's inquisitorial process that it leaves room for the exercise of administrative expertise in a way that generally eludes the courts. Frequently the ombudsman [and its staff . . .] will be drawn from the world of public administration, will have played a part in framing the principles that apply to the area of administration under investigation, and will have grappled in practice with similar circumstances in the course of their own organisational experience. The reticence that properly attends judicial examination of administrative practice is to that extent reduced when it is an ombudsman who is engaged in the work of adjudication.

Critical also is the functional flexibility of the ombudsman institution. The concept of maladministration is itself notoriously fluid [. . .] Ombudsmen have not habitually found it desirable to establish the precise boundaries of maladministration . . . Instead, they express a desire to achieve an equitable outcome, to do whatever is just and reasonable in the particular circumstances of the case. That conceptual fluidity at the heart of the ombudsman remit is matched by a significant measure of functional flexibility. [. . .] At the heart of ombudsman practice is the ambition of drawing upon the empirical experience of adjudication to identity patterns of maladministration and poor service, and to propose remedies that have systemic bite. [. . .]

It is this functional flexibility, comprising so-called 'fire-fighter', 'firewatcher', and 'fire-prevention' roles, that enables the ombudsman to address directly the key ambition of social rights: the future amelioration of large-scale violation. If the adversarial judicial process is essentially individualistic in its concerns, inherently preoccupied with the particular and the immediate, it falls to the ombudsman to take a more expansive adjudicative perspective, to look to the underlying causes of citizen grievance and, over time, and by way of a cumulative and iterative process, to make recommendations that will remedy not just the plight of the individual complainant but of others already, or yet to be, in the same or similar situation.

[O'Brien goes on to emphasize that a further important difference between ombudsmen and the courts lies in the nature of the outcome that is delivered.]

[The ombudsmen's outcome is] an authoritative but unenforceable contribution to a continuing debate about the merits of the case and of the policy and other factors that shaped it [. . .]. The ombudsman's word carries weight, but it is frequently far from the last word. It might be said that the ombudsman's 'style of control' is to that extent 'co-operative' rather than 'coercive', more a mandate of 'influence' than of 'sanction'.

Both the complainant and the authority can claim a sense of ownership in the outcome. This, O'Brien suggests, increases the likelihood that public bodies will find it easier to comply with recommendations of an ombud rather than decisions of courts.[87]

[87] See further M. Hertogh, 'Coercion, cooperation and control: Understanding the policy impact of administrative courts and the ombudsman in the Netherlands' (2001) 23 Law and Policy 47.

16.5.9 A SELF-ASSESSMENT: A CONSTITUTIONAL FORCE TO BE RECKONED WITH

Before her retirement, Ann Abraham reiterated the constitutional importance of the PHSO and the distinctive contribution it makes, as well as the need for some key reforms.

A. Abraham, The Parliamentary Ombudsman and Administrative Justice: Shaping the Next 50 Years, JUSTICE, Tom Sargant Memorial Annual Lecture, October 2011

Making the Vision a Reality

[. . . W]e have at times lost sight of the basic insights that shaped the Whyatt Report and indeed the Franks Report before it. In particular, we have failed to remember, that the Parliamentary Ombudsman has a constitutional role that cannot simply be confined to the function of dispute resolution, important though that is; that the Ombudsman system of justice is distinctive yet integral to a broader administrative justice system as a whole; and that the framework of values within which the work of the Ombudsman can be located is that of the protection and promotion of citizens' rights. From that recognition we can extrapolate a number of more concrete proposals.

First, I would echo the recommendations of the Law Commission that the MP filter [. . .] and other barriers to access such as the need to put complaints in writing, must go [. . .]

Secondly, I propose that the time has finally come to acknowledge the power of own initiative investigation, to accept that, in the absence of a specific individual complaint, the Ombudsman should not stand idly by. [. . .]

Thirdly, we must accept that if we are to achieve a genuine 'system' of administrative justice, with Ombudsmen as an integrated and coherent part, we must pay close attention to the currently fragmented structures of regulation, inspection and accountability throughout the UK and across the devolved administrations, protecting the Ombudsman 'brand' whenever necessary and making sense of the disparate and disjointed structures that so frustrate aggrieved citizens and at times defy all logic. [. . .]

And finally, if we are to maintain the distinctive qualities of the Ombudsman system of justice within that broader administrative justice landscape, we must resist any temptation to model the Ombudsman process on that of the courts. And resist also those changes that would reduce the Ombudsman function to just a form of dispute resolution, a mechanism of consumer redress devoid of systemic and structural bite.

What matters is that the Ombudsman is a just alternative—not just an alternative. In short, we must recognise that the origins of the Ombudsman system in the contested territory between individual and State are especially salient at a time when the boundaries of the State itself—and of the public services delivered in its name—are under daily scrutiny.

The need for a fundamental review of Ombudsmen in this country [. . .] is more urgent than ever. I suggest we get on with it. [. . .]

16.5.10 REFORM OF THE PUBLIC SECTOR OMBUDS

In the above extract Ann Abraham sets out a number of reforms that she believes are necessary if the PHSO is to fully fulfil its constitutional role. These include removal of the MP filter and other barriers to access; giving the PHSO the ability to investigate on its own initiative so that it does not have to wait for complaints to be made; and the need to create a more coherent ombuds system. The need to look again at reforming the PHSO and the other public sector ombuds was recognised by the government when it commissioned Robert Gordon[88] to review the work of these bodies. Robert Gordon's 2014 report, *Better to Serve the Public: Proposals to restructure, reform, renew and reinvigorate public services ombudsmen*, led to a Draft Public Sector Ombudsman Bill that was published in December 2016. This would create a single ombud replacing the Parliamentary, Health, and Local Government Ombuds[89] and abolish the MP filter for the parliamentary ombud. However, the Bill was not proceeded with and the government has subsequently indicated that while it will keep the matter under review it has no plans to resurrect the Bill and proceed with major reforms. The Public Administration and Constitutional Affairs Committee recently considered the Government's position and its response is set out in the following extract.

House of Commons Public Administration and Constitutional Affairs Committee, *Parliamentary and Health Service Ombudsman Scrutiny 2022–2023*, 27 February 2024, HC 198, para. 58

We renew our call for legislative reform of the PHSO, the principle of which enjoys widespread support among stakeholders and the ombudsmen that would be directly affected. The PHSO have outlined to us some concrete examples of the operational issues that are being caused, and exacerbated over time, by the lack of reform. Reforms are long overdue, and we do not agree with the Government that this is not an urgent issue; rather it has been neglected too long and further delay is no longer tenable.

QUESTIONS

1. Which of the following two statements in your view is the more accurate?
    - '*The parliamentary ombud is an "ombudsmouse": all squeak and no real power or influence.*'
    - '*The parliamentary ombud is a constitutional force to be reckoned with.*'
2. '*The parliamentary ombud is essentially part of the political process by which government is held to account. It is not necessary, and it may be undesirable, to give the ombud greater legal power to enforce its findings.*' Do you agree?
3. In what ways do courts and ombuds differ? Are there any lessons to be learnt by judges from the way in which ombuds work? For example, should judges issue press releases if their judgments are not respected by government?
4. Ann Abraham says that '*What matters is that the Ombudsman is a just alternative—not just an alternative [to courts].*' What do you think she means by this in concrete terms?
5. If you were asked to identify the main reforms that should be made to the PHSO what would these be and why?

[88] Robert Gordon CB had considerable experience as a senior civil servant in Scotland.

[89] While there has been some pre-legislative scrutiny of the draft Bill a final Bill has yet to appear. L. Maer and S. Priddy, *The Parliamentary Ombudsman: Role and Proposals for Reform* (House of Commons Briefing Paper, 21 June 2018).

16.6 WINDRUSH: A CASE STUDY IN THE FAILURE TO PROVIDE ADMINISTRATIVE JUSTICE

We end this chapter with a case study based on treatment of the so called 'Windrush generation' that displayed appalling failures to provide administrative justice. The name 'Windrush' derives from name of the 'HMT Empire Windrush', the ship which brought one of the first large groups of Caribbean people to the UK in 1948. The saga shows the wrongs that can occur when people are affected by a combination of government policy and poor administrative practices and procedures. It also illustrates how the various processes and institutions respond when redress is sought. While we touch on some of the deeply troubling issues the limitations of space mean that many matters that deserve further consideration are necessarily omitted or only briefly mentioned. Readers are therefore invited to extend their own research beyond what can be included here.[90]

16.6.1 THE BACKGROUND

Windrush Generation and the Home Office, House of Commons Public Accounts Committee, HC 1518, 6 March 2019

Between 1948 and 1973, nearly 600,000 Commonwealth citizens came to live and work in the UK with the right to remain indefinitely. But many were not given any documentation to confirm their immigration status, and the Home Office kept no records. In the last 10 years, successive governments have introduced the 'compliant environment' where the right to live, work and access services including benefits and bank accounts in the UK is only available to people who can demonstrate their eligibility to do so. Towards the end of 2017 the media began to report stories of members of the Windrush generation being denied access to public services, being detained in the UK or at the border, or being removed from, or refused re-entry to, the UK. This has been referred to as the Windrush scandal.

Because many of the Windrush generation arrived as children on their parents' passports, and the Home Office destroyed thousands of landing cards and other records, many lacked the documentation to prove their right to remain in the UK.[91] The Home Office also placed the burden of proof on individuals to prove their residency predated 1973 and demanded at least one official document from every year they had lived here. Attempting to find documents from decades ago created a huge, and in many cases, impossible burden on people who had done nothing wrong.

Falsely deemed as 'illegal immigrants'/'undocumented migrants' people began to lose their access to housing, healthcare, bank accounts, and driving licenses. Many were placed in immigration

[90] See British Library resources for more information on The Windrush Scandal (www.bl.uk). See also reports by Parliamentary committees, including: the House of Commons Home Affairs Committee, *The Windrush Generation*, HC 990, published on 3 July 2018 (the government response to this report was published on 3 July 2018), https://publications.parliament.uk/pa/cm201719/cmselect/cmhaff/1545/1545); the Joint Committee on Human Rights, *Windrush Generation Detention*, HC 1633, 18 October 2018, and the government's response, 21 September 2018, appended to the report: chrome-extension://efaidnbmnnnibpcajpcglclefindmkaj/https://publications.parliament.uk/pa/jt201719/jtselect/jtrights/1633/1633.pdf; Sheona York, 'The "hostile environment" – How Home Office immigration policies and practices create and perpetuate illegality' (2018) 32 JIANL 363; *Beyond the Scandal: Repairing the Harm from the Windrush Scandal*, (2023, Runnymede Trust).

[91] Windrush scandal explained by the Joint Council for the Welfare of Immigrants (JCWI): https://www.jcwi.org.uk.

detention, prevented from travelling abroad, and threatened with forcible removal, while others were deported to countries they hadn't seen since they were children.

This treatment provoked widespread criticism of government failings and calls for radical reform of the Home Office and the UK's immigration policy.[92] The injustices also highlighted the difficulties faced by ordinary people in dire situations when challenging government and seeking redress.

Here we consider two main aspects. We first consider how the institutional and systemic failings revealed by the saga were investigated and the steps taken to achieve reform. We then look briefly at how particular instances of injustice have been handled, including by the PHSO.

16.6.2 THE INSTITUTIONAL AND SYSTEMIC FAILINGS

In response to mounting criticism the then Home Secretary, Sajid Javid, apologized for the way people from the Windrush generation had been treated. He established a taskforce to provide urgent help with formalizing peoples' legal status and a Windrush Compensation Scheme.[93] In May 2018, the government announced the appointment of an independent 'Windrush Lessons Learned Review' to be led by Wendy Williams, Her Majesty's Chief Inspector of the Constabulary. When published on 19 March 2020 the review made it clear that the scandal was a direct consequence of a combination of government policy intended to make life in the UK impossible for those who could not produce the right papers coupled with serious administrative failings. The following extract provides a summary of the review's main findings.

Windrush Lessons Learned Review, an independent review
by Wendy Williams March 2020 HC 93

Executive Summary

Members of the Windrush generation and their children have been poorly served by this country. They had every right to be here and should never have been caught in the immigration net. The many stories of injustice and hardship are heart-breaking, with jobs lost, lives uprooted and untold damage done to so many individuals and families. However, despite the scandal taking the Home Office by surprise my report sets out that what happened [. . .] was foreseeable and avoidable. The causes of the Windrush scandal can be traced back through successive rounds of policy and legislation [. . . that aimed to . . .] restrict the eligibility of certain groups to live in the UK. The 1971 Immigration Act confirmed that the Windrush generation had, and have, the right of abode in the UK. But they were not given any documents to demonstrate this status. Nor were records kept. They had no reason to doubt their status, or that they belonged in the UK. [. . .] over time those in power forgot about them and their circumstances, which meant that when successive governments wanted to demonstrate that they were being tough on immigration by tightening immigration control and passing laws creating, and then expanding the hostile environment, this was done with a complete disregard for the Windrush generation.

[92] See Amelia Gentleman, *The Windrush Betrayal: Exposing the Hostile Environment* (2019, London: Guardian Faber 2019); Fiona Bawdon, 'Remember When "Windrush" Was Still Just the Name of a Ship?' in Devyani Prabhat (ed.), *Citizenship in Times of Turmoil? Theory, Practice and Policy* (2019, Guildford: Edward Elgar).

[93] See further: *Spotlight on the Windrush Compensation Scheme: your stories, your rights, PHSO; Windrush compensation scheme overhauled* (www.gov.uk); for an assessment of the scheme, see 'Falling through the gaps' Windrush Scandal Webinar—Administrative Justice Council (ajc-justice.co.uk); for data on use of the scheme, see Windrush Compensation Scheme data: April 2022 (www.gov.uk).

> [. . .] [This] report identifies the organisational factors in the Home Office which created the operating environment in which these mistakes could be made, including a culture of disbelief and carelessness when dealing with applications, made worse by the status of the Windrush generation, who were failed when they needed help most. The lessons are for both ministers and officials in the Home Office to learn. Ministers set the policy and the direction of travel and did not sufficiently question unintended consequences. [. . .] While I am unable to make a definitive finding of institutional racism within the department, I have serious concerns that these failings demonstrate an institutional ignorance and thoughtlessness towards the issue of race and the history of the Windrush generation within the department, which are consistent with some elements of the definition of institutional racism. This report makes 30 recommendations for change and improvement [. . .]

The recommendations urged the government to: go further to right the wrongs; to better understand and do more to tell the stories of empire, Windrush, and their legacy; to assess and limit the impact of the hostile environment on the Windrush generation; to engage meaningfully with stakeholders and communities to develop, implement, and evaluate policy; and, to better understand and provide internal training on the public sector equality duty and its intersection with immigration and nationality law.

The then Conservative government agreed that the Windrush scandal 'should never have happened' and initially accepted all of the review's recommendations.[94] However, to Williams's disappointment it later changed its mind and decided not to adopt several key recommendations. This decision she said:

> *. . . goes to the heart of how the department operates and is indicative of an organisation which was not yet confident enough to secure an increase in the type of independent insight and scrutiny that my recommendations envisaged.*[95]

The government's decision was challenged in judicial review. In the following extract the PHSO explains the background to the case.

Spotlight on the Windrush compensation scheme, PHSO, p. 8

> [. . .] In July 2020, Home Secretary Priti Patel said the actions that led to the Windrush generation's suffering were an 'ugly stain on the face of our country and on the Home Office'. The Home Office accepted all 30 recommendations [made by Wendy Williams]. It published a Comprehensive Improvement Plan in September 2020, which set out how it would implement them. In January 2023, Home Secretary Suella Braverman announced the Government was dropping three key recommendations from the review:
>
> - setting up a commissioner responsible for 'speaking up for migrants and those affected by the system directly or indirectly' [recommendation 9]

[94] *The Response to the Windrush Lessons Learned Review: A Comprehensive Improvement Plan*, September 2020, CP 293.
[95] *Windrush Lessons Learned Review: Progress Update*, Wendy Williams, March 2022, p. 10.

- giving new powers to the independent chief inspector of borders and immigration [recommendation 10]
- holding 'reconciliation events' with people affected to 'listen and reflect on their stories' [recommendation 3]

This decision has recently been challenged. In April 2024, the High Court heard a legal claim made by a man affected by the Windrush generation scandal. The claim said the decision to drop these recommendations was institutionally racist (discriminatory) and another example of broken promises made to the Windrush generation. The claim is being supported by the Black Equity Organisation and Unison.

While the challenge concerning recommendation 3 failed the court held that the decision not to adopt recommendations 9 and 10 after initially promising to do so was unlawful partly because Windrush community and Wendy Williams had a legitimate expectation that they would be consulted before the government reversed its decision to implement these recommendations and no consultation had occurred.[96] The court also held that the decision:

. . . amounted to indirect discrimination, given the particular impact on Windrush victims as compared to the rest of the population at large and that the Defendant had not shown that these policy decisions were a proportionate means of achieving a legitimate aim . . .[97]

The Labour Party's manifesto for the July 2024 general election included a promise to establish a Windrush Commissioner and in June 2025 Reverend Clive Foster MBE was appointed as the first Windrush Commissioner. The following is an extract from the government's announcement.

Reverend Clive Foster appointed as first Windrush Commissioner, 18 June 2025 https://www.gov.uk/government/news/reverend-clive-foster-appointed-as-first-windrush-commissioner

Home Secretary Yvette Cooper MP said:

The story of the Windrush generations is woven into the fabric of our nation and this government is absolutely determined to right the wrongs they suffered at the hands of the Home Office.

This is why I am delighted to welcome Reverend Clive Foster as our new Windrush Commissioner. His deep understanding through his own connections and dedicated community work makes him the perfect champion for those affected by this historic injustice.

I look forward to working closely with Reverend Foster as we continue our vital work to rebuild trust and deliver the justice that the Windrush generations so rightfully deserve.

You can read more about the work of the Windrush Commissioner at the Commissioner's website https://www.windrushcommissioner.uk/. In the following extract Reverend Clive Foster explains his key aims.

[96] *R (Donald) v Secretary of State for the Home Department* [2024] EWHC 1492. On legitimate expectations see Chapter 19.

[97] ibid para 291.

Reverend Clive Foster MBE, Windrush Commissioner

I'm committed to delivering justice for people affected by the Home Office Windrush Scandal through cultural change, accountability, and action. My aim is to deliver change that people can see and feel in their everyday lives. I act independently, without fear or favour, guided by the voices and needs of impacted people. I firmly believe that the legacy of the Windrush generations must be defined by their extraordinary contribution to the UK, not by a scandal.

One of the Commissioner's first concerns was to seek improvements in the compensation scheme and on 3 September 2025 the Commissioner wrote to Seema Malhotra MP, the then Minister for Migration and Citizenship, calling for urgent reform of the Windrush Compensation Scheme, improved support for those affected, and action to ensure everyone eligible receives their rightful status.[98] At the time of writing we do not know how government will respond to this call for reform and this is something worth keeping an eye on.

Reflecting on what we have read about the Windrush scandal in the context of this chapter we can see that achieving administrative justice demands serious commitment to recognise and understand errors and to correct wrongs. Doing so demands serious commitments to improving policy and cultures within government and an ability and willingness to alter how large government departments like the Home Office actually function on a daily basis. This includes ensuring that staff are properly trained and managed and that procedures are fair and properly followed. Achieving administrative justice requires appropriate cultures policies and systems that ensure just and high-quality administration. As Wendy Williams argued this also requires effective independent oversight. Providing redress and righting individual wrongs through ombuds, tribunals and courts is also an important element in achieving administrative justice.

16.6.3 INDIVIDUAL INJUSTICE AND THE OMBUDS

The Windrush scandal has given rise to many complaints to the PHSO.[99] We have already seen some examples.[100] The complaint made by Mr V's daughter to the PHSO is another example that highlights the personal cost of administrative failure. The then PHSO, Mr Rob Behrens CBE summarised the case and its implications in a letter to Willliam Wragg MP, Chair of the Public Administration and Constitutional Affairs Committee.[101]

[98] 20250903-Letter-from-the-Windrush-Commissioner-to-Minister-Malhotra(www.windrushcommissioner.uk).

[99] Including about the operation of the compensation scheme: see Spotlight on the Windrush Compensation Scheme: your stories, your rights, PHSO https://www.ombudsman.org.uk/publications/spotlight-windrush-compensation-scheme-your-stories-your-rights/guidance-and-facts-not-properly-considered.

[100] See Section 16.5.4.

[101] For the PHSO's report into Mr V's case, see: *An Investigation into UK Visas and Immigration's Handling of Windrush Man's Status* (ombudsman.org.uk). For the PHSO's report a complaint brought by Mr R, see *Windrush Applicant Waited Over a Year To Be Rejected*, Parliamentary and Health Service Ombudsman (PHSO).

Letter from Rob Behrens CBE, the PHSO, to William Wragg MP, Chair of the Public Administration and Constitutional Affairs Committee, 8 June 2021

Dear William

I am writing to share with you a case I have recently concluded regarding an application made by a Jamaican national (Mr V) to UK Visas and Immigration (UKVI) for a permit confirming the applicant's right to British citizenship. This led to a series of hostile actions by Immigration Enforcement over several years – including threats of imprisonment and deportation and the seizure of Mr V's passport and driving licence [. . .].

This happened despite Mr V having Indefinite Leave to Enter [. . .] Mr V was finally able to prove his right to live in the UK, after several attempts, but died in 2019—less than a year after being granted citizenship. As a result of the treatment he experienced, he lived his final years with severe depression and anxiety. Mr V's daughter brought the complaint to PHSO after UKVI failed to put things right. For his family, seeing their father and grandfather decline was very distressing.

We upheld the complaint, finding that maladministration led to: Flawed decision-making [. . .]; Inaccurate record-keeping [. . .]; UKVI requesting excessive evidence [. . .]; Unsatisfactory complaint handling by UKVI and Immigration Enforcement; Mr V being wrongly told by Immigration Enforcement that he had no status in the UK; [. . .] missed opportunities to put things right.

This case highlights the distressing experiences of one individual within the UK immigration system. It also highlights some of the issues experienced by the Windrush generation [. . .]

We are publishing this case [. . .] to encourage others affected by Windrush to bring their complaints to us if they have gone unaddressed. PHSO is committed to providing justice for complainants [. . .] Similarly, our role in improving the system for others is something I take very seriously.

Rob Behrens went on to explain that an apology had been provided together with a financial payment to Mr V's daughter in recognition of the emotional distress caused. He also said that the UKVI and Immigration Enforcement should share the lessons learnt from the complaint (and any actions) with the Public Administration and Constitutional Affairs Committee and the Home Affairs Committee to support Parliament in its scrutiny of the service provided by these bodies. The learning should, he said, also be shared with Wendy Williams. The PHSO's intervention here shows the value of having an independent mechanism to investigate and correct administrative harm—even when other avenues have failed.

16.6.4 JUDICIAL REVIEW

Judicial review also provides a potential route for redress.[102] An example is *R (Vanriel and Tumi) v Secretary of State for the Home Department*.[103] Here it was held that the inflexible nature of the British Nationality Act 1981, in not permitting the grant of citizenship to those who had not been physically present in the UK for five years prior to the application even when they had indefinite leave to remain

[102] See further Chapters 17–20.

[103] [2021] EWHC 3415 (Admin). Judicial review was less helpful in *Hubert Howard (deceased) v Secretary of State for the Home Department* [2022] EWCA 1068 and for a partially successful challenge concerning the compensation scheme see *R (Raymond Alfred Lee) v Secretary of State for the Home Department* [2025] EWHC 519 (Admin).

under the Windrush scheme was contrary to the claimants' rights under Art. 14 of the ECHR in conjunction with Art. 8 ECHR.[104]

16.6.5 SOME REFLECTIONS

We have only been able to touch on aspects of the Windrush scandal, but even this brief survey shows the scale of injustice caused by a combination of policy initiatives and attitudinal and administrative errors. A key lesson, in the context of this chapter, is that the delivery of administrative justice requires serious and determined efforts in relation to policy, administrative decision-making and procedures, as well as the provision of effective redress. The systemic problems identified by the Windrush scandal underline the need for various forms of accountability and scrutiny as well as the ability of different institutions to work together and to share knowledge and learning.

Before closing the case-study it is worth noting that Timothy Jacob-Owens and Professor Jo Shaw conclude their analysis of the quality of redress in relation to Windrush with the following comment.

T. Jacob-Owens and J. Shaw, 'Justice for Windrush? Redress, reform, repeat' (2022) 36(2) *Journal of Immigration Asylum and Nationality Law* 131, 143 (footnotes omitted)

> Finally, ongoing developments in immigration and citizenship law, including the post-Brexit treatment of EU citizens resident in the UK, indicate that the Windrush scandal is by no means an isolated historical incident, but rather part of a broader and ongoing regime of precarity for those whose rights and status go unrecognized. By creating and maintaining the (internal) border between 'citizens' and '(im) migrants', the law plays a central role in sustaining that regime [. . .] As the Windrush scandal showed, this is no guarantee of justice for those left on the wrong side of that border.

QUESTIONS

1. What do you consider to be the three main lessons to be learned from the Windrush scandal from the perspective of administrative justice?
2. 'It is impossible to have just administration if the policies being administered are unjust'. Discuss this comment.
3. 'Responses to the Windrush scandal show the importance of having institutions such as the PHSO that are willing to draw general lessons from individual complaints and to work with other institutions including Parliament to address broader systemic failings.' Looking back at this case study, what examples could be used to justify this comment?
4. 'The Windrush scandal shows that providing effective redress is necessary but not sufficient to achieve administrative justice: administrative justice cannot be secured by the "administrative justice system" alone.' Discuss this comment.
5. Could the injustices experienced by the Windrush generation have been prevented had the administrative justice system worked properly, or was the problem deeper?

[104] The Nationality and Borders Act 2022 permits some discretion in such cases.

16.7 CONCLUDING COMMENTS

We opened the Chapter by imagining that our disability benefits were wrongly denied. The Chapter shows that we don't necessarily need to go to court. We might:

- ask the government department to look again at the decision (mandatory reconsideration),
- appeal to a tribunal that specialises in benefit decisions,
- or make a complaint to an ombud, who can investigate whether the system has caused us injustice.
- But you've also seen that access to justice is not just about having options—it's about whether people can actually use those options. Do they know their rights? Do they trust the process? Do they have help, or feel heard?

In a fair system, people shouldn't have to fight to be treated fairly. That's the goal of administrative justice—not just to fix mistakes, but to make sure the system itself is just, inclusive, and accountable. A key message of the chapter and one that is graphically illustrated by the Windrush scandal is that achieving administrative justice requires attention not only to the quality of procedures for redress, important as these are, but also to the wider quality of government policy and government behaviour.

In the chapters that follow we look more closely at judicial review.

FURTHER READING

Adler, M. (ed.), *Administrative Justice in Context* (2010, Oxford and Portland, OR: Hart Publishing).

Buck, T., Kirkham R., and Thompson, B., *The Ombudsman Enterprise and Administrative Justice* (2011, Farnham: Ashgate).

Cane, P., *Administrative Tribunals and Adjudication* (2009, Oxford: Hart Publishing).

Creutzfeldt, N., *Ombudsmen and ADR: A Comparative Study of Informal Justice in Europe* (2018, London: Palgrave).

Doyle, M. and O'Brien, N., *Reimagining Administrative Justice: Human Rights in Small Places* (2020, London: Palgrave)

Harlow, C. and Rawlings, R., *Law and Administration*, 4th edn (2022, Cambridge: Cambridge University Press), esp. chs 13–14.

Hertogh, M., Kirkham, R., Thomas, R., and Tomlinson, J. (eds), *The Oxford Handbook of Administrative Justice* (2022, Oxford: OUP).

Palmer, E., Cornford, T., Marique, Y., and Guinchards A., *Access to Justice: Beyond* the *Policies and Politics of Austerity* (2016, Oxford and Portland, OR: Hart Publishing).

17

JUDICIAL REVIEW 1: THE IMPORTANCE AND ROLE OF JUDICIAL REVIEW

CENTRAL ISSUES

1. The High Court's inherent jurisdiction to judicially review decisions of public bodies is a principal means by which the rule of law is enforced. The jurisdiction is inherent in the sense that it is rooted in the common law and is not granted by Parliament and not dependent on statute.
2. Judicial review enables people to challenge the actions of public authorities on the grounds that authorities have misunderstood, exceeded, or abused their legal powers, or breached rights protected by the common law. It also provides a route for protecting rights under the Human Rights Act 1998 (HRA).
3. As well as providing redress, judicial review imposes legal accountability on public authorities that requires them to justify the legality of their actions to the courts.
4. Judicial review has grown in importance over the past few decades and in high-profile cases judges have shown increasing willingness to scrutinize the legality of government action and force government to rethink important decisions, including in areas as sensitive as the prevention of terrorism.
5. This has heightened debate about the constitutional foundations for judicial review in the UK system. From where do judges derive their authority to review the legality of government's decisions? How in a democracy can unelected judges justify questioning the actions of elected ministers and local authorities?
6. As well as the above issues, this chapter considers the statistics on the use of judicial review, the procedure by which judicial review is claimed, and the remedies that courts may grant when claims are successful.
7. The Chapter ends by looking at ways in which judicial review matters to government.

17.1 INTRODUCTION

17.1.1 OVERVIEW

Judicial review is a principal means by which the rule of law is enforced. It enables people to challenge the actions of public authorities when they have misunderstood, exceeded, or abused their legal powers, or breached rights protected by the common law. It also provides a route for protecting rights under the Human Rights Act 1998 (HRA). In providing redress, judicial review imposes legal accountability on public authorities that requires them to justify the legality of their actions to the courts. Importantly, the High Court's power to judicially review decisions of public bodies is 'inherent' which means that it is based on the common law and is not granted to the courts by Parliament. As judges have become more willing to question the legality of government decisions, including in high profile cases such as *Miller 1*[1] and *Miller 2*[2] there has been heightened debate about the constitutional justifications and foundations for judicial review in the United Kingdom system with government and others accusing the unelected judiciary of trespassing into the domain of the politically accountable branches of constitution—of 'judicial overreach'. This has resulted in a programme of reforms designed to limit the use and scope of judicial review. We return to these issues, but before doing so we need to note some more basic matters about the United Kingdom's system of judicial review.

In many other constitutional systems, 'judicial review' refers to the power of a constitutional or a supreme court to strike down legislation as being contrary to the (written) constitution. As discussed earlier, the courts in the United Kingdom have more limited powers when it comes to reviewing primary legislation than many of their counterparts in other countries.[3] In the United Kingdom, judicial review is therefore principally concerned with the legality of action taken by government ministers, local authorities, and other public bodies; as well as decisions of courts and tribunals with limited jurisdiction. It may also be used to challenge delegated legislation and legislation enacted by the devolved legislatures.[4]

The three separate territorial jurisdictions in the United Kingdom each have their own judicial review court processes. In Scotland, proceedings for judicial review are dealt with by the Court of Session. In Northern Ireland, applications for judicial review are heard in the High Court of Northern Ireland in Belfast. In England and Wales, judicial review claims are dealt with by the Administrative Court (part of the King's Bench Division of the High Court) in London or in regional centres in Birmingham, Cardiff, Leeds, and Manchester. A significant proportion of the caseload of the UK Supreme Court consists of appeals in judicial review cases from the three territorial jurisdictions.

While we concentrate on judicial review in the Administrative Court (and appeals from that court) it is worth noting that other courts also have a judicial review jurisdiction, although in these instances that jurisdiction is not inherent but is granted by legislation. For example, The Upper Tribunal has a judicial review jurisdiction in relation to decisions taken by the First-tier Tribunal and in exercising this jurisdiction, the Upper Tribunal must apply the same principles as the High Court and, broadly speaking, it may grant the same forms of relief as the High Court.[5] The county court also has a judicial review type jurisdiction in relation to homelessness appeals from decisions of local housing authorities, as does the Special Immigration Appeal Commission, in relation to challenges to decisions taken by the Home Secretary on grounds of national security.

[1] *R (on the application of Miller and another) v Secretary of State for Exiting the European Union* [2017] UKSC 5.

[2] *R (on the application of Miller) v The Prime Minister; Cherry and others v Advocate General for Scotland* [2019] UKSC 41.

[3] See Chapter 3 on the legislative supremacy of the UK Parliament.

[4] See Chapter 13. See *AXA General Insurance Ltd and others (Appellants) v The Lord Advocate and others (Respondents) (Scotland)* [2011] UKSC 46. Also, *R (on the application of The Greyhound Board of Great Britain) v The Welsh Ministers,* The Senedd, and Llywdd, [2026] EWHC 670.

[5] See Tribunals Courts and Also, *R (on the application of The Greyhound Board of Great Britain) v The Welsh Ministers,* The Senedd, and Llywdd, [2026] EWHC 670 Enforcement Act 2007, ss 15–21.

We look in more detail at the grounds of judicial review in the following two chapters. For the time being, it is sufficient to know that the underlying arguments that a judicial review claimant may make fall into the following broad types:

(a) that public bodies have exceeded or abused powers conferred upon them by statute, that duties conferred on a public body have not been carried out, or a statutory procedure for making a decision has not been followed;

(b) that the requirements of the common law have not been fulfilled: over the years, the courts have developed various principles, especially in relation to the way in which discretionary powers must be exercised and the need to adopt fair decision-making procedures;

(c) that there has been a breach of s. 6 of the HRA, which requires public authorities to comply with human rights.[6]

17.1.2 HISTORICAL DEVELOPMENT

Many of the underlying legal principles of judicial review are centuries old. For example, although not a judicial review case in the modern sense, *Entick v Carrington* (1765)[7] enunciated the core principle that continues to underpin judicial review—namely, that government bodies and others exercising public functions must have legal authority for their actions and must act in accordance with the law.[8] This principle continues to be developed and expanded upon by the judges. During the past few decades, judicial review has been one of the most dynamic and fascinating areas of law, as judges have created new grounds of review and applied principles of review to novel situations.

Commentators have been interested in why the courts have been more active since the 1960s and different explanations are given. Some have contrasted the more activist approach of recent years with the more cautious approach that dominated during the early part of the twentieth century.[9] Professors Wade and Forsyth, for instance, tell us that, during that period, the courts became reluctant to develop the principles of judicial review and '*showed signs of losing confidence in their constitutional function and they hesitated to develop new rules in step*'[10] with the growth in the scale of government. For these writers, then, whether judges take a more or less activist approach depends on judicial confidence. But what factors are likely to influence the confidence of judges to assert legal principles against government authorities?

Two factors were particularly important during the first half of the twentieth century. First, the two World Wars contributed greatly to a legal–political climate that encouraged judicial deference to the executive and discouraged judicial activism.

Perhaps the best-known example of the deferential approach is the infamous 1942 decision of the House of Lords in *Liversidge v Anderson*.[11] The date of this case is important, because it was decided at a stage of the Second World War during which the British war effort was at its most stretched and there was a widely held view that the institutions of the state needed to pull together. The Defence (General) Regulations 1939—a piece of delegated legislation[12]—enabled the executive to detain persons without trial '*if the Secretary of State has reasonable cause to believe*' that the person had hostile associations.

[6] See further Chapter 21. [7] (1765) 19 St Tr 1030. [8] See Chapter 4.

[9] There is evidence that the UK Supreme Court has recently become less interventionist: see Lewis Graham, *Judicial Individuality on the UK Supreme Court*, (Oxford: Hart Publishing, 2025) especially ch. 10. See also, Paul Craig, 'Judicial Review, Methodology and Reform', (2022) Public Law 19–37.

[10] H.W.R. Forsyth and C. Forsyth, *Administrative Law*, 11th edn (2014, Oxford: OUP), p. 11.

[11] [1942] AC 206. See further A.W.B. Simpson, *In the Highest Degree Odious: Detention without Trial in Wartime Britain* (1994, Oxford: OUP).

[12] On delegated legislation, see Chapter 13.

In using this wording, Parliament had deliberately rejected an alternative form of wording that would have given the Secretary wider (more subjective) power to detain 'if satisfied' that the person had hostile associations. Nonetheless, the majority of the House of Lords held that even though the matter concerned individual liberty and the legislation specifically said that the Secretary of State could only act if he had 'reasonable cause', the courts could not review the legality of a detention under this power and would not require the Secretary of State to show objective justifications for the detention. Lord Atkin disagreed and delivered a withering attack on the decision taken by the majority of his colleagues.

Liversidge v Anderson
[1942] AC 206

Lord Atkin (Dissenting)

I view with apprehension the attitude of judges who on a mere question of construction when face to face with claims involving the liberty of the subject show themselves more executive minded than the executive [...] In this country, amid the clash of arms, the laws are not silent. They may be changed, but they speak the same language in war as in peace. It has always been one of the pillars of freedom, one of the principles of liberty for which [...] we are now fighting, that the judges are no respecters of persons and stand between the subject and any attempted encroachments on his liberty by the executive, alert to see that any coercive action is justified in law. In this case I have listened to arguments which might have been addressed acceptably to the Court of King's Bench in the time of Charles I.

QUESTIONS

1. What do you think Lord Atkin means when he says that laws may be changed, '*but they speak the same language in war as in peace*'?
2. Why does he say that, in this case, he has '*listened to arguments which might have been addressed [...] to the Court of King's Bench in the time of Charles I*'?

Deference to the executive during times of war was one element—but other factors also gave rise to a lack of confidence among the judges and limited their willingness to review decisions of public bodies. The early years of the twentieth century saw an extension of the franchise, and a consequential growth in the democratic legitimacy of Parliament and of government itself. Government became increasingly concerned to step in and to develop systems that were designed to improve people's quality of life in areas such as education, health, land use planning, and the provision of general welfare. This inevitably led to a reassessment of older attitudes to concepts such as the rule of law.

In Chapter 2, we saw that those who adopt a 'legal constitutionalist' approach view the rule of law as a shield that protects people from government and as a brake on government powers that will prevent the executive from interfering with rights. Harlow and Rawlings have labelled this the 'red light' approach, because it emphasizes the law's role in controlling and limiting government.[13] As we noted,

[13] C. Harlow and R. Rawlings, *Law and Administration*, 4th edn (2022, Cambridge: Cambridge University Press), ch. 1.

some who adopt a legal constitutionalist approach would like the rule of law to have an even greater role as *the* controlling principle of the UK constitution, with the judges having power to review not only *government*, but also *Parliament*. If this change were ever to come about, it would mark a major departure from the principle of parliamentary supremacy.

During the twentieth century, an alternative approach evolved, which was much closer to that adopted by those favouring a political constitutionalist approach, stressing that legal principles have a role in enabling government to use its powers for the common good. Harlow and Rawlings call this the 'green light' approach. The 'red light' and 'green light' metaphors are still useful in summarizing two of the main ways of understanding the relationship between law and government, and the task of the judges in judicial review, and they continue to inform debate, with some writers and judges tending to lean towards one or other of the approaches.

The main point being made for now, however, is that, during the first half of the twentieth century, some of the leading judges were acutely aware of the growing democratic legitimacy of government and its social welfare programme. They were also aware of their own weak democratic credentials and of the limitations of the adjudication process in determining complex public interest issues. During this period, in a number of important cases, the judges explained the principles that the courts could apply when reviewing decisions of public bodies and the need to balance these principles with the needs of government. One of the best-known examples is *Associated Provincial Picture Houses Ltd v Wednesbury Corporation*[14] in which Lord Greene MR emphasized the limited ability of the judges to review the exercise of discretionary powers by local authorities.

The mood of the judiciary changed during the 1960s under the judicial leadership of judges such as Lord Denning and Lord Reid. Of particular importance was a series of extremely influential decisions of the House of Lords that rejuvenated the principles of judicial review and the constitutional standing of the courts. Three of the key decisions during the 1960s are summarized in Box 17.1.[15]

BOX 17.1 THREE KEY JUDICIAL REVIEW DECISIONS OF THE 1960S[16]

***Ridge v Baldwin* [1964] AC 40**

This case placed the principles of natural justice on a modern footing, so that they could be applied to a wide range of government decisions, and not only to decisions of courts and administrative actions that were 'judicial' in character. (The practical result was that Chief Constable Ridge was held to have a right to notice of allegations made against him and a right to respond before the police authority removed him from office.)

[14] [1948] 1 KB 223. See further Chapter 18.

[15] See further, TT Arvind, R. Kirkham, Daithi Mac Sitigh, and L. Stirton (eds), *Executive Decision-Making and the Courts: Revisiting the Origins of Modern Judicial Review* (2021, Oxford: Hart Publishing). Also J. Satvinder and M. Sunkin (eds) *Landmark Cases in Public Law* (2017, Oxford: Hart Publishing), chs 2, 3, and 4.

[16] See also *Burmah Oil Co (Burma Trading) Ltd v Lord Advocate* [1965] AC 75 and *Conway v Rimmer* [1968] AC 910.

***Padfield v Minister of Agriculture* [1968] AC 997**

This case showed that legislation never gives unfettered discretion to ministers. When ministers are given discretion by an Act of Parliament, they must use that discretion to further the 'policy and objects' of the Act. The courts and not ministers are the final arbiters of how an Act of Parliament is to be interpreted. (The result was that it was unlawful for the minister, solely for reasons of wanting to avoid political embarrassment, to refuse to set up an inquiry into the operation of a milk marketing scheme.)

***Anisminic v Foreign Compensation Commission* [1969] 2 AC 147**

This case held that the jurisdiction of the courts to review decisions of public bodies cannot be ousted by Parliament without the clearest words. Legislation saying that a 'determination' of a public body could not be '*called into question in any court of law*' was not clear. It was not clear that Parliament intended to prevent review of 'purported determinations' as well as valid determinations. Given this uncertainty the House of Lords interpreted the wording in a way that was compatible with access to justice so that courts retained ability to review a 'determination' of the Foreign Compensation Commission to ensure that it was lawful.[17]

These decisions, to which we return, mark the start of the modern phase of public law, which, during the past 50 or so years, has seen the courts develop the availability and scope of judicial review. While recognizing their limits the courts have become far more willing to examine the legality of government action.

The constitutional importance of judicial review has been given additional impetus by devolution and by the HRA—especially s. 6(1), which created a new ground of review providing that '*It is unlawful for a public authority to act in a way which is incompatible with a Convention right.*' These developments are discussed in more detail elsewhere.[18] As Aileen Kavanagh puts it: '*[R]ather than starting from the premise that review of democratically elected bodies is somehow constitutionally suspect, the courts now start from the premise that they have a democratic mandate to engage in strong constitutional review.*'[19]

This renewed judicial confidence, clearly illustrated by decisions in the two *Miller* cases discussed elsewhere in the book, has generated fresh and heated debate about the constitutional justifications for judicial review and the appropriate role of the judges.

17.2 THE CONSTITUTIONAL JUSTIFICATIONS FOR JUDICIAL REVIEW

As the courts have become more interventionist and public bodies have discovered that their actions are increasingly vulnerable to legal challenge, debate surrounding the legitimacy of judicial review has grown in intensity both in the political arena and among legal theorists.

[17] On *Anisminic* see further Chapter 20. [18] See especially Chapter 21.

[19] A. Kavanagh, *Constitutional Review under the UK Human Rights Act* (2009, Cambridge: Cambridge University Press), p. 347.

Anthony King, a political scientist, provides a feel of the growing antagonism within the UK government towards the judges during the 1980s and 1990s following a series of court decisions that were critical of ministerial actions. He goes so far as to liken the relationship between the UK government and the courts to a state of war. The following extract from his book *The British Constitution* picks up the story when Tony Blair's Labour government was elected in 1997.

A. King, *The British Constitution* (2007, Oxford: OUP), pp. 141–3 (footnotes omitted)

It might have been expected that the departure of the Major government and the election of the Blair government in 1997 would have ended the war between judges and ministers. Admittedly, Lord Irvine of Lairg, the incoming Lord Chancellor had, while Labour was still in opposition, defended elected governments' 'administrative autonomy' and counselled judges against saying or doing anything that smacked of 'judicial supremacism'. He had insisted that 'judicial self-restraint [. . .] must inform decision making in public law' [. . .] Lord Irvine was being true to Labour's historic suspicion of judicial activism [. . .] It turned out that the war between the Major government and the judges had not been a mere spat [. . .] it had been a manifestation of a relatively new but by now inbuilt constitutional tension between the claims of judges to defend the rule of law, including human rights, and the claims of ministers to be the sole and legitimate custodians of the country's long-term national interests. [. . .] The principal combatant on the government side was David Blunkett, home secretary between 2001 and 2004 [. . .] When one judge ruled that a recent piece of legislation violated the European Convention on Human Rights, Blunkett told the BBC, 'Frankly, I'm personally fed up with having to deal with a situation where parliament debates issues and the judges then overturn them.'

King is correct to observe that tension, or as he calls it 'war', between the judges and the Major government was more than a 'mere spat'. Indeed throughout the past three decades there have been many examples of situations in which courts have found government to have acted unlawfully and government has responded by accusing judges of overstepping their powers, arguing for the need to curtail the use of judicial review.

Such concerns have led to various government initiatives aimed at limiting the use and reach of judicial review. The 2010 Coalition government, responded to what it claimed to be the 'massive' growth in the use, and abuse, of judicial review by seeking to introduce reforms intended to protect public bodies from challenge.[20] The Joint Committee on Human Rights considered the justifications given by the government for these reforms and the following is an extract from its report.

Joint Committee on Human Rights, The Implications for Access to Justice of the Government's Proposals to Reform Judicial Review HL 174/HC 868, 2013–14 (notes omitted)

21. In an article in *The Daily Mail* on 6 September 2013 [. . .] the Lord Chancellor suggested that the rationale for the Government's proposed reforms is that judicial review is being used as 'a promotional tool by countless Left wing campaigners.' [. . .]

[20] For a critique of the government's justifications for reform, see M. Sunkin and V. Bondy, 'The Use and Effects of Judicial Review: Assumptions and the Empirical Evidence' in, J. Bell, M. Elliott, J. N.E. Varuhas, and P. Murray (eds), *Public Law Adjudication in Common Law Systems* (2016, Oxford:, Hart Publishing), ch. 14.

22. We recognise and accept that the Government has an entirely legitimate interest in ensuring that judicial review is not abused in a way which incurs unnecessary expense to the public purse and causes unwarranted delay to the implementation of decisions for which elected authorities have an electoral mandate. Nevertheless, the Lord Chancellor's energetic pursuit of reforms which place direct limits on the ability of the courts to hold the executive to account is unavoidably problematic from the point of view of the rule of law. Providing independent judges with the means to deal adequately with possible abuses is an important part of the constitutional arrangements.

The evidence base

24. The premise of the Government's . . . [reform proposals] . . . is that 'the use of judicial review' has expanded massively in recent years and it is open to abuse. Many of the submissions we received questioned this premise. Professor Maurice Sunkin's evidence in particular was that 'the statistics do not justify the claim that judicial review is being abused or that it is increasing'.[21] [. . .]

30. [. . .] We note that the number of judicial reviews has remained remarkably steady when the increase in the number of immigration judicial reviews is disregarded. [. . .] We therefore do not consider the Government to have demonstrated by clear evidence that judicial review has 'expanded massively' in recent years as the Lord Chancellor claims, that there are real abuses of the process taking place, or that the current powers of the courts to deal with such abuse are inadequate.

This phase of reforms led to some significant procedural changes,[22] but these did not satisfy those in government and elsewhere who argued that a wider range of reforms were needed to curtail the growth in judicial power.[23] This became a top priority for the Conservative Party which in its 2019 election manifesto promised:

[To . . .] update the Human Rights Act and administrative law to ensure that there is a proper balance between the rights of individuals, our vital national security and effective government. We will ensure that judicial review is available to protect the rights of the individuals against an overbearing state, while ensuring that it is not abused to conduct politics by another means or to create needless delays. In our first year we will set up a Constitution, Democracy & Rights Commission that will examine these issues in depth, and come up with proposals to restore trust in our institutions and in how our democracy operates.[24]

The broader Constitution, Democracy and Rights Commission did not happen, but two more specifically focused commissions were established: the Independent Review of Administrative Law (IRAL)[25] and the Independent Human Rights Act Review (IHRAR).[26] We consider the IHRAR when

[21] We consider the statistics on the use of judicial review in Section 17.3.1.

[22] Including a reduction of the time limit for bringing judicial review in planning cases and the introduction of s. 84 of the Criminal Justice and Courts Act 2015 which requires the courts to refuse to grant permission to seek judicial review or a remedy (on which see below) '. . . if it appears to the court to be highly likely that the outcome for the applicant would not have been substantially different if the conduct complained of had not occurred'. The intended purpose is to prevent the use of judicial review where a finding of illegality would not make a real difference to the claimant.

[23] Including the Judicial Power Project: https://judicialpowerproject.org.uk/.

[24] https://www.conservatives.com/our-plan/conservative-party-manifesto-2019, p. 48.

[25] https://www.gov.uk/government/groups/independent-review-of-administrative-law.

[26] https://www.gov.uk/guidance/independent-human-rights-act-review.

we look at the proposed repeal of the Human Rights Act 1998 in Chapter 21. Here we are interested in the IRAL which was established to consider some broad questions about judicial review, including whether common law principles of judicial review should be codified in statute and whether certain areas of policy making should be regarded as off-limits by the courts.[27] In the event IRAL recommended against fundamental changes[28] and the tangible reforms made following the IRAL have been much more modest than some will have hoped and others feared.[29] That said, the debates generated by the reform process have once again highlighted the contentious nature of judicial review and underscored the government's continuing concerns about so called judicial overreach, and may well return to the political agenda. The concerns may also influence judges to become more sensitive and cautious in certain cases.

It is clear that judicial review can be a significant irritant for government and it is perhaps understandable that government might wish to be protected from the threat of legal challenge. Clearly, there are serious constitutional issues here. Amongst the most basic is the question: from where do judges—who are not elected or politically accountable—acquire authority to review, and strike down, decisions that have been taken by ministers who are politically accountable to Parliament?

A similar question is asked in all constitutional systems in which a judicial review jurisdiction exists. Normally the answer is provided by the written constitution, which either expressly provides for judicial review of governmental powers or arguably implicitly does so. The latter situation is the case in the US Constitution. Although this does not expressly give the US Supreme Court a judicial review jurisdiction, it was held in *Marbury v Madison*[30] that the US Supreme Court must be able to review the legality of the actions of the other branches of government—including the legislature—in order to ensure compliance with the written Constitution. This jurisdiction was implicit in the existence of the written Constitution, because without it, the Constitution could not be enforced.

Nonetheless, even when a written constitution exists, debate over the appropriate scope of judicial review can be intense. In the USA, for instance, there has been longstanding discussion over whether the Supreme Court should be able to review legislation enacted by Congress and, if so, on what grounds.[31] Professor Mauro Cappelletti, a comparative lawyer, goes so far as to say that tension between judicial review and democratic theory poses a '*theoretically insoluble contradiction*'.[32]

[27] See T. Konstadinides, L. Marsons, and M. Sunkin, 'Reviewing Judicial Review: The constitutional importance of the Independent Review of Administrative Law 2020' (24 September 2020, UKCLA). Available at https://ukconstitutionallaw.org/2020/09/24/theodore-konstadinides-lee-marsons-and-maurice-sunkin-reviewing-judicial-review-the-constitutional-importance-of-the-independent-review-of-administrative-law-2020/.

[28] *The Independent Review of Administrative Law*, March 2021, CP 407.

[29] Judicial Review and Courts Act 2022, s. 1 created suspended and prospective-only quashing orders and s. 2 abolished *Cart* judicial reviews (the use of judicial review to challenge decisions of the Upper Tribunal not to allow appeals from the First-tier Tribunal in immigration and asylum matters), see further Chapter 20.

[30] 5 US (1 Cranch) 137 (1803).

[31] See, e.g., J.H. Ely, *Democracy and Distrust: A Theory of Judicial Review* (Cambridge, MA: Harvard University Press, 1980), where Ely argues that judicial review should be limited to supporting people's rights to democratic participation; and J. Waldron, 'The core of the case against judicial review' (2006) 115 Yale Law Journal 1346, where Waldron argues against judicial review of legislation in a liberal democracy.

[32] M. Cappelletti, *The Judicial Process in Comparative Perspective* (1989, Oxford: Clarendon Press), p. xvii.

17.2.1 DEBATE OVER THE CONSTITUTIONAL BASIS OF JUDICIAL REVIEW: THE INTENTION OF PARLIAMENT VS THE COMMON LAW

In the British context, debate among constitutional lawyers over the constitutional basis for judicial review has focused on the relationship between two fundamental principles of the constitutional system: the supremacy of the UK Parliament and the rule of law.[33] Some argue that while judicial review is an inherent jurisdiction that is not explicitly conferred by Parliament it is nonetheless implicitly based on Parliament's supremacy—that the role of judges is to give effect to the expressed or implied intention of Parliament, as expressed in the words of Acts of Parliament. Others argue that judicial review is rooted not in parliamentary intent (whether express or implied), but in common law principles that enshrine the rule of law and in the judges' role in developing common law rules. We need not deal with these competing arguments in great detail, but it is important to be aware of the main strands of the debate.

17.2.1.1 Judicial review is founded upon the supremacy of the UK Parliament

Those advocating this position (the main advocate has been Professor Christopher Forsyth) say that the essential task for the courts when asked to review the actions of public bodies is to ensure that these bodies have not exceeded the powers conferred upon them by Parliament, using the *ultra vires* ('beyond the powers') doctrine. This approach, often referred to as the '*ultra vires* approach', assumes that public bodies derive their legal powers expressly or implicitly from Parliament, and that when public bodies are challenged in judicial review proceedings, the task of the court is to check whether the body has acted in accordance with Parliament's intentions. From this perspective, then, the judicial review jurisdiction derives its authority from the principles of parliamentary democracy. While judges are not themselves elected, they play a crucial part in the democratic process by ensuring that public bodies act within the powers conferred by Parliament.

17.2.1.2 Judicial review is founded upon the common law

Other commentators, including Professors Dawn Oliver, Paul Craig, Jeffrey Jowell, and Sir John Laws argue that this approach does not provide a satisfactory basis for explaining the constitutional justification for judicial review.[34] Two levels of criticism are made.

The first focuses on the realities of current judicial review. At this level, the basic criticism is that since developments in judicial review have been judge-made, it is simply unrealistic to say that they have been driven by parliamentary intentions. Sir John Laws, for example, has observed that modern developments in administrative law '*are categorically, judicial creations. They owe neither their existence nor their acceptance to the will of the legislature. They have nothing to do with the intention of Parliament, save as a fig leaf to cover their true origins. We do not need the fig leaf any more.*'[35]

[33] On parliamentary supremacy, see Chapter 3, and for the rule of law, see Chapter 4. See also the argument against judicial review from a political constitutionalist perspective in R. Bellamy, *Political Constitutionalism: A Republican Defence of the Constitutionality of Democracy* (2007, Cambridge: Cambridge University Press).

[34] D. Oliver, 'Is *ultra vires* the basis of judicial review?' [1987] Public Law 543, 567. See also P. Craig, '*Ultra vires* and the foundations of judicial review' (1999) 58 Cambridge Law Journal 63; J. Jowell, 'Beyond the rule of law: Towards constitutional judicial review' [2000] Public Law 671; and more recently, J. Laws, *The Constitutional Balance* (2021, Oxford: Hart Publishing).

[35] Sir John Laws, 'Law and Democracy' [1995] Public Law 72, 79.

The more fundamental criticisms of the *ultra vires* approach have a political and a constitutional perspective. From the former, it may be argued that to justify judicial review on the basis that it serves Parliament, and therefore parliamentary democracy, relies on a concept of democracy that is too narrow. As we have seen, the track record of the UK Parliament in holding ministers to account, according to many commentators, is not good.[36] Moreover, there are concerns that elected politicians in Parliament and government may not respect the interests of unpopular minorities (such as asylum seekers, prisoners, members of traveller communities, and terrorist suspects). In other words, the democratic credentials of the *ultra vires* approach are tarnished by a system that Lord Hailsham (a former Conservative Lord Chancellor) famously described as being an '*elective dictatorship*'.[37] To quote Sir John Laws once again:

J. Laws, *The Constitutional Balance* (2021, Oxford: Hart Publishing), p. 96

> . . . the [. . .] notion of parliamentary intent and of the *ultra vires* theory of judicial review [. . .] undermine vital pillars of the constitution – reason, fairness and the presumption of liberty – because they deliver them to the whim of the legislators for the time being. They open the door to the false notion that the democratic power is [. . .] the mere creature of the legislative majority.

These observations echo the arguments of those who call for a reassessment of the very theory of parliamentary supremacy. Various points are made, but the essential claim is that the UK Parliament cannot have truly unlimited powers because its legal authority derives from the unwritten constitution (Sir John Laws refers to what he calls a '*higher order law*'). Parliament must act compatibly with the fundamental requirements of the unwritten constitution because it is this unwritten constitution that provides the foundation of Parliament's own authority. On this view, judicial review is also based on the unwritten constitution. In the last resort, as in *Marbury v Madison*, courts derive their authority from the constitution and have ultimate responsibility for ensuring that the constitution is applied. This might conceivably require them to judge whether the UK Parliament has acted unconstitutionally.[38]

Jackson v Attorney General
[2005] UKHL 56

> **Lord Steyn**
>
> 102. [. . .] In exceptional circumstances involving an attempt to abolish judicial review or the ordinary role of the courts, the [. . .] Supreme Court may have to consider whether this is a constitutional fundamental which even a sovereign Parliament acting at the behest of a complaisant House of Commons cannot abolish.

[36] On accountability of ministers, see Chapter 9.

[37] Lord Hailsham of St Marylebone, *The Dilemma of Democracy* (1978, London: Collins).

[38] Legislation enacted by the Scottish Parliament is subject to judicial review to ensure it complies with the Scotland Act 1998, but the courts cannot use common law grounds of judicial review in this context: see *AXA General Insurance Ltd and others (Appellants) v The Lord Advocate and others (Respondents) (Scotland)* discussed in Chapters 3 and 6.

More recently Lord Hope has commented that '*The question whether the principle of the sovereignty of the United Kingdom Parliament is absolute or may be subject to limitation in exceptional circumstances is still under discussion.*'[39] If it is conceivable that the courts may be able to review primary legislation of the UK Parliament at Westminster, albeit in very exceptional situations, the authority of the courts must be based on something more fundamental than Parliament's own sovereignty: otherwise, the courts would have to respect Parliament's will even when Parliament is seeking to act contrary to a constitutional fundamental.[40]

17.2.1.3 A middle way?

While it is tempting to try to draw clear lines between opposing arguments, in reality it would be an oversimplification to say that of the two claimed constitutional foundations for judicial review—the intention of Parliament and the common law—only one can be totally correct. Both sides of the argument accept that the reality is more complicated and subtle. This is not surprising. After all, judicial review has had a long history, and its roots predate current understandings of democracy and the modern role of Parliament. Many changes have occurred over the centuries and, as we saw when discussing the prerogative, caution must be exercised when looking at older understandings of the relationship between the courts and the other institutions of government through twenty-first-century spectacles. Craig, for example, is no doubt correct to say that seventeenth-century authorities would not have rooted judicial review in parliamentary intent—but, in those days, Parliament was a very different institution from Parliament today, the quantity of legislation was far less, and ideas of democratic legitimacy were also very different.

Another factor that adds to the complexity is that judicial review involves the courts in a very wide range of issues, from relatively routine disputes (over matters such as local authority licensing, planning, and housing) to high-profile and constitutionally important matters (such as the review of executive powers in relation to terrorism or the legal status of primary legislation). Much of the day-to-day work of the judicial review judge concerns interpreting and applying legislation, and checking to see whether public bodies have acted in accordance with the requirements set out in Acts of Parliament. In such cases, there can be no doubt that the *ultra vires* approach is dominant, both in terms of what the judges consider their role to be and in terms of what they are actually doing.

Equally, judges are now regularly called upon to make constitutional decisions that have a bearing both on legal powers of the executive and the legislature itself. In such situations, judicial review cannot be adequately justified in terms of parliamentary intention. In the following extract from the conclusion to his book, *The Constitutional Foundations of Judicial Review*, Mark Elliott responds to issues such as these by arguing that it is unrealistic to seek to base judicial review on a single foundation stone.[41]

[39] *AXA General Insurance Ltd and others (Appellants) v The Lord Advocate and others (Respondents) (Scotland)* [2011] UKSC 46, [50]. It may be noted in passing that the fundamental nature of the principle of parliamentary sovereignty was endorsed by the UKSC in *R (On the application of Miller and Another) v Secretary of State for Exiting the European Union* [2017] UKSC 5, at [43].

[40] For Professor Forsyth's response to these arguments, see: C. Forsyth, 'Of fig leaves and fairy tales: The *ultra vires* doctrine, the sovereignty of Parliament and judicial review' (1996) 55 Cambridge Law Journal 122. For Professor Craig's response to Forsyth, see P. Craig, '*Ultra vires* and the foundations of judicial review' (1998) 57 Cambridge Law Journal 63.

[41] Note also the argument that the relationship between courts and Parliament and the executive should be understood as a 'dialogue'. See further Chapter 21.

M. Elliott, *The Constitutional Foundations of Judicial Review* (2001, Oxford: Hart Publishing), pp. 252–3

The notion that judicial review rests on a set of constitutional foundations, rather than on a single foundation, captures two central truths about the juridical underpinnings of the supervisory jurisdiction.

In the first place, it emphasises that the ethos lying at the heart of orthodox ultra vires theory—that judicial review is based solely on the intention of the legislature—is fundamentally incorrect. In truth, judicial review's legitimacy is secured, and its ambit determined, by the rich set of constitutional principles most notably the rule of law, the separation of powers and the sovereignty of Parliament—on which the constitution is founded. It is in the interaction of those constitutional fundamentals, rather than in the legislative command of the sovereign, that the justification for judicial review is to be found. Secondly, the pluralism which inheres in the notion of constitutional foundations reflects the fact that judicial review must be justified in ways which are appropriate to the diverse areas within which it now operates. The search for a single doctrine capable of furnishing a juridical rationalisation of all judicial review is futile—albeit that this conclusion emphatically does not detract from the fact that review in all its contexts rests on a common normative basis.

QUESTIONS

1. Summarize the main arguments for and against the proposition that, in exercising the judicial review jurisdiction, judges give effect to the intention of Parliament.
2. If the courts are ultimately responsible for ensuring that the executive and the legislature act in accordance with the unwritten constitution, who is to ensure that the courts interpret the constitution correctly?
3. '*The search for a single doctrine capable of furnishing a juridical rationalization of all judicial review is futile—albeit that this conclusion emphatically does not detract from the fact that review in all its contexts rests on a common normative basis*' (Elliott). Discuss.

17.3 JUDICIAL REVIEW IN PRACTICE

Having looked at questions associated with the constitutional foundations of judicial review, we now turn to consider some practical aspects of the process.

Judicial review is often important in practice because it is a remedy of last resort. Claimants turn to judicial review when they have exhausted other avenues of appeal or when no such avenues exist (because they have not been created by any Act of Parliament). But even then, judicial review may only be a limited remedy. This is because, even if claimants are successful in their claims judges will rarely replace the decision that has been challenged with their own decision.[42] Judicial review is generally about the way in which decisions are made (for example, whether people were properly consulted) and the limits of a public authority's legal powers, rather than the *merits* of the decision

[42] Cf. s. 31(5)(b) of the Supreme Court Act 1981 which sets out the limited circumstances in which a judicial review court may substitute its own decision for the decision that was challenged.

(for example, whether it was the best or wisest decision in the circumstances). Judges often stress that, when reviewing a decision, it is irrelevant whether they agree or disagree with it. Even if a claimant succeeds, the matter will normally be sent back ('remitted') to the original decision-maker for a fresh decision to be made in the light of the court's judgment. When this happens, the decision-maker may reach the same decision as that which was originally challenged, but hopefully, this time, the decision-maker will have acted lawfully. Research suggests that this happens less often than has been assumed and that in practice judicial review often leads public authorities to alter their decisions in favour of claimants.[43]

A qualification to this concerns situations in which the judicial review procedure is used to protect 'Convention rights' under the HRA. If a court decides that a public authority has infringed Convention rights, the authority may not be able to reach the same decision after a reconsideration. This is considered in more detail in Chapter 21.

A value of judicial review is that it requires bodies to comply with the law in their decision-making. Judicial review case law also sets standards of good administration, so that public bodies and the wider community may know what the law expects. In this way, judicial review should help to improve the quality of government. To what extent it does so in practice is an important empirical question that has been examined by researchers, to which we shall return.[44]

17.3.1 THE SCALE OF JUDICIAL REVIEW

We have already seen that the scale of judicial review litigation has attracted much attention and has been one of the reasons why governments have wanted to reform the system. The graph in Figure 17.1, based on Official Statistics, shows that between 2000 and 2013 the overall number of civil judicial review applications annually in England and Wales grew from around 2,000 to around 15,594 in 2013.[45] These numbers include immigration and asylum cases which historically have made up the largest single category of case. The numbers dropped drastically after 2013 because in that year immigration judicial reviews started being dealt with by the Upper Tribunal rather than the Administrative Court.

The graph shows that beyond immigration there has been no significant increase in the judicial review caseload since at least 2000. It also shows that between 2000 and 2017 the actual numbers of non-immigration judicial reviews stayed at around 2,000 a year. More recent statistics show falls in the number of claims.[46] The overall picture is that despite assumptions that the use of judicial has been massively growing, in reality there has been no massive growth and the scale of judicial review remains tiny when compared with the overall scale of government decision-making. This suggests that rather than being concerned about the growth of judicial review we should rather be asking why judicial review is not being used more frequently?

[43] V. Bondy, L. Platt, and M. Sunkin, *The Value and Effects of Judicial Review: The Nature of Claims, their Outcomes and Consequences* (2015, Public Law Project).

[44] See generally M. Hertogh and S. Halliday (eds) *Judicial Review and Bureaucratic Impact* (2004, Cambridge: Cambridge University Press).

[45] L. Graham, L. Marsons, M. Sunkin, and J. Tomlinson, 'A guide to reading the Official Statistics on judicial review in the Administrative Court' (UKAJI, October 2020), https://administrativejusticeblog.files.wordpress.com/2020/10/a-guide-to-reading-the-official-statistics-on-judicial-review-in-the-administrative-court-october-2020.pdf.

[46] In the first quarter of 2025 there were 670 applications for judicial review, of which 240 were immigration and asylum cases, 390 were other civil cases, and 30 were criminal cases. This reflected 3 per cent, 11 per cent and 12 per cent respectively reductions compared with the first quarter of 2024. See Justice Statistics Quarterly: January to March 2025, (MoJ, 5 June 2025), https://www.gov.uk/government/statistics/civil-justice-statistics-quarterly-january-to-march-2025/civil-justice-statistics-quarterly-january-to-march-2025

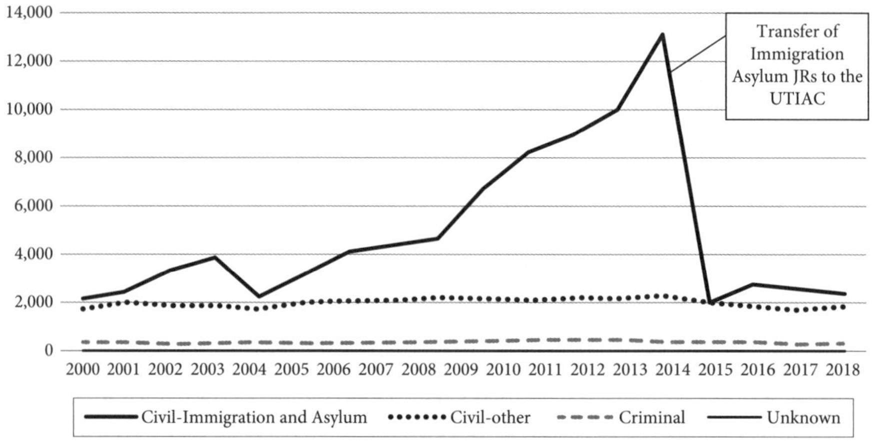

Figure 17.1 Annual Judicial Review Applications in England & Wales 2000–2017
Source: Ministry of Justice

> **QUESTIONS**
>
> 1. Does the graph in Figure 17.1 and more recent statistics suggest that judicial review is a growth industry that must be curtailed?
> 2. It can be argued that beyond immigration judicial review has been used less frequently than would have been expected given the effects of the Human Rights Act 1998 and expansion of the grounds of judicial review. What explanations might there be for this?

17.3.2 THE JUDICIAL REVIEW PROCEDURE

The three territorial jurisdictions in the United Kingdom each have different court procedures for claiming judicial review, and, as we noted earlier, a range of courts and tribunals exercise a jurisdiction that involves reviewing the legality of public actions. In this section of the chapter, we briefly examine the 'claim for judicial review' procedure, which applies in England and Wales.

The claim for judicial review procedure in England and Wales is set out in Pt 54 of the Civil Procedure Rules (CPR—delegated legislation made under the Civil Procedure Act 1997).

Civil Procedure Rules, Pt 54

Judicial Review

Scope and interpretation

54.1—(1) This Section . . . contains rules about judicial review.

(2) In this Section—

(a) a 'claim for judicial review' means a claim to review the lawfulness of—

(i) an enactment; or

(ii) a decision, action or failure to act in relation to the exercise of a public function.

The judicial review procedure consists of two basic stages.[47]

(a) Claimants must first obtain the permission of a judge to bring a claim.
(b) Only if permission is granted will the claim proceed to be dealt with by the court.

17.3.3 PERMISSION

In order to obtain permission,[48] the claimant will have to persuade the judge, usually in writing, that:

(a) the claim is arguable;
(b) the claim is made within the time limits (claims must be made promptly and in any event within three months of the decision being challenged);[49]
(c) the claimant has a sufficient interest in the case (standing);
(d) other potential avenues of redress have been exhausted (for example, an internal appeal) and that there is no other suitable way of challenging the decision (for example, a statutory appeal to the First-tier Tribunal); and
(e) that, if successful, the claim would make a difference to the claimant.[50]

17.3.4 THE LAWFULNESS OF AN ENACTMENT

You will have noticed that rule 54.1 of the Civil Procedure Rules (CPR) says that a claim for judicial review means a claim to review the lawfulness of an enactment, or the lawfulness of decisions or actions (or non-actions) in relation to the exercise of a public function.

The term 'enactment' means an item of legislation. The most common form of legislation to be challenged is delegated legislation made by ministers or local government.[51] Challenges may also be made to legislative provisions enacted by the National Assembly for Wales and (using judicial review in Scotland) legislation enacted by the Scottish Parliament.[52] Judicial review is also one route by which claimants may seek a declaration that legislation is incompatible with Convention rights under s. 4 of the HRA.[53]

It is also important to note that the judicial review procedure is concerned with questioning the 'lawfulness' of an enactment or a decision. We have already seen that when deciding judicial review claims judges are not being asked to overturn a decision because it is wrong or foolish in the circumstances. Instead they are asked to ensure that the decision has been lawfully made. Because judicial review focuses on questions of legality the procedure is not designed to deal with disputes about facts. So, for example, in judicial review the parties are much less likely to be able to cross examine witnesses or automatically obtain documentary evidence (discovery of documents) from

[47] The permission procedure was introduced in Scotland in September 2015 under powers contained in the Courts Reform (Scotland) Act 2014.

[48] For the background to the permission requirement, see A. Le Sueur and M. Sunkin, 'Applications for judicial review: The requirement of leave' [1992] Public Law 102.

[49] While the three-month time limit applies to most judicial review claims, a shorter period may apply for certain types of case, e.g., judicial reviews concerning planning must now be brought within six weeks (CPR 54.5).

[50] Section 84 of the Criminal Justice and Courts Act 2015 amended section 31 of the Senior Courts Act 1981 to provide that permission should be refused 'if it appears . . . to be highly likely that the outcome for the applicant . . . [assuming the claim were successful] . . . would not have been substantially different'.

[51] See Chapter 13. [52] See the *AXA* case at n. 39. [53] See Chapter 21,

opposing parties than they would in normal civil litigation.[54] This does not mean that facts are never relevant in judicial reviews and as Joanna Bell and Elizabeth Fisher have observed judicial reviews '*often deal with disputes about facts: the processes used to find them and the use made of them by decision-makers.*'[55] It is, however, another reminder of the limitations of the judicial review process for handling certain types of dispute.

17.3.5 THE LAWFULNESS OF DECISIONS OR ACTIONS IN RELATION TO THE EXERCISE OF A PUBLIC FUNCTION: AMENABILITY

Rule 54.1 of the CPR does not specify the bodies that may be challenged in judicial review proceedings (or, as is it is often put, the bodies that are amenable to judicial review). Instead, it says that judicial review claims are concerned with the exercise of 'public functions'. This recognises that judicial review may be used against any decision-maker that exercises 'public functions', even if that body is not a government body in the usual sense of that term. So, for example, private bodies, charities and self-regulatory organizations may find themselves subject to judicial review challenge in respect of their 'public functions'. As Lord Nicholls explains in the following extract, public, or government, functions are nowadays exercised by a wide range of bodies, including some in the private sector. While the *Aston Cantlow* case concerned the application of the HRA, rather than judicial review, Lord Nicholls' explanation is pertinent in the current context.

Aston Cantlow and Wilmcote with Billesley Parochial Church Council v Wallbank and anor
[2003] UKHL 37

Lord Nicholls of Birkenhead

9. [. . .] In the interests of efficiency and economy, and for other reasons, functions of a governmental nature are frequently discharged by non-governmental bodies. Sometimes this will be a consequence of privatisation, sometimes not. One obvious example is the running of prisons by commercial organisations. Another is the discharge of regulatory functions by organisations in the private sector [. . .]

The main way in which judges determine whether a body is amenable to judicial review is to look at the source of the body's powers. If the powers in question derive from statute or the prerogative, the decision will normally be reviewable. By contrast, decisions taken under powers contained in a contract are not considered to be reviewable, because in these cases the source of the legal power is a 'private' agreement between the contracting parties rather than a grant of power by Parliament or the common law.

[54] Discovery of documents may be ordered by the court and documents should be revealed in order to comply with the duty of candour: see, e.g Guidance on Discharging the Duty of Candour and Disclosure in Judicial Review Proceedings, Treasury Solicitor's Department, January 2010, *Administrative Court Judicial Review Guide, 2022*. Also, *R (Police Superintendents' Association) v Police Remuneration Review Body and the Secretary of State for the Home Department* [2023] EWHC 1838 (Admin); Elizabeth O'Loughlin, 'Government's Duty of Candour: On the Move?' (2023) Public Law 567–586.

[55] Joanna Bell and Elizabeth Fisher, 'Judicial Review of "Fact Work": Beyond the Law/Fact Distinction', in *Facts in Public Law Adjudication*, Joe Tomlinson and Anne Carter (eds) (Oxford: Hart 2023), ch. 7, p. 125.

Council of Civil Service Unions v Minister for the Civil Service
[1985] AC 374, 409

Lord Diplock

For a decision to be susceptible to judicial review the decision-maker must be empowered by public law (and not merely, as in arbitration, by agreement between private parties) to make decisions that, if validly made, will lead to administrative action or abstention from action by an authority endowed by law with executive powers, which have one or other of the consequences mentioned in the preceding paragraph. The ultimate source of the decision-making power is nearly always nowadays a statute or subordinate legislation made under the statute; but in the absence of any statute regulating the subject matter of the decision the source of the decision-making power may still be the common law itself, ie that part of the common law that is given by lawyers the label of 'the prerogative'.

It is clear that the exercise of statutory and prerogative power is reviewable, and that the use of contractual powers is not normally reviewable—but suppose that the source of a body's powers cannot be identified. This issue arose in the *Datafin* case. Although it performed important functions, the City Panel on Takeovers and Mergers appeared to have no formal legal powers at all. Did this mean that its decisions could not be challenged in the courts? The Court of Appeal held that the Panel could be reviewed because of the importance and impact of its functions.

R v Panel on Takeovers and Mergers, ex parte Datafin
[1987] QB 815, 824–36

Sir John Donaldson MR

The Panel on Take-overs and Mergers is a truly remarkable body. Perched on the 20th floor of the Stock Exchange building in the City of London, both literally and metaphorically it oversees and regulates a very important part of the United Kingdom financial market. Yet it performs this function without visible means of legal support.

The panel is an unincorporated association without legal personality and, so far as can be seen [. . .] It has no statutory, prerogative or common law powers and it is not in contractual relationship with the financial market or with those who deal in that market.

[. . .]

The issue is thus whether the historic supervisory jurisdiction of the . . . courts extends to such a body [. . .] Mr. Alexander, for the panel, submits that it does not. He says that this jurisdiction only extends to bodies whose power is derived from legislation or the exercise of the prerogative. Mr. Lever for the applicants, submits that this is too narrow a view and that regard has to be had not only to the source of the body's power, but also to whether it operates as an integral part of a system which has a public law character, is supported by public law in that public law sanctions are applied if its edicts are ignored and performs what might be described as public law functions [. . .] In all the reports it is possible to find enumerations of factors giving rise to the jurisdiction, but it is a fatal error to regard the presence of all those factors as essential or as being exclusive of other factors. Possibly the only essential elements are what can be described as a public element, which can take many different forms, and the exclusion from the jurisdiction of bodies whose sole source of power is a consensual submission to its jurisdiction.

This important decision showed that, in determining whether a body is amenable to judicial review, the courts would, if necessary, look not only at whether the body derives its powers from statute or prerogative, but also at whether the body performs functions that have a 'public element'. Sir John Donaldson MR says that the necessary public element can '*take many different forms*'. In *Datafin*, the Court of Appeal discerned the public element from the nature and impact of the Panel's functions, and the extent to which it was linked into a statutory scheme.[56] Here, it was clear that Parliament had enacted legislation on the assumption that the Panel existed. Had it not existed, Parliament would have needed to establish a statutory body to perform similar (public) functions.

The reference to the exercise of a public function in rule 54.1 CPR reflects the approach taken in *Datafin*. As we shall see in Chapter 21, similar wording is used in s. 6 of the HRA in order to identify which bodies are public authorities for the purposes of that Act.

The courts have not always found it easy to decide whether public functions are being exercised or not. Difficult issues, for example, have been raised in cases in which claimants have tried to use judicial review to challenge decisions taken by private companies and charities when performing functions that were previously undertaken by local authorities.

In *R v Servite Houses and Wandsworth LBC, ex parte Goldsmith*,[57] for example, a person was placed in a private care home by a local authority acting under powers in the National Assistance Act 1948 (NAA). The owner of the care home, Servite Homes, later decided to close the home. Could a resident challenge this decision in judicial review? The resident argued that although Servite Homes was not a government body, in providing accommodation and care to people who would have been previously looked after by a local authority under the NAA, it was exercising public functions. In essence, the claimant argued that these functions were public when exercised by a local authority and that they did not cease to be public when exercised by Servite Homes. The High Court rejected this argument. It held that the relationship between the resident and the care home was governed solely by contract, and therefore that judicial review was not appropriate; if a remedy existed, it should be in contract. In other words, the court looked not at the nature of the function—providing care to those in need under the terms of the NAA—but rather at the nature of the legal arrangements under which the functions were delivered to the individual. As we shall see, the approach in this decision was applied after the enactment of the HRA in cases in which claimants tried to argue that housing associations and charities in a similar position to Servite Homes were bound by the HRA.[58]

This discussion indicates that there is no definitive list of which bodies can be judicially reviewed. This reflects the fact that in the United Kingdom there is no precise definition of the state and no definitive list of bodies that constitute the state. It also means that there is no clear statement of which bodies must comply with the principles of judicial review and which bodies need not do so.

17.3.6 STANDING TO MAKE A JUDICIAL REVIEW CLAIM

In order to obtain permission to seek judicial review, claimants must show that they have a 'sufficient interest in the matter' to which the claim relates.[59] What constitutes a 'sufficient interest' is not defined in legislation and has been left to the judges to determine. In most cases, it is obvious that claimants have a sufficient interest, because they will be challenging decisions that clearly directly affect them.

[56] See *R (Warren) v Chartered Institute of Taxation* [2021] EWHC 1069 (Admin) holding that the Chartered Institute of Taxation is not amenable to judicial review because: it does not operate under statute; its relationship with its members is purely contractual; it exercises no disciplinary functions; and the government has no intention to intervene in the field.

[57] (2000) 3 Community Care Law Reports 325. [58] See Chapter 21.

[59] Senior Courts Act 1981, s. 31(3) (England and Wales); Judicature (Northern Ireland) Act 1978, s. 18; Courts Reform (Scotland) Act 2014, s. 89, introducing a new s. 27B into the Court of Session Act 1988. There had previously been no special standing rules for judicial review in Scotland: see Lord Hope of Craighead, 'Mike Tyson comes to Glasgow—a question of standing' [2001] Public Law 294.

The situation may be more problematic when claimants say that they are representing others (for example, a trade union representing its members) or where they claim to represent more general public interests (for example, claims made by a campaigning environmental organization). While some judges have preferred to take a 'closed' approach to such cases—insisting that claimants will only have a sufficient interest if they can show that they are directly adversely affected by the decision being challenged—subject to recent concerns to be discussed in a moment, the legal principles governing standing have tended to favour a much more open approach that allows claimants into court if they have an arguable case on the law.[60]

An important early decision on standing was *IRC v National Federation of the Self-employed and Small Businesses Ltd*[61] (the *IRC* case). The Federation, an interest group, wanted to challenge the legality of a decision by the tax authorities to grant a tax 'amnesty' to print workers employed on a casual basis by newspapers. The Federation was angered that the amnesty was granted when the Inland Revenue went to great lengths to collect tax from its members. The majority in the House of Lords held that, in order to determine whether the Federation had a sufficient interest in the matter, it was necessary to look at the substance of the claim. They therefore examined the legal and factual context. Having done so, the majority decided that the Federation did not have a sufficient interest in the matter: '*one taxpayer has no sufficient interest in asking the court to investigate the tax affairs of another taxpayer or to complain that the latter has been under-assessed*'. Moreover, '*an aggregate of individuals [such as the Federation] each of whom has no interest cannot of itself have an interest*'.[62]

Lord Diplock took a rather different approach. His view was that standing should be only a preliminary or threshold issue used to reject 'simple' cases. Once leave (now permission) was granted, the courts should concern themselves exclusively with the substance and quality of the arguments. He decided against the Federation, not on grounds of standing but because the Federation had failed to show that the Inland Revenue had acted unlawfully.

IRC v National Federation of the Self-employed and Small Businesses Ltd
[1982] AC 617, 644

Lord Diplock

It would, in my view, be a grave lacuna in our system of public law if a pressure group, like the federation, or even a single public-spirited taxpayer, were prevented by outdated technical rules of locus standi from bringing the matter to the attention of the court to vindicate the rule of law and get the unlawful conduct stopped.

Lord Diplock's approach became the dominant approach. For example in *R v Secretary of State for Foreign Affairs, ex parte World Development Movement Ltd*[63] The World Development Movement (WDM), a pressure group that campaigns to improve the quality of aid to developing countries, was granted standing to challenge the Foreign Secretary's decision to provide funding for the Pergau Dam project in Malaysia. WDM did not claim to represent a particular group of people in the United Kingdom who were adversely affected by the decision; rather, it claimed to represent broader public interests, including the interests of people in developing countries. Nonetheless, WDM was held to have a sufficient interest in the matter.

[60] For an argument that the courts should take a closed approach, see Sir Konrad Shiemann, '*Locus standi*' [1990] Public Law 342; also C. Harlow, 'Public law and popular justice' (2002) 65 Modern Law Review 1.

[61] [1982] AC 617. [62] *Per* Lord Wilberforce at 644.

[63] [1995] 1 All ER 611. Also *R v HMIP, ex parte Greenpeace Ltd* [1994] 1 WLR 570, [1994] 4 All ER 329.

R v Secretary of State for Foreign Affairs, ex parte World Development Movement Ltd
[1995] 1 All ER 611, 620

Rose LJ

. . . [T]here seem to me to be a number of factors of significance in the present case: the importance of vindicating the rule of law, as Lord Diplock emphasised in [*IRC*]; the importance of the issue raised [. . .] the likely absence of any other responsible challenger [. . .] the nature of the breach of duty against which relief is sought [. . .] and the prominent role of these applicants in giving advice, guidance and assistance with regard to aid [. . .] All, in my judgment, point, in the present case, to the conclusion that the applicants here do have a sufficient interest in the matter to which the application relates [. . .].

Some have argued that courts should confine themselves to protecting clear legal rights and directly affected interests and that they should not permit pressure groups to use the judicial review process as a platform for protest or to achieve political ends.[64] That said, certain decisions inevitably affect the legal interests of a very large number of people who may thereby have standing.

As we have seen elsewhere in the book in *Miller 1* the courts accepted that they had jurisdiction to determine whether the government could use its prerogative powers to serve notice under Art. 50 of the Treaty of European Union of the UK's intention to withdraw from the EU. Standing to bring the challenge was not an issue. As the then Lord Chief Justice, Lord Thomas of Cwmgiedd, put it:

It is not difficult to identify people with standing to bring the challenge since virtually everyone in the United Kingdom or with British citizenship will [. . .] have their legal rights affected if notice is given under Article 50.[65]

While the general trend has been towards accepting a liberal approach the IRAL stressed that standing is still something that the courts should consider even when the issue is not raised by the parties.[66] There are also signs in recent judgments of the courts taking a more restrictive approach, especially where the claims seem to be overtly political in character. As Lord Reed argued in *R (SC) v Secretary of State for Work and Pensions* [2021] UKSC 26:

In practice, challenges to legislation on the ground of discrimination have become increasingly common in the United Kingdom. They are usually brought by campaigning organisations which lobbied unsuccessfully against the measure when it was being considered in Parliament, and then act as solicitors for persons affected by the legislation, or otherwise support legal challenges brought in their names, as a means of continuing their campaign.[67]

[64] See, e.g., C. Harlow, 'Public law and popular justice' (2002) 65 Modern Law Review 1.
[65] [2016] EWHC 2768 (Admin), at [7].
[66] *The Independent Review of Administrative Law*, March 2021, CP 707, at 4.99.
[67] [2021] UKSC 26, at [162]. Similarly, in *R (All the Citizens) v Prime Minister* [2022] EWHC 960 (Admin) Singh LJ stressed that 'greater attention needs to be paid to the issue of standing in future cases and, as appropriate, should be considered at the permission stage before a claim for judicial review is allowed to proceed'. [152]. See also *R (Good Law Project and Runnymede Trust) v Secretary of State for Health* [2022] EWHC 298 (Admin) where Singh LJ noted that organizations could only have standing 'within their fields of interest' ([21]).

In this spirit the judiciary have expressed concern about judicial reviews including politicians as claimants, especially when there are already claimants with adequate standing. In *R (Good Law Project, Debbie Abrams, Caroline Lucas and Layla Moran) v Secretary of State for Health*[68] Chamberlain J concluded that:

> No doubt, the addition of politicians as parties may raise the profile of the litigation. It may make it easier to raise funds. But these are not proper reasons for adding parties. In a case where there is already a claimant with standing, the addition of politicians as claimants may leave the public with the impression that the proceedings are an attempt to advance a political cause, when in fact their sole legitimate function is to determine an arguable allegation of unlawful conduct.[69]

QUESTIONS

1. Consider the following scenario: a local authority proposes to grant a licence to a business to open a Vape shop. Who of the following would or should be able to bring a claim for judicial review?
   (a) The owners of the Vape shop (for example, because they dispute the legality of conditions that the local authority says it will impose on opening hours).
   (b) A local resident (for example, who objects to the opening of so many Vape shops and says that she was not properly consulted).
   (c) A national anti-Vaping campaign organization.
   (d) An individual who lives 250 miles away.
2. Would your answers have been different if, instead of granting a licence to open a Vape shop, the local authority decided to subsidize the provision of support for children with terminal illnesses? In this situation, who of the following would or should be able to bring a claim for judicial review?
   (a) A local resident who objects to the expenditure on the grounds that he was not properly consulted, has no children, and firmly believes that public money should not be spent on supporting those who are soon to die.
   (b) A national organization that campaigns for reductions in the level of taxation.
   (c) An individual who lives 250 miles away.

17.3.7 REMEDIES

Claimants for judicial review may seek various orders from the court. In England and Wales, the following main remedies may be granted.[70]

(a) A quashing order (such orders mean that, if the order is granted, the decision challenged will have no legal effect).[71] The effect of such an order may be suspended or only have effect in the future.[72]

[68] [2021] EWHC 346 (Admin), [107].
[69] [2021] EWHC 346 (Admin), at [107]. See also *R (Good Law Project) v Minister for the Cabinet Office and Public First Ltd* [2022] EWCA Civ 21.
[70] Senior Courts Act 1981, s. 31 and CPR Part 54. For a helpful overview and explanation of remedies available see also *The Administrative Court Judicial Review Guide 2025*, section 12.
[71] For an explanation see *R (Majera) v Secretary of State for the Home Department* [2021] UKSC 46, paras[27]–[32].
[72] Section 1 of the Judicial Review and Courts Act 2022.

(b) A quashing order is often combined with an order sending the matter back (remitting) to the original decision-maker '*with a direction to reconsider it and reach a decision in accordance with the findings*' of the court.

(c) A prohibiting order (prohibiting a public body from doing or continuing to do something).

(d) A mandating order (ordering the body to perform a duty).

(e) A declaration (a formal statement by the court about the legal rights of the parties).

(f) An injunction (injunctions can be temporary or permanent. They can stop something being done or a mandatory injunction can force something to be done).

(g) If the claim includes arguments about Convention rights, it may be appropriate for the court to make a 'declaration of incompatibility' under s. 4 of the HRA.[73]

(h) Damages may also be claimed. But damages will only be available if they could be obtained in non-judicial review proceedings. This means that damages cannot be sought in claims based only on the common law grounds of judicial review.

The grant of a remedy is discretionary, so the court may decide that even though the claimant has won on the legal arguments, no formal order should be made. This may happen, for example, if there has been delay in making the claim or if a remedy would serve no useful purpose.[74]

17.3.8 WHY JUDICIAL REVIEW MATTERS TO GOOD GOVERNMENT

A central question is whether judicial review matters, not only to the parties in the cases that are brought and fought in the courts, but also in a broader sense to the quality of government. While some of the discussions may suggest that there is an inevitable clash between judicial review and the interests of government, as we have already stressed judicial review is concerned with maintaining and improving the quality of government and administration. Both government and judges often refer to the link between judicial review and good administration.[75] This implies that judges are concerned both with providing just results in individual cases and with using judicial review to improve the quality of public administration.

The following are some general observations based on the findings of a research study on the impact of judicial review on the quality of local government services which indicate some ways that judicial review assists good government.

[73] See Chapter 21.

[74] Section 84 of the Criminal Justice and Courts Act 2015 amended s. 31 Senior Courts Act 1981 to provide that a judge should refuse relief 'if it appears . . . to be highly likely that the outcome for the applicant would not have been substantially different'. For a study of how this provision is applied, see Lia Lawton, 'Section 31(2A) of the Senior Courts Act 1981 in the Courts' [2025] Public Law 239–260. Also, Dave Cowan and Joe Tomlinson, 'Crisis Relief? Public Resources and Judicial Review Remedies' [2023] Public Law 495–509, discussing discretionary refusal of remedies when public authorities have limited resources to act.

[75] *JOYS The Judge Over Your Shoulder* (Government Legal Department, 6th edn 2022) Chapter 1. In *R v Lancashire CC, ex p Huddleston* [1986] 2 All ER 94 Lord Donaldson MR said that in judicial review the relationship between the courts and government was '*one of partnership based on a common aim, namely the maintenance of the highest standards of public administration . . .*'

M. Sunkin, L. Platt, T. Landman, and K. Calvo, 'Judicial Review litigation as an incentive to change in Local Authority Public Services in England & Wales' (2010) 20:I *Journal of Administration Research and Theory* 243–60

Local authorities do their best to implement judgments. As one respondent expressed it: 'they tend to respond ultimately to what the court orders them to do because that's how local authorities operate'. Respondents also noted that it helps to clarify legal duties. As one interviewee put it: 'I think as the law has been clarified we've been clearer as to what our advice to the client department should be and we'll be saying "you've got a duty to meet needs here" and the judicial review never gets off the ground'.

The researchers were also told that litigation can reshape internal balances of power and give new legitimacy to the claims and interests of marginalized sectors or groups. It was found that when responding to judicial decisions, authorities are motivated by a combination of considerations extending from concern to meet financial targets to desire to pursue other service oriented goals, including furthering the needs of client groups and respecting the law.

But, the pace and extent of implementation varies according to the nature of decisions, authorities' legal competence, organizational capacity and culture, and other contextual factors, such as local and national political considerations.

17.3.9 WHAT DIFFERENCE DO THE JUDGMENTS MAKE?

Judicial review judgments have the capacity to challenge local authorities and may do so from an awkward and often unpredictable angle. Respondents talked about decisions that '*came out of the blue*' and which were '*a shock to a lot of local authorities*'.

They may also create financial problems for authorities. Referring to a decision that held that a local authority had a wider range of duties than it had previously believed, a respondent said that the cost implications meant '[. . .] *it's sort of beyond the power of the local authority to implement the judgment*'.

Nevertheless, there was much that was regarded as positive about judgments. As well as clarification of responsibilities, certain judgments were regarded as enabling authorities to better meet clients' needs. Looking back on one decision that had been particularly critical of local authority practice, one interviewee described its initial devastating effect on officials and on the reputation of the authority. With hindsight, however, the judgment is seen to have had '*a massive effect*', and to have contributed substantially to the improvement of services. Certainly, many respondents emphasized that judicial review does not hinder them in their work. As one put it: '*As a general point we were not sitting around worrying about judicial review and it's not making us defensive, we're much more proactive about doing things right than defensive about trying to avoid making mistakes.*'

EXERCISE

You are a civil servant in the Ministry of Justice. The Ministry is writing an assessment of judicial review to help the Minister, who is newly appointed. You are asked to present a summary of the main reasons why judicial review may be viewed positively and negatively by government, and for your overall assessment. What points would you make?

17.4 CONCLUDING COMMENTS

In this Chapter we have looked at the recent historical development of judicial review in the United Kingdom. We have seen that the growing importance of judicial review has heightened debate about the constitutional justifications of courts interfering with decisions taken by the politically accountable branches of government and this has led to a programme of reforms aimed at limiting the use of judicial review. We have also looked briefly at what the statistics tell us about the scale of judicial review and seen that, contrary to some assumptions, aside from immigration, there has been no massive increase in use of judicial review. Indeed, it is perhaps surprising that more judicial reviews claims are not made. The reasons for this may lie in the costs of litigation and other factors, such as: the nature of the procedure; that use of judicial review is always a last resort; that courts cannot overturn decisions just because they are considered to be wrong; and, that even when successful claimants may not get the remedy they are seeking. We have also seen some of the reasons why judicial review assists in achieving good government. The next two chapters look more closely at the grounds of judicial review.

FURTHER READING

Arvind, T. T., Kirkham, R., Daithi Mac Sitigh, and Stirton, L., (eds), *Executive Decision-Making and the Courts: Revisiting the Origins of Modern Judicial Review* (2021, Oxford: Hart Publishing).

Bondy, V., Platt, L., and Sunkin, M., *The Value and Effects of Judicial Review* (October 2015, Public Law Project).

Bellamy, R., *Political Constitutionalism: A Republican Defence of the Constitutionality of Democracy* (2007, Cambridge: Cambridge University Press).

Elliott M., *The Constitutional Foundations of Judicial Review* (2001, Oxford: Hart Publishing).

Graham, L. *Judicial Individuality on the UK Supreme Court* (2025, Oxford: Hart Publishing).

Government Legal Department, *JOYS The Judge Over Your Shoulder* (2022, 6th ed).

HM Courts & Tribunals Judiciary, *The Administrative Court Judicial Review Guide* (August 2025, HM Courts & Tribunals Judiciary).

Juss S. and Sunkin M., (eds) *Landmark Cases in Public Law* (2017, Oxford: Hart Publishing).

Laws, J., *The Constitutional Balance* (2021, Oxford: Hart Publishing).

Nason, S., *Reconstructing Judicial Review* (2019, London: Bloomsbury).

Sedley, S., *Lions Under the Throne: Essays on the History of English Public Law* (2015, Cambridge: Cambridge University Press).

18

JUDICIAL REVIEW 2: THE GROUNDS OF JUDICIAL REVIEW

CENTRAL ISSUES

1. Judicial review operates through grounds developed by the courts rather than statutory codification. The absence of a fixed code means that grounds evolve through case law, with courts continuing to develop and refine principles. This chapter examines illegality and irrationality, two central grounds of review established by Lord Diplock in *GCHQ*.
2. Illegality requires decision-makers to understand their legal powers correctly and exercise them within statutory limits. This encompasses the obligation to exercise discretion rather than fetter it, to consider relevant factors while ignoring irrelevant ones, and to use powers only for their intended purposes. These principles ensure public authorities remain within the bounds of their statutory authority.
3. Irrationality permits courts to review decisions that no reasonable decision-maker could have reached. The *Wednesbury* test sets a deliberately high threshold, though academic and judicial criticism has questioned whether this standard provides adequate protection against arbitrary decision-making while remaining appropriately deferential to the government's discretionary powers.
4. Courts increasingly apply proportionality in human rights cases, raising questions about whether this more structured approach should replace *Wednesbury* unreasonableness in other contexts. This debate reflects broader constitutional tensions about the appropriate scope of judicial intervention in administrative decision-making and the relationship between legal and political accountability.

18.1 INTRODUCTION

Courts establish the grounds for reviewing the exercise of public functions through case law. The grounds derive from common law rather than statute, and Parliament has chosen not to codify them. The Independent Review of Administrative Law (IRAL) considered statutory codification but concluded that Parliament should not determine the scope of judicial oversight of government action, particularly where constitutional rights are involved.[1]

Lord Diplock's classification in *GCHQ* remains the standard framework for understanding judicial review grounds, despite subsequent doctrinal developments.[2]

Council of Civil Service Unions v Minister for the Civil Service
[1985] AC 374, 410–11

Lord Diplock

Judicial review has I think developed to a stage today when [. . .] one can conveniently classify under three heads the grounds on which administrative action is subject to control by judicial review. The first ground I would call 'illegality', the second 'irrationality' and the third 'procedural impropriety'. That is not to say that further development on a case by case basis may not in course of time add further grounds. I have in mind particularly the possible adoption in the future of the principle of 'proportionality' [. . .]

By 'illegality' [. . .] I mean that the decision-maker must understand correctly the law that regulates his decision-making power and must give effect to it. Whether he has or not is par excellence a justiciable question to be decided [. . . by judges . . .]

By 'irrationality' I mean what can by now be succinctly referred to as '*Wednesbury* unreasonableness' [see the *Wednesbury case* in the following section]. It applies to a decision which is so outrageous in its defiance of logic or of accepted moral standards that no sensible person who had applied his mind to the question to be decided could have arrived at it. [. . .] 'Irrationality' by now can stand on its own feet as an accepted ground on which a decision may be attacked by judicial review.

Since this judgment, the law has evolved, especially concerning the principles of illegality and irrationality. Lord Diplock's framework accommodates these developments, though specific arguments may span multiple grounds or resist neat categorisation. The three heads provide an analytical structure rather than rigid compartments.

18.2 ILLEGALITY: THERE MUST BE A LAWFUL EXERCISE OF DISCRETION

Lord Diplock explained that decision-makers '*must understand correctly the law that regulates his decision-making power and must give effect to it.*' Public authorities must operate within their legal powers and use those powers for the purposes Parliament intended. This includes several requirements: correctly understanding legal duties and powers, performing duties properly, and exercising discretion for proper purposes rather than extraneous considerations.

Parliament may impose duties requiring public authorities to act, or grant discretion allowing them to decide whether and how to act. Legislative language such as 'may' or 'think fit' generally indicates discretionary power. The scope varies from subjective discretion (where decision-makers may

[1] See Independent Review of Administrative Law, March 2021, paras 1.43; 3.17; 3.19; 3.34. For a discussion of the merits and disadvantages of codification in the light of codifications in other jurisdictions, see T.H. Jones, 'Judicial review and codification' (2000) 20 Legal Studies 517. Professor Jones concludes that codification would not be advantageous.

[2] For the background to the case, see Chapter 10, Section 10.2.6.1. For a very useful explanation of the grounds written for government officials see: *The Judge Over Your Shoulder* (JOYS) The Government Legal Department (GLD) 6th edn, 2022, London.

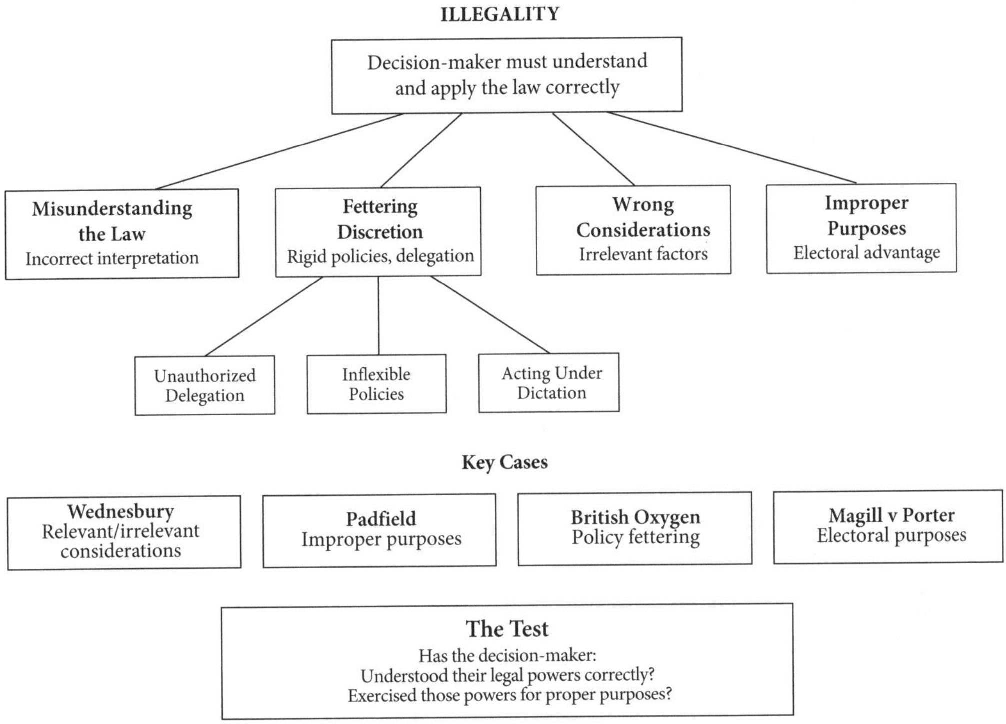

Figure 18.1 Types of illegality

act when 'satisfied' certain circumstances exist) to objective discretion (requiring that circumstances actually exist).

Discretion serves several purposes. It allows public bodies to adapt decisions to particular circumstances and changing conditions. It enables consideration of individual cases within broader policy frameworks. Parliament confers discretion on bodies it considers best placed to make particular decisions, which influences how courts approach judicial review of discretionary powers. Figure 18.1 outlines the main types of illegality.

18.2.1 THE *WEDNESBURY* CASE

In the early days of the cinema, 'picture houses', as they were then often known, were licensed by local authorities. Controversially, local authorities could allow picture houses to open on Sundays, but they had the freedom to impose '*such conditions as they thought fit*' (s. 1(1) of the Sunday Entertainments Act 1932). This broad discretion appeared to allow local authorities power to impose whatever conditions they considered desirable in the circumstances. In other words, it appeared to give councils complete or unfettered discretion.

Wednesbury Corporation granted the claimants a licence to open their cinema on Sundays, but, wanting to protect the moral welfare of children in its area, the Corporation imposed a condition that '*no children under the age of 15 years shall be admitted* [. . .] *whether accompanied by an adult or not*'.

The claimants feared that the condition would prevent families from going to the cinema on Sundays, making it uneconomic to open on that day, thereby undermining the value of the licence. They challenged the legality of the condition using two main arguments. First, they argued that, despite appearances, the local authority's discretion to impose conditions was not unfettered. In particular, it had to be used to further the purposes contemplated by the legislation by which it was conferred. The legislation concerned the licensing of cinemas, not the protection of children's moral welfare. The local authority had therefore used its power for reasons that were irrelevant in order to achieve purposes that were improper given the scope of the legislation.

Second, they argued that even if the authority could use its discretion to protect children's welfare, the condition imposed was unlawful because it was unreasonably wide. The moral welfare of children, they said, could be protected without a total exclusion of children from cinemas on Sundays: a narrower condition, such as requiring children to be accompanied by a parent or guardian, would have been just as effective and would have been less damaging to the plaintiffs.

The claimants lost their case. The Court of Appeal held that the local authority could take the moral welfare of children into account. In relation to the second argument, the court said it would have intervened if the condition had been so unreasonable that no reasonable authority could have imposed it. This, however, had not been established.

The decision, especially in relation to the second argument. has been cited over the years as an example of judicial restraint, and many commentators and judges have rightly said that judges should now be less cautious. Nonetheless, the following extract from Lord Greene MR's judgment contains a clear statement of principles that remain relevant and important to understand.

Associated Provincial Picture Houses Ltd v Wednesbury Corporation
[1948] 1 KB 223, 228

Lord Greene MR

[. . .] When [. . .] discretion is entrusted by Parliament to a body such as the local authority in this case, what appears to be an exercise of that discretion can only be challenged in the courts in a strictly limited class of case. As I have said, it must always be remembered that the court is not a court of appeal. When discretion of this kind is granted the law recognizes certain principles upon which that discretion must be exercised [. . .]. What then are those principles? They are well understood. [. . .] The exercise of [. . .] a discretion must be a real exercise of the discretion. If, in the statute conferring the discretion, there is to be found expressly or by implication matters which the authority exercising the discretion ought to have regard to, then in exercising the discretion it must have regard to those matters. Conversely, if the nature of the subject matter and the general interpretation of the Act make it clear that certain matters would not be germane to the matter in question, the authority must disregard those irrelevant collateral matters [. . .].

18.3 ILLEGALITY: FETTERING DISCRETION

Authorities granted discretionary power must exercise it themselves rather than surrender control to others. The obligation not to fetter discretion operates through several specific requirements:

- **Unauthorized delegation** is prohibited. Public bodies cannot transfer their decision-making power to other bodies without express statutory authorization. Parliament grants discretion to particular authorities because it considers them institutionally appropriate and democratically accountable for those decisions.

- **Rigid policies** that prevent individual consideration are unlawful. While authorities may adopt policies to guide decision-making, they must remain willing to depart from them when circumstances warrant different treatment. Policies become unlawful fetters when they operate as inflexible rules that preclude consideration of individual cases.
- **Acting under dictation** violates the obligation to exercise independent judgement. Authorities may properly consider the views of other bodies, central government, or interest groups, but cannot treat themselves as bound by such views.[3] The decision must ultimately rest with the body granted the discretion.

These requirements ensure that discretionary powers are exercised by the institutions Parliament intended, for the purposes Parliament contemplated, with appropriate consideration of individual circumstances.

18.4 ILLEGALITY: PERMITTED DELEGATION

While authorities cannot surrender their discretion to others through unauthorized delegation, the law recognises practical realities of modern administration. Large organizations cannot function if every decision requires personal attention from the named decision-maker. The law has developed different approaches to address this tension between legal principle and administrative necessity

The obligation not to delegate unlawfully raises important practical issues for large organizations such as local authorities or UK government departments. Legislation is drafted to place powers and duties on 'the authority' or 'the Secretary of State', but it would not be feasible for a full meeting of all elected councillors (in the case of local authorities) or a government minister personally to make every decision. The law therefore recognizes these realities.

In relation to local authorities, s. 101(1) of the Local Government Act 1972 provides that '*a local authority may arrange for the discharge of any of their functions—(a) by a committee, a sub-committee or an officer of the authority [. . .]*'. Every local authority adopts a 'scheme of delegation' that specifies by whom, within a local authority, a statutory power may be exercised. A failure to follow a scheme of delegation is unlawful and may be challenged by judicial review.

The approach to ministerial powers is quite different. The courts have simply recognised that while a minister may be formally responsible and accountable for the legal exercise of powers, in practice, the vast majority of decisions are taken by civil servants. There is, however, no need for a scheme of delegation to be adopted in each department. This is because of a principle referred to as the '*Carltona* doctrine', after the decision in *Carltona Ltd v Commissioner of Works*.[4] The Commissioners for Works, a central government department, had the power to requisition land (to demand that owners of land give up control of their land) '*if it appears necessary or expedient to do so*'. Although the power had been given to the Commissioners, in practice, decisions to requisition were made by officials. The Court of Appeal held that this was entirely lawful.

In the following extract, Lord Greene MR provides the classic statement of the principle.

[3] *Lavender v Ministry of Housing and Local Government* [1970] 1 WLR 1231.

[4] [1943] 2 All ER 560. Although widely referred to as a 'doctrine' it may be more accurate to refer to it as a 'principle'.

Carltona Ltd v Commissioner of Works
[1943] 2 All ER 560, 563

Lord Greene MR

In the administration of government in this country the functions which are given to ministers [. . .] are functions so multifarious that no minister could ever personally attend to them. To take the example of the present case no doubt there have been thousands of requisitions in this country by individual ministers. It cannot be supposed that this regulation meant that, in each case, the minister in person should direct his mind to the matter. The duties imposed upon ministers and the powers given to ministers are normally exercised under the authority of the ministers by responsible officials of the department. Public business could not be carried on if that were not the case. Constitutionally, the decision of such an official is, of course, the decision of the minister. The minister is responsible. It is he who must answer before Parliament for anything that his officials have done under his authority, and, if for an important matter he selected an official of such junior standing that he could not be expected competently to perform the work, the minister would have to answer for that in Parliament. The whole system of departmental organisation and administration is based on the view that ministers, being responsible to Parliament, will see that important duties are committed to experienced officials. If they do not do that, Parliament is the place where complaint must be made against them.

Although the Carltona principle is widely used, it is not always applicable. The principle reflects constitutional assumptions about ministerial accountability that may seem outdated in modern government—ministers rarely resign over civil service errors, and parliamentary scrutiny provides limited control over routine administrative decisions. Despite these concerns, the principle remains essential for government to function.

The principle's limits are significant. Courts examine the nature of the power, the level of official exercising it, and any statutory indications about personal exercise. In *ex p Oladehinde*,[5] the House of Lords held that even decisions affecting individual liberty could be delegated to civil servants, but emphasized that the seniority of the official should match the decision's importance. However, some powers are too significant to delegate. In *R v Adams (Northern Ireland)*,[6] the Supreme Court held that where the Secretary of State had been given power to imprison someone without trial, possibly for an indefinite period, that decision could not be delegated but had to be taken by the Secretary of State personally because of its 'momentous' nature.[7]

18.5 ILLEGALITY: FETTERING DISCRETION BY TREATING POLICIES AS BINDING

Public bodies routinely adopt policies to guide decision-making and achieve consistency.[8] A local authority with discretion to provide grants to shop owners might establish policies on the proportion of the costs to be funded, eligible streets, and application criteria. Such policies promote transparency and help officials make decisions fairly across similar cases.

[5] *R v Secretary of State for the Home Department, ex parte Oladehinde* [1991] 1 AC 254.
[6] [2020] UKSC 19.
[7] Ibid, esp. Lord Kerr at [38].
[8] See further C. Hilson, 'Judicial review, policies and the fettering of discretion' [2002] *Public Law* 111.

Policies remain lawful provided they meet certain requirements. The policy itself must be legal and, where published policies exist, unpublished internal guidance must not contradict them.[9] Most importantly, authorities must retain the willingness to depart from established policies where individual circumstances justify different treatment.[10]

The balance between consistency and flexibility was explained in *Venables*:

R v Secretary of State for the Home Department, ex parte Venables
[1998] AC 407, 497

Lord Browne-Wilkinson

When Parliament confers a discretionary power exercisable from time to time over a period, such power must be exercised on each occasion in the light of the circumstances at that time. In consequence, the person on whom the power is conferred cannot fetter the future exercise of his discretion by committing himself now as to the way in which he will exercise his power in the future. [. . .]

These considerations do not preclude the person on whom the power is conferred from developing and applying a policy as to the approach which he will adopt in the generality of cases [. . .] But the position is different if the policy adopted is such as to preclude the person on whom the power is conferred from departing from the policy or from taking into account circumstances which are relevant to the particular case in relation to which the discretion is being exercised. If such an inflexible and invariable policy is adopted, both the policy and the decisions taken pursuant to it will be unlawful.

British Oxygen Co. Ltd v Minister of Technology[11] is a leading decision on this issue. The Board of Trade had the discretion to grant funds to help firms with their capital expenditure. It adopted a policy not to pay grants for individual items costing less than £25. BOC spent £4 million buying new gas cylinders and applied for a grant. Its application was turned down on the basis that, despite the overall sum involved, each cylinder cost less than £25 and it would have been contrary to the Board's policy to confer a grant. The BOC unsuccessfully challenged the decision, arguing that the Board had applied its policy without considering the merits of its application. While this argument failed on the facts of the case, Lord Reid set out the key principles.

British Oxygen Co. Ltd v Minister of Technology
[1971] AC 610, 625

Lord Reid

In this Act Parliament has clearly laid down the conditions for eligibility for grants and it has clearly given to the Board a discretion so that the Board is not bound to pay to every person who is eligible to receive a grant. [. . .] It was argued on the authority of *Rex v Port of London Authority, Ex parte Kynoch Ltd.* [1919] 1 K.B. 176 that the Minister is not entitled to make a rule for himself as to how he will in future exercise his discretion. [. . .] The general rule is that anyone who has to exercise a statutory discretion must not

[9] See *Walumba Lumba v Secretary of State for the Home Department* [2011] UKSC 12.

[10] An exception is that the executive may be permitted to apply policy in a rigid manner when using prerogative powers: see *R (on the application of Sandiford) v The Secretary of State for Foreign and Commonwealth Affairs* [2014] UKSC 44 (see Chapter 10).

[11] [1971] AC 610.

> 'shut his ears to an application' [. . .] There may be cases where an officer or authority ought to listen to a substantial argument reasonably presented urging a change of policy. What the authority must not do is to refuse to listen at all. But a Ministry or large authority may have had to deal already with a multitude of similar applications and then they will almost certainly have evolved a policy so precise that it could well be called a rule. There can be no objection to that, provided the authority is always willing to listen to anyone with something new to say [. . .].

The key principle is that policies provide guidance rather than binding rules. Authorities must remain open to arguments that individual cases warrant departure from established policy, or that the policy itself requires reconsideration.

18.6 ILLEGALITY: RELEVANT AND IRRELEVANT CONSIDERATIONS AND IMPROPER PURPOSES

In *Wednesbury*, the legislation had not specifically set out the purposes to be achieved or the factors to be considered. These matters were determined by the judges by interpreting the legislation to work out Parliament's intention. A similar set of issues arose in the constitutionally more important context of judicial review of executive powers in *Padfield v Ministry of Agriculture, Fisheries and Food*,[12] one of the most important landmark decisions in modern judicial review. In this case, the House of Lords confirmed that members of the executive do not have unfettered discretion, even when their legislative powers appear unrestricted.

18.6.1 *PADFIELD V MINISTRY OF AGRICULTURE, FISHERIES AND FOOD*

The case arose out of a scheme designed to ensure that milk was available across the country at a broadly level cost. It involved farmers selling their milk to the Milk Marketing Board for a price set centrally, which could vary by region. The Milk Marketing Act 1958 provided for the establishment of a committee of investigation to look into disputes arising from the scheme. Section 19 of the Act said that disputes could be referred to a committee '*if the Minister in any case so directs*'. The section also gave the minister power to amend the scheme '*if he thinks fit to do so after considering*' a report of the committee.

Milk producers in the south-east of England complained that the pricing policy treated them unfairly, because it meant that they would be paid less for their milk than producers in other parts of the country. They therefore asked the minister to refer their complaint to an investigative committee. He refused to do so. His decision letter said that the matter was not suited for an investigation because it '*raised wide issues*'. It also indicated the minister's belief that he would be required to alter the scheme if the committee upheld the complaint. He was not prepared to do this, in part because it would be politically embarrassing.

[12] [1968] AC 997. See further, S. Juss and M. Sunkin (eds) *Landmark Cases in Public Law* (2017, Oxford: Hart Publishing), ch. 3. See also M. Sunkin, 'Judges and Parliamentary Democracy: The Lessons of *Padfield v Ministry of Agriculture, Fisheries and Food*', in T.T. Arvind, R, Kirkham, Daithi Mac Sitigh, and L. Stirton (eds), *Executive Decision-Making and the Courts: Revisiting the Origins of Modern Judicial Review* (2021, Oxford: Hart Publishing), ch. 4.

The producers applied for a mandamus (now a mandating order) to force the minister to refer their complaint. The minister responded by arguing that the legislation gave him complete discretion in the matter. In response to the claim that he had based his decision on irrelevant factors, he argued that since he was under no obligation to give reasons for his decision, he could not be found to have acted improperly on the basis of reasons that he had voluntarily given.

The majority of the House of Lords (Lord Morris dissenting) rejected the minister's arguments. It held that the minister had misconstrued his legal powers and acted for reasons that were irrelevant to the purposes of the legislation.

Padfield v Ministry of Agriculture, Fisheries and Food
[1968] AC 997, 1030–3

Lord Reid

The question at issue in this appeal is the nature and extent of the Minister's duty under . . . [the Act] . . . in deciding whether to refer to the committee of investigation a complaint as to the operation of any scheme made by persons adversely affected by the scheme. The respondent contends that his only duty is to consider a complaint fairly and that he is given an unfettered discretion with regard to every complaint either to refer it or not to refer it to the committee as he may think fit. The appellants contend that it is his duty to refer every genuine and substantial complaint, or alternatively that his discretion is not unfettered and that in this case he failed to exercise his discretion according to law because his refusal was caused or influenced by his having misdirected himself in law or by his having taken into account extraneous or irrelevant considerations.

In my view, the appellants' first contention goes too far. There are a number of reasons which would justify the Minister in refusing to refer a complaint. For example, he might consider it more suitable for arbitration, or he might consider that in an earlier case the committee of investigation had already rejected a substantially similar complaint, or he might think the complaint to be frivolous or vexatious. So he must have at least some measure of discretion. But is it unfettered?

[. . .] Parliament must have conferred the discretion with the intention that it should be used to promote the policy and objects of the Act, the policy and objects of the Act must be determined by construing the Act as a whole and construction is always a matter of law for the court. In a matter of this kind it is not possible to draw a hard and fast line, but if the Minister, by reason of his having misconstrued the Act or for any other reason, so uses his discretion as to thwart or run counter to the policy and objects of the Act, then our law would be very defective if persons aggrieved were not entitled to the protection of the court.

[. . .]

I must now examine the Minister's reasons for refusing to refer the appellants' complaint to the committee. [. . .]

Paragraph 3 of the letter of May 1, 1964, refers to the possibility that, if the complaint were referred and the committee were to uphold it, the Minister 'would be expected to make a statutory Order to give effect to the committee's recommendations.' If this means that he is entitled to refuse to refer a complaint because, if he did so, he might later find himself in an embarrassing situation, that would plainly be a bad reason. [. . .]

It was argued that the Minister is not bound to give any reasons for refusing to refer a complaint to the committee, that if he gives no reasons his decision cannot be questioned, and that it would be very unfortunate if giving reasons were to put him in a worse position. But I do not agree that a decision cannot be questioned if no reasons are given. If it is the Minister's duty not to act so as to frustrate the policy and objects of the Act, and if it were to appear from all the circumstances of the case that that has been the effect of the Minister's refusal, then it appears to me that the court must be entitled to act.

Lord Upjohn (at 1062)

[. . . I]f [the minister] does not give any reason for his decision it may be, if circumstances warrant it, that a court may be at liberty to come to the conclusion that he had no good reason for reaching that conclusion and order a prerogative writ to issue accordingly.

Following the decision, the minister established a committee. In due course, it upheld the complaint, as he had feared it would. The saga ended, however, when the minister told the House of Commons that he refused to accept the committee's decision and that he would not alter the pricing scheme.

QUESTIONS

1. What is the basic principle enunciated by Lord Reid in *Padfield*?
2. '*Discretionary powers conferred by Parliament can never be unfettered and purely subjective. They must always be exercised in accordance with the law*'. Explain this statement. Is the statement applicable in all circumstances? Consider a similarly wide discretion to take 'such steps as the minister considers necessary' in a (hypothetical) National Emergency Act.
3. Can it be argued that, in the *Padfield* case, the unfettered discretion of the minister became the unfettered discretion of the judges?
4. 'The outcome of the *Padfield* case confirms that judicial review is concerned with the process of decision-making and not the merits of governmental decisions. The decision delayed government, but it did not prevent it from doing what it wanted. Only political accountability could do this. This is how it should be'. Discuss.

18.6.2 WHERE LEGISLATION SPECIFIES FACTORS TO BE TAKEN INTO ACCOUNT

The *Wednesbury* and *Padfield* decisions concerned discretionary powers that were not expressly limited by the legislation. However, legislation often makes it clear that discretion must be exercised for particular reasons, or that public bodies must take account of certain factors.

Equality Act 2010

149 Public sector equality duty

1) A public authority must, in the exercise of its functions, have due regard to the need to—
   (a) eliminate discrimination, harassment, victimisation and any other conduct that is prohibited by or under this Act;
   (b) advance equality of opportunity between persons who share a relevant protected characteristic and persons who do not share it;
   (c) foster good relations between persons who share a relevant protected characteristic and persons who do not share it.

[. . .]

What exactly does the duty to have 'due regard' mean? The question was raised in a case supported by the Public Law Project (PLP, a national charity concerned with improving access to public law remedies) against the London Borough of Hammersmith and Fulham concerning similar wording in the Disability Discrimination Act 1995. The authority had previously decided to cut its council tax by 3 per cent. This inevitably meant that the council had less money to spend. As a result, it decided to charge disabled people for non-residential home-care services. The PLP challenged this decision, arguing, *inter alia*, that the authority had failed to have due regard for the need to take into account the needs of disabled persons. The challenge failed because the authority satisfied the court that it had properly taken into account its responsibilities under the legislation when making its decision. However, the court stressed that the duty to have '*due regard*' was a substantive requirement and not simply a matter of form.

R (Domb and Ors) v Hammersmith and Fulham London Borough Council
[2009] EWCA Civ 941

Rix LJ

52. [The cases show that . . .] the test of whether a decision maker has had due regard is a test of the substance of the matter, not of mere form or box-ticking, and that the duty must be performed with vigour and with an open mind; and that it is a non-delegable duty.

18.6.3 EXERCISING POWERS FOR IMPROPER PURPOSES

The cases so far discussed have concerned specific statutory powers. But the courts will also apply similar principles to impose broader obligations on public authorities. In *Magill v Porter*, for example, the House of Lords held that local authorities have a general obligation to act in the public interest and that powers cannot be used to serve the interests of the ruling political group. In this case, the Conservative-controlled local authority decided to use its statutory powers to sell its housing stock in a way that was intended to help the Conservatives win the next local election.

Magill v Porter; Magill v Weeks
[2001] UKHL 67

Lord Bingham

21. [. . .] Elected politicians of course wish to act in a manner which will commend them and their party (when, as is now usual, they belong to one) to the electorate. Such an ambition is the life blood of democracy and a potent spur to responsible decision-taking and administration. Councillors do not act improperly or unlawfully if, exercising public powers for a public purpose for which such powers were conferred, they hope that such exercise will earn the gratitude and support of the electorate and thus strengthen their electoral position. The law would indeed part company with the realities of party politics if it were to hold otherwise. But a public power is not exercised lawfully if it is exercised not for a public purpose for which the power was conferred but in order to promote the electoral advantage of a political party. The power at issue in the present case is s 32 of the Housing Act 1985, which conferred on local authorities the power to dispose of land held by them subject to conditions specified in the Act. Thus a local authority could dispose of its property, subject to the provisions of the Act, to promote any public purpose for which such power was conferred, but could not lawfully do so for the purpose of promoting the electoral advantage of any party represented on the council.

18.7 'IRRATIONALITY' OR '*WEDNESBURY* UNREASONABLENESS'

In the *Wednesbury* case, Lord Greene MR distinguished between two senses of unreasonableness. He explained that, on the one hand, the term may be used as '*a general description of the things that may not be done*'. In this sense, it would cover the grounds that we have already discussed. He went on to explain, however, that unreasonableness may also be used in a more specific way to refer to decisions that are 'absurd'.

Associated Provincial Picture Houses Ltd v Wednesbury Corporation
[1948] 1 KB 223, 229

Lord Greene MR

It is true the discretion must be exercised reasonably. Now what does that mean? [. . .] It has frequently been used and is frequently used as a general description of the things that must not be done. [. . .] Similarly, there may be something so absurd that no sensible person could ever dream that it lay within the powers of the authority. Warrington L.J. in *Short v Poole Corporation*[13] gave the example of the red-haired teacher, dismissed because she had red hair. That is unreasonable in one sense. In another sense it is taking into consideration extraneous matters. It is so unreasonable that it might almost be described as being done in bad faith; and, in fact, all these things run into one another [. . .]. It is true to say that, if a decision on a competent matter is so unreasonable that no reasonable authority could ever have come to it, then the courts can interfere. That, I think, is quite right; but to prove a case of that kind would require something overwhelming, and, in this case, the facts do not come anywhere near anything of that kind.

In the *GCHQ* case, Lord Diplock preferred to speak about 'irrationality', a term which he said '*applies to a decision which is so outrageous in its defiance of logic or of accepted moral standards that no sensible person who had applied his mind to the question to be decided could have arrived at it*'.

Whether we use the expression 'unreasonableness' or 'irrationality', this head of challenge recognises that courts can review the substance of decisions and are not limited to reviewing the process by which decisions are taken, although both Lord Greene and Lord Diplock conceived of this head of review as being limited to an exceptional class of case in which it could be shown that the public authority had very obviously stepped outside the range of decisions that it could reasonably make. Over the years, significant criticisms have been made of *Wednesbury* unreasonableness, both in academic commentaries and in judgments. The attack was led by Professor Jowell and Anthony Lester QC.

J. Jowell and A. Lester, 'Beyond Wednesbury: Substantive principles of administrative law'
[1987] *Public Law* 368, 371–2 (footnotes omitted)

We suggest that [the present *Wednesbury* unreasonableness test] it is unsatisfactory for three reasons. First, it is inadequate. The incantation of the word 'unreasonable' simply does not provide sufficient justification for judicial intervention. Intellectual honesty requires a further and better explanation as to

[13] [1926] Ch. 66, 90, 91.

why the act is unreasonable. The reluctance to articulate a principled justification naturally encourages suspicion that prejudice or policy considerations may be hiding underneath *Wednesbury's* ample cloak.

Secondly, the context of Wednesbury unreasonableness is unrealistic. Attempting as it does to avoid judicial intervention in the merits of decisions assigned to officials, it seeks to prevent review except in cases where the official has behaved absurdly or has 'taken leave of his senses.' In practice, however, the courts are willing to impugn decisions that are far from absurd and are indeed often coldly rational. Were the courts only to interfere with decisions verging on the insane, a zone of immunity would be drawn around many oppressive or improper decisions that are in reality vulnerable to judicial review. And public authorities which had taken leave of their senses could use the language of rationality to circumvent judicial review.

Thirdly, the Wednesbury test is confusing, because it is tautologous. It allows the courts to interfere with decisions that are unreasonable, and then defines an unreasonable decision as one which no reasonable authority would take. [. . .] One can understand that Lord Greene's definition of unreasonableness sought to make the judges think twice about interfering with the merits of official decisions, but a test which requires the official action not to be ordinarily reasonable, but only, in effect, extremely unreasonable, is unhelpful as a practical guide.

Judges have also been critical. Indeed, some have questioned whether *Wednesbury* was wrongly decided from the outset.

R v Secretary of State for the Home Department, ex parte Daly

[2001] UKHL 26

Lord Cooke of Thorndon

32. [. . .] I think that the day will come when it will be more widely recognised that [*Wednesbury*] was an unfortunately retrogressive decision in English administrative law, insofar as it suggested that there are degrees of unreasonableness and that only a very extreme degree can bring an administrative decision within the legitimate scope of judicial invalidation.

When the *Wednesbury* principle was first set out, it was intended to catch decisions that were so obviously outrageous that the decision fell outside the range of lawful decisions available to a public authority. In other words, situations where decisions were clearly unlawful without the need to consider whether they were tarnished by 'illegality'. In the years since, the courts have made the Wednesbury test more elaborate by positing a sliding scale of scenarios, with courts taking different approaches depending on where a case falls along that scale.

At one end are cases involving decisions by public authorities that affect fundamental rights or interests. In a 1996 case in which four members of the armed forces challenged the Ministry of Defence's blanket policy of dismissing any member discovered to be gay, Sir Thomas Bingham MR (as he then was) held that '*the more substantial the interference with human rights, the more the court will require by justification before it is satisfied that the decision is reasonable*'.[14] Note that Bingham suggests a presumption that decisions that infringe human rights are unreasonable, and that it is for the

[14] *R v Ministry of Defence, Ex p Smith* [1996] QB 517. The service personnel lost their judicial review in England, but secured victory in a subsequent application to the European Court of Human Rights, which forced the Ministry of Defence to change its policy.

authority to justify its actions as reasonable. This is very different to the situation envisaged by Lord Greene in *Wednesbury* when he made it clear that there is an 'overwhelming' burden *on claimants* to show unreasonableness. Since the HRA came into force, human rights cases have been approached not as *Wednesbury* unreasonableness cases, but instead using the proportionality test required by the European Convention on Human Rights (ECHR), so that infringements of human rights must be shown by the public authority to be proportionate.[15]

At one end of the scale are human rights cases; at the other are situations in which the decision under challenge involves broad policy or political judgements, for example, about setting levels of public expenditure or taxation. In such scenarios, the courts may decide not to intervene on the grounds that the matter is non-justiciable and not for the courts. If they do intervene, they are likely to apply only a 'light touch' review, intervening only where the public authority or minister has '*taken leave of his senses*'.[16]

In the middle of the scale are cases that do not directly involve human rights infringements or broader policy issues. In such situations, there has been much debate about whether the courts should continue to apply a *Wednesbury* approach or move beyond *Wednesbury* and use a proportionality test as in human rights cases.

18.8 PROPORTIONALITY

Proportionality requires balancing the public interest served by a decision against its impact on affected individuals. The means used must be no more restrictive than necessary to achieve the legitimate objective.

18.8.1 THE DEVELOPMENT OF PROPORTIONALITY (*GCHQ* TO *DALY*)

As we noted, in the mid-1980s in the *GCHQ* case, Lord Diplock suggested that proportionality might be growing into a separate ground of review. The courts have come to use proportionality in light of the requirements of European Union law and human rights law, although they have been reluctant to adopt it as a ground of review when rights issues are not involved.[17]

The difference between the *Wednesbury* and proportionality approaches was explained by Lord Steyn in *R v Secretary of State for the Home Department, ex parte Daly*. Daly, a long-term prisoner, challenged the legality of the Home Secretary's blanket policy that authorized cell searches in prisons and the examination of correspondence between prisoners and their legal advisers, in the absence of the prisoners. The House of Lords, reversing the Court of Appeal, held that the blanket policy infringed Daly's common law right to legal professional privilege. It also held that the infringement was disproportionate because it was greater than could be shown to be justified (for example, it was not always necessary to exclude prisoners during searches). In delivering his judgment, Lord Steyn 'clarified' (and effectively overruled) one of the very early judgements of the Court of Appeal under the HRA. Lord Phillips of Worth Matravers MR had said, in *R v Secretary of State for the Home Department, ex parte Mahmood*,[18] that the British courts should use '*anxious scrutiny*' irrationality as the test when reviewing whether one of the qualified Convention rights had been breached.

[15] See Chapter 21.

[16] *R v Secretary of State for the Environment, ex parte Nottinghamshire County Council* [1986] AC 240, 247–8, *per* Lord Scarman.

[17] See further Chapter 21. [18] [2001] 1 WLR 840.

R v Secretary of State for the Home Department, ex parte Daly
[2001] UKHL 26

Lord Steyn

26. The explanation of the Master of the Rolls [in *Mahmood*] requires clarification. It is couched in language reminiscent of the traditional *Wednesbury* ground of review [. . .] and in particular the adaptation of that test in terms of heightened scrutiny in cases involving fundamental rights as formulated in *R v Ministry of Defence, Ex p Smith*. There is a material difference between the Wednesbury and Smith grounds of review and the approach of proportionality applicable in respect of review where convention rights are at stake.

27. The contours of the principle of proportionality are familiar. In *de Freitas v Permanent Secretary of Ministry of Agriculture, Fisheries, Lands and Housing* [1999] 1 AC 69 [. . . T]he Privy Council adopted a three stage test. Lord Clyde observed, at p. 80 [. . .] that in determining whether a limitation (by an act, rule or decision) is arbitrary or excessive the court should ask itself:

> whether: (i) the legislative objective is sufficiently important to justify limiting a fundamental right; (ii) the measures designed to meet the legislative objective are rationally connected to it; and (iii) the means used to impair the right or freedom are no more than is necessary to accomplish the objective.

Clearly, these criteria are more precise and more sophisticated than the traditional grounds of review. What is the difference for the disposal of concrete cases? Academic public lawyers have in remarkably similar terms elucidated the difference between the traditional grounds of review and the proportionality approach: [he cites the work of Professors Jeffrey Jowell, Paul Craig, and David Feldman]. The starting point is that there is an overlap between the traditional grounds of review and the approach of proportionality. Most cases would be decided in the same way whichever approach is adopted. But the intensity of review is somewhat greater under the proportionality approach. [. . .] I would mention three concrete differences without suggesting that my statement is exhaustive. First, the doctrine of proportionality may require the reviewing court to assess the balance which the decision maker has struck, not merely whether it is within the range of rational or reasonable decisions. Secondly, the proportionality test may go further than the traditional grounds of review inasmuch as it may require attention to be directed to the relative weight accorded to interests and considerations. Thirdly, even the heightened scrutiny test developed in *R v Ministry of Defence, Ex p Smith* [. . .] is not necessarily appropriate to the protection of human rights. It will be recalled that in *Smith* the Court of Appeal reluctantly felt compelled to reject a limitation on homosexuals in the army. The challenge based on art 8 [ECHR . . .] foundered on the threshold required even by the anxious scrutiny test. The European Court of Human Rights came to the opposite conclusion: *Smith and Grady v United Kingdom* (1999) 29 EHRR 493. The court concluded, at p. 543, para. 138:

> the threshold at which the High Court and the Court of Appeal could find the Ministry of Defence policy irrational was placed so high that it effectively excluded any consideration by the domestic courts of the question of whether the interference with the applicants' rights answered a pressing social need or was proportionate to the national security and public order aims pursued, principles which lie at the heart of the court's analysis of complaints under article 8 of the Convention.

In other words, the intensity of the review, in similar cases, is guaranteed by the twin requirements that the limitation of the right was necessary in a democratic society, in the sense of meeting a pressing social need, and the question whether the interference was really proportionate to the legitimate aim being pursued.

28. The differences in approach between the traditional grounds of review and the proportionality approach may therefore sometimes yield different results. It is therefore important that cases involving convention rights must be analysed in the correct way. This does not mean that there has been a shift to merits review. On the contrary, as Professor Jowell [2000] PL 671, 681 has pointed out the respective roles of judges and administrators are fundamentally distinct and will remain so [. . .].

Note that Lord Steyn stresses that adopting a proportionality approach does not *'mean that there has been a shift to merits review'*. This is extremely important given that judicial review is not about the merits of decisions: whether decisions are right or wrong, good or bad. It is not for unelected judges to intervene in public decision-making because they dislike or disagree with the decision. Judicial review is about whether public authorities have the legal power to act as they have acted. Some argue that because proportionality requires judges to look closely at how decisions are made—including how various factors are considered and weighed—that it inevitably draws judges into the substance of decision-making and therefore the merits of decisions. Lord Steyn is at pains to say that this is not the case, but not everyone is convinced.

Certainly, the decision in *Daly* reinforced calls both among academics and some judges to extend the proportionality test beyond cases involving rights issues. The Court of Appeal in the *R (Association of British Civilian Internees: Far East Region) v Secretary of State for Defence* set out some strong reasons why proportionality should replace *Wednesbury* unreasonableness in cases in which a court has to consider whether the balance struck between public and individual interests was lawfully struck. But, as you will see, it did not see this as something that could be achieved by the Court of Appeal.

R (Association of British Civilian Internees: Far East Region) v Secretary of State for Defence
[2003] EWCA Civ 473

Dyson LJ

34. [. . .] It seems to us that the case for [recognizing a proportionality requirement beyond Convention rights issues] is indeed a strong one. As Lord Slynn points out, trying to keep the *Wednesbury* principle and proportionality in separate compartments is unnecessary and confusing. The criteria of proportionality are more precise and sophisticated: see Lord Steyn in the *Daly case* [. . .] It is true that sometimes proportionality may require the reviewing court to assess for itself the balance that has been struck by the decision-maker, and that may produce a different result from one that would be arrived at on an application of the *Wednesbury* test. [. . .] The *Wednesbury* test is moving closer to proportionality and in some cases it is not possible to see any daylight between the two tests [. . .] Although we did not hear argument on the point, we have difficulty in seeing what justification there now is for retaining the *Wednesbury* test. [. . .]

35. But we consider that it is not for this court to perform its burial rites. [. . .]

The burial rites were not performed by the House of Lords[19] and have yet to be performed by the UK Supreme Court, although there have been indications that proportionality could be accepted as a general ground of judicial review.

[19] See *Docherty and ors v Birmingham City Council* [2008] UKHL 57, [134]–[135], *per* Lord Mance.

18.8.2 EXTENSION BEYOND CONVENTION RIGHTS (*PHAM, UNISON, KENNEDY*)

In *Pham*,[20] three Supreme Court judges[21] endorsed Professor Craig's view[22] that reasonableness review and proportionality both involve considerations of weight and balance, with the intensity of scrutiny varying according to context. This suggests the tests may not be as distinct as often supposed. Lord Reed observed that: '*where Parliament authorises significant interferences with important legal rights, the courts may interpret the legislation as requiring that any such interference should be no greater than is objectively established to be necessary to achieve the legitimate aim of the interference: in substance, a requirement of proportionality*'.[23]

The *UNISON* case illustrates this development.[24] The Supreme Court invalidated employment tribunal fees that hindered access to justice, applying an analysis that resembled proportionality review. Lord Reed emphasized that courts exist to ensure that laws are properly applied and enforced, and that individuals have unimpeded access to them.[25] The decision regarded access to justice as a constitutional principle rather than an ordinary public service, requiring clear statutory wording before Parliament would be deemed to have authorised such interference.

R (UNISON) v Lord Chancellor
[2017] UKSC 51

Lord Reed

[68] At the heart of the concept of the rule of law is the idea that society is governed by law. Parliament exists primarily in order to make laws for society in this country. Democratic procedures exist primarily in order to ensure that the Parliament which makes those laws includes Members of Parliament who are chosen by the people of this country and are accountable to them. Courts exist in order to ensure that the laws made by Parliament, and the common law created by the courts themselves, are applied and enforced. That role includes ensuring that the executive branch of government carries out its functions in accordance with the law. In order for the courts to perform that role, people must in principle have unimpeded access to them. Without such access, laws are liable to become a dead letter, the work done by Parliament may be rendered nugatory, and the democratic election of Members of Parliament may become a meaningless charade. That is why the courts do not merely provide a public service like any other.

Courts will apply strict scrutiny when government action interferes with fundamental constitutional rights, even beyond the Convention rights context. Where common law rights are involved, courts may require that interference is no greater than necessary to achieve legitimate objectives.

Kennedy v Charity Commission examined how proportionality might apply to common law rights in domestic contexts. Lord Mance's judgment articulates a key argument regarding the proper starting point for legal analysis in rights cases:

[20] *Pham v Secretary of State for the Home Office* [2015] UKSC 19.
[21] Lord Carnwath, at [60]; Lord Mance, at [98]; Lord Sumption at [108]–[109].
[22] P. Craig, 'The nature of reasonableness' (2013) 66 *Current Legal Problems* 131.
[23] *Pham v Secretary of State for the Home Department* [2015] UKSC 19, [119].
[24] *R (UNISON) v Lord Chancellor* [2017] UKSC 51.
[25] *R (UNISON) v Lord Chancellor* [2017] UKSC 51 [68], per Lord Reed.

Kennedy v Charity Commission
[2014] UKSC 20

[46] Since the passing of the Human Rights Act 1998, there has too often been a tendency to see the law in areas touched on by the Convention solely in terms of the Convention rights. But the Convention rights represent a threshold protection; and, especially in view of the contribution which common lawyers made to the Convention's inception, they may be expected, at least generally even if not always, to reflect and to find their homologue in the common or domestic statute law. Not surprisingly, therefore, Lord Goff of Chieveley in *Attorney General v Guardian Newspapers Ltd* (No 2) [1990] 1 AC 109, 282–284 and the House in *Derbyshire County Council v The Times Newspapers Ltd* [1993] AC 534, 551E both expressed the view that in the field of freedom of speech there was no difference in principle between English law and article 10. In some areas, the common law may go further than the Convention, and in some contexts it may also be inspired by the Convention rights and jurisprudence (the protection of privacy being a notable example). And in time, of course, a synthesis may emerge. But the natural starting point in any dispute is to start with domestic law, and it is certainly not to focus exclusively on the Convention rights, without surveying the wider common law scene. As Toulson LJ also said in the *Guardian News and Media* case, para 88: 'The development of the common law did not come to an end on the passing of the Human Rights Act 1998. It is in vigorous health and flourishing in many parts of the world which share a common legal tradition'. Greater focus in domestic litigation on the domestic legal position might also have the incidental benefit that less time was taken in domestic courts seeking to interpret and reconcile different judgements (often only given by individual sections of the European Court of Human Rights) in a way which that Court itself, not being bound by any doctrine of precedent, would not itself undertake.

Lord Mance's analysis establishes several principles for understanding the interaction between common law and Convention rights. Convention rights provide minimum rather than maximum protections. The common law may provide more extensive safeguards than the Convention requires, as seen in areas like access to justice. A growing synthesis is developing between common law and Convention jurisprudence, with each system influencing the other. Courts should commence their analysis with domestic law rather than immediately turning to Convention rights. Lord Toulson similarly warned against allowing the Human Rights Act to render the common law an 'ossuary'.[26] These observations in *Kennedy* demonstrate how the Supreme Court approaches rights protection through domestic constitutional principles while recognising the complementary role of Convention jurisprudence. The decision reflects a broader judicial philosophy that centuries of common law development should not be abandoned but should evolve alongside Convention principles.

Although cases like *Kennedy* exemplify '*the common law's emphatic reassertion in recent years of the importance of constitutional rights*',[27] their broader applicability should not be overstated. Richard Clayton argues that the structural weaknesses of common law rights (their identification remains contestable and their status uncertain) means that '*common law rights cannot on current principles present replicate the positive rights created by the HRA*'.[28] As he observes:

[26] [2014] UKSC 20 [133].
[27] *D v Secretary of State for the Home Department* [2005] EWCA Civ 38; [2006 1 W.L.R. 1003 at 130], per Brooke LJ.
[28] R. Clayton, 'The Empire Strikes Back: common law rights and the Human Rights Act' [2015] *Public Law* 3–12, 4.

Richard Clayton QC, 'The Empire Strikes Back: common law rights and the Human Rights Act' [2015] *Public Law* 3–12, 10.

The upshot for the jobbing practitioner is that common law rights will ordinarily have less forensic impact than utilising positive Convention rights under the HRA. Ultimately, the doctrine of parliamentary sovereignty, the principle that rights are residual and the traditional status the common law accords to rights all combine to limit their impact.

While Lord Mance's approach marks a significant development, common law rights face inherent limitations compared to the positive obligations created by the HRA. This tension between the aspirational vision of common law constitutionalism and its practical constraints continues to shape debates about rights protection in UK public law. Indeed, Kirsty Hughes noted the irony that in *Kennedy* itself, the majority's support for common law rights ultimately led to the denial of access to information, with the proposed alternative route through judicial review being untested and uncertain.[29] These practical difficulties underscore the ongoing challenges in developing effective rights protection through common law principles alone.

Returning to *Kennedy,* Lord Mance explicitly addressed whether proportionality should apply in purely domestic cases:

Kennedy v Charity Commission
[2014] UKSC 20

Lord Mance

[54] . . .both reasonableness review and proportionality involve considerations of weight and balance, with the intensity of the scrutiny and the weight to be given to any primary decision maker's view depending on the context. The advantage of the terminology of proportionality is that it introduces an element of structure into the exercise, by directing attention to factors such as suitability or appropriateness, necessity and the balance or imbalance of benefits and disadvantages. There seems no reason why such factors should not be relevant in judicial review even outside the scope of Convention and EU law. Whatever the context, the court deploying them must be aware that they overlap potentially and that the intensity with which they are applied is heavily dependent on the context. In the context of fundamental rights, it is a truism that the scrutiny is likely to be more intense than where other interests are involved.

[55] But the right approach is now surely to recognize [. . .] that it is inappropriate to treat all cases of judicial review together under a general but vague principle of reasonableness, and preferable to look for the underlying tenet or principle which indicates the basis on which the court should approach any administrative law challenge in a particular situation. Among the categories of situation. . .are those where a common law right or constitutional principle is in issue. In the present case, the issue concerns the principles of accountability and transparency.

[29] Kirsty Hughes, 'The Limits of Freedom of Information and Human Rights, and the Possibilities of the Common Law' [2014] 73(3) *Cambridge Law Journal* 471–474.

Lord Mance proposed developing judicial review through case-by-case identification of relevant constitutional principles rather than wholesale replacement of *Wednesbury*. Under this approach, courts would calibrate review intensity according to the specific constitutional values engaged rather than applying universal tests.

A v BBC[30] and *Osborn v Parole Board*,[31] illustrate this methodology. In *A v BBC*, Lord Reed held that '*the common law principle of open justice remains in vigour, even when Convention rights are also applicable*',[32] prioritising domestic principles over Convention analysis. *Osborn* applied demanding scrutiny to protect common law procedural rights, with Lord Reed noting '*the importance of the continuing development of the common law in areas falling within the scope of the Convention guarantees*'.[33] Both cases suggest that courts focus on identifying underlying constitutional values rather than choosing between *Wednesbury* and proportionality as competing tests.

18.8.3 THE LIMITS OF COMMON LAW CONSTITUTIONALISM

The Supreme Court's approach to common law constitutionalism varies across different areas of public law. Courts consider factors including the nature of the right at stake, such as institutional competence, and separation of powers when determining the intensity of review. National security cases receive more deferential treatment even where fundamental interests are affected.

Begum illustrates these variations in approach.[34] The case concerned citizenship deprivation of a woman who had joined ISIS. The Court of Appeal applied proportionality-style analysis, concluding that fairness required allowing her to return to pursue her appeal. The Supreme Court unanimously overturned the decision, emphasising the limited judicial role in matters of national security and prioritising institutional competence over individual procedural rights.

Begum shows the Supreme Court's reluctance to extend proportionality beyond established context of Convention rights, even where citizenship is at stake. The case reflects the difficulty of applying Lord Mance's approach from *Kennedy*, where he advocated identifying the underlying constitutional principle in each case rather than applying universal tests. Despite this approach, different courts reached opposite conclusions about the appropriate level of review when applying ostensibly similar legal principles. Hayley Hooper identifies a constitutional concern about the common law's hierarchical approach to rights protection:

Hayley J. Hooper, 'Justice for one side alone? R. (on the application of Begum) v Special Immigration Appeals Commission'
[2022] *Public Law* 1–9, 8–9.

The *Begum* ruling exemplifies a worrying and under-scrutinized trend in the common law whereby substantive rights attract greater judicial protection according to their source, as opposed to their gravity. Although the right to citizenship is effectively a 'platform' right (much like access to justice) which can be used to give effect to other rights important to democracy (such as rights of residence and the right to vote) it is not recognised by the common law as 'fundamental'.[35] Instead, it belongs to a lower caste of

[30] [2014] UKSC 25. [31] [2013] UKSC 61; discussed in Ch.19. [32] [2014] UKSC 25 [56].
[33] [2013] UKSC 61 [61].
[34] *R (Begum) v Secretary of State for the Home Department* [2021] UKSC 7.
[35] *R. (on the application of Bancoult) v Secretary of State for Foreign and Commonwealth Affairs* [2008] UKHL 61; [2009] 1 A.C. 453 at [41].

'statutory' rights, which can be overridden or interfered with more readily. By contrast, access to justice, the other paradigm 'platform' right, is accorded fundamental status by the common law, resulting in stringent scrutiny of any legislative or practical obstacle placed in its path.[36] Of course, at the margins one man's fundamental right is merely another's political claim. However, case law on immigration generally, and on national security immigration in particular, illustrates the absurdity of a legal system that affords differing standards of procedural protection based on the arbitrary metric of the source from which a right is derived.

18.8.4 THE UNRESOLVED CONSTITUTIONAL QUESTION (*KEYU*)

In *Keyu*, Lord Neuberger considered whether '*the traditional Wednesbury rationality basis for challenging executive decisions should be replaced by a more structured and principled challenge based on proportionality*'.[37] He concluded that such a constitutional question should not be decided by a five-Justice panel but would require nine Justices because the question '*potentially has implications which are profound in constitutional terms and very wide in applicable scope*'.[38] The fact that the Supreme Court considered this question sufficiently important to require an enlarged panel reflects the constitutional significance of the unresolved debate.

Keyu itself demonstrated the complexity of these issues through divergent judicial approaches within the same case. Even an enlarged panel might struggle to resolve disagreements rooted in different conceptions of judicial review's proper scope.

J. Rylatt and J. Tomlinson, 'Something new in substantive review: Keyu v Secretary of State for the Home Department' (2016) 21(3) *Judicial Review* 204–208, 208

. . .it was clear that the terms each had different meanings to the different members of the Court. For example, Lord Neuberger stated that proportionality is distinct from *Wednesbury* in requiring the courts to consider the balance the decision-maker has struck between competing interests, and yet this is arguably what Lady Hale did in her application of *Wednesbury*. Unless unanimity between the Justices emerges on at least some of the myriad questions arising from the distinction between Wednesbury and proportionality, having nine Justices providing opinions on such a divisive issue may just open Pandora's Box.

The ongoing nature of these debates was confirmed in *Youssef v Secretary of State for Foreign and Commonwealth Affairs*,[39] where Lord Carnwath acknowledged that the question remained unresolved and expressed hope that 'an opportunity can be found in the near future for an authoritative review in this court of the judicial and academic learning on the issue . . . Such a review might aim for rather more structured guidance for the lower courts than such imprecise concepts as "anxious scrutiny" and "sliding scales".'[40]

[36] *R. (on the application of UNISON) v Lord Chancellor* [2017] UKSC 51; [2020] A.C. 869.
[37] *Keyu v Secretary of State for Foreign and Commonwealth Affairs* [2015] UKSC 69 [131].
[38] At [132]. [39] [2016] UKSC 3. [40] At [55].

18.8.5 COMMON LAW CONSTITUTIONALISM AS AN ALTERNATIVE FRAMEWORK

The Supreme Court appears to be developing a domestic approach to review intensity that avoids choosing definitively between *Wednesbury* and proportionality. Lord Mance's methodology in *Kennedy* suggests that courts should identify 'the underlying tenet or principle' that governs each case rather than applying universal tests. Courts would calibrate scrutiny according to the constitutional values engaged.

This approach offers certain advantages. It grounds review standards in domestic constitutional traditions rather than European frameworks, addressing concerns about judicial legitimacy while safeguarding rights protection. It allows context-sensitive analysis without forcing constitutional questions into fixed categories. It requires courts to articulate their reasoning more clearly.

The approach also creates difficulties. Review standards may become unpredictable if they depend on judicial identification of constitutional principles in each case. Consistency across courts cannot be assured without guidance about which principles take precedence. Courts may exercise excessive discretion in determining which constitutional values warrant protection and how much weight they deserve.

These developments reflect broader constitutional changes. The UK has moved from parliamentary supremacy tempered by political conventions to a system in which legal principles constrain political power. Whether this represents constitutional development or judicial overreach remains disputed.

QUESTIONS

1. The IRAL comment that:

> The issue most widely debated among respondents was the growth of so-called 'merits-based review'[. . .] The key area of expansion was generally held to be in the sphere of proportionality/reasonableness/irrationality. Opposing arguments coalesced around [. . .] whether proportionality was straying into the territory of 'merits-based review'. Respondents on both sides tended to recognise this as a potential risk but disagreed as to whether it had happened. There were a minority of respondents who agreed that judicial review was moving into the realms of merit-based review, but instead of seeing this as a judicial overreach, argued that this was a proper evolution of the role of the courts and that merits-based review should be expanded further.[41]

What view would you take on these issues and why? Does the common law constitutional approach discussed in section 18.8.2 avoid these concerns about 'merits-based review'?

2. Does common law constitutionalism provide a principled alternative to the *Wednesbury*/proportionality debate? Drawing on *Kennedy*, *A v BBC*, and *Osborn*, assess whether this approach resolves doctrinal difficulties or creates new forms of judicial discretion. Consider the advantages of domestic legitimacy and flexibility against potential problems of uncertainty and inconsistency.
3. Compare the Court of Appeal and Supreme Court approaches in *Begum*. How does this case illustrate the practical difficulties of Lord Mance's methodology of identifying underlying

[41] The Independent Review of Administrative Law, March 2021, Appendix C.

constitutional principles? What does the different treatment of citizenship rights reveal about judicial approaches to review intensity?

4. Evaluate Lord Mance's argument in *Kennedy* for context-sensitive constitutional analysis. Does this methodology represent constitutional development or risk unprincipled decision-making based on judicial preferences about constitutional values? How might courts maintain consistency under this approach?
5. Hayley Hooper argues that *Begum* illustrates 'the absurdity of a legal system which affords differing standards of procedural protection based upon the arbitrary metric of the source from which a right is derived.' Does the common law constitutional approach address this criticism or make it worse? Consider whether multiple sources of rights protection enhance or undermine constitutional coherence.
6. Given developments in common law constitutionalism, does the *Wednesbury*/proportionality question require definitive resolution? Lord Neuberger suggested a nine-justice panel would be needed in *Keyu*, while Lord Carnwath called for clearer standards in *Youssef*. What does judicial preference for case-by-case development suggest about UK constitutional adjudication?

18.9 CONCLUDING COMMENTS

This chapter has examined illegality and irrationality as grounds of judicial review. Illegality operates through established principles that require decision-makers to understand their powers, exercise discretion appropriately, consider relevant factors, and use those powers for proper purposes. Irrationality permits courts to review decisions that no reasonable authority could reach, though the *Wednesbury* test attracts criticism for setting the threshold too high.

The *Wednesbury*/proportionality debate remains unresolved. Courts have developed common law constitutional approaches that adjust the intensity of review according to the rights and principles at stake, as seen in *Kennedy*, *A v BBC*, and *Osborn*. This methodology avoids rigid adherence to either *Wednesbury* deference or European proportionality structures. Lord Mance's judgment in *Kennedy* exemplifies this approach, emphasising that domestic law provides the natural starting point for rights analysis, with the common law sometimes offering protections that go beyond Convention requirements. While this revival of common law constitutionalism faces inherent limitations, particularly compared with the positive obligations created by the HRA, it continues to shape how courts calibrate the intensity of review when fundamental constitutional principles are engaged.

Begum illustrates both the appeal and limitations of flexible constitutional analysis. Different courts reached opposite conclusions about citizenship rights using similar legal frameworks. *Keyu* confirms the constitutional importance of these questions, with Lord Neuberger suggesting that resolving the *Wednesbury*/proportionality debate would require an enlarged panel of the Supreme Court.

The grounds of judicial review continue to develop through case law. Courts must balance their supervisory role against democratic accountability while adapting legal doctrine to contemporary constitutional challenges. Whether judicial review achieves greater coherence or remains fragmented will depend on future Supreme Court guidance.

FURTHER READING

The Administrative Court Judicial Review Guide, October 2024.

Arden, M., 'Proportionality: the way ahead?' [2013] *Public Law* 498–518.

Government Legal Department, *The Judge Over Your Shoulder*, 6th edn (republished 2022, London: GLD).

Sales, P., 'Rationality, proportionality and the development of the law' (2013) 129 *Law Quarterly Review* 223–241.

Sayer, T. and Murray, CRG, 'A tale of two doctrines: Revaluating bifurcation in substantive review before the Supreme Court' [2021] *Public Law* 47–68.

Woolf, H., Jowell, J., Donnelly, C., and Hare I., *De Smith's Judicial Review*, 8th edn (2018, London: Sweet & Maxwell).

19

JUDICIAL REVIEW 3: PROCEDURAL IMPROPRIETY

CENTRAL ISSUES

1. Procedural impropriety encompasses both failures to follow statutory procedures and breaches of common law fairness requirements. Courts distinguish between mandatory procedural requirements (whose breach typically invalidates decisions) and directory requirements (whose breach may not be fatal if no prejudice results). The common law imposes procedural duties even where statute is silent, following the principle from *Cooper v Wandsworth* that '*the justice of the common law will supply the omission of the legislature*'.
2. Courts recognise both instrumental and non-instrumental justifications for procedural fairness. Instrumental justifications focus on improved decision-making through proper information gathering and testing. Non-instrumental justifications emphasize respect for human dignity and rule of law values. These dual justifications explain why procedural failures matter independently of whether different procedures would have changed outcomes.
3. Procedural requirements vary according to context rather than following rigid rules. Courts consider the importance of interests at stake, the nature of the decision-making body, statutory context, and practical constraints. Decisions affecting fundamental rights require more extensive procedures than routine administrative matters. Emergency situations may justify abbreviated procedures, though courts scrutinise such claims carefully.
4. Fair hearing requirements typically include notice of decisions, opportunities to make representations, and appropriate hearing formats. Whether oral hearings are required depends on factors such as factual disputes, complexity, and the impact of the decision. Consultation must meet the *Gunning* principles when required. The duty to give reasons depends on statutory requirements and the importance of interests affected.
5. Decision-makers must avoid both actual and apparent bias. The test asks whether a fair-minded observer would perceive a real possibility of bias. Courts distinguish pre-disposition (preliminary views open to change) from pre-determination (closed minds). Financial interests automatically disqualify, while policy commitments by elected officials require careful analysis.
6. Public body representations and practices can generate legitimate expectations. The *Coughlan* case distinguishes procedural expectations, substantive expectations, and mere considerations. Substantive expectations are enforceable

unless overriding public interest justifies a departure. Requirements include clarity, consistency with statutory powers, and consideration of the number affected.

7. Courts reject substantive fairness as an independent ground of review, as confirmed in *Gallaher*. Consistency and equal treatment remain relevant on the grounds of illegality, irrationality, and procedural impropriety rather than as free-standing principles. This approach reflects constitutional boundaries between judicial review of legality and political accountability for policy choices.

19.1 INTRODUCTION

Procedural impropriety forms one of the three grounds of judicial review established in *GCHQ*, alongside illegality and irrationality. This ground addresses how public bodies make decisions rather than what they decide. A public body may be challenged for procedural failures even if it reaches the correct substantive outcome.

In *GCHQ*, Lord Diplock identified two types of procedural impropriety: failure to follow procedures mandated by legislation, and failure to comply with the common law requirements of procedural fairness (or natural justice).

This distinction is important for practical application. Parliament sometimes specifies procedures that must be followed, such as requirements for consultation or public hearings. Where legislation is silent, the common law may impose procedural requirements based on principles of fairness. This dual source of procedural obligations means public bodies must consider both statutory and common law requirements when making decisions.

19.2 STATUTORY PROCEDURES

When Parliament creates a power for public bodies to make decisions, it often specifies particular procedures that must be followed. Understanding when these requirements are truly mandatory, and what happens when they are breached, is essential for both public administrators and those who might be affected by their decisions.

The following extract from *The Judge Over Your Shoulder* summarizes the main principles that apply when legislation requires certain procedures to be followed, and explains the distinction between 'mandatory' and 'directory' requirements.

Government Legal Department, *The Judge Over Your Shoulder*, 6th edn (republished 2022, London: GLD)

Mandatory versus directory requirements

2.57 Due process requires you to consider if any relevant legislation expressly imposes a procedural requirement that must be met before a power should be exercised. There is a presumption that a statutory requirement is 'mandatory'. Failure to comply with mandatory requirements will usually result in a decision being unlawful. Examples of legislative imposed procedural requirements include:

- consulting with local authority representatives
- publishing the decision in draft

- making due inquiry
- considering any objections before making a decision

2.58 Occasionally, the presumption of a mandatory requirement can be rebutted: for example, if the requirement is minor or technical; or the breach of the required procedure would not defeat the purpose of the statute, or is of insufficient importance in the context of the decision. In such a case, the requirement may be considered to be 'directory'.

2.59 Failure to satisfy a directory requirement will not necessarily cause the decision to be unlawful. For example, a statute requires a public body to carry out a function within a certain time limit but the public body performed the function slightly late. The court might find that there had been substantial compliance with the procedure and that the breach could therefore be overlooked.

2.60 There is no clear distinction between 'mandatory' and 'directory' requirements. These labels do not matter, but rather the court's view of the effect of noncompliance, any prejudice caused as a result, and the scope and purpose of the enactment as a whole. Complying with a statutory requirement is not a tick-box exercise: the requirement must be complied with in spirit as well as literally. It is therefore best practice to comply with any procedural requirement, including time limits, directory or otherwise.

The distinction between mandatory and directory requirements lacks bright-line rules. As the guidance states, the labels themselves '*do not matter*'—what matters is the court's assessment of the practical consequences of non-compliance. Courts examine several factors when making this determination:

- **The effect of non-compliance**: Courts ask whether the breach undermines the purpose of the statutory scheme or is merely a minor technical failure that causes no real harm. A breach that defeats Parliament's underlying objectives will likely render the decision invalid, while technical non-compliance may be overlooked.
- **Prejudice caused**: Has anyone been disadvantaged by the procedural failure? Courts are more likely to treat a requirement as directory where no one has suffered prejudice from the breach. Conversely, when individuals have lost opportunities to participate or influence decisions, courts tend to find the requirements mandatory.
- **The scope and purpose of the enactment**: Courts examine the overall statutory context to determine how important the particular requirement is to achieving Parliament's objectives. Requirements that go to the heart of the statutory scheme receive stricter enforcement than peripheral procedural steps.
- **The nature of the requirement**: Minor technical requirements (such as precise timing for administrative steps) may be directory, while requirements central to fair process (such as notice or consultation) are more likely to be mandatory.

Consider these practical applications:

Consulting 'interested parties' before making planning decisions is typically mandatory, as it helps ensure fair treatment and gather relevant information before decisions affecting property rights.

By contrast, a requirement to publish a decision within exactly seven days might be directory if the decision is published after ten days but no one is prejudiced by the delay. Courts would likely find '*substantial compliance*' with the procedural scheme if the delay caused no harm and the statutory purpose was still achieved.

The principle that compliance must be '*in spirit as well as literally*' prevents public bodies from treating procedures as mere formalities. They cannot simply go through the motions – they must engage with the purposes behind procedural requirements. For instance, a consultation that appears to comply with the timing requirements in which the authority has already made its decision would breach this principle. As the guidance notes state, best practice is to comply with all procedural requirements regardless of their potential classification as directory, to avoid litigation risk and ensure good administration.

19.3 PROCEDURAL FAIRNESS AS A REQUIREMENT OF THE COMMON LAW

Even where the statute says nothing about procedural requirements, the common law may impose duties of fairness. The recognition that fair procedures are legally required, not merely desirable, marks an important development in English administrative law.

Today, the expressions 'procedural fairness' and 'natural justice' are often used interchangeably to refer to two main requirements:

(a) that those adversely affected by decisions should be given a fair hearing at which they can present their side of the case;

(b) that decision-makers be neutral and impartial.

These requirements apply naturally in court proceedings, but their application to administrative decision-making raises questions. When local authorities allocate housing or community care, or when ministers apply policy, must they follow court-like procedures? The answer depends on understanding how the doctrine of procedural fairness developed beyond traditional judicial settings.

19.3.1 HISTORICAL DEVELOPMENT

The modern law of procedural fairness developed through judicial decisions that progressively expanded the scope of fair procedure requirements. This evolution explains both the doctrine's current flexibility and its application beyond traditional judicial settings.

The principle that fair procedures are required even where statute is silent has deep roots in English law. In the 19th-century decision *Cooper v Wandsworth Board of Works*,[1] Byles J established that '*although there are no positive words in the statute requiring that the party shall be heard, yet the justice of the common law will supply the omission of the legislature*'. This principle recognised that fairness could be a legal requirement independent of statutory specification. Parliament cannot anticipate every situation where fairness might be required, so the common law fills the gaps.

By the early twentieth century, courts had developed rigid categories to determine when fair procedures were required. The Donoughmore Committee (1932) distinguished between judicial functions (requiring full natural justice), administrative functions (requiring no procedural protections), and quasi-judicial functions (requiring some procedural protections).

This formalistic approach meant that procedural rights depended on classifying the function rather than assessing the impact on individuals. Many decisions affecting people's lives received no procedural protection because they were classified as 'administrative'.

[1] (1863) 143 ER 414 at 420.

This restrictive approach changed with *Ridge v Baldwin*.[2] The case concerned a Chief Constable dismissed without a hearing after being acquitted of criminal charges but criticized by the trial judge. The House of Lords held the dismissal unlawful because Ridge had not been given an opportunity to be heard.

Ridge v Baldwin rejected the formal distinctions that had limited procedural protection. The House of Lords held that the test for deciding whether a body must respect natural justice is not whether it must adopt a judicial procedure, but whether its decisions affect rights and important interests. The obligation to respect natural justice, or to adopt fair procedures, is not limited to situations where public bodies must follow court-like procedures; it may apply to all types of decision-making.

This meant that public bodies—from local councils making housing decisions to immigration officials determining visa applications—could be required to follow fair procedures, even if they were not acting like courts.

19.3.2 THE DEVELOPMENT OF 'FAIRNESS'

The expansion continued in *Re HK*,[3] where the Privy Council held that even immigration officers making routine administrative decisions must '*act fairly*'. This case introduced the modern term 'fairness' rather than 'natural justice', reflecting the recognition that administrative decisions required appropriate procedural protections even if they did not mirror court procedures.

R v Gaming Board, ex p Benaim and Khaida[4] developed this flexible approach. The case concerned gaming licence applications, in which the Gaming Board used confidential information in their decision-making. The Court of Appeal held that the Board had '*a duty to act fairly*' and must give applicants an opportunity to respond to concerns about their suitability. However, the court recognised that administrative fairness could be adapted to context: '*They must let him know what their impressions are so that he can disabuse them. But I do not think that they need quote chapter and verse against him as if they were dismissing him from an office . . . or depriving him of his property*'.[5]

This shows how procedural fairness became flexible rather than rigid—applicants needed a fair opportunity to respond, but the Gaming Board did not need to provide the detailed disclosure required in cases involving dismissal or property rights. The court confirmed that '*at one time it was said that the principles [of natural justice] only apply to judicial and not to administrative proceedings. That heresy was scotched in* Ridge v Baldwin'.[6]

These developments led courts to recognise that procedural fairness operates on a spectrum rather than through rigid categories.[7] At one extreme lies the full judicial process with oral hearings, legal representation, cross-examination, and detailed written reasons. At the other extreme are decisions requiring minimal procedural protections, such as a Prime Minister's decision to dismiss a minister, which involves political judgment unsuitable for judicial oversight.

Most administrative decisions fall between these extremes. An immigration tribunal might require oral hearings for complex asylum cases, while a licensing authority might satisfy fairness requirements through written representations. The position on the spectrum depends on the importance of the interests at stake, the nature of the decision-making body, and the impact of the decision on affected individuals.

This spectrum approach replaced the old formalistic categories with contextual analysis. Rather than asking whether a body is 'administrative' or 'quasi-judicial', courts ask what level of procedural protection the circumstances require.

[2] [1964] AC 40. [3] [1967] 2 QB 617. [4] [1970] 2 Q.B. 417. [5] Ibid. 429–432. [6] Ibid at 430.
[7] D.J. Mullan, 'Fairness: The New Natural Justice?' (1975) 25(3) *The University of Toronto Law Journal* 281–316.

The requirements of procedural fairness may overlap with Article 6 ECHR, which provides a right to have '*civil rights and obligations, or any criminal charge*' determined '*by a fair and public hearing within a reasonable time by an independent and impartial tribunal established by law*'.

Article 6 has both a narrower scope and a higher standard than common law fairness. It applies only to the determination of civil rights and criminal charges, but where it does apply, it may impose more stringent requirements. Article 6 generally requires an oral hearing, whereas the common law might accept written representations in some contexts. It also requires hearings before independent and impartial tribunals, which may set a higher standard than common law impartiality requirements. Article 6 guarantees public hearings and imposes reasonable time limits, creating enforceable constraints that common law does not always provide.

Understanding both sources of procedural protection matters because they can apply simultaneously, with claimants entitled to whichever provides stronger protection.

19.3.3 WHY DOES PROCEDURAL FAIRNESS MATTER?

The answer to this question may seem obvious: fairness matters because public functions should be executed fairly. Yet this response is circular and unhelpful. The reason for examining why procedural fairness matters is to help determine what fairness requires in concrete situations. If fairness is required simply to be fair, courts and officials lack practical guidance about what fairness demands.

One approach distinguishes between different justifications for requiring procedural fairness. Academic and judicial perspectives illuminate why fair procedures matter beyond administrative convenience.

P. Craig, 'Natural justice in English Law: continuity and change from the 17th Century'
[2022] *Liber Amicorum Per Marco D'Alberti* 3

> The general justification for process rights in modern academic discourse is based on instrumental and non-instrumental argumentation. . . . This is unsurprising, given that the instrumental and non-instrumental justifications are not time dependent. To the contrary they are expressive of enduring values that would have been understood and accepted in the 17th as well as the 20th century.
>
> The instrumental justification emphasizes the connection between procedural due process and the substantive justice of the final outcome. [. . .] The non-instrumental justification for hearing rights is grounded on commitment to formal justice and the rule of law, helping to guarantee objectivity and impartiality, and protect human dignity.

This distinction explains why procedural fairness matters even when the outcome might have been the same. The instrumental justification focuses on how fair procedures improve decision-making by ensuring all relevant information is considered and properly tested. The non-instrumental justification is grounded in a commitment to formal justice and the rule of law: fair procedures protect human dignity and respect individuals affected by decisions, regardless of whether those decisions change the outcome.

These issues were addressed by Lord Reed when the UK Supreme Court considered whether the Parole Board must hold oral hearings before determining whether a prisoner should be released or transferred to open conditions. The Supreme Court decided that oral hearings should be held whenever fairness to the prisoner required one, given the facts and the issues at stake. In the following extract, Lord Reed explains why fair procedures matter.

Osborn v The Parole Board
[2013] UKSC 61

Lord Reed

67. There is no doubt that one of the virtues of procedurally fair decision making is that it is liable to result in better decisions, by ensuring that the decision maker receives all relevant information and that it is properly tested. At least two other important values are also engaged.

68. The first was described by Lord Hoffmann (in *Secretary of State for the Home Department v AF (No 3)* [2009] UKHL 28 para. 72) as the avoidance of the sense of injustice which the person who is the subject of the decision will otherwise feel. [. . .] justice is intuitively understood to require a procedure which pays due respect to persons whose rights are significantly affected by decisions taken in the exercise of administrative or judicial functions. Respect entails that such persons ought to be able to participate in the procedure by which the decision is made, provided they have something to say which is relevant to the decision to be taken. [. . .]

70. This aspect of fairness [. . .] has practical consequences [. . .] In the present context, research has established the importance attached by prisoners to a process of risk assessment which provides for their contribution to the process (see Attrill and Liell, 'Offenders' Views on Risk Assessment', in *Who to Release? Parole, Fairness and Criminal Justice* (2007), ed Padfield). Other research reveals the frustration, anger and despair felt by prisoners who perceive the board's procedures as unfair, and the impact of those feelings upon their motivation and respect for authority (see Padfield, *Understanding Recall* 2011, University of Cambridge Faculty of Law Research Paper No 2/2013 (2013)). The potential implications for the prospects of rehabilitation, and ultimately for public safety, are evident.

71. The second value is the rule of law. Procedural requirements that decision makers should listen to persons who have something relevant to say promote congruence between the actions of decision-makers and the law which should govern their actions (see, e.g., Fuller, *The Morality of Law*, revised ed (1969), p. 81, and Bingham, *The Rule of Law* (2010), chapter 6).

Harlow and Rawlings refer to the *Osborn* case as the 'Grandchild of *Ridge v Baldwin*' for reasserting the importance of oral hearings.[8] Osborn's significance lies in both its practical outcome and theoretical foundation. Lord Reed's analysis identifies three interconnected justifications for procedural fairness:

1. **Better decision-making** (instrumental): Fair procedures help ensure decision-makers have all relevant information and that it is properly tested.
2. **Respect for human dignity** (value-based): People have a right to be heard on matters that affect them significantly, regardless of whether this changes the outcome.
3. **Rule of law**: Fair procedures help ensure that decision-makers act in accordance with law rather than on arbitrary grounds.

Understanding why procedural fairness matters has practical implications for judicial review. It explains why courts are often unsympathetic to arguments that procedural failures do not matter because the outcome would have been the same. The value-based justifications for fairness mean that people are entitled to fair treatment for its own sake, not just as a means to achieving particular outcomes. However, recent legislative changes require courts to refuse permission for judicial review if it appears '*highly likely*' that the outcome would not have been substantially different, unless there are

[8] C. Harlow and R. Rawlings, *Law and Administration* 4th edn (Cambridge: Cambridge University Press, 2022), 675.

reasons of exceptional public interest. This creates tension between procedural rights and administrative efficiency.

These justifications also have conceptual implications for democratic government. As Sir Jeffrey Jowell explains, modern democracy requires public authorities to justify their actions rather than simply assert their authority:

J. Jowell, Written Evidence to Parliament (ROL0099), 22 April 2025

> . . . the notion of access to legal rights requires also that restrictions on rights and liberties should not be made in a democracy without proper justification. The 'culture of justification', rather than the 'culture of authority', is a vital mark of the difference between democracy and despotism. Hence the need for procedural fairness is supplemented by the requirement for reasonableness and proportionality in all official decisions, as a substantive guard-rail against arbitrariness.

The theoretical justifications for procedural fairness extend beyond individual cases to constitutional principles about how public power should be exercised in a democracy. The instrumental and non-instrumental justifications work together: fair procedures both improve decisions and affirm the dignity of those affected by them. This dual foundation explains why courts treat procedural failures seriously even when outcomes might remain unchanged, though the statutory '*highly likely*' test now constrains this approach.

QUESTIONS

1. In light of what Paul Craig and Lord Reed say, should courts take a different view of the importance of being unable to make representations in the following situations?
   (a) X applies for a licence and is given no chance to make representations to the decision-maker. She is refused the licence for reasons that have nothing to do with the representations she wanted to make.
   (b) Y applies for a licence and is also given no chance to make representations. She is also refused the licence, but for reasons that she could have addressed had she been able to make representations.
2. The guidance in *The Judge Over Your Shoulder* notes that courts are now required to refuse permission for judicial review if it appears '*highly likely*' that the outcome would not have been substantially different, unless there are reasons of exceptional public interest. This legislative change (in sections 31(2A), (3C) and (3D) of the Senior Courts Act 1981) applies mainly to procedural failures and failures to consider relevant factors. Given the value-based justifications for procedural fairness discussed by Paul Craig and Lord Reed, do you think this statutory provision strikes the right balance between procedural rights and administrative efficiency? Consider whether there are some procedural failures that should lead to quashing regardless of outcome.
3. How does the duty of good administration, referenced throughout the guidance, relate to the different justifications for procedural fairness discussed in this section? Does the emphasis on '*good administration*' suggest courts should focus more on outcomes or procedures?

19.3.4 FAIRNESS DEPENDS ON CONTEXT

Procedural fairness is not a one-size-fits-all concept. What fairness requires varies depending on the circumstances of each case. This contextual approach reflects the practical reality that different types of decisions call for different procedures, and the recognition that standards of fairness evolve over time.

The precise requirements of procedural fairness depend on multiple interconnected factors: the interests involved, the nature of the decision, and the nature of the body making the decision. What seemed adequate procedural protection in the 1960s—perhaps a brief written notice and an opportunity to reply by letter—might fall short of contemporary expectations, given that technology enables more comprehensive communication and participation. What constitutes fair procedures for a routine administrative decision will be insufficient for matters affecting fundamental rights like liberty or livelihood. What is fair in some circumstances will be unfair in others, and what is fair to some participants may be unfair to others.

R v Secretary of State for the Home Department, ex parte Doody
[1994] 1 AC 531, 560

Lord Mustill

What does fairness require in the present case? [. . .] From [the decided cases] I derive that (1) where an Act of Parliament confers an administrative power there is a presumption that it will be exercised in a manner which is fair in all the circumstances. (2) The standards of fairness are not immutable. They may change with the passage of time, both in the general and in their application to decisions of a particular type. (3) The principles of fairness are not to be applied by rote identically in every situation. What fairness demands is dependent on the context of the decision, and this is to be taken into account in all its aspects. (4) An essential feature of the context is the statute which creates the discretion, as regards both its language and the shape of the legal and administrative system within which the decision is taken. (5) Fairness will very often require that a person who may be adversely affected by the decision will have an opportunity to make representations on his own behalf either before the decision is taken with a view to producing a favourable result; or after it is taken, with a view to procuring its modification; or both. (6) Since the person affected usually cannot make worthwhile representations without knowing what factors may weigh against his interests fairness will very often require that he is informed of the gist of the case which he has to answer.

Doody itself illustrates how this contextual approach works in practice. The case concerned prisoners serving mandatory life sentences who were not told why the Home Secretary had set particular minimum terms for their sentences. The House of Lords held that the gravity of the decision (affecting liberty) and the prisoners' need to understand the basis for their potential release meant that fairness required explanations.

Lord Mustill's framework in Doody provides guidance for understanding how contextual analysis works in practice. Several principles emerge from his analysis.

First, the concept of fairness evolves over time. What seemed fair in 1950 might not meet modern standards. This reflects changing social expectations and improved understanding of effective decision-making processes.

Second, the statutory context matters. The specific statute creating the power shapes what fairness requires. Some statutes anticipate formal procedures; others contemplate quick, informal decisions. Courts examine Parliament's intentions as expressed in the legislation to determine the appropriate level of procedural protection.

Third, there is a presumption that Parliament intends powers to be exercised fairly, even without specified procedures. Courts will read procedural requirements into legislation where necessary to ensure fair treatment. Even where legislation says the minister 'may' make a decision, courts require basic procedural protections unless Parliament has clearly excluded them. Parliament can override this presumption, but must do so explicitly—vague language will not suffice.[9]

19.3.4.1 The forfeiture/application/expectation framework

Courts have developed additional frameworks for determining what procedural fairness requires. In *McInnes v Onslow-Fane*,[10] Megarry V-C established a distinction between three categories of case requiring different levels of procedural protection.

Forfeiture cases involve decisions that remove an existing right or benefit, such as revoking a professional licence or expelling someone from an organization. These cases attract the highest level of procedural protection because something is being 'taken away'. The right to an unbiased tribunal, notice of the grounds for action, and an opportunity to be heard are *'plainly apt'* in such circumstances.[11]

Application cases involve refusal to grant a new right, licence, or benefit where the applicant has no existing entitlement. McInnes's unsuccessful application for a boxing manager's licence fell into this category. Since *'nothing is being taken away, and in all normal circumstances there are no charges'*, the procedural requirements are more limited. The decision-making body need only act *'honestly and without bias'*, and is generally not required to provide detailed reasons or an oral hearing.[12]

Expectation cases fall between the extremes of certainty and uncertainty, where applicants have a legitimate expectation that their application will be granted, such as in licence renewal cases or situations where similar applications have been routinely approved. These cases are 'more akin to the forfeiture cases than the application cases' because, although no formal right exists, the disappointed expectation creates a stronger claim to procedural protection.[13]

19.3.4.2 Factors influencing contextual analysis

When determining what fairness requires, courts consider numerous interconnected factors. The importance of the interests at stake is perhaps the most significant consideration. Decisions affecting fundamental rights such as liberty or livelihood require more extensive procedures than routine administrative matters. A decision to revoke someone's professional licence demands more elaborate procedures than a decision about routine administrative fees.

Courts also consider the nature of the decision-making body. They expect more formal procedures from bodies that regularly make similar decisions than from those making one-off policy decisions. A tribunal processing hundreds of similar cases each year is expected to have more developed procedural safeguards than a minister making a unique policy decision.

Practical constraints affect what procedures are feasible. Emergency situations may justify departing from ideal procedural standards, though courts scrutinise such claims carefully. In urgent deportation cases, courts may accept that national security concerns justify abbreviated procedures. Similarly, a local authority processing thousands of housing applications cannot provide the same individualised procedures as a professional disciplinary tribunal that hears only a few cases per year. The key is whether the constraints are genuine and whether reasonable alternatives exist.

Courts must also consider the impact on others of requiring extensive procedures. Sometimes extensive procedures for one person would delay decisions affecting many others. Immigration tribunals

[9] *R v Secretary of State for the Home Department, ex p Pierson* [1998] AC 539).
[10] [1978] 1 W.L.R. 1520.
[11] At p. 1529.
[12] At p. 1533.
[13] At p. 1529.

must balance thorough individual hearings against the need to process large caseloads. Courts recognise that administrative efficiency cannot trump basic fairness, but fairness requirements must be realistic given administrative constraints and the needs of other users of the system.

Given that the precise requirements of fairness depend on context and vary over time, we now examine what a fair hearing and a neutral and unbiased decision-maker require.

19.3.5 ELEMENTS OF A FAIR HEARING

While the content of fairness varies by context, certain elements recur across situations. Understanding these common elements helps predict what might be required in particular cases.

Fairness may require those adversely affected by a decision to have prior notice of the decision and knowledge of the case to be answered; an opportunity to be consulted and to make representations; a hearing either in writing or orally, depending on the issues; representation, possibly by a lawyer; and knowledge of the reasons for the decision, as this provides transparency and helps people decide whether to challenge or complain about decisions.

19.3.5.1 Prior notice and knowledge of the case

The principle that people should know the case against them is fundamental. You cannot defend yourself against accusations you do not know about. This does not always require detailed disclosure—sometimes '*the gist*' is sufficient—but people must have enough information to respond meaningfully.

This requirement can create tensions with other interests. In immigration cases, full disclosure might compromise intelligence sources. Courts must balance fairness to individuals against other legitimate interests.

19.3.5.2 The right to make representations

The opportunity to put your side of the story is central to fair decision-making. However, this does not always require an oral hearing. Written representations may suffice, particularly for straightforward factual matters.

Recent cases have emphasized that consultation must be genuine. In *R (Binder) v Secretary of State for Work and Pensions*,[14] the court found that the government's National Disability Strategy violated common law principles concerning fair consultation. The judgment emphasized that when government voluntarily embarks on consultation, it must satisfy duties to fairly consult interested and affected parties.

19.3.5.3 Consultation requirements

Where consultation is required (whether by statute, legitimate expectation, or common law fairness), it must meet established standards. The requirements for fair consultation were established in *R v Brent London Borough Council, ex p Gunning*[15] and are known as the Gunning principles:

First, consultation must begin when proposals are at a formative stage, not after minds are made up. Public bodies cannot consult on final decisions, though they may have a preferred option provided they remain open to change.

[14] [2022] EWHC 105 (Admin).

[15] [1985] 84 LGR 168.

Second, sufficient information must be provided to enable intelligent consideration. Consultees cannot respond intelligently to vague or incomplete information. As seen in *R (Moseley) v Haringey LBC*,[16] this may require explaining not just the preferred option but realistic alternatives, so consultees understand the full range of choices available.

Third, adequate time must be given for responses. What constitutes '*adequate time*' depends on the complexity of issues, the resources of consultees, and any urgency. A consultation period that works for well-resourced organizations may be inadequate for individuals or voluntary groups.

Fourth, responses must be conscientiously considered by the decision-maker. Decision-makers must engage with opposing views and explain why they have been rejected. A decision-maker who has already decided to ignore consultation responses will breach this requirement.

19.3.5.4 Oral vs written hearings

The choice between oral and written procedures depends on several factors. Where credibility is crucial in factual disputes, oral hearings allow for questioning and assessment of witnesses. Simple matters may be adequately addressed in writing, while complex issues may require oral discussion. More serious consequences generally justify more formal procedures. As noted in *JCWI v The President of the Upper Tribunal and the Lord Chancellor*,[17] an oral hearing should be allowed where facts are in issue and where the credibility and veracity of witnesses need to be tested by oral questioning.

19.3.5.5 Legal representation

The right to legal representation is not absolute in administrative proceedings, but may be required where legal complexity makes self-representation impractical, the individual lacks capacity to represent themselves effectively, or the consequences of an adverse decision are particularly serious.

19.3.5.6 Reasons for decisions

Giving reasons serves multiple purposes. Reasons demonstrate that the decision-maker has properly considered the issues rather than acting arbitrarily. They enable affected parties to understand the basis for adverse decisions, facilitating informed decisions about whether to appeal or seek judicial review. They also promote better decision-making by requiring decision-makers to articulate their reasoning.

The recent development of the duty to give reasons deserves emphasis. As recently as the 1980s, English law recognised no general duty for administrative decision-makers to provide reasons for their decisions. In 1988, the influential JUSTICE/All Souls Committee Report on Administrative Law recommended that Parliament should legislate to introduce a general duty to give reasons, noting that the absence of such a duty was increasingly anomalous.[18] The Committee regarded giving reasons as something '*demanded by our national sense of justice*' and referred to the right to reasons as '*the third principle of natural justice*'.[19] Yet even today, '*the common law does not as yet impose a general duty to give reasons for a decision*'.[20] The Committee's recommendation for legislation was never implemented. Instead, the duty to give reasons has developed incrementally through case law, with courts recognizing duties in specific contexts rather than as a general rule.

[16] [2014] UKSC 56. [17] [2020] EWHC 3103 (Admin).

[18] *Administrative Justice: Some Necessary Reforms* (Oxford, 1988), 71–72. [19] Ibid, pp.76, 80.

[20] William Wade, Christopher Forsyth, and Julian Ghosh, *Wade & Forsyth's Administrative Law* (12th edn, OUP, 2022) 391.

Courts have recognised a legal duty to provide reasons only in specific circumstances. This duty arises when a statute expressly requires it, or where the decision affects fundamental rights. The principle was established in *Doody*, where the House of Lords held that prisoners serving life sentences were entitled to know why particular minimum terms had been set for their release. The duty also applies where there is an established practice of giving reasons, where the decision appears inconsistent with established policy, or where Article 6 ECHR requires a fair hearing.

However, the duty to give reasons is not universal. In *R v Home Secretary, ex p Fayed*,[21] the court confirmed that while procedural rights like adequate notice cannot be excluded, there is no general obligation to provide detailed reasons for all administrative decisions. The existence and extent of the duty depend on the specific circumstances and the importance of the interests at stake.

The adequacy of reasons, where required, depends on context. Simple administrative decisions may require only brief explanations, while complex matters affecting fundamental rights typically need more detailed reasoning that addresses the main arguments raised.

QUESTIONS

1. Using Lord Mustill's framework in *Doody*, explain why a professional licensing tribunal might be required to provide more extensive procedural protections than a local authority making routine housing allocation decisions, even though both decisions significantly affect the individuals involved. In your answer, consider at least three factors that courts use to determine what fairness requires in different contexts.
2. A government department conducts a 3-week consultation on closing rural libraries, providing only a brief summary and failing to mention alternative funding options discussed internally. Which Gunning principles are breached and why?
3. An immigration tribunal faces large backlogs but an asylum seeker requests an oral hearing for a case involving disputed country conditions. How should courts resolve the tension between individual procedural rights and administrative efficiency?
4. A taxi licensing authority wants to revoke a driver's licence based on anonymous witness statements but refuses to disclose witness identities. What procedural protections should the driver receive and how should competing interests be balanced?
5. A local authority refuses a planning application for a new housing development. The decision letter states only: 'Application refused. The proposal is not in accordance with local planning policy'. The applicant argues they are entitled to more detailed reasons explaining which policies were breached and why their supporting evidence was rejected. Using the principles from *Doody* and *Fayed*, explain when public bodies have a legal duty to give reasons and whether more detailed reasoning would be required in this case.

19.3.6 THE NEED FOR NEUTRAL AND IMPARTIAL DECISION-MAKERS

Fair procedures are meaningless if decision-makers are biased or have already made up their minds. The requirement for impartiality is therefore fundamental to procedural fairness.

[21] [1997] 1 WLR 228.

There is no point in following a fair procedure if decision-makers have already made up their mind, are unable or unwilling to listen to those affected, or have conflicting interests. This applies not only to judges, who must be impartial and neutral, but also to administrative decision-makers. For example, officials employed by local authorities to review initial decisions made by housing officers must be open-minded when reviewing those decisions again.

Courts are concerned with apparent bias, where circumstances would lead a fair-minded observer to conclude there was a real possibility of bias. The modern test, established in *Porter v Magill*, asks '*whether the fair-minded and informed observer, having considered the facts, would conclude that there was a real possibility that the tribunal was biased*'.[22] This hypothetical observer is expected to be reasonably informed about legal processes and to consider all relevant circumstances before reaching a conclusion.

The test is objective: what matters is not whether bias actually occurred, but whether it might reasonably appear to have occurred. While actual bias (where evidence shows the decision-maker was influenced by improper considerations) can be proven, it is difficult to establish directly.

19.3.6.1 Categories of bias

Financial interests create automatic disqualification. The principle was established in *Dimes v Proprietors of the Grand Junction Canal*,[23] where the Lord Chancellor was disqualified from hearing a case involving a company in which he held shares. As the Privy Council later confirmed, '*any direct pecuniary interest, however small, does disqualify a person from acting as a judge in the matter*'.[24] This rule applies regardless of whether actual bias can be proven.

Personal relationships with affected parties may also create bias, though professional relationships do not automatically disqualify decision-makers. The *Porter v Magill* test is used to determine whether a relationship creates an appearance of bias.

Ideological bias represents a more complex category. *R v Bow Street Metropolitan Stipendiary Magistrate, ex p Pinochet Ugarte (No.2)*[25] established that strong ideological commitments can disqualify decision-makers even without financial interest. Lord Hoffmann was disqualified from the Pinochet case because of his unpaid role as chairman and director of Amnesty International, which had been granted leave to intervene and appeared by counsel before the appellate committee. The House of Lords found that this connection automatically disqualified him from sitting as a judge in the case, because he was '*in effect, acting as a judge in his own cause*'.

Policy commitments present challenges in administrative contexts. In *Franklin v Minister of Town and Country Planning*,[26] it was held that a government minister could be biased in favour of pursuing their own stated policy. This reflects the reality that politicians are expected to have policy positions. The question is whether they remain open to evidence and argument on specific applications.

19.3.6.2 The rule against pre-determination

Decision-makers must keep an open mind until they have heard all the evidence and arguments. The key distinction is between pre-disposition (holding preliminary views that might change in light of evidence) and pre-determination (having a closed mind that will not change regardless of evidence). Pre-disposition is acceptable; pre-determination is not.

[22] [2001] UKHL 67 [103], per Lord Hope.
[23] (1852), 10 E.R. 301, 3 H.L.C. 759.
[24] *R. v. Rand* (1866) L.R. 1 Q.B. 230, 232.
[25] [2000] 1 AC 119.
[26] [1948] AC 87.

This distinction is important for elected officials, who are expected to have policy positions while remaining open to evidence on specific applications. The challenge lies in distinguishing between legitimate policy commitment and illegitimate closed-mindedness.

19.3.6.3 Institutional bias

Sometimes the structure of decision-making creates inherent conflicts. If the same body that brings a prosecution also decides guilt, this may create an appearance of bias, even if individual decision-makers are personally impartial. Courts consider whether institutional arrangements create an unacceptable appearance of bias that undermines public confidence in the decision-making process.

19.4 LEGITIMATE EXPECTATIONS

The ground of judicial review called '*legitimate expectations*' arises when claimants argue that public bodies have said or done things that create an expectation that they will act in accordance with past practice, policies, promises, or representations.

The doctrine addresses a tension in administrative law: public bodies need flexibility to change policies and practices in the public interest, but people also need predictability and reliability in their dealings with government. Legitimate expectations provide a legal framework for balancing these competing needs.

In *GCHQ*, the unions claimed a legitimate expectation, based on past practice, that they would be consulted about proposed changes to the terms and conditions under which their members worked. The legitimate expectation was procedural: to be consulted. It was not a claim that the unions had a legitimate expectation that no changes would be made to the terms and conditions of their members' employment. This would have been a substantive legitimate expectation.

19.4.1 HISTORICAL DEVELOPMENT

Until recently, courts were only willing to accept procedural legitimate expectation claims. The view was that public authorities must remain free to make decisions in the public interest and therefore cannot be bound to provide discretionary substantive benefits to individuals on the grounds that they have indicated they would do so. In one case, the idea of a legitimate expectation requiring a public body to provide a substantive benefit was said to be a 'heresy'.[27]

The development of procedural legitimate expectations can be traced to cases like *R v Secretary of State for the Home Department, ex p Khan*.[28] Khan applied for entry clearance under the published immigration criteria, but was refused on grounds not specified in the policy. The Court of Appeal held that this was unlawful: a public body consulting those affected by its decisions cannot subsequently use unpublished criteria that were not discussed during consultation. This established that representations about procedure (what criteria would be used) could create enforceable expectations.

This restrictive approach reflected concerns about the separation of powers (courts constraining executive decision-making), democratic accountability (unelected judges preventing elected officials from changing policy), and administrative flexibility (the government needing to respond to changing circumstances).

[27] See *R v Secretary of State for the Home Department, ex parte Hargreaves* [1997] 1 All ER 397, 412. See Sedley LJ's judgment in *Niazi v Secretary of State* [2008] EWCA Civ 755.

[28] [1984] 1 WLR 1337.

However, that view has now changed. It is now accepted that substantive legitimate expectations may be generated by public bodies and that these ought to be respected, unless there is some overriding public interest in allowing the public body to go back on its word or conduct.[29]

This evolution reflects recognition that predictability and reliability in government action are constitutional values, even if they sometimes limit administrative flexibility.

19.4.2 *R V NORTH AND EAST DEVON HEALTH AUTHORITY, EX PARTE COUGHLAN*

The *Coughlan* case marked the acceptance of substantive legitimate expectations in English law. The facts illustrate both the human dimension of legitimate expectations and the legal principles at stake.

Miss Coughlan was seriously injured in a road accident and, as a result, was tetraplegic, doubly incontinent, and partially paralysed. In 1993, with her agreement, she was moved from a hospital that the health authority wished to close to Mardon House, an NHS facility for the long-term disabled. The health authority assured her and other residents that Mardon House would be their home for life. Despite this assurance, in 1998, following a public consultation, the health authority decided to close Mardon House. Miss Coughlan challenged the decision, in part, on the ground that the promise she had been given created a legitimate expectation that Mardon House would be her home for life. The decision to close the home breached this legitimate expectation and was therefore unlawful. The High Court agreed with her and said that the health authority had shown no overriding public interest that entitled it to break the promise. The health authority appealed unsuccessfully to the Court of Appeal.

The following is an extract from the judgment of the Court of Appeal, to which all members of the court contributed (Lord Woolf MR, Mummery LJ, and Sedley LJ). The principles outlined in the judgment have been followed in subsequent cases and are accepted as correct.[30]

R v North and East Devon Health Authority, ex parte Coughlan (Secretary of State for Health and Anor)
[2001] QB 213

The Promise of a Home for Life

50. The Health Authority appeals on the ground that the judge wrongly held that it had failed to establish that there was an overriding public interest which entitled it to break the 'home for life' promise.

[. . .]

Legitimate expectation—the court's role

55. [. . . I]t is necessary to begin by examining the court's role where what is in issue is a promise as to how it would behave in the future made by a public body when exercising a statutory function. In the past it would have been argued that the promise was to be ignored since it could not have any effect on how the public body exercised its judgment in what it thought was the public interest. Today such an argument would have no prospect of success [. . .]

[29] For further discussion, see Alison L. Young, 'Stuck at a crossroad? Substantive legitimate expectations in English law' (2021) 80 C.L.J. s.179–207; J. Bell, 'The doctrine of legitimate expectations: power-constraining or right-conferring legal standard?' [2016] Public Law 437; P. Reynolds, 'Legitimate expectations and the protection of trust in public officials' [2011] Public Law 330.

[30] *R (Reprotech (Pebsham) Ltd) v East Sussex County Council* [2002] UKHL 8, *per* Lord Hoffmann; also Lord Carswell in *R (Bancoult) v Secretary of State for Foreign and Commonwealth Affairs* [2008] UKHL 61, [133].

56. What is still the subject of some controversy is the court's role when a member of the public, as a result of a promise or other conduct, has a legitimate expectation that he will be treated in one way and the public body wishes to treat him or her in a different way. Here the starting point has to be to ask what in the circumstances the member of the public could legitimately expect. [. . .] Where there is a dispute as to this, the dispute has to be determined by the court [. . .] This can involve a detailed examination of the precise terms of the promise or representation made, the circumstances in which the promise was made and the nature of the statutory or other discretion.

57. There are at least three possible outcomes. (a) The court may decide that the public authority is only required to bear in mind its previous policy or other representation, giving it the weight it thinks right, but no more, before deciding whether to change course. Here the court is confined to reviewing the decision on *Wednesbury* grounds [. . .] This has been held to be the effect of changes of policy in cases involving the early release of prisoners (see *Findlay*'s case; *R v Secretary of State for the Home Dept, ex p Hargreaves* [1997] 1 All ER 397, [1997] 1 WLR 906). (b) On the other hand the court may decide that the promise or practice induces a legitimate expectation of, for example, being consulted before a particular decision is taken. Here it is uncontentious that the court itself will require *the opportunity for consultation* to be given unless there is an overriding reason to resile from it (see *A-G of Hong Kong v Ng Yuen Shiu* [1983] 2 All ER 346, [1983] 2 AC 629) in which case the court will itself judge the adequacy of the reason advanced for the change of policy, taking into account what fairness requires. (c) Where the court considers that a lawful promise or practice has induced a legitimate expectation of a *benefit which is substantive*, not simply procedural, authority now establishes that here too the court will in a proper case decide whether to frustrate the expectation is so unfair that to take a new and different course will amount to an abuse of power. Here, once the legitimacy of the expectation is established, the court will have the task of weighing the requirements of fairness against any overriding interest relied upon for the change of policy.

58. The court having decided which of the categories is appropriate, the court's role in the case of the second and third categories is different from that in the first. In the case of the first, the court is restricted to reviewing the decision on conventional grounds. The test will be rationality and whether the public body has given proper weight to the implications of not fulfilling the promise. In the case of the second category the court's task is the conventional one of determining whether the decision was procedurally fair. In the case of the third, the court has when necessary to determine whether there is a sufficient overriding interest to justify a departure from what has been previously promised.

60. [. . .] We consider that the judge was correct in regarding this case as coming into the third category.] Our reasons are as follows. First, the importance of what was promised to Miss Coughlan [. . .]; second, the fact that promise was limited to a few individuals, and the fact that the consequences to the health authority of requiring it to honour its promise are likely to be financial only.

Coughlan establishes a three-category framework for analysing legitimate expectations:

- **Category 1**: The representation is relevant but not binding. The public body need only consider it alongside other factors. Review is on normal Wednesbury irrationality grounds.
- **Category 2**: The representation creates a procedural legitimate expectation (e.g., to be consulted). The court will enforce this unless there are overriding reasons not to.
- **Category 3**: The representation creates a substantive legitimate expectation to a particular outcome. The court will enforce this unless there is sufficient overriding public interest to justify departure.

19.4.2.1 The proportionality test

The Court of Appeal in *Coughlan* explains when public bodies may act contrary to legitimate expectations. It will be unlawful to frustrate a substantive legitimate expectation if the court decides there has been an abuse of power. '*Here [. . .] the court will have the task of weighing the requirements of fairness against any overriding interest relied upon for a change of policy*' (at [57]).

In undertaking this weighing exercise, the court considered the importance of the promise and that it was made to a specific individual. It applied a proportionality test, which indicated that because the authority's interests were financial only, the promise should be enforced.[31] Where an authority says that an overriding public interest justified frustrating a substantive expectation, the court will expect to see evidence of this. If evidence is not forthcoming, or is considered unpersuasive, the court may not agree.[32]

This approach represents judicial intervention in administrative decision-making. Courts are not just checking whether decisions are rational; they also weigh competing interests and determine whether promises should be enforced.

This judicial intervention has attracted constitutional criticism. Mark Elliott argues that substantive legitimate expectations create an anomaly in the broader framework of judicial review:

M. Elliott, 'Coughlan: substantive protection of legitimate expectations revisited' (2000) 5(1) *Judicial Review* 27–32, 31–32.

> Against this background, *Coughlan* begins to look rather incongruous. The authoritative and highly influential line of case law on the level of protection afforded to human rights on judicial review is premised on the notion that, pending legislative intervention, the rationality doctrine delimits the jurisdiction of the courts vis-à-vis the substance of executive decisions. It is from this general philosophy of the current relationship between judges and decision-makers that the limited jurisdiction of the courts in human rights cases is derived. It is very difficult to see why that general philosophy does not prescribe precisely the same approach in the substantive expectation context.

This critique highlights the tension between legitimate expectations and traditional separation of powers principles. Elliott argues that substantive legitimate expectations are constitutionally problematic because they allow courts to override executive policy decisions based on judicial assessment of what is '*objectively justified*', rather than applying the traditional rationality test that respects executive discretion.[33] He contends that this results in an inconsistent approach, where courts apply strict rationality review even in fundamental human rights cases, yet exercise more intrusive scrutiny when government promises are at stake. This undermines the distinction between judicial review of legality and executive responsibility for policy choices. However, the doctrine has continued to develop, subject to certain requirements that limit its scope.

19.4.3 REQUIREMENTS FOR VALID LEGITIMATE EXPECTATIONS

Not every statement or practice by a public body will generate a legitimate expectation. The law has developed several requirements that must be met.

[31] In *Paponette* the Privy Council approved of the approach taken by Laws LJ in *R (Nadarajah and Abdi) v Secretary of State for the Home Department* [2005] EWCA Civ 1363.

[32] Lord Dyson, *Paponette v Attorney General of Trinidad and Tobago* [2010] UKPC 32, [42].

[33] M. Elliott, 'Coughlan: Substantive Protection of Legitimate Expectations Revisited' (2000) 5(1) Judicial Review 27–32, 30.

Where a legitimate expectation is claimed on the basis of a representation or promise, the representation or promise must not conflict with applicable statutory provisions. This reflects the principle that public bodies cannot exceed or contradict their statutory powers, even by making promises.

In *Begbie*[34] the applicant had been offered a place on the assisted places scheme, under which children were allowed places at independent schools with their fees paid from public funds. Following the 1997 general election, the new Labour government abolished the scheme. The applicant argued that this decision was in breach of her legitimate expectation of a place based on an offer made prior to the election. The claim failed on the ground that the offer could not create a legitimate expectation because that would conflict with legislative provisions that enabled (but did not require) the minister to allow children to take advantage of the assisted places scheme in exceptional situations. This was not the type of situation envisaged by the legislation.

This requirement prevents public bodies from amending legislation through informal promises. It also prevents individuals from using legitimate expectations to circumvent statutory limitations.

19.4.4 THE REPRESENTATION MUST BE CLEAR AND UNEQUIVOCAL

Vague or ambiguous statements cannot generate legitimate expectations.[35] This requirement reflects several policy concerns: fairness to public bodies (they should know when they are making binding commitments); legal certainty (clear rules about what creates expectations); and democratic accountability (formal decisions should generally be made through proper procedures).

In order to generate legitimate expectations, representations must be *'clear and unequivocal'*. *ABCIFER*[36] concerned a scheme set up to compensate British people who had been interned by the Japanese during the Second World War. Those eligible would receive an *ex gratia* payment of £10,000. The minister announced to Parliament that *'British civilians who were interned'* would benefit. The eligibility criteria were later changed so that payments would be made only to *'British subjects whom the Japanese interned and who were born in the UK, or had a parent or grandparent born here'*. Some ex-prisoners were therefore excluded and claimed judicial review on the ground that earlier announcements had created a legitimate expectation that they would benefit. The court held that the minister's announcement was not sufficiently clear and unequivocal to create a substantive legitimate expectation.

The requirement for clarity can be difficult to apply in practice. The decision of the House of Lords in *Bancoult*[37] illustrates that what is clear to some judges may be unclear to others.

The case concerned government statements about allowing the Chagos Islanders to return to their homeland. The Foreign Secretary had stated that the government would *'put in place a new Immigration Ordinance which will allow the Ilois to return to the outer islands'*.[38] When the government later prevented their return, the islanders claimed this breached a clear promise. The Court

[34] *R v Department of Education and Employment, ex parte Begbie* [1999] All ER (D) 983.

[35] Dyson LJ, *R (Association of British Civilians: Far Eastern region) v SS for the Defence* [2003] QB 1397, [62]; *R v IRC, ex parte MFK Underwriting Agents* [1990] 1 AC, 1569; *The United Policyholders Group and others v The Attorney General of Trinidad and Tobago* [2016] UKPC, Lord Neuberger, [37].

[36] *Association of British Civilian Internees: Far Eastern Region (ABCIFER) v Secretary of State for Defence* [2003] QB 1397.

[37] *R (Bancoult) v Secretary of State for Foreign and Commonwealth Affairs* [2008] UKHL 61; see Chapter 10, Section 10.2.7, 'Judicial Review of Prerogative Powers'.

[38] 3 November 2000; quoted in Richard Gifford, Chagos Refugees Group, 'Memorandum Concerning British Indian Ocean Territory', Submission to The Foreign Affairs Select Committee of the House of Commons, October 12, 2007.

of Appeal unanimously agreed that the statement was sufficiently clear to create a legitimate expectation. However, the House of Lords majority disagreed, finding no clear and unambiguous promise.

This case demonstrates the subjective nature of determining whether statements are '*clear and unequivocal*'. It also illustrates how political and policy considerations may influence judicial interpretation of seemingly factual questions.

19.4.5 FACTORS AFFECTING THE STRENGTH OF LEGITIMATE EXPECTATIONS

Even when the basic requirements are met, several factors influence whether legitimate expectations are enforceable and how strong the protection will be.

In *Coughlan*, one consideration for the Court of Appeal was that the promise had been made to a small group of people who were directly affected by it. This factor has been developed in subsequent cases.

In *Niazi v Secretary of State*,[39] Laws LJ explained that substantive legitimate expectations are more likely to be enforced when made to small groups rather than large classes of people: '*Though in theory there may be no limit to the number of beneficiaries of a promise for the purpose of such an expectation, in reality it is likely to be small, if the court is to make the expectation good*'.[40]

This reflects practical and constitutional considerations. Courts are more willing to enforce promises to small groups because the administrative burden is manageable and there are fewer competing public interests. Conversely, broad policy promises raise concerns about democratic accountability—courts are reluctant to enforce promises that could constrain the elected government or override competing public interests affecting large numbers of people.

Laws LJ refers to the likelihood that public interest factors will enable public bodies to break promises to a broad class of people. The broader the class affected, the more likely it is that policy and political factors will be involved, and courts will consider the matter to fall beyond their domain.

19.4.6 RELIANCE AND DETRIMENT

A traditional contract law approach might suggest that legitimate expectations should only be protected where individuals have relied on representations to their detriment. However, administrative law has taken a different approach.

While some judges suggest that a legitimate expectation will arise only if the claimant has relied on a promise or a representation to their detriment, the better view is that reliance is not necessary, although if it can be established that the claimant has relied on a promise to their detriment the claim will be strengthened.

Lord Justice Laws explained in *Niazi* that the obligation to respect legitimate expectations is rooted in the requirements of good administration and does not depend on whether individuals have relied on, or been adversely affected by, representations made by public bodies. This approach has been supported by the UK Supreme Court.

[39] [2008] EWCA Civ 755. [40] Ibid at [46].

In the matter of the application by Geraldine Finucane for Judicial Review
[2019] UKSC 7

Lord Kerr [With Whom Lady Hale, Lord Hodge, and Lady Black Agreed]

72. I would disagree with any suggestion that it must be shown that the applicant suffered a detriment before maintaining a claim for frustration of legitimate expectation for a fundamental reason. A recurring theme of many of the judgments in this field is that the substantive legitimate expectation principle is underpinned by the requirements of good administration. It cannot conduce to good standards of administration to permit public authorities to resile at whim from undertakings which they give simply because the person or group to whom such promises were made are unable to demonstrate a tangible disadvantage.

This approach emphasizes that legitimate expectations serve broader constitutional purposes beyond protecting individual reliance. They promote consistency in government (public bodies should honour their commitments), accountability (officials should be held to their public statements), and trust in government (reliable public administration depends on keeping promises).

However, evidence of detrimental reliance still strengthens claims significantly, as it demonstrates concrete harm from breaking promises and makes judicial intervention more justifiable.

QUESTIONS

1. The *Coughlan* case establishes that promises made by public authorities can be broken only where there is '*sufficient overriding public interest to justify departure*'. Using the three-category framework from *Coughlan*, explain how courts balance individual reliance on promises against broader public interests. Why might this balance be struck differently for promises made to individuals versus those made to large groups?
2. Substantive legitimate expectations allow courts to enforce the content of government promises, not just procedural rights. Does this represent an appropriate extension of judicial review beyond its traditional focus on decision-making processes, or does it risk courts becoming '*appeal courts*' from administrative decisions? Consider the constitutional implications of your answer.
3. A government department announces it will conduct individual interviews before refusing asylum applications, and follows this practice for 6 months. Due to a sudden increase in applications, the department wants to switch to a paper-based system to clear the backlog faster. Asylum seekers who have not yet had their interviews argue they have a legitimate expectation to individual interviews based on the announced practice. Can the department change its procedure to cope with increased caseload, or must it honor the expectation it created through its established practice? Using the *Coughlan* framework, explain what type of legitimate expectation this might be and how a court would balance the individual's expectation against the department's need for administrative flexibility to manage its workload.

19.4.7 SUBSTANTIVE FAIRNESS AND EQUAL TREATMENT

While procedural fairness is well-established, a key question remains: must public bodies also make decisions that are substantively fair, for instance by ensuring equal treatment of similarly situated individuals?

This question was addressed directly by the Supreme Court in *R (Gallaher) v Competition and Markets Authority*.[41] The case concerned whether the Competition and Markets Authority should withdraw findings against some companies because it had withdrawn similar findings against others. The claimants argued that fairness required equal treatment unless there was objective justification for different treatment.

The Supreme Court unanimously rejected this argument. Lord Carnwath explained:

> Whatever the position in European law or under other constitutions or jurisdictions, the domestic law of this country does not recognise equal treatment as a distinct principle of administrative law. Consistency, [. . .] is a 'generally desirable' objective, but not an absolute rule.[42]

The court's reasoning reflects fundamental constitutional principles. As Lord Hoffmann explained in an earlier case:

Lord Hoffmann in *Matadeen v Pointu*
[1999] 1 AC 98

> [9] . . . treating like cases alike and unlike cases differently is a general axiom of rational behaviour. [. . .] But what counts as a valid reason for treating them differently? And, perhaps more important, who is to decide whether the reason is valid or not? Must it always be the courts? The reasons for not treating people uniformly often involve [. . .] questions of social policy on which views may differ. These are questions which the elected representatives of the people have some claim to decide for themselves.

In other words, while equal treatment is important in a democracy, deciding what constitutes 'fair' treatment often involves policy choices that should be made by elected officials rather than unelected judges.

Gallaher establishes several principles. Simple unfairness is not, by itself, a ground for judicial review, whereas procedural fairness remains well-established within judicial review. Claims about unfair treatment must be channelled through existing grounds such as illegality, procedural impropriety, or irrationality. Courts should not become general appeal courts for administrative decisions.

This means that while a decision might seem unfair, it can only be challenged in judicial review where it violates statutory requirements (illegality), results from unfair procedures (procedural impropriety), is so unreasonable that no rational decision-maker could have reached it (irrationality), or breaches legitimate expectations where specific promises have been made.

The relationship between procedural and substantive fairness remains complex. Critics argue that the distinction is sometimes artificial: procedural failings often lead to substantively unfair outcomes. The doctrine of legitimate expectations, which can require substantively fair treatment, sits somewhat uneasily with the general rule that substantive fairness is not a ground of review.

[41] [2018] UKSC 25. [42] Ibid para. [24].

These tensions reflect deeper questions about the appropriate role of courts in a democratic system, balancing individual protection against democratic accountability and administrative effectiveness. Not all commentators accept the Supreme Court's approach in *Gallaher*. Mark Elliott argues that subsuming consistency within rationality review makes the law less transparent and predictable.

M. Elliott, 'A "principle" of consistency? The doctrinal configuration of the law of judicial review' (2018) 77(3) *The Cambridge Law Journal* 444–448

It might therefore be retorted that any criticism of *Gallaher* amounts to little more than taxonomical fetishism: does it really matter whether, like legitimate expectation, consistent/equal treatment is regarded as an administrative law 'principle' in its own right (in the sense of being a separate ground of review)?

For three reasons, it does matter. First, recognising consistent/equal treatment as a free-standing principle would be fitting recognition of its normative importance. Secondly, it would facilitate the development of a suitable doctrinal superstructure, as occurred with legitimate expectation. This would enable courts to approach in a more systematic and predictable manner such issues as the circumstances in which a policy or practice should be regarded as sufficiently clear and settled as to render deviations from it prima facie 'inconsistent'. Thirdly, carving out a principle of consistent/equal treatment from the generality of rationality review would place less weight on the latter and, as a result, would aid legal transparency.

This academic critique highlights a tension in administrative law between doctrinal simplicity and legal clarity. While the Supreme Court in *Gallaher* prioritized avoiding a multiplication of legal categories, critics argue this comes at the cost of transparency about the real reasons for judicial decisions. Whether future courts will move toward recognizing consistency as a distinct principle, or continue to channel such claims through existing grounds, remains to be seen. For now, students should understand that claims about unfair treatment must be formulated as challenges to legality, procedural impropriety, or irrationality.

QUESTIONS

1. A council gives housing priority to families with children but refuses to explain why single people are treated differently. A single applicant argues this is 'unfair discrimination'. Using the principles from *Gallaher*, explain whether this claim would succeed in judicial review and what legal grounds (if any) might be available.
2. The *Gallaher* decision establishes that 'simple unfairness as such is not a ground for judicial review', yet we have seen throughout this chapter that procedural fairness is well-established and legally enforceable. Explain the difference between procedural fairness and substantive fairness, using examples to illustrate why courts are willing to enforce one but not the other. In your answer, consider what this distinction reveals about the constitutional role of courts in reviewing administrative decisions.
3. A university changes its admissions criteria mid-year, disadvantaging students who have already applied under the old system. Some students argue this is 'unfair', while others claim it breaches their 'legitimate expectations'. Explain the difference between these two arguments and which is more likely to succeed in judicial review.

19.5 CURRENT DEVELOPMENTS AND FUTURE CHALLENGES

Procedural impropriety continues to evolve as courts grapple with new challenges and changing social expectations. Several trends merit attention:

19.5.1 DIGITAL GOVERNMENT AND FAIR PROCEDURES

The increasing digitization of government services raises new questions about what fair procedures require. *Bridges*[43] illustrates these challenges. The case concerned police use of automated facial recognition technology that scanned faces in crowds. The Court of Appeal found the legal framework inadequate because the criteria for watchlists were too vague and there was insufficient guidance on where the technology could be deployed.

Bridges demonstrates that traditional procedural fairness principles, such as adequate legal frameworks and clear decision-making criteria, still apply to new technologies, but may require adaptation to address automated decision-making systems.

19.5.2 RESOURCE CONSTRAINTS AND FAIRNESS

Public bodies increasingly argue that resource constraints limit their ability to provide extensive procedural protections. Courts must balance fairness requirements with practical constraints, particularly in high-volume areas like social welfare and immigration. The challenge is ensuring that administrative efficiency does not completely override basic procedural rights.

19.5.3 THE IMPACT OF HUMAN RIGHTS

The Human Rights Act 1998 continues to influence procedural requirements, particularly through Article 6 (fair trial) and Article 8 (private and family life). Where human rights standards exceed common law requirements, claimants may rely on the higher protection. This creates a complex interplay between different sources of procedural protection.

19.6 CONCLUDING COMMENTS

This chapter has considered procedural impropriety as a ground of judicial review. It has examined how courts distinguish between mandatory and directory statutory requirements, and how the common law imposes duties of procedural fairness even where the statute is silent. The chapter has shown how courts address questions about the scope of judicial review, including how far judges should go when questioning the legality and fairness of decisions by public bodies. While judges have expanded the grounds of review, they remain mindful of the need not to trespass into the policy or political domain. If judges are perceived as overreaching, the executive and legislature may impose constraints on their powers by limiting or excluding judicial review.

Procedural impropriety illustrates central tensions in modern administrative law. The development from rigid rule-based approaches to flexible, contextual fairness requirements demonstrates

[43] *R (Bridges) v Chief Constable of South Wales Police* [2020] EWCA Civ 1058.

how administrative law adapts to changing circumstances while maintaining core principles. The evolution of legitimate expectations from a 'heresy' to an accepted ground of review demonstrates how legal doctrine develops to meet new challenges.

The limits identified in cases like *Gallaher* remind us that judicial review operates within constitutional constraints. Courts must balance their role in ensuring fair treatment against respect for democratic decision-making and administrative effectiveness.

For students beginning their study of administrative law, procedural impropriety illustrates how legal principles develop through case law, how competing values must be balanced, and how constitutional considerations shape legal doctrine. Understanding these materials requires not just learning rules, but appreciating the broader context in which administrative law operates.

FURTHER READING

The Administrative Court Judicial Review Guide, 2024.

Government Legal Department, *The Judge Over Your Shoulder*, 6th edn (republished 2022, London: GLD).

Harlow, R. and Rawlings, R., *Law and Administration*, 4th edn, (2022, CUP), Ch. 16.

Woolf, H., Jowell, J., Donnelly, C., and Hare I., *De Smith's Judicial Review*, 8th edn (2018, London: Sweet & Maxwell).

20

JUDICIAL REVIEW 4: EXCLUSION AND LIMITATION OF JUDICIAL REVIEW

CENTRAL ISSUES

1. Governments recognise's' that compliance with judicial review helps achieve good administration. However, governments use various techniques to respond to judicial review when they dislike judgments or considers judicial review to be inappropriate. Professors Harlow and Rawlings refer to these techniques as 'striking back' and 'clamping down'.
2. Governments may also use legislation to limit or prevent (oust) judicial review
3. The courts have accepted that Parliament can exclude, or 'oust', judicial review, but have held that this can only be achieved with the clearest of words.
4. But the issues are not simply about the language of legislation. They concern fundamental questions of constitutional law. Can a supreme or sovereign Parliament prevent access to the courts and enforcement of the rule of law? Can the courts protect the rule of law by refusing to accept Parliament's ability to limit or prevent judicial review?

20.1 INTRODUCTION

Public bodies normally seek to comply with judicial review decisions and see judicial review as being important to achieving good administration. This, however, is not to say that judicial review is always welcome or that judgments are always well received, and over the years governments of all political complexions have taken steps to limit the use of judicial review and reduce or remove the effects of judgments. Professors Harlow and Rawlings refer to various strategies.[1] These include 'striking back' to remove the effects of judicial decisions that government dislikes or finds inconvenient and 'clamping down' to protect government from future judicial reviews by such things as reforming procedures to restrict access; altering how litigation is funded; restricting legal aid; granting very broad

[1] C. Harlow and R. Rawlings, 'Striking Back' and 'Clamping Down', An Alternative Perspective on Judicial Review', in J. Bell, M. Elliott, P. Murray, and J. Varuhas (eds) *Public Law Adjudication in Common Law Systems: Process and Substance* (2016, Oxford: Hart Publishing).

discretionary powers; or limiting judges' ability to fully consider issues A recent example of 'striking back' and 'clamping down' was s. 2(1) of the The Safety Rwanda (Asylum and Immigration) Act 2024. This provided that 'every decision – maker must conclusively treat Rwanda as a safe country' thus enabling the removal of asylum seekers to Rwanda and removing the effect of *R(AAA) v Secretary of State of State for the Home Department.*[2]

In the following extract the authors build on what Harlow and Rawlings say and identify the emergence of a third form of executive response to judicial review, that they call 'entrapment'.

J. Tomlinson, N. Coakley, and R. Gambroudes, 'It's a trap! The changing dynamics of executive engagement with judicial review', U.K. Const. L. Blog (28 July 2022) https://ukconstitutionallaw.org/

> Executive 'entrapment' of judicial review becomes possible when [government] . . . realise there is political advantage to be gained by routinely being critical of the judicial review system, including the courts, the lawyers representing claimants, and the claimants themselves. In such political conditions, government consciously then makes decisions or adopts controversial policies at serious risk of being found to be unlawful, which provoke legal challenge. The inevitable judicial review challenge, from the government's perspective, then creates a 'win-win' scenario: it either wins in court, overcoming 'meddling' courts, and being given licence to implement its 'bold' policy; or the government loses in court and does not get to implement its policy but secures popular political advantage through vocal complaining about courts and lawyers 'blocking' a government that is trying to implement 'bold' policies. Complaining can then, in turn, lay the groundwork for further striking back and clamping down. All of this is, of course, entirely possible within a constitutional system where the government is both the chief repeat player litigant within, and chief designer of, the judicial review system.

While it is important to be aware of the various ways governments respond to judicial review in this chapter we focus on one method of restricting access to the courts, namely the use of legislation to limit or totally exclude (oust) judicial review.

Given the recent heightened concerns in some quarters regarding judicial overreach and the inappropriate use of judicial review to question government decisions there is considerable constitutional interest in whether judicial review can be prevented. In particular, can an Act of Parliament actually oust the court's judicial review jurisdiction? Can it, in other words, prevent the courts from ensuring that governmental bodies, including ministers, comply with the requirements of legality set out in the three previous chapters? At the root of this contentious question lies a potential clash between two fundamental constitutional principles. Does the principle of parliamentary supremacy enable Parliament to prevent judicial review? If so, does this not undermine the ability of the courts to protect and enforce the rule of law? While these questions are posed throughout this Chapter it is worth repeating Lord Steyn's view in the *Jackson* case that in:

> *exceptional circumstances involving an attempt to abolish judicial review or the ordinary role of the courts, the [. . .] Supreme Court may have to consider whether this is a constitutional fundamental which even a sovereign Parliament acting at the behest of a complaisant House of Commons cannot abolish.*[3]

[2] [2023] UKSC 42. The Act was repealed in 2025.

[3] *Jackson v Her Majesty's Attorney General [2005] UKHL 56*, para 102.

Questions: Ousting judicial review—A clash of constitutional fundamentals?

Does Parliament's supremacy extend to excluding access to judicial review, or even abolishing judicial review altogether?

- If judicial review were excluded or abolished would this fundamentally conflict with the rule of law?
- If there was a conflict between the supremacy of Parliament and the rule of law which would prevail, and how would (or should) the conflict be resolved?

20.1.1 REMEMBER SOME BASICS: JUDICIAL REVIEW IS BASED ON THE COMMON LAW

Before going further it is important to remember that a distinction exists between appeals and the judicial review jurisdiction. As we saw in Chapter 17 while the opportunities to appeal only exist if they are permitted by statute the High Court's judicial review jurisdiction does not depend on statute but is based on the common law. While judicial review is not created by statute Parliament may try to use statute to limit or prevent its use, and there has been a long history of such attempts.[4] These have included the following provisions in statutes:

- *'as if they were enacted'* clauses indicating that decisions of ministers should be treated as if they were enacted in legislation and therefore not subject to judicial review (because UK judges cannot review the legality of statutory provisions). Such clauses have been held not to prevent judicial review of decisions that a minister had no power to make.[5]
- *'shall be final'* clauses indicating that a decision of a tribunal or body should be treated as final and for this reason not subject to judicial review. It has been held that here the word 'final' means final on the facts and not final on the law and therefore judicial review remains available.[6]
- *Time limit clauses* allowing appeal against a decision of a public authority within a limited period, but saying that after this period, decisions *'cannot be questioned in any legal proceedings whatsoever'*. Time limit clauses of this type will prevent legal challenge after the period has expired.[7] The difference between time limit clauses and the earlier examples is that courts accept that it is in the public interest to ensure that legal claims are brought within certain time limits.

One of the most important decisions on exclusion or ouster clauses was the decision in *Anisminic v Foreign Compensation Commission*[8] to which we now turn.

[4] See, e.g. the historical accounts in *R (on the application of Privacy International v Investigatory Powers Tribunal* [2019] UKSC 22, see below. Hayley Hooper notes that an early example is art 9 of the Bill of Rights Act 1689 which states that 'Freedoms of Speech and Debates or Proceedings in Parlyament ought not to be impeached or questioned in any Court . . .': see Hayley J. Hooper, 'No superior form of law? *R (Oceana) v Upper Tribunal* [2024] *Public Law*, 1 at 7.

[5] *R v Min of Health. ex p Yaffe* (1931) AC 494.

[6] *R v Medical Appeal Tribunal ex p Gilmore* [1957] 1 QB 574.

[7] *Smith v East Elloe* [1956] AC 736; for a more recent case, see e.g. *Derwent Holdings Ltd v Liverpool City Council* [2008] EWHC 3023. See also 'conclusive evidence' clauses, considered in *Johnstone v Chief Constable of the Royal Ulster Constabulary* [1987] QB 129.

[8] [1969] 2 AC 147. see D. Feldman, 'Anisminic in Perspective' in S. Juss and M. Sunkin (ed.), *Landmark Cases in Public Law*, (2017, Oxford: Hart Publishing); also D. Feldman, 'Anisminic in *Retrospect*' in Arvind, T.T., Kirkham, R. Daithi Mac Sitigh, and Stirton. L. (eds), *Executive Decision-Making and the Courts: Revisiting the Origins of Modern Judicial Review* (2021, Oxford: Hart Publishing).

20.2 *ANISMINIC V FOREIGN COMPENSATION COMMISSION*

The Foreign Compensation Commission (FCC) had been established by the Foreign Compensation Act 1950 to deal with compensation claims made by those whose property had been damaged or lost in fighting abroad. The fund from which the compensation was paid had a fixed amount of money in it, which was not necessarily sufficient to meet all potential claims. The FCC therefore had discretion when making of compensation payments which meant that claimants did not have a legal right to receive any money or to particular sums. In order to reinforce this aspect of the scheme s. 4(4) of the Foreign Compensation Act 1950 provided that:

> *The determination by the commission of any application made to them under this Act shall not be called in question in any court of law.*

Anisminic claimed compensation for property that was lost or damaged in Egypt during the Suez crisis. However, they were unsuccessful because the FCC found that they had sold the property to TEDO an Egyptian concern. The FCC said that this disqualified them because under the eligibility rules their 'successor in title' had to be British. There was no appeal allowed from decisions of the FCC, so they could not appeal. Did the wording of s 4(4) mean that they had no legal remedy?

Despite the wording of the ouster clause Anisminic decided to challenge the FCC's decision. Their core argument was that the FCC had made an error of law when they considered the nationality of TEDO. They said the nationality of TEDO would only have been relevant had TEDO actually been a 'successor in title', but TEDO was not a 'successor in title' because when they sold the property to TEDO they retained the right to claim compensation. This meant that TEDO was not a 'successor in title' to the right to claim compensation and therefore its nationality was irrelevant. This error, Anisminic said, meant that the FCC's determination had been unlawfully made and so was not protected by s. 4(4).[9] The FCC disputed that they had made an error of law and argued that in any case s 4(4) prevented a legal challenge.

At first instance, Brown J held that the courts were not excluded. His decision was overturned by a unanimous decision of the Court of Appeal. The House of Lords, by a majority of three to two, upheld Anisminic's appeal. The core reasoning of the majority is set out in the following extract from Lord Reid's judgment.

Anisminic v Foreign Compensation Commission
[1969] 2 AC 147

Lord Reid
The next argument was that, by reason of the provisions of section 4(4) of the [Foreign Compensation Act] 1950 [. . .], the courts are precluded from considering whether the respondent's determination was a nullity [. . .]

[He sets out s. 4(4) of the 1950 Act.]

The [FCC] maintains that these are plain words only capable of having one meaning. Here is a determination which is apparently valid: there is nothing on the face of the document to cast any doubt on its validity. If it is a nullity, that could only be established by raising some kind of proceedings in court.

[9] Similar to the reasoning in *R v Min of Health. ex p Yaffe* (1931) AC 494, above.

But that would be calling the determination in question, and that is expressly prohibited by the statute. The appellants maintain that that is not the meaning of the words of this provision. They say that 'determination' means a real determination and does not include an apparent or purported determination which in the eyes of the law has no existence because it is a nullity. Or, putting it in another way, if you seek to show that a determination is a nullity you are not questioning the purported determination—you are maintaining that it does not exist as a determination. It is one thing to question a determination which does exist: it is quite another thing to say that there is nothing to be questioned.

[Having summarised the core arguments Lord Reid continues . . .]

Statutory provisions which seek to limit the ordinary jurisdiction of the court have a long history. No case has been cited in which any other form of words limiting the jurisdiction of the court has been held to protect a nullity. If the draftsman or Parliament had intended to introduce a new kind of ouster clause so as to prevent any [such] inquiry [. . .] I would have expected to find something much more specific than the bald statement that a determination shall not be called in question in any court of law. Undoubtedly such a provision protects every determination which is not a nullity. But I do not think that it is necessary or even reasonable to construe the word 'determination' as including everything which purports to be a determination but which is in fact no determination at all [. . .] if that were intended it would be easy to say so [. . .]. I have come without hesitation to the conclusion that in this case we are not prevented from inquiring whether the order of the commission was a nullity.

The majority went on to hold that the FCC had made an error of law and that its decision was therefore a nullity. This raised the question whether all legal errors would result in a body's decision being a nullity or whether a body remained free to make certain errors without their subsequent decision being null and void? We need not go into this question here. The key point for us is that Anisminic had not argued that Parliament could never exclude judicial review; rather, it said—and Lord Reid agreed—that judicial review could be excluded only by clear words. The '*bald statement*' that '*a determination shall not be called into question*' was insufficiently clear: did it prevent the courts from declaring a purported determination to be a nullity, or did it only prevent them from questioning a valid determination? Faced with this ambiguity, the House of Lords gave the word 'determination' the meaning that was compatible with maintaining access to justice and the jurisdiction of the courts rather than the meaning that removed this jurisdiction. This may seem a rather artificial way of dealing with the issue: after all, how could the courts conclude that a 'purported determination' was a nullity without it being 'called into question' in the courts? It may have been artificial, but it was also a very orthodox approach to statutory interpretation: it enabled access to the courts in this particular case but left Parliament free in the future to oust judicial review using clearer language.

PAUSE FOR REFLECTION

The basic message of the decision in *Anisminic* is that Parliament can only prevent judicial review by using statutory language that is clear and unambiguous.

Saying that 'determinations' cannot be questioned in any legal proceedings is not clear because it does not clearly cover invalid or purported determinations.

To prevent judicial review of purported determinations Parliament would have to say something like: '*neither determinations nor purported. determinations can be questioned*' in the courts.

Parliament quickly responded by enacting the Foreign Compensation Appeals Act 1969. This established an appeal from the Foreign Compensation Commission to the Court of Appeal on points of law. It also provided a new definition of the term 'determination' in s. 3(3): *'In this section "determination" includes* [. . .] *anything which purports to be a determination.'*

Since the *Anisminic* saga, various other attempts have been made to find ways to exclude judicial review. One such example[10] is provided by the wording of the Regulation of Investigatory Powers Act 2000. Section 67(8) provides that:

> [. . .] determinations, awards, and other decisions of the [Investigatory Powers Tribunal] (including decisions as to whether they have jurisdiction) shall not be subject to appeal or be liable to be questioned in any court.

We will come back to s. 67(8) of the Regulation of Investigatory Powers Act 2000 in a moment. However, before doing so it is worth briefly considering Mr Cart's attempt to seek judicial review of the Upper Tribunal as this provides an example of how courts have balanced access to judicial review on the one hand with other rule of law interests such as the independence of the tribunal system.[11]

20.3 THE UPPER TRIBUNAL AND JUDICIAL REVIEW: THE *CART* LITIGATION

The Tribunals, Courts and Enforcement Act 2007 gives the Upper Tribunal a judicial review jurisdiction over the First-tier Tribunal, applying the same principles as the High Court,[12] but can judicial review be used to challenge decisions of the Upper Tribunal? This issue was considered when Mr Cart complained that a decision to vary his child maintenance payments was unfairly made without him being notified. He appealed to the First-tier Tribunal but was unsuccessful. The First-Tribunal refused him permission to appeal to the Upper Tribunal. The Upper Tribunal also refused him permission to appeal. Because legislation does not allow an appeal to the courts against a decision of the Upper Tribunal to refuse permission to appeal, Mr Cart's only remedy was to challenge the Upper Tribunal's refusal using judicial review. He applied for judicial review but was unsuccessful in the High Court, Court of Appeal[13] and UK Supreme Court.[14] While Cart lost in the UK Supreme Court it was accepted by all parties that the Upper Tribunal was not immune from judicial review. The *'real question'*, said Lady Hale, *'is what level of independent scrutiny outside the tribunal system is required by the rule of law'* (at [51]). The Supreme Court accepted that some limitation on judicial review was necessary, not least to avoid the courts being flooded with claims. In order to adopt an approach that was in the words of Lady Hale *'principled but proportionate'*, the court held that judicial review of non-appealable decisions (such as refusals to allow an appeal) should only be possible when there is

[10] Note also the Asylum and Immigration (Treatment of Claimants, etc) Bill that would have inserted a new s. 108A into the Nationality, Immigration and Asylum Act 2002 preventing judicial review of the Asylum and Immigration Tribunal. See A. Le Sueur, 'Three strikes and it's out? The UK Government's strategy to oust judicial review from immigration and asylum decision making' [2004] Public Law 225–33.

[11] See Chapter 16. [12] Section 15(4) and (5). [13] [2010] EWCA Civ 859.

[14] *R (Cart) v Upper Tribunal* [2011] UKSC 28. In the Supreme Court the case was joined by another: *R (MR (Pakistan)) v The Upper Tribunal* which raised the same issue but involving asylum. A case from Scotland was also dealt with by the same court: *Eba v Advocate General for Scotland* [2011] UKSC 29.

an important point of principle or practice involved, or when there is another compelling reason. This is the test used when considering whether appeals should be heard by the Court of Appeal.[15]

Following *Cart* it therefore became possible to use judicial review to challenge non-appealable, decisions of the Upper Tribunal where important issues of principle were involved and this became an important route for redress in certain situations. However, the Independent Review of Administrative Law was concerned that too many *Cart* judicial reviews were being made, saying that: '*the continued expenditure of judicial resources on considering applications for a Cart JR cannot be defended.*'[16] Its recommendation that *Cart* judicial reviews should be prevented was accepted by the government and implemented by s. 2 of the Judicial Review and Courts Act 2022.[17]

We now return to s. 67(8) of the Regulation of Investigatory Powers Act 2000 and the case brought by Privacy International seeking judicial review of the Investigatory Powers Tribunal (IPT).

20.4 THE *PRIVACY INTERNATIONAL* CASE

Privacy International is a group that campaigns to protect privacy arguing that '*privacy is essential to the protection of autonomy and human dignity, serving as the foundation upon which other human rights are built*'.[18] The IPT is a judicial body which operates independently of government to provide a right of redress for anyone who believes they have been a victim of unlawful action by a public authority using covert investigative techniques. It considers complaints about any conduct by or on behalf of the UK Intelligence Community, MI5, SIS, and GCHQ, as well as claims alleging the infringement of human rights by those agencies.

Privacy International complained to the IPT that GCHQ had been conducting unlawful computer network exploitation activity (i.e. hacking). It argued that GCHQ did not have authority to undertake generalized hacking because the Secretary of State under whose warrant it was acting only had power to grant warrants authorizing 'specified' acts in respect of 'specified' property,[19] but not general warrants. The IPT held that the grant of general warrants was permitted.

Privacy International claimed judicial review to challenge the IPT's decision. The High Court held that s. 67(8) of the Regulation of Investigatory Powers Act 2000 (see earlier for the wording of this provision) prevented judicial review. Privacy International appealed unsuccessfully to the Court of Appeal essentially relying on the approach taken in *Anisminic*.[20] The Court of Appeal, however, distinguished the *Anisminic* case on two main grounds. First, s. 67(8) expressly included decisions concerning the IPT's jurisdiction, and thereby prevented judicial review of '*a purported decision*' (para. 34). In other words, even assuming the IPT's decision had been tarnished by an error of law that meant the IPT had acted beyond its jurisdiction it could not be reviewed. Secondly, the Court of Appeal stressed the special characteristics and functions of the IPT, in particular that the IPT is a judicial body staffed

[15] For an overall assessment see E. Laurie, 'Assessing the Upper Tribunal's potential to deliver administrative justice' [2012] Public Law 288; J. Bell, 'The Relationship between judicial review and the Upper Tribunal: What have the courts made of Cart?' [2018] Public Law 394.

[16] *Independent Review of Administrative Law*, March 2021, para. 3.46. The statistical basis for this view has been convincingly challenged, see, e.g. J. Tomlinson and A. Pickup, 'Putting the *Cart* before the horse? The confused empirical basis for reform of *Cart* judicial reviews', U.K. Const. L. Blog (29 March 2021), available at https://ukconstitutionallaw.org/.

[17] Inserting s 11A into the Courts and Enforcement Act 2007. See *R (Oceana) v Upper Tribunal (Immigration and Asylum Chamber)* [2023] EWHC 791 (Admin).

[18] https://privacyinternational.org.

[19] Section 5 of the Intelligence Services Act 1994.

[20] *R (on the application of Privacy International) v Investigatory Powers Tribunal* [2017] EWCA 1868.

by senior judges that operates under special (closed) procedures because of the potential national security interests involved, such interests could, the Court of Appeal said, be prejudiced by judicial review proceedings. Lord Justice Sales (as he then was) went on to say that:

> . . . on its proper construction, section 67(8) does clearly mean that all determinations, awards, orders and decisions of the IPT 'shall not . . . be liable to be questioned in any court', including in the High Court on judicial review. This includes those determinations and decisions which the IPT may have made on the basis of what (if there were a judicial review or appeal) might have been found by a court to have been an erroneous view of the law. This interpretation is given clearly, in my view, by the language used in the provision as read in its legislative context.[21]

Privacy International further appealed to the UK Supreme Court.

R (on the application of Privacy International) v Investigatory Powers Tribunal and others
[2019] UKSC 22

> Two issues are identified [. . .]:
>
> i) whether section 67(8) of RIPA 2000 'ousts' the supervisory jurisdiction of the High Court to quash a judgment of the Investigatory Powers Tribunal for error of law?
>
> ii) whether, and, if so, in accordance with what principles, Parliament may by statute 'oust' the supervisory jurisdiction of the High Court to quash the decision of an inferior court or tribunal of limited statutory jurisdiction?

The first *question: does s. 67(8) oust the supervisory jurisdiction of the High Court?*

The Supreme Court, by a majority of four to three, disagreed with the Court of Appeal and held that s. 67(8) does not 'oust' the supervisory jurisdiction of the High Court. This view was taken by Lord Carnwath (who delivered the leading judgment for the majority: Lady Hale, Lord Kerr, and Lord Lloyd-Jones. Lords Sumption, Reed, and Wilson disagreed).

The key elements of Lord Carnwath's judgment on the first issue may be summarized as follows. He adopted an approach that was similar to that taken by the majority in *Anisminic*. In particular, he stressed the strong interpretative presumption against the exclusion of judicial review other than by the '*most clear and explicit words*' (para. 37). He also found there to be no justification for distinguishing *Anisminic* on the grounds that the Foreign Compensation Commission and the IPT are different types of body. For Lord Carnwath '*no principled distinction can be drawn between the Foreign Compensation Commission and the IPT, or indeed the Upper Tribunal in Cart. All were or are inferior jurisdictions, equally subject to the supervision of the High Court*' (para. 66). Thirdly, he said that there is no longer any justification in drawing a distinction between errors of law that are jurisdictional (and which therefore result in a decision being a nullity) and errors of law that are not jurisdictional. The practical effect of this is that any error of law would be capable of being challenged in judicial review.

[21] Para. [26].

Lord Carnwath's conclusions on the first issue are contained in the following extract.

R (on the application of Privacy International) v Investigatory Powers Tribunal and others
[2019] UKSC 22

Lord Carnwath

[99] [The precedents] ... reaffirm in no uncertain terms the continuing strength of the fundamental presumption against ousting the supervisory role of the High Court over other adjudicative bodies, even those established by Parliament with apparently equivalent status and powers of the High Court [...]

[104] [...] I can state my conclusions on the first issue relatively briefly.[...]

105. As Ms Rose [counsel for Privacy International] submits, our interpretation of [s. 67(8)] ... must be informed by the close parallel with the provision under review in *Anisminic*. [...] A determination vitiated by any error of law, jurisdictional or not, was to be treated as no determination at all. It therefore fell outside the reference in the ouster clause to a 'determination of the commission'. In other words, the reference to such a determination was to be read as a reference only to a legally valid determination.

106. On the other side, Sir James Eadie submits that the task of interpretation is to be approached, by reference, not simply to a general presumption against ouster clauses of any kind, but rather to careful examination of the language of the provision, having regard to all aspects of the statutory scheme, and the status or the body in question, [...] The special character and functions of the IPT, combined with the specific references to decisions relating to 'jurisdiction', show a clear intention to protect it from any form of review by the ordinary courts, even in cases to which the *Anisminic* principle would otherwise have applied.

107. The main flaw in this argument, in my view, is that it treats the exercise as one of ordinary statutory interpretation, designed simply to discern 'the policy intention' of Parliament, so downgrading the critical importance of the common law presumption against ouster. In that respect it echoes the unsuccessful argument of the Commission in *Anisminic*. [...] If one applies [Lord Reid's] approach to section 67(8) [...] the exclusion applies, not to all determinations, awards or other decisions whatever their status, but only to those which are 'legally valid' [...]

111 [...] Judicial review can only be excluded by 'the most clear and explicit words' (*Cart*, para. 31). If Parliament has failed to make its intention sufficiently clear, it is not for us to stretch the words used beyond their natural meaning. It may well be that the promoters of the 1985 Act thought that their formula would be enough to provide comprehensive protection from jurisdictional review of any kind. [...] But one is entitled to ask why they did not use more explicit wording. [...] excluding challenges to any determination or 'purported' determination as 'a nullity by reason of lack of jurisdiction, error of law, or any other matter'. The reason for not adopting that course may simply be that [...] it might not have been expected to survive Parliamentary scrutiny.

112. So far as concerns the features of the IPT regime on which the Court of Appeal relied, [...] I am unimpressed by arguments based on the security issues involved in many (though not all) of the IPT's cases. As this case shows, the tribunal itself is able to organise its procedures to ensure that a material point of law can be considered separately without threatening any security interests. The Administrative Court can also ensure that the grant of permission is limited to cases raising points of general significance, and that its proceedings are conducted without risk to security concerns. Further, in the case of the IPT, the potential for overlap with legal issues which may be considered by the ordinary courts [...] makes it all the more important that it is not able to develop its own 'local' law without scope for further review.

Lord Sumption delivered a dissenting judgment with which Lord Reed agreed. There is not space here to consider his arguments fully. Suffice to say, he argued that s. 67(8) must be interpreted having regard to the character of the IPT's functions as well as the nature of the error of law it is said to have committed. Like the Court of Appeal he stressed the special nature of the functions being performed, including the need to maintain confidentiality of secret material (para.196). He noted that the IPT's functions: '*are judicial in an altogether more significant sense than those of the Foreign Compensation Commission. A critical point is that the Tribunal exercises a power of judicial review which would otherwise be exercised by the High Court*' (para. 197).

So Lord Sumption draws a distinction between the FCC and the IPT stressing that the IPT is itself a judicial body. Since the IPT is a judicial body the rule of law is not necessarily threatened if the IPT is not reviewable. While accepting that judicial review is available if the IPT commits certain legal errors, such as if it breaches natural justice, he argues that judicial review is not available to question the merits of decisions taken by the IPT. In this case the alleged error made by the IPT, he argued, goes to the merits of the IPT's decision: the alleged error is one that the IPT can make without rendering its decision subject to judicial review. These points are explained in the following extract dealing with s. 67(8).

R (on the application of Privacy International) v Investigatory Powers Tribunal and others
[2019] UKSC 22

Lord Sumption

199 It is agreed on all sides that the meaning of this provision is a question of construction. It is also agreed that clear words are required if it is to be regarded as ousting the review jurisdiction of the High Court. However, we must not lose sight of the reason why clear words are required. The reason is, as all the authorities (and indeed Lord Carnwath in his judgment in the present case) agree, that Parliament is presumed not to legislate contrary to the rule of law. [. . .] There is nothing inconsistent with the rule of law about allocating a conclusive jurisdiction by way of review to a judicial body other than the High Court. The presumption against ouster clauses is concerned to protect the rule of law, which depends on the availability of judicial review. It is not concerned to protect the jurisdiction of the High Court in some putative turf war with other judicial bodies on whom Parliament has conferred an equivalent review jurisdiction. [. . .]

[Lord Sumption goes on to emphasize that while s. 67(8) excludes judicial review in some situations, it does not exclude judicial review in all situations. For example, it does not exclude review based on a breach of the rules of natural justice]

[205] [. . .] a statutory ouster clause may be clear enough to oust review of a judicial body's substantive decisions but not its procedural failings. In my opinion, section 67(8) is a provision of that kind. It ousts any kind of merits review of the Tribunal's decisions but nothing more than that. This is the narrowest meaning consistent with the language and manifest purpose of the subsection. It does not oust review of those procedural failings which if made out would deprive the Tribunal of its adjudicatory competence.

206. The appellant's complaint is that the Tribunal misconstrued section 5(2) of the Intelligence Services Act 1994 by holding that it authorised thematic warrants. If this was an error, then it seems to me to be clear that it was an error within the permitted field of interpretative power which Parliament has conferred on the Tribunal. [. . .] I conclude that the effect of section 67(8) of Investigatory Powers Act 2000 is that the High Court had no jurisdiction to entertain a challenge to the Tribunal's decision in the present case, whether by way of appeal or judicial review.

In Lord Sumption's view preventing judicial review of errors made within the IPT's 'permitted field of interpretative power' would not threaten the rule of law.[22]

The second question: *Whether and, if so, in accordance with what principles, may Parliament 'oust' the supervisory jurisdiction of the High Court to quash the decision of an inferior court or tribunal?*

The second question considered by the Supreme Court is an unusually general one that appears to seek the court's views on matters that are not specifically concerned with determining a legal dispute between the parties. Lord Sumption likened it to seeking '*an answer to an examination question posed in wholly general terms*' (para. 207). Lord Carnwath, for the majority, also recognised its breadth. Given his answer to the first question he said it was strictly unnecessary to deal with the second question. However, he thought that the principles discussed in his judgment '*have important implications beyond the form of ouster clause under consideration in this case*' and therefore '*some comment may be of value*' (para. 113). His comments on the second issue should be carefully read, but for present purposes it is sufficient to go immediately to his conclusion.

R (on the application of Privacy International) v Investigatory Powers Tribunal and others
[2019] UKSC 22

Lord Carnwath [on the Second Issue]

144. In conclusion on the second issue, although it is not necessary to decide the point, I see a strong case for holding that, consistently with the rule of law, binding effect cannot be given to a clause which purports wholly to exclude the supervisory jurisdiction of the High Court to review a decision of an inferior court or tribunal, whether for excess or abuse of jurisdiction, or error of law. In all cases, regardless of the words used, it should remain ultimately a matter for the court to determine the extent to which such a clause should be upheld, having regard to its purpose and statutory context, and the nature and importance of the legal issue in question; and to determine the level of scrutiny required by the rule of law.

QUESTIONS

1. If you were a Supreme Court justice deciding the *Privacy International* case would you have been more inclined to agree with the views of Lord Carnwath or those of Lord Sumption?
2. Suppose you were a parliamentary draftsman charged with drafting an amendment to s. 67(8) in the light of the Supreme Court's judgment in the *Privacy International* case. What changes would you make?
3. You are a government lawyer and have been asked by the minister to explain Lord Carnwath's conclusion on the second issue. In particular, the minister would like to know
   a) what is meant when Lord Carnwath says that '*binding effect cannot be given to a clause which purports wholly to exclude the supervisory jurisdiction of the High Court*'.

[22] This brings us back to one of the questions we posed when looking at *Anisminic*: how can a court tell whether an error is within or beyond a body's interpretative power (i.e. whether it is judicially reviewable or not) unless the court is able to look at the error?

b) Does this mean that the courts will not permit Parliament to exclude judicial review of a decision of an inferior court of tribunal? If so, what are the implications of this for Parliament's supremacy?

c) Bearing in mind that *Privacy International* concerned judicial review of a judicial body would Lord Carnwath's response to the second question have any relevance should Parliament attempt to exclude judicial review of decisions of a government minister?

d) Can Parliament prevent judges interpreting legislation?

4. Why, in the extract below, do you think in *Oceana* Saini J says that the rule of law '*applies as much to the courts as it does to anyone else*'?

20.4.1 OUSTER CLAUSES: ARE PARLIAMENTARY SUPREMACY AND THE RULE OF LAW COMPETING PRINCIPLES?

Our discussion of judicial reactions to Parliament's attempts to prevent judicial review highlights a potential clash between two basic constitutional principles: the supremacy or sovereignty of Parliament on the one hand and the rule of law on the other. The majority judgments in *Anisminic* and *Privacy International* appear to accept Parliament's ability to limit or even exclude judicial review. But as protectors of the rule of law the judges will only permit Parliament to oust judicial review if it uses language that the courts consider to be sufficiently clear. While it may be argued that this produces a clash between the supremacy or parliament and the rule of law, Dr Alexander Latham-Gambi, prefers to see these two key principles of the UK's constitution to be working together as two integrated principles. He writes that:

Dr Alexander Latham-Gambi, 'Sovereignty, the rule of law and the nature of legislation: reconceptualising the traditional ultra vires theory',
[2024] *Public Law* 109, at 129

> The very logic of government under law entails that both the scope of executive power and the identity of those entitled to wield it are legally defined. Since Parliament . . . governs through law, we cannot make sense of its enactments by holding that it intends to create power free of legal limits, as a literal reading of an ouster clause would suggest.

On this view judges need not take an overly technical literal approach to ouster clauses. They and Parliament should both accept that the courts are justified applying ouster clauses in the context of the overall legislative scheme and the nature and purpose of the decision maker and their powers. Rather than resort to technical approaches, judges should be transparent about the contextual factors that will be considered. By implication they should be ready to accept and explain that in certain situations ouster clauses will limit or prevent judicial review. Likewise Parliament should accept that the courts have a legitimate role in determining the effectiveness or otherwise of ouster clauses.

Hayley Hooper also emphasizes the need to interpret ouster clauses in their context:

Hayley J. Hooper, 'No superior form of law?' *R (Oceana) v Upper Tribunal*
[2024] *Public Law*, 1 at 7

> Different contexts compel different judicial interpretations. The emerging picture from the leading cases is more complex than a straightforward hierarchy of norms. An accurate picture becomes clear if we accept that the common law has a 'zone of tolerance' for ouster clauses. The boundaries of this zone are determined according to four considerations: the clarity of the statutory language in the clause, the extent to which the role of the court is curtailed, the nature of the institution and decision insulated from review, and the impact of the ouster clause on both fundamental rights and the legal system

These approaches steer us away from seeing judicial interpretation of ouster clauses in terms of a conflict between the courts and the rule of law on the one hand and Parliament and its supremacy on the other.[23] They suggest that while judges will interpret ouster clauses cautiously such clauses should not necessarily be seen as threats to the rule of law and may therefore be used by Parliament to further the policy of objects of particular legislative schemes. This view clearly accords with the approach taken by Lord Sumption in *Privacy International* when he argued that limiting judicial review of a judicial body such as the IPT was not necessarily a threat to the rule of law. A similar view was more recently taken by Saini J in In *Oceana*[24] when he accepted that s 11A of the Tribunals, Court and Enforcement Act 2007[25] prevented *Cart* judicial reviews.[26] In the following extract from his judgment Saini J stressed that the rule of law 'applies as much to the courts as it does to anyone else'.

Saini J in R *(Oceana) v Upper Tribunal*
[2023] EWHC 791 (Admin)

> [52] .... the courts must always be the authoritative interpreters of all legislation including ouster clauses. That is a fundamental requirement of the rule of law and the courts jealously guard this role. However, the rule of law applies as much to the courts as it does to anyone else. That means that under, our constitutional system, effect must be given to Parliament's will expressed in legislation. .... The common law supervisory jurisdiction of the High Court enjoys no immunity from these principles when clear legislative language is used, and Parliament has expressly confronted the issue of exclusion of judicial review ...

20.5 RECENT ATTEMPTS TO PREVENT JUDICIAL REVIEW

The failures to prevent judicial review in *Anisminic* and *Privacy International* have not stopped the use of statutory provisions aimed at preventing judicial review. We have already seen that Parliament has put a stop to *Cart* judicial reviews by providing that decisions, including purported decisions, of the Upper Tribunal refusing leave to appeal cannot be judicially reviewed.

[23] See also Jeffrey Goldsworthy, 'Is Parliamentary Sovereignty Alive, Dying or Dead?' [2023] Public Law 126, 137: '... a confrontation between Parliament and the Supreme Court concerning strong ouster clauses is best avoided. The outcome could not be confidently predicted, and institutional damage would likely be such that neither side could 'win'.

[24] *(Oceana) v Upper Tribunal* [2023] EWHC 791 (Admin).

[25] s. 2 of the Judicial Review and Courts Act 2022.

[26] See *Cart* in Section 20.3.

Another example is The Dissolution and Calling of Parliament Act 2022, which repeals the Fixed-term Parliament Act 2011,[27] contains provisions—set out in the following extract—that are clearly intended to prevent judicial review of decisions to dissolve Parliament and call a new Parliament. Note the language used and in particular the statement that the '*revived prerogative powers*' to call and dissolve Parliament are '*non justiciable*'. Note also that: '*A court or tribunal may not question*' '*purported*' exercises of power or '*purported*' decisions; or the '*limits or extent of those powers*'.

Dissolution and Calling of Parliament Act 2022

2 Revival of prerogative powers to dissolve Parliament and to call a new Parliament

(1) The powers relating to the dissolution of Parliament and the calling of a new Parliament that were exercisable by virtue of Her Majesty's prerogative immediately before the commencement of the Fixed-term Parliaments Act 2011 are exercisable again, as if the Fixed-term Parliaments Act 2011 had never been enacted.

[. . .]

3 Non-justiciability of revived prerogative powers

A court or tribunal may not question—

(a) the exercise or purported exercise of the powers referred to in section 2,

(b) any decision or purported decision relating to those powers, or

(c) the limits or extent of those powers.

Several authors have doubted whether the above wording is capable of excluding any judicial review. Professor Alison Young, for example, questions whether the wording would prevent judicial review in order to protect fundamental constitutional principles.[28]

20.6 CONCLUDING COMMENTS

This chapter has looked at various ways in which government and Parliament may attempt to restrict or even prevent the use of judicial review and at how the courts have responded. It has raised issues of profound constitutional importance relating to the rule of law and Parliament's supremacy and the practical relationships between executive, judicial, and legislative powers in the UK's system.

Clearly there is likely to be on-going debate, and potentially further litigation, over the desirability and effectiveness of provisions seeking to limit or exclude judicial review. We may well find that the

[27] See further Chapter 10 on prerogative powers and dissolution.

[28] A.L. Young, 'The Draft Fixed-term Parliaments Act 2011 (Repeal) Bill: Turning back the clock?', U.K. Const. L. Blog (4 December 2020), https://ukconstitutionallaw.org/. Young discusses clauses in the Draft Fixed-term Parliaments Act 2011 (Repeal) Bill which became the Dissolution and Calling of Parliament Act 2022 and the relevant wording remained unchanged. Also, Dr Alexander Latham-Gambi, 'Sovereignty, the rule of law and the nature of legislation: reconceptualising the traditional ultra vires theory', [2024] Public Law, 109, at 28 pointing out that there must be some limitation to the meaning of 'purported decision'.

attitudes of judges, including their willingness to accept limitations to their jurisdiction, changes so that new approaches are taken to cases such as *Privacy International*.[29] This is an area that students of public law will want to keep an eye on in the future.

FURTHER READING

Arvind, T. T., Kirkham, R., Daithi Mac Sitigh, and Stirton., L. (eds), *Executive Decision-Making and the Courts: Revisiting the Origins of Modern Judicial Review* (2021, Oxford: Hart Publishing).

Bondy, V., Platt, L., and Sunkin, M., *The Value and Effects of Judicial Review* (October 2015, Public Law Project).

Government Legal Department, *The Judge Over Your Shoulder*, 6th edn (republished 2022, London: GLD).

Graham, L., *Judicial Individuality on the UK Supreme Court* (2025, Oxford: Hart Publishing).

Harlow, C. and Rawlings, R., 'Striking Back' and 'Clamping Down', An Alternative Perspective on Judicial Review', in Bell, J. Elliott, M., Murray P., and Varuhas J. (eds), *Public Law Adjudication in Common Law Systems: Process and Substance* (2016, Oxford: Hart Publishing).

Juss S. and Sunkin, M. (eds), *Landmark Cases in Public Law* (2017, Oxford: Hart Publishing).

Laws, J., *The Constitutional Balance* (2021, Oxford: Hart Publishing).

Woolf, H., Jowell, J., Donnelly, C., and Hare I., *De Smith's Judicial Review*, 8th edn (2018, London: Sweet & Maxwell).

[29] Lewis Graham's research on the UK Supreme Court, for e.g. suggests that the court has become less interventionist and that Privacy International's claim might not even have got beyond the permission stage had the case been brought today: Lewis Graham, *Judicial Individuality on the UK Supreme Court*, (2025, Oxford: Hart Publishing), ch. 10.

21

PROTECTING RIGHTS: USING HUMAN RIGHTS IN THE UNITED KINGDOM COURTS

CENTRAL ISSUES

1. Any constitutional system faces the task of protecting fundamental rights. The Human Rights Act 1998 (HRA) altered how the UK approaches rights protection. Previously, protection depended on political processes and common law principles. The Act established legally enforceable Convention rights that individuals can pursue in domestic courts.

2. Public authorities must now act compatibly with 'Convention rights' from the European Convention for the Protection of Human Rights and Fundamental Freedoms (ECHR). The Act operates through three enforcement mechanisms: courts must interpret legislation compatibly with Convention rights 'so far as possible'; higher courts may issue declarations of incompatibility when compatible interpretation proves impossible; and individuals may bring direct claims against public authorities that breach Convention rights.

3. The obligation for UK courts to 'take account of' European Court of Human Rights (ECtHR) jurisprudence has proved contentious. Courts disagree whether they should simply 'mirror' Strasbourg decisions or develop distinctively British approaches to Convention rights. Recent Supreme Court decisions show increasingly restrictive interpretation of this duty.

4. Core public authorities (government departments, local authorities, police) clearly fall within the Act's scope. More problematic is the extension to private bodies exercising 'functions of a public nature'. Courts have interpreted this concept narrowly, limiting protection in privatized public services despite parliamentary and governmental concern.

5. Tensions persist about the proper balance between judicial and political power, particularly regarding national security, immigration, and social policy. When should courts defer to executive and legislative judgments? How should constitutional 'dialogue' between courts and Parliament operate? What limits constrain judicial review of legislation?

6. Political controversy surrounds the Act's future. The 2021 Independent Human Rights Act Review (IHRAR) concluded

the Act was working well but recommended improvements.[1] The Conservative government's 2022 Bill of Rights Bill would have restricted the Act's scope significantly, but was abandoned following political upheaval. Labour supports retaining the current framework, though academic and judicial developments continue to reshape the Act's operation.

7. The Act affects healthcare, education, family life, criminal justice, and social care. Empirical evidence suggests regular judicial use of the Act, but interpretive approaches often prove more conservative than the legislation might permit. Whether the HRA fulfills its intended purposes remains contested.

21.1 INTRODUCTION

The Human Rights Act 1998 marked a departure from traditional UK approaches to rights protection. Previously, rights depended on parliamentary democracy and common law principles. The Act introduced legally enforceable Convention rights that can be vindicated in domestic courts.

The change occurred within broader developments in international human rights law. The European Convention for the Protection of Human Rights and Fundamental Freedoms (ECHR) emerged from the Second World War, creating the first system in which individuals could enforce their rights against their own states before an international court.

The Act was designed '*to give further effect*' to the ECHR. It enables litigants to enforce most Convention rights in UK domestic courts, removing the need for lengthy and expensive proceedings before the European Court of Human Rights (ECtHR) in Strasbourg. This challenged traditional concepts of parliamentary supremacy and judicial restraint.

Previously, courts had reviewed public authority actions under common law grounds: illegality, irrationality, and procedural impropriety. Section 6(1) adds a new dimension by making it unlawful for public authorities to act incompatibly with 'Convention rights.' Human rights now operate as legally enforceable standards throughout public administration rather than merely political aspirations or judicial presumptions.

The Act's practical impact extends across modern governance. Leading decisions have addressed:

- Social care and vulnerable adults: Whether private care homes exercising public functions must respect residents' human rights, particularly regarding dignity and family life;[2]
- Religious freedom and property rights: The extent to which churches can be required to maintain historical buildings, balancing religious autonomy with heritage preservation;[3]
- Housing and family life: How human rights considerations affect tenant evictions and the protection of established family homes;[4]
- Education and religious expression: The balance between school autonomy and students' rights to religious expression, non-discrimination, and cultural identity;[5]
- Social security and bereavement: Whether state support systems adequately protect family life following the death of a partner.[6]

[1] Independent Human Rights Act Review, December 2021, CP 586.

[2] *YL (by her litigation friend the Official Solicitor) (FC) v Birmingham City Council and ors* [2007] UKHL 2.

[3] *Aston Cantlow and Wilmcote, with Billesley Parochial Church Council v Wallbank and anor* [2003] UKHL 37.

[4] *Pinnock v Manchester City Council* [2010] UKSC 45.

[5] The *Begum* case, see Chapter 22; *R (on the application of E) v The Governing Body of JFS and the Admissions Appeal Panel of JFS and ors* [2009] UKSC 15.

[6] *R (Jwanczuk) v Secretary of State for Work and Pensions* [2022] EWHC 2298.

These cases show how human rights law has moved from the constitutional periphery to everyday legal practice, affecting ordinary citizens' interactions with public authorities across government activity.

The Act's introduction created constitutional tensions that remain unresolved. At its core lies a fundamental question: how can a legal system committed to parliamentary supremacy accommodate judicially enforceable rights that may conflict with democratically enacted legislation?

Parliament addressed this tension through two key mechanisms. Section 3 requires courts to interpret legislation in a way that is compatible with Convention rights where possible. Section 4 enables higher courts to declare legislation incompatible with Convention rights without affecting its validity. Both mechanisms preserve parliamentary supremacy while enabling judicial protection of rights, though their operation has proved controversial.

Understanding the historical background remains important. Many concerns that initially motivated opposition to the Act—fears about judicial overreach, erosion of parliamentary supremacy, and the practical workings of rights protection—continue shaping political and legal debates. The constitutional arguments that led to the Act's distinctive design help explain its mechanisms and how they are intended to operate. These historical perspectives illuminate current discussions about the Act's future, including recent proposals for reform and academic debate about whether judicial developments have substantially altered the Act's operation.

The Act represents both a constitutional settlement and a constitutional experiment. Fundamental questions remain about the proper relationship between courts and Parliament, the scope of rights protection, and the balance between individual rights and collective democratic governance. These tensions have been shaped not only by formal legislative and judicial decisions, but also by shifts in judicial attitudes and interpretive approaches that may prove equally significant for the Act's constitutional trajectory.

This chapter examines how the Act operates in practice, exploring both its potential and its constitutional limitations. We begin by tracing the historical development that led to the Act's enactment, before analysing its key mechanisms and considering contemporary challenges to its operation and future.

21.2 THE BACKGROUND TO THE HUMAN RIGHTS ACT 1998: THE INTERNATIONAL PROTECTION OF HUMAN RIGHTS

After the Second World War, the newly formed United Nations sought to establish international machinery for protecting rights. The UN Charter committed member states to '*reaffirm faith in fundamental human rights, in the dignity and worth of the human person, in the equal rights of men and women and of nations large and small*'. This project aimed to prevent future conflicts by protecting '*succeeding generations from the scourge of war*'.[7]

The UN General Assembly adopted the Universal Declaration of Human Rights in 1948, defining basic human rights entitlements for the first time in international law. However, this groundbreaking document was not enforceable. Two International Covenants (on Civil and Political Rights, and on Economic, Social, and Cultural Rights) were opened for signature in 1966, and came into force in 1976. Together with the 1948 Declaration, these instruments form the 'International Bill of Rights'.

International law provides two essential features of human rights protection that domestic law often lacks. First, it imposes obligations on states to protect the rights of people in their jurisdictions—states cannot claim that treatment of their citizens is purely domestic business. States that failto provide adequate protection are accountable to international bodies.

[7] Preamble to the Charter of the United Nations 1945.

Second, international law provides victims with methods for bringing violations to international attention. The United Kingdom became a party to the Convention in 1953, but only accepted the right of 'victims' to bring complaints against it to the European Commission on Human Rights (now the European Court of Human Rights) in 1966. That right is now central to the protection of human rights in Europe.

21.3 THE EUROPEAN CONVENTION ON HUMAN RIGHTS

The ECHR emerged from the Second World War as European leaders sought to prevent state sovereignty from shielding those who committed crimes against humanity. The Convention created a system where individuals could enforce rights against their own states before an international court.[8]

British attitudes toward the ECHR were ambivalent. Although the UK was the first state to sign the ECHR, it opted out of the right to petition. The UK only accepted these rights in 1966, initially on a temporary basis. Individual petition is now compulsory and heavily used.

Andrew Moravcsik shows that while Britain supported human rights in principle, it strongly opposed enforcement mechanisms. The Foreign Office legal advisor stated: '*We attach the greatest importance to a well-drafted Convention of Human Rights but we are dead against anything like an international court to which individuals who think they are aggrieved could go.*' Officials worried about undermining parliamentary supremacy and feared a '*blank cheque*' allowing '*Communists, crooks, and cranks of every type to bring actions*'.[9] British opposition was overcome only by fears of resurgent totalitarianism abroad.

The main rights contained in the ECHR and its Protocols are shown in Box 21.1.

BOX 21.1 THE ECHR RIGHTS

- Article 2 Right to life
- Article 3 Prohibition of torture
- Article 4 Prohibition of forced labour
- Article 5 Right to liberty and security
- Article 6 Right to a fair trial
- Article 7 No punishment without law
- Article 8 Right to respect for private and family life
- Article 9 Freedom of thought, conscience and religion
- Article 10 Freedom of expression
- Article 11 Freedom of assembly and association
- Article 12 Right to marry
- Article 13 Right to an effective remedy
- Article 14 Prohibition of discrimination in the enjoyment of rights and freedoms

[8] Anthony Lester QC 'Human Rights and the British Constitution', in J. Jowell and D. Oliver (eds) *The Changing Constitution*, 7th edn (2011, Oxford: OUP), ch. 3, p. 74.

[9] A. Moravcsik, 'The origins of human rights regimes: Democratic delegation in postwar Europe' (2000) 54 International Organization 217, 238.

First Protocol

- Article 1 Protection of property
- Article 2 Right to education
- Article 3 Right to free elections

Sixth Protocol

- Article 1 Abolition of the death penalty
- Article 2 Death penalty in time of war

Other Protocols set out further rights, including the Fourth Protocol (rights in relation to civil imprisonment, freedom of movement, and expulsion) and the Twelfth Protocol, which establishes a free-standing right against discrimination. The United Kingdom has yet to agree to these rights.

QUESTIONS

1. Do the UK government's original concerns about the ECHR, particularly regarding parliamentary supremacy and individual petition rights, remain relevant today? How do these concerns relate to current debates about the HRA's future?
2. The ECHR focuses on civil and political rights but omits economic, social and cultural rights (like healthcare, housing, or employment). Why might this distinction have been made in the 1950s, and should it still apply today?
3. How does the current political climate toward human rights in the UK compare to the initial reluctance described by Moravcsik? What factors might explain similarities or differences?

21.3.1 ENFORCING RIGHTS IN THE EUROPEAN COURT OF HUMAN RIGHTS

Cases reach the European Court of Human Rights (ECtHR) through two routes. States may bring cases against other states for violations of the ECHR, though this procedure is rarely used. Notable examples include Greece v UK (concerning Cyprus) and Ireland v UK (concerning Northern Ireland).

More commonly, the individual petition procedure enables individuals, companies, groups, or NGOs claiming to be victims of state violations to bring claims. As of December 2025, there were 53,450 applications pending before the Court.[10] Turkey had the highest number at 18,464 (34.5 per cent of all applications), followed by Russia (7,177, under the Court's residual jurisdiction following expulsion from the Council of Europe), Ukraine (4,004), Romania (3,517), and Italy (2,787). These five states account for approximately two-thirds of pending applications.

The UK has a very low number of pending cases, maintaining the lowest per capita rate among all Council of Europe member states.

[10] Annual Report, ECHR, 2025.

21.4 THE CAMPAIGN TO INCORPORATE CONVENTIONS RIGHTS

By the 1990s, UK judges were becoming attuned to human rights issues, and the ECHR was being used more frequently as a source of argument in courts (although the provisions could not be relied on directly). Moreover, people were aware that if claimants lost their cases in UK courts, they could appeal to the ECtHR level. There were also a growing number of cases in which the Strasbourg Court found the United Kingdom to be in breach of the Convention, leading to government reconsideration and changes to UK law. The *Malone* case was one such example.[11] Having unsuccessfully challenged the legality of the surveillance before the High Court, Mr Malone successfully took the UK to the ECtHR, where his Art. 8 rights were held to have been infringed. This led to the enactment of the Interception of Telecommunications Act 1985, which placed the imposition of telephone taps on a statutory basis. As we will see in the case study on the right of prisoners to vote (see Chapter 22), the UK has not always been ready to implement decisions of the Strasbourg Court.

As Anthony King explains, despite courts gradually adapting British law to meet ECHR requirements, support for a UK bill of rights grew throughout the 1990s, including among eminent judges and the Labour Party. In the following extract, he lists three problems that advocates had identified with the existing system.

A. King, *The British Constitution* (2007, Oxford: OUP), pp. 129–30 (footnotes omitted)

One was the lack of entrenchment. Successive governments over the years had ratified the European convention and its various protocols, but a government at some time in the future could always un-ratify them. Another was that British judges, although increasingly disposed to interpret British law in the light of the European convention and the associated rulings of the European Court of Human Rights, were still reluctant to construe British law in its entirety as though it were subject to or conformed to the European convention's terms and the European court's rulings. [...]

But perhaps the main reason the human rights campaigners found the existing state of affairs so unsatisfactory—and certainly the part of their argument that they found easiest to deploy in public—was the seeming absurdity of people, whether British citizens or not, having to go to a court hundreds of miles away in Strasbourg to obtain rights under the European convention that were, or should have been, theirs already. It was expensive going to Strasbourg. It could be immensely time-consuming (it often took the commission and court years to settle cases). The European judges were often not familiar with local circumstances. If the court found against the UK government or one of its agencies, the UK government then had to change the law. Not least, the sight of UK citizens having to trek all the way to Strasbourg to obtain justice was just embarrassing. [...]

QUESTIONS

1. King identifies three main arguments for incorporating the ECHR into UK law: lack of entrenchment, judicial reluctance to fully apply ECHR standards, and the practical problems of the Strasbourg route. Which argument do you find most compelling and why?
2. How do these historical arguments for the HRA relate to current debates about its future? Are the same concerns still relevant today?

[11] See Chapter 4.

As Anthony King notes, not everyone agreed that reform was needed. Opposition came from the left (against giving judges more power), defenders of executive power, political constitutionalists (preferring political over judicial resolution of controversial issues), and those who argued the common law was preferable to the '*vague and uncertain provisions of the ECHR*'.

However, Labour fought the 1997 election on a promise to introduce human rights legislation. After winning, Tony Blair's government published *Rights Brought Home: The Human Rights Bill* in May 1997. The Human Rights Act 1998 received Royal Assent on 9 November 1998 and came fully into force on 2 October 2000.

Secretary of State for the Home Department, *Rights Brought Home: The Human Rights Bill*, Cm 3782 (October 1997)

Bringing Rights Home

We [. . .] believe that the time has come to enable people to enforce their Convention rights against the State in the British courts, rather than having to incur the delays and expense which are involved in taking a case to [. . .] Strasbourg and which may altogether deter some people from pursuing their rights. Enabling courts in the United Kingdom to rule on the application of the Convention will also help to influence the development of case law on the Convention by the European Court of Human Rights on the basis of familiarity with our laws and customs and of sensitivity to practices and procedures in the United Kingdom. [. . .] Enabling the Convention rights to be judged by British courts will also lead to closer scrutiny of the human rights implications of new legislation and new policies. [. . .] Our aim is a straightforward one. It is to make more directly accessible the rights which the British people already enjoy under the Convention. In other words, to bring those rights home.

21.5 THE HUMAN RIGHTS ACT 1998

The purpose of the HRA, as expressed in its long title, is '*to give further effect to the rights and freedoms guaranteed under the European Convention on Human Rights*'. The Act adds to the rights protection that is provided by the common law and statute[12] by enabling claimants to rely on most ECHR rights and freedoms in domestic legal proceedings.[13] This was a significant breakthrough. Until the HRA, the ECHR could be used in UK courts to support arguments that public bodies had acted *Wednesbury* unreasonably, or that ambiguously worded legislation should be interpreted in a manner that favoured human rights. But Convention rights were not part of domestic law and could not be relied on directly: public authorities could not be held to have acted unlawfully solely because they had acted contrary to the Convention. Convention rights could be enforced only through lengthy proceedings in Strasbourg after domestic avenues had been exhausted. The HRA, therefore, significantly improved people's ability to enforce human rights obligations. But the Act also has the broader aim of inculcating a general culture of respect for human rights within public authorities, which must comply with human rights in all of their activities, irrespective of whether legal challenges are involved.

[12] That the HRA does not supersede common law rights or statutory protection was stressed by Lord Reed in *Osborn v Parole Board* [2013] UKSC 61, [57].

[13] The Act does not apply to the right to a remedy in Art. 13, nor to the right not to be discriminated against in Protocol 12 of the ECHR, to which the United Kingdom has yet to agree.

21.5.1 BASIC SCHEME OF THE HUMAN RIGHTS ACT 1998

Before looking more closely at the provisions of the HRA it may be helpful to summarize its key elements.

- All legislation (both primary and secondary) '*must be read and given effect in a way which is compatible with Convention rights in so far as it is possible to do so*' (s. 3). This interpretative obligation is imposed on everyone who has to apply legislation, but is most important for judges.
- If legislation cannot be interpreted in a way that is compatible with Convention rights, the higher courts may issue '*a declaration of incompatibility*' (s. 4). This makes clear that the legislation conflicts with Convention rights, but does not affect the legislation's validity. Parliament's ability to legislate contrary to human rights is retained. Ministers must make a written statement that the bill is compatible with Convention rights or, if not, that the government nonetheless wishes to proceed (s. 19).
- Where legislation has been declared to be incompatible with Convention rights, ministers may make delegated legislation to amend provisions in an Act of Parliament to remove the incompatibility (s. 10(2) and (3)).
- It is unlawful for public authorities to act contrary to Convention rights (s. 6).
- Public authorities may have a defence if primary legislation requires them to act in the way that they did (s. 6(2)).
- Those claiming to be 'victims' of unlawful actions by public authorities can rely on Convention rights in any legal proceedings, including judicial review. If successful, courts have a wide range of remedies, including the ability to award damages (ss 7 and 8).

We now look more closely at the key provisions of the HRA.

21.5.2 THE DUTY 'TO TAKE INTO ACCOUNT' CONVENTION CASE LAW

Section 2(1) of the HRA imposes a duty on courts and tribunals to '*take into account*' the case law of the ECtHR.[14] This recognises that the HRA did not establish new free-standing rights, but rather gives domestic effect to rights and freedoms that are established by the ECHR and interpreted by the ECtHR. It enables '*. . . the rights and remedies available in the [ECtHR] to be asserted and enforced by domestic courts, rather than [. . .] provide a basis for development of rights of the domestic courts' own creation*'.[15]

There has been disagreement over what is meant by the requirement to 'take into account'. At one extreme, some, including Lord Hoffmann, have said that domestic courts are bound to follow the ECtHR.[16] However, Lord Irvine of Lairg, who steered the Human Rights Bill through Parliament as Lord Chancellor, has argued that this approach is wrong, pointing out that Parliament could have told courts that they must 'follow', or 'give effect to' or 'be bound by' ECtHR decisions if that was the intention.[17]

[14] The Bill of Rights Bill introduced to the House of Commons on 22 June 2022 would repeal the HRA and ensure that UK courts 'do not interpret rights more expansively than the ECtHR has or would'. Bill of Rights Bill Explanatory Notes, para. 6.

[15] *R (Elan-Cane) v Secretary of State for the Home Department* [2021] UKSC 56, [94], citing *In re G (Adoption: Unmarried Couples)* [2008] UKHL 38, at [54]–[59].

[16] See, e.g., Lord Hoffmann in *AF v Secretary of State for the Home Department and anor* [2009] UKHL 28, [70], extracted below at p. 612.

[17] Lord Irvine of Lairg, 'A British interpretation of Convention rights' [2012] Public Law 237, 239.

Lord Irvine of Lairg, 'A British interpretation of convention rights' [2012] *Public Law* 237, 239 (emphasis in original)

> Section 2 means that the domestic courts *always have a choice*. The domestic court is not only *entitled* to make the choice, its statutory duty under s. 2 *obliges* it to confront the question whether the relevant decision of the [ECtHR] is sound in principle and should be given effect domestically. Simply put, the domestic court must decide the case for itself.

In Lord Irvine's view, the proper approach is that set out by Lord Neuberger on behalf of the unanimous nine-justice UK Supreme Court in *Pinnock v Manchester City Council*:[18]

Pinnock v Manchester City Council
[2010] UKSC 45

> **Lord Neuberger**
>
> 48. [. . .] This court is not bound to follow every decision of the European court. Not only would it be impractical to do so: it would sometimes be inappropriate, as it would destroy the ability of the court to engage in the constructive dialogue with the European court which is of value to the development of Convention law [. . .] Of course, we should usually follow a clear and constant line of decisions by the European court: *R (on the application of Ullah) v Special Adjudicator* [in the following extract] [. . .] But we are not actually bound to do so [. . .]

This statement has been approved by the UK Supreme Court.[19] This debate about how closely domestic courts should follow Strasbourg raises a related question: even when courts do follow ECtHR decisions, should they be limited to existing Strasbourg jurisprudence, or can they extend Convention rights beyond what Strasbourg has already established?

21.5.3 CAN UK COURTS EXTEND CONVENTION RIGHTS?

Related to the obligation to take account of Strasbourg case law is the question of whether UK courts are free to take a more expansive approach to rights than that adopted by the Strasbourg Court: as commentators have put it, does the Strasbourg case law impose a ceiling on rights or does it provide a floor?

When we consider the decision of the House of Lords in the *Begum* case, we shall see that Lord Bingham said that the purpose of the HRA '*was not to enlarge the rights or remedies of those in the United Kingdom whose Convention rights have been violated but to enable those rights and remedies to*

[18] Cf. Sir Philip Sales, 'Strasbourg jurisprudence and the Human Rights Act: A response to Lord Irvine' [2012] Public Law 253; R. Clayton 'Smoke and mirrors: The Human Rights Act and the impact of the Strasbourg case law' [2012] Public Law 639; Lewis Graham, 'The modern mirror principle' [2021] Public Law 523.

[19] See, e.g., *R (Elan-Cane) v Secretary of State for the Home Department* [2021] UKSC 56, [101]; *R (AB) v Secretary of State for Justice (Equality and Human Rights Commission intervening)* [2021] UKSC 28; *Osborn v Parole Board* [2013] UKSC 61, [56]; and *In the matter of an application of James Clyde Reilly for Judicial Review (Northern Ireland)* [2013] UKSC 61, [56].

be asserted and enforced by the domestic courts of this country and not only by recourse to Strasbourg'[20]—echoing his statement in the earlier case, *Ullah*.

R (on the application of Ullah) v Special Adjudicator
[2004] UKHL 26

Lord Bingham

20. [. . .] It is of course open to member states to provide for rights more generous than those guaranteed by the Convention, but such provision should not be the product of interpretation of the Convention by national courts, since the meaning of the Convention should be uniform throughout the states party to it. The duty of the courts is to keep pace with the Strasbourg jurisprudence as it evolves over time: no more, but certainly no less.

This view is widely referred to as the 'mirror principle', which holds that domestic courts should do no more than accurately reflect the decisions of the ECtHR. This has generated much debate and has been challenged by those who argue that it is contrary to the HRA's intent and wording, which was designed to provide 'a floor of rights protection', but not to impose a ceiling on the ability of the courts to interpret rights dynamically.

Lord Hope agreed with Lord Bingham who said that: '. . .*Parliament never intended to give the courts of this country the power to give a more generous scope to those rights than that which was to be found in the jurisprudence of the Strasbourg Court.*'[21] However, Lord Dyson argued that where '*there is no clear and constant line of authority*' from Strasbourg,[22] the court's duty is to '*give effect to the domestically enacted Convention rights*'.[23] Lord Dyson indicates that under the HRA the Convention rights are to be interpreted and potentially extended as part of domestic common law.[24]

The following comments by Lords Kerr and Mance in *D v Commissioner of Police of the Metropolis (Liberty and others intervening) v Commissioner of Police of the Metropolis* indicate consensus around the situations in which domestic courts may be willing to expand on the rights set out in the ECHR.[25]

Commissioner of Police of the Metropolis (Liberty and others intervening) v DSD and another
[2018] UKSC 11

Lord Kerr

77. In . . . recent cases, a departure from the mirror principle can be detected. Thus, in *Rabone v Pennine Care NHS Trust* [2012] 2 AC 72 it was held that there was a positive obligation to protect the life of a mentally ill young woman [. . .] notwithstanding that there was no authority from ECtHR to that effect. In *Surrey County Council v P* [2014] AC 896, para 62 Lord Neuberger said that where there was

[20] *R (Begum) v Governors of Denbigh High School* [2006] UKHL 15 [29], see further Ch. 21.
[21] *Ambrose v Harris (Procurator Fiscal, Oban)* [2011] UKSC 43, [19]. Lord Brown agreed, [86]. The
[22] Ibid, [101]–[102].
[23] Ibid, [103].
[24] Also Lord Dyson, in *Al Rawi v The Security Service and Ors* [2011] UKSC 34, [68].
[25] [2018] UKSC 11.

no Strasbourg authority which dealt precisely with the issues before this court, this court could rely on principles expressed by ECtHR, even if only indirectly relevant, and apply them to the cases which it had to decide. And in *Moohan v Lord Advocate* [2015] AC 901 Lord Wilson suggested that there had been a 'retreat' from the *Ullah* principle. At para 105, he said:

> where there is no directly relevant decision of the ECtHR with which it would be possible (even if appropriate) to keep pace, we can and must do more. We must determine for ourselves the existence or otherwise of an alleged Convention right.

78. This seems to me to be inescapably correct. Reticence by the courts of the UK to decide whether a Convention right has been violated would be an abnegation of our statutory obligation under section 6 of HRA. This section makes it unlawful for a public authority, including a court, to act in a way which is incompatible with a Convention right.

Lord Mance

152. [. . .] The general aim of the Human Rights Act 1998 was to align domestic law with Strasbourg law. Domestic courts should not normally refuse to follow Strasbourg authority, although circumstances can arise where this is appropriate and a healthy dialogue may then ensue [. . .] Conversely, domestic courts should not. . .forge ahead, without good reason [. . .]

153. There are however cases where the English courts can and should, as a matter of domestic law, go with confidence beyond existing Strasbourg authority: see eg *Rabone*. If the existence or otherwise of a Convention right is unclear, then it may be appropriate for domestic courts to make up their minds whether the Convention rights should or should not be understood to embrace it. Further, where the European Court of Human Rights has left a matter to states' margin of appreciation, then domestic courts have to decide what the domestic position is, what degree of involvement or intervention by a domestic court is appropriate, and what degree of institutional respect to attach to any relevant legislative choice in the particular area [. . .]

The Court's restrictive stance reached its logical conclusion in *Elan-Cane*, where Lord Reed delivered a unanimous judgment that explicitly prioritized parliamentary supremacy over judicial innovation in human rights interpretation.[26]

R (Elan-Cane) v Secretary of State for the Home Department [2021] UKSC 56

Lord Reed

[After citing with approval Lord Neuberger's comments in *Pinnock* to the effect that UK domestic courts are not bound to 'slavishly' follow the ECtHR, Lord Reed continued.]

[101] . . . Nor are domestic courts prevented from developing the law in relation to Convention rights beyond the limits of the European case law. [. . .] the protection of Convention rights under the Human Rights Act can go beyond the situations previously considered by the European court, where the principles established by that court enable such a step to be taken. In these ways, domestic courts can

[26] In *R (Hallam) v Secretary of State for Justice* [2019] UKSC 2 Lord Reed said that: 'I find it difficult to accept that this court should deliberately adopt a construction of the Convention which it knows to be out of step with the approach of the European Court of Human Rights, established by numerous Chamber judgments over the course of decades, and confirmed at the level of the Grand Chamber, in the absence of some compelling justification for taking such an exceptional step.' at [175].

and do engage in dialogue with the European court and influence the development of its case law. It is also important to remember that, quite apart from the Human Rights Act, the Convention can influence statutory interpretation and the development of the common law. But it has generally been accepted that the domestic application of Convention rights under the Human Rights Act has to be based on the principles established in the case law of the European court, rather than upon a distinct domestic interpretation of Convention rights. Parliament can, of course, extend rights beyond those set out in the ECHR. The current position in relation to UK courts was summarized by the IRHRA as follows.

21.5.4 SUMMARY OF THE CURRENT POSITION ON SECTION 2 HRA

Elan-Cane reflects broader changes in the UK Supreme Court's constitutional approach under Lord Reed's leadership. Courts now use parliamentary supremacy as an active constraint on judicial power rather than merely a background constitutional principle. In *Elgizouli*,[27] the Court refused to recognise a contested common law right partly because '*it is parliamentary legislation rather than the common law which has created and delimits the right to life*.' In *Elan-Cane*,[28] the Court's restrictive interpretation of the duty to '*take into account*' Strasbourg case law was justified as avoiding '*encroachment upon Parliamentary sovereignty*'. The Court reasoned that allowing domestic courts to find Convention breaches where Strasbourg had recognised a margin of appreciation would improperly permit judicial reinterpretation of legislation contrary to both its ordinary meaning and established ECtHR jurisprudence.

This departs from earlier HRA cases that envisioned domestic courts contributing to the '*dynamic and evolving interpretation of the Convention*'. Lewis Graham argues that this reflects a systematic judicial strategy of using the supremacy doctrine to limit the interpretation of the HRA, the development of the common law, and the powers of the devolved governments.

Lewis Graham 'Has the UK Supreme Court Become more restrained in public law cases?
(2024) 87(5) *Modern Law Review* 1073–1110, 1082; 1109

Taking these cases together, it is clear that over the last few years the Court has adopted a particularly muscular conception of parliamentary sovereignty, no longer some background constitutional principle but in some cases almost a distinct legal tool in and of itself, the application of which has resulted, amongst other things, in greater limitations upon devolved governments, a stunting of the development of the common law, and a severely limited scope for review of legislation under the HRA.

[. . .] what the Court's case law reveals is a commitment to a kind of legal conservatism, and in particular, what might be called a kind of political constitutionalist outlook, in which elected politicians rather than the judges get the last word in constitutional disputes. This can be seen most clearly through the Court's tendency to afford greater deference to the legislature and (especially) the executive, and its allergy to policy considerations, as well as in its general approach to human rights cases. The Court adopts a wide understanding of forbidden 'political' territory and is anxious to stay away from it.

Parliament can, of course, extend rights beyond those set out in the ECHR. The current position in relation to UK courts was summarized by the IRHRA as follows.

[27] *R (Elgizouli) v Secretary of State for the Home Department* [2020] UKSC 10; [2021] AC 937 at [232].
[28] *R (Elan-Cane) v Secretary of State for the Home Department* [2021] UKSC 56; [2023] AC 559 [108].

Independent Human Rights Act Review 2021 Cp 586, p. 64 [footnotes omitted]

Section 2 - where we are now

- There is an order of priority of assessing rights protection: domestic statute; the common law; and then, finally, Convention rights.
- *Ullah* remains the starting point for an analysis of the approach to section 2 and ECtHR case law.
- Free-standing Convention rights cannot be developed by UK Courts. However, UK Courts may go beyond the ECtHR where doing so was a natural development from the ECtHR's case law or the ECtHR has not (yet) specifically resolved the issue.
- UK Courts are more confident in departing from ECtHR case law. [. . .] Specific instances where UK Courts have declined to follow the ECtHR are where: there is only one ECtHR decision on the issue; the ECtHR case law was criticised at the time it was made or is inconsistent with other ECtHR decisions; the ECtHR's decision is based on a misunderstanding of, or failed to take account of, UK law or constitutional principle.
- Common law rights protection can still be developed, and can be developed further than that provided by the Convention, subject (as always) to judicial restraint and Parliamentary Sovereignty.

Empirical analysis of judicial behaviour reveals substantial variance in how individual Supreme Court judges approach human rights claims. Graham's study of the UK Supreme Court's first decade found that in contested ECHR cases where judges disagreed, the likelihood of individual judges finding Convention breaches ranged from approximately 20 per cent to 96 per cent, with an average rate of around 62 per cent.[29] This spread persisted across different types of human rights claims, whether derived from the ECHR, EU law, or common law, suggesting that judicial attitudes toward rights protection generally, rather than toward specific sources, explain the variance. Some judges consistently sided with human rights claimants while others consistently adopted more restrictive interpretations, even when applying identical legal frameworks. The outcome of human rights cases may be significantly influenced by which judges happen to sit on a particular panel.

Understanding these evolving judicial approaches to Convention rights requires examining how they interact with a parallel development: the resurgence of common law constitutional rights as an alternative foundation for protecting rights.

QUESTIONS

1. Should Strasbourg case law provide a 'floor' or 'ceiling' for domestic rights protection? Explain the constitutional arguments for treating ECtHR jurisprudence as either minimum standards that UK courts may exceed, or maximum standards that constrain domestic interpretation. Which approach better serves the constitutional purposes underlying the Human Rights Act?
2. Section 2 HRA requires courts to '*take into account*' ECtHR decisions but does not mandate following them. How do judicial disagreements about this obligation reflect tensions

[29] L. Graham, *Judicial Individuality on the UK Supreme Court* (Oxford: Hart Publishing, 2025), Chapter 7.

between legal certainty (uniform interpretation across jurisdictions) and judicial flexibility (allowing domestic courts to develop rights protection suited to UK circumstances)?

3. The Supreme Court under Lord Reed has used parliamentary supremacy more assertively to constrain judicial power in human rights cases. Does this represent:
   (a) Appropriate constitutional restraint that preserves democratic legitimacy and prevents judicial overreach; or
   (b) Excessive judicial deference that undermines effective rights protection and the Human Rights Act's constitutional role? In your answer, consider specific examples of how this approach has affected the interpretation of Convention rights and the balance between individual rights and democratic governance.

21.5.5 COMMON LAW CONSTITUTIONAL RIGHTS AND THE HRA

The judicial emphasis on common law constitutional principles discussed in Chapter 18 (s.18.7.2) shows how domestic and international sources of rights protection have been recalibrated. When the HRA was enacted, Masterman and Wheatle describe a period of '*common law dormancy*',[30] as the Act's clear catalogue of enforceable rights, structured tests, and specific remedies proved appealing to judges and advocates. One senior judge later reflected that lawyers' attitude to Convention rights '*was not unlike that of a child to a new toy. As we became fascinated with the new toy, the old toy, the common law, was left in the cupboard*'.[31] This displacement reached its peak in *Watkins*,[32] where the House of Lords suggested that pre-HRA judicial references to '*constitutional rights*' had been '*heroic efforts*' to achieve incorporation's benefits without formal incorporation—efforts rendered 'unnecessary' by the HRA's provision of enforceable Convention rights.

The Supreme Court decisions examined in Chapter 18 (*Kennedy*, *A v BBC*, and *Osborn*) represent a deliberate constitutional strategy to restore common law rights as a primary foundation for rights protection. This approach establishes '*sequential primacy*' in human rights adjudication:[33] courts should begin with domestic common law constitutional principles before turning to Convention jurisprudence. This does not create hierarchical supremacy of common law over Convention rights. As Lord Reed acknowledged in *A v BBC*, where domestic and Convention approaches conflict, '*effect must be given to the Convention rights in accordance with the Human Rights Act*'.[34] Instead, it reflects constitutional subsidiarity that prioritizes domestic legal sources as the starting point for rights analysis.

R. Masterman and S. Wheatle, 'A common law resurgence in rights protection?'
(2015) 1 *European Human Rights Law Review* 57–65

In the face of calls for revision of the current statutory scheme for the protection of human rights. . .the common law is showing signs not only of resilience but also of its continuing ability to recalibrate itself in the face of new challenges and current needs. The recent case law encourages the conceptualisation

[30] R. Masterman & S. Wheatle, 'A Common Law Resurgence in Rights Protection?', (2015) 1 *European Human Rights Law Review* 57–65, 58.

[31] Lord Neuberger, 'The Role of Judges in Human Rights Jurisprudence: A Comparison of the Australian and UK Experience' (8 August 2014), at [29].

[32] *Watkins v Secretary of State for the Home Department* [2006] UKHL 17; [2006] 2 A.C. 395 [61]–[62].

[33] R. Masterman & S. Wheatle, 'A Common Law Resurgence in Rights Protection?', (2015) 1 *European Human Rights Law Review* 57–65, 64.

[34] *A v BBC* [2014] UKSC 25 [57].

of the common law as an autonomous track of rights protection; one that is not insulated from the Convention but which operates as an independent source of rights, and may, as it develops, be influenced by the ECHR.

In the ongoing debates over the perceptions of supremacy of national and international sources of law, the reiteration of the common law's vitality in the face of the Convention rights amounts to a partial rejoinder to calls for a UK Bill of Rights based on the dilution of domestic authority over rights. More broadly assessed, the above cases also contribute to the incremental development of the common law constitution. The potential of neither should be lightly dismissed; this 'gradual adaptation', to use Lord Toulson's phrase, 'has always been the way of the common law'.[35] Thus, while the HRA sought to 'bring rights home' from Strasbourg, the common law's resurgence, fuelled by its unique adaptability, protests that rights were already, and continue to be, a part of the British 'national inheritance'.[36]

Masterman and Wheatle observe that the common law resurgence '*amounts to a partial rejoinder to calls for a UK Bill of Rights based on the dilution of domestic authority over rights*' by demonstrating that robust rights protection can emerge from domestic sources without legislative reform. Common law constitutional rights complement the restrictive interpretive trends discussed in sections 21.5.2 and 21.5.3. Courts have become cautious about extending Convention rights beyond clear Strasbourg authority, but the resurgence of the common law provides an alternative avenue for constitutional development that may prove more politically sustainable.

These developments '*contribute to the incremental development of the common law constitution*'. The HRA's enduring legacy may lie less in importing European human rights culture and more in encouraging distinctly British constitutional evolution. The Supreme Court's emphasis on common law constitutional rights represents both continuity with historical constitutional development and adaptation to contemporary challenges. As Lord Toulson observed, '*gradual adaptation*' remains '*the way of the common law*'.

21.5.6 THE INTERPRETATIVE OBLIGATION

Human Rights Act 1998, s. 3

(1) So far as it is possible to do so, primary legislation and subordinate legislation must be read and given effect in a way which is compatible with the Convention rights.

(2) This section—

(a) applies to primary legislation and subordinate legislation whenever enacted;

(b) does not affect the validity, continuing operation or enforcement of any incompatible primary legislation; and

(c) does not affect the validity, continuing operation or enforcement of any incompatible subordinate legislation if (disregarding any possibility of revocation) primary legislation prevents removal of the incompatibility.

[35] *Kennedy* [2014] UKSC 20 at [133].

[36] Dinah Rose QC, 'Beef and Liberty: Fundamental Rights and the Common Law' (Atkin Memorial Lecture 2011), para. 37.

Section 3 says that primary and subordinate legislation '*must be read and given effect in a way which is compatible with Convention rights*', but only '*so far as it is possible to do so*'.[37] It also indicates that legislation will remain valid and enforceable in operation even if a human rights-compatible interpretation is not possible.[38]

In relation to subordinate legislation, s. 3(2)(c) indicates that the validity, operation, and enforcement of subordinate legislation that is incompatible with Convention rights may be rendered invalid, unless primary legislation prevents the removal of the incompatibility. In other words, if primary legislation dictates that subordinate legislation be incompatible with Convention rights, then that subordinate legislation will continue to be operative—but if not, the subordinate legislation that is incompatible with human rights may be rendered invalid.[39]

Prior to the HRA, judges had presumed that unclear or ambiguous legislative provisions should be interpreted in a way that was compatible with the United Kingdom's international human rights obligations and common law constitutional rights. This principle, 'the principle of legality', was stated by Lord Hoffmann in *R v Secretary of State for the Home Department, ex parte Simms*.[40]

The White Paper, *Rights Brought Home*, explained the interpretative obligation as follows:

Secretary of State for the Home Department, *Rights Brought Home*, Cm 3782 (October 1997), para. 2.7

[The interpretative obligation] goes far beyond the present rule which enables the courts to take the Convention into account in resolving any ambiguity in a legislative provision. The courts will be required to interpret legislation so as to uphold the Convention rights unless the legislation itself is so clearly incompatible with the Convention that it is impossible to do so.

This indicated that courts would be obliged to give human rights-compatible meanings both where legislation is ambiguous and where it is clear. Section 3 says that courts must do what is possible to give legislation a human rights-compatible meaning—but what is possible? Can judges rewrite legislation and insert new words into the legislation as if they were legislating? If so, how far should courts go and at what point would judges trespass upon the legislative function? These questions have been discussed by academic commentators and by judges.[41] And they were considered by the House of Lords in the leading decision on the interpretative obligation, *Ghaidan v Godin-Mendoza*.[42]

[37] See further *Independent Human Rights Act Review*, December 2021, CP 586, pp. 192–213.

[38] Compare the wording of s. 2(4) of the European Communities Act 1972, which provided that '*any enactment [. . .] shall be construed and have effect subject to [EU] law*'.

[39] For a case concerning subordinate legislation, see *Re P and ors* [2008] UKHL 38.

[40] [2000] 2 AC 115, 131.

[41] E.g. G. Marshall, 'The lynchpin of parliamentary intention: Lost, stolen, or strained?' [2003] Public Law 236; Lord Irvine, 'The impact of the Human Rights Act: Parliament, the courts and the executive' [2003] Public Law 308; A. Wagner and G. Barth, 'Judicial interpretation or judicial vandalism? Section 3 of the Human Rights Act 1998', (2016) 21(2) Judicial Review 99–104. See more generally, A. Kavanagh, *Constitutional Review under the UK Human Rights Act* (2009, Cambridge: Cambridge University Press) and see references given later in the chapter.

[42] [2004] UKHL 30.

21.5.6.1 *Ghaidan v Godin-Mendoza*

The main issue in *Ghaidan* was whether a same-sex partner who had for many years lived in a close and stable relationship with someone could succeed to the statutory tenancy under the Rent Act 1977 when the tenant died. The Act granted succession rights to the 'surviving spouse', extended in 1988 to include '*a person who was living with the original tenant as his or her wife or husband*'. In *Fitzpatrick v Sterling Housing Association*,[43] a case with the same facts that was decided before the HRA, the House of Lords had held that a same-sex survivor would *not* qualify under the wording of these provisions.

In *Ghaidan*, the House of Lords was unanimous that denying Mr Godin-Mendoza succession rights would breach Art. 14 (taken with Art. 8). The majority held that the 1977 Act could be read compatibly with Convention rights (see Box 21.2). Lord Millett disagreed, arguing that the approach taken by the majority involved rewriting the legislation and trespassing beyond permissible judicial interpretation into Parliament's legislative domain.

Ghaidan v Godin-Mendoza
[2004] UKHL 30

Lord Nicholls

26. Section 3 is a key section in the Human Rights Act 1998. It is one of the primary means by which Convention rights are brought into the law of this country. Parliament has decreed that all legislation, existing and future, shall be interpreted in a particular way. All legislation must be read and given effect to in a way which is compatible with the Convention rights 'so far as it is possible to do so'.

29. [. . .] It is now generally accepted that the application of s 3 does not depend upon the presence of ambiguity in the legislation being interpreted. Even if, construed according to the ordinary principles of interpretation, the meaning of the legislation admits of no doubt, s 3 may nonetheless require the legislation to be given a different meaning. [. . .]

30. From this it follows that the interpretative obligation decreed by s 3 is of an unusual and far-reaching character. Section 3 may require a court to depart from the unambiguous meaning the legislation would otherwise bear. In the ordinary course the interpretation of legislation involves seeking the intention reasonably to be attributed to Parliament in using the language in question. Section 3 may require the court to depart from this legislative intention, that is, depart from the intention of the Parliament which enacted the legislation. The question of difficulty is how far, and in what circumstances, s 3 requires a court to depart from the intention of the enacting Parliament.

32. [. . .] the mere fact the language under consideration is inconsistent with a Convention-compliant meaning does not of itself make a Convention-compliant interpretation under s 3 impossible. Section 3 enables language to be interpreted restrictively or expansively. But s 3 goes further than this. It is also apt to require a court to read in words which change the meaning of the enacted legislation, so as to make it Convention-compliant. In other words, the intention of Parliament in enacting s 3 was that, to an extent bounded only by what is 'possible', a court can modify the meaning, and hence the effect, of primary and secondary legislation.

33. Parliament, however, cannot have intended that in the discharge of this extended interpretative function the courts should adopt a meaning inconsistent with a fundamental feature of legislation. That would be to cross the constitutional boundary s 3 seeks to demarcate and preserve. Parliament

[43] [2001] 1 AC 27.

has retained the right to enact legislation in terms which are not Convention-compliant. The meaning imported by application of s 3 must be compatible with the underlying thrust of the legislation being construed. Words implied must, in the phrase of my noble and learned friend Lord Rodger of Earlsferry, 'go with the grain of the legislation'. Nor can Parliament have intended that s 3 should require courts to make decisions for which they are not equipped. There may be several ways of making a provision Convention-compliant, and the choice may involve issues calling for legislative deliberation.

[...]

Lord Steyn

[...]

49. [... T]here has sometimes been a tendency to approach the interpretative task under s 3(1) in too literal and technical a way. In practice there has been too much emphasis on linguistic features. If the core remedial purpose of s 3(1) is not to be undermined a broader approach is required. That is, of course, not to gainsay the obvious proposition that inherent in the use of the word 'possible' in s 3(1) is the idea that there is a Rubicon which courts may not cross. If it is not possible, within the meaning of s 3, to read or give effect to legislation in a way which is compatible with Convention rights, the only alternative is to exercise, where appropriate, the power to make a declaration of incompatibility. Usually, such cases should not be too difficult to identify. An obvious example is *R (Anderson) v Secretary of State for the Home Department* [2003] 1 AC 837, [2002] 4 All ER 1089. The House held that the Home Secretary was not competent under Article 6 of the ECHR to decide on the tariff to be served by mandatory life sentence prisoners. The House found a s 3(1) interpretation not 'possible' and made a declaration under s 4. Interpretation could not provide a substitute scheme. *Bellinger* is another obvious example. As Lord Rodger of Earlsferry observed '[...] in relation to the validity of marriage, Parliament regards gender as fixed and immutable': [2003] 2 WLR 1174, 1195, para 83. Section 3(1) of the 1998 Act could not be used.

50. Having had the opportunity to reconsider the matter in some depth, I am not disposed to try to formulate precise rules about where s 3 may not be used. Like the proverbial elephant such a case ought generally to be easily identifiable. What is necessary, however, is to emphasise that interpretation under s 3(1) is the prime remedial remedy and that resort to s 4 must always be an exceptional course. In practical effect there is a strong rebuttable presumption in favour of an interpretation consistent with Convention rights. Perhaps the opinions delivered in the House today will serve to ensure a balanced approach along such lines.

BOX 21.2 A SUMMARY OF THE APPROACH OF THE MAJORITY IN *GHAIDAN*

1. Courts must give legislation a Convention-compatible meaning where possible. When this is not possible, higher courts may make a declaration of incompatibility under s. 4.
2. Courts may depart from the unambiguous meaning of legislation and from the intention of the Parliament that enacted it.
3. Courts should not be limited to the words used, as this 'would make the application of s 3 something of a semantic lottery'.
4. Courts may '*read in words which change the meaning of the enacted legislation, so as to make it Convention-compliant*'.

5. Courts cannot *'adopt a meaning inconsistent with a fundamental feature of legislation'* as this would *'cross the constitutional boundary s. 3 seeks to demarcate and preserve'*.
6. Interpretations must not go *'against the grain of the legislation' and courts cannot make decisions 'for which they are not equipped'*.[44]

Lord Millett disagreed with the majority. While accepting the breadth of the interpretative obligation in s. 3, he emphasized that it is concerned with the *'process of interpretation alone'* and *'does not entitle the court to supply words which are inconsistent with a fundamental feature of the legislative scheme; nor to repeal, delete, or contradict the language of the offending statute'*.[45] He disagreed with the majority's alteration of the meaning of the specific legislative provisions. In his view, this amounted to rewriting legislation and usurped the role of Parliament. For Lord Millett, the only solution would be to consider declaring the legislative provisions to be incompatible with Convention rights—an option that he was disinclined to take.

Ghaidan v Godin-Mendoza
[2004] UKHL 30

Lord Millett

101. In my opinion all these questions are essentially questions of social policy which should be left to Parliament. [. . . I]t is in my view not open to the courts to foreclose them by adopting an interpretation of the existing legislation which it not only does not bear but which is manifestly inconsistent with it.

Courts use section 3 through various interpretive techniques. These range from minimal textual intervention to more substantial rewriting. Common approaches include adding words to statutory text (*'reading in'*), removing problematic language (*'reading out'*), or replacing specific terms with Convention-compatible alternatives. Lewis Graham's empirical study shows that courts prefer subtler techniques that avoid explicit textual modification. Most commonly, courts interpret provisions *'as if'* they had different meanings to achieve Convention compliance. *'Ultimately judges seem to prefer to adopt methods which do the least damage to the legislative text'*.[46]

This preference for minimal intervention reflects constitutional sensitivity about the proper limits of interpretation. Courts typically read statutes with implicit Convention-compatible limitations or apply strained but plausible meanings to problematic terms rather than dramatically rewriting legislation. Graham found that nearly half of all successful section 3 cases involved this *'reading as if'* approach. Despite the provision's potential, judges exercise considerable restraint in practice.

The choice of interpretive technique depends on the statutory context and the nature of the rights breach. Courts are more willing to make explicit textual changes when dealing with procedural provisions or technical drafting errors, but prefer interpretive techniques that preserve legislative language when addressing substantive policy choices.

[44] On this second limit, see further A.L. Young, '*Ghaidan v Godin-Mendoza*: Avoiding the deference trap' [2005] Public Law 23.

[45] *Ghaidan v Godin-Mendoza* [2004] UKHL 30, [68].

[46] Lewis Graham, 'Interpreting the Interpretive Obligation: Empirical Insights into the use of Section 3 of the Human Rights Act 1998' *Oxford Journal of Legal Studies* (forthcoming).

QUESTION

1. How do the majority and minority approaches in *Ghaidan* reflect different constitutional views about the proper relationship between judicial interpretation and legislative authority under the HRA?
2. Has section 3 achieved an appropriate constitutional balance, or has judicial restraint limited the provision's effectiveness?

21.5.6.2 Does the intention of Parliament still matter?

Ghaidan v Godin-Mendoza
[2004] UKHL 30

Lord Nicholls

30. In the ordinary course the interpretation of legislation involves seeking the intention reasonably to be attributed to Parliament in using the language in question. Section 3 may require the court to depart from this legislative intention, that is, depart from the intention of the Parliament which enacted the legislation.

[...]

32. [... T]he intention of Parliament in enacting s 3 was that, to an extent bounded only by what is 'possible', a court can modify the meaning, and hence the effect, of primary and secondary legislation.

Do these comments mean that the courts no longer have to heed the intention of Parliament as expressed in the words of the enactment being interpreted? Do they mean that once judges have decided that provisions are incompatible with Convention rights, they can disregard the wording used and the intention behind them? The most contentious judicial statements indicate that section 3 empowers courts to override both statutory language and parliamentary purpose. Lord Bingham's unqualified assertion in *Sheldrake* that section 3 'may require the court to depart from the legislative intention of Parliament' exemplifies this controversial position.[47] However, in *R (Wilkinson) v IRC*,[48] Lord Hoffmann explained that the wording of legislation still matters.

In this case, a widower claimed entitlement to a tax allowance available only to widows. Section 262 of the Income and Corporation Taxes Act 1988 provided that '*Where a married man whose wife is living with him dies, his widow shall be entitled [. . .] to an income tax reduction.*' He argued that to avoid unlawful discrimination, the court should apply the presumption '*that unless the contrary intention appears* [. . .] *words importing the feminine gender include the masculine*'.[49]

Lord Hoffmann rejected this argument, noting that the 1988 Act is 'brim-full' of indications that references to the feminine gender were not intended to include the masculine.[50] He then made the following observations on the interpretative obligation, stressing the need to focus on the actual words used by Parliament.

[47] Sheldrake v DPP [2004] UKHL 43; [2005] A.C. 264 at [28].
[48] [2005] UKHL 30.
[49] Interpretation Act 1978, s. 6.
[50] *R (Wilkinson) v IRC* [2005] UKHL 30, [15].

R (Wilkinson) v IRC
[2005] UKHL 30

Lord Hoffmann

17. [...] The important change in the process of interpretation which was made by section 3 was to deem the Convention to form a significant part of the background against which all statutes, whether passed before or after the 1998 Act came into force, had to be interpreted. Just as the 'principle of legality' meant that statutes were construed against the background of human rights subsisting at common law (see *R v Home Secretary, Ex p Simms* [...]), so now, section 3 requires them to be construed against the background of Convention rights. There is a strong presumption, arising from the fundamental nature of Convention rights, that Parliament did not intend a statute to mean something which would be incompatible with those rights. [...] It may have come as a surprise to the members of the Parliament which in 1988 enacted the statute construed in the *Ghaidan* case that the relationship to which they were referring could include homosexual relationships. In that sense the construction may have been contrary to the 'intention of Parliament'. But that is not normally what one means by the intention of Parliament. One means the interpretation which the reasonable reader would give to the statute read against its background, including, now, an assumption that it was not intended to be incompatible with Convention rights.

The meaning of the expression the 'intention of Parliament' has long been debated. In the following extract, Aileen Kavanagh summarizes her analysis of how this expression has been used since the enactment of the HRA.

A. Kavanagh, 'The role of parliamentary intention in adjudication under the Human Rights Act 1998' (2006) 26 *Oxford Journal of Legal Studies* 179 (footnotes omitted)

[In this paper w]e discovered that reference to the 'intention of Parliament' has many meanings. It may refer to Parliament's *enacted intention*, i.e. that which is manifest and expressed in the text of the statute. Alternatively, it may refer to the *legislative purposes* which Parliament may have sought to achieve by enacting the legislation. Finally, there are the *presumed intentions* which can be attributed to Parliament due to longstanding principles of the common law. We also discovered that although the HRA brings about some changes in the role of Parliamentary intention, it does not 'abolish' its relevance altogether. [...]

However, there is no denying that interpretation under s 3 brings about significant changes in the traditional role of Parliamentary intention in statutory interpretation. It shifts the interpretive focus away from what Parliament originally intended, towards fulfilling the overriding goal of achieving compatibility with the Convention. When interpreting under s 3, judges can detach legislative meaning from its original contextual setting. Moreover, within certain constraints, they can rectify the *enacted intention* of the statute, if to do so would render it Convention-compatible. Finally, if we view s 3 as introducing a new presumption of Parliamentary intention, it means that at least with reference to pre-HRA legislation, judges are applying a presumption which Parliament could not have known or foreseen when it enacted the original legislation. Even when an innovative decision is reached under s 3, the judiciary is nonetheless keen to emphasize the limits of that creativity, rather than its breadth. Judicial reference to 'the will of Parliament' is a way of expressing those limits. [...]

One final point: before the HRA ever came into force, judges have had at their disposal devices with which they could, in appropriate cases, rectify, improve and update statutory provisions. The familiar presumptions of statutory interpretation are just such a device. [. . .] Much of the alarm about the expanded judicial power under the HRA has perhaps been due to a mischaracterization of the nature of statutory interpretation which existed prior to it. The idea that the only task of the judge before 1998 was to ascertain 'the intention of Parliament' and apply the existing law, is [. . .] part of such a misrepresentation. [. . . W]e should not fall into the trap of characterizing pre-HRA interpretation in terms of a fairytale, in order to cast the HRA as the big bad wolf. The Act certainly brings about changes in the judicial law-making function, but it does not create that function anew. [. . .]

Graham's empirical study supports Kavanagh's analysis. Despite controversial dicta suggesting courts may '*depart from legislative intention*', judges rarely do so in practice. His review of 107 successful section 3 cases from 2000–2023 shows that courts typically seek to 'identify and preserve the intention of the legislature' rather than override it. Early concerns about systematic disregard for parliamentary purpose appear to have been overstated.

L. Graham, 'Interpreting the interpretive obligation: Empirical insights into the use of Section 3 of the Human Rights Act 1998' *Oxford Journal of Legal Studies* (forthcoming)

Section 3 is powerful, but is perhaps not as *radical* as it is sometimes portrayed as being. Indeed, some of the cases in which section 3 is invoked appear very *un*-radical indeed. The provision has been used, for example, in order to correct drafting errors and lacunas which escaped the legislature's attention, and the provisions are not being used – at least, on a regular basis – to radically depart from the intention of the legislature, or to completely re-write the meaning of a statute (it is telling that on the rare occasions where the courts have adopted a particularly radical interpretation, this has been at the insistence of all parties to the dispute). Finally, it is noteworthy that many of the limits to the use of section 3 recognised by the judges are entirely self-imposed. Where section 3 is not being used outside of its proper constitutional boundaries, the reason for that is largely because of the limits drawn up and adhered to by the judges themselves.

QUESTIONS

1. Kavanagh identifies different meanings of 'parliamentary intention' (enacted intention, legislative purposes, and presumed intentions). How do these distinctions help explain the constitutional tensions surrounding section 3 HRA?
2. Does the empirical evidence about section 3's actual use support or challenge concerns about judicial overreach under the HRA?

21.5.7 DECLARATIONS OF INCOMPATIBILITY

Section 4 of the HRA enables senior or higher courts to make a declaration that legislative provisions are incompatible with Convention rights. However, a declaration of incompatibility '*does not affect the validity, continuing operation or enforcement of the provision in respect of which it is given*',[51]

[51] Section 4(2)(a).

nor does it compel government or Parliament to change the law. Here, then, is another reminder of Parliament's legal supremacy: its legislation remains valid and effective even when a court has declared that it conflicts with Convention rights. Another important feature is that declarations of incompatibility are not binding on the parties to the proceedings. In this sense, declarations do not provide tangible remedies for claimants and do not impose legal obligations upon public authorities.

While Declarations of Incompatibility have limited formal effects, their symbolic and practical effects may be considerable. Professor Anthony Bradley, for instance, argued that although legislation is not formally invalidated, when declared incompatible with human rights, it is fatally wounded, and this does affect the sovereignty of Parliament.[52] For this reason, it is perhaps not surprising that the courts regard this remedy as being a last resort. As Lord Steyn emphasized in his judgment in *Ghaidan*, '*interpretation under s 3(1) is the prime remedial remedy and [. . .] resort to s 4 must always be an exceptional course*'.[53]

As you can see from the word 'may' in s. 4(2), judges have discretion whether or not to do so. Different judges take different approaches to this discretion, as illustrated by the disagreement between Lord Millett and Baroness Hale in *Ghaidan* about whether a declaration would serve any useful purpose when Parliament was already considering remedial legislation. The *Steinfeld* case illustrates the judicial approach to this discretion. The UK Supreme Court granted a declaration that the Civil Partnership Act 2004 was incompatible with Convention rights despite government promises of future reform:

R (Steinfeld and Keidan) v Secretary of State for International Development (in substitution for the Home Secretary and the Education Secretary)
[2018] UKSC 32

Lord Kerr (With the Agreement of Lady Hale, Lord Wilson, Lord Reed and Lady Black)

[54] This court was encouraged to refrain from making a declaration of incompatibility because, it was said, the decision not to take action about extending or abolishing civil partnerships was one which fell squarely within the field of sensitive social policy which the democratically-elected legislature was pre-eminently suited to make.[. . .]

[56] The starting point is that the court is not obliged to make a declaration of incompatibility when it finds that a particular provision is not compatible with a Convention right. [. . .]

[60] In this context, it is salutary to recall that a declaration of incompatibility does not oblige the government or Parliament to do anything. [. . .] [by] sending the message to Parliament that a particular provision is incompatible with the Convention, the courts do not usurp the role of Parliament, much less offend the separation of powers. [. . .] In other words, the courts say to Parliament, 'This particular piece of legislation is incompatible, now it is for you to decide what to do about it.' And under the scheme of the Human Rights Act 1998 it is open to Parliament to decide to do nothing.

[61] In my view, there is no reason that this court should feel in any way reticent about the making of a declaration of incompatibility. To the contrary, I consider that we have been given the power under s 4 of HRA to do so and that, in the circumstances of this case, it would be wrong not to have recourse to that power.

[52] A. Bradley, 'The Sovereignty of Parliament: Form or Substance?' in J. Jowell and D. Oliver (eds) *The Changing Constitution*, 7th edn (2011, Oxford: OUP), p. 65.

[53] See also, *R v A (Complainant's Sexual History)* [2001] UKHL 25, [44]–[45].

In order to help expedite responses to such declarations, the HRA enables ministers, if they consider there to be 'compelling reasons', to make 'remedial orders' that amend the legislation to remove the incompatibility. By this process, reforms may be made without the full parliamentary process, although a draft order must be approved by both Houses of Parliament.[54] While the purpose is to enable speedy amendment of legislation that is incompatible with human rights, the use of remedial orders to amend primary legislation is controversial. The Joint Committee on Human Rights has argued that remedial orders should not be used to amend primary legislation, unless there is a specific need, for example if rapid reform is required in order to protect the life, liberty, physical or mental integrity of a person and the parliamentary timetable does not permit the speedy introduction of a new Bill.[55] The Independent Human Rights Act Review agreed with this.

21.5.7.1 Declarations of incompatibility: Dialogue between the courts, Parliament, and government

The matters just mentioned raise an important question about the role of declarations of incompatibility and the relationship between the courts, on the one hand, and Parliament and government, on the other. As we have seen, the HRA '*was carefully drafted to ensure that Parliamentary Sovereignty was not weakened . . . the UK Parliament can always over-rule*' court decisions.'[56] However, while this may represent the formal constitutional position there can be little doubt that the HRA has affected the actual working relationships between the courts, government, and Parliament.

Lady Hale and Lord Kerr, for example, clearly see the courts as having a positive role in warning Parliament and informing debate on the content of future legislation. We have also seen judges call for constructive dialogue between courts and Parliament.[57] The general argument is that the relationship between courts and government can no longer be understood (if it ever could) as based either on judicial subservience or on conflict. On the contrary, the relationship is subtle and ongoing with government and Parliament taking account of judicial decisions in their discussion about sensitive policy issues.

21.5.7.2 *R (on the Application of Nicklinson and Another) v Ministry of Justice*

The issues we have been discussing were important to the Supreme Court's decision in *R (on the application of Nicklinson and another) v Ministry of Justice*. In Nicklinson, the key questions were whether s. 2 of the Suicide Act 1961, which makes it a criminal offence to assist another person to commit suicide, is incompatible with Art. 8 rights and, if so, whether the court should make a declaration of incompatibility? The court agreed that the ban on assisted suicide was incompatible with the ECHR and could not be rendered compatible by interpretation. However, there were differences over what should be done. The majority of the court (Lords Neuberger, Mance, Wilson, Lady Hale, and Lord Kerr) said that it was within the competence of the court to make a declaration of incompatibility, but only Lady Hale and Lord Kerr would actually do so. Lords Sumption, Clarke, Reed, and Hughes were of the view that the matter was for Parliament rather than for the courts.

[54] HRA, s. 10 and Sch. 2, paras 1 and 2. *Independent Human Rights Act Review*, December 2021, CP 586, ch. 10.

[55] *Independent Human Rights Act Review*, December 2021, CP 586, p. 419.

[56] *Independent Human Rights Act Review*, December 2021, CP 586, p. 224.

[57] There is now a large literature on dialogue, see, e.g., *Independent Human Rights Act Review*, December 2021, CP 586, ch. 4. Also: A. Kavanagh, *Constitutional Review under the UK Human Rights Act* (2009, Cambridge: Cambridge University Press); D. Nicol, 'Law and Politics after the Human Rights Act' [2006] Public Law 722; A.L. Young, 'Is dialogue working under the Human Rights Act 1998?' [2011] Public Law 773; R. Bellamy, 'Political constitutionalism and the Human Rights Act' [2011] International Journal of Constitutional Law 86; C. Chandrachund, 'Reconfiguring the discourse on political responses to declarations of incompatibility' [2014] Public Law 624.

R (on the application of Nicklinson and another) v Ministry of Justice
[2014] UKSC 38

Lord Neuberger

76. In these circumstances, [. . .] even under our constitutional settlement, which acknowledges parliamentary supremacy and has no written constitution, it is, in principle, open to a domestic court to consider whether section 2 infringes article 8. The more difficult question, to which I now turn, is whether we should do so.

[. . .]

100. Nonetheless it is self-evident that the mere fact that Parliament has recently enacted or approved a statutory provision does not prevent the courts from holding that it infringes a Convention right. By the 1998 Act, Parliament has cast on the courts the function of deciding whether a statute infringes the Convention. In a case such as the present, where the margin of appreciation applies, a court will only invoke this function where it has concluded that the issue is within its competence, in which case the fact that Parliament has recently considered the issue, while relevant, cannot automatically deprive the courts of their right, indeed their obligation, to consider the issue. [. . .]

[. . .]

112. [. . . W]hile I respect and understand the contrary opinion, so well articulated by Lord Sumption and Lord Hughes, I am of the view that, provided that the evidence and the arguments justified such a conclusion, we could properly hold that that section 2 infringed article 8. A court would therefore have to consider an application to make a declaration of incompatibility on its merits, and it seems to me that it would be inappropriate for us to fetter the judiciary's role in this connection in advance. More specifically, where the court has jurisdiction on an issue falling within the margin of appreciation, I think it would be wrong in principle to rule out exercising that jurisdiction if Parliament addresses the issue: it could be said with force that such an approach would be an abdication of judicial responsibility. [On this he expresses agreement with Lord Mance.] [. . .]

113. However, I consider that, even if it would otherwise be right to do so [. . .] it would not be appropriate to grant a declaration of incompatibility at this time. In my opinion, before making such a declaration, we should accord Parliament the opportunity of considering whether to amend section 2 so as to enable Applicants, and, quite possibly others, to be assisted in ending their lives [. . .] in the light of what may be said to be the provisional views of this Court, as set out in our judgments in these appeals.

Lord Sumption

Parliament or the Courts?

230. [. . .] The question whether relaxing or qualifying the current absolute prohibition on assisted suicide would involve unacceptable risks to vulnerable people is in my view a classic example of the kind of issue which should be decided by Parliament. [. . .] the issue involves a choice between two fundamental but mutually inconsistent moral values, upon which there is at present no consensus in our society. Such choices are inherently legislative in nature. The decision cannot fail to be strongly influenced by the decision-makers' personal opinions about the moral case for assisted suicide. This is entirely appropriate if the decision-makers are those who represent the community at large. It is not appropriate for professional judges. The imposition of their personal opinions on matters of this kind would lack all constitutional legitimacy.

233. [. . .] If it were possible to say that Parliament had abdicated the task of addressing the question at all, so that none of the constitutional organs of the state had determined where the United Kingdom stood on the question, other considerations might at least arguably arise. As matters stand, I think it clear that Parliament has determined that for the time being the law should remain as it is.

Lady Hale

300. Like everyone else, I consider that Parliament is much the preferable forum in which the issue should be decided. Indeed, under our constitutional arrangements, it is the only forum in which a solution can be found which will render our law compatible with the Convention rights. None of us consider that section 2 can be read and given effect, under section 3(1) of the Human Rights Act 1998, in such a way as to remove any incompatibility with the rights of those who seek the assistance of others in order to commit suicide. However, in common with Lord Kerr, I have reached the firm conclusion that our law is not compatible with the Convention rights. Having reached that conclusion, I see little to be gained, and much to be lost, by refraining from making a declaration of incompatibility. Parliament is then free to cure that incompatibility, either by a remedial order under section 10 of the Act or (more probably in a case of this importance and sensitivity) by Act of Parliament, or to do nothing. It may do nothing, either because it does not share our view that the present law is incompatible, or because, as a sovereign Parliament, it considers an incompatible law preferable to any alternative.

BOX 21.3 KEY ISSUES IN *NICKLINSON*—WHEN SHOULD COURTS MAKE DECLARATIONS OF INCOMPATIBILITY?

The Legal Question: Whether s. 2 of the Suicide Act 1961 (criminalizing assisted suicide) was incompatible with Art. 8 ECHR, and if so, whether the Court should make a declaration of incompatibility.

The Court's Agreement: All judges agreed the legislation was incompatible with Art. 8 and could not be made compatible through s. 3 interpretation.

The Disagreement: Should the Court make a declaration of incompatibility?

Majority Position (Lords Neuberger, Mance, Wilson): Courts have competence to make declarations on human rights issues, but should defer to Parliament when it is actively considering the issue.

Pro-Declaration (Lady Hale, Lord Kerr): Courts should make declarations to fulfil their constitutional role and warn Parliament of incompatibilities, regardless of parliamentary consideration.

Anti-Declaration (Lords Sumption, Clarke, Reed, Hughes): Assisted suicide involves fundamental moral choices that are 'inherently legislative in nature' and should be left entirely to Parliament.

Constitutional Principles:

- Declarations do not compel Parliament to act
- Courts can exercise discretion about when to make declarations
- The relationship between judicial competence and democratic legitimacy in controversial moral issues
- Parliamentary consideration of an issue does not automatically prevent judicial declarations

Outcome: No declaration made, but the Court signalled its 'provisional views' that the law was incompatible, leaving the door open for future individual challenges.

QUESTIONS

1. How do the different approaches in *Nicklinson* reflect constitutional tensions about the relationship between courts and Parliament under the HRA?
2. Does the disagreement between the judges in *Nicklinson* suggest that the HRA's framework for handling incompatible legislation is working as intended, or does it reveal fundamental problems with the Act's design?

21.5.7.3 Responses to declarations of incompatability

Government responses to declarations have been largely compliant. Ministry of Justice data shows that of 44 declarations made between 2000–2021, only one remained unaddressed.[58] Graham's study shows that section 3 interpretations, used roughly 4.6 times annually, far exceed declarations of incompatibility in frequency. Courts prefer judicial reinterpretation to formal constitutional dialogue.[59] This pattern raises questions about whether the 'dialogue' model functions as intended, or whether judicial restraint has shifted constitutional conversations away from the political arena of parliamentary response toward the technical realm of statutory interpretation. These concerns about the HRA's operation, particularly whether courts were using section 3 too aggressively to avoid constitutional dialogue and whether this was undermining parliamentary supremacy, became central to government proposals for reform.

Graham's empirical study documents a marked shift in the UK Supreme Court's approach to human rights claims following Lord Reed's appointment as President in 2020. Between 2020 and 2022, the Court sided with human rights claimants in just 29.4 per cent of cases involving Convention rights—a significant decline from the 41 per cent average for 2009–2019, and a dramatic fall from the 60 per cent success rate in 2019, which was Lady Hale's final year as President. The Court has increasingly characterized human rights issues as 'political' matters unsuitable for judicial determination, applying this label broadly to welfare schemes, immigration decisions, and cases involving 'competing interests' or 'sensitive moral and ethical issues'.[60] Graham identifies this trend as reflecting what he terms 'legal conservatism' combined with a political constitutionalist outlook in which elected politicians rather than judges get the final word in constitutional disputes.[61] The Court has adopted more deferential review standards in human rights cases, particularly where legislatures have already balanced competing interests, and has been notably reluctant to issue declarations of incompatibility or invoke strong interpretive powers under section 3.

QUESTIONS

1. '*The practical choice facing the House in* Ghaidan *was between breathing life into the legislation or making a declaration of incompatibility. The former was a far better option in the circumstances and fully justified the relatively minor legislative action that was undertaken.*' Discuss this statement in light of empirical evidence about how section 3 is actually used in practice.'

[58] Ministry of Justice, Report to the Joint Committee on Human Rights on the Government's Response to Human Rights Judgments 2020–2021 (December 2021) CP 562.

[59] Lewis Graham, 'Interpreting the Interpretive Obligation: Empirical Insights into the use of Section 3 of the Human Rights Act 1998' *Oxford Journal of Legal Studies* (forthcoming).

[60] L. Graham, *Judicial Individuality on the UK Supreme Court* (Oxford: Hart Publishing, 2025), 212–213.

[61] Ibid. p. 201; Ch.10.

2. What are the arguments against treating Declarations of Incompatibility as a last resort? Given that section 3 is used approximately 4.6 times annually compared to roughly 2 declarations per year, does judicial preference for interpretive solutions undermine the constitutional 'dialogue' the HRA was designed to facilitate?
3. Empirical evidence shows that individual Supreme Court judges' approaches to human rights claims vary substantially, with some finding ECHR breaches in over 90 per cent of contested cases while others do so in fewer than 20 per cent. What are the constitutional implications of this variance for the HRA's operation? Does it suggest problems with the Act's design, or is such variance an inevitable and acceptable feature of judicial decision-making?

21.5.8 PROPOSALS FOR REFORM OF SECTIONS 3 AND 4 HRA

The government set up an Independent Human Rights Act Review Panel to examine how the Act was operating in practice.[62] The Panel investigated concerns that UK courts were using section 3 to override Parliament's intentions when interpreting legislation. After reviewing the evidence, the Panel concluded that:

- there was no substantive evidence that courts had misused section 3;
- judges had exercised appropriate restraint in applying the interpretive obligation;
- empirical research showed section 3 was used infrequently and typically addressed unforeseen circumstances that aligned with Parliament's overall legislative purpose.

This finding addresses one of the most persistent criticisms of the HRA—that it allows judges to rewrite legislation beyond acceptable constitutional limits. The Panel's evidence-based conclusion suggests that these concerns, while politically salient, are not supported by the way courts actually apply section 3.

Despite this evidence-based conclusion, the Conservative government subsequently attempted to repeal section 3 entirely through the Bill of Rights Bill (BORB), proposing to limit courts to 'orthodox principles of construction' instead. The BORB was abandoned following political upheaval in 2022–2023. The current Labour government supports the existing HRA framework.

The HRA's interpretive provisions have faced sustained challenge through three developments that demonstrate how constitutional change can occur without formal repeal:

Legislative circumvention became as a direct threat. Although the Bill of Rights Bill was abandoned, the Conservative government continued pursuing similar objectives through what Stuart Wallace describes as 'piecemeal disapplication' of the HRA.[63] Three pieces of legislation—the Illegal Migration Act 2023, the Safety of Rwanda Act 2024, and the Victims and Prisoners Act 2024—directly disapplied section 3 HRA from their operation, preventing courts from interpreting these statutes compatibly with Convention rights.

This departure from established practice was unprecedented. The 2023–24 legislation was exceptional in issuing negative compatibility statements covering entire Bills rather than specific provisions, involving absolute non-derogable rights, and making no attempt to mitigate violations. The approach revealed what Wallace describes as the 'unique vulnerability' of the UK's rights protection regime, by which he means that the absence of constitutional guardrails made it possible to strip away fundamental protections 'at breakneck speed with very limited public consultation'.[64]

[62] Independent Human Rights Act Review—Executive Summary, December 2021, CP 587.
[63] Stuart Wallace, 'The Human Rights Act under Siege: The Vulnerability of Fundamental Rights Protection under the UK Constitution' [2025] *Public Law* 648–669, 660.
[64] Ibid 666.

Academic disagreement persists about whether strong-form interpretive obligations are constitutionally appropriate. Critics contend that section 3 empowers courts to resolve contentious social policy questions that exceed judicial competence and properly belong to elected representatives.[65] Defenders contend that the interpretive framework enhances democratic governance by embedding rights protection within ordinary legal processes, elevating normative standards in public decision-making, and creating additional accountability mechanisms for executive action.[66]

Judicial retrenchment under the Supreme Court's increasingly restrained approach under Lord Reed may have reduced political pressure for formal legislative reform by achieving through judicial evolution what legislative reform had sought to accomplish through statutory change. Conor Gearty observes that 'the Supreme Court is quietly editing the Human Rights Act out of existence'.[67] Gearty attributes the return to legal formalism and narrower conceptions of judicial review to the influence of the Court's President, Lord Reed. This raises important questions about whether recent developments represent organic constitutional evolution reflecting judicial restraint and respect for parliamentary democracy, or a deliberate retrenchment from the HRA, which is regarded by the current members of the UK Supreme Court as an 'unwelcome remnant of a past era'.[68]

C. Gearty, 'In the shallow end' (2022) 44(2) *London Review of Books*

> Reed's Supreme Court has reached some judgments strongly assertive of traditional civil liberties and others that insist on the importance of access to justice. But in some areas the tone is markedly different from the one taken by the court under Hale's leadership. This has been clear in a series of decisions that have been very helpful to government on issues of equality, social policy and human rights. It should not be assumed that the lines the court has taken are in response (conscious or subconscious) to government pressure; it is entirely possible – indeed probable – that the change in direction is primarily driven by the judicial philosophy espoused by Reed and his colleagues, and would have happened even if the court (and the system of the rule of law over which it presides) were not being threatened. Johnson's Brexit administration is in many ways an exercise in nostalgia, a search for a lost England, and the Supreme Court under Reed is similarly backward-looking. It has reverted to an approach rooted in legal formalism, an extremely narrow reading of the rule of law, while displaying an old-school lack of interest in the lived experiences of those whose plights have brought them to the judges' attention.

Sections 3 and 4 show that constitutional change can occur through judicial evolution as much as legislative intervention. Whether this represents constitutional maturity or retreat from the HRA's intended role remains contested in UK human rights protection.

21.5.9 THE SECTION 6 DUTY AND ITS ENFORCEMENT

Section 6 represents the HRA's core enforcement mechanism, making it unlawful for public authorities to act incompatibly with Convention rights. Every public body must respect human rights in everything it does.

[65] Philip Sales and Richard Ekins, '*Rights-consistent interpretation and the Human Rights Act 1998*' (2011) 127 LQR 217.
[66] Aileen Kavanagh, *The Collaborative Constitution* (CUP, 2023).
[67] Conor Gearty, 'Unwelcome Remnant' (2025) 47(18) *London Review of Books*. [68] Ibid.

Section 6 raises three questions that have shaped the HRA's practical impact: which relationships does it govern (vertical vs horizontal effect), which bodies must comply (the meaning of '*public authority*'), and who can enforce these obligations (the victim requirement). Each limitation reflects constitutional choices about the appropriate scope of human rights protection.

The section 6 duty differs from the other HRA mechanisms. While section 3 tells courts how to interpret legislation and section 4 provides a remedy when interpretation fails, section 6 directly regulates the conduct of public bodies. It applies to all public authority conduct, from major policy decisions to routine administrative actions. A local authority making housing allocations, a hospital deciding on treatment priorities, or a police officer conducting a search must all consider whether their actions respect Convention rights.

As the House of Lords explained in *Aston Cantlow*,[69] public authorities '*must act compatibly with Convention rights in everything [they] do*'. Rights considerations become part of everyday decision-making rather than an afterthought when legal challenges arise.

Section 6 operates through several features. Human rights arguments can be raised in any court or tribunal, not just through judicial review. A person challenging a school exclusion in an education appeal, contesting a benefit decision before a social security tribunal, or defending criminal charges can all rely on their Convention rights. This procedural flexibility makes human rights protection more accessible to ordinary people who might never consider bringing a judicial review claim.

The duty applies even when public authorities exercise private law powers. When a local authority enters into a contract to provide services or a government department purchases property, it remains bound by human rights obligations. This prevents public bodies from avoiding their human rights duties by acting through commercial arrangements rather than formal statutory powers.

Section 6 contains an important limitation that preserves parliamentary supremacy. Public authorities have a defence when primary legislation requires them to act in an incompatible way (section 6(2)). This ensures that public bodies cannot be held liable for carrying out what Parliament has instructed them to do. The defence is narrowly interpreted: it only applies when legislation mandates the incompatible action, not when it merely permits it.

The relationship between section 6 and the other HRA provisions creates an integrated system of rights protection. When public authorities face potentially incompatible legislation, they must first ask whether section 3 allows a compatible interpretation. Only if compatible interpretation is impossible can they rely on a section 6(2) defence. This ensures that human rights-compatible outcomes are pursued wherever possible while respecting Parliament's ultimate authority.

Section 6 has transformed UK public law by adding a human rights dimension to all actions by public authorities. Before the HRA, public bodies could violate human rights provided they stayed within their legal powers and followed proper procedures. Now they must also ensure their actions meet Convention standards. This has had practical consequences across government, including the need for human rights impact assessments, staff training, and proactive policies designed to protect Convention rights.

The section's effectiveness depends on how courts interpret key concepts like '*public authority*' and 'victim'. The narrow approach taken in cases like *YL v Birmingham City Council*[70] has limited the scope of the duty, while restrictive standing rules have reduced access to remedies. Understanding the Act requires seeing it as an integrated framework rather than separate legal tools.

[69] *Aston Cantlow and Wilmcote with Billesley Parochial Church Council v Wallbank* [2003] UKHL 37, [7] (Lord Nicholls).

[70] *YL v Birmingham City Council* [2007] UKHL 27.

21.5.9.1 Vertical and horizontal effects

The HRA follows international human rights law by imposing obligations on state actors rather than private parties directly. Since the UK lacks a unified legal concept of '*the state*', the Act targets '*public authorities*' as the domestic equivalent.

Private parties face no direct HRA obligations, regardless of their power or influence. They may acquire indirect obligations through contractual requirements imposed by public authorities, or through human rights standards incorporated into common law. Courts, as public authorities under s. 6, must develop common law compatibly with Convention rights, creating '*indirect horizontal effect*' between private parties alongside the primary '*vertical effect*' between individuals and public authorities.[71]

Campbell v MGN Ltd illustrates this approach, in which privacy rights developed through the common law's evolution under HRA influence, rather than through direct Convention application.

Campbell v MGN Ltd
[2004] UKHL 22

Lord Nicholls of Birkenhead

17. [. . .] The values embodied in articles 8 and 10 are as much applicable in disputes between individuals or between an individual and a non-governmental body such as a newspaper as they are in disputes between individuals and a public authority.

18. [. . .] This approach has been adopted by the courts in several recent decisions, reported and unreported, where individuals have complained of press intrusion. A convenient summary of these cases is to be found in Gavin Phillipson's valuable article 'Transforming Breach of Confidence? Towards a Common Law Right of Privacy under the Human Rights Act' (2003) 66 MLR 726, 726–728.

The HRA's vertical structure raises a practical question: which bodies count as 'public authorities' subject to human rights obligations? This definitional issue has proved contentious in the Act's operation.

21.5.9.2 The meaning of 'public authority'

While of central importance, the term 'public authority'[72] is not defined in the HRA. The Act tells us only that it includes the following.[73]

[71] For discussion of the horizontal effect of the HRA, see, e.g., M. Hunt, 'The "horizontal effect" of the Human Rights Act' [1998] Public Law 423; R. Buxton, 'The Human Rights Act and private law' (2000) 116 Law Quarterly Review 48; H.W.R. Wade, 'Horizons of horizontality' (2000) 116 Law Quarterly Review 217; A. Lester and D. Pannick, 'The impact of the Human Rights Act: The knight's move' (2000) 116 Law Quarterly Review 380; N. Bamforth, 'The true "horizontal effect" of the Human Rights Act 1998' (2001) 117 Law Quarterly Review 34; I. Hare, 'Verticality challenged: Private parties, privacy and the Human Rights Act' (2001) 5 European Human Rights Law Review 526; J. Morgan 'Questioning the "true effect" of the Human Rights Act' (2002) 22 Legal Studies 259; G. Phillipson and A. Williams, 'Horizontal effect and the constitutional constraint' (2011) 74 Modern Law Review 878.

[72] See also amenability to judicial review, Chapter 17 p. 490.

[73] The Bill of Rights Bill would apply to the same bodies as the HRA: Clause 34.

Human Rights Act 1998, s. 6(3)–(5)

(3) [. . .]

(a) a court or tribunal, and

(b) any person certain of whose functions are functions of a public nature, but does not include either House of Parliament or a person exercising functions in connection with proceedings in Parliament.

(4) In subsection (3) 'Parliament' does not include the House of Lords in its judicial capacity.

(5) In relation to a particular act, a person is not a public authority by virtue only of subsection (3)(b) if the nature of the act is private.

Note that neither of the Houses of Parliament are public authorities for the purpose of the Act. This means that they cannot be held to have acted unlawfully for participating in the enactment of legislation that breaches rights.

21.5.9.3 Core Public Authorities

Aston Cantlow and Wilmcote with Billesley Parochial Church Council v Wallbank and another
[2003] UKHL 37

Lord Nicholls of Birkenhead

7. [. . . T]he phrase 'a public authority' in section 6(1) is essentially a reference to a body whose nature is governmental in a broad sense of that expression. It is in respect of organisations of this nature that the government is answerable under the European Convention on Human Rights. Hence, under the Human Rights Act a body of this nature is required to act compatibly with Convention rights in everything it does. The most obvious examples are government departments, local authorities, the police and the armed forces. Behind the instinctive classification of these organisations as bodies whose nature is governmental lie factors such as the possession of special powers, democratic accountability, public funding in whole or in part, an obligation to act only in the public interest, and a statutory constitution: see the valuable article by Professor Dawn Oliver, 'The Frontiers of the State: Public Authorities and Public Functions under the Human Rights Act', [2000] PL 476.

21.5.9.4 Hybrid public authorities

Section 6(3)(b) extends the HRA to private bodies performing 'functions of a public nature': so-called 'hybrid' public authorities. This provision addresses modern governance, where many traditionally public services are delivered by private organizations through contracting out, privatization, and public-private partnerships. The Act does not define what constitutes a 'public function', generating legal and constitutional debate about the boundaries of human rights protection.

How should human rights obligations adapt to the changing architecture of public service delivery? As Lord Nicholls observed in *Aston Cantlow*, the phrase 'public authority' in section 6(1) is essentially a reference to bodies whose nature is governmental in a broad sense.[74] It is in respect of

[74] *Aston Cantlow and Wilmcote with Billesley Parochial Church Council v Wallbank* [2003] UKHL 37, [7].

such organizations that the government is answerable under the ECHR. Yet this broad formulation provides little guidance when applied to private bodies that may exercise some functions that appear governmental while retaining their fundamentally commercial character.

Two different approaches to defining 'public functions' have emerged in the case law:

Narrow approach: Public functions require the exercise of special statutory powers or coercive authority that would not be available to private actors. Under this approach, private prisons qualify as hybrid authorities because they exercise statutory powers of detention and control that ordinary private bodies cannot possess. Commercial relationships, even when involving public funding or regulatory oversight, remain outside the HRA's scope because they do not involve distinctively governmental powers.

Broad approach: The nature, importance, and public character of the function matter more than the specific legal powers used to deliver it. Essential services, such as healthcare, education, or social care should be subject to human rights obligations regardless of whether they are provided by public or private bodies, particularly when public authorities have statutory duties to ensure service provision and exercise significant control over delivery standards.

The tension between these approaches came to a head in *YL v Birmingham City Council*,[75] where the House of Lords adopted the narrow approach in a controversial 3-2 decision. The court considered whether a private care home providing publicly-funded accommodation to an elderly resident with Alzheimer's disease was exercising public functions. The majority held that the care home was not a hybrid public authority because its relationship with residents was fundamentally contractual and commercial, despite being heavily regulated and publicly funded.

The majority emphasized several factors that pointed away from public function status: the care home operated as a commercial business seeking profit; it had contractual relationships with both residents and local authorities; and the local authority had not 'delegated' its statutory functions but had instead arranged for their discharge through commercial contracts.[76] The majority rejected the argument that providing care and accommodation was inherently a governmental function, emphasizing instead the contractual and commercial context within which services were delivered.

The dissenting judgments of Lord Bingham and Baroness Hale advocated the broader approach. They argued that the statutory context, particularly the local authority's duty to arrange care and the detailed regulatory framework governing provision, created a sufficiently public character to attract HRA obligations. Baroness Hale emphasized that from the resident's perspective, the source of human rights protection should not depend on whether care happened to be provided directly by the local authority or through commercial arrangements.[77]

The *YL* decision proved controversial, prompting criticism from the Joint Committee on Human Rights and concern that privatization was creating gaps in human rights protection.[78] The government responded with legislation to reverse the decision's effects in the care home context, initially through the Health and Social Care Act 2008 and subsequently through the Care Act 2014, which explicitly extends HRA obligations to privately-provided care services arranged or funded by public authorities (section 73).

This legislative response addressed only the specific care home context without resolving the broader conceptual difficulties surrounding hybrid authorities. The narrow approach established in *YL* continues to limit the HRA's application to other privatized services, creating what critics describe

[75] *YL v Birmingham City Council* [2007] UKHL 27.

[76] Ibid, [11] (Lord Scott), [63] (Lord Mance).

[77] Ibid, [20] (Lord Bingham), [72] (Baroness Hale).

[78] Joint Committee on Human Rights, Eighth Report, Session 2007–08 (HL 46/HC 303).

as a 'postcode lottery' of human rights protection that depends on the specific contractual and regulatory arrangements used to deliver services rather than their essential public character.

S. Palmer, 'Public, private and the Human Rights Act 1998: An ideological divide'
(2007) 66(3) *Cambridge Law Journal* 559–573, 572

> The consequence of the *YL* decision is that the delivery of many formerly public services by way of contractual arrangements with private bodies is beyond the reach of human rights law and regulated solely by the private law of contract. This decision creates a lacuna for many public recipients of services. Occasions may arise where there will be no direct contractual relationship between the private service provider and the users of services. The Joint Committee on Human Rights described such recipients as 'stranded victims'.[79] Even if individuals can seek judicial review against local authorities who have arranged the care placements, this is hardly encouraging a culture of human rights to flourish. Human rights values must traverse the public-private boundary if there is to be a change of culture in our institutions delivering public services.

Stephanie Palmer's concept of '*stranded victims*' shows the human cost of the narrow approach to hybrid authorities, which prioritizes legal formalism and commercial freedom over substantive rights protection. The narrow approach ensures that private bodies do not acquire human rights obligations merely by providing publicly-funded services, but this creates the gaps Palmer identifies: situations where vulnerable individuals have no effective means of enforcing their rights. The broad approach, advocated by the dissenting judges, would prioritize functional considerations. Citizens should not lose human rights protection simply because public authorities choose to deliver services through private contractors.

This tension reflects constitutional questions about the boundaries of '*the state*' for human rights purposes and the balance between commercial freedom and public accountability. As public service delivery continues evolving through various forms of privatization, outsourcing, and partnership arrangements, these definitional questions become increasingly significant for determining the practical scope of human rights protection in the UK.

The narrow interpretation of '*public authorities*' in cases like *YL* limits who must comply with section 6. But even when clear public authorities are involved, a separate limitation restricts who can enforce these obligations. The HRA's 'victim' requirement significantly constrains access to human rights remedies.

21.5.10 THE VICTIM REQUIREMENT

The HRA imposes a restrictive standing requirement, requiring claimants to be '*victims of the unlawful act*' (s. 7(1)(b)). This reflects the European Convention's approach to standing, which differs from the more liberal '*sufficient interest*' test in judicial review.

Convention jurisprudence requires claimants to be directly affected by the alleged violation. The victim requirement serves constitutional purposes: ensuring human rights cases involve genuine disputes rather than abstract questions; preventing public authorities from claiming victim status; and maintaining the individual focus of rights protection.

[79] The Joint Committee on Human Rights, HL 39/HC 382, 'The Meaning of "Public Authority" under the Human Rights Act (2003–04), at [84].

Dudgeon v UK[80] illustrates the practical application. A gay man successfully challenged Northern Ireland's criminalization of homosexual conduct despite never being prosecuted. The European Court found the legislation directly affected him by criminalizing his conduct and creating a constant threat of prosecution. Actual enforcement is not required where the claimant's conduct falls within the prohibited category.

Family members may qualify as 'indirect victims' in some circumstances. In *Daniel v St George's Healthcare NHS Trust*,[81] the court applied a four-factor test considering: the legal/family relationship; personal ties; personal impact and suffering; and involvement in related proceedings. A foster mother qualified given her parental relationship with a child who died in NHS care, but a close friend did not, despite genuine emotional impact.

Public interest groups cannot claim victim status, though they may intervene. This contrasts with judicial review, where such organizations frequently bring challenges under the sufficient interest test.

The Supreme Court's approach in *Northern Ireland Human Rights Commission*[82] shows restrictive trends. The Commission sought to challenge Northern Ireland's abortion law in its own name to 'prevent any woman or girl from having to face the burden of doing so'.[83] Despite the Court finding the law incompatible with Convention rights, the majority denied standing on technical grounds concerning the distinction between HRA enforcement mechanisms.[84] As Lady Hale observed in dissent, this created an 'arid' situation where violations were identified but could not be remedied through the institution best placed to bring them to court's attention.[85]

The decision shows how the victim requirement can undermine systematic rights protection. Lord Mance acknowledged that if an individual victim challenged the legislation, a declaration of incompatibility would be 'inevitable',[86] yet refused to allow the Commission, which was established precisely to avoid forcing vulnerable individuals through such ordeals, to bring the challenge. This creates an anomaly where violations of fundamental rights may be subject to more restrictive access to justice than ordinary administrative law disputes.[87]

Jane Rooney argues that the majority's approach fundamentally misunderstood the constitutional arrangements established by the Good Friday Agreement.

J. Rooney, 'Standing of the Northern Ireland Human Rights Commission in the UK Supreme Court Abortion Decision', University of Bristol Law School Blog, 9 June 2018

The judgment represents a misunderstanding, and lack of regard, for the constitutional arrangement established by the Good Friday Agreement wherein the Commission was empowered with the right to bring judicial proceedings when human rights are stake, both in relation to the commission of an unlawful act by a public authority and judicial review of legislation. Lord Kerr is the only judge in the Supreme Court to consider the constitutional significance of a ruling finding against standing for the Commission, and reads both the Northern Ireland Act and Human Rights Act purposively to ensure that

[80] (1981) 4 EHRR 149. [81] [2016] EWHC 23 (QB).

[82] *In the Matter of an application by the Northern Ireland Commission for Judicial Review* [2018] UKSC 27.

[83] NIHRC, 'Northern Ireland Termination Law Breaches Women and Girls' Human Rights', 7 June 2018 (https://nihrc.org/news/detail/northern-ireland-termination-law-breaches-women-and-girls-human-rights).

[84] The majority's literal interpretation of statutory wording requiring identification of an 'unlawful act' prevented challenges to incompatible legislation itself.

[85] *In the Matter of an application by the Northern Ireland Commission for Judicial Review* [2018] UKSC 27 [11].

[86] Ibid [135].

[87] See Chapter 17, Section 17.3.6, 'Standing to Make a Judicial Review Claim'.

the mistake of denying standing to the Commission is not made. A literal interpretation of the Northern Ireland Act supports the proposition that the Commission should have standing and a purposive interpretation of the Human Rights Act ensures that its provisions are not used as an excuse to abdicate judicial responsibility in politically contentious cases.

The *NIHRC* decision shows how restrictive approaches to standing can undermine the institutional framework designed to protect human rights. The victim requirement serves constitutional functions by preventing abstract litigation and ensuring courts address genuine disputes. When applied inflexibly, it risks forcing vulnerable individuals to bear the burden of systemic challenges that representative institutions were specifically created to pursue. Whether this balance appropriately serves the HRA's constitutional purposes, or unduly restricts access to effective rights protection, remains contested among practitioners and scholars.

21.5.10.1 Remedies under the HRA

Section 8 provides courts with broad powers to grant remedies for human rights violations, stating that courts may grant 'such relief or remedy, or make such order within its powers as it considers just and appropriate' when finding HRA breaches. This flexible approach ensures that effective remedies are available across the diverse situations, in which human rights violations occur.

The remedial framework is comprehensive. Courts can use any remedy available in judicial review proceedings: quashing orders, mandatory orders, prohibiting orders, plus damages or compensation. Courts can issue declarations, injunctions, require public authorities to reconsider decisions, mandate specific actions, or award monetary compensation as circumstances require.

Damages under the HRA follow a distinctive '*just satisfaction*' test rather than ordinary tort principles. Section 8(4) requires courts to consider whether damages are necessary for '*just satisfaction*', taking into account all circumstances, including any other relief granted. Courts must also apply principles developed by the European Court of Human Rights.

This differs from tort damages, which aim to restore claimants to their pre-violation position. The 'just satisfaction' test is more limited, focusing on whether monetary compensation adequately acknowledges the rights violation rather than providing full compensation for all losses. The European Court has explained that the Convention's primary purpose is rights protection rather than victim compensation, and this philosophy influences domestic awards.

HRA damages awards have been notably modest, particularly for non-pecuniary losses. Awards for unlawful detention typically range from a few hundred to several thousand pounds, even for lengthy wrongful imprisonment. This reflects both the European Court's conservative approach and domestic courts' reluctance to award substantial sums for non-material harm.

The modest awards have generated academic criticism. Jason Varuhas argues that courts should adopt a '*vindicatory approach*' modelled on tort cases when basic rights are violated, rather than the current 'mirror' approach, which ties domestic awards to the European Court's notably modest compensation.[88] Kent Roach contends that '*the low quantum of damages awarded by many courts sends the wrong message about human rights*' and that courts should '*elevate damage awards better to vindicate rights that when violated do not typically result in pecuniary harms*'.[89]

The remedial framework faces practical limitations. The victim requirement means only those directly affected can claim remedies, preventing public interest organizations from seeking broader

[88] Jason Varuhas, *Damages and Human Rights *(Oxford: Hart Publishing, 2016).

[89] Kent Roach, The Disappointing Remedy? Damages as a Remedy for Violations of Human Rights (2019) 69(1) *The University of Toronto Law Journal* 33–63, 35.

relief. Modest damages may discourage litigation where legal costs exceed likely compensation. Constitutional constraints may prevent immediate relief, forcing claimants toward damages claims.

Carmichael[90] illustrates these limitations. Mr Carmichael's housing benefit was reduced under the '*bedroom tax*' (housing benefit reduction for 'spare' bedrooms) despite his wife's severe disability requiring separate accommodation. While his wife's judicial review reached the Supreme Court, which declared the regulation incompatible with ECHR rights, Mr Carmichael separately appealed to the First-Tier Tribunal. The Upper Tribunal ordered that his benefit be recalculated, but the Court of Appeal overturned the decision, holding that tribunals cannot disapply incompatible legislation. Mr Carmichael's remedy lay in a damages claim instead.

B. Fullbrook, 'Judicial remedies for Human Rights Act breaches: *Secretary of State for Work and Pensions v Carmichael* [2018] EWCA Civ 548'
(2018) 23(2) *Judicial Review* 119–123, 122–123

Following this judgment, it would appear clear that the FTT (and UT) is not permitted to disapply secondary legislation even where it has been declared incompatible with the HRA, provided that legislation is still in force. It would seem that the appropriate response in such a situation is for it to determine that there is incompatibility and to require the appellant to remedy any loss suffered by way of a claim for damages in the civil courts pursuant so s. 8(2) HRA (para. 67).

This judgment is a helpful authority on the interpretation and purpose of the HRA. It provides some support for the suggestion that the Act has, at its heart, respect for parliamentary supremacy as recognised in s. 6(6) and by Lord Wilson JSC in *R (T) v Chief Constable of Greater Manchester* [2014] UKSC 35 [. . .].

However, it is also arguably the most practical solution to this problem. As Sir Brian Leveson noted, there is a real risk that the UT's approach could result in different litigants seeking to persuade the tribunal to modify the language of regulations indifferent ways so as to achieve the result best suited to their situation. This situation would be difficult to sustain and would be vulnerable to the suggestion that it licensed judicial legislation.

Critics argue the HRA's remedial framework compares unfavourably with constitutional courts empowered to strike down incompatible legislation immediately. Varuhas shows that HRA damages are lower than awards for comparable intentional torts, and that courts fail to maintain real value over time. The combination of modest damages, narrow standing rules, and reliance on government cooperation creates limitations that undermine the HRA's effectiveness.

The debate reflects tensions between individual rights protection and parliamentary supremacy, and between accessibility through diverse remedies versus centralized enforcement effectiveness.

21.6 CONCLUDING COMMENTS

This chapter has examined how the Human Rights Act 1998 operates in practice, revealing both its achievements and limitations. The HRA marked a break in UK public law, but remains embedded within the domestic constitutional framework, creating ongoing tensions about the balance between judicial and political power.

Constitutional 'dialogue' between courts and Parliament continues to function, though differently than originally envisioned. Empirical evidence shows government responses to declarations of incompatibility have been largely compliant, but the far more frequent use of section 3 interpretations

[90] *Secretary of State for Work and Pensions v Carmichael* [2018] EWCA Civ 548.

indicates that constitutional conversation has shifted toward technical statutory interpretation rather than overt political dialogue. Contemporary debates have evolved from formal repeal attempts to questions about judicial evolution and practical application.

The most significant development has been the Supreme Court's increasingly restrictive approach under Lord Reed's leadership, which has adopted what Lewis Graham describes as a '*particularly muscular conception of parliamentary sovereignty*' that uses sovereignty doctrine as an active tool to constrain judicial power. This judicial evolution, combined with the experience of '*piecemeal disapplication*' through recent legislation, demonstrates both the HRA's constitutional vulnerability and its practical importance.

The HRA presents a tension: it continues to provide meaningful protection of human rights while operating within increasingly narrow judicial constraints. Whether this represents constitutional maturity that appropriately restrains judicial overreach or constitutional regression that undermines effective protection of rights remains contested.

Twenty-five years after its enactment, the HRA's significance lies in showing how constitutional innovation can occur within a parliamentary democracy. The lessons of the HRA's operation remain relevant for understanding how rights, democracy, and constitutional change interact within the UK's evolving constitution.

FURTHER READING

Amos, M., *Human Rights Law*, 3rd edn (2021, Oxford: Hart Publishing).

Constigan, R. and Stone, R., *Civil Liberties & Human Rights*, 11th edn (2017, Oxford: OUP).

Cowell, F., *Critically Examining the Case Against the 1998 Human Rights Act* (2018, Abingdon: Routledge).

Feldman, D. (ed.), *English Public Law*, 2nd edn (2009, Oxford: OUP), chs 7–12 and 19.

Independent Human Rights Act Review, December 2021, CP 586.

Kavanagh, A., *The Collaborative Constitution* (2023, Cambridge: Cambridge University Press).

Moores, C., *Civil Liberties and Human Rights in Twentieth-Century Britain* (2017, Cambridge University Press).

Wadham, J. et al., *Blackstone's Guide to the Human Rights Act 1998*, 8th edn (2024, Oxford: OUP).

Young, A. L., *Democratic Dialogue and the Constitution* (2017, Oxford: OUP).

WEBSITES

UN Human Rights Council	www.ohchr.org/en/pages/home.aspx
European Court of Human Rights	www.echr.coe.int/pages/home.aspx?p=home&c=
European Union and Human Rights	http://europa.eu
	www.consilium.europa.eu
Ministry of Justice	www.justice.gov.uk
UK Parliamentary Joint Committee on Human Rights	www.parliament.uk/business/committees/committees-a-z/joint-select/human-rights-committee/
Equality and Human Rights Commission	www.equalityhumanrights.com/

22

PROTECTING HUMAN RIGHTS CASE STUDIES: SCHOOL UNIFORMS, TERRORISM, AND PRISONER VOTING

CENTRAL ISSUES

1. The chapter considers three case studies that illustrate key issues in UK human rights law. The first is Shabina Begum's challenge to her school's decision not to permit her to dress in accordance with her religious belief. In this case, the House of Lords explained the difference between the approach to be taken by judges in human rights cases and that required by the common law grounds of judicial review.
2. The second case study deals with the most challenging issue in this area of law since the enactment of the HRA—the relationship between human rights and terrorism. The case study examines the landmark decision in the *Belmarsh* case and its aftermath.
3. The third case study considers prisoner voting. Here the UK's ban on prisoner voting was found to breach the ECHR but the UK refused to accept the decision. The case study illustrates how the human rights system established by the ECHR responds in such a situation.

22.1 CASE STUDY: THE *DENBIGH HIGH SCHOOL* CASE—SCHOOL UNIFORMS AND THE RIGHT TO MANIFEST ONE'S RELIGION

Shabina Begum was nearly 14 years old and had been a pupil at the Denbigh High School in Luton for two years. The school is a mixed-sex maintained secondary school for children aged between 11 and 16 years, and is open to people of all faiths, or no faith. At the time, four of six parent governors were Muslim, the chairman of the Luton Council of Mosques was a community governor, and three of the local education authority governors were Muslim. The head teacher was from a Bengali Muslim family and had grown up in India. It had a diverse intake, with 21 different ethnic groups and ten religious groupings represented. Approximately 79 per cent of its pupils were Muslim.

On 3 September 2002, the first day of the new school year, Shabina Begum went to school with her older brother and another man. She was wearing a jilbab,[1] which she wanted to wear to school. In her previous years at school, she had, in accordance with the school's uniform policy, worn a shalwar kameeze.[2] Given her age, Shabina now believed that her religion dictated that she should wear a jilbab in mixed company.

They asked to speak to the head teacher, but she was not available, and instead they spoke to the assistant head, Mr Moore. Mr Moore said that the school's policy on school uniforms did not permit pupils to wear a jilbab. In the words of one of the Law Lords, who was eventually to deal with the case, *'the men told Mr Moore at length and in forceful terms that Shabina was entitled under human rights law to come to school wearing a jilbab and that unless she was admitted they would sue the school'.*[3] Mr Moore responded by telling Shabina to go home and get changed. She, her older brother, and the other man left.

On the same day, the head teacher, who had been informed of the incident, wrote to Shabina's mother and brother (with whom she lived), setting out an account of the incident. The head teacher said that the uniform policy had been agreed with the governing body and the local education authority, and was, in her view, reasonable in taking into account the cultural and religious concerns of the community and the school population. But the matter did not end there: neither side was prepared to alter its position.

Shabina claimed that she had been excluded from the school and did not attend during that academic year. In the meantime, as the dispute continued, the school and the local education authority obtained independent advice on whether the school's uniform policy offended Islamic dress code. They were advised that it did not. Shabina also obtained an expert opinion that the jilbab was the accepted dress for mature Muslim women.

Shabina was urged to return to the school, or to seek a place at one of the other schools in the area. One of these was a single-sex girls' school, in which the jilbab would not have been necessary; the other two schools would have permitted the jilbab. In October 2003 (after the beginning of the next school year), she applied to the single-sex school, but was told that, by this date, it did not have a place available. Eventually, she went to another school that allowed her to wear the jilbab.

22.1.1 THE CLAIM

On 13 February 2004, Shabina Begum—advised by the Children's Legal Centre, then based at the University of Essex—issued a claim for judicial review arguing that the decisions to prevent her wearing the jilbab and to exclude her until she was prepared to dress in accordance with the school's uniform policy were contrary to her human rights, and therefore unlawful under s. 6 of the HRA.

22.1.2 THE ISSUES TO BE CONSIDERED

Pausing here, let us briefly consider some of the obstacles that Shabina and her lawyers confronted on these facts. The main preliminary issue was to identify legal arguments that could be made and whether the HRA applied to the situation. In order to answer this question, the lawyers had to look in particular at ss 6 and 7 of the Act. As we have seen, it is unlawful for 'a public authority' to act

[1] A long loose-fitting garment that includes a hijab, which covers the head and much of the face.

[2] A sleeveless, smock-like dress with a square neckline revealing the wearer's collar and tie, with loose trousers, tapering at the ankles, worn with a long-sleeved white shirt and pullover, depending on the weather.

[3] Lord Hoffmann, at [46].

incompatibly with a Convention right. In Shabina's case, it is clear that Denbigh High School, its governors, and the local education authority were public authorities. Had the school been a private school, the situation might have been more complex, because the school may then have been able to argue that its uniform policy was a matter of contract between it and those who paid fees, and therefore not within the scope of the HRA.[4]

Likewise, in this case, it is clear that Shabina was able to claim to be a victim under s. 7 of the HRA. By contrast, had the case been brought by her brother or her friend, for example, it is unlikely that they would satisfy this requirement on these facts.[5]

The lawyers next had to identify the Convention rights that were engaged. From the list of rights set out in Sch. 1 to the HRA 1998, the lawyers identified two that appeared directly relevant to Shabina. The first was Art. 9 on freedom of thought, conscience, and religion, and the second was the right to an education contained in Art. 2 of the First Protocol to the ECHR. We shall concentrate on Shabina's claim under Art. 9.

Article 9 Freedom of thought, conscience, and religion

(1) Everyone has the right to freedom of thought, conscience and religion; this right includes freedom to change his religion or belief and [. . .] freedom, either alone or in community with others and in public or private, to manifest his religion or belief, in worship, teaching, practice and observance.

(2) Freedom to manifest one's religion or beliefs shall be subject only to such limitations as are prescribed by law and are necessary in a democratic society in the interests of public safety, for the protection of public order, health or morals, or for the protection of the rights and freedoms of others.

In order to establish a breach of Art. 9, the lawyers had to look very carefully at its wording. Because of the duty in s. 2 of the HRA '*to take account of*' the jurisprudence developed by the ECtHR they also had to look carefully at this case law. They would have been aware of the following statement by the ECtHR stressing the importance of the rights contained in Art. 9 (but pointing out that the freedom to manifest one's religion, alone among the freedoms protected by Art. 9(1), may be limited on the grounds set out in Art. 9(2)).

Kokkinakis v Greece ECtHR,
25 May 1993, Series A No. 160-A, p. 17

31. As enshrined in Article 9, freedom of thought, conscience and religion is one of the foundations of a 'democratic society' within the meaning of the Convention. It is, in its religious dimension, one of the most vital elements that go to make up the identity of believers and their conception of life, but it is also a precious asset for atheists, agnostics, sceptics and the unconcerned. The pluralism indissociable from a democratic society, which has been dearly won over the centuries, depends on it.

While religious freedom is primarily a matter of individual conscience, it also implies, inter alia, freedom to 'manifest [one's] religion'. Bearing witness in words and deeds is bound up with the existence of religious convictions.

[. . .]

[4] See Chapter 21 for a discussion of hybrid public bodies.

[5] *Leigh v UK* (1984) 38 DR 74 (claimants not directly affected by the breach were not victims).

33. The fundamental nature of the rights guaranteed in Article 9 para 1 [. . .] is also reflected in the wording of the paragraph providing for limitations on them. Unlike the second paragraphs of Articles 8, 10 and 11 [. . .] which cover all the rights mentioned in the first paragraphs of those Articles, that of Article 9 refers only to 'freedom to manifest one's religion or belief'. In so doing, it recognises that in democratic societies, in which several religions co-exist within one and the same population, it may be necessary to place restrictions on this freedom in order to reconcile the interests of the various groups and ensure that everyone's beliefs are respected.

They would also have been aware that the decision of the European Commission on Human Rights in *Karaduman v Turkey*[6] (holding that a Turkish university could refuse to allow women to wear headscarves when having their graduation certificate photographs taken, in order to prevent people passing themselves off as graduates) was being challenged in the ECtHR, and that the decision was about to be given.[7]

QUESTIONS

Put yourself in the position of the lawyers and look again at Art. 9 with the following questions in mind.

(a) What freedoms are protected by Art. 9(1)?

(b) Which of these freedoms are most relevant to Shabina's claim?

(c) Which of these freedoms can be limited under Art. 9(2)?

(d) In what circumstances may limitations be imposed and do any of these appear relevant in Shabina's case?

Shabina's lawyers took the view that Shabina's strongest claim under Art. 9 would be in relation to her freedom to manifest her religion: the essence of her claim would be that, by stopping her from wearing the jilbab, the school had prevented her from manifesting her religion.

QUESTION

Were Shabina also to have argued that the school had limited her freedom of religion (rather than the freedom to manifest her religion), what obstacle(s) would she have faced?

22.1.2.1 Anticipating the school's response

The lawyers will have recognised that establishing a breach of Art. 9 was unlikely to be straightforward and they will have tried to anticipate the arguments that were likely to be used by the school. Two main arguments could have been anticipated.

[6] (1993) 74 DR 93.

[7] In fact, the decision of the ECtHR was delivered on 29 June 2004, upholding the legality of the ban on headscarves. This decision was confirmed by the Grand Chamber on 18 November 2005: *Leyla Sahin v Turkey*, App. No. 44774/98. The ban was justified in the interests of protecting the principle of secularism in Turkish society.

(a) The school was likely to argue that its uniform policy did not prevent Shabina from manifesting her religion; it only prevented her from wearing a jilbab at Denbigh High School. She could have chosen to go to one of the other schools in the area at which she would have been free to manifest her religion. In other words, it was her choice of school that led to her being unable to manifest her religion in this situation, and not the school's policy or its decision to apply the policy in her case.

(b) As we have seen, the freedom to manifest one's religion in Art. 9(1) is a qualified right that can be limited in the circumstances set out in Art. 9(2). The school was likely to argue that, even if it had infringed Art. 9(1), the infringement was justified under Art. 9(2). This was to become a central issue in the case and led to a serious difference between the Court of Appeal and the House of Lords.

22.1.2.2 Suppose that the HRA had not been enacted or was not applicable

Before moving on to see how the case fared in the courts, it is worth briefly considering how the case might have been presented had the HRA not been applicable or enacted. In this situation, Shabina could not rely directly on Art. 9 and the claim would have been much weaker. Shabina could still challenge the school's decision, but she would have had to rely on general principles of judicial review. She could, for example, have argued that the school had not taken proper account of her rights under Art. 9, or that its policy had been applied in an overly rigid fashion without giving sufficient attention to her particular situation.[8] It is unlikely that she could have successfully argued that the school's decision was *Wednesbury* unreasonable and irrational.[9]

Irrationality aside, these traditional arguments would have focused on the school's process of decision-making, but they would not have directly confronted the substance of Shabina Begum's real complaint—that is, that her human rights had been violated because she had been prevented from doing what her religious beliefs demanded.

22.1.3 THE ADMINISTRATIVE COURT

Shabina was unsuccessful in the Administrative Court.[10] Bennett J accepted that her claim engaged rights under Art. 9, but there was, he said, no breach of Art. 9(1): '*Although her refusal [to respect the school uniform policy] was motivated by religious beliefs, she was excluded for her refusal to abide by the school uniform policy rather than her religious belief as such.*'[11]

Although not necessary, given his decision, Bennett J went on to consider whether, had there been a breach of Art. 9(1), this would have been justified under Art. 9(2).

R (Begum) v The Headteacher and Governors of Denbigh High School
[2004] EWHC 1389 (Admin)

Bennett J

91. In my judgment the school uniform policy and its enforcement has, and continues to have, a legitimate aim and is proportionate. The legitimate aim was the proper running of a multi-cultural, multi-faith, secular school. The limitation was also proportionate to the legitimate aim pursued. The limitation was specifically devised with the advice of the Muslim community. Although it appears that there

[8] See Chapter 18. [9] Ibid.

[10] *R (Begum) v The Headteacher and Governors of Denbigh High School* [2004] EWHC 1389 (Admin).

[11] At [74].

is a body of opinion within the Muslim faith that only the jilbab meets the requirements of its dress code, there is also a body of opinion that the shalwar kameeze does as well. In my judgment, the adoption of the shalwar kameeze by the Defendant as the school uniform for Muslim (and other faiths) female pupils was and continues to be a reasoned, balanced, proportionate policy.

Shabina Begum and her lawyers decided to appeal against this judgment. In the Court of Appeal, her legal team was led by Cherie Booth QC, wife of Tony Blair who was Prime Minister when the HRA was enacted.

22.1.4 THE COURT OF APPEAL

The Court of Appeal (Brooke, Mummery, and Scott Baker LJJ) was unanimous in disagreeing with Bennett J and allowed Shabina's appeal.[12] It held that Shabina had been excluded from the school because she was not willing to comply with the school's uniform policy and that the policy had infringed her freedom to manifest her religion under Art. 9(1). It also held that the infringement of her right had not been justified under Art. 9(2). The lead judgment was delivered by Brooke LJ and the core of his reasoning on Art. 9 was as follows.

Begum v Denbigh High School
[2005] EWCA Civ 199

Brooke LJ

50. [. . .] SB's freedom to manifest her religion or beliefs may only be subject to limitations that are prescribed by law and are necessary in a democratic society in the interests of public safety, for the protection of public morals, or for the protection of the rights and freedoms of others. There was no suggestion that the protection of public morals had any relevance, and a justification on health and safety grounds was dismissed by the judge and not resurrected on the appeal once evidence had showed that other schools (including the local school which the claimant now attends) had been able to accommodate girls wearing the jilbab without any serious concern being raised on that ground.

[. . .]

74. The position of the School is already distinctive in the sense that despite its policy of inclusiveness it permits girls to wear a headscarf which is likely to identify them as Muslim. The central issue is therefore the more subtle one of whether, given that Muslim girls can already be identified in this way, it is necessary in a democratic society to place a particular restriction on those Muslim girls at this school who sincerely believe that when they arrive at the age of puberty they should cover themselves more comprehensively than is permitted by the school uniform policy.

75. The decision-making structure should therefore go along the following lines:

1) Has the claimant established that she has a relevant Convention right which qualifies for protection under Article 9(1)?
2) Subject to any justification that is established under Article 9(2), has that Convention right been violated?
3) Was the interference with her Convention right prescribed by law in the Convention sense of that expression?

[12] [2005] EWCA Civ 199.

4) Did the interference have a legitimate aim?
5) What are the considerations that need to be balanced against each other when determining whether the interference was necessary in a democratic society for the purpose of achieving that aim?
6) Was the interference justified under Article 9(2)?

76. The School did not approach the matter in this way at all. Nobody who considered the issues on its behalf started from the premise that the claimant had a right which is recognised by English law, and that the onus lay on the School to justify its interference with that right. Instead, it started from the premise that its uniform policy was there to be obeyed: if the claimant did not like it, she could go to a different school.

[...]

78. In my judgment [...] because it approached the issues in this case from an entirely wrong direction and did not attribute to the claimant's beliefs the weight they deserved, the School is not entitled to resist the declarations she seeks [...]

Not surprisingly, the decision received widespread attention in the media and not all views were positive. In the *Daily Telegraph*, for example, a comment on the case was headed, 'The school uniform case was a victory for bigots'.[13]

But criticism of the decision was not limited to the press coverage: there was also significant academic criticism of the Court of Appeal's approach. Thomas Poole, for example, wrote an article in *Public Law* that was extremely critical of the way in which the Court of Appeal had applied the proportionality test to the Art. 9(2) question.[14] He argued that in finding that the school had approached Shabina's case '*from an entirely wrong direction*', the Court of Appeal had focused on the procedure adopted by the school rather than on the substance of its decision. In other words, the Court of Appeal had approached the case using the traditional judicial review approach, rather than the approach required by the HRA. He said that the Court of Appeal implied that the way in which authorities decide things is more important than the impact that decisions have on people's rights—that is, that procedure is more important than substance.

T. Poole, 'Of headscarves and heresies: *The Denbigh High School* case and public authority decision-making under the Human Rights Act' [2005] *Public Law* 685, 689–91 (footnotes omitted)

There are problems [...] with the approach taken by the Court of Appeal in the *Denbigh High School* case. First and foremost, it rests on a basic mistake. Proportionality is a [test] to be applied by the court when reviewing decisions of public authorities after they have been made [...]. It is not a test which ought to mean that public authorities should themselves adopt a proportionality approach to the structuring of their decision-making [as they are being made].

There is nothing in the Human Rights Act, the European Convention or Convention jurisprudence which would seem to require public authorities to act in this way. [...] The wording of [s. 6] indicates that the obligations public authorities are required to fulfil relate to the substance of their policies, decisions and actions. As Ian Leigh observed [I. Leigh, 'Taking rights proportionately: Judicial review, the Human Rights Act and Strasbourg' [2002] Public Law 265, 283] the primary question asked by s. 6 is *result-orientated—were* the claimant's rights violated by the public authority?—and, if the answer to that question is affirmative, 'the *process* by which the public authority came to violate his or her Convention rights is irrelevant'. [...]

[13] *Daily Telegraph*, 6 March 2005.

[14] Also T. Linden and T. Hetherington, 'Schools and human rights: *Denbigh High School*' [2005] Education Law Journal 229.

QUESTION

Do you agree with this criticism of the Court of Appeal's approach, given what Brooke LJ said about the importance of protecting Shabina's rights under Art. 9?

The matter, however, did not end with the Court of Appeal. The school appealed to the House of Lords (the top appeal court at the time). At this stage, the Secretary of State for Education and Skills also appeared as an intervener, arguing that the approach adopted by the Court of Appeal revealed '*a fundamental misunderstanding of the 1998 Act*'.

22.1.5 THE HOUSE OF LORDS

The House of Lords allowed the appeal and reinstated the decision of Bennett J. All five Law Lords agreed with this result. There were, however, significant differences between them. Lords Bingham, Hoffmann, and Scott agreed with Bennett J that Shabina Begum's freedom to manifest her religion had not been limited by the school, and that even if it had been, the limitation would have been proportionate and justified under Art. 9(2). Lord Nicholls and Baroness Hale were inclined to the view that Shabina Begum's freedom to manifest her religion had been interfered with, but agreed that the interference was justified.

R (on the application of Begum) v Head Teacher and Governors of Denbigh High School
[2006] UKHL 15

Lord Bingham

2. [The] case concerns a particular pupil and a particular school in a particular place at a particular time. It must be resolved on facts which are now, for purposes of the appeal, agreed. The House is not, and could not be, invited to rule whether Islamic dress, or any feature of Islamic dress, should or should not be permitted in the schools of this country. That would be a most inappropriate question for the House in its judicial capacity and it is not one which I shall seek to address.

[He reiterated the fundamental importance of Art. 9 in a pluralistic, multicultural society and continued.]

21. It is common ground in these proceedings that [. . .] the respondent sincerely held the religious belief which she professed to hold. [. . . I]t is accepted, obviously rightly, that art 9(1) is engaged or applicable. That, in itself, makes this a significant case, since any sincere religious belief must command respect, particularly when derived from an ancient and respected religion. The main questions for consideration are, accordingly, whether the respondent's freedom to manifest her belief by her dress was subject to limitation (or, as it has more often been called, interference) within the meaning of art 9(2) and, if so, whether such limitation or interference was justified under that provision.

Interference

[. . .]

23. The Strasbourg institutions have not been at all ready to find an interference with the right to manifest religious belief in practice or observance where a person has voluntarily accepted an employment

or role which does not accommodate that practice or observance and there are other means open to the person to practise or observe his or her religion without undue hardship or inconvenience.

[...]

25. In the present case the respondent's family chose for her a school outside their own catchment area. It was a school which went to unusual lengths to inform parents of its uniform policy. The shalwar kameeze, and not the jilbab, was worn by the respondent's elder sister throughout her time at the school and by the respondent for her first two years without objection. It was, of course, open to the respondent, as she grew older, to modify her beliefs, but she did so against a background of free and informed consent by her and her family. It is also clear that there were three schools in the area at which the wearing of the jilbab was permitted. The respondent's application for admission to one of these was unsuccessful because the school was full and it was asserted in argument that the other two were more distant. There is, however, no evidence to show that there was any real difficulty in her attending one or other of these schools, as she has in fact done and could no doubt have done sooner had she chosen. On the facts here, and endeavouring to apply the Strasbourg jurisprudence in a reasonable way, I am of opinion that in this case [...] there was no interference with the respondent's right to manifest her belief in practice or observance. I appreciate, however, that my noble and learned friends Lord Nicholls and Lady Hale of Richmond incline to a different opinion. It follows that this is a debatable question, which gives the issue of justification under art 9(2) particular significance.

Justification

26. To be justified under art 9(2) a limitation or interference must be (a) prescribed by law and (b) necessary in a democratic society for a permissible purpose, that is, it must be directed to a legitimate purpose and must be proportionate in scope and effect. It was faintly argued for the respondent that the school's uniform policy was not prescribed by law, but both the judge [...] and the Court of Appeal [...] held otherwise, and rightly so. The school authorities had statutory authority to lay down rules on uniform and those rules were very clearly communicated to those affected by them. It was not suggested that the rules were not made for the legitimate purpose of protecting the rights and freedoms of others. So the issue is whether the rules and the school's insistence on them were in all the circumstances proportionate. This raises an important procedural question on the court's approach to proportionality and, depending on the answer to that, a question of substance.

27. In para [75] of his leading judgment in the Court of Appeal, Brooke LJ set out a series of questions to be asked and answered by a decision-maker resolving an issue raised under art 9. He observed (at [76]) that the school did not approach the matter in that way at all. Since, therefore, the school had approached the issues from an entirely wrong direction [...]

29. I am persuaded that the Court of Appeal's approach to this procedural question was mistaken for three main reasons. First, the purpose of the 1998 Act was not to enlarge the rights or remedies of those in the United Kingdom whose Convention rights have been violated but to enable those rights and remedies to be asserted and enforced by the domestic courts of this country and not only by recourse to Strasbourg. This is clearly established by authorities [...] But the focus at Strasbourg is not, and has never been, on whether a challenged decision or action is the product of a defective decision-making process, but on whether, in the case under consideration, the applicant's Convention rights have been violated. [... T]he House has been referred to no case in which the Strasbourg court has found a violation of Convention right on the strength of failure by a national authority to follow the sort of reasoning process laid down by the Court of Appeal. [...]

30. Secondly, it is clear that the court's approach to an issue of proportionality under the Convention must go beyond that traditionally adopted to judicial review in a domestic setting. The inadequacy of that approach was exposed in *Smith v UK* (1999) 29 EHRR 493 at 543 (para 138) and the new approach

required under the 1998 Act was described by Lord Steyn in *R v Secretary of State for the Home Dept, ex p Daly* [2001] UKHL 26 [. . .] in terms which have never to my knowledge been questioned. There is no shift to a merits review, but the intensity of review is greater than was previously appropriate and greater even than the heightened scrutiny test adopted by the Court of Appeal in *R v Ministry of Defence, ex p Smith* [1995] 4 LRC 300 at 307. The domestic court must now make a value judgment, an evaluation, by reference to the circumstances prevailing at the relevant time [. . .] Proportionality must be judged objectively by the court (see *R (on the application of Williamson) v Secretary of State for Education and Employment* [2005] 5 LRC 670 at [51]). As Davies observed, [in 'Banning the jilbab: Reflections on restricting religious clothing in the light of the Court of Appeal in *SB v Denbigh High School*' (2005) 1.3 European Constitutional Law Review 511], 'The retreat to procedure is of course a way of avoiding difficult questions'. But it is, in my view, clear that the court must confront these questions, however difficult. The school's action cannot properly be condemned as disproportionate, with an acknowledgement that on reconsideration the same action could very well be maintained and properly so.

31. Thirdly, and as argued by Poole [. . .] I consider that the Court of Appeal's approach would introduce 'a new formalism' and be 'a recipe for judicialisation on an unprecedented scale'. The Court of Appeal's decision-making prescription would be admirable guidance to a lower court or legal tribunal, but cannot be required of a head teacher and governors, even with a solicitor to help them. If, in such a case, it appears that such a body has conscientiously paid attention to all human rights considerations, no doubt a challenger's task will be the harder. But what matters in any case is the practical outcome, not the quality of the decision-making process that led to it.

[. . .]

34. On the agreed facts, the school was, in my opinion, fully justified in acting as it did. It had taken immense pains to devise a uniform policy which respected Muslim beliefs but did so in an inclusive, unthreatening and uncompetitive way. The rules laid down were as far from being mindless as uniform rules could ever be. The school had enjoyed a period of harmony and success to which the uniform policy was thought to contribute. On further inquiry it still appeared that the rules were acceptable to mainstream Muslim opinion. It was feared that acceding to the respondent's request would or might have significant adverse repercussions. It would, in my opinion, be irresponsible of any court, lacking the experience, background and detailed knowledge of the head teacher, staff and governors, to overrule their judgment on a matter as sensitive as this. The power of decision has been given to them for the compelling reason that they are best placed to exercise it and I see no reason to disturb their decision.

[. . .]

Lord Hoffmann

68. Quite apart from the fact that, in my opinion, the Court of Appeal would have failed the examination for giving the wrong answer to [the question whether the Art. 9(1) right has been violated] the whole approach seems to me a mistaken construction of art 9. In domestic judicial review the court is usually concerned with whether the decision-maker reached his decision in the right way rather than whether he got what the court might think to be the right answer. But art 9 is concerned with substance, not procedure. It confers no right to have a decision made in any particular way. What matters is the result: was the right to manifest a religious belief restricted in a way which is not justified under art 9(2)? The fact that the decision-maker is allowed an area of judgment in imposing requirements which may have the effect of restricting the right does not entitle a court to say that a justifiable and proportionate restriction should be struck down because the decision-maker did not approach the question in the structured way in which a judge might have done. Head teachers and governors cannot be expected to make such decisions with textbooks on human rights law at their elbows. The most that can be said is that the way in which the school approached the problem may help to persuade a judge that its answer fell within the area of judgment accorded to it by the law.

22.1.6 THE IMPACT OF THE DECISION

As with the earlier court decisions, the decision of the House of Lords attracted massive public attention, and was both widely applauded and widely criticized across the media. Many schools will have been relieved to know that the courts had upheld the legality of the uniform policy and the way in which it had been applied.

Aspects of their Lordships' decision have proved controversial. One of these is Lord Bingham's observation that courts should not use the HRA to expand on the scope of human rights protection—in other words, that the Act imposes a ceiling to human rights protection rather than a floor. It is notable that the House of Lords reversed a unanimous decision of the Court of Appeal upholding Begum's human rights claim, while criticizing that court for being overly concerned with process. The most important criticisms of the judgment, however, have come from those who believe that the outcome-based approach adopted by the House of Lords is misconceived and likely to have negative effects. David Mead, for instance, points to three main disadvantages with this approach.

D. Mead, 'Outcomes aren't all: Defending process-based review of public authority decisions under the Human Rights Act' [2012] *Public Law* 61, 76–8 (footnotes omitted)

First, *Denbigh* effects a shift towards court-based enforcement and judicial protection, away from protection by those best placed to do so [. . .] those on whom discretionary political power is conferred. [. . .] An internalised, prospective process-driven model of human rights protection creates—or at least has the potential to create—human rights equally for all. That is its beauty. The judicial enforcement of fair procedures, where decision-makers know they must ask the right questions in the right order for the right reasons should mean that your rights are as well protected as mine: protection is systemic and institutionalised. In contrast, a system in which outcomes are all mean that aggrieved citizens must pursue individualised one-off legal remedies to protect their rights, with the costs of enforcement and protection shifted onto them. [. . .]

Secondly, the House of Lords has removed any incentive for decision makers to reach decisions by a process that is Convention-sensitive. Why not just toss a coin? For a decision to survive scrutiny, a decision-maker needs only to demonstrate that the decision is what a panel of judges at some time in the future considers to be proportionate. There is a fifty-fifty chance it will. Such decisions are not hedged in shades of grey—they are either proportionate or they are not. That a decision-maker did not actually consider whether other less restrictive measures could have been employed will have no bearing on the result. In fact, [. . .] there is a double whammy here in favour of decision makers. They will be able to array evidence and arguments not necessarily before them or in their minds at the time. So long as they do not waver on the outcome, it matters not that wholly different arguments are paraded before the Administrative Court than were called upon by [the decision-maker at the time] [. . .] As Hickman notes, 'where reliance can be placed on an ex post facto justifications, it is also much more difficult for claimants to predict in advance their chances of success' [T. Hickman, *Public Law after the Human Rights Act*, p. 240]. [. . .]

Thirdly, [. . . c]hanging public service culture to one where human rights discourse permeates thinking at all levels was one of the government's avowed intentions in introducing the HRA. That objective is supported by process-based review but stunted by *Denbigh*.

The following comment by David Pannick QC (now Lord Pannick KC) summarizes some of the broader issues raised by the case in the light of the decision of the ECtHR in *Leyla Sahin v Turkey*,[15] which had, by now, been delivered.

[15] See n. 7.

D. Pannick QC, 'Drawing a jilbab over a schoolgirl's religious rights', *Times Online*, 14 February 2006

[. . .] Last November, the European Court of Human Rights decided, by 16–1, that it was not a breach of the right to religious freedom for a female university student in Turkey to be refused admission to lectures if she insisted on wearing an Islamic headscarf. The court emphasized that, in a multicultural society, restrictions on the manifestation of religion might be necessary to protect the interests of others. The university authorities were entitled to require the removal of the headscarf in order to protect female students who did not wish to wear such an item and who would otherwise come under severe pressure from extremist groups to comply with religious requirements.

The evidence on behalf of the school expressed similar concerns. A secular school is entitled to refuse to allow its female pupils to wear the more conservative jilbab if there is a reasonable basis for concern that girls who would wish to follow a more liberal tradition would then be pressured to conform to an extreme religious conception of the female role that they want to avoid. [. . .] *Shabina Begum v Denbigh High School* is not just a case about the rights of a schoolgirl to wear a jilbab. It is also a case about whether a secular school may protect other pupils from religious pressures that seek to dictate the role of women.

22.1.7 THE AFTERMATH

The decision in *Leyla Sahin v Turkey* no doubt influenced the decision not to take Shabina's case to the ECtHR.[16] Since the *Begum* case, courts in England and Wales have considered several other cases involving similar questions. In *R (X) v Headteachers of Y School and anor*,[17] Silber J held that a Muslim girl's rights under Art. 9 had not been infringed when she was prevented from wearing a niqab veil,[18] because she could have accepted an offer of a place at a similar school that would allow the veil and to which it was easy for her to travel. In *R (on the application of Playfoot) v Governing Body of Millais School*,[19] the High Court rejected a challenge to a school that had stopped a pupil from wearing a 'purity' ring (which was a symbol of the pupil's commitment to celibacy before marriage). The court held that her beliefs did not oblige her to wear the ring, that she had voluntarily accepted the school's policy, and that there were other means open to her to practise her beliefs.

Another significant decision is that of the High Court in *R (Watkins-Singh) v Governing Body of Aberdare Girls' High School*.[20] The claimant, a 14-year-old girl of Punjabi–Welsh heritage, was refused permission to wear a 'Kara' to school (a plain steel bangle), which she said was central to her ethnic identity as an observant member of the Sikh community. Silber J upheld her claim on the grounds that the school's decision had constituted indirect discrimination on grounds of race contrary to the Race Relations Act 1976 and on the grounds of religion under the Equality Act 2006, which the school had not been able to justify. An important aspect of this case is that it reminds us that human rights arguments are not limited to the HRA and that claimants may rely on other legislative provisions.

[16] See also *Eweida and others v United Kingdom*, App. Nos 48420/10, 59842/10, 51671/10 and 36516/10, 15 January 2013, where the ECtHR held that there had been a breach of Art. 9 when an employee of British Airways was prevented from wearing a cross at work. In *SAS v France*, App. No. 43835/11, 1 July 2014, the ECtHR held that the French ban on face-covering did not violate the ECHR.

[17] [2007] EWHC 298 (Admin).

[18] A veil that covers the entire face and head, except for the eyes.

[19] [2007] EWHC 1698 (Admin).

[20] [2008] EWHC 1865 (Admin). See also *SG v St Gregory's Catholic Science College* [2011] EWHC 1452 (Admin), where Collins J held that a school's ban of the cornrows hairstyle, insofar as it applied to the child in question, was unlawful. Collins J rejected the school's argument that a voluntary decision to have cornrows did not attract the protection of the discrimination legislation, holding that family and social customs can form 'part of ethnicity'.

QUESTIONS

1. Which of the following statements is the most accurate?
   (a) In *Begum*, the House of Lords decided that the school had acted lawfully because, when making its decision, it had paid sufficient attention to Shabina Begum's rights. (By contrast, the Court of Appeal had decided that insufficient attention had been paid to her rights.)
   (b) In *Begum*, the House of Lords agreed with the school that pupils should not be allowed to wear the jilbab.
   (c) In *Begum*, the House of Lords had no opinion as to whether the school was right or wrong, but it did accept that the school's policy was aimed at achieving a lawful objective, that its decision in this case furthered that policy, and that it did not unnecessarily limit Shabina's rights.
2. The core reason why the House disagreed with the Court of Appeal's approach in *Begum* is contained in Lord Bingham's comment that '*The school's action cannot properly be condemned as disproportionate, with an acknowledgement that on reconsideration the same action could very well be maintained and properly so.*' Discuss and explain the difference between the task of the courts in a judicial review case in which HRA issues are not involved and the approach to be taken when they are involved.
3. If you were a lawyer advising schools, what are the most important things that you would tell schools in relation to the *Begum* decision?
4. If you were advising the government, what principles of general application emerge from the decision?

22.2 CASE STUDY: HUMAN RIGHTS AND TERRORISM

22.2.1 BACKGROUND

This case study examines some of the litigation and legislation generated in the wake of the terrorist bombing of the World Trade Center in New York and the other related attacks on 11 September 2001. It is, however, important to remember the following.

A. T. H. Smith, 'Offences against the state', in D. Feldman (ed.) *English Public Law*, 2nd edn (2009, Oxford: OUP), ch. 27, p. 1161

> It would be a mistake to suppose that the UK law devoted to the suppression of terrorism is particularly modern, let alone a reaction to the events that convulsed the world following the attacks in the United States in September 2001. Continuing problems in Northern Ireland meant that the statute books were replete with offences directed against terrorist groups and their activities.[21]

[21] See also C. Walker, *Blackstone's Guide to the Anti-terrorism Legislation* (2002, Oxford: OUP).

The United Kingdom's legislative reaction to what President Bush called the 'war on terror', nonetheless has raised fundamental questions about the balance between the government's legitimate need to protect the public (and the corresponding right of the public to security), on the one hand, and the rights of individuals to be protected from state action, on the other. Coming so soon after the enactment of the HRA, reaction to terrorism was to test the effectiveness of the new Act; it would also profoundly test the relationship between the judges and the executive and Parliament. Would the judges adopt their traditional stance of deferring to the executive whenever the government justified breaching individual human rights in the interests of national security, or would the judges be more robust in their application of the HRA and the rights that it had brought home?

The responses to international terrorism have extended across a very broad range of activities, and have led to several extensive Acts of Parliament and, to much debate, as well as to a very substantial literature. In this case study, we shall principally focus on litigation generated in reaction to Pt IV of the Anti-terrorism, Crime and Security Act 2001, which permitted detention without trial and the control order regime initially established by the Prevention of Terrorism Act 2005 and later amended.

22.2.1.1 The legal response to events on 11 September 2001

On 11 November 2001, the Home Secretary made a Derogation Order under s. 14 of the HRA enabling the United Kingdom to take steps that would otherwise constitute a deprivation of liberty contrary to Art. 5 ECHR (the right to liberty).[22] The ECHR gives states limited power to derogate from (that is, act contrary to) some of the Articles in the Convention, including Art. 5, but not Art. 3 (the prohibition of torture and degrading treatment or punishment). Derogations can be made only '*in time of war or other public emergency threatening the life of the nation*' and derogations are only permissible '*to the extent strictly required by the exigencies of the situation*'.[23]

Parliament also swiftly enacted the Anti-terrorism, Crime and Security Act 2001 (ATCSA). The speed of enactment and the short time available for Parliament to consider the proposals have been summarized by the ECtHR.

A and ors v UK

Grand Chamber of the ECtHR, App. No. 3455/05, 19 February 2009

12. On 12 November 2001 the Anti-Terrorism Crime and Security Bill, containing the clauses which were to eventually become Part 4 of the Anti-Terrorism, Crime and Security Act 2001 [. . .] was introduced into the House of Commons. The Bill was passed by Parliament in two weeks, with three days of debate on the floor of the House of Commons set aside for its 125 clauses in a restrictive programming motion, prompting both the Joint Committee of Human Rights and the Home Affairs Select Committee to complain of the speed with which they were being asked to consider the matter.

13. The 2001 Act came into force on 4 December 2001.

In order to understand the relevant provisions of the ATCSA, we need to go back a step to the 1996 decision of the ECtHR in *Chahal v UK*.[24]

[22] The Human Rights Act 1998 (Designated Derogation) Order 2001 (SI 2001/3644). The United Kingdom also derogated from Art. 9 of the International Covenant on Civil and Political Rights 1966.

[23] Article 15 ECHR. [24] (1996) 23 EHRR 413.

22.2.1.2 *Chahal V UK*

Chahal was an Indian citizen resident in the United Kingdom. The Home Secretary believed that he had been involved in terrorist activities in support of Sikh separatism and he sought to deport him, believing that Chahal's presence in the United Kingdom was not conducive to the public interest on national security grounds. Under the Immigration Act 1971, a person subject to a deportation order on these grounds had no right to appeal to a court against the decision and no right to see the evidence upon which the Home Secretary had acted.[25] Instead, he or she could make representations, without a right to legal representations, to an advisory panel of 'three wise men'.

Chahal took his case to the ECtHR, making two lines of argument. He argued that the procedure adopted was unlawful because it infringed his right to a court hearing under Art. 5(4) (which requires those who are deprived of their liberty to have access to a court), as well as his right to an effective remedy in Art. 13.

Chahal also argued that if he were deported and returned to India, there was a real risk that he would be tracked down and killed by lawless Punjab police. This claim had been accepted in a separate case by the Immigration Appeal Tribunal, and was corroborated by reports of the US Department of State and by Amnesty International.[26] He argued that, in this situation, deportation would constitute a breach of Art. 3 of the ECHR.

The ECtHR upheld each of these claims. The decision was to have a very significant effect on the United Kingdom. It had two major implications. First, it meant that a new procedure had to be introduced that would enable people to challenge decisions to deport made on grounds of national security, but which would not enable the release of confidential information. In giving its judgment, the ECtHR referred to the practice adopted in Canada whereby the confidentiality of sensitive material was maintained by holding closed sessions in the absence of the person concerned and his or her legal representatives.

The decision in *Chahal* also led to the enactment of the Special Immigration Appeals Commission Act 1997 establishing the Special Immigration Appeals Commission (SIAC), modelled on the Canadian practice referred to by the Court.

22.2.1.3 The Special Immigration Appeals Commission

The SIAC is a superior court of record that was established to hear appeals against decisions to deport on national security grounds. It is composed of a High Court judge or some other holder of high judicial office, an expert on immigration matters, and an intelligence expert. It operates under procedural rules that allow it to hold closed hearings in the absence of the appellant or the appellant's lawyer. These procedures are exceptional and known as Closed Material Procedures or CMPs,[27] and in cases in which closed hearings take place, the Act enables the appointment of special advocates (experienced lawyers who have been security cleared) to represent the interests of appellants. The procedure is described by John Ip.

[25] Section 15(3); see *R v Secretary of State for the Home Department, ex parte Hosenball* [1977] 1 WLR 766.

[26] See K. Starmer, 'Setting the record straight: Human rights in an era of international terrorism' (2007) 2 European Human Rights Law Review 123.

[27] CMPs are used when Parliament provides for them: *Al-Rawi v Security Service* [2011] UKSC 34.

J. Ip, 'The rise and spread of the special advocate'
[2008] *Public Law* 717, 721 (footnotes omitted)

The appeal hearing is conducted in open and closed sessions. The open session, in which the appellant and his representatives can participate, occurs first; the special advocate is also present. During the closed session, all parties other than the Home Secretary and the special advocate leave. The special advocate may then challenge the government's case by, adducing evidence, cross-examining witnesses, and making representations to SIAC about the closed material. Although the special advocate is able to see all the closed material, the special advocate's ability to take instructions or communicate with the appellant is restricted once the advocate has seen the closed material. If the special advocate wishes to consult with the appellant or his or her lawyer, SIAC must authorise it after notifying the Secretary of State, who may object. The appellant may also communicate in writing with the special advocate via counsel.

As we shall see, there has been much litigation concerning the compatibility of SIAC procedures with human rights.

22.2.1.4 *Chahal* and Art. 3

While government and Parliament could respond to the procedural aspect of *Chahal* by reforming the process, it was less easy for them to respond to the decision on the effect of Art. 3. The rights in Art. 3 are absolute and they can neither be infringed nor derogated from. While the United Kingdom is a party to the ECHR, it is therefore bound to respect Art. 3, as interpreted by the ECtHR. The HRA also means that people in Chahal's situation can rely directly on Art. 3 before domestic courts.

The implications of the decision have been summarized by the government as follows:

'The implications of *Chahal* for the government's ability to deport or remove people whose presence in the UK threatens national security', Derogation lodged with the Secretary General of the Council of Europe on 18 December 2001

[. . . W]here the intention remains to remove or deport a person on national security grounds, continued detention may not be consistent with Article 5(1)(f) as interpreted by the Court in the *Chahal* case. This may be the case, for example, if the person has established that removal to their own country might result in treatment contrary to Article 3 of the Convention. In such circumstances, irrespective of the gravity of the threat to national security posed by the person concerned, it is well established that Article 3 prevents removal or deportation to a place where there is a real risk that the person will suffer treatment contrary to that article. If no alternative destination is immediately available then removal or deportation may not, for the time being, be possible [. . .] In addition, it may not be possible to prosecute the person for a criminal offence given the strict rules on the admissibility of evidence in the criminal justice system of the United Kingdom and the high standard of proof required.

The government has never liked this aspect of *Chahal*. Indeed, on 5 August 2005, the then Prime Minister Tony Blair suggested that unless the government could persuade courts to depart from *Chahal*, the government would consider amending the HRA to force domestic courts to do so. The government has intervened in litigation before the ECtHR to argue that the Court should alter its approach. To date the court has refused to do so.[28]

Suffice to say, the restrictions imposed by *Chahal* on the ability to deport people who constitute a threat to national security have significantly influenced the design of the anti-terrorist legislation.

QUESTION

If you were a government lawyer asked to advise on how the HRA might be amended to remove the effect of the *Chahal* case, what advice would you give?

22.2.2 PART 4 OF THE ANTI-TERRORISM, CRIME AND SECURITY ACT 2001

Part 4 of ATCSA allowed foreign nationals to be indefinitely detained without charge when the Home Secretary had certified them to be suspected international terrorists who could not be deported from the United Kingdom as a consequence of *Chahal*.[29] Those in this situation could choose to leave the United Kingdom, but if they chose not to do so, they would remain in detention, subject to a six-month review by the SIAC. As well as its duty to review certifications, the Act gave the SIAC exclusive jurisdiction to hear challenges to certifications and to deal with derogation matters, with further appeal on a point of law to the Court of Appeal. The government accepted that this form of detention was incompatible with Art. 5 of the ECHR, which would have been contrary to the ECHR but for the 11 November 2001 Derogation Order.

Sixteen people were certified and detained under Pt IV. These detentions generated challenges to:

(a) the legality of the derogation and the legislative scheme; and

(b) individual certifications.

We shall start by considering the challenges to the legality of the Derogation Order and the legislative scheme.

22.2.3 THE LEGALITY OF THE DEROGATION ORDER AND OF THE LEGISLATION

The broadest line of challenge was to the legality of the Derogation Order. If this could be successfully challenged, the legislative provisions infringing Art. 5 would be incompatible with the ECHR and would almost certainly have to be repealed or amended. Remember that derogation from the ECHR is only possible in situations in which there is an emergency that threatens the life of the nation. The government's position was that it was solely responsible for determining whether such an emergency existed and its judgement could not be upset by the courts.

If the court was not prepared to hold the derogation unlawful, a second line of challenge was to the proportionality of the legislative provisions. Even if there were an emergency that justified the

[28] In *Saadi v Italy*, the Grand Chamber of the ECtHR unanimously reaffirmed the absolute nature of Art. 3 and its approach in *Chahal* (App. No. 37201/06, Judgment of 28 February 2008). Also *A v Netherlands*, App. No. 4900/06; *N v Sweden*, App. No. 23505/09, Judgment of 20 July 2010; and *A.S. v France*, App. No. 46240/15, Judgment of 19 April 2018.

[29] ATCSA, ss. 21–23.

Derogation Order, the steps taken to meet the emergency must be 'strictly required' by the situation. Here, the claimants argued that the key provisions in Pt IV were not strictly required. Once again, the government would argue that this was not a matter for the courts, but for Parliament.

These arguments were first considered by the SIAC. After examining both open and closed material, and hearing submissions from special advocates as well as counsel for the parties and for Liberty (which had been joined as an interested party), the SIAC held, on the basis of the open material, that it was satisfied that the threat from al-Qaeda had created a public emergency threatening the life of the nation, within the meaning of Art. 15 of the Convention. The closed material confirmed this view.

The SIAC also held that while it was possible that the public could have been protected by other methods, this did not mean that the measures adopted were not strictly necessary. Moreover, that the detainees could leave the United Kingdom if they wished to do so demonstrated that the measures were properly tailored to the state of emergency.

The SIAC held, however, that the relevant provisions of Pt IV of the 2001 Act unjustifiably discriminated against foreign nationals, in breach of Art. 14 of the ECHR. For this reason, it quashed the Derogation Order of 11 November 2001 and issued a declaration of incompatibility in respect of s. 23 of the 2001 Act, under s. 4 of the HRA. It adjourned the applicants' individual appeals against certification, pending the outcome of any appeals that there may have been against its decision on the legality of the derogation and the legislative provisions.

The government successfully appealed against this decision to the Court of Appeal, which delivered its judgment on 25 October 2002.[30] The Court of Appeal held that the SIAC had been entitled to find that there was a public emergency threatening the life of the nation. Unlike the SIAC, however, it held that the approach adopted by the Secretary of State could be objectively justified. There was a rational connection between the detention of non-nationals, who could not be deported because of fears for their safety, and the purpose that the Secretary of State wished to achieve, which was to remove non-nationals who posed a threat to national security. In its view, there was no discrimination contrary to Art. 14 of the ECHR, because British suspect terrorists were in a different situation from that of foreign suspects who could not be deported because of Art. 3: foreign nationals have no right to remain in the country, but only a right, for the time being, not to be removed for their own safety. The Court of Appeal noted that, in international law, there are situations in which states can distinguish between nationals and non-nationals, especially in times of emergency.

We may note in passing that in May 2003, after the Court of Appeal's decision, the SIAC started to hear the individual challenges to certification under s. 21, but we shall return to the SIAC's decisions on these later.

22.2.4 *A V SECRETARY OF STATE FOR THE HOME DEPARTMENT* (THE *BELMARSH* CASE) IN THE HOUSE OF LORDS

The detainees appealed to the House of Lords.[31] Here, they once again argued that their detention was inconsistent with the obligations of the United Kingdom under the ECHR, that the Derogation Order was unlawful, and that the statutory provisions under which they were detained were incompatible

[30] *A and ors v Secretary of State for the Home Department* [2002] EWCA Civ 1502.

[31] Two of the appellants had, by the time the appeal was heard, exercised their right to leave the country (one went to Morocco and the other to France); one had been transferred to Broadmoor Hospital on grounds of mental illness; another had been released on bail.

with the ECHR. In what is probably the most significant human rights case yet decided by the UK courts, the House of Lords quashed the 2001 Derogation Order and made a declaration that s. 23 of the 2001 Act was incompatible with Arts 5 and 14 of the ECHR. The judgments of the nine judges[32] ran to 240 paragraphs and should be carefully read.

Here, we summarize the main findings, as follows.

1. *In relation to the legality of the Derogation Order, was there a public emergency that threatened the life of the nation?*[33]

While the United Kingdom had been the only party to the ECHR to derogate from Art. 5 in the wake of the attacks of 11 September 2001, the House of Lords—by a majority of eight to one—agreed with the SIAC that there was power to derogate from Art. 5. Lords Bingham and Scott reached this view with hesitation, and Lord Hoffmann dissented. In reaching their decision, the majority took account of an early decision of the ECtHR that had accepted that Ireland could derogate from the Convention even though it was not shown that a widespread loss of life or an attack on the territorial integrity of the state was involved.[34] The majority also attached great weight to the judgement of the Home Secretary and Parliament on whether there was a threat to the life of the nation.

A v Secretary of State for the Home Department
[2004] UKHL 56

Lord Bingham

29. [. . .] I would accept that great weight should be given to the judgment of the Home Secretary, his colleagues and Parliament on this question, because they were called on to exercise a pre-eminently political judgment. [. . .] I do not accept the full breadth of the Attorney General's argument on what is generally called the deference owed by the courts to the political authorities. It is perhaps preferable to approach this question as one of demarcation of functions or what Liberty in its written case called 'relative institutional competence'. The more purely political (in a broad or narrow sense) a question is, the more appropriate it will be for political resolution and the less likely it is to be an appropriate matter for judicial decision. The smaller, therefore, will be the potential role of the court. It is the function of political and not judicial bodies to resolve political questions. Conversely, the greater the legal content of any issue, the greater the potential role of the court, because under our constitution and subject to the sovereign power of Parliament it is the function of the courts and not of political bodies to resolve legal questions. The present question [whether a derogation order was necessary] seems to me to be very much at the political end of the spectrum [. . .]

Lord Hoffmann dissented on this point and held that the Derogation Order was unlawful because there was no threat to the life of the nation. It is worth setting out the following extract from his judgment, especially bearing in mind the way in which Lord Hoffmann had approached the issue of deference in the past.

[32] Lords Bingham of Cornhill, Nicholls of Birkenhead, Hoffmann, Hope of Craighead, Scott of Foscote, Rodger of Earlsferry, Walker of Gestingthorpe, Carswell, and Baroness Hale of Richmond.

[33] See also *Independent Human Rights Act Review*, December 2021, CP 586, ch. 6.

[34] *Lawless v Ireland (No. 3)* (1961) 1 EHRR 15.

A v Secretary of State for the Home Department
[2004] UKHL 56

Lord Hoffmann

93. The Home Secretary has adduced evidence, both open and secret, to show the existence of a threat of serious terrorist outrages. [. . . D]espite the widespread scepticism which has attached to intelligence assessments since the fiasco over Iraqi weapons of mass destruction, I am willing to accept that credible evidence of such plots exist. The events of 11 September 2001 in New York and Washington and 11 March 2003 in Madrid make it entirely likely that the threat of similar atrocities in the United Kingdom is a real one.

94. But the question is whether such a threat is a threat to the life of the nation. [. . .] Of course the government has a duty to protect the lives and property of its citizens. But that is a duty which it owes all the time and which it must discharge without destroying our constitutional freedoms. There may be some nations too fragile or fissiparous to withstand a serious act of violence. But that is not the case in the United Kingdom. [. . .]

95. This is a nation which has been tested in adversity, which has survived physical destruction and catastrophic loss of life. I do not underestimate the ability of fanatical groups of terrorists to kill and destroy, but they do not threaten the life of the nation. Whether we would survive Hitler hung in the balance, but there is no doubt that we shall survive Al-Qaeda. [. . .]

96. [. . .] The real threat to the life of the nation, in the sense of a people living in accordance with its traditional laws and political values, comes not from terrorism but from laws such as these. That is the true measure of what terrorism may achieve. It is for Parliament to decide whether to give the terrorists such a victory.

2. *The Derogation Order was lawful, but were the provisions of the 2001 Act relating to the powers of detention proportionate? Were they 'strictly required by the exigencies of the situation'?*

The House considered that proportionality was a question of law and therefore a matter for the courts. The powers of detention related only to foreign nationals who could not be deported. But the majority stressed that foreign nationals were not the only threat. Moreover, even when they were a threat, the 2001 Act left them free to leave the United Kingdom and carry on their activities from abroad. In other words, the legislative provisions infringed Art. 5 and the infringements were not rationally directed at the reasons for the emergency—that is, the prevention of terrorism. The House of Lords—by a majority of seven to one (Lord Walker of Gestingthorpe dissented and Lord Hoffmann expressed no view on this issue)—held that the proportionality requirement had not been met, essentially because s. 23 was not specifically focused on the actual threat posed. As Lady Justice Mary Arden, as she then was, has put it, '*in a word, s. 23 was irrational*'.[35]

A v Secretary of State for the Home Department
[2004] UKHL 56

Lord Bingham

37. [. . . T]he Attorney General [. . .] submitted that as it was for Parliament and the executive to assess the threat facing the nation, so it was for those bodies and not the courts to judge the response necessary

[35] M. Arden, 'Human rights in an age of terrorism' (2005) 121 Law Quarterly Review 604, 608. Mary Arden became a Justice in the UK Supreme Court. She retired in January 2022.

to protect the security of the public. These were matters of a political character calling for an exercise of political and not judicial judgment. Just as the European Court allowed a generous margin of appreciation to member states, recognising that they were better placed to understand and address local problems, so should national courts recognise, for the same reason, that matters of the kind in issue here fall within the discretionary area of judgment properly belonging to the democratic organs of the state. It was not for the courts to usurp authority properly belonging elsewhere. The Attorney General drew attention to the dangers identified by Richard Ekins in '*Judicial Supremacy and the Rule of Law*' (2003) 119 LQR 127. This is an important submission, properly made, and it calls for careful consideration.

[Lord Bingham reviewed the domestic and international authorities, and continued as follows.]

42. [. . .] I do not accept the full breadth of the Attorney General's submissions. I do not in particular accept the distinction which he drew between democratic institutions and the courts. It is of course true that the judges in this country are not elected and are not answerable to Parliament. It is also of course true [. . .] that Parliament, the executive and the courts have different functions. But the function of independent judges charged to interpret and apply the law is universally recognised as a cardinal feature of the modern democratic state, a cornerstone of the rule of law itself. The Attorney General is fully entitled to insist on the proper limits of judicial authority, but he is wrong to stigmatise judicial decision-making as in some way undemocratic. It is particularly inappropriate in a case such as the present in which Parliament has expressly legislated in s 6 of the 1998 Act to render unlawful any act of a public authority, including a court, incompatible with a Convention right, has required courts (in s 2) to take account of relevant Strasbourg jurisprudence, has (in s 3) required courts, so far as possible, to give effect to Convention rights and has conferred a right of appeal on derogation issues. The effect is not, of course, to override the sovereign legislative authority of the Queen in Parliament, since if primary legislation is declared to be incompatible the validity of the legislation is unaffected (s 4(6)) and the remedy lies with the appropriate minister (s 10), who is answerable to Parliament. The 1998 Act gives the courts a very specific, wholly democratic, mandate. [. . .]

43. The Appellants' proportionality challenge to the Order and s 23 is, in my opinion, sound, for all the reasons they gave and also for those given by the European Commissioner for Human Rights and the Newton Committee. The Attorney General could give no persuasive answer. [. . . T]he choice of an immigration measure to address a security problem had the inevitable result of failing adequately to address that problem (by allowing non-UK suspected terrorists to leave the country with impunity and leaving British suspected terrorists at large) while imposing the severe penalty of indefinite detention on persons who, even if reasonably suspected of having links with Al-Qaeda, may harbour no hostile intentions towards the United Kingdom. The conclusion that the Order and s 23 are, in Convention terms, disproportionate is in my opinion irresistible.

Lord Nicholls of Birkenhead

78. All courts are very much aware of the heavy burden, resting on the elected government and not the judiciary, to protect the security of this country and all who live here. All courts are acutely conscious that the government alone is able to evaluate and decide what counter-terrorism steps are needed and what steps will suffice. Courts are not equipped to make such decisions, nor are they charged with that responsibility.

79. But Parliament has charged the courts with a particular responsibility. It is a responsibility as much applicable to the 2001 Act and the Human Rights Act 1998 (Designated Derogation) Order 2001 as it is to all other legislation and ministers' decisions. The duty of the courts is to check that legislation and ministerial decisions do not overlook the human rights of persons adversely affected. [. . .]

80. In the present case I see no escape from the conclusion that Parliament must be regarded as having attached insufficient weight to the human rights of non-nationals. The subject matter

of the legislation is the needs of national security. This subject matter dictates that, in the ordinary course, substantial latitude should be accorded to the legislature. But the human right in question, the right to individual liberty, is one of the most fundamental of human rights. Indefinite detention without trial wholly negates that right for an indefinite period. With one exception all the individuals currently detained have been imprisoned now for three years and there is no prospect of imminent release. It is true that those detained may at any time walk away from their place of detention if they leave this country. Their prison, it is said, has only three walls. But this freedom is more theoretical than real. This is demonstrated by the continuing presence in Belmarsh of most of those detained. They prefer to stay in prison rather than face the prospect of ill treatment in any country willing to admit them.

3. *The third main issue was whether the detention powers in s. 23 violated Art. 14 of the ECHR by discriminating unjustifiably between British and foreign nationals.*

Disagreeing with the Court of Appeal, the House of Lords held that the appropriate comparators were UK nationals who were suspected terrorists, and not, as the government argued, non-UK nationals who were suspected terrorists, but who could be deported to third countries (that is, who did not fall within the *Chahal* class of case). For this reason, s. 23 was incompatible with Art. 14, read in conjunction with Art. 5. Again, Lord Walker of Gestingthorpe dissented and Lord Hoffmann expressed no view on this point, not wanting to suggest that the government could remedy the situation by extending the powers to UK citizens.

QUESTIONS

1. What do you understand by the term 'relative institutional competence' in the context of judicial review of executive and parliamentary decision-making?
2. According to Lord Hoffmann, who in the UK constitution should decide whether there is a threat to the life of the nation? Does this view appear to be compatible with his earlier statements on deference?
3. '*The* Belmarsh *decision illustrates the contentious nature of democracy in the UK constitution.*' Discuss.

22.2.5 THE IMPACT OF THE DECISION

Lady Arden considered the impact of the decision in an article in the Law Quarterly Review in which she said the following.

M. Arden, 'Human rights in an age of terrorism' (2005) 121 *Law Quarterly Review* 604, 605

The result in this case was remarkable. [. . .] The *A* case may well be the first time that a court of the United Kingdom has dealt such a body blow to legislation conferring powers on the executive to meet a threat to national security.

As Lady Arden has said, there was a 'startling difference' between the approach taken in the *Belmarsh* case[36] and that taken in *Liversidge v Anderson*.[37] In *Liversidge*, the majority had held that the balancing of the interests of national security against those of the individual was the sole prerogative of the Home Secretary. Here, the House held that the courts have a duty to review the way in which this balance is struck in order to ensure that both the Home Secretary and Parliament act in conformity with human rights requirements. The House took the view that there is no jurisdictional barrier to the review of national security decisions and that national security is not a 'no-go' area for the courts or the law.

M. Arden, 'Human rights in an age of terrorism' (2005) 121 *Law Quarterly Review* 604, 614 (footnotes omitted)

> [. . . T]he decision in the *A* case is a landmark decision that will be used as a point of reference by courts all over the world for decades to come, even when the age of terrorism has passed. It is a powerful statement by the highest court in the land of what it means to live in a society where the executive is subject to the rule of law. Even the Government, and even in times when there is a threat to national security, must act strictly in accordance with the law.

She went on to quote the following statement of President Barak in a decision of the Israeli Supreme Court.[38]

Public Committee Against Torture v Israel (the Ticking Time Bomb case)
26 May 1999, HC 5100/94(4)PD 817, 845

> **President Barak, President of the Israeli Supreme Court**
>
> We conclude this judgment by revisiting the harsh reality in which Israel finds itself [. . .] We are aware that this decision does not make it easier to deal with that reality. This is the fate of democracy, as not all means are acceptable to it, and not all methods employed by its enemies are always open before it. Sometimes, democracy must fight with one hand tied behind its back. Nonetheless, it has the upper hand. Preserving the rule of law and recognition of individual liberties constitute an important component of its understanding of security. At the end of the day, they strengthen its spirit and this strength allows it to overcome its difficulties.

From another perspective, the decision may provide further evidence of the judiciary using human rights arguments to frustrate government's attempts to protect the public from terrorism and of the way in which the HRA operates as a charter for terrorists and other undesirables.[39]

Criticisms of this sort are misplaced. Far from saying that government could not take steps to protect the public, the message given by the judges was that the route chosen by the government was irrational and, as Keir Starmer KC[40] explains, likely to be ineffective.

[36] Much has been written on the impact of this case, see e.g., T. Poole, 'Rights and opinion: or, the progress of sentiments', (2016) 10(2) Law & Ethics of Human Rights 453–78; M. Elliott in a three-part blog piece that can be accessed at https://publiclawforeveryone.com/?s=Belmarsh.

[37] [1942] AC 206, see Chapter 17. [38] Cited at p. 623.

[39] See e.g. Chapter 15, Section 15.2.2.2 (Home Secretary's criticism of the courts).

[40] Later the Director of Public Prosecutions. He was knighted in 2014 and is currently the Prime Minister.

K. Starmer, 'Setting the record straight: Human rights in an era of international terrorism' (2007) 2 *European Human Rights Law Review* 123, 124

> [. . . T]he Law Lords found that the 2001 Act did not rationally address the threat posed by Al-Qa'ida terrorists and their supporters because it did not address the threat presented by UK nationals. As the events of July 7, 2005 in London underlined, that was timely advice for which the Government ought to have been grateful. Secondly, the Law Lords were concerned that the 2001 Act, grounded as it was in immigration law rather than criminal law, permitted suspected terrorists to leave the United Kingdom on a voluntary basis and carry on their activities abroad. In one case the individual in question simply got the Eurostar to France. Thirdly, the Law Lords were concerned that the 2001 Act permitted the detention of individuals who sympathised with terrorist activity abroad but posed no threat to the United Kingdom. Against that background it can hardly be suggested that their Lordships were mischievously dismantling the Government's anti-terrorism strategy. They were simply pointing out that the Government's approach was discriminatory, irrational and, worst of all, ineffective.

22.2.5.1 Impact on the individuals concerned

Despite the constitutional importance of the principles enunciated by the House of Lords, the declaration of incompatibility did not affect '*the validity, continuing operation or enforcement*' of s. 23, nor did it bind the Home Secretary.[41] Immediately after the announcement of the decision, Mr Charles Clarke, then Home Secretary, told the House of Commons: '*My primary role as Home Secretary is to protect national security and to ensure the safety and security of this country. I will not be revoking the certificates or releasing the detainees, whom I have reason to believe are a significant threat to our security.*' The detainees would remain in prison, he said, until Parliament decided '*whether and how we should amend the law*'. He said that he would study the judgment to see whether it was possible to modify the legislation '*to address the concerns raised by the House of Lords*'.[42]

On 21 January 2005, those who were still detained started proceedings in the ECtHR. These led to the decision *A and ors v UK* which was given by the Grand Chamber of that Court four years later, on 19 February 2009.[43] In its judgment, the Grand Chamber agreed with the House of Lords in the *Belmarsh* case on the principal issues with which it had dealt. It also addressed the compatibility of the process used by the SIAC with the obligation to provide a fair hearing in Arts 6 and 5(4). We will consider this aspect of the decision later in the chapter.

22.2.5.2 The legislative response to the *Belmarsh* decision

On the 26 January 2005, Mr Charles Clarke made a statement to the House of Commons setting out proposals to repeal Pt 4 of the 2001 Act and to establish a new scheme. This would adopt a twin-track approach. Foreign nationals who were suspected of being involved in terrorist activities would be deported once assurances were obtained from the countries to which they would be sent that they would not be treated in a manner that contravened Art. 3. Those who could not be deported would be subject to a new system of control orders. The proposed control orders could be made irrespective of the person's nationality and would therefore also apply to British nationals suspected of terrorist activity.

[41] HRA, s. 4(6).

[42] Oral statement by Charles Clarke, Home Secretary, to the House of Commons, 26 January 2005. Two of the detainees elected to leave the United Kingdom and one was released on bail conditions that were equivalent to control order conditions.

[43] App. No. 3455/05.

The control orders would impose a range of controls restricting movement, including preventing people from leaving their residence (subjecting them to a curfew), preventing association between named individuals, tagging, and restricting access to telecommunications and the internet.[44]

22.2.6 CONTROL ORDERS

The Prevention of Terrorism Act 2005 (PTA) came into force on 11 March 2005.[45] This enabled the Secretary of State to make derogating and non-derogating control orders. The former would breach Art. 5 of the ECHR and would be imposed only if a derogation from that Article was in place. Such orders were intended to be used only for individuals considered to pose a high risk to public safety associated with the public emergency that justified the derogation. They would be made by a court on application by the Secretary of State and they would be reviewed by the court after six months. No derogating control orders were made.

Non-derogating control orders were intended to be compatible with Art. 5 of the ECHR and were made by the Secretary of State when he had '*reasonable grounds for suspecting*' that someone is or has been '*involved in terrorism-related activity*'[46] and he considered it '*necessary, for purposes connected with protecting members of the public from the risk of terrorism, to make a control order*'.

The making of control orders was supervised by the SIAC, which had the task of determining whether these requirements were satisfied.[47] As with its other national security-related tasks, including challenges to certifications under (the repealed) Pt IV of ATSCA, the SIAC is permitted by its rules of procedures to consider material in closed sessions and to use special advocates who are unable to reveal or discuss the contents of any closed material with the person concerned. The legislation was reviewed annually and the Joint Committee on Human Rights reported on the reviews.[48]

The appellants in the *Belmarsh* case who remained detained were released on 11 March 2005 and immediately made subject to non-derogating control orders. In response to this, Sangeeta Shah noted as follows.

S. Shah, 'The UK's anti-terror legislation and the House of Lords: The first skirmish' (2005) 5 *Human Rights Law Review* 403, 419

> Between 2001 and 2004, 17 individuals were certified as being a risk to national security and suspected international terrorists and as such warranted indefinite detention in prison. Yet by 2005 these individuals could be released subject to certain restrictions. Ha[d] the risk they pose diminished? Or [was] this further vindication that the measures under Part 4, ATCSA were [. . .] disproportionate?

On 11 August 2005, following negotiations, the UK government secured assurances from the Algerian and Jordanian governments that deportees would not be ill-treated if they were returned to these countries. With these assurances secured, the government served notices of intention to deport on seven people who had been taken into immigration custody pending removal to Algeria and Jordan. On 9 April 2008, the Court of Appeal[49] ruled that Omar Othman (known as 'Abu Qatada') could not

[44] HC Deb, 26 January 2005, vol. 430, col. 307.

[45] And the derogation order was withdrawn. [46] Section 2(1). [47] Section 3(10).

[48] See, e.g., *Counter-terrorism Policy and Human Rights (Fourteenth Report): Annual Renewal of Control Orders Legislation 2009*, Fifth Report, Session 2008–09.

[49] [2007] EWCA Civ 808, [2008] EWCA Civ 290.

be lawfully extradited to Jordan, because it was likely that, in Jordan, evidence that had been obtained by torture could be used against him, in flagrant violation of his right to a fair trial. Perhaps somewhat surprisingly, given the record of the House of Lords at the time, this decision was overturned by the House in February 2009.[50] Abu Qatada took his case to the ECtHR where he was successful.[51]

22.2.7 THE LEGALITY OF CONTROL ORDERS

The control order regime led to a large number of legal challenges, including several top-court decisions. Two main lines of argument were made. One focused on whether the non-derogating control orders infringed the Art. 5(1) right to liberty, even though they purported to be compatible with this right. It would, of course, be unlawful under s. 6(1) of the HRA for the Secretary of State to make control orders that were incompatible with Art. 5 of the ECHR. It would, on normal judicial review grounds, also be beyond the powers conferred by the PTA.

22.2.8 CONTROL ORDERS AND THE RIGHT TO LIBERTY

In *Secretary of State for the Home Department v JJ*,[52] the House of Lords agreed with the Court of Appeal[53] that a non-derogating control order that prevented a person from leaving a one-bedroom flat for 18 hours in every 24 (an 18-hour curfew) and imposed very restricted controls that effectively meant that the person's life was wholly regulated by the Home Office was contrary to Art. 5. After reviewing the jurisprudence of the ECtHR and UK law, Lord Bingham reached the conclusion that is set out in the following extract.

Note that in *Guzzardi v Italy*[54] to which Lord Bingham refers, the ECtHR held there to be a deprivation of liberty when a person was forced to stay on a small island, in dilapidated accommodation, without social intercourse. He was under almost constant supervision, had a nine-hour overnight curfew, and was obliged to report to the authorities twice a day and to inform them of any person whom he wished to telephone; he also had to obtain consent to visit Sardinia on the mainland.

Secretary of State for the Home Department v JJ
[2007] UKHL 45

Lord Bingham

24. [. . .] The effect of the 18-hour curfew, coupled with the effective exclusion of social visitors, meant that the controlled persons were in practice in solitary confinement for this lengthy period every day for an indefinite duration, with very little opportunity for contact with the outside world, with means

[50] *RB (Algeria) (FC) and anor (Appellants) v Secretary of State for the Home Department; OO (Jordan) (Original Respondent and Cross-appellant) v Secretary of State for the Home Department (Original Appellant and Cross-respondent)* [2009] UKHL 10. Julia Hall, for Human Rights Watch, said that '*The Law Lords have given the government a green light to send people back to places where they risk torture and ill-treatment*' (see www.hrw.org).

[51] *Othman v United Kingdom*, App. No. 8139/09 (2012) 55 EHRR 1, 32 BHRC 62. The Court held that since there remained a real risk that evidence obtained by torture would be used at a trial in Jordan, deportation would be contrary to the ECHR. That decision was applied by the SIAC (SC/15/2005) and the government's appeal against this decision was unsuccessful: [2013] EWCA Civ 277. Abu Qatada later agreed to be deported to stand trial in Jordan after a treaty between the UK and Jordan provided that evidence obtained by torture would not be used against him. At a trial in Jordan he was found not guilty of terrorism offences.

[52] [2007] UKHL 45; cf. *Secretary of State for the Home Department v E* [2007] UKHL 47, in which the House of Lords said that a control order imposing a curfew of 12 hours, with other less onerous restrictions, was held to be lawful.

[53] [2006] EWCA Civ 1141.

[54] (1980) 3 EHRR 533.

> insufficient to permit provision of significant facilities for self-entertainment and with knowledge that their flats were liable to be entered and searched at any time. [. . .] Their lives were wholly regulated by the Home Office, as a prisoner's would be, although breaches were much more severely punishable. The judge's analogy with detention in an open prison was apt, save that the controlled persons did not enjoy the association with others and the access to entertainment facilities which a prisoner in an open prison would expect to enjoy.

Lords Hoffmann and Carswell dissented. Lord Hoffmann said that the right to liberty was an unqualified right under the ECHR and that it was therefore essential not to give liberty an over-expansive interpretation. Article 5, he said, should apply only to literal physical restraint and not to restrictions of the type imposed.[55]

22.2.9 CONTROL ORDERS AND PROCEDURAL FAIRNESS

A second line of argument focused on the legality of the procedures adopted when the SIAC reviewed decisions of the Secretary of State. Two particular issues were raised: the first was whether the SIAC could use information that may have been obtained as a consequence of torture; the second concerned the use of secret material in closed hearings.[56]

22.2.9.1 The use of torture evidence

The House of Lords has unanimously decided that evidence obtained by torture cannot be used by the SIAC. In reaching this decision, the House overturned the Court of Appeal—but while the seven judges were agreed that torture evidence cannot be used, they disagreed about the approach to be taken when it is not certain that evidence has been obtained by torture. The majority (Lords Hope of Craighead, Rodger of Earlsferry, Carswell, and Brown of Eaton-under-Heywood) held that if the SIAC is in doubt as to whether the evidence was obtained by torture, then it should admit it, but bear its doubt in mind when evaluating the evidence. The minority (Lords Bingham, Nicholls, and Hoffmann) disagreed with this. They said that in cases in which there was doubt about the use of

[55] Cf *R (on the application of Gillan) v Commissioner of Police of the Metropolis* [2006] UKHL 12, in which the House of Lords held that the exercise of stop and search powers did not involve a deprivation of liberty. This case was taken to the ECtHR which held that the exercise of stop and search powers under the anti-terrorism legislation was unlawful: *Gillan and Quinton v United Kingdom*, App. No. 4158/05, 12 January 2010. See also *Austin and another v Commissioner of Police of the Metropolis* [2009] 1 AC 564 and *Austin v United Kingdom* (2012) 55 EHRR 14 where the House of Lords and the ECtHR held that 'kettling' (containment in a police cordon) of protestors for several hours was not a deprivation of liberty. Cf. *P v Cheshire West and Chester Council; P and Q v Surrey County Council* [2014] UKSC 19; where the UKSC held that disabled people living in residential homes were deprived of their liberty because they were under continuous supervision and control and not free to leave. See further S. Wilson Stark, 'Deprivations of Liberty: Beyond the Paradigm' [2019] Public Law 380.

[56] Note also *Ibrahim and others v UK* (Grand Chamber, 13 September 2016). Four individuals involved in attempting and supporting a terrorist conspiracy in London in 2005 complained that the restriction of their right to prompt legal advice whilst they were being questioned by police and the use of the evidence taken from those sessions at their trial was a breach of Art 6. The ECtHR rejected their claim. Their case was then heard by the Grand Chamber which found that the government had demonstrated, in the case of three applicants, that the proceedings as a whole were fair given that there was an urgent need to avert serious adverse consequences for the life and physical integrity of the public. In the case of the fourth applicant, the Grand Chamber found a violation of Art 6 because the Government had not shown compelling reasons for their actions. For details on the implications of this decision, see the Ministry of Justice, *Report on Responding to Human Rights Judgments*, 2016–2017, (December 2017 Cm 9535), pp. 19–20.

torture, the SIAC should refuse to admit the evidence. Given the fundamental nature of the obligation not to torture, the view of the minority must be correct in principle.

A, D and C v Secretary of State for the Home Department
[2005] UKHL 71

Lord Bingham

51. The Secretary of State is right to submit that SIAC is a body designed to enable it to receive and assess a wide range of material, including material which would not be disclosed to a body lacking its special characteristics. And it would of course be within the power of a sovereign Parliament (in breach of international law) to confer power on SIAC to receive third party torture evidence. But the English common law has regarded torture and its fruits with abhorrence for over 500 years, and that abhorrence is now shared by over 140 countries which have acceded to the Torture Convention. I am startled, even a little dismayed, at the suggestion (and the acceptance by the Court of Appeal majority) that this deeply rooted tradition and an international obligation solemnly and explicitly undertaken can be overridden by a statute and a procedural rule which make no mention of torture at all. [. . .] It trivialises the issue before the House to treat it as an argument about the law of evidence. The issue is one of constitutional principle, whether evidence obtained by torturing another human being may lawfully be admitted against a party to proceedings in a British court, irrespective of where, or by whom, or on whose authority the torture was inflicted. To that question I would give a very clear negative answer.

QUESTION

Why do you think the Law Lords differed in relation to situations in which it is uncertain whether evidence has been obtained by torture? Which approach do you think to be:

(a) the most principled?

(b) the most practical?

22.2.9.2 Closed hearings and secret evidence

AF was born in the United Kingdom in 1980 to an English mother who was divorced from his Libyan father. He had both UK and Libyan nationality. Although brought up in Libya, he had lived in England since 2004. A control order confining him to his flat for 18 hours a day was first imposed on him on 24 May 2006. That order was revoked following the Court of Appeal's decision in *JJ*. A new order was imposed on 11 September 2006. This reduced the curfew period from 18 hours to 14 hours.

AF initially argued that this control order was an unlawful infringement of his liberty, but this ultimately failed in the House of Lords.[57] His second challenge was directed against the procedure adopted by the SIAC and, in particular, the reliance on closed material that neither he, nor his lawyers, were able to see. He argued that this was fundamentally unfair and contrary to his right to a fair hearing, as required by Arts 6 and 5(4) of the ECHR.

This aspect of the case reached the House of Lords on two occasions. On the first, Lord Bingham decided that the procedure was unfair; Lord Hoffmann disagreed with him. The three other judges delivered judgments that fell between those of Lord Bingham and Lord Hoffmann. They expressed

[57] *Secretary of State for the Home Department v AF and MB* [2007] UKHL 45.

the view that, in some cases, it would be possible for the controlee, with the assistance of the special advocate, to have a fair trial notwithstanding the admission of closed material and that, in others, it would not. The fair trial issue was fact-specific and the trial judge was best placed to resolve it.

As a result, the case was remitted back to Stanley Burnton J, who held that, in the circumstances, the procedure was unfair. The Secretary of State appealed to the Court of Appeal which, by a majority, allowed the appeal and held that there was no absolute requirement to disclose the essence of the case against AF. Lord Justice Sedley dissented, saying that a hearing could not be fair unless the case against AF were disclosed to him so that he could answer it. AF appealed once again to the House of Lords.

22.2.9.3 Re-enter *Belmarsh*

On 19 February 2009, shortly before the House of Lords was to hear AF's appeal, the Grand Chamber of the ECtHR handed down its judgment in *A and ors v UK*,[58] the case that had been taken to Strasbourg four years earlier by those who remained detained after the decision of the House of Lords in the 2004 *Belmarsh* case.

As we have mentioned, the Grand Chamber reiterated the main conclusions reached by the House of Lords—but the Court also made important pronouncements on the fairness of the closed procedure used by the SIAC when it dealt with challenges to certifications made under Pt IV of the ATCSA. Although Pt IV has been repealed, the judgment is important because it is relevant to other aspects of the SIAC's work. The judgment also has a wider significance in explaining the requirements of fairness. The core conclusions on this aspect of the Grand Chamber's unanimous decision are set out in the following extract.

A and ors v UK

Grand Chamber of the ECtHR, App. No. 3455/05, 19 February 2009

216. The Court takes as its starting point that, as the national courts found and it has accepted, during the period of the applicants' detention the activities and aims of the al'Qaeda network had given rise to a 'public emergency threatening the life of the nation'. [. . .]

217. Balanced against these important public interests, however, was the applicants' right under Article 5 (4) to procedural fairness. [. . . I]n the circumstances of the present case, and in view of the dramatic impact of the lengthy—and what appeared at that time to be indefinite—deprivation of liberty on the applicants' fundamental rights, Article 5(4) must import substantially the same fair trial guarantees as Article 6(1) in its criminal aspect [. . .]

218. Against this background, it was essential that as much information about the allegations and evidence against each applicant was disclosed as was possible without compromising national security or the safety of others [. . .].

219. The Court considers that SIAC, which was a fully independent court [. . .] and which could examine all the relevant evidence, both closed and open, was best placed to ensure that no material was unnecessarily withheld from the detainee. In this connection, the special advocate could provide an important, additional safeguard through questioning the State's witnesses on the need for secrecy and through making submissions to the judge regarding the case for additional disclosure. On the material before it, the Court has no basis to find that excessive and unjustified secrecy was employed in respect of any of the applicants' appeals or that there were not compelling reasons for the lack of disclosure in each case.

The House of Lords immediately applied this judgment in *Secretary of State v AF and anor.*

[58] App. No. 3455/05.

Secretary of State for the Home Department v AF and anor
[2009] UKHL 28

Lord Phillips

59. [The decision of the Grand Chamber] establishes that the controlee must be given sufficient information about the allegations against him to enable him to give effective instructions in relation to those allegations. Provided that this requirement is satisfied there can be a fair trial notwithstanding that the controlee is not provided with the detail or the sources of the evidence forming the basis of the allegations. Where, however, the open material consists purely of general assertions and the case against the controlee is based solely or to a decisive degree on closed materials the requirements of a fair trial will not be satisfied, however cogent the case based on the closed materials may be.

[...]

62. [...] What is in issue in control order cases is whether there are reasonable grounds for suspecting involvement on the part of the controlee in terrorism-related activity. This is a low threshold to cross and there are, so it seems to me, bound to be cases where the closed evidence is so cogent that the judge can rightly form the conclusion that there is no possibility that the controlee would be able, if this evidence were disclosed to him, to dispel the reasonable suspicion. [...]

63. There are, however, strong policy considerations that support a rule that a trial procedure can never be considered fair if a party to it is kept in ignorance of the case against him. The first is that there will be many cases where it is impossible for the court to be confident that disclosure will make no difference. [...] Next [is that... r]esentment will understandably be felt, not merely by the controlee but by his family and friends, if sanctions are imposed on him on grounds that lead to his being suspected of involvement in terrorism without any proper explanation of what those grounds are. Indeed, if the wider public are to have confidence in the justice system, they need to be able to see that justice is done rather than being asked to take it on trust.

[Once again, Lord Hoffmann dissented.]

Lord Hoffmann

70. [...] I agree that the judgment of the European Court of Human Rights ('ECtHR') [...] requires these appeals to be allowed. I do so with very considerable regret, because I think that the decision of the ECtHR was wrong and that it may well destroy the system of control orders which is a significant part of this country's defences against terrorism. Nevertheless, I think that your Lordships have no choice but to submit. [He goes on to explain his view that the UK is bound to accept decisions of the ECtHR on the interpretation of the ECHR, see Section 2(b) of this chapter.]

QUESTIONS

1. Consider the two following perspectives.

   '[... T]here are [...] bound to be cases where the closed evidence is so cogent that the judge can rightly form the conclusion that there is no possibility that the controlee would be able, if this evidence were disclosed to him, to dispel the reasonable suspicion.' '[...] There are, however, strong policy considerations that support a rule that a trial procedure can never be considered fair if a party to it is kept in ignorance of the case against him' (Lord Phillips).

'A system of justice which allowed a thousand guilty men to go free for fear of convicting one innocent man might not adequately protect the public. Likewise, [. . .] that in theory there is always some chance that the Applicant might have been able to contradict closed evidence is not [. . .] a sufficient reason for saying [. . .] that control orders can never be made against dangerous people if the case against them is based "to a decisive degree" upon material which cannot in the public interest be disclosed' (Lord Hoffmann).

(a) Which of these two views is to be preferred?

(b) Given the importance of policy in these judgments, should fairness ultimately be determined by judges or by those who are politically accountable?

2. What do these judgments tell us about the nature of the duty upon UK judges 'to take account' (s. 2(1) HRA) of decisions of the ECtHR?

22.2.9.4 The aftermath of the decision

As Lord Hoffmann had predicted, following the decision the Home Secretary decided to free AF after three years 'under virtual house arrest' rather than disclose the secret intelligence case against him. As we shall see the decision also contributed to wider changes in the control order regime.

Note that in the situations we have been considering the Closed Material Procedures (CMP) were used in proceedings that affected liberty. Where such procedures are used in situations that do not affect liberty or other fundamental rights the UK Supreme Court has held both that legislation permitting the use of CMP is compatible with Art. 6 and that no obligation exists to provide the person concerned with the 'gist' of the case against them.[59]

Finally, in this context we may note that the UK Supreme Court has held that the courts do not have the jurisdiction to permit the use of CMP to be extended to ordinary civil cases for damages. The core reason is contained in Lord Dyson's leading judgment in *Al Rawi and ors v The Security Services.*

Al Rawi and ors v The Security Services
[2011] UKSC 34

Lord Dyson

47. Closed material procedures and the use of special advocates continue to be controversial. In my view, it is not for the courts to extend such a controversial procedure beyond the boundaries which Parliament has chosen to draw for its use thus far. It is controversial precisely because it involves an invasion of the fundamental common law principles [of openness and natural justice] [. . .]

48. The common law principles to which I have referred are extremely important and should not be eroded unless there is a compelling case for doing so. If this is to be done at all, it is better done by Parliament after full consultation and proper consideration of the sensitive issues involved. [. . .]

[59] *Tariq v Home Office* [2011] UKSC 35. Orders effectively preventing a bank from operating may be considered to affect interests equivalent to infringements upon fundamental rights: *Bank Mellat v Her Majesty's Treasury (No. 1)* [2013] UKSC 38. Here, by a majority, it was held that a CMP could be used in the Supreme Court on appeal from decisions which had been taken following CMP proceedings. For an analysis of the decision, see H.J. Cooper, 'Crossing the Rubicon' [2014] Public Law 171. More generally see J. Jackson, 'Justice, security and the right to a fair trial: Is the use of secret evidence ever fair?' [2013] Public Law 720.

Following that decision, the government issued a Green Paper, *Justice and Security*,[60] proposing legislation to permit the use of CMP in ordinary civil proceedings and, following considerable opposition, s. 6 of the Justice and Security Act 2013 now permits this.

22.2.10 THE IMPACT OF THE CONTROL ORDER LITIGATION

Different views exist on the implications of the litigation that we have described. Many commentators and human rights groups saw the legal challenges as the inevitable consequence of legislation that was hastily enacted with insufficient regard to the human rights consequences. Many will agree with Lord Hoffmann that the '*real threat to the life of the nation, in the sense of a people living in accordance with its traditional laws and political values, comes not from terrorism but from laws such as these*'.[61] From this perspective, the task of the courts has been to 'arrest the slide' from the principles enshrined in the HRA.[62] Others emphasized the potentially ameliorating influence of judgments, and the way in which the judges have drawn attention to weaknesses in legislative schemes and provided guidance for their improvement. This perspective arguably illustrates the existence of a dialogue between the courts and the other institutions of government, that we have discussed elsewhere in the book.[63]

In terms of the effects of the judicial decisions on the way in which the control order scheme functioned, the following is an assessment by Professor Clive Walker.

C. Walker, 'The threat of terrorism and the fate of control orders' [2010] *Public Law* 4–17 (footnotes omitted)

> It is arguable that the principal consequence has been to minimise the use of control orders [. . .] There were dire predictions when the PTA 2005 was passed that control orders could affect 'hundreds–thousands, who knows'. Yet, just 15 orders were in force at the end of 2008. This paltry total stands in stark contrast to the apocalyptic analysis in 2007 of Jonathan Evans, the Director of the Security Service, that there were 2,000 specific people who posed a direct threat to national security, plus as many again yet to be identified. Clearly, the meagre number of control orders is not for a want of customers but relates to their relative lack of security effectiveness and legal certainty compared to criminal prosecution. The application by the courts of arts 5 and 6 and their willingness to traduce the assertions of the state are significant factors in this outcome.

The then Labour government, while clearly frustrated by some of the judgments, put a positive spin on its experience in the courts, arguing that the case law confirmed that the control order regime was not fundamentally flawed from a human rights perspective stressing that the courts had adopted a nuanced approach that explained how individual circumstances should be handled.[64] However, the overwhelming view, reflected by the Joint Committee on Human Rights, was that the control order regime was unsustainable and required reform.[65]

[60] Cm 8194.

[61] *A v Secretary of State for the Home Department* [2004] UKHL 56, [96].

[62] D. McKeever, 'The Human Rights Act and anti-terrorism in the UK: One great leap forward by Parliament, but are the courts able to slow the steady retreat that has followed?' [2010] Public Law 110, 139.

[63] See especially Chapter 21.

[64] UK Government, *Reply to the Fifth Report from the Joint Committee on Human Rights*, Cm 7625 (May 2009).

[65] Joint Committee on Human Rights, *Counter-terrorism Policy and Human Rights (Fourteenth Report): Annual Renewal of Control Orders Legislation 2009*, Fifth Report, Session 2008–09 (HL Paper 37/HC 282). See also Joint Committee on Human Rights, *Counter-terrorism Policy and Human Rights (Seventeenth Report): Bringing Human Rights Back In*, Sixteenth Report, Session 2009–10 (HL Paper 86/HC 111).

Control Orders were replaced by a new regime known as Terrorism Prevention and Investigation Measures (TPIMs).[66] TPIMs were replaced by Enhanced Terrorism Prevention and Investigation Measures (ETPIMs).[67]

22.2.11 CONCLUSION ON THIS CASE STUDY

This case study has concerned a limited range of legal responses to the threat of terrorism and[68] has provided an opportunity to consider some of the impacts of the HRA in the context of strategies to counter terrorism. Professor Helen Fenwick concludes a survey of the control orders saga by considering what it means for the role and importance of the HRA. As you will see from the following extract she ends on a positive note.

H. Fenwick, 'Terrorism and the control orders/TPIMS saga: a vindication of the Human Rights Act or a manifestation of "defensive democracy"?' [2017] *Public Law* 609, 626 (footnotes omitted)

> [. . .] The varying iterations of control order-type measures considered here are illustrative of the post-9/11 struggle in the UK and elsewhere to reconcile international human rights norms with reliance on non-trial-based measures. The tension and interaction between security needs and such law partly explains [. . .] the changing iterations of the control orders model discussed which exhibit a human rights tempering of that model. Credit therefore should be given to the Human Rights Act, both for the under-use of these measures, and for their modification [. . .] The interaction discussed between the courts, the executive and Parliament [. . .] may be said to [. . .] represent a vindication of the Human Rights Act, even at a time of a rising terrorist threat. From this viewpoint this saga thus not only provides no support for the repeal of the HRA, but also underlines the folly of giving serious consideration to withdrawal from the ECHR.

PAUSE FOR REFLECTION

'*This case study shows both the effectiveness of the HRA and that there is a healthy democratic dialogue between the judiciary and the government and Parliament.*' Do you agree with this?

22.3 CASE STUDY: PRISONER VOTING: *HIRST V UK (NO. 2)* AND ITS AFTERMATH

In this case study we summarize the aftermath of *Hirst v UK (No. 2)*.[69] In this case the Grand Chamber of the ECtHR held that UK legislation preventing all convicted prisoners from voting in elections is contrary to the ECHR. This decision was not welcomed by the UK government and was unpopular

[66] The Terrorism Prevention and Investigation Measures Act 2011.

[67] Introduced by Part 2 of the Counter-Terrorism and Security Act 2015.

[68] For discussion of the wider range of measures that have been introduced, see e.g. Joint Committee on Human Rights report on counter-extremism, *2nd Report of Session 2016–17*, HL Paper 39, HC paper 105; S. Greer and L. Bell 'Counter-Terrorist Law in British Universities: A Review of the "Prevent" Debate' Public Law 84; C. Walker 'Counter-Terrorism and Counter-Extremism: The UK Policy Spirals' [2018] Public Law 725.

[69] App. No. 74025/01.

across a broad cross-section of MPs. So much so that over many years the UK government failed to introduce legislation implementing the decision, despite severe criticism from Parliament's Joint Committee on Human Rights and the Council of Europe's Committee of Ministers (the body responsible for ensuring that states implement decisions of the ECtHR).

From the perspective of the ECHR, a failure to implement a decision of the ECtHR is a breach of the Convention and flouts the rule of law. Others involved in the saga will see things rather differently. From the point of view of many in Parliament, the saga reflects the democratic power of a national legislature not to be forced to adopt law (especially, some would say, 'European law') that is considered to be wrong and unacceptable.

However the issues are viewed, the saga provides graphic insight into why the relationship between the United Kingdom and the ECtHR matters and is so contentious; and helps to explain why so much attention has been placed in recent years on the power of that Court. The episode also helps to explain some of the attitudes to reform of the HRA and whether the UK should continue to be a party to the ECHR. More broadly, it also raises important questions about the relationship between courts and politicians.[70]

The existing UK law is contained in s. 3 of the Representation of the People Act 1983, which provides: '(1) A convicted person during the time that he is detained in a penal institution in pursuance of his sentence [. . .] is legally incapable of voting at any parliamentary or local election.' The disqualification does not apply to persons imprisoned for contempt of court (s. 3(2)(a)) or to those imprisoned only for default in, for example, paying a fine (s. 3(2)(c)).

Section 3 re-enacted the provisions of s. 4 of the Representation of the People Act 1969. These dated back to the Forfeiture Act 1870, which in turn reflected earlier laws relating to the forfeiture of certain rights by a convicted 'felon' dating back to the time of King Edward III. The Representation of the People Act 2000 permitted remand prisoners and unconvicted people detained under the mental health legislation to vote.

Successive governments have taken the view that prisoners convicted of crimes warranting a sentence of imprisonment have lost the moral authority to vote. This view has been supported by many politicians, across a broad political spectrum.

In *Hirst v UK (No. 2)*[71] the Grand Chamber of the ECtHR held (by a majority of 12 to 5) that s. 3 breached the right to vote in Art. 3 of the First Protocol to the ECHR: It said that: '*Such a general, automatic and indiscriminate restriction on a vitally important Convention right had to be seen as falling outside any acceptable margin of appreciation.*'

It is important to note that the Court did not decide that prisoners could not be prevented from voting. What is unlawful is the imposition of a blanket ban that is applied automatically to all prisoners irrespective of their crime or their circumstances. While the Court indicated that states have a 'margin of appreciation', imposing an automatic and indiscriminate ban on the right to vote could not fall within that margin. This was an aspect of the decision that the UK government found particularly difficult to accept.

The decision clearly meant that s. 3 was incompatible with the ECHR and had to be amended or repealed.

[70] See further, S. Fredman, 'From dialogue to deliberation: Human rights adjudication and prisoners' right to vote' [2013] Public Law 29. There are also some excellent blogs commenting on the issues in this saga: e.g. the UK Constitutional Law Group's blog: C. O'Cinneide, 'Prisoners' Votes (Again) and the "Constitutional Illegitimacy" of the ECHR', http://ukconstitutionallaw.org; J. King, 'Should prisoners have the right to vote?', http://ukconstitutionallaw.org.

[71] App. No. 74025/01.

The UK government responded by commencing a public consultation on prisoner voting. That consultation initially ended in March 2007. Possibly because the consultation revealed significant support for reform, rather than using the results of the consultation to formulate a legislative response to *Hirst (No. 2)*, the government instead embarked on a second more detailed consultation, the outcome of which was not published until April 2009.[72] By this point the Labour government had accepted that: '*to meet the terms of the [ECtHR] judgment a limited enfranchisement of convicted prisoners in custody should take place, with eligibility determined on the basis of sentence length*', although it acknowledged that the final decision on the extension of the franchise to convicted prisoners must rest with Parliament.[73]

During the long period of consultation, the Joint Committee on Human Rights had asked the government to explain how it was intending to implement *Hirst (No. 2)*. In its 31st report of 2007–08 the Committee noted the government's delay and reiterated the need for urgent action to resolve the issue:

> 62. [. . . T]he Government's [. . .] failure to set a concrete timetable for its response raises serious questions about its reluctance to deal with this issue. In our previous reports, we have drawn attention to a number of cases where significant delay in implementation has tarnished the otherwise good record of the United Kingdom in responding to the judgments of the European Court of Human Rights. For the most part, these cases have been legally straightforward, but politically difficult. This case appears destined to join a list of long standing breaches of individual rights that the current Government, and its predecessors, have been unable or unwilling to address effectively within a reasonable time frame. The Government should rethink its approach.
> 63. [. . .] If the Government fails to meet this timetable, there is a significant risk that the next general election will take place in a way that fails to comply with the Convention and at least part of the prison population will be unlawfully disenfranchised.[74]

On 3 December 2009, the Council of Europe Committee of Ministers adopted a resolution calling for the UK government to lift the blanket ban on prisoners voting. In the resolution the Committee of Ministers expressed '*serious concern*':

> [. . .] that the substantial delay in implementing the judgment has given rise to a significant risk that the next United Kingdom general election, which must take place by June 2010, will be performed in a way that fails to comply with the Convention; [. . .]

At their meeting in March 2010, the Committee of Ministers issued a warning to the UK government to 'rapidly adopt' measures to enable prisoners to vote in the forthcoming general election.

Despite continuing pressure from the Joint Committee and the Committee of Ministers, the legal position remained unchanged and no convicted prisoners were able to vote in the May 2010 election.

In November 2010, the ECtHR, in *Greens and MT v UK*,[75] reiterated its decision in *Hirst (No. 2)* and gave the United Kingdom six months from the final decision in the case to introduce appropriate legislative proposals. Attempting to appeal against this deadline, the UK government asked for the case to be referred to the Court's Grand Chamber. This request was refused on 11 April 2011 and the six-month time limit for new legislation was triggered from that date.

[72] *Voting Rights of Convicted Prisoners Detained Within the United Kingdom: Second Stage Consultation*, Consultation Paper CP6/09, Ministry of Justice, 8 April 2009.

[73] Ibid, p. 21.

[74] The concerns of the Committee were repeated in its fourth report of 2008–09.

[75] App. Nos 60041/08 and 60054/08.

In the meantime, in December 2010 the then Minister for Political and Constitutional Reform, Mark Harper, told the Commons that the government was finally to propose legislation. This would give offenders sentenced to a custodial sentence of less than four years the right to vote in UK Westminster Parliamentary and European Parliament elections, unless the judge considered this inappropriate when making the sentence.

Following that announcement on 10 February 2011,[76] an all-day debate took place on the floor of the House of Commons on a motion put forward jointly by Jack Straw (former Labour Party minister) and David Davis (a Conservative and former Minister for Europe). The motion was:

> That this House, [. . .]conscious of the treaty obligations of the UK, is of the opinion that (a) legislative decisions of this nature should be a matter for democratically elected lawmakers and (b) that on the merits of the issue, the current policy by which no sentenced prisoner is able to vote except those imprisoned for contempt, default or on remand, is confirmed.

The motion was carried by 234 votes to 22.[77]

While the vote in the House of Commons was not binding, the government considered it provided a clear indication of the nature and strength of feeling in the House. The vote may have vindicated the government's general approach, but it also indicated that the government could not rely on the House to support its proposed amendment of the law: an issue that was becoming increasingly pressing given the timetable imposed in *Greens and MT.*

In the event, a further case on prisoner voting, *Scoppola v Italy (No. 3)*,[78] was referred to the Grand Chamber of the ECtHR and the Court agreed to an extension to the deadline of six months from the date of the judgment in the case. This was delivered by the Grand Chamber on 22 May 2012.

In *Scoppola (No. 3)* the Grand Chamber confirmed its decision in *Hirst (No. 2)* and reiterated that general, automatic, and indiscriminate restrictions on voting are contrary to the ECHR.[79] However, the Court accepted the United Kingdom's argument on the breadth of the margin of appreciation: states should have a wide discretion as to how they regulate a ban on prisoners voting '*both as regards the types of offence that should result in the loss of the vote and as to whether disenfranchisement should be ordered by a judge in an individual case or should result from general application of a law*'.[80]

Although the decision, predictably, attracted the ire of some sections of the media (the *Daily Mail*, for example, saw it as showing '*Contempt for Democracy*'), it has been said that the judgment effectively extended an olive branch to the UK government which it would be wise to accept.[81] However, not everyone was in favour of compromising.

In Parliament, Mr Nigel Dodds (Belfast North) (DUP) asked the Prime Minister whether he would: '*give an undertaking that he will not succumb to the diktat from the European Court of Human Rights in relation to prisoners voting, that he will stand up for the resolution that was agreed in this House by an overwhelming majority and that he will stand up for the sovereignty of this House and the British people?*'

[76] In November 2010 the ECtHR decided *Frodl v Austria* (App. No. 20201/04), holding that prisoners could only be deprived of their right to vote in very limited circumstances. On 17 January 2011 the Court of Appeal decided in *R (Chester) v Secretary of State for Justice and Another* (*The Times*, 17 January) that it was not for the courts to construe existing statutes so as to give prisoners a right to vote. This is a task for Parliament. In this instance, the legislation patently did not give this right and the judges would have been acting as a legislator.

[77] Government ministers and their official Opposition counterparts abstained from voting.

[78] App. No. 126/05. [79] Para. 102 of the judgment.

[80] European Court of Human Rights Press release, 22 May 2012.

[81] J. Rozenberg, *Law Society Gazette*, Opinion, 31 May 2012. Cited by C. O'Cinneide, 'Prisoners Votes (Again) and the "Constitutional Illegitimacy" of the ECHR', UK Constitutional Law Blog.

The Prime Minister replied:[82]

> The short answer to that is yes. I have always believed that when someone is sent to prison they lose certain rights, and one of those rights is the right to vote. Crucially, I believe that it should be a matter for Parliament to decide, not a foreign court. Parliament has made its decision, and I completely agree with it.[83]

On 22 November 2012, just before the deadline, the government published the Voting Eligibility (Prisoners) Draft Bill setting out three options: a ban for prisoners sentenced to four years or more; a ban for prisoners sentenced to more than six months; and a ban for all convicted prisoners. The bill was referred to a joint Committee of both Houses for pre-legislative scrutiny and the Committee reported in December 2013.

In its report the Committee referred to:

> grave implications of a refusal to comply with the [. . . judgments of ECtHR . . .] for the UK's relationship with the Court and for the future of the entire Convention system. A refusal to implement the Court's judgment, which is binding under international law, would not only undermine the standing of the UK; it would also give succour to those states in the Council of Europe who have a poor record of protecting human rights and who could regard the UK's action as setting a precedent for them to follow. We have also considered the implications of failure to comply with the European Court's ruling for the rule of law, which the UK has for so long upheld. The rule of law has been and should remain a fundamental tenet of UK policy. It is not possible to reconcile the principle of the rule of law with remaining within the Convention while declining to implement the judgment of the Court [. . .][84]

The Committee recommended that the government introduce a bill at the start of the 2014–15 session, which would entitle all prisoners serving sentences of 12 months or less to vote in all UK parliamentary, local, and European elections.

The following picks up the story following the Joint Committee's report.

Standard Note on Prisoners' Voting Rights, SN/PC/01764 (11 February 2015, Author: Alexander Horne and Isobel White, Section: Parliament and Constitution Centre)

> The Lord Chancellor and Justice Secretary, Chris Grayling, made a brief response to the Committee's report on 25 February 2014; but the Government have not responded substantively and did not bring forward a Bill with the 2014 Queen's Speech. On 16 October 2013 the UK Supreme Court dismissed the appeals of George McGeoch and Peter Chester, both prisoners serving life sentences for murder, who had brought domestic law proceedings in 2010 challenging the ban. The Supreme Court rejected a separate head of claim that the blanket ban was incompatible with European Union law. However, the Supreme Court also maintained the position determined in Strasbourg that the UK's blanket ban was

[82] The Prime Minister had earlier commented that the prospect of implementing a decision of the Strasbourg Court enabling prisoners to vote made him '*physically ill*': HC Deb., 3 November 2010, vol. 517, col. 921.

[83] HC Deb., 23 May 2012, col. 1127.

[84] The Joint Committee on the Draft Voting Eligibility (Prisoners) Bill, *Draft Voting Eligibility (Prisoners) Bill Report*, Session 2013–14 (HL Paper 103/HC 924), Executive Summary.

contrary to the European Convention on Human Rights; although it refused to make a further 'declaration of incompatibility' with the Human Rights Act 1998, considering that it was unnecessary in the circumstances. In two recent judgments in August 2014 and February 2015 (*Firth and others v UK* and *McHugh and others v UK*) relating to a large number of outstanding claims by prisoners, the European Court of Human Rights noted the continuing violation of Article 3 to Protocol No. 1 to the Convention, but did not award the applicants any compensation or legal expenses. In December 2014, the Government announced that prisoners would not be enfranchised prior to the General Election of 2015.

At meetings in September 2014 and again in September 2015, the Committee of the Council of Europe considered the United Kingdom's continued failure to give effect to the judgments of the ECtHR in *Hirst (No. 2)* and *Greens* and *MT*. At its September 2015 meeting, the Committee of Ministers, acting through their Deputies:

1. expressed their appreciation for the presence of the Minister for Human Rights and the assurances presented of the United Kingdom's support for the European Convention on Human Rights;
2. reiterated their serious concern about the on-going delay in the introduction of a Bill to Parliament (as recommended by the Parliamentary Committee in December 2013) leading to repetitive violations of the Convention (*Firth and Others* and *McHugh and Others*);
3. expressed profound regret that, despite their repeated calls, the blanket ban on the right of convicted prisoners in custody to vote remains in place and reiterated that concrete information is yet to be presented to the Committee on how the United Kingdom intends to abide by the judgment;
4. reiterated [. . .] their call upon the United Kingdom authorities to introduce a Bill to Parliament as recommended by the Parliamentary Committee without further delay, and to inform them as soon as this has been done;
5. decided to resume consideration of these cases at their . . . [meeting in December 2015] . . . and, in the event that no Bill has been introduced to Parliament in the meantime, instructed the Secretariat to prepare a draft interim resolution to be distributed with the revised draft order of business.

In the event no legislation has been introduced to remove or limit the ban on prisoner's voting rights and the following Briefing Paper updates the situation and points to the future implications for local and devolved elections.[85]

N. Johnston, Prisoners' voting rights: developments since May 2015, House of Commons Library Briefing Paper Number 07461, 19 November 2020 (pp. 4–5)

The solution

Following further calls from the Council of Europe's Committee of Ministers to resolve the impasse, [the then] Secretary of State for Justice, David Lidington, published proposals in November 2017. These

[85] Thierry Delvigne, a convicted murderer, sentenced to 12 years' imprisonment, claimed that a ban on him voting in European Parliament elections violated his civil and political rights under the Charter of Fundamental Rights of the EU. In a preliminary ruling, the Court of Justice held that the '*ban to which Mr Delvigne is subject is proportionate in so far as it takes into account the nature and gravity of the criminal offence committed and the duration of the penalty*': Case C-650/13 *Thierry Delvigne v Commune de Lesparre-Médoc*, Judgment 6 October 2015.

proposals were more limited in scope than those included in previous proposals. The main change proposed was to allow prisoners on Temporary Licence to vote. In December 2017 the Council of Europe welcomed the proposals, agreeing to them as an acceptable compromise that would address the criticisms raised by Hirst (No 2).

The Government intended to implement the proposed changes by the end of 2018. It agreed to report back to the Council of Europe's Committee of Ministers by September 2018. The Council of Europe confirmed that the case was closed at its meeting of September 2018.

Although the dispute between the UK and the EctHR appears to have been resolved, responsibility for local elections and elections to the Scottish Parliament and the Nationally Assembly of Wales, is devolved. In Scotland the Scottish Elections (Franchise and Representation) Act 2020 enables convicted prisoners serving a prison sentence of 12 months or less to register to vote in local and Scottish Parliamentary elections and to vote by proxy or post. Currently, convicted prisoners in Wales are still unable to register to vote.[86]

QUESTIONS

1. How would you respond to those who say that this saga displays the ECtHR's contempt for democracy?
2. What, if anything, does this saga tell us about the United Kingdom's attitude to the rule of law?
3. Who should have the final say on whether there should be a blanket ban on prisoner voting—a court or Parliament? Does it matter that the court is an international rather than a domestic court?
4. Does the saga suggest that the relationship between courts and government is one of conflict or dialogue?
5. What lessons does this saga have for the relationship between the Council of Europe and states which refuse to accept decisions of the ECtHR?

[86] See Neil Johnston, *Prisoners' Voting Rights*, House of Commons Library Research Briefing, 9 August 2023, especially section 5 (Scotland) and Section 6 (Wales).

PART V

THE EUROPEAN UNION

23

INSTITUTIONS OF THE EUROPEAN UNION

CENTRAL ISSUES

1. This chapter examines the story of European integration and analyses the government of the European Union. While the principal institutions are listed in Art. 13 TEU, this chapter focuses on those that exercise executive power—the European Council, the Council of the European Union, and the Commission.
2. These executive institutions operate through shared institutional responsibilities rather than traditional separation of powers. The European Union employs a system of '*institutional balance*'.
3. The chapter discusses the European Parliament, which has evolved from a consultative assembly into an equal partner with the Council in law-making. It possesses the strongest democratic mandate of any EU institution.
4. The chapter examines how the EU enacts legislation through the ordinary legislative procedure (OLP) and the two main types of legislation: regulations and directives.
5. A central theme is democratic legitimacy. The EU's executive institutions are not directly elected—does this make them undemocratic, or do alternative sources of legitimacy validate the EU's institutional architecture?

23.1 INTRODUCTION

This chapter introduces the European Union (EU), explains the role and functions of the EU institutions that wield executive powers, and touches on their different rationales. It will also examine the EU's law-making process.

The relationship between the United Kingdom and European integration has been challenging from the outset, even before the UK formally joined what is now the European Union in 1973. These tensions reached their climax with the 2016 EU withdrawal referendum and subsequent negotiations culminating in the Withdrawal Agreement (see Chapter 24). Does EU withdrawal render EU institutional study merely historical? Three compelling reasons suggest otherwise.

First, the EU remains an economic powerhouse and the UK's dominant trading partner. As the world's third-largest trading bloc alongside the USA and China, it accounted for 41 per cent of UK exports and 51 per cent of imports in 2024.[1] This economic interdependence requires the UK to

[1] House of Commons Library, Statistics on UK-EU trade, Research Briefing, 22 April, 2025.

maintain ongoing relationship with EU institutions, making the study of these institutions essential for understanding UK public law.

Second, complete legal divorce from the EU is neither possible nor practical. Historical ties, geographic proximity, and the realities of modern governance create what Sir Ivan Rogers, the UK's former permanent representative to the EU calls *'a state of permanent negotiation with the European Union'* in which the UK negotiates *'on everything from aviation to energy to phytosanitary [regarding plants] to financial services for ever more with our biggest neighbour'*.[2] The May 2025 UK-EU agreements on defence cooperation, border systems, and carbon markets exemplify this continuing institutional entanglement.[3]

Third, the EU serves as a constitutional comparator for UK public law. As the most developed supranational legal order, it offers unique insights into post-national governance, institutional balance, and democratic legitimacy beyond the state. Understanding how the EU manages executive power, legislative processes, and accountability mechanisms offers insight into the possibilities and limitations of constitutional design in an interconnected world.

Readers should study the EU institutions critically, but with an open mind. From a nation state's perspective, EU power structures are easily dismissed as bureaucratic, obscure, unaccountable, and detached from the popular will. This perception makes it all the more important to examine how EU decision-making processes measure up to the principles of good government, such as accessibility, accountability, transparency, and reasoned decision-making.

23.2 UNDERSTANDING THE TREATY STRUCTURE

Before examining the institutions themselves, we need to understand the legal foundations of the European Union. The EU and its predecessors were created through international treaties between member states. The United Kingdom participated from 1 January 1973 until 31 January 2020, followed by a transition period maintaining the status quo until 31 December 2020. Treaty development can be understood through three main phases (see Boxes 23.1 and 23.2).

BOX 23.1 THE EU TREATY FRAMEWORK

1950s–1993	1993–2009[4]	Since December 2009[5]
Treaty Establishing the European Coal and Steel Community Treaty Establishing the European Atomic Energy Community Treaty Establishing the European Economic Community[6] *Membership grows from six, to nine, to 12*	Treaty on European Union (TEU, or 'Maastricht Treaty') Treaty Establishing the European Communities (TEC). *Expansion from 15 to 25, and then to 27, members*	Treaty on European Union (TEU) (revised) Treaty on the Functioning of the European Union (TFEU) *28 members (from July 2013–January 2020)* *27 members (since February 2020)*

** Reformed by the Single European Act (a treaty) in 1987*
*** Reforms made by the Treaty of Amsterdam (1999) and the Treaty of Nice (2003)*
**** Reforms introduced by the Treaty of Lisbon 2009*

[2] Institute for Government, 'In conversation with Sir Ivan Rogers', 4 March 2019.
[3] Cabinet Office, Policy paper, UK-EU Summit—Common Understanding 19 May 2025. https://www.gov.uk/government/publications/ukeu-summit-key-documentation/uk-eu-summit-common-understanding-html [Accessed May 2025].
[4] *Reforms made by the Treaty of Amsterdam (1999) and the Treaty of Nice (2003).*
[5] *Reforms introduced by the Treaty of Lisbon 2009.*
[6] *Reformed by the Single European Act (a treaty) in 1987.*

BOX 23.2 DEVELOPMENT OF THE EU TREATY FRAMEWORK

There are currently two principal treaties under which the EU operates:

- the Treaty on the Functioning of the European Union (TFEU), which means the Treaty establishing (what was then called) the European Economic Community, signed at Rome on 25 March 1957 (as amended and renamed by the Treaty of Lisbon); and
- the Treaty on European Union (TEU), which means the Treaty on European Union signed at Maastricht on 7 February 1992 (as amended by the Treaty of Lisbon).

The Treaty of Rome created the European Economic Community (EEC) in 1957 and was originally signed by the heads of six European states (West Germany, Italy, France, the Netherlands, Belgium, and Luxembourg). The United Kingdom joined the EEC in January 1973. The Treaty of Rome was not substantially amended (apart from the various Accession Treaties) for the next 30 years. From 1986 until the Lisbon Treaty in 2009, amendments to the Treaty of Rome were frequent and far-reaching:

The Single European Act (signed in 1986, entered into force on 1 July 1987) is an international treaty and not—as its name might suggest—an Act of Parliament. Its objective was to accelerate the completion of the internal market, thereby broadening the scope of the common market introduced in 1958. To do so, it created new EEC powers in monetary policy, social policy, economic and social cohesion, research and technological development, the environment, and co-operation in foreign policy. The SEA also reformed the legislative process in two significant ways. First, it replaced many unanimous decision-making processes with Qualified Majority Voting (QMV) in order to facilitate the adoption of EU legislation by the end of 1992. Second, the SEA introduced a more collaborative legislative process, which gave the European Parliament (EP) real, albeit limited, legislative powers. The EP first emerged as a genuine co-legislator.

The Treaty on European Union (the 'Maastricht Treaty'; signed in 1992, entered into force on 1 November 1993) made a number of significant changes. The economic objectives of the Treaty of Rome and of the Single European Act were now being surpassed by a distinctive move towards social and economic cohesion and, ultimately, political union (note the introduction of EU citizenship). The Maastricht Treaty renamed the EEC as the 'European Community' (EC) and created a new body, the European Union (EU) that consisted of three pillars. In addition to the first 'Community' pillar, the Treaty on European Union (TEU) added two further policies and forms of cooperation to the EC—namely, a 'Common Foreign and Security Policy' and 'Justice and Home Affairs' (renamed after 2003 as 'Police and Judicial Cooperation in Criminal Matters'). A separate Protocol linked to the Maastricht Treaty led to the creation of a common currency, of which the United Kingdom opted out. The law-making process was reformed once more with the introduction of the co-decision procedure, under which the EP and the Council share legislative authority.

The Amsterdam Treaty (signed in 1997, entered into force on 1 May 1999) further extended QMV and co-decision, while allowing the UK and Ireland to opt out of the Schengen Agreement on border controls.

The Treaty of Nice (signed in 2001, entered into force on 1 February 2003) was designed to reform the EU institutions in the run-up to enlargement of the European Union.

23.3 THE ORIGINS OF THE EUROPEAN UNION

Before we examine the exercise of executive power in the EU, we need to remind ourselves of the story of the EU.

D. Dinan, *Europe Recast: A History of European Union*, 2nd edn (2014, Boulder, CO: Lynne Rienner), pp. 1–2

The idea of a united Europe is a recurring theme in the long and often violent history of the continent. The Holy Roman Emperors, Napoleon, Hitler, and others sought, in sometimes horrifying ways, to achieve a continental unity based variously on princely alliances, ethnic cohesion, ideology, or raw power. Ever since the emergence of the modern state, in the mid-seventeenth century, philosophers and political thinkers have also imagined a united Europe triumphing over narrow national interests and allegiances. Today's European Union (EU) is singular among these competing visions. Tempering the nationalist ethos that had become the ruling principle of European political development, the countries that formed the European Communities, the basis of the EU, chose to limit (but not eliminate) their own sovereignty, the hallmark of a modern nation-state, in favour of collective peace, economic integration, and supranational governance.

Their reasons for doing so were rooted in the disastrous decades of the early twentieth century. The miserable legacy of heroic European nationalism—two world wars, countless millions dead, and economic ruin—was not lost on the peoples of Europe, who were receptive to the idea of treaty-based and highly institutionalized economic and political integration after World War II. European politicians wanted above all to end international strife, foster social harmony, and promote economic well-being. They sought to build a better world, free of the hatreds and rivalries that had destroyed their countries in recent years. For their generation, European integration became synonymous with peace and prosperity.

Yet there was nothing inevitable about the emergence of European integration in the form with which we are now familiar. European politicians were (and still are) instinctively averse to sharing national sovereignty, despite rhetorical flourishes to the contrary. National leaders decided to share sovereignty in supranational organizations primarily because they perceived that it was in their countries' (and therefore their own) interests to do so. Ideas, intellectual fashion, opportunity, chance, conviction, calculation, personal predilection, and ambition all played a part. Ultimately, however, European integration emerged as it did because of a calculated response by politicians, businesspeople, and other actors to changing economic, political, and strategic circumstances, ranging from Germany's postwar recovery, to the fall of the Berlin Wall, to the acceleration of globalization. Despite growing public concern about the process and politics of European integration, Europeans generally acquiesced because the outcome seemed worthwhile and the alternatives less attractive.

The lessons of the Second World War and of the emerging Cold War (a period of intense political tension between the democratic capitalist West and the totalitarian communist Soviet Union that lasted from 1946 to 1990) demonstrated the urgent need for Western European unity. The USA actively supported integration from 1947,most notably through the Marshall Plan, administered by the Organization for European Economic Co-operation (OEEC) to strengthen Western Europe economically and create a bulwark against communism. The US envisioned a federal European structure modelled on its own political and economic system—an aspiration Winston Churchill famously articulated to students in Zurich in 1946: '*The cannons have ceased firing. The fighting has stopped; but the dangers have not stopped. If we are to form the United States of Europe, or whatever name it may take, we must begin now.*'

However, this federalist vision proved unrealistic for three fundamental reasons: Europe's geopolitical situation precluded simply replicating American federalism; Britain, still viewing itself as a global power, remained aloof; and France sought to restore its own continental leadership rather than submit to supranational authority.

Jean Monnet, head of France's General Planning Commission, offered a pragmatic alternative to American federalist ambitions: uniting Europe through incremental steps rather than immediate federation. 'This gradualist approach would begin with strategic, practical measures designed to make *"any war between France and Germany becomes not merely unthinkable, but materially impossible."*'[7] Monnet aspired to create '*the first concrete foundations of the European Federation which is indispensable to the maintenance of peace*'.[8]

The Treaty of Paris (1951), signed by France, Germany, Italy, Belgium, Luxembourg, and the Netherlands, embodied two crucial innovations. First, it established a common market for coal, iron, and steel—the key resources of war production—where prices operated freely and trade barriers were progressively eliminated. Second, it subjected these industries to supranational governance through the European Coal and Steel Community (ECSC), led by a 'High Authority' (a precursor to the European Commission) under Monnet's presidency, with political oversight by governmental and parliamentary representatives and legal review by an independent court.

But Monnet was not merely concerned with creating a federation of states. He famously declared that Europe's circumstances required '*that we unite Europeans and that we do not keep them separated. We are not joining states, we are unifying men*'.[9] This human-centred approach informed the next breakthrough: the economic union agreed in March 1957 and incorporated in the Treaty of Rome. The European Economic Community (EEC) aimed to create a common market—a free trade area for the factors of production (labour, goods, services, and capital). Beyond market integration, the EEC sought to harmonize the economic policies of the six member states, promote balanced economic development, establish frameworks for gradual economic expansion and stability, and improve citizens' living standards. The 1962 common agricultural policy, which standardized agricultural prices, became one of the EEC's first major achievements.

The integrationist logic of the EEC may seem obscure given its narrow focus on economic and trade development. Indeed, 'human rights', 'democracy', and 'rule of law' were notably absent from the Treaty of Rome's objectives. One explanation is that these fundamental rights and principles were already addressed by the Council of Europe, established in 1949, which had adopted the Convention for the Protection of Human Rights and Fundamental Freedoms—commonly referred to as the European Convention on Human Rights, or ECHR—in 1950. More fundamentally, however, the themes of integration, peace, and prosperity were gradually being operationalized through progressive market liberalization and the long-term possibility of political unity. The EEC and Schuman's gradualist strategy thus represented a distinctly European response to the challenge of continental unity, one that prioritised economic interdependence over constitutional blueprints[10] and offered a pragmatic *alternative* to American federalist models.[11]

Three concepts are essential for understanding the complex relationship between the EU and its member states: intergovernmentalism, supranationalism, and sovereignty. In some policy areas, the EU resembles a classic *intergovernmental* organization, accommodating member states' high-level geopolitical and diplomatic interests where they retain autonomous (or sovereign) powers and are simply working together. Foreign affairs, defence and security policies, and certain justice and home affairs issues, such as asylum or border control policies, are dominated by national governments

[7] Robert Schuman's proposal of 9 May 1950.

[8] J. Monnet, *Memoirs* (1978, New York: Doubleday and Company), p. 298.

[9] Speech of 30 April 1952, see J. Monnet, *Les États-Unis d'Europe ont Commencé: La Communauté Européene du Charbon et de l'Acier, Discours et Allocutions 1952–1954* (1955, Paris: Robert Laffont), p. 132.

[10] See now Art. 3(1) TEU: 'The Union's aim is to promote peace, its values and the well-being of its peoples'.

[11] E. Hobsbawm, Age of Extremes: The Short Twentieth Century 1914–1991 (1994, London: Michael Joseph), pp. 239–41.

working through the Council of Ministers and the European Council. Here the EU implements member states decisions through unanimity and intergovernmental negotiation, preserving national sovereignty through direct member state control.

Elsewhere, however, member states cooperate without retaining complete control over outcomes. In areas such as agriculture and trade, member states have pooled their sovereignty and delegated decision-making powers to EU institutions. The EU acts *supranationally*—autonomously from the member states, though under supervision by the Court of Justice of the EU. Consequently, member states may be bound by individual decisions to which they did not consent, effectively limiting national sovereignty.

Interstate cooperation on matters of mutual interest has increased through international organizations like the UN, WTO, and NATO, but the EU has developed a distinctive institutional architecture. As McCormick demonstrates:

J. McCormick, *Understanding the European Union*, 7th edn (2017, Basingstoke: Macmillan), p. 14

> [. . .] the EU has many of the typical features of an intergovernmental organization, in that membership is voluntary, the balance of sovereignty lies with the member states, decision making is consultative and the procedures used to direct the work of the EU are based on consent rather than compulsion. At the same time, it also has some of the qualities of a state: it has external borders that are harder than its internal borders, there is an EU system of law to which all member states are subject, it has administrative institutions with the authority to make law and policy, the balance of responsibility in many policy areas has shifted to the European level, and in some areas—such as trade—the EU functions as a unit.

This hybrid character—neither purely intergovernmental nor fully federal—explains many of the institutional tensions we see today. The third element in this constitutional equation is national *sovereignty*. Sovereignty is a loaded term that means different things to different people and in different states. As discussed in Chapter 3, UK parliamentary sovereignty encompasses two core principles: (i) the absence of legal limitation on the authority of Parliament; and (ii) the primacy of an Act of Parliament within the domestic legal order. Neil Nugent captures this broader significance, from its political resonance to its analytical utility:

N. Nugent, *The Government and Politics of the European Union*, 8th edn (2017, Basingstoke: Macmillan), p. 436

> *Sovereignty* is an emotive word, associated as it is with notions of power, authority, independence, and the exercise of will. Because of its emotiveness and its associations, it is a word to which several meanings are attached. The most common meaning, and the one which will be employed here, refers to the legal capacity of national decision-makers to take decisions without being subject to external restraints. This is usually called national, or sometimes state, sovereignty.

Having established these foundational concepts, we can now examine the main EU institutions: those exercising executive functions (the European Council, the Council of the European Union, and the Commission) and legislative functions (the Council of the European Union and the European Parliament). Three analytical challenges emerge from the sovereignty-intergovernmentalism-supranationalism nexus.

First, the EU's governing structure must balance supranational integration with member states' determination to retain policy control through intergovernmental cooperation—a tension embedded in its constitutional framework. Second, the EU requires a distinctive institutional architecture because it is neither an international organization nor a conventional state. Third, accountability mechanisms must address the democratic legitimacy of EU institutions and actors.

23.4 WHERE DOES EXECUTIVE POWER IN THE EUROPEAN UNION LIE?

Executive power refers to politicians' authority to develop policy initiatives and act in the public interest, with those decisions implemented by civil servants and officials. The European Union distributes executive authority across three institutions, two of which directly involve member state governments:

- The European Council brings together member states' heads of state or government, the Commission President, and the High Representative for Foreign Affairs and Security Policy, representing the apex of EU political cooperation.
- The Council of the European Union (commonly called the 'Council of Ministers' or simply 'the Council') provides a decision-making forum for ministers from member states with corresponding portfolios—health ministers, agriculture ministers, and so forth.
- The Commission operates through a College of Commissioners, with one representative from each member state.

EU policy-making also involves numerous other actors: non-member governments, subnational authorities, business corporations, and interest groups like trade unions and environmental organizations.

23.5 THE EU INSTITUTIONS

In this section, we turn to examine the institutions that exercise executive power.

23.5.1 THE EUROPEAN COUNCIL

The European Council emerged in 1974 as an informal leadership forum and remained outside the EU's formal institutional framework until the Lisbon Treaty. The Lisbon Treaty empowered it to set the Union's directions and priorities rather than merely provide guidelines, making it a central decision-making body.

Article 15 TEU

1. The European Council shall provide the Union with the necessary impetus for its development and shall define the general political directions and priorities thereof. It shall not exercise legislative functions.

From an EU perspective, the European Council:

- decides the overall direction and political priorities of the EU;
- resolves complex or sensitive issues that cannot be resolved at lower levels of intergovernmental cooperation;
- deliberates on EU common foreign and security policy;
- initiates cooperation in new areas of activity;
- nominates and appoints candidates for senior EU positions, including the European Central Bank and the Commission.

Composition and leadership: The European Council comprises the heads of state or government of all member states, its President, and the President of the Commission. The Lisbon Treaty formalized the European Council as an institution and created a dedicated President, elected by qualified majority for a term of two-and-a-half years (renewable once). The President cannot hold national office, chairs meetings, coordinates the workload with the Commission President, and ensures implementation of decisions, including reporting to the European Parliament after each summit.

Functions and operations: The European Council provides leadership across political and economic integration, internal economic matters, foreign policy issues, budget disputes, treaty revisions, membership applications, and institutional reform. Meeting typically seven times a year, and up to 13 times during crisis situations (e.g. the euro crisis or the Coronavirus pandemic), it has no formal legislative power but compensates by exercising agenda-setting authority over policy, resources, and institutional developments.

In July 2020, the European Council agreed on the EU's extraordinary recovery effort to ameliorate the economic consequences of the Coronavirus pandemic: the Next Generation EU recovery instrument, worth over €800 billion over 2021–2026.[12] This temporary facility authorizes the Commission to borrow on capital markets and distribute funds through grants (€390 billion) and loans (€360 billion) based on national recovery and resilience plans. The programme establishes the principle of joint EU borrowing backed by common guarantees, linking financial assistance to the EU's green and digital transitions.[13]

Institutional character: The European Council operates intergovernmentally through consensus, deferring decisions on unresolved issues. Despite this formal structure, it functions increasingly as a crisis manager, commanding media attention and generating unified responses during emergencies. While theoretically an intergovernmental forum, it actively leads EU institutional politics, creating tension between its formal status and practical influence.

The Council of the European Union handles day-to-day legislative and executive work.

23.5.2 THE COUNCIL OF THE EUROPEAN UNION

The Council of the European Union—informally called the 'Council of Ministers' or 'Council' in the Treaties—serves as the EU's primary decision-making institution. While the European Council handles 'high politics,' the Council manages day-to-day governance.

The Council operates with dual constitutional functions. Legislatively, it '*shall, jointly with the European Parliament, exercise legislative and budgetary functions*' (Art. 16(1) TEU). Executively, it

[12] In 2025 prices It amounts to €750 billion in 2018 prices.

[13] European Commission, *Recovery Plan for Europe*, https://commission.europa.eu/strategy-and-policy/recovery-plan-europe_en

'consists of '*a representative of each Member State at ministerial level, who may commit the government of the Member State in question and cast its vote*' (Art.16(2) TEU). These representatives defend national interests, making the Council primarily an intergovernmental institution that counterbalances the supranational Commission.

As a forum where national and EU-level politicians and officials negotiate and legislate, the Council aggregates national interests into a common 'Council position', which it then defends against the European Parliament as co-legislator. Although permanent, the Council lacks constant membership; its composition varies by the policy area under consideration. Ministers remain accountable to their national parliaments, providing the Council's decisions with indirect democratic legitimacy.

23.5.2.1 Functions

Although structurally intergovernmental, the Council adopts different operational modes depending on the policy procedure involved. Under the TFEU, the Council exercises five core responsibilities:

- Legislative co-decision: negotiating and enacting European legislation with the European Parliament through the ordinary legislative procedure (accounting for 90 per cent of all legislative acts);
- Policy coordination: harmonising member state policies in areas like economic and fiscal policy or education (typically requiring unanimity);
- External relations: managing EU foreign affairs alongside the European Council and High Representative;
- Treaty-making: concluding international agreements negotiated by the Commission (with EP and member state consent);
- Budgetary authority: approving the EU budget jointly with the European Parliament.

In legislative co-decision (see Section 23.5.7), the Council operates primarily *supranationally*, meaning that member states have delegated (or 'pooled') their decision-making powers to the European Union. Regular ministerial meetings (some monthly, others annually), informal contacts, and routine bargaining foster continual negotiation and close cooperation, generating shared understanding and collective identity among national executives.

Conversely, in economically sensitive areas like fiscal policy or foreign and security policy, the Council functions *intergovernmentally*. Here, member states retain sovereign control and decisions require unanimity, effectively granting each state veto power over outcomes.

23.5.2.2 Composition and structure

The Council operates through national representatives at the ministerial level who, while not directly elected to EU roles, are dispatched as ministers of their respective national government (occasionally regional ministers in federal states like Belgium and Germany). With 70–80 meetings annually lasting one to two days, the Council maintains a busy schedule between its Brussels headquarters and Luxembourg (where it meets in April, June, and October, honouring a 1965 institutional compromise). The Council meets in 10 different configurations, based on policy areas.[14]

(i) General Affairs (GAC)

(ii) Foreign Affairs (FAC)

[14] In the 1990s there were 22 configurations; this was reduced to 16 in June 2000 and then to nine in June 2002. Since the entry into force of the Treaty of Lisbon on 1 December 2009, there are ten configurations.

(iii) Economic and Financial Affairs (Ecofin)

(iv) Agriculture and Fisheries (Agrifish)

(v) Justice and Home Affairs Council (JHA)

(vi) Employment, Social Policy, Health and Consumer Affairs Council (EPSCO)

(vii) Competitiveness (COMPET)

(viii) Transport, Telecommunications and Energy (TTE)

(ix) Environment (ENV)

(x) Education, Youth, Culture and Sport (EYC).

Each configuration handles policy and legislation within its competence, with ministers empowered '*to commit the government of the Member State*'.[15] Though ministers derive legitimacy from national appointment, their collective Council responsibilities create ambiguity about representation and accountability.

QUESTIONS

1. **Supranational versus intergovernmental operation**: Using the five Council responsibilities listed above, identify which areas involve pooled sovereignty (supranational) and which preserve national vetoes (intergovernmental). Why might member states accept majority voting for legislative co-decision but insist on unanimity for fiscal policy?
2. **Democratic legitimacy**: The Council's ministers are accountable to national parliaments rather than directly elected to EU positions. Does this 'indirect' democratic legitimacy adequately represent EU citizens? Compare this model with the legitimacy claims of the directly elected European Parliament.
3. **Institutional balance**: The Council serves simultaneously as part of the EU's executive (alongside the European Council and the Commission) and as a co-legislator (alongside the Parliament). How does this dual role differ from the traditional separation of powers? Consider whether this overlap strengthens or weakens the Council's effectiveness in representing member state interests.

23.5.3 THE COMMISSION

While every political system requires institutions for agenda-setting and leadership—a role the European Council fulfils—the Commission serves as the EU's principal executive institution.

The Commission embodies a duality. As the EU's civil service, it comprises the Directorates-General (DGs)—the permanent bureaucracy that manages Union administrative and policy affairs, and assisted by national agencies that implement day-to-day tasks. Yet the Commission also resembles *cabinet* government: the Commission President leads the *College* of Commissioners, which is collectively accountable to the directly elected European Parliament. Appointed every five years following EP elections, the Commission is formally independent of member states (Art. 17(3) TEU). The two-sided nature of the Commission makes it arguably '*the strangest administration ever created*'.[16]

[15] Art. 16(2) TEU.

[16] J. Peterson, 'The College of Commissioners', in D. Hodson and J. Peterson (eds) *The Institutions of the European Union*, 4th edn (2017, Oxford: OUP), p. 109.

As a supranational institution independent of national governments, the Commission promotes '*the general interest of the Union and take appropriate initiatives to that end*' (Art. 17(2) TEU). It represents, according to its former Secretary General, '*the only organization that is paid to think European*'.[17] This European perspective underpins its exclusive right of legislative initiative: '*Union legislative acts may only be adopted on the basis of a Commission proposal, except where the Treaties provide otherwise*' Art. 17(2) TEU.

The Commission's executive functions span three core areas: initiating and drafting legislation, implementing decisions adopted by the Council and Parliament through co-decision, and ensuring that all member states comply with the law. In this latter capacity as 'guardian of the treaties', the Commission may launch formal infringement proceedings against non-compliant member states[18] and, ultimately, refer the case to the Court of Justice of the EU.

23.5.3.1 How does the Commission exercise power?

The Commission's executive authority resembles the powers of national governments in several respects. Like the UK government's near-monopoly on policy initiation, the Commission enjoys exclusive legislative initiative, while its executive responsibilities blur the traditional political-administrative divide. The Commission operates through three tiers:

- Political leadership: the College of Commissioners proposes policies, initiates legislation, arbitrates disputes, and negotiates international agreements;
- Administrative machinery: the Directorates-General handle legislative drafting, budget management (including Structural Funds designed to reduce regional disparities), and policy regulation in competition, agriculture, and trade;
- Implementation networks: committees and agencies that monitor and regulate compliance with EU primary and secondary law.

As European integration has deepened through successive treaty revisions, transferring national competences to the EU level, Commission powers have expanded across most governance functions. Key powers include:

- Legislative initiative: While the European Council and Parliament may request proposals,[19] the Commission retains ultimate discretion. Officials draft proposals for College approval before submission to Parliament and Council for decision.
- Implementation and enforcement: As treaty guardian, the Commission ensures institutional compliance and may initiate infringement proceedings against member states (Art. 258 TFEU).
- Mediation: Acting in the '*general interest of the Union*' (Art. 17(1) TEU), the Commission serves as an honest broker between member states and institutions.

Yet the Commission differs fundamentally from national governments, resembling a specialized regulatory agency instead. While possessing rule-making and policy powers, it lacks taxation authority, coercive enforcement mechanisms, or military capacity. As a former ECJ judge observed, '*the Community [now Union] is only able to exist as a Community of law. It has no weapons or armies, it is held together by the authority of law*'.[20] The Commission's competence covers 'regulatory policies'

[17] Interview with European Commission Secretary-General Catherine Day, *EurActiv*, 25 September 2006.

[18] Art. 258 TFEU. [19] Art. 225 TFEU.

[20] U. Everling, 'The *Maastricht* judgment of the Federal Constitutional Court and its significance for the development of the European Union' (1994) 14 Yearbook of European Law 1, 18. See also Sir Francis G. Jacobs, *The Sovereignty of Law: The European Way* (2007, Cambridge: Cambridge University Press), ch. 4.

(competition, agriculture, trade) rather than 'non-regulatory policies' (income redistribution), reflecting its financial dependence on member states and distinguishing it from traditional government models.

Constitutional law both *empowers* political institutions by defining their functions and *constrains* them through accountability mechanisms. The EU features a complex executive architecture—the Council, Commission, and (since Lisbon) the increasingly prominent European Council. Having examined how these institutions exercise authority, we must now address how that power is controlled and constrained.

QUESTIONS

1. **Distribution of executive power**: Identify which executive functions are performed by the European Council, the Council of the European Union, and the Commission. Using specific examples from the text, explain why executive power is divided among three institutions rather than concentrated in a single body.
2. **The European Council's evolution**: The text states that the European Council 'remained outside the EU's formal institutional framework until the Lisbon Treaty'. What powers did Lisbon grant it? Compare its role in the €800 billion COVID recovery package with its formal treaty powers under Art. 15 TEU.
3. **The Council's dual nature**: Using the Council's five responsibilities listed in the text, identify which involve intergovernmental decision-making (requiring unanimity) and which involve supranational decision-making (using qualified majority voting). What explains these differences?
4. **Democratic legitimacy**: The Commission is described as having 'exclusive legislative initiative' despite being unelected. Consider three potential sources of legitimacy for the Commission: (a) appointment by elected governments, (b) oversight by the European Parliament, and (c) its role as guardian of the treaties. Which provides the strongest democratic justification?

23.5.4 THE EUROPEAN PARLIAMENT

From Assembly to Parliament: The European Parliament traces its origins to the ECSC's assembly of 1952, when members were drawn from national parliaments. Since direct elections began in 1979, the EP has transformed from a consultative body to a co-legislator.

Evolution of legislative powers: Initially, the EP merely offered non-binding opinions before Council legislation. The institution persistently campaigned for genuine co-legislative status, achieved incrementally through successive treaty reforms. The Single European Act (1986) introduced the co-operation procedure, allowing the Council to adopt Commission proposals with EP support via QMV—though unanimous Council votes could override EP rejections.

The breakthrough came with the Maastricht co-decision procedure (1992), which was extended by Amsterdam and renamed the '*ordinary legislative procedure*' in Lisbon (Art. 289 TFEU). This established institutional parity: both EP and Council must consent before legislation can be adopted. The EU now operates a bicameral legislature: Council ministers represent member states and MEPs represent Union citizens.

Representative character and composition: Lisbon transformed the EP's representative basis from '*peoples of the States brought together in the Community*' to representatives of '*the Union's citizens*'

(Art. 14(2) TEU). These 705 MEPs (since UK withdrawal) are elected every five years '*by direct universal suffrage in a free and secret ballot*' (Art. 14(3) TEU), with EU citizens entitled to vote and stand as candidates in their state of residence.[21] Despite varied national electoral systems (closed lists, open lists, single transferable vote), the German Federal Constitutional Court recognised the EP as '*an additional independent source*' of democratic legitimacy for 450 million Europeans.[22]

The EP exercises three essential functions: co-legislating with the Council on most EU law, jointly controlling the EU budget, and holding the Commission accountable through questioning, hearings, and the power to dismiss the entire College of Commissioners.

Legitimacy challenges: Legitimacy requires public engagement, and the EP struggles with citizen disconnection and perceptions of irrelevance with largely unknown politicians. This raises questions about how the democracy and legitimacy deficits can be addressed, particularly the missing link in accountability between citizens and EU governance. These challenges remain central to contemporary debates about the EU's future constitutional development.

The European Parliament operates across three cities in an arrangement critics call a 'travelling circus'. While Brussels hosts the bulk of parliamentary work—committee meetings, political group sessions, MEP offices, and increasingly plenary sessions—Strasbourg remains the official seat for 12 mandatory four-day plenary sessions annually. The General Secretariat operates from Luxembourg.[23]

This monthly relocation of MEPs, staff, and EU bureaucracy incurs estimated annual costs of €156–204 million, and it also has environmental impacts that many parliamentarians consider unacceptable. The arrangement reflects historical compromise rather than functional logic, embedded in treaty protocols that require unanimous consent to change—effectively giving France a veto over any attempt to consolidate Parliament's operations in Brussels.

Unlike the UK Parliament's legislative supremacy, the EP operates within a system of shared institutional responsibility. While it has gained co-equal legislative status, it cannot initiate legislation (only the Commission can) and shares budgetary authority with the Council—illustrating how the EU's 'institutional balance' differs from Westminster's concentrated power model.

Figure 23.1 The European Parliament Building in Brussels (outside and interior)

[21] See further Art. 19(2) TEC (Art. 22(2) TFEU), and Directive 93/109/EC (OJ No. L329, 30 December 1993, p. 34).

[22] See Art. 10(2) TEU; quotes from the *Lisbon Treaty* decision in BVerfG, 2 BvE 2/08, 30 June 2009, at [271].

[23] Protocol (No. 6) on the location of the seats of the institutions and of certain bodies and departments of the European Communities and of Europol (1997).

Figure 23.2 The European Parliament Building in Strasbourg

Source: © x-drew/istockphoto.com.

QUESTIONS

1. **Treaty development**: Using the information provided, identify the three key treaty changes that transformed the European Parliament's role (Single European Act 1986, Maastricht 1992, Lisbon 2009). What specific powers did each treaty grant? Why might member states have agreed to strengthen an institution they cannot directly control?
2. **Democratic functions**: The text identifies three essential EP functions: co-legislation, budget control, and Commission oversight. Which of these provides the strongest democratic check on EU power? Consider that the EP cannot initiate legislation and must share budgetary authority with the Council.
3. **Practical challenges**: The Parliament's '*travelling circus*' between Brussels, Strasbourg, and Luxembourg costs €156–204 million annually. Beyond financial waste, how might this arrangement affect the Parliament's ability to connect with EU citizens? What does France's effective veto over consolidation reveal about member state priorities versus institutional efficiency?

23.5.5 THE LEGISLATIVE PROCESS

EU law-making once involved no fewer than 22 different legislative procedures. The Lisbon Treaty simplified this by establishing the '*ordinary legislative procedure*' (OLP)[24] as the principal method for adopting EU legislation, now covering around 85 policy areas.

Our focus centres on TFEU legislation. (Under the TEU, the Council adopts legislation after consulting Parliament through a process of consideration and negotiation.)

[24] Arts 289 and 294 TFEU.

Formal responsibility for initiating TFEU legislative proposals lies with the Commission across all areas subject to co-decision. This constitutes a 'right to propose' rather than a 'right to legislate'—the Council[25] and European Parliament[26] may request Commission proposals, though the Commission retains discretion over whether to comply. The European Council's agenda-setting role increasingly shapes not only broad EU directions but also specific legislation, creating a principal-agent relationship with the Commission in certain areas.[27]

While theoretically exclusive, the Commission's initiative power operates within a complex web of influences. Though no single source drives proposals, the Commission's annual work programme demonstrates real legislative power. As Art. 294(2) TFEU states: '*The Commission shall submit a proposal to the European Parliament and the Council.*' Once submitted, proposals proceed to the legislature under the ordinary legislative procedure.

23.5.6 THE DECISION-MAKING PROCESS IN THE ORDINARY LEGISLATIVE PROCEDURE

The OLP operates through up to four stages—first reading, second reading, conciliation, and third reading—though legislation may be adopted whenever Council and Parliament reach agreement. This flexibility distinguishes EU law-making from the rigid UK parliamentary procedures where Bills must complete all stages:

- **First reading**: The Commission simultaneously submits proposals to Council and Parliament. Parliamentary committees (20 specialized committees of 28–86 MEPs) examine proposals, appointing rapporteurs to draft reports with amendments for plenary consideration. Without time constraints, the first reading encourages early agreement—legislation adopts immediately if the Council approves Parliament's amendments or Parliament proposes none. Where disagreement persists, the Council adopts a '*common position*' triggering a second reading.
- **Second reading**: Under strict time limits (three months, extendable to four), Parliament may adopt, reject (by absolute majority), or amend (by absolute majority) the Council position. Parliament alone can improve texts at this stage, though amendments are more likely to succeed when limited to procedural changes rather than fundamental alterations. Council approval enables qualified majority adoption; rejection terminates the procedure. Opposition to the Commission requires Council unanimity to proceed. Parliament's veto power—though rarely exercised—operates through threat rather than implementation, as the binary choice (accept/reject) offers no middle ground for compromise.
- **Conciliation and third reading**: Where the second reading fails, the Conciliation Committee (equal Council and Parliament representatives, plus the Commission as mediator) convenes within six weeks. Successful conciliation produces joint texts that require adoption within six weeks; Parliament retains final veto power even at this stage. Without agreement, proposals die automatically.
- **Constitutional maturation**: EU legislative politics has evolved into a system recognisable to observers of bicameral democracies worldwide. The OLP provides comprehensible and accessible decision-making through clear institutional procedures. EU legislation emerges through a slow, transparent, and rule-governed process in which every law is scrutinized by 27 national governments, the directly elected Parliament, and the Commission. With supermajority thresholds

[25] See Art. 241 TFEU. [26] Art. 225 TFEU.

[27] P. Boquillon and M. Dobbels, 'An Elephant on the 13th Floor of the Berlaymont? European Council and Commission relations in legislative agenda setting' (2014) 21 Journal of European Public Policy 20–38.

The ordinary legislative procedure step by step (Article 294 TFEU)

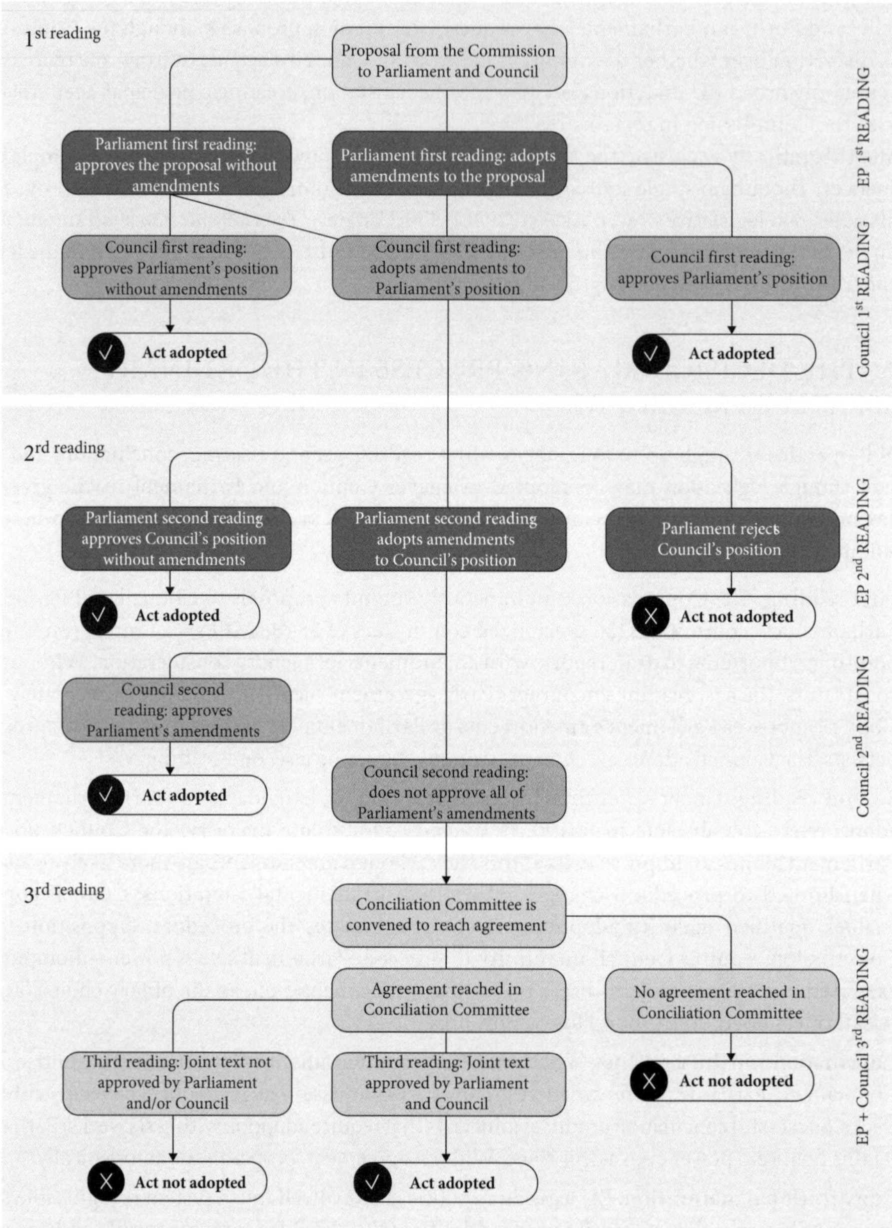

Figure 23.3 Presentation of the OLP

Source: European Parliament, *Handbook on the Ordinary Legislative Procedure: A Guide To How the European Parliament Co-legislates* (November 2017), p. 12.

(55–65 per cent) and two democratically accountable institutions (excluding the Commission), the system embeds multiple sources of legitimacy.

- **Legitimacy challenges**: Low EP electoral turnout potentially undermines the process's democratic credentials. This challenge reveals the complexity of legitimacy and democracy beyond the nation-state context. Supranational organizations like the EU require an understanding of legitimacy's multiple dimensions—input, output, and throughput—that extend beyond traditional democratic theory.

QUESTIONS

1. **Legislative initiative**: The Commission holds the exclusive right to propose legislation under Art. 294(2) TFEU. Using examples from the text, explain the difference between the Commission's '*right to propose*' and a '*right to legislate*'. How can the Council (Art. 241 TFEU) and Parliament (Art. 225 TFEU) influence what the Commission proposes?
2. **Co-decision principle**: The ordinary legislative procedure requires both Council and Parliament to agree before legislation is adopted. How does this differ from: (a) the UK system, where the Commons can override the Lords, and (b) international treaties that typically require unanimous state consent?
3. **First reading comparison**: In the EU's first reading, legislation can be adopted immediately if Council and Parliament agree. In the UK Parliament's first reading, the Bill's title is simply read out with no debate. What does this difference suggest about where the real legislative work happens in each system?
4. **Conciliation mechanism**: When Council and Parliament cannot agree after second reading, the Conciliation Committee has six weeks to find a compromise. Given that this committee has equal representation from both institutions plus Commission mediation, why might Parliament still retain 'final veto power' at this stage?

23.5.7 INCORPORATING EU LEGISLATION INTO NATIONAL LAW

The legislative process produces five types of legislative acts (regulations, directives, decisions, recommendations, and opinions), though only regulations and directives are important for our purposes (see Box 23.3 for some examples).

Article 288 TFEU

A regulation shall have general application. It shall be binding in its entirety and directly applicable in all Member States.

A directive shall be binding, as to the result to be achieved, upon each Member State to which it is addressed, but shall leave to the national authorities the choice of form and methods.

[...]

This legislation constitutes 'secondary legislation', while the treaties form 'primary legislation'. Once adopted by the Council, the question becomes how regulations and directives integrate with domestic legal systems—a process that differs fundamentally between these two instruments.

23.5.7.1 Regulations

Regulations automatically become legally effective in domestic law upon EU institutional approval under the TFEU. As '*directly applicable*' instruments, they require no further action to create legal effects—national parliaments play no role in transposing them into domestic law. Indeed, national implementation through domestic legislation may violate EU law, even where governments consider such action desirable.[28]

23.5.7.2 Directives

Directives target member states rather than citizens or businesses directly. While binding as to objectives, they grant member states discretion over implementation methods and administrative arrangements. Member states must amend their domestic laws to achieve the directive's specified results through a process known as 'transposition' or 'implementation', typically within twelve to eighteen months.

BOX 23.3 EXAMPLES OF REGULATIONS AND DIRECTIVES

- Regulation No. 2016/679 General Data Protection Regulation (GDPR) is a regulation in EU law on data protection and privacy for all individuals within the European Union.
- Directive 2003/88/EC (the Working Time Directive), which gives workers the right to paid annual leave, daily and weekly rest periods, and limits the working week to 48 hours.
- Directive 2000/43/EC on implementing the principle of equal treatment between persons irrespective of racial or ethnic origin (aka the Race Directive).

Regulations and directives range from constitutionally significant measures (such as equal treatment in employment) and politically consequential policies (like automotive emission standards) to technical specifications (such as maximum design speeds for forestry tractors).

QUESTIONS

1. **Commission's role**: Article 294(2) TFEU states '*The Commission shall submit a proposal to the European Parliament and the Council*'. Why does the Commission have the exclusive right to propose legislation? What problems might arise if the Parliament or Council could directly introduce legislation?

[28] See Case 39/72 *Commission v Italy* [1973] ECR 101.

2. **Comparing legislative systems:** The UK Parliament can pass legislation even if the House of Lords objects (using the Parliament Acts). The EU requires both Council and Parliament to agree through the OLP. Which system provides stronger democratic legitimacy? Consider both efficiency and representation in your answer.
3. **Strategic behaviour in the OLP:** At second reading, Parliament can only accept or reject the Council's position by an absolute majority. Why might Parliament sometimes prefer to accept imperfect legislation rather than risk the conciliation process? Use the information about time limits and voting thresholds in your answer.
4. **Regulations versus directives:** A regulation becomes law immediately across all member states, while a directive requires national implementation. When might the EU choose one instrument over the other? Consider the examples given (GDPR as a regulation, Working Time as a directive) to support your analysis.
5. **Democratic input:** Trace how a Commission proposal becomes law through the OLP. At which stages can democratically elected representatives (MEPs and national ministers) modify or block legislation? Does this provide sufficient democratic control over EU law-making?

23.6 CONCLUDING COMMENTS

This chapter has examined the constitutional frameworks through which the European Union's executive functions are exercised and how the EU is held to account. We have seen that executive power is distributed across three institutions—the European Council, the Council of the European Union, and the Commission—each serving distinct but overlapping functions. This distribution reflects the EU's fundamental tension between supranational integration and member state sovereignty.

The legislative process, particularly through the ordinary legislative procedure, demonstrates how the EU has evolved from an international organization into a sophisticated law-making system with its own democratic mechanisms. The European Parliament's transformation from consultative assembly to co-legislator represents a significant, if incomplete, democratization of EU governance.

Key questions remain about the EU's democratic legitimacy. While the Parliament provides direct electoral representation and the Council represents member state governments, the Commission's unelected status and exclusive right of legislative initiative continue to generate debate about the EU's democratic credentials.

Understanding EU institutions remains essential for UK lawyers. The continuing need for UK-EU cooperation on trade, security, and regulatory matters means these institutions will continue to influence UK law and policy, albeit from outside rather than within.

To carry on exploring the European Union, turn to Chapter 24. To explore the executive functions related to the UK government, turn to Chapter 10, which looks at the use of prerogative powers.

FURTHER READING

Anderson, P., *Ever Closer Union?: Europe in the West* (2021, London: Verso).

Hodson, D., Puetter, U., Saurugger, S., and Peterson, J., (eds) *The Institutions of the European Union*, 5th edn (2021, Oxford: OUP).

Kenealy, D., Hadfield, A., Corbett, R., and Peterson, J., *The European Union: How Does It Work?*, 6th edn (2022, Oxford: OUP).

McCormick, J., *Understanding the European Union: A Concise Introduction*, 8th edn (2020, Basingstoke: Macmillan).

Nugent, N., *The Government and Politics of the European Union*, 8th edn (2017, Basingstoke: Macmillan).

Pinder, J. and Usherwood, S., *The European Union: A Very Short Introduction*, 4th edn (2018, Oxford: OUP).

24

JOINING AND LEAVING THE EUROPEAN UNION

CENTRAL ISSUES

1. This chapter examines the key European Union (EU) principles of direct effect and supremacy. Neither principle appears in the Treaty on the Functioning of the European Union (TFEU) but was developed by the European Court of Justice (ECJ), which understood the EU as constituting 'a new legal order'. Direct effect allows individuals to rely on EU law directly in national courts, though its precise scope remains contested. The doctrine of supremacy requires national courts to apply EU law when it conflicts with domestic legislation. Both principles continue to apply in specific circumstances after Brexit through the Withdrawal Agreement.
2. The chapter then examines how the UK joined and left the EU. We consider the UK's accession to the European Economic Community in 1973, focusing on parliamentary supremacy and the European Communities Act 1972, before discussing how UK courts responded to EU law. This includes landmark cases such as Factortame and their constitutional implications, as well as the Supreme Court's analysis of fundamental constitutional principles in HS2.
3. We examine the complex withdrawal process following the 2016 referendum. This covers the Article 50 mechanism, the legislative framework including the European Union (Withdrawal) Act 2018 and the European Union (Withdrawal Agreement) Act 2020, and the concept of 'retained EU law'. The chapter analyses the particular challenges posed by devolution, including the Scottish Continuity Bill reference and the breach of the Sewel Convention.
4. The chapter addresses specific constitutional challenges arising from EU withdrawal. These include the Protocol on Northern Ireland/Ireland and its creation of differential legal arrangements within the UK, the Internal Market Act 2020 and its impact on devolution, and the ongoing process of legal divergence from EU law. We examine how these developments have created tensions within the UK's territorial constitution.
5. Finally, we consider the broader constitutional implications of the UK's relationship with EU law. This includes how EU withdrawal has affected parliamentary supremacy, the role of the courts in mediating between different legal orders, and the challenges of managing a multi-level constitutional system after EU withdrawal. The chapter demonstrates how leaving the EU has proven constitutionally more complex than joining it.

24.1 INTRODUCTION

Although the UK left the European Union in 2020, EU law continues to influence the UK constitution. EU membership between 1973 and 2020 altered UK constitutional law in three respects. First, EU law introduced legal principles that challenged parliamentary supremacy. Second, UK courts had to develop new approaches when the UK joined the EU in 1973. Third, the UK's withdrawal from the EU in 2020 created constitutional complexities that remain unresolved.

BOX 24.1 TIMELINE: KEY DATES IN UK-EU CONSTITUTIONAL RELATIONS

- 1957: Treaty of Rome signed (before UK membership)
- 1960s: ECJ establishes direct effect (van Gend end Loos 1963) and supremacy (Costa 1964)
- 1973: UK joins EEC; European Communities Act 1972 comes into force
- 1975: First UK referendum on EEC membership (67 per cent vote to remain)
- 1986: Single European Act signed (major constitutional change expanding EU powers)
- 1991: *Factortame* decision: UK courts disapply an Act of Parliament for the first time
- 1992: Maastricht Treaty creates the European Union
- 2009: Lisbon Treaty enters into force (consolidates EU constitutional framework)
- 2016: EU referendum: 51.9 per cent vote to leave EU 2017 - UK triggers Article 50 (29 March)
- 2017: *Miller I*: Supreme Court rules Parliament must authorize Article 50
- 2018: European Union (Withdrawal) Act 2018 passed
- 2019: *Miller II*: Supreme Court rules prorogation unlawful
- 2020: UK formally leaves EU (31 January); Withdrawal Agreement enters into force
- 2020: Internal Market Act 2020 passed without devolved consent
- 2023: Retained EU Law (Revocation and Reform) Act 2023 transforms retained EU law into 'assimilated law'.

24.2 DIRECT EFFECT AND SUPREMACY: HOW EU LAW CHALLENGED PARLIAMENTARY SUPREMACY

Two legal principles define the relationship between EU law and national law, creating the EU's 'supranational' legal order. While these principles shaped UK law for nearly five decades, their general application ended with EU withdrawal, though they continue to apply in specific areas under the Withdrawal Agreement.

Direct effect means that individuals can rely on EU law directly in their national courts, without waiting for their government to pass implementing legislation. If EU law gives you a right, you can enforce it immediately before a UK judge. The supremacy of EU law means that when EU law conflicts with national law, EU law overrides it. National courts must set aside conflicting domestic legislation, including Acts of Parliament.

This represented a significant constitutional change because it gave UK courts a power they had never possessed: the ability to 'disapply' Acts of Parliament. While UK courts still cannot declare

Acts of Parliament 'unconstitutional' and void (unlike constitutional courts in other countries), they could set aside conflicting statutes to give effect to EU law.

These principles cannot be found anywhere in the EU treaties themselves.[1] Instead, they were created by the European Court of Justice (ECJ) in two landmark cases from the early 1960s, before the UK even joined the EU. This judge-made law fundamentally changed the nature of European integration.

The first landmark case involved a Dutch transport company called van Gend en Loos. The case raised a fundamental question: could the rules in the Treaty of Rome create rights that individuals could enforce directly in national courts? In deciding in favour of the company against the Dutch authorities, the ECJ delivered a landmark judgment that established the principle of direct effect.

Case 26/62 NV Algemene Transporten Expeditie Onderneming van Gend en Loos v Nederlandse Administratie der Belastingen

[1963] ECR 1, 12

> The European Economic Community constitutes a new legal order of international law for the benefit of which the States have limited their sovereign rights, albeit within limited fields, and the subjects of which comprise not only the Member States but also their nationals.
>
> Independently of the legislation of Member States, Community law not only imposes obligations on individuals but is also intended to confer upon them rights which become part of their legal heritage. These rights arise not only where they are expressly granted by the Treaty but also by reason of obligations which the Treaty imposes in a clearly defined way upon individuals as well as upon the Member States and upon the institutions of the Community.
>
> [. . .]
>
> According to the spirit, the general scheme and the wording of the EEC Treaty, [Article 30 TFEU] must be interpreted as producing direct effects and creating individual rights which national courts must protect.

You will recall from Chapter 23 that under Art. 288 TFEU EU regulations are 'directly applicable' in each member state. 'Directly applicable' means that certain provisions of EU law (such as regulations and some Treaty provisions) become part of national law without the need for further enactment. This should not be confused with direct effect, which is a doctrine developed by the ECJ in *van Gend en Loos*. Certain provisions of EU law (Treaty provisions, regulations, and directives) are directly effective in that they create '*individual rights that the national courts have to protect*' without any implementing measure in the member state in question.[2] In short, the subjects of EU law are not only the member states (as recognised under public international law), but also EU citizens. To be enforced against a member state by an EU citizen, any EU obligation must meet two conditions. It must be (i) clear and precise (that is, the concepts contained in the provision must not leave to the member states an element of discretion in applying EU law), and (ii) 'unconditional', i.e. it must not depend on the control, judgement, or discretion of an EU institution or another member state.

[1] This principle of supremacy (or primacy) was made express by Art. I-6 of the Draft Constitutional Treaty, and is now moved to a footnote in Declaration No. 17 to the Lisbon Treaty.

[2] Case 26/62 van Gend en Loos [1963] ECR 1, 2.

The concepts of direct applicability and direct effect operate differently depending on the type of EU law. An EU directive may be directly effective (if it is clear, precise, unconditional, and creates rights), but not directly applicable (an EU directive requires further implementation). A Treaty provision may be directly applicable, but not directly effective (because it does not satisfy the conditions of direct effect). A regulation may be both directly applicable and directly effective.[3] An EU regulation on product safety is both directly applicable (automatically becomes part of national law) and directly effective (consumers can enforce it in court). An EU directive on workers' rights may be directly effective (workers can enforce rights) but requires national implementation to be fully operative.

The second landmark case, *Costa v ENEL*, established the supremacy of EU law over national law. Since the purpose of the EEC was to create a common market among different states, the ECJ argued that this aim would be undermined if Community law were deemed subordinate to the national laws of the member states. *Costa* involved a challenge to the legality of an electricity bill issued by the newly nationalized Italian state electricity authority. The Court echoed its ruling in *van Gend en Loos*, but also went one step further.

Case 6/64 Flaminio Costa v ENEL

[1964] ECR 585, 593–4

By contrast with ordinary international treaties, the EEC Treaty has created its own legal system which, on the entry into force of the Treaty, became an integral part of the legal systems of the member states and which their courts are bound to apply.

By creating a Community of unlimited duration, having its own institutions, its own personality, its own legal capacity and capacity of representation on an international plane and, more particularly, real powers stemming from a limitation of sovereignty or a transfer of powers from the states of the Community, the member states have limited their sovereign rights, albeit within limited fields, and have thus created a body of law which binds both their nationals and themselves.

[...]

It follows from all these observations that the law stemming from the Treaty, an independent source of law, could not, because of its special and original nature, be overridden by domestic legal provisions, however framed, without being deprived of its character as Community law and without the legal basis of the Community itself being called into question.

The ECJ's reasoning in Costa established that EU law is fundamentally different from ordinary international law. According to the Court, EU law creates an autonomous legal system with its own institutions exercising '*real powers*'—making it distinct from other international organizations where states retain full control.

The Court concluded that member states cannot pass later legislation that contradicts EU law. Without this supremacy principle, the ECJ argued, EU law would be '*quite meaningless*' and member states' treaty obligations would be '*merely contingent*'—depending on whether national governments chose to respect them.

[3] J. A. Winter, 'Direct applicability and direct effect: Two distinct and different concepts in Community Law' (1972) 9(4) Common Market Law Review 425–38.

In the following extract, Paul Craig identifies four different rationales that justify the supremacy of EU law:

P. P. Craig, 'Constitutionalising constitutional law: HS2 (case comment)'
[2014] *Public Law* 373–92, 376–7

[The reasoning of the ECJ in *Costa* provides] justificatory rationales for the supremacy of EU law over national law that were contractarian, functional, egalitarian and analytical. The contractarian argument was that EU law should be accorded primacy because it flowed from the agreement made by the Member States when they joined the European Union through which they limited their sovereign rights. This was reinforced by a more functional argument, to the effect that the aims of the Treaty could not be achieved unless primacy was accorded to EU law. A level playing field was integral to a common market and would be undermined if a Member State could choose not to accept an EU law, since it would thereby jeopardise the uniformity that was central to realisation of the EEC's objectives. The egalitarian argument was related to but distinct from the functional. Ratification of a multilateral treaty is akin to joining a club, from which the recipient gains benefits and accepts constraints on autonomous individual action. This is indeed the logic of collective action. Viewed from this perspective if a Member State claims that its law should be accorded priority in the event of a conflict with EU law it is seeking unequal treatment in its favour, by continuing to take all benefits of membership while refusing to accept the attendant obligations. This was reinforced by an analytical argument that the obligations undertaken by the Member States in the Treaty would be merely contingent rather than unconditional if they were to be subject to later legislative acts by Member States that could trump EEC law.

The combined effect of *van Gend en Loos* and *Costa* meant that national courts had to apply EU law and set aside conflicting national law. This worked well for technical areas like customs duties or product standards, where harmonization made obvious sense. But what should happen when EU law conflicted with fundamental national constitutional principles?

The ECJ's answer was uncompromising. In *Internationale Handelsgesellschaft*,[4] the Court held that no national law—not even fundamental constitutional principles—could override EU law. In *Simmenthal*,[5] the Court reinforced this, ruling that national courts must apply EU law even when it conflicts with later national legislation. Member states could not use the principle of implied repeal to undermine EU law.

The relationship between UK law and EU law became more complex after withdrawal, not simpler. While EU law supremacy no longer applies to new UK legislation passed after withdrawal, it continues to operate through the Withdrawal Agreement, particularly regarding Northern Ireland and citizens' rights.[6] The European Union (Withdrawal) Act 2018 initially established a complex transitional framework in which retained EU law took precedence over pre-withdrawal UK statutes and UK courts were required to interpret pre-withdrawal domestic law 'as far as possible' in accordance with EU law. However, this framework has now been largely superseded by the Retained EU Law (Revocation and Reform) Act 2023, which transformed retained EU law into 'assimilated law' and removed most of these continuing obligations.

[4] Case 11/70 *Internationale Handelsgesellschaft mbH v Einfuhr- und Vorratsstelle für Getreide und Futtermittel* [1970] ECR 1125.

[5] Case 106/77 *Amministrazione delle Finanze dello Stato v Simmenthal SpA* [1978] ECR 629.

[6] Article 4 of the Withdrawal Agreement is given domestic effect by s. 7A of the European Union (Withdrawal) Act 2018 (as inserted by s. 5 of the European Union (Withdrawal Agreement) Act 2020).

Article 4 Agreement on the withdrawal of the United Kingdom of Great Britain and Northern Ireland from the European Union

Methods and principles relating to the effect, the implementation and the application of this Agreement

1. The provisions of this Agreement and the provisions of Union law made applicable by this Agreement shall produce in respect of and in the United Kingdom the same legal effects as those which they produce within the Union and its Member States.
2. Accordingly, legal or natural persons shall in particular be able to rely directly on the provisions contained or referred to in this Agreement which meet the conditions for direct effect under Union law.
3. The United Kingdom shall ensure compliance with paragraph 1, including as regards the required powers of its judicial and administrative authorities to disapply inconsistent or incompatible domestic provisions, through domestic primary legislation.

Article 4 requires that the provisions of the Withdrawal Agreement and the provisions of EU law made applicable by the Agreement produce '*the same legal effects*' in the UK as those which they produce within the EU and its member states. It allows private parties to invoke EU rights under the withdrawal agreement before national courts, and it instructs the UK to ensure compliance with its obligations by requiring UK courts to '*disapply*' any domestic legislation that is inconsistent with EU law. In short, the doctrine of supremacy is still relevant, and will continue to apply in UK courts in some future cases.

24.3 THE PROCESS OF THE UK JOINING THE EUROPEAN ECONOMIC COMMUNITY

The United Kingdom, Ireland, and Denmark joined the European Economic Community (EEC) on 1 January 1973,[7] after the UK had overcome significant political obstacles. The UK's path to membership was tortuous—it had first applied in 1961 under Harold Macmillan's Conservative government, recognising that Britain could not afford to remain outside Europe's emerging economic bloc. France vetoed the UK's applications twice (1963 and 1967), with President Charles de Gaulle arguing that Britain was too closely tied to the USA and insufficiently committed to European integration.

The UK also had to overcome its own ambivalence about European integration. As a former colonial power, Britain viewed its legal and political system as superior to, rather than subject to, its Continental counterparts. Many British politicians still believed in the 'special relationship' with the United States and Commonwealth ties as alternatives to European integration.

When Edward Heath's Conservative government finally secured membership in 1972, it faced the challenge of selling EU membership to a skeptical Parliament and public. Crucially, the UK government presented membership primarily as an economic necessity, deliberately deflecting attention from the constitutional changes that membership would bring. As one commentator observed, '*no country was constitutionally as ill-prepared for what was to come as the UK*'.[8]

This was not because the government was unaware of the constitutional implications. The principles of direct effect and supremacy were already well-established by 1973, and senior legal figures

[7] See the Treaty of Accession (1972) Cmnd 7461.

[8] J. Cornford, 'On writing a constitution' (1991) 44 Parliamentary Affairs 558.

had warned of their constitutional consequences. In 1960, Lord Kilmuir, the Lord Chancellor, had advised that EU membership would affect UK sovereignty in three ways:

> Adherence to the [1957] Treaty of Rome would, in my opinion, affect our sovereignty in three ways: Parliament would be required to surrender some of its functions to the organs of the Community; the Crown would be called on to transfer part of its treaty-making power to those organs; our courts of law would sacrifice some degree of independence by becoming subordinate in certain respects to the European Court of Justice . . . In the long run we shall have to decide whether economic factors require us to make some sacrifice of sovereignty. . . .[9]

Despite these warnings, the government chose to focus solely on economic benefits and repeatedly assured Parliament that membership would not affect parliamentary supremacy. Government White Papers insisted there was '*no question of any erosion of essential national sovereignty*'.[10] This deliberate obfuscation would have long-term consequences—the unresolved tension between EU law supremacy and parliamentary supremacy would resurface repeatedly throughout the UK's membership, ultimately contributing to the EU withdrawal debate decades later.

In the context of Community membership, the doctrine of parliamentary supremacy was both an advantage and a source of difficulty.

Parliamentary supremacy offered a practical advantage: whereas other countries, such as Ireland, had to amend their constitutions to accommodate EU law supremacy, the United Kingdom needed only to pass an Act of Parliament—the European Communities Act 1972. Parliamentary supremacy meant the UK could join without complex constitutional amendment procedures.

However, the same doctrine that made joining easier also created ongoing constitutional tension. The European Communities Act 1972 had to give effect to Community law and recognise its supremacy over national law, but could only do so through the obscure language of the statute rather than explicit constitutional amendment. This created ambiguity about whether parliamentary supremacy had actually been limited or merely suspended.

While other member states had clear constitutional frameworks for EU membership, the UK was left with an unresolved tension between parliamentary supremacy and EU law supremacy that would persist throughout its membership.

European Communities Act 1972, s. 2 (repealed)

General Implementation of Treaties

(1) All such rights, powers, liabilities, obligations and restrictions from time to time created or arising by or under the Treaties [. . .] are without further enactment to be given legal effect or used in the United Kingdom [. . .].[11]

(2) [. . .] any enactment passed or to be passed [. . .] shall be construed and have effect subject to the foregoing provisions of this section [. . .].

[9] Public Records Office (PRO), FO 371/150369.

[10] In 1967, on *Legal and Constitutional Implications of United Kingdom Membership of the European Communities* (Cmnd 3301); in 1971, on *UK and European Communities* (Cmnd 4715), para. 29.

[11] This provision has been preserved by s. 7A European Union (Withdrawal) Act 2018.

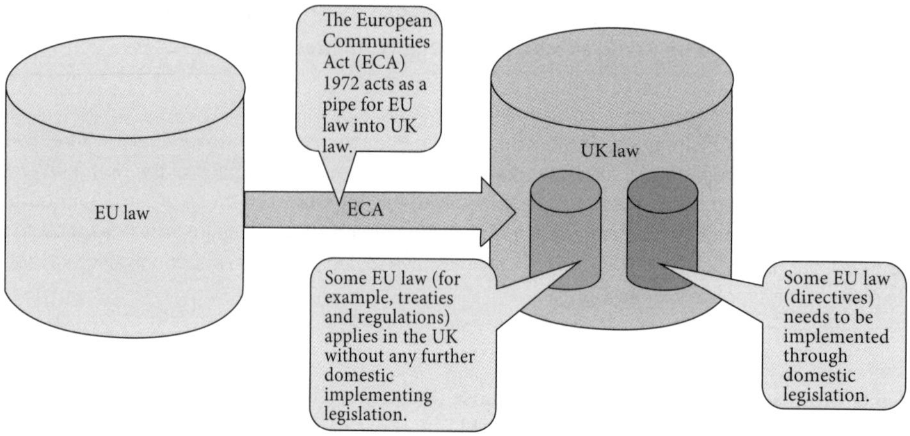

Figure 24.1 The operation of s. 2(1) ECA 1972 as the 'gateway' or 'conduit' to give domestic legal effect to EU law

Source: European Union (Withdrawal) Act: Explanatory Notes, p. 9.

Section 2 was a carefully drafted provision that had to reconcile opposing constitutional forces. It operated as the gateway through which EU law entered the UK legal system, shaped by the requirements of EU law, particularly the pre-existing principles of direct applicability, direct effect, and supremacy that we examined earlier.

As Figure 24.1 shows, EU regulations (which are directly applicable) took immediate effect in UK law under s. 2(1) without any need for further domestic implementing legislation, whether by Act of Parliament or delegated legislation.

Since EU law took priority over national law, section 2(4) had to ensure that directly effective EU law was given priority over all existing and all future statutes ('*passed or to be passed*'). This forward-looking language was essential because Parliament might legislate in future (deliberately or accidentally) in ways that conflicted with EU law.

Section 2 of the European Communities Act 1972 appeared to violate fundamental principles of UK constitutional law. Section 2(1) contradicts Dicey's rule that '*no person or body*' may override an Act of Parliament[12]—yet EU institutions could now do exactly that. Section 2(4) contradicted the principle that Parliament cannot bind its successors[13]—yet future Parliaments were now constrained not to legislate contrary to EU law.

However, these apparent violations could be answered: Parliament remained free to '*make or unmake any law whatsoever*'—including repealing the European Communities Act 1972 itself. Dicey's 'positive' limb of parliamentary supremacy remained intact.

The European Communities Act 1972 created a constitutional problem regarding the source of law in the UK. While the Act provided the legal gateway for EU law, the Supreme Court in

[12] A.V. Dicey, *Introduction to the Study of the Law of the Constitution* (1885; 10th edn 1959, London: Macmillan & Co), pp. 39–40.

[13] Ibid, pp. 41–3. H.W.R. Wade, 'The basis of legal sovereignty' (1955) Cambridge Law Journal 172, 174.

Miller I recognised that this created a more complex relationship than simple domestic authorization:

R (Miller) v Secretary of State for Exiting the European Union
[2017] UKSC 5

> [61] In one sense, of course, it can be said that the 1972 Act is the source of EU law, in that, without that Act, EU law would have no domestic status. But in a more fundamental sense and, we consider, a more realistic sense, where EU law applies in the United Kingdom, it is the EU institutions which are the relevant source of that law. The legislative institutions of the EU can create or abrogate rules of law which will then apply domestically, without the specific sanction of any UK institution. It is true that the UK government and UK-elected members of the European Parliament participate in the EU legislative processes and can influence their outcome, but that does not diminish the point. Further, in the many areas of EU competence which are subject to majority decision, the approval of the United Kingdom is not required for its legislation to take effect domestically. It is also true that EU law enjoys its automatic and overriding effect only by virtue of the 1972 Act, and thus only while it remains in force. That point simply reflects the fact that Parliament was and remains sovereign: so, no new source of law could come into existence without Parliamentary sanction — and without being susceptible to being abrogated by Parliament. However, that in no way undermines our view that it is unrealistic to deny that, so long as that Act remains in force, the EU Treaties, EU legislation and the interpretations placed on these instruments by the Court of Justice are direct sources of UK law

This analysis reveals a tension in the UK's constitutional arrangements during EU membership. While Parliament remained sovereign in principle—retaining the power to repeal the 1972 Act—in practice it had authorized a new source of law that operated independently of ongoing parliamentary control. This helps explain why the process of EU withdrawal proved constitutionally more complex than the process of joining.

The following extract argues that while the European Communities Act 1972 was formally just an ordinary Act of Parliament, its constitutional effects were extraordinary:

G. Phillipson, 'EU Law as an agent of national constitutional change: Miller v Secretary of State for Exiting the European Union' (2017) 36(1) *Yearbook of European Law*, pp. 46–93, 81–3

> Thus the effect of the European Communities Act—the conduit that carries EU law into the UK—was profound indeed. Not only did a vast flood of EU law in the form of thousands of pages of Regulations, and of foundational principles in the Treaties like non-discrimination, flow into the UK legal system, in such quantity and significance that it is widely acknowledged that unpicking it will take government lawyers many years of work. But at the same time the constitution itself was radically changed: the traditional doctrine of parliamentary sovereignty—its very bedrock—was, as we have just seen, significantly modified; dualism was overcome, hierarchies of statutes were established for the first time, and British courts [under s.3(1) European Communities Act] became bound when applying EU law by the rulings of an international court.

The European Communities Act 1972 represented a constitutional watershed that altered the UK's legal order. While presented by the government as a technical measure to facilitate trade, it proved to be one of the most significant Acts in British history—creating tensions between parliamentary supremacy and EU law supremacy that would persist throughout the UK's membership and ultimately contribute to the decision to withdraw.

QUESTIONS

1. Can you explain the difference between 'directly applicable' and 'direct effect'?
2. Explain how the European Communities Act 1972 acted as the 'gateway' to give domestic legal effect to EU law.
3. What constitutional problems did section 2 of the European Communities Act 1972 create for the doctrine of parliamentary supremacy?
4. The Supreme Court in *Miller I* described EU law as having two different constitutional roles: the 1972 Act as the formal 'source' of EU law's domestic status, but EU institutions as the 'more realistic' source of legal rules. Analyse this constitutional paradox and explain why it created tensions for parliamentary supremacy.
5. Both Phillipson and the Supreme Court in Miller I recognise that EU membership changed the UK constitution, yet Parliament retained the power to repeal the European Communities Act 1972. How do you reconcile the view that EU membership created 'profound constitutional change' with the principle that Parliament remained sovereign?

24.4 THE RECEPTION OF EU LAW BY THE UK COURTS

When the European Communities Act 1972 was passed, UK courts faced a new challenge: how to navigate between traditional parliamentary supremacy and the new requirement to apply EU law. They developed two main approaches.

Initially, courts tried to avoid direct conflicts by interpreting UK law to comply with EU law wherever possible. This 'construction' approach involved examining relevant EU Treaty principles, considering EU directives, and interpreting UK legislation to give effect to EU obligations. This worked well in cases like *Pickstone v Freemans*[14] and *Litster v Forth Dry Dock*,[15] where courts could imply words into UK law to achieve EU compliance. A purposive construction of domestic law was justified to give effect to EU law.

But what happened when UK law directly contradicted EU law and could not be reinterpreted? The answer came in the landmark Factortame case.

Spanish fishing companies were 'quota-hopping', i.e. registering boats as British to fish under UK quotas. The UK government passed the Merchant Shipping Act 1988 with nationality requirements designed to stop this practice. Section 14 required fishing vessels to be British-owned,[16] managed

[14] [1989] AC 66. [15] [1990] 1 AC 546.

[16] According to s. 14(2). A fishing vessel was deemed to be British-owned if the legal title to the vessel was vested wholly in one or more qualified persons or companies and if the vessel was beneficially owned by one or more qualified companies or, in relation to not less than 75 per cent, by one or more qualified persons.

from the UK, and operated by British persons or companies.[17] Officials and ministers were aware of the discriminatory nature of their economic policy and the risk that their legislation could constitute a sufficiently serious breach of EC law, giving rise to damages for Factortame. This created a conundrum: what would happen if UK courts were required to choose between applying an Act of Parliament and complying with EU law?

The government's concerns proved justified. After the Merchant Shipping Act 1988 came into force, the United Kingdom was successfully challenged at Community level by the Commission, which brought infringement proceedings under Art. 258 TFEU for a declaration that s. 14 breached the right of freedom of establishment.[18]

Freedom of establishment is one of the fundamental freedoms in the Treaty. Article 49 TFEU allows self-employed persons who legally operate a business in one member state to carry on an economic activity in a stable and continuous way in another member state. Establishment entails a permanent link with another member state for economic purposes, unlike providing services in another member state. Business mobility is further achieved by eliminating discrimination on the grounds of nationality and through the harmonization of national rules.

More significantly for UK constitutional law, Spanish fishing companies sought an interim injunction in British courts to prevent their boats from being deregistered while the legal challenge proceeded. However, under s. 21 of the Crown Proceedings Act 1947, UK courts were prevented from granting injunctions against government ministers. This created a direct conflict between UK law (which prohibited the remedy) and EU law (which, the ECJ would rule, required UK courts to provide effective protection for EU rights).

EU law required UK courts to grant interim relief to protect EU rights, even if this meant setting aside an Act of Parliament. The ECJ's ruling was wholly in line with the earlier case of *Simmenthal*,[19] in which it had ruled that any conflicting provision of national law was deemed '*automatically inapplicable*' by Community law. Nonetheless, its decision in *Factortame I*[20] provoked strong reactions regarding the demise of parliamentary supremacy. Jonathan Aitkin MP described the ruling as 'an historical surrender of some constitutional significance';[21] Teddy Taylor MP said that the decision was 'one of the most frightening things that has happened since the time of King Charles'.[22] In light of the constitutional difficulties that the ECJ's ruling unearthed, would the House of Lords respond by strengthening Parliament's legislative supremacy or by accepting the ECJ's supremacy doctrine?

R v Secretary of State for Transport, ex parte Factortame Ltd (No. 2)
[1991] 1 AC 603, 658

Lord Bridge

Some public comments on the decision of the Court of Justice, affirming the jurisdiction of the courts of the member states to override national legislation if necessary to enable interim relief to be granted in protection of rights under Community law, have suggested that this was a novel and dangerous invasion

[17] According to s. 14(7), 'qualified person' meant a person who was a British citizen resident and domiciled in the United Kingdom, and 'qualified company' meant a company incorporated in the United Kingdom and having its principal place of business there, at least 75 per cent of its shares being owned by one or more qualified persons or companies, and at least 75 per cent of its directors being qualified persons.

[18] Case C-246/89R *EC Commission v United Kingdom (Re Merchant Shipping Rules)* [1989] ECR 3125.

[19] Case 106/77 *Amministrazione delle finanze dello Stato v Simmenthal SpA* [1978] ECR 629.

[20] *R v Secretary of State for Transport, ex parte Factortame Ltd and ors (No. 1)* [1990] 2 AC 85.

[21] Quoted in 'European Court Order Criticized', *The Times*, 27 October 1989.

[22] Quoted in R. Ford and F. Gibb, 'Law officers prepare reply to EC ruling on UK laws', *The Times*, 21 June 1990.

> by a Community institution of the sovereignty of the United Kingdom Parliament. But such comments are based on a misconception. If the supremacy within the European Community of Community law over the national law of member states was not always inherent in the EEC Treaty it was certainly well established in the jurisprudence of the Court of Justice long before the United Kingdom joined the Community. Thus, whatever limitation of its sovereignty Parliament accepted when it enacted the European Communities Act 1972 was entirely voluntary. Under the terms of the 1972 Act it has always been clear that it was the duty of a United Kingdom court, when delivering final judgement, to override any rule of national law found to be in conflict with any directly enforceable rule of Community law. Similarly, when decisions of the Court of Justice have exposed areas of United Kingdom statute law which failed to implement Council directives, Parliament has always loyally accepted the obligation to make appropriate and prompt amendments. Thus there is nothing in any way novel in according supremacy to rules of Community law in areas to which they apply and to insist that, in the protection of rights under Community law, national courts must not be prohibited by rules of national law from granting interim relief in appropriate cases is no more than a logical recognition of that supremacy.

The construction approach reached its limits in *Factortame* because it was impossible to interpret the Merchant Shipping Act 1988 as compatible with EU law. The ECJ therefore required the conflicting national law to be '*set aside*', meaning the statute was rendered 'inoperative' in the specific circumstances of the case.

Disapplication does not make the statute 'null', 'void', or 'repealed'. The Act remains on the statute book and applies in other situations. This approach is formally reconcilable with parliamentary supremacy because courts do not invalidate Acts of Parliament—they simply decline to apply them when they conflict with EU law.

Factortame represented the inevitable clash between two competing constitutional principles: EU law supremacy and parliamentary supremacy. The case involved a direct conflict between EU Treaty provisions (1957), the European Communities Act 1972, and the Merchant Shipping Act 1988.

Why did the normal rule of implied repeal not apply? Under traditional doctrine, the later Act (1988) should have overridden the earlier Act (1972). The House of Lords in *Factortame* provided little analysis of this basic constitutional problem. Lord Bridge simply observed that any limitation on parliamentary sovereignty was '*entirely voluntary*', but this raised more questions than it answered. Constitutional scholars have since offered competing explanations for what happened.

Lord Bridge's view was that the UK voluntarily accepted limitations on parliamentary supremacy when it passed the 1972 Act. Parliament knew what it was doing and deliberately chose to be bound by EU law. Courts should presume Parliament intends to comply with EU obligations unless it explicitly states otherwise. This preserves Dicey's principle that Parliament can enact any law, which of course also includes the repeal of the 1972 Act.

Professor Wade's view was that the courts fundamentally changed the UK constitution by prioritizing the 1972 Act over the 1988 Act. This violated the basic constitutional principle that courts recognise the supremacy of the current Parliament. Wade argues this was a '*legal revolution*' that changed the Grundnorm (fundamental rule) of the constitution.[23] The Parliament of 1972 had successfully bound its successors—something orthodox theory said was impossible. As Wade put it: '*While Britain remains in the Community we are in a regime in which Parliament has bound its successors successfully, and which is nothing if not revolutionary*'.[24]

[23] H.W.R. Wade, 'Sovereignty and the European Communities' (1972) 88 Law Quarterly Review 1, 5.

[24] H.W.R. Wade, 'Sovereignty: Revolution or evolution?' (1996) 112 LQR 568, 571.

This theoretical disagreement had practical implications. If Wade was correct that *Factortame* represented a constitutional revolution, it suggested the UK constitution had fundamentally changed. If Lord Bridge was right about voluntary limitation, parliamentary supremacy remained intact in principle, even if temporarily constrained in practice.

QUESTIONS

1. Explain what is meant by 'disapplication' of an Act of Parliament. How does this differ from declaring an Act 'null and void'?
2. Do you agree with Lord Bridge in *Factortame* that '*there is nothing in any way novel in according supremacy to rules of [EU] law in areas to which they apply*'?
3. Do you think that the UK government acted in bad faith in passing the Merchant Shipping Act 1988?
4. What does Professor Wade mean by the following statement: '*While Britain remains in the Community we are in a regime in which Parliament has bound its successors successfully, and which is nothing if not revolutionary*'?
5. Do you think that, in relation to directly applicable EU law, UK courts acted like a constitutional court? What are the key differences between disapplication and constitutional review?

24.5 CONSTITUTIONAL LIMITS ON EU LAW SUPREMACY: THE *HS2* CASE

While Factortame showed courts willing to disapply Acts of Parliament, the UK Supreme Court's decision in *R (HS2 Action Alliance Ltd) v Secretary of State for Transport*[25] raised fundamental questions about whether EU law supremacy has constitutional limits. While no actual conflict occurred, the case forced the Supreme Court to consider what would happen if EU law directly challenged the UK's fundamental constitutional principles.

HS2 (High Speed 2) is a planned high-speed railway in England. The government chose to authorize this £100+ billion project using Parliament's 'hybrid bill procedure', a centuries-old legislative process that combines elements of public and private bill procedures for projects affecting both general and specific interests.

Environmental campaigners challenged this approach, arguing that the hybrid bill procedure failed to provide adequate public participation as required by EU Directive 2011/92/EU on environmental impact assessments. The directive mandates meaningful public consultation for major infrastructure projects to ensure environmental concerns are properly considered.

The claimants' argument created a potential constitutional conflict. Success would have required UK courts to scrutinize Parliament's own internal legislative procedures, declare them incompatible with EU law, and potentially order Parliament to change how it conducts its legislative business. This directly threatened Article 9 of the Bill of Rights 1689, which protects parliamentary proceedings from judicial interference: '*freedom of speech and debates or proceedings in Parliament ought not to be impeached or questioned in any court or place out of Parliament*'.[26]

[25] [2014] UKSC 3, [2014] 2 All ER 109, discussed in Chapter 3.

[26] Lord Reed [78]; see also Lord Neuberger and Lord Mance [206].

The case thus presented a direct conflict between EU law supremacy (requiring courts to enforce EU environmental law) and parliamentary privilege (protecting Parliament's internal procedures from judicial review).

The Supreme Court rejected the claimants' argument, but the judicial reasoning went much further than necessary. Rather than simply finding no violation of EU law, the judges explored fundamental questions about constitutional hierarchy. Lord Reed JSC distinguished this case from *Factortame*, emphasizing that parliamentary supremacy remains the UK's cardinal constitutional principle:

R (HS2 Action Alliance Ltd) v Secretary of State for Transport
[2014] UKSC 3

[79] Contrary to the submission made on behalf of the appellants, that question cannot be resolved simply by applying the doctrine developed by the Court of Justice of the supremacy of EU law, since the application of that doctrine in our law itself depends upon the 1972 Act. If there is a conflict between a constitutional principle, such as that embodied in article 9 of the Bill of Rights, and EU law, the conflict must be resolved by our courts as an issue arising under the constitutional law of the United Kingdom. Nor can the issue be resolved, as was also suggested, by following the decision in *R v Secretary of State for Transport, Ex p Factortame Ltd (No 2)* [1991] 1 AC 603, since that case was not concerned with the compatibility with EU law of the process by which legislation is enacted in Parliament.

Lords Neuberger and Mance JSC went even further, suggesting that some constitutional principles might be so fundamental that Parliament couldn't have intended to authorize their abrogation:

[207] The United Kingdom has no written constitution, but we have a number of constitutional instruments. They include Magna Carta, the Petition of Right 1628, the Bill of Rights and (in Scotland) the Claim of Rights Act 1689, the Act of Settlement 1701 and the Act of Union 1707. The European Communities Act 1972, the Human Rights Act 1998 and the Constitutional Reform Act 2005 may now be added to this list. The common law itself also recognises certain principles as fundamental to the rule of law. It is, putting the point at its lowest, certainly arguable (and it is for United Kingdom law and courts to determine) that there may be fundamental principles, whether contained in other constitutional instruments or recognised at common law, of which Parliament when it enacted the European Communities Act 1972 did not either contemplate or authorise the abrogation.

The judges identified potential sources of principles that might limit EU law supremacy: historic constitutional statutes like Magna Carta (1215), the Bill of Rights (1689), and the Act of Union (1707); modern constitutional legislation including the Human Rights Act 1998 and Constitutional Reform Act 2005; and common law principles such as the rule of law, access to courts, and parliamentary privilege. These judicial comments suggest a hierarchy of constitutional norms in which some principles may be so fundamental that even EU law cannot override them.

The judicial comments in *HS2* built on earlier suggestions that EU law supremacy might have limits. In *Thoburn*,[27] Laws LJ had suggested that general statutory words might not suffice to incorporate EU measures that violated fundamental domestic rights. The *HS2* judges took this reasoning further, suggesting a broader doctrine of constitutional limits.

[27] [2002] EWHC 195 Admin; [2003] QB 151 [69].

Lord Reed JSC also drew on approaches from other EU member states. He cited approvingly the German Federal Constitutional Court's view that '*as part of a co-operative relationship, a decision of the [ECJ] should not be read by a national court in a way that places in question the identity of the national constitutional order*'.[28]

Crucially, no actual constitutional conflict arose in *HS2*. The Supreme Court found that the hybrid bill procedure provided adequate public participation under EU law; even if it had not, this would not necessarily have violated fundamental constitutional principles, and that Article 9 parliamentary privilege had not been threatened.

The HS2 case suggests UK courts might recognise what constitutional theorists call 'constitutional identity'—a core of fundamental principles that cannot be compromised even by international legal obligations. However, this idea conflicts with the doctrine of parliamentary supremacy.

The judicial reasoning in HS2 implies a shift in the understanding of parliamentary supremacy. The traditional Diceyan view holds that Parliament has unlimited legislative authority—including power to pass laws that bind future Parliaments (as the European Communities Act 1972 appeared to do).

But the HS2 judges suggested something more nuanced: while Parliament could authorize EU law supremacy over 'ordinary' domestic legislation, it may not have contemplated authorizing the abrogation of the fundamental constitutional principles. This creates a distinction between ordinary constitutional arrangements that Parliament can modify or abandon, and fundamental constitutional principles that form the irreducible core of UK constitutional identity.

The constitutional difficulty is determining who decides which category applies. If courts can identify principles that Parliament '*did not contemplate*' abandoning when it passed the European Communities Act 1972, this gives judges significant power to determine the scope of parliamentary authority and possibly undermine the very parliamentary supremacy they claim to protect.

This represents a shift from traditional constitutional doctrine toward a model where some constitutional principles are so fundamental that they cannot be compromised, even by a supreme Parliament acting through clear statutory language. The *HS2* approach was not isolated. Indeed, the Supreme Court has developed similar themes in cases like *Osborn v Parole Board* and *Kennedy v Charity Commission* (discussed in Ch.18), which suggests a broader judicial project to recognise constitutional principles beyond formal statutory frameworks. Constitutional scholar Mark Elliott argues that this approach amounts to a reconceptualization of the UK's constitutional order that moves beyond simply recognising different categories of legislation:

M. Elliott, 'Constitutional legislation, European Union law and the nature of the United Kingdom's contemporary constitution' (2014) 10(3) *European Constitutional Law Review* 379–392, 391–392

The importance of HS2 is thus not confined to the acknowledgment of a hierarchy of statutes. Important though that aspect of the case is, its deeper significance lies in its embrace of a constitutional order that accommodates a hierarchy of norms—owing neither their existence nor their status to an exercise of legislative will—within a single framework that also acknowledges parliamentary sovereignty. In this

[28] Counter Terrorism Database Act, 1 BvR 1251/07, para. 91.

way, the Diceyan gulf between the legal realm, in which Parliament reigns supreme, and the political or moral realm, which may operate in practice to constrain the uses to which legislative authority may be put, is bridged. This is so because, on the view adopted in HS2, constitutional norms operate as legal constraints upon Parliament's legislative capacity, denying it the authority to effect their disturbance other than through express or specific provision.

QUESTIONS

1. What constitutional conflict did the HS2 case present between EU law and parliamentary privilege? Why did the Supreme Court suggest this conflict might have limits that didn't apply in Factortame?
2. The HS2 judges identified three categories of potential constitutional constraints on EU law supremacy: historic statutes, modern constitutional legislation, and common law principles. Give examples of each category and explain why courts might view them as more fundamental than ordinary legislation.
3. Mark Elliott argues that *HS2* forms part of a wider series of Supreme Court decisions—including *Osborn v Parole Board* and *Kennedy v Charity Commission*—that together sketch '*a particularly rich vision of the UK's unwritten constitutional order*'.[29] He suggests that the endorsement of constitutional statutes in *HS2* and the renaissance of common-law constitutional rights in these other cases '*form part of a single constitutional endeavour which rests upon a normative-hierarchical vision of the constitutional order.*'[30]

Analyse how this '*normative-hierarchical vision*' challenges traditional Diceyan constitutional theory. In your answer, consider:

(a) How does Elliott's concept of a '*hierarchy of norms*' differ from simply recognising different categories of legislation?

(b) What does Elliott mean when he argues that HS2 helps bridge '*the Diceyan gulf between the legal realm, in which Parliament reigns supreme, and the political or moral realm*'?

(c) Elliott suggests that this approach means '*constitutional norms operate as legal constraints upon Parliament's legislative capacity, denying it the authority to effect their disturbance other than through express or specific provision.*'[31] How does this differ from the traditional view that parliamentary supremacy can only be limited by political constraints? What are the implications for the separation of powers between Parliament and the courts?

[29] M. Elliott, 'Constitutional Legislation, European Union Law and the Nature of the United Kingdom's Contemporary Constitution' (2014) 10(3) *European Constitutional Law Review* 379–392, 390.

[30] Ibid, 391. [31] Ibid. 392.

24.6 THE PROCESS OF LEAVING THE EU

The process of leaving the EU proved far more complex than the simple question put to voters in 2016. The referendum asked: 'Should the United Kingdom remain a member of the European Union or leave the European Union?' The result was narrow but clear: EU referendum results and turnout

UK total

	Leave	Remain
Percentage	51.89%	48.11%
Votes	17.4m	16.1m
Nation results		
England	53.4% (15.2m)	46.6% (13.2m)
Northern Ireland	44.2% (350,000)	55.8% (440,000)
Scotland	38% (1m)	62% (1.6m)
Wales	52.5% (850,000)	47.5% (770,000)
Total Electorate:	46.5m	
Turnout:	72.2%	

However, the referendum result only answered whether to leave—not how to leave. The statute authorizing the referendum provided no guidance on what withdrawal would actually mean. This left fundamental questions unresolved about the UK's future relationship with the EU unresolved.

Before withdrawal could begin, the Supreme Court in *Miller I*[32] confirmed that triggering Article 50 required parliamentary authorization. The Court emphasized that the European Communities Act 1972 had operated as a '*conduit pipe*' allowing EU law to take effect domestically, and removing this conduit was a decision of such constitutional significance that it required explicit parliamentary approval rather than executive action alone.[33] The legal mechanism for leaving the EU is set out in Article 50 of the Treaty on European Union:

Article 50 of the Treaty on European Union

(1) Any Member State may decide to withdraw from the Union in accordance with its own constitutional requirements.

(2) A Member State which decides to withdraw shall notify the European Council of its intention. In the light of the guidelines provided by the European Council, the Union shall negotiate and conclude

[32] *R (Miller) v Secretary of State for Exiting the European Union* [2017] UKSC 5.

[33] Ibid. [80]–[88].

> an agreement with that State, setting out the arrangements for its withdrawal, taking account of the framework for its future relationship with the Union [. . .] It shall be concluded on behalf of the Union by the Council, acting by a qualified majority, after obtaining the consent of the European Parliament.
>
> (3) The Treaties shall cease to apply to the State in question from the date of entry into force of the withdrawal agreement or, failing that, two years after the notification referred to in paragraph 2, unless the European Council, in agreement with the Member State concerned, unanimously decides to extend this period.

In essence, Article 50 stipulates the following sequence. A member state may decide to leave the EU in accordance with its own constitutional requirements. A member state must serve notice under Art. 50(2) of its intention to withdraw (which the UK did on 29 March 2017). Once notice is served, a two-year countdown begins under Art. 50(3). Unless an agreement is reached sooner or time is extended by mutual agreement, the EU Treaties cease to apply to the withdrawing member state at the end of the two-year period, regardless of whether an agreement on future relations has been concluded. The original 'exit day' of 29 March 2019 for the UK was extended three times until 31 January 2020, when the UK formally withdrew from the EU.

The default position under Article 50 is that the withdrawing member state becomes a third country (i.e. non-EU) at the end of the two-year negotiation period. The subsequent relationship with the EU is governed by a new agreement. Any rights and obligations that previously derived from EU law are no longer enforceable in the UK under the European Communities Act 1972, which has been repealed, but are now enforceable under the European Union (Withdrawal) Act 2018 and by the European Union (Withdrawal Agreement) Act 2020.

The European Union (Withdrawal) Act 2018 had two main purposes. It provides for a clean break with the European Union, by repealing the European Communities Act 1972, leaving the customs union and the internal market, ending the free movement of people and the Charter of Fundamental Rights, and ending the automatic jurisdiction of the European Court of Justice. But it also provides for continuity. The European Union (Withdrawal) Act 2018 converts the entire corpus of EU law into domestic law, which can then be repealed, amended, or retained. The House of Lords' Delegated Powers and Regulatory Reform Committee called the Act '*one of the most important . . . in the constitutional history of the United Kingdom*'.[34] Before we look at the EUWA in more detail, we need to note that it was passed without the consent of the Scottish Parliament—the first time that the Sewel Convention had been breached by the UK Parliament, but not the last. The European Union (Withdrawal Agreement) Act 2020 and the Internal Market Act 2020 (see 23.6.4) were also enacted without the consent of the devolved legislatures.

24.6.1 RETAINED EU LAW AND ITS TRANSFORMATION

Consider a simple example: EU regulations on food labelling that require allergen warnings on packaging. On exit day, should these rules suddenly disappear, creating confusion for manufacturers and posing a risk to consumers? The concept of retained EU law was designed to prevent exactly this kind of 'cliff edge' scenario.

[34] House of Lords Delegated Powers and Regulatory Reform Committee, *European Union (Withdrawal) Bill* (3rd Report 2017–19, HL 22), para. 1.

Retained EU law operated as a legal 'snapshot' taken at the moment of leaving the EU. The European Union (Withdrawal) Act 2018 essentially took a photograph of all EU law applying in the UK on 31 January 2020 and converted it into domestic law. This included approximately 20,000 pieces of EU legislation—everything from environmental standards to worker protections. The 2018 Act preserved EU law in three forms: EU-derived domestic legislation (s.2)—UK laws that implemented EU obligations; direct EU legislation (s.3)—EU regulations (approximately 5,000 pieces); and directly effective EU law (s.4)—EU Treaty rights that individuals could enforce.

The Retained EU Law (Revocation and Reform) Act 2023 fundamentally altered this system. The government renamed retained EU law as 'assimilated law'—but this was not just cosmetic rebranding. These laws lost their special constitutional status and no longer have supremacy over conflicting UK legislation. UK courts must now interpret them as purely domestic legislation, without reference to EU legal principles or ECJ case law. The government can also now modify former EU regulations through secondary legislation, rather than requiring full Acts of Parliament.

Most retained EU law expired on 31 December 2023 unless specifically preserved, giving the government broad powers to revoke EU-derived law and replace it with domestic alternatives. This removal of EU law supremacy and interpretive principles represents a fundamental shift in UK law, creating legal uncertainty while providing regulatory autonomy.

The move from retained to assimilated law affects thousands of legal provisions across employment, environment, consumer protection, and other areas. It demonstrates how EU withdrawal continues to reshape the UK constitution. However, the 2023 Act has created interpretive uncertainty about how courts should interpret laws originating from an EU source.

F. Barth, 'How will the retained EU Law (Revocation and Reform) Act 2023 affect the principle of EU-law conforming construction in UK law?' (2023) 44 *Statute Law Review* 1–7, 7

> The Revocation Act 2023 does not explicitly address the question whether and to what extent it affects the principle of conforming construction [that requires UK courts to interpret domestic legislation in a way that aligns with EU law, even after the UK's exit from the EU: see s. 23.4]. On the one hand, it abolishes retained EU treaty rights and obligations as well as the supremacy of EU law, which arguably both constitute the legal foundation for applying a conforming construction post-withdrawal. On the other hand, it leaves intact the binding nature of most case law, including that which establishes those principles. Depending on how much emphasis is placed on each angle, one may read the Revocation Act 2023 as not affecting conforming construction, as radically abolishing it, or as somewhere in between.
>
> In a nutshell, it appears on balance most likely and reasonable that the courts will find a middle-ground. This could be that a conforming construction will, in the future, only apply where it is already the subject of binding case law for the specific provision one seeks to construe, or where there is a genuinely identifiable intention by Parliament for the enactment to fully comply with EU law. In other cases however, the principle of conforming construction likely may no longer be available as a tool to interpret domestic statutes, not even for the ones which originate from EU law and will become 'assimilated law'.

The interpretive uncertainty created by the 2023 Act was foreshadowed by earlier Supreme Court disagreement about how retained EU law operates. In *Lipton v BA Cityflyer*,[35] the Supreme Court split on fundamental questions about the legal status of pre-withdrawal EU rights, with the majority and minority offering competing analyses of how the European Union (Withdrawal) Act

[35] *Lipton v BA Cityflyer* [2024] UKSC 24.

2018 was intended to work. The disagreement among senior judges illustrates the ongoing constitutional complexity of interpreting the withdrawal legislation and managing the legal transition from EU membership.

24.6.2 EU WITHDRAWAL AND DEVOLUTION: THE SCOTTISH CONTINUITY BILL

EU withdrawal created significant tensions between Westminster and the devolved governments. The European Union (Withdrawal) Act 2018 allowed UK Ministers to restrict how devolved legislatures could modify retained EU law in devolved areas—effectively reducing devolved powers without consent. This was constitutionally significant because it meant Westminster could override the devolution settlements without following the normal conventions of seeking consent, thereby altering the balance of power between the UK government and the devolved administrations.

The Scottish Parliament voted 93-30 to withhold consent for the Withdrawal Bill. In response, the Scottish Government passed its own version—the UK Withdrawal from the European Union (Legal Continuity) (Scotland) Bill. Section 17 of this Bill directly challenged Westminster by stating that UK ministerial regulations affecting devolved EU law would be '*of no effect unless the consent of the Scottish Ministers was obtained*'. This provision would have given Scotland an effective veto over UK government policy in devolved areas, something that would have reversed the UK's constitutional hierarchy by making Westminster subordinate to Edinburgh in certain policy areas.

The UK Supreme Court ruled in December 2018 that while the Scottish Parliament had legal power to pass most of the Bill, Section 17 was invalid because it would make UK law conditional on Scottish consent.[36]

Specifically, the Supreme Court confirmed '*that, notwithstanding the conferral of legislative authority on the Scottish Parliament, the UK Parliament remains sovereign, and its legislative power in relation to Scotland is undiminished*'.[37] It confirmed the power of the UK Parliament to authorize Ministers to make subordinate legislation, and nullified the effect of cl. 17, which would have made the legal effect of such subordinate legislation conditional upon the consent of the Scottish Ministers.

The UK Withdrawal from the European Union (Legal Continuity) (Scotland) Bill
[2018] UKSC 64 [52]

> An enactment of the Scottish Parliament which prevented such subordinate legislation from having legal effect, unless the Scottish Ministers gave their consent, would render the effect of laws made by the UK Parliament conditional on the consent of the Scottish Ministers. It would therefore limit the power of the UK Parliament to make laws for Scotland, since Parliament cannot meaningfully be said to 'make laws' if the laws which it makes are of no effect. The imposition of such a condition on the UK Parliament's law-making power would be inconsistent with the continued recognition, by section 28(7) of the Scotland Act, of its unqualified legislative power.

The constitutional importance of this case extends beyond the immediate legal issues. While the UK government secured a legal victory, the case highlighted fundamental tensions about how the UK's territorial constitution should work in practice. The Scottish Government argued that EU withdrawal

[36] *The UK Withdrawal from the European Union (Legal Continuity) (Scotland) Bill* [2018] UKSC 64.

[37] At [41].

was being used to centralize powers that had previously been exercised at EU level, rather than allowing them to flow naturally to the devolved administrations. Westminster's willingness to proceed without devolved consent—the first breach of the Sewel Convention—set a precedent that would be repeated with subsequent legislation. The UK government's tactical use of the Supreme Court reference procedure to prevent the Scottish Bill from reaching the statute book first also raised questions about whether Westminster was playing fair within the devolution settlement. As Aileen McHarg noted, this approach may have secured short-term legal advantage at the cost of longer-term political damage to inter-governmental relations:

A. McHarg, 'The Scottish Continuity Bill Reference', Centre on Constitutional Change, University of Edinburgh, 18 December 2018

> After all, the Supreme Court's decision reinforces the narrative that Withdrawal Act amounted to a 'power grab': the competence that Holyrood previously enjoyed to regulate the consequences of Brexit in relation to devolved matters was removed by the Withdrawal Act, and this was done without its consent. The UK's Government's ability to halt the progress of the Continuity Bill by using its Supreme Court reference powers, and thereby to rig the race to the statute book decisively in its favour, further underlines the weakness of the devolved institutions within the current territorial constitution. In choosing to press its tactical advantage, the UK Government may yet find that it has committed a(nother) strategic error in its handling of the devolved aspects of Brexit.

24.6.3 THE NORTHERN IRELAND PROTOCOL: AN IMPOSSIBLE TRIANGLE

EU withdrawal created an impossible situation for Northern Ireland. The UK government had three objectives that could not all be achieved: no hard border between Northern Ireland and Ireland; no border in the Irish Sea between Northern Ireland and Great Britain; and leaving the EU's internal market and customs union. It is possible to achieve any two of these, but not all three.

When the UK left the EU, the Irish border became an external EU frontier. Normally, this would require customs checks and controls. But a 'hard border' with physical infrastructure would disrupt highly integrated economies where 30,000 people cross the border daily, undermine the peace process that had removed military checkpoints and security installations, and create massive practical problems across nearly 300 border crossing points.

After failed attempts to achieve all three objectives, the Protocol chose objectives (a) and (c) but sacrificed (b). Northern Ireland remains formally part of UK customs territory but must follow EU rules on goods—with 286 EU legal instruments applying—effectively creating a 'soft regulatory border' in the Irish Sea.

The practical result of the Protocol is that goods moving from Great Britain to Northern Ireland are subject to customs checks, while the Irish land border remains open. UK politicians promised there would be no Irish Sea border and that Northern Ireland would have '*unfettered access*' to the UK market. Legally, this amounted to '*nothing short of misleading advertising*'—the Protocol clearly requires checks between Great Britain and Northern Ireland.[38] This constitutional arrangement is

[38] S. Weatherill, 'The Protocol on Ireland/Northern Ireland: Protecting the EU's Internal Market at the expense of the UK's' (2020) 45(2) European Law Review 222, 224.

unprecedented in UK history. No part of the UK has ever before operated under a different regulatory regime from the rest of the country, creating a form of 'differentiated integration' within the UK itself.

Colin Harvey argues that this political contradiction reflects deeper structural problems with the Protocol arrangements.

C. Harvey, 'The Irish Border', in F. Fabbrini (ed.) *The Law & Politics of Brexit: Volume II: The Withdrawal Agreement* (2020, Oxford: OUP), p. 160, p. 166

> ... in reality [Northern Ireland] will be following the EU customs regime, as well as a broad range of relevant EU rules, and whatever has been said and promised politically by politicians in the UK, the law clearly requires that there will be checks within the UK. The scale of the alignment is significant, with Annex 2 to the Protocol containing hundreds of EU regulations and directives. These provisions will be governed and enforced by many of the traditional methods of EU law, albeit subject to a democratic consent mechanism in Northern Ireland [...].
>
> It is plain that close alignment between the UK and the EU in the future is the optimal solution if the aim is to the reduce tensions, challenges, and difficulties in Northern Ireland and across these islands. In practice the signs are that the UK government desires a more divergent future and this will cause on-going problems for Northern Ireland. The more that the UK attempts to drift away from the EU the more tensions will arise in the practical operation of the Protocol.

The Protocol created a new constitutional reality: a border that divides the UK into two regulatory zones. Northern Ireland follows EU rules on goods and customs, while Great Britain can set its own tariffs and regulations. This means products made in Northern Ireland operate under different rules than those made in Great Britain, requiring checks on trade between the two parts of the UK. To avoid a hard Irish land border, the Protocol placed a soft regulatory border in the Irish Sea.

In February 2023, the UK and EU agreed the Windsor Framework, which significantly modified the Northern Ireland Protocol arrangements while maintaining its core structure. The Green Lane/Red Lane System means goods staying in Northern Ireland follow a simplified 'green lane' with minimal checks, while goods potentially moving to the EU follow the 'red lane' with full customs procedures. The Stormont Brake allows the Northern Ireland Assembly to object to new EU laws applying in Northern Ireland, though this power is limited and subject to safeguards. The ECJ's role has been more narrowly defined, though it retains the final say on the interpretation of EU law.

The Windsor Framework demonstrates ongoing evolution in post-withdrawal arrangements. While it reduces practical friction, it maintains the fundamental constitutional challenge: Northern Ireland continues to operate under different rules than Great Britain, preserving the regulatory border in the Irish Sea. The Framework shows how international agreements continue to shape the UK's internal constitutional arrangements, with Northern Ireland's status remaining distinct from the rest of the UK.

What happens if the UK fails to comply with the obligations under the Protocol? The Commission may pursue infringement proceedings (Article 12 of the Protocol) and the Court of Justice of the European Union has the jurisdiction to interpret and apply the provisions of the Protocol referring to EU law (Article 13 of the Protocol). Moreover, the EU principles of direct effect and supremacy apply to the entire Withdrawal Agreement, including over Acts of Parliament. Article 4 of the Withdrawal Agreement provides that UK courts are authorized to hear cases brought by legal individuals who are '*able to rely directly on the provisions contained or referred to in this Agreement which meet the conditions for direct effect under Union law*' (see Section 24.2, above). The application of EU law and the relevance of the Court of Justice continue behind the scenes. It is surely only a matter of time before a Factortame-type conflict between a post-withdrawal Act of Parliament and the Withdrawal

Agreement is adjudicated by the domestic courts. As Paul Craig observes, this complexity reflects the broader challenge of legal 'unravelling' after nearly five decades of integration.

P. Craig, 'The Ratifications', in F. Fabbrini (ed.), *The Law & Politics of Brexit: Volume II: The Withdrawal Agreement* (2020, Oxford: OUP), p. 166

Nothing about Brexit has been simple. This is true for the politics and the economics. It is no less true for the law. The twin UK domestic statutes that pave the way for the UK's exit from the EU are both fearsomely complex. This is in certain respects unsurprising, given the very fact that the UK has been a Member State of the EU for nearly 50 years. EU law has permeated every aspect of UK law, albeit to varying degrees. The complexity of the legal unravelling is thus to be expected. This does not render it any easier from a legal perspective. This is more especially so because there are a number of other statutes that will shape legal relations between the UK and the EU in a post-Brexit world. It should not moreover be forgotten that we have not yet begun to see the case law that will inevitably emerge wherein the courts grapple with the more intractable provisions of the European Union (Withdrawal Agreement) Act 2020 and the European Union (Withdrawal) Act 2018.

The Protocol demonstrates how international legal obligations continue to shape the UK's internal constitutional arrangements post-withdrawal. Rather than achieving constitutional autonomy, EU withdrawal has created new forms of external constraint that may prove more constitutionally disruptive than EU membership itself.

QUESTIONS

1. Is withdrawing from the EU a matter that should be decided by the electorate in a referendum? Is it a matter of high politics, namely foreign affairs, that is properly reserved to the UK government? Is it about the removal of a legal source, which requires prior authorization by Parliament? Or is it a matter of constitutional reform, which requires a shared intergovernmental process of negotiation across the United Kingdom's four regions tied together by a multi-level constitutional settlement?
2. What was the main purpose of the European Union (Withdrawal) Act 2018, and how did it attempt to balance 'clean break' with 'continuity'?
3. Explain why the concept of retained EU law represented a fundamental re-shaping of law and regulation post-EU withdrawal. Given that most retained EU law has now been converted to 'assimilated law' under the 2023 Act, was this always intended as a temporary measure?
4. Why did the Scottish Government attempt to pass the UK Withdrawal from the European Union (Legal Continuity) (Scotland) Bill? Do you agree with the UK Supreme Court's assessment in its judgment on the Scottish Continuity Bill that 'the UK Parliament remains sovereign, and its legislative power in relation to Scotland is undiminished'?
5. Is it possible for the UK to leave the EU in order to take back regulatory control of its trade policy while also avoiding a hard border between Northern Ireland and Ireland and between Northern Ireland and Great Britain?
6. How does the Northern Ireland Protocol demonstrate the continuing relevance of EU law principles (direct effect and supremacy) in post-withdrawal UK law?

24.6.4 THE INTERNAL MARKET ACT 2020: CENTRALIZATION V DEVOLUTION

Following the UK's withdrawal from the European Union, the UK government returned hundreds of regulatory powers from the EU to the UK and devolved governments. This created a dilemma: how to maintain free trade across the UK while allowing devolved administrations to regulate differently.[39] Any federal system faces the same fundamental tension: how to allow regional governments to regulate differently while maintaining free trade across the federation. If Scotland, Wales, and Northern Ireland set different product standards, they might inadvertently create barriers to trade between the different parts of the UK.

The United States Constitution addresses this through the 'interstate commerce clause',[40] which gives Congress power to regulate trade between states. The UK faced the same challenge after EU withdrawal—but without a clear constitutional framework for resolving it.

The Internal Market Act 2020 addresses this through two key principles: mutual recognition (goods that are legal in one part of the UK can be sold anywhere) and non-discrimination (against goods from other parts of the UK). However, the Act was passed without consent from the Scottish Parliament and the Welsh Senedd, violating the Sewel Convention. Devolved governments saw it as a '*power grab*' that reduced their regulatory autonomy, undermining the point of devolution by imposing what the Scottish Government called '*a new, unilaterally designed and imposed regime*'.[41] They also feared it would give English market dominance since England's market is much larger.

In his foreword to the White Paper, the Secretary of State explained the need for the Internal Market Act.

UK Internal Market: Presented to Parliament by the Secretary of State for Business, Energy and Industrial Strategy, CP 278, July 2020

[F]rom 1 January 2021, hundreds of powers previously exercised at EU level will flow directly to the UK government and the devolved administrations in Edinburgh, Cardiff, and Belfast. Devolved administrations will have unprecedented regulatory freedom within new UK frameworks, allowing them to benefit from opportunities to innovate. To allow each home nation to take full advantage of these new opportunities, and ensure businesses can continue to trade freely across the UK as they do now, we are consulting on legislating for a UK Internal Market.

Northern Ireland sells more to the rest of the UK than to all EU member states combined. Scotland sells more to the rest of the UK than to the rest of the world put together. And in some parts of Wales, a quarter of workers commute in from England on a daily basis.

Under the plans in this white paper, the UK will continue to operate as a coherent Internal Market. A Market Access Commitment will guarantee UK companies can trade unhindered in every part of the United Kingdom—ensuring the continued prosperity and wellbeing of people and businesses across all four nations. At the same time, we will maintain our high standards for consumers and workers.

This will give business certainty. If a baker sells bread in both Glasgow and Carlisle, they will not need to create different packaging because they are selling between Scotland and England. Likewise,

[39] Although Northern Ireland is technically included in the Internal Market Act 2020, the market rules governing Northern Ireland are set out in the Protocol discussed in Section 24.6.3.

[40] Article 1, Section 8, Clause 3, US Constitution.

[41] Scottish Government, 'After Brexit: The UK Internal Market Act and devolution', 8 March 2021 [57].

engineering firms in Scotland using parts made in Wales will know that the parts are compliant with regulations across other home nations.

By enshrining the principle of mutual recognition into law, our proposals will ensure regulations from one part of the UK are recognized across the country. The principle of non-discrimination will support companies trading in the UK, regardless of where in the UK they are based.

These principles will not undermine devolution, they will simply prevent any part of the UK from blocking products or services from another part while protecting devolved powers to innovate, such as introducing plastic bag minimum pricing or introducing smoking bans.

The Internal Market Act 2020 applies market access principles to regulatory powers that returned to the UK from the EU after withdrawal. They are designed to create a level playing field across the UK by preventing new trade barriers.[42] Mutual recognition means that a good that can be lawfully sold in the part of the United Kingdom where it was produced or imported into can also be sold in other parts of the United Kingdom. (Northern Ireland operates under different rules due to the Protocol (see Section 24.6.3)). The objective is to allow a baker who produces and sells bread in Scotland and adheres to the Scottish rules on bread production to automatically sell their bread in England and Wales without needing to comply with English and Welsh requirements. Any local discriminatory rules concerning how a good is sold or service is provided (e.g. one which regulates against a product from a specific region within the UK) would violate the principle of non-discrimination and impede cross-border trade.

EU withdrawal also returned significant powers to devolved governments. In the White Paper, the UK government called it 'the single biggest transfer of powers to the devolved administrations in history' [12]—covering 160 policy areas including agriculture, fisheries, food standards, environmental protection, and transport. In the House of Commons, the Business Secretary said 111 powers would 'flow back' to Scotland, as well as around 70 to Wales and around 150 to Northern Ireland.[43] This created a constitutional dilemma: if Scotland, Wales, and Northern Ireland use these new powers to set different standards, they might accidentally create barriers to trade within the UK.

There was an alternative approach that devolved governments preferred: 'common frameworks'—consensual agreements between all four UK governments on how to regulate specific policy areas.[44] This would have ensured UK market coherence while allowing policy divergence where appropriate and requiring consent from all devolved administrations. Both sides agreed this was the ideal approach.[45] However, in practice, the UK government identified only 22 policy areas (out of 154) as suitable for common frameworks. This left 115 areas unregulated, creating potential for trade barriers.[46]

The alternative is to apply the Internal Market Act 2020 to enable the joint market to function across England, Scotland, Wales, and Northern Ireland. The problem is not technical—the UK

[42] The mutual recognition principle and the non-discrimination principle do not apply to requirements that were in force in a part of the UK before 31 December 2020 and remain unchanged.

[43] HC Debate, UK Internal Market: White Paper, Hansard vol. 678, col. 1705, 16 July 2020. The returning competences are primarily in areas involving agriculture and fisheries, food standards, economic development, public procurement and transport, animal welfare and environmental protection, as well as for Scotland and Northern Ireland aspects of justice and home affairs.

[44] Scottish Government, 'After Brexit: The UK Internal Market Act and devolution', 8 March 2021 [60].

[45] The UK government views common frameworks as '*the mechanism most advanced in its development to address regulatory coherence*': UK Internal Market: Presented to Parliament by the Secretary of State for Business, Energy and Industrial Strategy, CP 278, July 2020, p. 20.

[46] Frameworks Analysis, *2020 Breakdown of Areas of EU Law that Intersect With Devolved Competence in Scotland, Wales and Northern Ireland*, September 2020.

government is seeking an integrated approach to market access and the seamless operation of the UK internal market. Indeed, according to the government's own analysis, common frameworks are 'most advanced' atsecuring those outcomes. Rather, the problem is political and stems from the UK government's underlying assumptions about the UK as a state and as a market, which the devolved administrations regard as a deliberate choice to centralize power rather than work collaboratively. The result is a recurring cycle of centralized regulation and decentralized distrust.

This has given rise to competing constitutional narratives. The UK Government argues the Act manages '*the biggest transfer of powers in the history of devolution*',[47] while the Scottish Government calls it '*a shameless grab on Scotland's democratic powers and an assault on devolution*',[48] and the Welsh Government describes it as an '*outrageous attack on [the Senedd's] legislative competence*'.[49]

While the UK Parliament has legal power to legislate without devolved consent (as discussed in Chapter 6), doing so for UK-wide market regulation violates the spirit of devolution. The result has been a constitutional crisis, with observers noting '*we have never known relations between the Welsh and Scottish Governments on the one hand, and the UK Government on the other, to be as poor as they are today*'.[50]

The deeper constitutional problem stems from market economics. While mutual recognition sounds egalitarian, the economic reality is that England's market far exceeds Scotland and Wales in size. This means English market rules effectively become the default, diluting devolved regulatory power and undercutting the social, environmental, and health objectives of smaller jurisdictions.

S. Weatherill, 'Will the United Kingdom survive the United Kingdom Internal Market Act?'
UKICE Working Paper 03/2021, p. 26

> For example, one could imagine the Scottish Government pursuing a campaign against obesity which involves obligations to label foodstuffs and beverages to make clear their more harmful ingredients and to add warnings about the consequences of consumption for obesity. This would fall within the scope of the Act and it would seem to be subject to the mutual recognition principle. No exception or justification is available for such a general public health measure. So, assuming there are no rules of this type in force in England, the requirements would not apply to non-compliant goods imported from England. Given that most UK production takes place in England, this would rob the Scottish rules of any worthwhile purpose, unless the measure were targeted at a niche product which unusually is not mostly produced in England (Irn-Bru perhaps).

The Internal Market Act 2020 must be understood as part of a wider pattern of post-withdrawal constitutional tension. Like the Scottish Continuity Bill dispute (Section 24.6.2), it represents what devolved governments see as a '*unilaterally imposed and highly centralized regime that does not allow for adequate consideration of fundamental policy choices*'.[51]

The Act also cannot deliver on its core promise of '*unhindered trade across the United Kingdom*'. Under the Northern Ireland Protocol (Section 24.6.3), Northern Ireland follows EU rules while Great

[47] HC Deb, 16 July 2020, col 1705.

[48] SNP, *Westminster Power Grab: Explained*, 8 December 2020.

[49] Welsh Counsel General, Written Statement: Possible Legal challenge to the UK Internal Market Bill, 16 December 2020.

[50] Centre on Constitutional Change, 'UK Internal Market Bill: Devolution and the Union', University of Edinburgh, October 2020.

[51] Scottish Government, 'After Brexit: The UK Internal Market Act and devolution', 8 March 2021 [57].

Britain can diverge. The more Great Britain moves away from EU standards, the greater the friction on trade between Great Britain and Northern Ireland.

The Internal Market Act illustrates how EU withdrawal has strained the UK's territorial constitution, creating tensions between legal power and constitutional propriety, market integration and devolved autonomy, and unitary state governance and federal-style cooperation.

S. Weatherill, 'Will the United Kingdom survive the United Kingdom Internal Market Act?'
UKICE Working Paper 03/2021, p. 26

What sort of internal market has the UK chosen for itself, and why?

It has chosen a *divided* and a *divisive* one. It is an internal market which is *divided* between Great Britain and Northern Ireland. Northern Ireland is unwillingly excluded from the market rules enacted in London in the areas covered by the Protocol attached to the EU-UK Withdrawal Agreement. It is moreover an internal market marked by a *divisive* relationship between Scotland and Wales, on the one hand, and on the other England. Scotland and Wales are likely to be unwillingly included in the application of market rules enacted in London, to the detriment of the regulatory autonomy promised under their devolution settlements. The Act aims to sustain the UK as an integrated trading area but dissatisfaction surrounds Northern Ireland's place *outside* it and Scotland and Wales's place *inside* it.

The Internal Market Act illustrates a fundamental constitutional dilemma created by EU withdrawal. While the UK government achieved its goal of regulatory autonomy from the EU, it has struggled to manage the resulting tensions within its own territorial constitution. The Act demonstrates how withdrawal has not restored simple parliamentary supremacy, but has created new forms of constitutional complexity. Rather than resolving the tensions between different legal orders that characterized EU membership, withdrawal has relocated these tensions to the relationships between different parts of the UK itself. The continuing application of EU law in Northern Ireland, combined with centralized market regulation for Great Britain, suggests that 'taking back control' has proven more constitutionally disruptive than EU membership itself.

QUESTIONS

1. The UK government argues the Internal Market Act 2020 ensures '*unhindered trade across the United Kingdom*'. Given the Northern Ireland Protocol's continuing operation and the constitutional tensions with devolved governments, does the Act succeed in achieving seamless UK market integration?
2. According to the Scottish Parliament's Constitution Committee, the Internal Market Act 2020 places more emphasis on open trade than on regulatory autonomy. Is the Internal Market Act 2020 properly calibrated to the distinctive features of the UK's territorial constitution?
3. The Internal Market Act creates a tension between market integration and devolved autonomy. Given that both the UK government and devolved administrations agreed that 'common frameworks' were the ideal approach, why did the UK government choose the more divisive Internal Market Act? What does this reveal about competing visions of the UK's territorial constitution?

4. Using Weatherill's obesity labelling example, analyse how the mutual recognition principle might undermine devolved policy objectives. How does this illustrate the broader constitutional problem of England's market dominance within the UK's federal-style arrangements?
5. Weatherill argues the UK has chosen a '*divided and divisive*' internal market. How does the Internal Market Act 2020 demonstrate that EU withdrawal has relocated rather than resolved the constitutional tensions between different legal orders? What are the implications for the UK's long-term territorial integrity?

24.7 CONCLUSION: CONSTITUTIONAL COMPLEXITY AND CONTINUITY

The UK's relationship with European Union law demonstrates a key feature of constitutional change: it is easier to join a legal order than to leave one. When the UK joined the EEC in 1973, the European Communities Act 1972 provided a relatively straightforward gateway for EU law to become part of the domestic legal system. The constitutional tensions this created—between parliamentary supremacy and EU law supremacy—remained largely theoretical for two decades.

By contrast, EU withdrawal has proven far more constitutionally complex. Rather than restoring a simple Diceyan constitution, withdrawal has created new forms of constitutional fragmentation. The UK now operates several legal regimes at once assimilated EU law governs much domestic regulation; the Withdrawal Agreement maintains EU law supremacy in specific areas; Northern Ireland follows EU rules while Great Britain diverges; and the Internal Market Act attempts to keep an increasingly divided territorial constitution together.

The cases examined in this chapter—ranging from *Factortame* to *HS2* to *Miller I*—show how UK courts have gradually developed constitutional theories to manage legal pluralism. The Supreme Court's recognition of constitutional hierarchy in *HS2*, its articulation of the limits of parliamentary supremacy in the *Scottish Continuity Bill* case, and its analysis of legal sources in *Miller I* all demonstrate judicial recognition of constitutional complexity.

Most significantly, EU withdrawal has not ended the constitutional challenges posed by legal pluralism. Instead, it has relocated them. The tensions between different legal orders that characterized EU membership now exist within the UK's own territorial constitution. The continuing relevance of EU law principles through the Withdrawal Agreement, combined with growing friction between Westminster and the devolved governments, suggests that constitutional complexity has become a permanent feature of the modern UK constitution rather than a temporary consequence of EU membership.

FURTHER READING

Bogdanor, V., *Beyond Brexit: Towards a British Constitution* (2019, London: I.B. Tauris).

Craig, P., 'The withdrawal agreement: Content, complexity and consequences' (2019) 82 (2) *Modern Law Review* 319–366.

Craig, P., 'Brexit and the UK Constitution', in Jowell, J. and O'Cinneide, C. (eds), 9th edn *The Changing Constitution* (2019, OUP).

Dougan, M. (ed.), *The UK After Brexit: Legal and Policy Challenges* (2017, Cambridge: Intersentia).

Elliott, M., 'The Supreme Court's judgment in Miller: In search of constitutional principle' (2017) 76(2) *Cambridge Law Journal* 257–288.

Elliott, M. and Tierney, S., 'Political pragmatism and constitutional principle: The European Union (Withdrawal) Act 2018' [2019] *Public Law* 36–60.

Elliott, M., Williams, J., and Young, A.L. (eds.), *The UK Constitution after Miller: Brexit and Beyond* (2018, Oxford: Hart Publishing).

Fabbrini, F., (ed.), *The Law & Politics of Brexit* Vols I-V (2017–2024, Oxford: OUP).

Gordon, M., 'Referendums in the UK constitution: Authority, sovereignty and democracy after Brexit' (2020) 16(2) *European constitutional law review* 213–248.

Whitten, L.C., *Brexit and the Northern Ireland constitution* (2023, OUP).

INDEX

Tables, figures, and boxes are indicated by an italic *t*, *f*, and *b* following the page number.

C

D

E

Y